International Business

Environments and Operations

FOURTEENTH EDITION

John D. Daniels
University of Miami

Lee H. Radebaugh
Brigham Young University

Daniel P. Sullivan
University of Delaware

PEARSON

Boston   Columbus   Indianapolis   New York   San Francisco   Upper Saddle River
Amsterdam   Cape Town   Dubai   London   Madrid   Milan   Munich   Paris   Montréal   Toronto
Delhi   Mexico City   São Paulo   Sydney   Hong Kong   Seoul   Singapore   Taipei   Tokyo

Editorial Director: Sally Yagan
Acquisitions Editor: Brian Mickelson
Editorial Project Manager: Sarah Holle
Director of Marketing: Maggie Moylan
Senior Marketing Manager: Nikki Ayana Jones
Marketing Assistant: Ian Gold
Senior Managing Editor: Judy Leale
Production Project Manager: Ann Pulido
Senior Operations Supervisor: Arnold Vila
Operations Specialist: Cathleen Petersen
Creative Art Director: Blair Brown
Senior Art Director: Steve Frim
Interior and Cover Designer: Judy Allan
Cover Images: bluehand/Shutterstock.com,
    Aleksandar Todorovic/Shutterstock.com,
    Sam DCruz/Shutterstock.com,
Jeremy Richards/Shutterstock.com,
Pedro Rufo/Shutterstock.com, Martin
Mette/Shutterstock.com, David Koester/
Shutterstock.com, Philip Lange/Shutterstock.
com, yui/Shutterstock.com, Losevsky
Pavel/Shutterstock.com, Ragnarock/
Shutterstock.com
Lead Media Project Manager: Lisa Rinaldi
Editorial Media Project Manager: Denise
    Vaughn
**Full-Service Project Management
    and Composition:** Integra
Printer/Binder: R.R. Donnelley/Willard
Cover Printer: Lehigh-Phoenix Color/
    Hagerstown
Text Font: 10/12 Palatino

Credits and acknowledgments borrowed from other sources and reproduced, with permission, in this textbook appear on the appropriate page within text.

Library of Congress Cataloging-in-Publication Data

Daniels, John D.
    International business : environments and operations/John D. Daniels, Lee H. Radebaugh,
    Daniel P. Sullivan.—14th ed.
        p. cm.
    Includes bibliographical references and indexes.
    ISBN-13: 978-0-13-266866-8
    ISBN-10: 0-13-266866-1
    1. International business enterprises.   2. International economic relations.   3. Investments,
        Foreign.   I. Radebaugh, Lee H.   II. Sullivan, Daniel P.   III. Title.
    HD2755.5.D35 2013
    658.1'8—dc23
                                                                                2011045707

10 9 8 7 6 5 4 3 2 1

ISBN 10:   0-13-266866-1
ISBN 13: 978-0-13-266866-8

brief contents

contents

■ **PART FIVE**   GLOBAL STRATEGY, STRUCTURE, AND IMPLEMENTATION   397

11   The Strategy of International Business   397

12 Country Evaluation and Selection   441

13 Export and Import   479

chapter opening and closing cases

industry. Highlights the managerial dimensions of developing and implementing an innovative strategy that disrupts industry structure.

Value Chains: Where, When, and Why 434

Evaluates the perspectives that guide how MNEs in developed and emerging market configure and coordinate value chains. Highlights the changing standards of excellence, given business circumstances in each type of market, that shape MNE's choices.

CHAPTER 12

Carrefour: Crossroads at a Crossroads 442

Inspects the location, pattern, and reasons for Carrefour's international operating locations.

Burger King® Beefs Up Global Operations 470

Overviews Burger King's international expansion history with particular emphasis on its reasons for choice of countries for operations.

CHAPTER 13

SpinCent: Starting-Up Export 480

Examines a small U.S. manufacturer's efforts to expand its exports into the fast-growing Asian market. Highlights the role played by decision-making processes, strategic goals, market opportunities, and public assistance programs. Pays particular attention to the learning process that shapes managers' interpretation and actions in starting-up export.

A Little Electronic Magic at Alibaba.com 513

Looks at how online trading forums in general, as well as the specific situation of Alibaba.com, are changing the means and methods of import and export for small and medium-sized companies around the world. Highlights the implication of emerging technologies platforms to the mechanics of export and import.

CHAPTER 14

The Fizz Biz: Coca-Cola 520

Demonstrates how a range of operating forms, especially alliance and partnership programs with U.S. and non-U.S. companies, have helped Coca-Cola compete better both domestically and internationally.

Connecting within oneworld 546

Discusses the nonequity joint venture between American Airlines and Japan Airlines across the Pacific Ocean along with methods by which members of the oneworld airline alliance cooperate.

CHAPTER 15

Building an Organization at Johnson & Johnson 558

Explores the philosophy and approaches that Johnson & Johnson uses to organize its international operations. Explores the idea of "decentralized centralization" within the loosely coupled network of the company's worldwide operations. Highlights the systemic choices managers make regarding structure, systems, and culture in designing an organization.

Infosys: The Search for the Best and the Brightest 588

Profiles the founding legacy and organization format of a leading Indian information technology company. Examines particular features of its recruitment, training, and socialization programs in building an organization that can serve clients worldwide. Raises the questions about how an MNE organizes operations in ways that fits it founding legacies.

CHAPTER 16

Tommy Hilfiger 598

Examines a company with a globally recognized brand that, nevertheless, alters marketing practices to fit specific country needs.

special features

Looking to the Future

Does Geography Matter?

MAPS

Designed to help improve students' geographic literacy, the book's many maps add interest and illustrate facts and topics discussed in the text. Many case maps zero in on the case company's home country or market region to give students a close-up look at foreign locales. A complete atlas with index is available following Chapter 1.

preface

This textbook is one of the best-selling international business textbooks in both the United States and the rest of the world. Widely used in both undergraduate and MBA level courses, this text has had authorized translations into Spanish, Chinese, Thai, and Russian, and it will soon be in Albanian and Macedonian as well. This textbook set the global standard for studying the environments and operations of international business. The elements of success that have driven this performance anchor our efforts to make this edition the best version yet. We believe these efforts result in a textbook that provides you and your students the best possible understanding of what is happening and is likely to happen in the world of business.

New to This Edition:

- All cases have been updated to reflect the current global business environment.
- Ten entirely new cases. We have added a broad range of new cases. Some evaluate environmental aspects of global business while others look at firm-level features of international business.
- Expanded coverage of the emerging economies, especially the BRICs.
- Discussion of the impact of the earthquake and tsunami in Japan in March 2011 on financial markets, the Japanese yen, the competitive position of Japanese companies like Sony, and the global supply chain. Update of challenges to the global financial system, especially the budget crises in Europe and the United States.
- New cases to reflect important changes in the global economy, such as the rise in importance of the Chinese yuan and its gradual liberation in foreign exchange trading.
- Updated and expanded Test Item File and PowerPoints.

Authoritative, Relevant, Current

Students, faculty, and managers praise this book for its compelling balance between rigorous, authoritative theory and meaningful practice within the context of a fresh, current analysis of the international business environment. Indeed, this book not only describes the ideas of international business but also uses contemporary examples, scenarios, and cases to make sense of what managers do and should do. We include multiple insights and real-world examples, which we base on our research, discussions with managers and other stakeholders, opinions of students and professors, and observations from traveling the world. In 2010–2011 alone, the authors traveled individually to 33 countries, only a few of which overlapped. We traveled to every region and nearly every continent, which provided significant insights we were able to use in this edition. We believe no other textbook comes close to successfully blending a comprehensive review of international business theory with exhaustive attention to what happens in the many parts of the global market. We are confident that this new edition, by making international business ideas and practices more meaningful than ever before, will give students a comprehensive, current view of international business in the twenty-first century.

Relevant Materials That Engage Students

AUTHOR-WRITTEN CASES

An enduring strength of this text is its in-depth case profiles of cutting-edge issues in international business. This edition introduces new cases and updates and revises the remaining. (Please see pages xxi–xxiv for a complete list of cases.) All 40 cases are unique and, with two exceptions, are personally researched and written by the text's authors. As such, we believe they set the standard for integration of theory and practice in an international business textbook on the following three levels:

1. *Level of Analysis*: Cases engage an extensive range of topics from environmental, institutional, country, industry, company, and individual perspectives. No one perspective dominates; all are represented and, hence, create a meaningful representation of the world of international business.
2. *Scope of Geographic Coverage*: Cases cover topics in settings that span the globe; no region is unaddressed, no major market is neglected.
3. *Scope of Company Coverage*: Cases look at various issues from a range of company perspectives, notably companies headquartered in all regions of the world, from large MNEs to small exporters, from old-line manufacturers to emergent cyber businesses, from companies that make products to those that deliver services.

Opening Business Case   Each chapter starts with a provocative case written to set the stage for the major issues covered in the chapter. Designed to grab the student's attention, these cases look at fascinating issues in a way that makes students want to understand the ideas and concepts of international business. These cases, by variously taking the point of view of individuals, companies, and institutions, give a great sense of the richness of the ensuing chapter. Material from the opening cases is then integrated with chapter discussions that we highlight in the text.

Closing Business Case   Each chapter closes with a rich, elaborate case that integrates the ideas and tools presented in the chapter. The closing cases aim to put the student into a situation that asks, given certain circumstances, what should be done. Called on to analyze issues and decisions for which the chapter prepares them, students can then grapple with many of the opportunities and challenges of international business.

New Cases in This Edition

We have extensively updated *all* the cases from the previous edition so that students will find them relevant and rigorous. In addition, we have included several entirely new cases:

- Chapter 2: Shifting Sands of Saudi Society
- Chapter 3: It's a Knockoff World

LOOKING TO THE FUTURE

Each chapter offers future scenarios that are important to managers, companies, or the world. The topic of each *Looking to the Future* feature alludes to ideas discussed in the chapter in a way that prompts students to engage their imagination about the future of the world.

POINT/COUNTERPOINT

To reinforce our strong applications orientation, we have included a separate feature in every chapter that brings to life a major debate in contemporary international business and globalization. We use a point/counterpoint style to highlight the diversity of perspectives that managers and policymakers use to make sense of vital issues. The give-and-take between two sides reinforces this textbook's effort to link theory and practice in ways that will undoubtedly energize class discussion.

GEOGRAPHY AND INTERNATIONAL BUSINESS

In appropriate chapters, we have included "Does Geography Matter?" sections. Some of the geographic variables we include to help explain the chapters' content are country location, location of population and population segments within countries, natural resources and barriers, climate, natural disasters, and country size.

NEW TOPICS AND CHAPTER CHANGES

Although it is a tired cliché, every instructor of international business knows the world is changing in many and often unpredictable ways. We wake up to the same challenges you do, trying to make sense of what we read, hear, and see in the global press. Our effort to make sense of this leads to an unconditional effort to improve and update the text to reflect the latest knowledge and practice of international business. Most notably, among the many changes in this edition are the following:

PART ONE: BACKGROUND FOR INTERNATIONAL BUSINESS

- Updated opening case, such as the extension of global competition (World Cup, Olympics, Commonwealth Games) to new countries, foreign investor purchase of professional soccer teams, and the NBA's development of youth talent in India (Chapter 1)
- Brought in difficulty of determining product origins because of their mixed composition, such as Apple iPhones with made in China labels even though less than 4 percent of value is from China (Chapter 1)

- Illustrated interdependence with new examples, such as the rescue of Chilean miners through technology coming from various countries (Chapter 1)
- Extended discussion of economic uncertainties (oil prices and economic recession), especially as they affect present and future globalization and business (Chapter 1)
- Introduced additional downsides of offshoring, such as the loss of higher skilled jobs and the possible inattention to process techniques as an alternative to cheap labor (Chapter 1)
- Initiated coverage of the effects of natural occurrences on globalization, such as an Icelandic volcanic eruption's closure of airports in Europe and the melting of polar ice shortening some international transport routes (Chapter 1)
- Revised the ending case, such as by inclusion of the cruise line's response to the global economic crisis (Chapter 1)

PART TWO: COMPARATIVE ENVIRONMENTAL FRAMEWORKS

- Created a new case on the background and dynamics of Saudi Arabian culture and the adaptation of local and foreign business to it (Chapter 2)
- Emphasized the concept of cultural dynamics because of other conditions, such as economic ones that have shifted the Chinese preference for male to female offspring (Chapter 2)
- Explained how differences in workforce composition among countries affect work motivation (Chapter 2)
- Brought in new information on the interplay between culture and genetics, especially as it impacts perception (Chapter 2)
- Expanded the concept that companies need to learn abroad, especially by examining economies and companies that are doing well (Chapter 2)
- Introduced opinion that multiculturalism has failed (Chapter 2)
- Updated economic and demographic data in the closing case (Chapter 2)
- Revised opening case to reflect China's political and legal evolution and the implication to foreign investors (Chapter 3)
- Restructured sequence of materials; increased emphasis of political freedom as the basis for political analysis (Chapter 3)
- Stronger statement of the business implications of individualism and collectivism (Chapter 3)
- Briefer discussion of the idea of the constituent ideologies of a political spectrum as well as more focused discussion of the construct of political ideology (Chapter 3)
- Streamlined presentation of the principles and practices of democracy and totalitarianism; emphasis given to their respective business implications (Chapter 3)
- Extended discussion of the standard of political freedom Chapter 3)
- Discussion of the ongoing recession and reported retreat in political freedom; anchored in reports by Freedom House and the Economist Intelligence Unit (Chapter 3)
- Profile trends in democracy and totalitarianism given the consequences of global financial crisis (Chapter 3)
- Expanded coverage of the Third Wave of Democratization (Chapter 3)
- Coverage of democracy's ongoing retreat and emergent recession (Chapter 3)
- Identification of the engines of democracy and totalitarianism (Chapter 3)

- New Looking to the Future insert that develops the idea of the Washington Consensus, Beijing Consensus, Clash of Civilizations, and their respective implications to political ideologies and business environments facing MNEs (Chapter 3)
- New summary chart of the types of political risk; organized to directly support corresponding discussion in chapter (Chapter 3)
- Streamlined discussion of the types of legal systems of prevailing world (Chapter 3)
- Refined discussion of the rule of man versus the rule of law (Chapter 3)
- Focused consideration of the implication of the legal environment to managerial choice and action (Chapter 3)
- Tighter specification of the operational concerns and strategic concerns posed by variation in legal systems among countries (Chapter 3)
- Revised discussion of intellectual property rights, their protection, and their violation; streamlined profile of their implication from a Western versus emerging market perspective (Chapter 3)
- Updated statistics throughout chapter (Chapter 3)
- New end-of-chapter case that profiles the economic, political, and social dynamics of counterfeiting and intellectual property piracy; introduces angles of political and legal ambiguity that reflect location effects (Chapter 3)
- Revised chapter structure based on reviewer feedback and student commentary (Chapter 4)
- Updated and enriched opening case, emphasizing the ongoing and accelerating comeback of emerging economies and its growing scope of implication to Western economies (Chapter 4)
- Revised chapter sequence to anchor it in terms of the concept of economic freedom; this helps illustrate the ongoing change in the nature of market activity as well as to integrate discussion with its analog, political freedom, presented in Chapter 3 (Chapter 4)
- Inclusion of a geographic consideration of the Arctic ice cap and its implication to economic development (Chapter 4)
- Streamlined discussion of the types of market systems; discussion now oriented toward the implication of each to the corresponding practice of economic freedom (Chapter 4)
- Evaluation of the ongoing pushback against economic freedom (Chapter 4)
- Refined discussion and extended application of state capitalism (Chapter 4)
- Adjustment of chapter material to evolving implication of global financial crisis (Chapter 4)
- Streamlined presentation of the traditional measures of economic performance and potential (Chapter 4)
- Expanded discussion of broader conceptions of economic performance and potential, with emphasis given toward sustainability and stability (Chapter 4)
- Additional development of topics such as green economics and happynomics (Chapter 4)
- Refined presentation of the Point/Counterpoint, "Is Growth Good?" (Chapter 4)
- Expanded discussion of inflation, with attention to the matters of chronic inflation, hyperinflation, deflation, and reflation and their implication to managerial decision making (Chapter 4)

- Expanded discussion of the Base of the Pyramid framework in understanding the opportunity of poverty in both emerging as well as Western markets (Chapter 4)
- Linkage of the Base of the Pyramid to the economic consequences of austerity movements in Western economies (Chapter 4)
- Improved discussion of the types of economic systems with greater consideration of features of a mixed economy (Chapter 4)
- Updated and expanded profile of emerging economies throughout chapter (Chapter 4)
- Updated statistics throughout chapter (Chapter 4)
- New end-of-chapter case that relates the causes and consequences of the global financial crisis; calls for the student to apply many of the perspectives and observations discussed throughout the chapter (Chapter 4)
- Updated GE's "Green" strategy and potentially new markets. Updated the information in the closing case on efforts to control HIV/AIDS in South Africa. (Chapter 5)
- Eliminated discussion of the economic impact of the MNC with more focus on the foundations of ethical behavior in a global context (Chapter 5)
- Updated initiatives by the UN and EU to combat bribery as well as expanded coverage on U.S. anticorruption efforts (Chapter 5)
- Added new examples of global sustainability initiatives by SMEs (Chapter 5)

PART THREE: THEORIES AND INSTITUTIONS: TRADE AND INVESTMENT

- Updated trade and demographic figures for the opening case and added map showing Costa Rican trade directions (Chapter 6)
- Added discussion on how factor mobility changes countries' production capabilities (Chapter 6)
- Enhanced competitive reasons for adopting a strategic trade policy (Chapter 6)
- Supplemented data on returning immigrants because of the global economic downturn (Chapter 6)
- Brought in 3D printing as a possible factor affecting shifts in where products will be made in the future (Chapter 6)
- Introduced new closing case on rose exports from Ecuador (Chapter 6)
- Updated figures in opening case on U.S. dependence on seafood imports, especially catfish imports (Chapter 7)
- Discussed the complexity of U.S. import restrictions on Chinese goods because of U.S. dependence on China for essential rare-earth elements (Chapter 7)
- Included current subsidy disagreements, such as on commercial aircraft (Boeing and Airbus) and cotton (Brazil versus the United States) (Chapter 7)
- Augmented export restrictions by including examples of recent export bans of agricultural products (Chapter 7)
- Brought up to date the ending case, such as how, on one hand, U.S. easing of travel bans might stimulate U.S.–Cuban trade, but, on the other hand, how U.S. 2010 mid-term elections might result in an even more hard-line trade stance (Chapter 7)
- Updated the Toyota case to reflect its expansion into Europe, and revised the Walmart case to reflect its expansion into Central America and the consolidation of its regional operations with its Mexican operations (Chapter 8)
- Updated the Doha Round discussion to reflect the progress that has been made (Chapter 8)

- Discussion on antitrust investigations and the EU's aggressive enforcement of their laws (Chapter 8)
- Update of the differences between the EU and NAFTA regarding rules-of-origin (Chapter 8)
- Updated the predictions and outcomes for NAFTA (Chapter 8)
- Update of the trends in the ASEAN, APEC, PAFTA, and AU (Chapter 8)

PART FOUR: WORLD FINANCIAL ENVIRONMENT

- Revised opening case to include information on sources and destinations of migration as well as the role of remittances of foreign workers in Dubai (Chapter 9)
- Update of players on the foreign-exchange market to demonstrate the changes that have occurred (Chapter 9)
- Addition of how to trade in foreign exchange to illustrate the options available (Chapter 9)
- Updated foreign exchange instruments to reflect the current definitions (Chapter 9)
- Updated size, composition, and location of the foreign-exchange market according to the latest BIS survey (Chapter 9)
- Added a new end-of-chapter case on China's revaluation of the yuan and the role of the yuan in the global financial system (Chapter 9)
- Added to the discussion on the quota system in the IMF to reflect the changes that occurred in 2010 and 2011 (Chapter 10)
- New information on the global financial crisis in 2010 and 2011 and the focus on Europe (Chapter 10)
- Update of exchange rate agreements to fit with the new definitions (Chapter 10)
- Discussion of the Greek financial crisis and the efforts of the European Union to find a resolution (Chapter 10)
- Elimination of the discussion on the Chinese yuan and creation of a new case on the yuan for Chapter 9 (Chapter 10)
- Update Looking to the Future to reflect the changes in relative strength among currencies (Chapter 10)
- Updated the closing case to reflect the affect the 2011 earthquake and tsunami in Japan on the Japanese yen and Sony's competitive position (Chapter 10)

PART FIVE: GLOBAL STRATEGY, STRUCTURE, AND IMPLEMENTATION

- Updated opening case for latest performance data and strategic moves; streamlined presentation of materials. (Chapter 11)
- Reset the sequence of first few sections of chapter to reflect feedback from reviewers and students (Chapter 11)
- Streamlined profile of industry structure and its linkage to the of the five fundamental forces model (Chapter 11)
- Profile of key examples that link generic concepts of strategy and industry structure to the activities of MNEs (Chapter 11)
- Shorter overview of the two dominant strategy perspectives (Chapter 11)
- Refined discussion of the cost leadership and differentiation strategy in international markets (Chapter 11)
- Streamlined specification of the value chain and anchored more directly within the context of global operations (Chapter 11)
- Developed additional graphics to better communicate the concept of the value chain (Chapter 11)

- Updated profile of key factors that shaped the configuration of value chains (Chapter 11)
- Emphasized the geographic aspect of global strategy by profiling the notion of business clusters (Chapter 11)
- Moved material in other sections of the book, most notably labor rates and productivity, to Chapter 11 to better communicate configuration choices (Chapter 11)
- Reset the linkage of international strategy trends and ideas from the Base of the Pyramid framework (Chapter 11)
- Updated the profile of Samsung and Sony, as a means to illustrate the dynamic give-and-take of strategy and global markets (Chapter 11)
- Expanded profile of the dynamic of change in competitive competencies, and position (Chapter 11)
- Streamlined and updated the closing chapter case to better compare and contrast the idea of the value chain within established versus emerging markets (Chapter 11)
- Provide summary chart to integrate and organize the key characteristics of the international, multi-domestic, global, and transnational strategies (Chapter 11)
- Brought opening case up-to-date, such as by showing how performance problems have altered Carrefour's priority among countries (Chapter 12)
- Bolstered discussion of the importance of historical ties for companies' choice of operating locations (Chapter 12)
- Enhanced discussion on lack of accuracy on countries' presentation of data, including examples of Greece's presenting false statistics and Bolivian contraband that distorts trade figures (Chapter 12)
- Updated closing case on Burger King's international expansion to include its new entries into Morocco, Russia, and Slovenia (Chapter 12)
- New opening case: SpinCent: Starting-Up Export (Chapter 13)
- Completely reset structure and sequence of chapter material; as a result, have effectively developed a new chapter (Chapter 13)
- Disaggregated treatment of the concepts of export and import (Chapter 13)
- Expanded sections on who are exporters and why do they export (Chapter 13)
- Refined coverage of export development perspectives, paying particular mind to the incremental internationalization and the born global perspectives (Chapter 13)
- Expanded discussion of the primary approaches to exporting (Chapter 13)
- Expanded sections on who are importers and why they import (Chapter 13)
- New section on the pitfalls and problems that challenge importers and exporters (Chapter 13)
- Identification of key points of difficulty that complicate international trade from the perspective of small and medium-sized enterprises (Chapter 13)
- Reset chapter structure to better organize discussion of the resources available to international traders (Chapter 13)
- Tighter construction of the dimensions that guide developing an export plan (Chapter 13)
- Updated profile of the technology of trade and its application to potential and practicing exporters and importers (Chapter 13)
- Refined coverage of the documentation demands of international trade (Chapter 13)
- Streamlined coverage of countertrade and it role as a facilitator of international trade (Chapter 13)

- Complete re-edit of closing case with the goal of streamlining the presentation of material (Chapter 13)
- Update opening case with Coca-Cola's newer operating figures and alliances (Chapter 14)
- Introduced concept of transport cost dynamics because of fuel prices, infrastructure, risk factors, and climate change (Chapter 14)
- Brought in the concept of market failure as a reason for non-collaboration (Chapter 14)
- Discussed the need to acquire management skills as a motive for international expansion via acquisition (Chapter 14)
- Presented examples of trademark squatting (Chapter 14)
- Elaborated on differences in national and corporate cultures as impediments to successful international collaboration (Chapter 14)
- New ending case on collaboration among members of the oneworld Alliance, with particular emphasis on the non-equity joint venture between American Airlines and Japan Airlines for trans-Pacific traffic (Chapter 14)
- Streamlined opening case to better accentuate key elements of organizational design that are then discussed throughout the chapter (Chapter 15)
- Reset and updated discussion of macro environmental trends that influence contemporary interpretations of organization in the MNE (Chapter 15)
- Updated company examples regarding adoption or abandonment of organizational structure (Chapter 15)
- Reset earlier discussion of contemporary structures in terms of the standard of of neoclassical structures to better reflect the academic literature (Chapter 15)
- Reorganized discussion of neoclassical structures to emphasize key points of forms and functions (Chapter 15)
- Streamlined interpretation of coordination and control systems; developed richer explanations within the context of MNE's practices (Chapter 15)
- Reset discussion of organization culture regarding its forms, functions, and connection to company strategy (Chapter 15)
- Updated profile of the rise of corporate universities and their role in developing and sustaining organization in the MNE (Chapter 15)
- Streamlined profile of Infosys in the closing case (Chapter 15)

PART SIX: MANAGING INTERNATIONAL OPERATIONS

- Updated operating figures in the opening case along with discussion of Hilfiger's flagship store concept (Chapter 16)
- Added examples of social marketing, such as those by Tesco and Coca-Cola (Chapter 16)
- Enhanced companies' approaches to sell simultaneously to different income levels (Chapter 16)
- Added the importance of word of mouth in product acceptance, especially where uncertainty avoidance is high (Chapter 16)
- Launched a new ending case on a social business international joint venture in Bangladesh (Chapter 16)
- Updated the opening case to include information regarding Samsonite's IPO in Hong Kong in June 2011 (Chapter 17)
- New example of innovation and quality strategies to introduce the idea of 3D printing (Chapter 17)

- New examples for regional manufacturing and multidomestic manufacturing (Chapter 17)
- Revised case about car quality to include more discussion about Toyota (Chapter 17)
- Update to ISO 9000 and ISO 14000 standards (Chapter 17)
- Discussion of principles from *The World Is Flat* to illustrate offshoring, outsourcing, and supply-chaining and other ways information technology is changing global supply chains (Chapter 17)
- Eliminated the closing case on Ventus (Chapter 17)
- Replaced the ending case on Ventus in Chapter 17 with a new case on Nokero to highlight its opportunities and challenges regarding its supply chain in an entrepreneurial and environmentally responsible setting (Chapter 17)
- Update of opening case to reflect how Parmalat has recovered from its corporate corruption scandal (Chapter 18)
- Revised the discussion on balance sheet formats to coincide with IFRS (Chapter 18)
- Update of macro versus micro systems to enhance the discussion of the governments influence (Chapter 18)
- Updated trends in the convergence of accounting standards through IFRS and negotiations with the U.S. FASB (Chapter 18)
- Update of the European response to the adoption of IFRS (Chapter 18)
- Discussion of comparing a budget with actual results translated at the actual exchange rate (Chapter 18)
- Updated the closing case to reflect Ericcson's adoption of IFRS and the impact on its financial statements.
- Updated the opening case to enhance the discussion of future challenges GPS faces and how they are coping strategically (Chapter 19)
- Revised discussion on leveraging to illustrate how the structures of companies are changing in different countries (Chapter 19)
- Discussion on the European crisis and how debt has been involved (Chapter 19)
- Update of interest rates in the Eurocurrency market and the attractiveness of those markets (Chapter 19)
- Addition of how corporations use Eurobonds to fund expansion (Chapter 19)
- Eliminated the closing case on Dell Mercosur and the Brazilian real (Chapter 19)
- Added a new closing case on Prada's IPO in Hong Kong in June 2011 (Chapter 19)
- Refined and expanded the idea of globalizing your career as reported in opening case; includes greater diversity of viewpoints of the expatriate experience (Chapter 20)
- Profile of trends in expatriate processes given consequences of global financial crisis and the call to economize expatriate management (Chapter 20)
- Highlighted implications of the changing workplace of globalization to the use of third-country nationals, reverse expatriates, and different genders and demographics (Chapter 20)
- Improved specification of the approaches to global staffing (Chapter 20)
- Streamlined discussion of the linkage of expatriate selection and professional and personal characteristics (Chapter 20)
- Reported survey data identifying key competencies and key concerns of expatriates (Chapter 20)

- Fuller explanation of the causes and consequences of expatriate failure (Chapter 20)
- Profile of changing compensation patterns given globalization of compensation standards as well as growing pressures to economize (Chapter 20)
- Updated and improved coverage of the Indian market as well as its moderating characteristics (Chapter 20)
- Enriched the presentation of material closing case by including photos of the candidates for the country manager (Chapter 20)

Engaging In-Text Learning Aids

We believe a powerful textbook must teach as well as present ideas. To that end, we use several in-text aids to make this book an effective learning tool. Most notably, each chapter uses all of the following features:

CHAPTER OBJECTIVES AND SUMMARY

Each chapter begins with learning objectives and ends with a summary that tie directly to the chapter material. This linkage helps students prepare for the major issues within each chapter, appreciate their general relationships, and reinforce the important lessons of the chapter material.

CONCEPT LINKS

Throughout each chapter, as warranted by discussion in the corresponding text, we highlight in the margin how ideas from previous chapters link to the ideas being discussed. This cumulative series of concept links helps the student build an understanding of the connections among concepts across chapters. This feature also facilitates student understanding when instructors do not assign all chapters.

CASE LINKS

Another effort to help students better interpret the connections among ideas and practices is encompassed in our latest innovation. Specifically, as warranted by discussion in the corresponding text, we highlight with text shading and icons how those ideas being discussed elaborate ideas that were presented in the opening and closing cases of that chapter.

KEY TERMS AND POINTS: BOLDING, MARGINAL NOTES, AND GLOSSARY

Every chapter highlights key terms; each key term is put in bold print when it first appears. Key learning points are also highlighted in the adjoining margin. These terms and others are then assembled in an end-of-chapter list and into a comprehensive glossary at the end of the book.

CASE QUESTIONS

The closing case of each chapter stipulates several questions to guide how students apply what they have learned in the chapter to the reality of international business. We have found in our classes that the questions at the end of the case go a long way toward putting the case into perspective for students. In addition, they make for great assignment activities, directing students to respond to questions with information presented in the specific case as well as the chapter.

POINT/COUNTERPOINT

This feature, as we have already discussed, is compelling not only for class discussion, but also for specific assignments. These assignments may include requiring students to take sides in debates or to apply arguments to specific countries.

MAPS

Geographic literacy is essential in international business. Thus, we have not only included a map section between Chapters 1 and 2, but we incorporate maps throughout that show both locations and other information.

Currency and Readability

We have always prided ourselves on being current in the research and examples we cite in the chapters. The 14th edition is no exception; in fact, we believe our coverage goes beyond that of any other IB text. If you examine the endnotes for any chapter, you will see that we include both classic and the most up-to-date materials from both scholarly treatises and the popular press. If you examine the list of companies in the "Company Index and Trademarks," you will see that our citations are numerous and include large and small firms from a variety of industries based in countries throughout the world. These citations illustrate to students the practical reality of the theories and alternative operations we describe.

We have made a special effort in this edition to improve the readability of the extensive materials we present. First, we make a point of putting authors' names (except for classics such as Adam Smith) only in the reference section rather than in the chapters' prose. We have simply seen too many students try to remember names rather than concepts. Second, we have engaged a copy editor to improve the language and flow of materials.

Instructors can access downloadable supplemental resources by signing into the Instructor Resource Center at www.pearsonhighered.com/educator.

> *It gets better.* Once you register, you will not have additional forms to fill out or multiple user names and passwords to remember to access new titles and/or editions. As a registered faculty member, you can log in directly to download resource files and receive immediate access and instructions for installing Course Management content to your campus server.

> *Need help?* Our dedicated Technical Support team is ready to assist instructors with questions about the media supplements that accompany this text. Visit http://247pearsoned.custhelp.com/ for answers to frequently asked questions and toll-free user support phone numbers. The following supplements are available to adopting instructors.

The helpful Instructor's Manual includes sample syllabi, lecture outlines, and answers to all end-of-chapter case questions.

Test Item File

The Test Item File boasts over 100 questions per chapter, including multiple choice, true/false, short answer, and essays. The Test Item File includes questions that are tagged Learning Objectives, Learning Outcomes and to AACSB Learning Standards to help measure whether students are grasping the course content that aligns with AACSB guidelines.

TestGen Software

Pearson Education's test-generating software is available from www .pearsonhighered.com/irc. The software is PC/MAC compatible and preloaded with all of the Test Item File questions. You can manually or randomly view test questions and drag and drop to create a test. You can add or modify test-bank questions as needed. All of our TestGens are converted for use in Blackboard and WebCT and are available for download from www.pearsonhighered.com/irc.

Learning Management Systems

BLACKBOARD/WEBCT

BlackBoard and WebCT Course Cartridges are available for download from www .pearsonhighered.com/irc. These standard course cartridges contain the Instructor's Manual, TestGen, Instructor PowerPoints, and when available, Student Powerpoints and Student Data Files.

PowerPoint Slides

INSTRUCTOR POWERPOINTS

This presentation includes basic outlines and key points from each chapter. It includes figures from the text but no forms of rich media, which makes the file size manageable and easier to share online or via email.

AUDIO POWERPOINTS

Pearson's MyIBLab also offers the instructor PowerPoints in an audio format for students taking classes online or as a supplemental teaching aid to the classroom lectures.

Videos

Exciting and high-quality video clips help deliver engaging culture, country, and business programs to the classroom to help students better understand the world around them. Please contact your local representative to receive a copy of these videos.

MyIBLab

MyIBLab gives students the opportunity to test themselves on key concepts and skills, track their own progress through the course, and use personalized study plan activities—all to help them achieve success in the classroom.

To order MyIBLab with this text, use ISBN 0132886057.

CourseSmart eTextbooks Online

CourseSmart eTextbooks were developed for students looking to save the cost on required or recommended textbooks. Students simply select their eText by title or author and purchase immediate access to the content for the duration of the course using any major credit card. With a CourseSmart eText, students can search for specific keywords or page numbers, take notes online, print out reading assignments that incorporate lecture notes, and bookmark important passages for later review. For more information or to purchase a CourseSmart eTextbook, visit www.coursesmart.com

Acknowledgments

Every author relies on the comments, critiques, and insights of reviewers. It is a tough task that few choose to support. Therefore, we want to thank the following people for their insightful and helpful comments on the thirteenth edition of *International Business: Environments and Operations*, which helped guide us in preparing the fourteenth edition.

MARK BAYLOR, University of Delaware
ALI KARA, Pennsylvania State University
LOUIS MELBOURNE, Florida International University
SHAD MORRIS, Ohio State University
JOHN O'BRIEN, University of Denver
AJAYI RICHARD, University of Central Florida
SHIRI TERJESEN, Indiana University
ANTHONY PAPUZZA, University of Colorado, Boulder

In addition, we have been fortunate since the first edition to have colleagues who have been willing to make the effort to critique draft materials, react to coverage already in print, advise on suggested changes, and send items to be corrected. Because this is the culmination of several previous editions, we would like to acknowledge everyone's efforts. However, many more individuals than we can possibly list have helped us. To those who must remain anonymous, we offer our sincere thanks.

We would also like to acknowledge people whom we interviewed in writing cases. These are Brenda Yester (Riding the Tide of Growth: Carnival Cruise Lines), Omar Aljindi, Nora al Jundi, and Talah Tamimi (Shifting Sands of Saudi Society), Mauricio Calero (Ecuador: A Rosy Export Future?), Raul Arguelles Diaz Gonzales and Francisco Suarez Mogollon (Walmart Goes South), Jonathan Fitzpatrick, Julio A. Ramirez, Arianne Cento, and Ana Miranda (Burger King Beefs Up Global Operations), several executives at American Airlines and oneworld who wish to remain anonymous (Connecting within oneworld) and Ali R. Manbien (GPS: In the Market for an Effective Hedging Strategy). In addition, we would like to thank Manuel Serapio at the University of Colorado at Denver for his excellent case at the end of Chapter 17, Nokero: Lighting the World, and Jon Jungbien Moon at Korea University who co-authored the ending case for Chapter 16, Marketing at the Base of the Pyramid (BoP) in Bangladesh: Grameen Danone Foods. Additionally, others who helped with administrative and research matters are Melanie Hunter, Yifan Xu, Tyler Gill, Hongbin Hu, Mathias Gardner, Adriane Moline, and Maddison DeWolf.

It takes a dedicated group of individuals to take a textbook from first draft to final manuscript. We would like to thank our partners at Pearson Prentice Hall for their tireless efforts in bringing the fourteenth edition of this book to fruition. Our thanks go to Editorial Director, Sally Yagan; Acquisitions Editor, Brian Mickelson; Director of Editorial Services, Ashley Santora; Marketing Manager, Nikki Jones; Senior Managing Editor, Judy Leale; Project Manager, Production, Ann Pulido; Project Manager from Integra-Chicago, Kristin Jobe.

about the authors

From left to right: **Daniel Sullivan, Lee Radebaugh, John Daniels**

Three respected and renowned scholars show your students how dynamic, how real, how interesting, and how important the study of international business can be.

John D. Daniels, the Samuel N. Friedland Chair of Executive Management at the University of Miami, received his Ph.D. at the University of Michigan. His dissertation won first place in the award competition of the Academy of International Business. Since then, he has been an active researcher and won a decade award from the *Journal of International Business Studies.* His articles have appeared in such leading journals as *Academy of Management Journal, Advances in International Marketing, California Management Review, Columbia Journal of World Business, International Marketing Review, International Trade Journal, Journal of Business Research, Journal of High Technology Management Research, Journal of International Business Studies, Management International Review, Multinational Business Review, Strategic Management Journal, Transnational Corporations,* and *Weltwirtschaftliches Archiv.* Professor Daniels co-edited with Jeffrey Krug three volumes, *Multinational Enterprise Theory,* and three volumes, *International Business and Globalization.* On its 30th anniversary, *Management International Review* referred to him as "one of the most prolific American IB scholars." He served as president of the Academy of International Business and dean of its Fellows. He also served as chairperson of the international division of the Academy of Management, which named him Outstanding Educator of the Year in 2010. Professor Daniels has worked and lived a year or longer in seven different countries, worked shorter stints in approximately 30 other countries on six continents, and traveled in many more. His foreign work has been a combination of private sector, governmental, teaching, and research assignments. He was formerly a faculty member at Georgia State University and The Pennsylvania State University, director of the Center for International Business Education and Research (CIBER) at Indiana University, and holder of the E. Claiborne Robins Distinguished Chair at the University of Richmond.

Lee H. Radebaugh is the Kay and Yvonne Whitmore Professor International Business and Director of the Whitmore Global Management Center/CIBER at Brigham Young University. He received his M.B.A. and doctorate from Indiana

University. He taught at The Pennsylvania State University from 1972 to 1980. He also has been a visiting professor at Escuela de Administracion de Negocios para Graduados (ESAN) in Lima, Peru. In 1985, Professor Radebaugh was the James Cusator Wards visiting professor at Glasgow University, Scotland. His other books include *International Accounting and Multinational Enterprises* (John Wiley and Sons, 6th edition) with S. J. Gray and Erv Black; *Introduction to Business: International Dimensions* (South-Western Publishing Company) with John D. Daniels; and seven books on Canada-U.S. trade and investment relations, with Earl Fry as co-editor. He has also published several other monographs and articles on international business and international accounting in journals such as the *Journal of Accounting Research, Journal of International Financial Management and Accounting, Journal of International Business Studies,* and the *International Journal of Accounting.* He is the former editor of the *Journal of International Accounting Research* and area editor of the *Journal of International Business Studies.* His primary teaching interests are international business and international accounting. Professor Radebaugh is an active member of the American Accounting Association, the European Accounting Association, the International Association of Accounting Education and Research, and the Academy of International Business, having served on several committees as the president of the International Section of the AAA and as the secretary treasurer of the AIB. He is a member of the Fellows of the Academy of International Business. He is also active with the local business community as past president of the World Trade Association of Utah and member of the District Export Council. In 2007, Professor Radebaugh received the Outstanding International Accounting Service Award of the International Accounting Section of the American Accounting Association, and in 1998, he was named International Person of the Year in the state of Utah and Outstanding International Educator of the International Section of the American Accounting Association.

Daniel P. Sullivan, Professor of International Business at the Alfred Lerner College of Business of the University of Delaware, received his Ph.D. from the University of South Carolina. He researches a range of topics, including globalization and business, international management, global strategy, competitive analysis, and corporate governance. His work on these topics has been published in leading scholarly journals, including the *Journal of International Business Studies, Management International Review, Law and Society Review,* and *Academy of Management Journal.* In addition, he serves on the editorial boards of the *Journal of International Business Studies* and *Management International Review.* Professor Sullivan has been honored for both his research and teaching, receiving grants and winning awards for both activities while at the University of Delaware and, his former affiliation, the Freeman School of Tulane University. He has been awarded numerous teaching honors at the undergraduate, M.B.A., and E.M.B.A. levels—most notably, he has been voted Outstanding Teacher by the students of 14 different Executive M.B.A. classes at the University of Delaware and Tulane University. Professor Sullivan has taught, designed, and administered a range of graduate, undergraduate, and nondegree courses on topics spanning globalization and business, international business operations, international management, strategic perspectives, executive leadership, and corporate strategy. In the United States, he has delivered lectures and courses at several university sites and company facilities. In addition, he has led courses in several foreign countries, including China, Bulgaria, the Czech Republic, France, South Korea, Switzerland, Taiwan, and the United Kingdom. Finally, he has worked with many managers and consulted with several multinational enterprises on issues of international business.

chapter 1

Globalization and International Business

Objectives

1. To define *globalization* and *international business* and explain how they affect each other

2. To show why companies engage in international business and why its growth has accelerated

3. To discuss globalization's future and the major criticisms of it

4. To illustrate the different ways a company can accomplish its global objectives

5. To apply social science disciplines to understanding the differences between international and domestic business

Access a host of interactive learning aids to help strengthen your understanding of the chapter concepts at www.myiblab.com.

MyIBLab

The world's a stage; each plays his part, and takes his share.

—*Dutch proverb*

Source: Allstar Picture Library / Alamy

1

CASE

Global Games for Fun and Business

The Fédération Internationale de Football Association (FIFA) has more country members than the United Nations has, and it administered the competition that brought 32 national teams to the 2010 World Cup in South Africa after months of qualifying games.[1] (The preceding photo shows part of the opening ceremony.) You were likely part of the record global television audience for at least some of the Cup and remember the droning of vuvuzela horns throughout the matches. While FIFA's membership has long been global, the 2010 Cup was the first in Africa, thus contributing toward the rapid global diffusion of major sports competition. In addition, the 2010 Commonwealth Games were played for the first time in India, the first Olympics in South America is scheduled for Brazil, and the first World Cup in the Middle East is confirmed for Qatar.

Sports, according to one political historian, is now "the most globalized [legitimate] business in the world." Historically, most players and teams in most sports competed only on their own home turf. Today, however, fans everywhere demand to see the best, and "best" has become a decidedly global standard. Satellite TV now brings live events from just about anywhere in the world to fans just about anywhere else in the world. Thus the key players in the sports-promotion business—team owners, league representatives, and sports associations—have broadened audience exposure, expanding fan bases and augmenting revenues, especially through advertising that cuts across national borders.

Likewise, because more fans expect to see the world's best teams and players, the search for talent has become worldwide. You can now find U.S. and European professional basketball scouts in remote areas of Nigeria looking for high-potential tall youngsters. Baseball agents have opened live-in training camps for teenagers in the Dominican Republic in exchange for a percentage of any of their future professional signing bonuses. However, keep in mind that assembling talent is necessary but insufficient to make a sports business successful. Shrewd marketing and financial management are crucial too. For instance, the Barcelona football club, arguably the best professional soccer team in recent years, nevertheless has had financial problems. It has turned to young business graduates to turn things around.

THE INTERNATIONAL JOB MARKET

Today's top-notch players in just about every sport are willing to follow the money wherever it may take them. For instance, many of the best Brazilian soccer players are with European teams that offer much higher payrolls than their Brazilian counterparts. England's professional soccer league (Premiership) includes players from about 70 countries, which helps to improve the caliber of play and increase the TV fan base outside England. Interestingly, fans continue to follow national favorites even after they've taken their talents elsewhere. About 300 million Chinese tuned in to watch local basketball legend Yao Ming's first game in America's National Basketball Association (NBA).

How the ATP Courts Worldwide Support

If you're a fan of individual sports, you've probably noticed that players are globe hoppers. Take tennis. No single country boasts enough interested fans to keep players at home for year-round competition. In any case, today's top-flight tennis pros come from every continent except Antarctica, and tennis fans everywhere want to see the top players compete on local courts. For 2012, the Association of Tennis Professionals (ATP) sanctioned 66 tournaments in 30 countries. It also requires member pros to play in a certain number of events—and thus stop over in a number of countries—to maintain international rankings.

Because no tennis pro can possibly play in every tournament, organizers must attract enough top draws to fill stadium seats and land lucrative TV contracts. Tournaments, therefore, compete for top-billed stars, not only with other tournaments but also with such regular international showcases as the Olympics and the Davis Cup. Prizes for two weeks' worth of expert serving and volleying can be extremely generous (about U.S. $2.2 million for the 2011 singles champions of the Australian Open).

Remember, too, that tournaments earn money through ticket sales, corporate sponsorship agreements, television contracts, and leasing of advertising space. The more people in the stadium and TV audience, the more sponsors and advertisers will pay to get their attention. Moreover, international broadcasts attract sponsorship from international companies. The sponsor list for the 2011 Australian Open tennis tournament included a South Korean automaker (Kia), a Dutch brewer (Heineken), a Swiss watchmaker (Rolex), a French clothing company (Lacoste), and a U.S. sporting goods firm (Wilson).

From National to International Sports Pastimes

Some countries have legally designated a national sport as a means of preserving traditions, and some others effectively have one. Map 1.1 shows a sample of these. However,

MAP 1.1 Examples of National Sports

Some 33 countries have either defined a national sport by law or de facto have a national sport. Some national sports are shared by more than one country, such as cricket by six former British colonies in the Caribbean. Some others have been established to protect an historical heritage, such as tejo in Colombia. Note also that Canada has two designations, one for winter and one for summer.

Source: The information on sports was taken from Wikipedia, http://en.wikipedia.org/wiki/National_sport (accessed March 3, 2009)

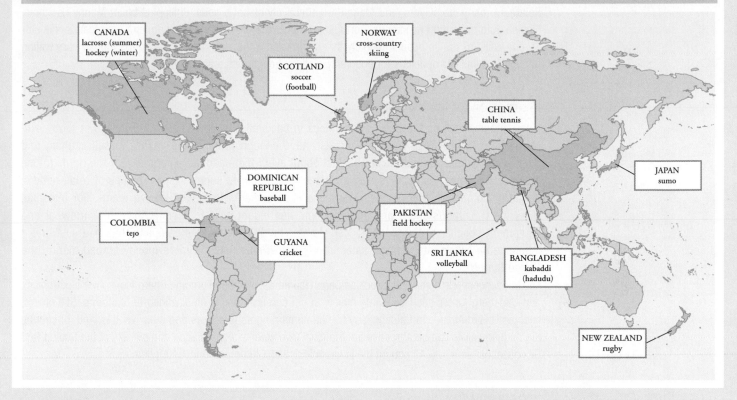

other sports have sometimes replaced national sports in popularity, such as cricket's replacement of field hockey as India's most popular sport.

Further, the International Baseball Federation now has over 100 member countries, even though baseball was popular only in its North American birthplace for most of its history. As TV revenues flattened in North America, Major League Baseball (MLB) began broadcasting games to international audiences. Increased exposure not only broadened the global fan base, but it also showed youngsters all over the world how the game was played. As late as 1986, only 14 percent of MLB players were born outside the United States; by 2010, that number had climbed to almost 28 percent. The average MLB clubhouse is now a bastion of multilingual camaraderie, with players and coaches talking baseball in Spanish, Japanese, and Korean as well as English.

THE WIDE WORLD OF TELEVISED SPORTS

Not surprisingly, other professional sports groups have expanded their global TV coverage (and marketing programs). Most viewers of Stanley Cup hockey watch from outside North America. Fans watch National Association for Stock Car Auto Racing (NASCAR) races in more than 120 countries and NBA games in about 200. If you lived in Tunisia and enjoyed simultaneous access to multiple TV channels, you could watch more hours of NBA action than there are hours in the year.

And TV isn't the only means by which sports organizations are seeking foreign fan bases and players. For several years, the National Football League (NFL) of the United States sponsored a now-defunct professional league in Europe. It continues to underwrite flag-football programs in Chinese schools, and it is playing some regular NFL games in Europe. The NBA has appointed a director of basketball operations for India to help build youth leagues there. With the growth of broadband, we'll soon enter the realm of thousand-channel TV, where we'll be able to tune into sporting events that currently appeal only to highly localized niche markets. How about Thai boxing or Japanese sumo wrestling?

The Top-Notch Pro as Upscale Brand

Relatedly, many top players (and teams) are effectively global brands. Philippine boxer Manny Pacquiao, Finnish auto racer Kimi Raikkonen, Portuguese soccer player Cristiano Ronaldo, and American tennis star Serena Williams are so popular globally that companies within and outside the sports industry are willing to pay them millions of dollars for endorsing clothes, equipment, and other products.

Promotion as Teamwork

A few teams, such as the New York Yankees in baseball, the New Zealand All Blacks in rugby, and Manchester United (Man U) in soccer also have enough brand-name cachet to sell clothing and other items to fans around the world. Just about every team can get something for the rights to use its logo, and some teams have enough name recognition to support global chains of retail outlets. Similarly, companies both sponsor and seek endorsements from well-known teams. For instance, Nike, the U.S. sports shoes and apparel giant, has fought hard to become the top sportswear and equipment supplier to European soccer teams. The success of this campaign has had such a big influence on Nike's international sales efforts that it now takes in more money abroad than in the United States.

Many nonsports companies, such as Canon (cameras, office equipment), Sharp (consumer electronics), and Carlsberg (beer), sponsor teams mainly to get corporate logos emblazoned on uniforms. Still others, such as United Airlines in Chicago, pay for the naming rights to arenas and other venues. And, of course, teams themselves can be attractive international investments. For instance, the owners of the Boston Red Sox baseball team (U.S.A.) bought the Liverpool Football Club of the United Kingdom.

Sports and You

What does all this mean to you as a sports fan? Chances are—especially if you're a male—you fantasized at one time about going pro in some sport, but you've probably given up that fantasy and settled into the role of spectator. Now that pro sports has become a global phenomenon (thanks to better communications), you can enjoy a greater variety—and a higher level of competition—than any generation before you.

That's the upside, but we must point out that people don't always take easily to another country's sport. Despite many efforts, cricket has never become popular in the United States. It became popular in many countries during centuries of British colonialism, but it has made no recent inroads internationally. Nor has American football gained much popularity outside the United States. A former NFL lineman expressed a reason: that rules for American football and cricket are so complicated that one must learn them as children. However, basketball and soccer have traveled to new markets more easily because they are easier to understand and require no specialized equipment.

Further, there is disagreement about the economic effect of successfully winning a bid to host big international competitions such as the World Cup and Olympics. On the one hand, the events bring in tourists and they publicize to the world (especially potential investors) the opportunities that might exist in the host location. They also help spur the construction of infrastructure that will speed future economic growth. On the other hand, hosts may spend on stadiums and facilities that have no use afterward. Finally, few competitions have ended without substantially increasing local and national debt.

Nor is everyone happy with the unbridled globalization of sports—or at least with some of the effects. Brazilian soccer fans lament the loss of their best players, and U.S. fans and public officials protested the sale of the MLB Seattle Mariners to a foreign investor.

Introduction

In its broadest sense, **globalization** refers to the widening set of interdependent relationships among people from different parts of a world that happens to be divided into nations. The term can also refer to the integration of world economies through the elimination of barriers to movements of goods, services, capital, technology, and people.[2] Throughout recorded history, human connections over ever-wider geographic areas have expanded the variety of available resources, products, services, and markets. We've altered the way we want and expect to live, and we've become more deeply affected (positively and negatively) by conditions outside our immediate domains.

The opening case shows how far-flung global contact allows the world's best sports talent to compete—regardless of nationality—and the fans to watch them, from almost anywhere. The changes that have led firms to consider ever more distant places as sources of supplies and markets affect almost every industry and their consumers. We may not always know it, but we commonly buy products from all over the world. "Made in" labels do not tell us everything about product origins. So many different components, ingredients, and specialized business activities go into products that it's often a challenge to say exactly where they were made. For example, because Apple's iPhones are shipped from China they appear to be Chinese products, but less than 4 percent of their value is performed in China.[3]

Here's an interesting example of interdependent relationships. One of 2010's biggest stories and one that was watched on TV worldwide was the rescue of Chilean miners, but the rescue would have been impossible without the innovations and products from a variety of countries—the Center Rock drill bit from the United States, a high-strength cable from Germany, a super-flexible fiber optics communications cable from Japan, and a special cell phone from South Korea.[4]

HOW DOES *INTERNATIONAL BUSINESS* FIT IN?

Globalization enables us to get more variety, better quality, or lower prices. Our daily meals contain spices that aren't grown domestically and fresh produce that's out of season in one local climate or another. Our cars cost less than if all the parts were made and the labor performed in one place. All of these connections between supplies and markets result from the activities of **international business,** defined as all commercial transactions, including sales, investments, and transportation, that take place between two or more countries. Private companies undertake such transactions for profit; governments may undertake them either for profit or for other reasons.

> International business consists of all commercial transactions between two or more countries.
>
> • The goal of private business is to make profits.
> • Government business may or may not be motivated by profit.

The Study of International Business Why should we study international business? Simply, it comprises a large and growing portion of the world's total business. Global events and competition affect almost all companies, large and small, regardless of industry, as a result of selling output to and securing supplies and resources from foreign countries, as well as competing against products and services from abroad. Thus, most managers need to approach their operating strategies from an international standpoint. Recall the NBA teams in the opening case, which are looking globally for human resources—on-court talent—and additional markets that exist abroad. As a manager in almost any industry, you'll need to consider (1) where to obtain the inputs you need of the required quality and at the best possible price and (2) where you can best sell the product or service you've put together from those inputs.

CRN
Case Review Note

Understanding the Environment/Operations Relationship The best way of doing business abroad may not be the same as the best way at home. Why? First, when your company operates internationally, it will engage in *modes* of business, such as exporting and importing, that differ from those in which it engages domestically. Second, physical,

FIGURE 1.1   Factors in International Business Operations

The conduct of a company's international operations depends on two factors: its objectives and the means by which it intends to achieve them. Likewise, its operations affect, and are affected by, two sets of factors: physical/social and competitive.

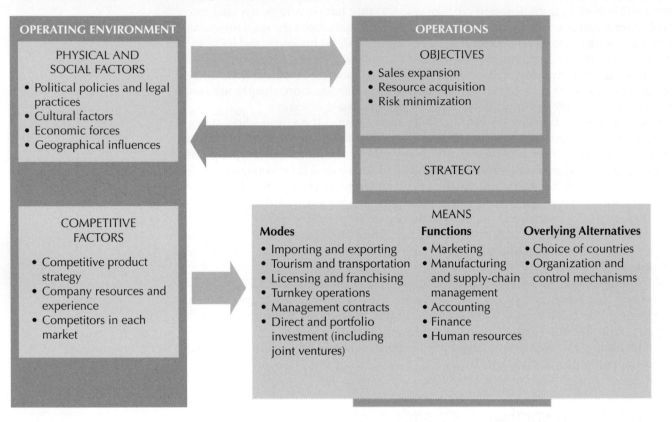

Studying international business is important because

- Most companies either are international or compete with international companies.
- Modes of operations may differ from those used domestically.
- The best way of conducting business may differ by country.
- An understanding helps you make better career decisions.
- An understanding helps you decide what governmental policies to support.

Globalization

- Has been growing.
- Is less pervasive than generally thought.
- Has economic and non economic dimensions.
- Is stimulated by several factors.

social, and competitive conditions differ among countries and affect the optimum ways to conduct business. Thus, companies operating internationally have more diverse and complex operating environments than those that conduct business only at home. Figure 1.1 outlines the complex set of relationships among conditions and operations that may occur when a firm decides to conduct some of its business on an international scale.

Even if you never have direct international business responsibilities, understanding some of the complexities may be useful to you. Companies' international operations and their governmental regulations affect overall national conditions—profits, employment security and wages, consumer prices, and national security. A better understanding of international business will help you make more informed operational and civic decisions, such as where you want to operate and what governmental policies you want to support.

The Forces Driving Globalization

Measuring globalization is problematic, especially for historical comparisons. First, a country's interdependence must be measured indirectly.[5] Second, when national boundaries shift, such as in the breakup of the former Soviet Union or the reunification of East and West Germany, domestic business transactions can become international transactions and vice versa. Nevertheless, various reliable indicators assure us that globalization has been increasing, at least since the mid-twentieth century. Currently, over 20 percent of world production is sold outside its country of origin, compared to about 7 percent in 1950. Restrictions on imports have generally been decreasing, and output from foreign-owned investments as a percentage of world production has increased. In almost every year since World War II, world trade has grown more rapidly than world production. However, in recessionary periods, global trade and investment contract even more than the global economy, such as a fall in world trade of 21 percent between April 2008 and May 2009.

At the same time, however, globalization is less pervasive than you might suppose. In much of the world (especially poor rural areas), people lack the resources to establish more than the barest connection with anyone beyond the outskirts of their isolated domains. Only a few countries—mainly very small ones—either sell over half their production abroad or depend on foreign output for more than half their consumption. This means that most of the world's goods and services are still sold in the countries in which they're produced. Moreover, the principal source of capital in most countries is domestic rather than international.

Granted, these measurements address only *economic* aspects of global interdependence. Various studies have relied on different indicators for comparison.[6] One of the most comprehensive is the A.T. Kearney/Foreign Policy Globalization Index, which shows not only that some countries are more globalized than others but also that a given country may be highly globalized on one dimension and not another. This index ranks countries across four dimensions:

- *Economic*—international trade and investment
- *Technological*—Internet connectivity
- *Personal contact*—international travel and tourism, international telephone traffic, and personal transfers of funds abroad
- *Political*—participation in international organizations and government monetary transfers

In recent years, the index has ranked Singapore and Hong Kong as the most globalized countries and India and Iran as the least. The U.S. ranking shows how globalization can differ by dimension: first on the technological scale but almost last on the economic.[7]

FACTORS IN INCREASED GLOBALIZATION

What factors have contributed to the growth of globalization in recent decades? Most analysts cite the following seven factors:

1. Increase in and application of technology
2. Liberalization of cross-border trade and resource movements
3. Development of services that support international business
4. Growing consumer pressures
5. Increased global competition
6. Changing political situations
7. Expanded cross-national cooperation

These factors are, of course, interrelated, and each deserves a closer look.

Increase in and Application of Technology   Many of the proverbial "modern marvels" and efficient means of production have come about from fairly recent advances in technology that have occurred in many different countries. Thus, much of what we trade today did not exist a decade or two ago and cannot easily be produced in our own countries. The increased demand due to rising productivity means, on average, people produce and can buy more by working the same number of hours. In addition, more than half the scientists who have ever lived are alive today. One reason, of course, is population growth. But another is economic growth, which frees up more people to *develop* new products because fewer people can *produce* them. As the base of our technology expands, new product development accelerates and we need more scientists and engineers to work on technical applications.

Further, much new technical innovation takes so much financial and intellectual resources that companies must cooperate to take on portions of development. These efforts may necessitate collaboration among firms in different countries that have financial resources and specialized capabilities. Once new products are developed, the optimum scale size of production seldom corresponds with the market demand in a single country. Consequently, companies must sell both domestically and internationally in order to spread the fixed developmental and production costs over more units of production.

Advances in Communications and Transportation   Strides in communications and transportation now permit us to learn about and want products and services developed in other parts of the world. Moreover, the costs of these improvements have risen more slowly in most years than costs in general. A three-minute phone call from New York to London that cost $10.80 in 1970 costs less than $0.20 today, while a call using Voice over Internet Protocal (VoIP) is virtually free.

Innovations in transportation mean that more countries can compete for sales to a given market. For example, the sale of foreign-grown flowers in the United States used to be impractical; today, however, flowers from as far away as Ecuador, Israel, the Netherlands, and New Zealand compete with each other for the U.S. market because growers can ship them quickly and economically.

Case Review Note

Or recall the opening case. Innovations allow individual athletes and teams to go head to head at venues around the world and sports media to broadcast competitions to fans everywhere. If it weren't for modern means of transportation, a tennis pro couldn't play in Morocco right after finishing a tournament in Miami. And if it weren't for modern means of advertising to fans around the globe, the prize money wouldn't be big enough to induce players to do all that traveling.

Improved communications and transportation not only speed up interactions, they also enhance a manager's ability to oversee foreign operations. Thanks to the Internet, even small companies can reach global customers and suppliers. Atlanta's Randy Allgaier, for example, has established a partnership in Taiwan that contracts a Chinese factory to manufacture lighting fixtures for him—all this without his need for costly on-site contact with people in either Taiwan or China.[8]

Liberalization of Cross-Border Trade and Resource Movements   To protect its own industries, every country restricts the movement across its borders of not only goods and services but also the resources—workers, capital, tools, and so on—needed to produce them. Such restrictions, of course, set limits on international business activities and, because regulations can change at any time, contribute to a climate of uncertainty. Over time, however, most governments have reduced such restrictions, primarily for three reasons:

1. Their citizens want a greater variety of goods and services at lower prices.
2. Competition spurs domestic producers to become more efficient.
3. They hope to induce other countries to lower their barriers in turn.

Development of Services That Support International Business   Companies and governments have developed a variety of services that facilitate international business. Take the sale of goods and services in a foreign country and currency. Today, because of bank credit agreements—clearing arrangements that convert one currency into another and insurance that covers such risks as nonpayment and damage en route—most producers can be paid relatively easily for goods and services sold abroad. What happens, for instance, when Nike sells sportswear to a French soccer team? As soon as the shipment arrives at French customs (probably from somewhere in Asia), a bank in Paris collects payment in euros from the soccer team and pays Nike in U.S. dollars through a U.S. bank.

Growing Consumer Pressures   Not only do consumers know more today about products and services available in other countries, but also many more can afford to buy products that were once considered luxuries. We want more, newer, better products, and we want them more finely differentiated. As usually occurs, such greater affluence is spread unevenly, both among and within countries as well as from year to year, but more and more companies are now responding to those markets where incomes and consumption are growing most rapidly, such as China.

Greater affluence has also spurred companies to spend more heavily on research and development (R&D) and to search worldwide—via the Internet, industry journals, trade fairs, and trips abroad—for innovations and products they can sell to ever-more-demanding consumers. By the same token, consumers are more proficient today at scouring the globe for better deals; such as U.S. consumers' Internet-searches for lower-priced prescription drugs abroad.

Greater Global Competition The present and potential pressures of increased foreign competition can persuade companies to buy or sell abroad. For example, a firm might introduce products into markets where competitors are already gaining sales, or seek supplies where competitors are getting cheaper or more attractive products or the means to produce them.

In recent years, many companies have merged or acquired firms to gain operating efficiencies that enable them to compete with or become global leaders, such as the merger between the Brazilian firms Perdigão and Sadia to create BRF-Brasil Foods, a major exporter of chilled and frozen foods.[9] So-called **born-global companies** start out with a global focus because of their founders' international experience[10] and because advances in communications give them a good idea of where global markets and supplies are. Many new companies locate in areas with numerous competitors and suppliers—a situation known as **clustering** or **agglomeration**—where they quickly learn of foreign opportunities and gain easier access to the resources needed for international moves.[11]

Regardless of industry, firms and individuals have to become more global; in today's competitive business environment, failure to do so can be catastrophic. (Figure 1.2 shows this humorously.) Once a few companies have responded to foreign opportunities, others inevitably follow suit. And they learn from each other's foreign experiences. As the opening case suggests, for example, the early success of foreign-born baseball players in U.S. leagues undoubtedly spurred American basketball and football organizations to begin looking for and developing talent abroad.[12]

CRN
Case Review Note

FIGURE 1.2 International Business as a Two-Edged Sword

Although global competition promotes efficiency, it obliges both companies and their employees to spend time and effort on a greater range of activities.

Source: © 1998 The New Yorker Collection, Roz Chast, from cartoonbank.com. All rights reserved.

Changing Political Situations   A major reason for growth in international business is the end of the schism between Communist countries and the rest of the world. For nearly half a century after World War II, business between the two camps was minimal. Today, only a few countries do business almost entirely within a political bloc.

Another political factor is the willingness of governments to support programs, such as improving airport and seaport facilities, that have fostered speed and cost efficiencies for delivering goods internationally. Governments now also provide an array of services to help domestic companies sell more abroad, such as collecting information about foreign markets, furnishing contacts with potential buyers, and offering insurance against nonpayment in the home-country currency.

Expanded Cross-National Cooperation   Increasingly, governments have come to realize that their own interests can be addressed through international cooperation by means of treaties, agreements, and consultation. The willingness to pursue such policies is due largely to these three needs:

1. To gain reciprocal advantages
2. To attack problems jointly that one country acting alone cannot solve
3. To deal with areas of concern that lie outside the territory of any nation

Gain Reciprocal Advantages   Essentially, companies don't want to be at a disadvantage when operating internationally, so they petition their governments to act on their behalf. Thus, governments join international organizations and sign treaties and agreements for a variety of commercial activities, such as transportation and trade.

Some treaties and agreements allow the countries' commercial ships and planes to use certain seaports and airports in exchange for reciprocal port use. Some cover commercial-aircraft safety standards and flyover rights; some protect property, such as foreign-owned investments, patents, trademarks, and copyrights. Countries also enact treaties for reciprocal reductions of import restrictions (remaining prepared, of course, to retaliate when another party interferes with trade flows by raising trade barriers or cutting diplomatic ties).

Multinational Problem Solving   Countries often act to coordinate activities along their mutual borders, building highways and railroads or hydroelectric dams that serve the interests of all parties. They also cooperate to solve problems that they either cannot or will not solve by themselves, for several reasons. First, the resources needed to solve the problem may be too great for one country to manage; sometimes no single country is willing to pay for a project that will also benefit another country, as witnessed by Japan and the United States sharing the costs of ballistic-missile defense technology. In any case, many problems are inherently global—think of, for example, global climate change or nuclear proliferation—and can't be easily addressed by a single country. That's why cooperative efforts have developed to fight the spread of diseases such as malaria, to set warning systems against such natural disasters as tsunamis, and to take actions affecting environmental problems such as global warming.

Second, one country's policies may affect those of others. Higher real-interest rates in one country, for example, can attract funds very quickly from individuals and firms in countries with lower rates, thus creating a shortage of investment funds in the latter. Similarly, companies may change suppliers in one country for those in another as costs change, thus contributing to unemployment in the country where they abandon suppliers. To coordinate economic policies in these and other areas, the most economically important countries meet regularly to share information and pool ideas.[13]

Areas Outside National Territories   Three global areas belong to no single country: the noncoastal areas of the oceans, outer space, and Antarctica. Until their commercial viability was demonstrated, they excited little interest for either exploitation or multinational cooperation. The oceans, however, contain food and mineral resources and constitute the surface over which much international commerce passes. Today, we need agreements to specify the amounts and methods of fishing to be allowed, to address questions of oceanic mineral rights (such as on oil resources below the Arctic Ocean), and to deal with piracy of ships.

Likewise, there is disagreement on the commercial benefits to be reaped from outer space. Commercial satellites, for example, pass over countries that receive no direct benefit from them but argue that they should. If that sounds a little far-fetched, remember that countries do charge foreign airlines for flying over their territories.[14]

Antarctica, with minerals and abundant sea life along its coast, attracts thousands of tourists each year, has a highway leading to the South Pole, and has thus been the subject of agreements to limit commercial exploitation. However, there is still disagreement about the continent's development—how much there should be and who does it.

Much of the cooperation we've described has been undertaken by international organizations, which we discuss in more detail in later chapters, especially in Chapter 8.

The Costs of Globalization

Although we've discussed seven interrelated reasons for the rise in international business and globalization, we should remember that the consequences of the rise remain controversial. To thwart the globalization process, *antiglobalization* forces regularly protest international conferences and governmental policies—sometimes violently. The adjacent photo shows such a protest. We focus here on three issues: *threats to national sovereignty, growth and environmental stress,* and *growing income inequality and personal stress.* We revisit these and others in more depth later; watch for them also in several of our Point-Counterpoint features.

◄ This is part of an antiglobalization protest in London, England in 2011.

Source: © photocritical/iStockphoto.com

THREATS TO NATIONAL SOVEREIGNTY

Critics of globalization claim
- Countries lose sovereignty.
- The resultant growth hurts the environment.
- Some people lose both relatively and absolutely.

You've probably heard the slogan "Think globally, act locally." In essence, it means that local interests should be accommodated before global ones. Some observers worry that the proliferation of international agreements, particularly those that undermine local restrictions on how goods are produced and sold, will diminish a nation's **sovereignty**—its freedom to "act locally" and without externally imposed restrictions.

The Question of Local Objectives and Policies   Countries seek to fulfill their citizens' economic, political, and social objectives by setting rules reflecting national priorities, such as those governing worker protection and environmental practices. However, some critics argue that individual countries' priorities are undermined by opening borders to trade. For example, if a country has stringent regulations on labor conditions and requires clean production methods, companies may produce where they can cut costs because of less rigorous rules. The result, if imports can enter freely, may be that the strict country must forgo its priorities or face the downside of fewer jobs and tax receipts.

The Question of Small Economies' Overdependence   In addition, critics say that small economies depend so much on larger ones for supplies and sales that they are vulnerable to foreign demands, including everything from defending certain positions at the United Nations to supporting a large economy's foreign military or economic actions. Nobel economist George Akerlof has noted that consequences of this dependence are intensified by poor countries' inadequate administrative capacity to deal with globalization.[15] These countries are also concerned that large international companies are powerful enough to dictate their operating terms (say, by threatening to relocate), exploit legal loopholes to avoid political oversight and taxes, and counter the small economies' best interests by favoring their home countries' political and economic interests.

The Question of Cultural Homogeneity   Finally, critics charge that globalization homogenizes products, companies, work methods, social structures, and even language, thus undermining the cultural foundation of sovereignty. In Chapter 2 we'll see that, as international differences diminish, countries find it harder to maintain the traditional ways of life that unify and differentiate their cultures. Recall in our opening case that despite countries' designation of national sports to maintain tradition, some are losing out to imported sports anyway. Fundamentally, many critics feel helpless when it comes to stopping the incursion of foreign influences by such means as satellite television, print media, and Internet sites.[16]

Case Review Note

ECONOMIC GROWTH AND ENVIRONMENTAL STRESS

Much criticism of globalization revolves around the economic growth it brings. According to one argument, growth consumes more nonrenewable natural resources and increases environmental damage—despoliation through toxic runoffs into rivers and oceans, air pollution from factory and vehicle emissions, and deforestation that can affect weather and climate.

The Argument for Global Growth and Global Cooperation   Not everyone agrees with such a conclusion. Others argue that globalization has positive results for both sustaining natural resources and maintaining an environmentally sound planet. Global cooperation, they say, fosters superior and uniform standards for combating environmental problems, while global competition encourages companies to seek resource-saving and eco-friendly technologies, such as automobiles that use less gas and emit fewer pollutants. However, unless the positive results of globalization are seen as outpacing the negative, sustaining economic growth will remain a problem in the future.

The pursuit of global interests may even conflict with what a country's citizens think is best for themselves. Consider, for instance, the effect of global pressure on Brazil to curtail logging activity in the Amazon region to help protect the world's climate. Unemployed Brazilian workers have felt that job creation in the logging industry is more important than climate protection outside Brazil.

GROWING INCOME INEQUALITY AND PERSONAL STRESS

In measuring economic well-being, we look not only at our absolute situations but also compare ourselves to others. We generally don't find our economic status satisfactory unless we're doing better *and* keeping up with others.

Income Inequality   By various measurements, income inequality has been growing both among and within a number of countries. Critics claim that globalization has affected this disparity by helping to develop a global superstar system, creating access to a greater supply of low-cost labor, and developing competition that leads to winners and losers.

The superstar system is especially apparent in sports, where global stars earn far more than the average professional player or professionals in sports with a more limited worldwide following. It also carries over to other professions, such as business, where charismatic top people can command many times what others can.

Although globalization has brought unprecedented opportunities for firms to profit by gaining more sales and cheaper or better supplies, critics argue that profits have gone disproportionately to the top executives rather than to the rank and file. Nobel economist Robert Solow supports this criticism by arguing that greater access to low-cost labor in poor countries has reduced the real wage growth of labor in rich countries.[17] And even if overall worldwide gains from globalization are positive, there are bound to be some losers in either an absolute or relative sense (who will probably become critics of globalization). The speed with which technology and competition expand globally affects the number of winners and losers along with the relative positions of individuals, companies, and countries. As an example, relocation of U.S. manufacturing jobs to China and India have helped the latter grow more rapidly than the United States, thus lessening the U.S.'s *relative* economic leadership over those countries.[18] Likewise, some displaced workers have lost economic and social standing relative to workers whose jobs were not moved. The challenge, therefore, is to maximize the gains from globalization while simultaneously minimizing the costs borne by the losers.

Personal Stress   Certain repercussions of globalization can't be measured in strictly economic terms. What about the stress imposed on the people whose relative economic and social status suffers, or those who fear the loss of their jobs?[19] There is some evidence that the growth in globalization goes hand in hand not only with increased insecurity about job and social status but also with costly social unrest.[20] Further, although few of the world's problems are brand new, we may worry about them more now because globalized communications bring exotic sagas of misery into living rooms everywhere.[21]

Point ▶   **Is Offshoring Good Strategy?**

Point   **Yes** **Offshoring** is the shifting of production to a foreign country. *If offshoring succeeds in reducing costs, it's good.* This is happening with many companies. Most branded clothing companies offshore to have work done by cheaper sewing machine operators. Many investment companies, such as Fidelity in India, are hiring back-office workers in poor countries to cut the cost of industry research. What good are cost savings? It's basic. If you can cut your costs, you can cut your prices or improve your product. For example, by offshoring work to India, Claimpower, a small U.S. medical-insurance billing company, cut costs, lowered the prices it charges doctors,

quadrupled its business in two years, and hired more U.S. employees because of the growth.[22]

What's the main complaint about offshoring? Too many domestic jobs end up abroad. As we discuss this, keep in mind that employment results from offshoring are difficult to isolate from other employment changes. Sure, unemployment in most high-income countries increased substantially in the 2008–2009 period, but this was probably due mainly to improvements in production technology and the global recession. However, I'll try to pinpoint direct results of offshoring.

IBM is a good example. Over 70 percent of its nearly 400,000 employees are based outside the United States.

By shipping some of its programming work abroad, IBM saves a tidy $40 an hour per worker—which comes out to $168 million a year.[23] Analysts agree that IBM's competitors in low-wage countries, such as Infosys from India, can underprice IBM with competitive products and services if IBM fails to offshore.[24] Moreover, when you become price-competitive, you sell more at home and in foreign countries by exporting to them. You may also increase sales abroad if you locate near foreign customers. As you *create* jobs in this process, you improve your chances of survival.[25] For instance, IBM is actually saving jobs by offshoring. Again, it's basic business: Cost savings generate growth, and growth creates more jobs.[26]

And not just any jobs: This process lets companies create more *high-value* jobs at home—the ones performed by people like managers and researchers, who draw high salaries. When that happens, demand for qualified people goes up. In the United States, that process has already resulted in a higher percentage of white-collar and professional employees in the workforce. These are *high-income* people, and more of them are employed as a result of sending *low-income* jobs to countries with lower labor costs.[27]

Further, offshoring is a natural extension of *outsourcing*, the process of companies contracting work to other companies so that they can concentrate on what they do best.[28]

This contributes to making a company more efficient. What is the difference, then, of outsourcing to a domestic versus a foreign company?

Admittedly, workers do get displaced from offshoring, but *aggregate* employment figures show that these workers find other jobs the same as do workers who get displaced for other reasons. In a dynamic economy, people are constantly shifting jobs. Doing so because of outsourcing is no different from doing so for any other reason, such as a company deciding to invest in some laborsaving technology. In any case, because there are bound to be upper limits on the amount of outsourcing work a country can do, the direst predictions about job loss are exaggerated: There simply aren't enough unemployed people abroad who have the needed skills *and* who will work at a sufficiently low cost.

Offshoring isn't for all companies or all types of operations. Some companies are bringing many operations *back* from abroad because of such factors as poor quality, consumer pressure, and concerns about competitive security. In fact, about a fifth of the companies that have gone to offshoring now say that the savings are less than they expected.[29] And that brings us back to what we said explicitly at the outset: Offshoring works when you cut operating costs *effectively.*

Is Offshoring Good Strategy?

Counterpoint

Counterpoint   **No** Some things are good for some of the people some of the time, and that's *almost* the case with offshoring, which unfortunately is good for only a *few* people but not for *most.* I keep hearing about the cost savings, but when I buy goods or services I rarely find anything that's cheaper than it used to be. Whether buying a Ralph Lauren shirt, getting medical services from a doctor who is saving money through Claimpower, or having Fidelity manage my assets, I have seen no lower prices for me. Further, Claimpower's growth had to be at the expense of other companies in the business, not because of growth in the number of people getting medical services because of price decreases.

I know of one study that took a close look at 17 high-income countries and found that, in aggregate, the percentage of national income going to labor has gone down while the percentage of national income going to profits has gone up.[30]

Here's one of the key problems: When you replace jobs by offshoring, you're exchanging *good* jobs for *bad* ones. Most of the workers who wind up with the short end of the offshoring stick struggled for decades to get reasonable work hours and a few basic benefits, such as healthcare and retirement plans. More important, their incomes al-

lowed them to send their kids to college, and the result was an upwardly mobile—and productive—generation.

Now many of these employees have worked long and loyally for their employers and what do they have to show for it in the offshoring era? Yes, I know that governments give them unemployment benefits but these never equal what the employees had before, and they run out.[31] On top of everything else, they may have no other usable skills, and at their ages, who's going to foot the bill for retraining them? The increase in what you call "high-value jobs" doesn't do *them* any good.

Offshoring may lead to short-term cost savings, but many studies indicate that it merely diverts companies' attention from taking steps to find innovative means of more efficient production, such as better operating techniques and machinery.[32] Concentrating on these latter alternatives may cut costs, increase production, and maintain the jobs that are going abroad.

While we're on the subject of job "value," what kinds of jobs *are* we creating in poor countries? Because countries are competing with lower wages, it encourages them to keep wages from rising, a sort of race to the bottom. However, MNEs no doubt pay workers in low-wage countries more than they could get otherwise, and I'll grant that some of these jobs—the white-collar and technical jobs—are pretty good. But for most people, the hours are long, the working conditions are barbaric, and the pay is barely enough to survive on. There is also little job security. As salaries creep up where companies are offshoring, the companies merely move to even cheaper places to get the job done. For instance, this is what happened to workers in the island country of Mauritius. As soon as Mauritians began to think they might expect a better way of life, MNEs found workers elsewhere to do their sewing.[33]

Admittedly, in a dynamic economy, people have to change jobs more often than they would in a stagnant economy—*but not to the extent caused by offshoring*. There's still some disagreement about the effects of off-shoring on a country's employment rate. Researchers are still looking into the issue, but what they're finding are that more of the so-called better jobs are also being outsourced. A study of 2,700 major U.S. and European organizations showed that 700,000 finance, IT, and other high level jobs were outsourced in 2009 and that another 250,000 per year will be outsourced through 2014.[34] Researchers are finding data like these: About 11 percent of U.S. jobs are at risk of being offshored—nearly 2 million of them in accounting-related fields alone.[35] So are we really creating higher-level jobs? Here's the bottom line: In countries like the United States, workers simply aren't equipped to handle the pace of change when it means that jobs can be exported faster than the average worker can retrain for different skills.

Why Companies Engage in International Business

Let's now focus on some of the specific ways firms can create value by going global. Take another look at Figure 1.1, where you'll see three major operating objectives that underlie the reasons for engaging in international business:

- Expanding sales
- Acquiring resources
- Reducing risk

Normally, these three objectives guide all decisions about whether, where, and how to engage in international business. Let's examine each of them in more detail.

EXPANDING SALES

A company's sales depend on the desire and ability of consumers to buy its goods or services. Obviously, there are more potential consumers in the world than found in any single country. Now, higher sales ordinarily create value, but only if the costs of making the additional sales don't increase disproportionately. Recall, for instance, the opening case. Televising sports competitions to multiple countries increases costs only marginally while generating advertising revenue in excess of these marginally increased costs. In fact, additional sales from abroad may enable a company to reduce its per-unit costs by covering its fixed costs—say, up-front research costs—over a larger number of sales. Because of lower unit costs, it can boost sales even more.

So increased sales are a major motive for expanding into international markets, and many of the world's largest companies—such as Volkswagen (Germany), Ericsson (Sweden), IBM (United States), Michelin (France), Nestlé (Switzerland), and Sony (Japan)—derive more than half their sales outside their home countries.[36] Bear in mind, however, that international business is not the purview only of large companies. In the United States, 41 percent of export value is by small and mid-sized firms (SMMs) from a combination of their direct exports plus their sales of components to large companies, which install them in finished products slated for sale abroad.[37]

CRN
Case Review Note

Pursuing international sales usually increases the potential market and potential profits.

ACQUIRING RESOURCES

Producers and distributors seek out products, services, resources, and components from foreign countries—sometimes because domestic supplies are inadequate (as with crude oil shipped to the United States). They're also looking for anything that will create a

Foreign sources may give companies

- Lower costs.
- New or better products.
- Additional operating knowledge.

competitive advantage. This may mean acquiring a resource that cuts costs, such as Rawlings' reliance on labor in Costa Rica—a country that hardly plays baseball—to produce baseballs.

Sometimes firms gain competitive advantage by improving product quality or differentiating their products from those of competitors; in both cases, they're potentially increasing market share and profits. Most automobile manufacturers, for example, hire design companies in northern Italy to help with styling. Many companies establish foreign R&D facilities to tap additional scientific resources.[38] Companies also learn while operating abroad. Avon, for instance, applies know-how from its Latin American marketing experience to help sell to the U.S. Hispanic market.[39]

REDUCING RISK

International operations may reduce operating risk by

- Smoothing sales and profits.
- Preventing competitors from gaining advantages.

Operating in countries with different business cycles can minimize swings in sales and profits. The key is the fact that sales decrease or grow more slowly in a country that's in a recession and increase or grow more rapidly in one that's expanding economically. During 2008, for example, General Motors' U.S. sales fell 21 percent, but this was partially offset by its sales growth of 30 percent in Russia, 10 percent in Brazil, and 9 percent in India.[40] Moreover, by obtaining supplies of products or components both domestically and internationally, companies may be able to soften the impact of price swings or shortages in any one country.

Finally, companies often go international for defensive reasons. Perhaps they want to counter competitors' advantages in foreign markets that might hurt them elsewhere. By operating in Japan, for instance, Procter & Gamble (P&G) delayed foreign expansion on the part of potential Japanese rivals by slowing their amassment of resources needed to expand into other international markets where P&G was active.

Similarly, British-based Natures Way Foods followed a customer, the grocery chain Tesco, into the U.S. market. This move expanded its sales and its relationship with Tesco. Moreover, it reduced the risk that Tesco would find an alternative supplier who might then threaten Natures Way's relationship with Tesco in the U.K. market.

Modes of Operations in International Business

When pursuing international business, an organization must decide on one of the suitable *modes of operations* included in Figure 1.1 In the following sections, we discuss each of these modes in some detail.

MERCHANDISE EXPORTS AND IMPORTS

Merchandise exports and imports are usually a country's most common international economic transactions.

Exporting and importing are the most popular modes of international business, especially among smaller companies. **Merchandise exports** are tangible products—goods—that are sent *out* of a country; **merchandise imports** are goods brought *into* a country. Because we can actually *see* these goods as they leave and enter the country, we sometimes call them *visible exports* and *imports*. The athletic shoes that an Indonesian plant sends to the United States are exports for Indonesia and imports for the United States. For most countries, the export and import of goods are the major sources of international revenues and expenditures.

SERVICE EXPORTS AND IMPORTS

The terms *export* and *import* often apply only to *merchandise*. For non-merchandise *international earnings*, we use the terms **service exports** and **service imports**. The provider and receiver of payment makes a *service export*; the recipient and payer makes a *service* *import.* Services constitute the fastest growth sector in international trade. Service exports and imports take many forms, and in this section we discuss the most important:

- Tourism and transportation
- Service performance
- Asset use

Tourism and Transportation   Let's say that the Williams sisters, Venus and Serena, take Air France from the United States to Paris to play in the French Open tennis tournament. Their tickets on Air France and travel expenses in France are service exports for France and service imports for the United States. Obviously, then, tourism and transportation are important sources of revenue for airlines, shipping companies, travel agencies, and hotels.

The economies of some countries depend heavily on revenue from these sectors. In Greece and Norway, for example, a significant amount of employment and foreign-exchange earnings comes from foreign cargo carried by Greek and Norwegian shipping lines. Tourism earnings are more important to the Bahamian economy than earnings from export of merchandise. (As we'll see in our closing case, year-round good weather enables Caribbean countries to benefit from passengers arriving on cruise ships.)

Service Performance   Some services, including banking, insurance, rental, engineering, and management services, net companies earnings in the form of *fees:* payments for the performance of those services. On an international level, for example, companies may pay fees for engineering services rendered as so-called **turnkey operations,** which are construction projects performed under contract and transferred to owners when they're operational. The U.S. company Bechtel currently has turnkey contracts in Peru and Saudi Arabia to build respectively a copper concentrator and aluminum smelter. Companies also pay fees for **management contracts**—arrangements in which one company provides personnel to perform general or specialized management functions for another. Disney receives such fees from managing theme parks in France and Japan.

Asset Use   When one company allows another to use its assets—such as trademarks, patents, copyrights, or expertise—under contracts known as **licensing agreements,** they receive earnings called *royalties.* For example, Adidas pays a royalty for the use of the Real Madrid football team's logo on jackets it sells. **Royalties** also come from franchise contracts. **Franchising** is a mode of business in which one party (the *franchisor*) allows another (the *franchisee*) to use a trademark as an essential asset of the franchisee's business. As a rule, the franchisor (say, McDonald's) also assists continuously in the operation of the franchisee's business, perhaps by providing supplies, management services, or technology.

INVESTMENTS

Dividends and interest paid on foreign investments are also considered service exports and imports because they represent the use of assets (capital). The investments themselves, however, are treated in national statistics as different forms of service exports and imports. Note that *foreign investment* means ownership of foreign property in exchange for a financial return, such as interest and dividends, and it may take two forms: *direct* and *portfolio.*

Direct Investment   In **foreign direct investment (FDI),** sometimes referred to simply as *direct investment,* the investor takes a controlling interest in a foreign company. When, for example, U.S. investors bought the Liverpool Football Club, the football club became a U.S. FDI in the United Kingdom. Control need not be a 100 percent or even a 50 percent interest; if a foreign investor holds a minority stake and the remaining ownership is widely dispersed, no other owner may effectively counter the investor's decisions. When two or more companies share ownership of an FDI, the operation is a **joint venture.**

Case Review Note

Case Review Note

Although the world's 100 largest international companies account for a high proportion of global output, the vast number of companies using FDI indicates that it's also common among smaller firms. Today, about 79,000 companies worldwide control about 790,000 FDIs in all industries.[41]

Portfolio Investment   A **portfolio investment** is a *noncontrolling* financial interest in another entity. It usually takes one of two forms: stock in a company or loans to a company (or country) in the form of bonds, bills, or notes purchased by the investor. They're important for most companies with extensive international operations, which routinely move funds from country to country for short-term financial gain.

TYPES OF INTERNATIONAL ORGANIZATIONS

Basically, an "international company" is any company that operates internationally, but we have a variety of terms to designate different types of operations. Highly committed international companies usually draw on multiple operating types. Companies work together—in *joint ventures, licensing agreements, management contracts, minority ownership,* and *long-term contractual arrangements*—all of which are known as **collaborative arrangements.** The term **strategic alliance** is sometimes used to mean the same, but it usually refers either to an agreement that is of critical importance to one or more partners or to an agreement that does not involve joint ownership.

Multinational Enterprise   A **multinational enterprise (MNE)** usually refers to any company with foreign direct investments. This is the definition we use in this text. However, some writers reason that a company must have direct investments in some minimum number of countries to be an MNE. The term **multinational corporation or multinational company (MNC)** is often used as a synonym for MNE, while the United Nations uses the term **transnational company (TNC).**

Does Size Matter?   Some definitions require a certain size—usually giant. A small company, however, can have foreign direct investments and adopt any of the operating modes we've discussed. Of course, a small international company, if successful, becomes a large company. Vistaprint is a good example. Founded in 1995, its sales in 120 countries for 2010 were U. S. $670 million, of which 45 percent came from outside its U.S. domestic market.

Why International Business Differs from Domestic Business

Let's now turn to the conditions in a company's *external environment* that may affect its international operations. Smart companies don't form or develop the means to implement international strategies without examining these conditions indicated in the left-hand side of Figure 1.1 and organized into the following categories:

• *Physical factors* (such as a country's geography or demography)
• *Social factors* (such as its politics, law, culture, and economy)
• *Competitive factors* (such as the number and strength of a company's suppliers, customers, and rival firms)

In examining these categories, we delve into the realm of the *social sciences*, which helps in explaining how external conditions affect patterns of behavior in different parts of the world.

PHYSICAL AND SOCIAL FACTORS

The physical and social factors we show above can affect how companies produce and market products, staff operations, and even maintain accounts. Remember that any of these factors may require a company to alter its operation abroad (compared to domestically) for the sake of efficiency.

Geographic Influences Managers who are knowledgeable about geography are in a position to determine the location, quantity, quality, and availability of the world's resources, as well as ways to exploit them. The uneven distribution of resources throughout the world helps explain why different products and services are produced in different places. Further, countries differ in size of landmass and population. Because smaller countries have less access to varied domestic resources and large markets, they are usually more dependent on international trade than larger countries are.

Again, take sports. Norway fares better in the Winter Olympics than in the Summer Olympics because of its climate, and except for the well-publicized Jamaican bobsled team (whose members actually lived in Canada), tropical countries don't even compete in the Winter Olympics. East Africans' domination in distance races is due in part to their ability to train at higher altitudes than most other runners.

Geographic barriers—mountains, deserts, jungles, and so forth—often affect communications and distribution channels. And the chance of natural disasters and adverse climatic conditions (hurricanes, floods, droughts, earthquakes, volcanic eruptions, tsunamis) can make business riskier in some areas than in others, while affecting supplies, prices, and operating conditions in far-off countries, such as the one illustrated in the photos on page 20. Again, we can look ahead to our ending case, which shows that cruise-line operators must adjust their ports-of-call when hurricanes threaten. Keep in mind also that climatic conditions may have short- or long-term cycles. For instance, recent melting of Arctic ice floes along with new ship technologies have allowed more ships to use a Northwest Passage to cut transport costs by saving as much as 15 days at sea.[42]

Finally, population distribution and the impact of human activity on the environment may exert strong future influences on international business, particularly if ecological changes or regulations cause companies to move or alter operations.

Political Policies Not surprisingly, a nation's political policies influence how international business takes place within its borders (indeed, *whether* it will take place). For instance, Cuba once had a minor-league baseball franchise, which went the way of diplomatic relations between Cuba and the United States back in the 1960s. Several Cuban baseball players are now members of professional U.S. teams, although most of them had to defect from Cuba to play abroad.

Obviously, political disputes—particularly military confrontations—can disrupt trade and investment. Even conflicts that directly affect only small areas can have far-reaching effects. The terrorist bombing of a hotel in Indonesia resulted in a decrease in tourism revenue and investment capital because individuals and businesses abroad perceived Indonesia as too risky.

Legal Policies Domestic and international laws play a big role in determining how a company can operate overseas. *Domestic law* includes both home- and host-country regulations on such matters as taxation, employment, and foreign-exchange transactions. British law, for example, determines how the U.S.-investor owned Liverpool Football Club is taxed and which nationalities of people it employs. Meanwhile, U.S. law determines how and when the earnings from the operation are taxed in the United States.

International law—in the form of legal agreements between countries—determines how earnings are taxed by *all* jurisdictions. International law may also determine how

Natural conditions affect where different goods and services can be produced.

Case Review Note

Politics often determines where and how international business can take place.

Each country has its own laws regulating business. Agreements among countries set international law.

Source: © Jon Helgason/iStockphoto.com

Source: Fedor Selivanov/Shutterstock.com

A 2010 volcanic eruption in Iceland (above) affected business over a wide area, such as closing the airport in Zurich, Switzerland (below).

Case Review Note

(and whether) companies can operate in certain places. As we point out in our closing case, for example, agreements permit ships' crews to move about virtually anywhere without harassment.

Finally, the ways in which laws are *enforced* also affect a firm's foreign operations. In the realm of trademarks, patented knowledge, and copyrights, most countries have joined in international treaties and enacted domestic laws dealing with violations. Many, however, do very little to enforce either the agreements or their own laws. This is why companies not only must understand agreements and laws but must also determine how fastidiously they're enforced in different countries.

The interpersonal norms of a country may necessitate a company's alteration of operations.

Behavioral Factors   The related disciplines of anthropology, psychology, and sociology can help managers better understand different values, attitudes, and beliefs. In turn, such understanding can help managers make operational decisions abroad.

Let's return once again to the opening case. Although professional sports are spreading internationally, the popularity of specific sports differs among countries. Interestingly, these differences affect the way the U.S. film industry treats sports as subject matter. As a rule, U.S. producers spare no expense to ensure that movies generate the greatest possible international appeal (and revenue). When it comes to sports-themed movies, however, they typically cut costs. Why? Because people in one country are usually lukewarm about other countries' sports, and moviemakers see little point in spending extra money trying to attract foreign audiences and revenues with these films.[43]

We should also point out that sports rules sometimes differ among countries. The Japanese *do* care about U.S. baseball, but Japanese culture values harmony more than U.S. culture does, whereas U.S. culture values competitiveness more than the Japanese do. This is reflected in different baseball rules: A game in the United States continues until there is a winner, while Japanese are content with a tie if neither team is ahead after 12 innings.

Economic Forces Economics explains why countries exchange goods and services, why capital and people travel among countries in the course of business, and why one country's currency has a certain value compared to another's. Recall from our opening case that the percentage of non-U.S.-born players on major-league rosters has been increasing. Players from the Dominican Republic form the largest share of non-U.S.-born players, but even though baseball is quite popular in the Dominican Republic, the idea of putting a major-league baseball team there simply isn't feasible. Why? Because too few Dominicans can afford the ticket prices necessary to support a team. Obviously, higher incomes in the United States and Canada enable major league teams to offer higher salaries that attract Dominican players.

Economics also helps explain why some countries can produce goods or services for less. And economics provides the analytical tools to determine the impact of an international company's operations on the economies of both host and home countries, as well as the impact of the host country's economic environment on a foreign firm.

> Economics explains country differences in costs, currency values, and market size.

THE COMPETITIVE ENVIRONMENT

In addition to its physical and social environments, every globally active company operates within a competitive environment. Figure 1.1 highlights the key competitive factors in the external environment of an international business: product strategy, resource base and experience, and competitor capability.

Competitive Strategy for Products Products compete by means of *cost* or *differentiation strategies*, the latter usually by:

- Developing a favorable *brand image,* usually through advertising or from long-term consumer experience with the brand; or

- Developing *unique characteristics,* such as through R&D efforts or different means of distribution.

Using either approach, a firm may mass-market a product or sell to a niche market (the latter approach is called a *focus strategy*). Different strategies can be used for different products or for different countries, but a firm's choice of strategy plays a big part in determining how and where it will operate. Take Fiat, an Italian automobile brand that competes mostly with a cost strategy aimed at mass-market sales. This strategy has influenced Fiat to locate engine plants in China, where production costs are low, and to sell in India and Argentina, which are cost-sensitive markets. Interestingly, Fiat also owns Ferrari, which competes with a focus strategy toward very high-income consumers. Whereas the competitive U.S. market has not been conducive to a mass-market Fiat brand strategy, Fiat sells over a quarter of all its Ferraris in the United States. With Fiat's

> A company's situation may differ among countries by
> - Its competitive ranking.
> - The competitors it faces.

investment in Chrysler, it plans to also sell the Fiat 500 (a sort of boutique car) with a focus strategy.

Company Resources and Experience   Other competitive factors are a company's size and resources compared to those of its competitors. A market leader, for example—say, Coca-Cola—has resources for much more ambitious international operations than a smaller competitor like Royal Crown. Royal Crown sells in about 60 countries, Coca-Cola in more than 200.

In large markets (such as the United States), companies have to invest many more resources to secure national distribution than in small markets (such as Ireland). Further, they'll probably face more competitors in large markets; in a European country, especially in retailing, a firm is likely to face three or four significant competitors, compared to the 10 to 20 it will face in the United States.[44]

Conversely, national market share and brand recognition have a bearing on operating in a given country. A company with a long-standing dominant market position uses operating tactics quite different from those employed by a newcomer. Such a company, for example, has much more clout with suppliers and distributors. Remember, too, that being a leader in one country doesn't guarantee being a leader anywhere else. In most markets, Coca-Cola is the leader, with Pepsi-Cola coming in a strong second; in India, however, Coke is number three, trailing both Pepsi and a locally owned brand called *Thums Up*.[45]

Competitors Faced in Each Market   Finally, success in a market (whether domestic or foreign) often depends on whether the competition is also international or local. Commercial aircraft makers Boeing and Airbus, for example, compete almost only with each other in every market they serve. What they learn about each other in one country is useful in predicting the other's strategies elsewhere. In contrast, the British grocery chain Tesco faces different competition in almost every foreign market it enters.

Looking to the Future   Three Ways of Looking at Globalization

At this juncture, there's a big difference of opinion on the future of international business and globalization. Basically, there are three major viewpoints:

- Further globalization is inevitable.
- International business will grow primarily along regional rather than global lines.
- Forces working against further globalization and international business will slow down the growth of both.

Globalization Is Inevitable

The view that globalization is inevitable reflects the premise that advances in human connectivity are so pervasive that consumers everywhere will know about and demand the best products for the best prices regardless of their origins. Those who hold this view also argue that because MNEs have built so many international production and distribution networks, they'll pressure their governments to place fewer restrictions on international movements of goods and means to produce them.

Even if we accept this view, we must still meet at least one challenge to riding the wave of the future: Because the future is what we make of it, we must figure out how to spread the benefits of globalization equitably while minimizing the hardships placed on those parties—both people and companies—who suffer from increased international competition.

The *Wall Street Journal* posed a question to all living Nobel Prize winners in economics: "What is the greatest economic challenge for the future?" Several responses addressed globalization and international business. Robert Fogel said it's the problem of getting available technology and food to people who are needlessly dying. Both Vernon Smith and Harry Markowitz specified the need to bring down global trade barriers. Lawrence Klein called for "the reduction of poverty and disease in a peaceful political environment." John Nash felt we must address the problem of increasing the worldwide standard of living while the amount of the earth's surface per person is shrinking.[46] Clearly, each of these responses projects both managerial challenges and opportunities.

More Regional Than Global Growth

The second view—that growth will be largely regional rather than global—is based on studies showing that almost all of the companies we think of as "global" conduct most of their business in home and neighboring countries.[47] Most world trade is regional, and many treaties to remove trade barriers are regional. Transport costs favor regional over global business. And regional sales may be sufficient for companies to gain scale economies to cover their fixed costs adequately. Nevertheless, regionalization of business activity may be merely a transition stage. In other words, companies may first promote international business in nearby countries and then expand their activities once they've reached certain regional goals.

Globalization and International Business Will Slow

The third view argues that the pace of globalization will slow down, or may already have begun collapsing.[48] In light of the antiglobalization sentiments mentioned earlier, it's easy to see that some people are adamant and earnest in voicing their reservations. The crux of the antiglobalization movement is the perceived growing schism between parties (including MNEs) who are thriving in a globalized environment and those who aren't. For example, during 2009, hungry (undernourished) people increased by about 100 million from 2008 and reached about 20 percent of the world's population.[49]

Antiglobalists pressure governments to promote nationalism by raising trade barriers and rejecting international organizations and treaties. Historically, such groups have often succeeded (at least temporarily) in obstructing either technological or commercial advances that threatened their well-being. Recently, antiglobalization sentiments have grown in many countries, such as a state law change in Arizona to restrict undocumented aliens, the deportation by France of ethnic Roma (gypsies), the evacuation in Italy of immigrants to protect them against local residents, and gains by Sweden's anti-immigration Democrat's Party.[50] In Brazil and South Africa, voters have authorized domestic companies to copy pharmaceuticals under global patent protection. Bolivia and Venezuela have nationalized some foreign investments, and the United States prevented China from purchasing a U.S. oil company. The sparring between pro- and anti-globalists is one of the reasons why the globalization process has progressed in fits and starts.

Other uncertainties may hamper globalization. First is the question of oil prices, which affect international transportation because they can constitute more than 75 percent of operating costs on large ships.[51] In early 2008 global oil prices rose 44 percent, fell 74 percent by the end of the year, and then more than doubled by the end of 2010. Many U.S. companies, such as furniture manufacturers, have responded by returning to domestic production bases rather than facing transport cost uncertainty.[52] Second, the economic recession and lingering unemployment since 2008 have led countries to enact measures to protect their work forces. Third, safety concerns—property confiscation, terrorism, piracy of ships, and outright lawlessness—may inhibit companies from venturing as much abroad.

Finally, one view holds that for globalization to succeed, efficient institutions with clear-cut mandates are necessary; however, there is concern that neither the institutions nor the people working in them can adequately handle the complexities of an interconnected world.[53]

Going Forward

Only time will tell, but one thing seems certain: If a company wants to capitalize on international opportunities, it can't wait too long to see what happens on political and economic fronts. Investments in research, equipment, plants, and personnel training can take years to pan out. Forecasting foreign opportunities and risks is always challenging. Yet, by examining different ways in which the future may evolve, a company's management has a better chance of avoiding unpleasant surprises. That's why each chapter of this book includes a feature that shows how certain chapter topics can become subjects for looking into the future of international business. ■

 **CASE** Riding the Tide of Growth: Carnival Cruise Lines

I must go down to the seas again, for the call of the running tide
Is a wild call and a clear call that may not be denied

—*John Masefield,* The Seekers

The call of the sea spurs the cruise business.[54] Sea voyages have had an aura of mystique for centuries, but only in recent decades has the experience of the open sea and exotic ports of call been available to a mass market.

Historically, the recreational sea voyage was an essentially elitist endeavor. Certainly, members of the lower classes occasionally found themselves on the open sea, but usually as displaced job seekers or crew members aboard ships. In recent years, however, the cruise industry has undergone a sea of change of sorts, and the demographic groups it now targets include the working middle class as well as the idle rich.

What's a Cruise, and What Happened to the Cruise Industry?

A "cruise" is a sea voyage taken for pleasure (as opposed to, say, passage on a whaling ship, an assignment in the navy, or a ferry ride to get you from point A to point B). Typically, passengers enjoy cabin accommodations for the duration of a fixed itinerary that brings them back to their original point of embarkation.

There was a time when ships (called *passenger liners*) transported people across oceans and seas for business or pleasure, but the advent of transoceanic air service after World War II offered a speedier and less expensive alternative, and airlines captured passengers from ocean liners. The competitive balance tipped decisively in the 1960s, when advances in jet technology made air travel a viable option for a growing mass market of budget-minded international travelers. Converting more shipboard space to low-priced accommodations, shipping lines countered with the reminder that "getting there is half the fun," but one by one, they retired the great luxury liners that had plied the seas for decades.

The Contemporary Cruise Industry

Today, the cruise industry is dominated by three companies—Carnival, Royal Caribbean, and Star—which command a combined 91 percent of the market. By far, the largest of the three is Carnival, which operates a number of lines that it calls *brands*. Map 1.2 shows the headquarters of these brands. Carnival offers cruises to every continent on the globe, including Antarctica.

Carnival Corporation was born when Ted Arison, a former partner in Norwegian Cruise Lines, saw an opportunity to expand mass-market sea travel by promoting the idea of the "Fun Ship" vacation—an excursion designed to be a little less formal and luxurious than the traditional ocean liner. The timing was right. Sea travel still projected a certain aura, and more people could afford an ocean-borne vacation. Further, a lot of these vacationers gravitated to holidays—group tours, theme-park visits, and sojourns in Las Vegas—that were compatible with the Fun Ship concept. Arison bought a retired liner at a good price, refurbished it in bright colors, rigged it with bright lights, and installed discos and casinos. On its maiden voyage from Miami in 1972, the *Mardi Gras* ran aground with 300 journalists on board, but, fortunately, neither the ship nor Arison's business concept was severely damaged. Embarking from Miami to such destinations as Jamaica, Puerto Rico, and the U.S. Virgin Islands, the *Mardi Gras* soon became successful.

Over time, Arison added not only ships but also whole cruise lines to his fleet. Today, each brand operates primarily in a designated area of the world and is differentiated from other Carnival brands in terms of geographically pertinent themes (based in Italy, for instance, Costa boasts a Mediterranean flavor) and in terms of cost per cruise (the cost per night on Cunard and Seabourne cruises is much higher than that on Carnival cruises).

MAP 1.2   Where Carnival's Cruise Lines (Brands) Are Headquartered

Countries designated on the map denote headquarters locations of each company/brand (e.g., four lines operate out of North America and three out of the United Kingdom). Carnival has the most recognized brands in North America, the United Kingdom, Germany, France, Italy, and Spain—areas that account for 85 percent of the world's cruise-line passengers.

Source: Data come from Carnival Corporation/Corporate Information/Our Brands at http://phx.corporate-ir.net/phoenix.zhtml?c=200767&p=irol-products (accessed June 25, 2009)

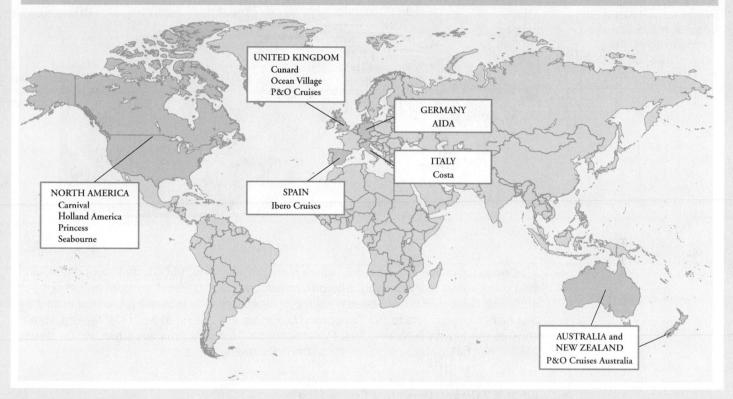

Doing Business in International Waters

Given the nature of its business, the whole cruise-line industry is international in scope. Take the nationality of competitors. Companies can obtain so-called *flags of convenience* from about 30 different countries. By registering as, say, a Liberian legal entity, a company can take advantage of lower taxes and less stringent employment rules. Legally, Carnival is a Panamanian company, even though it's listed on the New York Stock Exchange, has operating headquarters in Miami and London, and caters mainly to passengers who set sail from the United States. Although cruise-line revenue is subject to neither Panamanian nor U.S. income taxes, Carnival does have to pay substantial "port fees" wherever its ships drop anchor. In fact, ports compete for cruise stopovers because of fees and tourist expenditures. For instance, Port Everglades (Fort Lauderdale) agreed in 2010 to spend U.S. $34 million to improve terminals in order to divert embarkation from the port of Miami, and estimates are that it will generate U.S. $500 million over a 10-year period. The photo shows cruise ships docked in Cozumel, Mexico, a popular stop in the Caribbean.

Only a few cruise-line offerings—such as excursions along the Mississippi River, around the Hawaiian Islands, or among the Galapagos Islands—can be characterized as purely domestic. Even trips from the U.S. West Coast to Alaska are "international" because they stop in Canada. By far the most popular destination for cruise passengers is the Caribbean/Bahamas, largely because the area boasts balmy weather year round. During summer months, Carnival shifts some of its ships from Caribbean/Bahamas to Alaskan and Mediterranean routes.

Ports compete for cruise line arrivals, largely because they bring thousands of tourists to spend in local shops. Here we see passengers disembarking from two cruise ships in Cozumel, Mexico, a popular Caribbean port of call.

Source: Jim Lopes/Shutterstock.com

Obviously, cruise ships go only where there are seaports, but Carnival cooperates with (and owns some) tour operators who provide almost 2,000 different onshore excursions (for additional fees), which have been a source of recent revenue increases. Carnival estimates that half its passengers to the Caribbean take shore excursions to such sightseeing attractions as the Mayan ruins in Belize. Passengers on Carnival's Princess Lines, which serves Alaska, can helicopter to a glacier for a little dogsledding.

What It Takes to Operate a Cruise Line

Ship Shopping

Not surprisingly, ships constitute the biggest investment for cruise lines. Shipyards in several countries are capable of building ships that meet cruise-industry needs. To add to its global fleet, Carnival secures bids from all over the world. Because shipbuilding employs so many people and uses so much locally produced steel, governments often subsidize the industry—a practice that works to the benefit of the cruise-line industry by offering less expensive prices for ships. For instance, the Italian government awarded the shipyard Fincantieri about $50 million in subsidies to build five ships sold to Carnival for $2.5 billion. In 2010, Carnival ordered another ship from Fincantieri for about $820 million, negotiating for payment in U.S. dollars rather than euros to protect itself from rises in the value of euros.

Where to Find Able-Bodied Seamen

Shipping companies—including cargo and cruise lines—scour the world for crew members who not only can perform specialized tasks but who are properly certified (by international agreement, a registered crew member can enter virtually any port in the world). Cruise lines, of course, have special staffing needs—notably, crew who can interact with passengers. About a third of all the world's ship crews are from the Philippines, not only because of reasonable labor costs but because Filipinos are generally fluent in English. On a typical Carnival ship, crew members hail from over 100 countries, and Carnival maintains a range of employee-training programs, including instruction in English as a foreign language.

Casinos and Other Amenities

Although Carnival has thrived with the concept of informal cruises for a mass market, each of its cruises offers one or two formal nights per week; theme-based dinners centering on national cuisines; a variety of musical entertainment, games, and contests; and spas and athletic facilities. Because cruises operate outside the jurisdiction of any national authority, they're not subject to any national laws restricting gambling. Casinos, therefore, are on-board fixtures.

Passengers can also shop for merchandise from all over the world. Indeed, art dealers occasionally hold shipboard auctions and seminars, and one dealer sells about 300,000 pieces of art per year on cruise ships. As you might expect, the pricier the cruise, the pricier the average objet d'art.

The Overseas Environment

Because Carnival operates around the world, it has the advantage of treating the whole world as a source of both customers and supplies. In addition, because its chief assets are ocean-borne, Carnival can ship capital and other assets to places where they can best serve the company's needs. However, it's also vulnerable to a wide range of environmental disturbances. Let's take a look at a few of these.

Safety Issues

After terrorists seized a cruise ship in the Mediterranean in 1985, the major cruise lines instituted a policy of strict security checks for boarding passengers. Even before 9/11, then, the cruise-line industry has had in place a security protocol that the airline industry didn't establish until afterward.

In the wake of 9/11, when cancellations started to exceed bookings, Carnival increased the number of U.S. ports from which its ships embarked so that passengers with a heightened fear of flying could reach points of departure by land. Carnival also redeploys cruises to avoid areas in which passengers might face danger from political upheaval or crime, such as suspending cruises to St. Croix in the U.S. Virgin Islands because of its high crime rate. Further, Carnival does not stop in Cuba, a popular tourist destination, because the U.S. government limits travel there by U.S. citizens.

Fortunately, shipboard emergencies are infrequent, but when they do occur, they are problematic. For example, in 2010 a Carnival cruise ship became disabled on a voyage to Mexico. This caused a three-day delay in returning 4500 passengers to San Diego. During this time, lighting went out, toilets backed up, and food became limited.

Sporadically, cruise ships are stricken with a virus that causes diarrhea and vomiting. These outbreaks are hard to control because of the close contact among people on board a ship. More than once, Carnival has had to take an infected ship out of service to eradicate all traces of the virus; the process involves sanitizing virtually every object on board. When the H1N1 flu (swine flu) hit Mexico in 2009, Carnival modified itineraries temporarily to avoid Mexican ports.

Economic Issues

Buying a cruise is generally considered discretionary rather than priority spending. During recessions, people are more apt to take shorter cruises and to embark from nearby ports rather than flying to faraway points of departure. Interestingly, however, in comparison with other segments of the tourist industry, cruise lines have fared well during economic downturns. Why? This is due in part to their all-inclusive per diem prices that are often bargains when compared with the cost of travel to major cities and popular resorts. In addition, fixed cruise-line prices spare passengers the added risk of encountering unforeseen unfavorable exchange rates. Nevertheless, in 2009, Carnival began offering discounts because of the global recession, which attracted more passengers but lower profits per passenger.

But there is some concern in the industry over uncertain gasoline prices and mortgage interest rates, which might leave more households with too little discretionary income for taking cruises. In addition, oil price increases have upped Carnival's fuel costs at a time when many potential passengers want lower prices.

The Weather

Whenever there are hurricanes, Carnival may have to cancel trips, switch embarkation points, or change destinations, such as for Hurricane Earl in 2010. Typically, passengers on canceled trips receive full refunds and those on shortened cruises partial refunds.

Concluding Remarks

Overall, the outlook for Carnival and the cruise-line industry is sunny. With prospects for growing incomes (despite a global recession) in many countries (such as China), more people will have discretionary income to spend on tourism. There are still relatively untapped cruise destinations, such as Indonesia, which Carnival plans to exploit. Only 16 percent of the U.S. population has yet to take a cruise—a potential two-edged sword. On the one hand, this number indicates growth potential. On the other hand, people who have taken a cruise continue to be repeat customers, and the percentage of first-time customers is in fact declining. On the downside, then, industry observers worry that experienced cruisers will tire of visiting one port that's pretty much like another and that noncruisers will still prefer such destinations as resorts to ports of call.

QUESTIONS

1. What global forces have contributed to the growth of the cruise-line industry?
2. What specific steps has Carnival Cruise Lines taken to benefit from global social changes?
3. What are some of the national differences that affect the operations of cruise lines?
4. Although most cruise-line passengers are from the United States, the average number of annual vacation days taken by U.S. residents is lower than that of workers in most other high-income countries (13 days, compared with 42 in Italy, 37 in France, 35 in Germany, and 25 in Japan). How might cruise lines increase sales to people outside the United States?
5. What threats exist to the future performance of the cruise-line industry and, specifically, of Carnival Cruise Lines? If you were in charge of Carnival, how would you (a) try to prevent these threats from becoming reality and (b) deal with them if they were realized?
6. Discuss the ethics of cruise lines regarding the avoidance of income taxes while buying ships built with governmental subsidies.

MyIBLab   Now that you have finished this chapter, go back to www.myiblab.com to continue practicing and applying the concepts you've learned.

SUMMARY

- Globalization is the ongoing process that deepens and broadens the interdependence among countries. International business is a mechanism to bring about globalization.

- International business has been growing rapidly in recent decades because of technological expansion, the liberalization of government policies on cross-border movements (goods, services, and the resources to produce them), the development of services to facilitate international transactions, consumer pressures to buy foreign products and services, increased global competition, changing political situations, and cooperation in dealing with transnational problems and issues. Because of these factors, foreign countries increasingly are a source of both production and sales for companies.

- Globalization has many critics who feel that it weakens national sovereignty, promotes growth that is detrimental to the earth's environment, and skews income distributions.

- Offshoring—the transferring of production abroad—is controversial in terms of who benefits when costs are reduced and whether the process exchanges good jobs for bad ones.

- Companies engage in international business to expand sales, to acquire resources, and to diversify or reduce their risks.

- A company can engage in international business through various operating modes, including exporting and importing merchandise and services, direct and portfolio investments, and collaborative arrangements with other companies.

- Multinational enterprises (MNEs) are companies with foreign direct investments. Sometimes they are referred to as multinational corporations or companies (MNCs) or transnational companies (TNCs).

- When operating abroad, companies may have to adjust their usual methods of carrying out business. This is because foreign conditions often dictate a more suitable method, and the operating modes used for international business differ somewhat from those used on a domestic level.

- To operate within a company's external environment, its managers not only must understand business operations but must also have a working knowledge of the basic social sciences: geography, political science, law, anthropology, sociology, psychology, and economics.

- A company's competitive strategy influences how and where it can best operate. Likewise, from one country to another, its competitive situation may differ in terms of its relative strength and which competitors it faces.

- There is disagreement about the future of international business—that globalization is inevitable, that it will be primarily regional, and that the growth will slow.

KEY TERMS

agglomeration (p. 9)
born-global company (p. 9)
clustering (p. 9)
collaborative arrangement (p. 18)
foreign direct investment (FDI) (p. 17)
franchising (p. 17)
globalization (p. 5)
international business (p. 5)
joint venture (p. 17)

licensing agreement (p. 17)
management contract (p. 17)
merchandise export (p. 16)
merchandise import (p. 16)
multinational corporation
  or company (MNC) (p. 18)
multinational enterprise
  (MNE) (p. 18)
offshoring (p. 13)

portfolio investment (p. 18)
royalty (p. 17)
service export (p. 16)
service import (p. 16)
sovereignty (p. 12)
strategic alliance (p. 18)
transnational company
  (TNC) (p. 18)
turnkey operation (p. 17)

ENDNOTES

1 *Sources include the following:* Andrew Zimbalist, "Is It Worth It?" *Finance & Development* 47:1 (March 2010): 6–11; Harald Dolles and Sten Söderman (eds.), *Sport as a Business: International Professional and Commercial Aspects* (Houndsmills, UK: Palgrave Macmillan, 2011); Mark Mulligan, "Football, Funding and MBAs," *Financial Times* (December 13, 2010): 11; Roger Blitz, "Sports Organisers Play High Stakes Games," *Financial Times* (September 29, 2010): 7; Jeremy Kahn, "N.B.A. in India, In Search of Fans and Players," *New York Times* (December 28, 2010): B13; George Vecsey, "When the Game Absorbs the Globe," *New York Times* (April 1, 2007): A+; "Percentage of Foreign-Born," *Dominican Today* (April 1, 2008), www.dominicantoday.com/dr/sports/2008/4/1; Simon Kuper, "Lost in Translation," *Financial Times* (February 2–3, 2008): p. life & arts 2; "Percentage of Foreign-Born Major League Baseball Players Drops," Dominican Today.com/dr/sports/2008/4/1 (accessed March 3, 2009); C3; Matthew Graham, "Nike Overtakes Adidas in Football Field," *Financial Times* (August 19, 2004): 19; L. Jon Wertheim, "The Whole World Is Watching," *Sports Illustrated* (June 14, 2004): 73–86; Wertheim Jon, "Hot Prospects in Cold Places," *Sports Illustrated* (June 21, 2004): 63–66; Grant Wahl, "Football vs. Fútbol," *Sports Illustrated* (July 5, 2004): 69–72; Wahl, "On Safari for 7-Footers," *Sports Illustrated* (June 28, 2004): 70–73; André Richelieu, "Building the Brand Equity of Professional Sports Teams," Paper presented at the annual meeting of the Academy of International Business, Stockholm, Sweden (July 10–13, 2004); Brian K. White,

"Seattle Mariners Justify Losing Streak as 'Cunning,'" GlossyNews .com (July 15, 2004) (accessed November 6, 2004).

2 For a good discussion of the versatility of the term *globalization*, see Joyce S. Osland, "Broadening the Debate: The Pros and Cons of Globalization," *Journal of Management Inquiry* 10:2 (June 2003): 137–54.

3 Andrew Batson, "Not Really 'Made in China,'" *Wall Street Journal* (December 16, 2010): B1–B2.

4 Daniel Henninger, "Capitalism saved the Miners," *Wall Street Journal* (October 14, 2010): A19.

5 Günther G. Schulze and Heinrich W. Ursprung, "Globalisation of the Economy and the Nation State," *The World Economy* 22:3 (May 1999): 295–352.

6 For example, see OECD, *Measuring Globalisation: OECD Economic Globalisation Indicators* (Paris: OECD, 2005); Pim Martens and Daniel Zywietz, "Rethinking Globalization: A Modified Globalization Index," *Journal of International Development* 18:3 (2006): 331–50.

7 "The Globalization Index," *Foreign Policy* (November–December 2007): 68–76.

8 Betty Liu, "Cross-Border Partnerships," *Financial Times* (March 14, 2003): 9.

9 Antonio Regalado and Lauren Etter, "Brazil Food Merger Creates Export Giant," *Wall Street Journal* (May 20, 2009): B2.

10 See Rodney C. Shrader, Benjamin M. Oviatt, and Patricia Phillips McDougall, "How New Ventures Exploit Trade-Offs among International Risk Factors: Lessons for the Accelerated Internationalization of the 21st Century," *Academy of Management Journal* 43:6 (2000): 1227–47; Ian Fillis, "The Internationalization Process of the Craft Microenterprise," *Journal of Developmental Entrepreneurship* 7:1 (2002): 25–43; Michael Copeland, "The Mighty Micro Multinational," *Business 2.0 Magazine* (July 28, 2006): n.p.

11 Stephanie A. Fernhaber, Brett Anitra Gilbert, and Patricia P. McDougall, "International Entrepreneurship and Geographic Location: An Empirical Examination of New Venture Internationalization," *Journal of International Business Studies* 39:2 (2008): 267–90.

12 Dan McGraw, "The Foreign Invasion of the American Game," *The Village Voice* (May 28–June 3, 2003) (accessed June 4, 2007).

13 For a long time, the group was the G7, including Canada, France, Germany, Italy, Japan, United Kingdom, and United States; it became the G8 when Russia started to attend meetings. There is also the G20, which includes the G8 plus Argentina, Australia, Brazil, China, India, Indonesia, Mexico, Saudi Arabia, South Africa, South Korea, Turkey, and one seat for the European Union.

14 Susan Carey, "Calculating Costs in the Clouds," *Wall Street Journal* (March 6, 2007): B1+.

15 His views are discussed in Joellen Perry, "Nobel Laureates Say Globalization's Winners Should Aid Poor," *Wall Street Journal* (August 25, 2008): 2.

16 Lorraine Eden and Stefanie Lenway, "Introduction to the Symposium Multinationals: The Janus Face of Globalization," *Journal of International Business Studies* 32:3 (2001): 383–400.

17 His views are discussed in Joellen Perry, "Nobel Laureates Say Globalization's Winners Should Aid Poor," *Wall Street Journal* (August 25, 2008): 2.

18 Steve Lohr, "An Elder Challenges Outsourcing's Orthodoxy," *New York Times* (September 9, 2004): C1+; Paul A. Samuelson, "Where Ricardo and Mill Rebut and Confirm Arguments of Mainstream Economists Supporting Globalization," *Journal of Economic Perspectives* 18:3 (Summer 2004): 135–47.

19 An examination of this subject may be found in Arne Kalleberg, "Precarious Work, Insecure Workers: Employment Relations in Transition," *American Sociological Review* 74:1 (2009): 1–22.

20 Bernhard G. Gunter and Rolph van der Hoeven, "The Social Dimension of Globalization: A Review of the Literature," *International Labour Review* 143:1/2 (2004): 7–43.

21 Jagdish Bhagwati, "Anti-Globalization: Why?" *Journal of Policy Modeling* 26:4 (2004): 439–64.

22 Craig Karmin, "Offshoring Can Generate Jobs in the U.S.," *Wall Street Journal* (March 16, 2004): B1.

23 William M. Bulkeley, "IBM Documents Give Rare Look at 'Offshoring,'" *Wall Street Journal* (January 19, 2004): A1+; William M. Bulkeley, "IBM to Cut U.S. Jobs, Expand in India," *Wall Street Journal* (March 26, 2009): B1.

24 Richard Waters, "Big Blueprint for IBM," *Financial Times* (March 3, 2009): 14.

25 N. Gregory Mankiw and Phillip Swagel, "The Politics and Economics of Offshore Outsourcing," NBR Working Paper No. 12398 (July 2006); Kristien Coucke and Leo Sleuwaegen, "Offshoring as a Survival Strategy: Evidence from Manufacturing Firms in Belgium," *Journal of International Business Studies* 39:8 (2008): 1261–77.

26 Matthew J. Slaughter, "Globalization and Employment by U.S. Multinationals: A Framework and Facts," *Daily Tax Report* (March 26, 2004): 1–12; Olivier Bertrand, "What Goes Around, Comes Around: Effects of Offshore Outsourcing on the Export Performance of Firms," *Journal of International Business Studies* 42:2 (February/March 2008): 334–44.

27 Robert C. Feenstra and Gordon H. Hanson, "The Impact of Outsourcing and High-Technology Capital on Wages: Estimates for the United States, 1979–1990," *Quarterly Journal of Economics* 114:3 (1999): 907–40.

28 Alan S. Brown, "A Shift in Engineering Offshore," *Mechanical Engineering* 131:3 (2009): 24–29.

29 Timothy Aeppel, "Coming Home: Appliance Maker Drops China to Produce in Texas," *Wall Street Journal* (August 24, 2009): B1+; Linda Tucci, "Offshoring Has Long Way to Go," *CIO News Headlines* (June 2, 2005): n.p.; Alexandra Harney, "Travel Industry," *Financial Times* (September 2, 2004): 11; Paulo Prada and Niraj Sheth, "Delta Air Ends Use of India Call Centers," *Wall Street Journal* (April 18–19, 2009): B1+.

30 Marcus Walker, "Just How Good Is Globalization?" *Wall Street Journal* (January 25, 2007): A10, referring to data from Morgan Stanley Research.

31 Deborah Solomon, "Federal Aid Does Little for Free Trade's Losers," *Wall Street Journal* (March 1, 2007): A1+.

32 Paul Windrum, Andreas Reinstaller, and Christopher Bull, "The Outsourcing Productivity Paradox: Total Outsourcing, Organisational Innovation, and Long Run Productivity Growth," *Journal of Evolutionary Economics* 19:2 (2009): 197–232.

33 Carlos Tejada, "Paradise Lost," *Wall Street Journal* (August 14, 2003): A1+

34 "The Hackett Group, Inc. *Investment Weekly News* (December 18, 2010): 1040.

35 Alan S. Blinder, "Offshoring: The Next Industrial Revolution," *Foreign Affairs* 85:2 (March–April 2006): 113–22; David Wessel and Bob Davis, "Working Theory," *Wall Street Journal* (March 28, 2007): A1+ (discussing studies by Alan S. Binder); A. Hilsenrath, "Forrester Revises Loss Estimates to Overseas Jobs," *Wall Street Journal* (May 17, 2004): A8; J. Kirkegaard, "Offshoring, Outsourcing, and Production Relocation—Labor-Market Effects in the OECD Countries and Developing Asia," Working Paper No. 07–2 (Washington: Peterson Institute for International Economics, 2007).

36 United Nations Conference on Trade and Development, *World Investment Report 2001: Promoting Linkages* (New York and Geneva: United Nations, 2001): 90–92.

37 Small Business Export Association, 'New Report: SME Exports Support 4 Million Jobs," (December 6, 2010) www.nsba.biz /content/3647.shtml (accessed December 21, 2011).

38 Heather Berry, "Leaders, Laggards, and the Pursuit of Foreign Knowledge," *Strategic Management Journal* 27 (2006): 151–68; and Jaeyong Song and Jongtae Shin, "The Paradox of Technological Capabilities: A Knowledge Sourcing from Host Countries of Overseas R&D Operations," *Journal of International Business Studies* 39:2 (2008): 291–303.

39 Nery Ynclan, "Avon Is Opening the Door to Spanglish," *Miami Herald* (July 23, 2002): E1.

40 Sharon Terlep, "GM Sales Fell 11% in '08," *Wall Street Journal* (January 22, 2009): B3.

41 United Nations Conference on Trade and Development, *World Investment Report 2008: Transnational Corporations, and the Infrastructure Challenge* (New York and Geneva: United Nations, 2008): xvi.

42 "Ships Take to Arctic Ocean as Sea Ice Melts," www.msnbc.com /id/39394645/ns/world_news-worldenvironment (accessed September 28, 2010).

43 Linn Hirschberg, "Is the Face of America That of a Green Ogre?" *New York Times Magazine* (November 14, 2004): 90–94.

44 John Willman, "Multinationals," *Financial Times* (February 25, 2003): Comment & Analysis, ii.

45 Edward Luce, "Hard Sell to a Billion Consumers," *Financial Times* (April 25, 2002): 14.

46 David Wessel and Marcus Walker, "Good News for the Globe," *Wall Street Journal* (September 3, 2004): A7+.

47 Alan M. Rugman and Cecelia Brain, "Multinational Enterprises Are Regional, Not Global," *Multinational Business Review* 11:1 (2004): 3.

48 John Ralston Saul, "The Collapse of Globalism," *Harpers* (March 2004): 33–43; James Harding, "Globalisation's Children Strike Back," *Financial Times* (September 11, 2001): 4; Bob Davis, "Wealth of Nations," *Wall Street Journal* (March 29, 2004): A1; Harold James, *The End of Globalisation: Lessons from the Great Depression* (Cambridge, MA: Harvard University Press, 2001).

49 "Hunger on the Rise," *Finance & Development* (March 2010): 40–41.

50 Peter Mayer, "Yearender: Europe Toughens Attitudes on Immigrants," *McClatchy – Tribune Business News* (December 15, 2010): n.p.

51 D. Ronen, "The Effect of Oil Price on Containership Speed and Fleet Size," *The Journal of the Operational Research Society* 62:1 (January 2011): 211–16.

52 Larry Rohter, "Shipping Costs Start to Crimp Globalization," *New York Times* (August 3, 2009): 1+.

53 On the schism between those who thrive in a globalized environment and those who don't, see Jagdish Bhagwati, "Anti-Globalization: Why?" *Journal of Policy Modeling* 26:4 (2004): 439–64; Roger Sugden and James R. Wilson, "Economic Globalisation: Dialectics, Conceptualisation and Choice," *Contributions to Political Economy* 24:1 (2005): 13–32; J. Ørstrøm Møller, "Wanted: A New Strategy for Globalization," *The Futurist* (January–February 2004): 20–22.

54 *Sources include the following:* We'd like to acknowledge the invaluable assistance of Brenda Yester, vice president of Carnival Cruise Lines. Other sources include Elliot Spagat, "Passengers Disembark 'Nightmare' Cruise Amid Cheers," www.msnbc.msn.com/id/40126918/ns/travel-cruise_travel?GT1=43001 (accessed November 11, 2010); Martha Brannigan, "Port Everglades Makes Big Push for Cruise Business," *McClatchy – Tribune News* (April 7, 2010): n.p.; Martha Brannigan, "Confident Carnival Orders New Cruise Ship," *McClatchy – Tribune News* (December 2, 2009): n.p.; Pan Kwan Yuk, "Carnival Outlook Down on Discounts," *Financial Times* (March 25, 2009): 16; Tom Stieghorst, *McClatchy-Tribune Business News* (March 21, 2008): n.p.; "Carnival Cruise Lines; Carnival Experiencing Dramatic Increase on On-Line Shore Excursion Sales," *Entertainment & Travel* (March 26, 2008): 168; "The Wave Rolls On; Carnival Cruise Lines Reports Record Booking Week," *PR Newswire* (March 3, 2009): n.p.; Martha Brannigan, "Cruise Lines Aim for Wider Appeal," *Knight Ridder Tribune Business News* (March 14, 2007): 1; Cruise Lines International Association, "Cruise Industry Overview," Marketing Edition 2006, www.cruising.org/press/overview%202006.cfm (accessed May 9, 2007); Donald Urquhart, "Greed and Corruption Rooted in Flag of Convenience System," *The Business Times Singapore* (March 9, 2001): n.p.; Daniel Grant, "Onboard Art," *American Artist* (March 2003): 18; Nicole Harris, "Ditching the Cruise Director," *Wall Street Journal* (April 22, 2004): D1+; Rana Foroohar et al., "The Road Less Traveled," *Newsweek* (May 26, 2003): 40.

An Atlas

Satellite television transmission now makes it commonplace for us to watch events as they unfold in other countries. Transportation and communication advances and government-to-government accords have contributed to our increasing dependence on foreign goods and markets. As this dependence grows, updated maps are a valuable tool. They can show the locations of population, economic wealth, production, and markets; portray certain commonalities and differences among areas; and illustrate barriers that might inhibit trade. In spite of the usefulness of maps, a substantial number of people worldwide have a poor knowledge of how to interpret information on maps and even of how to find the location of events that affect their lives.

We urge you to use the following maps to build your awareness of geography.

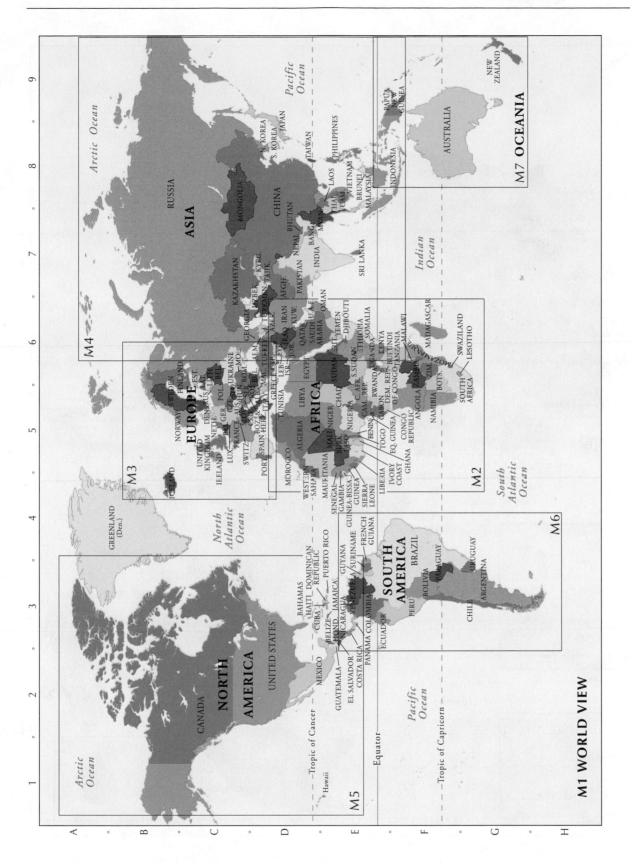

M1 WORLD VIEW

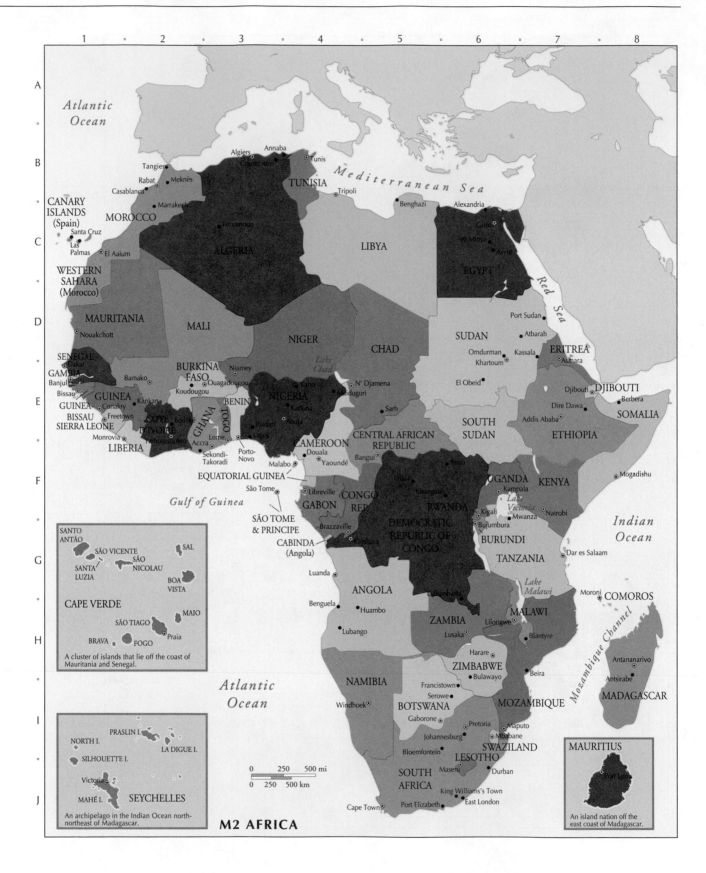

Atlantic Ocean

Mediterranean Sea

Algiers • Annaba
Constantine •   • Tunis
Tangier •
Rabat •   • Meknès   **TUNISIA**
Casablanca •   Tripoli •
• Marrakech   Benghazi •

CANARY ISLANDS (Spain)
Santa Cruz •
Las Palmas •
• El Aaium

MOROCCO

ALGERIA
Timimoun •

LIBYA

EGYPT
Cairo •
Al Minya •
Asyut •

Red Sea

Alexandria •

WESTERN SAHARA (Morocco)

MAURITANIA
• Nouakchott

MALI

NIGER
Niamey •

CHAD
N' Djamena •

SUDAN
Port Sudan •
Atbarah •
Omdurman •   • Kassala
Khartoum •
El Obeid •

ERITREA
Asmara •

DJIBOUTI
Djibouti •   • Berbera
Dire Dawa •

SOMALIA

SENEGAL
Dakar •
GAMBIA
Banjul •
Bissau •
GUINEA-BISSAU

Bamako •

BURKINA FASO
Ouagadougou •
Koudougou •

NIGERIA
Kano •
Kaduna •
Maiduguri •
Abuja •

BENIN

Sarh •

CENTRAL AFRICAN REPUBLIC
Bangui •

SOUTH SUDAN

Addis Ababa •

ETHIOPIA

• Mogadishu

GUINEA
Conakry •
Kankan •
Freetown •
SIERRA LEONE
Monrovia •
LIBERIA

CÔTE D'IVOIRE
Bobo •
Yamoussoukro •

GHANA
Accra •
Sekondi-Takoradi •

TOGO
Lomé •
Ibadan •
Lagos •
Porto-Novo •

CAMEROON
Douala •
Yaoundé •
Malabo •

EQUATORIAL GUINEA
São Tomé •

SÃO TOME & PRINCIPE

CABINDA (Angola)

Libreville •
GABON
CONGO REP.
Brazzaville •
Kinshasa •

DEMOCRATIC REPUBLIC OF CONGO
Lisala •
Kisangani •

UGANDA
Kampala •
Kigali •
RWANDA
Bujumbura •
BURUNDI
Mwanza •

Lake Victoria

KENYA
Nairobi •

Indian Ocean

Gulf of Guinea

Luanda •
ANGOLA
Benguela •   • Huambo
Lubango •
Lubumbashi •

TANZANIA
Dar es Salaam •

Lake Malawi

Moroni •   **COMOROS**

ZAMBIA
Lilongwe •
Lusaka •
MALAWI
Blantyre •

Harare •
Bulawayo •   • Beira
ZIMBABWE

Antananarivo •
Antsirabe •
MADAGASCAR

Mozambique Channel

Atlantic Ocean

NAMIBIA
Francistown •
Serowe •
Windhoek •
BOTSWANA
Gaborone •
Pretoria •   Maputo •
Johannesburg •   • Mbabane
Bloemfontein •   **SWAZILAND**
LESOTHO
Maseru •   • Durban
SOUTH AFRICA
King Williams's Town •
Cape Town •   Port Elizabeth •   East London •

MOZAMBIQUE

Inset — Cape Verde:
SANTO ANTÃO
SÃO VICENTE   SAL
SÃO NICOLAU
SANTA LUZIA
BOA VISTA
CAPE VERDE
MAIO
SÃO TIAGO
BRAVA   FOGO
Praia •
A cluster of islands that lie off the coast of Mauritania and Senegal.

Inset — Seychelles:
PRASLIN I.
NORTH I.
LA DIGUE I.
SILHOUETTE I.
Victoria •
MAHÉ I.   **SEYCHELLES**
An archipelago in the Indian Ocean north-northeast of Madagascar.

Inset — Mauritius:
MAURITIUS
Port Louis •
An island nation off the east coast of Madagascar.

Scale: 0   250   500 mi
0   250   500 km

M2 AFRICA

1   2   3   4   5   6   7   8

JAN MAYEN IS.
(Denmark)

*Arctic
Ocean*

Denmark Strait

Barents Sea

• Murmansk

ICELAND
⊕ Reykjavik

*Norwegian
Sea*

FAEROE IS.
(Den.)

SWEDEN   FINLAND   R U S S I A

*Lake
Ladoga*

• Kostroma

SHETLAND IS.
(U.K.)

NORWAY   • Helsinki   ⊕ Tallinn   • St. Petersburg

ORKNEY IS.   Bergen •   ESTONIA

Oslo •   Stockholm⊕   • Moscow
*North
Sea*   • Göteborg   • Riga   • Tula

Glasgow   • Edinburgh   LATVIA   • Smolensk
•   *Baltic*   LITHUANIA
Belfast•   UNITED   DENMARK   *Sea*   RUS.   Vilnius⊕
          KINGDOM   Copenhagen • Malmö   • Minsk   • Orel
Dublin ⊕ *Irish*   Kaliningrad•   • Kursk
          Sea • Manchester   Gdansk•   BELARUS
IRELAND   • Liverpool   • Bydgoszcz   Homyel'•

          • Birmingham   Hamburg •   • Kiev
                      NETHERLANDS   Berlin⊕   POLAND   UKRAINE   • Dnipropetrovsk
          • London⊕ Amsterdam•   • •   • Warsaw
                      The Hague   GERMANY   Leipzig•   • Lódz
*Atlantic   BELGIUM   Essen• • Dresden • Wroclaw   L'vov•   • Mykolaiv
Ocean*   *English Channel* Brussels⊕ Liège•Düsseldorf• • Prague • Krakow   MOLDOVA
          Le Havre•   •Bonn   • Chernivtsi
              LUXEMBOURG • Frankfurt CZECH   • Brno
          Paris⊕ Luxembourg•   •Stuttgart REP. SLOVAKIA   Chisinau⊕   • Odesa
          Le Mans•   • Vienna   • Debrecen
                              Munich• Linz• ⊕Bratislava   ROMANIA
          FRANCE   Zurich• LIECHTENSTEIN   HUNGARY   • Arad
                    Geneva• SWITZERLAND AUSTRIA • Budapest   • Timisoara
*Bay of   • Limoges   Bonn•   SLOVENIA   Belgrade• • Bucharest *Black Sea*
Biscay*   Lyon•   Milan• Padova Ljubljana⊕   BULGARIA
          Bordeaux• St. Etienne• Turin•   Venice• Zagreb⊕ BOSNIA &
                                SAN   CROATIA HERZE-   SERBIA &
          A Coruña•   MARINO   GOVINA   MONTE-   • Sofia
Porto•   Nîmes•   Monaco• Genoa• Florence•   NEGRO MACEDONIA • Istanbul
          Toulouse•   • Livorno Sarajevo• KOSOVO
PORTUGAL   ANDORRA   Marseille•   ITALY   *Adriatic* ⊕ Pristina
                            Rome•   *Sea* ⊕ Skopje   TURKEY
Lisbon• • Madrid⊕ • Barcelona   CORSICA VATICAN   Tirana⊕ ALBANIA Thessaloniki•
          SPAIN   CITY   MACEDONIA
       • Valencia   SARDINIA Naples•   Bari•   GREECE   *Aegean
Sevilla• • Granada   BALEARIC IS.   Taranto•   Sea*
Málaga• • Cartagena   *Tyrrhenian   *Ionian*   Piraiévs•⊕ •Athens
          Strait of   Sea   Sea*
          Gibraltar*   Palermo• •Messina   CYPRUS
                              SICILY   CRETE

0   300 mi
0   300 km   MALTA ⊕ Valetta

Mediterranean Sea

M3 EUROPE

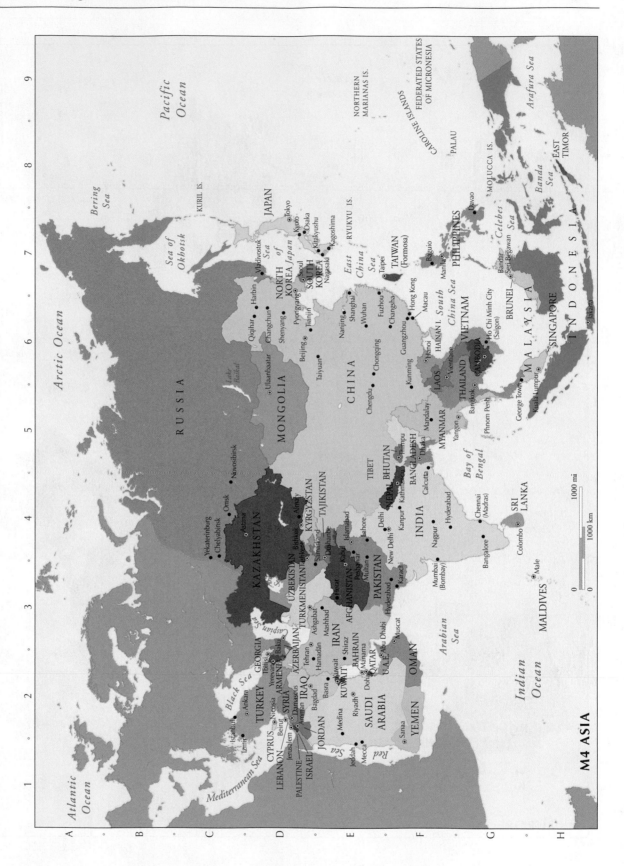

M4 ASIA

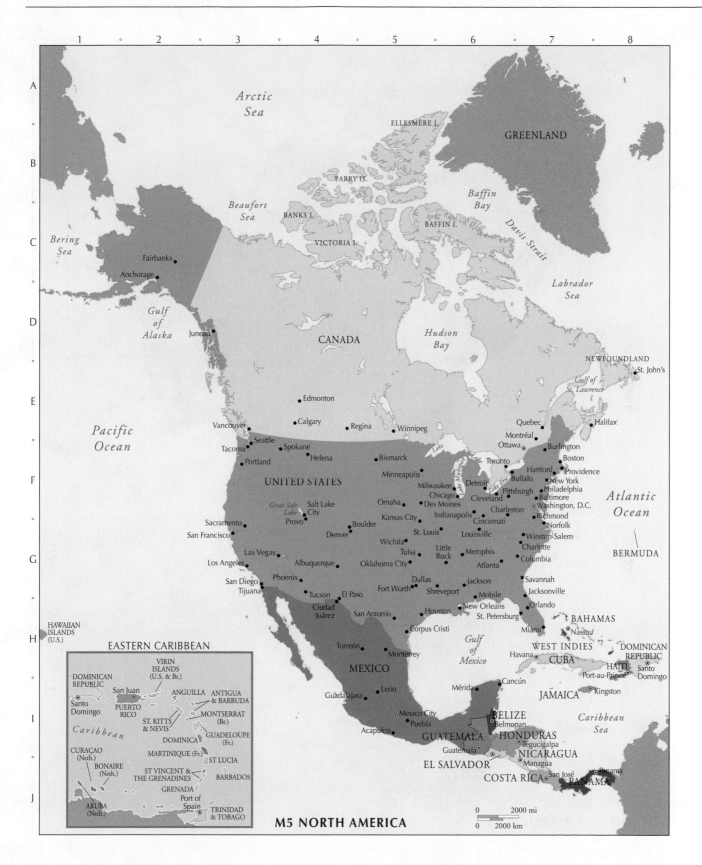

1   2   3   4   5   6   7   8

A

Arctic Sea

ELLESMERE I.

GREENLAND

B

PARRY IS.

Baffin Bay

Beaufort Sea

BANKS I.

BAFFIN I.

Davis Strait

C

Bering Sea

VICTORIA I.

Labrador Sea

Fairbanks

Anchorage

D

Gulf of Alaska

Juneau

CANADA

Hudson Bay

NEWFOUNDLAND

St. John's

Gulf of St. Lawrence

E

Pacific Ocean

Edmonton

Calgary   Regina   Winnipeg   Quebec   Halifax

Vancouver   Montréal   Burlington

Seattle   *Lake*   Ottawa   Boston

Tacoma   Spokane   Toronto   Hartford   Providence

Portland   Helena   Bismarck   Buffalo   New York

F

UNITED STATES   Minneapolis   Milwaukee   Detroit   Pittsburgh   Philadelphia

Lake Michigan   *Lake Erie*   Chicago   Cleveland   Baltimore

Great Salt Lake   Salt Lake City   Omaha   Des Moines   Charleston   Washington, D.C.

Sacramento   Provo   Kansas City   Indianapolis   Cincinnati   Richmond

San Francisco   Boulder   St. Louis   Louisville   Norfolk

Denver   Wichita   Winston-Salem   *Atlantic Ocean*

Las Vegas   Charlotte

G   Los Angeles   Albuquerque   Oklahoma City   Little Rock   Memphis   Columbia   BERMUDA

Phoenix   Tulsa   Atlanta

San Diego   Tucson   El Paso   Fort Worth   Dallas   Jackson   Savannah

Tijuana   Shreveport   Jacksonville

Ciudad   San Antonio   Houston   Mobile   Orlando

Juárez   New Orleans

H   HAWAIIAN ISLANDS (U.S.)   Corpus Cristi   St. Petersburg   Miami   BAHAMAS   Nassau

Torreón   *Gulf of Mexico*   WEST INDIES   DOMINICAN REPUBLIC

EASTERN CARIBBEAN   Monterrey   Havana   CUBA   HAITI

MEXICO   Cancún   JAMAICA   Santo Domingo

VIRGIN ISLANDS (U.S. & Br.)   Guadalajara   León   Mérida   Port-au-Prince   Kingston

DOMINICAN REPUBLIC   San Juan   ANGUILLA   ANTIGUA & BARBUDA

I   Santo Domingo   PUERTO RICO   MONTSERRAT (Br.)   Mexico City   *Caribbean Sea*

ST. KITTS & NEVIS   GUADELOUPE (Fr.)   Puebla   BELIZE   Belmopan

Caribbean   DOMINICA   Acapulco   GUATEMALA   HONDURAS

CURAÇAO (Neth.)   MARTINIQUE (Fr.)   ST LUCIA   Guatemala   Tegucigalpa

BONAIRE (Neth.)   ST VINCENT & THE GRENADINES   BARBADOS   EL SALVADOR   NICARAGUA

J   GRENADA   Managua

ARUBA (Neth.)   Port of Spain   TRINIDAD & TOBAGO   COSTA RICA   San José   Panama   PANAMA

0   2000 mi

0   2000 km

M5 NORTH AMERICA

M6 SOUTH AMERICA

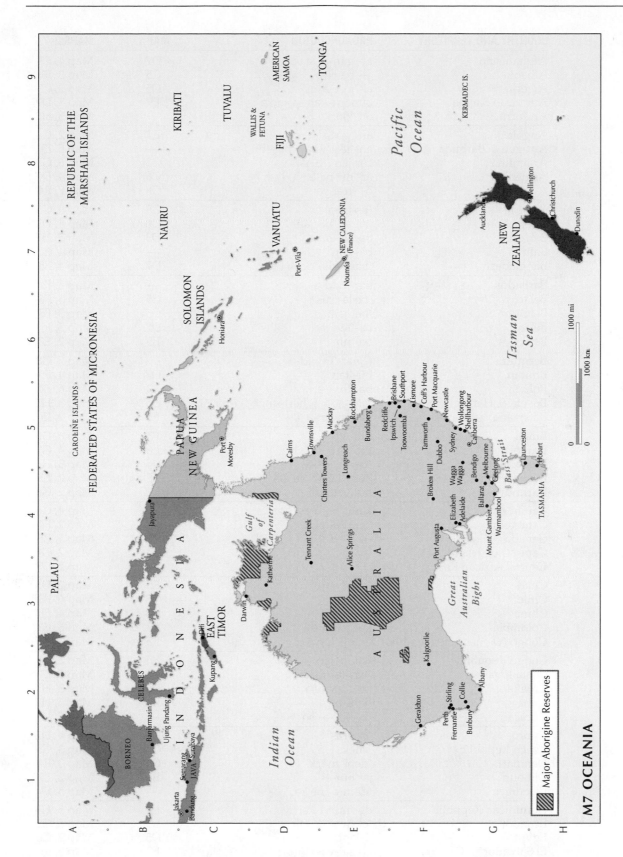

REPUBLIC OF THE
MARSHALL ISLANDS

CAROLINE ISLANDS

FEDERATED STATES OF MICRONESIA

PALAU

KIRIBATI

NAURU

TUVALU

WALLIS &
FETUNA

AMERICAN
SAMOA

TONGA

FIJI

SOLOMON
ISLANDS

VANUATU

NEW CALEDONIA
(France)

Pacific
Ocean

KERMADEC IS.

Honiara

Port-Vila

Nouméa

Auckland
Wellington

Christchurch

NEW
ZEALAND

Dunedin

Tasman
Sea

BORNEO

CELEBES

Banjarmasin

Ujung Pandang

I N D O N E S I A

Jakarta
Semarang
JAVA Surabaya
Bandung

Kupang

EAST
TIMOR

Dili

Jayapura

PAPUA
NEW GUINEA

Port
Moresby

Gulf
of
Carpenteria

Darwin

Katherine

Tennent Creek

Alice Springs

A U S T R A L I A

Kalgoorlie

Geraldton

Perth Stirling
Fremantle Collie
Bunbury

Albany

Indian
Ocean

Cairns

Townsville

Charters Towers

Longreach

Rockhampton

Mackay

Bundaberg

Redcliffe
Brisbane
Ipswich Southport
Toowoomba Lismore
Coff's Harbour
Port Macquarie
Tamworth
Newcastle
Dubbo Sydney Wollongong
Shellharbour
Wagga Canberra
Wagga
Broken Hill
Bendigo
Elizabeth Ballarat Melbourne
Adelaide Warrnambool Geelong Bass Strait
Mount Gambier
Port Augusta
Launceston
Hobart

TASMANIA

Great
Australian
Bight

1000 mi

1000 km

Major Aborigine Reserves

M7 OCEANIA

COUNTRY AND TERRITORY	PRONUNCIATION	MAP 1	MAPS 2–7
Afghanistan	af-´gan-ə-,stan	D7	Map 4, E3
Albania	al-´bā-nē-ə	C5	Map 3, I6
Algeria	al-´jir-ē-ə	D5	Map 2, C3
American Samoa	ə-mer´i-kən sə-mō´ə	F9	Map 7, D9
Andorra	an-´dȯr-ə	—	Map 3, H2
Angola	an-´gō-lə	E5	Map 2, G4
Antigua & Barbuda	an-´tē-g(w)ə / bär-´büd-ə	—	Map 5, I3
Argentina	,,är-jen-´tē-nə	G3	Map 6, G3
Armenia	är-´mē-ne-ə	C6	Map 4, D2
Australia	ȯ-´strāl-yə	G8	Map 7, E4
Austria	´ȯs-trē-ə	C5	Map 3, G5
Azerbaijan	´az-ər-´bī-´jän	D6	Map 4, D2
Bahamas	bə-hä´-məz	D3	Map 5, H7
Bahrain	bä-´rān	—	Map 4, E2
Bangladesh	´bänJ-glə-´desh	D7	Map 4, F5
Barbados	bär-´bād-əs	—	Map 5, J3
Belarus	´bē-lə-´rüs	C5	Map 3, F6
Belgium	´bel-jəm	C5	Map 3, F3
Belize	bə-´lēz	D2	Map 5, I6
Benin	bə-´nin	E5	Map 2, E3
Bermuda	(´)bər-´myüd-ə	—	Map 5, G8
Bhutan	bü-´tan	D7	Map 4, F5
Bolivia	bə-´liv-ē-ə	F3	Map 6, E4
Bosnia & Herzegovina	´bäz-nē-ə / ´hert-sə-gō-´vē-nə	D5	Map 3, H5
Botswana	bät-´swän-ə	F5	Map 2, I5
Brazil	brə-´zil	F3	Map 6, D6
Brunei	brōo-nī´	E8	Map 4, G7
Bulgaria	´bəl-´gar-ē-ə	D5	Map 3, H6
Burkina Faso	bu´r-´kē-nə-´fa´-sō	E5	Map 2, E2
Burundi	bu´-´rün-dē	E6	Map 2, G6
Cambodia	kam-´bd-ē-ə	E7	Map 4, G6
Cameroon	´kam-ə-´rün	E5	Map 2, F4
Canada	´kan-əd-ə	C2	Map 5, E5
Cape Verde Islands	´vard	—	Map 2, G1
Central African Rep.		E5	Map 2, E5
Chad	´chad	E5	Map 2, D5
Chile	´chil-ē	G3	Map 6, F3
China	´chī-nə	D8	Map 4, E5
Colombia	kə-´ləm-bē-ə	E3	Map 6, B3
Congo (Democratic Republic)	´känJ(´)gō	E5	Map 2, G5
Congo Republic	´känJ(´)gō	E5	Map 2, F4
Costa Rica	´käs-tə-´rē-kə	E2	Map 5, J7
Croatia	krō-´ā-sh(ē)ə	D5	Map 3, H5
Cuba	´kyü-bə	E3	Map 5, H7
Curaçao	´k(y)ür-ə-´sō	—	Map 5, J1
Cyprus	´sī-prəs	D6	Map 4, D2
Czech Republic	´chek	C5	Map 3, G5
Denmark	´den-´märk	C5	Map 3, E4
Djibouti	jə-´büt-ē	E6	Map 2, E7
Dominica	´däm-ə-´nē-kə	—	Map 5, I3
Dominican Republic	də-´min-i-kən	E3	Map 5, H8
Ecuador	´ek-wə-´dȯ(ə)r	E3	Map 6, C2
Egypt	´ē-jəpt	D5	Map 2, C6
El Salvador	el-´sal-və-´dȯ(ə)r	E2	Map 5, I6
Equatorial Guinea	ē-kwa´-tōr-ēal `gi-nē	E5	Map 2, F4
Eritrea	´er-ə-´trē-ə	E6	Map 2, D7
Estonia	e-´stō-nē-ə	C5	Map 3, D6

COUNTRY AND TERRITORY	PRONUNCIATION	MAP 1	MAPS 2–7
Ethiopia	´ē-thē-´ō-pē-ə	E6	Map 2, E7
Falkland Islands	´fȯ(l)-klənd	—	Map 6, J4
Fiji	´fē-jē	—	Map 7, D8
Finland	´fin-lənd	B5	Map 3, C6
France	´fran(t)s	C5	Map 3, G3
French Guiana	gē-´an-ə	E3	Map 6, B5
Gabon	ga-´bōⁿ	E5	Map 2, F4
Gambia	´gam-bē-ə	E4	Map 2, E1
Georgia	´jȯr-jə	C6	Map 4, D2
Germany	´jerm-(ə-)nē	C5	Map 3, F4
Ghana	´gän-ə	E5	Map 2, E2
Greece	´grēs	D5	Map 3, I6
Greenland	´grēn-lənd	A4	Map 5, B7
Grenada	grə-nā´də	—	Map 5, J3
Guatemala	´gwät-ə-´mäl-ə	E2	Map 5, I6
Guinea	´gin-ē	E4	Map 2, E1
Guinea-Bissau	´gin-ē-bis-´au˙	E4	Map 2, E1
Guyana	gī-´an-ə	E3	Map 6, B4
Haiti	´hāt-ē	E3	Map 5, H8
Honduras	hän-´d(y)u̇r-əs	E2	Map 5, I7
Hong Kong	´hänJ-´känJ	—	Map 4, F6
Hungary	´hənJ-g(ə)rē	C5	Map 3, G5
Iceland	´ī-slənd	B4	Map 3, B1
India	´in-dê-ə	D7	Map 4, F4
Indonesia	´in-də-´nē-zhə	E8	Map 4, H7; Map 7, B3
Iran	i-´rän	D6	Map 4, E3
Iraq	i-´räk	D6	Map 4, D2
Ireland	´ī(ə)r-lənd	C5	Map 3, F1
Israel	´iz-rē-əl	D6	Map 4, D2
Italy	´it-əl-ē	D6	Map 3, H4
Ivory Coast (Cote D'Ivoire)	ī´və-rē	E5	Map 2, E2
Jamaica	jə-´mā-kə	E3	Map 5, I7
Japan	jə-´pan	D8	Map 4, D7
Jordan	´jȯrd-ən	D6	Map 4, D2
Kazakhstan	kə-´zak-´stan	D7	Map 4, D4
Kenya	´ken-yə	E6	Map 2, F7
Kiribati	kîr-ì-bàs´	—	Map 7, B8
Korea, North	kə-´rē-ə	D8	Map 4, D7
Korea, South	kə-´rē-ə	D8	Map 4, D7
Kosovo	´Ko-sō-vō	C5	Map 3, H6
Kuwait	kə-´wāt	D6	Map 4, E2
Kyrgyzstan	kîr-gē-stän´	D7	Map 4, D4
Laos	´lau˙s	D7	Map 4, F5
Latvia	´lat-vē-ə	C5	Map 3, E6
Lebanon	´leb-ə-nən	D6	Map 4, D2
Lesotho	lə-´sō-(´)tō	F6	Map 2, J6
Liberia	lī-´bir-ē-ə	E5	Map 2, F2
Libya	´lib-ē-ə	D5	Map 2, C4
Liechtenstein	lìk´tən-stīn´	—	Map 3, G4
Lithuania	´lith-(y)ə-´wā-nē-ə	C5	Map 3, E6
Luxembourg	´lək-səm-´bərg	C5	Map 3, G3
Macedonia	´mas-ə-´dō-nyə	D6	Map 3, H6
Madagascar	´mad-ə-´gas-kər	F6	Map 2, I8
Malawi	mə-´lä-wē	F6	Map 2, H6

COUNTRY AND TERRITORY	PRONUNCIATION	MAP 1	MAPS 2–7
Malaysia	mə-ˈlā-zh(ē-)ə	E8	Map 4, G6
Maldives	môlˈdīvz	—	Map 4, H3
Mali	ˈmäl-ē	D5	Map 2, D2
Malta	ˈmȯl-tə	—	Map 3, J5
Marshall Islands	märˈshəl	—	Map 7, A8
Mauritania	ˈmȯr-ə-ˈtā-nē-ə	D5	Map 2, D1
Mauritius	mȯ-ˈrishˈəs	—	Map 2, J8
Mexico	ˈmek-si-ˈkō	D2	Map 5, I5
Micronesia	mīˈkrō-nēˈzhə	—	Map 7, A5
Moldova	mälˈdō-və	D6	Map 3, G7
Mongolia	mänˈgōl-yə	D8	Map 4, D5
Morocco	mə-ˈräk-(ˈ)ō	D5	Map 2, B2
Mozambique	ˈmō-zəm-ˈbēk	F6	Map 2, H6
Myanmar	ˈmyänˈmär	E7	Map 4, F5
Namibia	nə-ˈmib-ē-ə	F5	Map 2, I4
Naura	näˈü-rü	—	Map 7, B7
Nepal	nə-ˈpȯl	D7	Map 4, F4
Netherlands	ˈneth-ər-lən(d)z	C5	Map 3, F3
New Caledonia	ˈkal-ə-ˈdō-nyə	—	Map 7, E7
New Zealand	ˈzē-lənd	G9	Map 7, H7
Nicaragua	ˈnik-ə-ˈräg-wə	E3	Map 5, I7
Niger	ˈnī-jər	E5	Map 2, D4
Nigeria	nī-ˈjir-ē-ə	E5	Map 2, E4
Norway	ˈnȯ(ə)r-ˈwā	C5	Map 3, D4
Oman	ō-ˈmän	E6	Map 4, F2
Pakistan	ˈpak-i-ˈstan	D7	Map 4, E3
Palau	pä-louˈ	—	Map 7, A3
Palestine	pa-lə-ˈstīn	—	Map 4, D1
Panama	ˈpan-ə-ˈmä	E3	Map 5, J8
Papua New Guinea	ˈpap-yə-wə	F9	Map 7, C5
Paraguay	ˈpar-ə-ˈgwī	F3	Map 6, E4
Peru	pə-ˈrü	F3	Map 6, D2
Philippines	ˈfil-ə-ˈpēnz	E8	Map 4, F7
Poland	ˈpō-lənd	D5	Map 3, F5
Portugal	ˈpōr-chi-gəl	D5	Map 3, I1
Puerto Rico	ˈpōrt-ə-ˈrē(ˈ)kō	E3	Map 5, I2
Qatar	ˈkät-ər	D6	Map 4, E2
Romania	rō-ˈā-nē-ə	D5	Map 3, H6
Russia	ˈrəsh-ə	C7	Map 3, D7; Map 4, C5
Rwanda	ruˈ-ˈän-də	E6	Map 2, F6
St. Kitts & Nevis	ˈkits / ˈnē-vəs	—	Map 5, I3
St. Lucia	sānt-ˈlü-shə	—	Map 5, I3
St. Vincent and the Grenadines	grènˈə-dēnzˈ	—	Map 5, J3
San Marino	sàn mə-rēˈnō	—	Map 3, H4
São Tomé and Príncipe	soun tōə-mèˈprēnˈ-sēpə	—	Map 2, F3
Saudi Arabia	ˈsauˈd-ē	E6	Map 4, E2
Senegal	ˈsen-i-ˈgˈl	E4	Map 2, D1
Serbia & Montenegro	ˈsər-bē-ə / ˈmän-tə-ˈnē-grō	D5	Map 3, H6
Seychelles	sā-shèlzˈ	—	Map 2, J1
Sierra Leone	sēˈer-ə-lēˈōn	E4	Map 2, E1
Singapore	ˈsinJ-(g)ə-ˈpō(ə)r	—	Map 4, H6
Slovakia	slō-ˈväk-ē-ə	C5	Map 3, G5
Slovenia	slō-ˈvēn-ē-ə	C5	Map 3, H5
Solomon Islands	ˈsäl-ə-mən	—	Map 7, C6
Somalia	sō-ˈmäl-ē-ə	E6	Map 2, F8

COUNTRY AND TERRITORY	PRONUNCIATION	MAP 1	MAPS 2–7
South Africa	´a-fri-kə	F6	Map 2, J5
South Sudan	sü-´dan	E6	Map 2, E6
Spain	´spāpn	C5	Map 3, I1
Sri Lanka	(´)srē-´länJ-kə	E7	Map 4, G4
Sudan	sü-´dan	E6	Map 2, E6
Suriname	su˙r-ə-´näm-ə	E3	Map 6, B5
Swaziland	´swäz-ē-´land	F6	Map 2, I6
Sweden	´swēd-ən	B5	Map 3, C5
Switzerland	´swit-sər-lənd	C5	Map 3, G4
Syria	´sir-ē-ə	D6	Map 4, D2
Taiwan	´tī-´wän	D8	Map 4, E7
Tajikistan	tä-´ji-ki-´stan	D7	Map 4, E4
Tanzania	´tan-zə-´nē-ə	F6	Map 2, G6
Thailand	´tī-land	E8	Map 4, F5
Togo	´tō(´)gō	E5	Map 2, E3
Tonga	´tän-gə	—	Map 7, D9
Trinidad & Tobago	´trin-ə-´dad / tə-´bā-(´)gō	—	Map 5, J3
Tunisia	t(y)ü-´nē-zh(ē-)ə	D5	Map 2, B4
Turkey	´tər-kē	D6	Map 4, D2
Turkmenistan	tûrk´-men-i-stàn´	D6	Map 4, D3
Tuvalu	tü´-vä-lü	—	Map 7, C9
Uganda	(y)ü-´gan-də	E6	Map 2, F6
Ukraine	yü-´krān	C6	Map 3, F7
United Arab Emirates	yoo-nī´tid à r´əb i-mîr´its	D6	Map 4, E2
United Kingdom	king´dəm	C5	Map 3, F2
United States	yu˙-´nīt-əd-´stāts	D2	Map 5, F5
Uruguay	´(y)u˙r-ə-gwī	G3	Map 6, G5
Uzbekistan	(´)u˙z-´bek-i-´stan	C6	Map 4, D3
Vanuatu	van-ə-´wät-(´)ü	—	Map 7, D7
Vatican City	vàt´ ì-kən	—	Map 3, H4
Venezuela	´ven-əz(-ə)-´wā-lə	E3	Map 6, A4
Vietnam	vē-´et-´näm	E8	Map 4, G6
Western Sahara	sə-hâr´ə	D4	Map 2, C1
Yemen	´yem-ən	E6	Map 4, F2
Zambia	´zam-bē-ə	F5	Map 2, H5
Zimbabwe	zim-´bäb-wē	F6	Map 2, H6

chapter 2

The Cultural Environments Facing Business

PART TWO

Objectives

1. To understand methods for learning about cultural environments

2. To analyze the major causes of cultural difference and change

3. To discuss behavioral factors influencing countries' business practices

4. To understand guidelines for cultural adjustment

Access a host of interactive learning aids to help strengthen your understanding of the chapter concepts at www.myiblab.com.

MyIBLab

Source: Darren Baker/Shutterstock.com

If you see men stroking their beards, stroke yours.

—*Arab proverb*

CASE

Shifting Sands of Saudi Society

Saudi Arabia (see Map 2.1), a land of contrasts and paradoxes, can be perplexing to foreign managers as they try to exercise acceptable personal and business behavior.[1] This is because of Saudi Arabia's mixture of strict religious convictions, ancient social customs, and governmental moves to modernize and grow the country economically. The result includes laws and customs—sometimes shifting with little advanced notice—that vary by industry and region as dominant forces evolve. In some ways, these laws and customs are an extreme contrast to those found in the countries whose companies dominate international business. Thus, foreign companies and their employees must determine what these differences are and how to adjust to operate successfully to them. Although we cannot cover all aspects of this adjustment process, a brief discussion of the roots of Saudi traditions and a sample of both cultural norms and foreign operating adjustments to them should help you understand the importance of culture in international business.

A LITTLE HISTORY AND BACKGROUND

Although the land encompassing the Kingdom of Saudi Arabia has a long history, until recently most inhabitants' loyalty was primarily tribal rather than national. In most times past, the land was divided and under the control of invaders. Nevertheless, the inhabitants have shared a common language (Arabic) and religion (Islam), while being the birthplace of Islam and location of its two holiest cities, Mecca and Medina. Beginning in 1745, the Wahabi movement swept across and united most of the peninsula by calling for the purification of Islam through a literal view of the Koran. King Ibn Saud (1882–1953), a descendant of Wahabi leaders, took power in 1901, merged independent areas, created an entity that was both political and religious, and legitimized his monarchy and succession by being the defender of Islamic holy areas, beliefs, and values.

The growing importance of oil revenue for Saudi Arabia, particularly since the 1970s, has led to rapid urbanization

MAP 2.1   Saudi Arabia and the Arabian Peninsula

The kingdom of Saudi Arabia comprises most of the Arabian Peninsula in Southwest Asia. The capital is Riyadh. Mecca and Medina are Islam's holiest cities. Jeddah is the most important port. All of the country's adjacent neighbors are also Arabic—that is, the people speak Arabic as a first language. All the nations on the peninsula are predominantly Islamic.

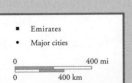
- ■ Emirates
- • Major cities

0 ———— 400 mi
0 ———— 400 km

and has given the government means to offer social services such as free education. These changes have furthered its citizens' sense of a national identity and their diminished traditional ways of living. Since 1950, the rural population has decreased from over 80 percent (about half nomadic) to less than 20 percent. Cities have also modernized physically. However, below the physical surface, Saudis hold attitudes and values that are neither like the norm elsewhere nor easily discerned.

Modernization has been controversial within Saudi Arabia. On the one hand, there is a liberal group. It is supported by an elite segment that has traveled abroad, wants the trappings from economic growth, and fancies greater choices in products and lifestyles. On the other hand, there is a conservative group. It is supported by religious leaders and people fearful that modernization will upset traditional values and adherence to strict Koranic teachings. In turn, the government (the Royal Family) must balance these viewpoints, but it has been particularly careful not to overstep the acceptable boundaries of conservatives lest it become vulnerable to being replaced. For instance, it is well aware that Iran's Islamic Revolution was spearheaded in part by dissenters who viewed the Shah's modernization movements as corrupt and too secular. Additionally, in 1979, a group, largely marginalized by modernization, seized the Grand Mosque of Mecca, which brought questions about the Royal Family's ability to protect Islam's holiest site. Meanwhile, liberals have been largely pacified by taking well-paid government jobs and by slowly gaining the transformation they wish. The government has sometimes made tradeoffs to appease conflicting groups, such as requiring women to wear longer robes (women must wear *abayas* and men customarily wear *thobes*) in exchange for increasing women's education.

THE RELIGIOUS FACTOR

If your country maintains more or less strict separation between religion and the state, you will probably find the pervasiveness of religious culture in Saudi Arabia daunting. For example, religious proscriptions prohibit the sale or use of pork products and alcohol, and restaurants must ensure that customers do not bring their own black market alcohol, lest they lose their operating licenses. During the holy period of Ramadan, when people fast during the day, restaurants serve customers only in the evening. Because Muslim men are called to prayer five times per day, restaurants such as McDonald's dim their lights and close their doors during those periods. Many companies convert revenue-generating space to prayer areas. Saudi Arabian Airlines does this in the rear of its planes, and the British-retailer Harvey Nichols does this in its department store. One importer had to halt the sales of the children's game Pokémon because Saudi authorities feared it might encourage the un-Islamic practice of gambling.

However, there are regional differences. In the capital, Riyadh, women traditionally wear *garhas* that cover their faces; in the port city of Jeddah, which has more contact with foreigners and is less conservative, dress codes are more relaxed and fewer women wear them. Nevertheless, merchants routinely remove the heads and hands of mannequins and keep them properly clad to prevent public objections. Starbucks franchises altered the company logo and Coty Beauty its point-of-purchase exhibits in order not to display women's faces.

Rules of behavior may also be hard to comprehend because of the ways in which religious and legal rules have been adapted to contemporary situations. Islamic law, for instance, forbids charging interest and selling accident insurance (strict doctrine holds there are no accidents, only preordained acts of God). In the case of mortgages, the Saudi government gets around this proscription by offering interest-free loans. As for accident insurance, the government has simply eliminated the prohibition because Saudi businesses, like businesses elsewhere, need the coverage.

Nor are expected behaviors necessarily the same for locals and foreigners. Non-Muslim foreign women are not required to wear head scarves, although religious patrols may admonish them for not doing so. Saudi Arabian Airlines disallows Saudi women from working as flight attendants (being in direct contact with men might tempt promiscuous behavior), but it allows women from other Arab nations to do so. In addition, there are compounds inhabited largely by Americans and Europeans, who have come to Saudi Arabia to work in specialized positions for which there are insufficient numbers of Saudis to fill them. To attract these outsiders, Saudi Arabia allows compound dress and most behaviors to emulate what the residents were accustomed to back home (alcohol, pornography, and drugs are still prohibited). However, in an example of a reverse dress code, some compounds prohibit residents and their visitors from wearing *abayas* and *thobes* in public areas.

TRADITIONAL FACTORS

Some of Saudi Arabian traditions are probably the outgrowth of a tribal and nomadic past. For instance, an oft-quoted saying, "Me against my brother, my brothers and me against my cousins, then my cousins and me against strangers," illustrates a family-centered society where trust of others is highly correlated with the degree of familiarity with them.

Given the trust factor, most Saudi businesses have historically been family owned and operated. They prefer to hire family members or people they know well, even though they could hire others who are better qualified. However, these companies have seen the need to partner with foreign companies to gain expertise. Yet, the process of partnering is usually lengthy because Saudis take time to know the foreigners well and because they are reluctant to make full financial disclosures outside the family. Saudis generally prefer to get to know you well, perhaps inviting you into their homes and developing a certain level of friendship, before ever turning to business details.

This process of getting to know someone with whom to do business is illustrated by the example of a British publisher, which dispatched two salesmen to Saudi Arabia. Because of being paid on commission, they moved aggressively, figuring they could make the same number of calls—and sales—per day as they made in Britain. Back home, they were used to punctual schedules, the undivided attention of potential clients, and conversations devoted only to business transactions. To them, time was money. In Saudi Arabia, however, they soon found that appointments seldom began on time and usually took place at local cafés over casual cups of coffee. As far as they were concerned, Saudis spent too much time in idle chitchat, and to make matters worse, they would turn their attention to personal acquaintances rather than continuing with business. Eventually, both salesmen began showing their irritation. Before long, their Saudi counterparts came to regard them as rude and impatient, and their employer had to recall them.

Saudis' preference to deal with people they know has led to a system known as *wasta*, that roughly translates into English as "connections." Thus, who one knows helps a great deal in almost everything, such as moving a résumé to the top of a pile, gaining approval of a zoning request, getting a passport, and obtaining a visa to bring in a visitor from headquarters.

Gender Roles

Perhaps the most baffling aspect of Saudi culture to many outsiders is the expected role of people by gender. Based largely on a Koranic prescription whereby daughters receive only half the inheritance that sons receive, females are placed in a separate and often subservient position. Their role has been to be virtuous, marry young, and have offspring. In turn, males are responsible to be protectors of females and breadwinners for the family. Not only is female virtue required, but also the appearance of it. Because of family importance, a negative perception of one member reflects on all. These beliefs have led to a number of practices, e.g., women cannot obtain driver's licenses, travel abroad without permission of a male relative, and study abroad without a male relative escort. (In 2011 a group of women drove autos in protest, with little intimidation. Further, women were granted future rights to vote and hold political offices.) Basically, non-kin males and females may interact personally only in "open areas," or in "closed areas" when females are accompanied by a male relative. However, applying this restriction may seem a bit confusing to outsiders. For instance, restaurants are considered closed areas, and proprietors must maintain separate dining rooms and entrances for men without female companions. However, the food malls at most shopping centers are considered open areas where members of both sexes intermingle.

A 2008 royal decree lifted a ban on mixing men and women in the workplace, but the situation is complex. Male and female employees within the public sector work in separate buildings. When they must meet together, they do so within meeting rooms in the Governor's office, in which males and females must use separate entrances. However, within the private sector, males and females may work together, but there are other limitations.

Although there are now more female than male university graduates in Saudi Arabia, only about 7 percent of the workforce is female. Why? The answer is partially cultural. Some women prefer traditional family roles. Some find driving restrictions to be too much of a hassle. Finally, some families prohibit women members from working because of family honor, i.e., "What will people think?"

Economic factors blend with cultural ones as well. Companies must incur the cost of providing separate entrances and toilet facilities for males and females. But once in, the genders do interact, especially in multinational companies. For example, Unilever's female brand managers, who as long they adhere to dress codes, interact with male colleagues and meet with male personnel from other companies. However, female employees are limited in traveling abroad on company business because they need permission from male relatives. Some multinationals ease this problem by paying the travel costs for a male relative to accompany a female employee abroad.

At one time, visas for single women to enter Saudi Arabia were nearly unobtainable. However, the Saudi Arabian General Investment Authority (SAGIA) has successfully attracted investments by MNEs that need visas to send female executives to Saudi Arabia for short- and long-term assignments. While these visas are not given automatically, they can be obtained—more easily for women over 40, but also possible for younger women, especially with the use of *wasta*. For instance, the U.S. consulting company, Monitor Group, brought in American women in their twenties, and L'Oreal has sent its female human resources manager to Saudi Arabia.

The restrictions on gender interactions also lead to other adjustments. For instance, four young Saudis who had lived and studied abroad researched the market potential for opening an up-scale restaurant (the Java Lounge) in Jeddah. Ordinarily, such research can be difficult in Saudi Arabia because limitations on male-female interactions restrain family-focused interviews. In this case, researchers interviewed families who appeared to be affluent by approaching them in restaurants. They deduced who was affluent by noting how they comported themselves, whether they wore custom-made versus off-the-rack robes, the quality of wristwatches showing beneath long sleeves, and the care with which men kept their beards. These were all indicators that people from outside the society would probably overlook.

At upscale U.S.- and U.K.-based department stores like Saks Fifth Avenue and Harvey Nichols, mixed shopping is allowed only on the lower floors. There, all salespeople are men (even those specializing in such products as cosmetics and lingerie), and there are no changing rooms or places to try cosmetics. Meanwhile, the upper floors are for women only, and female shoppers can check their *abayas* and shop in jeans or whatever they choose. (Meanwhile, males who drove the women can relax in space that the stores have put aside for them.) One problem: Because male managers can visit these floors only when a store is closed, they are limited in their ability to observe operations.

CULTURAL DYNAMICS

Almost all aspects of culture evolve, and Saudi Arabia is no exception. Take the case of women in the workplace. In terms of preparation, the first public school for girls did not open until 1960, and the government had to provide troops in one city because of protests that the schooling would negatively affect girls' religion, social values, and norms. Since then, there has been a gradual increase in years of study and curriculum offered for females. Economic need has spurred both changes in education and the use of education within the workforce. At the same time, critics have had to be persuaded that changes are compatible with women's role. For example, one of the first acceptances of working women (and alongside men) was in the medical field because of the shortage of doctors, the high cost of separate male and female specialists, and the compatibility of healing with women's role as nurturers.

Within the conservative-liberal struggle, a 2003 incident (religious police prevented male firefighters from rescuing girls in a school fire because they were without *abayas* and head coverings) shifted more public opinion toward liberal views and provided the government the authority to reduce religious authorities' power. In addition, Saudi opinion and policy has been to reduce the heavy dependence on and cost of foreign workers. Thus, the Saudi government pays for foreign university education of its citizens. At the same time, there has been growing recognition that much female talent is being underutilized.

There has been much change in the Saudi business world. For instance, as of this writing, women own about 20 percent of all Saudi businesses (most of which must have a male manager and sell only to female customers), and the CEO of one of the country's largest concerns, the Olayan Financing Company, is a woman. Further changes are particularly apparent in the book *Leaders of Saudi Arabia*, which highlights the backgrounds and philosophies of 140 Saudi leaders, both male and female. Three things will likely increase Saudi female workforce participation: (1) increase in inward foreign investment, (2) increase in women studying abroad, and (3) women's psychological drive to prove themselves. Bear in mind, however, that changes tend to be uneven, particularly differing among geographic areas of the country and among people of certain income and educational levels.

Introduction

Concept Check

In Chapter 1, we explained that behavioral factors, values, attitudes, and beliefs can be studied as keys both to cultural conditions and to ways of developing suitable business practices.

Our opening case illustrates companies' need to understand and be sensitive to ever-changing operating environments. Figure 2.1 shows how **culture**—learned norms based on the values, attitudes, and beliefs of a group of people—is an integral part of a nation's operating environment. Culture is sometimes an elusive topic to study. Why? Because people belong to different groups, based on nationality, ethnicity, religion, gender, work organization, profession, age, political party membership, and income level, and each group comprises a culture. In this chapter, we emphasize the nature of *national cultures*; we also discuss other cultural memberships, especially as they differ from country to country.

THE PEOPLE FACTOR

Concept Check

Keep in mind our definition of *international business* in Chapter 1, where we stress that it involves "all commercial transactions"—sales, investments, transportation, and so forth.

Business involves *people*. Every business employs, sells to, buys from, and is owned and regulated by people. International business, of course, involves people from different national cultures. Every business function, therefore—managing a workforce, marketing and transporting output, purchasing supplies, dealing with regulators, securing funds—is subject to potential cultural differences.

Cultural Diversity   Chapter 1 explained that companies become international to create value for their organizations, and a means to this end is acquiring foreign assets, including knowledge-based resources. Another means of gaining global competitive

FIGURE 2.1   Cultural Factors Affecting International Business Operations

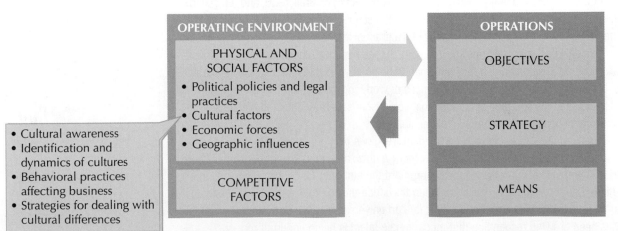

advantage is fostering cultural diversity. By bringing together people of diverse back-grounds, perspectives, and experience, companies often gain a deeper knowledge of products and services and how to create and deliver them. At companies like PepsiCo and IBM, executives report that much of their recent growth has been a result of greater workforce diversity.[2] However, as we shall see, bringing all these people together is difficult.

Cultural Collision   **Cultural collision** occurs when divergent cultures come in contact. In international business, the major problems of *cultural collision* arise under two conditions:

- When a company implements practices that are less effective than intended
- When a company's employees encounter distress because of difficulty in accepting or adjusting to foreign behaviors

Sensitivity and Adjustment   A firm doing business in another country must deter-mine which of that nation's business practices differ from its own and then decide what adjustments, if any, are necessary for operating efficiently. In this chapter, we first examine *cultural awareness,* especially the need for building it, and discuss the causes of cultural differences, rigidities, and changes. Next, we describe the major behavioral factors that affect the conduct of international business. Finally, we take a look at the reasons why some businesses—and some individuals—do or don't adjust to other cultures.

Cultural Awareness

Most cultural variables—daily routines and rules, codes of social relations, language, emo-tive expression, concepts of luck—are universal. The forms of these variables, however, differ among cultures, and not everyone responds to them in the same way. Every culture, for instance, features some form of dance, but types of and participation in dancing vary among and even within cultures.[3]

There is no foolproof method for building cultural awareness.[4] Travelers remark on cultural differences, experts write about them, and international businesspeople see how they affect operations. Even so, people tend to disagree on just what they are, whether they're widespread or limited, and whether they're deep-seated or superficial. Nor is it easy to isolate culture from such factors as economic and political conditions. A survey measuring people's entrepreneurial attitudes, for example, could be influenced by eco-nomic conditions along with basic risk-taking values. China's changing preference for male versus female offspring offers an example of how cultural and economic factors interplay. Under the country's one-child policy, millions of female fetuses have been aborted, while infanticide and adoption of female babies has been widespread. Why? This has been a combination of males' carrying on a family name (cultural), helping to work fields in rural areas (economic), and caring for parents in old age (cultural and eco-nomic). Recently, however, there has been a shift toward preference for female offspring. Why? Urbanization requires fewer male workers on farms (economic). Further, rising property values (economic) have created hardships on families' tradition (cultural) of buying living quarters for sons before they can marry.[5]

Some cultural differences, such as acceptable attire, are fairly obvious; others aren't. And people in every culture often react to given situations by expecting the same re-sponses they would likely get in their own cultures. In our opening case, PRI's British sales reps expected their potential Saudi customers to be punctual and to give them their undivided attention. In fact, the reps' compensation system discouraged them from spending much time on each business transaction. The Saudis, meanwhile, had no com-pulsion to wrap things up, regarded time spent in a café as worthwhile, and considered small talk a good way to identify good business partners. They regarded business deal-ings as less urgent than conversing with friends.

Almost everyone agrees that national cultures differ, but they disagree on what the differences are.

Problem areas that can hinder managers' cultural awareness are

- Subconscious reactions to circumstances.
- The assumption that all societal subgroups are similar.

CRN

Case Review Note

A LITTLE LEARNING GOES A LONG WAY

Some people seem to have an innate ability to say and do the right thing at the right time, while others offend unintentionally or seem ignorant. Experts agree, however, that businesspeople can learn to improve awareness and sensitivity and, by educating themselves, enhance the likelihood of succeeding abroad. Gathering some basic research on another culture can be instructive. However, managers must assess information to determine if it perpetuates unwarranted stereotypes, covers only limited facets of a country and its culture, or is obsolete. They should also observe the behavior of those people who have garnered the kind of respect and confidence they themselves will need.

Of course, cultural variations are so numerous that managers cannot memorize everything. Just consider how many different ways there are to address people. Should you use a given name or a surname? Does a surname come before or after a given name? Do people take a parent's name as a surname? If so, is it taken from a parent's first or last name? If so, is it from one or both parents? Does a wife take her husband's name? What titles are appropriate for different professions? Moreover, many languages have pronouns and verb forms (familiar and polite) that reflect status and how well people know each other. These can even vary among countries using the same language. Mistakes that may seem humorous can also be perceived as the result of ignorance or rudeness, thus jeopardizing a business deal. Fortunately, there are country guidebooks based on people's experiences, including those by international managers. You can also consult with knowledgeable people at home and abroad, whether in a governmental or private capacity.

There is another side to the cultural coin: Too often when we can't explain some difference—say, why the Irish consume more cold cereal than the Spanish do—we tend to attribute it to culture without trying to understand it. (Perhaps the difference is simply that cereal companies have marketed more in Ireland.) Fortunately, we now have access to many recent studies on cross-cultural attitudes and practices that concern businesspeople.[6] Nevertheless, many attitudes, practices, and cultures remain unstudied.

Before reporting major research findings throughout this chapter, we should emphasize a few common shortcomings:

1. Comparing countries by what people say can be risky. For one thing, responses may be colored by the culture you're trying to understand. Some groups of people, for example, may be happiest when they're complaining, or they respond with what they think you want to hear.

2. When researchers are focused on national differences in terms of *averages*, they may overlook specific variations within countries and believe in unrealistic stereotypes. (The average Scandinavian may be uncomfortable with bargaining, but it could be a grave mistake to assume that an Ikea [Swedish] buyer doesn't expect to bargain on prices.[7]) And, of course, personality differences make some people outliers in their own cultures, with no certainty that they'll eventually integrate and conform to cultural norms.[8] (You may score yourself on some common cultural comparison tests—ethnocentrism, individualism versus collectivism, and power distance—to see how you compare with your national norm.[9])

3. Because cultures evolve, behavior reflecting "current" attitudes may well change in the future. Our opening case, for instance, details some changing Saudi attitudes toward women.

The Idea of a "Nation": Delineating Cultures

We begin here by showing why the idea of a "nation" is a useful but imperfect cultural reference when talking about international business. Afterward, we explain why cultures develop and change and discuss how language and religion influence culture.

THE NATION AS A POINT OF REFERENCE

The idea of a *nation* provides a workable definition of a *culture* because the basic similarity among people is often both the cause and effect of national boundaries. Laws governing business operations also apply largely along national lines. Within its borders, a nation's people chiefly share such essential attributes as values, language, and race. The feeling of "we" casts foreigners as "they." National identity is perpetuated through rites and symbols—flags, parades, rallies—and the preservation of national sites, documents, monuments, and museums promotes a common perception of "we."

The Nation as Cultural Mediator   Obviously, the existence of shared attributes doesn't mean everyone in a country is alike, or that each country is unique in all respects. Nations usually include various subcultures, ethnic groups, races, and classes. However, a national culture must be flexible enough to accommodate such a mixture. In fact, a nation legitimizes itself by mediating its diversity;[10] those that fail to do so often dissolve. Yet a nation's shared and mediated characteristics constitute its national identity and affect the practices of any company that does business under its jurisdiction.

Nevertheless, certain cultural attributes can link groups from different nations more closely than groups in a given nation. People in urban areas differ in certain attitudes from people in rural areas. Managers have different work attitudes than do production workers; thus, Country A managers may hold work values closer to those of Country B managers than to those of Country A production workers. As a consequence, when international businesspeople compare nations, they must be careful to examine *relevant groups*—differentiating between, say, the typical attitudes of rural and urban dwellers, or between young and old people.

The nation is a useful definition of society because

- Similarity among people is a cause and an effect of national boundaries.
- Laws apply largely along national lines.

Managers find country-by-country analysis difficult because

- Subcultures exist within nations.
- Similarities link groups from different countries.

Cultural value systems are set early in life but may change through

- Choice or imposition.
- Contact with other cultures.

How Cultures Form and Change

Culture is transmitted in various ways—from parent to child, teacher to pupil, social leader to follower, peer to peer. Developmental psychologists believe that most people acquire their basic value systems as children, such as concepts of evil versus good, dirty versus clean, ugly versus beautiful, unnatural versus natural, abnormal versus normal, paradoxical versus logical, and irrational versus rational. These values are not easily changed later on.[11]

SOURCES OF CHANGE

Both individual and collective values and customs, however, may evolve. Examining this evolution may tell us something about the process by which a culture comes to accept (or reject) certain business practices—knowledge that could be useful to international companies attempting to introduce changes (e.g., new products or operating methods) into a culture. The important thing here is *change*, which may result from either *choice* or *imposition*.

Change by Choice   Change by choice may occur as a reaction to social and economic situations that present people with new alternatives. When rural people choose to accept factory jobs, for example, they change some basic customs—notably, by working regular hours that don't allow the sort of work-time social interactions that farm work allowed.

Change by Imposition   Change by imposition—sometimes called **cultural imperialism**—involves imposing certain elements from an alien culture, such as a forced change in laws by an occupying country that, over time, becomes part of the subject culture.

As a rule, contact among countries brings change; this is known as *cultural diffusion*. When the change results in mixing cultural elements, we have *creolization*. In many Asian countries, for example, ethnic Chinese embody a mixture of Chinese and local cultures.[12]

This photo shows people in traditional dress in Bhutan, arguably the world's most isolated national culture.

Source: Attila JANDI/Shutterstock.com

Some groups and governments have tried to protect national cultures but have not succeeded entirely because people travel and access foreign information through a variety of sources. Further, protecting a culture may result in other disadvantages. For instance, Bhutan, arguably the world's most isolated national culture has required national dress in public (see photo), a primary national language, and preservation of traditions (e.g., folksongs, marriage celebrations, house blessings, archery contests). It has also limited Bhutanese contact with foreigners. However, because these constraints isolated Bhutan from global economic growth, it has permitted some satellite TV since 2007 and will increase the number of permitted foreign tourists from 30,000 to 100,000 between 2010 and 2012.[13]

Language as Both a Diffuser and Stabilizer of Culture

A common language within countries is a unifying force.

Like national boundaries and geographic obstacles, language limits people's contact with other cultures. Map 2.2 shows the distribution of the world's major language groups. Not surprisingly, when people from different areas speak the same language, culture spreads more easily. This helps explain the greater cultural homogeneity among English-speaking and among Spanish-speaking countries, than between English-speaking and Spanish-speaking countries.

The map omits most of the world's approximately 6,000 languages because they are spoken by proportionately few people. When people understand only one language that has relatively few users—especially concentrated in a small geographic area—they tend to cling to their culture because they have little meaningful contact with others.

Such languages as English, French, and Spanish have such widespread acceptance (they're the most prevalent in 52, 21, and 21 countries and territories, respectively) that, as a rule, native speakers don't feel the same need to learn other languages as do speakers of languages that, like Armenian or Bulgarian, are found in only limited geographic areas. Among nations that share the same language, commerce is easier because translating everything isn't necessary. Thus, when people study second languages, they usually choose the ones that are most useful in interacting with other countries, especially in the realm of commerce.

MAP 2.2   Distribution of the World's Major Languages

The people of the world speak thousands of different languages, but only a few of them remain important in the dissemination of culture. A significant portion of the world, for example, speaks English, French, or Spanish. In those countries labeled "Regional," the predominant language is not dominant anywhere else; Japanese, for example, is dominant only in Japan. But take a look at China: It's the only place where people speak Mandarin, but it's important in international business because the population of China comprises a lot of people. The classification "Regional" actually takes in two categories: (1) countries in which the dominant language is not dominant anywhere else (e.g., Japan) and (2) countries in which several different languages are spoken (e.g., India).

Sources: www.udon.de/sprachk.htm. The number of native speakers is taken from World Almanac and Book of Facts (Mahwah, NJ: Primedia Reference, 2002).

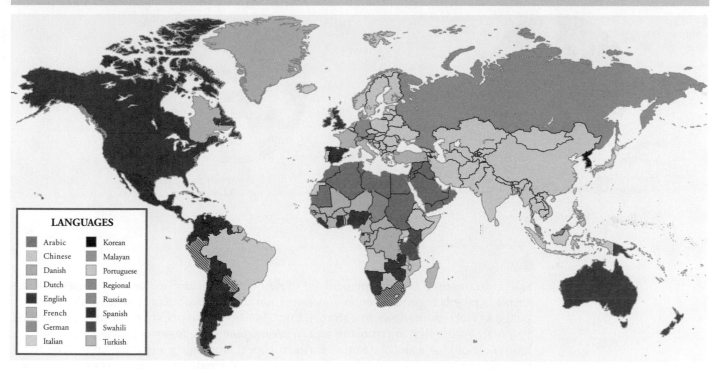

LANGUAGES

Arabic	Korean
Chinese	Malayan
Danish	Portuguese
Dutch	Regional
English	Russian
French	Spanish
German	Swahili
Italian	Turkish

WHY ENGLISH TRAVELS SO WELL

In Figure 2.2, the pie chart on the right shows portions of worldwide output by language. As you can see, native English speaking countries account for a third of the world's production, much more than any other language group—a fact that goes a long way toward explaining why English is the world's most important *second* language. Remember, too, that MNEs—which are largely headquartered in English-speaking countries—decide on the language to use for communicating among their employees in different countries. Not surprisingly, it's usually English, because many of their managers either speak only English or have English as a second language, and they need a common means for managers from different countries to communicate with each other. In addition, many MNEs from non-English-speaking countries have adopted English—the "international language of business"—as their operating language.[14]

However, at least one prominent linguist predicts that monolingual English speakers will eventually experience more difficulty in communicating worldwide. Why? Because the percentage of those people will decrease, while the languages of such countries as China and India will grow rapidly along with their economies.[15] As is so often the case, history may also have a thing or two to teach us in this matter: Latin and French, once the languages of scholarship and diplomacy, respectively, have long since been supplanted.

Nevertheless, for some time now, English words—especially American English—have been entering other languages, such as an estimated 20,000 into Japanese. English travels so well partly because the U.S. media are so influential and because the United

FIGURE 2.2   Major Language Groups: Population and Output

Native speakers for just a few languages—notably English—account for much more of the world's economic output than their population would indicate. Only 8 percent of the world's people speak English as their native (first) language, but the countries and territories where English is the most spoken native language account for 33 percent of global economic output, which helps to explain the prevalence of English as a second language when conducting international business.

Sources: The data for constructing the pie chart on the left came from by List of Languages by Number of Native Speakers," http://en.wikipedia.org/wiki/List_of_languages_by_number_of_native_speakers (accessed February 26, 2011); For constructing the pie chart on the right, the primary language by country came from "Languages Spoken in Each Country of the World," http://www.infoplease.com/ipa/A0855611.html (accessed February 26, 2011). The output per country and territory came from Central Intelligence Agency, The World Factbook, at www.cia.gov.

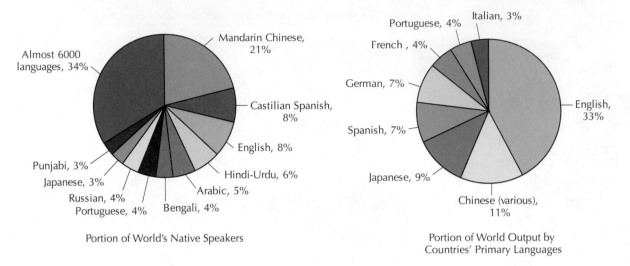

Portion of World's Native Speakers

Portion of World Output by Countries' Primary Languages

States originates a healthy percentage of new products and technology. When, for example, a new U.S. product enters a foreign market, its vocabulary usually enters the language as well—sometimes in a strange form. In a Spanish-speaking country, for instance, you might see a sign announcing that *Vendemos blue jeans de varios colores* ("We sell various colors of blue jeans"). At other times, the local language gives it an Anglicized twist; thus, the French call a self-service restaurant *le self.* Finally, the intrusion of English into another language may result in the development of a hybrid tongue, such as "Spanglish" (Spanish and English) or "Chinglish" (Mandarin Chinese and English), which may ultimately become a distinct language.[16]

Note that some countries, such as Finland, prefer to coin their own new words rather than accept Anglicized items into their vocabularies. Because many countries see language as an integral part of culture, they regulate linguistic changes. In the business arena, for example, they may require that all public signs be in the local language.

Religion as a Cultural Stabilizer

| Many strong values are the result of a dominant religion.

Map 2.3 shows the approximate distribution of the world's major religions. In many countries, the practice of religion has declined significantly; indeed, a few nations in northern Europe are sometimes called "post-Christian" societies. At the same time, religion has been a cultural stabilizer because centuries of profound religious influence continue to shape cultural values even in these societies.[17] Among people with strong religious convictions, the role of religion in shaping behavior is even stronger.

Many of these religions—Buddhism, Christianity, Hinduism, Islam, and Judaism—influence specific beliefs that may affect business, such as inhibiting the sale of certain products or the performance of work at certain times. McDonald's, for example, serves neither beef nor pork in India to offend neither its Hindu nor Muslim populations. El Al, the Israeli national airline, does not fly on Saturday, the Jewish Sabbath. In fact, religion impacts almost every business function. If companies do not take these into account, they may not be viewed legitimately by people where they are operating.[18]

MAP 2.3 Distribution of the World's Major Religions

Most countries are home to people of various religious beliefs, but a nation's culture is typically influenced most heavily by a dominant religion. The practices of the dominant religion, for instance, often shape customary practices in legal and business affairs.

Source: The numbers for adherents are taken from "List of Religious Populations," http://en.wikipedia.org/wiki/list_of_religious_populations **

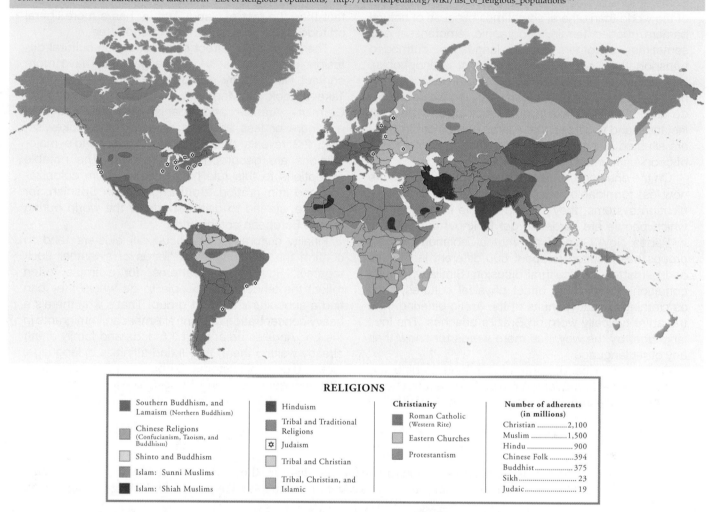

RELIGIONS

			Number of adherents (in millions)
Southern Buddhism, and Lamaism (Northern Buddhism)	Hinduism	**Christianity** Roman Catholic (Western Rite)	Christian 2,100
Chinese Religions (Confucianism, Taoism, and Buddhism)	Tribal and Traditional Religions	Eastern Churches	Muslim 1,500
Shinto and Buddhism	Judaism	Protestantism	Hindu 900
Islam: Sunni Muslims	Tribal and Christian		Chinese Folk 394
Islam: Shiah Muslims	Tribal, Christian, and Islamic		Buddhist..................375 Sikh............................23 Judaic........................19

Of course, not all nations that practice the same religion impose the same constraints on business. In predominantly Muslim countries, for example, Friday is a day of worship, whereas in Turkey (a secular Muslim country that adheres to the Christian work calendar to keep in step with European business activity) it is a workday. In places where rival religions or factions are vying for political control, the resulting strife can cause so much upheaval that business activity suffers, whether from property damage, broken supply chains, or breaches in customer connections. Unfortunately, the problem is substantial. In recent years, religious violence has erupted in such countries as India, Iraq, Sudan, and Northern Ireland.

Behavioral Practices Affecting Business

We have indicated that culture affects every business function. Attitudes and values constitute *cultural variables*, which both researchers and businesspeople define differently, attaching various names to slightly different and sometimes overlapping concepts. Because of all

Concept Check

In Chapter 1, we emphasize the importance of studying the behavioral factors that affect business conditions to help managers decide why and how they may need to alter operations in different countries.

Does Ge🌐graphy Matter? Birds of a Feather Flock Together

Some groups of people are more isolated from the rest of the world than others, sometimes because of natural barriers (rugged terrain, geographic remoteness) and sometimes by others (unique languages, outmoded transportation and communications, xenophobia). Historically, natural barriers—and natural advantages—have been quite important in determining where people do and don't live. Take a quick look at any map, for instance, and you'll see that a large portion of big cities are situated where waterways facilitate the interaction of people and interchange of goods.

On the one hand, although many natural barriers are now less formidable because of airplanes and communication systems, they still play a role in determining which people are harder to get to know than others. In Papua New Guinea, the mutual isolation of tribal groups has resulted in about 800 different languages and permitted little cultural diffusion. Similarly, natural conditions continue to affect physical cultures, such as clothing for native Inuits of the Arctic differing from the attire typically worn on Brazil's beaches. The Inuit language, by the way, has more words for snow than any other language.

On the other hand, some places have traditionally enjoyed more-than-average outside contact than others. As we saw in our opening case, the Saudi port of Jeddah, having long experienced more external contact than the rest of Saudi Arabia, has a more liberal attitude toward dress than the interior area.

Then there's the effect of proximity on cultural diffusion: Understandably, people generally have more contact with nearby groups than with remote ones. Take a look at Map 2.2. As you can see, most German-, Arabic-, and Spanish-speaking countries are more or less adjacent to each other. Likewise, Map 2.3 reveals that virtually all the world's major religions are geographically clustered. The notable exceptions to this rule have resulted from colonization and immigration. Both English and Spanish, for instance, spread to distant parts of the world during eras of European colonization.

Finally, cultural (and subcultural) clusters tend to confirm the old adage that "Birds of a feather flock together." Immigration patterns, for example, often reflect the tendency of people to go where they can find a subcultural support group. That's why there's a heavy concentration of Central American immigrants in the Los Angeles area; even if friends and family aren't already waiting there, they'll find affinities in language, diet, and general customs. Globally, we find many such patterns, such as Hong Kong Chinese in Vancouver, Canada, and Algerians in Marseilles, France. ●

these nuances in terms and concepts, there are thousands of possible ways to relate culture to business—far too many to cover in one chapter. We'll settle for hitting the highlights.

ISSUES IN SOCIAL STRATIFICATION

Every culture ranks some people more highly than others. Such *social stratification* dictates a person's class, status, and financial rewards within that culture. In business, this practice may entail ranking members of managerial groups more highly than production group members. Social stratification is determined by (1) individual's achievements and qualifications and (2) individual's affiliation with or membership in certain groups. These two factors interact, but the importance of one versus the other varies by business function and by culture.

Individual Qualifications and Their Limitations   In most societies, individual achievement is important, such as in choosing a successful athlete as a spokesperson to advertise sportswear. Similarly, in some nations, such as the United States, companies tend to base a person's eligibility for employment and promotion largely on individual achievements and qualification. However, we shall see that this is not always the case even in the United States.

Just as companies look for individual qualifications for choosing spokespersons for advertising, they also match spokespersons with the audience (group membership) they wish to reach, such as using older models for products aimed at the group of older

Concept Check

In the opening case of Chapter 1, we discussed that many top sports players are effectively global brands as companies pay them to use and endorse their products.

Businesses reward competence highly in some societies.

consumers. In addition, societies look at these group affiliations differently, thus causing certain business functions to be carried out differently. Companies in Japan, for instance, generally place more weight on seniority for employee promotion than companies in the United States (thus favoring older employees) because Japan stresses cooperation over competition in the workplace.[19] Similarly, a study of hiring, promotion, compensation, and staff-reduction practices at a number of banks showed that employers differed by nationality on all four functions. When needing to make staff reductions, for example, British banks were most prone to save costs by discharging on a performance-to-salary basis (targeting, say, a middle-aged manager with a high salary and average performance), whereas German banks were more concerned with minimizing personal hardship (targeting younger managers, regardless of performance, because they could find new jobs more easily).[20]

The above examples dealt with group memberships based largely on age affiliations, but there are many more as well. Those determined by birth are known as **ascribed group memberships** and include those based on gender, family, age, caste, and ethnic, racial, or national origin. **Acquired group memberships** include those based on religion, political affiliation, and professional and other associations.

The more egalitarian, or "open," a society, the less the importance of group membership in determining rewards. In less open societies, however, laws may be designed to reinforce or undermine rigid stratification based on group membership. In other cases, group memberships deny large numbers of people equal access to the preparation needed to qualify for jobs, such as to education that results in a much lower literacy rate for women than for men in much of sub-Saharan Africa. The Nobel economist, Amartya Sen, referred to this type exclusion of people from the workforce as *unfreedom* and pointed out its negative effect on economic advancement.[21]

Even when individuals qualify for given positions and no legal barriers exist to hold them back, certain social obstacles—say, public opposition to the use of child labor in the company's home country—can make it wary of adopting certain practices in host countries. In addition, opposition to certain groups may come from other workers, customers, local shareholders, or government officials.

The following sections focus on some of the group memberships that influence a person's social ranking from country to country. Two additional factors are often important: *education* (especially how much and where) and *social connections* (who you know and in what places).[22] This latter point corresponds to the old adage that "It's *who* you know, not *what* you know." (This is a point we pursue in our chapter-ending case, which details a U.S. company's adventures in Uganda. Here, we'll see not only that effective opposition can come from small ad hoc groups, but also that the people you need to know can sometimes be found in unexpected places.)

Ethnic and Racial Groups

In less open societies, laws may be designed to reinforce or undermine rigid stratification. Racial or ethnic quotas to counter discrimination are a good example. Malaysia, for example, has long maintained employment quotas for three ethnic groups—Malays, Chinese, and Indians—primarily to upgrade the economic position of Malays because, at the time of the country's independence, the Chinese and Indian minorities dominated business ownership and the professions, respectively.[23] The Malaysian system requires companies to maintain expensive record-keeping systems of their hiring practices; in fact, it has recently come under increasing criticism from within the country.[24] Likewise, Brazil, which has more than 300 terms to designate skin color, has proposed racial quotas in universities, government jobs, and even television soap operas.[25] (It plans no quotas for the national football team, where only competence counts.)

Gender-Based Groups

Country-specific differences in attitudes toward gender are sometimes quite pronounced. (Figure 2.3 looks at the difference humorously.) Some of these probably seem paradoxical, at least to the outsider. As you'll recall from our opening case, there are more than 13 employed men for every employed woman in Saudi Arabia.

Group affiliations can be
- Ascribed or acquired.
- A reflection of class and status.

Egalitarian societies place more importance on acquired group memberships.

Case Review Note

Country-by-country attitudes vary toward
- Male and female roles.
- Respect for age.
- Family ties.

Case Review Note

FIGURE 2.3   Gender roles vary substantially among national cultures

Source: Bruce Eric Kaplan/Cartoon Bank

"You know, in some cultures the male does things."

Compare that figure with the United States, where only 1.2 men are employed for every woman.[26] In Lithuania, more than 50 percent of both males and females agreed with the following statement: "When jobs are scarce, men have a better right to a job than women"; in Sweden and Iceland, the number was under 10 percent.[27]

In many parts of the world, however, barriers to gender-based employment practices are coming down, due to changes in both attitudes and work requirements. In the United States, one noticeable change is reflected in the number of people of one gender employed in occupations previously dominated by the other, such as more male nurses.[28] The cause of this change may be as much economic as cultural. The decrease in production jobs requiring brawn and increase in jobs for people with specialized education, such as X-ray technology and psychiatric casework, has caused shifts in the relative demand for female employees and the type of jobs for both genders.

Age-Based Groups   Countries treat age groups differently, and each country expresses its attitudes toward age in different ways. All enforce age-related laws such as statutes applying to employment, driving privileges, rights to obtain products and services (alcohol, cigarettes, certain pharmaceuticals, bank accounts), and civic duty (voting, serving in the military or on juries). Sometimes the logic of these laws seems contradictory. In the United States, for example, people can vote, marry, drive, and die for their country before they can legally buy alcohol at age 21. In parts of Switzerland, you can legally buy alcohol at age 14.[29] U.S. firms bombard children with TV advertising, but Sweden prohibits ads targeted to children.

National differences toward age of employment practices are substantial. Both Finland and the Netherlands, for example, enforce mandatory retirement ages, but with few exceptions (say, airline pilots), U.S. law (in response to lobbying by senior citizens) specifically prohibits the practice. In contrast, the photo shows French protests against raising the retirement age. In Britain, age discrimination laws apply to everyone, regardless of age, whereas U.S. law is designed to protect only people over age 40.[30] When the proposition "When jobs are scarce, people should be forced to retire early" was put to people in different countries, almost three-quarters of Bulgarians agreed, but only 10 percent of Japanese.[31] Why this latter difference? For one thing, Japanese hold strongly to the assumption that there's a significant correlation between age and wisdom.

In 2010, French marchers protested against proposals to raise the retirement age.
Source: Olga Besnard/Shutterstock.com

Family-Based Groups In some cultures, such as in much of Latin America, the most important group membership is the family. A person's position in society depends heavily on the family's social status or "respectability" rather than on individual achievement. Because family ties are so strong, there may also be a tendency to cooperate more closely within the family unit than in other relationships. In such cultures, not surprisingly, small family-run companies are quite successful; conversely, however, they often encounter difficulties in growing because owners are reluctant to share responsibility with professional managers hired from outside the family. When its business culture is hampered by this state of affairs, a country (or region) may lack the indigenously owned *large-scale* operations that are usually necessary for long-term economic development.[32]

WORK MOTIVATION

Not surprisingly, motivated employees are normally more productive than those who aren't. On an aggregate basis, of course, this influences companies' efficiency and countries' economic development. The following discussion summarizes studies showing major differences in how and why people in different nations are motivated to work.

Materialism and Motivation When developing his *Protestant ethic* theory, Max Weber observed that predominantly Protestant countries were the most economically developed. He attributed this "ethic" to an outgrowth of the Protestant Reformation in sixteenth-century Europe, which reflects the belief that work is a pathway to salvation and that material success does not impede salvation. Although we no longer accept a strict distinction between Protestant and non-Protestant attitudes toward work and material gain, we do tend to adhere to the underlying values of Weber's concept: namely, that self-discipline, hard work, honesty, and a belief in a just world foster work motivation and, thus, economic growth.[33] As a matter of fact, on one hand there is evidence indicating a positive correlation between the intensity of religious belief per se (regardless of

The desire for material wealth is

- A prime motivation to work.
- Positive for economic development.

specific belief systems) and adherence to some attributes that lead to economic growth (say, confidence in the rule of law and belief in the virtue of thrift).[34] Moreover, there's strong evidence that the individual desire for material wealth is a prime incentive to perform the kind of work that leads to community-wide economic development.[35] On the other hand, there are societies such as Myanmar and Bhutan where a large portion of the population vanish from the economic work force temporarily or permanently in order to live in monasteries and nunneries while being supported by others.

The Productivity/Leisure Trade-Off   Some cultures place less value on leisure time than others. Their people work longer hours, take fewer holidays and vacations, and generally spend less time and money on leisure activities. In a study of OECD (fairly high-income) countries, France and the United States offered an example of contrast. The French had 30 days mandated vacation, spent on average 135 minutes per day eating and drinking and 530 minutes sleeping, whereas Americans had no mandated vacation and spent only an average of 74 minutes per day eating and drinking and 518 minutes sleeping.[36] In the United States, there is still some disdain for people who fall on either end of the work/leisure spectrum: people of privilege who appear to contribute nothing to society and people who appear to be satisfied with a lifestyle that can be maintained by unemployment benefits. Americans who give up work (primarily retirees) often complain that they're no longer allowed to contribute anything useful to society, one of the reasons for laws prohibiting mandatory retirement.

In parts of some poor countries, meanwhile, such as rural India, living "the simple life"—that is, without benefit of much material comfort—seems to be a desirable end in itself. When productivity gains afford them the choice, people may choose to take at least part of the gains in leisure rather than all of it in earnings to buy more.[37] By and large, however, in most countries, most people today, whether rich or poor, regard personal economic advancement as a worthwhile goal in life.

Expectation of Success and Reward

Motivation toward work is influenced by the perceived likelihood of success and its rewards versus failure. Generally, people have little enthusiasm for effort when the likelihood of success seems too easy or too difficult. Few of us would care to run a race against either a snail or a racehorse; in either case, the outcome is too predictable. Our enthusiasm peaks when uncertainty of success is high, such as the challenge of racing another human of roughly equal ability. Likewise, the reward for a successfully completed task—say, winning a fair footrace—may be high or low, and most of us usually work harder the more we expect success to lead to a higher reward.

> People are more eager to work if
>
> • Rewards for success are high.
> • There is some uncertainty of success.

Success and Reward across Borders   Performed in different countries, the same tasks come with different probabilities of success, different rewards for success, and different consequences for failure. In cultures in which the probability of economic failure is almost certain and the perceived rewards of success are low, people tend—not surprisingly—to view work as necessary but unsatisfying, mainly because they foresee little benefit to themselves. This attitude may prevail in harsh climates, in very poor areas, or in subcultures subject to discrimination. Likewise, if there is little difference in reward between working hard or not, there is less motivation to work hard. In Cuba, for instance, where public policy allocates output from productive to unproductive workers, there is not much enthusiasm for work. When high uncertainty of outcome is combined with the likelihood of a positive reward for success and little or no reward for failure, we find the greatest work enthusiasm.[38]

Performance and Achievement

The Masculinity–Femininity Index   One study found significant differences around the world by using a so-called **masculinity–femininity index** to compare the attitudes of employees in 50 countries toward work and achievement. Employees with a high "masculinity score" admired successful work achievers, harbored little sympathy for the unfortunate, and preferred to be better than others rather than on a par with them. They shared a money-and-things orientation rather than a people orientation, a belief that it's better "to live to work" than "to work to live," and a preference for performance and growth over quality of life and the environment.[39]

Similarly, the degree to which people are assertive, confrontational, and aggressive in their relationships with others varies across borders. Such differences help explain why an international company may encounter managers abroad who behave differently than expected, or preferred. Let's say a company in a high-masculinity country, such as Austria, sets up operations in a high-femininity country such as Sweden. Typical purchasing managers in Sweden probably prefer smooth social relationships and amiable, ongoing dealings with suppliers to, say, lower costs or faster delivery. They may also place such organizational goals as employee and social welfare ahead of a typical Austrian firm's goals of growth and efficiency.

Hierarchies of Needs   According to the **hierarchy-of-needs theory** of motivation, people try to fulfill lower-level needs before moving on to higher-level ones.[40] As you can see from Figure 2.4, the most basic needs are *physiological*: food, water, and sex. We have to satisfy (or nearly satisfy) those before *security* needs—safe physical and emotional environments—become a sufficiently powerful set of motivators. Then we must satisfy our security needs before triggering the motivational effect of *affiliation* or social needs, such as peer acceptance. Once we have those, we're motivated to satisfy our *esteem* needs—bolstering our self-image through recognition, attention, and appreciation. The highest-order need calls for *self-actualization*—self-fulfillment, or (to quote Robert Lewis Stevenson) "becom[ing] all that we are capable of becoming." Finally, the theory also implies that we'll typically work to satisfy a need, but once satisfied, its value as a motivator diminishes.

> The ranking of needs may differ among countries.

What can the hierarchy-of-needs theory tell us about doing business in foreign countries? For one thing, research has shown that different cultures not only attach different degrees of importance to various needs, they also rank higher-order needs differently. Thus, the theory can help in distinguishing among the reward preferences of employees in different parts of the world. This is important because of differences in workforce composition.[41] In very poor countries, for example, a larger portion of workers are likely engaged in manual jobs, thus a company can motivate a larger portion of them simply by providing enough compensation to satisfy their needs for food and shelter. Elsewhere, a larger portion of workers are motivated by other needs.

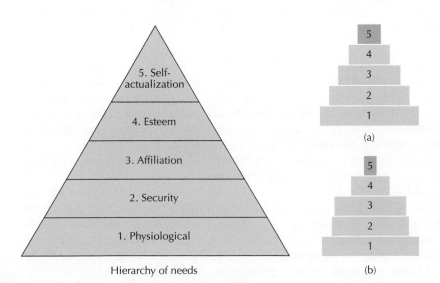

Hierarchy of needs

(a)

(b)

FIGURE 2.4 The Hierarchy of Needs and Need-Hierarchy Comparisons

The pyramid on the left represents the five-level hierarchy of needs formulated by Maslow. The two block pyramids on the right (a, b) represent two different groups of people—say, the populations of two different countries. Note that the block representing affiliation needs (level 3) is wider in (b) than in (a); conversely, the block representing self-actualization needs (level 5) is wider in (a) than in (b). In other words, even if we rank various needs in the same order (or hierarchy), the people in one country may regard a given higher-order need as more important (wider) than do people in another country.

However, compensation (even at low levels of income) cannot fully explain differences in work motivation. For example, a long-term ethnographic study among a U.S. airline's back-office employees in three countries found that those in the United States and the Dominican Republic saw the job as a stepping-stone to higher-level positions. However, few in Barbados wanted a promotion because it would change their relationships with friends. U.S. workers usually dressed very casually because they would not be seen by outsiders in the back office, but Barbadians dressed up to be seen going to what was considered a prestige job. In fact, the company offered Barbadian employees free company-owned bus transport, but the employees preferred to pay for slower public transportation where others could see them. The largely female staff in Barbados had low absenteeism and turnover rates because Barbados has a history of working women. In the Dominican Republic, however, most female employees stayed on only until they married.[42]

RELATIONSHIP PREFERENCES

So far, we've discussed two categories of behavioral practices affecting business: social stratification systems and work motivation. Next, we discuss some of the values underlying interpersonal differences in behavior.

There are national variations in the preference for autocratic or consultative management.

Power Distance   From country to country, employee preferences tend to differ in terms of interacting with bosses, subordinates, and peers. Considerable evidence suggests that people perform better when the nature of their interactions fits their preferences. That's why companies are well advised to align management styles with superior-subordinate interaction preferences, which are know in general as **power distance.**

With *high* power distance, people prefer little consultation between the two tiers and one of two management styles: *autocratic* (ruling with unlimited authority) or *paternalistic* (regulating conduct by supplying needs). With *low* power distance, they prefer "consultative" styles.[43] What might happen, therefore, if a Dutch company assigned domestic managers, who typically prefer low power distance, to improve productivity at a facility in Morocco, where workers typically prefer high power distance? The Dutch managers might consult with Moroccan subordinates in an attempt to improve employee productivity. Unfortunately, subordinates may lose confidence in their superiors (e.g., Why don't they know what to do?), so that performance deteriorates rather than improves.

Interestingly, managers who prefer an autocratic style of superior–subordinate relationship are also quite willing to delegate and accept decision making by a majority of subordinates. What they don't accept well is consultative interaction between the two tiers, which implies a more equal relationship between them. Clearly, worker-participation methods may need to be adjusted to fit different countries.

"Safe" work environments motivate collectivists. Challenges motivate individualists.

Individualism versus Collectivism   *High* **individualism** describes an employee's preference to fulfill leisure time and improve skills outside the organization, receive direct monetary compensation as opposed to fringe benefits, engage in personal decision making and on-the-job challenges. *High* **collectivism,** in contrast, typifies an employee's penchant for dependence on the organization thorough training, satisfactory workplace conditions, and good benefits. In countries with high individualism, self-actualization opportunity is a prime motivator because employees want challenges. In those with high collectivism, fulfilling security needs is a prime motivator.[44]

Degrees of individualism and collectivism also influence employee interactions. Consider Levi Strauss, which introduced team-based production into several U.S. plants because its management had observed high productivity when the system was used in the highly collectivist culture of Japan. U.S. employees, especially the most skilled workers, detested the system, productivity went down, and Levi returned to a more individualistic system that was more suitable to the culture of its U.S. workforce.

Situational Differences: The Family   Applying any measure of *individualism versus collectivism* is complex and imprecise because preferences may vary by situation.[45] Although Japan and Mexico are both characterized as collectivist cultures, Mexico's collectivist preference is based more on kinship relations that do not carry over easily into the workplace.[46] Moreover, the Mexican concept of family sometimes includes not only the *nuclear family* (husband, wife, and minor children) but also the *vertically extended family* (members of several generations) and the *horizontally extended family* (aunts, uncles, and cousins).

Such differences can affect business in a variety of ways:

- Individualists may be less motivated to receive material rewards from their work because of dividing the rewards among more family members.

- Because relocation means that family members must also find new jobs, a worker's geographic mobility is limited. Even when extended families don't live together, mobility may be reduced because people prefer to remain near relatives.

- Interrelated familial roles may complicate purchasing decisions.

- Security and social needs may be met more effectively at home than in the workplace.

RISK-TAKING BEHAVIOR

Cultures differ in people's willingness to accept things the way they are and their belief about control over their destiny. The following discussion examines four types of *risk-taking behavior* that reflect these attitudes: *uncertainty avoidance, trust, future orientation,* and *fatalism.*

Nationalities differ in

- Ease of handling uncertainties.
- Degree of trust among people.
- Future orientation.
- Attitudes of self-determination and fatalism.

Uncertainty Avoidance   In countries where **uncertainty avoidance** is high, most employees prefer to follow set rules even if breaking them may be in the company's best interests. They also tend to stay with current employers for a long time, preferring the certainty of present positions over the uncertainty of their future elsewhere.[47] When uncertainty avoidance is high, superiors may need to be more precise in their directions to subordinates, who typically don't want to be responsible for actions that counter the company's interests.

Moreover, fewer consumers are prepared to risk being early product adopters. Gillette, for example, depends heavily on introducing new products, so it is likely better off to enter markets like Denmark and the United Kingdom, which rate low on uncertainty avoidance, before venturing into Belgium and Portugal, which rate high.

Trust   Surveys measure *trust* and find country differences by asking respondents to evaluate such statements as "Most people can be trusted" and "You can't be too careful in dealing with people." Many more Norwegians than Brazilians, for example, regard most people as trustworthy.[48] Where trust is high, the cost of doing business tends to be lower because managers don't spend much time fussing over every possible contingency and monitoring every action for compliance with certain business principles. Instead, they can spend time producing, selling, and innovating.[49]

Future Orientation   Cultures differ in their perceptions of the risks from delaying gratification. For example, **future orientation** (living for the future) is more pronounced in Switzerland, the Netherlands, and Canada than in Russia, Poland, and Italy.[50] In the former cultures, companies may find it easier to motivate workers through such delayed-compensation programs as retirement plans.

Fatalism   If people believe strongly in self-determination, they may be willing to work hard to achieve goals and take responsibility for performance. But if they're *fatalistic*—if they believe every event in life is inevitable—they're less likely to accept the basic cause-and-effect relationship between work and reward. In countries that rate high on fatalism, people do less planning for contingencies, such as buying insurance. Religious differences play a significant role in this regard. Conservative or fundamentalist groups, for instance, are more likely to view occurrences as "the will of God." Thus, managers are less apt to sway them with cause-and-effect logic than by making personal appeals or offering them rewards for complying with requests.[51]

INFORMATION AND TASK PROCESSING

"Beauty," we're often told, "is in the eye of the beholder." So, apparently, are perceptions and judgments on cultural and personal levels. Both are based on what people perceive as accurate *information,* and different cultures handle information in different ways. The following discussion examines some of the ways in which different cultures perceive, obtain, and process information.

Perception of Cues   As a rule, we're selective in perceiving *cues*—features that inform us about the nature of something. We may identify things through any of our senses, and each sense can provide information in various ways; through vision, for example, we sense color, depth, and shape. The cues that people rely on are partly physiological, and there is growing evidence that evolution and genetics play a role in how different groups perceive.[52] Genetic differences in eye pigmentation, for instance, allow some people to differentiate colors more precisely than others.

Cultural differences, especially language, also reflect differences in perception of cues. The richness of a descriptive vocabulary allows its speakers to note and express very subtle differences that exist from place to place. Thus different cultures perceive certain subjects more precisely than others. For instance, the Arabic language has more than 6,000 different words for camels, their body parts, and the equipment associated with them,[53] and Arabic speakers can express nuances about camels that just about everybody else will probably overlook.

It helps managers to know whether cultures favor

- Focused or broad information.
- Sequential or simultaneous handling of situations.
- Handling principles or small issues first.

Obtaining Information: Low-Context versus High-Context Cultures   Researchers classify some countries (including the United States and most of northern Europe) as **low-context cultures,** in which people generally regard as relevant only firsthand information that bears directly on the subject at hand. Businesspeople spend little time on small talk and tend to get to the point. In **high-context cultures** (such as most countries in southern Europe), people tend to regard seemingly peripheral information as pertinent and to infer meanings from things said either indirectly or casually.

When people from the two types of cultures have to deal with each other, low-context people may perceive high-context people as inefficient in their use of time, while the latter may perceive the former as overly aggressive.

Information Processing   Insofar as all cultures categorize, plan, and quantify, information processing is a universal activity. However, every culture has its own systems for ordering and classifying information. In U.S. telephone directories, entries appear in alphabetical order by last (family) name; in Iceland, they're organized by first (given) names. (Icelandic last names are derived from the father's first name: Jon, son of Thor, is Jon *Thorsson,* and his sister's last name is *Thorsdottir,* "daughter of Thor"). To perform efficiently and work amicably in a foreign environment, you need to understand such differences in processing systems. Perhaps more important, different processing systems create challenges in sharing global data. Even the use of global personnel directories is problematic because of different alphabets and alphabetizing systems.

Monochronic versus Polychronic Cultures   Cultural differences also affect the degree of multitasking with which people are comfortable. For example, northern European cultures are often seen as **monochronic:** People prefer to work sequentially, such as finishing transactions with one customer before dealing with another. Conversely, **polychronic** southern Europeans are more comfortable when working simultaneously on a variety of tasks, such as dealing immediately with multiple customers who need service.[54] Imagine the potential misconceptions when businesspeople from northern Europe see their southern European counterparts as uninterested in doing business with them because they don't bother to give them their undivided attention.

Idealism versus Pragmatism Whereas some cultures tend to focus first on the whole and then on the parts, others do the opposite. When asked to describe an underwater scene in which one large fish was swimming among some smaller fish and other aquatic life, most Japanese first described the overall picture, whereas most Americans first described the large fish.[55] Similarly, some cultures prefer to establish overall principles before they try to resolve small issues—an approach sometimes labeled **idealism.** Cultures in which people focus more on details than on abstract principles are said to be **pragmatic.**

These different approaches can affect business in a number of ways. In a culture of pragmatists (as in the United States), labor negotiations tend to focus on well-defined issues—say, hourly pay increases for a specific bargaining unit. In an idealist culture (as in Argentina), labor disputes tend to blur the focus on specific demands as workers tend to rely first on mass action, such as general strikes or political activities, to publicize basic principles.

Communications

We now look at problems in *communications*—especially translating spoken and written language. Problems occur not only when you shift from one language to another, but also when you communicate with someone from another country with the same official language. Finally, we discuss communications that occur by means other than spoken and written language—a so-called "silent language."

Cross-border communications do not always translate as intended.

SPOKEN AND WRITTEN LANGUAGE

Translating one language directly into another is not as straightforward as it may seem. Some words simply don't have direct translations. In English, for example, *children* may mean either "young people" or "offspring." In Spanish, *niños* and *hijos* distinguish between the two.

In addition, language, including common word meanings, is constantly evolving. When Microsoft purchased a thesaurus code for its Spanish version of Word, the connotations of many synonyms had shifted by the time it implemented the software; some, in fact, were transformed into outright insults that alienated potential customers.[56] Of course, in any language words mean different things in different contexts. A U.S. company once described itself as an "old friend" of China; unfortunately, the Chinese word it chose for *old* meant "former" instead of "long-standing."[57]

Finally, remember that grammar is complex and the seemingly slight misuse (or even placement) of a word can substantially change the meaning. All of the following, each originally composed to assist English-speaking guests, have appeared on signs in hotels around the world:

FRANCE: "Please leave your values at the desk."

MEXICO (to assure guests about the safety of drinking water): "The manager has personally passed all the water served here."

JAPAN: "You are invited to take advantage of the chambermaid."

NORWAY: "Ladies are requested not to have children in the bar."

SWITZERLAND: "Because of the impropriety of entertaining guests of the opposite sex in the bedroom, it is suggested that the lobby be used for this purpose."

GREECE (at check-in line): "We will execute customers in strict rotation."

These examples offer a comical look at language barriers that usually result in only a little embarrassment. Poor translations, however, can have much graver consequences, such as structural collapses of buildings and airplane crashes.[58] So choose your words carefully. Although there's no foolproof way of ensuring translations, experienced international businesspeople rely on such following suggestions:

- Get references for the people who will do your translating.
- Make sure your translator knows the technical vocabulary of your business.
- For written work, do *back translations:* Have one person go from, say, English to French and a second from French back to English. If your final message says what you said originally, it's probably satisfactory.
- For written work, make sure that the tone, not just the words, fit both your own intentions and the expectations of recipients.
- Use simple words whenever possible (such as *ban* instead of *interdiction*).
- Avoid slang. American slang, especially words or phrases originating from sports— *off base, out in left field, threw me a curve, ballpark figure*— are probably meaningless to most businesspeople outside the United States.
- When either you or your counterpart is dealing in a language other than your first language, clarify communications in several ways (repeat things in different words and ask questions) to ensure that all parties have the same interpretation.
- Recognize the need and budget from the start for the extra time needed for translation and clarification.

Be careful with humor because some lacks a universal appeal. A Microsoft executive quipped to Indian executives that he really didn't have the qualifications to speak because he did not complete his MBA. The comment was badly received because Indians place high importance on education and on persevering rather than dropping out.[59]

Finally, even when all parties to a communication come from countries that share an official language, don't assume that understanding will go smoothly. Table 2.1, for instance, lists just some of the approximately 4,000 words that have different meanings in British and American English. What could go wrong? When Hershey's launched its Elegancita candy bar in Latin America, its expensive advertising campaign boasted about the *cajeta* in the product. Unfortunately, although *cajeta* means "goat's-milk caramel" in Mexico, in much of South America it's vulgar slang for a part of the female anatomy.[60]

TABLE 2.1   Dangers of Misspeaking the Language(s) of Business

Below are a couple of short lists containing words whose meanings are different in the United States and the United Kingdom—"two countries separated by a common language," as the British playwright G.B. Shaw once quipped. There are approximately 4,000 words with the potential to cause problems for people who—in theory—speak the same language.

United States	United Kingdom
turnover	*redundancy*
sales	*turnover*
inventory	*stock*
stock	*shares*
president	*managing director*
paperback	*limp cover*

SILENT LANGUAGE

Of course, spoken and written language is not our only means of communicating. We constantly exchange messages through a host of nonverbal cues that form a **silent language.**[61] Our opening case offers a good example. Recall that in the process of conducting market research for the Java Lounge, researchers depended on several non-verbal cues to deduce who was affluent.

Colors   Colors are an interesting aspect of a culture's silent language. For a product to succeed, its colors obviously must be consistent with the consumer's frame of reference. Colors invoke distinct associations in different countries, such as being lucky or unlucky or being associated with specific business (e.g., yellow cabs in the United States and black ones in the United Kingdom). In most Western countries, black is a color for mourning death; in parts of Africa, it's white; in Thailand, it's purple. In the United States, pink is used to denote femininity, while in Japan, it denotes masculinity. United Airlines' promotion of a new passenger service in Hong Kong is an example of an effort that backfired because of color. Why? It handed out white carnations to its best customers, but white carnations are given in Hong Kong only in sympathy for a death in the family.

Distance   Another aspect of silent language is the accustomed distance people maintain during conversations. In the United States, it is 5 to 8 feet for a business discussion and 18 inches to 3 feet for private conversations.[62] Thus, U.S. managers conducting business in Latin America may find themselves constantly moving backward to avoid the closeness their Latin American counterparts are accustomed to maintain. At the end of the discussion, both parties may well feel uneasy about each other without realizing why.

Time and Punctuality   Different perceptions of time and punctuality also may create confusion internationally. U.S. businesspeople usually arrive early for business appointments, a few minutes late for dinner at someone's home, and a bit later still for large social gatherings. In another country, the concept of punctuality in any or all of these situations may be different. A Latin American host may find it surprising and perhaps discourteous if a U.S. guest arrives only a few minutes later than the stated time for dinner.

Culturally speaking, there are different ways of looking at time. People in English-speaking, Germanic, and Scandinavian countries tend to value time as a scarce commodity; if it's lost, it can't be recouped.[63] They tend to stick to schedules, even if taking longer would yield better results. In contrast, people who view time as an event prefer to take as long as necessary to complete the event. In one case, a U.S. company competed for a contract, and its managers were so confident of winning on the basis of better technology that they scheduled a tight, one-day meeting in Mexico City. They thought this was plenty of time for their presentation and questions. Unfortunately, the Mexican team arrived one hour after the scheduled start. Then, when one member of the Mexican team was called out of the room for an urgent phone call, the whole group got upset when the U.S. team tried to proceed without him. The competing French team, in contrast, allocated two weeks for discussions and won the contract even though its technology was clearly less sophisticated.[64]

Body Language   Body language, or *kinesics*—the way people walk, touch, and move their bodies—also differs among cultures. Indeed, very few gestures have universal meanings. A Greek, Turk, or Bulgarian may indicate "yes" with a sideways movement of the head that could be construed as "no" in the United States and much of Europe. As Figure 2.5 shows, certain gestures may have several, even contradictory meanings.

Prestige   Another factor in silent language relates to a person's status, particularly in an organizational setting. A U.S. manager who places great faith in physical things as cues to prestige may underestimate the status of foreign counterparts who don't have large, plush corner offices on high floors. A foreigner may underestimate U.S. counterparts who

Silent language includes color associations, sense of appropriate distance, time and status cues, body language, and prestige.

FIGURE 2.5 Body Language Is Not a Universal Language

The fine line between approval and put-down: Very few gestures have universal meanings. In the United States, you'd probably be safe in approving of another person's statement by forming an O with your thumb and index finger (the so-called high sign). In Germany, Greece, and France, however, you'd be expressing a very different opinion.

Source: The meanings are based on descriptions in Roger E. Axtell, *Gestures* (New York: John Wiley, 1998). Reprinted by permission of John Wiley & Sons, Inc.

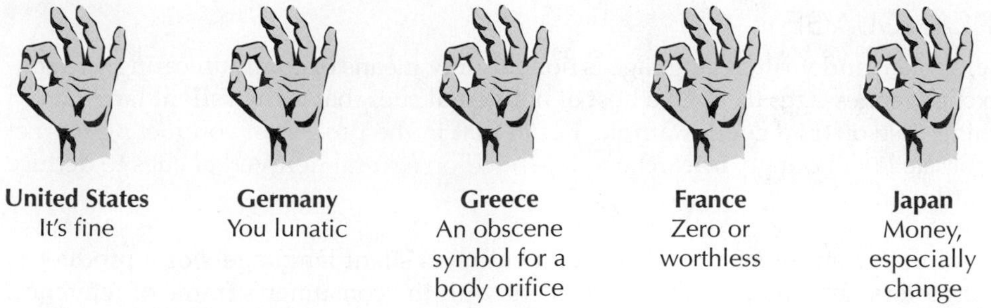

United States
It's fine

Germany
You lunatic

Greece
An obscene symbol for a body orifice

France
Zero or worthless

Japan
Money, especially change

perform their own services, such as opening their own doors, fetching their own coffee, and answering unscreened phone calls.

Dealing with Cultural Differences

After managers identify key cultural differences where they intend to do business abroad, must they alter their customary practices to succeed there? Can people overcome culturally related adjustment problems when working abroad? There are no easy answers to these questions, but the following discussion highlights four issues that affect *degrees* of successful adjustment:

1. The extent to which a culture is willing to accept the introduction of anything foreign
2. Whether key cultural differences are small or great
3. The ability of individuals to adjust to what they find in foreign cultures
4. The general management orientation of the company involved

The following sections address each of these issues in some depth.

HOST SOCIETY ACCEPTANCE

> Host cultures do not always expect foreigners to adjust to them.

Although our opening case illustrates the advantages of *adjusting* to a host country's culture, international companies sometimes succeed in introducing new products, technologies, and operating procedures with relatively little adjustment. They pull it off either because what they're introducing does not run counter to deep-seated attitudes or because the host culture is willing to accept the foreign product or practice as an agreeable trade-off. Bahrain, for instance, because it needs non-Muslim workers, permits the sale of pork products (ordinarily prohibited by religious law) as long as transactions are limited to special grocery store departments in which Muslims can neither work nor shop.

Sometimes the local society regards foreigners and domestic citizens differently. When staying overnight in Jeddah, Western female flight attendants can wear types of clothing publicly that local women cannot.[65] In other instances, local citizens may actually feel their cultures are being mocked when foreigners bend over backward to make adjustments, such as dressing in local traditional garb.[66]

DEGREE OF CULTURAL DIFFERENCES

> When doing business in a similar culture, companies
> - Usually have to make fewer adjustments.
> - May overlook subtle differences.

Obviously, some countries are much like other countries, usually because they share many characteristics such as language, religion, geographic location, ethnicity, and level of economic development.

Cultural Distance A Human Values study compared 43 societies on 405 cultural dimensions,[67] and by averaging the **cultural distance** separating them (number of countries apart) on each dimension, researchers could determine their *cultural proximity*. For instance, the United Kingdom is culturally close to the United States while China is culturally distant. Map 2.4 clusters 58 countries from another study on a fairly specific dimension—namely, the values and attitudes of middle managers toward leadership characteristics. When a company moves into a culturally similar foreign country, it should expect to encounter fewer cultural adjustments than when entering a dissimilar country. An Ecuadorian company doing business in Colombia, for instance, should expect to adjust more easily than if it were to do business in Thailand.

Even among similar countries, however, significant cultural differences could still affect business dealings. Moreover, managers may assume that closely clustered countries are more alike than they really are. If they become too confident about the fit between their own and another nation, they may well overlook important subtleties. Women's roles and behavior, for example, differ substantially from one Arab country to another even though the countries overall are culturally similar.

Hidden Cultural Attitudes   Even if a home and host country have seemingly similar cultures, people in the host country may reject the influx of foreign practices because they see them as additional steps that threaten their self-identities.[68] Further, there may be operating impediments that are not easily discerned by comparing countries on broad cultural dimensions. For example, Disney had much more success in opening a theme park in Japan than in France, even though France is culturally closer to the United States. Why? First, at the time of Disney's French entry, there was much concern within France about its separate identity, especially vis-à-vis the United States—e.g., addition of American English words into the French language, U.S. fast-food restaurants' threat to customary long lunches with traditional cuisine, and U.S. companies' acquisition of French firms considered focal to French distinctiveness. Thus, many French viewed Disney's entry as threatening. Next, there were some subtle differences separating the Japanese from the French. The Japanese were more receptive to Disney because (1) both Japanese children and adults perceived Mickey Mouse as a wholesome, nonthreatening figure; (2) the Japanese had a tradition of buying souvenirs on family excursions; and (3) Disney's reputation for super-cleanliness and smiling faces fit well with Japanese preferences for harmony and order. The French, in contrast, knew Mickey Mouse only as a comic-book conniver who'd been reformulated for the French market. They regarded Disney souvenirs as tacky and policies requiring personnel to dress uniformly and smile mindlessly as violations of personal dignity.[69]

ABILITY TO ADJUST: CULTURE SHOCK

International companies send personnel abroad for both short and long periods of time, subjecting them to potentially traumatic foreign practices. In fact, cultural practices all over the world are considered by many outsiders as downright wrong, such as polygamy, child marriage, and the punishment of people (sometimes severe) for activities not considered crimes at home. Both companies and individuals must decide if they're ready to do business in places that countenance such practices.

Even in countries whose practices aren't necessarily traumatic to them, workers who go abroad often encounter **culture shock**—the frustration that results from having to absorb a vast array of new cultural cues and expectations. Even such seemingly simple tasks as using a different type of toilet or telephone, getting a driver's license, or finding where to buy specific merchandise can at first be taxing experiences.

According to researchers, some people working in a culture that's significantly different from their own may pass through certain stages in the process of adjustment. At first, much like tourists, they're delighted with quaint differences. Later, however, they grow depressed and confused (the *culture shock* phase), so their effectiveness in the foreign environment suffers. Fortunately for most people, culture shock begins to ebb after a month or two as they grow more comfortable. In fact, some people experience **reverse**

Some people get frustrated when entering a different culture.

MAP 2.4
A Synthesis of Country Clusters

As you can see, this map illustrates a key finding of the GLOBE study in the early 2000s of middle manager attitudes and values: namely, that managers in different countries share different ideas about the nature of leadership—ideas that, not surprisingly, tend to affect domestic business practices. Note that cluster labels (e.g., "Nordic Europe," "Confucian Asia") reflect the attitudes of a majority of countries comprising each cluster. Thus note the inclusion of Turkey—where Arabic is not the dominant language—in the "Arab" cluster and the inclusion of Costa Rica and Guatemala in the "Latin American" cluster even though attitudes there tend to be closer to those in countries grouped in the "Latin European" cluster.

Source: The map is prepared from data shown in Vipin Gupta, Paul J. Hanges, and Peter Dorfman, "Cultural Clusters: Methodology and Findings," *Journal of World Business* 37 (Spring 2002): 13. Reprinted with permission from Elsevier.

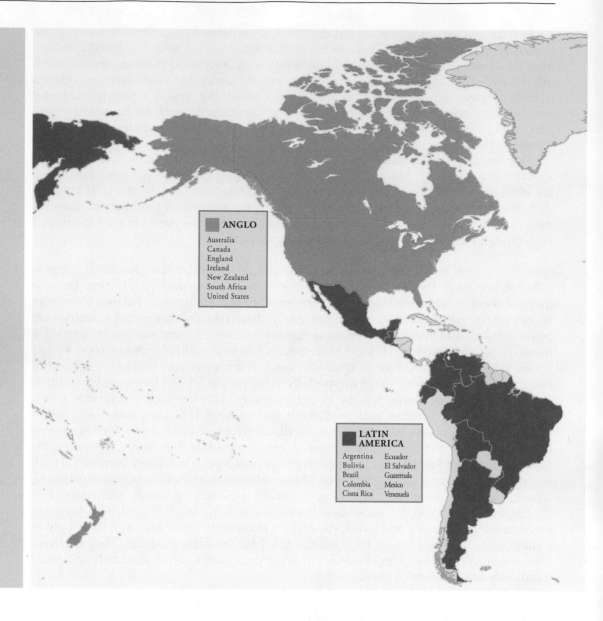

ANGLO
Australia
Canada
England
Ireland
New Zealand
South Africa
United States

LATIN AMERICA
Argentina   Ecuador
Bolivia   El Salvador
Brazil   Guatemala
Colombia   Mexico
Costa Rica   Venezuela

culture shock when they go back home, having become partial to aspects of life abroad that are not options back home.

COMPANY AND MANAGEMENT ORIENTATIONS

Whether and how a company and its managers adapt abroad depends not only on the host-country culture but also on their own attitudes. The following sections discuss three such attitudes or orientations: polycentrism, ethnocentrism, and geocentrism.

Polycentrism   A *polycentric* organization or individual tends to believe that their business units abroad should act like local companies. Given the unique problems often inherent in foreign ventures, it's not surprising that many companies develop polycentric perspectives. In some respects, however, polycentrism may be an overly cautious response to cultural variety. A firm whose outlook is too rigidly polycentric may shy away from certain countries or avoid transferring home-country practices or resources that will actually work well abroad.

Look at it this way. To compete effectively, an international company—and its foreign units—must usually perform some functions differently from the competitors it encounters

Polycentrist management may be so overwhelmed by national differences that it won't introduce workable changes.

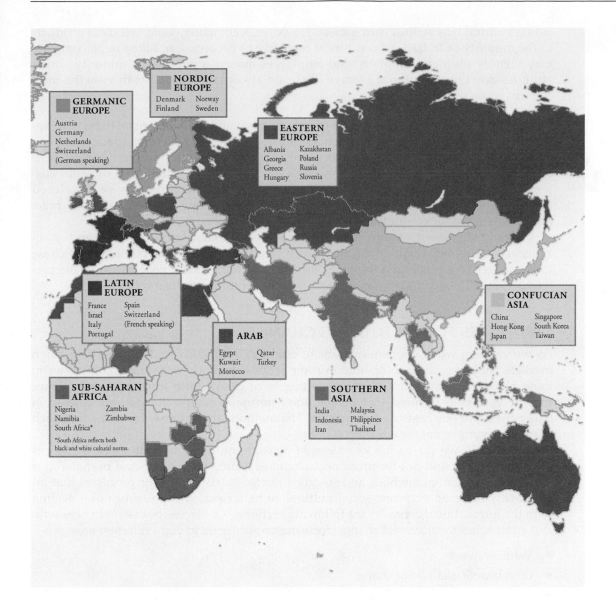

GERMANIC EUROPE
Austria
Germany
Netherlands
Switzerland
(German speaking)

NORDIC EUROPE
Denmark Norway
Finland Sweden

EASTERN EUROPE
Albania Kazakhstan
Georgia Poland
Greece Russia
Hungary Slovenia

LATIN EUROPE
France Spain
Israel Switzerland
Italy (French speaking)
Portugal

ARAB
Egypt Qatar
Kuwait Turkey
Morocco

CONFUCIAN ASIA
China Singapore
Hong Kong South Korea
Japan Taiwan

SUB-SAHARAN AFRICA
Nigeria Zambia
Namibia Zimbabwe
South Africa*
*South Africa reflects both black and white cultural norms.

SOUTHERN ASIA
India Malaysia
Indonesia Philippines
Iran Thailand

abroad in order to have an advantage over them. They may, for instance, need to sell and market new products or produce old ones differently. Because the overly polycentric firm is less receptive to the idea of risking such innovation in an unfamiliar market, it may rely too heavily on imitating proven host-country practices and, in the process, lose the innovative edge it has honed at home.

Ethnocentrism   *Ethnocentrism* reflects the conviction that one's own culture is superior to that of other countries. In international business, the term is usually applied to a company (or individual) so strongly committed to the principle of "what works at home will work abroad" that its foreign practices tend to ignore differences in cultures and markets. In turn, it underestimates the complexity of introducing new management methods, products, or marketing means, and the underestimation likely leads to poor performance

Before we go any further, we should point out that ethnocentrism isn't entirely an inappropriate way of looking at things. Obviously, much of what works at home will in fact work abroad. Further, concentrating on national differences in terms of *averages* overlooks specific variations within countries. A company may be able to deal with outliers even though the *average* person in the country has a strong cultural bias against what the company does in its home country. For example, the average person in India has a

Ethnocentrist management overlooks national differences and

- Ignores important factors.
- Believes home-country objectives should prevail.
- Thinks acceptance by other cultures is easy.

strong cultural bias against eating meat. However, a company could sell meat products to the minority of Indians who eat meat regularly or on occasion. Likewise, a company may identify partners, suppliers, and employees among a population minority whose attitudes don't fit the cultural average (there are always individualists in even the most collectivist societies).

Geocentrism   Between the extremes of polycentrism and ethnocentrism, there is an approach to international business practices called *geocentrism*, which integrates company and host-country practices as well as some entirely new ones.[70] In our opening case, both Saks Fifth Avenue and Harvey Nichols, for example, have adjusted to Saudi customs (such as by setting aside women-only floors). At the same time, they've introduced home-country merchandising practices (what they sell) along with entirely new practices (providing lounges for the drivers of female customers).

Geocentrism requires companies to balance informed knowledge of their own organizational cultures with home- and host-country needs, capabilities, and constraints. Because it encourages innovation and improves the likelihood of success, geocentrism is the preferred approach for companies to succeed in foreign cultures and markets.

Case Review Note

Geocentric management often uses business practices that are hybrids of home and foreign norms. Because people do not necessarily accept change readily, the management of change is important.

STRATEGIES FOR INSTITUTING CHANGE

As we've seen, when companies want to establish competitive advantages in foreign markets, they may need to operate in some ways differently from other companies in those markets, i.e., they introduce some degree of change into foreign markets. Thus, they need to bear in mind that people don't normally accept change very readily, in either the home- or host-country market. The methods they choose for managing such changes are important for ensuring success.

Fortunately, we can gain a lot of insight by examining the international experiences of both for-profit and not-for-profit organizations. Moreover, a great deal of material is available on potential methods and so-called *change agents* (people or processes that intentionally cause or accelerate social, cultural, or behavioral change), much of it dealing with the international arena. In the following sections, we discuss both experiences with and approaches to successful change, focusing on strategies in eight different areas:

- Value systems
- Cost-benefit analysis of change
- Resistance to too much change
- Participation
- Reward sharing
- Opinion leadership
- Timing
- Learning abroad

We conclude with a discussion on the importance of learning as a two-way process—one in which companies transfer knowledge to and from both domestic and foreign markets.

Value Systems   The more something contradicts our value system, the harder it is to accept. In Eritrea, for example, people eat less seafood than people in a lot of other countries, despite having suffered several periods of agricultural famine in recent years even while boasting a long coastline rich in seafood. In trying to persuade Eritrean adults to eat more seafood, however, the Eritrean government and the United Nations World Food Program have faced formidable opposition. There are religious taboos against eating fish without scales and insect-like sea creatures (including shrimp and crayfish), and most Eritreans have grown up believing that seafood has a foul taste. Among schoolchildren, however, whose value systems and habits are still flexible, officials have faced little opposition.[71]

Point

Yes The idea is pretty well accepted: International business influences globalization and globalization influences culture. Now, I have nothing against international business or globalization—at least part of it. What I don't like is *modern cultural imperialism,* which is what happens when the West, especially the United States, imposes its technical, political, military, and economic supremacy on developing countries.[72]

For years now, U.S. firms have been in the business of exporting U.S. culture—mostly through tactics that are rarely in the best interests of the national cultures it targets for economic domination. Because U.S. companies nearly monopolize the international entertainment media, people all over the world are stuck with CNN, MTV, and the Disney Channel and bombarded with U.S. movies. Moreover, the same viewers are barraged with ads for the products—everything from non-nutritious soft drinks to fattening fast foods—that pop up in the TV shows and movies they can't escape, even in the privacy of their own homes.

And what about the hordes of U.S. tourists who plop down more for a night's lodging in a developing country than the hotel maid makes in a year? They'll tell you they're just taking a look at how the other half lives, but the fact is they're selling the U.S. lifestyle to a market that can't afford it and that's probably better off without it. Thanks to canned entertainment, nonstop advertising, and a sales force posing as tourists, culture shoppers in developing countries can sample U.S. possessions and practices to their hearts' content. Never mind that they come from a place, at least

according to TV and the movies, that's populated mostly by the superwealthy and by cops and psychotic malcontents whose daily lives are taken up with bullet-spattered body parts, round-the-clock sex, and inane family relationships. The lifestyle is seductive and promotes everything that's "Made in the U.S.A." That's why people everywhere are starting to behave and even talk like fictional Americans—after all, every speech from Manila to Managua is now peppered with U.S. slang. Along the way, people are letting their own cultural identities slip away.

Once they have a foot in the door, Western companies barge in to exploit the demand they've created, further destabilizing local cultures. In Mexico, Walmart thinks nothing of putting up a superstore virtually next door to ancient ruins—eradicating the nearby street market in the process. What's more, because MNEs tend to cluster in urban markets, they drag workers away from rural areas to work hours—under managers who speak only English—that don't even allow time to go home for lunch.[73]

I admit, if a country is rich enough, it can afford to resist cultural exploitation. Canada, for instance, says no to foreign investment in culturally sensitive industries and makes sure there's Canadian content in local entertainment media. Finland discourages architecture that runs counter to tradition, and the French government discourages outside languages and subsidizes a national motion picture industry. In the developing world, however, where there's precious little cash for fighting off cultural extinction, people are at the mercy of foreign culture brokers.

Does International Business Lead to Cultural Imperialism?

Counterpoint

No You imply that people in poor countries passively accept everything they see in movie theaters and on TV. But they've turned their backs on a lot of products that international companies have promoted. Like most of us, they pick and choose.[74] You also imply that cultures in developing countries are the same. They aren't. They interpret what they see and hear—and what they buy—quite differently.

Like cultural purists everywhere, you've overlooked how cultural diffusion works. With contact, culture heads in both directions and evolves. Way back between 100 BCE (BC) and 400 CE (AD), about 50 Mediterranean languages disappeared when people took up reading and writing in Latin and Greek.[75] Today, of course, very few of us converse in Latin, but that doesn't mean it's completely disappeared; it's evolved—namely, into the "Romance" languages.

I agree that many languages are in trouble today, and it's important to study them while they're still around. But the thing to remember is this: Most of them are giving way to dominant languages in the countries where they're spoken, such as Spanish, Mandarin, or Arabic. Of course, American English is seeping into other languages, but Americans have recently added a lot of foreign words as well. If you're a macho (Spanish) guy in charge of the whole enchilada (Spanish), for example, you're probably called the head honcho (Japanese).

Similarly, although U.S.-style fast food is almost everywhere, it has not entirely displaced local foods anywhere. When it comes to food, the result of international business is greater diversity for everybody. What we're witnessing is not "cultural imperialism" but cultural hybridization. In most countries, U.S. hamburgers, Japanese sushi, Italian pizza,

Mexican tacos, and Middle Eastern pita bread coexist with the local cuisine.

Also, just because people in developing countries have taken a liking to soft drinks and fast food doesn't mean they have scrapped their traditional values. Moreover, some evidence suggests that, although young people are most likely to adopt elements from a foreign culture, they tend to revert to traditional values and habits as they get older. If that's the case, it's hard to argue that they're spearheading any permanent changes in their local cultures.[76]

As people seek to fulfill different wants, they must make trade-offs. But are people (and societies) worse off because they give up, say, lunch with the family to be able to afford certain consumer goods that will satisfy the whole family's needs? Globalization simply gives people more options.

And tourism is also a two-edged sword. Rather than having a primarily negative effect, quite often it has helped maintain certain features of a traditional culture, such as the revival of traditional Balinese dancing because tourists want to see it.

A successful business, whether local or foreign-owned, must accommodate itself sufficiently to the culture in which it operates. This may mean revising plans to respond to local demands. Before Walmart finalized its construction plans in Mexico, executives consulted with anthropologists, reduced the store's height, and decided on a stone facade in a subdued color. Now it can be seen only from atop the pyramids. And while we're on the subject, you also failed to mention that the so-called traditional street market in question was peddling imported plastic goods rather than indigenous Mexican handicrafts.

Cost-Benefit Analysis of Change   Companies' introduction of desired practices abroad may be costly or inexpensive. Some result in greatly improved performance, whereas others improve performance only marginally. Thus, a company must consider the expected *cost-benefit relationship* of what it does abroad. For example, U.S.-based Cummins Engine wanted to improve employee commitment in its Mexican plant. It achieved success by shutting down one day a year so workers may observe a religious holiday. On that day, it hosts a celebration for employees and families. The cost to Cummins has been much less than the benefits resulting from improved performance.

Resistance to Too Much Change   When the German magazine publisher Gruner + Jahr (G+J) bought U.S.-based *McCall's*, it immediately overhauled the magazine's format: changed editors, eliminated long stories and certain features, increased celebrity coverage, made layouts more robust, supplemented articles with sidebars, and refused discounts for big advertisers. Before long, morale declines led to greater turnover. More important, revenues fell because advertisers saw the change in format as too radical.[77] According to most observers, G+J might have obtained more employee and advertiser acceptance had it phased in its plans for change a little more gradually.

Participation   One way to avoid problems like those encountered by G+J is to discuss proposed changes with stakeholders (employees, suppliers, customers, and the like) in advance. The company might perceive the strength of the resistance it faces, stimulate stakeholders to recognize the need for change, and ease their fears about the consequences. People might be satisfied that management has at least listened to them, regardless of the decisions it ultimately makes.[78]

Companies sometimes make the mistake of thinking that stakeholder participation in decision making is effective only in countries with sufficiently educated people who are willing to speak up to make substantial contributions. Anyone who has had to deal with foreign aid programs can tell you that participation can be extremely important even in countries where education levels are low and power distance and uncertainty avoidance high.

Reward Sharing   Sometimes a proposed change may have no foreseeable benefit for those whose support is needed. Production workers, for example, may have little incentive to try new work practices unless they see some more or less immediate benefit for themselves. What can an employer do? It might develop bonus or profit-sharing programs based on the new approach, which may affect stakeholders both within and outside the company. For example, China National Petroleum has faced property damage from angry Iraqi farmers who have perceived problems without gains from living near drilling operations.[79] In contrast, a U.S.-Peruvian gold-mining venture won the support of skeptical Andean villagers simply by donating sheep to them.[80]

Opinion Leadership   By making use of local channels of influence, or *opinion leaders*, a firm may be able to facilitate the acceptance of change. Opinion leaders may emerge in unexpected places. When, for example, Ford wanted to instill U.S. production methods in a Mexican plant, managers relied on Mexican production workers, rather than on either Mexican or U.S. supervisors, to observe operations at U.S. plants. What was the advantage of this approach? The workers had more credibility with the Mexican workforce who would have to implement the new methods.[81] (Our closing case, which concerns a dam construction project in Uganda, tells the story of a fairly unusual opinion leader—one whose leadership techniques include the performance of elaborate religious rituals.)

CRN

Case Review Note

Timing   Many well-conceived changes fail simply because they're ill-timed. A proposed labor-saving production method, for example, might make employees nervous about losing their jobs no matter how much management tries to reassure them. If, however, the proposal is made during a period of labor shortage, the firm will likely encounter less fear and resistance.

In certain cases, of course, crisis precipitates the acceptance of change. In Turkey, for example, family members have traditionally dominated business organizations. Indeed, family members sometimes continue to exert substantial influence even after they no longer have any official responsibilities. In more and more instances, however, poor performance has stimulated a rapid change in this practice: Many families no longer "run" the business, but rather serve in "advisory capacities" (often on the board of directors).

Learning Abroad   Remember that, as companies gain more experience in overseas operations, they may learn as well as impart valuable knowledge—knowledge that proves just as useful in the home country as in a host country. Such learning may concern any business function; however, access to researchers is a particularly potent advantage in operating abroad.

Finally, companies should examine economies and companies abroad that are performing well in order to determine whether there are practices that they may emulate. For example, recently some large Indian companies have performed extremely well, not in spite of but because of placing social missions and heavy investments in their employees.[82]

Looking to the

Future   What Will Happen to National Cultures?

Scenario 1: New Hybrid Cultures Will Develop and Personal Horizons Will Broaden

International contact is increasing at a rate few could have imagined a few decades ago—a process that should lead to a certain mixing and greater similarity among national cultures. At first glance, that's exactly what's happening.[83] The mixing seems evident when one sees, say, a group of Japanese tourists listening to a Philippine band perform an American pop song in a British hotel in Indonesia. Likewise, combination languages such as "Spanglish" have emerged. The growing mix seems evident when people in every corner of the world wear similar clothing and listen to international recording stars alongside other people wearing local styles and listening to local recording artists. Competitors headquartered in far-flung areas of the globe are increasingly copying each other's operating practices, thus creating a competitive work environment that's more global than national. As companies and people get used

(continued)

to operating internationally, they should continue to become more confident in applying the benefits of cultural diversity and globally inspired operating procedures to explore new areas in both workplace productivity and consumer behavior.

We'll also likely see people taking advantage of greater mobility, broadening their concepts of what it means to enjoy global citizenship.[84] Historically, most people who immigrated to foreign countries were able to return to their homelands perhaps once in their lives. They were thus compelled to accept the cultures of their adopted countries, sacrificing much of their native cultural identity in the process. Today, however, many immigrants who come to high-income countries to find work often obtain dual citizenship and maintain contact with their native cultures through travel, direct-dial phone calls, and Internet communications. On the one hand, these immigrants may tend to transfer culture in both directions, bringing greater diversity to both host and home countries. In addition, there is some evidence that children of these immigrants are becoming bi- or multicultural. A result is that a class of international managers is emerging whose traditional ties to specific cultures are much looser than those of most people. Educated in France, for instance, CEO Carlos Ghosn of Japan's Nissan and France's Renault is a Brazilian of Lebanese extraction.[85] On the other hand, there is evidence that multiculturalism is failing because immigrants no longer have to assimilate into the culture of their new residency, thus this could lead to more cultural strife within nations.[86]

Scenario 2: Although the Outward Expressions of National Culture Will Continue to Become More Homogeneous, Distinct Values Will Tend to Remain Stable

Beneath the surface of the visual aspects of culture (including most of the elements touched on in the previous section), people continue to hold fast to some of the basics that make national cultures different from one another. In other words, although certain material and even behavioral facets of cultures will become more universal, certain fundamental values and attitudes will remain much the same. Religious differences, for instance, are as strong as ever, and language differences still bolster ethnic identities. What's

important is that differences in these areas are still powerful enough to fragment the world culturally and to stymie the global standardization of products and operating methods.

Scenario 3: Nationalism Will Continue to Reinforce Cultural Identity

If people didn't perceive the *cultural* differences among themselves and others, they'd be less likely to regard themselves as distinct *national* entities. That's why appeals to cultural identity are so effective in mobilizing people to defend national identity. Typically, such efforts promote the "national culture" by reinforcing language and religion, subsidizing nationalistic programs and activities, and propagandizing against foreign influences on the national culture. Further, even though people will be more internationally mobile, peer pressure will force them to adapt to their national cultures.

Scenario 4: Existing National Borders Will Shift to Accommodate Ethnic Differences

In several countries, we're seeing more evidence of subcultural power and influence. Why? Basic factors include immigration and the rise of religious fundamentalism. Equally important seems to be the growing desire among ethnic groups for independence from dominant groups where they reside. Both Yugoslavia and Czechoslovakia have broken up for this reason, while in Sudan and Afghanistan ethnic groups are currently pitted against one another in bloody wars. Meanwhile, some subcultures—such as the Inuits in the Arctic and the Kurds in the Middle East—simply resist identity by established national boundaries. Because they have less in common with their "countrymen" than with ethnic brethren in other countries, it's hard to assign them a national identity on the basis of geographic circumstances.

Regardless of the scenario that unfolds in any given arena, international businesspeople must learn to examine specific cultural differences if they hope to operate effectively in a foreign environment. In the future, analysis based only on national characteristics won't be sufficient; business will have to pay attention to all the other myriad factors that contribute to distinctions in values, attitudes, and behavior. ∎

Charles Martin in Uganda: What to Do When a Manager Goes Native

CASE

James Green, a vice president at U.S.-based Hydro Generation (HG), pondered a specific question: Should he retain Charles Martin for the construction and operation phases of a major dam project in Uganda?[87] (See Map 2.5 for the location of Uganda in Africa and of the dam project in Uganda.) Martin had already completed his assignments on the preliminary construction phases of the project, and he'd finished every task on time and within budget.

Green, however, was a little concerned with the means by which Martin tended to achieve his ends. In Green's opinion, Martin was too eager to accommodate Ugandan ways of doing business, some of which ran counter both to HG's organizational culture and to its usual methods of operating in foreign environments. In particular, Green worried that some of Martin's actions might have unforeseen repercussions for the company's presence in Uganda.

He also knew the philosophy and values of founder and current CEO Lawrence Lovell, who had been instrumental in shaping HG's mission and culture. A devout Christian and regular attendee of the National Prayer Breakfast, Lovell believed strongly that business activities, though secular, should embody Christian values. As a manager, he believed that subordinates should be given full responsibility for making and implementing decisions but that they should also be held accountable for the results.

Martin, however, wanted to stay in Uganda, and HG would be hard-pressed to find someone else with his combination of professional training, experience with HG, and familiarity with the host country. (Martin, although only 29, had already proved effective in using his knowledge of local development issues to disarm many critics of the power plant.)

Hiring Martin as a project liaison specialist represented a new approach for HG. In this capacity, Martin had been given a threefold task:

1. To gain local support for the project by working with both Ugandan authorities in the capital of Kampala and villagers in the vicinity of the construction site.

MAP 2.5 Uganda

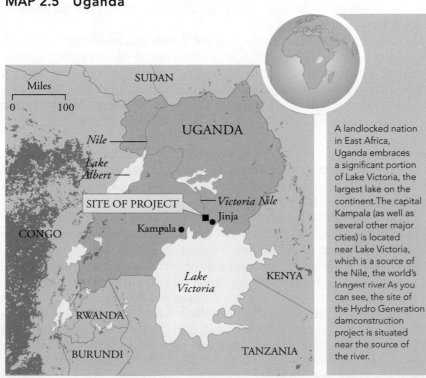

A landlocked nation in East Africa, Uganda embraces a significant portion of Lake Victoria, the largest lake on the continent. The capital Kampala (as well as several other major cities) is located near Lake Victoria, which is a source of the Nile, the world's longest river. As you can see, the site of the Hydro Generation dam construction project is situated near the source of the river.

2. To set up an office and hire office personnel to take charge of local purchasing (including lower-level hiring), clearing incoming goods through customs, securing immigration permissions for foreigners attached to the project, overseeing plans for the logistics of getting materials going from the airport in Kampala to the dam site, and keeping inventory and accounting records.

3. To help foreign personnel (mainly engineers) get settled and feel comfortable living and working in Uganda.

Martin was also responsible for establishing an operating structure that would spare incoming managers the hassles of such mundane start-up activities as obtaining licenses, installing telephones and utilities, and finding local people to hire for the wide range of jobs that would be needed. In addition, although HG specialized in power plants (it had built plants in 16 countries and retained ownership shares in about half of them), the Uganda project was its first African venture.

Dam construction anywhere requires huge amounts of capital, and projects often face opposition from groups acting on behalf of such local parties as the people who will need to move because of subsequent flooding. Thus, to forestall adverse publicity and, more importantly, activity that could lead to costly work stoppages, HG needed as many local allies as it could get. Getting (and keeping) them was another key facet of Martin's job.

Martin, although still young by most standards, was well suited to the Ugandan project. After high school, he'd entered the University of Wisconsin, where he became fascinated with Africa through a course in its precolonial history. Graduating with a major in African studies, he served with the Peace Corps in Kenya, where he worked with small business start-ups and took side trips to Ethiopia and Tanzania. Although he loved working in Kenya, Martin developed a disdain for the Western managers and workers who isolated themselves in expatriate ghettos and congregated in the capital's first-class hotels. His own creed became "Don't draw attention to yourself and, above all, learn and respect the culture."

At the end of his Peace Corps stint, Martin was determined to return to and work somewhere in Africa. After earning an MBA at the University of Maryland, he took a job with HG, where he worked for two years on project bidding and budgeting. Both when he was hired and when HG became involved in the Ugandan project, Martin made sure his superiors knew he wanted an African assignment.

Not surprisingly, HG saw the advantage of someone who possessed both a home-country corporate perspective and a knowledge of the host country's economics, politics, and culture. In Uganda, a country of about 25 million, English is the official language, but many people speak only an indigenous language—mainly Bantu or Nilotic languages. Although about two-thirds of Ugandans are Christians (about evenly split between Roman Catholics and Anglicans), there are large numbers of Muslims and adherents of various animistic religions.

Since gaining independence in 1962, Uganda has had a largely unhappy history. The ruthless dictatorship of Idi Amin included mass murder among its policies, and, more recently, Uganda has been forced to absorb huge numbers of refugees fleeing bloodshed in Rwanda, Zaire, and the Sudan. Nepotism is the norm, and the government is considered one of the most corrupt in the world. On the positive side, foreign companies that want to do business in Uganda aren't heavily regulated, and because few people have access to electricity, the Ugandan government strongly favored the HG power plant project.

Now, as the pre-construction phase of the project was coming to an end, Green reviewed Martin's performance. Specifically, he was concerned not only about some of Martin's business practices but also about certain aspects of his lifestyle, not the least of which was his participation in local tribal rituals. HG had no formal guidelines on the lifestyles of expatriate managers in its employ, but the company culture tended to encourage standards of living that were consistent with the values of a prosperous international company. With what HG paid him, Martin could certainly afford to live in one of the upscale neighborhoods that were home to most foreign managers working in and around Kampala. Martin, however, preferred a middle-class Ugandan neighborhood and declined to frequent the places where fellow expatriates typically gathered, such as churches and clubs.

As far as Green was concerned, not only was Martin's lifestyle inconsistent with HG culture, but his preference for isolating himself from the expatriate community also made him of little use in helping colleagues adapt to the kind of life that would be comfortable for them in the alien environment of Uganda. During dam construction, foreign managers and engineers would be moving in with their families.

As for Martin's business-related practices, Green was ready to admit that business in Uganda usually moved at a leisurely pace. It could take months to get a phone installed, supplies delivered, or operating licenses issued. Martin, however, had quickly learned that he could speed things up by handing out tips in advance. Nor could Green argue that such payments were exorbitant: In a country where per capita GDP is about $1,200 a year, people tended to take what they could get.

It was also a fact of local life that unemployment was high and so-called job searches were generally conducted through word of mouth, especially among family members. Martin had developed the practice of mentioning openings to local people and then interviewing and hiring the relatives they recommended. In a country like Uganda, he reasoned, such family connections could come in handy. Hiring the niece of a high-ranking customs officer couldn't hurt when it came to getting import clearances.

To Green, however, although such practices were both normal and legal in Ugandan business dealings, they bordered on the unethical in a U.S. organization. He also worried about a variety of long-term practical consequences. For instance, what if word got out that HG was paying extra for everything (and, inevitably, it would)? Wouldn't everyone start to expect bonuses for every little service?

What's worse, if word reached the higher echelons of the Ugandan government, HG would probably find itself dealing with people in a position to demand large payments for such services as, say, not finding some excuse to hinder efficient operation of the project. Not only would these payments start to get costly, but they might be illegal under U.S. law. What about adverse international publicity that could negatively affect HG's operations in other countries?

Finally, Green wasn't comfortable with Martin's hiring practices. He had no reason to doubt the competence of any given hire, but nepotism comes with risks. An employee's close connection with some government official, for example, might encourage the employee to participate more actively in the extortion process. What if a woman hired to work on import clearances decided to go into business with her uncle, the customs officer, to charge a little extra for every import approval? In addition, given Uganda's history of political instability, the company ran the risk that today's friends in high places might be tomorrow's enemies of the state.

Then there was the issue of the tribal rituals. The dam would displace about 700 villagers, and during early negotiations with the Ugandan government (and before Martin's transfer to Uganda), HG assembled a resettlement package that included the renovation of schools and health centers in the new location. (The photo shows the Bujagali Falls.) HG executives understood that the package, valued at millions of dollars, was acceptable to the people who were affected. Shortly after Martin's arrival, however, two tribes living close to the Bujagali Falls site of the dam proclaimed the river home to sacred spirits. One leader likened the site to the tribe's Mecca.

As news of the claims reached the international press, worldwide support for the tribes began to grow. With permission from HG headquarters, Martin hired a specialist in African religions, who advised HG to work with the religious caretakers of the falls to find a solution. When contacted, the official caretaker revealed that, although the spirits could not be moved, they could be appeased at the right price. For a fee of $7,500, he sacrificed a sheep, two cows, four goats, and a slew of chickens, pinning them down on hot coals while 40 diviners prayed and danced. For the finale, blood was sprinkled on some sacred trees. Unfortunately, the spirits were not appeased. It seems that Martin had not participated in the ceremony. So Martin paid another fee of about $10,000 to repeat the ceremony, in which he took part, evidently appeasing the spirits.

The Bujagali falls of Uganda, around which people are displaced with dam construction.

Source: Pecold/Shutterstock.com

Green was concerned about Martin's part in the second ceremony, which he himself considered pagan and probably a sham. Granted, Martin's participation had allowed work to continue, but Green worried that the episode could not only damage HG's image but could also offend Uganda's Christian majority and the many Christian missionaries in the country. In this respect, Evangelicals (recently growing rapidly in numbers) were pressuring for national action against anything "un-Christian," such as requesting a death penalty for homosexuals. On top of everything, Martin's participation might be construed in some quarters as a mockery of tribal customs, thereby contributing to a hostile environment for HG.

Having thoroughly considered the Charles Martin case, James Green now had to make decisions about staffing the operational phase of the project. He knew he needed to transfer a number of managers and engineers to Uganda, and he'd already begun interviewing some. But he was still left with one critical question: How much would the new expatriates benefit from the presence of an American who, like Martin, could be a valuable source of advice about Ugandan culture? And if he had to have someone in that role, was Martin still right for the part? ■

QUESTIONS

1. Describe Ugandan cultural attributes that might affect the operations of a foreign company doing business there.
2. How would you describe the respective attitudes of Martin and Green: ethnocentric, polycentric, or geocentric? What factors do you suspect of having influenced their respective attitudes?
3. Who was right, Green or Martin, about Martin's more controversial actions in facilitating the project? How might things have turned out if Martin had not been a member of the project team?
4. In the next phase of the project—building the power plant—should HG employ someone whose main function is that of liaison between its corporate culture and the culture of its host country? If so, is Martin the right person for the job?

Now that you have finished this chapter, go back to www.myiblab.com to continue practicing and applying the concepts you've learned.

SUMMARY

- *Culture* includes norms based on learned attitudes, values, and beliefs. Almost everyone agrees there are cross-country differences in culture, but most experts disagree as to exactly what they are.

- International companies and individuals must evaluate their business and personal practices to ensure that their behavior may fit with national norms.

- In addition to being part of a *national* culture, people are simultaneously part of other cultures, such as a professional or organizational one.

- Distinct societies are often found within a given country. People also may have more in common with similar groups in foreign countries than with groups in their own countries.

- Cultural change may take place as a result of choice or imposition. Isolation from other groups, especially because of language, tends to stabilize cultures.

- People fall into social-stratification systems according to their *ascribed* and *acquired group memberships,* which determine their level of access to economic resources, prestige, social relations, and power. Individuals' affiliations may determine their qualifications and access to certain jobs.

- Some people work far more than is necessary to satisfy their basic needs for food, clothing, and shelter. They're motivated to work for various reasons, including the preference for material possessions over leisure time, the belief that work will bring success and reward, and the desire for achievement.

- There are national differences in norms that influence people's behavior. Such norms determine whether they prefer autocratic or consultative working relationships, whether

they prefer their activities to follow set rules, and how much they prefer to compete or cooperate with fellow workers.

- There are national differences in norms determining such behavioral factors as trust, belief in fate, and confidence in planning for the future.

- Failure to perceive subtle distinctions in culturally determined behavior can result in misunderstandings in international dealings.

- People communicate through spoken, written, and silent language—all governed by culturally determined cues. Cultural background also plays a major role in how people process information.

- Host cultures don't always expect foreign companies or individuals to conform to their norms. Sometimes they accommodate those companies, and sometimes they apply different standards to foreigners' behavior.

- A company usually needs to make fewer adjustments when entering a culture similar to its own, but it must be quite careful to heed subtleties both in host-country behaviors and in host-country perceptions of foreigners' behaviors.

- People living and working in foreign environments should be sensitive to the dangers of excessive *polycentrism* and excessive *ethnocentrism.* Usually, *geocentrism* is a safer approach.

- In deciding whether to make changes in either home- or host-country operations, a company should consider several factors: the importance of the proposed changes to every party involved, the cost and benefit to the company of each proposed change, the value of opinion leaders in implementing the changes, and timing.

KEY TERMS

acquired group membership (p. 59)
ascribed group membership (p. 59)
collectivism (p. 64)
cultural collision (p. 51)
cultural distance (p. 70)
cultural imperialism (p. 53)
culture (p. 50)
culture shock (p. 71)
future orientation (p. 65)

hierarchy-of-needs theory (p. 63)
high-context culture (p. 66)
idealism (p. 67)
individualism (p. 64)
low-context culture (p. 66)
masculinity-femininity
index (p. 62)
monochronic (approach to
multitasking) (p. 66)

polychronic (approach to
multitasking) (p. 66)
power distance (p. 64)
pragmatism (p. 67)
reverse culture shock
(p. 72)
silent language (p. 69)
uncertainty avoidance
(p. 65)

ENDNOTES

1 We are particularly appreciative of personal insights given us by the following people in Saudi Arabia: Nora al Jundi, lecturer at Effat University; Omar Aljindi, consultant at Saudi Diyar Consultants; and Talah Tamimi, former executive at Saudi Investment General Authority. *Additional Sources include the following:* "Saudi Arabia: The Western Compound," http://americanbedu.com/2011/03/07 /saudi-arabia-the-western-compound/ (Accessed March 15, 2011); Summer Said, "Saudi Activism Accelerates As Women Dare to Drive," *Wall Street Journal* (June 18-19, 2011): A9; Abeer Allam, "Saudi Women Bridle at Business Rules," *Financial Times* (May 22, 2009): 4; Karen Elliott House, "Pressure Points," *Wall Street Journal* (April 10, 2007): A1+; Karen Elliot House, "For Saudi Women, a Whiff of Change," *Wall Street Journal* (April 7, 2007): A1+; Roula Khalaf, "Saudi Women Carve a Place in the Future of Their Country," *Financial Times* (January 25, 2002): 3; Steve Jarvis, "Western-Style Research in the Middle East," *Marketing News* (April 29, 2002): International section, 37; Barbara Slavin, "U.S. Firms' Saudi Offices Face Manpower Issues," *USA Today* (May 13, 2002): 5A; Colbert I. King, "When in Saudi Arabia…Do as Americans Do," *Washington Post* (February 2, 2002): A25; Donna Abu-Nasr, "Saudis Begin to Show Wear and Tear of Life under Feared Religious Police," *AP Worldstream* (April 28, 2002): n.p.; Cecile Rohwedder, "The Chic of Arabia," *Wall Street Journal* (January 23, 2004): A11+.

2 Jeanne Brett, Kristin Behfar, and Mary C. Kern, "Managing Multicultural Teams," *Harvard Business Review* 84 (November 2006): 84–91; Yaping Gong, "The Impact of Subsidiary Top Management Team National Diversity on Subsidiary Performance: Knowledge and Legitimacy Perspectives," *Management International Review* 46:6 (2006): 771–98; Carol Hymowitz, "Leadership," *Wall Street Journal* (November 14, 2005): R1.

3 David E. Brown, "Human Universals, Human Nature and Human Culture," *Daedalus* 133:4 (Fall 2004): 47–54.

4 Tomasz Lenartowicz and Kendall Roth, "The Selection of Key Informants in IB Cross-Cultural Studies," *Management International Review* 44:1 (2004): 23–51.

5 Patti Waldmeir, "Property Bubble Erodes China's Traditional Preference for Sons," *Financial Times* (November 2, 2010): 1.

6 Three of the most significant are Geert Hofstede, *Cultures and Organizations: Software of the Mind* (New York: McGraw-Hill, 1997), which explores attitudes in 50 countries, primarily those concerning workplace relationships; Ronald Inglehart, Miguel Basañez, and Alejandro Moreno, *Human Values and Beliefs: A Cross-Cultural Sourcebook* (Ann Arbor: University of Michigan Press, 1998) analyzes political, religious, sexual, and economic norms in 43 countries; Robert J. House, Paul J. Hanges, Mansour Javidan, Peter W. Dorfman, and Vipin Gupta, eds., *Culture, Leadership, and Organizations* (Thousand Oaks, CA: Sage, 2004) examines leadership preferences in 59 countries.

7 Mary Lou Egan and Marc Bendick, Jr., "Combining Multicultural Management and Diversity into One Course on Cultural Competence," *Academy of Management Learning & Education* 7:3 (2008): 387–93.

8 Geert Hofstede and Robert R. McCrae, "Personality and Culture Revisited: Linking Traits and Dimensions of Culture," *Cross-Cultural Research* 38:1 (February 2004): 52–88.

9 James W. Neuliep, *International Communication: A Contextual Approach*, 4th edition (Thousand Oaks, CA: Sage Publishing, 2009).

10 Robert J. Foster, "Making National Cultures in the National Acumen," *Annual Review of Anthropology* 20 (1991): 235–60, discusses the concept and ingredients of a national culture.

11 Harry C. Triandis, "Dimensions of Cultural Variation as Parameters of Organizational Theories," *International Studies of Management and Organization* 12:4 (Winter 1982–1983): 143–44.

12 See Aihwa Ong, *Flexible Citizenship: The Cultural Logics of the Transnationality* (Durham, NC: Duke University Press, 1999); Leo

Paul Dana, *Entrepreneurship in Pacific Asia* (Singapore: World Scientific, 1999).

13 Larry Habegger, "Bhutan: Restrictions on tourist Numbers Easing," September 22, 2010, www.worldtravelwatch.com/10/09 /bhutan-restrictions-on-tourist-numbers-easing.html (accessed February 23, 2011).

14 Yadong Luo and Oded Shenkar, "The Multinational Corporation as a Multilingual Community: Language and Organization in a Global Context," *Journal of International Business Studies* 37 (2006): 321–39.

15 David Crystal, *English as a Global Language* (Cambridge: Cambridge University Press, 1997): 1–23; Jon Boone, "Native English Speakers Face Being Crowded Out of Market," *Financial Times* (February 15, 2006): 8.

16 Evelyn Nien-Ming Ch'ien, *Weird English* (Boston: Harvard University, 2004).

17 Inglehart et al., *Human Values and Beliefs,* 21.

18 Matthew Coy Mitchell, "Corporate Legitimacy across Cultural Contexts: Mapping the Cultural Schemata of Religio-Institutional Actors," (Columbia, SC: unpublished PhD dissertation, Moore School of Business Administration, 2010).

19 "When Culture Masks Communication: Japanese Corporate Practice," *Financial Times* (October 23, 2000): 10; Robert House et al., "Understanding Cultures and Implicit Leadership Theories across the Globe: An Introduction to Project GLOBE," *Journal of World Business* 37 (2002): 3–10.

20 Michael Segalla, "National Cultures, International Business," *Financial Times* (March 6, 1998): mastering global business section, 8–10.

21 Amartya Sen, *Development As Freedom*, (Oxford: Oxford University Press, 1999): 192.

22 Fons Trompenaars, *Riding the Waves of Culture* (Burr Ridge, IL: Richard D. Irwin, 1994): 100–116.

23 "Putting the Malaise into Malaysia," *Asia Times Readers Forum*, at forum.atimes.com/topic.asp?topic_ID=9002& whichpage=10 (accessed May 27, 2007).

24 John Burton, "Cracks Appear in Malaysia's Multi-ethnic Settlement," *Financial Times* (January 10, 2008): 11.

25 Larry Rohter, "Multiracial Brazil Planning Quotas for Blacks," *New York Times* (October 2, 2001): A3; "Out of Eden," *The Economist* (July 5, 2003): 31+.

26 Robert F. Szarfran, "Age-Adjusted Labor Force Participation Rates, 1960-2045," *Monthly Labor Review* 125:9 (2002): 25–38.

27 Inglehart et al., *Human Values and Beliefs*, question V128.

28 "The New Workforce," Economist.com (November 1, 2001) (accessed March 12, 2005).

29 "Minimum Legal Ages for Alcohol Purchase or Consumption around the World," at www.geocities.jp/m_kato_clinic /mini-age-alcohol-eng-l.html (accessed May 28, 2007).

30 "The Employers Forum on Age," *Legal: Europe*, at www.efa.org .uk/legal/europe.asp (accessed May 27, 2007); Cindy Wu, John J. Lawler, and Xiang Xi, "Overt Employment Discrimination in MNC Affiliates: Home-Country Cultural and Institutional Effects," *Journal of International Business Studies* 39:5 (2008): 772–94.

31 Inglehart et al., *Human Values and Beliefs*, questions V129.

32 Francis Fukuyama, *Trust: The Social Virtues and the Creation of Prosperity* (New York: Free Press, 1995).

33 For a good overview of the literature on the Protestant ethic, see Harold B. Jones Jr., "The Protestant Ethic: Weber's Model and the Empirical Literature," *Human Relations* 50:7 (1997): 757–86.

34 Luigi Guiso, Paola Sapienza, and Luigi Zingales, "People's Opium? Religion and Economic Attitudes," *Journal of Monetary Economics* 50:1 (2003): 225–38.

35 See, for example, David S. Landes, *The Wealth and Poverty of Nations* (New York: Norton, 1998).

36 David Gauthier-Villars, "France Wrests Title of Sleeping Giant," *Wall Street Journal* (May 5, 2009): A8.

37 David Gardner, "Indians Face 10m Rupee Question: Do You Sincerely Want to Be Rich?" *Financial Times* (July 15–16, 2000): 24.

38 Triandis, "Dimensions of Cultural Variation as Parameters of Organizational Theories," 159–60.

39 Hofstede, *Cultures and Organizations*.

40 Abraham Maslow, *Motivation and Personality* (New York: Harper & Row, 1954).

41 F. Pichler and C. Wallace, "What Are the Reasons for Differences in Job Satisfaction Across Europe," *European Sociological Review* 25: (2009): 535–49.

42 Richard Metters, "A Case Study of National Culture and Offshoring Services," *International Journal of Operations & Production Management* 28:8 (2008): 727–47.

43 Hofstede, *Cultures and Organizations* 49–78; House et al., *Culture, Leadership, and Organizations*.

44 Hofstede, *Cultures and Organizations*.

45 Maxim Voronov and Jefferson A. Singer, "The Myth of Individualism-Collectivism: A Critical Review," *The Journal of Social Psychology* 142:4 (August 2002): 461–81.

46 See John J. Lawrence and Reh-song Yeh, "The Influence of Mexican Culture on the Use of Japanese Manufacturing Techniques in Mexico," *Management International Review*, 34:1 (1994): 49–66; P. Christopher Earley, "East Meets West Meets Mideast: Further Explorations of Collectivistic and Individualistic Work Groups," *Academy of Management Journal* 36:2 (1993): 319–46.

47 Hofstede, *Cultures and Organizations*.

48 Inglehart et al., *Human Values and Beliefs*, question V94.

49 Srilata Zaheer and Akbar Zaheer, "Trust across Borders," *Journal of International Business Studies*, 37:1 (2006): 21–29.

50 Examples in this section come from the GLOBE (Global Leadership and Organizational Behavior Effectiveness) project. See Bakacsi et al., "The Germanic Europe Cluster: Where Employees Have a Voice," *Journal of World Business* 37 (2002): 55–68; Jorge Correia Jesino, "Latin Europe Cluster: From South to North," *Journal of World Business* 37 (2002): 81–89.

51 Ping Ping Fu, Jeff Kennedy, Jasmine Tata, Gary Yuki, Michael Harris Bond, Tai-Kuang Peng, Ekkirala S. Srinivas, Jon P. Howell, Leonel Prieto, Paul Koopman, Jaap J. Boonstra, Selda Pasa, Marie-François Lacassagne, Hiro Higashide, and Adith Cheosakul, "The Impact of Societal Cultural Values and Individual Social Beliefs on the Perceived Effectiveness of Managerial Influence Strategies: A Meso Approach," *Journal of International Business Studies* 35:4 (2004): 284–304.

52 Shirley Wang, "The Science Behind Why We Love Ice Cream," *Wall Street Journal* (November 9, 2010): D1+; and Nicholas Wade, "Human Culture, an Evolutionary Force," *New York Times* (March 2, 2010): D1+.

53 Benjamin Lee Whorf, *Language, Thought and Reality* (New York: Wiley, 1956): 13.

54 For an examination of subtle differences among northern European cultures, see Malene Djursaa, "North Europe Business Culture: Britain vs. Denmark and Germany," *European Management Journal* 12:2 (June 1994): 138–46.

55 Richard E. Nisbett et al., "Culture and Systems of Thought: Holistic versus Analytic Cognition," *Psychological Review* 108:2 (April 2001): 291–310.

56 Don Clark, "Hey, #@*% Amigo, Can You Translate the Word 'Gaffe'?" *Wall Street Journal* (July 8, 1996): B6.

57 René White, "Beyond Berlitz: How to Penetrate Foreign Markets through Effective Communications," *Public Relations Quarterly* 31:2 (Summer 1986): 15.

58 Mark Nicholson, "Language Error Was Cause of Indian Air Disaster," *Financial Times* (November 14, 1996): 1.

59 Manjeet Kripalani and Jay Greene, "Culture Clash," *Business Week* (February 14, 2005): 9.

60 Christina Hoag, "Slogan Could Offend Spanish Speakers," *Miami Herald* (March 8, 2005): C1+.

61 Much of the discussion on silent language is based on Edward T. Hall, "The Silent Language in Overseas Business," *Harvard Business Review* (May–June 1960). Hall identified five variables—time, space, things, friendships, and agreements—and was the first to use the term *silent language.*

62 Fulford, "The China Factor."

63 For an excellent explanation of four ways to view time, see Carol Saunders, Craig Van Slyke, and Douglas Vogel, "My Time or Yours? Managing Time Visions in Global Virtual Teams," *Academy of Management Executive* 18:1 (2004): 19–31. See also Lawrence A. Beer, "The Gas Pedal and the Brake: Toward a Global Balance of Diverging Cultural Determinants in Managerial Mindsets," *Thunderbird International Business Review* 45:3 (May–June 2003): 255–270.

64 Trompenaars, *Riding the Waves of Culture*, 130–131.

65 Daniel Pearl, "Tour Saudi Arabia: Enjoy Sand, Surf, His-and-Her Pools," *Wall Street Journal* (January 22, 1998): A1.

66 June N. P. Francis, "When in Rome? The Effects of Cultural Adaptation on Intercultural Business Negotiations," *Journal of International Business Studies* 22:3 (1991): 321–22.

67 Inglehart, *Human Values and Beliefs,* 16.

68 Amin Maalouf, *In the Name of Identity* (New York: Penguin Group, 2000): 26 asserts that people pinpoint the aspect of their identity that is most under threat.

69 Mary Yoko Brannen, "When Mickey Loses Face: Recontextualization, Semantic Fit, and the Semiotics of Foreignness," *Academy of Management Review* 29:4 (2004): 593–616.

70 Mary Yoko Brannen and Yoko Salk, "Partnering across Borders: Negotiating Organizational Culture in a German-Japanese Joint Venture," *Human Relations* 53:4 (June 2000): 451–87; Baruch Shimoni and Harriet Bergman, "Managing in a Changing World: From Multiculturalism to Hybridization—The Production of Hybrid Management Culture in Israel, Thailand, and Mexico," *Academy of Management Perspectives* (August 2006): 76–89.

71 Geraldine Brooks, "Eritrea's Leaders Angle for Sea Change in Nation's Diet to Prove Fish Isn't Foul," *Wall Street Journal* (June 2, 1994): A10.

72 John Tomlinson, *Globalization and Culture* (Chicago: University of Chicago Press, 1999).

73 "In Mexico, Ancient Life vs. Walmart," *Miami Herald* (September 6, 2004): 6A.

74 Nader Asgary and Alf H. Walle, "The Cultural Impact of Globalisation: Economic Activity and Social Change," *Cross Cultural Management* 9:3 (2000): 58–76; Tyler Cowen, *Creative Destruction: How Globalization Is Changing the World's Cultures* (Princeton, NJ: Princeton University Press, 2002): 128–52.

75 Clive Cookson, "Linguists Speak Out for the Dying Languages," *Financial Times* (March 26, 2004): 9.

76 Adrian Furnham and Stephen Bochner, *Culture Shock* (London: Methuen, 1986): 234.

77 Patrick M. Reilly, "Pitfalls of Exporting Magazine Formulas," *Wall Street Journal* (July 24, 1995): B1; James Bandler and Matthew Karnitschnig, "Lost in Translation," *Wall Street Journal* (August 19, 2004): A1+.

78 Mzamo P. Mangaliso, "Building Competitive Advantage from Ubuntu: Management Lessons from South Africa," *Academy of Management Executive* 15:3 (August 2001): 23–34.

79 Gina Chon, "China Faces Unexpected Problem Drilling for Oil in Iraq—Farmers," *Wall Street Journal* (May 22, 2009): A6.

80 Sally Bowen, "People Power Keeps Peru's Investors in Check," *Financial Times* (February 6, 1998): 6.

81 Roberto P. Garcia, "Learning and Competitiveness in Mexico's Automotive Industry: The Relationship between Traditional

and World-Class Plants in Multination Firm Subsidiaries," unpublished Ph.D. dissertation (Ann Arbor, MI: University of Michigan, 1996).

82 Peter Capelli, Harber Singh, Jitendra Singh, and Michael Useem, "The Indian Way, Lessons for the U.S.," *The Academy of Management Perspectives* 24:2 (May 2010): 6–24.

83 Philippe Rosinski, *Coaching across Cultures: New Tools for Leveraging National, Corporate & Professional Differences* (London: Nicholas Brealey, 2003). Philippe Rosinski, *Coaching across Cultures: New Tools for Leveraging National, Corporate & Professional Differences* (London: Nicholas Brealey, 2003).

84 Aihwa Ong, *Flexible Citizenship: The Cultural Logics of Transnationality* (Durham, NC: Duke University Press, 1999).

85 James Mackintosh, "A Superstar Leader in an Industry of Icons," *Financial Times* (December 16, 2004): 10.

86 James Wilson and Quentin Peel, "Multicultural attempts 'Failed,' Claims Merkel," *Financial Times* (October 18, 2010): 3.

87 *Sources include the following:* Khadija Sharife, "Damnation for Africa's Big Dams?" *African Business* 352 (April 2009): 52–54; "Uganda Economy: Back to Basics," *EIU Newswire* (June 19, 2009): n.p.; "AES Begins Compensation for the Bujagali Project Affected Residents," *The Bujagali Power Project Update* 1:3 (October 2001): 1+; Deepak Gopinath, "The Divine Power of Profit," *Institutional Investor* 35:3 (March 2001): 39–45; Probe International home page, "World Bank Campaign," at www.probeinternational.org (accessed November 3, 2004); Taimur Ahmad, "We Are Devo," *Project Finance* 216 (April 2001): 39–44; "Give Us Freedom and Kampala: The Baganda on the March," *The Economist* (February 8, 2003): 64; "Uganda: Harnessing the Power of the Nile," IrinNews.org (March 21, 2003); Stephen Linaweaver, "A Case Study of the Bujagali Falls Hydropower Project, Uganda," Occasional Paper No. 42 (London: London School of Economics and Political Science, July 2002); "AAGM: Bujagali: A Dream That Ugandans Love to Hate," *Financial Times Information* (June 23, 2002); Charlotte Denny, "Nile Power Row Splits Uganda," *The Guardian* [London] (August 15, 2001), at www.guardian.co.uks; Marc Lacey, "Traditional Spirits Block a $500 Million Dam Plan in Uganda," *New York Times* (September 13, 2001): B1+; Mark Turner, "Uganda's Dam-Builders Search for Consensus," *Financial Times* (October 1, 2001): 15; "Appeasing the Spirits," *The Irish Times* (January 5, 2002): 62; "Face Music—History of Uganda," at www.music.ch/face/inform/history_uganda (accessed March 7, 2005); "Uganda," Lonely Planet World Guide, at www.lonelyplanet.com/destinations/africa/uganda/culture.htm (accessed March 7, 2005). The people in the case are fictitious, but some of the incidents are based on the experiences of U.S.-based AES Electric, Ltd., the world's largest independent power producer, which contracted with the Ugandan government to build a $520 million dam on the Bujagali Falls of the Nile River in 2001. Citing diminishing returns, AES withdrew from the project in 2003. The Blackstone Group announced in 2007 that it would resume the project.

chapter 3

The Political and Legal Environments Facing Business

Source: Daniel Sullivan

Objectives

1. To discuss the philosophy and practices of the political environment

2. To profile trends in contemporary political systems

3. To explain political risk and approaches to managing it

4. To discuss the philosophy and practices of the legal environment

5. To profile trends in contemporary legal systems

6. To examine legal issues facing international companies

Access a host of interactive learning aids to help strengthen your understanding of the chapter concepts at www.myiblab.com.

MyIBLab

Every road has two directions.

—*Russian proverb*

87

CASE

China—Complicated Risks, Big Opportunities[1]

From 1949 to the late 1970s, China's was autarkic, championing a self-sufficient economy that relied entirely on its own resources. Communist Party leaders believed contact with foreigners would corrupt the nation's political structure and pollute its cultural life; hence, they prohibited foreign direct investment and restricted foreign trade.[2] Near the end of the 1970s, however, the Chinese leadership began rethinking its economic strategy. In 1978, realizing it was lagging much of the world, China enacted the Law on Joint Ventures Using Chinese and Foreign Investment. This law effectively began China's reintegration into the global economy.

Since then, Chinese economic policy has been marked by market liberalization fueling its accelerating entry into the world of foreign trade and investment. Unquestionably, the Chinese Communist Party (CCP) maintains an absolute monopoly on political power. Observed a Beijing scholar, "The Party (CCP) is like God. He is everywhere. You just can't see him."[3] Free market principles, however, shape the country's business environment. This transformation has yielded astonishing results. Over the past 30 years, China has prospered more from globalization than any other country. Its people have moved from mud huts to high rises, companies have moved from woefully run state-owned enterprises to world-class multinationals, it has accumulated the greatest financial reserves in the world, and it has outsmarted, outlasted, and outperformed many on the world stage. Consequently, many see China's ascendency as a global event without parallel.

THE SIREN CALL OF CHINA

Compelling incentives attract foreign investors to China. The 1980s saw a gold rush by MNEs, ranging from manufacturing ventures and export processing to licensing

MAP 3.1 China: The Inscrutable Market

With more than 1.3 billion consumers and a labor force of just over 800 million workers, China is attractive to foreign investors. One of every five people in the world lives in China, but the population is unevenly distributed. In fact, 50 percent of all Chinese live on 8.2 percent of the country's total land. Even so, maintaining centralized control over the nation's political and economic affairs has traditionally been difficult. The vast distances between seats of authority ensure that local officials are often free to run things the way they want to.

agreements and service relationships. This rush has run strong for more than 30 years. Despite the global financial crisis, FDI in China increased by $162 billion in 2010. Total FDI in China—representing more than 600,000 ventures opened by companies from around the world—was $1,476 trillion in 2010 (up from $19 billion in 1990).[4] Why have so many rushed to China? Quite simply, they see stunning opportunities:

- *Market Potential* China, with a population of more than 1.34 billion people, has seen its economic growth reduce the number of poor by more than half-billion since 1981. Hundreds of millions more, although poor, see a brighter future. In 2010, 91 percent of Chinese saw their economic situation as "good"; in 2002, 52 percent had.[5] Many domestic markets are in early, high growth stages. Many MNEs that came for low-cost workers stay for increasingly well-off shoppers.

- *Market Performance* Rapid economic development catapulted China from an also-ran in 1978 to the world's second-largest economy in 2011; estimates put it as the world's largest sometime between 2016 and 2036.[6] Growing income powers consumer spending. During the industrialization of the United States and Great Britain in the nineteenth century, their real incomes per capita doubled in 50 years. China's did the same in nine years.

- *Infrastructure* China is in a multiyear program to build its infrastructure. It is investing trillions of dollars on housing, offices, highways, airports, seaports, waterways, dams, power plants, telecom grids, high-speed trains, and communication networks.

- *Resources* China's well-educated population creates an immense pool of productive labor. Wage rates are far less those in many other countries—perhaps 5 percent of comparable costs in the United States, Japan, Europe and a third of those in Mexico and Turkey.[7] Besides efficient factory workers, China boasts a large and growing number of productive, low-cost brainworkers.

- *Strategic Positioning* MNEs see investment and operation in China as fundamental strategic themes. Like the United States a hundred years ago, China is on the rise. MNEs from the four corners of the globe respond accordingly. Bluntly put, "you are not a global player unless you are in China."[8]

THE COMPLICATION OF REALITY

Notwithstanding the hype and its hyperactive performance, complications tarnish China's appeal. Its unique political and legal systems make business operations a complex, frustrating process. In a nutshell, China applies state capitalism whereby the government manipulates market activities to achieve political goals. Consequently, MNEs doing business in China often find themselves at a disadvantage. Ambitious Western firms such as Exxon Mobil, ABB, and Vodafone, for example, purchased material stakes in Chinese companies, seeing them as a shortcut to market share and industry position. Political ambiguities and legal difficulties short-circuited their plans. Eventually, many sold their stakes and reset their strategies.[9]

China's rapid emergence has created obstacles. Many reflect a mix of ancient and contemporary political and legal outlooks. Some observers argue that, when it comes to doing business in China, the number one rule is to throw away the rulebook. Sage foreign investors abandon the notion that Western ideas automatically work in China. In the West, for instance, you can form a corporation "for any valid business purpose." This principle does not exist in China. Incorporating in China requires telling the government—in excruciating detail—who you are, what you want to do, how do you plan to do it, how much you intend to invest, and how many jobs you will create.

Traditionally, centralized authority determined the path and pace of economic development. This situation is hardly unique to China. Many once-government-controlled economies like India, Vietnam, and Turkey deal with the legacies of centralized decision making. China, however, is a particularly tough case given that its political and legal systems impose many time-consuming tasks. Moreover, it tends to stack the odds against foreigners who are bold enough to forge ahead in the face of an elaborate government bureaucracy and a fledgling legal system.[10]

DRAGONS AND SNAKES

"If the great invention of European civilization was a legal system," quipped an observer, "then China's was bureaucracy."[11] Frustrated investors blame China's treacherous terrain on a bureaucratic system that regulates activity based more on arbitrary agendas than objective standards. Connections, not competencies, sometimes matter more. Those who believe that economics should determine the efficient means of generating prosperity see this as illogical. Still, it is utterly logical to Chinese leaders that regard state control of business activity as the most reliable path toward harmonious prosperity—and, they might add, staying in charge of the show.

Foreign investors navigate often-mysterious political channels. MNEs endure protracted negotiations in obtaining permission to open local operations. At each stop of the long march, national, provincial, and local officials ask how the investment encourages capital formation, promotes exports, creates jobs, and transfers technology. The long-running conflict between central and local Chinese authorities further confuses issues. The vastness of the country means that local officials, whether headquartered in the smallest village or the largest city, are largely left alone by their comrades in Beijing. There are rules and laws, but how they move from Beijing to the provinces is a different story. "The center," notes one observer, often "has no control over the provinces. When it sends people to investigate illegal pirating of CDs, local governors block access to the factories."[12] A sixteenth-century Chinese proverb, "The mightiest dragon cannot crush the local snake," captures the spirit of this enduring power struggle. Essentially, even though the central government in Beijing may appear to be all-powerful, its practical reach is limited by the politics of local fiefdoms.

PRECISE LAWS OR AMBIGUOUS GUIDELINES?

China had no formal legal system in 1978 when it launched one of the greatest campaigns of legal reform in history. Development has stabilized what had been an unpredictable legal environment. Still, China faces challenges, including legislative gaps, hazy interpretation, lax enforcement, and philosophical disagreements. The goal is not judicial independence. Rather, the Chinese chief justice advocates out-of-court mediation as a favored means of settling civil disputes in ways that enhance social harmony.[13] "Chinese legislation is chock-full of ambiguities," says one Beijing-based lawyer, who thinks it will take 10 to 15 years to iron out many wrinkles. Some are less optimistic, comparing the state of the Chinese legal system with that of the United States in the 1920s—then an antiquated composite of statutes and codes that took several decades to modernize. Even to this day, it remains a work in progress.

Others note that, in the case of the Chinese system, even bigger problems reflect a difference in the conception of legality in a society. Western legal systems rest on the rule of law and its doctrine of legitimate regulations administered by public officials who are held accountable for their just enforcement. In contrast, China practices the philosophy of the rule of man, seeing the right of the "man," today in the form of the CCP, to act free of checks and balances. Besides being the law, the CCP is seen above the law.[14] Criminal defendants, for example, have limited access to legal counsel, few rights to call their own witnesses, or even opportunities to contest testimony. Rare is the Chinese criminal-core proceedings that ends with anything other than a guilty verdict. Rather, said an FBI Special Agent and legal attaché at the U.S. Embassy in Beijing, "there is really no rule of law here...they (CCP) make a decision ahead of time to make a point."[15]

THE LEGALITY OF ILLEGALITY

China's legal practices, combined with the growing pains of its fledgling legal institutions and evolving political norms, create problems for MNEs. A flashpoint is the theft of intellectual property—the product of someone's intellect that has commercial value such as patents, trademarks, or copyrights. MNEs complain that the relentless, widespread, and sophisticated theft of their intellectual property fuels China's economic surge. Aggressive estimates attribute nearly a third of the Chinese economy to piracy.[16] In the United States, the FBI estimates that American companies lose up to $250 billion annually to counterfeiting, half of it because of China's illegal practices. In 2009, almost 80 percent of the seized counterfeit goods in the United States were made in China.[17] In frustration, the United States has accused the Chinese of counterfeiting software, videos, pharmaceuticals, and other goods—sometimes with the open encouragement of state officials—and falling short in punishing pirates.[18]

The United States, as has other countries, fights back. It has complained to the World Trade Organization (WTO), a global institution that sets rules for international trade and intellectual property rights, about "inadequate enforcement." China's failure to curb piracy costs software, music, and book publishers billions of dollars in lost sales, argued the United States, as well as makes it unfairly hard for legitimate firms to operate there. Expressing "great regret and strong dissatisfaction at the decision," a Chinese official responded that the U.S. charge was "not a sensible move."[19]

Meanwhile, on the city streets and country roads of China, counterfeiting is never far away. What accounts for China's status as the world's premier number-one counterfeiter? Most analysts point to the mix of China's quest to catch the west, collectivist orientation, rule-of-man legacy, and dubious enforcement of ambiguous laws. These conditions create an unprecedented political and legal morass. Noted an observer, "We have never seen a problem of this size and magnitude in world history...There's more counterfeiting going on in China now than we've ever seen anywhere."[20] The problem threatens to escalate. Government policies have "left a deep impression on companies that intellectual property is there for anyone to use it." Local and provincial economies rely heavily on pirates to power growth. Moreover, make no mistake about it, China excels in making high-quality knockoffs. As they say in Shanghai, "We can copy everything except your mother."[21]

WHERE TO NOW?

The siren call of China continues attracting MNEs. Still, investors question how an opaque, single-party political system and a murky legal system can protect their rights. Some believe that external institutions will improve transparency. China's 2001 ascension to the WTO, for example, required it to accept rules on all sorts of business matters, including tariffs, subsidies, and intellectual property. China has steadily amended its legal codes to comply with WTO standards. Today, the problem is not a shortage of regulations. The problem is China's sluggish enforcement.

Despite intimidating political difficulties and confusing legal questions, foreign investors head to China. Perhaps driven by optimism, perhaps by confidence in continued progress, or perhaps by desperation to ride this megatrend, companies leave the sanctuary of predictable markets for the unique ways of the Middle Kingdom. And, once they cross the modern-day Rubicon, they face the daunting task of interpreting China's political and legal systems.

CRN
Case Review Note

Introduction

Chapter 2 showed that the cultural issues facing international businesses differ from those facing domestic firms. This chapter carries analysis forward, emphasizing that once a company leaves its home country, it operates in markets with different political and legal systems. Certainly, some countries are similar (Australian companies will not find many surprises in New Zealand). In other cases, the differences are profound (an unprepared U.S. company will encounter shocks in Russia). Navigating among countries requires MNEs study how their political and legal circumstances overlap and differ. Determining where, when, and how to adjust business practices without undermining the basis for success is an enduring challenge.

Consider that a domestic company operates in a single national environment where institutional policies are reasonably predictable. Operating internationally exposes its managers to diverse and conflicting pressures from wide-ranging groups in different nations. Variations increase the political and legal risk of navigating different philosophies,

FIGURE 3.1   Political and Legal Factors Influencing International Business Operations

The political and legal environment are broad-stroke concepts that defy straightforward classification. Nevertheless, managers emphasize key points, principally those identified here, to develop a useful perspective to evaluate each.

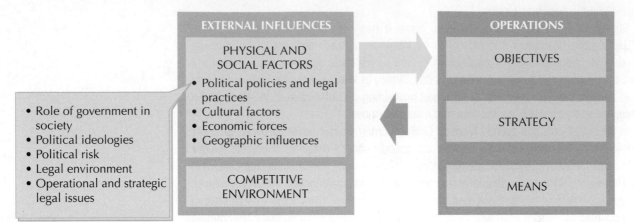

laws, and attitudes concerning political freedom, property rights, and social responsibility. Consequently, effective managers begin with the realization that when it comes to politics and laws, countries' different ideas result in different political and legal environments. They position themselves to compete by understanding these differences, rather than ignoring or, worse, resisting them.

No matter the degree of difference, the prevailing politics and laws in any country influence MNEs. China's political and legal environments, for example, require MNEs rethink the best ways to acquire resources, make investments, adapt operating modes, and manage risk. Figure 3.1 identifies the political policies and legal practices that define a nation's business environment. Throughout this chapter, we will discuss how they reflect the prevailing political ideology, shape the role of government, moderate the degree of political risk, and pose legal complexities.

Managers study political and legal environments in order to adjust company activities to local circumstances.

Case Review Note

Case Review Note

The Political Environment

Our profile of China shows that its evolving political and legal systems create a thriving business environment. Today, foreign investors enter its market, establish operations, manage activities, and earn profits. Still, the Chinese political system imposes hardships, while its legal system complicates attempts to right wrongs. This situation is not unique to China. The interplay of political ideologies, conceptions of political freedoms, legacies of legality, presumptions of fairness, and the exercise of power make for many challenging political environments around the world.

Consider Russia. It is the world's largest country in terms of territory, possesses vast natural resources, has over 140 million people, and has a government that wants to modernize its energy-dependent economy. Still, foreign investors face hurdles. Explained an executive at Swedish retailer IKEA, the Russian political environment is "a bit of a roller coaster.... [Y]ou don't know exactly what will happen tomorrow."[22] The roster of horror stories features well-known names. Authorities arbitrarily confiscated products of Motorola, charged PwC Russia with tax evasion on flimsy evidence, and arguably expropriated Yukos.[23] Overall, doing business in Russia means you had better be "big enough to defend yourself against bureaucratic attacks [and]...ready to hold your nose when elections are rigged and political opposition is crushed."[24] Ironically, Russian Prime Minister Vladimir Putin has promised a "dictatorship of the law" but some see Russia trapped in lawlessness and legal nihilism.[25] Accordingly, in 2010 Transparency International rated Russia 154 out of 178 nations in its Corruption Perceptions Index, alongside Cambodia, Kenya, and Laos.

Consequently, executives evaluate, monitor, and forecast political environments. They study how government officials exercise authority, legislate policies, regulate enterprise, and punish wrongdoers. They monitor how politicians are elected, if, and how they depart. They assess whether the rule of law or the rule of man prevails. They gauge whether freedom is a practical ideal or a wishful abstraction. Then, based on their analyses, they forecast business scenarios, always mindful that political stability rewards investment, political uncertainty penalizes it.[26]

No matter whether they target Afghanistan, Zimbabwe, or the 206 markets in between, managers study how its politics work.[27] This directs their attention to a nation's **political system,** namely the structural dimensions and power dynamics of its government that (1) specify institutions, organizations, and interest groups and (2) define the norms and rules that govern political activities. The purpose of a political system is clearcut: integrate different groups into a functioning, self-sustaining, and self-governing society. Likewise, its test is sustaining society in the face of divisive viewpoints. Success supports peace and prosperity, as we see in Sweden, Botswana, and Australia. Failure leads to instability, insurrection, and, ultimately, disintegration of the sort seen in Somalia, Sudan, Afghanistan, and Libya.

> The goal of the political system is integrating the diverse elements of a society.

> The test of a political system is uniting a society in the face of divisive viewpoints.

Individualism versus Collectivism

Political systems share similarities and demonstrate differences. Explaining the rhyme and reason of these characteristics has intrigued a long line of philosophers, beginning with Plato and Confucius and moving on to such thinkers as Niccolò Machiavelli, Adam Smith, Jean-Jacques Rousseau, Mohandas Gandhi, and Milton Friedman. Each wrestled with enduring questions: How should society balance individual rights versus the needs of the community to sustain a rational, righteous, and harmonious system? Should society guarantee individual freedom in the pursuit of economic self-interest? Does society fare better when individual rights are subordinated to collective goals? Should society champion equality or institute hierarchy? Are individual rights inalienable or conferred by the collective? Engaging these and like-minded questions anchors interpretation of the political systems in terms of **individualism** versus **collectivism.**

Concept Check

Chapter 2 showed that culture moderates the practices of international business. Many points of interpretation, both from an academic and managerial perspective, follow from the pervasiveness of collectivism or individualism in a country.

INDIVIDUALISM

This doctrine emphasizes the primacy of individual freedom, self-expression, and personal independence—think of the declaration that all men have "certain inalienable Rights, that among these are Life, Liberty and the pursuit of Happiness."[28] Individualism champions the exercise of one's ambitions and desires while opposing the rules and regulations that a political system uses to constrain them. The political system encourages a government that protects the liberty of individuals to act as they wish, as long their actions do not infringe on the liberties of others.

The business implications of individualism hold that each person has the right to make economic decisions free of rules and regulations. Countries with an individualistic orientation, like Australia, Canada, Netherlands, New Zealand, United States, and the United Kingdom, shape their marketplace with the idea of **laissez-faire.** Literally meaning, "leave things alone," laissez-faire holds that the government should not interfere in business affairs. Instead, people behave and the market operates according to the neoliberal principles of market fundamentalism. People, left to their own devices, are self-regulating in promoting economic prosperity and growth, acting fairly and justly to maximize personal performance without threatening the welfare of society.

Gaps between philosophical ideals and opportunistic behaviors often fan an adversarial relationship between governments and business in individualistic societies. Recent events dramatize this circumstance. The global financial crisis revealed that some firms had maximized their interests at the expense of society's welfare. Businesses' support of

> Individualism refers to the primacy of the rights and role of the individual. Collectivism refers to the primacy of the rights and role of the group.

deregulation, privatization, and trade liberalization—advocated with the goal of maximizing individuals' freedom of choice—destabilized the marketplace and jeopardized system sustainability. In response, governments reset regulations to reduce market inefficiencies (such as insufficient consumer knowledge or excessive producer power) that had distorted competition. Ongoing market problems in Japan, United States, Ireland, Greece, and Portugal, among others, push governments to rein in the individualism of market fundamentalism in order to protect the welfare of the collective.

COLLECTIVISM

Collectivism stresses the supremacy of human interdependence within the context of the community.

This doctrine emphasizes the primacy of the collective, such as a group, party, community, class, society, or nation, over the interests of the individual. No matter the importance of the individuals that comprise the collective, the whole of the collective is ultimately greater than the sum of its individual parts. Today we see collectivism in a range of countries, including Argentina, China, Vietnam, Japan, South Korea, Egypt, Brazil, Taiwan, and Mexico.

Collectivism in the business world holds that the ownership of assets, the allocation of resources, the structure of industries, the conduct of companies, and the actions of managers improves societal welfare. Business decisions are made by the group. Its members assume joint responsibility to improve the lot of everyone. Political systems that exhibit a collectivist orientation hold that government regulates the market to ensure that business benefit society. Similarly, governments in collectivist societies promote social equality, labor rights, income equality, and workplace democracy so that the "welfare of the nation takes precedence over the selfishness of the individuals."[29] In extreme cases, such as Venezuela or Saudi Arabia, political leaders limit property rights and regulate the mass media in order to control the business environment.

Political Ideology

The orientation toward individualism or collectivism shapes a nation's political system. Understanding how directs managers' attention to the idea of political ideology. In theory, an ideology is an integrated vision that defines a holistic conception of an abstract ideal and its normative thought processes. For example, the ideal of freedom carries with it ideas about related principles, doctrines, goals, practices, and symbols. Hence, a **political ideology** stipulates how society ought to function and outlines the methods by which it will do so.

A political ideology encapsulates the doctrine of political behavior and change. It outlines the procedures for converting ideas into actions.

In the United States, for example, the liberal principles of the Democratic Party and the conservative doctrine of the Republican Party define their respective political ideologies—i.e., the former favors collectivist measures such as progressive taxation and strict environmental standards whereas the latter champions individualistic measures such as flat taxes and minimal regulation. Japan has a similar situation whereby its Democratic Party champions social liberalism and its Liberal Democratic Party advocates conservatism. Practically, a political ideology moves beyond describing a vision of a better, brighter future; it specifies the means to achieve that ideal.

In Japan and the United States, as in many other countries, there are political parties that list smaller memberships than do primary parties. Consequently, most nations are pluralistic in which different political groups champion competing ideologies.[30] **Pluralism** also arises when two or more groups in a country differ in terms of language (Belgium), class structure (United Kingdom), ethnic background (South Africa), tribal legacy (Afghanistan), or religion (India).

Pluralism holds that there are multiple opinions about an issue, each of which contains part of the truth, but none that contain the entire truth.

Competing ideologies requires governments, lacking the authority to act unilaterally, negotiate solutions. The resulting ambiguity complicates decision making for MNEs. Pluralism requires managers assess the interplay among groups. The bargaining process between competing groups means that politics and decision making follow multiple, shifting lines. Hence, companies often try to shape policy. In the United States, for example, some companies support political action committees that support preferred candidates or shape the legislative process.

SPECTRUM ANALYSIS

Figure 3.2 outlines a **political spectrum** of the various forms of political ideologies. By specifying a basic conceptual structure, spectrum analysis guides the assessment of a complex issue—in this case, political ideology. Configuring ideologies along the central axis lets us model different ones in relation to others. This task calls for specifying credible ideas to anchor the endpoints. Reasonably set, one then positions other options.

The standard of "reasonably set" is treacherous. The world exhibits a diversity of ideologies, including anarchism, conservatism, secularism, environmentalism, liberalism, feminism, nationalism, socialism, and theocracy. Cultural perspectives also moderate interpretation of these choices. From a Western perspective, for example, one commonly sees the endpoints defined as conservative versus liberal interpretations of democracy—i.e., Republican versus Democrat. Other endpoints command greater relevance in other contexts. A political spectrum in an Islamic country, such as Iran or Saudi Arabia, is likely bounded by theocracy versus secularism to reflect the role of the clergy in the government. In the case of Taiwan, parties that endorse Chinese reunification oppose those that champion Taiwanese independence. Similarly, in Belgium, ends would reflect the ethnic and socioeconomic tensions between the Dutch-speaking Flanders region and the French-speaking Walloon region.

Although varied, these situations share a common theme, namely what degree of political freedom prevails in the country. **Political freedom** measures the degree to which fair and competitive elections occur, the extent to which individual and group freedoms are guaranteed, the legitimacy ascribed to the rule of law, and the existence of freedom of the press. For managers, a key concern is how the political system determines the freedom they have to make investments choices and operational decisions. The matters of where, how, and why a company invests, and once there, how its managers run operations are not inalienable freedoms. They are determined by the political system. Therefore, with the notion of political freedom in mind, Figure 3.2 sets the political spectrum with democracy, with its call to preserve, protect, and defend freedom, anchoring one endpoint and totalitarianism, with its call to control, constrain, and, suppress freedom, the other. [31]

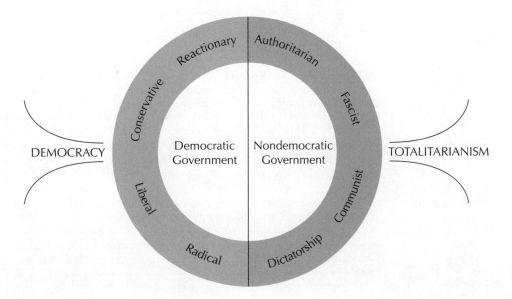

FIGURE 3.2 The Political Spectrum

In practice, purely democratic and totalitarian systems are exceptions. Looking around the world, one sees many variations. For example, democratic systems range from radical on one side (advocates of extreme political reform) to reactionary (advocates of a return to past conditions). Likewise, totalitarian systems emphasize different degrees of state control. Fascism aims to control people's minds, souls, and daily existence, whereas authoritarianism confines itself to political control of the state.

Figure 3.2 indicates that the ideologies that fall between these endpoints interpret **freedom** differently. Liberal political ideologies, for instance, advocate the right of individuals whereas authoritarianism subordinates individual freedoms to the welfare of the collective. In the former, managers have many investment and operating options. In the latter, they have far fewer. Similar examples reinforce the chief point: Freedom is the distinguishing characteristic of political ideologies. Some stress its primacy, others oppose it, and throughout all, MNEs study how it affects them.

Each political ideology in Figure 3.2 is notable; space constraints prevent us from covering each. However, understanding the ideals and means of the two endpoints, democracy and totalitarianism, helps explains the others.

DEMOCRACY

> Democracy calls for participation by citizens in a fair and just decision-making process.

Abraham Lincoln held that **democracy** is a government "of the people, by the people, and for the people." Modern-day democracies translate this ideology into the principles that all citizens are politically and legally equal; all are equally entitled to freedom of thought, opinion, belief, speech, and association; and all equally command sovereign power over public officials.[32] These principles and practices institutionalize political freedoms and civil liberties that endorse individualism.

> Democracy and individualism are intrinsically related and mutually reinforcing; democracy legitimates standards of individualism and individualism supports principles of democracy.

The scale and scope of modern society limits the practice of democracy, particularly when population size makes it impossible for all voters to participate directly. Table 3.1 shows that countries respond with different types of democracies. Notwithstanding variance, all champions the power of the many over the few. A democratic government protects personal and political rights, civil liberties, fair and free elections, and independent courts of law.[33] In the future, we may see a resurgence of direct democracy, whereby a virtual assembly of citizens let's all express their votes directly through electronic signature gathering or online polling processes.

Business Implications   Democracy supports individualistic attitudes that permit MNEs to invest and operate based on economic, not political, standards. It creates business environments that promote commerce, expand trade, and streamline exchange, both within the country as well as across countries. The signaling devices of market activities, not bureaucratic regulation, develop a productive business environment. Managers and consumers are free to do as they see fit. In political terms, freedom sanctions rights and liberties; in economic terms, freedom legitimates profits and prosperity. Brazil, India, Indonesia, and Turkey provide cases in point. Belief in central planning run by a strong

TABLE 3.1   Prominent Types of Democracies

Representative	Originates in a constitution that protects individual freedoms and liberties. The law treats all citizens, both public and private, equally. Elected representatives hold ultimate sovereignty but must act in the people's interest. Officials represent voters and, while mindful of voters' preferences, have the authority to act as they see fit. Examples include the United State and Japan.
Multiparty	A political system whereby three or more parties govern, whether separately or as part of a coalition. The leadership of a single party cannot legislate policy without negotiating with the opposition parties. Examples include Canada, Germany, Italy, and Israel.
Parliamentary	Citizens exercise political power by electing representatives to a legislative branch called a parliament. The legislature is the source of legitimacy for the various ministers that run the executive branch. Examples include India and Australia.
Social	Applies democratic means to power the transition from capitalism to socialism. Government regulates capitalism to control its tendency toward injustice. Examples include Norway and Sweden.

state had led to stagnant, if not failing, economies 20 years ago. Now, these countries are converting the energy of "messy" democracy into dynamic business environments.[34]

TOTALITARIANISM

A **totalitarian system** subordinates the individual to the interests of the collective. A single agent in whatever form, such as an individual, an assembly, a committee, a junta, or a party, monopolizes political power and uses it to regulate many, if not all, aspects of public and private life. Fair game includes a person's occupation, income level, personal interests, religion, and even family structure.[35] A totalitarian government eliminates dissent within the state through indoctrination, persecution, surveillance, propaganda, censorship, and violence. It tolerates few to no ideas, interests, or activities that run counter to state ideology—e.g., bookstores in China may only stock only works of which the Chinese Communist Party (CCP) approves.[36] There is no alternative because none is allowed to exist. In extreme situations, personal survival is linked to that of the ruling regime. Collectively, these conditions merge the interests of individuals with those of the state. Table 3.2 profiles types of totalitarian systems.

The dynamics of change in a totalitarian state highlight the means used to enforce its ideology. Rejecting the preceding forms of society as corrupt, immoral, and beyond reform or redemption, a single leader advocates a new society that corrects wrongs, redresses injustice, and supports harmony. The state uses propaganda, indoctrination, and incarceration to make citizens conform.[37] State-controlled media filters information, state-controlled education filters ideas, and state-controlled security suppresses dissent. The cumulative result is a "virtual mind prison" in which the leader and the state fuse.[38]

Although remote to citizens in western democracies, forms of totalitarianism prevail throughout the world. Presently some 2.5 billion people, roughly one-third of the world population, live in totalitarian systems. Whether calling home Madagascar, Turkmenistan, Afghanistan, China, Iran, North Korea, or Saudi Arabia, the citizens of these countries have few personal freedoms and civil liberties. The reemergence of powerful, single-party states worldwide, notably in Russia, Venezuela, and Iran reinforces totalitarianism; Russia suppresses individual freedoms, Venezuela nationalized media

> **Concept Check**
>
> Recall our discussion in Chapter 2 of "Behavioral Factors Affecting Business." These variables change as people change—or as state authority influences them. To shape people's behavior to support the state's interests a totalitarian government manipulates norms governing work motivation, risk taking, communication practices, and consumption preferences.

> A totalitarian system consolidates power in a single agent who then controls the political, economic, and social activities.

> Totalitarianism and collectivism are intrinsically related and mutually reinforcing; totalitarianism legitimates standards of collectivism and collectivism supports principles of totalitarianism.

TABLE 3.2 Prominent Types of Totalitarianism

Authoritarianism	Tolerates no deviation from state ideology. Day-to-day life reflects obedience to state authority; resistance incurs punishment. Officials regulate the political environment but pay less attention to the economic and social structure of society. Often lacks an ideology to politicize public and private life. Examples include Kazakhstan, Chad, and Turkmenistan.
Fascism	Organizes a nation based on corporatist perspectives, values, and systems. Advocates a single-party state that controls, through force and indoctrination, people's minds, souls, and daily existence. Examples include North Korea and Burma.
Secular	Single-party government controls elections, tolerates dissent as long as it does not challenge the state, and suppresses other ideologies. The state does not prescribe an all-encompassing ideology. It grants individual freedoms provided one does not contest state authority or disrupt social harmony. Examples include China, Vietnam, and Venezuela.
Theocratic	Government is an expression of the preferred deity. Leaders claim to represent its interests on earth. Applies ancient dogma in place of modern political or legal principles. Strict social regulation and gender regimentation typically ensue. Examples include Iran, Afghanistan, and Saudi Arabia.

Hail to the Ruler ▶

Supporters of Venezuelan President Hugo Chavez cheer as they parade by his larger than life image during a rally in Caracas. Pro-Chavez rallies often attract tens of thousands onto the streets. Many see Chavez's message of self-styled revolution for the poor legitimating his authoritarian presidency.

Source: © Camilo Delgado Castilla / Demoti/Demotix/Demotix/Corbis

that urged democracy; and Iran corrupted its electoral process. Lastly, some see China's rise endorsing authoritarianism.[39]

Business Implications   Managers in totalitarian systems face markets that are radically different from those found in democracies. Totalitarianism endorses a statist approach to economic management. Private capitalism plays a supporting role to state control of economic activities. For instance, the Chinese government, under the direction of the CCP, claims majority ownership and management control of immense sections of the economy. The state is the majority owner of 99 of the 100 largest publicly listed Chinese companies—39 of these are among the 500 biggest firms in the world.[40] Similarly, 129 huge conglomerates in finance, media, mining, metals, transportation, communication, and so on answer directly to the CCP.[41] Furthermore, China's provinces and cities run thousands of medium-sized and smaller ones. Add it all up and you have an authoritarian system that rejects many of the practices found in a democracy.

Managers operating in these sorts of markets must adjust decision making to account for the intricacies of political activities. Bluntly put, the government's imperative is sustaining state power. Economics and markets are tools to do so. The situation affects all companies. It typically hits foreign investors hardest. The state favors local companies at the expense of their foreign competitors.[42] Unbeatable financial assistance, special tax programs, and relaxed work regulations are just some of the benefits offered to local companies. In recourse, MNEs often strike deals that would be unthinkable elsewhere. In China, getting along with the system requires foreign enterprises tolerate, if not facilitate, setting up of Communist Party cells in their local operations.

Case Review Note

Consider, for example, General Electric's 50–50 joint venture with Aviation Industry, a Chinese military-jet maker, to produce avionics, the electronic brains of aircraft. The deal required GE take the risky but potentially lucrative step of folding pieces of its global operations into partnerships with a state-owned enterprise. Earlier such deals had proved troublesome, souring over concerns that Chinese partners, after gaining access to Western technology and expertise, became potent new rivals.[43] Even so, seeing China as "our second home market," GE reasoned the risks outweigh the cost of missing the fast-growing Chinese aviation market.

The Standard of Freedom

Freedom House stipulates, "Freedom is possible only in democratic political systems in which the governments are accountable to their own people; the rule of law prevails; and freedoms of expression, association, and belief, as well as respect for the rights of minorities and women, are guaranteed."[44] Since 1972, Freedom House has annually assessed political and civil freedom around the world.[45] It uses measures derived from the Universal Declaration of Human Rights to analyze countries.[46] Map 3.2 shows the distribution of freedom worldwide. Freedom House identifies three types:

- A *free country* exhibits open political competition, respect for civil liberties, independent civic life, and independent media. There are inalienable freedoms of expression, assembly, association, education, and religion. Examples include Australia, Brazil, India, and the United States.

- A *partly free country* exhibits limited political rights and civil liberties, corruption, weak rule of law, ethnic and religious strife, unfair elections, and censorship. Often, democracy is a convenient slogan for the single political party that dominates within a façade of regulated pluralism. Examples include Guatemala, Pakistan, and Tanzania.

- A *not free country* has few to no political rights and civil liberties. The government allows minimal to no exercise of personal choice, relies on the rule of man as the basis of law, constrains religious and social freedoms, and controls a large share, if not all, of business activity. Examples include China, Russia, Saudi Arabia, and Vietnam.

> Freedom House classifies three types of political systems:
> - Free.
> - Partly free.
> - Not free.

MAP 3.2 Map of Freedom, 2010

Freedom House identifies three types of political systems—Free, Partly Free, and Not Free. If you live in a country classified as "free," you enjoy a high level of political rights and civil liberties. If you are a citizen of a "partly free" nation, your share of rights and liberties ranges anywhere from average to just below average. If your homeland is "not free," you enjoy very few rights and liberties.

Source: Freedom House, "Map of Freedom 2010," at www.freedomhouse.org.

Note: Given that this is a Mercator projection, the scale approximates east-west distance at the equator; however, the farther you move from the equator, the more the east-west distance is distorted.

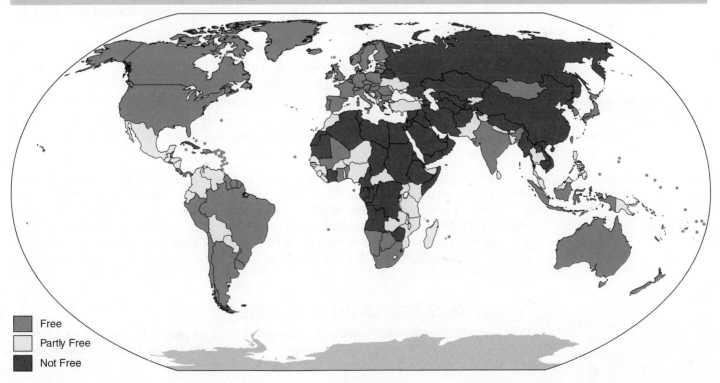

- Free
- Partly Free
- Not Free

Trends in Political Ideologies

THE THIRD WAVE OF DEMOCRATIZATION

The second half of the twentieth century saw the steady diffusion of the democratic ideology. The number of democratic political systems grew from 22 out of 154 countries (14 percent) in 1950 to 90 out of 193 countries (47 percent) in 2009. The number of nations that made the transition, particularly during the 1970s and 1980s, gave rise to the **Third Wave of Democratization.**[47] Countries throughout Africa, Asia, Latin America, South America, and Eastern Europe abandoned totalitarianism for democracy. The quest for individual freedoms and civil liberties transformed the world. Societies began building fairer civic institutions, independent media, objective judiciaries, and stronger property rights.[48] Today, one-half of the world's population lives in a democracy of some sort. Alternatively, more people live in countries with democratic governments than at any time in history.

In doubling the number of democracies in two decades, the Third Wave of Democratization helped topple the Berlin Wall in 1989, collapse the Communist Bloc, and end the Cold War. Some saw democracies' surge symbolizing the "end of history." The universalization of Western liberal democracy, reinforced by the market fundamentalism of capitalism, represented the endpoint of mankind's ideological evolution and the final stage of human government.[49]

Engines of Democracy   Several engines powered the Third Wave of Democratization. Notably:

1. The failure of totalitarian regimes to deliver economic progress undermined their legitimacy. Aggrieved citizens contested the right of officials to govern. The fall of the Berlin Wall punctuated this epic change. Formerly Communist countries adopted democracy en masse.

2. Improved communications eroded totalitarian states' control of information. Images of resistance and rebellion had snowball effects on pro-democracy campaigns worldwide. Where once it took weeks for word of mouth of protests to spread, improving connections circulated news within hours.[50] Technologies integrated disenfranchised people into the global village.

3. Freedom yielded economic dividends.[51] The median per capita gross domestic product, a measure of the standard of living, rose nearly seven times higher for the freest countries than for those that are not free. Growing wealth strongly correlates with property rights, the rule of law, more education, gender equality, a free press, and social tolerance.[52] In many countries, economic advances fostered the expansion of the middle class worldwide. Rising prosperity supported the political stability and faith in the future that anchors democracy.[53]

The multi-decade march toward greater political freedoms and expansive civil liberties fueled a belief in the inevitability of democracy—again, the so-called "end of history" phenomenon. For MNEs, this trend stabilized operating conditions and encouraged them to expand their investment horizon to more countries in more parts of the world. This, in turn, accelerated the globalization of business as MNEs entered more markets to sell more goods to more people who had more resources to buy them.

DEMOCRACY: RECESSION AND RETREAT

Democracy retains appeal worldwide. Surveys show that people in most countries want it. Increasing wealth and education, along with an expanding middle class, energize its

---

The Third Wave of Democratization refers to the third major surge of democracy in the 20th century that began in 1974. It ultimately doubled the number of countries led by a democratic government.

Concept Check

In profiling "The Forces Driving Globalization" in Chapter 1, we noted the power of changing political situations. Until recently, we have witnessed the diffusion of democracy and the corresponding decline in totalitarianism. The acceptance of democracy and its advocacy of freedom accelerated the expansion of international business.

Powering the rise of democracy over the past three decades has been:

• Failure of totalitarian regimes to deliver prosperity.
• Improving communication technology.
• Economic dividends of political freedom.

Concept Check

Chapter 1 identifies the "Expansion of Technology" as a driving force of globalization. Advances in telecommunications liberated the flow of information, thereby helping to change social and political attitudes in many countries.

Over the past five years, gains in freedom have given way to declines.

The End of an Era
Following weeks of protest, Tunisians celebrate the resignation of President President Zine El Abidine Ben Ali on January 14, 2011. For 23 years, his authoritarian party held power, relying on shadowy politics, skewed elections, and nefarious security agencies to impose a police state.

allure. Troubling data, however, question its momentum. Managers increasingly qualify their interpretation of political environments with the possibility that "history," rather than ending, is just beginning.

A few years ago, longitudinal data on the slowing momentum of democracy indicated a "democracy recession." Now, data indicate democracy is in retreat worldwide. In 1987, there were 66 electoral democracies in the world; in 1997, there were 117; 2006 saw 123; by 2010, it was 115 (see Figure 3.3).[54] Moreover, Figure 3.4 indicates an ominous shift over the past few years. Gains in freedom have given way to declines in freedom. Sham elections, police crackdowns, kangaroo courts, and persecution of dissidents have

> Several indicators show slowing adoption of democracy.

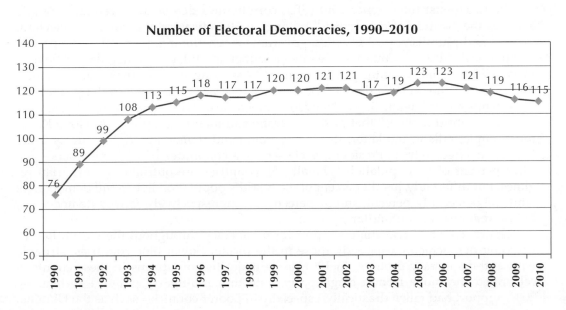

Number of Electoral Democracies, 1990–2010

FIGURE 3.3   Freedom in the World: Number of Electoral Democracies

Freedom House's Annual Survey of Political Rights and Civil Liberties reports there were 115 electoral democracies in 2010 versus 76 in 1990. Democracy's growth curve began flatlining in the mid-1990s. It started declining in 2007. A continuing downward trend signifies democracy's retreat or, alternatively, totalitarianism's advance.

Source: Freedom House, "Freedom in the World 2011," at www.freedomhouse.org (accessed May15, 2011).

FIGURE 3.4   Freedom in the World: Gains and Declines

The past decade shows a disturbing reversal. Early on, gains in freedom exceeded declines. The past five years have seen the opposite.

Source: Freedom House, "Freedom in the World 2011: The Authoritarian Challenge to Democracy," www.freedomhouse.org.

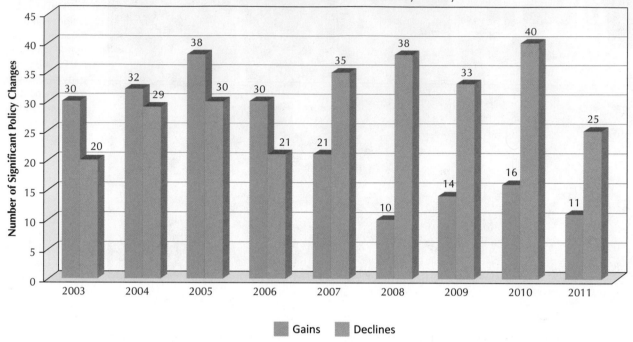

Total Gains and Declines in Freedom by Country

gained traction. All speak to the stance, as President Lukashenka of Belarus declared on the heels of a rigged election victory, that "there will be no more mindless democracy in this country."[55] Worldwide, increasingly powerful totalitarian regimes impose "forceful measures designed to suppress democratic reformers, international assistance to those reformers, and ultimately the very idea of democracy itself."[56] As a result, 2010 marked the fifth consecutive year in which global freedom declined—the longest consecutive period of setbacks in nearly 40 years.

The Economist Intelligence Unit classifies four types of political systems:

- Full democracy.
- Flawed democracy.
- Hybrid regime.
- Authoritarian regime.

The Economist Intelligence Unit (EIU) corroborates **democracy's retreat.** The EIU assesses the "texture of democracy," relying on 60 indicators of a country's electoral process and pluralism, civil liberties, government functioning, political participation, and political culture.[57] Countries are rated as either as a full democracy, flawed democracy, hybrid regime, or authoritarian regime.[58] Assessing 167 countries, the EIU found that many of the world's democracies are "democracies" in name only; just 26 are "full democracies," while 53 are "flawed democracies." Of the remaining, 33 are classified as "hybrid regimes" that mix democratic and totalitarian practices. Hong Kong, for example, falls in the latter; its citizens command democratic rights but its Chief Executive, effectively its President, is chosen by a committee of 1,200 members—just 0.017 percent of its population.[59] Finally, 55 countries are outright authoritarian regimes. Put differently, just 12 percent of the world's population live in full democracies while 37 percent, 14 percent, and 37 percent live in, respectively, flawed democracies, hybrid regimes, and authoritarian regimes.[60]

Reports confirm weakening support for democracy throughout the world. Recent fledgling democracies, especially those in the former Soviet bloc countries, struggle with anti-democracy protests. In 1991, large majorities of citizens in these countries celebrated the move from a single-party state to a multiparty political system. By 2009, support had fallen drastically, especially in poorer countries such as the Ukraine,

Hungary, and Lithuania.[61] Events in other areas slowed democracy. In the United States, the terrorist attacks of September 11, 2001 reset the standards of personal freedom. Resulting restrictions raised questions about the legitimacy of democratic ideals. Collectively, trends throughout the world signal a surge in totalitarianism. More precisely, the EIU concluded,

> Authoritarian trends have become even more entrenched in the Middle East and much of the former Soviet Union. Democratisation in Sub-Saharan Africa is grinding to halt, and in some cases is being reversed. A political malaise in east-central Europe has led to disappointment and questioning of the strength of the region's democratic transition. Media freedoms are being eroded across Latin America and populist forces with dubious democratic credentials have come to the fore in a few countries in the region. In the developed West, a precipitous decline in political participation, weaknesses in the functioning of government and security-related curbs on civil liberties are having a corrosive effect on some long established democracies.[62]

Engines of Totalitarianism   Several engines powered the Third Wave of Democratization. Likewise, today the following forces promote totalitarianism.

Economic Development   There is growing uncertainty of the relationship between the level of economic development and democracy. The classic modernization hypothesis holds that economic development is a pre-condition of democracy.[63] This is longer universally accepted. Big case in point: China's economic performance since 1979 endorses its authoritarian, one-party system as an alternative to liberal, multiparty democracies. The Chinese model of a "people's democratic dictatorship" has steadily gained credibility.

Inconsistencies and Double Standards   Democracy setbacks in Italy, France, UK, and the United States, for example, give pause to the 70 strategically important countries at the political crossroad—if democracy can't work there, how could it work here?[64] Charges of hypocrisy against Western countries (owing to incursions in Iraq, Libya, and Afghanistan, along with the implications of its antiterrorist activities to

Powering the resurgence of totalitarianism is

- Economic development.
- Inconsistencies.
- Economics problems.
- Standards of democracy.

FIGURE 3.5   The Agents of Totalitarianism Gain Ground

A comic, yet frightful, take on the political forces compelling the retreat of democracy.

Source: May 12, 2011, *The Economist.*

political freedoms and civil liberties), slowly delegitimize democracy. Double standards in foreign policy (i.e., some countries run by autocrats can be friends, such as Saudi Arabia, whereas others are foes, like Venezuela) eroded the credibility of democracy-promoters.[65]

Economic Problems   The global financial crisis has complicated matters. High unemployment, slow growth, and rising debt, by threatening the middle class, weakened democracy. Confidence in institutions has declined throughout the West. The International Labour Organization reports fewer believe that political policies in democratic states lead to a fairer and better future.[66] History shows that right-wing totalitarian movements generally draw popular support from the middle class seeking to preserve the status quo. Those who fall into poverty are politically hazardous. In the United States, for example, the worse the economy, the more people describe themselves as "right-wing."[67] On the other hand, left wing totalitarianism often develops from working class movements seeking to overthrow wealthy oppressors—think of the tension between the proletariat and bourgeois in Marxism. Unless reversed, unemployment, debt, and anxiety encourage totalitarianism.[68]

Who Defines Democracy?   The legitimacy of Western notions of democracy travels poorly to societies with different ideals and institutions. Hu Jintao, CCP chief and China's president, speaks of "democracy" with a different meaning from the one understood by Westerners. In his view, calls for multiparty democracy are taboo, opposition cannot officially organize, reform must obey the "correct political orientation," and "orderly" change must respect and preserve the authority of the CCP.[69] Similarly, Prime Minister Vladimir Putin, proclaiming himself "a true democrat," argues the West misinterprets Russia's authoritarianism. He criticizes the West, charging that the "largest complexity today is that some of the participants in the international dialogue believe that their ideas [of democracy] are the ultimate truth."[70] Likewise, Brazil's former president, Luiz Inacio Lula da Silva, says countries like the United States, UK, Germany, France, Canada, and Japan—the primary advocates of Western-style democracy—no longer speak for the world. They have, he adds, lost the moral authority to dictate solutions to developing countries.[71]

The engines of totalitarianism, considered in the context of democracy's retreat, raise the question: Has democracy, at least in the form advocated by the world's veteran democracies, run its course? If so, as we consider in our "Looking to the Future" box, what then might become of political ideologies and how might MNEs respond?

Looking to the Future   Political Ideology and MNEs' Actions

As a rule, managers wonder what a political map of the world might look like in the next decade. Will democracy spread? Will totalitarianism make a comeback? Will new political ideologies arise? It is tempting to regard these questions as academic straw men. The latest data indicate they are anything but. Faltering freedom and resurgent authoritarianism accelerate democracy's retreat. Trends highlight the political ideologies competing for supremacy—namely, the Washington Consensus, the Beijing Consensus, and the Clash of Civilizations. Let's look at each.

The Washington Consensus

Coined after the Cold War for the free-market, pro-trade, and pro-globalization policies promoted by United States, the Washington Consensus champions democracy, freedom, the rule of law, and human rights.[72] The collapse of the Soviet Empire led to an American-dominated unipolar world with Washington its philosophical center. The Washington Consensus, promoted by executives, politicians, generals, journalists, and institutions, called upon advanced and developing countries to reform in ways that reflected the political economy of the United States. Powering the Washington Consensus was the belief that right-minded reform led to economic growth, which in turn created a middle class that supported property rights. This, in turn, began institutionalizing the rule of law, the key precondition for democracy.

Successfully navigating this sequence, reasoned the United States, resulted in countries that championed prosperity and peace. These compelling virtues, within the context of a world practicing U.S.-style liberal democracy, arguably signified the ultimate form of government and the endpoint of humanity's socio-cultural evolution.[73] Ironically, noted some, promoting and protecting the Washington Consensus required a powerful military; the United States' defense spending, at nearly $700 billion, exceeds that of the next 17 countries combined.[74]

The Beijing Consensus

Some link the decline of Western-style democracy to the growing appeal of the Beijing Consensus.[75] A euphemism for China's self-proclaimed system of a "people's democratic dictatorship," the Beijing Consensus calls for a one-party system in which elected representatives, preapproved by the ruling party, oversee a nominal democratic system whose citizens, though granted the right to vote, cannot participate in decision making.[76] The CCP aspires to rule by consent, preferring benevolent persuasion to the iron fist. Still, it is quick to suppress threats to its authority. As party official routinely note, "stability trumps everything."[77]

Unlike the ideologically interventionist Washington Consensus, the Beijing Consensus is ideologically agnostic. It prizes economic development and international trade as the means to generate growth, create wealth, and build a harmonious society. It uses fast-growing prosperity to subvert political choice. It does not pass judgment on another country's political model and expects not to be judged in turn. It advocates trade "with no strings attached" (which, in the case of the Washington Consensus, are democracy, freedom, human rights, and the rule of law).

China's political ideology of harmonious stability has gained credibility worldwide, particularly given its strong economic performance in the wake of the global economic crisis. Said one analyst, the "China model of authoritarian capitalism is gaining currency. Governments from Syria to Vietnam (along with Sudan, Burma, Uzbekistan, North Korea, and Zimbabwe, to name just a few others) have sung its praises."[78] Some argue state control that marries liberal economics with authoritarian politics in the style of China, not the union of liberal economics and democracy markets in the style of the United States, now represents the superior path to prosperity and harmony.

The Clash of Civilizations

Spreading democracy in the Arab world, which is regularly rated the world's least free region, has been a long-running goal of the West. Indeed, an aim of the Iraq War was to build the luminous "city upon a hill" that set the foundation for peaceful democracy in the region. Efforts there, as well as movements in Tunisia, Egypt, Afghanistan, Bahrain, Yemen, and Libya, for example, have met limited success. Moreover, Western military involvement has raised questions about the legitimacy of democratic ideals throughout the region. Faltering institutions and changes in political sentiments hinder the transition to democracy in several Islamic nations, including Kuwait, Iran, Saudi Arabia, and the Palestinian areas.

Upheaval in Tunisia, Egypt, Jordan, Libya, Syria, and Yemen highlight the difficulty of promoting democratic political cultures, to say nothing of a functioning democracy. The discontent of the economically and politically disadvantaged, particularly among youth suffering extreme unemployment, mobilized the massive pro-democracy protests of the so-called Arab Spring. Data on the determinants and consequences of democratic transitions advise caution. Violent uprisings are less likely to lead to a regime change and, if a shift takes place, they may lead to worse democracies when coupled with weak consensus for property rights and civil liberties.[79]

Strong economies in the oil-rich Persian Gulf, furthermore, stall the spread of democracy given that it no longer appears vital to prosperity. Oil-based revenue entrenches autocracy given that it removes the need to levy taxes, thereby reducing state accountability. Consequently, moderate Arab leaders contend that the transition from totalitarianism to democracy is, at best, "a slow process." All the while, hardliners vilify any and all aspects of democracy.[80]

The reluctance of Islamic states to adopt democracy introduces the "clash-of-civilizations" scenario. Irreconcilable cultural and religious differences between Islam and the West, goes this scenario, will trigger a backlash against Western political ideals and their crystallization in the ideologically interventionist

(continued)

Washington Consensus.[81] Some speculate that an epic clash between different civilizations will usher in a new political ideology based on cultural and religious ideals.

What's Next, Managers Ask?

Democracy's ongoing retreat questions long-cherished ideals. Managers ask which direction political ideologies might track. Will liberal democracy, in the form of the Washington Consensus, regain the commanding heights? Developments worldwide, such as those in Egypt and Tunisia, powered by poverty and supported by social networking channels, suggest possibly.[82] Or, will the one-party trademark of the Beijing Consensus set political standards? China's growing involvement in a politically receptive Asia, Africa, and Middle East suggests possibly. To that end, asked, "How satisfied are you with the country's direction," in 2010, 87 percent of Chinese reported being so versus 31 percent in Britain, 30 percent in the United States, and 20 percent in Japan.[83] Last, if countries bypass the American Way or the Chinese Path, might a clash of civilizations give rise to new ideas of freedom and liberty?[84] Ongoing tensions in hotspots worldwide do not bode well.

Whatever the scenario, history reminds us that it matters. The first and second waves of democratization (1828–1926 and 1943–1962, respectively) were followed by periods of freedom backlash and democracy retreat. The end of the second wave saw more than 20 countries revert from democracy to totalitarianism, epitomized in the ensuing ideological contest in the bipolar world of Washington versus Moscow. Hence, the question arises: Are we facing once again a cycle of transition, consolidation, and regression?[85]

Whatever the answer, few managers underestimate political change. If the Washington Consensus proves resilient, they must adjust operations to the growing pains of countries that champion freedom, advocate human rights, and adopt the rule of law. Prosperity may be difficult, but there will be prosperity for many. If the Beijing consensus predominates, they must rethink business in a world that uses state controls to generate economic growth at the price of freedom. Prosperity may be easier, but its price will include individual freedoms. If ideologies transform as civilizations clash, the resulting social and religious orders will reset systems. Prosperity may be a wild card as opposing ideologies battle for the commanding heights. ■

Political Risk

Politics, if anything, is dynamic. At different times, different parties champion different ideologies that endorse different political systems. Difference inevitably create unpredictability. Consequently, investing and operating internationally exposes companies to risks that arise from a country's political system. This class of risk, referred to as **political risk,** is the potential loss arising from a change in government policy. More precisely, it is the risk that political decisions, events, or conditions will affect a country's business environment in ways that force investors to accept lower rates of return, cost them some or all of the value of their investment, or threaten the sustainability of the operation. Table 3.3 identifies leading causes of political risk.

Two trends are increasing political risk around the world. First, many fast-growing, emerging markets are rife with the flashpoints of political risks, notably weak legal systems, makeshift institutions, volatile cities, and fragile regimes. Many companies in these countries are state-run, pursuing political goals that complicate economic situations. Worse yet, political risks differ from market to market. In Venezuela, one faces economic nationalism; in Brazil, one need to understand Congress's multi-party alliances; in China, the task is interpreting the power and play of the CCP; in Saudi Arabia, one must make sense of the internal relations of the ruling family. Hence, operating in these markets is quite different from the comparatively more predictable politics in Western democracies.

Political risk refers to the threat that decisions or events in a country will negatively affect the profitability of an investment.

TABLE 3.3 Characteristics of Political Risk

Scale	Class	Type	Outcome
Micro		Financial Anomalies	Regulatory policies that make it difficult for the company to get credit or arrange overseas loans.
	Systemic	Competing Perspectives	The host government's interpretations of issues, such as human rights or environmental sustainability, creates problems for a foreign company in its home market.
		Unilateral Breach of Contract	The host government repudiates a contract negotiated with a foreign company or approves a local firm's doing the same.
	Procedural	Tax Discrimination	A foreign company is saddled with a higher tax burden than a local competitor.
		Restrictions on Profit Repatriation	The host government arbitrarily limits the amount of profit that a foreign company can remit from its local operations.
	Distributive	Destructive Government Actions	Imposing unilateral trade barriers (say, in the form of revised local-content requirements) let's the host government interferes with the distribution of products to local consumers.
		Harmful Action Against People	Local employees of a foreign company are threatened by kidnapping, extortion, or terrorist actions.
	Catastrophic	Expropriation/Nationalization	The host government or a political faction seizes a company's local assets. Compensation, if any, is usually trivial. Resurgent totalitarianism and resource nationalism increase this risk.
Macro		Civil Strife, Insurrection, War	Military action damages or destroys a company's local assets.

Second, the global credit crisis aggravates political risk in both developed and developing markets. Upon the fall of the Berlin Wall, globalization steadily standardized the inconsistencies of politics across markets. Certainly, countries evolved at different rates. However, as each developed in the broad context of the Washington Consensus, managers could reasonably assume that the laws of economics, not local quirks, would shape national politics. The global credit crisis reset the equation. Now, political motivations influence the performance of global markets and the actions of international companies on a scale not seen in decades. If the global financial crisis continues to shake people's faith in democracy, companies face growing political risk at home and abroad.

CLASSIFYING POLITICAL RISK

The evaluation of political risk often relies on a macro-micro criterion. Macro risks affect all companies in a given country; micro risks are project-specific and affect individual, usually foreign-owned, companies. We follow this logic, as seen in Table 3.3, but disaggregate the macro-micro division into *systemic, procedural, distributive,* and *catastrophic* classes of political risk.

Systemic Political Risk   As a rule, a country's political processes do not arbitrarily punish specific companies. If they did, few would hazard the investment. More often, investors face political risk that follow from shifts in public policy. New political leadership, for instance, may adopt policies that differ from its predecessor's—say, reducing the individual benefit of business activity by increasing tax rates to improve collective welfare. In that case, new regulations will alter the macro-environment for all. Similarly, a government may target an economic sector that it sees dominated by foreign interests, such as Venezuela's program to nationalize energy and media companies.[86] In both situations,

Concept Check

In Chapter 1, we note that interest groups often fear that the globalization of the local business environment will weaken national sovereignty—that is, its freedom from external control and the right to act in its own interests. Here, we observe that this attitude itself often contributes to political risk. Foreign companies and investors face higher risks when a host government becomes increasingly sensitive to aspects of its national sovereignty.

The primary types of political risk, from least to most disruptive, are

- Systemic.
- Procedural.
- Distributive.
- Catastrophic.

politically motivated polices alter the macro-environment, thereby creating *systemic risks* that affect all firms. If democracy continues faltering, the likely rise in corruption, weakened property rights, arbitrarily enforced laws, and freedom restrictions will increase systemic political risk in many countries.

Systemic risks do not necessarily reduce potential profits. In fact, elections and policy shifts can create opportunities for foreign investors. In the past few years, for example, newly elected governments in Vietnam, Malawi, Estonia, and Guinea have deregulated and privatized their previously state-controlled economies. Investors who accepted the risk that public policy might suddenly reverse and pursued the emerging opportunities prospered as freer markets developed in these countries. Our opening case traces a similar market pattern and profit potential in China. Political trends encouraged pro-market reforms that reduced risks and created opportunities. Still, taking advantage of such opportunities, whether in China or elsewhere, calls for tough-minded analysis the risk-return relationship.

Case Review Note

> Systemic political risks affect all firms.

Procedural Political Risk

Around the clock, people, products, and funds move from point to point in the global market. Each move creates a *procedural transaction* between companies or countries. Political actions sometimes impose frictions that slow or stop these transactions. The repercussions of, say, public fraud or a partisan judicial system can raise business costs; corrupt officials, for instance, might pressure a foreign firm to pay additional monies to clear goods through customs or obtain a permit to open a factory. For example, Nigeria's notoriously challenging business environment is laced with procedural risks. Said an observer, "the entire state machinery exists to siphon off cash. Many functions of government have been adapted for personal gain. . . . A universe of red tape engulfs the economy. . . . In some Nigerian states, governors must personally sign off on every property sale; many demand a fee."[87] Politically motivated interference escalates expenses, thereby lowering returns. Procedural political risk is often classified as a micro risk—that is, it affects some but not all companies. Monitoring industry developments, minding the relative contribution of their firms to the local economy, and promoting solid citizenship helps MNEs manage it.

Distributive Political Risk

Countries see foreign investors as agents of prosperity. As they generate greater profits in the local economy, the host country may begin to question the distributive justice of rewards. More to the point, officials question whether they are getting their "fair" share of the MNEs growing profits. In some situations, change is immediate. For example, rapidly rising silver prices led the Bolivian government to "dismantle the privatization model" governing its mining industry and expropriate all assets owned by private, largely foreign-owned, mining companies; explained a Bolivian official, "the government is recovering all the privatized companies."[88] Foreign MNEs, like Coeur d'Alene Mines and Pan American Silver, besides watching their share price plummet on the news, were given two weeks to prepare for state takeover of their Bolivian mines.

More often, political officials launch programs of creeping expropriation whereby they slowly take a bigger share of the rewards. Methods take various forms, such as increasing barriers to transferring personnel into or profits out of the country. Creeping expropriation rests on gradually eliminating MNEs' local property rights. Generally, vigilance helps MNEs minimize exposure. Too, they can fight back—one way is to create global supply chains that diversify operations. Chrysler, for example, escaped creeping expropriation in Peru because its local factory made about half the parts needed to assemble a car; importing the rest meant the local facility was useless if the government interfered with operations.

Sometimes MNEs have few practical options given the importance of the market. For instance, few see the United States as a hotbed of distributive political risk. If you're in the cigarette business, however, you know that the United States arguably has the highest degree of political risk in the world.[89] Its government battles cigarette makers (both domestic, like

> The dynamic of distributive political risk is the gradual elimination of the local property rights of foreign companies.

Philip Morris, and foreign, like British American Tobacco) on matters of taxation, regulation, business practice, and liability. Preserving market access requires companies accept hard limits on promotional campaigns along with high compliance costs.

Catastrophic Political Risk   Catastrophic political risk includes political developments that adversely affect the operations of every company in a country. Catastrophic risk typically arises from flash points, such as ethnic discord, illegal regime change, civil disorder, or insurrection, which disrupt society. Anti-state activities in Egypt in early 2011, for example, paralyzed its economy. Foreign commerce and domestic business all but halted, markets seized-up, and supplies of all sorts vanished. Auspiciously, Egypt pulled back from the brink. In other situations, such as seen in failed states like Chad, Haiti, Afghanistan, or Zimbabwe, spiraling disruptions led to political fallout that devastated the business environment.[90]

> Catastrophic political risk devastates companies and countries.

Point ▶ **Should Political Risk Management Be an Active Strategy?**

Point **Yes** Companies need to take politics seriously—it's no secret that the actions of host governments affect the business environment. Consequently, MNEs face threats that demand political risk management strategies. They have a choice in how they do so: They can take an active or passive approach. Those who advocate active political risk management believe proactive is the way to go—essentially, the best defense is a good offense. In my opinion, they're right. Take charge, predict political problems, and control risks is the ticket to success.

WHAT TO DO: Seasoned managers rely on two battle-tested tactics to pull this off. First, they apply state-of-the-art statistical modeling to quantify political risks. Second, they stress test their models, consulting experts on the political maneuverings in a particular country. This two-pronged approach, like good management in general, is based on cold, hard analysis and objective interpretation. It is anchored in the assumption that neither positive nor negative political events in any country are independent or random events. Civil strife, creeping expropriation, regime change, ethnic tension, terrorism, and the like do not happen randomly. There are patterns, provided one can apply rigorous tools that parse the signal from the noise. That is, political events and trends unfold in observable patterns that let bright folks estimate the odds of future outcomes. Objective models that detect, measure, and predict scenarios moves MNEs ahead of the curve, predict change, and manage their political risk exposure.

WHAT TO WATCH: Measuring the right set of discrete events is the key precondition of estimating political risks. Granted, this approach requires identifying valid risk indicators that one can measure reliably. Typically, identification and measurement are reasonable tasks. Research identifies useful indicators, such as the number of generals in political power, pace of urbanization, frequency of government

crises, degree of literacy, or ethno-lingual fractionalization. The challenge is not identifying individual measures, but rather identifying the right mix. Once done, however solid data coupled with skillful statistical modeling objectively estimates the company's risk exposure. Increasingly, this task gets easier. Political risk management services monitor developments in national and regional markets. Managers apply data they've collected in one country to benchmark analysis in others.

WHAT TO ADD: Naturally, we are not so confident to argue this approach is flawless. Spreadsheet estimation, no matter how rigorous or extensive, carries analysis so far. Reaching this limit does not halt analysis, however. Improving analytics calls for complementing quantitative measures with in-depth, country-specific qualitative indicators. How does this approach work? A popular tactic entails polling country experts to tap their judgment. These folks are mindful of quantitative factors. The best, however, bring the power of personal insight to the table. They enhance analyses with their expertise on the subjective conditions in a country, adding a bit of wisdom to interpret what appears to most as idiosyncratic circumstances but, in their eyes, is a systematic pattern of political activities. Enriching interpretation requires perspectives and perceptions that intuitively understand a country's political drama in ways that numbers struggle to represent.

Integrating expert assessments into your overall political risk strategy is straightforward. Begin by running standardized interviews with experts to assess a country's political environment. If stuck, a useful starting point is the Internet; entering the search string "political risk management" generates many resources. Collectively, they support projecting realistic scenarios and logically assigning probabilities to reasonable outcomes—the hallmarks of active political risk management.

Should Political Risk Management Be an Active Strategy?

Counterpoint

No Unquestionably, an active approach sounds like the hallmark of good management—proactive, confident, and controlling. However, it fails to explain why many MNEs do the exact opposite, choosing to manage political risk passively. That is, they treat political risk as an unpredictable hazard, reasoning that no model, regardless of how brilliantly it has been conceptualized, how systematically it has been specified, and how precisely it has been administered, can predict political risk. Granted, shrewd models extrapolate from economic, political, and social reports meaningful insights about who may take office, what polices may pass, and how these sorts of political events might affect business. Unquestionably, these insights make the political system and its risks understandable. They do not, however, make it predictable.

WHAT TO HEDGE: Insights do not qualify as predictions precisely because of the intrinsic impossibility of reliably measuring messy, ill structured situations. The political world is complex, its inalienable feature is ambiguity, and its tendency to change is high. Complicating matters are the many variables and their interaction that shape a political system. This situation becomes more difficult as companies venture into emerging markets, each with its own political peculiarities. Going from the United States to Mexico may be a stretch, but that pales in comparison to expanding from the United States to Indonesia. No matter how powerful the spreadsheet or insightful the expert, the dimensions and dynamic of a political environment defy precise specification. Certainly, developing broad frameworks that anticipate unpredictable hazards is fair game. However, prudently managing the risks of politics start by rejecting the delusion that one can. The objective is explanation, not prediction.

HOW TO HEDGE: This, of course, poses an immediate question: How then do I hedge my company's exposure? Typically, MNEs applying a passive approach outsource the political risk-management process. They reason the best shield is buying political risk insurance—essentially, the best offense is a good defense. Consider the flexibility they get through this approach. They can purchase coverage that protects operations from an array of political risks, including government expropriation, involuntary abandonment, and damage due to political violence. Furthermore, companies are not limited to a few carriers. A range of public agencies, international organizations, and private companies provide a variety of insurance coverage. Leading insurers include:

- Multilateral development banks (MDBs) are international financial institutions (such as the African Development Bank, the Asian Development Bank, and the World Bank Group) that are funded and owned by member governments. They promote growth in member countries by providing financial incentives to potential investors. Reducing the capital at risk encourages firms to expand into otherwise unacceptably risky environments.

- The Overseas Private Investment Corporation (OPIC) encourages U.S. investment projects overseas by protecting ventures against various forms of risk, including civil strife, expropriation, and currency inconvertibility. Increasingly, OPIC promotes investments in emerging markets that support U.S. foreign policy priorities.

- Private insurance companies underwrite political risk protection. Many cover "routine" distributive and procedural risks that involve property and income, such as contract repudiation and currency inconvertibility. Private insurers are reluctant to cover catastrophic risks that result from civil strife, insurrection, or war.

WHAT TO REALIZE: Ultimately, we have no quarrel with the notion that prediction and control are touchstones of competent management. Still, politics are anything but predictable and controllable. Indeed, few, if any, predicted the political turmoil of the Arab Spring and the surprisingly swift collapse of the Mubarak regime. Furthermore, who would have called democracy's retreat a decade ago, especially when leading analysts were celebrating the "end of history?" Not to put too sharp of an edge on it, but if one cannot predict these mega-events, then exactly what can one predict? Therefore, it just makes better sense, and we might add more cents, to resist the delusion of active management and opt for the practicality of passively managing political risk.

The Legal Environment

Businesspeople champion consistency in laws from country to country. Uniform, transparent laws make it easier to plan where to invest and, once there, how to compete on competencies, not connections. In theory, legitimate rules that apply without prejudice to individual or institutional behavior, regardless of political, cultural, or economic status, anchor legal environments. In reality, just as political ideologies differ among countries, so do legal systems. Thus, a key aspect of the business environment is how a country develops, interprets, and enforces its laws. Done legitimately, individuals and companies can make lawful decisions that support peace and prosperity. Done arbitrarily, all suffer because "to distrust the judiciary," reasoned Honoré de Balzac, "marks the beginning of the end of society."

LEGAL SYSTEMS

The **legal system** specifies the rules that regulate behavior, the processes by which laws are enforced, and the procedures used to resolve grievances. Legal systems differ across countries due to variations in tradition, precedent, usage, custom, or religious precepts. But, *ceteris paribus*, a legal system aims to institute rules that support business formation, regulate transactions, and stabilize relationships. Successfully doing so ensures that a society can pursue economic development and, when disagreements arise, resolve them without resorting to lawlessness.

The legal system is the mechanism for creating, interpreting, and enforcing the laws in a formal jurisdiction.

Modern legal systems share three components:

Modern legal systems are composed of constitutional law, criminal law, and civil and commercial law.

- *Constitutional law* that translates the country's constitution into an open and just legal system, setting the framework for the system of government, and defining the authority and procedure of political bodies to establish laws.

- *Criminal law* that safeguards society by specifying what conduct is criminal and prescribing punishment to those who breach these standards.

- *Civil and commercial laws* that ensure fairness and efficiency in business transactions. It speaks to private rights and remedies in regulating relations and conduct between individuals and/or organizations.

Aspects of each class influence MNEs' actions in a host country. [91] Our opening case, for example, shows how China's legal traditions and practices attract, retain, and deter foreign investment. For instance, Western investors are accustomed to transparent bankruptcy laws that protect creditors. In China, however, this investment-oriented tradition has not taken hold; hence, Chinese law presently protects debtors.

Case Review Note

Types of Legal Systems The type of legal system in a country determines the conduct of business transactions, who has which rights and obligations, and what legal redress is open to those who believe they have been wronged. Understanding the nuances of the legal system highlights several issues: Are laws based on abstractions or practicality? Do judges or juries pass judgment? Is justice the matter of man or the province of divinity? Do personal connections trump case facts? Peculiar as these questions sound, international business puts managers into situations where these issues influence the legality of their actions.

Managers face five types of legal systems in the world today:

- Common law.
- Civil law.
- Theocratic law.
- Customary law.
- Mixed.

Map 3.3 identifies the legal systems that prevail worldwide. Managers face five types: *common law, civil law, theocratic law, customary law,* or *mixed.*

Common Law A common law system relies on tradition, judge-made precedent, and usage. It respects established case law in resolving disputes. Judicial officials refer to statutory codes and legislation, but only after considering the rules of the court, custom, judicial reasoning, prior court decisions, and principles of equity. Common-law courts base their decisions on prior judicial pronouncements rather than on legislative codes. The doctrine of *stare decisis* (or precedent) by courts is a distinguishing feature of the common law system. The common law system has Anglo-American legacies; it prevails in, among others, Canada, the United States, India, Hong Kong, England, New Zealand, and Australia.

Common law is based on judicial precedents.

Civil Law A civil law system relies on systematic codification of accessible, detailed laws. It assigns political officials, not government-employed judges, the responsibility to translate legal principles into a compendium of statues. Rather than create law, as in the common law system, judges apply the relevant statues to resolve disputes. In contrast to *stare decisis*, judicial officers in a civil law system are unbound by precedent.[92] However,

Civil law is based on statutory laws.

MAP 3.3   The Wide World of Legal Systems

The globalization of business practices drives the standardization of laws, regulations, and policies across countries. Still, enduring philosophical outlooks and practical orientations result in different types of legal systems.

Source: University of Ottawa, "World Legal Systems," at: http://www.juriglobe.ca/eng/index.php

Note: Given that this is a Mercator projection, the scale approximates east-west distance at the equator; however, the farther you move from the equator, the more the east-west distance is distorted

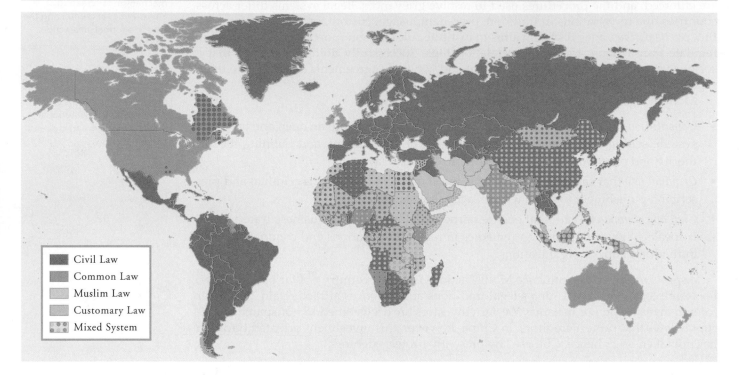

Civil Law
Common Law
Muslim Law
Customary Law
Mixed System

precisely stipulated statutory codes constrain their authority to interpret the law. Civil law is the most widespread type of legal system in the world, applied in various forms in approximately 150 countries such as Germany, France, Mexico, and Japan.

| Theocratic law is based on religious teachings.

Theocratic Law   A theocratic law system relies on religious doctrine, precepts, and beliefs. Ultimate legal authority is vested in religious leaders, who regulate business transactions and social relations based on their interpretation of the sacred text. For instance, Iran's president, Mahmoud Ahmadinejad, must defer to Iran's supreme leader, Ayatollah Ali Khamenei, who has the final say in matters of national import. Theocratic laws see no separation of church and state; government, law, and religion are one. The most prevalent theocratic system, Muslim or Islamic law (or *Shari'a*), is based on the Qur'an, the *Sunnah* (decisions and sayings of the Prophet Muhammad), the writings of Islamic scholars, and the consensus of legal communities in Muslim countries.[93] Muslim law prevails in the Middle East and Northern Africa. Modernists (e.g., Turkey, Indonesia), traditionalists (e.g., Kuwait, Malaysia), and fundamentalists (e.g., Iran, Saudi Arabia), however, advocate different interpretations of *Shari'a*.

| Customary law is based on norms of behavior practiced over a long period.

Customary Law   A customary law system reflects the wisdom of daily experience or, more elegantly, spiritual legacies and philosophical traditions. It anchors the law in many indigenous communities, defining the rights and responsibilities of members. Legitimacy follows not from a powerful person or institution but from individuals recognizing the benefits of conforming to community standards. Offenses are treated as torts—i.e., private wrongs or injuries rather than crimes against the state or society. Customary law prevails in many developing countries, particularly those in Africa.[94] Few nations operate under a wholly customary legal system. Rather, it plays a role in many countries that have a mixed legal system.

Mixed System A mixed legal system emerges when a nation uses two or more of the preceding types. Map 3.3 shows that the majority of these nations are found in Africa and Asia. For example, Nigeria has a mixed legal system comprising common, theocratic, and customary law. Pakistan blends common (a legacy of British colonial influence) and theocratic law. Indonesia, on the other hand, blends theocratic law with its civil codes. Officially, the U.S. legal system is categorized as common law. Technically, it is mixed due to Louisiana's use of French civil law with English criminal law.

TRENDS IN LEGAL SYSTEMS

As the Third Wave of Democratization rolled through the world, it promoted norms of justice and instituted practices of due process. Consequently, the law became more transparent, courts became more impartial, and officials became more accountable in many countries. Presently, democracy's retreat, by signaling the advance of totalitarianism, pushes managers to pinpoint likely changes in legal systems. Analysis begins by accepting that totalitarian governments use the legal system to regulate business activity so that it unconditionally supports and sustains the state. There is no separation of law and state; law is an instrument of the state that it uses to control public and private matters. Bluntly put, justice is not blind but arbitrary, oppressive, and state serving. Recall earlier observations on justice in China. Doing business there, said an observer, means dealing with "a society that had...plenty of rules, but they were seldom enforced. China appeared to be run by masterful showmen: appearances mattered more than substance, rules were there to be distorted." Moreover, the CCP's status above the law further complicates determining what is right and what is wrong.[95]

The Basis of Rule Once on the periphery of the global economy, emerging markets command center stage. Their accelerating development increasingly frames managers' interpretation of legal systems. Most notably, the strong performance of emerging economies pushes managers to reassess their philosophical basis of law in order to understand how they apply it. Specifically, the rise of emerging economies, along with their dissimilar conceptions of legality, requires managers ask, "What is the *basis of rule* in a given country—is it the rule of man or the rule of law?

Concept Check

As we saw in Chapter 1, business environment vary. Granted, there are points of convergence, but conducting international business means recognizing the existence of fundamental differences across countries. Here, we stress the differences in legal systems.

Case Review Note

Concept Check

As developed in Chapter 2, a country's cultural orientation toward standards of accountability, equity, and fairness influences the prevailing principles in its legal environment.

◀ Lady Justice, here seen at Römer Square in Frankfurt, Germany, is an allegorical personification of the moral force of the rule of law
Source: interlight/Shutterstock.com

The rule of man holds that the ruler, in whatever form, commands authority that is not bound by law.

The Rule of Man   The **rule of man** holds that ultimate power resides in a person whose word and whim, no matter how unfair or unjust, is law. For much of history, rulers and law were synonymous—the law was the will of the ruler, whether called king, queen, emperor, empress, shogun, czar, raj, chief, caliph, etc.[96] Today, these titles have largely given way to others, such as chairman, emir, comandante, generalissimo, dictator, supreme leader, or, in the case of North Korea, "Dear Leader." The rule of man defines a legal system in which the actions of the man, in whatever form and with whatever title, are not restricted by a constitution, regulated by criminal codes, or open to opposition. In China, for example, top-ranked party members answer to the CCP first, not to the law of the land, if accused of wrongdoing precisely because "the Party sits outside, and above the law."[97]

The rule of man anchors the legal system in totalitarian states.

The rule of man is an instrumental device of totalitarianism. A legal system grounded in it gives government free rein to suppress threats to, or reward support for, state authority. Constitutional issues are discretionary, criminal law is arbitrary, and opportunism taints commercial and civil matters. The law is an apparatus of the state. Rather than deficient, justice is absent.

The Rule of Law   The **rule of law** is a hallmark of a democracy; absent, democracy cannot exist.[98] The rule of law institutes a just political and social environment, guarantees the enforceability of commercial contracts and business transactions, and safeguards property rights and individual freedom. Citizens and companies rely on it to validate laws, codes, and statutes. The rule of law regulates the behavior of the "man" as symbolized by public officials. Constitutional standards are absolute, criminal law is legitimate, and commercial/civil matters are anchored in principle. The law is independent of the state.

The rule of law holds that no individual is above laws that are clearly specified, commonly understood, and fairly enforced.

The rule of law holds that governmental authority is legitimately exercised in accordance with written, publicly disclosed laws. No one, whether a public official or private citizen, is above the law. Thomas Jefferson, for instance, wrote in the United States' Declaration of Independence, "all men are created equal," to convey the belief that all people, from kings to peasants, are subject to the same laws.[99] More symbolically, in front of courthouses worldwide stands a statue of a woman, carrying a sword and measuring balances, sometimes wearing a blindfold, sometimes with eyes shut closed. Her sword stands for the power of the court, her scales for the competing claims of the petitioners, and her blindfold indicate that justice is meted out objectively, without fear or favor, regardless of identity, power, or weakness. Justice is blind so that justice is impartial.

The rule of law sets unequivocal standards. First, officials are accountable to the law of the land. Second, laws are clear, publicized, regarded as legitimate, and protect fundamental rights. Third, laws are developed, administered, and enforced transparently. Finally, all citizens have access to a competent, independent, and ethical judiciary.[100] Rather than absent, justice is omnipresent.

IMPLICATIONS FOR MANAGERS

Originating in the Magna Carta of 1215, the concept of the rule of law anchored the legal evolution of many developed economies, most notably Great Britain, the United States, France, and Germany. Consequently, in the West, property rights, namely the exclusive authority to determine how a resource is used, are taken so for granted that they rarely cross our minds. We cannot say the same for many countries in Asia, Africa, Middle East, and South America. There, the rule of law is an abstraction that has influenced few institutions. At best, it has a negligible legacy in the legal traditions of many long-developing, now-emerging countries. Consequently, property rights in countries like China, as we saw in our opening case, Venezuela, Saudi Arabia, Russia, and Vietnam are so arbitrarily, if at all, protected that they are an enduring concern.[101]

Map 3.4 indicates that the rule of law prevails in wealthier, westernized countries—i.e., the United States, Canada, Japan, New Zealand, Australia, and most of Europe.[102] In contrast, the countries that fall in the long crescent that starts in northern Russia, cuts

MAP 3.4   The Worldwide Distribution of the Rule of Law

The rule of law holds that government authority is legitimate only when it is exercised according to written laws and established enforcement procedures. The coding of this map is based on the degree a country does so. Therefore, for example, the United States at the 90th percentile indicates the pervasiveness of the rule of law. Conversely, Venezuela's classification below the 10th percentile indicates the pervasiveness of the rule of man.

Source: Based on methods and statistics reported in: (1) Kaufmann, Daniel & Kraay, Aart & Mastruzzi, Massimo, 2010. "The Worldwide Governance Indicators : Methodology and Analytical Issues," *Policy Research Working Paper Series 5430,* The World Bank (2) Kaufmann, Daniel & Kraay, Aart & Mastruzzi, Massimo, 2009. "Governance Matters VIII : Aggregate and Individual Governance Indicators 1996–2008," *Policy Research Working Paper Series 4978,* The World Bank.

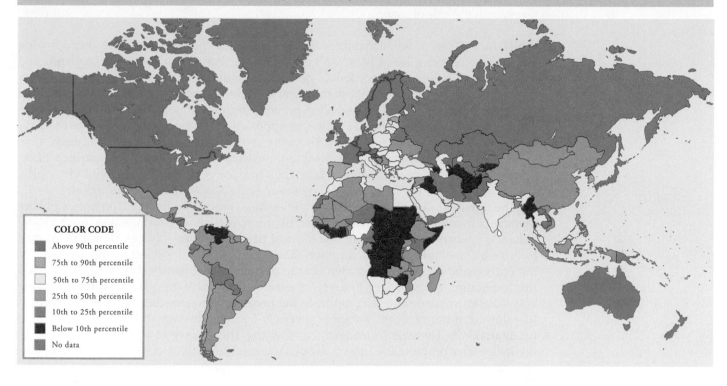

COLOR CODE

Above 90th percentile
75th to 90th percentile
50th to 75th percentile
25th to 50th percentile
10th to 25th percentile
Below 10th percentile
No data

southward through China, circles down to South East Asia, moves on toward the Middle East, and extends through Africa over to South America show the far greater pervasiveness of the rule of man. Conclusion? The rule of man anchors the legal systems of many emerging countries. Managers, eyeing these fast-growing markets, realize that where there is no formal law officially in place, there is another law in place—the rule of man.

The tendency toward totalitarianism in many developing countries complicates matters. Again, look at Map 3.4. Every country that Freedom House rates as "Partly Free" or "Not Free" falls in the "rule of man crescent." The same goes for countries rated as Hybrid or Authoritarian regimes by the EIU. Uncertainty about the basis of law and the goals of government in much of the world creates a perplexing situation for managers. Operating in Western economies grants them the benefit of a consistent and systematic application of legitimate laws. Few developing countries offer such safeguards. In Germany, for example, action taken by foreign firms against local companies that counterfeit their products consistently proves decisive. Violators are stopped and punished. In Vietnam, the same sorts of legal actions have proven powerless. There, as in other rule-of-man systems, writs, injunctions, and lawsuits are trapped in a slow-grinding legal machine that answers to the man, not to legitimate legal standards.[103] Violators in the good graces of the "man" flourish.

Certainly, a prudent MNE could simply choose to avoid markets dominated by the rule of man. This had long been the case. From about 1850 or so until 2000, the question of the basis of law in developing countries was inconsequential. Markets in the West provided a wealth of opportunities for productive, profitable activity. Developing markets were on the periphery of the global economy, serving mainly as sources of raw materials. The occasional dispute between the adventurous Western company and the locals was

Uncertainty about the basis of law in a particular country challenge decision making.

typically resolved in the favor of the former. Now, slowing growth in the West, aggravated by the aftermath of the financial crisis, moves the fast-growing emerging economies to the center of the global market. Their supply of inexpensive, productive resources along with accelerating consumer demand power is a siren call few MNEs can resist. As GE's CEO reasoned, "we've globalized around markets…Today we go to Brazil, we go to China, we go to India because that's where the customers are."[104] As a result, and as suggested in our opening profile of China, MNEs long accustomed to the rule of law come to terms with the rule of man.

Which Rule When?   Some hypothesize that developing countries, especially fast-growing emerging economies like China, Argentina, Russia, Peru, Saudi Arabia, Thailand, and Malaysia, will follow the precedent of developed countries and recognize the rule of law as the basis of legitimacy. As Western countries moved from an agrarian to an industrial economy, society increasingly respected property rights. Economic development eventually called for a legal system that no longer appealed to the man in power but to the written law for guidance and resolution. Therefore, extrapolating from Western history, some presume that the shift from agrarianism to industrialism in developing countries will accelerate their adoption of the rule of law. The Third Wave of Democracy, with ideological change anchored in the Washington Consensus, had supported this presumption.

The retreat of democracy along with the emergence of the Beijing Consensus pushes managers to adjust their forecasts. Now, the more realistic scenario is one in which developing countries migrate from one basis of rule to another—that is, from rule of man to "rule *by* law" and its implicit notion that even the ruler is subject to the law. Ideally, the corresponding adoption of democratic principles will fortify this transition, laying the foundation for a society to accept the rule *of* law. Still, trends spiral in surprising ways. Recent circumstances complicate the projected progression. Democracy's retreat has slowed, if not reversed, progress precisely because the rule of law is antithetical to totalitarianism. Therefore, managers monitor the Third Wave of Democratization, hoping its legacies promote the rule of law or, conversely, fearful that its retreat prolongs the rule of man.

Legal Issues in International Business

Differences in political ideologies often pose operating problems. Aggravating this situation is the fact that countries use any one of five types of legal systems to regulate the business environment. In addition, new forms of business activity along with changing patterns of trade and investment put MNEs in uncertain legal situations. The following profile identifies principles that guide their day-to-day decision-making.

OPERATIONAL CONCERNS

Companies comply with local laws on starting, running, and closing a business. Furthermore, activities such as employing workers, obtaining credit, protecting investors, paying taxes, trading across borders, and enforcing contracts, comply with applicable laws. In theory, business regulations are efficiently designed, easily accessible, and straightforwardly administered. MNEs often experience the opposite.

One entrepreneur recalls his experience in starting up his first company in his home country, Brazil. He found that getting the authorizations, licenses, and permits to start a new business—from seven different ministries—took about 150 days. When he started a U.S.-based business, however, "within a week I had formed an LLC (limited liability corporation), incorporated in Delaware, and set up bank accounts."[105] The latter situation is increasingly the norm. The legacies of Democracy's Third Wave, fortified by the push to improve the efficiency of globalization, have standardized many features of legal environments.

Operational concerns that managers face worldwide include

- Starting a business.
- Entering and enforcing contracts.
- Hiring and firing workers.
- Closing down the business.

Concept Check

Chapter 1 suggests that democratic political systems grant MNEs the freedom to engage in their preferred "modes of international business." Note, however, that democracy's retreat creates uncertainty about operating in particular countries. When it comes to dealing with certain modes of international business, nations rely on their legal system to encourage, regulate, or prohibit them.

Table 3.4 shows how some countries regulate business operations. Let's look at some specifics.

Getting Started   Starting a business involves activities such as registering its name, choosing the appropriate tax structure, obtaining licenses and permits, arranging credit, and securing insurance. Some countries expedite this process. Others do not. For example, starting a business is a straightforward process in Australia, requiring one registration procedure that encompasses tax, labor, and administrative declarations. Conversely, India imposes 13 procedural requirements, including regulations for bank deposits, court registration, health benefits, and so on. The upshot: it takes about two days to start a business in Australia but about 30 days in India. Still, at least one can take comfort in avoiding the same in Suriname—there one must satisfy 13 procedures spanning 694 days before starting a business.

Making and Enforcing Contracts   Once up and running, companies enter and enforce contracts with buyers and sellers. A contract is a binding legal agreement that formally exchanges promises, the breach of which triggers legal actions. The sanctity of a contract is vital to business transactions. The United Nations Convention on Contracts for the International Sale of Goods sets guidelines for negotiating and enforcing contracts. Still, standards vary across the types of legal systems. Countries using a common law system, for instance, encourage precise, detailed contracts, whereas those with a civil law system encourage less specific ones.

Concept Check

Chapters 1 and 2 discuss income and wealth as national resources. They also show how the availability of such resources influences the actions that countries, both rich and poor, take to develop their business environments. These factors also influence countries' approach to regulating MNEs local operations.

TABLE 3.4   The Rules of the Game

Economy	Starting a Business			Enforcing Contracts			Closing a Business		
	Number of Procedures[1]	Time (Days)	Cost (% of income per capita)	Number of Procedures[2]	Time[3] (Days)	Cost[4] (% of Claim)	Recovery rate (Cents on the dollar)	Time (Years)	Cost[5] (% of Estate)
Australia	2	2	0.7	28	395	20.7	81.8	1	8
Brazil	15	120	7.3	45	616	16.5	17.1	4	12
Canada	1	5	0.4	36	570	22.3	91.2	0.8	4
Chad	13	75	226.9	41	743	45.7	0	PNP[6]	PNP
China	14	38	4.5	34	406	11.1	36.4	1.7	22
France	5	7	0.9	29	331	17.4	45.2	1.9	9
Germany	9	15	4.8	30	394	14.4	53.1	1.2	8
Guatemala	12	37	49.1	31	1459	26.5	27.5	3	15
India	12	29	56.5	46	1420	39.6	16.3	7	9
Japan	8	23	7.5	30	360	22.7	92.7	0.6	4
Korea, Rep.	8	14	14.7	35	230	10.3	81.7	1.5	4
Russian Federation	9	30	3.6	37	281	13.4	25.3	3.8	9
England	6	13	0.7	28	399	23.4	88.6	1	6
United States	6	6	1.4	32	300	14.4	81.5	1.5	7

Source: Compiled from "Doing Business 2011," The World Bank.

Notes

[1] Number of procedures to complete before starting a business.

[2] Number of procedures that require interaction between the parties to the dispute or between them and the judge or court officer.

[3] Number of days from when the plaintiff files the lawsuit in court until settlement.

[4] Cost incurred during dispute resolution, including court fees and attorney fees.

[5] Cost of bankruptcy process, including court costs, insolvency practitioners' costs, and associated expenses.

[6] Presently, no practice.

Similar tendencies show up in contract-enforcement policies. Australia, Norway, and the United Kingdom impose the fewest number of enforcement procedures. Burundi, Angola, Bolivia, Cameroon, El Salvador, Mexico, and Panama require many procedures. Countries vary in the time span required to enforce a contract; Singapore, the speediest enforcer, needs 150 days, the United States about 300 days, and Timor-Leste, the slowest, 1,800 days. On average, across 185 countries, one is looking at 615 days to settle a contract dispute.

Hiring and Firing   No matter where you are operating, you will have to hire and, when necessary, fire workers. One would think that common sense would guide legally appropriate decisions. Legal issues around the world, however, are rarely straightforward. Singapore, New Zealand, and the United States are among the countries with the most flexible labor-regulation statutes. China has the most flexibility in hiring and firing plus the greatest discretion in setting employment conditions (work hours, minimum wages, and benefits). In contrast, Angola, Belarus, and Paraguay restrict firing employees and impose generous severance payments. India's national government imposes 55 labor laws while its states add another 150 or so that regulate hiring and firing. Its Industrial Disputes Act, for example, requires any company employing 100 or more workers to get the state's permission, even if it company's has hit hard times, before firing anyone.[106]

Richer countries regulate business activities less whereas poorer countries regulate more.

Getting Out or Going Under   Closing a business involves more than padlocking the doors. In the United States, the Internal Revenue Service requires reporting the sale of assets, payments to subcontractors, and termination of retirement plans. In the West, the bankruptcy process is anchored in the English bankruptcy law of 1732, the first modern law to address this issue, and its revision by the United States in 1800.

Ireland, Japan, Canada, and Hong Kong make closing the doors both fast (between four to eight months) and cheap (between 1 and 10 percent of the estate). The situation differs in developing countries. India's lack of a comprehensive bankruptcy code complicates dealing with creditors, officials, and courts. This limitation discourages bankruptcy. Consequently, 4 of every 10,000 firms go bankrupt in India, compared with 350 per 10,000 firms in the United States. Bankruptcy in Indonesia, Vietnam, and Ecuador is slow (between five to eight years) and expensive (between 10 and 30 percent of the estate). Several countries, including Burundi, Sudan, Cambodia, Afghanistan, Guinea-Bissau, and Dominica stipulate no standards to govern dissolution.

Key Relationships   The data indicate an inverse relationship between a nation's general wealth and its tendencies to regulate business activity. Overall, richer countries regulate less and poorer countries regulate more. In high-income countries (e.g., the United States, France, Japan), the average number of procedures to start a new business is seven; its 10 in upper-middle-income countries (e.g., Mexico, Poland, Malaysia), 12 in lower-middle-income countries (e.g., Brazil, Jamaica, China), and 11 in low-income countries (e.g., Angola, Ghana, Vietnam). Moreover, legal systems in wealthier nations tend to regulate operational activities more consistently than do those in poorer countries—as one would expect, given the prevalence of the rule of law in the former and the rule of man in the latter.[107]

Table 3.5 identifies the top-ranked and bottom-ranked countries whose legal policies make for the most or least supportive business environments. In terms of the former, Singapore has developed a comprehensive legal code that fosters the most favorable business environment in the world. Conversely, the Central African Republic's legal shortcomings create the world's least favorable business environment. These rankings confirm an important relationship. Most of the top-ranked countries in Table 3.5 have a democratic political system, a common or civil law legal system, and rule of law doctrine. In contrast, most of the bottom-ranked countries have a totalitarian political system, a mixed (largely civil, customary, and theocratic) legal system, and rule of man orientation.

TABLE 3.5   The Regulation of Business Operations in Select Countries

The World Bank ranks 183 countries on their respective ease of doing business—high scores signify favorable business environments, low score indicate the opposite. Technically, the ease of business index averages the country's percentile rankings on ten dimensions: starting a business, dealing with construction permits, employing workers, registering property, getting credit, protecting investors, paying taxes, trading across borders, and enforcing contracts.

Country	Ranking	Country	Ranking
Singapore	1	Niger	174
Hong Kong SAR, China	2	Timor-Leste	175
New Zealand	3	Congo, Dem. Rep.	176
United Kingdom	4	Guinea-Bissau	177
United States	5	Congo, Rep	178
Denmark	6	São Tomé and Principe	179
Canada	7	Guinea	180
Norway	8	Eritrea	181
Ireland	9	Burundi	182
Australia	10	Central African Republic	183

Source: Doing Business 2011, The World Bank.

Strategic Concerns

Routine concerns focus managers' attention on day-to-day operations. Strategic concerns shift managers' interest to long-term issues. A county's legal environment influences MNEs' strategic decisions on making a product, marketing it, and protecting its unique features.

> Strategic concerns that managers face worldwide include
>
> - Product origin and local content.
> - Marketplace behavior.
> - Legal jurisdiction.
> - Product safety and liability.

COUNTRY OF ORIGIN AND LOCAL CONTENT

National laws affect the flow of products across borders. To determine charges for the right to import a product, host governments devise laws that consider the product's **country of origin**—the country where it was grown, produced, or manufactured. Some countries apply this policy to product labels, under the title COOL (country-of-origin labeling), to inform consumers and support local producers.

Governments prefer MNEs make a greater share of a product in the local market. To spur reluctant companies, governments resort to **local content** regulations. For example, Nigeria required foreign oil companies to increase their level of activities in the country. At the time, only about 5 percent of their activities took place in Nigeria. The government aimed to boost this to 40 percent with the expectation that it would train locals for engineering jobs as well as procure newer technologies.

Worries about slowing markets following the global financial crisis have boosted the popularity of country-of-origin and local-content regulations, as well as their populist cousin, *buy-local campaigns*.[108] Indonesia, for example, penalized public officials who did not buy locally produced food, drinks, shoes, clothes, music, and films. Consumers in Hangzhou, China, got a subsidy if they bought locally made appliances. The United States included "Buy American" provisions in stimulus-funded infrastructure projects, requiring iron and steel purchases from American suppliers. Similar policies called for mandating that the $20 billion allocated to digitize medical records go exclusively to U.S. companies as well as requiring the Defense Department buy solar panels from U.S. companies.[109]

Politicians mandate buy-local programs and impose local-content regulations to protect jobs, appease voters, placate special interests, and preserve tax revenue. Consequently, escalating political risk in the local business environment typically penalizes international companies.[110] Governments, aware of this problem, try to finesse solutions. For example, even though it imposed local content regulations regarding the purchase of solar panels (in tacit violation of free trade norms), U.S. officials discouraged legal challenges by formulating provisions of the bill to satisfy the spirit of WTO regulations.

MARKETPLACE BEHAVIOR

National laws stipulate permissible practices in all forms of business activities, including sourcing, distributing, advertising, and pricing products. MNEs adjust their manufacturing configuration, supply chain coordination, and marketing strategy accordingly. In France, for example, transport trucks may not use motorways on Sundays, and shops may hold sales twice annually on dates set by the government.[111]

High-profile cases highlight the consequences for the MNEs that disregard local regulations on marketplace behavior. The European Commission fined Intel a record U.S. $1.45 billion for abusing its dominance in the computer chip market to exclude rival Advanced Micro Devices. Intel's marketplace behavior, by violating consumers' rights and undermining innovation, breached competition law in the European Union. The EU Competition Commissioner explained that Intel used "illegal anticompetitive practices to exclude its only competitor and reduce consumers' choice—and the whole story is about consumers."[112] Coming on the heels of decisions against General Electric and Microsoft, Intel's punishment highlighted European regulators' role as leading enforcers of antitrust law.

In countries where the rule of man is the basis of law, acceptable marketplace behavior is unpredictable. MNEs often complain of trumped-up charges, solicitation of bribes, and favoritism for local rivals. Especially controversial in legal systems where the rule of man prevails is the issue of the protection—or lack thereof—of intellectual property. Finally, the global financial crisis has spurred governments to reshape their regulatory environments, effectively tightening the rules of the game. These regulatory initiatives, by increasing the degree of systemic political risk, affect both domestic and foreign firms.

PRODUCT SAFETY AND LIABILITY

International companies customize products to comply with local standards. Similarly, countries often impose product-safety and liability laws that require a company to adapt a product or else forsake market access. Wealthier countries impose stringent standards, whereas poorer countries, reflecting underdeveloped legal codes and rule-of-man legacies, apply inconsistent ones. The European Union's product-liability directive shapes global standards.[113] It outlines the legal responsibility of manufacturers and stipulates the process of product-liability compensation claims. Then again, some MNEs proactively preempt the risk. Lego, the Danish toy maker, realized consumers' fear of the possible toxicity of plastic toys made in China discouraged opening a factory there. Instead, Lego opted for factories in comparatively higher-costs but higher regarded Mexico and Eastern Europe.[114]

LEGAL JURISDICTION

Countries stipulate the criteria for litigation when agents—whether legal residents of the same or of different countries—are unable to resolve a dispute. Usually, in the face of a cross-national dispute, each company petitions its home-country court to claim jurisdiction in the belief that it will likely receive more favorable treatment. This situation is especially pressing when a MNE from a rule-of-law system has legal problems in a rule-of-man environment. Worry about legal proceedings in certain legal systems leads MNEs to specify a **choice-of-law clause** in contracts. This clause stipulates whose laws, if necessary, govern dispute resolution. Importantly, it obliges both parties to negotiate a compromise in the event the law changes.

INTELLECTUAL PROPERTY: RIGHTS AND PROTECTION

In Adam Smith's time, countries drew strength from their agricultural prowess. Later, smokestack industries defined a nation's prosperity and power. Now countries look to their brainpower to create might, prestige, and wealth. We call the output of this brainpower **intellectual property**—the creative ideas, innovative expertise, or intangible insights that give an individual, company, or country a competitive advantage. The growing power of ideas in the global economy has made the protection of intellectual property rights a flash point of controversy.

International Property Rights The right to claim ownership of intellectual property, goes mainstream thought, stimulates creation, innovation, and inventiveness. Transnational institutions notably, the World Intellectual Property Organization (WIPO), along with governments and industry associations, push for stronger protections. The primary safeguard is an **intellectual property right** (IPR) that grants the registered owner of inventions, literary and artistic works, and symbols, names, images, or designs the right to determine the use of his or her property. In other words, an IPR grants the registered owner of a copyright the legal authority to decide who may use the property and under what circumstances. Essentially, an IPR constitutes a legally enforceable but limited monopoly granted by a country to the innovator. It specifies a period during which other parties may not copy an idea so that the innovator can commercialize it. MNEs invest great effort to safeguard intellectual property, relying on tools like patents, trademark registrations, and copyrights.

The pervasiveness of piracy worldwide shows how hard it is to enforce IPRs. Poor enforcement in some countries, particularly those marked by rule-of-man bias and totalitarian politics, impose obstacles. Other problems arise because not all countries support the various agreements that protect IPRs. The primary regulatory codes are the Paris Convention for the Protection of Industrial Property and the Berne Convention for the Protection of Literary and Artistic Works, both created in the 1880s and updated periodically. More recently, the WTO's Trade-Related Aspects of Intellectual Property Rights (TRIPS) broadens protection.

Matters of jurisdiction complicate protection. IPR protection by U.S. patent, for example, extends only to the United States and its territories and possessions. It does not carry to a foreign country. Furthermore, there's no shortcut to worldwide protection; companies cannot register a "global" patent, trademark, or copyright. Moreover, countries often interpret and enforce agreements arbitrarily. Until recently, Indian patent law regarding pharmaceuticals, for example, protected only the "processes" by which drugs are made, not the drugs themselves. Applying a process that differed from that recorded by the registered owner permits Indian companies to make drugs patented in other countries.[115]

As difficult as IPR protection sounds, it falls short of the task of IPR enforcement. In the United States, companies can go after makers and sellers, not the users, of counterfeit goods. Unlike in the case of illegal narcotics, for example, existing law does not prohibit consumers from buying counterfeit products.[116] Worldwide, governments claim to abide by these agreements and enforce IPRs. However, piracy increasingly threatens popular or pricey products.

Big Business, Big Money Intellectual property theft is big business.[117] The expanding scale of globalization and scope of the Internet benefits legitimate business as well as pirates. The costs of counterfeit intellectual property—in terms of lost sales, eroded consumer confidence, ruined brand reputation, dangerous products, enforcement expenses, and legal costs—is stunning. The International Anti-Counterfeiting Coalition (IACC) estimates that international trade in illegitimate goods runs more than U.S. $600 billion a year—approximately 5 to 7 percent of world trade.[118] Furthermore, piracy has grown over 10,000 percent in the past two decades—it was $5.5 billion in 1982.

Piracy grows because counterfeiting is astoundingly profitability; gross margins of 500 to 5,000 percent are common. Counterfeit medicines are more profitable than heroin,

Intellectual property is the general term for creative ideas, expertise, or intangible insights that grant its owner a competitive advantage.

Intellectual property rights refer to the right to control and derive the benefits from writing (copyright), inventions (patents), processes (trade secrets), and identifiers (trademarks).

copywatches may run a couple of bucks to make but sell for $20 in Beijing's Silk Market and $250 on Internet sites, and copies of high-end counterfeit software rival the return from cocaine.[119] For example, the notorious Mexican drug cartel, "La Familia," sold counterfeit Microsoft software through kiosks, markets, and stores in the Michoacan region. Adding insult to injury, it stamped counterfeit Office discs with its "FMM" logo.[120] Globally, Microsoft's number two competitor is not another software company. It is counterfeiters.

Microsoft's predicament in China highlights common problems. In China, copies of the latest versions of Microsoft's Office and Windows programs are openly peddled on street corners for $1 to $3, a fraction of their retail price. Rampant software piracy means Microsoft's revenue in China in 2011 is just 5 percent of its U.S sales—even though personal-computer sales in the two countries are almost equal. Explained its CEO, Microsoft's total revenue in China, with its population of 1.34 billion, is less than what it collects in the Netherlands, a country of fewer than 17 million.[121] This, by the way, comes in the face of a long-running war on piracy by Microsoft, industry associations, the U.S. government, and transnational institutions. Moreover, this situation is not merely Microsoft's particular problem; thousands of companies in tens of countries are caught in the same trap. Our closing case, "It's a Knockoff World," profiles the problems of piracy and counterfeiting.

Case Review Note

Legacies, Economics, and Orientations   Many local issues pose reasonable challenges that can be met with improved international laws.[122] One cannot say the same for IP violations. Its roots in elemental facets of life in many countries create intricate ambiguities. Not only are some countries less inclined to protect intellectual property, but prevalent attitudes, anchored in *legal legacies*, *economic conditions*, and *cultural orientations*, encourage, if not legitimize, piracy.

The predominant share of counterfeit products is made in countries in which the rule of man prevails.

Legal Legacies   Most counterfeit goods are made in markets in which the rule of man is the *de facto* legal system. A return trip to China, given its legal tradition, its influence, and its sluggishness in protecting intellectual property, highlights the scope of the problem. Officially, China has a battery of laws that comply with international standards for market access, nondiscrimination, and transparency. However, many Chinese citizens and officials question the legitimacy of laws passed by foreign governments. Hence, foreign-made laws are inconsistently enforced in the local marketplace. This gap between domestic traditions and foreign standards, explained a Chinese jurist, means that intellectual property laws "exist to protect Chinese intellectual property from foreign intellectual property."[123] This situation is not unique to China. The Asian Development Bank evaluated the performance of Indonesia, Malaysia, the Philippines, South Korea, and Thailand relative to the rest of the world, on measures of good governance: accountability, political stability, government effectiveness, regulatory quality, control of corruption, and rule of law. Over the past decade, their performance had deteriorated on nearly every dimension.[124]

Countries that observe the rule of law, as opposed to the rule of man, more aggressively protect intellectual property rights.

Calls for China (as well as Vietnam, Russia, Chad, India, Malaysia, to name just a few of the many who behave similarly) to protect intellectual property in the context of the rule of law may one day prove successful. Still, few managers anticipate quick progress. Advised Mr. Hu, partner of Jones Day Shanghai, the "trend in China is toward more transparency, but it's likely to be a 20 year process....even then, it will be far from the standards in the United States."[125] For China, the legal legacy of two millennia of the rule of man, or, in its current form, the rule of the CCP, suggests that such a change may be "one of the largest social infrastructure projects in the history of mankind."[126]

Generally, poorer countries protect intellectual property less vigilantly than do wealthier countries.

Wealth, Poverty, and Protection   The vigor of intellectual property protection often reflects a country's stage of economic development. Just as poorer countries regulate operating conditions less rigorously than richer countries, so too do they provide weaker protection of intellectual property.[127] Why? Developed countries largely reason that protecting intellectual property is the best way to energize innovation. "If the stuff you create can be misappropriated," noted an analyst, "your incentive for continuing to create valuable intellectual property diminishes significantly."[128] Strong protection has created extensive intellectual property in the West. Companies and individuals from developed countries world control virtually all intellectual property rights. Presently, they hold nearly 95 percent of all patents worldwide. In addition, 80 percent of patents granted in developing countries belong to residents of industrial countries.[129]

The evolving world economy, especially the market changes wrought by emerging economics, alters transnational institutional structures and legal outlooks.[130] Popular perspectives in developing countries advocate less-stringent protection, arguing that intellectual property rights are better thought of as intellectual monopoly rights that impose costs by:

- stifling the creativity, innovation, and emulation that supports technological and cultural advance.

- inhibiting local development and lowering global welfare by constraining the use of existing knowledge.

- creating intellectual monopolies that protect business interests, bestow monopoly profits, and lessen the efficiency gains of free trade.

- inflating the prices that poor nations pay for products and processes that are available only from wealthy nations.

- stipulating licensing fees and regulatory burdens that increase the cost of idea creation and slow the diffusion of innovations.

> Critics of intellectual property protection argue that granting monopoly rights imposes hardships, creates inefficiencies, and slows innovation.

In sum, goes this argument, property rights are state-created privilege that impoverishes the majority in order to concentrate wealth and power among the privileged.[131]

This debate will twist and turn for many years. In the meantime, hard economics is likely the key determinant of a country's protection of IPRs. Poor people have little money to spend on necessities, let alone for expensive branded goods sold by foreign companies. In Kenya, where the average annual income is about $1,600 and some people earn less than $300, it should not come as a surprise that many Kenyans "think you have to cheat to survive."[132] One means of survival is buying pirated copies of products that improve productivity (i.e., software), fight illness (medicines), or provide relief (consumer products).

Cultural Orientation Different attitudes toward intellectual property protection ultimately trace to cultural orientations. Individualist countries, such as the United States and Australia, regard individual ownership as intrinsically legitimate; if you create something, you should have the right to say who can use it or copy it for any given purpose. In contrast, collectivist countries, such as South Korea, Thailand, and China, extol the virtue of sharing over individual ownership; if you create something, it should improve the welfare of society. Asked about piracy in his country, a South Korean diplomat explained, "historically, Koreans have not viewed intellectual discoveries or scientific inventions as the private property of the discoverers or inventors. New ideas or technologies [are] 'public goods' for everybody to share freely. Cultural esteem rather than material gain [is] the incentive for creativity."[133]

> Cultural attitudes influence the protection of intellectual property rights. Individualist societies are more vigilant than collectivist societies.

Today, technologies challenge the interplay of individualism and collectivism in the use and abuse of intellectual property. Among some demographics, whether in collectivist China or individualist United States, piracy is an increasingly mainstream behavior. On one hand, economics spurs piracy; more poor people seek affordable solutions—legality notwithstanding. Alternatively, the prevalence of piracy among teenagers and young adults in rich and poor countries reflects evolving attitudes and technological opportunism. Said the general counsel for NBC Universal, "Young people, in particular, conclude that if it's so easy, it can't be wrong." Improving technologies, by making piracy cheaper and easier, accelerate violations of intellectual property rights.

Countries that generate intellectual property are strong advocates of ownership rights.

Improving Protection   Convincing countries to protect intellectual property confronts a potent mix of legal legacies, economic conditions, and cultural orientations. Institutional initiatives try to expedite stronger enforcement. The WTO, for example, gives wealthy countries a year to comply with its latest rules on intellectual property but grants poorer countries five- to 10-year grace periods. Longer grace periods, the thinking goes, support gradual awareness of the benefits of protecting intellectual property while acknowledging economic realities. Rising piracy rates suggest these programs struggle to make a difference.

Ironically, hopes for stronger protection hinge on the future success of companies in currently lax countries. History shows that countries that create intellectual property— no matter their legal legacy, economic state, or cultural orientation—ultimately enforce property rights.[134] As countries evolve from idea consumers to idea creators, they market products based on their own intellectual property. At some point, the benefits of protection exceed the gains from piracy. Observers note that the United States was a notorious IPR violator when it was a developing country in the eighteenth century. An analyst explained, "American political independence was founded on the notion of economic self-sufficiency. And technology piracy became the premier tool to industrial development."[135] Inventing its own intellectual property eventually led the United States to endorse the Paris and Berne Conventions, both of which originated in the 1880s. From then on, the United States has steadfastly advocated strong property rates.

Trends in China signal the start of this process. Long the factory floor of the world, China aims to be the new product lab. Presently, its patent office leads the world in patent applications, with more than 1.2 million filed in 2010.[136] Although many registered minor modifications, a growing share is significant "invention" patents that grant the holder 20 years of protection (the same as in the West). Abroad, Chinese firms are similarly ramping up, registering 2,270 patents in 2009 in the United States (up from 90 in 1999).[137] Going forward, the Chinese government has a goal of 2 million domestic patent applications annually by 2015. It aims to be one of the top two patent-owning countries by 2020.[138] Besides claiming new markets, Chinese firms will likely protect their intellectual property worldwide. Right now, the signals from Chinese officials and companies are confusing—increasing piracy yet increasing patent activity.[139] The resolution of this conundrum—will China stay a pirate's paradise or become a property protector—will shape intellectual property practices throughout the world.[140]

 CASE   It's a Knockoff World

I stride toward ground zero of counterfeiting—the notorious Silk Market of Beijing. As do more than 10 million people a year, I enter a 35,000-square-meter, seven-level piracy temple, packed with nearly 2,000 small stalls, staffed by thousands of hard-charging, take no prisoner vendors, offering cheap knockoffs of the leading branded products in the world. Navigating a surreal bazaar gone wild, I stroll by stalls boldly displaying bogus Prada purses, Hugo Boss shirts, and Hermes scarves; depending on how well you negotiate, each can be had for an absurd fraction of the price of the genuine version. Moving on, stall after stall offers infamous "copywatches," Nike gear, Sony Jump Drives, Wii Remotes, Gillette razors, Oakley sunglasses, Zeiss binoculars, Nikon lenses, North Face jackets—one after another, in a seemingly endless

procession of premier brand names. Despite spot-on cosmetic resemblance, virtually all is counterfeit. Moving around, one comes to digital zones, Finding copies of software, music, games, and movies. Rack upon rack displays products from some of the best and the brightest minds of the world, now selling for ludicrously low prices—Microsoft Windows 7 for about a buck, Microsoft Office for $0.75, Wii Guitar Hero for a buck, Photoshop for two bucks, AutoCAD for five dollars. Each stall is packed with an ever-changing collage of customers—Germans, Indians, Canadians, Brazilians, British, and Americans, and so on—each getting past the initial shock, and many buying multiple titles.
— DPS's stroll through the Silk Market, Beijing, March 2011

Companies are dogged by piracy—the illegal imitating, copying, or counterfeiting of their registered products. It's a tense issue given that it cuts right to issues of innovation, culture, politics, and prosperity. Making matters worse is that pirates, besides being everywhere, come in every form. Individuals making unauthorized copies at work, imitators laboring in dingy sweatshops, and hardened criminals running global networks power the knockoff world.

The problem, basically, is this: Intellectual property in the form of books, music, product designs, brand names, process innovations, software, film, and the like, is tough to conceive but easy to copy. Notwithstanding their moral shortcomings, pirates do not lack initiative or imagination. In our knockoff world, if it's being made, it's being faked. Counterfeiters leave no product category untouched. Fair game includes, for example, books, printer cartridges, music CDs, brake pads, DVDs, aircraft parts, cigarettes, wristwatches, razor blades, batteries, medicine, motorcycles, handbags, jewelry, automobiles, shampoo, pens, toys, wine, shoes, clothing, luggage, foods, beer, perfume, cleaning supplies, pharmaceuticals, and healthcare supplies. And, for the kicker, knockoffs sell for a fraction of the price of the real thing to eager buyers worldwide.

Big Money, Big Risks

Counterfeiting is big business.[141] Globalization and the Internet fuel the perfect storm. The cost of intellectual property theft is stunning, with estimates up to U.S. $600 billion a year. Besides a significant chunk of percent of world trade, piracy has grown over 10,000 percent since 1982.[142] Piracy grows because counterfeiting is astoundingly profitability; gross margins of 500 to 5,000 percent are common. [143]

◀ **Gateway to the Silk Market**
Given many of the activities conducted inside, all ye who enter are well-advised to check your ethical sensitivities.
Source: Courtesy of Daniel Sullivan

The lucrative rewards of piracy entice even notorious drug cartels to diversify. Mexico's La Familia and Los Zetas, for example, generate hundreds of millions of dollars in counterfeit DVDs. Their expanding operations have made Mexico the pirate capital of Latin America. The cartels export so many bootleg movies to Central America, for example, that major studios have stopped shipping their products there. Too, whether buying it in Cancun, Cozumel, Monterrey, or Tijuana, the bootleg DVD more than likely bears a stamp indicating it was distributed by La Familia (a butterfly) or Zetas (a stallion).[144]

Most think piracy is the problem of snobbish, expensive brands. Certainly, fakes target high-end brands—the top 10 brands counterfeited are Microsoft, Nike, Adidas, Burberry, Louis Vuitton, Sony, Lacoste, Reebok, Viagra, and Benson & Hedges. Luxury fakes, however, are just 4 percent of the counterfeit problem. The remaining 96 percent includes everyday, ordinary products. Nothing is off-limits; "If it's making money over here in the U.S., it's going to be reverse-engineered or made overseas."[145]

Increasingly, counterfeiting threatens global health and safety. The Food and Drug Administration estimates that counterfeits account for 10 percent of all drugs sold in the United States. Studies of anti-infective treatments in Africa and South-East Asia peg more than a quarter as fake. The United Nations estimates that half of the anti-malarial drugs sold in Africa are counterfeits. Imitations of Pfizer's best-selling drugs have been found in the legitimate supply chains of at least 44 countries.[146] Counterfeit pills annually kill tens of thousands.

Waging a Multifront War

Companies, industry associations, and governments use a battery of weapons to battle piracy. An enduring approach relies upon dispatching squads of lawyers to search and destroy. Big companies "lawyer-up" to train customs officials on the nuances of their product, monitor the Web, prod Internet providers to takedown copycat sites, and file lawsuits against illegal sellers. Ugg Australia, the popular boot brand, began aggressively enforcing its intellectual property after realizing the prevalence of counterfeit boots. In 2009, the company shut down 2,500 Web sites selling fake Uggs and blocked 20,000 eBay listings and 150,000 listings on other trading sites. Liz Claiborne Inc., owner of the Juicy Couture and Kate Spade brands, fought legions of Web sites selling counterfeits. It removed 27,000 auction listings of counterfeits in just a few months.

Some companies prefer high-tech assault. One approach embeds radio frequency identification (RFID) chips in the product packaging to allow precise tracking; IBM, 3M, and Abbot Laboratories are pacesetters. Others, like Oracle, provide software programs that track products from factories to consumers. In Ghana, mPedigree lets consumers use their mobile phones to check if the product is genuine or fake; buyers call in a special code embossed inside the package to the vendor who then verifies its authenticity.[147]

MNEs lobby governments to enact tougher intellectual property protection. The European Union, for example, ranks intellectual property theft as a high priority.[148] The United States elevated software piracy from a misdemeanor to a felony (if 10 or more illegal copies were made within a six-month period and if those copies were worth more than U.S. $2,500). Also, it has boosted enforcement efforts, threatening to sanction notorious pirates with records of "onerous and egregious" IPR violations such as China, Russia, Argentina, India, Thailand, Turkey, and the Ukraine. Other ramp up the rhetoric. The U.S. Trade Representative, for instance, declared, "We must defend ideas, inventions, and creativity from rip-off artists and thieves." Industry associations, like the International Anti-Counterfeiting Coalition, spearhead efforts to toughen laws. Governments worldwide provide global services in public policy, business development, and consumer education.

MNEs, officials, and trade associations lobby transnational institutions to devise stronger weapons. The World Intellectual Property Organization (WIPO) fortifies intellectual property treaties and spurs members to bolster antipiracy efforts. Likewise, the WTO applies TRIPS to regulate enforcement. TRIPS require all member nations of the WTO to protect and enforce IPRs according to global, not local, standards.

One would think that this fusillade of legal assaults, novel technologies, consumer education, stronger intellectual property policies, aggressive law enforcement, and concerted political, commercial, and institutional action would prove more than sufficient. Then, to make things a bit more interesting, add in the firepower of the global reach of vigilant MNEs, high-profile legal proceedings, increased government cooperation, criminalization of piracy, and tougher trade agreements. Arguably, one would think this shock and awe campaign would devastate the pirates. Surprise, surprise: Piracy keeps increasing at an increasing rate.

"The Bandits Are Everywhere"

The global cat-and-mouse game between MNEs and pirates, far from winding down, escalates. Booming piracy in big, fast-growing emerging markets like China and India spells big, fast-growing trouble. As more people enter the global market, many of them are eager to consume Western brands despite income constraints. Experts warn their quest for low prices turbocharges piracy.

In addition, clever and crafty pirates quickly overcome defense. They crack licensing codes, duplicate holograms, falsify email headers, set up anonymous post office boxes, and devise crypto-currencies like bitcoins. Pirates seem to stay one step ahead of the intellectual property police. "Like drug trafficking, the counterfeiting problem is so massive [that] you don't know how to get a handle on it. The bandits are everywhere."[149] Worrisomely, successful pirates evolve into sophisticated entrepreneurs. "When you are dealing with high-end counterfeits, you are talking about organizations that have a full supply chain, a full distribution chain, a full set of manufacturing tools all in place and it is all based on profits."[150]

Piracy gets huge boost from the increasing availability of counterfeit goods through Internet channels, such as P2P file-sharing sites and mail order or auction sites. Outgunned and outfoxed, some companies surrender. Foley & Corinna, a high-end handbag maker, explained that as it noticed more and more Internet fakes, it stopped looking altogether. "It's just too frustrating. You can try to do something, but it's so big and so fast."[151] Then again, there are those who treat IPR as the price of doing business. Despite everyday piracy of his products in the Chinese market, an executive reasoned that the profitability of his legal sales more than offset the losses due to counterfeits.[152]

Is Piracy Inevitable?

The pervasiveness of piracy, in the face of aggressive lawyering, sophisticated tracking and tagging technologies, database software, and security controls, poses profound questions for protecting IPRs. Some worry that the different legal legacies and political ideologies among countries complicate basic issues. TRIPS, by standardizing codes and norms, should have settled such troublesome issues. Legal and operational boundaries have limited its impact.

Others fear that the antipiracy war may already be lost. Evidently, a not-too-small number of consumers and businesses around the world have few ethical qualms about using counterfeits. Take software, for instance. Global software piracy is rampant. In 2008, the worldwide PC software piracy rate rose for the second year in a row—from 38 to 41 percent. In 2010, it hit 42 percent. Put differently, of all the packaged software installed on PCs worldwide in 2009, 42 percent was obtained illegally, at a cost of U.S. $52 billion in lost revenue (up from losses of $29 billion in 2003). For many nations, such as Armenia, Libya, Ukraine, Bolivia, China, and Zambia, software piracy rates top 80 percent. Even the best-behaved nations, like the United States and Japan, report software piracy rates north of 20 percent.[153] Consequently, Microsoft's number two competitor is not another software company. It is counterfeiters.

The global financial crisis pushes more people to seek counterfeits. Similarly, some in collectivist cultures reason that intellectual property holders should honor society by abandoning their profit-maximizing business models. Sharing knowledge, not protection, is the moral imperative. But, counters others, without protection, ultimately there will be no intellectual property to share. ∎

QUESTIONS

1. Collectivism and individualism, democracy and totalitarianism, rule of law and rule of man: What do these concepts say about IPRs and the legitimacy of protection?
2. What is the relationship among governments, transnational institutions, organizations, and MNEs fighting piracy?
3. Can companies stop piracy without government help? Why would companies dislike greater government assistance?
4. Do you think consumers in wealthier countries versus those in poorer countries justify piracy with similar rationalizations? Why?
5. Can you envision a scenario where developers and consumers of intellectual property form a relationship that eliminates the profitability of piracy?

MyIBLab   Now that you have finished this chapter, go back to www.myiblab.com to continue practicing and applying the concepts you've learned.

SUMMARY

- Political and legal systems converge and vary across countries in terms of guiding principles and practical routines.

- Two standards anchor assessment of a political system: the degree to which it emphasizes individualism vs. collectivism and the degree to which it is democratic vs. totalitarian.

- Individualism endorses the primacy of personal freedoms in the political, economic, and cultural realms. It champions the interests of the individual over those of society.

- Collectivism holds that the needs of society take precedence over the needs of the individual. Collectivism encourages state intervention to improve the welfare of the group at the expense of the individual.

- Political officials and agencies play an extensive role in a collectivist society. They play a limited role in an individualistic society.

- Democracy champions the power of the many over the few. A democratic government protects personal and political rights, civil liberties, fair and free elections, and independent courts of law.

- Totalitarianism champions the power of the few over the many. The government exercises control over many to all aspects of life, the individual is subordinated to the state, and opposing political and cultural expression is suppressed.

- Political freedom measures the degree to which fair and competitive elections occur, the extent to which individual and group freedoms are guaranteed, the legitimacy ascribed to the rule of law, and the existence of freedom of the press.

- Recent data on the spread of democracy indicate it is in retreat. Democracy's retreat coupled with growing freedom stagnation signals resurgent totalitarianism.

- Political risk is the likelihood that political decisions, events, or conditions will affect a country's business environment in ways that (1) cost investors some or all of the value of their investments, (2) force them to accept lower-than-projected rates of return, and (3) threatens the sustainability of local activities

- The legal system specifies the rules that regulate behavior, the processes that enforce the laws of a country, and the procedure used to resolve grievances.

- Modern legal systems share a system of constitutional law that preserves an open and just political order, a system of criminal law that safeguards the social order, and a system of civil and commercial laws that promote fairness.

- A common law system is based on tradition, precedent, custom, usage, and interpretation by the courts; a civil law system relies on a systematic collection of codes and statues that judges must follow; a theocratic legal system is based on religious precepts; a customary legal system follows the wisdom of daily experience; and a mixed legal system combines elements of the other systems.

- The rule of law endorses systematic and objective laws applied by public officials who are held accountable for their just administration.

- The rule of man holds that legal rights derive from the individual who commands the power to impose them.

- We see an inverse relationship between a nation's wealth and its tendency to regulate business activity.

- Primary legal issues in international business include product safety and liability, marketing practice, rule of origin, jurisdiction, and intellectual property protection.

- Intellectual property is the creative ideas, innovative expertise, or intangible insights that give an individual, company, or country a competitive advantage. Its protection within a country is moderated by its legal legacies, economic development, and cultural orientation.

KEY TERMS

collectivism (p. 93)
country of origin (p. 119)
choice-of-law clause (p. 120)
democracy (p. 96)
democracy's retreat (p. 102)
freedom (p. 96)
individualism (p. 93)
intellectual property (p. 121)

intellectual property rights
  (IPR) (p. 121)
laissez-faire (p. 93)
legal system (p. 111)
local content (p. 119)
pluralism (p. 94)
political freedom (p. 95)
political ideology (p. 94)

political risk (p. 106)
political spectrum (p. 95)
political system (p. 93)
rule of law (p. 114)
rule of man (p. 114)
Third Wave of Democratization
  (p. 100)
totalitarianism (p. 97)

ENDNOTES

1 Regarding our opening photo, the issue is 'What would Confucius say?' On 11 January 2011, the Chinese installed this 9.5-metre-high bronze statue of Confucius on the east side of Tiananmen Square in Beijing. Some now wonder might one perhaps understand Chinese politics and law by better understanding the teachings of Confucius. Then, as the *New York Times* reported on 22 April 2011, "Apparently, someone extremely powerful has taken the saying to heart, having decided that a 31-foot bronze statue of the ancient Chinese sage that was unveiled near Tiananmen Square four months ago did not belong on the nation's most hallowed slice of real estate. The sudden disappearance of the statue Confucius, which took place under cover of darkness early Thursday morning, has stoked outrage among the philosopher's descendants, glee among devoted Maoists and much conjecture among analysts who seek to decipher the intricacies of the Chinese leadership's decisions" (See www.nytimes.com/2011/04/23/world/asia/23confucius.html?_r=1)

2 *Sources include the following:* Michael Sylvester, "Flaming Hoops," *Corporate Counsel: Market Report China* 11:10, (2004): 171; Mure Dickie, "A Call for More Chinese Walls: Foreign Companies Are Angered by Beijing's Inability to Tackle Piracy," *The Financial Times* (September 21, 2004): 9; Honglin Zhang, "What Attracts Foreign Multinational Corporations to China?" *Contemporary Economic Policy* (July 2001): 336; Jiang Xueqin, "Letter from China," *The Nation* (March 4, 2002): 23; "A Disorderly Heaven," *The Economist* (March 20, 2004): 12, US; "Bulls in a China Shop," *The Economist* (March 20, 2004): 10; "China Slams US Piracy Complaint," *BBC News* (April 10, 2007); *The Economist*, Country Briefings: China, www.economist.com/countries/China/ (Retrieved September 26, 2009); U.S. Department of State, Background Note: China, www.state.gov/r/pa/ei/bgn/18902.htm (Retrieved June 29, 2009); Central Intelligence Agency, World Factbook, www.cia.gov/library/publications/ the-world-factbook/geos/ch.html (Retrieved June 28, 2009). The pace of change in China's business environment makes any discussion of it hazardous. Regard this case as a set of educated generalizations about the kinds of problems encountered by would-be foreign investors in China from the 1990s to date.

3 Richard McGregor, *The Party: The Secret World of China's Communist Rulers* (Harper Collins, 2010): 1.

4 China SAFE Reports Monetary Gold Holdings Increased by $11 Billion, or 30%, in 2010, as Gross Foreign Financial Assets Pass $4 Trillion, www.zerohedge.com (Retrieved June 1, 2011).

5 Pew Global Attitudes Project, Country's Economic Situation. Specific query: "Is the country's economic situation good or bad?" www.pewglobal.org/database/?indicator=5&survey=12&response=Good&mode=chart (Retrieved April 21, 2011).

6 For example, the IMF and Nobel Prize winner Robert Fogel pegs 2016, Angus Madison of the OECD targets 2020, Price Waterhouse Cooper claims 2025, Goldman Sachs targets 2027, and the National intelligence Council of the United States targets 2036.

7 According to research published in the Monthly Labour Review of the US Bureau of Labour Statistics in April 2009, compensation of Chinese manufacturing workers was only $0.81 per hour in 2006—just 2.7% of comparable costs in the US, 3.4% of those in Japan, and 2.2% of compensation rates in Europe. While these figures are now A bit out of date, they underscore the magnitude of the gap between China and the developed world. Moreover, as of May 2011, Apple has contracted with Foxconn to make their iPad 2s in China, where employees are reportedly paid 1,200 Yuan/month, or about $185 at current exchange rates (y/$ = 0.154), or, if we assume an average 8-hour/day, 250-day/year, (probably unrealistic assumptions), $1.11/hour. In contrast, the average U.S. manufacturing/mining/construction compensation is $32.53/hour as of December 2010 according to the Bureau of Labor Statistics.

8 Personal Conversation, Daniel Sullivan and Peter Leung, Director, Nalco China, Beijing, March 1, 2011.

9 "Foreign investment in China: Even harder than it looks," *The Economist*, www.economist.com/node/17046627 (Retrieved March 23, 2011).

10 Chinese Negotiation: The Long Kiss Goodnight, www.chinesenegotiation.com/page/2/ (Retrieved May 14, 2009).

11 "A survey of business in China: A disorderly heaven," The Economist," www.economist.com/node/2495184 (Retrieved March 24, 2011).

12 "Foreign investment in China: Even harder than it looks," 8.

13 Willy Lam, "Beijing Tightens Control over Courts," *Asia Times*, http://atimes.com/atimes/China/MF25Ad02.html (Retrieved August, 4, 2011).

14 McGregor, *The Party*, 2.

15 Personal Conversation, Daniel Sullivan and Kathy Stearman, Beijing (March 4, 2011).

16 "Oded Shenkar, *The Chinese Century: The Rising Chinese Economy and Its Impact on the Global Economy, the Balance of Power, and Your Job* (Upper Saddle River, NJ: Pearson Prentice Hall, 2006).

17 "Economic Indicator: Even Cheaper Knockoffs - CNBC," www.cnbc .com/id/38504 is such 275/Economic_Indicator_Even_Cheaper _Knockoffs (Retrieved March 24, 2011).

18 Steven Weisman, "Before Visit to China, a Rebuke," *New York Times* (December 12, 2006): A-1.

19 Ibid.

20 "The World's Greatest Fakes," *60 Minutes*, quote by Dan Chow, www.cbsnews.com/stories/2004/01/26/ 60minutes/main595875 .shtml (Retrieved June 15, 2006).

21 "The Sincerest Form of Flattery," *The Economist* (April 4, 2007): 67.

22 "Business in Russia: Dancing with the Bear," *The Economist* (February 1, 2007): 23.

23 "BP in Russia: Dancing with Mr. Putin," *The Economist*, www .economist.com/node/17967066?story_id=17967066 (Retrieved February 14, 2011).

24 "Business in Russia: Dancing with the Bear," *The Economist* (February 1, 2007): 23.

25 "Crocodile Tears," *The Economist* (April 28, 2007): 44. Andrew Osborn, *Russia's Rule of Lawlessness*, WSJ.com, online.wsj.com /article/SB123758426519199313.html (Retrieved January 20, 2011).

26 Daniel Kaufmann, Aart Kraay, and Massimo Mastruzzi, "Governance Matters IV: Governance Indicators for 1996–2004," *World Bank Policy Research Working Paper Series No. 3630* (May 2005).

27 The World Bank Group, www.worldbank.org/data/ databytopic /class.htm. See also "How Many Countries Are in the World?" geography.about.com/cs/countries/a/ numbercountries.htm (Retrieved July 24, 2009).

28 Statement from the Declaration of Independence of the United States of America.

29 In Germany, before the adoption of liberal western economic ideas, its economic policy, so named "Gemeinnutz geht vor Eigennutz," held that that "the welfare of the nation takes precedence over the selfishness of the individuals" (www.stephenhicks.org/tag /gemeinnutz-geht-vor-eigennutz/).

30 Pluralism rests upon ideas drawn from the sociology of small groups. Translated to the level of a society, these ideas interpret the relationships and interactions between and within groups as they champion and contest political ideologies.

31 Hannah Arendt, "Totalitarianism," Part three of *The Origins of Totalitarianism* (New York: Houghton Mifflin Harcourt, 1968), p. 164.

32 Practically, the ideology of democracy anchors a political system that grants voters the power to alter the laws and structures of government, to make decisions (either directly or through representatives), and to participate directly in elections.

33 More specifically, any and all democracies accept the legitimacy of (1) freedom of opinion, expression, press, religion, association, and access to information; (2) free, fair, and regular elections; (3) majority rule coupled with protection of individual and minority rights; and (4) subordination of government to the rule of law.

34 Patrick French, *India: A Portrait* (London: Allen Lane, 2011).

35 In China, for example, the One Child Policy prohibits a family from having more than a single child; a couple that has a second child may be fined the equivalent of $1,300—a steep penalty in rural areas where most annual incomes are a fraction of that sum.

36 "China's Future: Rising Power, Anxious State," *The Economist*, Special Report: China (June 25, 2011): 3.

37 For example, during the rule of Hugo Chavez, Venezuela's prison population has increased from 22,000 to 50,000—of whom 60 percent have never been sentenced. Imprisoning dissidents stabilizes the regime. "The Fifth Circle of Hell," *The Economist*, (July 16, 2011): 40.

38 Anne-Marie Brady, *Marketing Dictatorship: Propaganda and Thought Work in Contemporary China* (Lanham, MD: Rowman & Littlefield, 2007).

39 "China's Future: Rising Power, Anxious State," *The Economist*, Special Report: China (June 25, 2011): 3.

40 "The Long Arm of the State," *The Economist*, Special Report: China (June 25, 2011): 14

41 Willy Lam, "China's State Giants too Big to Play with," *Asia Times Online*, www.atimes.com/atimes/China_Business/MA22Cb01.html (Retrieved May 26, 2011).

42 Keith Brasher, "Solar Panel Maker Moves Work to China," *NYTimes.com*, www.nytimes.com/2011/01/15/business /energy-environment/15solar.html?pagewanted=2&hpw (Retrieved February 11, 2011).

43 "China Squeezes Foreigners for Share of Global Riches - WSJ.com," online.wsj.com/article/SB100014240529702037310045760456840683 08042.html?mod=rss_whats_news_us_business (Retrieved December 29, 2010).

44 Extracted from Mission Statement, Freedom House, www .freedomhouse.org/template.cfm?page=2 (Retrieved June 28, 2009). For example, classical liberal philosophy holds that freedom is the absence of coercion of one person by others; jurisprudence holds that one has the right to determine one's own actions autonomously; environmentalism advocates constraints on the use of ecosystems in any definition of freedom. Others take a more abstract approach, discussing notions of positive versus negative freedom (the right to fulfill one's own potential vs. freedom from restraints).

45 Adrian Karatnycky, *Freedom in the World 2001–2002: The Democracy Gap* (New York: Freedom House, 2002), www.freedom house.org (Retrieved February 11, 2011).

46 Specifically, on December 10, 1948, the General Assembly of the United Nations adopted the Universal Declaration of Human Rights and has since called on all member countries to publicize the text and "to cause it to be disseminated, displayed, read, and expounded principally in schools and other educational institutions, without distinction based on the political status of countries or territories," For the full text of the Declaration, go to www.un.org/Overview/rights.html.

47 Samuel P. Huntington, *The Third Wave: Democratization in the Late Twentieth Century* (Norman: University of Oklahoma Press, 1991).

48 Ibid.

49 Francis Fukuyama, *The End of History and the Last Man* (New York: Free Press, 1992).

50 "Sledge Hama," *The Economist*, (July 9, 2011): 45.

51 *The Economist Intelligence Unit's Index of Democracy 2008*, graphics .eiu.com/PDF/Democracy percent 20Index percent 202008.pdf (Retrieved June 24, 2009).

52 Ronald Bailey, "Does Disease Cause Autocracy?" *Reason Magazine* (June 1, 2011).

53 Christian Haerpfer, Patrick Bernhagen, Ronald Inglehart, and Christian Welzel (eds.), *Democratization* (Oxford: Oxford University Press, 2009); Two Billion More Bourgeois," *The Economist* (February 14, 2009): 18.

54 "Freedom in the World: The Annual Survey of Political Rights and Civil Liberties" *Freedom House*, ww.freedomhouse.org/template .cfm? (Retrieved February 11, 2011):15.

55 Arch Puddington, "Freedom in the World 2011: The Authoritarian Challenge to Democracy," *Freedom House*, freedomhouse.org: Freedom in the World 2011 Survey Release," www.freedomhouse .org/template.cfm?page=594 (Retrieved April 21, 2011).

56 "Freedom in the World 2011," 48, 49.

57 *"Democracy Index 2010: Democracy in Retreat, "Economist Intelligence Unit,"* www.eiu.com/public/topical_report.aspx?campaignid=demo2010 (Retrieved February 7, 2011). Laza Kekic, "A Pause in Democracy's March," *The Economist*, The World in 2007 (Annual Review, 2007): 59–60.

58 The EIU stipulates the following characteristics:
- *Full democracies*: Countries in which not only basic political freedoms and civil liberties are respected, but these will also tend to be underpinned by a political culture conducive to the flourishing of democracy. The functioning of government is satisfactory. Media are independent and diverse. There is an effective system

of checks and balances. The judiciary is independent and judicial decisions are enforced. There are only limited problems in the functioning of democracy.

- *Flawed democracies*: These countries also have free and fair elections and even if there are problems (such as infringements on media freedom), basic civil liberties will be respected. However, there are significant weaknesses in other aspects of democracy, including problems in governance, an underdeveloped political culture and low levels of political participation.

- *Hybrid regimes*: Elections have substantial irregularities that often prevent them from being both free and fair. Government pressure on opposition parties and candidates may be common. Serious weaknesses are more prevalent than in flawed democracies—in political culture, functioning of government and political participation. Corruption tends to be widespread and the rule of law is weak. Civil society is weak. Typically, there is harassment of and pressure on journalists and the judiciary is not independent.

- *Authoritarian regimes*: In these states political pluralism is absent or heavily circumscribed. Many countries in this category are outright dictatorships. Some formal institutions of democracy may exist, but these have little substance. Elections, if they do occur, are not free and fair. There is disregard for abuses and infringements of civil liberties. Media are typically state-owned or controlled by groups connected to the ruling regime. There is repression of criticism of the government and pervasive censorship. There is no independent judiciary.

59 "Monsoon of their Discontent," *The Economist*, (July 9, 2011): 40.

60 "World" population refers to the total population of the 167 countries covered by the index. Since this excludes only microstates, this is nearly equal to the entire actual estimated world population in 2010, *Economist Intelligence Unit*.

61 "Public Opinion in Eastern Europe: The Glow Fades," *The Economist*, www.economist.com/research/articlesBySubject/displaystory .cfm?subjectid=7933596&story_id=14792427 (Retrieved January 31, 2011).

62 "Freedom in the World 2011," 48, 49.

63 Julian Wucherpfennig, "Modernization and Democracy: Theories and Evidence Revisited, *Living Reviews in Democracy* (2009): 1.

64 "Countries at the Crossroads," freedomhouse.org, www.freedomhouse .org/template.cfm?page=139&edition=9 (Retrieved April 18, 2011).

65 Scott Shane, February 5, 2011 "America's Journeys with Strongmen NYTimes.com," www.nytimes.com/2011/02/06/weekinreview /06shane.html?_r=1&ref=us (Retrieved February 7, 2011).

66 ILO, "World of Work Report 2010. From one crisis to the next?" www.ilo.org/global/publications/books/WCMS_145259/lang–en /index.htm (Retrieved February 7, 2011).

67 Richard Florida, "The Conservative States of America," *The Atlantic*, www.theatlantic.com/politics/archive/2011/03/the-conservative -states-of-america/71827/ (Retrieved March 30, 2011).

68 "The Global Crisis and the Poor," *The Economist* (March 14, 2009): 62–64.

69 "Democracy? Hu Needs It," *The Economist* (June 28, 2007): 44; "A Warning for Reformers," *The Economist* (November 17, 2007): 67.

70 "'I am a True Democrat': G-8 Interview with Vladimir Putin," *Spiegel Online* www.spiegel.de/international/ world/0,1518,486345,00.html (Retrieved June 4, 2007).

71 "Brazil's President Lula Says G7 Nations No Longer Speak for the World," *The Telegraph* (March 16, 2009): A-1.

72 Roger Cohen, November 11, 2006. "China vs. U.S.: Democracy Confronts Harmony. Stay Tuned." New York Times, select.nytimes .com/iht/2006/11/22/world/IHT-22globalist.html (Retrieved February 7, 2011).

73 "Freedom in the World," 48, 49.

74 "Military spending: Defence costs," *The Economist*, www.economist .com/blogs/dailychart/2011/06/military-spending (Retrieved June 8, 2011).

75 James Mann, *The China Fantasy: Why Capitalism Will Not Bring Democracy to China*, (London: Penguin 2007); Eamonn Fingleton, *In the Jaws of the Dragon: America's Fate in the Coming Era of Chinese Hegemony* (New York: Thomas Dunne Books, 2008); Martin Jacques, *When China Rules the World: The End of the Western World and the Birth of a New Global Order* (London: Penguin Press, 2009); Stefan Halper, *The Beijing Consensus: How China's Authoritarian Model Will Dominate the Twenty-First Century* (New York: Basic Books, 2010).

76 "Banyan: On the defensive," *The Economist* (April 7, 2011): 49; Jacob Talmon, *The Origins of Totalitarian Democracy* (London: Secker & Warburg, 1952). "China: Democratic Dictatorship," *Time*, www.time .com/time/magazine/article/0,9171,800834,00.html (Retrieved May 16, 2011).

77 "Where do you live?" *The Economist*, Special Report: China (June 25, 2011): 12.

78 "China's Modern Authoritarianism - WSJ.com," online.wsj.com /article/SB124319304482150525.html (Retrieved February 10, 2011).

79 Matteo Cervellati, Piergiuseppe Fortunato, and Uwe Sunde, "Democratization and Civil Liberties: The Role of Violence during the Transition," IZA DP No. 5555 (March 2011).

80 Hassan Fattah, "Democracy in the Arab World, a U.S. Goal, Falters," *New York Times* (April 10, 2006): C-1.

81 Samuel Huntington, *The Clash of Civilizations and the Remaking of World Order* (New York: Simon & Schuster, 1996); Huntington, *Who Are We? The Challenges to America's National Identity* (New York: Simon & Schuster, 2004).

82 "US tells Egypt to unblock Facebook, Twitter," www.todayonline .com/World/EDC110128-0000197/US-tells-Egypt-to-unblock -Facebook,-Twitter (Retrieved January 31, 2011). Edward Wong and David Barboza, "Wary of Egypt Unrest, China Censors Web,"- NYTimes.com, www.nytimes.com/2011/02/01/world /asia/01beijing.html?_r=1&hp (Retrieved January 31, 2011). For example, Iranian leaders in 2009 and Egyptian authorities in 2011 struggled to quash anti-government protests by blocking social networking sites that had been used to organize protests. Meanwhile, in the initial days of the Egyptian rebellion, wary Chinese officials instructed Sina.com and Netease.com — two of the country's biggest online portals — to blocked keyword searches of the word "Egypt"; Weibo, the Chinese equivalent of Twitter, did the same.

83 Category, Satisfaction with Country's Direction, Specific Query, "How satisfied are you with the country's direction?" Pew Global Attitudes Project, pewglobal.org/database/?indicator=3&survey=12 &response=Satisfied&mode=chart (Retrieved April 21, 2011).

84 Aubrey Belford, 2011. "Indonesia's Political Landscape Offers Path for Egypt," *The New York Times*, www.nytimes.com/2011/02/17 /world/asia/17iht-indo17.html?partner=rss&emc=rss (Retrieved February 16, 2011).

85 "Freedom in the World," 48, 49.

86 "Venezuelan Bluster? Hugo Chávez Threatens to Seize Banks and a Steel-Maker," *The Economist Intelligence Unit* (May 8, 2007): 57.

87 "Nigeria's Prospects: A Man and a Morass" *The Economist* (May 28, 2011): 24.

88 "Will Silver Surge Following the Nationalization of Bolivia's Silver Mines by Embattled President Evo Morales?," www.zerohedge.com (Retrieved April 15, 2011).

89 Duff Wilson, "Cigarette Giants in Global Fight on Tighter Rules," NYTimes.com, www.nytimes.com/2010/11/14/business /global/14smoke.html?_r=1 (Retrieved February 1, 2011).

90 "The 2010 Failed States Index | Foreign Policy," www.foreignpolicy .com/failedstates (Retrieved February 8, 2011).

91 For example, consider the legal concept of due diligence, which requires that the statements in a firm's security-registration forms be true and omit no material facts. Companies rely on due diligence to manage the risk of cross-border acquisitions; it enacts a legally binding process during which a potential buyer, say an Indian software designer, evaluates the assets and liabilities of a potential acquisition in say, Germany. Hence, due diligence is often the difference between success and failure—provided the local legal codes permit the full examination of operations and management and the verification of material facts. In the European Union, data protection rules can interfere with assessing important elements of a potential acquisition, such as managers' physical or mental health, patterns of trade union membership, and criminal histories. Hence, prudent companies considering cross-border acquisitions pinpoint issues, the country or countries involved, and the citizenship and identity of people involved from the pre-due-diligence phase to the close of the deal. These decisions inevitably reference aspects of constitutional law, (i.e., what philosophies anchor ownership rights?), criminal law, (i.e., what are the procedures and penalties for malfeasance?), and civil/commercial law, (i.e., do regulations promote disclosure and verification of information?).

92 *Stare Decisis.* Latin, "to stand by that which is decided." The principle that the precedent decisions are to be followed by the courts.

93 Denis Wiechman, Jerry Kendall, and Mohammad Azarian, "Islamic Law: Myths and Realities," muslimcanada.org/Islam_myths.htm (Retrieved June 22, 2009).

94 Andorra and the Guernsey and Jersey Islands, both of which belong to the United Kingdom, apply customary law only. The codification of civil law developed out of legal customs that evolved in particular communities and, over time, were collected and recorded by local jurists.

95 "A Disorderly Heaven," *The Economist* (March 20, 2004): 75.

96 Ian Morris, *Why the West Rules…For Now* (New York: Farrar, Strauss and Giroux, 2010).

97 Quote, He Weifang, p. 22. Ibid, 43.

98 Paul Collier, *Wars, Guns, and Votes: Democracy in Dangerous Places* (New York: HarperCollins, 2009).

99 Similarly, Thomas Paine wrote "in America, the law is king" in contrast to the view that the king was the law, *Common Sense*, www.ushistory.org/paine/commonsense/singlehtml.htm (Retrieved March 26, 2011).

100 "Rule of Law Index | World Justice Project," worldjusticeproject.org/rule-of-law-index (Retrieved February 8, 2011).

101 Hernando De Soto, *The Mystery of Capital: Why Capitalism Triumphs in the West and Fails Everywhere Else* (Basic Books, 2000).

102 See profile of the World Justice Project, reported in "The Paper Chase," The Economist, (June 25, 2011): 40

103 "Business in Russia: Dancing with the Bear," 18.

104 "Big US Firms Shift Hiring Abroad," *Wall Street Journal* (April 19, 2011): B1.

105 Geoff Lewis, "Who in the World Is Entrepreneurial?" *Fortune: Small Business* (June 1, 2007): 24.

106 "Economics focus: The Himalayas of hiring," *The Economist* (August 7, 2010): 76.

107 "Doing Business - Measuring Business Regulations," *World Bank Group,* www.doingbusiness.org (Retrieved June 8, 2011).

108 "Business in Asia: The Next Great Wall," *The Economist* (March 12, 2009): 67–68.

109 "Trade Policy: Buying American," *The Economist* (January 29, 2009): 40. Keith Bradsher, "Pentagon Must 'Buy American,' Barring Chinese Solar Panels," *The New York Times* (January 9, 2011): B2.

110 Keith Bradsher, "Foreign Companies Chafe at China's Restrictions," *NYTimes.com,* www.nytimes.com/2010/05/17/business/global/17lobby.html?_r=2&hp (Retrieved March 30, 2011).

111 "Vive la difference! The French Model," *The Economist* (May 7, 2009): 31.

112 James Kanter, "Intel Fined Record $1.45 Billion in Antitrust Case," *New York Times* (May 13, 2009): A-1.

113 Duncan Fairgrieve and Geraint Howells, "Is Product Liability Still a Global Problem?," *Managerial Law* 49:1/2 (2007): 6–9.

114 "Lego: Bricks and Flicks," *The Economist* (May 7, 2011): 70.

115 Evans, Nathan, "India's New Patent Regime and its Impact on the Global Pharmaceutical Industry," *Pharmaceutical Law Insight,* (September 2007).

116 "Stephanie Clifford, "Recession? Knockoffs Go Downmarket" *NYTimes.com,* www.nytimes.com/2010/08/01/business/economy/01knockoff.html (Retrieved February 14, 2011).

117 "Inside the Knockoff-Tennis-Shoe Factory," NYTimes.com, www.nytimes.com/2010/08/22/magazine/22fake-t.html?_r=2&adxnnl=1&emc=eta1&adxnnlx=1282932069-1merRjlswb8WDMPz0lEG1w (Retrieved February 14, 2011).

118 "Homepage | International AntiCounterfeiting Coalition," www.iacc.org/ (Retrieved February 14, 2011).

119 Stephanie Sutton, "EFCG: Counterfeit Medicines More Profitable than Heroin," pharmtech.findpharma.com/pharmtech/Ingredients/EFCG-Counterfeit-Medicines-More-Profitable-than-He/ArticleStandard/Article/detail/635540 (Retrieved February 16, 2011).

120 "Pirated Microsoft software funded Mexican drug cartel," www.digitaltrends.com/computing/pirated-microsoft-software-funded-mexican-drug-cartel/ (Retrieved February 16, 2011).

121 Owen Fletcher and Jason Dean, "Ballmer Decries Huge China Sales Holes," *Wall Street Journal, WSJ.com* (May 27, 2011): A-1.

122 "India: Cipla Launches 3-in-1 AIDS Pill," October 14, 2006, www.medindia.net/news/view_news_main.asp?x=15038 (Retrieved September 15, 2008).

123 Veronica Weinstein and Dennis Fernandez, "Recent Developments in China's Intellectual Property Laws," *Chinese Journal of International Law* 3:1 (2004): 227.

124 "Gold from the Storm," *The Economist* (June 28, 2007): 65.

125 Personal Conversation, Daniel Sullivan and Mr. Patrick Hu, Shanghai (March 2, 2011).

126 Zhenmin Wang, "The Developing Rule of Law in China," *Harvard Asia Quarterly* (2000):4.

127 Robert Ostergard, "The Measurement of Intellectual Property Rights Protection," *Journal of International Business Studies* 31 (Summer 2000): 349.

128 Stephanie Sanborn, "Protecting Intellectual Property on the Web—The Internet Age Is Making Digital Rights Management Even More Important," *InfoWorld* (June 19, 2000): 40.

129 "Executive Summary: Genetics, genomics and the patenting of DNA," World Health Organization, (www.who.int/genomics/publications/background/en/index.html (Retrieved May 16, 2011).

130 "Economists Say Copyright and Patent Laws Are Killing Innovation; Hurting Economy," Washington University, www.newswise.com/articles/view/549822/sc=dwhn (Retrieved May 10, 2009).

131 Jack Coats, "Intellectual property: an unnecessary evil," CSMonitor.com, www.csmonitor.com/Business/The-Adam-Smith-Institute-Blog/2011/0428/Intellectual-property-an-unnecessary-evil (Retrieved April 28, 2011). Stephan Kinsella, "Against Intellectual Property," Ludwig von Mises Institute, mises.org/resources/3582/Against-Intellectual-Property (Retrieved April 28, 2011).

132 "Going Up or Down?" *The Economist* (June 7, 2007): 45.

133 "A High Cost to Developing Countries," *New York Times* (October 5, 1986): D2.

134 "A Gathering Storm," *The Economist* (June 7, 2007): 67.

135 Doron S. Ben-Atar, *Trade Secrets: Intellectual Piracy and the Origins of American Industrial Power* (New Haven, CT: Yale University Press, 2004).

136 "China grants more patents in 2010," *IPR in China*," www.chinaipr .gov.cn/newsarticle/news/government/201101/1185432_1.html (Retrieved March 24, 2011).

137 "China Claims #9 Rank in United States Patents," www.defence .pk/forums/china-defence/55892-china-claims-9-rank-united -states-patents.html (Retrieved April 23, 2011).

138 Raja Murthy, "China on Patent Overdrive," *Asia Times Online*, www.atimes.com/atimes/China_Business/MA07Cb01.html (Retrieved March 24, 2011).

139 "U.S. Customs and Border Protection," *Trade*, www.cbp.gov /xp/cgov/trade/priority_trade/ipr/pubs/seizure/ (Retrieved February 14, 2011).

140 "Battle of Ideas: Intellectual property in China," *The Economist* (April 25, 2009): 73. "China on Patent Overdrive" Asia Times Online, www.atimes.com/atimes/China_Business/MA07Cb01 .html (Retrieved February 14, 2011).

141 "Inside the Knockoff-Tennis-Shoe Factory," NYTimes.com, www .nytimes.com/2010/08/22/magazine/22fake-t.html?_r=2&adxnnl =1&emc=eta1&adxnnlx=1282932069-1merRjlswb8WDMPz0lEG1w (Retrieved February 14, 2011).

142 "International AntiCounterfeiting Coalition," www.iacc.org /(Retrieved February 14, 2011).

143 Stephanie Sutton, "EFCG: Counterfeit Medicines More Profitable than Heroin," pharmtech.findpharma.com/pharmtech/Ingredients /EFCG-Counterfeit-Medicines-More-Profitable-than-He/Article Standard/Article/detail/635540 (Retrieved February 16, 2011).

144 William Booth, "Drug Cartels Muscle into Piracy Business," *The Washington Post* (June 1, 2011): A-1.

145 Ibid, Quote by Jonathan Erece, a trade enforcement coordinator for United States Protection.

146 "Fake drugs: Poison Pills," *The Economist*, www.economist.com /node/16943895?story_id=16943895 (Retrieved February 14, 2011).

147 Ibid.

148 Benoit Godart, "IP crime: the new face of organized crime," *Journal of Intellectual Property Law & Practice*, jiplp.oxfordjournals.org /content/5/5/378.full (Retrieved February 14, 2011).

149 "Software piracy takes toll on global scale," Hack in the Box: Keeping Knowledge Free, www.hackinthebox.net/modules.php? op=modload&name=News&file=article&sid=2951 (Retrieved April 23, 2011).

150 "Microsoft says software piracy continues to grow," | TG Daily, www.tgdaily.com/hardware-brief/13603-microsoft-says-software -piracy-continues-to-grow (Retrieved February 14, 2011).

151 Ibid.

152 "Business in China and the West: A Tale of Two Expats," *The Economist* (December 29, 2010):73.

153 "Business Software Alliance - Global Software Piracy Study," portal .bsa.org/globalpiracy2009/index.html (Retrieved February 16, 2011).

chapter 4
The Economic Environments Facing Businesses

Objectives

1. To communicate the importance of economic analysis

2. To discuss the idea of economic freedom

3. To profile the characteristics of the types of economic systems

4. To introduce the notion of state capitalism

5. To profile indicators of economic development, performance, and potential

Access a host of interactive learning aids to help strengthen your understanding of the chapter concepts at www.myiblab.com.

MyIBLab

Source: Stéphane Bidouze/Shutterstock.com

A man is rich who owes nothing.

—French proverb

CASE

The Comeback Accelerates[1]

In the world of globalization, one often struggles to separate the rhetoric from reality. Some view it in the extreme, as in the transformation of everything. Others see it as just the latest stage in the evolution of the market. Some see it as the final phase before forces of deglobalization usher in the inevitable return to local enterprise. Despite wide-ranging opinions, few doubt the ongoing integration of national economies into the global market resets the business environment.

Discussions have taken a far more dramatic tone the past few years. Some commentators see the flattening of the world whereby advances in institutions, communications, and technology fundamentally change the economics of globalization. They speak of "distributed tools of innovation and connectivity empowering individuals from anywhere to compete, connect, and collaborate."[2] Powered by hardware and software innovations, companies operate anywhere, anytime.

Others emphasize the entry of billions of people into the global marketplace. Some reason that the world is experiencing a two-part transformation.

> Three billion new people—billion and a half Chinese, billion Indians, half a billion people from former Soviet bloc—have suddenly come into the global economy all at one time. Within these three billion people is a population as big as the United States, bigger than anybody in Europe or Japan, who are every bit as skilled and can do anything that could be done in the U.S. or Japan or any of the developed countries for ten cents on the dollar.[3]

Rarely do such changes take place. Inevitably, the entry of billions of low-wage, skilled workers radically resets how we interpret capital and labor in the production of goods and services.

Finally, the consequences of the global economic meltdown raises the specter of slowing markets triggering deglobalization. Rising trade barriers, risk-adverse companies, and nationalistic consumers slow the cross-national movement of information, people, products, capital, and jobs. Governments constrain the animal spirits of capitalism, regulating what had become hazardously free markets. Economic freedom, as we saw with political freedom in Chapter 3, is under siege from surging state intervention.

WHAT'S NEXT?

Provocative in their own right, these interpretations suggest that, in the opening decades of the twenty-first century,

globalization reinforced long-running developments and initiated powerful trends. Combined, they challenge one's lifestyle, job, company, country, and future. The possibility that globalization has reached an inflection point—namely a time where old strategic patterns give way to the new—signals the need for managers to rethink economic principles and practices.

Understanding where we are heading calls for highlighting where we have come from. Initially, attention turns to how the world economy evolved from 1950 through 2000. During this time, the diffusion of democracy and free market principles powered growing trade among the richer, developed nations. It also spilled over to many poorer, developing countries. Institutions like the IMF, WTO, and World Bank stabilized the playing field. Companies from the United States, Western Europe, and Japan—the so-called Triad—ruled international business and globalized the world in their image.

The precedents from this era increasingly fall short in helping managers interpret today's puzzles. Indeed, focusing on the tried-and-true indicators of the past distort interpreting today's global economy. Unquestionably, measures of the performance and potential in developed countries matter. However, they no longer matter decisively. Unfolding trends direct attention toward an epochal shift in the center of gravity of the global economy.

THE EMERGENCE

By 2050, four of the six largest economies in the world—Japan, China, India, and Russia—will be in greater Asia. Their growth will create a second tier of robust economies among their Asian neighbors, such as Singapore, South Korea, Indonesia, Taiwan, Kyrgyzstan, Vietnam, Thailand, and Australia. Countries in other parts of the world, like Brazil in South America, South Africa in Africa, and Israel and Saudi Arabia in the Middle East, will develop along with their Asian counterparts. (See Map 4.1). All, although each at a different pace, are inexorably moving from the periphery to the center of the global economy.

Extrapolating from 2012 out to 2050 is, unquestionably, more speculation than estimation. Still, these countries are implementing powerful pro-growth policies. Hard data confirm their success so far. In 1980, the combined output of emerging economies accounted for 36 percent of global GDP. They crossed a milestone in 2009, accounting for more

MAP 4.1   Leading Emerging Markets

There are various types of market designations, including advanced, industrial, postindustrial, and developing. Here we identify those markets that are commonly referred to as emerging economies. These 24 countries earn this designation given the status of their market development and high rate of economic growth.

Source: Compiled from *The Economist* and the Morgan Stanley Emerging Markets Index.

Note: Given that this is a Mercator projection, the scale approximates east-west distance at the equator; however, the farther you move from the equator, the more the east-west distance is distorted.

than half of total world GDP.[4] Similarly, emerging economies' share of world exports is nearly 50 percent (up from 20 percent in 1970). Their share of the world's foreign-exchange reserves is 70 percent (up from net deficits in the mid-1990s). China alone holds more than 28 percent of total reserves in the world. Institutionally, the G-7, long a developed market stronghold, expanded into the G-20, thereby giving new members, like China, India, Brazil, Mexico, and South Korea, greater say in the premier global policy forum. These new stakeholders advocate different views of trade and investment regulation. Collectively, the accelerating rise of emerging economies signaled that the wealthy countries of the twentieth century would not dominate the global economy in the twenty-first century.[5]

The economics in emerging markets suggests the revolution has only begun. Ambition to improve infrastructure, increase productivity, create jobs, and alleviate poverty has put into motion what will likely be the biggest economic stimulus in history. The last transformation of similar magnitude—the Industrial Revolution—involved far fewer people in far fewer nations but still produced a century-and-a-half economic expansion that altered lives everywhere. Today's revolution spans the globe and includes far more people in far more countries. The transfer of the leadership baton from wealthy countries to emerging markets, for better and for worse, resets our interpretation of economic environments.

PRECEDENTS AND PREDICTIONS

Making sense of the situation moves some to review a broader span of history. Tracking the past millennium, they say, puts the current economic drama into perspective. Before the steam engine and the power loom drove the transfer of economic might from Asia to the West, today's emerging economies dominated world output. From 1000 to the mid-1880s, they produced, on average, 70 to 80 percent of world output (see Figure 4.1). Over this span, China and India were the world's two biggest economies; China alone generated one-third of the world's gross domestic product in 1820.

FIGURE 4.1   Emerging Markets Make a Comeback

Over most of the past millennium, today's emerging economies, most notably China and India, accounted for about 70 percent of global economic output. By the twentieth century, today's developed economies, such as the United States, Germany, and Japan, generated more than half of global economic output. Trends suggest that, by 2050, if not sooner, emerging economies will again account for more than 70 percent of global economic output, thereby culminating their comeback.

Sources: Based on *The World Economy: A Millennial Perspective, Angus Maddison.* Paris: OECD Development Centre Studies, 2001; IMF; The Economist.

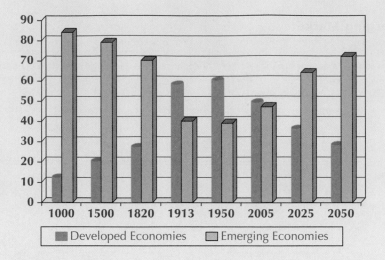

In 1850, China produced the highest percent of all the goods consumed in the world. Britain, on the basis of the Industrial Revolution, soon claimed this title before ceding the top spot to the United States around the beginning of the 20th century. By 1950, emerging economies' share of global output had fallen to 40 percent; China's share had fallen to 5 percent. They lost their lead (temporarily, trends now suggest) as internal political failure, aggravated by colonial exploitation and unfair trade agreements, spurred isolationism and xenophobia. Consequently, the Industrial Revolution benefited the West while bypassing them.

Today, their ambition is straightforward: Restore their historic stature as the engine of the global economy. Since 2001, annual growth in emerging markets has averaged 6.4 percent; in contrast, the rich economies have averaged 1.6 percent. While they expand, the **global financial crisis** slows and shrinks many developed economies. Over the next decade, emerging economies will grow at an average of 6.8 percent a year. In addition, nearly 70 percent of the world growth over the next few years will come from emerging markets, with 40 percent coming from China and India and another 15 percent from Brazil, Indonesia, Russia, and South Korea.[6] In contrast, most developed economies will be fortunate just to grow. If these trends persist, in 20 years or so, today's emerging economies will complete their comeback, again accounting for more than 70 percent of global output.[7] Symbolizing this process, China reclaimed the top spot it last held in 1850—it produced 19.8 percent of all the goods consumed in the world in 2009; the United States, leader for the previous 110 years, produced 19.4 percent and fell to second.[8]

The diminishing role of today's rich economies, coupled with the accelerating scope of emerging economies, changes investment, trade, consumption, wealth, poverty, fiscal, and monetary patterns. For some, these shifts pose threats. For others, they create opportunities. Figure 4.2 shows who sees which. Noted one observer, "No visitor to the emerging world can fail to be struck by its prevailing optimism, particularly if his starting point is the recession-racked West... [emerging markets] see opportunities in every difficulty rather than difficulties in every opportunity."[9] Put differently, strategic inflection points do not necessarily lead to disaster, as cellphones to land lines or the Internet to print-centric newspapers. Change creates prospects for players, whether newcomers or incumbents, who are adept at operating in the new economy, such as those who applied computer chips to cell phones or publishers that migrated to the Web.

HERE AND NOW

Megatrends such as the Comeback are rare events. And, unquestionably, trends often go awry. Still, at this point, the odds are that policymakers, executives, workers, and investors will wrestle with this shift for decades. Against this backdrop, this chapter profiles the frameworks that interpret the brave,

FIGURE 4.2   Is the Country's Economic Situation Good or Bad?

Surveys regularly tap citizens' sense of their nation's economic situation. These results, the latest in a long running series, suggest folks in emerging economies have greater confidence in their current situation then do their counterparts in developed markets.

Source: Adapted from Pew Global Attitudes Project: Country's Economic Situation, 2011.[i]

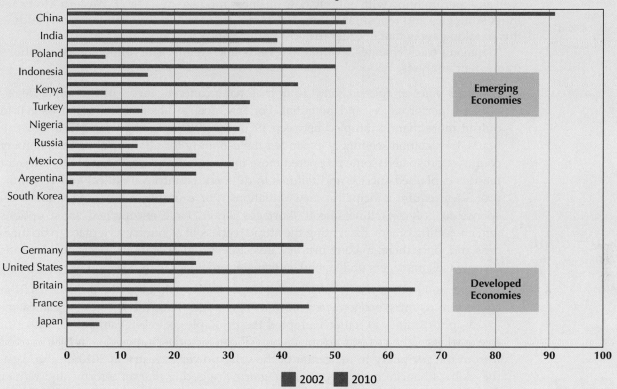

new world. Economic change, particularly the sort we have seen during the global financial crisis, seems unpredictable. Nevertheless, as this chapter shows, there is rhyme and reason that helps managers interpret the development, evaluate the performance, and assess the potential of CRN economic environments.

Introduction

Cultural, political, and legal systems influence a company's decisions on where, when, and how to do business. This chapter completes our macro-profile. It presents the perspectives and tools that managers use to interpret economic environments.[10]

Although easily overdramatized, this task has perhaps not been more important in our lifetimes given the opportunities and challenges currently facing individuals, companies, and countries. For example, consider the following situation. In 2007, shortage of polycrystalline silicon—the main raw material for solar panels—threatened China's nascent solar-energy industry. Polysilicon prices soared tenfold in a year, hitting $450 a kilogram in 2008. Foreign companies then dominated production and passed high costs onto Chinese producers. Beijing's response was swift: The development of domestic polysilicon supplies was declared a national priority. State-owned banks, along with China's sovereign-wealth fund, poured money into local polysilicon manufacturers. Local governments expedited approvals for new plants. In the West, polysilicon factories require lengthy reviews that results in years to build a plant. In China, Zhu Gongshan raised $1 billion for a plant, built it, and started production within 15 months. Since then, he has created one of the world's biggest polysilicon makers, GCL-Poly Energy—which counts China's sovereign wealth fund as a key owner. Today, China makes about a quarter of the world's polysilicon and supplies roughly half the global market for finished solar-power equipment.[11]

Rather than an isolated situation, the tale of GCL-Poly Energy increasingly is the norm. Emerging economies are reinventing systems of production and distribution as well as experimenting with entirely new business models. As a result, Western MNEs rethink strategies and reposition assets. Policymakers worldwide watch the game, adding this or taking away that in order to boost performance.

Managers track changes, evaluating events and trends. The following assumptions frame their analyses.

> *Countries differ in different ways.* Countries have different levels of economic development, performance, and potential. For instance, in absolute terms, gross world output more than quintupled between 1970 and 2010, growing from $12 to $61 trillion. Globalization seemingly expanded the economy for all. In relative terms, many countries prospered, some prospered more than others, and a few not at all. Different reasons explained success and failures in different countries. Political and economic processes require anticipating new situations. For example, forecasting China's response to polycrystalline silicon shortages would have encouraged some options while rejecting others. Estimating the attractiveness of a country as a place to do business and, once there, making prudent investment and operational decisions depends on how well managers understand, anticipate, and adapt to its economic environment.

> *Economic and political changes alter market circumstances.* Although the pace varies from country to country, economic environments change. Since the 1980s, companies enjoyed opportunities as nations adopted the principles of capitalism and practices of free markets. China's fast tracking its polysilicon factories, impossible in 1980, moved it from the periphery to the center of the solar power industry in 2010. In the West, the global financial crisis has reset the game, triggering market reforms and tighter regulation. In the East, it has endorsed growing government involvement in allocating resources.

> In both worlds, changing economic policies reveal government ambitions. They also spotlight implications for economic freedom. For example, in mid-2011, Bolivia dismantled its privatization model that governed the mining industry and expropriated all assets owned by private, largely foreign owned mining companies. Executives worldwide had to determine if this was an isolated example or the start of a trend. Consequently, managers study changes, both big and small, both here and there, that shape economic environments. And, in the back of their minds, managers realize that steps taken in Ireland, Thailand, Australia, or Mexico differ from those taken in China, Brazil, Estonia, or South Africa. The task is distinguishing common trends from unique events.

> *Connections, Change, and Consequences.* Besides assessing the foreign markets in which they operate, managers monitor those in which they do not. Globalization connects countries. Change in one country has consequences in others. Companies also monitor changes in countries where improving performance or revised policies strengthen local competitors. In Boston, for example, aided by $43 million in public assistance, Evergreen Solar became one of the largest makers of solar panels in the United States by 2009. In 2011, it shut its Massachusetts factory, laid off 800 workers, and shifted production to a joint venture with a Chinese company in Wuhan, China. Evergreen Solar cited the superior location economics and higher government support for solar activity in China.[12] On the larger scale, the United Nations estimates there are approximately 22,000 multinationals based in the emerging world; few of these existed

Managers study a country's economic environment to assess its development, explain its performance, and estimate its potential.

Studying an economic environment helps managers make better investment choices and operating decisions.

Case Review Note

Concept Check

"The Forces Driving Globalization" explained how an economic environment responds to technology, trade, competition, consumer attitudes, and cross-border relationships. The scope of the connections among these conditions spurs MNEs to examine them as individual and interdependent factors.

10 years ago.[13] The number of companies from Brazil, India, China, or Russia on the *Financial Times 500* moved from 15 in 2006 to 77 in 2010. Too, for the first time, a Chinese company, PetroChina, dethroned Exxon Mobil as the world's most valuable company.

Challenges of the Comeback. The rise of emerging economies distorts traditional economic indicators. Greater competition for scarce resources increases prices of commodities but decreases costs of manufactured goods; more people are working worldwide but poverty is increasing; and recycling massive foreign exchange reserves means capital is too cheap here, too expensive there.[14] More than 70 percent of the world's growth over the next few years will be in emerging markets. Managers' macroeconomic instincts, tried and tested for the past decades in the West, adapt to the changing, sometimes confusing, circumstances.

Choices of Citizens, Policymakers, and Institutions. Economics is vital to citizens, policymakers, and institutions. By 2000, the apparent triumph of free markets over state-controlled economies had led countries to launch bold development programs. Free market reforms increased investment, consumption, employment, and wealth. However, the global financial crisis cast doubt on the **sustainability** of market-led change. Free markets, the crisis showed, can also misallocate capital and fan opportunism. Governments, particularly those in the West, increasingly constrain the animal spirits of unbridled capitalism through expanding regulations. New market standards reset asset valuation and resource allocation, reshape trade and investment, and reconfigure industries. All of which, as we see, rapidly happened in the solar power industry. Hence, a fuller understanding of economic transitions and market evolution helps citizens, policymakers, and institutions make better decisions.

Case Review Note

Concept Check

A principle of globalization is the broadening network of relationships among people, companies, countries, and institutions. Philosophically, the same principle applies to the emergence and evolution of economies.

Does Ge🌐graphy Matter? Change and Consequence of Arctic Sea Ice

Understanding economic environments moves managers to mind the changing dimensions of the world. For example, **economic geography** is the study of the location, distribution, and spatial organization of economic activities across the earth. One would think that the terrain of our planet had been thoroughly mapped over the past millennium given the relentless expansion of trade and investment. However, for both good and bad reasons, we see interesting developments in the geography of globalization.

Today, the bulk of goods between Eastern United States, Northern Europe, and Asia travel through the Panama Canal to navigate between the Atlantic and the Pacific. Similarly, most goods between Asia and southern Europe travel through the South China Sea, cut past Singapore, round the bottom of India, pass through the Suez Canal, cross the Mediterranean, and head up the west coast of Europe.

Now, just as the Panama and Suez Canal changed the flow of trade, so too might global warming do the same. Satellite images show the consequences of global warming in northerly latitudes. The shrinking polar ice cap is turning the forbidding waters at the top of the world into new shipping routes. Companies and countries evaluate the implications of emerging shipping routes linking the Atlantic and Pacific along Russia's Arctic coast (the Northeast Passage) or through Canada's Arctic Archipelago (the Northwest Passage).[15]

Traveling these fabled passages, rather than the Panama or Suez Canals, alters shipping logistics and trade routes. The voyage from Vladivostok in the Russian Far East to Rotterdam, Germany, via the Northeast Passage takes less than a month. The traditional route through the Panama Canal runs at least six weeks. Similarly, shipping goods from South Korea to the Netherlands via the Suez Canal travels 14,000 nautical miles (about 15,000 miles). Traveling the Northwest Passage shaves around 3,000 nautical miles (3,452 miles) and 10 days off the journey. And

(continued)

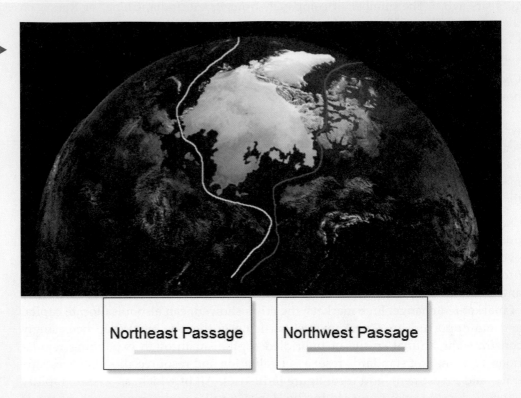

Northeast Passage

Northwest Passage

since time is money, the shorter trip significantly reduces the cost per ship per trip.[16]

Presently, ships can feasibly ply the Northwest or Northeast Passage at the end of the summer melt season.[17] However, by mid-century, scientists predict these waterways could remain ice-free year round. Accelerating ice loss may bring that date forward. Scientists tracking the annual maximum extent of Arctic sea ice reported that 2011 was among the lowest ice extents measured. "For the first 20 years of the satellite record, the average annual maximum was basically uniform," said NASA. "Then, in 2011, we see an abrupt decline."[18]

The shrinking arctic ice is, at best, a mixed blessing. Improving conditions for traveling the Northwest or Northeast Passages depend upon worsening conditions for the planet. As climate change resets the Arctic ice cap, to say nothing of radically redrawing the world's coastlines, it yields new trade routes, markets, and resources. Nevertheless, an increasingly hotter world poses innumerable side effects that may trump the benefits of shorter trade routes. ●

International Economic Analysis

The World Bank identifies 208 discrete economic environments in the world today—194 countries and 14 other economies with populations of more than 30,000.[19] Few MNEs can fund and run operations in all 208 markets. Resource constraints mean managers must prioritize their options, operating in countries that offer the greatest return with the least risk. Improving decisions depends on assessing the development, performance, and potential of an economy. In particular, although economics champions many scientific principles it still relies on a variety of behavioral assumptions to interpret activity.[20] As a result, assessments are often more conditional than universal because:

| Given resource constraints, managers ask which countries in the world warrant investment.

1. The complexity of even the simplest economic system defies straightforward classification. Stipulating indicators that definitively represent a country's economic performance and potential is difficult. Managers can consult an ever-expanding set

FIGURE 4.3   Economic Factors Affecting International Business Operations

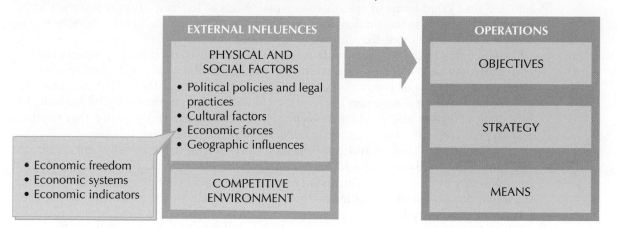

of economic indicators. The challenge is identifying the measures that matter, mapping them onto a market, and monitoring their performance.

2. Marketplace dynamism means that today's valid measures may prove invalid tomorrow. In the wake of the global financial crisis, some indicators that worked in 2007 were flawed by 2009 and remained dubious in 2011.

3. Just as no man is an island, no country is isolated. The consequence of connections is an integrated system of markets in which actions in one influences outcomes in others. Interdependencies complicate interpretations. Adjusting analysis for actions and reactions across a broad scope of markets is difficult.

Figure 4.3 shows how managers overcome these constraints. It identifies economic conditions that shape a country's development, performance, and potential. Too, it highlights elements, namely economic freedom and system type, which guide assessment. Figure 4.3 also suggests that linkages among elements mean that a change in one affects others; a systems perspective, therefore, proves useful. Consider, for example, the consequences of a reduction in interest rates; a cut spurs more borrowing that fans greater demand that boosts inflation that erodes purchasing power that creates wage pressure that reduces profits that lowers savings and so on. Clarifying interactions among elements of an economy help estimate its development path and performance potential. Therefore, managers typically integrate insights from company activities, analysts' reports, and news articles in developing a mosaic profile that represents an economy's features and estimates its interactions.

Managers apply three perspectives to improve their sense of economic environments. First, they estimate how much freedom they will have to make investments and run operations as they see fit. Second, they evaluate the type of economic system in the country, studying how current policies shape development and performance. Third, they investigate the points of change that drive economic change, assessing the conditions that moderate economic freedom as well as move a country from one economic system to another. Collectively, these insights pinpoint where investments should go and, perhaps more importantly, where they should not.

Economic Freedom

Chapter 3 used political freedom to organize discussion for a simple reason: Any discussion of politics, no matter the terminology, dimensions, or dynamics, ultimately takes one to the issue of what one is free to do in a political system. We reapply the same logic here. Although managers monitor a range of economic issues, analysis ultimately centers on what they are free to do as economic agents: What investments can they make? How can they allocate

Concept Check

Chapter 1 notes changing environmental variables promote and constrain globalization, Chapter 2 notes changing cultural identities, and Chapter 3 notes changing political philosophies and legal outlooks. The same perspective applies here as well—namely, the changing economic environments of international business create opportunities and impose constraints.

resources? What property rights can they claim? How can they compete? Whom can they hire and fire? What forms of operations can they engage? In many countries, these sorts of freedoms are taken so for granted, they rarely cross one's minds. In many others, however, these freedoms are so rare, they are ongoing points of fascination and conflict.

Against this backdrop, **economic freedom** is the "absolute right of property ownership, fully realized freedoms of movement for labor, capital, and goods, and an absolute absence of coercion or constraint of economic liberty beyond the extent necessary for citizens to protect and maintain liberty itself."[21] Rather than the state, individuals decide how they wish to work, produce, consume, save, and invest. Importantly, that freedom is both protected by the state as well as unconstrained by the state.

The **Economic Freedom Index** estimates the extent to which a government constrains free choice and free enterprise for reasons that go beyond the need to protect property, liberty, safety, and efficiency. This index rests on Adam Smith's notion that "basic institutions that protect the liberty of individuals to pursue their own economic interests result in greater prosperity for the larger society."[22] The Economic Freedom Index is made up of 50 indicators organized into 10 dimensions (see Table 4.1). Analysts apply this index to 183 countries, grading each's performance. The higher the score on a factor, within the range of 0 to 100 percent, the higher the degree of economic freedom (or, conversely, the lower the level of government interference)

ECONOMIC FREEDOM TODAY

Worldwide, economic freedom advanced in 2011, regaining some momentum it had lost during the great financial crisis and ensuing global recession. In 2011, the average freedom score was 59.7 percent among the 183 sampled countries; it was 59.4 in 2010.[23] Worldwide, governments reiterated the importance of sound finances, open markets, regulatory reform, and property rights. Still, economic freedom remains down from the pre-crisis high of 60.2 percent in 2007.

Economic freedom varies across regions, with people in North America and Europe enjoying more than do others elsewhere. Economic freedom on a regional basis shows higher degrees in Western countries and lower degrees in Eastern countries. Population data indicate that most people live in countries with lower degrees of economic freedom (see Figure 4.4). Approximately 1.2 billion people live with high to moderate degrees of

TABLE 4.1   Dimensions of the Economic Freedom Index

Business Freedom	**Property Rights**
The ability to start, operate, and close a business that represents the overall burden of regulation as well as the efficiency of government in the regulatory process.	Ability of individuals to accumulate private property, secured by clear laws that are fully enforced by the state.
Monetary Freedom	**Trade Freedom**
The degree of price stability and the extent to price controls.	The absence of tariff and non-tariff barriers that affect imports and exports of goods and services.
Fiscal Freedom	**Government Size**
Tax burden imposed by government on its citizens.	Government expenditures as a percentage of GDP.
Investment Freedom	**Financial Freedom**
Ability of individuals and firms to move resources, without restriction, into and out of activities both internally and across the country's borders.	Efficiency of banking as well as the independence of the financial sector from government control and interference.
Freedom from Corruption	**Labor Freedom**
Degree that corruption introduces insecurity and uncertainty into economic relationships.	Aspects of the legal and policy framework that regulates the country's labor market.

Source: Based on The Economic Freedom Index, The Heritage Foundation and the *Wall Street Journal*.

FIGURE 4.4 Economic Freedom by Region, with Population

The relationship between economic freedom and population indicates that the vast majority of the world, approximately 5.5 billion people, live in countries whose governments constrain their choice om how they wish to work, produce, consume, save, and invest.

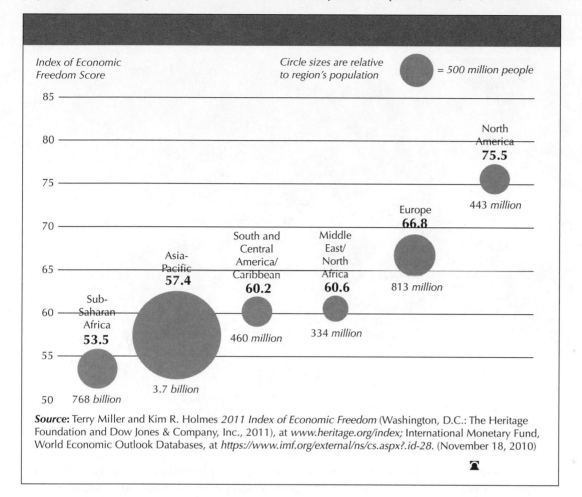

Index of Economic Freedom Score

Circle sizes are relative to region's population = 500 million people

- North America **75.5** — 443 *million*
- Europe **66.8** — 813 *million*
- Asia-Pacific **57.4** — 3.7 *billion*
- South and Central America/Caribbean **60.2** — 460 *million*
- Middle East/North Africa **60.6** — 334 *million*
- Sub-Saharan Africa **53.5** — 768 *billion*

Source: Terry Miller and Kim R. Holmes *2011 Index of Economic Freedom* (Washington, D.C.: The Heritage Foundation and Dow Jones & Company, Inc., 2011), at *www.heritage.org/index;* International Monetary Fund, World Economic Outlook Databases, at *https://www.imf.org/external/ns/cs.aspx?.id-28.* (November 18, 2010)

economic freedom. The majority of the world, roughly 5.2 billion people, lives in countries where the state grants them low degrees of economic freedom.

Map 4.2 profiles economic freedom around the world. It indicates six countries have free economies, 27 are rated mostly free, 57 are moderately free, 57 are mostly not free, and 32 are repressed.[24] The freest economies are Hong Kong, Singapore, Australia, New Zealand, Switzerland, and Canada. The least free economies include North Korea, Cuba, Zimbabwe, Eritrea, and Venezuela. The United States dropped to ninth place in 2011 largely due to increased government spending, debt, and regulations. Its score of 77.8 placed it in the "mostly free" category. In 2007, the United States ranked fifth with a score of 81.2 and placed in the "Free" category.

THE VALUE OF ECONOMIC FREEDOM

Economic freedom helps explain a country's development, performance, and potential. Higher-rated countries generally outperform laggards on a variety of measures. Countries with high economic freedom have higher rates of growth and productivity. Income is higher in countries with higher economic freedom; it more than

Economically free countries tend to have higher per capita income, standards of living, and social stability than do less-free or repressed countries.

MAP 4.2 Global Distribution of Economic Freedom

The Index of Economic Freedom classifies a country as either: *free, mostly free, moderately free, mostly unfree,* and *repressed* given the degree to which its government regulates individual's economic choices.

Source: Terry Miller and Kim Holmes, *2011 Index of Economic Freedom,* Washington, DC: The Heritage Foundation and Dow Jones & Co., Inc. 2011 (www.heritage.org, retrieved June 1, 2011). Reprinted by permission of The Heritage Foundation.

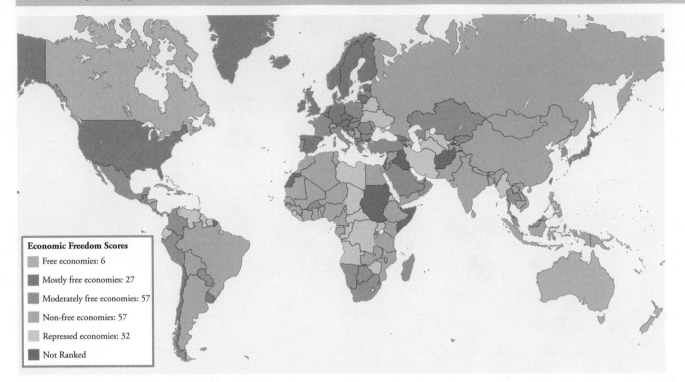

Economic Freedom Scores

- Free economies: 6
- Mostly free economies: 27
- Moderately free economies: 57
- Non-free economies: 57
- Repressed economies: 32
- Not Ranked

> The track record of free markets around the world indicates that economic freedom is positively related with financial prosperity, economic stability, and standards of living.

doubles the worldwide average and is seven times higher than in mostly unfree and repressed economies (see Figure 4.5). Positive relationships exist between economic freedom, inflation, and employment. Economic freedom pays social dividends. Life expectancy, literacy, political openness, and environmental sustainability show positive relationships with economic freedom. Collectively, the data indicate a positive relationship between economic freedom and various measures of economic performance and quality of life.[25] The data support the argument that liberating resources from government control improves financial performance, economic stability, and standards of living.

TRENDS IN ECONOMIC FREEDOM

For the past few decades, managers could reasonably presume that countries would adopt reforms that increased economic freedom. Free markets had consistently outperformed "not free" countries. Large and growing majorities believed that people's lives benefited from more, not less, economic freedom. The fall of the Berlin Wall in 1989, in signifying the triumph of capitalism over communism, symbolized the supremacy of economic freedom.

Increasingly, countries abandoned the policies of state control and adopted the principles of capitalism and the practices of economic freedom. Throughout the world, governments deferred to the laws of supply and demand—the invisible hand of the marketplace rather than the visible hand of politicians—to anchor the philosophy and regulate the practices of their economic environments.

FIGURE 4.5   Economic Freedom and Leading Economic Indicators

Economic Freedom has notable relationships with a variety of market, social, and political measures. Here we see that economically free countries, on average, have higher incomes, lower inflation, and lower unemployment.

Source: Adapted from data reported by the Heritage Foundation and the *Wall Street Journal, The 2011 Index of Economic Freedom,* at www.heritage.org (accessed June 6, 2011). Reprinted by permission of The Heritage Foundation.

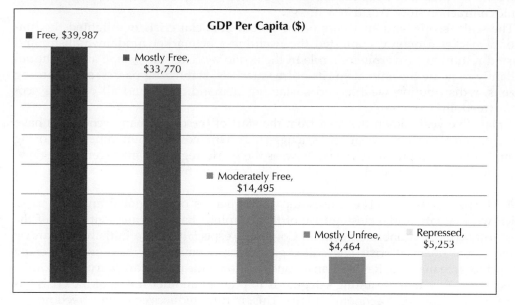

GDP Per Capita ($)

- Free, $39,987
- Mostly Free, $33,770
- Moderately Free, $14,495
- Mostly Unfree, $4,464
- Repressed, $5,253

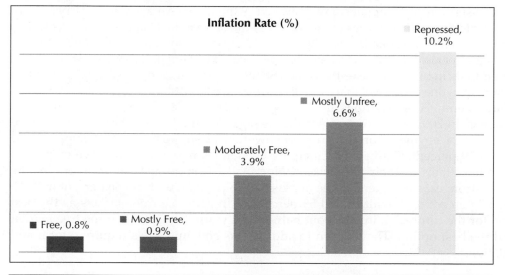

Inflation Rate (%)

- Repressed, 10.2%
- Mostly Unfree, 6.6%
- Moderately Free, 3.9%
- Free, 0.8%
- Mostly Free, 0.9%

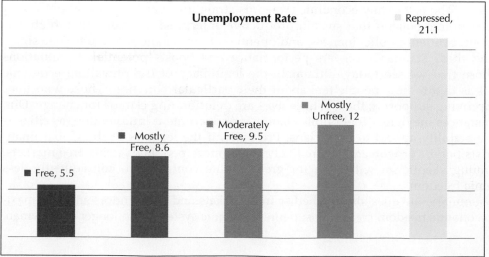

Unemployment Rate

- Repressed, 21.1
- Mostly Unfree, 12
- Moderately Free, 9.5
- Mostly Free, 8.6
- Free, 5.5

The global financial crisis, by spurring a resurgence of state intervention, has interrupted the decades-long march of economic freedom.

Changing marketplace conditions and unfolding political trends indicate that MNEs face increasingly uncertain economic times. The global financial crisis has disrupted the expansion of economic freedoms. Its immediate aftermath saw industrial production, exports, and equity valuations tracking or doing worse than during the Great Depression.[26] Stubborn downturns in many economies signaled the biggest global economic contraction since World War II.

The scale, scope, and swiftness of the global financial crisis highlighted the limits of a market economy, contested the usefulness of market fundamentalism, and spurred rethinking government's role in the economy. The state, some argue, should vigilantly regulate the animal spirits of free markets, stabilizing panics, safeguarding citizens, redistributing wealth, and sustaining demand. Each and all decrease economic freedom.

Today, five years down the road from the start of the crisis, many economies have stabilized. Still, sovereign debt crises, sluggish growth, costly commodities, and rising unemployment complicate recovery. Now, as the world regroups, managers struggle to pinpoint the implication of these trends to their economic freedom.

Fear of Freer Markets   The causes and consequences of the global financial crisis, which we evaluate in the closing case of this chapter, challenge the legitimacy of the quest to maximize economic freedom. Countries, especially those initially hit hardest by the global financial crisis and still experiencing anemic growth, show weakening support for free markets. Rather than an unconditional ideal, they are wary of maximizing economic freedom. Resulting safeguards to prevent another round of the crisis has increased state control of economic affairs. This, in turn, reduces economic freedom.

Dissatisfaction with capitalism prevails across the globe. An average of 11 percent of respondents across 27 countries reportedly held the opinion that capitalism works well.[27] Some 23 percent saw capitalism fatally flawed. Many called for a new economic system—including 43 percent in France, 38 percent in Mexico, 35 percent in Brazil, and 31 percent in Ukraine. Only in two countries—the United States (25 percent) and Pakistan (21 percent)—did more than one in five feel that capitalism works well as it stands.[28]

Case Review Note

Our opening case cautions qualifying attitudes in developed versus emerging economies. In 2002, 80 percent of Americans regarded the free market as the best economic system for the future—then the bellwether of support. By 2010, support had fallen to 59 percent. Conversely, emerging economies now match or have overtaken the United States in their enthusiasm. Nominally, Communist China is one of the world's strongest supporters of free markets, at 68 percent, up from 66 percent in 2002. Some 67 percent of Brazilians and 59 percent of Indians see free markets as the best option for the future. All in all, about half of the "world" reasons that the free market is still the best option. They hasten to add that its endemic flaws require reform and regulation.[29]

The Test   The test of any economic system is straightforward: It must apply sound macroeconomic policies that sustain productive enterprise. Low inflation, high employment, prudent public finances, and openness to trade and FDI are telltale signs. Meeting these standards powers performance and boosts potential. In situations like those that we see today, ultimately the legitimacy of the prevailing economic outlook is tied to how people feel about their particular situation. Those who lives are improving support it; those whose lives are deteriorating clamor for change. Dire circumstances inevitably fuel public clamor for government intervention, as citizens seeking stability appeal to politicians. Presently, if the legacies of the global financial crisis persist or worsen, we are likely to see more people question free markets. Continuing skepticism will push for greater state control and, consequently, less economic freedom.

In summary, the question of whether free markets and their endorsement of maximum economic freedom create the superior economic system is no longer a strawman.

The global financial crisis, besides disrupting markets, has disrupted interpretations.[30] In many countries, notably western markets, praise for the virtues of economic freedom has turned to criticism of its deficiencies. In others, notably emerging economies, the exact opposite takes place. Their evolution and interplay will alter the relationship between markets and governments.

Types of Economic Systems

Wherever they go, managers question how the host government might regulate the economy, authorize property rights, implement fiscal and monetary policies, and ultimately, interpret economic freedom. Managers often begin analysis by evaluating the **economic system** in a country. This leads them to investigate the structures and processes that guide resource allocation and business conduct. Three types of economic systems stand out: the *market, mixed*, and *command* economies (see Figure 4.6).

MARKET ECONOMY

A system whereby individuals, rather than the government, make most economic decisions is a **market economy**. It is anchored in the philosophy of **capitalism** and its principle that private ownership confers inalienable property rights that legitimize profits earned by one's initiative, investment, and risk. Optimal resource allocation follows from consumers exercising their freedom to choose and producers responding accordingly. A market economy of the sort seen in Hong Kong, Singapore, Australia, Switzerland, Canada, and the United States grants people the economic freedom to decide where to work, what to do and for how long, how to spend or save money, and whether to consume now or later.[31] Ultimately, individuals' free choice in a market economy powers a country's progress toward prosperity.

An economic system organizes the production, distribution, and consumption of goods and services.

Concept Check

Chapter 3 notes that the individual voter is the cornerstone of a democracy. Here we add that the individual, as a consumer, is the key factor in a free market. Whereas democracy recognizes the supremacy of voter sovereignty, the market economy recognizes the supremacy of consumer sovereignty.

Capitalism is based on the principle of private ownership of capital.

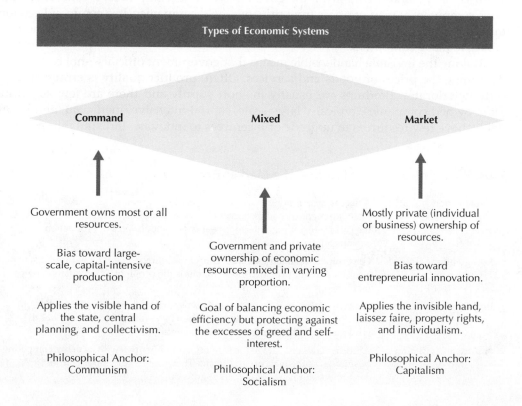

FIGURE 4.6 Types of Economic Systems

The three predominant types of economic systems rest on different principles, apply different approaches, and endorse different philosophies.

Laissez-faire refers to a policy of governmental noninterference in economic affairs.

The market economy champions the principle of **laissez-faire.** Literally translated, it suggests, "let do." More broadly, it advises "let it be" or "leave it alone." Whatever the translation, laissez-faire opposes government intervention in business affairs. Rather, it sees the "invisible hand" of self-interested consumers as the foundation of efficient activity. Consumers, through their interactions with producers, optimally determine relationships among price, quantity, supply, and demand. As Adam Smith observed, a market economy pushes producers, spurred by the profit motive, to make products that consumers, spurred by their need to maximize purchasing power, buy. Consequently, by virtue of what they do and do not buy, consumers direct the efficient allocation of resources and the optimal valuation of assets.

The invisible hand of a market economy, due to the need to provide public goods and protect society, is made visible by government involvement.

There is an enduring bias toward minimal government intervention in market economies. The more visible the "hand" becomes due to government intervention, the less efficiently the market works. Still, the invisible hand is not infallible. The need for public goods (e.g., traffic lights, national defense) and protections (e.g., minimum wage, financial regulation, environmental standards) that preempt those inclined to maximize personal gain at the expense of society's welfare requires some governmental involvement. Therefore, a market economy calls upon the state to enforce contracts, protect property rights, ensure fair and free competition, regulate certain sorts of economic activities, and provide general safety and security (see Table 4.2). Nevertheless, the anchor of the market economy remains the invisible hand of economically free agents driving growth and prosperity.

COMMAND ECONOMY

In a command economy, the visible hand of the state supersedes the invisible hand of individuals.

In theory, **communism** champions state ownership of resources and control of all economic activity. Although nominally a socioeconomic structure and political ideology, communism calls for an egalitarian, classless, and ultimately stateless society based on the government's command of the economy.[32] This reasoning results in a **command economy** in which the government owns and controls resources, commanding the authority to decide what products to make, in what quantity, at what price, and in what way. For example, in a market economy, if the government wants computers, it collects taxes and buys computers at market prices from privately-held companies. In a command economy, the visible hand of the government, with little regard for price, orders state-owned companies to make computers.[33]

Making the invisible hand visible means that government officials—not consumers—determine the prices of goods and services. Often, product quality is erratic and typically deteriorates. Products are usually in short supply and there are few substitutes. State-owned companies, typically large-scale, capital-intensive, inefficient, and unprofitable, have few resources to upgrade or incentives to innovate. Indisputably, command

TABLE 4.2   Means and Methods of a Market Economy

Privatization	A necessary condition of a market economy is the state's sale and legal transfer of government-owned resources to private interests. Privatization, by letting the private sector regulate supply and demand, improves production and consumption decisions.
Deregulation	Government regulations reduce individual choice—i.e., "Government is not a solution to our problem. Government is the problem." Deregulation helps markets optimize productivity.
Property Rights	Property rights give entrepreneurs ownership of their idea, effort, and risk. Protection boosts economic freedom by assuring individuals, not the government, will prosper from their ingenuity.
Antitrust Legislation	Antitrust laws encourage the formation of industries with as many competing businesses as the market can sustain. They prevent monopolies from exploiting consumers and restraining market growth.

economies can perform well for short periods. Controlling everything and everybody lets the state mobilize idle resources, usually labor, to generate growth spurts. High productivity continues as long as the state can utilize idle resources. Above all, the bias toward political stability and social control suppresses economic freedom.

Command economies have included the Soviet Union (which was for a time the world's second-largest economy), China during its Great Leap Forward era beginning in 1958, India prior to its economic reforms in 1991, and Afghanistan during the rule by Soviet occupation and the Taliban. Today, we see few pure examples, notably Cuba, Iran, North Korea, and Burma. More often, managers operate in economies that exhibit many but not all methods of state control. These sorts, such as Iran, Venezuela, Turkmenistan, Belarus, Zimbabwe, Ethiopia, Vietnam, Russia, and China, fall in the "mostly unfree" and "repressed" categories of the Economic Freedom Index.

MIXED ECONOMY

Most economies, broadly labeled **mixed economies,** fall between the market and command economies. A mixed economy is a system in which economic decisions are principally market-driven and ownership is largely private, but the government intervenes, from slightly to extensive, in allocating resources. For example, U.S. President Obama reasoned that it is the government's responsibility to make "strategic decisions about strategic industries."[34]

The mixed economy integrates elements of the command and market systems. Regarding the former, the state intermingles ownership of some resources, centralizes economic planning, and extensively regulates the market. Regarding the latter, the interaction of supply and demand, signaled to producers through the price system, determines production.[35] For example, the government may own companies that manufacture computers. Rather than instructing the state-owned firm how many computers to make, the government permits market forces to influence quantity.

A country's adoption of the socialist philosophy explains its decision to forsake the market or command economy. **Socialism** advocates regulating economic activity with an eye toward social equality and fair distribution of wealth. It utilizes the market to allocate resources, as does capitalism, but it subjects investment to social control largely directed by the government, as does communism. Socialism holds that a fair and just economy, besides optimizing efficiencies, also defends the weak by supporting low unemployment, prevents the consolidation of wealth and power, helps the impoverished by fairly distributing income, stabilizes the system by responding to market failures, and protects society by limiting abuses of market power. This mandate requires a country to achieve the efficiencies, productivity, and innovativeness found in free markets yet grants the state the authority to prevent individualism from harming the welfare of society. Governments, as opposed to the market, are presumed to far more conscientiously instill an egalitarian ethos into the economy.

The aftermath of the global financial crisis supported many of these principles. Countries that favored a strong state presence, higher taxes, heavier regulation, tougher job-protection laws, and generous social safety programs better navigated the economic upheaval than had their free market counterparts.[36] As the free market British economy cratered, France's mixed economy perservered. As the economically free United States regrouped and wondered what next, the socialism of Denmark supported its steady economic performance and citizens' status as the happiest people in the world.[37]

Advocates of the mixed economy do not unconditionally endorse state intervention as a panacea. Political agendas, the slate of officials, and social circumstances shape how the government balances economic freedom and state control.[38] Hence, the extent and nature of government intervention differs from country to country. At present, countries commonly classified as mixed economies include South Africa, Japan, South Korea,

A mixed economic system combines elements of the market and command economic systems; both government and private enterprise influence production, consumption, investment, and savings.

A market economy is anchored in capitalism, a command economy is anchored in communism, and a mixed economy is anchored in socialism.

Sweden, Austria, France, Brazil, Germany, and India. They typically fall in the "mostly" and "moderately" free categories of the Economic Freedom Index.

Looking to the

Future   Is State Capitalism a Detour or Destination?

Managers question, will free markets prevail, protecting hard-won economic freedoms? Or, will governments reclaim the commanding heights of the economy, taking control of development, regulating performance, and determining potential? For decades, economies had steadily adopted the free market model given the success of countries that had migrated from command and mixed to market economies. However, the global financial crisis has thrown markets into disarray. Now, buffeted by the meltdown, we see countries enforcing greater state control of the economy.

So, managers watch and wait as the contest between the siren call of free markets and the surge of state power determine the sort of economy that works best in the modern world. As they do, many reflect on a perplexing feature of the economic environment. Notwithstanding its dividends, so few countries maximize economic freedom. Map 4.2 shows that 6 of 183 countries have free economies while another 27 are mostly free. Put differently, 33 countries, or 18 percent of all, grant individuals substantial economic freedom. The rest do not. Some of these have a command economy—notably, North Korea and Cuba. Most, like China, Russia, United Arab Emirates, Mexico, Venezuela, and Saudi Arabia, practice State Capitalism.

State Capitalism

State capitalism is an economic system whereby the state decides how, when, and where assets will be valued and resources allocated.[39] The state develops national champions, manages trade relations and exchange rates to promote exports and discourage imports, leverages control of the financial system to provide low-cost capital to domestic industries, and runs pro-business legal and regulatory systems. Recall our earlier profile of GCL-Poly Energy of China. Zhu Gongshan, the owner, relied on quick approvals, cheap government loans, and state support to build a world-class company in 15 months. China's disruption of the solar power industry prompted many firms to shut down; some, such as Evergreen Solar, relocated to China.

Some may contend that state capitalism sounds a lot like a mixed or command economy. In some ways it is. But, in others, it is not. Foremost, state capitalism is a system whereby the government explicitly manipulates market outcomes for political purposes. Politics has a profound and pervasive impact on the performance of markets. The government uses markets to promote stability and growth, thereby creating the prosperity and wealth that maximize state power and supports its continued rule. State capitalism does not have an ideological component—the government manages markets for long-term political survival and power projection, not to enforce an abstract ideal or promote the cult of personality. Instead of politicized revolutionaries promising a brighter future, state capitalism relies upon pragmatic technocrats whose goal is developing a world-class economy that reinforces the power of the typically one-party state.

Visible as Needed

Moreover, the invisible hand is visible—but only when necessary. Under normal circumstances, the state stays in the shadows, influencing activities and shaping outcomes. In the event plans go awry, the state steps in, revises policies, resets funding, and redirects activities. National, provincial, and local officials control resources to fund investments, shape operations, and direct market development.

The government promotes the growth of particular industrial sectors and companies in order to speed economic development. The state attracts innovative foreign companies, using state-owned banks to provide cheap loans, favorable regulations, and stable industry settings. Bolstering its developing solar power industry, for example, led China to recruit Evergreen Solar, a technology-rich U.S. company.

Who Owns Whom

For the most part, the state owns its national champions. For instance, China is the majority owner of 99 of the 100 largest publicly listed Chinese companies, including all major banks, its three major oil companies, its three telecom carriers, and its major media firms. Collectively, 129 huge conglomerates in finance, media, mining, metals, transportation, communication, and so on answer directly to the Chinese central government.[40]

Furthermore, China's provinces and cities run thousands of medium-sized and smaller ones. At all levels, "the tentacles of state-owned enterprises extend into every nook where profits can be made."[41]

Telltale Marks

State capitalist economies, whether in the Middle East, Asia, Eastern Europe, or South America, have telltale marks. Public investment, public wealth, and public enterprise prevail. Officials fan economic nationalism. The state promotes domestic markets as sanctuaries for national champions. No matter the question, the state favors local companies at the expense of their foreign competitors. Its goal is developing national companies into global leaders. State capitalism has little need for an independent judiciary; the state typically treats the legal system as an apparatus that legitimates, as needed, its policies. The state games the system, capturing competitive advantages through whatever means necessary. Officials install barriers to trade and investment in order to generate local development and prosperity. Regulations restrict foreign companies from entering strategic industries.

Gaining Momentum

The global financial crisis has expanded the scale and scope of state capitalism. Countries that favored a larger state presence, higher taxes, heavier regulation, tougher job-protection laws, and more generous social safety programs dealt more successfully with market disruptions than did their free-market counterparts.

State capitalism professes to better protect social values, equalize income distribution, and prevent the accumulation of vast wealth and powerful self-interests that threaten social harmony. Allowed to run free, market economies encourage the psychology that greed is good. Only a strong state, goes the reasoning, stops it from devolving into psychosis.[42]

Presently, some 70 strategically important countries worldwide are at a critical crossroads in determining their political and economic future.[43] Whether they advocate economic freedom or state capitalism remains to be seen. Many see China as the bellwether; where it goes, both good and bad, many will follow. Over the past 32 years, the Chinese renaissance has shown that Western-style economics is no longer the only viable route to modernization.[44] China has used state capitalism to develop and direct the world's fastest growing economy that has powered the swiftest, most extensive rise out of poverty any nation has ever seen. It relative success, not just surviving but prospering during the great financial crisis, further "persuaded the Chinese leadership that state control of much of the country's economic development is the steadiest path toward prosperity—and, therefore, domestic tranquility."[45]

Given economic circumstances in the world today, one should not be surprised if others, particularly authoritarian, one-party political systems, find state capitalism attractive. Arcing though Asia, the Middle East, Africa, and Latin America, authoritarian governments emulate China's model of state capitalism.[46] Democracy's retreat, covered in Chapter 3, along with the surging success of state capitalism, helps explain why 80 percent of the countries in the world are moderately free, mostly unfree, or repressed in terms of economic freedom. ∎

Measuring Economic Development, Performance, and Potential

Managers use various measures to assess a country's economic development, performance, and potential. They also monitor indicators of the direction and dynamic of transition from one type of economic system to another. Some measures may be informal or idiosyncratic: i.e., number of wireless subscriptions, amount of electrical power generated, internet searches for telltale terms, or military officers running companies.[47] Typically, convention dominates practice. Matters of income and wealth often anchor analysis. Managers elaborate their analyses with indicators of sustainability and stability.

Before reviewing each, a brief note regarding how we classify countries is in order. We follow the World Bank's lead in labeling low- and middle-income nations as *developing countries*. This type has low per capita income—an average of $2,963 in 2009. The vast majority of their citizens have a low standard of living with limited access to few goods and services. Developing countries comprise the largest number of countries (151 or so, according to the World Bank) and have the highest number of inhabitants (a combined 5.5 billion) in the world.

Broad classes of countries include

- Developing countries.
- Emerging economies.
- Developed countries.

TABLE 4.3   The Emerging Economy Alphabet

Commonly, one comes across terms that describes various sets of emerging economies. As different countries develop, observers have coined a variety of shorthand codes.	
Acronym	**Members**
BRIC	B for Brazil, R for Russia, I for India, C for China
BRICS	Add S for South Africa
BRICK	Adds K for South Korea
BRIIC	Adds I for Indonesia
BRICIT	Adds I for Indonesia, T for Turkey
BRIMC	Adds M for Mexico
BRICET	Adds E for Eastern Europe, T for Turkey
BRICA	Adds A for Arab countries—Saudi Arabia, Qatar, Kuwait, Bahrain, Oman, and the United Arab Emirates
N-11 (The Next 11)	Bangladesh, Egypt, Indonesia, Iran, Mexico, Nigeria, Pakistan, Philippines, South Korea, Turkey, and Vietnam
CIVETS	C for Colombia, I for Indonesia, V for Vietnam, E for Egypt, T for Turkey, S for South Africa

The faster growing, relatively prosperous developing countries such as China, Brazil, and India are referred to as *emerging markets* or *emerging economies*. Currently, there are approximately 30 or so **emerging economies** in the world (see Map 4.1). Table 4.3 lists some of the acronym used to sort them. Notwithstanding the variability, the core group consistently includes Brazil, Russia, India, and China. Typically, when one speaks of the emerging economies, one speaks principally of the **BRICs.** Although much larger in scale and scope than other emerging economies, the BRICs are the vanguard of change. Many presume that where the BRICs go, both good and bad, others will follow.

In contrast, *developed countries* are those with high per capita income—an average of $37,970 in 2009. Their citizens have a high standard of living with access to a variety of goods and services. Developed countries include Japan, Australia, New Zealand, Canada, the United States, and many in Western Europe. Less commonly, these countries are called high-income countries, advanced markets, or industrial countries. In the future, we may see the United States and similar countries called established market economies (EMEs), given their high per capita income, high standard of living, and sophisticated institutional framework but comparatively slower growth.

Concept Check

In discussing "Growing Consumer Pressures" among the drivers of globalization, Chapter 1 notes that worldwide consumption grew sixfold in the second half of the twentieth century. Such information improves managers' investment choices and operating decisions.

Gross National Income

GNI is the broadest measure of economic activity for a country.

Gross national income (GNI) is the broadest measure of a country's economy. It measures the value of all production in the domestic economy together with the income that the country receives from other countries (mainly interest and dividends), less similar payments it has made to other countries. Thus, the value of, say, a Samsung TV built in South Korea as well as the portion of the value of a Samsung TV made in Japan using Samsung's resources is counted in South Korea's GNI. Similarly, the portion of the value of a Sony TV built in South Korea using Sony's resources counts in the GNI of Japan. Last, if Samsung's Japanese subsidiary repatriates profits to headquarters in Seoul, it increases South Korea's GNI. Table 4.4 identifies the 15 largest economies in the world in terms of GNI.

GNP is the total value of all final goods and services produced within a nation in a particular year.

Gross national product (GNP) is the value of all final goods and services produced within a nation in a given year, plus the income earned by its citizens abroad, minus the income earned by foreigners from domestic production. Conceptually, world GNP and world GNI are equal. However, their slightly different calculation can result in small discrepancy at the country level.[48] Consequently, managers crosscheck their analyses, noting the assumptions of the measure and characteristics of a particular country.

TABLE 4.4   The 15 Largest Economies by GNI, 2009

Rank	Country	GNI (US$, billions)[i]
1	United States	14,233
2	Japan	4,857
3	China	4,856
4	Germany	3,476
5	France	2,750
6	United Kingdom	2,558
7	Italy	2,114
8	Brazil	1,557
9	Spain	1,476
10	Canada	1,416
11	India	1,367
12	Russian Federation	1,324
13	Korea, Rep.	966
14	Mexico	962
15	Australia	957
**	World	$59,132

[i]Data calculated with the *Atlas Method*, which smoothes exchange rate fluctuations by applying a three-year moving average, price-adjusted conversion.

Source: Based on World Bank Development Indicators 2009. Copyright 2011 by the World Bank. Reproduced with permission of the World Bank.

GROSS DOMESTIC PRODUCT

The total value of all goods and services produced within a nation's borders, no matter whether domestic or foreign-owned companies make the product, is reported as the *gross domestic product* (GDP).[49] It helps assess countries in which the output of the multinational sector is a significant share of activity. For example, almost 90 percent of Irish exports are made by foreign-owned firms; GDP, not GNI, more accurately measure its performance. Technically, GDP plus the income generated from exports, imports, and the international operations of a nation's companies equals GNI. Therefore, both Samsung and Sony TVs made in South Korea contribute to South Korea's GDP, but TVs made in Japan by Samsung do not.

> GDP is the total market values of goods and services produced by workers and capital within a nation's borders.

IMPROVING ANALYSIS

GNI and its offshoots estimate an economy's absolute performance. They can mislead managers when comparing countries. For example, economic powers like the United States, Japan, and Germany consistently claim the top rankings when sorted by GNI. Some may mistakenly presume that they are also more productive and faster growing than lower-ranked countries. Often, the opposite is true. Managers improve GNI's usefulness by adjusting it for the rate of economic growth, size of the population, and purchasing power of the local currency.

> Managers improve the usefulness of GNI by adjusting it for the
> - Growth rate of the economy.
> - Number of people in a country.
> - Local cost of living.

Rate of Economic Growth   Gross figures are a snapshot of one year. They do not measure the rate of change in an indicator. Interpreting present and forecasting future performance requires pinpointing an economy's growth rate. Looking at countries in terms of their growth rate shows a wide range. For example, between 2000 and 2008, China grew more than 11 percent per annum. Meanwhile, Japan averaged 1.2 percent growth over the same span. Figure 4.7 reports the real GDP growth rates for various developed and developing economies.[50]

Case Review Note

FIGURE 4.7   GDP: Real Growth Rates for Select Countries, 2010

Nominal GDP increases from year to year partly because a country produces more goods and services and partly because of increasing prices. Real GDP strips out price effects in order to estimate the annual growth in the actual production of goods and services. This conversion shows that many developing countries are growing faster than developed countries.

Source: Compiled from the Central Intelligence Agency, *The World Factbook*, at www.cia.gov

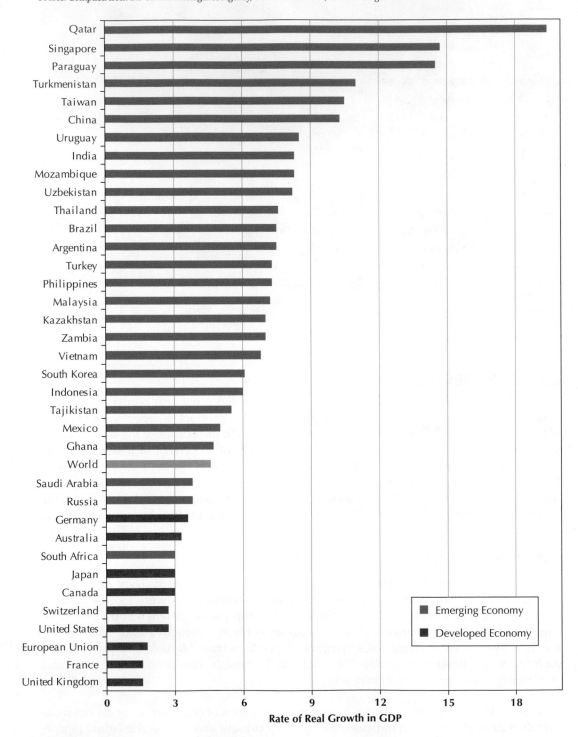

The growth rate of GNI indicates a country's economic potential: If it grows faster (or *slower*) than its population, the country's standards of living are rising (or *falling*).[51] It also indicates business opportunities. For example, China has been one of the fastest growing economies over the past 30 years, averaging double-digit growth for many. It has seen the swiftest, most extensive rise out of poverty in history. Commensurately,

China's GNI has gone from $1.68 trillion in 2000 to $5.700 trillion in 2010. Rising income has fueled consumer demand, thereby attracting foreign investment.

CRN
Case Review Note

Population Size Managers adjust GNI, like many other economic indicators, by the number of people who live in a country.[52] This conversion is common sense, given how unevenly the world's population of 6,967,367,182, as of October, 2011, is distributed across countries; e.g., from a high of 1.34 billion in China to the low of 50 in the Pitcairn Island. Adjusting GNI by population, therefore, measures a country's relative performance.

For example, GNI may be low in absolute terms, such as is the case for Monaco whose 33,000 citizens put it among the smaller economies of the world. However, Monaco ranked first in the world by GNI per capita in 2009, with a value of $203,900. In comparison, the United States ranked 18th ($46,360), Japan 32nd ($38,080), Brazil 84th ($8,040), China 125th (3,650), and India 154th ($1,180). GNI per capita was $9,097 in 2010 up from $7,995 in 2007, $7,011 in 2005 and $5,500 in 2003.[53]

Map 4.3 shows that high-income countries are clustered in a few regions of the world. They account for about 15 percent of world population but more than 70 percent of global GNI. On average, they report an average GNI per capita in the mid-tens of thousands ($). Lower-income countries are spread throughout the world. They comprise a large share of world population, but have a small share of the world's GNI. They report GNI per capita from the mid-hundreds to low thousands ($).

Purchasing Power Parity The calculation of GNI per capita does not account for the cost of living from one country to another. Instead, it presumes that a dollar of income in Minneapolis has the same purchasing power as a dollar of income in Mumbai, even though the cost of living differs between the United States and India. Consequently, GNI

MAP 4.3 GNI Per Capita, 2009

GNI per capita measures a country's performance in terms of its population. A country's GNI performance can change significantly when we control for the size of its population. For instance, China is the world's second largest economy according to GNI. It ranks in the lower-middle income tier for GNI per capita given its immense population.

Source: Based on data Gross National Income Per Capita 2010, Atlas Method and PPP <http://siteresources.worldbank.org/DATASTATISTICS/Resources/GNIPC.pdf> reported at (1) http://www.nationsonline.org/oneworld/GNI_PPP_of_countries.htm and (2) https://secure.wikimedia.org/wikipedia/en/wiki/List_of_countries_by_GNI_%28nominal,_Atlas_method%29_per_capita

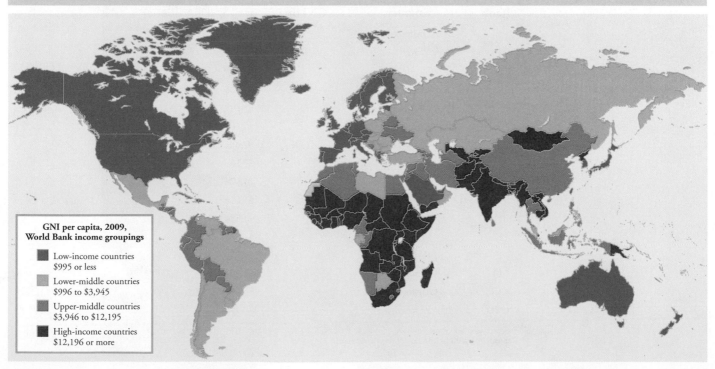

GNI per capita, 2009,
World Bank income groupings

- Low-income countries
  $995 or less
- Lower-middle countries
  $996 to $3,945
- Upper-middle countries
  $3,946 to $12,195
- High-income countries
  $12,196 or more

PPP provides a method of measuring the relative purchasing power of different countries' currencies for the same basket of goods and services.

per capita is unable to tell us much about how many goods and services one can buy with a unit of income in one country relative to how much one can buy with a unit of income in another. Therefore, managers adjust GNI in terms of **purchasing power parity (PPP)**, specifically the number of units of a country's currency required to buy the same amount of goods and services in the domestic market that one unit of income would buy in the other country. Basically, it lets us determine how much "stuff" a dollar will buy in another country.

We calculate PPP between countries by estimating the value of a universal "basket" of goods (e.g., soap and bread) and services (e.g., telephone and electricity) that can be purchased with one unit of a country's currency. For example, a loaf of bread that sells for 49.16 rupees in India should cost U.S. $1.00 in the United States given an exchange rate between India and the United States of 49.16 INR to U.S. $1.[54]

Table 4.5 shows the impact of adjusting a country's performance for PPP. Notably, the raw country rankings by GNI reported in Table 4.4 change. China, India, Russia, Mexico, and Canada, for instance, move up. Japan, the United Kingdom, France, and Italy drop down. Second, PPP reduces some of the otherwise extreme variability in many country-to-country comparisons. Revisiting our comparison of the United States and India finds that India's GNI per capita in 2009 is $1,180 but rises to $3,250 when adjusted for local purchasing power.[55] The opposite occurs in the case of countries with expensive standards of living, such as Monaco. Its GNI per capita falls from $203,900 to $131,694 when adjusted for the reduced purchasing power a unit of currency has in high-priced Monaco. Map 4.4 profiles the countries of the world in terms of GNI per capita adjusted for PPP.[56]

BROADER CONCEPTIONS OF PERFORMANCE AND POTENTIAL

Measures of gross national income emphasize monetary aggregates. As a result, GNI, GNP, and GDP, including adjustments for growth, population size, and cost of living, partially profile a country's performance and potential. Managers enrich assessment by estimating an economy's sustainability and stability.

TABLE 4.5   The 15 Largest Economies, 2009: GNI Adjusted for PPP

Rank	Country	GNI by PPP (U.S. $, 000 trillions)
1	United States	$14,011
2	China	$9,170
3	Japan	$4,269
4	India	$3,758
5	Germany	$3,011
6	Russian Federation	$2,603
7	United Kingdom	$2,302
8	France	$2,189
9	Brazil	$1,976
10	Italy	$1,888
11	Mexico	$1,514
12	Spain	$1,464
13	Korea, Rep.	$1,331
14	Canada	$1,262
15	Turkey	$1,025
**	World	$71,845

Source: Based on World Bank Development Indicators 2009. Copyright 2011 by the World Bank. Reproduced with permission of the World Bank.

MAP 4.4 GNI per Capital Adjusted for Purchasing Power Parity

Adjusting raw income data for purchasing power parity essentially creates an international dollar that has the same purchasing power as a dollar has in the United States. It lets managers compare economic differences between nations by taking into account the relative cost of living. And, as international travelers well know, costs can vary dramatically from country to country.

Source: Based on World Development Indicators database, World Bank, May 1, 2011.

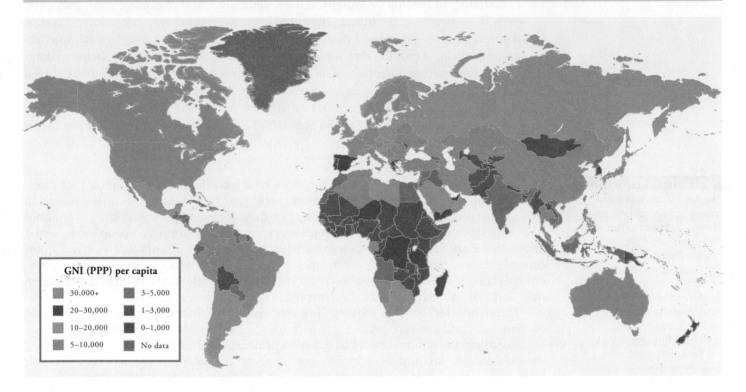

GNI (PPP) per capita

- 30,000+
- 20–30,000
- 10–20,000
- 5–10,000
- 3–5,000
- 1–3,000
- 0–1,000
- No data

Sustainability Concern for the ecological welfare of the world spurs calls for green measures of growth that look beyond narrow measures of monetary aggregates. **Green economics** holds that each country is a component of, and dependent on, the natural world. Measuring the monetary quantity of market activity without accounting for the associated social and ecological costs misrepresents performance.

Consequently, narrow indicators, notably GNI, GNP, and GDP, only partially represent current performance and long-term potential. Furthermore, **sustainable development** calls for economic activity that "meets the needs of the present without compromising the ability of future generations to meet their own needs."[57] As such, it endorses a broader accounting of the gains and costs of growth to better gauge an economy.

Presently, there is no consensus on how to 'greenify' GNI, GNP, or GDP for sustainability concerns. Current candidates include:

- *Net National Product (NNP):* Calls for measuring the depletion of natural resources and degradation of the environment that results from generating GNI. As a company must depreciate its tangible and intangible assets when making a product, goes this reasoning, so too should countries. NNP does so by depreciating the country's assets commensurate with their use to generate growth.[58]

- *Genuine Progress Indicator (GPI):* Starts with the same accounting framework used to calculate GDP but then adjusts for values assigned to environmental quality, population health, livelihood security, equity, free time, and educational attainment. For example, unlike GDP, GPI values unpaid voluntary and household work as paid work and subtracts the costs of crime, pollution, and family breakdown. Effectively, GDP

> Green measures gauge economic performance in terms of the effect of current choices on long-term sustainability.

> Sustainability and stability perspectives hold that the objective of economic activity is to create an enabling environment for people to enjoy long, healthy, and happy lives.

versus GPI is analogous to the difference between the gross profits versus net profits of a company—net is gross less the costs incurred. Accordingly, GPI will be zero if the costs of pollution, crime, and family breakdown, holding all other factors constant, equal the monetary gains from the production of goods and services.

- *Human Development Index (HDI)* Matters of human development do not show up immediately in income or growth figures. Ultimately, the reasoning goes, they will, given that improving the human condition improves economic performance. So, estimating a country's degree of human development, in terms of the physical, intellectual, and social standards that shape a country's overall quality of life, helps managers measure market potential.[59] The United Nations translates this view into the HDI and its components, *Longevity,* as measured by life expectancy at birth, *Knowledge,* as measured by the adult literacy rate and the combined primary, secondary, and tertiary gross enrollment ratio, and *Standard of living,* as measured by GNI per capita expressed in PPP for U.S. dollars.

Concept Check

Chapter 1 notes that some groups oppose globalization, Chapter 2 discussed cultural objections, and Chapter 3 identified political reasons that inspire opposition. Here, we add that critics charge overly emphasizing monetary measures misrepresents economic performance. Understanding grows growth, progress, and prosperity fully, demands considering sustainability and stability.

An ongoing paradox is that people in rich countries are not significantly happier than people in poor countries.

Stability　For several decades, policymakers have puzzled over a paradox that questions the validity of monetary aggregates as performance measures.[60] Namely, people in rich countries do not appear to be any happier than people in poor countries. No matter how high income rose, there has been little evidence that it improved peoples' reported happiness. Furthermore, the emerging science of happiness reports that nearly 70 percent of personal satisfaction is determined by the quantity and quality of relationships, not by economic output or wealth creation.[61] Consequently, there is growing criticism that GNI and its offshoots are at best, misleading, and at worst, flawed.[62]

"Happynomics" calls for moving "from the concept of financial prosperity to the idea of emotional prosperity."[63] Assessing a country's performance and potential depends on measuring the national well-being beyond financial performance. Rather, evaluation should take into account the happiness of a society and peoples' satisfaction with their lives. For example, rated by monetary measures, the United States is far in front of France and Germany. Accounting for life expectancy, leisure time, and income equality, however, makes living standards in France and Germany about the same as those in the United States.[64] Granted, some may say worrying about happiness unnecessarily confuses economic analysis. However, an unhappy citizenry may be a leading indicator of change in government policy that alters the economic environment.

Presently, estimation is difficult. Defining happiness, like beauty, is often in the eye of the beholder. Potential items, such as love, friendship, family relations, and actualization, are tough to pin down. In addition, how does one value indicators, like safe streets and clean air, which can be measured? The intricacies of happiness capture increasing attention; insight should clarify measures. In the meantime, managers can consider:

- *Gross National Happiness (GNH):* Progressive society presumes material and spiritual development occur side by side; one must reinforce the other or both suffer. GNH measures a country's ability to promote equitable and sustainable socioeconomic development, preserving and promoting cultural values, conserving the natural environment, and establishing good governance.
- *Happy Planet Index (HPI):* Reflects the utilitarian view that most people wish to live long, healthy, happy lives. Therefore, a country's economic performance and potential is represented by how well it helps its citizens do so while not infringing on the opportunity of future generations, and people in other countries, to do the same. The HPI advocates measuring the environmental costs of growth while emphasizing that maximizing happiness and health, not monetary wealth, is the objective.
- *Your Better Life Index (YBLI)* This index measures well-being and perceptions of living conditions by evaluating 11 areas: housing, incomes, employment, social

FIGURE 4.8

Source: Edward Koren/Cartoon Bank

"I totally agree with you about capitalism, neo-colonialism, and globalization, but you really come down too hard on shopping."

relationships, education, the environment, the administration of institutions, health, general satisfaction, security, and the balance between work and family. Developed by the Organization for Economic Cooperation and Development (OECD), it advocates evaluating economic performance in terms of matters that people worldwide believe are important but that fall beyond the narrow scope of monetary measures. Explained the OECD, YBLI pushes the "boundaries of knowledge and understanding in a pioneering and innovative manner....It has extraordinary potential to help us deliver better policies for better lives."[65] Incidentally, YBLI indicates that the 10 happiest countries in the world, beginning with the leader, are Denmark, Canada, Norway, Australia, the Netherlands, Sweden, Switzerland, Finland, Israel, and Austria.[66]

Point ▷ **Is Growth Good?**

Point

Yes Growth is not only good, it is a fundamental necessity. Growth is life, creating the basis for individuals, communities, institutions, and society. Growth provides long-term benefits to everyone in every country. It morally stabilizes society. It liberates those trapped in poverty. It reduces violent conflict. It raises living standards. It funds safety nets and government backstops. It creates material improvements that comfort life. It creates jobs, income, wealth, and prosperity for individuals and society. Let's take a closer look each.

Moral Stability Growth affects social attitudes and political institutions, the keystone to the moral stability of society. People experiencing rising incomes and improving economies are commensurately tolerant of and benevolent toward each other. In a word, wealth engenders humanity. Growth creates the resources that promote transparency of authority, openness of opportunity, tolerance of diversity,

pathways of social mobility, fair and just laws, and virtues of democracy.

Poverty Reduction Notwithstanding the kindness of strangers, growth is the only means to alleviate poverty for the billions struggling to sustain life. Growth in many impoverished countries has reduced the number of people living in abject poverty. In 1990, 34 percent of the global population survived on less than $1 a day. By 2008, freer markets had fueled economic growth, reducing it to 22 percent of the world—about 1.6 billion people. Without growth, humanity loses the war against poverty. Billions, presuming they survive, suffer physically and psychologically.

Business Dividend Growth stimulates higher employment, capital investment, and profits. Rising asset valuations, stabilizing wealth effects, and resolute confidence in surviving tough times supports the prosperity of individuals and companies. Moreover, amidst the panic of the recent global crisis, people endorsed the virtue of growth. Some 76 percent of Americans agreed that U.S. strength is "mostly based on the success of American business" and that 90 percent admired people who "get rich by working hard."[67]

Fiscal Dividend   Government finances are ultimately at the mercy of growth. A thriving economy boosts tax revenues, thereby providing local, state, regional, and national governments the monies to finance spending projects that support, enrich, and sustain society. Although appealing, history shows cheap government does not translate into good government.

Peace Dividend   Growth creates more opportunities for more people in more places. People who see the potential for prosperity behave peacefully. Moving poor people into the middle class, for example, enables them to think and behave differently. Free from the tyranny of ceaselessly seeking sustenance and shelter, they become more open-minded, more concerned about their children's future, more influenced by abstract values than traditional norms, more inclined to settle conflicts peacefully, more supportive of free markets and democracy, and more inclined to have faith in the future.

Environmental Benefits   Growth encourages innovations. People specialize in what they do best and, courtesy of pro-growth policies, outsource the rest. Together, these drive

the efficient allocation of resources. The falling ratio of energy consumption per unit of GDP over the past 40 years, in the face of the growing abundance of goods and services, testifies to the benefits of growth. By making resources valuable, growth spurs us to consume them wisely.

Quest to Excel   Growth incents people to bring to bear their ingenuity, their imagination, and their industriousness to find a better way, every day, to make a difference. Pushing back the frontier of human experience—whether it involves the trivial (e.g., forms of entertainment) or the substantive (e.g., alternative energy)—is powered by the quest to grow. Eliminating the pursuit of progress leaves society stuck in sloth.

Life   Growth supports longer lives. In 1900, life expectancy at birth was 47 years in the United States. By 2011, after a century of growth, it was 78.4 years. Moreover, people now need work just half the time they once had to, relying on new tools to boost productivity, finding comfort in the rising quality-of-life standards, and taking solace in improving health care.

Progress or Decline   Unquestionably, as the Counterpoint argues, growth imposes costs on individuals, humanity, and the planet. Moreover, we fully agree that these costs are striking. Still, our position is crystal clear: No matter the costs of growth, they pale in comparison to the unacceptable price of not growing. Put bluntly, when growth stops, decay starts.

Is Growth Good?

Counterpoint ◀ **Counterpoint**

Counterpoint   **No** We accept the premise that growth supports life, fostering morality, transparency, tolerance, mobility, justice, and liberty. However, ignoring or worse, denying, the costs of these benefits—costs that seem to grow faster than growth itself—imperils civil society and, ultimately, the survival of humanity and the planet. Once you untangle the strands of half-truths, falsehoods, and self-interests that lace insidious pro-growth arguments, the promise of endless milk and honey for all devolves into a bitter delusion. The problems of growth span the immediate and the future. Where one stops and the other starts is tough to pinpoint. Still, as this list shows, each hits society hard.

Growth Privileges Few   The defining benefit of growth is that "a rising tide lifts all boats." In theory, as an economy grows, it generates higher wages, income, and wealth for all. In reality, the benefits of growth are unevenly distributed, creating extreme inequalities of income, wealth, and power. We agree that over the long run, increasing growth has lifted

the tide. However, a share of the global population has seen their patchwork-rafts capsize, many struggle to keep their leaky boats afloat, and a minute fraction upgraded their yachts.

Growth Is Misleading   Despite the hype and hoopla, growth does not deliver the benefits it promises. It rewards the financially strong but punishes the economically weak. It liberates people from old routines but enslaves them to new habits. It creates free time to spend with family and community but then demands mobility and migration that fracture groups. It promises newer, cooler products to enable self-fulfillment but then restarts a never-ending cycle of hope and deception. In a phrase, economic growth oversells and underdelivers, condemning people to "spiritual despair scarcely concealed by the frantic pace of life."[68] People, trapped on hedonic treadmills in the quest for newer, shinier, better, bigger, faster, or fancier, confuse consumption of the latest and greatest as the path toward actualization. In actuality, the destination is alienation.

Growth Threatens Life Polluted air, poisoned water, and toxic land—let alone global warming, biodiversity collapse, and resource depletion—are the by-products of growth. Granted, we need some production and consumption; however, overproduction and overconsumption destabilize the basis for life. Ironically, when we measure the value created by an economy—say, in GNI—no costs are tallied. Rather, they are mysteriously called "externalities," understood to impact society but conveniently excluded while we sing praise of the wondrous "benefits" of growth. Effectively, since "nobody" is responsible for the costs of externalities, "nobody" pays for them, and the growth engine chugs merrily along. Ultimately, "everybody" pays with a despoiled environment, warped society, and financial servitude.

Growth Destroys Individuality Growth's mandate to optimize efficiency requires massification—mass production, mass consumption, mass distribution, mass markets, mass media, and so on. Massification delivers great benefits, but at high cost. Noted one observer, "a part of the price that people in the West pay for this unending procession of shiny assembly-line products is the concomitant loss of those now rarer things that once imparted zest and gratification—the loss of individuality, uniqueness and flavor; the loss of craftsmanship, local variety and richness; the loss of intimacy and atmosphere, of eccentricity and character."[69]

Current Growth Is Unsustainable Humanity plunders the earth at an unprecedented rate. Presently, human consumption is 30 percent larger than nature's capacity to regenerate. By 2050, at current trends, humanity will require five planets of natural resources just to keep the game going. "For more than 20 years we have exceeded the Earth's ability to support a consumptive lifestyle that is unsustainable and we cannot afford to continue down this path," warned the Worldwatch Institute.[70] Barring black-swan innovation in mining, agriculture, and manufacturing, no matter how hard we wish otherwise, Mother Earth is going to stop current growth patterns sooner than later.

Change the Game In summary, our position is straightforward. Epic poverty for billions, slow-motion death spiral of the ecosystem, false hope of actualization by consumption, the alienation of binge-buying, and the transformation of nominal democracies into functional oligarchies puts the world at the proverbial fork in the road. We can remain blissfully ignorant of the price of growth, lost in the endless rush of apparent gains but continually surprised by inevitable and underestimated externalities. Alternatively, we can face the issue full on and radically reset the equation so that growth "meets the needs of the present without compromising the ability of future generations to meet their own needs."[71]

Features of an Economy

Narrow (e.g., GNI, GDP, and GNP) and broad (e.g., HDI, HPI, NPP) estimators profile absolute and relative economic condition. They meaningfully indicate a country's performance and potential. Managers study other features to refine analyses and elaborate interpretation. Leading indicators include inflation, unemployment, debt, income distribution, poverty, and the balance of payments. Let's take a closer look at each.

INFLATION

Inflation is the sustained rise in prices measured against a standard level of purchasing power. We estimate it by comparing two sets of products at two points in time and computing the increase in cost that is not due to quality improvement. Mainstream economics holds that inflation results when aggregate demand grows faster than aggregate supply—essentially, too many people try to buy too few goods, thereby creating demand that exceeds supply that increases prices faster than incomes. Other theories, such as the Austrian School of Economics, hold that inflation results from increasing supply of money by central banks.[72] Last, some define inflation as the continuous fall in the value of the currency.[73] No matter the explanation, managers watch inflation given its influence on, among others, interest rates, living costs, consumer confidence, and political stability.[74] Regarding the latter, for example, discontent with rising prices sparked China's Tiananmen Square protests of 1989.[75]

Inflation measures the increase in the cost of living.

Inflation and the Cost of Living Consider the impact of inflation on the cost of living. Unless incomes rise at the same pace or faster, consumers struggle to buy groceries, gas, and so forth. Sometimes just buying stuff is practically impossible. For example, during periods of rapid inflation, or "hyperinflation" as seen in Brazil, Yugoslavia, and Turkmenistan in the 1990s, consumers spent their money as fast as they got it or else watched it turn worthless. More pointedly, in Zimbabwe over the past few years, prices increased up to 95 percent per day; by 2009, the annual inflation rate hit an astounding 79,600,000,000 percent and prices doubled every 25 hours.[76] Noted one Zimbabwean, "There's a surrealism here that's hard to get across to people. If you need something and have cash, you buy it. If you have cash, you spend it today, because tomorrow it's going to be worth 5 percent less. Normal horizons don't exist here."[77] Even in normal circumstances, inflation is a decisive economic condition. For example, inflation in the United States, like most Western markets, significantly changes the cost of products. For instance, an item that cost $10.00 in 1913, 1960, or 2000 would cost you, respectively, $227.18, $57.97, or $13.06 in 2011.[78]

History shows that chronic inflation—high inflation for a prolonged period—erodes confidence in a country's currency and spurs people to seek other ways to store value. Chronic inflation has bleak implications for companies. Neither they nor their customers can plan long-term investments. There is no incentive to save, and ordinary investment instrument like insurance policies and long-term bonds become speculative. Inflation pressures governments to control it, through policies that raise interest rates, regulate wages and prices, or impose protectionism. These measures slow performance and erode potential.

A country experiencing rising prices for a prolonged period of time suffers chronic inflation.

Measuring Inflation   The measurement of inflation highlights a common difficulty: namely, what a country measures when estimating an economic variable. Price indices are sensitive to decisions about their scope and the calculations applied.[79] For instance, the United States uses the Consumer Price Index (CPI). In the European Union, it is the Harmonized Index of Consumer Prices (HICP). Unlike the CPI, the HICP surveys the rural population and excludes owner-occupied housing. Consequently, managers mind the estimation process.[80]

If Not Inflation, Then Deflation   A nagging consequence of the global financial crisis has been the movement of deflation from conjecture to concern. For the first time in generations, deflation, not just inflation, poses a menacing risk. Overcapacity, systematic deleveraging, shrinking credit, reduced corporate spending, declining real estate values, and falling consumer demand fan deflationary dynamics. **Deflation** is the opposite of inflation—prices for products go down, not up. Technically, it occurs when the annual inflation rate is less than zero.

Deflation, a decrease in the general price level of goods and services, is often caused by a reduction in the supply of money or credit.

Deflation results from rather ordinary circumstances. Reduction in the money or credit supply contracts personal and investment spending. Declining demand and growing supply trigger increasing quantity and falling prices. Unchecked, economies fall into deflationary spirals wherein companies increasingly struggle to sell products. In recourse, they discount prices to appeal to consumers who delay purchases in order to exploit tomorrow's cheaper price. Explained a Japanese analyst, "Profits fall, then wages come down, then consumers stop shopping. And because people aren't shopping, companies lower prices.... It isn't easy to break out of."[81]

Deflation and unemployment are intricately linked. Lower demand slows company activity, which then fires workers, which then lowers demand, and so on. At present, central banks and governments rely on **reflation**—increasing the money supply and reducing taxes to accelerate economic activity—to combat deflation. For example, the OECD urged the Bank of Japan to keep pumping cash into the economy "until underlying inflation is firmly positive."[82] Likewise, the Federal Reserve of the United States has implemented quantitative easing programs, essentially printing money to stimulate demand, in order to achieve inflation targets.

UNEMPLOYMENT

The *unemployment rate* is the share of unemployed workers seeking employment for pay relative to the total civilian labor force. Countries that cannot create jobs suffer sluggish growth, social pressures, and political instability. The proportion of employed workers in a country shows how well it productively uses its human resources. People gainfully employed testify to the competency of policymakers to sustain a productive economy. Persistent unemployment symbolizes the ineptitude of the government in managing domestic affairs.

Some economists advise tracking the **misery index,** which is the sum of a country's inflation and unemployment rates. The higher the sum, the greater the economic misery, and the more likely consumers and companies curtail spending and investment. In addition, researchers confirm that misery loves company; as the misery index increases so too do social costs, such as crime, despondency, and family stress.[83]

Measuring Unemployment   As with inflation, measuring the number of unemployed workers seeking work in various countries is difficult. Different assumptions and exclusions alter measurements. [84] Often, the unemployment rate underestimates the scale and scope of the jobless. Technically, it indicates how many are not working for pay but seeking employment for pay. However, it does not count the number of people who are not working at all, are working without pay, or have stopped looking for work. Unemployment measures in many poorer nations routinely underestimate the true degree of joblessness.[85]

Measures often underreport worker productivity. in Asia, Africa, and South America commonly face economic, political, and social problems due to underemployment. That is, even though officially employed, people work only part time, thereby reducing productivity, lowering incomes, and decreasing social stability. Besides measurement issues, the unemployment rate means different things in different countries due to different social policies.[86] Some countries, such as France and Germany, provide generous unemployment protection, whereas countries like China, Kenya, or Jordan offer little to none.

DEBT

Debt, the total of a government's financial obligations, measures what the state borrows from its citizens, foreign organizations, foreign governments, and international institutions. The larger the total debt, the more uncertain an economy's performance and potential. In the present, interest expenses divert money from more productive uses. Regarding the future, worries about the ability of coming generations to repay saps consumer confidence and constrains government activity.

The national debt for many countries had been steadily, albeit slowly, increasing. This changed dramatically as governments responded to the global financial crisis. Company bailouts, unemployment benefits, and macroeconomic stimulus led to unprecedented debt creation. The IMF estimates that the debt of the 10 wealthiest countries will rise from 78 percent of their GDP in 2007 to nearly 115 percent by 2014; these governments, on average, will then owe approximately $50,000 for each citizen.[87] Our closing case—The Global Financial Crisis: Causes and Consequences— develops these issues.

Internal and External Debt   A country's debt has two parts: internal and external. **Internal debt** results when the government spends more than it collects in revenues. Deficits occur for several reasons, such as when an imperfect tax system under-collects revenue, security and social programs exceed tax revenues, or state-owned enterprises run deficits.[88] Consequently, governments struggle with spending priorities, budget management, and tax policy. Pressures to revise policies to deal with growing internal debt create economic uncertainties for consumers, investors, and companies. For

Unemployment measures the number of workers who want to work but do not have jobs.

Underemployment occurs when individuals work fewer hours a day than they would prefer or when individuals work below the level for which they have been trained.

Case Review Note

Internal debt: Portion of the government debt that is denominated in the country's own currency and held by domestic residents.

External debt: Debt owed to foreign creditors and denominated in foreign currency.

If Horses Were Wishes...
Protestors march in London against the government's spending cuts and austerity measures. Coming to terms with its escalating public debt increasingly constraints Britain's economy.
Source: godrick / Shutterstock.com

consumers, growing public debt is usually an early indicator of austerity measures and tax increases.

External debt results when a government borrows money from lenders outside the country, such as private commercial banks, other governments, or international financial institutions (e.g., the IMF or World Bank). Interest on the debt, and eventually the debt itself, is repaid in the currency in which the loan was made. Hence, the borrowing country may have to export its goods to the lender's country to earn that currency or to convert its currency into that of its creditor. Dreaded debt crises often occur when a weak economy is unable to do this, or can do so only at high political, economic, and social cost. In this situation, the economy grinds to a halt. Stress and loss usually precede its reboot to an efficient, smaller-scale version.

Growing public debt is a leading indicator of

- Tax increases.
- Reduced growth.
- Rising inflation.
- Increasing austerity.

INCOME DISTRIBUTION

Income distribution estimates the proportion of population that earns various levels of income.

Income distribution often defines a market's performance and potential. GNI, even when adjusted for population size or purchasing power, can misestimate the relative wealth of a nation's citizens. That is, GNI per capita reports how much income the average person earns. But, since not everyone is average, it does not tell us what share of income goes to what segments of the population. For example, the GNI of the United States exceeds $14 trillion, a performance that ranks first among nations. Similarly, its GNI per capita was an impressive $7,140 in 2010.[89] However, its performance looks less awe-inspiring when qualified by its income distribution. Presently, the richest one percent of Americans receives more income than the bottom 40 percent—the widest gap in 70 years. The top 1 percent own 37 percent of all privately held stock, 65 percent of financial securities, and 62 percent of business equity.[90] The top 10 percent of Americans own 85 to 90 percent of stocks, bonds, trust funds, and business equity, and over 75 percent of non-home real estate. Essentially, approximately 10 percent of U.S. citizens "own" the country.[91] The United States is not the exception; dozens of countries exhibit similar income distributions.

Worldwide, inequality grows. In 1960, the wealthiest 20 percent of the world's population had 30 times the income of the poorest 20 percent. This grew to 32 times in 1970, 45 times in 1980, 60 times in 1990, and 75 times in 2000. In addition, the richest 1 percent claim as much income as the bottom 57 percent—in other words, the 50 million richest people in the world receive as much income as do the 3.8 billion poorest people. On average, the income of the richest 10 percent of the population is about nine times that of the poorest 10 percent in most countries; we see bigger multiples in Israel, Turkey, the United States, Chile, and Mexico.[92]

> There is a growing gap between the rich and poor in virtually every country in the world

Benefits and Costs Some income inequality is useful in rewarding effort, talent, and innovation. However, widening inequality threatens the stability that supports growth as it "fans tensions that wear down the social fabric."[93] Countries that are more unequal have worse social indicators, poorer human-development records, and higher degrees of insecurity. Rising income disparities between booming cities and impoverished countryside threaten social stability and economic performance.[94] China's steadfast commitment to a "harmonious society," for instance, reflects the CCP's fear of growing income inequality between the 800 million people living on its coastal plain and the 500 million who populate its interior.[95] Whereas one sees Lexus, Lamborghini, and Bentley dealerships in Shanghai, many in rural China rely on bicycles and animals for transportation.

Widening inequality eventually triggers destructive outcomes, including shrinking opportunity, resource inefficiencies, and excessive individualism.[96] Ultimately, income inequality erodes a country sense of identity, in which fair play and equality of opportunity power economic performance and unleashes productive potential. For example, people with incomes below $20,000 in the United States have increasingly lost confidence in the free market; support dropped from 76 percent to 44 percent between 2009 and 2010.[97]

> The Gini coefficient measures the extent to which the distribution of resources deviates from a perfectly equal distribution.

Gini Coefficient Managers estimate the degree of inequality in the distribution of income in a country with the **Gini coefficient**. A score of zero implies perfect equality (everybody has the same income). A score of one implies perfect inequality (one person has all the income). Most countries range between 25 and 60 percent. The Gini coefficient presumes that there is a reasonable degree of income within a country. If not, then it partially represents income distribution. One controls for this error by assessing the scale and scope of poverty.

Consider India. It reports a Gini coefficient of 36.8 percent (Sweden, Japan, United States, China, and Brazil, respectively, report 23, 38.1, 41.5, 45, and 56.7 percent). India's score does not reflect enlightened ideals of equality. Rather, it represents the cheerless fact that most Indians are poor: 80 percent of its population lives on less than $2 per day.[98] So income may be distributed evenly on a relative basis, but there is very little to distribute in absolute terms. India, although extreme, is not the exception.

Concept Check

As we suggest in Chapters 1 and 3, both income inequality and poverty should diminish as international business improves the efficiency of resource allocation. The historic record of globalization, Chapter 1 suggested showed that the productive use of liberated capital creates jobs and fosters income growth.

POVERTY

Poverty prevails throughout the world. Managers fine-tune their study of income and wealth by considering its conditions and consequences. **Poverty** is a multidimensional condition in which a person or community lacks the essentials for a minimum standard of well-being and life.[99] These essentials can be life-sustaining resources such as food, clean water, and shelter; they may be social resources such as access to information, education, and healthcare; they may be the opportunity to sustain extended families or connect with people to build communities.

Extreme poverty, according to the World Bank, is living on less than $1.25 per day (PPP). Moderate poverty is less than $2 per day (PPP). Approximately 1.5 billion people live in extreme poverty.[100] Today, the world population is roughly 80 percent poor, 10 percent middle income, and 10 percent rich. The historical record adds an important perspective. While dramatic income inequality is a recent phenomenon, widespread poverty is not.[101]

Prevalence of Poverty   Poverty grows worldwide. Granted, estimates of the number of people in extreme poverty have fallen by approximately 200 million since 1990. However, this reduction has been concentrated in essentially one country. Removing China from the tally reveals that the number of poor in the developing world has remained constant, roughly 1.2 billion between 1981 and 2005. The global financial crisis has threatened many more; some saw it pushing 200 million people deeper into poverty.[102] Presently, rising food prices imperil millions more.[103]

Consequences   Poverty shapes economic environments. People struggle for food, shelter, clothing, clean water, and health services, to say nothing of safety, security, and education. Failure to find them results in malnutrition, mental illness, death, epidemics, famine, and war. For example, 100 percent of Canadians have access to clean water, compared to 13 percent of Afghans; the per capita dietary protein supply in the United States is 121 grams but 32 grams in Mozambique; the average life expectancy is 83 years in Japan yet 32 years in Swaziland.[104]

The growth of business activity and economic progress ultimately depends on alleviating poverty. Economies experiencing extreme poverty require MNEs reassess many taken-for-granted aspects of an economy. Market systems may not exist, national infrastructures may not work, crime may be pervasive, and governments may struggle to regulate society consistently or adopt prudent economic policies.

The Potential of the Poor   Managers monitor the buying potential of today's poor. For example, in 2002, India had fewer than 15 million mobile phone subscribers. By 2006, it had 136 million subscribers. It was fast approaching 700 million by 2011 even though more than 80 percent of Indians are poor, scraping by on less than $2 a day. Today, however, Indian companies offer the cheapest mobile services in the world while still earning profits. India and China (its state-owned mobile carriers report more than 800 million subscribers) account for more than half the world's increase in wireless subscriptions over the past five years. Similar developments with computers (e.g., the XO-1 programs of low-cost laptops for children) and automobiles (the development of functional cars such as Tata's Nano, priced at US$2,900) and housing (Idealab's program to provide functional homes for about $2,500) highlight finding opportunities in the face of dire circumstances. More dramatically, one manager noted, "A billion customers in the world are waiting for a $2 pair of eyeglasses, a $10 solar lantern, and a $100 house."[105]

This perspective alerts managers to the **Base of the Pyramid** phenomenon—the billions of poor people that are seen as inaccessible and unprofitable yet arguably represent the next market frontier of the global economy.[106] Narrowly defined, the Base includes the 2.5 billion people who live on less than $2.50 per day. Boosting the threshold

An Icon of Frugal Innovation
The Tata "Nano" is the world's least expensive production car. Its frugal engineering speaks to the economics of the Base of the Pyramid.
Source: paul prescott / Shutterstock.com

highlights its potential. For example, people earning U.S. $8 per day or less had an aggregate income of nearly U.S. $3 trillion in 2011. If growth rates remain steady, they will earn U.S. $4 trillion annually by 2015.

Accelerating income growth in emerging economies will move many of today's poor into their already expanding middle class.[107] Presently, the middle class includes about two billion people in a dozen emerging economies who collectively spend $6.9 trillion a year. During the next decade, their annual spending will rise to $20 trillion—twice-current U.S. consumption.[108] By 2030, the global middle class will include 5 billion people, a surge unseen since the Industrial Revolution that will reset markets around the world.

CRN
Case Review Note

Success Standards   As the world moves from being mostly poor to mostly middle class, the contours of the Base of the Pyramid will change. This multi-year process creates immense opportunities. Serving the Base of the Pyramid has two preconditions. First, "seeing" opportunity calls for market pioneers that have a particular mindset. More pointedly, "When you look behind the success stories of leading globalizers, you find companies that have learned how to think differently from the herd. They seek out different information, process it in a different way, come to different conclusions, and make different decisions. Where others see threats and complexity, they see opportunity. Where others see a barren landscape, they see a cornucopia of choices."[109]

Second, the task at hand is developing affordable, easily used, eco-sensitive products that work in harsh environments. For example, Nokia, Samsung, and Motorola offer phones with sealed faceplates (for water and dirt resistance), 400 hours of standby time on one battery charge, and larger screens that work in reflected light, use no internal lamp, and are specially enabled for text messaging. Kenya's Safaricom takes these technologies to the next level, pioneering money-transfer by mobile phone in remote locations that lack efficient means to exchange funds. At the grassroots level, similar initiatives have built a refrigerator from clay (which uses no electricity yet keeps vegetables fresh for several days) and a cheap crop duster (a sprayer mounted on a motorcycle).[110]

Concept Check
Although the Base of the Pyramid is attractive in terms of economic potential, managers heed the discussions of Chapters 2 and 3 concerning the different cultural, political, and legal environments found in developing countries. Still, Chapter 1 notes the drivers of globalization steadily narrow the gap between developed and developing countries.

Increasingly, these changes benefit the rich. MNEs translate frugal innovations into new products that serve Western consumers. Chinese firms have introduced reusable sutures—versus the old approach of higher cost, disposable ones—as well as heart stents that run 40 percent cheaper than those in the West.[111] GE developed a low-cost electro-cardiograph machine for rural India. Its efficiency and performance soon led to units marketed in Germany and the United States.[112]

The standards of the Base of the Pyramid—low-cost, high-powered, resource-minimizing, lifestyle-sensitive innovations—increasingly appeal to price-conscious consumers in Western markets. Declining affluence and slowing upward mobility in many rich countries results in growing number of *nouveaux pauvres*, namely former middle-class folks who face tightening budgets. The dawning age of austerity in the United States, Ireland, Spain, England, Greece, and fellow rich countries creates opportunities for frugal shops, notably Wal-Mart and Aldi, pre-paid service providers, such as Leap Wireless and TracFone, and new business designs, such as "collaborative consumption" that lets people share or rent, rather than own, as seen in Zipcar. In sum, the Base of the Pyramid is far wider and far more diffused than most realize. Frugal innovators, like Aldi, Tata, Haier, Wal-Mart, see natural markets spanning Dresden, Delhi, Dongguan, and Detroit.[113]

THE BALANCE OF PAYMENTS

A country's **balance of payments (BOP),** officially known as the *Statement of International Transactions*, reports its trade and financial transactions (as conducted by individuals, businesses, and government agencies) with the rest of the world.[114] The BOP has two main accounts:

- The **current account,** which tracks merchandise trade
- The **capital account,** which tracks both loans given to foreigners and loans received by citizens.

Table 4.6 lists the components of each account. Technically, exports generate positive sales abroad while imports generate negative sales domestically. Positive net sales, resulting when exports exceed imports, create a *current account surplus.* Conversely, importing more than exporting creates a *current account deficit.* Table 4.7 lists the five countries with the largest current account surpluses and those with the largest current account deficits.[115]

TABLE 4.6   Components of a Country's Balance of Payments

Current Account

- Value of exports and imports of physical goods, such as oil, grain, or computers (also referred to as *visible trade*)
- Receipts and payments for services, such as banking or advertising, and other intangible goods, such as copyrights and cross-border dividend and interest payments (also referred to as *invisible trade*)
- Private transfers, such as money sent home by expatriate workers
- Official transfers, such as international aid, on which the government expects no returns

Capital Account

- Long-term capital flows (i.e., money invested in foreign firms as well as profits made by selling those investments and returning the money home)
- Short-term capital flows (i.e., money invested in foreign currencies by international traders as well as funds moved around the world for business purposes by companies with international operations)

TABLE 4.7   Current Account Balances: The Top and the Bottom Five

Top 5	Country	Current Account Surplus (in millions of US$)
1	China	$272,500
2	Japan	$166,500
3	Germany	$162,300
4	Russia	$68,850
5	Norway	$60,230
Bottom 5	**Country**	**Current Account Deficit (in millions of US$)**
159	Brazil	–$52,730
160	France	–$53,290
161	Italy	–$61,980
162	Spain	–$66,740
163	United States	–$561,000

Source: Central Intelligence Agency, "Country Comparison—Current Account Balance," *The World Factbook* (2011), at www.cia.gov (accessed June 2, 2011).

Causes and Consequences of the Global Credit Crisis

CASE

No other economic event, since perhaps the 1930s' Great Depression, has proven more decisive than the global financial crisis of 2008. Although we are now down the road a bit, its legacies continue shaping economic policy, influencing market performance, and shaping countries' potential. Managers grapple with events and outcomes, trying to come up with reasonable interpretations. Increasingly, as events play out, three scenarios frame analysis. Some argue that liquidity is the problem, some point toward balance sheets and solvency, and some argue the need to reboot the system. Each has different implications for MNEs' investment choices and operating decisions.

Scenario One: Leaky Pipes

Initial analysis of the crisis focused on the realization that something had gone terribly awry with the financial plumbing of world's economy. Panic hit a high point in the fall of 2008 as the expanding liquidity freeze, owing to rising dread and mistrust, increasingly stopped money moving from institution to institution and from country to country. Despite anxieties, many reasoned that the credit crisis was not systemic. Certainly, countries' economies were shaken. Problems were, however, contained within the financial system.

Critically, the crisis revealed problems in the pipes that move money from lenders to debtors. However, it did not indicate structural flaws in the financial system. Snags followed from distorted flow dynamics—money was not moving efficiently or effectively through the elaborate channels that connect markets. So, like water moving through leaky pipes in a house, money was being lost along the way.

Granted, leaky pipes are not a big deal if fixed. But, if neglected, they will collapse the house. Officials and agencies quickly turned to fixing the financial pipes, resetting regulatory standards, applying technical solutions, reevaluating the linkages among economies and capital markets, and patching holes. Then, restoring economic vitality and getting countries moving again required refilling the money pipes with, in the words of U.S. Treasury Secretary Geithner, "capital, capital, capital."[116]

Subsequently, countries injected massive capital flows into financial markets. The United States launched its Troubled Asset Relief Program and purchased $700 billion of troubled

asset from banks and other financial institutions. The European Union added €500 billion of liquidity to its banking system. The Federal Reserve acted in kind, expanding its balance sheet by trillions as it bought troubled assets from banks around the world. As its Chairman explained, "a return to strong and stable economic growth will require appropriate and effective responses from economic policymakers across a wide spectrum."[117] Slowly, the financial pipes were patched, stabilized, and apparently returning to normality. Nevertheless, years later, consumers, companies, and countries wondered why capital flows still moved slowly.

Scenario Two: Broken Pumps

As markets struggled for traction, some argued that the financial system was more deeply broken. No one doubted that the pipes had been leaking. Now, some questioned whether larger difficulties overwhelmed the repaired money pumps to restore capital flows. Driving this line of thought was that, in the past, countries usually rebounded from a recession within a year or two. Now some four years later, and despite massive governmental intervention, economic prospects remain bleak for many.

Explanation centered on the fact that most past recessions had been caused by high interest rates associated with tight monetary policy. Loosening monetary policy typically led to demand rebounding, economies growing, and the recession ending. The current recession however, resulted from exceptionally loose monetary policy, further aggravated by aggressive leveraging, that culminated in the epic global crisis. For now, for whatever reason, flooding markets with "capital, capital, capital" seem unable to do the trick.

Officials, while still fixing the pipes, began overhauling the money pumps. In the United States, the Dodd-Frank financial reform legislation tackled issues that precipitated the crisis and seemed to confound the recovery. Its passage resulted in the most sweeping change to financial regulation in the United States since the Great Depression. Similar legislation elsewhere tried to correct flaws in the financial system by regulating opportunistic behaviors, perverse incentives, and agency conflicts.

Slowing progress, however, was the philosophical quandary of the "too-big-to-fail" (TBTF) status of many financial players. A precept of capitalism is that all firms, no matter how big or small, live or die by their wits, not by government protection. Competencies, not connections, drive the ruthless efficiency of capitalism. Now, the fact that institutions like

Citibank, Goldman Sachs, J.P. Morgan Chase, UBS, Dexia, Société Générale, and HSBC were seen as TBTF aggravated incentive problems. Some believed they were again taking excessive risks in the expectation that governments would would backstop them, as they had in 2008, if their bets went bad.

Scenario Three: The House Is Collapsing

No matter the dreadfulness of the broken pumps profile, it pales in comparison to the third scenario, namely the debt-plagued West had to shut down, take pause, and reboot. Unquestionably, the financial system accelerated the global collapse. However, it did not solely determine it. Rather, the "house is collapsing" view held that the pipes were sieves, the pumps busted, that the collapse signalled a systemic crisis. The financial system, given its extreme leverage and exposure, delivered the front half of the hurricane. Now, as the eye slowly passed and the second half began unfolding, there was the troubling resignation that the Western economic system might be fundamentally flawed.

Capitalism, allowed to run free, promotes the psychology that greed is good. Running too free, the global financial crisis suggested, had amplified it into a destructive psychosis that intensified distortions.[118] Its aftermath highlighted these problems, showing that free markets poorly protected social values, skewed income distribution, and concentrated vast wealth and powerful self-interests that threatened social harmony. Noted a leading analyst, "We (the USA) created a situation that caused a recession that wiped out the net worth of about 15 million households. That's a mistake. Many of these people have virtually no other savings. So there was something wrong with the system.[119]

Concerns, Precedents, and Questions

In fall 2010, the outgoing chair of the U.S. Council of Economic Advisers, confessed that she had "no idea how bad the economic collapse would be….still does not understand exactly why it was so bad…and doesn't have much of an idea about how to fix things…." Characterizing situations in the United States as well as throughout the West, she remarked, "Terrible recession…. Incredibly searing…. Dramatically below trend…. Suffering terribly…. Risk of making high unemployment permanent…. Economic nightmare."[120] Then, in April 2011, something a decade earlier most would have thought impossible, Standard & Poor's put a "negative" outlook on the U.S. AAA credit rating, citing rising budget deficits and debt.[121] "More than two years after the beginning of the recent crisis, U.S. policymakers have still not agreed on how to reverse recent fiscal deterioration or address longer-term fiscal pressures," said the S&P.[122]

Instead of a credible plan, the United States, through quantitative easing programs, had opted to print money to solve its problems. Already the largest indebted nation in history, the United States' debt headed higher. Elsewhere, Great Britain, Portugal, Ireland, Italy, Greece, Spain, Japan, among others, were in the same, if not worse shape. All continued underperforming past recovery benchmarks, especially given the unprecedented amount of policy stimulus.

Historical Precedents

Scholars began studying analogous situations, identifying insights and lessons learned from previous crises. In particular, *This Time Is Different: Eight Centuries of Financial Folly* assessed economic crises from 66 countries across five continents over the past 800 years.[123] It found financial fallouts strike with surprisingly consistent frequency, duration, and ferocity. Each time, experts had chimed, "this time is different." Claiming that the old rules of valuation no longer apply and that the new situation bears little similarity to past disasters. Reality consistently rejected this thesis. Confirming that the rules are the same, and even though the situation appears unprecedented, we have been here before. No matter how different the latest financial crisis always appears, it echos previous experiences.

Analysis found a recurring lesson across countries and across centuries: Debt is always dangerous, and excessive debt accumulation is perilous. Furthermore, the aftermath of financial crises tends to be nasty, brutish, and long. Financial crises are typically followed by deep recessions, and these recessions are followed by slow, disappointing recoveries. As such, economies, particularly those in the West that were caught in the bubble dynamics of the global financial crisis, might struggle for years.[124]

Possibly Something More

Others argued that ongoing shortfalls and struggles are the outcome of deep structural problems. Excessive debt, prolonged income inequality, and unscrupulous lenders who exploited consumers' insecurity all came to a head in the worldwide housing bubble. Housing problems highlighted the dangers of the credit bubble, threatened free-market capitalism, and signaled the advent of state capitalism.

Global labor markets made it become harder for people with common-place skills to build a secure middle-class future for their families. Technologies proved wonderful in entertaining us but less than ideal in generating jobs. In wealthier Western countries, unionized jobs, well-paying assembly line work, and prosperous small-business niches faded. In the United States, the share of the working population fell to its lowest level since women began entering the workforce three decades ago. Only 45.4 percent of Americans had jobs in 2010, the lowest rate since 1983 and down from a peak of 49.3 percent in 2000. Similar problems existed elsewhere. Britain stared into the face of harsh austerity, Spain's jobless rate surged pass 20 percent, German inflation accelerated, Portugal shrank, French consumer spending dropped, Greeks took to the streets, Ireland fell into a funk, Swedish sentiment slumped, and Italy's manufacturing sector shrank.[125] All, to some degree, tried to deal with deteriorating balance sheets and accelerating deleveraging. Meanwhile, in the emerging economies, hit hard by the fury of the crisis, billions of people feverishly worked to get ahead. Moreover, the great financial crisis reinforced strong tendencies toward state capitalism in many emerging markets.

Which Scenario?

The crystal ball remains cloudy as of this writing. Summer 2011 saw both gloomy and optimistic views. Regarding the gloomy take, looming risks are glaring and global. In the United States, slowing growth, a fragile recovery, diminishing dollar, waning consumer confidence, rising inflation, successive rounds of quantitative easing, persistent unemployment, and

Simmering concerns and criticisms of the financial system began to boil in the fall of 2011. Here we see a street shot of demonstrators participating in the Occupy Wall Street movement. This development moved people—the so-called "We are the 99%"—to contest the transparency, accountability, and integrity of the free market.

Source: Lev Radin/Shutterstock.com

escalating government debt suggested tough times ahead. Public sentiment seems to think along those lines; some 27 percent believed the economy is growing, 16 percent saying it is slowing down, 26 percent said it is in a recession, and 29 percent said the economy is in a depression.[126] The IMF warned the world's wealthiest nations to curb their surging public debt, saying it could drag down growth needed for economic recovery.[127] Unless abated, rising government debt will compound the fact that economies take a significant number of years to regain momentum following financial crises.[128] To top it off, in August, 2011 the United States lost its coveted triple-A credit rating following an S&P downgrade. Adding insult to injury, China, called upon the United States to "cure its addiction to debts" and "learn to live within its means."[129]

In Europe, the sovereign debt crisis questions the fate of the European Union (EU). Regional growth was steadily slowing as Europe reined in government spending. Japan faced monumental financial challenges, compounded by earthquake, tsunami, and nuclear plant failure. The Middle East uprisings fanned political turmoil. Developing countries throughout Asia and Africa faced rising food prices given inflationary policies in the West. Countries warned of austerity. Cuts in public support, healthcare, pension benefits, and potential opportunities triggered protests worldwide.

To some, the issues leading to the crises were still present and worsening in some places. Decisions made had not turned out as planned, perhaps unavoidably given the scale and scope of the crisis. Reflected U.S. Treasury Secretary Geithner, "Things were falling apart. We had no playbook and no tools.... Life's about choices. We had no good choices.... We allowed this huge financial system to emerge without any meaningful constraints.... The size of the shock was larger than what precipitated the Great Depression."[130]

Still, the world is stuck with global, regional, sectoral, and national imbalances in incomes, earnings, wealth, trade, and financial health as well as excessive levels of, and excessively narrow concentrations of, debt in Western economies. In many countries, the fact that the financial sector of the economy had grown from below a tenth to more than a third of total economic activity gave pause. To top it off, some argued the apparent solution to the crisis has been to implement many of the same policies that caused the crisis. This concern, Secretary Geithner suggested was not far-fetched, conceding, "It will come again. There will be another storm, but it's not going to come for a while."[131]

Rays of optimism pierced the gloom. Stable market conditions and improving growth prospects were apparent in many countries. Germany had rebounded strongly, while Sweden, Great Britain, the United States, France, and others slowly gained traction. The United States, for example, by midyear 2011 had recorded seven straight consecutive quarters of economic growth, was watching its unemployment rate steadily drop, and enjoyed a powerful stock market rally. Loose monetary policy promised to keep economies growing; analysts anticipated accelerating industrial production and improving consumer confidence. The road to recovery, while bumpy, was evident. ∎

QUESTIONS

1. Which scenario do you think best explains the global financial crisis? Why?

2. How does each scenario influence the policies that governments adopt, the strategies that companies pursue, and the choices that consumers make?

3. How might the various scenarios influence economic freedom?

4. The case points out the crises produce winners and losers. Who are the winners and losers for Scenario 1? Scenario 2? Scenario 3?

5. Say you were asked which economic indicator would confirm the end of the crisis. Which would you nominate?

6. Interpreting economic environments, estimating scenarios, and positioning the firm to prosper are the jobs of managers worldwide. How would you advise one to do so with respect to the global financial crisis?

MyIBLab Now that you have finished this chapter, go back to www.myiblab.com to continue practicing and applying the concepts you've learned.

SUMMARY

- Economic freedom measures the absence of government coercion or constraint on the production, distribution, or consumption of goods and services beyond the extent necessary for citizens to protect and maintain liberty.

- Economically free countries tend to have higher per capita income, standards of living, and social stability than do less-free or repressed countries.

- The global financial crisis challenges the legitimacy of free markets. Governments in many countries have expanded their regulation of the economy to deal with the resulting problems.

- Managers watch key events to gauge the contest between economic freedom and state control. These include how the government regulates the economy, protects property rights, sets fiscal and monetary policies, and enforces antitrust regulation.

- In a market economy, private interests own resources, and price and quantity, conveyed via the invisible hand, determine supply and demand.

- In a command economy, the government plans what goods and services a country produces, the quantity in which they are produced, and the price at which they are sold.

- A mixed economy includes some elements of market and command economies. Both influence investment activities and consumption behavior.

- A market economy requires accepting the doctrine of capitalism, its principles of the invisible hand and laissez-faire, and the goal of maximizing economic freedom.

- A mixed economy requires accepting the doctrine of socialism, its principle of the partly visible hand of an activist government that commands and controls some factors of production, and the goal of regulating economic freedom.

- A command economy requires accepting the doctrine of communism, its principle of an activist government that commands and controls most if not all factors of production, and the goal of constraining economic freedom.

- State capitalism is a system whereby the government explicitly manipulates market outcomes for political purposes.

- Managers assess markets in terms of size (GNI, GNP, GDP), income (GNI, GNP, or GDP per capita), stability (HDI, HPI), and sustainability (NNP, GPI).

- Green measures of economic performance call for considering ecological aspects that support sustainable development.

- Concern that monetary measures misestimate economic performance leads to calls to expand the concept of financial prosperity to include aspects of happiness.

- Managers use several indicators to assess the performance and potential of an economy, including, income distribution, inflation, unemployment, debt, balance of payments, and poverty.

- The Base of the Pyramid is the largest, but poorest socio-economic group in the world. Although poor in terms of individual wealth, the collective income of the Base arguably makes it the next market frontier.

KEY TERMS

balance of payments (BOP) (p. 170)
Base of the Pyramid (p. 168)
BRICs (p. 154)
capital accounts (p. 170)
capitalism (p. 149)
command economy (p. 150)
communism (p. 150)
current accounts (p. 170)
debt (p. 165)
deflation (p. 164)
economic freedom (p. 144)
Economic Freedom Index (p. 144)
economic geography (p. 141)

economic system (p. 149)
emerging economies (p. 154)
external debt (p. 166)
Gini coefficient (p. 167)
global financial crisis (p. 138)
green economics (p. 159)
gross national income (GNI) (p. 154)
gross national product (GNP) (p. 154)
happynomics (p. 160)
income distribution (p. 166)
inflation (p. 163)
internal debt (p. 165)
laissez-faire (p. 150)

market economy (p. 149)
mixed economy (p. 151)
misery index (p. 165)
poverty (p. 168)
purchasing power parity (PPP) (p. 158)
reflation (p. 164)
socialism (p. 151)
state capitalism (p. 152)
sustainability (p. 141)
sustainable development (p. 159)

ENDNOTES

1 **Sources include the following:** Thomas Friedman, *The World Is Flat: A Brief History of the of the Twenty-first Century"* (Farrar, Straus and Giroux, 2005); Clyde V. Prestowitz, *Three Billion New Capitalists: The Great Shift of Wealth and Power to the East* (New York: Basic Books, 2006); Clyde Prestowitz, "Three Billion New Capitalists," video transcript, *News Hour* (August 15, 2005), www.pbs.org/newshour /bb/economy/july-dec05/prestowitz_8-15.html; Kenneth Rogoff, "Betting with the House's Money," *Project Syndicate*, Retrieved May 7, 2007, from www.project-syndicate.org/commentary /rogoff27; Anne O. Krueger, "Stability, Growth, and Prosperity:

The Global Economy and the IMF," Retrieved June 7, 2006, from www.imf.org/external/np/speeches/2006/060706.htm; Angus Maddison, *The World Economy, 1–2030 AD* (London: Oxford University Press, 2007); *The World Economy: Volume 1: A Millennial Perspective* (Paris: Development Centre, 2001); *Volume 2: Historical Statistics* (Paris: Development Centre, 2003); "BRICs, Emerging Markets and the World Economy: Not Just Straw Men," *The Economist* (June 18, 2009): 45; "Government v. Market in America: The Visible Hand," *The Economist* (May 28, 2009): 25–28, Retrieved August 12, 2009, from www.economist.com/displaystory.cfm?story_id=13743310; "The Next Billions: Unleashing Business Potential in Untapped Markets," *World Economic Forum* (January 2009): 44; "A Special Report on Innovation in Emerging Markets: The World Turned Upside Down," *The Economist*, Retrieved April 21, 2011, from www.economist.com/node/15879369; "China Claims #9 Rank In United States Patents!" Retrieved April 23, 2011, from www.defence.pk/forums/china-defence/55892-china-claims-9-rank-united-states-patents.html Ian Morris, *Why the West Rules… For Now* (New York, Farrar, Straus and Giroux, 2010).

2 Thomas Friedman, *The World Is Flat: A Brief History of the Twenty-first Century* (Farrar, Straus and Giroux, 2005).

3 Clyde V. Prestowitz, *Three Billion New Capitalists: The Great Shift of Wealth and Power to the East,* (New York: Basic Books, 2006).

4 "Global Economic Outlook," The Conference Board," Retrieved April 11, 2011, from www.conference-board.org/data/globalout look.cfm. They moved to 50.4 percent in 2010. "Global Development Horizons 2011—Multipolarity: The New Global Economy," *The World Bank* (Retrieved May 19, 2011).

5 So, for example, in May 2011, Chinese central bank governor Zhou Xiaochuan said "The new IMF leadership needs to reflect changes in the world economic order and be more representative of emerging market economies."

6 "A Special Report on Innovation In Emerging Markets: The World Turned Upside Down," *The Economist*, Retrieved April 21, 2011, from www.economist.com/node/15879369; James Politi, "World Bank Sees End to Dollar's Hegemony," *Financial Times* (May 17, 2011).

7 Ibid.

8 Dustin Ensinger, "China Takes the Crown, Economy in Crisis," Retrieved April 13, 2011, from www.economyincrisis.org/content/china-takes-crown.

9 Ibid.: 5.

10 Clyde Prestowitz, "Three Billion New Capitalists," video transcript, *News Hour* (August 15, 2005), Retrieved July 18, 2007, from www.pbs.org/newshour/bb/economy/july-dec05/prestowitz_815.html

11 Jason Dean, Andrew Browne, and Shai Oster, "China's 'State Capitalism' Sparks a Global Backlash - WSJ.com" (November 16, 2010).

12 Ibid.: 16.

13 "A Special Report On Innovation In Emerging Markets: The World Turned Upside Down."

14 Stephen King, *Losing Control: The Emerging Threats to Western Prosperity,* (New Haven, CT: Yale University Press, 2010).

15 Kim Murphy, "Melting ice caps open up shipping routes," *Los Angeles Times* (October 13, 2009).

16 Simon Wilson, "Global Trade: The Opening of the Northeast Passage," *MoneyWeek* (September 25, 2009). Retrieved April 17, 2011, from www.moneyweek.com/news-and-charts/economics/global-trade-the-opening-of-the-northeast-passage-45402

17 Ships attempting the Northeast or Northwest Passages face hundred-mile long swathes of shifting pack ice, even during the two months or so each summer when safe passage is feasible.

18 "NASA—Arctic Ice Gets a Check Up," Retrieved April 18, 2011, from www.nasa.gov/mission_pages/icebridge/multimedia/arcticseaice-max2011.html

19 The World Bank Group, www.worldbank.org/data/ databytopic/class.htm. See also "How Many Countries Are in the World?" Retrieved July 24, 2009, from geography.about.com/cs/countries/a/ numbercountries.htm

20 See, for example, www.econlib.org/library/Enc/Behavioral Economics.html.

21 William W. Beach and Marc A. Miles, "Explaining the Factors of the Index of Economic Freedom," *2005 Index of Economic Freedom*, Retrieved August 14, 2006, from www.heritage.org/research/features/index:33.

22 Quotation extracted from *The Wealth of Nations*. Reported in "Executive Summary," Index of Economic Freedom (15 January 2008). Retrieved February 4, 2008, from www.heritage.org/research/features/index/chapters/pdf/index2008_execsum.pdf

23 *The 2011 Index of Economic Freedom.* www.heritage.org/Index

24 Counts for 2009 were: 7 countries had free economies, 23 were rated mostly free, 53 were moderately free, 67 were mostly nonfree, and 29 were repressed. Sample was 179 countries.

25 E.g., Robert Lawson "Measuring Economic Freedom," Cato Institute. Retrieved April 13, 2011, from www.cato.org/pub_display.php?pub_id=6101

26 Barry Eichengreen and Kevin H. O'Rourke, "A Tale of Two Depressions," (June 4, 2009). Retrieved June 5, 2009, from www.voxeu.org/index.php?q=node/3421

27 Data drawn from 12,884 interviews across 25 countries. "Sharp Drop in American Enthusiasm for Free Market," *Globescan*, Retrieved April 19, 2011, from www.globescan.com/news_archives/radar10w2_free_market; "Capitalism's waning popularity," *The Economist*, Retrieved April 19, 2011, from www.economist.com/node/18527446?story_id=18527446&CFID=168796516&CFTOKEN=46679551

28 Ibid.

29 Ibid.

30 Anatole Kaletsky, *"Capitalism 4.0: The Birth of a New Economy in the Aftermath of Crisis* (New York:Public Affairs, 2010).

31 Strictly speaking, none of them is a "pure" market economy because their governments intervene in the marketplace. Still, their historic advocacy of economic freedom endorses the philosophy of capitalism and the principle of laissez-faire.

32 Only then, the thinking goes, are the proletariat (the social class that does manual labor or work for wages) protected from exploitation by the bourgeois (the social class that owns the factors of production).

33 Companies in centrally planned economies exhibited a particular quirk. The absence of competition and bankruptcy in this sort of economic system meant that once an enterprise was up and running, it survived indefinitely, irrespective of performance.

34 "The global revival of industrial policy: Picking winners, saving losers," *The Economist*, Retrieved April 27, 2011, from www.economist.com/node/16741043

35 Michael Todaro, *Economic Development*, 6th edition (Reading, MA: Addison Wesley, 1996):705.

36 "The French Model: Vive la Différence!" *The Economist*, May 7, 2009.

37 "Denmark 'happiest place on earth,'" BBC News, 28 July 2006. Retrieved April 18, 2011, fromnews.bbc.co.uk/2/hi/health/5224306.stm; see also Russell Shorto, "Going Dutch: How I learned to love the welfare state," *New York Times*. Retrieved April 17, 2011, from www.nytimes.com/2009/05/03/magazine/03european-.html

38 Most worrisome to free market proponents is that, once a crisis passes, government control sometimes shrinks, but it never returns to its original size. Indeed, some argue that a mixed economy is essentially a move toward a socialist state.

39 "Q&A with Ian Bremmer on State Capitalism," Foreign Affairs, retrieved April 13 2011, from www.foreignaffairs.com/discussions/interviews/qa-with-ian-bremmer-on-state-capitalism?page=show

40 Michael Wines, "Make No Mistake: In China, State-run Firms Rule," *The New York Times* (August 31, 2010).

41 "China's Future: Rising Power, Anxious State," *The Economist*, Special Report: China (June 25, 2011): 14.

42 The state essentially prevents systemic distortions threatening the stability of the system and promoting societal welfare—or, as Marx prophesied, capitalism eventually is destroyed by its own contradictions.

43 "Countries at the Crossroads," freedomhouse.org. Retrieved April 18, 2011, from www.freedomhouse.org/template .cfm?page=139&edition=9

44 Eric Li, "How China broke the West's monopoly on modernization," CSMonitor.com, retrieved April 28, 2011, from www.csmonitor.com /Commentary/Global-Viewpoint/2011/0428/How-China-broke -the-West-s-monopoly-on-modernization

45 Ian Bremmer, "State Capitalism and the Crisis," *McKinsey Quarterly*, (July, 2009): 4.

46 Ian Bremmer, *The End of the Free Market: Who Wins the War Between States and Corporations?* (New York: Portfolio, 2010). Stefan Halper, *The Beijing Consensus: How China's Authoritarian Model Will Dominate the Twenty-First Century* (New York: Basic Books, 2010).

47 Regarding the informal, the Economist reported that "When Alan Greenspan was chairman of the Federal Reserve, he monitored several unusual measures. One favourite, supposedly, was sales of men's underwear, which are usually pretty constant, but drop in recessions when men replace them less often." See Fast Food for Thought," *The Economist* (July 30, 2011): 12.

48 For example, Indonesia's GNP is larger than its GNI—the former was $706 billion in 2010, while the latter was $599 billion. The same held for its neighbor, Thailand, with a GNI of $286 billion versus GNP of $318 billion the same year. In contrast, the GNI of the United States in 2010 was $14.60 trillion, while its GNP was $14.66 trillion. This discrepancy results from the fact that the net foreign factor income was negative for Indonesia and Thailand (i.e., a net outflow), but roughly balanced for the United States. Since GNI takes net flows into account, we have the resulting variance between GNI and GNP. As a rule, many developing countries produce more value than they receive as income, thereby leading to a higher GNP than GNI.

49 Historically, GNI was referred to as gross national product. The definition and measurement of GNI and GNP are analogous, but institutions such as the World Bank and International Monetary Fund now use the term GNI.

50 Ibid.

51 For example, Latin America has seen income per capita drop five times since the 1980s. The current global credit crisis has triggered a sixth occurrence—population in the region is growing 1.3 percent a year but the economy "grew" –2.2 percent in 2009. As expected, consumer demand, public finances, financial reserves, and currency valuations tumbled. This calamity is not unique to Latin America; at least 60 developing markets suffered income drops in 2009, with especially hard times for Central and Eastern Europe and sub-Saharan Africa.

52 Technically, we compute per capita GNI by taking the GNI of a country and converting it into a standard currency—say, the U.S. dollar at prevailing exchange rates—and then dividing this sum by population size.

53 U.S. and World Population Clocks—POPClocks, retrieved October 9, 2011. Check www.census.gov/main/www/popclock.html for current statistic.

54 Exchange rates as of October 9, 2011.

55 World Bank, 2007 Survey (Atlas methodology for GNI per capita). Typically, the prices of many goods are considered and weighted according to their importance in the economy of the particular country.

56 The most common PPP exchange rate comes from comparing a basket of goods and services in a country with an equivalent basket in the United States.

57 "Process of Preparation of the Environmental Perspective to the Year 2000 and Beyond," General Assembly Resolution 38/161" (December 19, 1983), retrieved May 27, 2007, from www.un.org /documents/ga/res/38/ a38r161htm

58 Joseph Stiglitz, "Good Numbers Gone Bad: Why Relying on GDP as a Leading Economic Gauge Can Lead to Poor Decision-Making," *Fortune* (September 25, 2006).

59 Some maintain that the purpose of development is to enlarge people's choices. In principle, these choices can be infinite and can change over time. People often value achievements that do not show up at all, or not immediately, in income or growth figures: greater access to knowledge, better nutrition and health services, more secure livelihoods, security against crime and physical violence, satisfying leisure hours, political and cultural freedoms, and sense of participation in community activities. The objective of development is to create an enabling environment for people to enjoy long, healthy, and creative lives. Statement by Dr. Mahbub ul Haq, co-conceiver, with Amartya Sen of HDI.

60 Richard Easterlin, "Does Economic Growth Improve the Human Lot?" in Paul A. David and Melvin W. Reder, eds., *Nations and Households in Economic Growth: Essays in Honor of Moses Abramovitz* (New York: Academic Press, 1974); Richard Easterlin, "Income and Happiness: Towards a Unified Theory," *The Economic Journal* (2001): 465–84.

61 Eric Weiner, "The Happiest Places in the World," *Forbes* (April 23, 2008). Retrieved July 16, 2009, from 2011 www .forbes.com/2008/04/23/happiest-places-world-opedcx _ewe_0423happiest.html

62 Mark Whitehouse, "GDP Can Be a Poor Measure of Success," *WSJ.com*, retrieved January 17, 2011, from http://online.wsj.com /article/SB10001424052748704064504576070343252409876.html

63 Roger Cohen, "The Happynomics of Life," *NYTimes.com*, retrieved April 27, 2011, from nytimes.com/2011/03/13/opinion/13cohen .html?_r=1

64 Charles Jones and Peter Klenow, *Beyond GDP? Welfare across Countries and Time*, NBER Working Papers 16352, National Bureau of Economic Research (2010).

65 "OECD Launches Happiness Index, *AFP*, retrieved May 26, 2011, from www.google.com/hostednews/afp/article/ALeqM5jj15a9ZCL 9ETVD9UAn18y7MlrG_g?docId=CNG.b86506f095cbf61164e88f98b0 d5d21c.2a1

66 The Happiest Countries in the World," 24/7 Wall St, retrieved June 4, 2011, from http://247wallst.com/2011/06/01/the-happiest -countries-in-the-world/2

67 "Government v. Market in America: The Visible Hand," *The Economist* (May 28, 2009): 25–28.

68 E. Mishan, *The Costs of Economic Growth* (New York: Praeger, 1967).

69 Ibid.

70 Jerome Glenn, Theodore Gordon, and Elizabeth Florescu, *2009 State of the Future, The Millennium Project*, retrieved May 15, 2011, from www.millenniumproject.org/millennium/sof2009.html; "Humans using Earth's Resources at Unsustainable Rate, Conservation Group Claims," retrieved June 2, 2011, from www.naturalnews .com/020873.html

71 *Process of Preparation of the Environmental Perspective to the Year 2000 and Beyond.* General Assembly Resolution 38/161 (December 19, 1983), retrieved May 27, 2007, from www.un.org/documents/ga /res/38/a38r161htm

72 Murray Rothbard, "Ludwig von Mises (1881–1973)," retrieved May 27, 2009, from www.mises.org/content/mises.asp

73 See www.usinflationcalculator.com/frequently-asked-questions-faqs

74 Economists use different types of indexes to measure inflation, but the one they use the most is the *Consumer Price Index (CPI)*. The CPI

measures a fixed basket of goods and compares its price from one period to the next. A rise in the index indicates inflation.

75 "China's Future: Rising Power, Anxious State," *The Economist*, Special Report: China (June 25, 2011): 9

76 Steve H. Hanke and Alex K. F. Kwok, "On the Measurement of Zimbabwe's Hyperinflation," *Cato Journal*, (Spring/Summer 2009).

77 Michael Wines, "How Bad Is Inflation in Zimbabwe?," *New York Times* (May 2, 2006): B1.

78 Ibid.: 73.

79 Kevin Phillips, "Numbers Racket: Why the Economy Is Worse than We Know," Harper's Magazine, retrieved April 26, 2001, from www.harpers.org/archive/2008/05/0082023; "Economics focus: Botox and bean counting," *The Economist* (April 30, 2011): 84; Rick Hampson, "U.S. Changes how it Measures Long-Term Unemployment," retrieved December 29, 2010, from USA TODAY.com

80 For instance, as of 2003, only three countries had annual inflation rates in excess of 40 percent, the level above which it is generally considered to be acutely damaging to an economy. All major industrial countries had inflation under 3 percent (and in Japan, deflation persisted). Moreover, inflation in many middle- and lower-income countries, once stuck with extreme inflation pressure, had fallen well into single digits in the early twenty-first century. Many credited the fall in inflation to a combination of the price pressures of globalization along with more vigilant central bankers and economic policymakers. See Ken Rogoff, "The IMF Strikes Back," *Foreign Policy* (January/February 2003): 39–48.

81 View of Junko Nishioka, Chief Japan economist at RBS Securities Japan Ltd. in Tokyo. From "Japan Succumbs to Deflation as Consumer Prices Fall Record 1.1 percent," Bloomberg.com, retrieved June 29, 2009, from www.bloomberg.com/apps/news?pid=newsarchive&sid=aaQyqjERBorM

82 Ibid.

83 Presently, the wealthier countries of the world are watching their working-age population shrink from approximately 740 to 690 million people between 2000 and 2025. However, over the same time, the working-age population will increase across poorer countries from about 3 to 4 billion people. In China alone, the population above the age of 16 will grow by 5.5 million annually on average in the next 20 years. The total population of working-age Chinese will reach 940 million by 2020. Presently, the youth of the world suffer the highest rates of unemployment in most countries, with rates twice that of adult (ages 25–65) unemployment. China, for example, sees the age structure of its population creating severe employment pressure within the next two decades.

84 Ibid.: 83.

85 Ibid.: 60.

86 See Constance Sorrentino, "International Unemployment Rates: How Comparable Are They?" *Monthly Labor Review* (June 2000): 3–20.

87 See U.S. National Debt Clock, www.brillig.com/debt_clock.

88 For example, arguably the U.S. fiscal system is plugged with many tax loopholes that cause inefficiencies, misallocation of resources, and lost revenues. Hence, eliminating the deficit requires eliminating these distortions.

89 GNI data is adjusted by purchasing power parity (data as of April 26, 2011).

90 Bob Herbert, "Losing Our Way - NYTimes.com," retrieved April 12, 2011, from www.nytimes.com/2011/03/26/opinion/26herbert.html?_r=1

91 William Domhoff, "Wealth, Income, and Power," retrieved May 5, 2009, from sociology.ucsc.edu/whorulesamerica/power/wealth.html; see "Gap between Rich and Poor: World Income Inequality," retrieved July 4, 2009, from www.infoplease.com/ipa/A0908770.html

92 "Growing Income Inequality in OECD Countries: What Drives It and How Can Policy Tackle It?," www.oecd.org/els/social/inequality (May 2010). Finally, income inequality is accelerating between top executives and the average employee. In 2010, the average CEO in the United States made 343 times more money than the average American did last year. In 2007, for example CEOs of the 15 largest companies earned 520 times more than the average worker. This is up from 360 times more in 2003. We see similar patterns Australia, Germany, Hong Kong (China), the Netherlands, and South Africa.

93 "Inequality: Unbottled Gini," *The Economist*," retrieved April 18, 2011, from www.economist.com/node/17957381

94 "Chinese Scholars Warn Growing Wealth Gap Likely to Trigger Social Instability," *Sina*, retrieved July 8, 2006, from english.sina.com/china/1/2005/0822/ 43237.html

95 "China's Urban, Rural Income Gap Widens Despite Economic Recovery," *People's Daily Online*, retrieved April 19, 2011, from english.people.com.cn/90001/90778/90862/6875693.html

96 Joseph Stiglitz, "Of the 1 Percent, by the 1 Percent, for the 1 Percent," *Vanity Fair* (May 2011).

97 Ibid.: 26.

98 "80 Percent of Indians Live on Less than $2 a day—World Bank," livemint.com, retrieved April 17, 2011, from www.livemint.com/articles/2007/10/16235421/80-of-Indians-live-on-less-th.htm

99 "A Wealth of Data: A Useful New Way to Capture the Many Aspects of Poverty," *The Economist*, Retrieved April 18, 2011, from www.economist.com/node/16693283

100 "Impossible Architecture," *Social Watch Report 2006*, retrieved May 27, 2007, from www.socialwatch.org/en/portada.htm

101 Noted Jeffery Sachs, "The world is more unequal than at any time in world history. There's a basic reason for that which is that 200 years ago everybody was poor. A relatively small part of the world achieved what the economists call a modern economic growth. Those countries represent only about one-sixth of humanity, and five-sixths of humanity is what we call the developing world. It's the vast majority of the world. The gap can be 100 to 1, maybe a gap of $30,000 per person and $300 per person. And that's absolutely astounding to be on the same planet and to have that extreme variation in material well-being." Transcript, Chapter 18, "Episode Three: The New Rules of the Game," *Commanding Heights: The Battle for the World Economy*, retrieved June 28, 2007, from www.pbs.org/wgbh/commandingheights/lo/index.htm

102 "Joseph Stiglitz, Wall Street's Toxic Message," *Vanity Fair*, retrieved June 15, 2009, from www.vanityfair.com/politics/features/2009/07/third-worlddebt200907; "The Poor and the Global Crisis: The Trail of Disaster," *The Economist* (June 18, 2009): 24.

103 Sandrine Rastello and Wendy Pugh, "Food Surge Is Exacerbating Poverty, World Bank Says," retrieved May 10, 2011, from www.bloomberg.com/news/2011-02-15/food-price-jump-pushes-44-million-into-extreme-poverty-world-bank-says.html

104 The Food and Agriculture Organization of the United Nations translates the food commodities available for human consumption in a country into their protein equivalent. This measure compensates for differences in protein supplied by different foods across countries (go to www.fao.org).

105 Donald McNeil Jr., "Design That Solves Problems for the World's Poor," *New York Times* (May 29, 2007): B-2.

106 "The Next Billions: Unleashing Business Potential in Untapped Markets," *World Economic Forum* (January 2009): 44; C. K. Prahalad and S. L. Hart, "The Fortune at the Bottom of the Pyramid," *Strategy+Business* (2002) 26: 54–67.

107 Christa Case Bryant, "Surging BRIC middle classes are eclipsing global poverty," CSMonitor.com, retrieved May 25, 2011, from

www.csmonitor.com/World/2011/0517/Surging-BRIC-middle-classes-are-eclipsing-global-poverty

108 David Court and Laxman Narasimhan, "Capturing the World's Emerging Middle Class," *McKinsey Quarterly* (July 2010): 67.

109 Jane Fraser and Jeremy Oppenheim, "What's New about Globalization," *The McKinsey Quarterly* (May 1997): 178.

110 See, for example, www.nextbillion.net.

111 "Medical technology: Frugal healing," *The Economist*," retrieved April 19, 2011, from www.economist.com/node/17963427

112 "Innovations to Create New Streams of Profitable Growth," *Accenture Outlook*, retrieved June 9, 2009, from www.accenture.com/in-en/outlook/Pages/outlook-journal-2010-less-is-new-more-innovation.aspx

113 "The Tata Group: Out of India," *The Economist* (March 5, 2011): 76–78; "The Bottom of the Pryamid," *The Economist* (June 25, 2011): 80.

114 The notion of *balance* means that all BOP transactions have an offsetting receipt. For instance, a country might have a surplus in merchandise trade (indicating that it is exporting more than it is importing) but may then report a deficit in another area, such as its investment income. In other words, because the current account and the capital account add up to the total account—which is necessarily balanced—a deficit in the current account is accompanied by an equal surplus in the capital account and vice versa. A deficit or surplus in the current account cannot be explained or evaluated without simultaneous explanation and evaluation of an equal surplus or deficit in the capital account.

115 Retrieved October 2, 2009, from www.cia.gov/library/publications/the-world-factbook/rankorder/2187rank.html

116 "Geithner Pushes New Financial Rules; GOP Skeptical: NPR," retrieved April 13, 2011, from www.npr.org/templates/story/story.php?storyId=102416414

117 "Tax Cuts to Job Creation: Will It Work?," retrieved August 8, 2011 from http://seekingalpha.com/article/240610-tax-cuts-to-job-creation-will-it-work.

118 The state essentially prevents systemic distortions threatening the stability of the system and promoting societal welfare—or, as Marx prophesied, capitalism eventually is destroyed by its own contradictions.

119 Jennifer Schonberger, "Robert Shiller Sees More Housing Pain Ahead," *Kiplinger's Personal Finance*, retrieved April 13, 2011, from www.kiplinger.com/columns/dekaser-practical-economics/archives/robert-shiller-shares-his-view-on-the-housing-market.html

120 Dana Milbank, "Economist Christina Romer serves up dismal news at her farewell luncheon" (September 1, 2010), retrieved April 13, 2011, from washingtonpost, www.washingtonpost.com/wp-dyn/content/article/2010/09/01/AR2010090106148.html?hpid=news-col-blog

121 Shannon D. Harrington and Cordell Eddings, "Standard & Poor's Puts 'Negative' Outlook on U.S. AAA Rating," retrieved April 18, 2011, from www.bloomberg.com/news/2011-04-18/standard-poor-s-puts-negative-outlook-on-u-s-aaa-rating.html.

122 "Jim Rogers Says the US Will Certainly Lose Its AAA Credit Rating," *Business Intelligence Middle East*, retrieved April 28, 2011, from www.lewrockwell.com/rogers-j/rogers-j139.html

123 Carmen Reinhart and Kenneth Rogoff, *This Time Is Different: Eight Centuries of Financial Folly*, (Princeton University Press, 2010).

124 Most will average annual real GDP growth in the low single digits for a decade or more. Stock markets will drop 50 to 80 percent in real value. The Dow Jones Industrial Average, for example, may see 4000 before 2030. This sounds utterly inconceivable until one considers that the Nikkei fell from its all-time high 38,915 on December 12, 1989 to 7,054 on March 10, 2009. Key cause of the 82 percent drop—the Japanese housing bubble of the 1980s. Interest rates will remain low for a long time; in the United States, we may see the federal funds rate below 0.5 percent until at least 2020. Persistently high unemployment will reflect persistently sluggish growth. Cycles of falling prices and wages will power deflationary dynamics. And, to top it off, the average home prices around the world will fall further. In the United States, some look for existing homes to fall to $100k (from $240k in 2006) before 2030; new homes will do the same, falling from $320K in 2007 to $125K by 2030. Combined, all signs point to a secular shift from over-leveraged, credit-driven consumption to compelling frugality that border for many on raw austerity. Closer inspection of 15 severe financial crises since World War II as well as the worldwide economic contractions that followed the 1929 stock market crash, the 1973 oil shock, and the 2007 implosion of the subprime mortgage market clarifies likely events and trends. In the decade following the crises, growth rates were significantly lower and unemployment rates were significantly higher. Housing prices took years to recover. It took households and companies about seven years on average for to reduce their debts and restore their balance sheets. Consistently, the crises were preceded by decade(s)-long expansions of credit and borrowing, and were followed by lengthy periods of retrenchment that lasted nearly as long.

125 Arthi Gupta, "German Jobless Rate at Record Low; French Consumer Spending Drops," Market Update, retrieved April 28, 2011, from www.123jump.com/market-update/German-Jobless-Rate-at-Record-Low;-French-Consumer-Spending-Drops/44005

126 David Morgan, "Most Americans say U.S. in recession despite data: poll," *Reuters*, Results from April 20-23 Gallup survey of 1,013 U.S. adults, retrieved April 28, 2011, from www.reuters.com/article/2011/04/28/us-usa-economy-gallup-idUSTRE73R3WW20110428?feedType=RSS&feedName=domesticNews

127 Ominously, at a time when debt levels in the United States and other countries at the center of the financial crisis are rapidly approaching the 90 percent threshold. Gross government debt in the United States, for example, stood at 85 percent of GDP in 2009 and will reach 108 percent of GDP by 2014, according to IMF projections. The U.K.'s gross government debt stood at 69 percent of GDP in 2009 and is expected to reach 98 percent of GDP by 2013.

128 "No Full Recovery until 2015, Says the IMF," *The Telegraph*, retrieved September 22, 2009 from www.telegraph.co.uk/finance/financetopics/ recession/6220089/No-full-recovery-until-2015-says-the-IMF.html

129 David Pierson, "China Demands U.S. 'Live within its Means,'" *Los Angeles Times* (August 6, 2011): A-1.

130 Lloyd Grove, "Too Big to Fail? Timothy Geithner Says No," The Daily Beast, retrieved May 19, 2011, from www.thedailybeast.com/blogs-and-stories/2011-05-18/too-big-to-fail-timothy-geithner-says-no-at-hbo-movie-screening/#

131 Ibid.

chapter 5

Globalization and Society

Objectives

1. To examine the broad foundations of ethical behavior

2. To demonstrate the cultural and legal foundations of ethical behavior

3. To discuss the importance of social responsibility when operating internationally, especially in the areas of sustainability

4. To discuss some key issues in the social activities and consequences of globalized business

5. To examine corporate responses to globalization in the form of codes of conduct, among other things

Access a host of interactive learning aids to help strengthen your understanding of the chapter concepts at www.myiblab.com.

MyIBLab

When the last tree has been cut down, the last river has been polluted and the last fish has been caught— only then do you realize that money can't buy everything.

—**Native American proverb**

Source: Yegor Korzh/Shutterstock.com

181

CASE

Ecomagination and the Global Greening of GE

As noted on Map 5.1, a recent TV ad opens by inviting viewers to take up the perspective of a small green frog as it does a little globe hopping from one exotic location to another.[1] The frog, however, doesn't seem intent on hitting the usual tourist spots: He prefers stopovers at such places as a solar farm in South Korea, a water-purification plant in Kuwait, and a wind farm in Germany. To begin the second leg of his tour, he hops on a GE90 Aircraft engine flying over China and, from there, takes viewers to a "clean" coal-powered facility somewhere in Florida. As he boards a GE Evolution locomotive in the Canadian Rockies, a voiceover explains the point of all this seemingly ordinary sightseeing: "At GE, we're combining imagination with advanced technology around the world to make it a better place to live for everyone." The journey's end finds our frog in the midst of a lush—and very green—tropical rain forest.

"GREEN IS GREEN"

The ad is part of a major promotional campaign by General Electric Company (GE) for its Ecomagination Initiative. Announced in 2005 by CEO Jeffrey Immelt, Ecomagination is an ambitious strategy designed to demonstrate that an ecologically conscious conglomerate can cultivate the bottom line while doing its duty toward the global environment. Hence the campaign motto "Green Is Green." The clever promotional campaign has highlighted several interesting Ecomagination initiatives, such as the 2011 Super Bowl ad on Biogas Technology featuring cows at a rock concert (see footnote 1 for links to the YouTube ads). Based in Fairfield, Connecticut, GE is the world's second largest corporation (in terms of market capitalization) and operates in over 100 countries through six core businesses: commercial finance,

MAP 5.1 Global Travels of GE's "Green Frog," Its Symbol of Commitment to the Environment

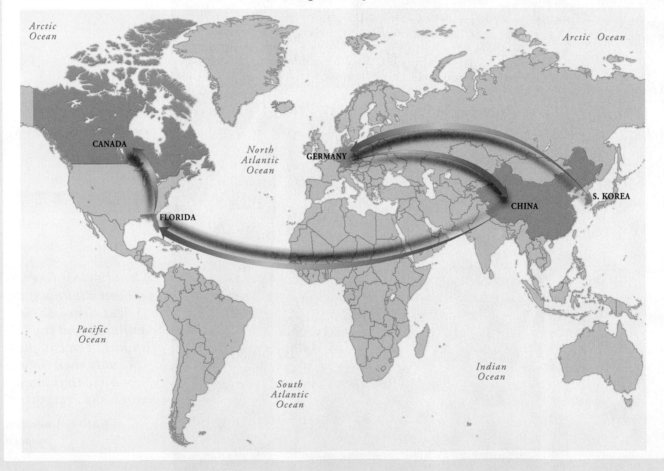

consumer finance, industrial manufacturing, infrastructure, healthcare, and communications. It sells, among other things, appliances, aircraft engines, consumer electronics, energy-related products such as solar panels and wind generators, locomotive engines, and nuclear products and services through a venture with GE Hitachi. GE's media division also includes 49 percent ownership of NBC Universal, following the completion of its sale of the majority ownership to Comcast Corporation in the first quarter of 2011.

When the company announced its plan to launch an internal green revolution, GE surprised both investors and industrial customers who had long seen the firm as an ally in the struggle against environmental activists and lobbyists. But as more and more evidence piles up to support the claim that carbon dioxide emitted from human-made sources is heating up average global temperatures, GE has decided to take a more conciliatory stance, allying itself with a growing number of companies that regard investor and environmental interests as intrinsically interlocked rather than diametrically opposed.

Commitments and Goals

Its new initiative represents five basic commitments on the part of GE:

- To reduce greenhouse emissions and improve the energy efficiency of operations
- To double investment in the research and development of "clean" technologies
- To increase revenues from those same technologies
- To reduce its global water use by 20 percent from 2006 to 2012
- To keep the public informed

GE now evaluates business unit managers not only on profitability and return on capital but also on success in reducing emissions of carbon dioxide, the chief greenhouse gas (GHG) attributed to global warming. Energy-intensive divisions, such as those catering to the power and industrial sectors, are responsible for the largest cuts, but even the financial-services and communications units are required to reduce whatever emissions they produce.

The company's overall target is a 1 percent reduction from 2004 levels by 2012. At first glance, that goal doesn't seem overly ambitious, but that number represents a significant improvement if you take into account the fact that, given GE's projected growth, levels would otherwise soar to 40 percent above 2004 levels. Immelt also committed the company to reducing the intensity of GHG emissions—its level of emissions in relation to the company's economic activity—30 percent by 2008 and to improving energy efficiency 30 percent by 2012. To ensure that these goals are met, Immelt has assembled a cross-business, cross-functional team to oversee planning and monitor progress. In 2007, GE reduced GHG emissions by 8 percent compared to 2004 levels. GE surpassed its goal by reducing GHG and intensity by 34 and 33 percent, respectively, in 2007. By 2009, GE has reduced GHG emissions by 22 percent compared to the 2004 baseline, ahead of schedule to achieve its goals for 2012.

A Little Consensus Seeking

In addition to instituting the internal changes necessary to curb GHG emissions, Immelt has taken a close look at GE's global political environment. He's traveled to Brussels and Tokyo to enlist the Belgian and Japanese governments in the global ecological discussion, and he's allied GE with other environmentally minded corporations to lobby American lawmakers on such matters as mandatory GHG reductions, essentially calling for regulations similar to those endorsed by the Kyoto Protocol, which calls for member countries to reduce emissions by 8 percent below 1990 levels by 2012. Working with the Environmental and Natural Resources Defense Council and the Pew Center on Global Climate Change, GE has also joined the likes of BP, DuPont, and Duke Energy to form the U.S. Climate Action Partnership, which seeks to help shape the international political debate over global warming.

Now, bear in mind that neither GE nor its corporate allies claim to be acting strictly from civic-minded motives: As usual—and as to be expected—they're pursuing their own best interests, particularly the idea that ecologically proactive firms are fashioning a strategic advantage over companies that are still dragging their feet. With other countries already enforcing limits stipulated by the Kyoto Protocol, and with other jurisdictions (such as the state of California) beginning to set their own limits, global corporations have much more to consider when it comes to developing forward-looking strategies and making long-term investments in an increasingly fragmented regulatory environment. With half of its markets located outside of the United States, GE is already under the jurisdiction of foreign governments that are more active than the United States in addressing environmental issues.

TECHNOLOGICAL TACTICS AND ECOFRIENDLY PRODUCTS

Under Immelt's direction, GE is also gearing up to double R&D investment in clean technologies, including renewable-energy and water-purification processes and fuel-efficient products, from $700 million in 2005 to $1.5 billion in 2010. However, as of 2009, GE has already reached its goal of $1.5 billion, one year ahead of schedule and despite the global recession. In turn, GE expects significant revenue growth. Its Ecomagination products earned $6 billion in 2004, $12 billion in 2006, $14 billion in 2007, and $18 billion in 2009. The company hopes to increase that total to $20 billion by 2010—and the way things are going, its projections appear to be on track.

Back in 2005, when the Ecomagination initiative was first launched, GE marketed only 17 products that met its own Ecomagination criteria; by 2008, there were 70 such products, and by 2009 that number has increased to 90. Some of these products include the Jenbacher Biogas Engine, which converts biological waste into electricity and heat, as well as all of GE's EnergyStar-approved consumer products.

On GE's main corporate Web site, it also discusses how its other standard products—such as clothes washers, refrigerators, and light bulbs—are energy efficient too. GE also intends to establish itself as an "energy-services" consultant and to bid on contracts for maintaining water-purification plants and wind farms, a venture that could be five times as lucrative as simply manufacturing the products needed for such projects. The use of its Web site to communicate information about its green products and efforts to improve its own reduction of GHG emissions is an example of commitment number 5, listed above, to keep the public informed.

"Solving Environmental Problems Is Good Business"

GE insists that the markets for such products and services are both growing and profitable, and Immelt is convinced that taking advantage of them not only helps the environment but also strengthens GE's strategic position with major profit opportunities. As one GE executive puts it, "Solving environmental problems is good business...and constitutes a significant growth strategy for the company."

GE also regards its Ecomagination strategy as a necessary response to customer demand. Before embarking on this initiative, GE spent 18 months working with industrial customers, inviting managers to two-day "dreaming sessions" to imagine life in 2015 and to discuss the kinds of products they'd need in such an environment. The result? GE came out of the talks with the indelible impression that both its customers and the social and political environments in which it conducted business would be demanding more environmentally "clean" products.

Going on the Offensive

"This is not just GE jamming environment down their throats," insisted former GE vice chairman David Calhoun. "We decided that if this is what our customers want, let's stop putting our heads in the sand, dodging environmental interests, and go from defense to offense." In fact, many of GE's Asian and European competitors had already begun investing in cleaner technologies, and GE knew it couldn't risk falling behind. Currently, the company is focusing on burgeoning markets in such developing countries as China and India, where rapid economic growth has spurred the need for expanded infrastructures, such as water and sewage systems, and for means of curbing appallingly high levels of pollution. China alone, which is home to no fewer than 16 of the world's 20 most polluted cities, has already earmarked $85 billion for environmental spending.

MIXED REACTIONS

Not surprisingly, GE has received its share of praise for its efforts to go green. It reached the ninth spot on Fortune magazine's list of the "Most Admired Companies" for 2009, and it has earned a place on the Dow Jones Sustainability Index, which identifies the 300 firms that perform best according to combined environmental, social, and financial criteria.

At the same time, however, the company has generated a certain amount of skepticism. What happens, for example, if the markets that it's betting on don't materialize fast enough (or at all)? Back in the 1980s and 1990s, for instance, a number of firms—including DuPont and such British and French water companies as Suez—predicting double-digit growth in clean-technology markets, invested heavily in the area, only to be forced to scale back considerably when demand didn't take off as expected.

Another potential risk revolves around the participation of developing nations in the clean-technology push. In particular, will they be willing to pay prices that developed countries pay for the technology that reaches the market? Even GE's Calhoun admitted that, at least in the key Chinese market, margins were already tight. And GE is still faced with the challenge of implementing the internal changes entailed by its fledgling green strategy. Traditionally, GE's culture has become accustomed to strategies of incremental change in time-tested products and services. In fact, its highly touted Six Sigma program, championed by ex-CEO Jack Welch, inherently discourages radical deviation and unnecessary risk taking. Management may have its work cut out when it comes to persuading marketing, sales, and production teams that untested, early-stage Ecomagination products are worth the risk.

Then, of course, there are clients and shareholders. Many of GE's customers work out of the utility sector, which has assumed a leadership role in disregarding warnings of climatic change and opposing ecofriendly regulation. In 2007, GE was presented with a shareowner resolution calling for top management to document the projected costs, benefits, and profits of the Ecomagination initiative. Some investors seemed particularly concerned about the company's newfound activism and the potential of newly instituted greening initiatives to alienate industrial customers. Given the enormous growth in revenue from the Ecomagination product line, generating more than $70 billion in revenue since 2005, it seems that GE's management made both a wise and profitable decision.

Ultimately, time will be the judge of GE's green strategy: whether it will bring about sufficient ecological and economic results to satisfy a worldwide constituency of customers, shareholders, CRN governments, and societies.

Case Review Note

Introduction

As we learned in Chapter 1, the globalization of business has not only been positive, but it has also resulted in three major criticisms: threats to national sovereignty, growth and environmental stress, and growing income inequality and personal stress. It is not easy to do business abroad. The greater the "distance" from one's home country, the more complicated it is to do business. Distance can be described in many different ways, but one way to identify distance is cultural (also known as psychic distance), administrative (such as political and institutional policies), geographic, and economic, or CAGE.[2] Given the criticisms of globalization and the challenge of companies and individuals doing business in areas of the world that are quite distant as defined above, how can companies and individuals be successful or at least not create serious mistakes?

In this chapter we will examine globalization and society from the standpoint of ethics and social responsibility. Initially, we'll examine ethics in a global context, especially in issues surrounding bribery and corruption, the environment, and corporate codes of conduct. Then we'll look at corporate social responsibility more broadly and examine how individuals as well as companies are trying to improve the human condition.

STAKEHOLDER TRADE-OFFS

Companies must satisfy
- Shareholders.
- Employees.
- Customers.
- Society.

To prosper (indeed, to survive), a company must satisfy different groups of **stakeholders** including shareholders, employees, customers, suppliers, and society at large. Obviously, this juggling act is often quite tricky. The stockholder-versus-stakeholder dilemma pits the demands of one stakeholder—the stockholder—against all the other stakeholders. The basic idea of focusing on stakeholders more broadly is that companies are able to take into consideration various socially important stakeholders as they make decisions.[3] In the short term, for example, group aims often conflict. *Stockholders* want additional sales and increased productivity (which result in higher profits and returns). *Employees* want safer workplaces and higher compensation. *Customers* want higher-quality products at lower prices. *Society* would like to see more jobs, increased corporate taxes, more corporate support for social services, and more trustworthy behavior on the part of corporate executives.

In the *long* term, all of these aims must be adequately met. If they aren't, there's a good chance that none of them will, especially if each stakeholder group is powerful enough to bring operations to a standstill. In addition, pressure groups, which may reflect the interests of any stakeholder group, lobby governments to regulate MNE activities both at home and abroad.

As we noted in our opening case, for example, GE's Ecomagination initiative has generated pressure from various constituencies, including clients and shareholders concerned about profitability, various governments concerned with drafting regulations, employees concerned about changes in the company's strategies and goals, and environmental lobbyists, NGOs (non-governmental organizations), and fellow businesses concerned with preserving the environment. Each of these groups has a powerful influence on how GE does business and on how successful it is in the marketplace.

Case Review Note

The Foundations of Ethical Behavior

Many actions elicit universal agreement on what is right or wrong, but other situations are less clear.

Companies and individuals who work for them must act *responsibly* wherever they go. However, when we look at ethical behavior, we tend to focus on the individual rather than the company, because individuals are the ones who finally make the decision on how they are going to behave. Top management in a company can determine the values the company espouses and expects its employees to adhere to. These values are generally included in Codes of Conduct, which we will discuss at the end of the chapter and in the behavior of other individuals in the organization, especially peers and superiors. In order to ensure those values are adhered to, companies will try to hire individuals who are willing to work in the type of ethical environment they are trying to create. However, people still have the make the decision about how they are going to act in any given situation.

There are three levels of moral development
- Preconventional.
- Conventional.
- Postconventional, autonomous, or principled.

In the sections below, we'll examine the cultural and legal dimensions to ethical behavior in a global context, but first let's briefly examine broad foundations of ethical behavior. One researcher has identified three levels of moral development.[4] Level 1, the *preconventional level*, is where children learn what is right and wrong, but they don't necessarily understand *why* their behavior is right or wrong. Level 2, the *conventional* level, we learn role-conformity, first from our peers (including parents) and then from societal laws. One could argue that company codes of conduct are also part of the *conventional* level of behavior in the narrow context of a company rather than a society. However, it is likely that these codes also reflect the values of the company's home country. In level 3, the *postconventional, autonomous,* or *principled,* level, individuals internalize moral behavior, not because they are afraid of sanctions, but because the truly believe that such behavior is right. It is possible that behavior under Level 2 and Level 3 are the same as long as individuals accept the laws where they live or the codes of conduct of the companies they work for as consistent with what they believe are correct.[5]

When individuals are confronted with ethical decisions, they enter the realm of moral reasoning. They examine their moral values, especially as related to levels 2 and 3 described above, and decide what to do. One approach, the **teleological approach,** is based on the idea that decisions are based on the consequences of the action. **Utilitarianism** is a consequences-based approach to moral reasoning, and it means that "an action is right if it produces, or if it tends to produce, the greatest amount of good for the greatest number of people affected by the action. Otherwise, the action is wrong."[6]

A second approach, the **deontological approach,** asserts that we make moral judgments or engage in moral reasoning independent of consequences. It implies that actions are right or wrong *per se*.[7] Another way to say this is ethics teaches that "people have a responsibility to do what is right and to avoid doing what is wrong."[8] When individuals engage in moral reasoning, they use one or the other approach, or possibly some mixture of the two.

When one moves abroad, moral reasoning becomes very complicated. Consequences may vary due to legal differences and what is right or wrong may depend to an extent on local values. Individuals need to figure out how make moral decisions, and so do the companies they work for. The first question is, why should companies and individuals care about ethical behavior, and then what are the cultural and legal foundations of ethical behavior as they consider how to adapt to a foreign environment?

WHY DO COMPANIES CARE ABOUT ETHICAL BEHAVIOR?

First, let's take a brief look at a preliminary but fairly important question: Why should companies worry about ethical behavior at all? As we discuss later, there are cultural and legal reasons to behave ethically. Also, individuals may have high standards of ethical behavior that can be translated into company policy. From a business standpoint, ethical behavior can be instrumental in achieving one or both of two possible objectives:

1. To develop competitive advantage
2. To avoid being perceived as irresponsible

As for the first objective, some analysts argue that responsible behavior contributes to strategic and financial success because it fosters trust, which in turn encourages commitment.[9] As our opening case indicates, for instance, GE's Ecomagination program reflects the belief of top managers that by actively responding to social concerns about global warming, GE can gain a strategic advantage over competitors, hoping to develop an edge in emerging markets facing severe environmental problems.

As for the second objective, companies are aware that more and more nongovernmental organizations (NGOs) are becoming active in monitoring—and publicizing—international corporate practices. The Interfaith Center on Corporate Responsibility (ICCR), for example, is an NGO that represents nearly 300 faith-based institutional investors, including national denominations, religious communities, pension funds, foundations, hospital corporations, economic development funds, asset management companies, colleges, and unions.[10] Initially organized to protest the policies of apartheid in South Africa, ICCR has become involved in a number of different projects, such as ranking companies in different industry sectors according to their carbon emissions, or introducing a resolution at the annual shareholders' meeting to adopt principles for healthcare reform. This is just one of many examples of NGOs that focus on country and industry issues. However, behaving irresponsibly, whether perceived or not has its costs as well. NGOs are not the only institutions that monitor the behavior of companies and their employees. Governments want to ensure that individual and corporate behavior are consistent with the best interest of the broader community and also want to be sure that laws are being followed. Breaking the law can have serious consequences.

The Cultural Foundations of Ethical Behavior

In the early 2000s, many companies (some based in the United States and others based in other countries) faced severe financial problems and even dissolution because of their managers' unethical or illegal actions. Enron, a U.S.-based energy company with operations

Case Review Note

Teleological Approach: Decisions are based on the consequences of the action.

Utilitarianism: An action if right if it produces the greatest amount of good.

Deontological Approach: Moral judgments are made and moral reasoning occurs independently of consequences.

NGOs are active in prodding companies to comply with certain standards of ethical behavior.

Values differ from country to country and sometimes between employees and companies.

worldwide, was one of the first companies forced into bankruptcy because of the illegal acts of some of its employees. They were followed by other U.S. companies, and then similar problems occurred in companies outside of the United States, such as Parmalat, which will be discussed in greater detail in Chapter 18. Some had hidden these actions for a number of years through their international operations. The results of these revelations included public outrage, investor anxiety, and, in general, a heightened interest in the activities of companies and the people who run them. (See Figure 5.1). Is this type of behavior universal, or is it more likely to occur in some countries or cultures than others?

RELATIVISM VERSUS NORMATIVISM

Chapter 2 discusses culture and how it varies from country to country. In spite of the differences discussed in that chapter it is tempting to assume that there is almost universal agreement on what's right and wrong when it comes to ethical and socially responsible behavior in business, especially if you follow the deontological approach described above.[11] In the real world, however, managers face situations in which the application of cultural values in differences is less than crystal clear. For example, people have different ideas about right and wrong that are influenced by family and religious values, laws and social pressures, one's own observations and experiences, and even economic circumstances. Because ethical convictions tend to be deep-seated, people can be avid in defending their views.

Even within a given country there are starkly contrasting views on ethical matters. To complicate things even more, our own personal values may differ from our employers' policies, prevalent social norms, or both. Finally, everything that complicates dilemmas in the domestic business environment tends to complicate them even further in the international arena. Does ethical behavior vary by country, or are there uniform values that everyone should share?

Relativism   One point of view is to accept the fact that there are significant differences from country to country that might affect our behavior. "When in Rome, do as the Romans do" is an oft-quoted expression that dates to the fourth century AD in a letter to St. Augustine from St. Ambrose, the bishop of Milan, and really has nothing to do with ethical behavior. In fact, it was a statement that "when I go to Rome, I fast on Sunday, but here in Milan I do not."[12] In other words, adjust to what make sense in different

---

Concept Check

Recall from Chapter 2 our discussion of "Cultural Awareness" and the various ways in which social and cultural distinctions can characterize a country's population. We also observed that companies doing business overseas need to be sensitive to internal diversity: They should remember that people in most nations are often members of multiple **cultures** and in some cases have more in common with certain foreign groups than with domestic groups.

Relativism: Ethical truths depend on the groups holding them.

FIGURE 5.1   What's Right and What's Wrong?

Sometimes businesspeople face ethical dilemmas: They must consider cultural, moral, legal, and political factors in choosing between acceptable but opposing alternatives. On the other hand, of course, there are questions of right versus wrong—whether or not to do something that's unethical or downright illegal.

Source: Mike Shapiro, Cartoonstock.com.

"Don't worry about doing the right thing. They'll be plenty of time for that when you're fired, retired, or reincarnated."

environments. In has been translated, retranslated, and adapted to many different contexts over the years. At its most basic level, it means that you adapt to local customs out of respect for them. A more aggressive application of the phrase is "if it's okay to bribe in country X, I guess I need to bribe when I'm in country X." But the phrase need not be an excuse for ethical lapses. The application of this expression in an international environment may depend on whether we assume that decisions are based on the consequences of our actions or on a strongly held view of right and wrong. Relativism holds that ethical truths depend on the values of a particular society and may vary from one society or country to another.[13] The implication is that it would not be appropriate to inject or enforce one's ethical values on another or that differences in local values or moral behavior can or must be adopted by foreigners in that country, whether or not they are consistent with your own values and beliefs.

Normativism Normativism, on the other hand, holds that there are indeed universal standards of behavior that, although influenced differently by different cultural values, should be accepted by people everywhere. Even in a pluralistic society, such as the United States, there is a large core of commonly held values and norms.[14] However, there are other values and norms that people adopt as their own. The key is to distinguish between what is common to all and what is unique to the individual. As suggested in Chapter 2, these commonly held values and norms are part of what distinguishes one culture (or country) from another. From this perspective, *nonintervention* is unethical. Not surprisingly, then, companies and their employees are always struggling with the problem of how to implement their own ethical principles in foreign business environments: Are they reflections of universally valid "truths" (the normative approach)? Or should the company be willing to adapt to local conditions on the assumption that every place has its own "truths" and needs to be treated differently (the relative approach)?

Walking the Fine Line between Relative and Normative Often, a company faces certain pressures to comply with local norms. These may take the form of laws that permit—or even require—only certain practices that grant competitive advantages to firms accepting local norms while throwing up roadblocks in front of companies that try to impose home-country practices in the local arena. Conversely, firms may face certain pressures *not* to comply from its home-country government, or even from constituencies that threaten retaliatory action if it submits to objectionable foreign practices.

Many individuals and organizations have laid out minimum levels of business practices that they say a company (domestic or foreign) must follow regardless of the legal requirements or ethical norms prevalent where it operates.[15] One could consider this as behavior based on principles of honesty and fairness, or what can be called "ordinary decency."[16] They argue that legal permission for some action may be given by uneducated or corrupt leaders who do not understand or care about the consequences, and that MNEs are obligated to set good examples that may become the standard for responsible behavior.

Negotiating between Evils Another potential complication derives from the fact that both societies and companies must often choose between the lesser of two evils. Consider the following illustration. As most of us know by now, the pesticide DDT is dangerous to the environment (especially to birds), and high-income countries have banned its use. At the same time, companies headquartered in those countries have been chided for selling DDT to lower-income countries that need it to fight malaria, one of the world's worst diseases.[17]

The Legal Foundations of Ethical Behavior

Dealing with *ethical dilemmas* is often a balancing act between *means* (the actions we take, which may be right or wrong) and *ends* (the consequences of our actions, which may also be right or wrong). There are legal foundations for ethical behavior that provide guidance in establishing ethical behavior, but legal justification is more rooted in the teleological approach to moral reasoning and moral behavior (consequences) instead of the deontological approach—a behavior is either right or wrong. However, there are good reasons to consider the law as a foundation of ethical behavior, just as there are limitations to using the law.

LEGAL JUSTIFICATION: PRO AND CON

Indeed, some experts suggest that legal justification for ethical behavior is the only important standard. According to this theory, an individual or company can do anything that isn't illegal. Opponents respond that there are five good reasons why this is inadequate:

1. Because some things that are *unethical* are not *illegal,* the law is not an appropriate standard for regulating *all* business activity. Some forms of interpersonal behavior, for example, can clearly be wrong even if they're not against the law.

2. The law is slow to develop in emerging areas of concern, and it takes time to pass laws and test them in courts. Moreover, because laws are essentially responses to issues that have already surfaced, they can't always anticipate dilemmas that will arise in the future. Countries with well-developed systems of civil law rely on specificity, and it isn't feasible to enact laws dealing with every possible ethical issue.

3. The law is often based on imprecisely defined moral concepts that can't be separated from the legal concepts they underpin. In other words, we must in any case consider moral concepts whenever we're considering legal ones.

4. The law often needs to undergo scrutiny by the courts. This is especially true of case law, in which the courts create law by establishing precedent.

5. The law simply isn't very efficient. "Efficiency" in this case implies achieving ethical behavior at a very low cost, and it would be impossible to solve every ethical behavioral problem with an applicable law.[18]

Those who support the legal-justification standard reply that there are also several good reasons for using the law as a justification for ethical behavior:

1. Because the law embodies many of a country's moral principles, it is in fact an adequate guide for proper conduct.

2. The law provides a clearly defined set of rules, and following it at least establishes a good precedent for acceptable behavior.

3. The law contains enforceable rules that apply to everyone.

4. Because the law represents a consensus derived from widely shared experience and deliberation, it reflects careful and wide-ranging discussions.[19]

EXTRATERRITORIALITY

When, however, you're trying to use the law to govern behavior in different countries, you'll soon run into a very basic problem—namely, that laws vary from country to country. Recall the challenges faced by GE in its efforts to deal with international variations in environmental laws. GE has actually lobbied the U.S. government to enact legislation more closely aligned to Europe's, reasoning that having to deal with a shifting array of regulations and limitations will not only impede its strategy but also become unnecessarily costly.

In addition, strong home-country governments may adopt a practice known as **extraterritoriality**: imposing domestic legal and ethical practices on the foreign subsidiaries of companies headquartered in their jurisdictions. This has become very controversial and, as argued by some, inconsistent with increased globalization and the need to collaborate across national boundaries.[20]

Legal justification for ethical behavior may not be sufficient because not everything that is unethical is illegal.

The law is a good basis for ethical behavior because it embodies local cultural values.

As countries tackle similar ethical issues, laws will become more similar.

Concept Check

Recall our explanation in Chapter 3 of a civil law system as one based on a systematic and extensive codification of laws.

Concept Check

As we explain in Chapter 3, the continued democratization of countries has led to the diffusion of the rule of law in place of the rule of man, which is more symbolic of totalitarian regimes. However, the global economic crisis may have slowed that process for a while.

CRN
Case Review Note

ETHICS AND CORPORATE BRIBERY

Granted, we've gone from con to pro and back again in our introduction to the relationship between ethics and the law. Nevertheless, let's return once more to a pro-law argument for certain types of behavior. Why? Because despite all the problems that arise, considering the law is still a good place to start when studying ethics. The reason shouldn't be surprising: As countries find themselves searching for common solutions to common problems—problems like those discussed in the following sections—they find themselves taking common legal steps. And in the effort to tackle important problems, they encounter certain externalities that must be solved in the public arena: by-products of activities that affect the well-being of people or the health of the environment even if those effects don't show up in market prices.

From our discussion of the cultural and legal foundations of ethical behavior, you have some tools for assessing worldwide corporate behavior. Let's examine some key ethical issues that companies must confront in doing business in foreign countries.

Corruption and Bribery

The first issue is *bribery,* which is actually one facet of the much bigger issue of *corruption.* The multifaceted determinants of corruption include cultural, legal, and political forces.[21] As defined by Transparency International, corruption is "the misuse of entrusted power for private gain."[22] There are some variations on this basic definition, but it is as good as any. Here we'll focus more on bribery, because it is at the heart of corrupt behavior on the part of MNEs.

Congressional investigations of U.S. MNEs in the 1970s yielded anecdotal information that questionable payments to foreign government officials had long been business as usual in both industrial and developing countries. How much money was involved in payouts from U.S. MNEs and firms based in other countries? Reports indicated that 400 corporations had admitted making questionable or illegal payments in excess of $300 million. In comparison, the U.S. government reported that between 1994 and 2001 it learned of cases in which foreign firms from more than 50 countries had offered bribes to buyers in more than 100 countries, involving more than 400 competitions for contracts valued at $200 billion.[23] It may be impossible to assess the true value of bribery, but it is huge.

Figure 5.2 also offers some interesting insight into the perceived levels of public-sector corruption, identifying how likely companies are to offer bribes in the countries

> Bribery of public officials takes place to obtain government contracts or to get officials to do what they should be doing anyway.

FIGURE 5.2 Where Bribes Are (and Are Not) Business as Usual

Transparency International asked country experts, nonresidents, and residents about the overall extent of corruption (frequency and/or size of bribes) in the public and private sectors. The scale runs from 0 to 10, with 10 least likely to pay a bribe. The figures include a sample of countries.

Source: Transparency International, "TI Corruption Perceptions Index" (2010), at http://transparency.org (accessed February 7, 2011).

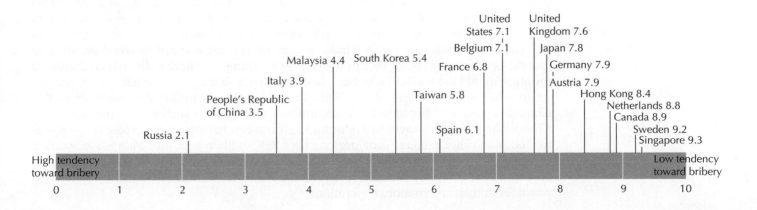

listed. Although no country is free of corruption, poverty is obviously a strong factor. Moreover, corruption requires someone to give a bribe in order for someone to take a bribe, and for intermediaries, from bankers to accountants, to facilitate the transactions. Transparency International not only publishes a Corruption Perceptions Index but also a Bribe Payers Index, which recently found that individuals from Belgium and Canada were least likely to pay bribes and individuals from Russia, China, and Mexico were most likely to pay bribes. The United States fit somewhere in between.[24]

THE CONSEQUENCES OF CORRUPTION

Bribes are payments or promises to pay cash or anything of value.

What's wrong with bribery? A number of things. First, it affects both company performance and country economies. Higher levels of corruption, for instance, correlate strongly with lower national growth rates and lower levels of per capita income.[25] Corruption can also erode the authority of governments that condone it. Over the years, bribery-based scandals have led to the downfall of numerous heads of state, along with many government officials and numerous business executives imprisoned, fined, or forced to resign. In an extreme case, China's former head of the State Food and Drug Administration, convicted of accepting bribes in return for approving certain medicines, was executed.[26] Moreover, disclosures of corruption not only damage the reputations of companies and whole countries, they also compromise the legitimacy of MNEs in the eyes of local and global communities.[27] Finally, corruption is expensive, inflating a company's costs and bloating its prices. And yet, corruption persists as one of the most challenging concerns in international business and politics in the world today and in some cases, reaches to the uppermost levels of international MNEs.

One such example of corruption in international business comes from the recent case of Rio Tinto in China. In July 2009, four executives of Rio Tinto's Chinese operations were arrested on suspicion of stealing state secrets and corruption during negotiations for iron ore pricing and distribution among China's largest steel mills. The charges were eventually reduced to stealing commercial secrets related to the benchmark prices being negotiated with the China Iron and Steel Association and bribe-taking, and for supposedly working illegally with private steel mill directors trying to gain an advantage in negotiations with Rio Tinto.

The four executives and Rio's top iron ore sales executive in China pleaded guilty to the charges of taking bribes from Chinese business partners in March 2010 and were each sentenced to prison terms of seven to 14 years. Rio Tinto quickly cut ties with the convicted employees in order to disconnect itself from the allegations and negative exposure internationally and to restore trust with the Chinese government, the company's single largest customer for iron ore, having accounted for 24 percent of Rio's 2009 global revenue. While the case is seemingly closed and Rio Tinto and China are moving on, it illustrates several of the key consequences of corruption in international business.

First, the Rio Tinto case in China has far-reaching implications for the environment of doing business in China for MNEs. The combination of China's opaque judicial process and reluctance to make its policies on the illegality of corruption uniform across the board make it difficult for companies to adapt to the behavior of businesses in China. Along these same lines, the relationship between countries with vested interests in Chinese business, such as Australia in this case, must attempt to stand on shifting ground on issues of corruption in businesses working internationally, which threatens the stability of business and economic relations between the two countries.

In addition, the failure of Rio Tinto to cultivate a corruption-free environment in China is a very real threat to the company as a whole. With such a large investment in Chinese iron ore sales (over $10 billion), Rio Tinto can hardly afford to lose its competitive edge to other mineral providers such as BHP Billiton Ltd. and Vale SA in gaining contracts with Chinese steel producers. However, equally important to the long-term success of the company is its ability to work within the Chinese law and eliminate illicit practices in their international operations.[28]

WHAT'S BEING DONE ABOUT CORRUPTION?

Many efforts are underway to slow the pace of bribery as an international business practice at global, regional, and national levels. International multilateral accords for combating bribery at the global rather than regional level include those established by the OECD (Organization for Economic Cooperation and Development), the ICC (International Chamber of Commerce), and the United Nations through UNCAC (United Nations Convention against Corruption).

The OECD comprises 34 mostly high-income countries from around the world. Its Anti-Bribery Convention, signed in 1997, establishes legally binding standards to criminalize bribery of foreign public officials in international business transactions and provides recommendations to the 38 signatory countries, which adopted the 2009 Anti-Bribery Recommendation. Of course, the member countries have to implement the recommendations into national law in order for them to have any weight. A 2010 study by Transparency International found that member countries' enforcement of the recommendations was uneven at best. In fact, they found active enforcement by only seven countries, moderate enforcement in nine, and little or no enforcement by 20 countries.[29]

The ICC issued a code of rules against corrupt practices in 1999 and has since been active in supporting other multilateral approaches to combating bribery, including codes of conduct issued by the OECD and the United Nations (UN). Whereas the OECD Convention targets the supply side of companies bribing officials in the public sector, the ICC is particularly interested in the private sector and the demand side of cross-border economics, where extortion of companies by public officials is a favorite criminal practice.[30]

The United Nations Convention against Corruption (UNCAC) covers a broad range of corruption issues and does not focus solely on bribery. In November 2009, representatives of the 148 member governments having ratified the UNCAC met in Doha, Qatar, to discuss a review mechanism to see if member governments are applying UNCAC standards to combat corruption. The conference concluded with the creation of a more specific review mechanism to measure implementation of UNCAC initiatives in ratifying member states over successive four-year periods. Thus, in 2010, implementation progress reviews were conducted for 28 UNCAC ratifying members by both regional and international peers. The second session of the Implementation Review Group took place from May 30 to June 3, 2011 for another 42 members of the convention. Once again, enforcement is a major issue because the UN has no power to enforce its provisions—this must be done by member governments.[31]

In addition to the broader global efforts to combat corruption, regional efforts in Africa and Latin America are addressing specific regional issues. However, the key is national legislation and enforcement. Changes in behavior take time.

Regional Initiative: The European Union The European Commission, the executive branch of the EU, confirmed its support for strong anti-corruption measures within the EU in a 2007 communication to the European Council, Parliament, and Economic and Social Committee. This included the adoption of the UN's official definition of corruption and support for many of the policies contained within international agreements. The communication also sanctions the work of the Commission's office of antifraud, OLAF, which conducts the affairs of the EU relevant to corporate and individual corruption, as well as an internal auditing service, which monitors the activities of all of the commission's departments. However, one of the lingering concerns within the EU is the lack of uniformity and transparency of laws across the national membership, as most antibribery provisions are left up to the member governments, which tend to be more strongly influenced by the OECD and the international conventions sponsored by the UN. Thus, regional approaches to antibribery within the EU remain relatively ineffective.[32]

National Initiative: The U.S. Foreign Corrupt Practices Act An example of a national approach is the **Foreign Corrupt Practices Act (FCPA)** in the United States. The FCPA

> The Foreign Corrupt Practices Act is U.S. legislation that makes bribery illegal. It applies to domestic or foreign operations and to company employees as well as their agents overseas.

outlaws bribery payments by U.S. firms to foreign officials, political parties, party officials, and political candidates. In 1998, its coverage was extended to include bribery by foreign firms operating in any U.S. territory. The FCPA applies not only to companies registered in the United States but also to any foreign company quoted on any stock exchange in the United States.

There is an apparent inconsistency in the provisions of the FCPA—namely, the fact that although it's legal to make payments to officials to expedite otherwise legitimate transactions (officially called *facilitating payments* but sometimes referred to as *speed money* or *grease money*), payments can't be made to officials who aren't directly responsible for the transactions in question. In 1988, an amendment to the FCPA actually excluded facilitating payments from the definition of *bribery*. Now, for example, payment to a customs official to clear legitimate merchandise is legal, whereas paying a government minister to influence a customs official is not. What's the difference? In the former case the FCPA recognizes that officials can delay legal transactions indefinitely or until they receive payments. However, sometimes behaviors that might be considered inappropriate by individuals in one country would be considered appropriate in another. A survey of Chinese managers found that gift giving is considered a normal part of the high-context Chinese culture and not a bribe, unless the gift is perceived as being so big that it results in contracts and favors in a business transaction.[33] The problem is in establishing the size of the gift. In 2007, the U.S. Justice Department levied a $2.5 million fine against U.S. telecommunications company Lucent Technologies Inc. for improperly recording millions of dollars in travel to Disney World and Las Vegas for about 1,000 Chinese employees of state-owned telecom companies.[34] Apparently, the Justice Department didn't consider the trips as mere gifts.

An interesting twist to the FCPA is that the U.S. Justice Department is aggressively pursuing U.S. companies that make payments made to executives at companies owned by governments, especially Chinese state-owned enterprises, under the assumption that they are really government employees. This goes beyond the intent of the law, which was to pursue payments made to government officials to abuse their power.[35]

The U.S. government continues to step up anticorruption efforts both at home and abroad. As of December 2010, The United States Department of Justice had filed at least 140 cases at various stages of investigation of violations of the FCPA compared to only 43 in 2007.[36] Additional legislation has been enacted since the FCPA that indirectly affects the crackdown on corporate bribery. Most notable, perhaps, is the Sarbanes-Oxley Act (SOX). Passed in 2002, SOX was a response to an epidemic of well-known corporate scandals involving such companies as Enron and Tyco International. It toughened standards with regard to corporate governance, financial disclosure, and oversight of accounting and auditing practices. With the passage of SOX, the Justice Department began to use the FCPA more aggressively to combat bribery.

In addition to the U.S. government, other governments worldwide are starting to crack down harder on bribery. Although the European Union does not have an FCPA/SOX-type law against bribery, many of its countries have begun to move more aggressively against bribery. Until recently, many of them allowed companies to deduct commissions paid to win foreign contracts as tax-deductible expenses. However, France (in 2000) and Germany (in 2003) have now outlawed such practices, although Britain does not have a formal anticorruption law.[37]

Industry Initiatives   Finally, various industries have recently stepped up their own efforts against bribery and corruption. In 2005, for example, in conjunction with the World Economic Forum, nearly 50 multinational construction and natural-resources companies, representing at least $300 billion in annual revenues, signed a "zero-tolerance" pact against extortion by bribery. By 2010, the number of signatory companies had risen to 150. This voluntary effort, called the Partnering Against Corruption Initiative (PACI), calls for member firms to set up "extensive internal programs to educate and oversee company officials and business partners and also [to] prohibit political contributions and

Sarbanes-Oxley legislation in the United States is helpful in combating corruption through more effective corporate governance, financial disclosure, and public accounting oversight.

A zero-tolerance pact against bribery was signed by companies at the 2005 World Economic Forum.

charitable gifts designed to curry favor."[38] Although many firms still adhere to their own antibribery standards, participants hope that the PACI will encourage companies within the industry to monitor each other.

Relativism, the Rule of Law, and Responsibility Obviously, avoiding bribe payments when they're regarded as business as usual is a challenge, especially when business is being held up by foreign government officials. Although it might be easier to fall back on the standard of cultural **relativism** (and, for example, simply pay bribes where they're accepted and/or expected), the international initiatives described in this section have made some headway in introducing the rule of law into more and more international business activity. Companies are now freer to establish policies and procedures that are consistent with both their own domestic laws and those of other countries. As the principles laid down by the OECD and the UN are incorporated into national statutes, companies are finding that laws and practices that once varied radically from country to country have become more uniform and easier to implement.

Concept Check

In Chapter 3, we explain how important it is for a nation's political process to generate rational laws that companies and individuals can follow. We also explain that, unfortunately, laws are based on cultural values that are bound to vary from country to country. Finally, we point out that laws, rational or otherwise, aren't necessarily enforced with the same rigor in every country.

Point — **Are Top Managers Responsible When Corruption Is Afoot?**

Point **Yes** In November 2006, German police raided the offices of the giant electrical engineering and electronics company Siemens AG. They netted nearly 36,000 documents to support allegations that Siemens regularly diverted funds filed under bogus consulting contracts into a network of "black accounts" for bribing officials in countries like Italy, Greece, Argentina, and Saudi Arabia, where Siemens was seeking lucrative public-sector contracts. Following the raid, the company itself announced it had uncovered over €420 million (U.S. $570 million) in suspicious payments going back as far as the early 1990s. Several managers caught up in the probe insisted that corruption was endemic to the company's culture and that they had acted with the knowledge—even the approval—of CEO Klaus Kleinfeld and board chief (and former CEO) Heinrich von Pierer.[39]

Now, nobody will deny that what Siemens employees did was misguided and wrongheaded, but let's be realistic: Step 1 in every textbook on foiling fraud is to follow the money, and in this case you can follow the money back to a culture that condones financial shenanigans. That means the real blame for the company's mess rests with top management.

Here's a little background on the business world in which Siemens is a leading corporate citizen. Compared to some other countries, Germany was slow to enact laws prohibiting bribery. In fact, up until 1999, German law allowed executives to write off overseas bribes as legitimate business expenses. Until 2002, it was still legal to bribe employees of foreign companies for anyone willing to absorb the cost without the tax break.[40] Even when the laws began to change, German businesses were slow to catch on. In 2005 alone, they racked up roughly 90,000 corporate crimes.[41]

The point? Like a lot of other German companies, Siemens was hanging onto a corporate culture that was perfectly comfortable with bribery and other forms of corrupt behavior. One senior executive says it even had an encryption code for itemizing bribe payments. The same exec says that he himself got a call from a Saudi contractor demanding $910 million in commission payments or else they'd send incriminating documents to certain U.S. authorities. When the exec alerted his superiors—including Kleinfeld and von Pierer—they replied that $910 million was perhaps a little high but suggested that a deal for $17 million in "past obligations" and $33 million in "hush money" wasn't beyond reason. According to this insider, most of his colleagues tossed off bribe payments as mere "peccadilloes" because, after all, "it was all for the good of the company."[42]

All of this transpired on von Pierer's and Kleinfeld's watch. To say the goings-on completely escaped their notice is unrealistic. It's top management's responsibility to lay out the ethical boundaries at a company and see that no one crosses them. Siemens management wasn't guarding its own ethical borders.

On top of everything else, Kleinfeld's management style of "fix, sell, or close"[43] was hardly the right approach for a company with a dirty-tricks chapter in its playbook. Once he became CEO, Kleinfeld immediately set high profit targets and began spinning off divisions that apparently weren't sufficiently inspired by the profit motive. His motto was "go for profit and growth," and when a team of managers failed to deliver, he just took an axe to the whole division.[44] Under top-down pressure like that, what other choice did employees really have? If the answer is "none," you have to admit that ultimate responsibility for company-wide behavior rests in the executive suite.

Are Top Managers Responsible When Corruption Is Afoot?

Counterpoint

Counterpoint

No Granted, Siemens was up to its corporate neck in a culture of corruption. But is that supposed to excuse the actions of the individual grown-ups directly involved in the present case? Or, to put it in more legal-sounding, Latinate terms: Does it mitigate their culpability? At the end of the business day, the actions of individuals, more than the official codes and theoretical due diligence of top managers, actually shape a company's culture.

Even so, back when he was CEO, von Pierer not only authorized a strict company-wide code of conduct, he also hired a few hundred compliance officers to enforce it.[45] When his turn came, Kleinfeld instituted a "zero-tolerance" policy toward corruption.[46] But more importantly, for a far-flung, highly decentralized conglomeration with 11 business units run by separate boards as virtually independent operating entities, it's hardly reasonable to expect top executives back home in Munich to know everything that's going on from Siemens Turkey to Siemens Taiwan. Former CEO von Pierer is absolutely right in arguing that under such circumstances, "deducing a political responsibility" would be absurd. As most of us learned in business school, the job of senior executives is strategic planning; it doesn't involve auditing the books and double-checking every suspicious double entry.[47]

And while we're on the subject of top-level managers, it's true that a bunch of former employees who are in trouble with the law claim that top Siemens managers knew all about the bribery and other underhanded activities. So far, however, no one, including an independent law firm that's looking into the matter, has found any solid evidence that they're telling the truth. Plus, neither Kleinfeld nor von Pierer has been officially accused of any wrongdoing.

As for the question of whether dragging its governmental feet on antibribery legislation has anything to do with the resilience of corruption in Germany, there's little question that adapting to or passing new laws may take quite some time. But that doesn't justify breaking them until you're good and ready to obey them. Regardless of the company's approach to adapting to a new legal environment, those of its employees who perpetuated the practice of paying bribes fully understood what the law said and that they were violating it. Besides, creating false consulting contracts and diverting company money into slush funds has come under the heading of legally dubious behavior for a long time just about everywhere. And no matter when a law goes into effect, it always comes with a pretty clear list of "dos and don'ts." It's obvious that certain individuals at Siemens took it on themselves to ignore those guidelines.

Finally, what about the argument that employees had no choice but to violate the law because they had to protect their jobs? The fact that many of them faced criminal charges and jail time with no hope of continuing their careers at Siemens or anywhere else attests to the faulty logic of that claim. Meanwhile, their former employer, which is still responsible for nearly half a million paychecks worldwide, has already paid out €63 million (U.S. $85.7 million) to outside auditors and investigators and still faces a court-ordered fine of €38 million (U.S. $51.4 million) following the conviction of just one finance officer and one consultant.[48] By the end of 2008, U.S. and German authorities had levied $1.6 billion in fines against Siemens. Why the United States? Because Siemens lists its stock there and is therefore subject to the FCPA. Siemens also risks being banned from contract bidding in any one of the 190 countries where it does business and generates wealth.

Ethics and the Environment

If for no other reason, environmental problems are important because they're a matter of life or death, either now or in the future. As we saw in our opening case, GE has come to see eco-responsibility as a matter of protecting not only the future of the environment but also its own future. Like GE, companies contribute to environmental damage in a variety of ways. Some, for example, endanger the environment by contaminating the air, soil, or water during manufacturing, or by making products such as automobiles or electricity that release fossil-fuel contaminants into the environment.

In extracting natural resources, other companies also have a direct and unmistakable impact on the environment. But even in these cases, the issue isn't necessarily clear-cut. Granted, although some resources (such as minerals, gas, and oil) may not be renewable, others (such as timber) are, and some observers even suggest that resources can never really become scarce. Why? Because as they become less available, prices go up and technology or substitutes compensate.

Case Review Note

Companies that extract natural resources, generate air or water waste, or manufacture products such as autos that generate pollution need to be concerned with their environmental impact.

◀ Wind energy is truly a global business. Suzlon, headquartered in India and one of the world's leading suppliers of wind turbines, supplied these turbines to Wasatch Wind to construct a wind farm in Spanish Fork, Utah (USA). The farm harvests primarily the southeasterly nightly canyon wind resource considered to be one of the most reliable winds in the United States. Suzlon is one of GE's main competitors in producing wind turbines.

WHAT IS "SUSTAINABILITY"?

Despite a lot of confusion and disagreement over the term, we assume here that **sustainability** means meeting the needs of the present without compromising the ability of future generations to meet their own needs. Proponents of the concept argue that sustainability considers what's best for both people and the environment. Nevertheless, it remains a controversial concept—one whose definition is subject to different interpretations, from environmentalists to businesspeople.[49] It is important that, regardless of how they feel about the principle of sustainability, businesses that affect the environment establish policies for responsible behavior toward the earth—a responsibility that has both cultural and legal ramifications.

But is it possible that sustainability is not only a good business practice, but also good business? Can a company succeed by exclusively offering environmentally friendly products in the modern competitive world of business? Anecdotal evidence seems to suggest that the answer is a resounding yes. To explore this idea further, let's take a look at a company that combines the idea of environmental responsibility and profitability.

In the modern world of business, sustainability is not merely a standard for international enterprises, but a surging industry of its own. Sustainability is no longer merely an internal concern of large companies, but an entirely new category of business of its own. Multinational companies are emerging to address the needs of international businesses and society as a whole by offering solutions and services that address some of the world's pressing environmental concerns. These companies function in a wide range of activities from renewable energy services and production to environmental cleanup and recycling. These companies devoted exclusively to sustainability are all attempting to find a niche in the world market for clean products and services as consumers become more environmentally conscious.

One such company, based in Shepherd, Montana, is called Floating Island International. FII was founded by Bruce Kania in 2000, when a combined concern for the environment and a clever business concept formed the opportunity for a valuable business venture. After several years of research and development, Kania and a team of engineers and scientists created their primary product, BioHaven Islands, made from post-consumer recycled materials and native plants and soils. The islands have more than 30 identified applications for use including wetland treatment and preservation, erosion control, and habitat creation and are designed to mimic natural biological processes that encourage restoration of food chains and maintain a clean environment.[50]

Sustainability involves meeting the needs of the present without compromising the ability of future generations to meet their own needs while taking into account what is best for the people and the environment.

Sustainability is no longer just good business practice. New businesses are emerging that are combining the idea of environmental responsibility and profitability.

Within the first five years of operations, from 2005 to 2010, FII produced and sold over 4,000 of its floating islands around the world, including the United States, Canada, Australia, UK, Korea, Singapore, and New Zealand. The company licenses its products to regional dealers across the United States, but also has licensees in China, New Zealand, and South Africa. Clearly, this is an example of a company that is making its mark internationally by focusing exclusively on filling the demand for environmentally oriented products, which are also profitable.[51]

GLOBAL WARMING AND THE KYOTO PROTOCOL

To illustrate some of the challenges faced by these companies, we start by examining the issue of *global warming,* including the role of the *Kyoto Protocol* and its potential impact on corporate behavior.

Global warming results from the release of greenhouse gases that trap heat in the atmosphere rather than allowing it to escape.

The Kyoto Protocol   At the core of the international treaty called the Kyoto Protocol is the theory that global climate change results from an increase in carbon dioxide and other gases that act like the roof of a greenhouse, trapping heat that would normally be radiated back into space and thereby warming the planet. If carbon dioxide emissions aren't reduced and controlled, rising temperatures could have catastrophic consequences, including melting the polar ice cap, flooding coastal regions, shifting storm patterns, reducing farm output, causing drought, and even killing off plant and animal species.[52] Most observers agree that the world is warming; however, there's no clear consensus on the cause or scope of the problem, much less the solution.[53]

The Kyoto Protocol was signed in 1997 to require countries to cut their greenhouse gas emissions to 5.2 percent below 1990 levels between 2008 and 2012. Some countries have adopted stricter requirements, and others, such as the United States, China, and India, have not ratified the Protocol.

The **Kyoto Protocol,** an extension of the UN Framework Convention on Climate Change of 1994, was born of the need to reduce greenhouse gas (GHG) emissions from burning fossil fuels and methane. Signed in 1997, the Protocol committed signatory countries to reduce the emissions to 5.2 percent below 1990 levels between 2008 and 2012.

As of October 2010, 193 nations and regional economic organizations had ratified the Protocol.[54] The United States, which generated 19 percent of the world's greenhouse gases in 2008, initially signed the agreement in 1998 but withdrew in 2001, citing concerns about domestic economic growth and exemptions for rapidly growing developing countries like China and India.[55] According to statistics compiled by the International Energy Agency, China's 2008 greenhouse gas emissions made up 22 percent of the world total, outpacing the United States for the second straight year (although production of greenhouse gases per capita in the United States remained nearly four times that of China.)[56] Why is the United States reluctant to get on board? Basically, it's banking on the development of low-carbon technologies to solve the problem and would prefer not to meet mandatory reductions for fear that reduced economic growth would create domestic employment problems. Although U.S. President Barack Obama is moving aggressively to implement new policies to reduce GHG emissions, he prefers to work on the new framework for climate control that will replace the existing Kyoto Protocol in 2012 rather than sign the existing Protocol. In addition, the G8 Summit that was held in July 2009 agreed to a broad mandate to reduce GHG emissions by 80 percent by 2050, but it failed to agree to set short-term, more concrete goals or to agree on the start date for the 80 percent cut. Germany and other European countries wanted emissions cut from 1990 levels, and President Obama wanted emissions cut from current levels—a significant difference. The resolution read that the reductions would be counted against 1990 levels "or later years" (a concession to the United States).[57]

One approach favored by many, including President Obama, is to invest more in alternative and renewable energy, such as nuclear, wind, and solar energy. The dramatic rise in oil prices in 2007–2008 spurred a lot of interest in renewable energy, but enthusiasm waned when energy prices fell. Renewable energy still has a bright future, and suppliers are truly global. Germany, for example, produces more energy from wind than any other country, and its companies have a head start in penetrating global markets.

However, suppliers from India, Spain, and Denmark are also major suppliers of wind turbines and other parts.[58]

Nuclear energy is an important source of electricity in many countries, supplying 75 percent of France's domestic energy production, for example, compared with 29 percent in Japan and 20 percent in the United States. However, the future of nuclear energy was dealt a stunning blow on March 11, 2011, when Japan was rocked by a 9.0 earthquake off the coast of Sendai, followed by a massive tsunami, and serious damage to the Fukushima Dai-ichi nuclear power station. The initial disruption to power in Japan was serious enough, but the long-term impact on nuclear energy as an alternative to carbon fuels is uncertain. However, it is obvious that the nuclear energy option will be an important dimension to electricity generation for the foreseeable future as countries struggle with environmental and safety issues.

National and Regional Initiatives   Meanwhile, firms operating in countries that have adopted the Kyoto Protocol are under pressure to take one of two steps: Reduce emissions or buy credits from companies that have reduced emissions below target levels. The choice isn't terribly attractive because they'll have to invest in new technologies, change the way they do business, or pay for others to clean up their acts. In addition, MNEs (such as GE) are now forced to reconsider their global strategies, particularly because firms with operations in countries that have adopted the Protocol are required to adhere to the same standards as local companies. The European Union has set a target of an 8 percent reduction from 1990 levels—a figure that's more aggressive than Protocol target levels. The Germans have gone one step further, setting a target of 21 percent (based on the assumption that they'd be able to close down coal-fired power plants still operating in the former East Germany).[59]

Case Review Note

Company-Specific Initiatives   As a result, of course, U.S. companies operating in Europe share the same stringent requirements with European-based firms. Not surprisingly, many U.S.-based MNEs, though not bound by Protocol targets at home, are preparing for what they believe is inevitable. Between 2000 and 2005, for example, when GM took part in a voluntary emissions-reduction program, it achieved a 10 percent reduction in North American plant emissions. It is now trying to determine what it needs to do to make its 11 European plants comply with EU standards.[60] DuPont has cut emissions by 65 percent since 1990,[61] and Alcoa exceeded its 2010 goal of a 25 percent reduction of 1990 levels by some 11 percent.[62] Thus, companies are clearly changing the way they do business, regardless of whether they're bound by Protocol standards. Our opening case provides a good example: Recall that GE set a target of reducing greenhouse gas emissions at all levels of its operations to 1 percent below 2004 levels.

U.S.-based MNEs must comply with the Kyoto Protocol in compliance countries where they may have operations.

Finally, bear in mind that many MNEs, based in the United States or elsewhere, also face the task of adapting to different standards in different countries. A European-based MNE with operations in, say, the United States, Germany, and China and a U.S.-based MNE with plants in the same countries are faced with a smorgasbord of regulatory environments. On the one hand, the *legal* approach to responsible corporate behavior says an MNE can settle for operating in accord with local laws. The *ethical* approach, on the other hand, urges companies to go beyond the law to do whatever is necessary and economically feasible to reduce GHG emissions, given that they still have multiple stakeholders to satisfy.

Case Review Note

Ethical Dilemmas and Other Business Practices

In addition to the ethical challenges resulting of bribery and reactions to global warming, we examine two other examples of ethical dilemmas and socially responsible behavior. Sometimes the dilemmas are industry-specific, such as pharmaceuticals. Other times they deal with issues that cross industries, such as labor conditions in developing countries. We have chosen these two examples to demonstrate how companies have to

Does Geography Matter? How to See the Trees in the Rain Forest

When it comes to the emission of carbon dioxide (and other gases), the whole world is one big greenhouse. From Pago Pago to Peoria, we're affected by GHG emissions. So what difference does it make if the emissions also affect, say, the city of Porto Velho in western Brazil? Porto Velho, situated on the Madeira River, a major tributary of the Amazon River, happens to be in the Amazon rain forest, which accounts for a third of the world's remaining tropical forest. Covering about 60 percent of Brazil, the Amazon rain forest is home to no less than 30 percent of the world's animal and plant species. As forests go, it's quite large—roughly the size of Western Europe and a little smaller than the United States (including Alaska and Hawaii). The Amazon River runs nearly 4,000 miles across South America, carrying 20 percent of all river water discharged into the Earth's oceans.[63]

Rain forests may provide a key to solving the problem of global warming. The reason is simple: Trees absorb carbon dioxide. That's why one of the approaches to the reduction of GHG emissions proposed by the Kyoto Protocol involves reforestation. Given its size, the Amazon rain forest is obviously key to the success of any global reforestation project; unfortunately, it's currently under a twofold human-made assault: logging and burning. Logging is an important source of revenue for Brazil, which suffers from high rates of unemployment and underemployment. In addition, Brazilians are cutting down and burning large tracts of rain forest to make room for farming and cattle ranching. In some cases, ranchers turn around and sell their land to agricultural interests, clear additional land for pastures, and sell the lumber to the timber industry.

Not only does the burning of rain forest land add to the volume of carbon dioxide emissions, but also the destruction of the forests eliminates a vast carbon dioxide "sink" that could benefit the rest of the world by disposing of an immense amount of GHG emissions. Brazil, then, is a major front in the war against GHG pollution. Burning alone accounts for 75 percent of its greenhouse gas emissions (5.38 percent of the world's total), making the country one of the world's top 10 polluters. Moreover, the huge timber potential has already attracted heavy investment from many multinational logging firms that plan to harvest even more trees in the future. The Brazilian government has tried to bring order to chaos by issuing land titles in an area of the Amazon about the size of France. In doing so, it hopes to reduce illegal land trade, make it easier to police the rain forest, and require the new landowners (which must be individuals, not companies) to pay taxes and follow environmental regulations.[64] In addition, two major droughts in the Amazon region (in 2005 and 2010) add to the problem since they result in the release of GHG emissions and lower the region's ability to absorb carbon dioxide.[65]

Climate control is a multifaceted issue. On one side, the world needs to engage in strong efforts to reduce global warming. On the other side, the world needs to work together to preserve regions like the Amazon rain forest that are so essential to absorbing GHG emissions. The challenge is to do what is right to protect the global environment while preserving Brazilians' sovereignty over their own resources. And Brazil needs to balance its own development needs with its responsibility to the rest of the world. ●

examine their ethical conduct as they spread internationally. Because the pharmaceutical industry and developing country labor conditions are prominent in the news, they should give you an idea of what you might face and how you can resolve the conflicts satisfactorily. We finish this section and the chapter by discussing the importance of corporate codes of conduct.

ETHICAL DILEMMAS IN THE PHARMACEUTICAL INDUSTRY

GlaxoSmithKline (GSK), one of the largest research-based pharmaceutical companies in the world, focuses on two lines of business: pharmaceuticals (prescription drugs and vaccines) and consumer healthcare products. With annual revenues of $28.4 billion, the U.K.-based company operates in 114 countries and sells in more than 150. It employs about 100,000 people, with 35,000 working at 80 manufacturing sites in 37 countries, about 15,000 of them in R&D.

To continue developing new products, GSK spends 14 percent of its revenues on R&D.[66] And like most research-based pharmaceutical companies, it is involved in the R&D, manufacturing, and sales ends of the patented-pharmaceuticals industry. In order to fund their large R&D budgets, and because so many of the drugs they try to develop take so long to get to market or never make it there, these companies sell their successful drugs at high prices as long as the drugs are covered by patents. After a patent expires (after 17 years, in the United States), the proven drug becomes generic and is manufactured at lower costs and sold at a much lower price.

Tiered Pricing and Other Price-Related Issues   There are some exceptions to this pricing structure. Only 3 percent of GSK's revenues, for instance, come from the Middle East and Africa, where GSK offers preferential prices for vaccines. This practice is known as *tiered pricing*, in which consumers in developed countries pay higher prices and those in developing countries—especially low-income ones—pay lower, subsidized prices. If a government buyer is still unsatisfied with the high cost of patented drugs, it may resort to substituting generics, which are legitimate *if* the countries in which they're produced extend patent protection to patent holders. (One more point about generics: Often they're simply pirated versions of the real thing, and pirated versions—about 10 percent of medicines sold worldwide, according to the World Health Organization [WHO]—often lack key ingredients.[67])

> Tiered pricing for pharmaceuticals means that companies charge a market price for products sold in industrialized countries and a discounted price for products sold in developing countries.

Here's an example of the kinds of problems that can arise when the cost of pharmaceuticals becomes a point of contention in the marketplace. AIDS is a major health problem in Brazil, where the government, at substantial cost, distributes AIDS drugs to anyone who needs them. In 2007, when drugmaker Merck offered to provide an AIDS drug at a 30 percent discount, the Brazilian government said thanks but no thanks, and instead made it lawful for Brazilian firms to manufacture or buy generic versions of the drug while paying Merck only nominal royalty fees.[68] Brazil has also resorted to the tactic of *reverse engineering* certain key drugs so they can be produced at lower prices.

Our closing case includes a similar illustration, which involves the efforts of GSK to offer steep discounts on AIDS drugs to an MNE attempting to provide free treatment to workers in South Africa.

Case Review Note

Taking TRIPS for What It's Worth   The WTO Agreement on Trade-Related Aspects of Intellectual Property Rights (TRIPS) allows poor countries to counter the high cost of patented drugs by doing either of two things: (1) producing generic products *for local consumption* or (2) importing generic products from other countries *if they themselves don't have the capacity to produce generics.* In both cases, the developing nation is compelled to license patented drugs from legal patent holders, rather than buy them from pirated sources, so that the patent holders generate revenue on the drugs they developed. However, in claiming that health problems such as HIV/AIDS and heart disease are "national emergencies," Brazil and Thailand have permitted local companies to make *unlicensed* generics and thus take advantage of a TRIPS clause that allows them to avoid paying the royalties, even though some companies and countries dispute that decision.[69]

> **Concept Check**
>
> In Chapter 3, we define *intellectual property rights (IPRs)* as intangible property rights resulting from intellectual effort. Note, however, that an IPR registered in one country doesn't necessarily confer protection in another.

Not surprisingly, this tactic is a major concern for pharmaceutical companies. For one thing, they worry that these generic products will find their way back into the developed countries where they generate the majority of patent holders' revenues. They also worry about fakes for the same reason.

> Legal generic products allow countries to purchase drugs at lower costs and comply with drug patents, whereas illegal generic products are fakes that may or may not be of high quality.

R&D and the Bottom Line   Drugs are *very* expensive to develop, and much more so in high-income countries. It's estimated, for example, that the cost of developing a new drug is close to $1 billion in the United States but as little as $100 million in a country like India.

As it happens, India, which is now home to a thriving industry in *unlicensed* generic drugs, once enjoyed hefty FDI in pharmaceuticals. But when it refused to secure patents on drugs made there by foreign companies, those companies chose to leave the country rather than give away all their secrets to local competitors. Today, however, a new

> Countries with health crises, such as African countries with high rates of AIDS, are allowed by TRIPS to manufacture or import generic drugs.

patent-protection law has brought India into line with WTO guidelines and fostered a whole new environment for pharmaceuticals. Many Indian R&D facilities have sprung up to develop drugs that can be legitimately produced and sold by Indian companies, and foreign pharmaceutical firms are now looking at different strategies for penetrating the Indian market—from FDI to licensing agreements with generic manufacturers.

In this arena, then, the issue of social responsibility comes down to cultivating ways in which drugmakers can generate enough revenues to create new products (which is, after all, their major source of competitive advantage) while at the same time responding to the needs of developing countries that are long on diseases and short on funds. Is finding solutions the responsibility of drugmakers or of developing nations, perhaps in conjunction with industrialized countries in global forums such as the WHO? Should drugmakers encourage the development of generic products long before patents expire, or will they thereby run the risk of promoting a flood of cheaper products that will come back to haunt them in their home markets?

India is a major manufacturer of generic drugs and is now moving to R&D of new drugs.

ETHICAL DIMENSIONS OF LABOR CONDITIONS

A major challenge facing MNEs today is the twofold problem of globalized supply chains and the labor conditions of foreign workers. Labor issues—which involve companies, governments, trade unions, and NGOs alike—include wages, child labor, working conditions, working hours, and freedom of association. They're especially critical in retail, clothing, footwear, and agriculture—industries in which MNEs typically outsource huge portions of production to independent companies abroad, usually the developing countries of Asia, Latin America, and Africa.

Major labor issues that MNEs get involved in through FDI or purchasing from independent manufacturers in developing countries are fair wages, child labor, working conditions, working hours, and freedom of association.

Figure 5.3 highlights the multiple pressures external stakeholders place on companies to force them to adopt responsible employment practices in their overseas operations. A more specific listing of worker issues was developed by the Ethical Trading Initiative (ETI), a British-based organization that focuses on MNEs' employment practices. Its members include more than 70 corporate members plus trade unions and NGOs. Its corporate members include companies such as Gap Inc., Inditex, Marks & Spencer, and The Body Shop International. The objective of ETI is to get companies to adopt ethical employment policies and then monitor compliance with their overseas suppliers. ETI's trading initiative base code identifies nine clauses which reflect best labor practices as identified by the International Labour Organisation.[70]

FIGURE 5.3   Sources of Worker-Related Pressures in the Global Supply Chain

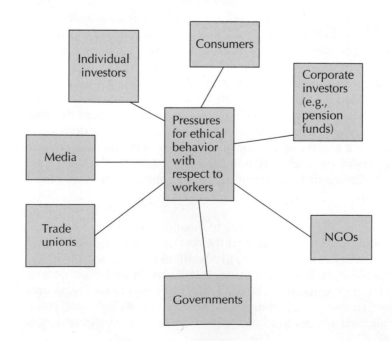

Although all issues identified by ETI are important, we focus on the one that, for a variety of good reasons, receives the most attention: *child labor.*

The Problem of Child Labor   Let's start by considering several very brief cases:

- There are two arguments for the use of children in the Indian carpet industry: (1) They're better suited than adults to perform certain tasks, and (2) if they weren't employed, they'd be even worse off. In fact, children in India are often put to work because parents don't earn enough to support families; if parents can't pay off debts, their children are often *indentured* to creditors.

- In the 1990s, the impoverished Asian nation of Bangladesh was pressured to stop employing thousands of child workers or face U.S. trade sanctions. In this case, the plight of the children did in fact go from bad to worse. Between 5,000 and 7,000 young girls, for example, went from factory work to prostitution.[71]

According to the International Labor Organization (ILO), a UN institution, 250 million children between the ages of 5 and 17 are working worldwide. Of those, according to one report, 180 million are "young children or in work that endangers their health or well-being, involving hazards, sexual exploitation, trafficking, and debt bondage."[72] ILO guidelines state that children who are at least 13 years old may be employed in "light" work that's not harmful to their health and doesn't interfere with school. All children under the age of 18 should be protected against the most abusive labor conditions.

For MNEs, the basic challenge is negotiating a global labyrinth of business environments with different cultural, legal, and political rules than those they're used to at home. In addition, they typically rely on local suppliers who are subject to specifically local pressures. Under these conditions, MNEs clearly can't solve all the problems revolving around child labor, especially given the fact that only about 5 percent of child labor worldwide occurs in industries supported by MNEs.[73] Most underage workers can be found in the informal sectors of an economy—especially agriculture—where it's difficult to protect them.

What MNEs Can and Can't Do   This doesn't mean that MNEs are powerless when it comes to labor-related matters in overseas facilities. When the Swedish retailer

An estimated 250 million children between 5 and 17 years old are working, but only about 5 percent of child labor is involved in export industries.

Some companies avoid operating in countries where child labor is employed, whereas others try to establish responsible policies in those same countries.

MNEs may not be willing to hire local workers who want to work long hours, due to concerns about exploitation.

◀ Young worker in a small factory in Old Delhi. Contributing to India's growing economy, but at what cost?

Source: Paul Prescott/February 2008

IKEA ran into trouble in India for buying carpets from local companies that relied heavily on extensive child labor, it identified and tackled two different problems rather than try to force suppliers to stop exploiting the children. First, it helped working mothers increase family earning power so they could escape the clutches of the loan sharks to whom they were putting up their children as collateral. Second, IKEA set up "bridge schools" to enable working children to enter mainstream education channels within a year.[74]

Frequently, MNEs operating in countries with very different labor policies succumb to the pressure to simply leave the market. Usually, this turns out to be a shortsighted decision. Research shows, for instance, that companies like Nike have substantially improved the conditions of workers in overseas facilities. Granted, MNEs are in no position to revolutionize the employment practices of the countries in which they operate, but they can improve conditions at subcontract facilities and even influence the guidelines set by other foreign investors. In the case of IKEA, carpets make up a small percentage of sales, and it would have been easy to simply give up the product line and move out of India. But officials at IKEA felt a responsibility to the children and decided to do as much as possible to make a difference. As IKEA got more involved in India, it set up the IKEA Foundation and partnered with UNICEF, contributing over $190 million in cash and in-kind donations to UNICEF programs to help children and their families. IKEA's work with UNICEF went beyond the issues of the supply chain and moved more into the humanitarian aspect of how to help the children. The IKEA Foundation targets South Asia, especially India, because of its supply chain issues, but it also targets that region because of the tremendous need that exists to help the children.[75]

Corporate Codes of Ethics: How Should A Company Behave?

So far, we've discussed numerous issues related to the impact of globalization on business, the role of businesses in the globalization process, and the impact of MNEs on society. But now we come to a qualitatively different question: How *should* a company behave? The United Nations Global Compact is a good start since it identifies 10 broad principles in the areas of human rights, labor, environment and anti-corruption—all of which we have described in this chapter.[76] The Global Compact is not legally binding, but it is a good guide for companies in establishing a code of conduct. Launched in 2000, the initiative has more than 8,000 participants, of which more than 6,000 are businesses representing 135 countries. The UN Global Compact Web site allows you to search participating companies by country. It is interesting to note that on June 30, 2009, there were 624 French companies actively participating in the initiative, compared to 275 from the United States, 173 from the United Kingdom, and 155 from Germany. Brazil leads the BRIC countries with 251 active business participants, and China has more than Germany with 160 business signatories.[77]

MOTIVATIONS FOR CORPORATE RESPONSIBILITY

Companies generally experience four strong motivations for acting responsibly:

1. Unethical and irresponsible behavior can result in *legal headaches,* especially in such areas as financial mismanagement, bribery, and product safety.
2. Such behavior could also result in *consumer action* such as boycotts.
3. Unethical behavior can affect *employee morale.* Conversely, responsible behavior can have a positive influence on a workforce, both at corporate headquarters and in overseas facilities.

4. You never know when *bad publicity* is going to cost you sales. Perhaps this concern is one reason why Nike and other apparel and clothing companies responded so quickly to criticism about allegedly unfair employment practices in developing countries.

DEVELOPING A CODE OF CONDUCT

A major component of most companies' strategies for ethical and socially responsible behavior is a **code of conduct.** In the context of international operations, we can take up two perspectives on codes of conduct: external and internal.

Bear in mind that external codes of conduct are useful only insofar as they give companies some general guidance on how to operate. The practical challenge for the company is familiarizing itself with the codes of many different organizations and use them to fashion its own *internal code of conduct.*

> A major component in a company's strategy for ethical and socially responsible behavior is a code of conduct.

What Makes a Good Internal Code of Conduct? Here are four criteria for an effective internal code of conduct:

1. *It sets global policies with which everyone working anywhere for the company must comply.* A good example is the code promulgated by the Finnish cell-phone company Nokia, which discusses how its code was set, who approved it, how it is communicated to its employees, and what its foundation values are.

2. *It communicates company policies not only to all employees but to all suppliers and subcontractors as well.* Gap, for example, maintains an education program to help subcontractors develop their own compliance programs that meet the objectives of Gap's code.[78]

3. *It ensures that the policies laid out in the code are carried out.* There are a variety of ways to approach this task:

   - GSK requires employees to confirm in writing that they've read and understand the company's code of conduct, then sign off that they understand and will follow the policies.

   - Syngenta, an Anglo-Swiss agrochemicals group, found out through press reports that child labor was being used in its supply chain. To ensure that suppliers were adhering to its policies in the matter, the company arranged with the Fair Labor Association, a nonprofit NGO, to submit its operations to external monitoring.[79]

4. *It reports the results to external stakeholders.* This can be a complicated and sometimes tricky process, as Nike found out. Up until a few years ago, Nike was willing to provide a lot of information about its labor practices. In 1998, however, when a lawsuit charged that the report constituted false advertising, Nike was forced to pay $1.5 million to the Fair Labor Association. Ever since the ruling came down in 2001, the giant shoe and apparel company has been less forthcoming about labor-related activities. Gap, however, has begun providing *more* information about its worldwide monitoring activities, including details about its code of conduct and practices; the Gap report also discusses its challenges—and failures—in getting subcontractors to act in accord with company policies.[80]

> Codes of conduct involve four dimensions:
> - Setting a global policy that must be complied with wherever the company operates.
> - Communicating the code to employees, suppliers, and subcontractors.
> - Ensuring that policies are carried out.
> - Reporting results to external stakeholders.

There's no reason to believe that governments won't continue to compete for larger shares of the wealth and other benefits to be gained from the activities of MNEs. In the short term, most countries will probably work to create more favorable environments for foreign investors, for several good reasons. Investment inflows provide developing countries with ways to deal with debt burdens and capital-accounts problems. Meanwhile, industrial nations struggling with trade-deficit problems, like the United

States, are more inclined to welcome FDI. The European Union, for example, will probably continue to welcome foreign investment as a means of fueling the growth it hopes to attain through unification.

The long term, however, may tell a different story. Historically, attitudes toward FDI have tended to fluctuate, with governments tending to favor restrictions when economies are thriving and incentives when they're struggling. But according to some observers, if they don't experience the rate of rapid growth they're expecting from the substantial FDI they've already attracted, developing countries may make the same about-face that such nations as Russia and Iran have already made—that is, place new restrictions on the flow of foreign investment.

Worse still, growing disappointment with the net results of foreign investment may lead some nations to attribute such problems as weakened sovereignty, increasing poverty, and cultural disintegration to overdependence on FDI. If this reaction to foreign investment is paired with growing criticism from NGOs and other external stakeholders, the ability of companies to operate globally will be further compromised.

Looking to the Future   Increased Globalization and the Effect on Ethical Behavior

In this chapter, we have continued the discussion from Chapter 1 on the effects of globalization. However, we've focused more on the ethical issues surrounding globalization and how companies can be more responsible as they operate abroad. Chapter 1 identified three scenarios on the future of globalization:

- Further globalization is inevitable.
- International business will grow primarily along regional rather than global lines.
- Forces working against further globalization and international business will slow down the growth of both.

Regardless of what happens, the more companies expand abroad, the greater the likelihood they will encounter ethical dilemmas that will make life challenging for the companies and, especially, the people who work for them. However, two things will have an impact on future ethical behavior. First, as countries confront common problems, such as corruption and bribery, and try to work together to solve those problems, there will be a greater convergence of proper ethical conduct. Will bribery and corruption disappear? Probably not, because there will always be differences due to the values and attitudes of individuals as well as the cultures in which these individuals operate. Second, as individuals and companies gain more experience abroad, they will develop skills surrounding ethical behavior. Sometimes you need experience in a country to learn how to make ethical decisions. As more companies encourage management to gain international experience, the greater the likelihood they will figure out how to behave ethically.

In addition, social media will have a greater impact on ethical behavior in the future. Historically, we have always thought that one of the keys to transparency is an independent press willing to investigate and report on wrong-doings. But now social media, such as Facebook, Twitter, YouTube, etc., have added an important new dimension to transparency. Even in countries where the press is controlled, news can go viral through the use of social media, as we learned in Egypt in 2011. This will be an important source of influence on future behavior.

However, there is more to responsible behavior than just not doing bad things. An important part of the impact of globalization on society is doing good things. Today's students, who will be tomorrow's future business and government leaders, are very interested in helping to solve some of the world's greatest problems though social innovation, microfranchising, volunteering, and other activities. They are willing to go around the world to build homes and schools in areas devastated by natural disasters or help the poor learn how to be effective entrepreneurs. Although some of these individuals will go on to work for NGOs or other not-for-profit ventures, others will work in the for-profit sector but with a different attitude to the problems of the world than their predecessors. They are more likely to help initiate and get involved in humanitarian ventures sponsored by their companies. These activities will continue to grow, in spite of or maybe because of difficult economic times, and employees who support and get involved in these activities will be changed through what they do. ■

Anglo American PLC in South Africa: What Do You Do When Costs Reach Epidemic Proportions?

CASE

By now it should be obvious that, regardless of where it chooses to do business, an MNE is going to face quite a variety of threats and disruptions—ranging from bureaucratic corruption and political instability to terrorism and even war—to its plans and operations. In 2007, Anglo American PLC, at that time one of the world's largest gold miners, found itself facing a threat that, although by no means new, defies most traditional categories of things that complicate business overseas—an HIV/AIDS epidemic in South Africa, the world's largest gold producer.[81]

In 2002, Anglo American made a landmark decision to provide free antiretroviral therapy (ART) to HIV-infected employees at its South African operations. Surprisingly, however, this commitment has met with mixed reactions from various stakeholders and achieved only controversial results, and the U.K.-based company is now asking itself, "Where do we go from here?"

AIDS in South Africa

How bad does a disease have to be to be accorded the status of an "epidemic"? Here's some background information. Sub-Saharan Africa, the portion of Africa lying south of the Sahara Desert, is home to just over 10 percent of the world's population and to 60 percent of all people infected with HIV, the virus that causes AIDS. Located at the southernmost tip of the African continent, the nation of South Africa has the highest number of people living with HIV/AIDS and suffers one of the world's highest rates of HIV infection—approximately 5.7 million cases (2007 estimate) in a population of 49 million (2009 estimate). Every day, almost 1,000 South Africans die from HIV/AIDS. Moreover, the UN and the World Health Organization say the epidemic has a long way to go before it reaches its peak.

◀ With about 5.7 million out of the 50 million people living in South Africa infected with HIV, government officials are doing more to make people aware of the treatments available. Throughout South Africa, members of the community are also finding ways to encourage others to get treated.

Source: REUTERS/Mike Hutchings

Needless to say, the spread of the disease has, over the past decade, had a profound impact on both the people of South Africa and their economy. Life expectancy is 48.98 years compared to, say, 75.63 years in Poland, a country with a similar population size and GDP per capita.

AIDS has also had a devastating effect on the country's economy. Between 1992 and 2002, the South African economy lost $7 billion annually—around 2 percent of GDP—as a result of AIDS-related worker deaths. Experts predict that, as AIDS spreads throughout sub-Saharan Africa, it will continue to reduce per capita growth by 1 to 2 percent per year and, in the worst-affected countries, cut annual GDP growth by as much as 0.6 percent by 2010. The consequences include both diminishing populations and shrinking economies, with GDPs deflating anywhere from 20 to 40 percent of the sizes they would have reached in the absence of AIDS.

Anglo American Operations in South Africa

Anglo American PLC is a diversified mining conglomerate operating in 45 countries and employing 107,000 permanent employees to produce precious metals (platinum and diamonds), base metals (copper, nickel, zinc, and phosphates), and bulk metals (for ferrous metals and coal). Founded in 1917 as the Anglo American Corporation of South Africa, it was South Africa's first home-based public limited company. Anglo American is a multinational firm headquartered in London, with its primary listing in London and secondary listing in Johannesburg. Anglo American has a presence in Europe, Africa, Asia, North America, and South America. In spite of its global spread, the company dominates South Africa's domestic economy through direct employment, contractors, and its supply chain. Through majority-share ownership of subsidiaries and associate companies, Anglo American controls over 25 percent of all shares traded on the South African stock market. Anglo American is huge: It is one of the world's largest mining companies, trailing such giants as BHP Billiton (dual-listed in Melbourne and London), Vale (Brazil), and Rio Tinto (Australia). Recently, Anglo avoided being taken over by Switzerland-based Xstrata PLC, which would have created the third largest mining conglomerate in the world. With the rapid rise in commodity prices followed by their collapse during the global financial crisis in 2008, it has been an interesting period for the mining industry.

Anglo American and ART

With such a huge investment in South Africa, Anglo American has been hit hard by the HIV/AIDS epidemic that's descended on the country. Having recognized the threat as far back as the early 1990s, Anglo American was one of the first corporations to develop a comprehensive, proactive strategy to combat the ravages of the disease on its workforce and the repercussions for its operations.

Originally, the program consisted of prevention initiatives aimed at education and awareness, the distribution of condoms, financial and skill-related training to alleviate poverty, and a survey system to monitor the prevalence of the infection. Eventually, these policies were expanded to include voluntary counseling, testing, and care-and-wellness programs, and the services of all programs were extended to cover not only the families of employees but also the populations of surrounding communities. Anglo American also became a member of the Global Business Council on HIV/AIDS, an organization of multinational companies that focuses on alleviating the effects of AIDS throughout the world and on protecting the rights of infected workers.

By adopting these strategies so early, Anglo American became a de facto leader in the private-sector fight against HIV/AIDS in Africa. Many other MNEs—including Coca-Cola, Ford, Colgate-Palmolive, and Chevron Texaco—soon followed Anglo American's example and initiated prevention, education, and wellness programs of their own. Even then, however, the majority of companies operating in South Africa still hesitated, and that's why Anglo American's 2002 announcement that it would provide ART to its South African workforce (at company expense) was met with a good deal of excited approval from such interested parties as the WHO, the Global Business Council on HIV/AIDS, and a host of other NGOs.

The Costs of Operating in an Epidemic

The incentive for Anglo American's ART program largely came from the failure of its AIDS-prevention efforts to make much headway in stemming the spread of the disease. By 2001, according to Brian Brink, senior VP of the firm's medical division, the prevalence of HIV-positive workers had risen to an average of 21 percent across all operations—a figure that was climbing steadily at a rate of 2 percent annually. Bobby Godsell, CEO and chairman of the subsidiary AngloGold, reported that HIV/AIDS was adding as much as $5 to the cost of producing one ounce of gold, thereby tacking on $11 million a year to the company's production costs in addition to the $7 million it was spending annually to combat such AIDS-related illnesses as tuberculosis (which was five times as prevalent as it had been just a decade earlier).

Finally, in addition to losses in productivity, the company had to bear the costs entailed by high levels of absenteeism, the constant retraining of replacement workers, and burgeoning payouts in health, hospitalization, and death benefits. Studies conducted at the time indicated not only that the costs of AIDS could reach as much as 7.2 percent of the company's total wage bill but also that the costs of leaving employees untreated would be even higher than those of providing ART.

Nine years after it rolled out its ART program, Anglo American now finds itself struggling to please various stakeholders and to determine whether all of its efforts are making a difference in the underlying problem or merely masking its effects. By the end of 2009, for instance, although 3,211 employees—approximately 27 percent of the HIV-infected workforce—were receiving ART, the company still struggled with high rates of non-adherence and dropout from treatment regimens. Thus, despite the relatively high rate of employees—82 percent as of the end of 2009—involved in voluntary counseling and testing (VCT), the proportion of employees engaged in treatment remains discouragingly low. However, the company remains encouraged by the increasing rate of participation in VCT, rising from 63 percent in 2006 to the current rate of 82 percent. The company anticipates a continuing increase in this number and eventually 100 percent annual participation in voluntary testing among its entire South African workforce.

◀ This monument in Durban, South Africa, is a testament to the devastation of HIV/AIDS to the South African economy and the need to combine forces in the public and private section to combat the disease.

Source: Hemis/Alamy

Anglo American also faces the problem of spiraling costs for the program itself. Even though the prices of most of the necessary drugs have been decreasing, the cost of distributing them remains high, and the treatment regime costs the company an estimated $4,000 per year per employee—quite expensive, especially when compared with the wages and benefits that Anglo American typically offers mineworkers. (Average monthly wages in the South African mining industry are about 5,100 rand, or U.S. $830.) Meanwhile, as Anglo American officials continue to remind investors that treating workers ultimately serves the bottom line, recent estimates project a total cost to the company of $1 billion or more over 10 years.

On the upside, cost per patient should decrease as the number of workers participating in the program increases. Unfortunately, one of the biggest challenges facing Anglo American is encouraging participation among a migrant and largely uneducated workforce laboring under harsh conditions in an unstable environment. In South Africa, HIV/AIDS still carries a severe stigma, and many South Africans refuse to be tested or to admit they've been infected for fear of discrimination by managers, fellow employees, and even society at large.

Moreover, many of those who had agreed to participate were confused by rumors and misinformation into assuming that they could stop using condoms once they were on the drugs—a situation, of course, that only exacerbated the prevalence of unsafe behavior. ART is in fact a lifelong regimen that can lead to various side effects and needs to be administered under strict supervision. Anglo American, however, continues to struggle with high levels of nonadherence. At one point, for example, supervisors were reporting that all workers undergoing treatment were taking medications as directed; urine tests, however, revealed that only 85 percent were actually doing so. By 2008, the company was forced to report that about 10 percent of participants had dropped out because of inability or unwillingness to adhere to the regimen. Now, physicians have to worry that extensive patterns of nonadherence pose a risk of fostering new drug-resistant strains of the virus.

In addition, harsh working conditions often make it hard for workers to take medications on time or to deal with certain side effects. Finally, migrant workers—about four-fifths of the total workforce—come from isolated villages located hundreds of miles away. They're 2.5 times more likely to contract the disease, which they take with them back to their villages.

Constituencies and Critics

Then there's the problem of pressure from various stakeholders. The National Union of Mineworkers has been hesitant to voice its support, citing the company's limitations on health-insurance benefits and lack of cooperation with national agencies. The union has also accused the company of helping to foster working conditions that exacerbate the problem. Even then-CEO Brian Gilbertson of BHP Billiton, another large mining concern operating in South Africa, charged Anglo American with merely trying to contain the problem instead of attacking its underlying causes: "You don't approach the problem by just throwing drugs at it," said Gilbertson.

Anglo American has countered many of these criticisms by insisting that it's beyond the resources and capacity of a single company to combat the overall problem and has called for more involvement on the part of the South African government. Instead of cooperation, however, the company has encountered outright opposition from political leaders. Indeed, the South African government has proved to be one of Africa's least committed to a program of effective intervention. Over the course of two years, the government diverted only 0.6 percent of the national budget to the HIV/AIDS crisis and has even resisted the wide distribution of antiretroviral drugs on the grounds that it's too expensive and too difficult to implement.

Matters weren't helped any when former President Thabo Mbeki publicly questioned the link between the HIV virus and the onset of AIDS. Then the country's health minister decried the Anglo American initiative as a "vigilante" move designed to place unreasonable burdens on the government, which would, after all, have to pick up the tab for treatments once workers had retired or left the company's employment.

In addition, dealing with pharmaceutical companies has proved a tricky proposition. On the one hand, Anglo American has a deal with GlaxoSmithKline allowing it to purchase anti-retroviral drugs at a tenth of the market price in the industrialized world (the same that

GSK charges not-for-profit organizations). At the same time, however, other drugmakers have been hesitant and unreliable at best, promising price cuts and then reneging over fears of violating intellectual property rights. As a matter of fact, several of these companies, complaining that cheap generic drugs made available in Africa will eventually be resold by profiteers on higher-priced Western markets, have put their energies into suing the South African government for what they claim to be generally poor enforcement of their patent rights.

Given the many challenges it's faced, not to mention the opposition from unexpected quarters, some observers have gone so far as to suggest that Anglo American would be better off by simply pulling back on its HIV/AIDS treatment program rather than pouring more resources into the effort to make it work. In the long run, however, the company must consider the continued pressure it will get from ethically minded shareholders as well as its own sense of moral responsibility.

There are also indications that the future may not be as bleak as it often appears. Of the workers who faithfully adhere to the drug regime, 95 percent have responded well to treatment and are working productively. The South African government may also be undergoing a gradual change of heart, having recently launched a National Strategic Plan for combating HIV/AIDS, which includes the aggressive goal of cutting the number of HIV infections in half by 2011. And in June 2009, the company's subsidiary, Anglo-Coal South Africa, was recognized by the Global Business Coalition on HIV/AIDS, Tuberculosis and Malaria, as best-in-class for the private sector for the success of its VCT programs with 94 percent of employees, having undergone testing.

Anglo American's strategy for HIV/AIDS intervention has in some ways become a model closely followed by other companies with operations in regions heavily affected by HIV/AIDS, including its industry rival, Rio Tinto PLC. Rio Tinto introduced a community intervention plan for HIV/AIDS as early as 2003 for all of its sub-Saharan operations, which included similar objectives of providing outreach activities and treatment options to employees, as well as family members and members of the community.[82] For their efforts, the Global Business Coalition on HIV/AIDS, Tuberculosis and Malaria recognized Rio Tinto's program in the Limpopo region of South Africa in 2008 as "Best in Business Action."[83] So, perhaps the criticism for such interventions is waning as companies continue to adopt responsible and effective initiatives for HIV/AIDS treatment.

QUESTIONS

1. Who are the various stakeholders that Anglo American needs to consider as it adopts an effective HIV/AIDS strategy?

2. What are the pros and cons of Anglo American's adoption of an aggressive strategy in combating HIV/AIDS among its South African workforce? What recommendations would you give the company concerning its HIV/AIDS policy?

3. Because such a large percentage of its workforce consists of migrant workers who are more likely to acquire and spread HIV/AIDS, should Anglo American adopt the policy of not hiring migrant workers? Should the South African government close the doors to migrant workers?

4. What role do pharmaceutical companies play in responding to the HIV/AIDS epidemic in South Africa? What policies or courses of action would you recommend to a company that produces HIV/AIDS drugs?

Now that you have finished this chapter, go back to www.myiblab.com to continue practicing and applying the concepts you've learned.

MyIBLab

SUMMARY

- MNEs must balance the interests of different constituencies that have different objectives.

- Companies create Codes of Conduct to help their employees understand how they are expected to act. However, ultimately individuals are the ones that make decisions, so companies must make sure that they hire ethical employees.

- Behaving ethically can help a company develop competitive advantage and avoid being seen as irresponsible.

- Relative behavior implies that we act according to the norms of the countries where we operate. Normative behavior implies that there are universal standards for ethical conduct that should be followed everywhere.

- The law is an important basis for ethical behavior, but not all unethical behavior is illegal. Thus, ethical behavior must go beyond the law to include common decency.

- Bribery is a form of unethical behavior being addressed at the multilateral level, such as at the UN and the OECD, and at the national level, such as with the Foreign Corrupt Practices Act in the United States.

- Environmental concerns are raised with extractive industries and those that generate air and water pollution or that produce products such as automobiles that use fossil fuels.

- The Kyoto Protocol, which requires the reduction of the emission of greenhouse gases, has not been adopted by all countries and is therefore still limited in its total global impact. However, companies must adapt to countries that have implemented the Protocol.

- Pharmaceutical companies face challenges on how to make enough money to fund R&D into new drugs and how to help provide critical drugs to developing countries at lower prices.

- A major challenge facing MNEs is the globalization of the supply chain and the impact on workers, especially in the areas of fair wages, child labor, working conditions, working hours, and freedom of association.

- Companies respond to the pressures for greater corporate social responsibility by establishing codes of conduct, distributing them to suppliers and subcontractors internationally, and ensuring compliance with the codes through effective training and auditing programs.

KEY TERMS

code of conduct (p. 205)
deontological approach (p. 187)
extraterritoriality (p. 190)
Foreign Corrupt Practices Act
  (FCPA) (p. 193)

Kyoto Protocol (p. 198)
normativism (p. 189)
relativism (p. 195)
stakeholder (p. 186)
sustainability (p. 197)

teleological approach (p. 186)
utilitarianism (p. 187)

ENDNOTES

1 *Sources include the following:* General Electric Co. home page, at www.ge.com/en/company (accessed May 16, 2011); GE Ecomagination home page, at http://ge.ecomagination.com /site/ index.html (accessed May 16, 2011); "A Lean, Clean Electric Machine," *The Economist* (December 10, 2005): 77–79; *GE 2010 Annual Report*, General Electric Co. (2007); Alan Murray, "Business: Why Key Executives Are Warming to Legislation on Climate Change," *Wall Street Journal* (February 7, 2007): A10; Rachel Pulfer, "Gambling on Green," *Canadian Business* (April 24, 2006): 35; Kara Sissell, "Major Corporations Form Advocacy Group to Curb Climate Change," *Chemical Week* (January 31, 2007): 12; "Safety, Health & the Environment at GE," *Professional Safety* Des Plaines (December 2006),. 51(12): 18; Anne Fisher, "America's Most Admired Companies," *Fortune* (March 19, 2007): 88–94; Neal St. Anthony, "'Green' Strategy Has GE Investor Seeing Red," *Minneapolis-St. Paul Star Tribune* (February 3, 2006): 1; Brendan Murray and Kim Chipman, "Bush Opposes Limits on Pollution Linked to Global Warming," *Pittsburgh Post-Gazette* (January 23, 2007): A5; John Teresko, "Technology of the Year: Connection Profits and Preservation," Industryweek.com (December 2005); *GE ecomagination Report 2007*, 2–8, at www.ge.com; GE *2008 Annual Report,* pages 4, 108, at www.ge.com; "GEs 2008 ecomagination revenues to rise 21%, cross $17 bn," *Mist News* (October 30, 2008); *Indexes Update March 2009*, page 5, 9, 10, at www.sustainability-index.com.

2 Pankaj Ghemawat, "Distance Still Matters: The Hard Reality of Global Expansion," *Harvard Business Review* (September 2001): 137–47.

3 Bradley R. Agle, Thomas Donaldson, R. Edward Freeman, Michael C. Jensen, Ronald K. Mitchell, and Donna J. Wood, "Dialogue toward Superior Stakeholder Theory," *Business Ethics Quarterly* 18:2 (2008): 153–90.

4 Lawrence Kohlgerg, "The Claim to Moral Adequacy of a Highest Stage of Moral Judgment," *Journal of Philosophy*, 70 (1973): 630–46.

5 Richard T. DeGeorge, *Business Ethics*, 7th edition (Upper Saddle River, NJ, 2010): pp. 22–24.

6 Ibid., 39 and 44.

7 Ibid.

8 Alfred Marcus, *Business & Society: Ethics, Government, and the World Economy* (Homewood, IL: Irwin, 1996).

9 David J. Vidal, *The Link between Corporate Citizenship and Financial Performance* (New York: Conference Board, 1999).

10 "Interfaith Center on Corporation Responsibility," retrieved March 28, 2011, from www.iccr.org.

11 Ronald Berenbeim, "The Search for Global Ethics," *Vital Speeches of the Day* 65:6 (1999): 177–78.

12 Trivia-Library.com, "Origins of Sayings – When in Rome, Do As the Romans Do," accessed on March 30, 2011. Reproduced with

permission from the People's Almanac series of books, 1975–1981 by David Wallechinsky & Irving Wallace.

13 See John M. Kline, *Ethics for International Business: Decision Making in a Global Political Economy* (London and New York: Routledge, 2005).

14 DeGeorge, *Business Ethics*, 33.

15 S. Prakash Sethi, "Standards for Corporate Conduct in the International Arena: Challenges and Opportunities for Multinational Corporations," *Business and Society Review* (Spring 2002): 20–39.

16 "The Ethics of Business," in "A Survey of Corporate Social Responsibility," *The Economist* (January 22, 2005): 20.

17 See "Indonesia's Plague," *Far Eastern Economic Review* (July 12, 2001): 8; John Danley, "Balancing Risks: Mosquitos, Malaria, Morality, and DDT," *Business and Society Review* 107:1 (Spring 2002): 145–70.

18 John R. Boatright, *Ethics and the Conduct of Business* (Upper Saddle River, NJ: Prentice Hall, 1993): 13–16.

19 Ibid., 16–18.

20 Austen L. Parrish, "The Effects Test: Extraterritoriality's Fifth Business," *Vanderbilt Law Review* 61:5 (October 2008): 1453+.

21 See A. M. Ali and I. H. Saiad, "Determinants of Economic Corruption," *Cato Journal* 22:3 (2003): 449–66; H. Park, "Determinants of Corruption: A Cross-National Analysis," *Multinational Business Review* 11:2 (2003): 29–48.

22 Transparency International, "How Do You Define Corruption? (in Frequently Asked Questions about Corruption), retrieved July 7, 2009, from www .transparency.org/news_room/faq/corruption_faq

23 "The Short Arm of the Law—Bribery and Business," *The Economist* (March 2, 2002): 78.

24 Transparency International, "Bribe Payers Index 2008," retrieved April 4, 2011, from http://transparency.org/news_room/latest _news/press_releases/2008/bpi_2008_en

25 See The World Bank, *World Development Report 2002: Building Institutions for Markets*; M. Habib and L. Zurawicki, "Country -Level Investments and the Effect of Corruption—Some Empirical Evidence," *International Business Review* 10:6 (2001): 687–700.

26 "China Execution Warning to Others," Aljazeera.net (July 11, 2007), retrieved August 20, 2007, from http://english.aljazeera.net (accessed August 20, 2007).

27 S. Ghoshal and P. Moran, "Towards a Good Theory of Management," in J. Birkinshaw and G. Piramal, eds., *Sumantra Ghoshal on Management: A Force for Good* (Upper Saddle River, NJ: Financial Times/Prentice Hall, 2005): 1–27.

28 "Spotlight: The Rio Tinto Scandal," *Time* (August 3, 2009), retrieved March 10, 2011, from www.time.com/time; James T. Areddy, "Rio Tinto China Employees Get Jail Terms for Bribery," *Wall Street Journal* (March 30, 2010): B1, 6; James T. Arredy, "China Schedules Rio Tinto Trial for Monday," *Wall Street Journal* (March 18, 2010): A12; James T. Arredy, "Rio Tinto Officials Admit Taking Bribes," *Wall Street Journal* (March 23, 2010): A11; Patty Waldmeir, Peter Smith, "Rio Sacks Staff Jailed by China for Bribery," *Financial Times* (March 30, 2011): 1

29 Fritz Heimann and Gillian Dell, *Progress Report 20010: Enforcement of the OECD Convention on Combating Bribery of Foreign Public Officials in International Business Transactions* (Transparency International, July 28, 2010): 12.

30 International Chamber of Commerce, "Extortion and Bribery in International Business Transactions" (1999), revised version, re-trieved April 23, 2005, from www.iccwbo.org/home/statements _rules/rules/1999/briberydoc 99.asp.

31 UN Convention Against Corruption (UNCAC), retrieved March 9, 2011, from www.unodc.org/unodc/en/treaties/CAC/index.html

32 A comprehensive EU anti-corruption policy, retrieved March 11, 2011, from http://europa.eu/legislation_summaries/fight_against _fraud/index_en.htm

33 Qing Tian, "Perception of Business Bribery in China: The Impact of Moral Philosophy," *Journal of Business Ethics* 80 (2008): 437–45.

34 Dionne Searcey, "U.S. Cracks Down on Corporate Bribes," *Wall Street Journal* (May 26, 2009): 1, 4.

35 Stuart Pfeifer, "Bribes to Foreign Firms are Targeted; Federal Authorities Step Up Prosecution of Businesses That Make Payments to Officials to Win Deals," *Los Angeles Times* (March 11, 2011): B1.

36 U.S. Department of Justice: Foreign Corrupt Practices Act, retrieved March 9, 2011, from www.justice.gov/criminal/fraud/fcpa/cases /a.html); Dionne Searcey, "U.S. Cracks Down on Corporate Bribes." *Wall Street Journal* (May 26, 2009): 1, 4.

37 Nicola Clark, "In Europe, Sharper Scrutiny of Ethical Standards," *New York Times* (May 7, 2008): C8.

38 Glenn R. Simpson. *Wall Street Journal (Eastern edition)* (January 27, 2005): A.2

39 Colleen Taylor, "U.S., Japan Authorities Join in Siemens' 'Black Money' Probe," *Electronic News* (February 12, 2007): 7; David Crawford and Mike Esterl, "Room at the Top: German Giant Siemens Faces Leadership Crisis," *Wall Street Journal* (April 26, 2007); Crawford and Esterl, "Widening Scandal: At Siemens, Witnesses Cite Pattern of Bribery," *Wall Street Journal* (January 31, 2007): A.1.

40 "The Hollow Men," *The Economist* (March 17, 2007): 71.

41 Michael Connolly, "Germany Inc. under a Cloud," *Wall Street Journal* (November 24, 2006).

42 Crawford and Esterl, "Widening Scandal."

43 Konstantin Richter, "The House of Siemens," *Wall Street Journal* (April 27, 2007): 13.

44 Jack Ewing, "Siemens' Culture Clash: CEO Kleinfeld Is Making Changes, and Enemies," *Business Week* (January 29, 2007): 42–46.

45 Richter, "The House of Siemens," 13.

46 David Crawford and Mike Esterl, "Siemens to Decide if New Leader Is Needed amid Widening Probes," *Wall Street Journal* (April 25, 2007): A3.

47 Ewing, "Siemens' Culture Clash," 42–46; Richter, "The House of Siemens," 13.

48 G. Thomas Sims, "Siemens Struggles to Regain Equilibrium," *New York Times*, online edition (April 27, 2007); Sims, "Two Former Siemens Officials Convicted for Bribery," *New York Times*, online edition (May 15, 2007).

49 Josef Jabareen, "A New Conceptual Framework for Sustainable Development," *Environment, Development and Sustainability* 10:5 (April 2008): 29.

50 Floating Island International, retrieved March 10, 2011, from www .floatingislandinternational.com, "Products" and "Applications."

51 Floating Island International, retrieved March 10, 2011, from www .floatingislandinternational.com, "Company Profile" and "Licensing Opportunities."

52 John Carey, "Global Warming," *Business Week* (August 16, 2004): 60–69.

53 "Hotting Up," *The Economist* (February 5, 2005): 73–74; Richard S. Lindzen, "The Climate Science Isn't Settled," *The Wall Street Journal* (December 1, 2009): A19.

54 UNFCC home page, retrieved June 19, 2009, from http://unfccc.int /kyoto_protocol/ status_of_ratification/items/2613.php

55 Alison Graab, "Greenhouse Gas Market to Slow Global Warming," CNN.com (accessed April 12, 2005).

56 International Energy Agency, retrieved February 17, 2011, from www.iea.org/index.asp

57 Jonathan Weisman, "G-8 Climate-Change Agreement Falls Short," *Wall Street Journal* (July 9, 2009): A.8.

58 Jack Ewing, "The Wind at Germany's Back," *Business Week* (February 11, 2008): 68.

59 Mark Lander, "Mixed Feelings as Kyoto Pact Takes Effect," *New York Times* (February 16, 2005).

60 Lander, "Mixed Feelings as Kyoto Pact Takes Effect."

61 Carey, "Global Warming," 62.

62 "Alcoa Inc.; Alcoa Volunteers Set to Contribute to a More Sustainable Future," *Biotech Week* (May 13, 2009): 2792.

63 Rebecca Lindsey, "Amazonia," on Earth Observatory, retrieved April 13, 2011, from http://earthobservatory.nasa.gov/Features/LBA

64 "Brazil Legalizes Rain-forest Ownership in France-Size Area," *Montreal Gazette* (June 27, 2009): A18.

65 "Amazon Droughts Increase Climate Change Fears," CNN.com, retrieved February 4, 2011, from www.cnn.com/2011/WORLD/Americas/02/04/brazil.amazon.drought/index.html

66 *GlaxoSmithKline 2010 Annual Report,* various pages, at www.gsk.com/index.htm.

67 Frederik Balfour, "Fakes!" *Business Week* (February 7, 2005): 56.

68 Miriam Jorda, "Brazil to Stir Up AIDS-Drug Battle," *Wall Street Journal* (September 5, 2003): A3; "Brazil to Break Merck AIDS Drug Patent," *Associated Press* story on MSNBC Web site (May 4, 2007).

69 "A Gathering Storm: Pharmaceuticals," *The Economist* (June 9, 2007): 73.

70 Ethical Trading Initiative, retrieved August 20, 2007, from www.ethicaltrade.org

71 Ans Kolk and Rob van Tulder, "Child Labor and Multinational Conduct: A Comparison of International Business and Stakeholder Codes," *Journal of Business Ethics* (March 2002), 36(3): 291–301.

72 Frances Williams, "Economic Case Made for Ending Child Labour," *Financial Times* (February 4, 2004): 5.

73 Kolk and van Tulder, "Child Labor and Multinational Conduct."

74 Edward Luce, "Ikea's Grown-Up Plan to Tackle Child Labour," *Financial Times* (September 15, 2004): 7.

75 UNICEF's Corporate Partnerships: IKEA, retrieved May 19, 2011, from www.unicef.org/corporate_partners/index_25092.html

76 United Nations, *United Nations Global Compact,* retrieved October 1, 2009, from www.unglobalcompact.org/AboutTheGC

77 Participants&Stakeholders, retrieved February 18, 2011, from www.unglobalcompact.org/ParticipantsAndStakeholders

78 Amy Merrick, "Gap Offers Unusual Look at Factory Conditions," *Wall Street Journal* (May 12, 2004): A1.

79 "Syngenta Opens Up to Independent Scrutiny," *Financial Times* (May 12, 2004): 8.

80 Sarah Murray and Alison Maitland, "The Trouble with Transparent Clothing," *Financial Times* (May 12, 2004): 8.

81 *Sources include the following: UNAIDS 2008 Report on the Global AIDS Epidemic; HIV and AIDS in South Africa,* www.avert.org/aidssouthafrica.htm; *Delivering Real Excellence: Annual Report 2010,* Anglo American; *Making a Difference Report to Society 2008,* Anglo American; *Delivering Real Excellence: Annual Report 2010,* Anglo American; "HIV/AIDS Co-Infection: Anglo American's Coal Division in South Africa Wins Global Business Coalition Award for Top International Workplace HIV and AIDS Programmed, *Law & Health Weekly* (July 11, 2009): 849; Alec Russell, "Answers to an AIDS Epidemic: New Initiatives to Help Infected Workers Mark a Big Shift in Attitude and Approach at Some of South Africa's Largest Companies," *Financial Times* (October 4, 2007): 14; Mark Schoofs, "Anglo American Drops Noted Plan on AIDS Drugs," *Wall Street Journal* (April 16, 2002): A19; World Health Organization/AFRO, "Southern African Health Challenges Intensify," press release (September 13, 2004): 1–2; Mark Schoofs, "New Challenges in Fighting AIDS—Enlisting Multinationals in Battle," *Wall Street Journal* (November 30, 2001): B1; "AIDS in the Workplace," *Business Africa* (July 1, 2001): 1–2; "The Corporate Response," *Business Africa* (September 1, 2001): 4; Schoofs, "South Africa Reverses Course on AIDS Drugs," *Wall Street Journal* (November 20, 2003): B1; "Anglo American to Provide HIV/AIDS Help for Workers," *American Metal Market* (August 7, 2002): 4; Bruce Einhorn and Catherine Arnst, "Why Business Should Make AIDS Its Business—Multinationals Are Taking Baby Steps to Control the Disease in Their Workforce," *Business Week* (August 9, 2004):83; "Digging Deep," *The Economist* (August 10, 2002): 55; James Lamont, "Anglo's Initiative," *Financial Times* (August 8, 2002):10; "Anglo American to Give Mineworkers AIDS Drugs Free," *Wall Street Journal* (August 7, 2002): A13; Matthew Newmann, Scott Hensley, and Scott Miller, "U.S. Reaches Patent Compromise to Provide Drugs to Poor Nations," *Wall Street Journal* (August 28, 2003): A3; Statistics South Africa, "Labour Statistics Survey of Average Monthly Earnings," *Statistical Release P0272* (February 2002): 3; Central Intelligence Agency, *The World Factbook,* www.cia.gov/library/publications/the-world-factbook/index.html; Julia Werdigier "Xstrata Ends Bid for Rival in London," *New York Times* (October 16, 2009): B8; *Delivering Sustainable Value Report to Society 2009,* Anglo American.

82 Rio Tinto, retrieved March 1, 2011, from www.riotinto.com, Rio Tinto HIV/AIDS strategy.

83 Global Business Coalition on HIV/AIDS, TB, and Malaria, retrieved March 1, 2011, from www.gbcimpact.org, member profiles: Rio Tinto.

Theories and Institutions:
Trade and Investment

PART THREE

chapter 6

International Trade and Factor-Mobility Theory

Objectives

1. To understand theories of international trade

2. To explain how free trade improves global efficiency

3. To identify factors affecting national trade patterns

4. To explain why a country's export capabilities are dynamic

5. To understand why production factors, especially labor and capital, move internationally

6. To explain the relationship between foreign trade and international factor mobility

Access a host of interactive learning aids to help strengthen your understanding of the chapter concepts at www.myiblab.com.

MyIBLab

A market is not held for the sake of one person.

—*African (Fulani) proverb*

Source: traveler_no1 /iStockphoto.com

CASE

Costa Rica: Trading Up Through Foreign Trade

Map 6.1 shows Costa Rica, a Central American country of about 4.5 million people, which borders the Pacific Ocean and the Caribbean arm of the Atlantic. Its name, "Rich Coast," refers to its fertile soil and bountiful biodiversity.[1] Costa Rica possesses some attributes we associate with developed countries and some that we associate with developing countries. With a per capita GDP of $11,300 (based on purchasing price parity in 2010), Costa Rica depends on agricultural commodities—primarily bananas, pineapples, and coffee—for about one-quarter of its merchandise export earnings. However, its tourism earnings are higher than those from these top three agricultural exports combined. (The opening photo is in a bio-diverse park that attracts ecotourism.) Map 6.1 shows Costa Rica's location and major export markets. It has a fairly high level of external debt, a literacy rate of about 95 percent, a life expectancy at birth of 78 years, and a fairly even income distribution (the highest 10 percent of the population earns about 36 percent of its income). It has also enjoyed a long history of democracy and political stability.

FOUR ERAS

Like all countries, Costa Rica relies on international trade and factor-mobility policies—strategies related to the movement of goods, services, and production factors across borders—to pursue its economic objectives. In any country, these two sets of policies change over time, as both domestic and foreign conditions evolve. They're also politically sensitive, especially when it comes to the economic priorities and judgments of the nation's leaders.

For Costa Rica, it's convenient to trace policy evolution through four historical periods, each characterized by particular strategies regarding international trade and factor mobility:

- *Late 1800s–1960: Liberal trade*—a policy calling for minimal government interference in trade and investment
- *1960–1982: Import substitution*—a policy calling for the local production of goods and services that would otherwise be imported

MAP 6.1   Costa Rica

In 2009, about 50 percent of Costa Rica's exports went to three countries.

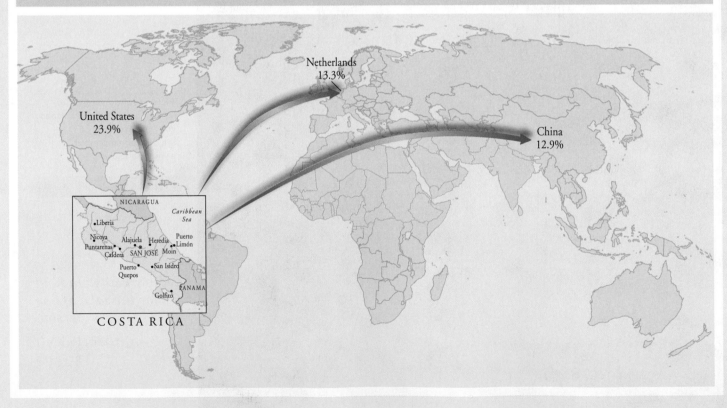

United States
23.9%

Netherlands
13.3%

China
12.9%

NICARAGUA
Liberia
Nicoya   Alajuela Heredia Puerto
Puntarenas   Limón
Caldera SAN JOSE Moin
Puerto   San Isidro
Quepos
Golfito
PANAMA
Caribbean Sea

COSTA RICA

- *1983–early 1990s: Liberalization of imports,* export promotion, and incentives for most types of foreign investments

- *Early 1990s–present: Strategic trade policy* (also called an *industrial policy*) calling for the production of specific types of products—and openness to imports

LATE 1800s–1960

In the latter part of the 1800s, most nations permitted goods, capital, and people to move with relative freedom from one country to another. Governments tended to interfere only minimally, and the general result was an economic environment in which individual producers determined what to produce and where to produce it. Trade flourished and countries tended to specialize in selling what they could best produce.

Most Latin American countries, including Costa Rica until the early 1960s, specialized in either a single or a few commodities (raw materials or agricultural products), which they exported in exchange for other commodities and manufactured goods. Costa Rican farmers specialized first in coffee and later, after the development of refrigerated ships, in bananas as well. For most of the period, the country was well served by this policy, primarily because commodity prices, especially coffee prices, remained high.

Eventually, however, three factors convinced Costa Rican leaders to encourage more diversified production and economic self-sufficiency:

- Two world wars disrupted Costa Rica's ability to export its commodities and import products it did not produce.

- Coffee and banana prices dropped relative to the prices of manufactured products, particularly as new commodity producers (especially in Africa) entered world markets.

- Latin American countries with less-open international markets had insulated themselves more from adverse international conditions.

As a result of these developments, Costa Rica turned to policies centered on the idea of import substitution.

1960–1982

In the early 1960s, Costa Rican authorities reasoned that if they limited imports (say, by taxing them heavily), they'd provide both Costa Rican and foreign investors with an incentive to produce more things within Costa Rica to sell there. They also realized that, unfortunately, the Costa Rican market was too small to support investments requiring large-scale production.

To address this problem, Costa Rica joined with four other countries—El Salvador, Guatemala, Honduras, and Nicaragua—to form the Central American Common Market (CACM), which allowed goods produced in any member country to enter freely into the market of any other member. Thus, a company located in a member country could serve a five-country market rather than a one-country market.

Miscalculations and Mixed Results

The results were mixed. Costa Rica's economic dependence on agriculture was already declining before the import substitution policy, from 40.9 percent to 25.2 percent of GDP between 1950 and 1960. Thus, the decline to 18 percent by 1980 could not be attributed completely to the policy change.

Likewise, most investors earmarked their new manufacturing to sell domestically and in not the larger CACM market. For example, import substitution helped attract pharmaceutical investment, but the availability of a larger market was not the primary reason; in this case, the strategy worked basically because small-scale packaging and processing are efficient within this industry.

So why was the strategy of import substitution, even coupled with a complementary regional trade agreement, less successful than CACM leaders had hoped? Quite simply, investors were convinced that the CACM was not destined to last, and as it turned out, they were right. By the late 1970s, civil wars in both El Salvador and Guatemala stifled those economies, and a new regime in Nicaragua was ideologically committed to complete governmental control of all aspects of the economy, including trade.

In some cases, import substitution did lead to increased exports, such as for Costa Rican processed coffee and cottonseeds. Many economists and prospective investors, however, began to worry that policies designed to protect local production—including price controls, import prohibitions, and subsidies— were channeling the country's resources toward inefficient production. For example, Costa Rica became nearly self-sufficient in rice production, but only because government policies kept lower-cost foreign-produced rice out of the market.

Moreover, the government held down consumer rice prices by subsidizing domestic rice producers. And where did the money for these subsidies come from? They came in part from higher taxes on efficient industries—industries that, in turn, found it hard to expand because they were strapped for cash. Finally, some inefficient producers survived because they reaped the benefits of high consumer prices, leaving consumers with less disposable income to spend on any products, domestic or foreign.

At this point, Costa Rican policymakers concluded that the country must emphasize the production of goods that could compete in international markets. For one thing, they had the example of Asian countries that were achieving rapid growth by competing internationally. In 1983, therefore, Costa Rica shifted to a policy of promoting exports.

1983–EARLY 1990s

First, to help ensure that only internationally competitive companies and industries were likely to survive, the government began removing import barriers. Rice imports, for example, rose substantially.

CINDE

Policymakers also decided to seek more outside capital and expertise to support economic reforms. Luckily, the United States launched its Caribbean Basin Initiative, which allowed products originating in the Caribbean region (including Costa Rica) to enter the United States at lower tariff (or import tax) rates than those originating elsewhere. To capitalize on this new opportunity, Costa Rica formed CINDE (Coalición Costarricense de Iniciativas de Desarrollo), a private organization funded by the government and grants from the U.S. government. The purpose of CINDE was to aid in economic development, and one of its top priorities was attracting foreign direct investment.

To augment CINDE's work, Costa Rica established an export processing zone (EPZ) that allowed companies exporting finished output to import all inputs and equipment tax free. They were also exempted from paying Costa Rican income tax for eight years and allowed to pay at a 50 percent discount for the next four years. By 1989, 35 companies—mainly textile and footwear producers seeking to take advantage of Costa Rica's pool of inexpensive labor—had located in the EPZ.

By this time, however, CINDE officials were beginning to worry about two potential problems facing its ambitious new initiatives:

1. That Costa Rica could not remain cost competitive in the type of products exported from the EPZ because other countries (mainly Mexico) were benefiting from even lower U.S. tariffs
2. That Costa Rica's highly skilled and educated workforce was being underutilized by the types of industries attracted to the EPZ

CINDE officials decided to work with the Costa Rican government to identify and attract investors who matched up better with Costa Rican resources.

EARLY 1990s–PRESENT

The Costa Rican government targeted industries for international competition that promised high growth potential and could pay higher wages and salaries than most of those that had already invested in the EPZ. The targeted industries included medical instruments and appliances, electronics, and software.

Costa Rican officials also identified characteristics of developing countries that were attracting significant amounts of foreign investment: a highly educated and largely English-speaking workforce (especially the availability of engineers and technical operators), political and social stability and relatively high levels of economic freedom, and a quality of life that would appeal to the managers and technical personnel that foreign investors would bring in to work in the facilities. The conclusion? In its targeted industries, Costa Rica should be able to compete on the international market.

What CINDE Recommended

CINDE also hired the Foreign Investment Advisory Service (FIAS) of the International Finance Corporation (an arm of the World Bank) to study the feasibility of attracting companies in these industries and the best means of attracting them to Costa Rica. FIAS concluded that attracting the right number of the right companies was well within Costa Rica's reach.

It also suggested areas within this selection of targeted industries, such as power technologies, that best fit with Costa Rica's main advantage—a labor force that was well educated in relation to its cost—and recommended that officials target industries that supported the electronics and computer industries, such as plastics and metalworking. Finally, FIAS noted that Costa Rica needed to improve protection of intellectual property rights and English proficiency among technicians and engineers. In response, Costa Rica put English language skills in a revised curriculum for training mid-level technicians and set up Spanish-language training for the personnel brought in by foreign investors.

Progress Report

Setting out to attract investments in electronics and software, Costa Rica landed such high-tech investors as Reliability, Protek, Colorplast, and Sensortronics. By far the largest investment, however, has been by the computer-chip giant Intel. CINDE officials drew up a list of all the questions and concerns that Intel might have, and they prepared knowledgeable responses to them. They also involved top governmental and company leaders in meetings with Intel executives, even enlisting the country's president, José Figueres, to pilot them on a helicopter survey of plant sites.

Since then, Costa Rica has turned its attention to medical devices, and it has attracted investments by such companies as Abbott Laboratories, Baxter, and Procter & Gamble. Although exports of coffee and bananas are still important to the nation's economy, about two-thirds of Costa Rica's merchandise exports are now manufactured goods, with high-tech products constituting the backbone of the **CRN** economy and export earnings.

Case Review Note

Introduction

The preceding case shows how Costa Rica has used trade and factor mobility (movement of capital, technology, and people) to help achieve its economic objectives. Figure 6.1 shows that trade in goods and services and the movement of production factors are means by which countries are linked internationally. Like Costa Rica, other countries wrestle with the questions of what, how much, and with whom their country should trade. These questions are intertwined with considerations of what they can produce efficiently and if and how they can improve their competitiveness by boosting the quality and quantity of capital, technical competence, and worker skills.

LAISSEZ-FAIRE VERSUS INTERVENTIONIST APPROACHES TO EXPORTS AND IMPORTS

Once countries set economic and political objectives, officials enact policies—including trade policies—to achieve the desired results. These policies influence which countries can produce given products more efficiently and whether countries will permit imports to compete against their domestically produced goods and services. Some nations

Trade theory helps managers and government policymakers focus on these questions:

- What products should we import and export?
- How much should we trade?
- With whom should we trade?

FIGURE 6.1   International Operations and Economic Connections

To meet its international objectives, a company must gear its strategy to trading and transferring its means of operation across borders—say, from (Home) Country A to (Host) Country B. Once this process has taken place, the two countries are connected economically.

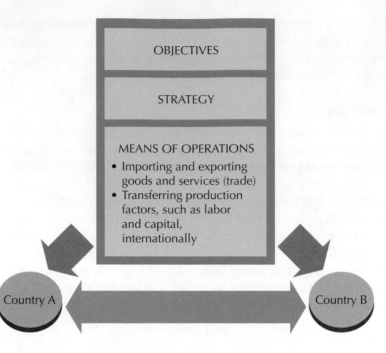

OBJECTIVES

STRATEGY

MEANS OF OPERATIONS
• Importing and exporting goods and services (trade)
• Transferring production factors, such as labor and capital, internationally

Country A   Country B

Concept Check

Compare Figure 6.1 with Figure 1.1, which outlines certain conditions that may affect a firm's operations when it decides to do business on an international scale. Here the graphic focuses in on operational adjustments that a company faces when it takes specific strategic actions to go international—namely, to trade and transfer means of production.

Some trade theories prescribe that governments should influence trade patterns; others propose a laissez-faire treatment of trade.

take a more *laissez-faire* approach, one that allows market forces to determine trading relations. *Free-trade theories* (absolute advantage and comparative advantage) take a complete laissez-faire approach because they prescribe that governments should not intervene directly to affect trade. At the other extreme are *mercantilism* and *neomercantilism*, which prescribe a great deal of government intervention in trade. Whether taking a laissez-faire or interventionist approach, countries rely on trade theories to guide policy development.

THEORIES OF TRADE PATTERNS

After taking a look at theories dealing with trade intervention, we examine those that help explain trade patterns (how much countries depend on trade, in what products, and with whom), including theories of *country size, factor proportions,* and *country similarity.* We then consider theories dealing with the dynamics of countries' trade competitiveness for particular products, which include the *product life cycle theory* and the *diamond of national competitive advantage theory.*

TRADE THEORIES AND BUSINESS

Table 6.1 summarizes the major trade theories and their emphases. These different theories expand our understanding about how government trade policies might affect business competitiveness. For instance, they provide insights on favorable locales and products for exports, thereby helping companies determine where to locate their production facilities when governments do or do not impose trade restrictions.

FACTOR-MOBILITY THEORY

Because the stability and dynamics of countries' competitive positions depend largely on the quantity and quality of their production factors (land, labor, capital, technology), we conclude the chapter with a discussion of factor mobility.

TABLE 6.1　What Major Trade Theories Do and Don't Discuss: A Checklist

A check mark indicates that a theory of trade concerns itself with the question asked at the head of the column; if there's a dash, it doesn't. In columns 4–7, you can see how each theory responds to the specific question; again, a dash indicates that the theory does not address the question.

Theory	Description of Natural Trade			Prescription of Trade Relationships			
	How Much Is Traded	What Products Are Traded?	With Whom Does Trade Take Place?	Should Government Control Trade?	How Much Should Be Traded?	What Products Should Be Traded?	With Whom Should Trade Take Place?
Mercantilism	—	—	—	yes	✓	✓	✓
Neomercantilism	—	—	—	yes	✓	—	—
Absolute advantage	—	✓	—	no	—	✓	—
Comparative advantage	—	✓	—	no	—	✓	—
Country size	✓	✓	—	—	—	—	—
Factor proportion	—	✓	✓	—	—	—	—
Country similarity	—	✓	✓	—	—	—	—
Product life cycle (PLC)	—	✓	✓	—	—	—	—
Diamond of national competitive advantage	—	✓	—	—	—	—	—

Interventionist Theories

Let's begin with mercantilism because it is the oldest trade theory, out of which neomercantilism has more recently emerged. These theories are based on some of the reasons for governmental intervention, but there are other reasons as well that we discuss in the next chapter.

MERCANTILISM

Mercantilism holds that a country's wealth is measured by its holdings of "treasure," which usually means its gold. According to this theory, which formed the foundation of economic thought from about 1500 to 1800,[2] countries should export more than they import and, if successful, receive gold from countries that run deficits. Nation-states were emerging during this period, and gold empowered central governments to raise armies and invest in national institutions so as to solidify the people's primary allegiances to the new nations.

According to mercantilism, countries should export more than they import.

Governmental Policies　To export more than they imported, governments restricted imports and subsidized production that otherwise could not compete in domestic or export markets. Some countries used their colonies to support this trade objective by having them supply commodities that they would otherwise have to purchase from a nonassociated country and by running trade surpluses with them as an additional way to obtain gold. They did this not only by monopolizing colonial trade but also by forcing the colonies to export less highly valued raw materials to them and import more highly valued manufactured products from them.

As the influence of the mercantilist philosophy weakened after 1800, the governments of colonial powers seldom directly intended to limit the development of industrial capabilities within their colonies. However, their home-based companies had technological leadership, ownership of raw material production abroad, and usually some degree of protection from foreign competition—a combination that continued to make colonies dependent on raw material production and tie their trade to their industrialized mother countries. We still see vestiges of these relationships.

The Concept of Balance of Trade   Some terminology of the mercantilist era has endured. For example, a **favorable balance of trade** (also called a **trade surplus**) still indicates that a country is exporting more than it imports. An **unfavorable balance of trade** (also known as a **trade deficit**) indicates the opposite. Many of these terms are misnomers. For example, the word *favorable* implies "benefit," and the word *unfavorable* suggests "disadvantage." In fact, it is not necessarily beneficial to run a trade surplus, nor is it necessarily detrimental to run a trade deficit. A country with a favorable balance of trade is, for the time being, supplying people in foreign countries with more than it is receiving from them.[3]

In the mercantilist period, the difference was made up by a transfer of gold; today it is made up by granting credit to the deficit country by holding its currency or investments denominated in that currency. If that credit cannot eventually buy sufficient goods and services, the so-called favorable trade balance actually may turn out to be disadvantageous for the country with the surplus.

NEOMERCANTILISM

The term **neomercantilism** describes the approach of countries that try to run favorable balances of trade in an attempt to achieve some social or political objective. A country may try to achieve full employment by setting economic policies that encourage its companies to produce in excess of the demand at home and send the surplus abroad. Or it may attempt to maintain political influence in an area by sending more merchandise there than it receives from it, such as a government granting aid or loans to a foreign government to use for the purchase of the granting country's excess production.

Free-Trade Theories

Thus far, we have intentionally ignored the question of why countries need to trade at all. Why can't Costa Rica (or any other country) be content with the goods and services produced within its own territory? In fact, many countries following mercantilist policy did try to become as self-sufficient as possible. In this section, we discuss two theories supporting free trade: *absolute advantage* and *comparative advantage*.

Both theories hold that nations should neither artificially limit imports nor promote exports.[4] The market will determine which producers survive as consumers buy those products that best serve their needs. Both free trade theories imply *specialization*. Just as individuals and families produce some things that they exchange for things that others produce, national specialization means producing some things for domestic consumption and export while using the export earnings to buy imports of products and services produced abroad.

THEORY OF ABSOLUTE ADVANTAGE

In 1776, Adam Smith questioned the mercantilists' assumptions by stating that the real wealth of a country consists of the goods and services available to its citizens rather than its holdings of gold. This theory of **absolute advantage** holds that different countries produce some goods more efficiently than others, and questions why the citizens of any country should have to buy domestically produced goods when they can buy them more cheaply from abroad.

Smith reasoned that if trade were unrestricted, a country would specialize in those products that gave it a competitive advantage. Its resources would shift to the efficient industries because it could not compete in the inefficient ones. Through specialization, it could increase its efficiency for three reasons:

1. Labor could become more skilled by repeating the same tasks.
2. Labor would not lose time in switching production from one kind of product to another.
3. Long production runs would provide incentives for developing more effective working methods.

The country could then use its excess specialized production to buy more imports than it otherwise could have produced. But in what products should a country specialize? Although Smith believed the marketplace would make the determination, he thought that a country's advantage would be either *natural* or *acquired*.

Natural Advantage   A country's **natural advantage** in creating a product or service comes from climatic conditions, access to certain natural resources, or availability of certain labor forces. As we saw in our opening case, Costa Rica's climate and soil support the production of bananas, pineapples, and coffee, while its biodiversity supports a thriving ecotourism industry. Costa Rica imports wheat. If it were to increase its wheat production, for which its climate and terrain are less suited, it would have to use land now devoted to the cultivation of bananas, pineapples, and coffee, or convert some of its bio-diverse national park areas to agricultural production, thus reducing the earnings from these products or services.

Conversely, the United States could produce coffee (perhaps in climate-controlled buildings), but at the cost of diverting resources away from products such as wheat, for which its climate and terrain are naturally suited. Trading coffee for wheat and vice versa is a goal more easily achieved than if these two countries were to try to become self-sufficient in the production of both. The more the two countries' natural advantages differ, the more likely they will favor trade with one another.

Variations among countries in natural advantages also help explain where certain manufactured or processed items might best be produced, particularly if a company can reduce transportation costs by processing an agricultural commodity or natural resource prior to exporting. Processing coffee beans into instant coffee reduces bulk and is likely to reduce transport costs on coffee exports; producing canned latte could add weight, lessening the industry's internationally competitive edge.

Acquired Advantage   Most of today's world trade is of manufactured goods rather than agricultural goods and natural resources. Countries that are competitive in manufactured goods have an **acquired advantage,** usually in either product or process technology. An advantage of *product technology* is that it enables a country to produce a unique product or one that is easily distinguished from those of competitors. For example, Denmark exports silver tableware, not because there are rich Danish silver mines but because Danish companies have developed distinctive products.

An advantage in *process technology* is a country's ability to efficiently produce a homogeneous product (one not easily distinguished from that of competitors). Japan has exported steel despite having to import iron and coal—the two main ingredients for steel production—because its steel mills have encompassed new labor- and material-saving processes. Thus, countries that develop distinctive or less expensive products have acquired advantages, at least until producers in another country emulate them successfully.

Acquired advantage through technology has created new products, displaced old ones, and altered trading-partner relationships. The most obvious examples of change are production and export of new products and services, such as computers and software. Products that existed in earlier periods have increased their share of world trade because of technological changes in the production process. For example, early hand-tooled automobiles reached only elite markets, but a succession of manufacturing innovations, from assembly lines to robotics, has enabled automobiles to reach an ever-widening mass market.

In other cases, companies have developed new uses for old products, such as aloe in sunscreen. Other products, such as artificial fibers, have partially displaced traditional ones. Finally, technology may be used to overcome natural advantages. Iceland now exports tomatoes grown near the Arctic Circle, while Brazil exports quality wine produced near the equator—both of which were impossible until the development of fairly recent technology.[5]

Natural advantage considers climate, natural resources, and labor force availability.

Case Review Note

Acquired advantage consists of either product or process technology.

Free trade will bring

- Specialization.
- Greater efficiency.
- Higher global output.

How Does Resource Efficiency Work?   We can demonstrate absolute trade advantage here by examining two countries (Costa Rica and the United States) and two commodities (coffee and wheat). Because we are not yet considering the concepts of money and exchange rates, we define the cost of production in terms of the resources needed to produce either coffee or wheat. This example is realistic because real income depends on the output of goods compared to the resources used to produce them.

Start with the assumption that Costa Rica and the United States are the only countries and each has the same amount of resources (land, labor, and capital) to produce either coffee or wheat. Using Figure 6.2, let's say that 100 units of resources are available in each country. In Costa Rica, assume that it takes four units to produce a ton of coffee and 10 units per ton of wheat. The purple Costa Rican production possibility line shows that Costa Rica can produce 25 tons of coffee and no wheat, 10 tons of wheat and no coffee, or some combination of the two.

In the United States, it takes 20 units per ton of coffee and five units per ton of wheat. The green U.S. production possibility line indicates that the country can produce five tons of coffee and no wheat, 20 tons of wheat and no coffee, or some combination of the two. Costa Rica is more efficient (that is, takes fewer resources to produce a ton) in coffee production, while the United States is more efficient in wheat production.

How can production be increased through specialization and trade? Consider a situation in which the two countries have no foreign trade. We could start from any place on each production possibility line; for convenience, however, assume that if each country devotes half of its 100 resources to production of each product, Costa Rica can produce 12.5 tons of coffee (divide 50 by 4) and five tons of wheat (divide 50 by 10), which are shown as point A in Figure 6.2, while the United States can produce 2.5 tons of coffee (divide 50 by 20) and 10 tons of wheat (divide 50 by 5), shown as point B in Figure 6.2.

Because each country has only 100 units of resources, neither can increase wheat production without decreasing coffee production, or vice versa. Without trade, the combined production is 15 tons of coffee (12.5 + 2.5) and 15 tons of wheat (5 + 10). If each country specialized in the commodity for which it had an absolute advantage, Costa Rica could then produce 25 tons of coffee and the United States 20 tons of wheat (points C and D in the figure).

FIGURE 6.2   Production Possibilities under Conditions of Absolute Advantage

In short, specialization increases output.

ASSUMPTIONS
for Costa Rica

1. 100 units of resources available
2. 10 units to produce a ton of wheat
3. 4 units to produce a ton of coffee
4. Uses half of total resources per product when there is no foreign trade

ASSUMPTIONS
for United States

1. 100 units of resources available
2. 5 units to produce a ton of wheat
3. 20 units to produce a ton of coffee
4. Uses half of total resources per product when there is no foreign trade

PRODUCTION	Coffee (tons)	Wheat (tons)
Without Trade:		
Costa Rica (point A)	12½	5
United States (point B)	2½	10
Total	15	15
With Trade:		
Costa Rica (point C)	25	0
United States (point D)	0	20
Total	25	20

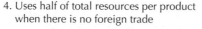

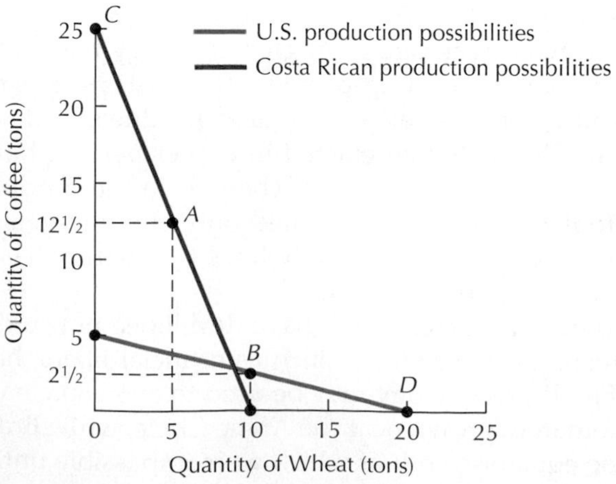

— U.S. production possibilities

— Costa Rican production possibilities

You can see that specialization increases the production of both products. By trading, global efficiency is optimized, and the two countries can have more coffee and more wheat than they would without trade.

THEORY OF COMPARATIVE ADVANTAGE

We have just described absolute advantage, which is often confused with and called *comparative advantage*. In 1817, David Ricardo examined the question, "What happens when one country can produce all products at an absolute advantage?" His resulting theory of **comparative advantage** says that global efficiency gains may still result from trade if a country specializes in what it can produce most efficiently—regardless of whether other countries can produce those same products more efficiently.

Gains from trade will occur even in a country that has absolute advantage in all products, because the country must give up less efficient output to produce more efficient output.

Comparative Advantage by Analogy   Although this theory may seem initially incongruous, an analogy should clarify its logic. Imagine that the best physician in town also happens to be the best medical administrator. It would not make economic sense for him or her to handle all the administrative duties of the office, because he or she can earn more money by concentrating on medical duties, even though that means having to employ a less-skilled medical administrator for the office. In the same manner, a country gains if it concentrates its resources on the commodities it can produce most efficiently. It then trades some of those for commodities for others produced abroad. The following discussion clarifies why this theory is true.

Production Possibility   In this example, assume the United States is more efficient in producing coffee and wheat than Costa Rica is, thus having an absolute advantage in the production of both.[6] Take a look at Figure 6.3. As in our earlier example, it assumes that there are only two countries, each with a total of 100 units of resources available, and half of each used in each product. It takes Costa Rica 10 units of resources to produce either a ton of coffee or a ton of wheat, whereas it takes the United States only five units to produce a ton of coffee and four for a ton of wheat. Costa Rica can produce five tons of coffee and five tons of wheat (point A on the purple line), and the United States can produce 10 tons of coffee and 12.5 tons of wheat (point B on the green line). Without trade, neither country can increase its coffee production without sacrificing some wheat production, or vice versa.

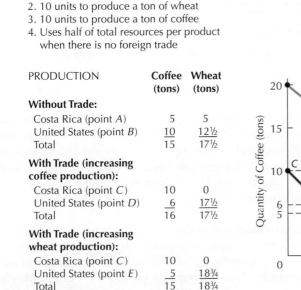

ASSUMPTIONS
for Costa Rica

1. 100 units of resources available
2. 10 units to produce a ton of wheat
3. 10 units to produce a ton of coffee
4. Uses half of total resources per product
   when there is no foreign trade

PRODUCTION	Coffee (tons)	Wheat (tons)
Without Trade:		
Costa Rica (point *A*)	5	5
United States (point *B*)	10	12½
Total	15	17½
With Trade (increasing coffee production):		
Costa Rica (point *C*)	10	0
United States (point *D*)	6	17½
Total	16	17½
With Trade (increasing wheat production):		
Costa Rica (point *C*)	10	0
United States (point *E*)	5	18¾
Total	15	18¾

ASSUMPTIONS
for United States

1. 100 units of resources available
2. 4 units to produce a ton of wheat
3. 5 units to produce a ton of coffee
4. Uses half of total resources per product
   when there is no foreign trade

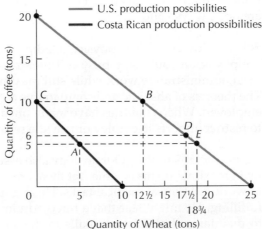

FIGURE 6.3 Production Possibilities under Conditions of Comparative Advantage

There are advantages to trade even if one country enjoys an absolute advantage in the production of all products.

Although the United States has an absolute advantage in producing both commodities, it has a comparative advantage only in wheat. This is because its advantage in wheat production is 2.5 times that of Costa Rica, but its advantage in coffee is only twice that of Costa Rica. Although Costa Rica has an absolute disadvantage in the production of both products, it has a comparative advantage (or less of a comparative disadvantage) in coffee. Why? Because its production is half as efficient as the United States in coffee and only 40 percent as efficient in wheat.

Without trade, the combined production is 15 tons of coffee (five in Costa Rica plus 10 in the United States) and 17.5 tons of wheat (5 plus 12.5). Through trading, the combined production of the commodities within the two countries can be increased. For example, if the combined wheat production is unchanged from when there was no trade, the United States could produce all 17.5 tons by using 70 units of resources (17.5 tons times 4 units per ton). The remaining 30 units could be used for producing six tons of coffee (30 units divided by 5 units per ton). This production possibility is point D in Figure 6.3. Costa Rica would use all its resources to produce 10 tons of coffee (point C). The combined wheat production has stayed at 17.5 tons, but the coffee production has increased from 15 to 16 tons.

If the combined coffee production is unchanged from the time before trade, Costa Rica could use all its resources to produce coffee, yielding 10 tons (point C in Figure 6.3). The United States could produce the remaining five tons of coffee by using 25 units, with the remaining 75 U.S. units being used to produce 18.75 tons of wheat (75 divided by 4). This production possibility is point E. Without sacrificing any of the coffee available before trade, wheat production has increased from 17.5 to 18.75 tons.

If the United States were to produce somewhere between points D and E, both coffee and wheat production would increase over what was possible before trade took place. Whether the production target is a rise in coffee or wheat or a combination of the two, both countries can gain by having Costa Rica trade some of its coffee production to the United States for some U.S. wheat output.

Don't Confuse Comparative and Absolute Advantage   Most economists accept the comparative advantage theory and its influence in promoting policies for freer trade. Nevertheless, many government policymakers, journalists, managers, and workers confuse comparative advantage with absolute advantage and do not understand how a country can simultaneously have a comparative *advantage* and absolute *disadvantage* in the production of a given product.

THEORIES OF SPECIALIZATION: SOME ASSUMPTIONS AND LIMITATIONS

Both absolute and comparative advantage theories are based on increasing output and trade through specialization. However, these theories make assumptions, some of which are not always valid.

| Full employment is not a valid assumption of absolute and comparative advantage. |

Full Employment   The physician/administrator analogy we used earlier assumed that the physician could stay busy full time practicing medicine. If he cannot, he may perform administrative work while still maximizing earnings from serving as a physician. The theories of absolute and comparative advantage both assume that resources are fully employed. When countries have many unemployed or unused resources, they may seek to restrict imports to employ or use idle resources.

| Countries' goals may not be limited to economic efficiency. |

Economic Efficiency   Our analogy also assumes that the physician is interested primarily in maximizing his income. Yet there are a number of reasons why he might choose not to work full time at medical tasks. He might find administrative work relaxing and self-fulfilling. He might fear that a hired administrator would be unreliable. He might wish to maintain administrative skills in the somewhat unlikely event that administration, rather than medicine, commands higher wages in the future. Often, countries also pursue objectives other than output efficiency. They may avoid overspecialization because of the vulnerability created by changes in technology and by price fluctuations.

Division of Gains Although specialization brings potential economic benefits to all trading countries, the earlier discussion did not indicate how countries will divide increased output. In the case of our wheat and coffee example, if both the United States and Costa Rica receive some share of the higher output, both will be better off economically through specialization and trade. However, many people are concerned with relative as well as absolute economic growth. If they perceive that a trading partner is gaining too large a share of benefits, they may prefer to forgo absolute gains for themselves so as to prevent others from gaining a relative economic advantage.[7]

Two Countries, Two Commodities As in our examples, both Smith and Ricardo assumed, for simplicity's sake, a simple world composed of only two countries and two commodities. Now although this simplification is unrealistic, it does not diminish the usefulness of either theory. Economists have applied the same reasoning to demonstrate efficiency advantages in multiproduct and multicountry trade relationships.

Transport Costs If it costs more to transport the goods than is saved through specialization, the advantages of trade are negated. In other words, in our two-country scenario, some workers would need to forgo producing coffee or wheat in order to work in transporting the coffee and wheat abroad. However, as long as the diversion reduces output by less than what the two countries gain from specialization, there are still gains from trade.

Statics and Dynamics The theories of absolute and comparative advantage address countries' statically—that is by looking at them at one point in time. However, the relative conditions that give countries production advantages and disadvantages change. For example, the resources needed to produce coffee or wheat in either Costa Rica or the United States could change because of advancements in and acceptance of genetically modified crops. In fact, most trade today is due to acquired advantage; thus, technical dynamics cause countries to gain or lose both absolutely and relatively.[8]

In addition, as we show in our opening case, when Costa Rica focused on goods that could compete in international markets, it developed and enhanced a competitive advantage in some promising high-tech industries. Thus, we should not assume that future absolute or comparative advantages will remain as they are today. We return to this theme later in the chapter as we examine theories to explain the dynamics of competitive production locations.

Services The theories of absolute and comparative advantage deal with products rather than services. However, with a growing portion of world trade made up of services, the theories apply because resources must also go into service production. For instance, the United States sells an excess of such services as education to foreign countries (many foreign students attend U.S. universities), as well as credit card systems and collections. At the same time, it buys an excess of foreign shipping services. To become more self-sufficient in international shipping, the United States might have to divert resources from its more efficient use in higher education or in the production of competitive products.

Production Networks Both theories deal with trading one product for another. Increasingly, however, portions of a product may be made in different countries. A company might conduct R&D in Country A, secure components in Countries B and C, assemble final products in Country D, manage finances in Country E, and carry out call-center services in Country F. Although this type of development adds complexity to the analysis, it fits well with the concept of advantages through specialization. In other words, costs are saved by having activities take place in those countries where there is an absolute or comparative advantage for their production.

Case Review Note

Mobility These theories assume that resources can move domestically from the production of one good to another—and at no cost. But this assumption is not completely valid. For example, steelworkers might not move easily into software development jobs because of different skill needs. Even if they do, they may be less productive than before.[9] The theories also assume that resources cannot move internationally. Increasingly, however, they do, and the movement affects countries' production capabilities. For instance, Nicaraguans account for a growing percent of Costa Rica's population.[10] Further, foreign companies have moved both personnel and capital to support their investments there, which has contributed to changing Costa Rican capabilities. Such movement is clearly an alternative to trade, a topic discussed later in the chapter. However, it is safe to say that resources are more mobile domestically than they are internationally.

Case Review Note

Trade Pattern Theories

The free trade theories demonstrate how economic growth occurs through specialization and trade; however, they do not deal with trade patterns such as the amount, product composition, or partners a country will have if it follows a free trade policy. In this section, we discuss the theories that help explain these patterns.

HOW MUCH DOES A COUNTRY TRADE?

Free-trade theories of specialization neither propose nor imply that only one country should or will produce a given product or service. **Nontradable goods**—products and services (such as haircuts and retail grocery distribution) that are seldom practical to export because of high transportation costs—are produced in every country. However, among tradable goods, some countries import and export more than others. We will now examine theories that help explain country differences.

Bigger countries differ in several ways from smaller countries. They

• Tend to export a smaller portion of output and import a smaller part of consumption.

• Have higher transport costs for foreign trade.

Theory of Country Size The **theory of country size** holds that large countries usually depend less on trade than small ones. Countries with large land areas are apt to have varied climates and an assortment of natural resources, making them more self-sufficient than smaller ones. Most large countries (such as Brazil, China, India, the United States, and Russia) import much less of their consumption needs and export much less of their production output than do small nations (such as Uruguay, the Netherlands, and Iceland).

Furthermore, distance to foreign markets affects large and small countries differently. Normally, the farther the distance, the higher the transport costs, the longer the inventory carrying time, and the greater the uncertainty and unreliability of timely product delivery. The following example illustrates why distance is more pronounced for a large country than for a small one.

Assume that the normal maximum distance for transporting a given product is 100 miles because prices rise too much at greater distances. Although almost any location in tiny Belgium is within 100 miles of a foreign country, the same isn't true for its two largest neighbors, France and Germany. Thus, Belgium's dependence on trade as a percentage of its production and consumption is greater than the comparable figures in either France or Germany, a fact that can be partially explained by the distance factor due to country size.

Size of the Economy Although land area is the most obvious way to measure a country's size, countries can also be compared by economic size. The world's top 10 exporters and importers in 2010 were dominated by developed countries (eight out of 10). Similarly, developed countries account for well over half of the world's exports.

Simply, developed countries produce so much that they have more to sell, both domestically and internationally. In addition, because they produce so much, incomes are high and people buy more from both domestic and foreign sources. At the same time, little of the trade of developing countries is with other developing countries.

WHAT TYPES OF PRODUCTS DOES A COUNTRY TRADE?

In our discussion of absolute advantage, we indicated that this advantage might be either natural or acquired. Here, we discuss theories that help explain what types of products result from these natural and acquired advantages. We won't delve again into those factors we've already discussed (climate and natural resources) that give a country a natural advantage; however, we will examine the factor endowment theory of trade. For acquired advantage, we discuss the importance of production and product technology.

Factor-Proportions Theory   Eli Heckscher and Bertil Ohlin developed the **factor-proportions theory,** maintaining that differences in countries' endowments of labor compared to land or capital endowments explain differences in the cost of production factors. For instance, if labor were abundant in comparison to land and capital, labor costs would be low relative to land and capital costs; if scarce, the costs would be high. These relative factor costs would lead countries to excel in the production and export of products that used their abundant—and therefore cheaper—production factors.[11]

> According to the factor-proportions theory, factors in relative abundance are cheaper than factors in relative scarcity.

People and Land   Factor-proportions theory appears logical. In countries that have many people relative to the amount of land, such as Hong Kong and the Netherlands, land price is very high because it's in such demand. Regardless of climate and soil conditions, neither Hong Kong nor the Netherlands excels in the production of goods requiring large amounts of land, such as wool or wheat. Businesses in countries such as Australia and Canada produce these goods because land is abundant compared to the number of people.

Manufacturing Locations   Casual observation of manufacturing locations also seems to substantiate the theory. The most successful industries in Hong Kong are those in which technology permits the use of a minimum amount of land relative to the number of people employed. Its clothing production occurs in multistory factories where workers share minimal space, but it does not compete in the production of automobiles, which requires much more space per worker.

Capital, Labor Rates, and Specialization   In countries where little capital is available for investment and the amount of investment per worker is low, managers might expect to find cheap labor rates and export competitiveness in products that need large amounts of labor relative to capital. An example would be agricultural products requiring a lot of labor for picking and packing, such as roses from Ecuador, which we discuss in the ending case.

> Production factors, especially labor, are not homogeneous.

Case Review Note

However, because the factor-proportions theory assumes production factors to be homogeneous, tests to substantiate the theory have been mixed.[12] Labor skills, in fact, vary within and among countries because of training and education differences. Training and education require capital expenditures that do not show up in traditional capital measurements, which include only plant and equipment values. When the factor-proportions theory accounts for different labor groups and the capital invested to train them, it seems to explain many trade patterns.[13] For example, because developed countries embody a higher proportion of professionals such as scientists and engineers than do developing economies, they use their abundant production factors to maintain their lead in exports. Low-income countries, though, show a high intensity of less-skilled labor in exports.[14]

This variation in labor skills has led to more international task specialization to produce a given product. For example, a company may locate its R&D and management functions primarily in countries with a highly educated population, while locating its production work in countries where it can employ less educated and less expensive workers.

Process Technology   Factor-proportions analysis becomes more complicated when the same product can be created by different methods, such as with labor or capital. The photos show, for instance, that in Pakistan labor instead of machines are harvesting wheat, whereas in the United States, mechanized methods require few workers. In the final analysis, the optimum location of production depends on comparing the cost in each locale based on the type of production that minimizes costs there.

> Companies may substitute capital for labor, depending on the cost of each.

Source: Jeff Zenner Photography/Shutterstock.com

The wheat harvesting is capital extensive in this US photo because of high labor costs. It is labor intensive in the Pakistani photo because of low labor costs.

▶

Source: Rubengutierrez | Dreamstime.com

Bigger countries depend more on products requiring longer production runs.

However, not all products lend themselves to such trade-offs in production methods. Some require huge amounts of fixed capital and long production runs to spread the fixed capital costs over more output units, usually resulting in development in large countries with large markets.[15] However, companies may locate long production runs in small countries if they expect to be able to export from them.[16] In industries where long

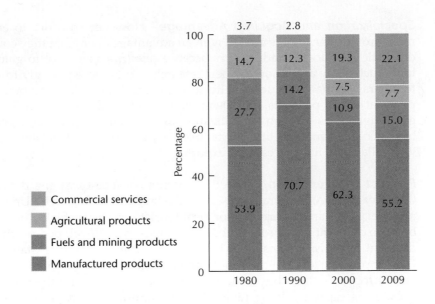

FIGURE 6.4 **Worldwide Trade by Major Sectors**

As a percentage of total world trade, manufactured products are more important than products in any other category. Services, however, constitute the fastest-growing category.

Source: From World Trade Organization, *Annual Report* (Geneva, various years).

production runs reduce unit costs substantially, companies tend to locate production in only a few countries, using these locations to export. Where long production runs are less important, we find a greater prevalence of multiple production units scattered around the world in different countries so as to minimize transportation costs through exporting.

In addition, high R&D expenditures create high up-front fixed costs. Therefore, a technologically intensive company from a small nation may need to sell more abroad than a company with a large domestic market. It may, in turn, pull resources from other industries and companies within its domestic market, which means the country will have more national specialization than one finds in a larger nation.[17]

Product Technology Figure 6.4 shows the changing composition of world trade. Manufacturing is by far the largest sector, with commercial services the fastest-growing sector. Manufacturing competitiveness depends largely on technology to develop new products and processes. The technology depends, in turn, on a large number of highly educated people (especially scientists and engineers) and a large amount of capital to invest in R&D.

Because developed countries have an abundance of these features, they originate most new products and account for most manufacturing output and trade. Developing countries depend much more on the production of primary products; thus, they depend more on natural advantage.

| Most new products originate in developed countries.

WITH WHOM DO COUNTRIES TRADE?

We have already noted that developed countries account for the bulk of world trade. They also trade primarily with each other, whereas developing countries mainly export primary and labor-intensive products to developed countries in exchange for new and technologically advanced products. Below, we discuss the roles that country similarity and distance play in determining trading partners.

Country-Similarity Theory The theories explaining why trade takes place have focused so far on the differences among countries in terms of natural conditions and factor endowment proportions. That most trade takes place among developed countries can be further explained by the **country-similarity theory.** This theory says that companies create new products in response to market conditions in their home market. They then turn to markets and consumer economic levels they see as most similar to what they are accustomed to.[18]

| Developed countries trade primarily with each other because they
- Produce and consume more.
- Emphasize technical breakthroughs in different industrial sectors.
- Produce differentiated products and services.

Specialization and Acquired Advantage   However, in order to export, a company must provide consumers abroad with an advantage over what they could buy from their domestic producers. Trade occurs because *countries* specialize to gain acquired advantage, such as by apportioning their research efforts more strongly to some sectors than to others. Germany is traditionally strong in machinery and equipment, Switzerland in pharmaceutical products, and Denmark in food products.[19] Even developing countries gain advantages through specialization in very narrow product segments. Bangladesh has succeeded in exporting shirts, trousers, and hats, but not bed linens or footballs, which Pakistan has successfully exported.[20]

Product Differentiation   Trade also occurs because *companies* differentiate products, thus creating two-way trade in seemingly similar products. The United States is both a major exporter and a major importer of tourist services, vehicles, and passenger aircraft because different firms from different countries have developed product variations with different appeals. For instance, both Boeing from the United States and Airbus from Europe produce large jet passenger aircraft that will fly from point A to point B, but U.S. and European airlines buy both companies' aircraft because their models differ in such features as capacity, flying range, fuel consumption, and perceived reliability.[21] As a result, Boeing and Airbus sell them within their own and each other's home markets as well as within countries that produce no aircraft.

Trading partners are affected by
• Cultural similarity.
• Political relations between countries.
• Distance.

The Effects of Cultural Similarity   Importers and exporters find it easier to do business in countries they perceive as being culturally similar to home, such as those that speak a common language. Likewise, historic colonial relationships explain much of the trade between specific developed and developing economies. For instance, France's colonial history in Africa has given Air France an edge in serving the continent's international air passenger markets.[22] Similarly, the lack of extensive trade among nations in the Southern Hemisphere is due partly to the absence of historic ties. Importers and exporters find it easier to continue business ties than to develop new distribution arrangements in countries where they are less experienced.

The Effects of Political Relationships and Economic Agreements   Political relationships and economic agreements among countries may discourage or encourage trade between them. Witness the political animosity between the United States and Cuba that has diminished their mutual trade for about five decades. An example of trade encouragement is the agreement among many European countries to remove all trade barriers with each other, thereby causing a greater share of the countries' total trade to be conducted with each other.

Concept Check

In discussing "Cultural Distance" in Chapter 2, we show that "distance" is an index of similarities between countries based primarily on such shared cultural attributes as language, ethnicity, or values. We indicate that, by and large, a company from one country should expect fewer adjustments when moving to a country whose culture is close to that of its home base, but we also caution that, even in these cases, executives should be aware of subtle cultural differences.

The Effects of Distance   Although no single factor fully explains specific pairs of trading relationships, the geographic distance between two countries is an important factor. In essence, greater distances usually mean higher transportation costs; that's why Intel's cost to ship semiconductors from Costa Rica to the United States is lower than if it had to bring them from, say, Argentina. However, the available transportation mode is also important. Wine exports from Australia can reach the United Kingdom (UK) by container ship for about the same cost as wine exports shipped overland to the UK from southern France.[23]

Overcoming Distance   Transport cost is not the only factor in trade partner choice. New Zealand competes with Chile, Argentina, and South Africa for out-of-season sales of apples to the Northern Hemisphere—but with a disadvantage in freight costs to the United States and Europe. It has countered this disadvantage by boosting yields, developing new premium varieties, bypassing intermediaries to sell directly to supermarkets abroad, and consolidating efforts through a national marketing board. However, such methods to overcome distance drawbacks are difficult to maintain. For example, rival orchardists have smuggled new strains of apple tree cuttings out of New Zealand.[24]

Does Ge🌍graphy Matter? Variety Is the Spice of Life

As you study this chapter, you'll see that geography plays a role in many of the theories and questions on trade. We pull them together in this discussion.

Part of a country's trading advantage is explained by its natural advantage—climate, terrain, arable land, and natural resources. Thus, Saudi Arabia trades oil, a natural resource, for U.S. rice, which needs huge wet areas for production. Remember that technology (acquired advantage) may often negate natural advantage, as in the development of substitutes (synthetic nitrate for natural nitrate) and the development of different production methods (Chile is not using traditional bogs for growing cranberries). Nevertheless, a country's geography—particularly the ease of moving goods to markets in other countries—may give it an advantage or disadvantage. For instance, landlocked countries have a considerable transport cost disadvantage relative to countries with seacoasts.[25]

Factor-proportions theory helps explain where certain goods may be more efficiently produced, such as labor-intensive goods where labor is plentiful in relation to capital and land. Bangladesh excels in producing clothing that requires lots of labor in relation to either capital or land. However, these factors can change in both quantity and quality. Hong Kong, with its very high population density, used to excel in the production of labor-intensive goods. But because it has accumulated capital and upgraded the education of its workforce, its competitive production and exports now encompass more capital intensity and skilled labor.

Usually, small countries need to trade more than large countries, primarily because they are apt to have less variety of natural advantages. There are exceptions, though. Small countries that also have low incomes tend to depend little on trade because they produce and consume so little. Distance from foreign markets also plays a role. Geographically isolated countries such as Fiji trade less than would be expected from their size because transportation costs raise the price of traded goods substantially.[26]

Conversely, Canada is a large developed country whose dependence on trade and trade per capita are not only among the world's highest but also much higher than we would expect from the theory of country size. This may be explained largely by Canada's population dispersion. Ninety percent of its population is within 100 miles of the U.S. border, so shipping goods between, say, Vancouver and Seattle or Toronto and Cleveland is often more feasible than between Vancouver and Toronto.

Although distance helps us understand the importance of pairs of trading partners, political relationships and cultural similarity are important factors as well. Consider the large amount of trade within regional trading organizations and between former colonizers and their former colonies. Most important, though, is the preponderance of world trade among developed countries because they produce and consume more. Further, they engage in technological specialization and product differentiation to fit market niches.

This begs the question of why some countries are developed and others are not—a very complex issue we cannot hope to answer. Nevertheless, some of the factors affecting income levels, and thus trade, are geographic. One study showed that 70 percent of countries' differences in per capita income can be accounted for by four factors: malaria, hydrocarbon endowments, coastal access, and transportation costs—all of which relate to geography.[27] •

The Statics and Dynamics of Trade

Although we've alluded to the fact that trading patterns change, due to such factors as political and economic relations among countries and the development of new product capabilities, we now discuss two theories—the product life cycle theory and the diamond of national advantage—that help explain how countries develop, maintain, and lose their competitive advantages.

PRODUCT LIFE CYCLE (PLC) THEORY

The international **product life cycle (PLC) theory** of trade states that the production location of certain manufactured products shifts as they go through their life cycle. The cycle consists of four stages: *introduction, growth, maturity,* and *decline*.[28] Table 6.2 highlights these stages.

According to the PLC theory of trade, the production location for many products moves from one country to another depending on the stage in the product's life cycle.

TABLE 6.2   Life Cycle of the International Product

During its life cycle, focus on a product's production and market locations often shifts from industrial to developing markets. The process is accompanied by changes in the competitive factors affecting both production and sales, as well as in the technology used to produce the product.

Life Cycle Stage

	1: Introduction	2: Growth	3: Maturity	4: Decline
Production location	• In innovating (usually industrial) country	• In innovating and other industrial countries	• Multiple countries	• Mainly in developing countries
Market location	• Mainly in innovating country, with some exports	• Mainly in industrial countries • Shift in export markets as foreign production replaces exports in some markets	• Growth in developing countries • Some decrease in industrial countries	• Mainly in developing countries • Some developing country exports
Competitive factors	• Near-monopoly position • Sales based on uniqueness rather than price • Evolving product characteristics	• Fast-growing demand • Number of competitors increases • Some competitors begin price cutting • Product becoming more standardized	• Overall stabilized demand • Number of competitors decreases • Price is very important, especially in developing countries	• Overall declining demand • Price is key weapon • Number of producers continues to decline
Production technology	• Short production runs • Evolving methods to coincide with product evolution • High labor input and labor skills relative to capital input	• Capital input increases • Methods more standardized	• Long production runs using high capital inputs • Highly standardized • Less labor skill needed	• Unskilled labor on mechanized long production runs

Changes over the Cycle   Companies develop new products primarily because they observe nearby needs for them, thus a U.S. company is most apt to create a new product for the U.S. market, a French company for the French market, and so on. At the same time, almost all new technology that results in new products and production methods originates in developed countries,[29] which have most of the resources to develop new products and most of the income to buy them.

Introduction   Once a company has created a new product, theoretically it can manufacture it anywhere in the world. In practice, however, the early-production stage, called the *introductory stage,* generally occurs in a domestic location so the company can obtain rapid market feedback and save on transport costs, since most sales are domestic. Any export sales are mainly to other developed countries because of more affluent customers there.

Production is apt to be more labor-intensive than in later stages because more labor-saving machinery may be introduced only when sales begin to expand rapidly and the product becomes highly standardized. Although production is in developed countries with high labor rates, their education and skills usually make this labor efficient in non-standardized production. Even if production costs are high because of expensive labor, companies can often pass costs on to consumers who are unwilling to wait for possible price reductions later.

Growth   Sales growth attracts competitors to the market, particularly in other developed countries. Let's say the innovator is in the United States and a competitor puts a manufacturing unit in Japan. The Japanese production is sold mainly in Japan for several reasons:

The introduction stage is marked by

• Innovation in response to observed need.
• Exporting by the innovative country.
• Evolving product characteristics.

Growth is characterized by

• Increases in exports by the innovating country.
• More competition.
• Increased capital intensity.
• Some foreign production.

1. The growing demand there does not allow for much attention to other markets.
2. Producers there stay occupied in developing unique product variations for Japanese consumers.
3. Japanese costs may still be high because of production start-up problems.

Sales growth creates an incentive for companies to develop labor-saving process technology, but this incentive is partly offset because competitors are differentiating their products, especially to fit the needs of different countries. Thus the capital intensity, though growing, is less than will come later. The original producing country will increase its exports, especially to developing countries, but will lose certain key export markets in which local production commences.

Maturity   In the *maturity stage,* worldwide demand begins to level off, although it may be growing in some countries and declining in others. Typically, there is a shakeout of producers, more standardized production, and increased importance of price as a competitive weapon. Capital-intensive production reduces per-unit cost, thus creating even more demand in developing economies. Because markets and technologies are widespread, the innovating country no longer commands a production advantage. Firms have incentives to shift production to developing economies where they can employ less skilled and less expensive labor efficiently for standardized (capital-intensive) production. Exports decrease from the innovating country as foreign production displaces it.

> Maturity is characterized by
> - A decline in exports from the innovating country.
> - More product standardization.
> - More capital intensity.
> - Increased competitiveness of price.
> - Production start-ups in emerging economies.

Decline   As a product moves into the *decline stage,* those factors occurring during the mature stage continue to evolve. The markets in developed countries decline more rapidly than those in developing economies as affluent customers demand ever newer products. By this time, market and cost factors have dictated that almost all production is in developing economies that export to the declining or small-niche markets in the developed world. In other words, the country in which the innovation first emerged—and was exported from—then becomes the importer.

> Decline is characterized by
> - A concentration of production in developing countries.
> - An innovating country becoming a net importer.

Verification and Limitations of PLC Theory   The PLC theory holds that the location of production facilities that serve world markets shifts as products move through their life cycle. Such items as ballpoint pens and hand calculators have followed this pattern. They were first produced in a single developed country and sold at a high price. Then production shifted to multiple developed country locations to serve those local markets. Today, most production has located in developing countries, and prices have declined.

There are many types of products for which production locations usually do not shift. Such exceptions include the following:

> Not all products conform to the dynamics of the PLC.

- Products with high transport costs that may have to be produced close to the market, thus never becoming significant exports.
- Products that, because of very rapid innovation, have extremely short life cycles, making it impossible to reduce costs by moving production from one country to another. Some fashion items fit this category.
- Luxury products for which cost is of little concern to the consumer. In fact, production in a developing country may cause consumers to perceive the product as less luxurious.
- Products for which a company can use a differentiation strategy, perhaps through advertising, to maintain consumer demand without competing on the basis of price.
- Products that require specialized technical labor near the production so as to move the products into their next generation. This seems to explain the long-term U.S. dominance of medical equipment production and German dominance in rotary printing presses.

Regardless of product, the trend is for international companies to introduce new products at home and abroad almost simultaneously. In other words, instead of merely observing needs within their domestic markets, companies develop products and services for observable worldwide market segments. In so doing, they eliminate delays as a product is diffused internationally, and they choose an initial production location (which may or may not be in the innovating company's home market) that will minimize costs for serving markets in multiple countries.

THE DIAMOND OF NATIONAL COMPETITIVE ADVANTAGE

Why have countries developed and sustained different competitive advantages? The **diamond of national competitive advantage** is a theory showing four features as important for competitive superiority: demand conditions; factor conditions; related and supporting industries; and firm strategy, structure, and rivalry[30] (see Figure 6.5).

We have largely discussed these conditions in the context of other trade theories, but how they combine affects the development and continued existence of competitive advantages. The framework of the theory, therefore, is a useful tool for understanding how and where globally competitive companies develop and sustain themselves.

Facets of the Diamond   Usually, all four conditions need to be favorable for an industry within a country to attain and maintain global supremacy.

Demand Conditions   *Demand conditions* are the first feature in the theory. Both PLC theory and country-similarity theory show that new products (or industries) usually arise from companies' observation of need or demand, which is usually in their home country, where they start up production. This was the case for the Italian ceramic tile industry after World War II: In a postwar housing boom, consumers wanted cool floors (which tile would provide) because of the hot Italian climate.

Factor Conditions   Continuing our example, the second feature—*factor conditions* (recall natural advantage within the absolute advantage and factor-proportions theories)—influenced both the choice of tile to meet consumer demand and the choice of Italy as the production location. Wood was less available and more expensive than tile, and most production factors (skilled labor, capital, technology, and equipment) were available within Italy on favorable terms.

Related and Supporting Industries   The third feature—the existence of nearby *related and supporting industries* (enamels and glazes)—was also favorable. Recall, for instance,

---

According to the diamond of national competitive advantage theory, companies' development of internationally competitive products depends on favorable

- Demand conditions.
- Factor conditions.
- Related and supporting industries.
- Firm strategy, structure, and rivalry.

Concept Check

In discussing the concept of the market economy in Chapter 4, we explain that such a system encourages an open exchange of goods and services among producers and consumers, both of which groups consist of "individuals" who make their own economic decisions; in this respect, then, the interaction among producers and consumers determines what products will be produced and in what quantities.

FIGURE 6.5   The Diamond of National Competitive Advantage

The interaction of these conditions must usually be favorable if an industry in a country is to develop and sustain itself. The theory was developed with domestic conditions in mind, but globalization results in favorable conditions that may come from anywhere.

Source: Based on Michael E. Porter, "The Competitive Advantage of Nations," Harvard Business Review, Vol. 68, No. 2, March-April 1990.

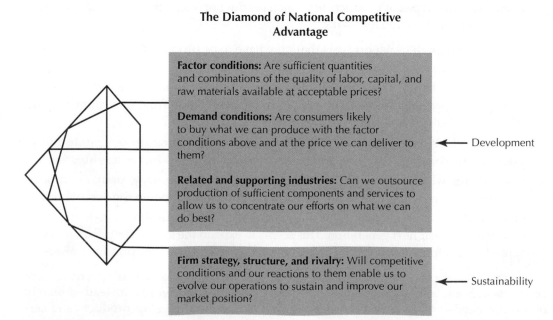

The Diamond of National Competitive Advantage

Factor conditions: Are sufficient quantities and combinations of the quality of labor, capital, and raw materials available at acceptable prices?

Demand conditions: Are consumers likely to buy what we can produce with the factor conditions above and at the price we can deliver to them? ← Development

Related and supporting industries: Can we outsource production of sufficient components and services to allow us to concentrate our efforts on what we can do best?

Firm strategy, structure, and rivalry: Will competitive conditions and our reactions to them enable us to evolve our operations to sustain and improve our market position? ← Sustainability

the importance of transport costs in the theory of country size, in assumptions of specialization, and in the limitation factors of the PLC theory.

Firm Strategy, Structure, and Rivalry The combination of three features—demand, factor conditions, and related and supporting industries—influenced companies' decisions to initiate production of ceramic tiles in postwar Italy. The ability of the companies to develop and sustain a competitive advantage required favorable circumstances for the fourth feature: *firm strategy, structure, and rivalry.*

Barriers to market entry were low in the tile industry (some companies started up with only three employees), and hundreds of companies initiated production. Rivalry became intense as companies tried to serve increasingly sophisticated Italian consumers. These circumstances forced breakthroughs in both product and process technologies, which gave the Italian producers advantages over foreign firms and enabled them to gain the largest global share of tile exports.

Limitations of the Diamond of National Advantage Theory The existence of the four favorable conditions does not guarantee that an industry will develop in a given locale. Entrepreneurs may face favorable conditions for many different lines of business. In fact, comparative advantage theory holds that resource limitations may cause a country's firms to avoid competing in some industries despite an absolute advantage. Conditions in Switzerland would seem to have favored success if companies in that country had become players in the personal computer industry. However, Swiss companies preferred to protect their global positions in such product lines as watches and scientific instruments rather than downsize innovation efforts in those industries by moving their highly skilled people into developing a new industry.

A second limitation concerns the growth of globalization. The industries on which this theory is premised grew when companies' access to competitive capabilities was much more domestically focused. We can see how globalization affects each of the four conditions:

1. Observations of foreign or foreign-plus-domestic demand conditions have spurred much of the recent Asian export growth. In fact, such Japanese companies as Uniden and Fujitech target their sales almost entirely to foreign markets.[31]

2. Companies and countries do not depend entirely on domestic factor conditions. For example, capital and managers are now internationally mobile, and companies may depend on foreign locations for portions of their production.

3. If related and supporting industries are not available locally, materials and components are now more easily brought in from abroad because of transportation advancements and relaxed import restrictions. In fact, many MNEs now assemble products with parts supplied from a variety of countries.

4. Companies react not only to domestic rivals but also to foreign-based rivals they compete with at home and abroad. Thus the prior domestic absence of any of the four conditions from the diamond may not inhibit companies and industries from gaining these conditions and becoming globally competitive.

Using the Diamond for Transformation By expanding the diamond of national advantage theory to include changes brought about by globalization, we can see the validity for countries' economic policies. In our opening case, Costa Rica diversified its economy from agricultural products to modern high-tech products by satisfying the market entry conditions of the diamond. This transformation could not have occurred had Costa Rican authorities looked only at what was available within their own borders. In Costa Rica itself, there was (and still is) very little demand for the high-tech products, such as microchips and medical devices, that it now produces; good transportation, however, makes efficient export possible. Similarly, the country initially lacked some of the factor conditions necessary for producing high-tech products, especially trained personnel. Eventually, however,

Domestic existence of all conditions

- Does not guarantee an industry will develop.
- Is not necessary with globalization.

Case Review Note

Point   **Yes** What's so important about acquiring advantage in world trade? For one thing, if you're a country that wants to compete in today's globalized business environment (and you have to), you obviously must develop and maintain some industries that will be internationally competitive. But those industries also must grow and earn sufficient revenues to keep your domestic economy performing. What's the role of your government in the process of going global? It should be central to your whole effort; after all, we're talking about national economies here.

A government's role is rarely neutral. The government may claim that its economic policies don't affect the performance of specific domestic industries on the world stage, but a lot of those policies are bound to have precisely that effect. Who will argue that U.S. efforts to "improve agricultural productivity" and "enhance defense capabilities" have nothing to do with the fact that the United States does a healthy business in the export of farm and aerospace products?

Moreover, just about every government policy designed to help one industry will have a negative effect on another. European airlines complain (with some justification) that government support for high-speed rail traffic in Europe deprives them of the revenue they need to compete with U.S. overseas carriers, which don't have much to worry about from railroad passenger traffic at home. In other words, national policymakers everywhere face trade-offs. So if every government policy will help one party while hurting another, why shouldn't a country's practices call for taking special care of the industries that will likely give it its best competitive advantage?

Executing such a plan can be pretty simple. First, target a growth industry and figure out what factors make it competitive (or potentially competitive). Next, identify your country's likely competitive advantages (and make sure you know why you have them). Finally, develop a little synergy between the strong points you've uncovered during both processes: Target the resources needed to support the industries that fit best with your country's advantages.

This program—which comes under the general heading of *strategic trade policy* or *industrial policy*—is particularly effective if you're a developing country. Why? Because you've probably already decided that (1) you need to integrate yourself into the global economy and (2) you need to figure out the best way of performing well in the international game. If your competitive countries support high-potential start-ups and you don't, your new industries will be disadvantaged.[32] So far, so good, but you need to remember that simply opening up your borders to foreign competition doesn't necessarily mean that domestic producers will have an easier time competing either abroad or at home.

When you throw open your borders, the first companies to take you up on the invitation will be foreign competitors with considerable advantages over the homegrown industries you're trying to develop. They've had a head start that's allowed them to develop not only certain internal efficiencies but cozy relations with everybody in the international distribution channel.

Moreover, no matter how promising your targeted industries may be, or how carefully you've tried to match up your industries with your competitive advantages, as a developing country, your companies probably lack the technology and marketing skills they'll need to compete. So, why not help them?[33]

This brings us back to why strategic trade policy is your optimal choice if you're a developing country: Your government must protect your local industries—say, by helping them get the skills and technology they'll need. You could also focus your efforts to attract foreign investment on companies that have the marketing and technical skills you need; that's one good way of bringing in the kind of production you need. And it wouldn't hurt to extend incentives to the industries you're counting on.

Want some evidence that strategic trade policy is effective in helping developing nations go global? Look at Singapore, which not only managed to attract companies with experience in consumer-electronics production but eventually emerged as a global competitor because it also had the advantage of low wages.[34] By the same token, we have ample evidence that laissez-faire often doesn't work in developing countries. In sub-Saharan Africa, for example, government institutions are so deeply rooted that it's almost impossible for anyone—either individuals or multinationals—to make a move without getting entangled in the bureaucratic undergrowth.[35]

Moreover, because no single institution in developing countries has much in the way of resources, all of them are better off focusing their collective efforts on specific industries that have some potential for international competitiveness; otherwise, all you have is a bunch of under-resourced agencies and ministries aiming at markets scattered all over the economic landscape.[36]

it altered its educational system to fit human resource development to production needs and allowed companies to bring in foreign managers and technicians to fill personnel gaps. Finally, it developed local factors, such as additional power and metalworking expertise,

Should Nations Use Strategic Trade Policies?

Counterpoint

No Of course, countries should try to become most competitive in the industries that promise the best returns and have the most potential for going global. Obviously, they're the ones most likely to add value (in the form of high profits and good wages) to national production. However, strategic trade policy is not the best way to achieve the goals—about which nearly everybody agrees.

I'll make a concession: Under limited circumstances a targeting program will work, particularly for small countries such as Costa Rica. Because Costa Rica's GDP amounts to less than 10 percent of the value of Walmart's annual sales, parties involved can manageably work together to reach mutually beneficial agreements with minimal frustration. But in a large economy? Impossible.

However, it's debatable just how much Costa Rica's economic success is due to strategic trade policy and how much goes back to conditions that existed before the government started the whole process of targeting industries. Costa Rica already had a well-educated workforce, a relatively high level of economic freedom, a large population of English-speaking workers, a quality of life that had some appeal to foreign personnel, and a high level of political stability. Yes, Costa Rica landed Intel, but it's only fair to point out that Intel had already decided to put a plant somewhere in Latin America. Costa Rica's job, then, was basically convincing Intel it was a better choice than certain countries, such as Brazil and Chile, which were at a distance disadvantage when it came to sending output to the United States.

An alternative is for a country to focus on conditions affecting its attractiveness to profitable companies in general instead of targeted industries in particular. In other words, a government can alter conditions affecting, say, factor proportions, efficiency, and innovation by upgrading production factors—improving human skills, providing an adequate infrastructure, encouraging consumers to demand higher-quality products, and promoting an overall competitive environment—for any industry interested in doing business within its borders.

Let's turn to your comments about sub-Saharan Africa. I'll even make another concession: Institutional inertia is indeed a way of life in the area, and there's no reason to expect that it will go away any time soon.[37] But what if we looked at things from another perspective? Rather than trying to focus on a specific industry in, say, the global high-tech universe, wouldn't all these bureaucratic agencies and ministries find it easier to review (and enforce) their own laws, take steps to stabilize their populations, rectify their most glaring economic, social, and gender inequities, and support entrepreneurial activity in the informal sectors of their economies? Wouldn't they find it more productive to foster an environment of trust—one in which, say, the government helps cut transaction costs so local firms will be willing to work with other companies, domestic and foreign, to acquire a little of the knowledge and a few of the resources they need to compete?[38]

Again, instead of picking and haggling over special industries, wouldn't they be better advised to improve the investment environment in which, after all, everybody will ultimately have to operate anyway?

At this point, I might as well take the offensive in this debate. Strategic trade policies typically result in no more than small payoffs—primarily because most governments find it difficult to identify and target the right industries.[39] What if a country targets an industry in which global demand never quite lives up to expectations? That's what happened to the United Kingdom and France when they got together to underwrite supersonic passenger planes. Or what if the domestic companies in a targeted industry simply fall short of being competitive? That's what happened when Thailand decided to get into the steel business.[40]

What if too many nations target the same global industries, thereby committing themselves to excessive competition and inadequate returns?[41] What if two countries compete to support the same industry, as happened when both Brazil and Canada decided to produce regional jets in the same hemisphere?[42] Finally, what if a country successfully targets an industry only to find unexpected conditions? Should it stay the course by reacting to various pressures, such as the pressure to support employment in a distressed industry?[43]

Finally, even if a government can identify a future growth industry in which a domestic firm is likely to succeed—a very big if—it doesn't follow that a company deserves public assistance. History recommends that nations permit their entrepreneurs to do what they do best: take risks that don't jeopardize whole sectors of the economy. The upshot will probably be the same as always: Some will fail, but the successful ones will survive and thrive competitively.

and attracted enough high-tech companies to ensure a vibrant competitive environment. Thus, understanding and having the necessary conditions to be globally competitive is important, but these conditions are neither static nor purely domestic.

Factor-Mobility Theory

As both the quantity and quality of countries' factor conditions change, their relative capabilities change as well, possibly because of internal circumstances. For instance, if savings rates increase, countries have more capital relative to their factors of land and labor. If they spend relatively more on education, they improve the quality of the labor factor.

Currently, one of the biggest changes underway concerns relative population numbers. At present rates, 33 countries, including Japan and Italy, are projected to have smaller populations in 2050 than today, primarily because of low fertility rates. They are also encountering aging populations, leaving fewer people to provide output and needing large immigration increases just to maintain the present ratios of employed people to retirees. Concomitantly, nine countries are expected to account for half of the world's population increase, with India, Pakistan, and Nigeria leading the pack.[44]

These changes, of course, are important in understanding and predicting changes in export production and import market locations. At the same time, the mobility of capital, technology, and people affect trade and relative competitive positions. Here we address the **factor-mobility theory** of trade patterns, which focuses on why production factors move, the effects of that movement on transforming factor endowments, and the impact of international factor mobility (especially people) on world trade.

WHY PRODUCTION FACTORS MOVE

Capital and labor move internationally to

- Gain more income.
- Flee adverse political situations.

Capital Capital, especially short-term capital, is the most internationally mobile production factor. Companies and private individuals primarily transfer capital because of differences in expected return (accounting for risk). They find information on interest-rate differences readily available, and they can transfer capital by wire instantaneously at a low cost. Short-term capital is more mobile than long-term capital, such as direct investment, because there is more likely to be an active market through which investors can quickly buy foreign holdings and sell them if they want to transfer capital back home or to another country.

Political and economic conditions affect investors' perceptions of risk and where they prefer to put their capital. At the same time, companies invest long-term abroad to tap markets, improve quality, and lower operating costs. However, businesses do not make all the international capital movements. Governments give foreign aid and loans. Not-for-profit organizations donate money abroad to relieve worrisome economic and social conditions. Individuals remit funds to help their families and friends in foreign countries. Regardless of the donor or motive, the result affects factor endowments.

People People are less mobile than capital. Some, of course, travel to other countries as tourists, students, and retirees; however, this does not affect factor endowments because the travelers do not work in the destination countries. Unlike funds that can be cheaply transferred by wire, people usually must incur high transportation costs to work abroad. If they move legally, they must get immigration papers, which most countries provide sparingly. Finally, they may have to learn another language and adjust to a different culture away from their customary support groups. Despite such barriers, people do endure hardships and risks to move to another country.

Migration was the major engine of globalization during the late nineteenth and early twentieth centuries, and at present it is important again. About 3 percent of the world's population (over 200 million people) have migrated to another country.[45] Because this 3 percent is spread unevenly, the percentage is much greater in some countries than in others; in the United States, it represents about 11 percent of the population.[46]

Of the people who go abroad to work, some move permanently, some temporarily. Some might emigrate to another country, become citizens, and plan to reside there for the rest of their lives. In contrast, MNEs may assign some to work abroad for periods ranging from a few days to several years (usually to a place where they also transfer capital), while some countries allow workers to enter on temporary work permits, usually for short periods. For instance, about two-thirds of the population in the United Arab Emirates are temporary workers.[47] In many cases, workers leave their families behind in the hopes of returning home after saving enough money working in the foreign country. Some move legally, others illegally (that is to say, they are undocumented).

Economic Motives People work in another country largely for economic reasons. Indonesian laborers work in Malaysia because they can make almost 10 times as much per day as they can at home.[48] Many Western executives take employment contracts with state-enterprise hotels in China that seek them out to improve performance.[49] After the economic downturn of 2008, substantial numbers of immigrants worldwide returned to their native countries, such as an estimated 60,000 Indonesians who had been working in wealthier Asian nations.[50]

Political Motives People also move for political reasons—for example, because of persecution or war dangers, in which case they are known as refugees and usually become part of the labor pool where they live. Sometimes it is difficult to distinguish between economic and political motives for international mobility because poor economic conditions often parallel poor political conditions. In the early twenty-first century, hundreds of thousands of Colombians left the country, fleeing both a civil war and unemployment. Map 6.2 highlights recent global immigration.

MAP 6.2 Global Immigration

Net gain and loss figures are in thousands and reflect annual average numbers of immigrants. Note that movement is primarily from developing to developed countries and that movement *into developing nations* consists largely of immigrants from neighboring countries. All in all, about 3 percent of the world's population—nearly 200 million people—live outside their nations of birth.

Source: Adapted from "Snapshots: Global Migration," *New York Times* (June 24, 2007): 8. Data from United Nations Population Division, The World Bank, and the International Monetary Fund.

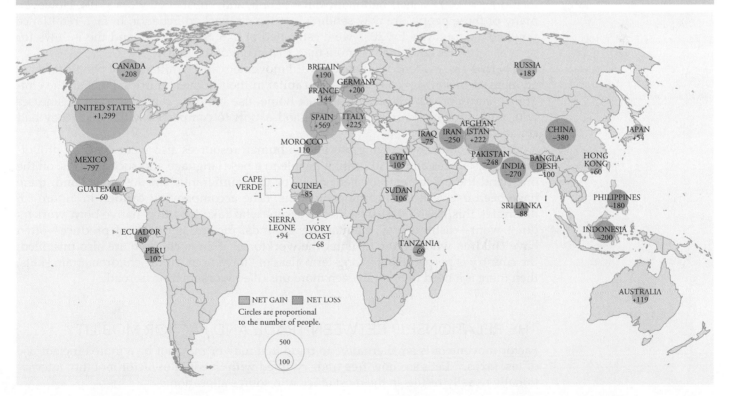

EFFECTS OF FACTOR MOVEMENTS

Factor movements alter factor endowments.

Neither international capital nor population mobility is a new occurrence. For example, had it not been for historical mass immigration, Australia, Canada, and the United States would have a greatly reduced population today. Further, many immigrants brought human capital with them, thus adding to the base of skills that enabled those countries to be newly competitive in an array of products they might otherwise have imported. Finally, these same countries received foreign capital to develop infrastructure and natural resources, which further altered their competitive structures and international trade.

What Happens When People Move?   Recent evidence is largely anecdotal. Nevertheless, factor movements are substantial for many countries and insignificant for others. Thus, the foreign-born as a percentage of total population is over 20 percent for Luxembourg, Australia, Switzerland, New Zealand, and Canada, but no more than 2 percent in South Korea, the Slovak Republic, Hungary, and Japan.[51]

The United States is currently an example of a country whose recent immigration is largely concentrated at the high and low ends of human skills. Over a third of all people with doctoral degrees in the United States are foreign-born. At the other extreme, much recent U.S. immigration has been made up of low-skilled workers. At both extremes, the United States—at least before the 2008 economic downturn—has had shortages of native-born workers, which has been partially alleviated through immigration.

Isolating a particular aspect of labor mobility is fraught with difficulty. Although labor and capital are different production factors, they are intertwined. For instance, Singapore has transformed itself from a labor-intensive and low-wage country to a capital-intensive and high-wage country largely because of capital accumulation that has come from abroad.[52] Much of its capital accumulation has been in human capital—the import of skilled foreigners and the education of its own workforce.

A controversial issue is the effect of outward migration on countries. On the one hand, countries lose potentially productive resources when educated people leave—a situation known as a **brain drain.** On the other hand, they may receive money from those people. Ecuador lost almost 5 percent of its population between 1999 and 2001, including 10,000 teachers and many other people with substantial work skills. However, many of these people are now sending remittances back to Ecuador. In fact, remittance flows to all countries for 2007 were estimated at U.S. $337 billion, and the inflows for several countries amounted to more than 15 percent of their GDP.[53]

There is also evidence that the outward movement and remittances of people leads to an increase in start-up companies and capital in their home countries. Further, the emigrants learn abroad, transfer ideas back home, use remitted capital to start businesses with family members or on their own, and export to companies with which they had connections abroad.[54]

Finally, countries receiving productive human resources also incur costs by providing social services and acculturating people to a new language and society. Thus, on the one hand there is an employment need for the immigrants. On the other hand, there have been backlashes concerning the costs. (The accompanying cartoon in Figure 6.6 illustrates this clash.) The unskilled workers who take jobs that native-born workers don't want—dishwashing, maintaining grounds, picking agricultural produce—often have children who eventually enter the workforce. If these children are also unskilled, the country is perpetuating a long-term class of "have-nots." If the children attain skills, then there is a need to bring in even more unskilled workers from abroad.

THE RELATIONSHIP BETWEEN TRADE AND FACTOR MOBILITY

Factor movement is an alternative to trade that may or may not be a more efficient use of resources.[55] Let's see how free trade coupled with freedom of factor mobility internationally usually results in the most efficient resource allocation.

FIGURE 6.6

On the one hand, countries place barriers to the entry of immigrants. On the other hand, they need the immigrants for specialized jobs.

Source: Gary Patterson/Cartoon Bank.

"You fellas need a job?"

Substitution When the factor proportions vary widely among countries, pressures exist for the most abundant factors to move to countries with greater scarcity, where they can command a better return. In countries where labor is more abundant than capital, laborers tend to be unemployed or poorly paid. If permitted, many in the labor pool go to countries that have full employment and higher wages.

> There are pressures for the most abundant factors to move to areas of scarcity.

Similarly, capital tends to move away from countries in which it is abundant to those in which it is scarce, such as Mexico getting capital from the United States, which gets labor from Mexico.[56] If finished goods and production factors were both free to move internationally, the comparative costs of transferring goods and factors would determine production location.

However, as is true of trade, there are restrictions on factor movements that make them only partially mobile internationally—such as both U.S. immigration restrictions and Mexican foreign capital ownership restrictions in the petroleum industry.

A hypothetical example, shown in Figure 6.7, should illustrate the substitutability of trade and factor movements under different scenarios. Assume the following:

- The United States and Mexico have equally productive land available at the same cost for growing tomatoes.
- The cost of transporting tomatoes between the United States and Mexico is $0.75 per bushel.
- Workers from either country pick an average of two bushels per hour during a 30-day picking season.

The only differences in price between the two countries are due to variations in labor and capital cost. In the United States the labor rate is $20.00 per day, or $1.25 per bushel; in Mexico it is $4.00 per day, or $0.25 per bushel. The capital needed to buy seeds,

FIGURE 6.7   Unrestricted Trade, Factor Mobility, and the Cost of Tomatoes

Costs are lowest when trade is unrestricted and production factors are mobile.

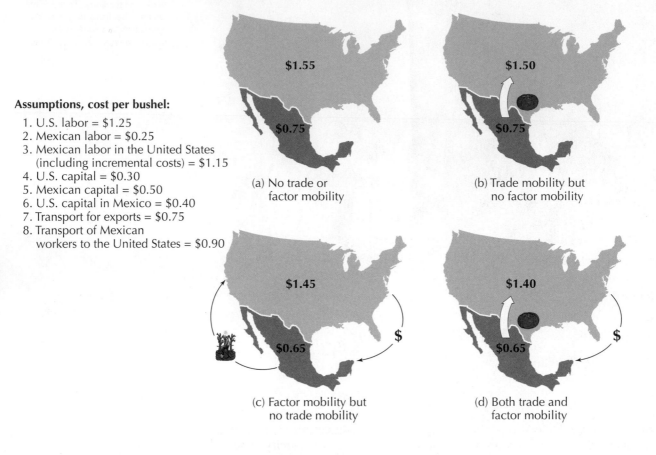

Assumptions, cost per bushel:

1. U.S. labor = $1.25
2. Mexican labor = $0.25
3. Mexican labor in the United States (including incremental costs) = $1.15
4. U.S. capital = $0.30
5. Mexican capital = $0.50
6. U.S. capital in Mexico = $0.40
7. Transport for exports = $0.75
8. Transport of Mexican workers to the United States = $0.90

(a) No trade or factor mobility

(b) Trade mobility but no factor mobility

(c) Factor mobility but no trade mobility

(d) Both trade and factor mobility

fertilizers, and equipment costs the equivalent of $0.30 per bushel in the United States and $0.50 per bushel in Mexico.

If neither tomatoes nor production factors can move between the two countries (see Figure 6.7[a]), the cost of tomatoes produced in Mexico for the Mexican market is $0.75 per bushel ($0.25 of labor plus $0.50 of capital), whereas those produced in the United States for the U.S. market cost $1.55 per bushel ($1.25 of labor plus $0.30 of capital). If the two countries eliminate trade restrictions on tomatoes between them (Figure 6.7[b]), the U.S. will import from Mexico because the Mexican cost of $0.75 per bushel plus $0.75 for transporting the tomatoes will be $0.05 less than the $1.55-per-bushel cost of growing them in the United States.

Consider another scenario in which neither country allows the importation of tomatoes but both allow certain movements of labor and capital (Figure 6.7[c]). Mexican workers can enter the United States on temporary work permits for an incremental travel and living expense of $14.40 per day per worker, or $0.90 per bushel. At the same time, U.S. companies will invest capital in Mexican tomato production, provided the capital earns more than it would earn in the United States—say, $0.40 per bushel, which is less than the Mexican going rate.

In this scenario, Mexican production costs per bushel will be $0.65 ($0.25 of Mexican labor plus $0.40 of U.S. capital), and U.S. production costs will be $1.45 ($0.25 of Mexican labor plus $0.90 of travel and incremental costs plus $0.30 of U.S. capital). Each country would reduce its production costs—from $0.75 to $0.65 in Mexico and from $1.55 to $1.45 in the United States—by bringing in abundant production factors from abroad.

With free trade *and* the free movement of production factors (Figure 6.7[d]), Mexico will produce for both markets by importing capital from the United States. According to

The lowest costs occur when trade and production factors are both mobile.

the three assumptions just stated, doing this will be cheaper than sending labor to the United States. In reality, because neither production factors nor the finished goods they produce are completely free to move internationally, slight changes in the extent of restrictions can greatly alter how and where goods may be produced most cheaply.

In some cases, however, the inability to gain sufficient access to foreign production factors may stimulate efficient methods of substitution, such as the development of alternatives for traditional production methods.[57] For example, at one time U.S. tomato growers in California depended almost entirely on Mexican temporary workers under what was known as the *bracero program*. Since the termination of this program, the California tomato harvests have quadrupled, while mechanization has replaced 72 percent of the number of workers.

However, not all harvesting jobs can reasonably be mechanized. Because cantaloupes ripen at different times, pickers go through a cantaloupe field about 10 times. A robot would have to be able to distinguish colors so as to leave green cantaloupes behind.[58] At the same time, many other jobs that defy mechanization—such as bussing tables at restaurants and changing beds in hotels—are largely filled by unskilled immigrants in developed countries.

Complementarity In our tomato example for the United States and Mexico, we showed that factor movements may substitute for or stimulate trade. Companies' investments abroad often stimulate exports from their home countries. In fact, about a third of world exporting takes place among companies' controlled entities, such as from companies' parents to their subsidiaries, from their subsidiaries to the parents, and from subsidiary to subsidiary.

Many of the exports would not occur without foreign investments, partly because a company may export equipment as part of its foreign investment. Another reason is that domestic operating units may export materials and components to their foreign facilities for use in a finished product, such as Coca-Cola's exports of concentrate to its bottling facilities abroad. Finally, a company's foreign facility may produce part of the product line while serving as sales agent for exports of its parent's other products.

> Factor mobility through foreign investment often stimulates trade because of
> - The need for components.
> - The parent's ability to sell complementary products.
> - The need for equipment for subsidiaries.

Looking to the Future   In What Direction Will Trade Winds Blow?

When countries have few restrictions on foreign trade and factor mobility, companies have greater latitude in reducing operating costs. For example, fewer trade restrictions give them opportunities to gain economies of scale by servicing markets in more than one country from a single base of production. Fewer restrictions on factor movements allow them to combine factors for more efficient production. However, government trade and immigration restrictions vary among countries, over time, and under different circumstances.

Nevertheless, it's probably safe to say that trade restrictions have been diminishing, primarily because of the economic gains that countries foresee through freer trade. Further, restrictions on the movement of capital and technology have become freer, but whether restrictions on the movement of people are freer is questionable.

There are uncertainties as to whether the trend toward the freer movement of trade and production factors will continue. Groups worldwide question whether the economic benefits of more open economies outweigh some of the costs, both economic and noneconomic. Although the next chapter discusses import restrictions (protectionism) in detail, it is useful at this point to understand the overall evolution of protectionist sentiment.

One key issue is the trade between developed and developing economies. As trade barriers are being lowered, some developing economies with very low wage rates are growing economically more rapidly than developed countries. Concomitantly, as companies shift production to developing economies, they displace jobs at home. These displaced workers need to find new jobs. But it is uncertain how fast

(continued)

new jobs will replace old ones and how much developed countries will tolerate employment displacement and job shifts. If they become intolerant, they may enact protectionist measures that would stifle trade.

Another key issue is the future of factor endowments. If present trends continue, relationships among land, labor, and capital will continue to evolve. For example, the population growth rate is expected to be much higher in developing economies than in developed ones. This could result in continued shifts of labor-intensive production to developing economies and pressures on the developed countries to accept more immigrants.

Urbanization will likely grow faster in developing than in developed countries, which are already heavily urbanized. Considerable evidence indicates that productivity rises with urbanization because firms can more likely find people with the exact skills they need, because there are economies in moving supplies and finished products, and because knowledge flows more easily from one company and industry to another. Thus we might expect higher growth in some developing countries due to their pace of urbanization. Such growth should also help them account for a larger share of world trade.

At the same time, the finite supply of natural resources may lead to price increases for these resources, even though oversupplies have often depressed prices. The limited supply may work to the advantage of developing economies, because their supplies have been less fully exploited.

We will probably see the continued trend toward a more finely tuned specialization of production among countries to take advantage of specific country conditions. Although part of this will be due to wage and skill differences, other factors are important as well. For instance, country differences in property right protection may influence companies to locate more of their technologically intensive activities within countries that offer more protection. Or they may disperse portions of production to different countries in order to hinder potential competitors from gaining the full picture needed to pirate their products and processes.

Four interrelated factors are worth monitoring because they could cause product trade to become relatively less significant in the future:

1. As economies grow, efficiencies of multiple production locations also grow because they can all gain sufficient economies of scale. This may allow country-by-country production to replace trade in many cases. For example, most automobile producers have moved into China and Thailand—or plan to do so—as a result of those countries' growing market size.

2. Flexible, small-scale production methods, especially those using robotics, may enable even small countries to produce many goods efficiently for their own consumption, thus eliminating the need to import those goods. For example, before the development of efficient minimills that can produce steel on a small scale, steel production took larger capital outlays that needed enormous markets.

3. Output from 3D printers has already reached the point whereby 20 percent is of final products (e.g., medical implants, jewelry, lampshades, car parts, mobile phones) and some predict that this figure will reach 50 percent by 2020. Basically, what this does is to permit a user to choose plans and use software for the printer to produce the product. It involves an additive technology (building a product up from raw materials) rather than a traditional subtractive technology (cutting, drilling, and bashing of raw materials). As this develops, products can be fabricated efficiently where they are used rather than traded from one country to another.[59] However, there will still be a need to trade production-grade metals and plastics as inputs to the computers.

4. Services are growing more rapidly than products as a portion of production and consumption within developed countries. Part of this change involves technology, such as the substitute of digitalized products, such as music and reading material, for traditionally manufactured products. Thus, one buys the right to copy (a service sale) from anywhere in the world with no need to ship products. Consequently, product trade may become a less important part of countries' total trade. Further, many of the rapid-growth service areas, such as retail gasoline distribution and dining out, are not easily traded, so trade in goods plus services could become a smaller part of total output and consumption. ■

Ecuador: A Rosy Export Future?

Rose is a rose is a rose is a rose - Gertrude Stein, "Sacred Emily"

Stein intended her line to illustrate that a word invokes imageries and emotions. Given the many real and symbolic uses of "rose" throughout the ages, the word brings a nearly unique image and emotion to each of us.[60] It has been a name for daughters, an adornment for a garden or vase, a representation of a deceased versus living mother on Mother's Day, a mark of love on Valentine's Day, an ingredient for perfume and medicine, a confetti when the petals are strewn, and even the symbol of opposing armies during the War of the Roses.

Some Global Changes

Rose cultivation probably began in China about 5000 years ago, and fossil evidence indicates that roses have existed for 35 million years. Although growers have sold roses for centuries, their perishability (they should usually be sold within three to five days of being cut) prevented extensive export before there was timely, dependable, and economical air service. Today, roses comprise about half the multi-billion dollar a year cut-flower export industry. Developing countries, many without significant domestic cut flower markets, have accounted for most recent export growth. The world's largest exporter is Colombia, with Ecuador and Kenya running neck and neck for the second and third positions. Given that consumers purchase roses as discretions rather than as necessities, most exports are to high-income countries. Given the need to reach markets quickly and inexpensively, most exports are regional. For instance, Kenya sends most of its flowers to Dutch auctions, Taiwan to Japan, and Colombia and Ecuador to the United States. Although Ecuador is just south of Colombia, its transport cost for roses to the United States averages 20-30 percent more. Map 6.3 shows Ecuador's location and its major rose export markets.

MAP 6.3 The Major Markets for Ecuadoran Rose Exports, 2009

Over 60 percent of Ecuador's rose exports go to two countries, the United States and Russia

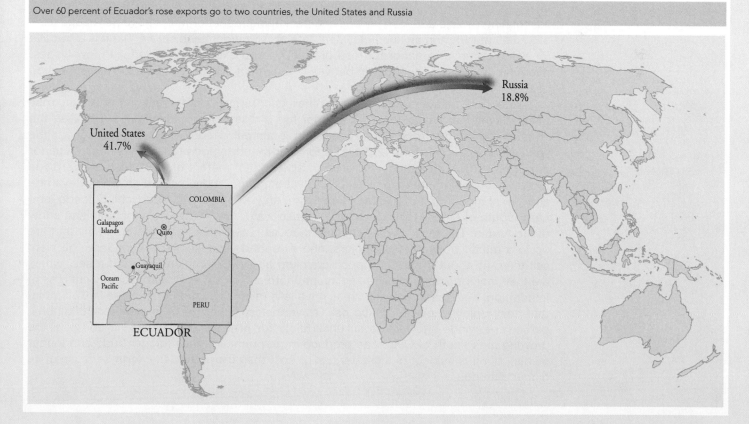

In addition to feasible air service, other logistical improvements have speeded the connection between growers and consumers. Take flower imports into the United States, of which about 85 percent of the $1.4 billion annual market enters by air through Miami where there are more than 50 wholesalers and importers. These flowers, mainly from Latin America, are packaged where they are cut and air freighted the same day by such carriers as UPS, Fedex, and American Airlines. This packaging often includes address labels and tracking information so as to avoid the costly and time-consuming process of re-packaging for transshipment. On arrival in Miami, they are placed at once in refrigerated warehouses (averaging 2 degrees Celsius) where U.S. government inspectors—customs and agriculture—clear shipments by spot-checking packages straight away to ascertain their adherence to invoice accuracy and the absence of insects, i.e. whether the packages contain roses and nothing else. They expedite clearance for companies certified by the Business Alliance for Secure Commerce (BASC), which is a nonprofit private coalition that examines the entire production and shipping process for exporters to the United States. BASC operates in 12 Latin American and Caribbean countries including Ecuador and its major Latin American rose export competitors.

Of course, long before the growth in export markets, many countries produced flowers for nearby sale, and some are still domestically focused. China and India, for example, have larger land areas under flower cultivation than any other countries, but their purchasing power is too low for sizable imports and their own quality insufficient to compete much internationally. Japan, the world's second largest cut flower market, has purchasing power, but it fills most demand with domestic production. However, in many other countries, imports have largely displaced domestic output. For instance, the United States now imports more than twice the value of U.S. domestic flower production.

Ecuadoran Advantages

Although most countries grow roses, sometimes within hot houses in cold climates, developing countries have a labor cost advantage because production is very labor intensive at almost every stage—planting, fertilizing, fumigating, pruning, removing thorns, assembling by size and rose variety, and packaging. Ecuador had a 2010 per capita GDP of $7,800 at PPP and an unemployment rate of 7.6 percent, indicators that it is attractive for hiring competitive labor for rose production and exportation. Even with low wages, direct labor costs in Ecuador run between 45 percent and 60 percent of total production costs.

Aside from nearness to market, other geographic factors are important in rose competitiveness. In this respect, Ecuador has almost unique advantages. Because the equator runs through the country, the sun is almost directly overhead throughout the year, which speeds growth and allows for year-round temperature consistency. Ecuador grows roses at high altitudes (averaging about 2000 meters or 6561 feet) that provide the very cool nights that are ideal for cultivation, e.g., 70 percent are grown in Cayambe and Tabacundo, north of the capital of Quito, and 30 percent in Machachi, Salcedo, and Lazo, south of Quito. These areas also obtain water from the mineral-rich melting snow of the Andes. The result is that Ecuadoran roses have very large buds on stems that are up to a meter in length, vivid colors, and extended vase life. Thus Ecuadoran growers sell them at about a one-third price premium above Colombian exported roses, which are their major competition. (The adjacent photo shows a worker with recently cut roses.) In addition, Ecuadoran growing areas have less rainfall variation than those in Colombia, thus they enjoy a lower climatic risk. Nevertheless, damage from weather conditions, particularly winds and rain, is an uncertainty for growers everywhere. In addition, the growing area south of Quito can produce more premium roses (bigger buds and longer stems), but it is subject to a greater risk of frost than the area to the north because of its higher altitude.

A worker shows recently picked roses within an Ecuadoran greenhouse. Note that the stems are approximately a meter in length.

Market Structure

Ecuador's cut flower exports, consisting mainly of roses, have become very important to its economy. The export value is exceeded only by its petroleum and banana exports. About 700 companies employ about 70,000 people directly in the flower industry and 250,000 in supporting industries.

Ecuador has about 300 rose farms. Typically, individual families own these farms and diversify their risk by also owning other types of businesses. These farms engage in a mixture of cooperation and competition. In terms of the former, they cooperate through a producers' association, Expoflores, to negotiate better airline carriage rates and to find means to improve production methods. In terms of the latter, they compete vigorously with each other for customers abroad, and it is common for them to sell below cost if they are short of cash and have excess supplies that might otherwise perish.

For Ecuador's largest market, the United States, growers sell to importers and wholesalers. The importers sell to large customers, such as wholesalers, mass market retailers (such as grocery chains), and hotels. Wholesalers, in turn, sell to mass market retailers or to florists, who then sell to final consumers. The farms have been trying to sell more directly to wholesalers in order to capture some of the margin now present in sales between importers and wholesalers; however, too much effort to bypass importers could jeopardize their existing sales to importers on whom they depend. Given final distribution fragmentation, it is impractical for farmers to sell directly to retailers abroad.

Sales to importers and wholesalers are generally highly personalized, handled via verbal agreement rather than written contract, and dependent on trust. In most instances, there is a buyers' market for cut flowers, thus exporters seek to develop confidence and trust among buyers so as to help secure repeat sales. For instance, if a farm cannot supply what it has promised, such as because of adverse weather conditions, it will typically try to buy supplies from other producers in order to fulfill its commitment and build buyer confidence. Negotiations take place largely via email, but exporters make occasional visits to importers and wholesalers to help cement personal relations. Contacts, both in person and via email, also help the growers to plan the quantity of future production by date and rose variety. Growers generally extend credit to the importers and wholesalers; however, if importers do not pay as agreed, then exporters require payment by letter of credit in future sales. Sales are f.o.b. Quito, which means that growers keep title only until the roses are loaded on the aircraft and thus do not have legal responsibility if roses arrive damaged or no longer fresh. (They are responsible for damage caused by disease and if they send a different variety of rose than was ordered.) However, the personal relationship in transactions means that importers, wholesalers, and growers work out responsibility in such circumstances. Although wholesalers and importers try to maintain high quality on roses sold to final consumers, there is an underground market for older and damaged roses that is difficult to control.

Fluctuations in Demand

Planning rose production is difficult because of demand changes during business cycles, during periods of the year, and by variety of rose. This planning is further complicated by unforeseen supply situations.

The demand for roses, especially the high-end market for Ecuador's large long-stemmed roses has been particularly sensitive to income changes in importing countries. For instance, the recent global economic recession caused the value of Ecuador's cut-rose exports to fall 42 percent between 2007 and 2009. This decrease occurred as consumers bought fewer flowers of any kind, replaced some rose purchases by buying less expensive flowers, and switched in part to less premium roses. The demand change was most noticeable through florists' sales, which depend more on the most expensive roses, whereas mass market sales, such as through supermarkets, of mixed flower bouquets held up fairly well.

Demand during the calendar year changes substantially in both volume and rose type. The biggest spike in sales by far is for red roses on Valentine's Day. They account for between 25 and 30 percent of Ecuadoran rose exports, are primarily office gifts, and must usually be presented on February 14, e.g., when Valentine's Day falls on the weekend rather than on a week day, sales drop substantially. Since the growth period for a rose stem is between 90 and 100 days, the farms must keep clipping stems so that they start growing and then mature on the right date for shipment. However, this 10-day margin between 90 and 100 days is due to uncontrollable weather conditions. When there is more sunlight, the roses mature faster. When weather is colder, they mature slower. Farms can warm growing areas artificially (at a cost). Slowing down maturity when temperatures rise is even more costly inasmuch as agronomists must paint rose encasements with mud or cover entire greenhouses with black fabric. The second biggest spike is for Mother's Day, but the demand is spread among different colors of roses. During the whole month of June, demand increases again because it is a big month for weddings, and this demand is primarily for cream-colored roses. During the remainder of the year, the export demand is fairly steady in both volume and color of rose, and growers try to get standing orders to assure steady sales. However, growers must make decisions on how much effort to put into production for the high-demand periods versus for sales in the remainder of the year. Further, individual growers must make these decisions without knowing what other growers are doing, thus there may be over- or under-supply at any given time.

Although Shakespeare said that "a rose by any other name would smell as sweet," our discussion thus far indicates that not all roses are the same. They vary by such characteristics as color, fragrance, size, stem length, and the way they open. In fact, there are about 6,500 varieties of roses, and a farm cannot grow them all. The variety per farm varies, depending largely on the farm's size. For instance, Hoja Verde, one of the largest Ecuadoran producers, grows 404 rose varieties. However, a more typical Ecuadoran rose farm, such as Grupo Vegaflor, grows about 60 varieties. Whether a farm is large or small, its managers must choose which varieties to grow, how much area to allocate to each, and when to bring different quantities to maturity. They base their decisions on what they think the market will demand. Of course, growers depend largely on a few fairly standard but distinct roses for which there is demand throughout the year and in ongoing years, such as the La Sevillana and Topsy Turvy roses. Despite depending a lot on standard roses from year to year, the industry depends on innovation. Growers are pressured, like producers in a fashion industry, to sell new varieties each year. Rose breeders, almost all in developed countries, such as Rosen Tantau in Germany and E. G. Hills in the United States, develop new rose varieties that they promote to distributors, such as florists. At the same time, growers must predict the success of new varieties in order to choose which to grow. In turn, growers pay a fixed licensing fee to the breeders for the rights to grow the new varieties and use their names.

Another factor affecting the rose market is the emergence of demand for fair-traded products, including cut flowers, from developing countries. For instance, TransFair, a not-for-profit organization, certifies if flowers are grown by using techniques promoting the environment and providing sufficient benefits to workers and communities. Once certified, the flowers sell for about a 10 percent premium, and the premium is used for the workers and community. While reliable figures are unavailable on the size of this market, some estimates put it as high as 10 percent of the rose export market. As of 2011, less than 10 percent of Ecuadoran rose farms had been certified.

Present and Future Market

The above discussion implicitly indicates that Ecuadoran rose growers could benefit by having consumers treat flowers as a less expendable purchase, choose roses over other flowers, preference Ecuadoran roses, increase rose buying during non-peak periods, and better align their rose partiality with the varieties that growers have chosen to produce. However, the growers presently have little influence on final consumers. In effect, Ecuadoran growers depend on distributors to promote sales to final consumers. In fact, many florists advertise through various media, and a quick perusal of the Internet indicates that some specifically promote Ecuadoran roses. Thus, for growers to increase exports, they must convince importers and wholesalers to promote final demand, such as through retailers, for the differentiated Ecuadoran roses that sell at a premium price. This is difficult because the number of players (growers, importers, wholesalers, and retailers) is so large and fragmented that no single player at any point in the distribution chain has much influence on final consumers.

Many Ecuadoran growers are putting more emphasis on some countries than on others. Although Ecuador exports roses to over 90 countries, its sales are highly concentrated in the United States and Russia, which account for over 60 percent of its export market. The world's largest rose importing country is the Netherlands, but this figure is highly misleading because most of its imports are transshipped to other countries. The United States and Russia are actually the largest final consumer markets for imported cut roses. Ecuador and Colombia dominate the rose export sales to these countries. For example in 2009, Ecuador accounted for 20.2 percent and Colombia 76.5 percent of the U.S. import market, and they accounted for 61.5 percent and 16.2 percent respectively for the Russian import market. Observers believe this discrepancy in market share between the two leading markets is due to Russian consumers' preference for premium roses at premium prices that Ecuador produces, whereas U.S. mass market consumers' preference, such as through supermarket sales, is for less expensive roses that Colombia can sell.

Ecuador and Colombia together dominate the export sale of cut roses to some other markets as well, such as Canada and Spain, but these markets are small in comparison with those in the United States and Russia. Thus, there is a question of whether there are some fairly untapped markets. Some Ecuadoran growers are considering the Middle East as a possibility for sales expansion because new air service links Ecuador with Iran via Venezuela. Other growers, however, believe that most future growth must come from traditional export locations, either through an increase in total rose sales within those locations or by picking up market share from Colombian and other countries' producers. At any rate, whether Ecuador's future cut rose export sales will be rosy or not seems to have nothing to do with its production ability; rather, it will depend on the penchant of consumers in other countries to buy its roses. ■

QUESTIONS

1. Explain each of the trade theories that help to explain Ecuador's competitive position in exporting roses.

2. What trade theories do *not* help explain Ecuador's competitive position in exporting roses? Why do these theories fail to explain?

3. Look back in Chapter 1 to the factors in increased globalization and explain which factors have influenced the growth of world trade in cut roses and why.

4. Think back to the external environmental conditions (cultural, legal-political, and economic) discussed in Chapters 2 through 4 and discuss how these have affected and might affect future demands for Ecuadoran cut roses.

5. There are a number of ways that Ecuadoran growers might increase demand for their cut roses. Among these are (a) to try to get more consumers to move up-market by buying premium roses, (b) to promote more rose demand for a different special day, and (c) to promote sales in relatively untapped markets, such as the Middle East. Compare these and any other alternatives that you can think of.

6. Some countries have had success by promoting the nationality of their products, such as the Juan Valdez campaign for Colombian coffee and the "If it's Danish it's good" campaign for Danish agricultural products. Discuss the viability of a national campaign to promote Ecuadoran roses abroad.

MyIBLab   Now that you have finished this chapter, go back to www.myiblab.com to continue practicing and applying the concepts you've learned.

SUMMARY

- Some trade theories examine what will happen to international trade in the absence of government interference. Other theories prescribe how governments should interfere with trade flows to achieve certain national objectives.

- Trade theory is useful because it helps explain what might be produced competitively in a given locale, where a company might go to produce a given product efficiently, and whether government practices might interfere with the free flow of trade among countries. Other theories address the explanation of trade patterns.

- Mercantilist theory proposed that a country should try to achieve a favorable balance of trade (export more than it imports) to receive an influx of gold. Neomercantilist policy also seeks a favorable balance of trade, but its purpose is to achieve some social or political objective.

- The theory of absolute advantage proposes specialization through free trade because consumers will be better off if they can buy foreign-made products that are priced more cheaply than domestic ones.

- According to the theory of absolute advantage, a country may produce goods more efficiently because of a natural advantage (e.g., raw materials or climate) or because of an acquired advantage (e.g., technology or skill for a product or process advantage).

- Comparative advantage theory also proposes specialization through free trade because it says that trade can increase total global output even if one country has an absolute advantage in the production of all products.

- Policymakers have questioned some of the assumptions of the absolute and comparative advantage theories: that full employment exists, output efficiency is always a country's major objective, countries are satisfied with their relative gains, there are no transport costs among countries, advantages appear to be static, and resources move freely within countries but are immobile internationally. Although the theories use a two-country analysis of products, the theories hold for multicountry trade and for services as well.

- The theory of country size holds that because countries with large land areas are apt to have varied climates and natural resources, they are generally more self-sufficient than smaller countries. A second reason for this greater self-sufficiency is

that large countries' production and market centers are more likely to be located at a greater distance from other countries, raising the transport costs of foreign trade.

- The factor-proportions theory holds that a country's relative endowments of land, labor, and capital will determine the relative costs of these factors. These factor costs, in turn, determine which goods the country can produce most efficiently.

- According to the country-similarity theory, most trade today occurs among developed countries because they share similar market characteristics and because they produce and consume so much more than developing economies.

- Much of the pattern of two-way trading partners may be explained by cultural similarity between the countries, political and economic agreements, and the distance between them.

- Manufactured products comprise the bulk of trade among high-income countries. This trade occurs because countries apportion their research and development differently among industrial sectors. It also occurs because consumers from high-income countries want and can afford to buy products with a greater variety of characteristics than are produced in their domestic markets.

- The international product life cycle (PLC) theory states that companies will manufacture products first in the countries in which they were researched and developed. These are almost always developed countries. Over the product's life cycle, production will shift to foreign locations, especially to developing economies as the product reaches the stages of maturity and decline.

- The diamond of national competitive advantage theory shows that four conditions are important for gaining and maintaining competitive superiority: demand conditions; factor conditions; related and supporting industries; and firm strategy, structure, and rivalry.

- Production factors and finished goods are only partially mobile internationally. The cost and feasibility of transferring production factors rather than exporting finished goods internationally will determine which alternative is better.

- Although international mobility of production factors may be a substitute for trade, the mobility may stimulate trade through sales of components, equipment, and complementary products.

KEY TERMS

absolute advantage (p. 222)
acquired advantage (p. 223)
brain drain (p. 242)
comparative advantage (p. 225)
country-similarity theory (p. 231)
diamond of national competitive
   advantage theory (p. 236)

factor-mobility theory (p. 240)
factor-proportions theory (p. 229)
favorable balance of trade (p. 222)
mercantilism (p. 221)
natural advantage (p. 223)
neomercantilism (p. 222)
nontradable goods (p. 228)

product life cycle (PLC)
   theory (p. 233)
theory of country size (p. 228)
trade deficit (p. 222)
trade surplus (p. 222)
unfavorable balance of
   trade (p. 222)

ENDNOTES

1 *Sources include the following:* World Trade Organization, "Trade Profiles: Costa Rica," retrieved July 16, 2007, from http://stat.wto.org/CountryProfile/ WSDBCountryPFView .aspx?Language=E&Country=CR; Debora Spar, *Attracting High Technology Investment: Intel's Costa Rican Plant* (Washington, DC: The World Bank, Foreign Investment Advisory Service Occasional Paper No. 11, 1998); CIA Factbook, retrieved July 7, 2009, from http://CIA .GOV/CIA/publications/ factbook/geos/cs.html; Gail D. Triner, "Recent Latin American History and Its Historiography," *Latin American Research Review* 38:1 (2003): 219–38; John Weeks, "Trade Liberalisation, Market Deregulation and Agricultural Performance in Central America," *The Journal of Development Studies* 35:5 (June 1999): 48–76; Niels W. Ketelhöhn and Michael E. Porter, "Building a Cluster: Electronics and Information Technology in Costa Rica," *Harvard Business School Case 9703422* (November 7, 2002); John Schellhas, "Peasants against Globalization: Rural Social Movements in Costa Rica," *American Anthropologist* 103:3 (2001):862–863; Jose Itzigsohn, *Developing Poverty: The State, Labor Market Deregulation, and the Informal Economy in Costa Rica and the Dominican Republic* (University Park, IL: Pennsylvania University Press, 2000); Roy Nelson, "Intel's Site Selection Decision in Latin America," *Thunderbird International Business Review* 42:2 (2001): 227–49; Andrés Rodríguez-Clare, "Costa Rica's Development Strategy Based on Human Capital and Technology: How It Got There, The Impact of Intel, and Lessons for Other Countries," *United Nations Human Development Report 2001* (New York: United Nations Development Programme, 2001).

2 For a good survey of mercantilism and the mercantilist era, see Gianni Vaggi, *A Concise History of Economic Thought: From Mercantilism to Monetarism* (New York: Palgrave Macmillan, 2002).

3 For reviews of the literature, see Jordan Shan and Fiona Sun, "On the Export-Led Growth Hypothesis for the Little Dragons: An Empirical Reinvestigation," *Atlantic Economic Review* 26:4 (1998): 353–71; George K. Zestos and Xiangnan Tao, "Trade and GDP Growth: Causal Relations in the United States and Canada," *Southern Economic Journal* 68:4 (2002): 859–74.

4 For a good discussion of the history of free trade thought, see Leonard Gomes, *The Economics and Ideology of Free Trade: A Historical Review* (Cheltenham, UK: Edward Elgar, 2003).

5 "Year Round Production of Tomatoes in Iceland," retrieved July 16, 2007, from www .freshplaza.com/news_detail.asp?id=3791; "The History of Wine Production in Brazil," retrieved July 16, 2007, from www.brazilianwines.com/en/brazilie_histoire.asp.

6 For simplicity's sake, both Smith and Ricardo originally assumed a simple world composed of only two countries and two commodities. Our example makes the same assumption. Now, although this simplification is unrealistic, it does not diminish the usefulness of either theory. Economists have applied the same reasoning to demonstrate efficiency advantages in multiproduct and multicountry trade relationships. Smith's seminal treatise remains abundantly in print; for a reliable recent edition, see *An Inquiry into the Nature and Causes of the Wealth of Nations* (Washington, DC: Regnery Publishing, 1998). Like Smith's *Wealth of Nations*, Ricardo's seminal work on comparative advantage, originally published in London in 1817, is continuously reprinted; see, for example, *On the Principles of Political Economy and Taxation* (Amherst, NY: Prometheus Books, 1996).

7 For a good discussion of this paradoxical thinking, see Paul R. Krugman, "What Do Undergraduates Need to Know about Trade?" *American Economic Review Papers and Proceedings* (May 1993):23–26. For a discussion of some developing countries' views that monopolistic conditions keep them from gaining a fair share of gains from international trade, see A. P. Thirwell, *Growth and Development*, 6th ed. (London: Macmillan, 1999).

8 Thomas I. Palley, "Institutionalism and New Trade Theory: Rethinking Comparative Advantage and Trade Theory," *Journal of Economic Issues* 42:1 (2008): 195–08.

9 Murray Kemp, "Non-Competing Factor Groups and the Normative Propositions of Trade Theory," *International Review of Economics and Finance* 17 (2008): 388–90.

10 Andrew Avery Herring, Roger Enrique Bonilla-Carríon, Rosilyne Mae Borland, and Kenneth Hailey Hill, "Differential Mortality Patterns Between Nicaraguan Immigrants and Native-born Residents of Costa Rica," *Immigrant Minority Health* 12 (2010): 33-42.

11 Eli J. Heckscher, *Heckscher-Ohlin Trade Theory* (Cambridge, MA: MIT Press, 1991).

12 For a discussion of ways in which the theory does not fit the reality of trade, see Antoni Estevadeordal and Alan M. Taylor, "A Century of Missing Trade?" *The American Economic Review* 92:1 (2002): 383–93. For a study supporting the theory, see Yong-Seok Choi and Pravin Krishna, "The Factor Content of Bilateral Trade: An Empirical Test," *The Journal of Political Economy* 112:4 (2004): 887–915.

13 See, for example, Donald R. Davis and David E. Weinstein, "An Account of Global Factor Trade," *The American Economic Review* 91:5 (2001): 1423–53; Oner Guncavdi and Suat Kucukcifi, "Foreign Trade and Factor Intensity in an Open Developing Country: An Input-Output Analysis for Turkey," *Russian & East European Finance and Trade* 37:1 (2001): 75–88.

14 See, for example, P. Krugman and A. J. Venables, "Globalization and the Inequality of Nations," *Quarterly Journal of Economics* 110 (1995): 857–80.

15 See Paul Krugman, "Scale Economies, Product Differentiation, and the Patterns of Trade," *The American Economic Review* 70 (1980): 950–59; James Harrigan, "Estimation of Cross-Country Differences in Industry Production Functions," *Journal of International Economics* 47:2 (1999): 267–93.

16 Drusilla K. Brown and Robert M. Stern, "Measurement and Modeling of the Economic Effect of Trade and Investment Barriers in Services," *Title Review of International Economics* 9:2 (2001): 262–86, discuss the role of economies of scale and trade barriers.

17 See Gianmarco I. P. Ottaviano and Diego Puga, "Agglomeration in the Global Economy: A Survey of the 'New Economic Geography,'" *The World Economy* 21:6 (1998): 707–31; Gianmarco I. P. Ottaviano, Takatoshi Tabuchi, and Jacques-François Thisse, "Agglomeration and Trade Revisited," *International Economic Review* 43:2 (2002): 409–35.

18 Stefan B. Linder, *An Essay on Trade Transformation* (New York: Wiley, 1961).

19 Dirk Pilat, "The Economic Impact of Technology," *The OECD Observer* 213 (August–September 1998): 5–8.

20 Anthony J. Venables, "Shifts in Economic Geography and Their Causes," *Economic Review—Federal Reserve Bank of Kansas City* 91:4

(2006): 61–85, referring to work by R. Hausmann and D. Rodrik, "Economic Development as Self Discovery" (2003), Harvard Kennedy School working paper.

21 Two discussions of intraindustry trade are: Don P. Clark, "Determinants of Intraindustry Trade between the United States and Industrial Nations," *The International Trade Journal* 12:3 (Fall 1998): 345–62; H. Peter Gray, "Free International Economic Policy in a World of Schumpeter Goods," *The International Trade Journal* 12:3 (Fall 1998): 323–44.

22 Daniel Michaels, "Landing Rights," *Wall Street Journal* (April 30, 2002): A1+.

23 Christopher A. Bartlett, "Global Wine Wars: New World Challenges Old," Harvard Business School Case 9-303-056 (July 21, 2003).

24 Terry Hall, "NZ Finds Pirated Varieties in Chile," *Financial Times* (January 21, 1999): 24.

25 Anthony J. Venables, "Shifts in Economic Geography and Their Causes.

26 Jeffrey A. Frankel and David Romer, "Does Trade Cause Growth?" *The American Economic Review* 89:3 (June 1999): 379–99.

27 J. L. Gallup and J. Sachs, "Geography and Economic Development," in B. Pleskovic and J. E. Stiglitz, eds., *Annual World Bank Conference on Development Economics* (Washington, DC: The World Bank, 1998).

28 See Raymond Vernon, "International Investment and International Trade in the Product Life Cycle," *Quarterly Journal of Economics* 80 (May 1996): 190–207; David Dollar, "Technological Innovation, Capital Mobility, and the Product Cycle in North–South Trade," *American Economic Review* 76:1 (1986): 177–90.

29 This is true according to various indicators. See, for example, International Bank for Reconstruction and Development, "Science and Technology," *The World Development Indicators* (Washington, DC: International Bank for Reconstruction and Development, 2000): 300.

30 Michael E. Porter, "The Competitive Advantage of Nations," *Harvard Business Review* 68:4 (1990): 73–93.

31 Kiyohiko Ito and Vladimir Pucik, "R&D Spending, Domestic Competition, and Export Performance of Japanese Manufacturing Firms," *Strategic Management Journal* 14 (1993): 61–75.

32 Jeremy Wiesen, "The U.S. Needs Its Own Industrial Policy," *Wall Street Journal* (September 13, 2010): A19.

33 Hubert Schmitz, "Reducing Complexity in the Industrial Policy Debate," *Development Policy Review* 25:4 (2007): 417–28.

34 James Kynge and Elisabeth Robinson, "Singapore to Revise Trade Priorities," *Financial Times* (January 21, 1997): 6.

35 Sonny Nwankwo and Darlington Richards, "Institutional Paradigm and the Management of Transitions: A Sub-Saharan African Perspective," *International Journal of Social Economics* 31:1/2 (2004): 111.

36 Jeffrey Sachs, "Institutions Matter, but Not Everything," *Finance and Development* (June 2003): 38–41.

37 Nwankwo and Richards, "Institutional Paradigm and the Management of Transitions," 111.

38 Andrés Rodríguez-Clare, "Clusters and Comparative Advantage: Implications for Industrial Policy," *Journal of Development Economics* 82 (2007): 43–57.

39 Paul Krugman and Alasdair M. Smith, eds., *Empirical Studies of Strategic Trade Policies* (Chicago: University of Chicago Press, 1993);

Howard Pack and Kamal Saggi, "Is There a Case for Industrial Policy?" *The World Bank Research Observer* 21:2 (2006): 267.

40 Paul M. Sherer, "Thailand Trips in Reach for New Exports," *Wall Street Journal* (August 27, 1996): A8.

41 Richard Brahm, "National Targeting Policies, High-Technology Industries, and Excessive Competition," *Strategic Management Journal* 16 (1995): 71–91.

42 Andrea E. Goldstein and Steven M. McGuire, "The Political Economy of Strategic Trade Policy and the Brazil-Canada Export Subsidies Saga," *The World Economy* 27:4 (2004): 541.

43 Theresa M. Greaney, "Strategic Trade and Competition Policies to Assist Distressed Industries," *The Canadian Journal of Economics* 32:3 (1999): 767.

44 Department of Economic and Social Affairs, Population Division, *World Population Prospects: The 2008 Revision Highlights* (New York: United Nations, 2009): xi.

45 "Global Estimates and Trends," *World Migration 2008: Managing Labour Mobility in the Evolving Global Economy*, International Organization for Migration, retrieved October 7, 2009, from www.iom.int/jahia/Jahia /about-migration/facts-and-figures/global estimates

46 Ron Hutcheson, "Defining 'American,'" *Miami Herald* (April 2, 2006): 16A.

47 Richard B. Freeman, "People Flows in Globalization," *Journal of Economic Perspectives* 20:2 (2006): 145–70.

48 John Salt, "The Future of International Labor Migration," *Migration Review* 26:4 (2002): 1077.

49 Ben Dolven, "China Recruits Foreign Talent," *Wall Street Journal* (April 15, 2004): A13.

50 Patrick Barta and Joel Millman, "The Great U-Turn," *Wall Street Journal* (June 6–7, 2009): A1.

51 *Trends in International Migration,* retrieved March 18, 2005, from oecd .org/dataoecd/7/49/24994376

52 See C. Chris Rodrigo, "East Asia's Growth: Technology or Accumulation?" *Contemporary Economic Policy* 18:2 (2000): 215–27; Paul Krugman, "The Myth of Asia's Miracle," *Foreign Affairs* 73:6 (1994): 62–78.

53 World Bank's Migration and Development Brief 5 (July 10, 2008).

54 Paul M. Vaaler and R. Isil Yavuz, "Immigrant Remittances and the Venture Investment Environment in Developing Countries," paper presented at the Academy of International Business, San Diego, CA (June 27–30, 2009).

55 Keith Head and John Ries, "Exporting and FDI as Alternative Strategies," *Oxford Review of Economic Policy* 20:3 (2004): 409–29.

56 See Frank D. Bean et al., "Circular, Invisible, and Ambiguous Migrants: Components of Differences in Estimates of the Number of Unauthorized Mexican Migrants in the United States," *Demography* 38:3 (2001): 411–22; United Nations Conference on Trade and Development, *World Investment Report 2000: Cross-Border Mergers and Acquisitions and Development* (New York and Geneva: United Nations, 2000): 312.

57 Paul Windrum, Andreas Reinstaller, and Christopher Bull, "The Outsourcing Productivity Paradox: Total Outsourcing, Organisational Innovation, and Long Run Productivity Growth," *Journal of Evolutionary Economics* 19:2 (2009): 197–229.

58 June Kronholtz, "Immigrant Labor or Machines?" *Wall Street Journal* (December 19, 2006): A4.

59 "Print Me a Stradivarius," *Economist* (February 10, 2011), retrieved February 17, 2011, from www.economist.com/node/18114327?story _id=18114327&fsrc=nwl; J. M. Pearce, C. Morris Blair, K. J. Laciak, R. Andrews, R. Nosrat, and I. Zelenika-Zovko, "3-D Printing of Open Source Appropriate Technologies for Self-Directed Sustainable Development," *Journal of Sustainable Development* 3:4 (December 2010): 17–29.

60 We wish to thank Mauricio Calero, former manager of two Ecuadoran rose farms, for granting us interviews and supplying additional data. We would also like to thank Tyler Gill, who while an undergraduate student at the University of Miami, worked diligently in gathering information on the world's and particularly Ecuador's export market in roses. Other information came from Jo H. M. Wijnands, Jos Bijman, and Ruud B. M. Huirne, "Impact of Institutions on the Performance of the Flower Industry in Developing Countries," paper presented at the ISNIE Conference, Reykjavik, Iceland, June 21–23, 2007; University of Illinois Extension, "Our Rose Garden: The History of Roses," retrieved December 8, 2010, from http://urbanext.illinois.edu/roses /history.cfm; Sector Publicatons, "The World Cut Flower Industry: Trends and Prospects," retrieved September 12m 2010, from www.ilo.org/public/english/dialogue/sector/papers /ctflower/139e1.htm; www.cia.gov/library/publications/ the-world-factbook/geos/ec.html; International Trade Center (ITC) "Trade Map—International Trade Statistics: List of Importing Markets for a Product Exported by Ecuador," retrieved February 4, 2011, from www.trademap.org/tradestat/Country _SelProductCountry_TS.aspx; TransFair Canada, "Hoja Verde: The Flower of Ecuador," retrieved February 3, 2011, from http://transfair.ca/en/producers/profiles/hoja-verde.

chapter 7

Governmental Influence on Trade

Objectives

1. To explain the rationales for governmental policies that enhance and restrict trade

2. To show the effects of pressure groups on trade policies

3. To describe the potential and actual effects of government intervention on the free flow of trade

4. To illustrate the major means by which trade is restricted and regulated

5. To demonstrate the business uncertainties and business opportunities created by governmental trade policies

Access a host of interactive learning aids to help strengthen your understanding of the chapter concepts at www.myiblab.com.

MyIBLab

Charity begins at home.

—*English proverb*

Source: © Anka Kaczmarzyk / iStockphoto.com

CASE

A Catfish by Any Other Name...?

Shakespeare said, "A rose by any other name would smell as sweet." But, what about catfish?[1] By giving them different names, are they the same or different? This question has spurred disagreements on fish import restrictions between Vietnam and the United States, due in part to the existence of more than 3,000 fish species that fall into the overall family of catfish. Their appearances vary, except that all have whiskers, which give them a catlike appearance. They are found mainly in freshwater in places all over the world.

IMPORTANCE OF THE INDUSTRY

Catfish have long been part of the Deep South U.S. diet. The U.S. catfish industry processed 492 million pounds of catfish in 2010, a figure that has been contracting for some time. In the meantime, U.S. catfish imports, mainly from Vietnam,

have been increasing. For instance, the U.S. share of frozen fillets (most of the market) from U.S. sources fell from 80 percent to 43 percent between 2005 and 2010. (Map 7.1 shows the production areas.) The U.S. industry is centered in poor areas of four states (Alabama, Arkansas, Louisiana, and Mississippi), which account for over 90 percent of U.S. production. At its height, it employed about 10,000 people. Likewise, the Vietnamese industry is located in one of the poorer areas of the country, the Mekong Delta. (The opening photo shows small boats there.) The Vietnamese catfish industry employs about 1 million people and accounts for about 2 percent of the country's economy.

Humans have always depended on marine life for part of their food consumption, and during most of history this marine life grew faster than human's consumed it. However, in the last half century, there has been such an increase in

MAP 7.1   Areas of Major U.S. and Vietnam Catfish Production

The catfish production for both the United States and Vietnam are near deltas of major rivers, the Mississippi and the Mekong respectively. Both areas have a great deal of poverty.

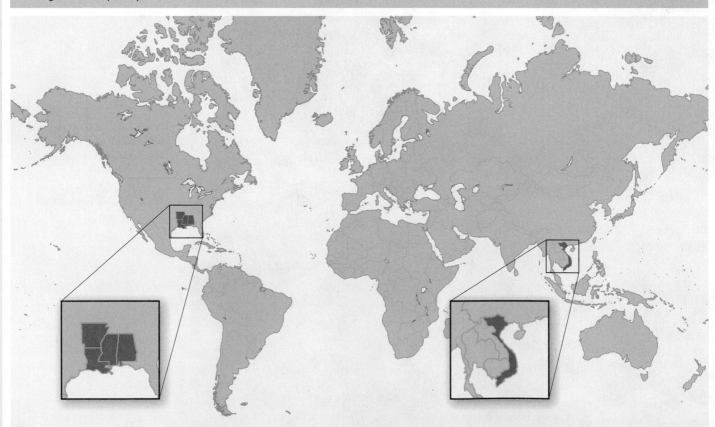

marine catch (overfishing) that the numbers of many species are not being replenished. The increase in catch has been due to a higher world population coupled with technology that enables fishing vessels to locate and land fish like never before. Fishing vessels must now go farther offshore, which increases fuel consumption at the same time that fuel prices are rising. One of the factors countering the overfishing has been the rise in aquaculture, which is called fish farming. (The 2010 U.S. revenue from commercial fishing and aquaculture combined was about $10 billion.) The catfish industry in both the United States and Vietnam has been part of the aquaculture revolution. In other words, instead of being caught in the wild by using nets or fish line with hooks, catfish are grown in ponds and harvested when the fish grow to a certain size. As this change has taken place, the catfish have ceased to be traditional scavengers; instead, they are fed corn and soybean feed. Catfish growers in the United States, in turn, have publicized the feeding change to promote sales to consumers who do not want to eat scavenger fish.

THE VIETNAMESE ADVANTAGE

The U.S. catfish industry has largely been developed by converting unproductive cotton lands to fishponds. That is, much of the land previously used for growing cotton is so high in clay content that, although it will not grow much cotton, it will hold pumped-in water very well. Meanwhile, the Vietnamese production has some competitive advantages that enable it to export. To begin with, the winterless Vietnamese climate permits the fish to grow faster. One of the Vietnamese catfish species, the tra, can go to the surface to breathe air; thus fish can be grown in greater density. Further, U.S. governmental regulations limit the discharge of fishpond waters into rivers, whereas Vietnam has no restrictions. This difference also allows for a greater density of production in Vietnam. Finally, labor rates are lower in Vietnam than in the United States, an important factor in the cost of filleting and freezing the fish.

THE U.S. INDUSTRY FIGHTS BACK

Alarmed by the loss of market, U.S. catfish growers convinced their congresspeople to push successfully in 2002 to disallow Vietnamese imports to be called catfish. Their argument was that the Vietnamese fish were of a different variety than those farmed in the United States. Thus, the Vietnamese varieties had to be imported as tra, basa, or pangasius. (The Maine lobster industry and European Union sardine fisheries were unsuccessful respectively in having Chilean langostino lobsters called crabs and Peruvian sardines called pilchards.) The U.S. producers reasoned that consumers, mainly in the Deep South, were not likely to buy some strange-sounding and unknown fish in lieu of the catfish that was part of their regular diet. Although the name change may have slowed the Vietnamese inroad, it did not prevent it. One of the problems the U.S. industry encountered was that few U.S. locales have truth-in-menu laws. Thus, the names for tra, basa, and pangasius were changed on menus to be "catfish," a more expensive grouper, or just plain "fish." Clearly, the U.S. catfish producers needed a different means to stifle the imports.

In the meantime, in addition to sales losses because of Vietnamese imports, the U.S. industry was facing a problem of diminished profit because of increased costs. In essence, the price of corn and soybean feed was rising faster than costs could be pushed onto consumers. The feed price increase was due to a combination of harvest shortfalls, increased grain demands in Asia, and the use of corn and soybeans to produce ethanol. In order to raise prices and increase demand, one of the associations representing catfish growers, the Catfish Institute, decided to change the fish's name. Basically, the name catfish has had a negative connotation for many people. (The catfish has been referred to in many ways over the years, including some ways that would be unprintable in this textbook.) The Institute noted how the change of name had recently helped sales of other previously unpopular fish, such as the name slimehead to that of orange roughy and the name Patagonian toothfish to that of Chilean sea bass. After market testing various names, the Institute has decided on "delacata" as a name for premium catfish At this writing, it is too early to tell if the change-of-name strategy will work or not.

However, let's get back to the import question. Because the U.S. industry was losing jobs and sales, it petitioned for increased taxes on the imported Vietnamese fish, claiming that they were being sold below the cost of production. Given that Vietnam is a command economy, it was difficult to establish what the true production costs were; however, these were estimated on the basis of Bangladesh production costs, and antidumping taxes (tariffs) of 64 percent were placed on the importation of the Vietnamese fish. The industry has since petitioned for estimates to be based on higher Philippine costs.

HEALTH ISSUES: A BOON FROM ADVERSITY

Despite the higher prices, the Vietnamese fish kept increasing their share of the U.S. market. Then, in 2007, the U.S. catfish industry seemed ironically to have found salvation when about 39,000 U.S. dogs and cats were sickened or killed after consuming imported Chinese pet food. This led to an alert and negative attitude toward imported food products in general, especially seafood originating anywhere in Asia. The U.S. catfish farmers have responded quickly with several initiatives. First, they have publicly implied that imported fish may be contaminated. For instance, the Catfish Institute has put out publicity saying, "U.S. farm-raised catfish: Safety you can trust." It has pushed for and gotten several states to require country-of-origin labeling on food and menus by advocating that consumers have the right to know whether the fish and seafood they buy could be contaminated. However, studies on changes in consumer purchases indicate that the labeling had no effect on demand.

Second, catfish farmers have worked through their congresspeople to legislate for increased inspections of fish from Vietnam. Given the food scare, emotions helped gain support. The Food and Drug Administration (FDA) has long been in charge of the safety of overseas food, but has had little budget to check the safety. Less than 2 percent of U.S. imported seafood shipments get inspected, as opposed to about 20 percent in the European Union.) However, during the congressional debates on the safety of food imports, there was a suggestion to upgrade inspection of all types of imported fish from all places. This suggestion was not well received because of the cost, and there was little support to simply single out one kind of fish from only one country. So, the congresspeople representing the catfish industry took a different approach by burying a provision deeply within the $300 billion farm bill of 2008, which called for the Department of Agriculture—rather than the FDA—to be in charge of catfish safety. Supporters' rationale was that aquaculture is a form of agriculture. Basically, the provision requires inspection at the production source, which is particularly difficult in Vietnam because its highly fragmented production would require an army of inspectors.

OPPOSITION AND THE FUTURE

As with most regulatory changes, there has been opposition to the effective protection of the U.S. catfish industry. Some have worried about how Vietnam would respond to restrictions on its fish exports. For instance, Montana senator Max Baucus, who hails from a beef-producing state, worried that Vietnam (the third largest export market for U.S. beef) would respond by buying its beef elsewhere.

Although the above describes what seems to be a possible means for the U.S. catfish producers to limit foreign competition, a particular problem prevents its implementation. The legislation calls for inspection of imported catfish, but the U.S. industry had earlier been successful in getting a legal ruling that Vietnam was exporting basa, tra, and pangasius rather than catfish. Thus, is a catfish by any other name a catfish?

An old adage is that if you give a man a fish, he will have food for a day. But if you teach him to fish, he will have food for a lifetime. However, the U.S.–Vietnamese catfish controversy illustrates that knowing how to fish is insufficient, especially in international competition. One also needs to know how to influence and maneuver through a maze of government regulations that affect competition.   CRN

Case Review Note

Introduction

At some point, you may work for or own stock in a company whose performance, or even survival, depends on governmental trade policies. These policies may affect the ability of foreign producers to compete in your home market. They may limit or enhance your company's ability to sell abroad or acquire needed foreign supplies. Collectively, such governmental restrictions and competitive support are known as **protectionism.**

The restrictions illustrated in the opening case are common; all countries regulate the flow of goods and services across their borders. Figure 7.1 illustrates the pressures

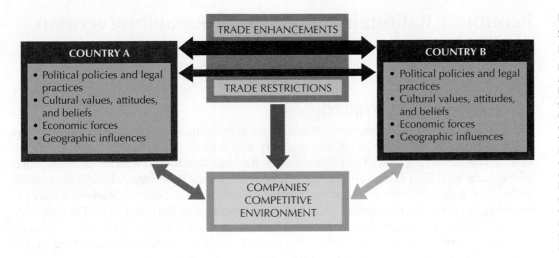

FIGURE 7.1 Physical and Social Factors Affecting the Flow of Goods and Services

In response to a variety of physical and social factors (i.e., political/legal, behavioral, economic, and geographic), governments enact measures designed to either enhance or restrict international trade flows. These measures invariably affect the competitive environment in which companies operate, either enhancing or hindering their capacity to compete on an international scale. To an extent, of course, the converse is also true: Companies influence government trade policies that affect their activities.

on governments to regulate trade and the subsequent effect of regulation on companies' competitiveness. This chapter reviews the economic and noneconomic rationales for trade protectionism and explains the major forms of trade controls and their effects on companies' operating decisions.

All countries seek to influence trade, and each has economic, social, and political objectives:

- Conflicting objectives.
- Interest groups.

Conflicting Results of Trade Policies

Despite free-trade benefits, governments intervene in trade to attain economic, social, or political objectives. Officials apply trade policies that they reason will have the best chance to benefit their nation and its citizens—and, in some cases, their personal political longevity. Determining whether and how to influence trade is complicated by uncertain and conflicting policy outcomes. For example, catfish importing was restricted to help workers in depressed areas, but the restrictions forced consumers in those same areas to pay higher prices. In general, governments would also like to help their struggling companies and industries without penalizing those that are doing well. This goal is often impossible, however, especially if other countries retaliate against their protectionist actions by limiting their own imports.

Concept Check

As we demonstrate in Chapter 6, specialization (coupled with trade) can increase a country's output of certain products; we also observe that the theories of both absolute and comparative advantage support the contention that free trade encourages specialization and more efficient output. Here we point out that protectionist policies, though sometimes warranted, can impede the process that revolves around specialization.

THE ROLE OF STAKEHOLDERS

Proposals on trade regulations often spark fierce debate among people and groups that believe they will be affected—the so-called *stakeholders.* Of course, those most directly affected are most apt to speak out, such as the U.S. stakeholders (workers, owners, suppliers, and local politicians) whose livelihoods depend on growing catfish. Displaced workers see themselves as being unemployed for the long term or forced to take new jobs in new industries, perhaps even in new towns at lower wages. People threatened in this way tend to object often and loudly.

Concept Check

In Chapter 5, we define **stakeholders** as all the groups—shareholders, employees, customers, society at large—with which a company must make satisfactory trade-offs if it is to survive.

The Role of Consumers In contrast, consumers (who are also stakeholders) typically buy the best product they can find for the price, often without knowing or caring about its origin. They often don't realize how much retail prices rise in aggregate because of import restrictions. Further, because consumer costs are typically spread out among many people, over time, they take little notice. For example, U.S. import restrictions on peanuts and sugar add to the price of peanut butter and confectionary products in the United States.[2] Even if consumers knew about this surcharge, they would likely not see enough incentive to band together and push their government leaders to rectify the situation.

Economic Rationales for Governmental Intervention

Governmental trade intervention may be classified as either economic or noneconomic, as shown in Table 7.1. Let's begin by analyzing some leading *economic rationales*.

FIGHTING UNEMPLOYMENT

There's probably no more effective pressure group than the unemployed; no other group has the time and incentive to protest publicly and contact government representatives. Workers displaced because of imports are often the least able to find alternative work, such as the fairly unskilled catfish workers in depressed regions. When they do find alternative work, they generally earn less in their new jobs than they did before.[3] Moreover, they often need to spend their unemployment benefits to survive in the short term. Further, they put off retraining because they hope to be recalled to their old jobs. When they do seek retraining, many workers, especially older ones, lack the educational background necessary to gain required skills. Or they train for jobs that do not materialize.

What's Wrong with Full Employment as an Economic Objective?   Although every country desires full employment, using trade policy to achieve it is problematic. From a practical standpoint, gaining jobs by limiting imports may not fully work as expected. Even if successful, the costs may be high and need to be borne by someone.

The Prospect of Retaliation   One difficulty with restricting imports to create jobs is that other countries, whose production may typically drop as a result, normally retaliate with their own restrictions. Our opening case addressed the concern that Vietnam would respond to U.S. catfish import restrictions by buying less U.S. beef.

However, large trading countries are more important in the retaliation process. If the United States were to limit clothing imports in general, China would have more power to retaliate than, say, Mauritius. And the United States is less apt to retaliate against Mauritian than Chinese trade restrictions because of the lesser effect on the U.S. economy. Even if no country retaliates, the restricting country may gain jobs in one sector only to lose them elsewhere. Why? There are three factors to consider:

1. Fewer imports of a product mean fewer import-handling jobs, such as those in the container-shipping industry.

2. Import restrictions may cause lower sales in other industries because they must incur higher costs for components. (When U.S. import restrictions on steel raised automobile manufacturing costs, auto producers united to convince authorities to remove the restrictions.[4])

3. Imports stimulate exports, though less directly, by increasing foreign income and foreign-exchange earnings, which foreign consumers then spend on new imports. Thus, restricting earnings abroad will have some negative effect on domestic earnings and employment.

Sidebar notes

The unemployed can form an effective pressure group for import restrictions.

Import restrictions to create domestic employment
- May lead to retaliation by other countries.
- Are less likely retaliated against effectively by small economies.
- Are less likely to be met with retaliation if implemented by small economies.
- May decrease export jobs because of price increases for components.
- May decrease export jobs because of lower incomes abroad.

CRN
Case Review Note

TABLE 7.1   Why Governments Intervene in Trade

Economic Rationales	Noneconomic Rationales
Fighting unemployment	Maintaining essential industries
Protecting infant industries	Promoting acceptable practices abroad
Promoting industrialization	Maintaining or extending spheres of influence
Improving comparative position	Preserving national culture

Analyzing Trade-Offs   In deciding whether to restrict imports to create jobs, governments must face the difficult task of comparing the costs of limiting imports with the costs of unemployment from freer trade. It is hard to put a price on the distress suffered by people who lose their jobs due to import competition. It is also difficult for working people to understand that they may be better off financially because of lower prices even if they must pay higher taxes to support unemployment or welfare benefits for the people who lose their jobs.

In summary, persistent unemployment pushes many groups to call for protectionism. However, evidence suggests that efforts to reduce unemployment through import restrictions are usually ineffective.[5] Unemployment in and of itself is better dealt with through fiscal and monetary policies.

> Possible costs of import restrictions include higher prices and higher taxes. Such costs should be compared with those of unemployment.

PROTECTING "INFANT INDUSTRIES"

One of the oldest arguments for protectionism, the **infant-industry argument,** holds that a government should shield an emerging industry from foreign competition by guaranteeing it a large share of the domestic market until it can compete on its own. Many developing countries use this argument to justify their protectionist policies, especially if entry barriers are high and foreign competition is formidable.

> The infant-industry argument says that production becomes more competitive over time because of
> - Increased economies of scale.
> - Greater worker efficiency.

Underlying Assumptions   The infant-industry argument presumes that the initial output costs for an industry in a given country may be so high as to make its output noncompetitive in world markets. Eventual competitiveness is the result of the efficiency gains that take time. Therefore, the industry's government needs to protect it long enough for its fledgling companies to gain economies of scale and their employees to translate experience into higher productivity, enabling efficient production and international competitiveness. The government can then recoup the costs of trade protection through benefits like higher domestic employment, lower social costs, and higher tax revenues.

Risks in Designating Industries   Although it's reasonable to expect production costs to decrease over time, they may never fall enough to create internationally competitive products. This risk poses two problems.

Determining Probability of Success   First, governments must identify those industries that have a high probability of success. Some industries grow to be competitive because of governmental protection; automobile production in Brazil is a good example. However, in many other cases, such as automobile production in Malaysia, the protected industries remain inefficient even after years of government aid.

If infant-industry protection fails to reduce costs enough to compete against imports, chances are its owners, workers, and suppliers will constitute a formidable pressure group that may prevent the importation of competing lower-priced products. Also, the security of government protection against import competition may deter managers from adopting the innovations needed to compete globally and to provide their own consumers with high-quality products at a low price.

Who Should Bear the Cost?   Second, even if policymakers can determine those infant industries likely to succeed, it does not necessarily follow that those companies therein should receive governmental assistance. Some segment of the economy must incur the higher cost when local production is still inefficient, such as consumers paying higher prices for the protected products or taxpayers paying for subsidies. Further, when taxes go to pay subsidies, governments can spend less elsewhere, such as on education and infrastructure, to improve overall competitiveness. There are many examples of entrepreneurs who endured early losses to achieve future benefits, without public help from consumers or taxpayers.

DEVELOPING AN INDUSTRIAL BASE

Countries with a large manufacturing base generally have higher per capita GDPs than those that do not. Some, such as the United States and Japan, developed an industrial base while largely restricting imports. Many developing countries try to emulate this strategy, using trade protection to spur local industrialization. Specifically, they operate under the following set of assumptions:

1. Surplus workers can increase manufacturing output more easily than agricultural output.

2. Inflows of foreign investment in the industrial sector promote sustainable growth.

3. Prices and sales of agricultural products and raw materials fluctuate very much, which is a detriment to economies that depend on few of them.

4. Markets for industrial products grow faster than markets for commodities.

5. Industrial growth reduces imports and/or promotes exports.

6. Industrial activity helps the nation-building process.

In the sections that follow, we review each of these assumptions in some detail.

Surplus Workers   Disguised unemployment is high in many developing countries' rural areas, where people are effectively contributing little, if anything, to the agricultural output. Consequently, many can move into the industrial sector without significantly reducing agricultural output. Like the infant-industry argument, the **industrialization argument** presumes that the unregulated importation of lower-priced products prevents the development of a domestic industry. Although proponents of this argument explain the advantages of developing an inefficient industrial sector, they nevertheless assert that there will be economic growth even if domestic prices do not become globally competitive. In other words, growth occurs because the underemployed gain jobs.[6]

Shifting people out of agriculture, however, can create at least two problems:

1. In rural areas, the underemployed may lose the safety net of their extended families, while many migrating to urban areas cannot find enough suitable jobs, housing, and social services. For example, millions of Chinese have moved to cities and not prospered. In fact, China's urban unemployment rate may run three to five times the officially reported rate.[7]

2. Improved agriculture practices may be a better means of achieving economic success than a drastic shift to industry. Typically, few developing countries farm their land efficiently, losing out on great benefits at low cost.[8] Many developed countries continue to profit from exports of agricultural products and maintain high per capita income with a mix of industry and efficient agricultural specialization.

Investment Inflows   Import restrictions, applied to spur industrialization, also may increase FDI, which provides capital, technology, and jobs. Barred from an attractive foreign market by trade restrictions, foreign companies may transfer manufacturing to that country to avoid the loss of a lucrative or potential market.

Diversification   Export prices of many primary products, such as oil and coffee, fluctuate markedly. Price variations due to uncontrollable factors—such as weather affecting supply or business cycles abroad affecting demand—can wreak havoc on economies that depend on the export of primary products. This is especially true for many developing countries that must rely on only a few commodities. Frequently, they are caught in a feast-or-famine cycle, as it were: able to afford foreign luxuries one year but unable to find the funds for replacement parts for essential equipment the next. Contrary to expectations, a greater dependence on manufacturing does not guarantee diversification of export earnings. The population of many developing economies is small; a move to

---

Countries seek protection to promote industrialization because that type of production

- Brings faster growth than agriculture.
- Brings in investment funds.
- Diversifies the economy.
- Brings more income than primary products do.
- Reduces imports and promotes exports.
- Helps the nation-building process.

When a country shifts from agriculture to industry,

- Demands on social and political services in cities may increase.
- Output increases if the marginal productivity of agricultural workers is very low.
- Development possibilities in the agricultural sector may be overlooked.

If import restrictions keep out foreign-made goods, foreign companies may invest to produce in the restricted area.

manufacturing may shift dependence from one or two agricultural commodities to one or two manufactured products, which face competitive risks and potential obsolescence.

Growth in Manufactured Goods The quantity of imports that a given quantity of a country's exports can buy—say, how many bananas Country A must sell to Country B to purchase one refrigerator from Country B—is referred to as **terms of trade.** Historically, the prices of raw materials and agricultural commodities have not risen as fast as those of finished products, although they have risen faster during short periods. Over time, therefore, it takes more low-priced primary products to buy the same amount of high-priced manufactured goods.

In addition, the quantity of primary products demanded does not rise as rapidly as manufactured products and services, due partly to people spending a lower percentage of income on food as their incomes rise and partly to raw-material-saving technologies. A further explanation is that because commodities are hard to differentiate, producers must compete on price, whereas the prices of manufactured products can stay high because competition is based more on differentiation.

Import Substitution and Export-Led Development Traditionally, developing countries promoted industrialization by restricting imports in order to boost local production and consumption of products they would otherwise import. However, if the protected industries do not become efficient—an all-too-frequent outcome—local consumers may have to support them by paying higher prices or taxes. In contrast, some countries, such as Taiwan and South Korea, have achieved rapid economic growth by promoting the development of industries that export their output, an approach known as **export-led development.** In reality, it's not easy to distinguish between import substitution and export-led development. Industrialization may result initially in import substitution, yet export development of the same products may be feasible later.

Nation Building There may be a strong relationship between industrialization and aspects of the nation-building process. Industrialization helps countries build infrastructure, advance rural development, and boost workforce skills. Ecuador and Vietnam maintain that industrialization has helped them move from feudal economies suffering chronic food shortages to nations with improved food security and budding export competitiveness.[9]

ECONOMIC RELATIONSHIPS WITH OTHER COUNTRIES

Every nation monitors its absolute economic welfare, compares its performance to that of other countries, and enacts practices aimed at improving its relative position. Among these many practices, four stand out: making balance-of-trade adjustments, gaining comparable access to foreign markets, using restrictions as a bargaining tool, and controlling prices.

Balance-of-Trade Adjustments A trade deficit creates problems for nations with low foreign exchange reserves—the funds that help finance the purchase of priority foreign goods and maintain the trustworthiness of a currency. So if balance-of-trade difficulties arise and persist, a government may act to reduce imports or encourage exports to balance its trade account. Basically, two options affect its competitive position broadly:

1. Depreciate or devalue its currency, which makes basically all of its products cheaper in relation to foreign products

2. Rely on fiscal and monetary policy to bring about lower price increases in general than those in other countries

---

Terms of trade for emerging economies may deteriorate because

- Demand for primary products grows more slowly.
- Production cost savings for primary products will be passed on to consumers.

Concept Check

In the opening case of Chapter 6, we explain import substitution as a policy of calling for the local production of goods and services that would otherwise have to be imported. We also demonstrate why this policy failed to achieve certain goals of one country's long-term trade strategy.

Industrialization emphasizes either

- Products to sell domestically or
- Products to export.

Concept Check

In Chapter 4, we explain why a trade deficit usually indicates that a country's currency— along with its debt—is piling up around the world; we go on to explain why a country afflicted with a burgeoning trade deficit needs to reconsider key areas of its economic policy.

Both of these options take time. Furthermore, they aren't selective; for instance, they make both foreign essentials and foreign luxury products more expensive. Thus, a country may use protection more effectively so as to affect only certain products. Doing so is really a stopgap measure that gives the country time to address its fundamental economic situation—the perceived quality, characteristics, and prices of its products—that is causing its residents to buy more abroad than they are selling.

As an example, since the 1970s the United States has run a trade deficit with Japan, largely because of automobile trade. The U.S. government has tried to correct the imbalance by limiting the number of Japanese vehicle imports, persuading Japanese auto companies to locate more production within the United States, and convincing Japan to ease the entry of U.S.-made cars. Nevertheless, the trade deficit continues.

Comparable Access or "Fairness"   Companies and industries often use the **comparable access argument,** which holds that they are entitled to the same access to foreign markets as foreign industries and companies have to their markets. Economic theory supports this idea for industries, such as semiconductors and chemicals, with substantial production cost decreases through economies of scale. Companies that lack equal access to a competitor's market will struggle to gain enough sales to be cost-competitive.[10]

> Domestic producers may be disadvantaged if their access to foreign markets is less than foreign producers' access to their market.

The argument for comparable access is also presented as one of fairness. For instance, the U.S. government permits foreign financial service firms to operate in the United States, but only if their home governments allow U.S. financial service firms equivalent market access. There are, however, at least two practical reasons for rejecting the idea of fairness:

1. Tit-for-tat market access can lead to restrictions that may deny one's own consumers lower prices.

2. Governments would find it impractical to negotiate and monitor separate agreements for each of the many thousands of different products and services that might be traded.

Restrictions as a Bargaining Tool   The threat or imposition of import restrictions may be a retaliatory measure for persuading other countries to lower their import barriers. The danger is that each country then escalates its restrictions, creating, in effect, a trade war that has a negative impact on all their economies. To use restrictions successfully as a bargaining tool, you need to be very careful in targeting the products you threaten to restrict. In particular, you need to consider two criteria:

> Countries levy trade restrictions to coerce other countries to change their policies.

- *Believability:* Either you have access to alternative sources for the product or your consumers are willing to do without it. The EU successfully retaliated against U.S. import restrictions by threatening to impose trade restrictions on U.S.-grown soybeans when Brazil had a surplus.

- *Importance:* Exports of the product you're restricting are significant to certain parties in the producer country—parties influential enough to prompt changes in their own country's trade policy. This consideration was emphasized after the United States had placed restrictions on the importation of steel. The EU threatened to restrict the importation of apples from the state of Washington and oranges from Florida. Given the importance of these two states in a close presidential election, the United States soon removed the steel import restrictions.

> Export restrictions may
>
> - Keep up world prices.
> - Require more controls to prevent smuggling.
> - Lead to substitution.
> - Keep domestic prices down by increasing domestic supply.
> - Give producers less incentive to increase output.
> - Shift foreign production and sales.

Price-Control Objectives   Countries sometimes withhold goods from international markets in an effort to raise prices abroad. This is most feasible when a few countries hold a monopoly or a near-monopoly control of certain resources and can limit supply so consumers must pay a higher price. However, this policy often encourages smuggling (such as emeralds and diamonds), the development of technology (such as synthetic rubber in place of natural rubber), or different means to produce the same product (such as caviar from farm-grown rather than wild sturgeons).[11] Export controls are especially ineffective for digital products because they are so easily copied abroad. In addition, if prices are too high or supplies too limited, people will seek substitutes, such as ethanol for petroleum.

A country may also limit exports of a product that is in short supply worldwide to favor domestic consumers. Typically, a greater supply drops local prices beneath those in the intentionally undersupplied world market. Egypt and India have pursued this strategy by limiting exports of rice; Canada has considered doing it with patented prescription drugs.[12] Favoring domestic consumers usually disfavors domestic producers, so they lack an incentive to maintain production when prices are low.

There is also the fear that foreign producers will price their exports so artificially low that they will drive producers out of business in the importing country. If they succeed, there are two potential adverse consequences for the importing economy:

1. The foreign producers may be shifting their countries' unemployment abroad, but their own taxpayers are subsidizing the purchases by consumers abroad.

2. If there are high entry barriers, surviving foreign producers can charge exorbitant prices once their competitors go out of business. However, competition among producers from different countries usually limits anyone's ability to charge exorbitant prices. Low import prices have eliminated most U.S. production of consumer electronics; still, the U.S. has some of the lowest prices in the world for consumer electronics because so many companies make them in so many countries.

Dumping Companies sometimes export below cost or below their home-country price—a practice called **dumping.** Most countries prohibit imports of dumped products, but enforcement usually occurs only if the imported product disrupts domestic production. If there is no domestic production, then host-country consumers get the benefit of lower prices. Companies may dump products to introduce them and build a market abroad—essentially, a low price encourages consumers to sample the foreign brand—after which they can charge a high enough price to make a profit. Recall in our opening case that the United States placed antidumping taxes on Vietnamese catfish.

Companies can afford to dump products if they can charge high prices in their home market or if their home-country government subsidizes them. Ironically, exporting-country consumers or taxpayers seldom realize that paying high prices or taxes results in lower prices for foreign consumers. An industry that believes it's competing against dumped products may appeal to its government to restrict the imports. U.S. companies in such industries as shrimp, candles, and furniture have done so in recent years.[13]

However, determining a foreign company's cost or domestic price is difficult because of limited access to the foreign producers' accounting statements, fluctuations in exchange rates, and the passage of products through layers of distribution before reaching the end consumer. The result is that governments allegedly restrict imports arbitrarily through antidumping provisions of their trade legislation and are slow to dispose of the restrictions if pricing situations change. Companies caught by antidumping restrictions often lose the export market they labored to build.

Optimum-Tariff Theory The **optimum-tariff theory** states that a foreign producer will lower its prices if the importing country places a tax on its products. If this occurs, benefits shift to the importing country because the foreign producer lowers its profits on the export sales.

Let's examine a hypothetical situation. Assume an exporter has costs of $500 per unit and is selling abroad for $700 per unit. With the imposition of a 10 percent tax on the imported price, the exporter may choose to lower its price to $636.36 per unit, which, with a 10 percent tax of $63.64, would keep the price at $700 in the foreign market.

Import restrictions may

- Prevent dumping from being used to put domestic producers out of business.
- Get foreign producers to lower their prices.

Case Review Note

The exporter may feel that a price higher than $700 would result in lost sales and that a profit of $136.36 per unit instead of the previous $200 is better than no profit at all. Consequently, an amount of $63.64 per unit has thus shifted to the importing country.

As long as the foreign producer lowers its price by any amount, some shift in revenue goes to the importing country and the tariff is deemed an optimum one. There are many examples of products whose prices did not rise as much as the amount of the imposed tariff; however, it is difficult to predict when, where, and which exporters will voluntarily reduce their profit margins.

Noneconomic Rationales for Government Intervention

Although noneconomic arguments are used to influence trade, many of these also have economic undertones and consequences. Figure 7.2 shows this humorously. However, let's look at the major noneconomic rationales:

- Maintaining essential industries (especially defense)
- Promoting acceptable practices abroad
- Maintaining or extending spheres of influence
- Preserving national culture

MAINTAINING ESSENTIAL INDUSTRIES

In protecting essential industries, countries must

- Determine which ones are essential.
- Consider costs and alternatives.
- Consider political and economic consequences.

Governments apply trade restrictions to protect essential domestic industries during peacetime so the country is not dependent on foreign supplies during war. This is called the **essential-industry argument.** As an example, the U.S. government subsidizes the domestic production of silicon so domestic computer-chip producers will not need to depend on foreign suppliers. Because of nationalism, this argument has much appeal in rallying support for import barriers. However, in times of real (or perceived) crisis or military emergency, almost any product could be deemed essential.

FIGURE 7.2

While using trade policies to influence acceptable political practices abroad, governments are also concerned about their implications on business.

Source: Mick Stevens/Cartoon Bank

"My government is very concerned about your government's torture and maiming of potential consumers."

Because of the high cost of protecting an inefficient industry or a higher-cost domestic substitute, the essential-industry argument should not be (but frequently is) accepted without a careful evaluation of costs, real needs, and alternatives. It is difficult to remove protection, once given, because the protected companies and their employees support politicians who support their continued protection—even when the rationale for the subsidies has long since disappeared. This is why the United States continued to subsidize its mohair producers more than 20 years after mohair was deemed no longer essential for military uniforms.[14]

In addition, governments buy and stockpile supplies of essential raw materials that might be in future short supply. For example, the U.S. military needs weapons, jet engines, high-powered magnets, and other gear that require imported raw materials for their domestic manufacture. It needs lasers and high-powered magnets that require rare-earth elements, and China controls over 90 percent of global production of these elements.[15]

PROMOTING ACCEPTABLE PRACTICES ABROAD

Governments limit trade to promote changes in foreign countries' political policies or capabilities. For instance, they use national defense arguments to prevent the export, even to friendly countries, of strategic goods that might fall into the hands of potential enemies. For example, the United States prevented exports of data-encryption technology until U.S. high-tech companies and privacy advocacy groups convinced the government to relax the curbs and allow them to export encryption products to various allies.[16]

Export constraints may be valid if the exporting country assumes there will be no retaliation preventing it from securing even more essential goods from the potential importing country. Even then, the latter may find alternative supply sources or develop a production capability of its own, in which case the former is the economic loser. (Our ending case discusses U.S. barriers to trade with Cuba as a means of weakening the Communist nation's economy, and Cuba's shift to imports from other countries.)

Case Review Note

◀ Although ivory trade is largely illegal, the photo shows that demand continues to stimulate elephant poaching.
Source: © Blueice69caddy/ Dreamstime.com

Import trade controls also may be used as a foreign policy weapon. When the United States found that nine Chinese companies and an Indian businessman had sold technology that Iran used for its chemical and conventional weapons programs, it imposed sanctions that barred these firms from doing business with the U.S. government and from exporting goods into the United States.[17]

Finally, trade controls are used to pressure foreign governments to alter their stances on a variety of issues ranging from human rights to environmental protection. For instance, many countries restrict importation of ivory to protect elephants.[18] However, the adjacent photo shows that, although restrictions may have slowed elephant slaughter, poaching still continues. A country's trade restrictions may coerce governments to follow certain political actions or punish companies whose governments do not. For example, China delayed permission for Allianz, a German insurance group, to operate in China after Germany gave a reception for the Dalai Lama, the exiled Tibetan spiritual leader.[19]

> **Point**

Should Governments Impose Trade Sanctions?

Point   **Yes** Let's face it: We're now living in a global society where actions in one country can spill over and affect people all over the world. For instance, the development of a nuclear arsenal in one nation can escalate the damage that terrorists can do elsewhere. The failure of a country to protect endangered species can have long-term effects on the whole world's environment. We simply can't sit back and let things happen elsewhere that will come back to haunt us.

At the same time, some pretty dastardly things occur in some countries that most of the world community would like to see stopped: human rights violations in Myanmar, child slaves harvesting cocoa in the Ivory Coast, diamond production in Sierra Leone financing revolutions, to name a few. Even if we can't stop such occurrences, we have a moral responsibility not to participate even if it costs us. I may get some economic benefits by buying from a criminal, and I may not stop his activity by withholding my business. However, I refuse to deal with him because, in effect, that makes me a criminal's associate.

Although not all trade sanctions have been successful, many have at least been influential in achieving their

objectives. These included UN sanctions against Rhodesia (now Zimbabwe), U.K. and U.S. sanctions against the Amin government of Uganda, and Indian sanctions against Nepal.[20] U.S. sanctions against Cuba may have slowed that country's ability to create revolutions elsewhere. The oil export embargo to Iran led to fuel rationing and resultant protests that have weakened the regime.[21]

Finally, when a nation breaks international agreements or acts in unpopular ways, what courses of action can other nations take? Between 1827 and World War I, nations mounted 21 blockades, but these are now considered too dangerous. Military force has also been used, as for the overthrow of the Saddam regime in Iraq, but such measures have little global support. Thus, nations may take such punitive actions as withholding diplomatic recognition, boycotting athletic and cultural events, seizing the other country's foreign property, and eliminating foreign aid and loans. These may be ineffective in and of themselves without the addition of trade sanctions. Moreover, countries may give incentives rather than taking punitive actions. This has occurred with North Korea to curb its nuclear program and has been suggested for Iran for the same purpose.[22]

Should Governments Impose Trade Sanctions?

> **Counterpoint**

Counterpoint   **No** Every time I turn around, I see my government imposing a new sanction. Although some don't affect my trade, others do, causing me to lose business that took me years to develop. A few years back, my company had worked hard to develop a market for office machinery in Iraq. Then, suddenly, we could not export there and were left holding inventory we had on the loading dock ready to ship. Thus,

the trade sanctions aimed at hurting the government of Iraq ended up hurting us even though we'd never engaged in any objectionable behavior.

Besides, I really question whether these sanctions even work. When the United States was maintaining its 20-year trade embargo on Vietnam, Vietnamese consumers were still able to buy U.S. products such as Coca-Cola, Kodak film, and Apple computers through other countries that did not enforce the sanctions.[23] Similarly, the Western oil export embargo you mentioned on Iran simply caused its government to turn to China for supplies. The U.S. trade embargo with Panama only made Panama's Noriega government more adamant in its opposition to the United States, requiring a military invasion to depose him. Oil embargoes against South Africa, because of its racial policies, merely spurred South African companies to become leaders in converting coal to oil.[24]

Even if trade sanctions succeed at weakening the targeted countries' economies, who really suffers? You can bet that the political leaders will still get whatever they need, so the costs of sanctions are borne by innocent people. This occurred in Iraq, where there were widespread reports of

children's deaths because of sanction-induced supply shortages of food and medicine. Moreover, the people adversely affected usually blame their suffering not on their internal regime but on the countries carrying on the sanctions. Despots are very good at manipulating public opinion.[25]

Finally, governments sometimes seem to impose trade sanctions based on one issue rather than on a country's overall record. For instance, some critics have suggested using trade policies to press Brazil to restrict the cutting of Amazon forests, even though its overall environmental record—particularly its limiting of adverse exhaust emissions by converting automobile engines to use methanol instead of gasoline—is quite good.

MAINTAINING OR EXTENDING SPHERES OF INFLUENCE

Governments also use trade to support their spheres of influence. Governments give aid and credits to, and encourage imports from, countries that join a political alliance or vote a preferred way within international bodies. The EU and the 77 members of the African, Caribbean, and Pacific Group of States signed the Cotonou Agreement to formalize preferential trade relationships that also strengthened political ties.[26] Venezuela has exported oil at low cost and with long-term financing to targeted Latin American countries to gain influence in the region.[27]

PRESERVING NATIONAL CULTURE

Countries are held together partly through a unifying sense of identity that sets their citizens apart from those in other nations. To sustain this collective identity, they prohibit exports of art and historical items that they deem to be part of their national heritage. In addition, they limit imports of certain foreign products and services that may either conflict with their dominant values, such as morality, or replace domestic sources of production that uphold these traditional values. The relevance of culture has been confirmed through several UNESCO conventions aimed at preserving cultural diversity, and the concern has been largely focused, but not entirely, on media (print, visual, and audio).[28] For many years, Japan, South Korea, and China maintained an almost total ban on rice imports, largely because rice farming has been a historically cohesive force in each nation.[29] Canada relies on a "cultural sovereignty" argument to prohibit foreign ownership or control of publishing, cable TV, and bookselling.[30] South Korea requires theaters to show Korean films a certain number of days per year.[31]

Instruments of Trade Control

Governments use many rationales and seek a range of outcomes when they try to influence exports or imports. The choice of trade-control instrument is crucial because each type may incite different responses from domestic and foreign groups. One way to understand trade-control instruments is by distinguishing between two types that differ in their effects:

- Those that indirectly affect the amount traded by directly influencing the *prices* of exports or imports

- Those that directly limit the *amount* of a good that can be traded

Let's review these instruments.

> **Concept Check**
>
> We observe in Chapter 2 that a primary function of culture is to support a nation's sense of its uniqueness and integrity. We also explain that—especially in developing countries— many people fear that the escalation and influence of global business interaction is a prelude to another era of **cultural imperialism** in which weaker nation-states will be weakened even further. Finally, we note that similar concerns are raised by the prospect of cultural diffusion—a process by which elements of a foreign culture may infiltrate themselves into a local culture.

TARIFFS

Tariff barriers directly affect prices, and *nontariff barriers* may affect either price or quantity. A **tariff** (also called a **duty**), the most common type of trade control, is a tax that governments levy on a good shipped internationally. That is, governments charge a tariff on a good when it crosses an official boundary—whether it be that of a nation or a group of nations that have agreed to impose a common tariff on goods crossing the boundary of their bloc.

Tariffs collected by the exporting country are called **export tariffs;** if they're collected by a country through which the goods pass, they're **transit tariffs;** if they're collected by importing countries, they are called **import tariffs.** Because import tariffs are by far the most common, we discuss them in some detail.

Import Tariffs   Unless they're *optimum tariffs* (discussed earlier in the chapter), import tariffs raise the price of imported goods by placing a tax on them, thereby giving domestically produced goods a relative price advantage. A tariff may be protective despite no domestic production in direct competition if the tariff raises the price of some foreign production in order to curtail overall demand for imports.

Tariffs as Sources of Revenue   Tariffs also serve as a source of governmental revenue. Import tariffs are of little importance to developed countries, usually costing more to collect than they yield.[32] However, in many developing countries they are a major source of revenue, potentially giving the governments more control over determining the amounts and types of goods crossing their borders and collecting a tax on them than over determining and collecting individual and corporate income taxes. Although revenue tariffs are most commonly collected on imports, some countries charge export tariffs on raw materials.[33] Transit tariffs were once a major source of countries' revenue, but governmental treaties have nearly abolished them.

Criteria for Assessing Tariffs   A government may assess a tariff on a per unit basis, in which case it is applying a **specific duty.** A tariff assessed as a percentage of the item's value is an **ad valorem duty.** If both types are assessed on the same product, the combination is a **compound duty.** A specific duty is more straightforward for customs officials to assess because they do not need to determine a good's value on which to calculate a percentage tax.

A tariff controversy concerns developed countries' treatment of manufactured exports from developing countries that seek to add manufactured value to their raw material exports. Raw materials frequently enter developed countries free of duty (say, coffee beans); however, if they are processed (instant coffee), developed countries then assign an import tariff. Because an ad valorem tariff is based on the total value of the product (say, $5 for a jar of instant coffee), meaning the raw materials and the processing combined ($2.50 for the coffee beans and $2.50 for the processing), developing countries argue that the **effective tariff** on the manufactured portion turns out to be higher than the published tariff rate. In other words, a tariff rate of 10 percent is effectively 20 percent on the manufactured portion. This anomaly further challenges developing countries to find markets for their manufactured products. At the same time, the governments of developed countries cannot easily remove barriers to imports of developing countries' manufactured products, largely because these imports are more likely to displace workers who are least equipped to move to new jobs.

NONTARIFF BARRIERS: DIRECT PRICE INFLUENCES

Now that we've shown how tariffs raise prices and limit trade, let's turn to a discussion of other ways that governments alter product prices to limit their trade.

Subsidies   **Subsidies** are direct assistance to companies to make them more competitive. (The photo shows a Colombian protest against subsidized European milk imports.)

A woman collects milks spilled under a truck that was handing out milk during a protest against the signature of a 2010 free trade agreement with the European Union in Medellin, Colombia. Colombian milk producers argue that the local dairy industry will be unable to compete with the heavily-subsidized European dairy producers.

Source: AP Photo/Luis Benavides

Although this definition is straightforward, disagreement on what constitutes a subsidy causes trade frictions. In essence, not everyone agrees that companies are being subsidized just because they lose money, nor that all types of government loans or grants are subsidies. One long-running controversy involves commercial aircraft. Airbus Industrie and the EU claim that the U.S. national and state governments subsidize Boeing respectively through R&D contracts for military aircraft that also have commercial applications and tax breaks to secure employment from Boeing's facilities. Meanwhile, Boeing and the U.S. government claim that the EU subsidizes Airbus Industrie through low-interest government loans.[34]

An area that may well raise future questions about subsidies is governmental support to shore up floundering companies and industries during the global recession. For instance, several countries have bailed out banks and acted on behalf of their automobile industries with help such as generous loans and support for consumers to replace their old cars. Other countries have eliminated taxes on their companies' export earnings.[35] In turn, these actions are altering international competitiveness.[36]

Agricultural Subsidies The one area in which everyone agrees that subsidies exist is agricultural products in developed countries. The official reason for granting subsidies to farmers is that food supplies are too critical to be left to chance. Although subsidies lead to surplus production, surpluses are argued to be preferable to the risk of food shortages. The question of food shortages came to the forefront during 2010 droughts when a number of countries limited or banned exports of such agricultural commodities as rice and wheat in order to maintain supplies for their own consumers.[37]

Although this official reason seems compelling, it does not explain agricultural subsidies for non-food products, such as U.S. subsidies for cotton that have disadvantaged Brazilian production.[38] There is an unofficial reason as well. Within the EU, Japan, and the United States, rural areas have a disproportionately high representation in government decision making. In the United States, for instance, there is one senator per 300,000 people in Vermont, a state with a 68 percent rural population, and one senator per 18 million in California, which is 93 percent urban. The result is that internal politics effectively prevents the dismantling of such instruments as price supports for farmers, government agencies to improve agricultural productivity, and low-interest loans to farmers.

What is the effect? Developing countries are disadvantaged in serving the developed markets with competitive agricultural products. Further, much of the surplus production from developed countries is exported at prices below those in the products' domestic markets, thus distorting trade and disadvantaging production from developing countries.[39]

Overcoming Market Imperfections   Another subsidization area is less contentious. Most countries offer potential exporters many business development services, such as market information, trade expositions, and foreign contacts. From the standpoint of market efficiency, these sorts of subsidies are more justifiable than tariffs because they seek to overcome, rather than create, market imperfections. There are also benefits to disseminating information widely because governments can spread the costs of collecting information among many users.

Aid and Loans

Governments also give aid and loans to other countries. If the recipient is required to spend the funds in the donor country, which is known as *tied aid* or *tied loans*, some products can compete abroad that might otherwise be noncompetitive. For instance, tied aid helps win large contracts for infrastructure, such as telecommunications, railways, and electric power projects.

However, there is growing skepticism about the value of tied aid, because it requires the recipient to use suppliers in the donor country who are shielded from competition and may not be the best. Tied aid can also slow the development of local suppliers in developing countries. These concerns led OECD members to untie financial aid to developing countries, no longer obliging aid-recipient countries to purchase equipment from suppliers in the donor country.[40] However, China is using tied aid for nearly all its foreign projects.[41]

Because it is difficult for customs officials to determine the honesty of import invoices,

- They may arbitrarily increase value.
- Valuation procedures have been developed.
- They may question the origin of imports.

Customs Valuation

Tariffs for imported merchandise depend on the product, price, and origin. The temptation exists for exporters and importers to declare these wrongly on invoices to pay less duty. Generally, most countries have agreed to use the invoice information unless customs officers doubt its authenticity. Agents must then assess on the basis of the value of identical goods. If not possible, agents must assess on the basis of similar goods arriving in or about the same time.

For example, there is no sales invoice when imported goods enter for lease rather than purchase. Customs officials must then base the tariff on the value of identical or similar goods. If this basis cannot be used, officials may compute a value based on final sales value or on reasonable cost. Similarly, agents sometimes use their discretionary power to assess the value too high, thereby preventing the importation of foreign-made products.[42]

Valuation Problems   The fact that so many different products are traded creates valuation problems, especially since new products are coming on the market all the time and must be classified within existing tariff categories. It is easy (by accident or intention) to misclassify a product and its corresponding tariff. Administering more than 13,000 categories of products means a customs agent must use professional discretion to determine, say, if silicon chips should be considered "integrated circuits for computers" or "a form of chemical silicon." In our opening case, we saw the controversy of whether the Vietnamese fish are catfish or whether they are basa, tra, or pangasius. The classification will become even more complex as both U.S. and Vietnamese scientists develop fish hybrids that combine, for example, fast-growing with good-tasting fish. The differences among products in tariff schedules are also minute. For example, the United States has a different tariff on athletic footwear than on sports footwear, and these are further categorized by whether the sole overlaps the upper part of the shoe or not. Each type of accessory and reinforcement of the shoes' uppers have different tariffs.

Case Review Note

Although classification differences may seem trivial, the disparity in duties may cost companies millions of dollars. Some contentious examples are whether the French company Agatec's laser leveling device would be used primarily indoors or outdoors as well,[43] whether Marvel's X-Men Wolverines were toys or dolls, and whether sport utility vehicles—such as the Suzuki Samurai and the Land Rover—were cars or trucks. Because of a much higher U.S. tariff on trucks than on automobiles, Ford imports autos from Turkey and then removes the rear seats and replaces the rear windows with solid metal in order to turn them into trucks.[44]

Because countries treat products from different countries differently, customs must also determine products' origins. This is neither cheap nor easy. However, officials have uncovered many instances of transshipping products—shoes, cigarette lighters, garlic, lightbulbs—from China through Cambodia to overcome quantity limitations and higher duties.[45]

Other Direct-Price Influences   Countries use other means to affect prices, including special fees (such as for consular and customs clearance and documentation), requirements that customs deposits be placed in advance of shipment, and minimum price levels at which goods can be sold after they have customs clearance.

NONTARIFF BARRIERS: QUANTITY CONTROLS

Governments use other nontariff regulations and practices to affect the quantity of imports and exports directly. Let's take a look at the various forms these typically take.

Quotas   The **quota** is the most common type of quantitative import or export restriction, limiting the quantity of a product that can be imported or exported in a given time frame, typically per year. *Import quotas* normally raise prices for two reasons: (1) to limit supply and (2) to provide little incentive to use price competition to increase sales. A notable difference between tariffs and quotas is their effect on revenues. Tariffs generate revenue for the government. Quotas generate revenue only for those companies that are able to obtain and sell a portion of the intentionally limited supply of the product. (Sometimes governments allocate quotas among countries, based on political or market conditions.)

> A quota may
> - Set the total amount to be traded.
> - Allocate amounts by country.

To circumvent quotas, companies sometimes convert the product into one for which there is no quota. For instance, the United States maintains sugar import quotas that result in its sugar prices averaging about double the world market price. As a result, many U.S. candy producers have moved plants to Mexico where they can buy lower-cost sugar and import the candy duty-free to the United States.[46]

Finally, import quotas are not necessarily imposed to protect domestic producers. Japan has maintained quotas on many agricultural products from outside the country. It has then allocated import rights to competing suppliers as a means of bargaining for sales of Japanese exports and preventing excess dependence on any one country for essential foods.

Voluntary Export Restraint   A variation of an import quota is the so-called **voluntary export restraint (VER)**. Essentially, Country A asks Country B to voluntarily reduce its companies' exports to Country A. The term *voluntarily* is somewhat misleading; typically, either Country B volunteers to reduce its exports or else Country A may impose tougher trade regulations. Procedurally, VERs have unique advantages. They are much easier to switch off than an import quota, and the appearance of a "voluntary" choice by a particular country to constrain its shipments can do less damage to political relations than an import quota.

A country may establish *export quotas* to assure domestic consumers a sufficient supply of goods at a low price, to prevent depletion of natural resources, or to attempt to raise export prices by restricting supply in foreign markets. To restrict supply, some countries band together in various commodity agreements, such as OPEC for petroleum, which then restrict and regulate exports from the member countries.

Embargoes   A specific type of quota that prohibits all trade is an **embargo**. As with quotas, countries or groups of countries may place embargoes on either imports or exports, on whole categories of products regardless of origin or destination, on specific products with specific countries, or on all products with given countries. Governments impose embargoes in an effort to use economic means to achieve political goals. As we explain in our closing case, the U.S.-imposed embargo on Cuba was conceived to weaken the Cuban economy and thus induce a demoralized populace to overthrow the Communist regime.

"Buy Local" Legislation   Another form of quantitative trade control is so-called *buy local legislation*. Government purchases are a large part of total expenditures in many countries; typically, governments favor domestic producers. Sometimes they specify a domestic content restriction—that is, a certain percentage of the product must be of local origin. For example, the U.S. economic stimulus package of 2009 to counter the economic recession required any funded project to use only U.S.-made steel, iron, and manufactured goods.[47] Sometimes governments favor domestic producers through price mechanisms, such as permitting an agency to buy a foreign-made product only if the price is at some predetermined margin below that of a domestic competitor. Sometimes governments favor domestic purchases indirectly, such as the U.S. prohibition of foreign Medicare payments for elderly Americans except in emergency situations, a regulation that limits U.S. foreign purchases in the fast growing area of medical tourism.

Standards and Labels   Countries can devise classification, labeling, and testing standards to allow the sale of domestic products but obstruct foreign-made ones. Consider product labels. The requirement that companies indicate on a product where it is made informs consumers who may prefer to buy products from certain nations. In our opening case, we saw that the U.S. catfish industry sought country-of-origin labeling on fish. Countries also may dictate content information on packaging that is not required elsewhere. These technicalities add to a firm's production costs, particularly if the labels must be translated for different export markets. In addition, raw materials, components, design, and labor increasingly come from many countries, so most products today are of such mixed origin that they are difficult to sort out.

The professed purpose of standards is to protect the safety or health of the domestic population. However, some companies argue that standards are just another means to protect domestic producers. For example, some U.S. and Canadian producers have contended that EU regulations and labeling requirements on genetically engineered corn and canola oil are merely means to keep out the products until their own technology catches up.[48] In another case, following U.S. publicity about contaminated Chinese foods, China upped its rejection of foodstuffs from the United States, citing contamination with drugs and salmonella.[49]

In reality, there's no way of knowing to what extent products are kept out of countries for legitimate safety and health reasons rather than arbitrarily to protect domestic production. Nevertheless, the U.S. FDA publishes a monthly summary of rejected food import shipments by country, a list that is substantial. For example, in April 2011 it rejected over a thousand shipments from 73 different countries. Most of the rejections, in order, were from China, India, and Mexico.[50]

Specific Permission Requirements   Some countries require that potential importers or exporters secure permission from government authorities before conducting trade transactions. This requirement is known as an **import or export license.** A company may have to submit samples to government authorities to obtain such a license. The procedure can restrict imports or exports directly by denying permission or indirectly because of the cost, time, and uncertainty involved.

Case Review Note

Through "buy local" laws

- Government purchases give preference to domestically made goods.
- Governments sometimes legislate a percentage of domestic content.

Other types of trade barriers include

- Arbitrary standards.
- Licensing arrangements.
- Administrative delays.
- Reciprocal requirements.
- Service restrictions.

Case Review Note

A **foreign-exchange control** is similar. It requires an importer to apply to a government agency to secure the foreign currency to pay for the product. As with an import license, failure to grant the exchange, not to mention the time and expense of completing forms and awaiting replies, obstructs foreign trade.

Administrative Delays Closely akin to specific permission requirements are intentional administrative delays or those caused by inefficiency, which create uncertainty and raise the cost of carrying inventory. Competitive pressure, however, moves countries to improve their administrative systems. Chinese trade authorities, for example, cut the time from one week to one day for goods manufactured by Hong Kong firms in Guangdong to pass through internal customs checks. Improved processes, such as electronic submission of cargo manifests, affected 68,000 non-mainland firms and reduced administrative costs more than US$70 million.[51]

Reciprocal Requirements Because of government regulations in the importing countries, exporters sometimes must take merchandise or buy services in lieu of receiving cash payment. This requirement is common in the aerospace and defense industries—sometimes because the importer does not have enough foreign currency. For instance, Indonesia bought Russian jets in exchange for commodities such as rubber.[52]

Countertrade **Countertrade** or **offsets** are government requirements in the importing country whereby the exporter, usually in sales (especially military ones) to a foreign government must provide additional economic benefits such as jobs or technology as part of the transaction. When McDonnell Douglas sold helicopters to the British government it had to equip them with U.K.-made Rolls Royce engines as well as transfer much of the technology and production work to the United Kingdom.[53] Countertrade has been criticized because large defense contractors usually keep their own sales in tact while transferring their purchases from smaller domestic contractors to those in foreign countries, thus weakening domestic defense capabilities.[54]

Reciprocal requirements often mean that exporters must find markets for goods outside their lines of expertise or engage in complicated organizational arrangements that require them to relinquish some operating control. All things being equal, companies avoid these transactions. However, some have developed competencies in these types of arrangements in order to gain competitive advantages.

Restrictions on Services Service is the fastest-growing sector in international trade. In deciding whether to restrict service trade, countries typically consider four factors: *essentiality, not-for-profit preference, standards,* and *immigration.*

Essentiality Countries judge certain service industries to be essential because they serve strategic purposes or provide social assistance to citizens. Governments may prohibit private companies, foreign or domestic, in some sectors because they feel the services should not be sold for profit. In other cases, they set price controls or subsidize government-owned service organizations that create disincentives for foreign private participation. Some essential services in which foreign firms might be excluded are media, communications, banking, utilities, and domestic transport.

Not-for-Profit Services Mail, education, and hospital health services are often not-for-profit sectors in which few foreign firms compete. When a government privatizes these industries, it customarily prefers local ownership and control.

Standards Some services require face-to-face interaction between professionals and clients. At the same time, governments limit entry into many service professions to ensure practice by qualified personnel. The licensing standards for these personnel vary by country and include such professionals as accountants, actuaries,

Concept Check

In Chapter 1, we define service exports and imports and discuss the significance of services for some companies and countries. We also divide them into three categories: tourism and transportation, service performance, and asset use.

Three main reasons for restricting trade in services are

- Essentiality.
- Preference for not-for-profit operations
- Standards.
- Immigration.

architects, electricians, engineers, gemologists, hairstylists, lawyers, medical personnel, real estate brokers, and teachers.

At present, there is little reciprocal recognition in licensing from one country to another because occupational standards and requirements differ substantially. This means that an accounting or legal firm from one country might face obstacles in another, even to serve its domestic clients' needs. The firm must hire professionals within each foreign country or else try to earn certification abroad. The latter option can be difficult because the professionals may have to take examinations in a foreign language and study materials different from those in their home country. There also may be lengthy prerequisites for taking an examination, such as internships, time in residency, and coursework at a local university.

Immigration   Satisfying the standards of a particular country is no guarantee that a foreigner can then work there. In addition, governmental regulations often require an organization—domestic or foreign—to search extensively for qualified personnel locally before it can even apply for work permits for personnel it would like to bring in from abroad.[55]

Dealing with Governmental Trade Influences

Government intervention in trade affects the flow of imports and exports of goods and services among countries. When companies face possible losses because of import competition, they have several options, four of which stand out:

1. Move operations to another country.
2. Concentrate on market niches that attract less international competition.
3. Adopt internal innovations, such as greater efficiency or superior products.
4. Try to get governmental protection.

There are costs and risks with each option. Nevertheless, the records of many companies show that they undertake different ones. For example, competition from Japanese imports spurred the U.S. automobile industry to move some production abroad (such as subcontracting with foreign suppliers for cheaper parts), developing niche markets through the sale of minivan and sport utility vehicles (SUVs) that initially had less international competition, and adopting innovations such as lean production techniques to improve efficiency and product quality. General Motors and Chrysler eventually received substantial government funding to survive.

Tactics for Dealing with Import Competition

Granted, these methods are not realistic for every industry or every business. Companies may lack the managerial, capital, or technological resources to shift their own production abroad, and finding qualified foreign suppliers may be problematic. They may not be able to identify more profitable product niches. Even if they manage to develop niches or improve efficiency, foreign competitors may quickly copy their innovation. In such situations, companies often ask their governments to restrict imports or open export markets. As our opening case shows, U.S. catfish farmers have successfully gained government support to limit import competition, such as changing the name of the imported competitive fish.

Case Review Note

CONVINCING DECISION MAKERS

Governments cannot try to help every company that faces tough international competition. Likewise, helping one industry may hurt another. Thus, as a manager, you may propose or oppose a particular protectionist measure. Inevitably, the burden falls on you and your company to convince officials that your situation warrants particular policies. You must identify the key decision makers and convince them by using the economic and noneconomic arguments presented in this chapter. In any situation, companies must convey to public officials that voters and stakeholders support their position.[56]

INVOLVING THE INDUSTRY AND STAKEHOLDERS

A company improves the odds of success if it can ally most, if not all, domestic companies in its industry. Otherwise, officials may feel that its problems are due to its specific inefficiencies rather than the general import challenges or difficulty in gaining export sales. Similarly, involving other stakeholders can help, such as the taxpayers and merchants in the communities where it operates. Finally, it can lobby decision makers and endorse the political candidates who are sympathetic to its situation.

PREPARING FOR CHANGES IN THE COMPETITIVE ENVIRONMENT

Companies can take different approaches to deal with changes in the international competitive environment. Frequently, their attitudes toward protectionism are a function of the investments they have made to implement their international strategy. Those that depend on freer trade and/or have integrated their production and supply chains among countries tend to oppose protectionism. In contrast, those with single or multidomestic production facilities, such as a plant in Japan to serve the Japanese market and a plant in Taiwan to serve the Taiwanese market, tend to support protectionism.

Companies also differ in their self-perception of being able to compete against imports. In nearly half the cases over a 60-year period in which U.S. firms proposed protecting a U.S. industry, one or more companies in that industry opposed it, typically commanding competitive advantages in terms of scale economies, supplier relationships, or differentiated products. Thus, they reasoned that not only could they successfully battle international rivals, they also stood to gain even more as their weaker domestic competitors failed to do so.[57]

> **Concept Check**
>
> As we point out in Chapter 3, although representative democracies tend to share many features, the process whereby citizens select representatives to make decisions on their behalf varies from country to country, especially when it comes to the centralization or decentralization of authority. Among other things, the task of locating decision makers for business purposes thus differs from one country to another.

Looking to the

Future Dynamics and Complexity

When trade restrictions change, there are winners and losers among countries and among companies and workers within them. So it's probably safe to say that we'll see mixtures of pushes for freer trade and greater protection.

In addition, gains to consumers from freer trade may be at the expense of some companies and workers—people who see themselves as big losers. They are not apt to lose without a struggle; they'll garner as much support for protection as they can, and they may win. This support may well come from alliances that cross national borders, such as clothing companies in various developing nations uniting to push governments to enact quota agreements to protect their markets in developed countries against Chinese and Indian competition. Thus, if you are a manager in an industry that may be affected by changes in governmental protection, you must watch closely to predict how the politics may affect your own economic situation.

Finally, the international regulatory situation is becoming more, rather than less, complex—a situation that challenges companies to find the best locations in which to produce. New products are coming onto the market regularly, thus making the task of tariff classification more complex. Services available over the Internet, such as international online gambling, challenge governments to find means of regulation and

(continued)

tax collection. Heightened concerns about terrorism and product safety compound considerations of what should or should not be traded and with whom.

In Chapter 8, we discuss the trade agreements countries are reaching; nevertheless, it's useful at this point to say a word or two about the impact these have on decision making. Every time countries negotiate a trading agreement (and these agreements are proliferating), there is the possibility that a new optimum production location emerges. When the United States and Mexico negotiated a free trade pact, it caused some U.S. imports to shift from Taiwan to Mexico. However, with an additional free trade agreement between the United States and Central America, some of the production that developed in Mexico shifted to Central American countries. Another free trade agreement might cause another shift in the future. All of this creates uncertainties and dynamics for companies' operations. ■

CASE   U.S.–Cuban Trade: When Does a Cold War Strategy Become a Cold War Relic?

The U.S. embargo of Cuba has been a resilient foreign policy, able to weather a variety of political leaders, economic events, and historical eras for over 50 years.[58] In 2011, the Obama administration rescinded earlier restrictions by allowing licensed organizations to grant U.S. citizens permission to make purposeful (academic, cultural, and humanitarian) travel to Cuba. In addition, the Cuban government announced in 2011 that it was easing restrictions on Cubans' ability to buy and sell houses and automobiles and to travel abroad. On the one hand, these moves led to speculation that commercial relations would grow between the two countries. On the other hand, 2010 U.S. mid-term elections gave more power to hard-liners in the U.S. House of Representatives and Senate, who want stricter restrictions on U.S.-Cuban relations, such as by limiting the number of flights between the United States and Cuba and revoking visas for executives from non-U.S. companies doing business in Cuba. Many U.S. observers want normal commercial relations with Cuba and many do not. The opposing positions are straightforward and similar to those that have prevailed for over five decades. On the one hand, proponents of normal relations argue that the long embargo has not worked and that U.S. companies have been forced to lose business to competitors from other countries. On the other hand, opponents of normal relations argue that a demoralized Cuban population will overthrow the regime if economic conditions deteriorate just a little more. Further, they argue that there is a moral obligation not to do business with a regime that has been so economically and politically repressive. For instance, Cuba is on the official U.S. list of countries sponsoring terrorism and the list refusing to do enough to prevent child prostitution. Let's first look at the history of the situation.

Before and After the Revolution

Since Cuba's independence from Spain in 1899, it has depended on a succession of "sugar daddies." Until Fidel Castro overthrew the Batista government in 1959, more than two-thirds of Cuba's foreign trade took place with the United States. The U.S. bought Cuban sugar at a price well above the world market price, which was a disguised form of foreign aid that extended the U.S. sphere of political influence. Later, the Soviet Union poured aid into Cuba and Venezuela has followed by subsidizing oil exports to Cuba.

After Castro came to power in 1959, he threatened to incite revolutions elsewhere in Latin America. The United States countered by canceling its agreements to buy Cuban sugar, and

Cuba retaliated by seizing U.S. oil refineries. The oil companies refused to supply Cuba with crude oil. Cuba then turned to the Soviet Union for replacement supplies.

The Cold War Sets In

This conflict occurred at the height of the Cold War tension between the United States and the Soviet Union. In 1962, the United States severed diplomatic relations and initiated the full trade embargo of Cuba. In 1963, the Treasury Department set forth regulations that prohibited all unlicensed financial transactions, forbade direct or indirect imports from Cuba, and imposed a total freeze on Cuban government assets held in the United States. Trade between the United States and Cuba stopped.

The incidents that strained relations during the next decades are too numerous to detail. Some threatened peace; others bordered on the absurd. They included the U.S. sponsorship of an invasion by Cuban exiles at the Bay of Pigs, the placement and removal of Soviet missiles in Cuba, the deployment of Cuban forces to overthrow regimes the United States supported (such as in Nicaragua and Angola), and exposés claiming the CIA had tried to air-lift someone to assassinate Castro and had tried to develop a powder to make his beard fall out. Figure 7.3 gives a time line of major events in U.S.-Cuban relations.

Enacting the Embargo

During this period, the U.S. trade embargo endured as originally set. Despite the collapse of communism in most of the world in the early 1990s, the U.S. Congress passed the Cuban Democracy Act in 1992. This policy codified the ban on American travel to Cuba and extended the embargo to the foreign subsidiaries of U.S. companies operating abroad—there would be no trade, direct or otherwise, between the United States and Cuba. The act also required Cuba to hold democratic elections before the U.S. executive branch could repeal the embargo.

Shifting Sympathies

Over time, the U.S. role in the Cuban drama has played to a less sympathetic audience worldwide. Initially, many countries supported the U.S. embargo. All members of the Organization of American States (OAS) except Mexico agreed in 1964 to endorse it. Gradually, countries began trading with Cuba anyway. In 2011, the United Nations voted 186 to 2 against the U.S. embargo. Only Israel voted with the United States. In 2009, the OAS lifted a 47-year suspension of Cuba as a member, basically by redefining democracy to include Marxist–Leninist ideology and not requiring property rights, transparent elections, and free speech as part of the definition.

The Cold War Thaws

Events increasingly created questions about the rationale for continuing the embargo. The fall of the Berlin Wall and the end of the Cold War in the early 1990s triggered many changes.

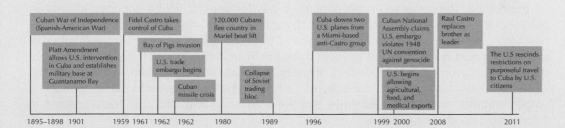

FIGURE 7.3   The Saga of U.S.-Cuba Relations

Relations between the United States and the island nation of Cuba have been embroiled in the vicissitudes of international politics for more than a century—and especially since Fidel Castro took power in 1959.

The attendant collapse of the Soviet Union deprived Cuba of annual subsidies that sustained its feeble economy. Before long, the export of revolution from Cuba seemed less of a threat. In 2000, congressional legislation allowed certain exports of U.S. agricultural, food, and medical products. After the passage of this act, the United States has become the fourth largest exporter to Cuba after Venezuela, China, and Spain.

The Argument for Policy Change

Those in favor of establishing diplomatic relations with Cuba argue that hard-liner policies caused adversity for over 11 million Cubans without weakening either Fidel Castro's or Raúl Castro's political power. (Raúl replaced his older brother in 2008 and turned 80 in 2011.) In fact, they point to the Cuban government's past actions against the Cuban people in retaliation for new, stringent U.S. economic policies. These have included the raising of prices in Cuba for foreign-produced goods and the elimination of the U.S. dollar as an official currency.

Moreover, they warn that Cuban economic problems merely aggravate U.S. immigration tensions with Cuba. A growing number of leaders in the United States (including heads of major firms, Democratic and Republican members of Congress, and labor leaders) have publicly favored normalization of U.S.–Cuban trade. In essence, they believe that increasing exposure to the United States, not the embargo, would be a more promising force of change.

Are There U.S. Business Advantages in Cuba?

Repealing the embargo might help many U.S. industries and companies inasmuch as companies from other countries have already found advantages in tapping Cuba's highly qualified workforce and near-perfect literacy rate. (The Cuban government has announced elimination of a half million state jobs, thus creating a substantial labor supply.) Further, there is a Cuban demand for foreign products and services.

Groups in the United States have noted Cuba's market potential for U.S. companies within the tourism and transportation sectors. Cuba received over 2.5 million international arrivals in 2010. Even with travel bans, there were about 300 sanctioned flights per month between Miami and Cuba. Further, many Americans defied U.S. travel bans by entering Cuba from non-U.S. embarkation points. There are also some bright spots for the Cuban economy. Venezuela has been supplying Cuba with about 100,000 barrels per day of petroleum products at preferential terms, paid for in part by receiving about 30,000 Cuban medical professionals. Further, there are estimates of large oil reserves off the north Cuban coast only 65 miles from the United States. U.S. companies are currently not allowed to bid for exploration rights, and environmentalists worry that the use of Chinese-made rigs by the Spanish company Repsol may increase dangers of spills that enter U.S. waters. In addition, Cuba receives substantial remittances from its citizens working abroad and from relatives of Cuban residents.

At the same time, many argue that the potential for business with Cuba is highly limited. Cuba's per capita GDP is low, which when coupled with its small population (a little over 11 million) does not amount to much purchasing power. This is evident by the prevalence of 1950s U.S.-made cars in Cuba even though European and Asian auto companies face no embargoes on their sales. (See the photo on page 283.)

In addition, Cuba has to export enough to pay for imports. Cuba depends heavily on commodity exports—sugar, nickel, tobacco, citrus, coffee—for which the United States has ample alternative supplies. In fact, the U.S. sugar quota system with a number of countries would surely cause a political backlash in those countries if part of their sugar quotas were given to Cuba. Certainly, there is the possibility of tourism, but there is disagreement about the unused capacity of its hotels. Further, there has been concern in some countries, such as the Bahamas and the Dominican Republic, that tourist growth in Cuba would be at their expense.

◄ US autos from the 1950s are commonly seen in Havana because funds are lacking to import new vehicles.
Source: © Roxana Gonzalez/ iStockphoto.com

Is the Embargo a Cold War Relic?

Finally, there has been debate over the basis for the pro-embargo position. Some argued that, in an age when China is a member of the WTO and nations like Vietnam are trading with the United States, the Cuban embargo looked like a Cold War relic. Moreover, the Cuban embargo is the longest and harshest embargo by one state against another in modern history.

However, a change in U.S. commercial policy toward Cuba does not necessarily mean that Cuba would welcome or accept it. For example, U.S. trade actions have given the Cuban government something other than inept policies to blame for economic blunders. Further, when the OAS allowed Cuba's reentry, Cuba rejected the overture by calling the OAS "totally anachronistic." Fidel Castro has said that the OAS will end up "in the garbage dump of history." Further, Raúl Castro purged Cuba's political leadership in 2009 by referring to former aides as foreign lackeys and indicating that he would not allow any cozying up to foreigners. ■

QUESTIONS

1. Should the United States seek to tighten the economic grip on Cuba? If so, why?
2. Should the United States normalize business relations with Cuba? If so, should the United States stipulate any conditions?
3. Assume you are Cuba's leader. What kind of trade relationship with the United States would be in your best interest? What type would you be willing to accept?
4. How does the structure and relationships of the U.S. political system influence the existence and specification of the trade embargo?
5. Much U.S. tourism, especially via cruise ships, goes to the Caribbean. Do you think that the end of U.S. travel restrictions to Cuba will add or displace tourism going to other Caribbean countries?

Now that you have finished this chapter, go back to www.myiblab.com to continue practicing and applying the concepts you've learned.

MyIBLab

SUMMARY

- Despite the documented benefits of free trade, no country permits an unregulated flow of goods and services across its borders.

- It is difficult to determine the effect on employment from protecting an industry due to the likelihood of retaliation and the fact that imports as well as exports create jobs.

- Policymakers continue to struggle with the problem of income redistribution due to changes in trade policy.

- The infant-industry argument for protection holds that governmental prevention of import competition is necessary to help certain industries evolve from high-cost to low-cost production.

- Government interference is often argued to be beneficial if it promotes industrialization, given the positive relationship between industrial activity and certain economic objectives.

- Trade controls to improve economic relations with other countries include objectives of improving the balance of payments, raising prices to foreign consumers, gaining fair access to foreign markets, preventing foreign monopoly prices, assuring that domestic consumers get low prices, and shifting revenue from foreign producers to domestic tax receipts.

- Considerable government interference in international trade is motivated by political rather than economic concerns, including maintaining domestic supplies of essential goods and preventing potential enemies from gaining goods that would help them achieve their objectives.

- Trade controls that directly affect price and indirectly affect quantity include tariffs, subsidies, arbitrary customs valuation methods, and special fees.

- Trade controls that directly affect quantity and indirectly affect price include quotas, VERs, "buy local" legislation, arbitrary standards, licensing arrangements, foreign-exchange controls, administrative delays, and reciprocal requirements.

- A company's development of an international strategy will greatly determine whether it will benefit more from protectionism or from some other means for countering international competition.

KEY TERMS

ad valorem duty (p. 272)
comparable access argument (p. 266)
compound duty (p. 272)
countertrade (p. 277)
dumping (p. 267)
duty (p. 272)
effective tariff (p. 272)
embargo (p. 276)
essential-industry argument (p. 268)

export-led development (p. 265)
export tariffs (p. 272)
foreign-exchange control (p. 277)
import (or export) license (p. 276)
import tariff (p. 272)
industrialization argument (p. 264)
infant-industry argument (p. 263)
offsets (p. 277)
optimum-tariff theory (p. 267)

protectionism (p. 260)
quota (p. 275)
specific duty (p. 272)
subsidy (p. 272)
tariff (or duty) (p. 272)
terms of trade (p. 265)
transit tariff (p. 272)
voluntary export restraint
  (VER) (p. 275)

ENDNOTES

1 Terry Hanson and Dave Sites, "U.S. Farm-Related Catfish Industry 2009 Review and 2010 Outlook" Unpublished report, department of Fisheries and Allied Aquacultures, Auburn University (March 2011); Fred Kuchler, Barry Krissoff, and David Harvey, "Do Consumers Respond to Country-of-Origin Labelling?" *Journal of Consumer Policy* 33:4 (December 2010): 323–37; "Catfish Industry Maintains Support for USDA," *The Mississippi Business Journal* 31:31 (August 3, 2009): 16; "Fishy Diplomacy with Hanoi," *Wall Street Journal (Online)* (September 21, 2010), accessed November 30, 2010; Bartholomew Sullivan, "Stakes High in Catfish Fight," *McClatchy – Tribune Business News* (October 31, 2010) accessed November 30, 2010; "Fishy Tales; Charlemagne," *The Economist* 387: 8584 (June 14, 2008): 53; Jeffrey H. Birnbaum, "Companies Start to Lift Veil on Political Spending," *Washington Post* (May 13, 2008): A13; Paul Greenberg, "A Catfish by Any Other Name," *New York Times* (October 12, 2008): 72; Ben Evans, "Catfish Plan Risks Trade War," *Miami Herald* (July 2, 2009): 4C; Jeffrey H. Birnbaum, "House Floats Idea for Fish Inspections, But No One Is Biting," *Washington Post* (March 11, 2008): A17; Taras Grescoe, "Catfish with a Side of

Scombroid," *New York Times* (July 15, 2007): WK13; David Streitfeld, "Soaring Grain Prices Put Catfish Farms on the Endangered List," *New York Times* (July 18, 2008): A1.

2 Hans S. Nichols, "Taking the Fix out of Farm Subsidies," *Insight on the News* (August 13, 2001): 20.

3 Lori Kletzer, *Job Loss from Imports: Measuring the Costs* (Washington, DC: Institute for International Economics, 2001); Alan M. Field, "WTO Approves Sanctions against U.S." *Journal of Commerce– Online* (August 31, 2004): WP.

4 Greg Hitt, Paul Glader, and Mike Spector, "Trade Ruling on Steel May Boost Auto Industry," *Wall Street Journal* (December 15, 2006): A3.

5 Fuat Sener, "Schumpeterian Unemployment, Trade and Wages," *Journal of International Economics* 54 (2001): 119.

6 This argument is most associated with the writings of Raul Prebisch, Hans Singer, and Gunnar Myrdal in the 1950s and 1960s. For a recent discussion, see P. Sai-wing Ho, "Arguing for Policy Space to Promote Development: Prebisch, Myrdahl, and Singer," *Journal of Economic Issues* 42:2 (June 2008): 509–16.

7 Jiang Xueqin, "Letter from China," *The Nation* (March 4, 2002): n.p.

8 Steve Padgittm, Peggy Petrzelka, Wendy Wintersteen, and Eric Imerman, "Integrated Crop Management: The Other Precision Agriculture," *American Journal of Alternative Agriculture* 16 (January 2001): 16.

9 Hou Hexiang, "Vietnam to Accelerate Industrialization and Modernization of Rural Areas," *Xinhua News Agency* [China] (June 2, 2002): 1008; "Pushing Ecuador into the 21st Century," *Latin Finance* (March 2002: 30), retrieved July 17, 2002, from http://web.lexis -nexis.com/universe; "Is Inequality Decreasing? Debating the Wealth and Poverty of Nations," *Foreign Affairs* (August 2002): 178.

10 Gerald K. Helleiner, "Markets, Politics, and Globalization: Can the Global Economy Be Civilized?" *Global Governance* (July–September 2001): 243; Marina Murphy, "EU Chemicals Need Flexibility: A Level Playing Field Should Be Established between the EU and U.S. Chemicals Industries," *Chemistry and Industry* (July 1, 2002): 9; Lisa Schmidt, "How U.S. Sees Trade Rows," *Calgary Herald* [Canada] (June 25, 2002): A2.

11 Annie Gowen, "U.S. Caviar with a Russian Accent," *Washington Post* (December 31, 2004): Metro, B1.

12 Alan Beattie and Javier Blas, "Precious Grains," *Financial Times* (April 14, 2008): 9; Randall Palmer, "Canada Mulls Nonprescription-Drug Tactic," *Seattle Times* (February 19, 2005): A13.

13 Edward Alden and Raphael Minder, "EU and Canada Impose Retaliatory Duties on U.S. Imports," *Financial Times* (April 1, 2005): 6.

14 Stephen Moore, "Tax Cut and Spend: The Profligate Ways of Congressional Republicans," *National Review* (October 1, 2001): 19.

15 Liam Pleven, "Pentagon in Race for Raw Materials," *Wall street Journal* (May 3, 2010): A3+.

16 George Leopold, "U.S. Eases Regulations on Cryptography Exports," *Electronic Engineering Times* (July 24, 2000): 43.

17 James Dao, "U.S. to Punish 10 Businesses for Iran Sales," *New York Times* (July 20, 2002): D1.

18 Andrew M. Lemieux and Ronald V. Clarke, "The International Ban on Ivory Sales and Its Effects on Elephant Poaching in Africa," *The British Journal of Criminology* 49:4 (July 2009): 451–71.

19 Tony Walker, "China Warns Australia over Dalai Lama Visit," *Financial Times* (September 18, 1996): 1; Ying Ma, "China's America Problem," *Policy Review* (February 2002): 43–57.

20 Lance Davis and Stanley Engerman, "Sanctions: neither War nor Peace," *Journal of Economic Perspectives* 17:2 (Spring 2003): 187–97.

21 Javier Blas, "Squeeze on Iran Fuels Debate over Sanctions," *Financial Times* (March 8, 2010): 3.

22 "Leaders: A Grand Bargain with the Great Satan? Testing Iran's Nuclear Intentions," *The Economist* (March 12, 2005): 10.

23 Philip Shenon, "In Hanoi, U.S. Goods Sold but Not by U.S.," *New York Times* (October 3, 1993): A1.

24 Patrick Barta, "Black Gold," *Wall Street Journal* (August 16, 2006): A1+

25 Jacob Weisberg, "Sanctions Help to Sustain Rogue States," *Financial Times* (August 3, 2006): 11.

26 "EU/Latin America/Caribbean: Leaders Aim to Revive Ties," *European Report* (May 15, 2002): 501.

27 Vanessa Bauza, "In Struggle for Influence, It's Better to Give," *Knight Ridder Tribune Business News* (March 24, 2007): 1.

28 Rostram J. Neuwirth, "The 'Culture and Trade Debate' Continues: The UNESCO convention in Light of the WTO Reports in China— Publications and Audiovisual Products: Between Amnesia or Déjà Vu?" *Journal of World Trade* 44:6 (December 2010): 1333–56.

29 Gail L. Cramer, James M. Hansen, and Eric J. Wailes, "Impact of Rice Tariffication on Japan and the World Rice Market," *American Journal of Agricultural Economics* 81 (1999): 1149.

30 Matthew Fraser, "Foreign Ownership Rules Indefensible: And There Appears to Be Appetite for Change," *Financial Post* (May 28, 2001): C2.

31 John Larkin, "Now Playing: Korea's Movie Industry Prevents Investment Pact with the U.S.," *Wall Street Journal* (March 20, 2002): A19.

32 "Futile Fortress," *Financial Times* (August 26, 2003): 16.

33 Bernard Hoekman and Kym Anderson, "Developing-Country Agriculture and the New Trade Agenda," *Economic Development & Cultural Change* 49 (October 2000): 171.

34 Neil King, Jr., Scott Miller, Daniel Michaels, and J. Lynn Lunsford, "U.S., Europe Sue Each Other at WTO over Aircraft Subsidies," *Wall Street Journal* (October 7, 2004): A2+; John W. Miller and Daniel Michaels, "Boeing Received Illegal Aid, WTO Says," *Wall Street Journal* (September 16, 2010): B1.

35 John W. Miller, "WTO Warns Members Not to Undermine Trade," *Wall Street Journal* (March 27, 2009): A8.

36 Josept Stiglitz, "The Global Crisis, Social Protection and Jobs," *International Labour Review* 148:1/2 (June 2009): 1–13.

37 Andrew E. Kramer, "Russia, Crippled by Drought, Bans Exports of Grains," *New York Times* (August 6, 2010):A1; and Javier Blas, "Export Bans Prompt Reviews of Security of Supplies," *Financial Times* (October 15, 2010): World Food, 1.

38 James Politi, "Brazil Moves Closer to Showdown over US Cotton Subsidies," *Financial Times* (March 8, 2010): 4.

39 G. Chandrashekhar, "Should India Demand Farm Subsidy Cuts by Developed Nations?" *Businessline* (January 4, 2006): 1.

40 Chi-Chur Chao and Eden S. H. Yu, "Import Quotas, Tied Aid, Capital Accumulation, and Welfare," *Canadian Journal of Economics* 34 (2001): 661; Mark Rice, "Australia Must Join Other Countries in Untying Overseas Aid," *Australian Financial Review* (April 4, 2002): 59.

41 Jamil Anderlini, "China 'Ties' 5 B[illio]n Aid to Africa," *Financial Times* (June 26, 2007): 8.

42 Mohsin Habib and Leon Zurawicki, "Corruption and Foreign Direct Investment," *Journal of International Business Studies* 33 (2002): 291–308.

43 "National Import Specialist Addresses Outreach to the Public," *U.S. Customs Border Protection Today* (October–November 2006), retrieved July 13, 2007, from www.customs.ustreas.gov /xp?CustomsToday/2006/october_nove mber/import_article; *Customs Bulletin and Decision* (June 27, 2007): 58.

44 Matthew Dolan, "To Outfox the Chicken Tax, Ford Strips Its Own Vans," *Wall Street Journal* (September 22, 2009): A1+.

45 John W. Miller, "Why Some China Exports Are Taking Illegal Detours," *Wall Street Journal* (May 25, 2007): B1+.

46 Jeremy Grant, "Signs of Decay as Companies Desert the U.S. Candy Capital," *Financial Times* (January 21, 2004): 14; Christopher Swann, "Shielding Sugar Industry 'Costs Thousands of Jobs,' " *Financial Times* (February 15, 2006): 6.

47 Sarah O'Connor, "Tug of War over Buy American," *Financial Times* (June 24, 2009): 4.

48 Jeremy Grant and Ralph Minder, "Comment & Analysis: Agribusiness," *Financial Times* (February 1, 2006): 11.

49 Anita Chang, "Food Safety," *Miami Herald* (July 15, 2007): 18A.

50 "Import Refusal Report: May 2009," retrieved August 12, 2011, from www.accessdata.fda.gov/scripts/ImportRefusals/ir_byCountry.

51 Peggy Sito, "Guangdong to Slash Internal Customs Delays," *South China Morning Post* (May 16, 2002): 1.

52 Devi Asmarani, "MPs Criticise Jakarta for Buying Pricey Russian Jets," *Singapore Straits Time* (June 19, 2003).

53 "McDonnell and Partner Win $4 Billion British Copter Deal," *New York Times* (July 14, 1995): C5.

54 Mark J. Nackman, "A Critical Examination of Offsets in International Defense Procurements: Policy Options for the United States," *Public Contract Law Journal* 40:2 (Winter 2011): 511–29.

55 Sara Robinson, "Workers Are Trapped in Limbo by I.N.S.," *New York Times* (February 29, 2000): A12.

56 Ralph G. Carter and Lorraine Eden, "Who Makes U.S. Trade Policy?" *International Trade Journal* 13:1 (1999): 53–100.

57 Eugene Salorio, "Trade Barriers and Corporate Strategies: Why Some Firms Oppose Import Protection for Their Own Industry," unpublished DBA dissertation, Harvard University, 1991.

58 *Sources include the following:* Randal C. Archibold, "Cuban Government Outlines Steps Toward a Freer Market," *New York Times* (May 10, 2011): A2; Lesley Clark, "Cuba Travel," *Miami Herald* (February 18, 2011): 5A; "Cuba Politics: US Report on Human Trafficking Enrages Cuba," *EIU ViewsWire* (2010); "Cuba: Country Fact Sheet" (2011); Andres Schipani, "Legislators Aim to Make Oil Prospectors Choose between Cuba and US," *Financial Times* (February 25, 2011): 6; "Cuba Economy: Food Sales, Tourism Grow in 2010," *EIU ViewsWire* (2011); "Cuba Politics: Easing of US Restrictions Welcomed," *EIU ViewsWire* (2011); John Paul Rathbone, "Cash-Strapped Cuba Weighs the Costs of Political Reform," *Financial Times* (July 12, 2010): 6; Patricia Treble, " 'Putrid' OAS Attacked for Cuba Invite," *Maclean's* 122:23 (June 22, 2009): 33; Mary Anastasia O'Grady, "Latin America's Brave New World," *Wall Street Journal* (June 8, 2009): A15; Will Weissert, "Can Cuba Cope with an Onslaught of Americans?" *Yahoo News* (April 13, 2009), retrieved July 15, 2009, from http://news.yahoo .com/s/ap_travel_brief_cuba_american_tourism; Joel Millman, "Cuba Receives More Cash from Workers Abroad," *Wall Street Journal* (March 5, 2009): A12; "CIA World Factbook—Cuba," retrieved May 3, 2011, from www.cia.gov/library/publications /the-world-factbook/geos/ cu.html; William M. Leo Grande, "From Havana to Miami: U.S. Cuba Policy as a Two-Level Game," *Journal of Interamerican Studies and World Affairs* 40:1 (1998): 67–86; Kathleen Parker, "Exposure, Not Embargoes, Will Free Fidel's Cuba," *Seattle Times* (March 14, 2001): B6; Timothy Ashby, "Who's Really Being Hurt?" *Journal of Commerce* (January 31, 2005): 1; "The Web Site of Cuban Industry," retrieved October 5, 2009, from www.cubaindustria.cu/ English (accessed October 5, 2009).

chapter 8

Cross-National Cooperation and Agreements

Objectives

1. To identify the major characteristics and challenges of the World Trade Organization

2. To discuss the pros and cons of global, bilateral, and regional integration

3. To describe the static and dynamic impact of trade agreements on trade and investment flows

4. To define different forms of regional economic integration

5. To compare and contrast different regional trading groups

6. To describe other forms of global cooperation such as the United Nations and OPEC

Marrying is easy, but housekeeping is hard.

—German proverb

Source: Shamukov Ruslan Itar-Tass Photos/Newscom

CASE

Toyota's European Drive

Anna Kessler put the key into the ignition of her brand-new Toyota Yaris, started the engine, and began to navigate her way home from work through the crowded streets of Berlin, Germany.[1] Having owned the car for just over a week, she was already satisfied with her decision. She liked the car's distinctive European look, the generous warranty it had come with, and its low fuel consumption.

Her decision the previous week marked the first time Anna had ever owned a vehicle manufactured by an Asian company; in fact, it was the first time she had considered one. When she had made her last car purchase, the thought of buying a car from Toyota—then known for its lackluster designs, limited options, and seven-month-long waiting lists—had not even entered her mind. However, as she was researching different vehicles, she found that Toyota had ranked the highest in several categories in a recent quality survey and that the Yaris had achieved an outstanding four-star Euro NCAP safety rating, which led her to investigate the car more thoroughly.

With her purchase, Anna became another one of the millions of Toyota vehicle owners located around the globe, contributing to the Japanese automaker's rapid growth over the past two decades. In 1990, the company possessed 20 production facilities in 14 countries; now it has 53 manufacturing facilities in 27 countries, including eight located in Western and Eastern Europe, along with 14 logistics and parts centers serving the European region's distributors. Known for its low-cost, efficient production operations, Toyota finally surpassed General Motors as the largest car manufacturer in the world in 2008. Given Toyota's steady increase in market share, it is hard to believe that before 2002, Toyota had not posted a profit for its European operations for three decades and had suffered from consistently low market share and growth in the region. So why has it taken Toyota so long to crack into the competitive European market, and why are European companies only now beginning to feel the pressure from Asian manufacturers? Many analysts have pointed to an agreement between the Japanese government and the European Economic Community (EEC)—predecessor to the European Union (EU)—in which the two negotiated a quota each year for the number of Japanese cars imported into Europe. The quota amounts agreed upon each year depended on such factors as the level of consumer demand and sales growth in the region and were fixed at 11 percent of the European market.

The arrangement was set up to allow European carmakers to become more competitive as the EC made the transition to a common market; previously, several independent European nations possessed their own import and registration restrictions on Japanese cars. Italy, for example, limited the number of imported Japanese vehicles to 3,000, while France kept them at a 3 percent share of its market. Britain, Spain, and Portugal imposed similar restrictions. This policy goes back to the end of World War II when the Japanese government asked the European automakers to curtail exports to Japan to help Japan rebuild its industry. The Europeans reciprocated by limiting the access of Japanese autos to their market. At the time, that wasn't a problem. However, when the Japanese auto companies became export conscious, they wanted access to the European markets. The quota system helped protect the domestic industry.

Under the new system, these countries had to abandon their individual policies, but French carmakers fought to include an 80 percent local-content rule and an allowance to export 500,000 cars a year to Japan, five times the then-current level. In the end, the EC disregarded these additional requests, and in the first year of the agreement, 1.089 million Japanese cars were allowed to be imported.

The quota, however, also fixed separate caps for each participating country and then divided this amount among the Japanese automakers according to their historic market shares. The caps essentially prevented the Japanese from being able to transfer their excess imports from countries where their quotas weren't being met to ones where they were unable to meet demand due to having already reached the maximum limits. It was primarily for this reason that they never actually met their quota for the EC; during the seven years the quota system was in effect, Toyota was held to a 2 to 3 percent market share in most EU countries.

Although the system seemed to be having the desired effect, even some French auto officials admitted that the eventual opening of the market was inevitable. One noted, "Can we put off change for years? Officially, yes. But honestly, I don't think so." That statement proved prophetic when the EU lifted the import quota in 1999 and additionally made it easier for the Japanese auto manufacturers to expand distribution and to sign up dealers. Although this move did not necessarily cause the Japanese to flood the European market with their products, it did open the way for them to invest more heavily in design and manufacturing facilities in the EU, to broaden the range of products they marketed there, and to customize their offerings to better appeal to European tastes.

Toyota responded to the drop in barriers by introducing a new strategy of designing vehicles targeted specifically at

European customers. The new strategy involved setting up a European Design and Development center in southern France and allowing design teams across the globe to compete for projects. The Yaris, Toyota's best-selling vehicle in the EU, was designed by a Greek and was the first to be developed within the region. It subsequently was named Car of the Year 2000 in both Europe and Japan. In addition, it received five stars in the Euro NCAP (New Car Assessment Programme) tests for adult occupant protection in 2008.

As another key element of its European strategy, Toyota has also set up additional production centers in the region and now manufactures all of its best European-selling vehicles in Europe. The new-generation Toyota Corolla, voted 2002 European Car of the Year, and the Avensis, the first Toyota vehicle to be exported from Europe to Japan, were both designed and built in Europe. In December 2006, Toyota celebrated its one millionth made-in-Europe Yaris at its Valenciennes plant in France.

Manufacturing facilities in Eastern Europe allow the Japanese automaker to lower production costs due to lower wages. For example, workers in Toyota's plant in Turkey earn only $3.60 an hour, giving Toyota a distinct cost advantage over European competitors such as Volkswagen, which pays as much as $40.68 per hour to the workers in its plants in Germany.

The difference in wages, in addition to its efficient operations, has allowed Toyota to remain profitable while others are undergoing layoffs and industry-wide restructuring. Volkswagen cut nearly 20,000 jobs and introduced longer shifts in its German factories. GM's European unit cut 13,000 jobs to help it reduce costs and restore profitability after seven consecutive years of losses in the region. Additionally, Ford, Fiat SpA, and Volkswagen have undergone substantial management changes as they've sought to rein in operations to keep costs from running over in the new competitive market in which they are slowly losing market share.

The situation seems even bleaker as Japanese competitors continue to open up facilities in the Eastern bloc countries recently admitted to the EU as well as in other low-wage areas such as China. Toyota has already set up state-of-the-art production plants in the Czech Republic and Poland—the one in the Czech Republic being established in cooperation with France's PSA Peugeot Citroën to develop good relationships with PSA's local suppliers. Because of the elimination of internal tariffs in the EU, Toyota can manufacture automobiles anywhere within the EU and ship them to all markets duty-free. Before the reduction in tariff barriers, this would not have been possible.

Other recent trends in the EU have also favored Toyota since the quotas were eliminated. In light of a sluggish European economy facing high unemployment and low growth, Europeans are becoming less loyal to European brands in their search for more economical, higher-quality vehicles. In recent J.D. Power customer surveys in the United Kingdom and Germany, Toyota ranked first overall and scored the highest in three of seven categories; Ford, Renault, and Volkswagen all ranked below average. In addition, Toyota's environmentally friendly hybrid vehicle, the Prius, was voted the 2005 European Car of the Year. In light of its growing presence in Europe, the company's application to become a full member of the European Automobile Manufacturers' Association has been accepted.

Riding on its success in Europe up to 2007 and its growth internationally, Toyota had ambitious goals for the future. However, the global financial crisis and the ongoing difficulties posed by international recalls of more than 9.5 million vehicles have put a crimp in those plans. Although Toyota overtook GM for global leadership of sales in 2008, worldwide sales dropped nearly 22 percent in FY 2009 compared with FY 2008, and Toyota posted a ¥436.9 billion loss in FY 2009 compared with net income of ¥1,717.8 billion in FY 2008. In 2010, Toyota's global revenues were down an additional 7.7 percent from 2009 levels and unit sales uniformly decreased around the world for the second straight year.

Toyota's European Division saw unit sales decrease by 19.2 percent from 2009 levels, from 1,062,000 to 858,000, continuing a downward trend since 2007. However, corresponding decreases in production costs in Europe, due to cost-cutting measures, resulted in an operating loss of ¥33 billion, a relatively small loss compared to 2009's operating loss of ¥143.3 billion. Toyota's market share in Europe has also been damaged by the financial crisis and its ongoing struggle to re-establish its quality image after the global recalls. In Europe, Toyota saw its market share fall to 4.4 percent in 2010, down from its peak of 5.9 percent in 2007. This dropped Toyota to the number 9 position in European market share, being overtaken by Daimler and Korean rival Hyundai Kia AG, with Hyundai Kia capturing a 4.8 percent market share by late 2010.

Despite difficulties posed by the present market conditions, and the necessity of having to lay off people worldwide, Toyota has so far resisted the move to shut down plants. Toyota is continuing its push to increase its share of the European market by restructuring its Brussels-based European division, including devolving more decision-making power from Japan and focusing on the values of European consumers. This includes placing renewed focus on hybrid technology in Europe, in which the company still retains a comparative advantage over its global rivals.

As the decade continues and many areas of the world begin to emerge from the financial crisis of the past several years, it will be interesting to see if Toyota can recapture the success it enjoyed up until three years ago. Will its strategy of manufacturing directly in Europe and through partnerships with PSA Peugeot-Citroën return the company to profitability in the region? Can the company continue to impress European consumers with its "green" technology and more localized attention? Given all of the uncertainty of the last few years, you have to wonder if Anna Kessler is still driving her Yaris, or if she has traded it in for another Yaris or something else.

CRN$
Case Review Note

Introduction

Concept Check

Recall from Chapter 6 our discussion of the ways in which the mobility of capital, technology, and people affects a country's trade and the relative competitive positions of domestic firms and industries. Imbalances in the mobility of factors of production are often addressed in strategies for cross-national integration.

In the mid- to late 1940s, many nations decided that if they were going to emerge from the wreckage of World War II and promote economic growth and stability within their borders, they would have to assist—and get assistance from—nearby countries. In some respects, the United States is the perfect example of such economic integration: the largest economy in the world comprising 50 states in continental North America and a few Pacific islands, with a common currency and labor and capital mobility. However, it is just one country. What about the rest of the world? How do its nations and regions combine forces to give and gain the assistance they need to prosper together?

Economic integration is a term used to describe the political and monetary agreements among nations and world regions in which preference is given to member countries. There are three ways to approach such agreements:

- **Bilateral integration**—Two countries decide to cooperate more closely together, usually in the form of tariff reductions
- **Regional integration**—A group of countries located in the same geographic proximity decide to cooperate, as with the European Union
- **Global integration**—Countries from all over the world decide to cooperate through the World Trade Organization (WTO)

Approaches to economic integration—political and economic agreements among countries in which preference is given to member countries—may be

- Bilateral.
- Regional.
- Global.

Why do you need to understand the nature of these agreements? Trade groups, whether bilateral, regional, or global, are an important influence on MNE strategies. They can define the size of the regional market and the rules under which a company must operate. In fact, an increase in market size is their single most important reason for existing.[2] A company in the initial stages of foreign expansion must be aware of how the groups encompass countries with good manufacturing locations or market opportunities. Recall from our opening case that Toyota has been able to find success in Europe by taking advantage of changes in EU policy that allow it to adjust its design and production strategies to meet the unique needs of European consumers. Similarly, in the ending case we'll see how NAFTA affected Walmart's expansion into Mexico and Central America. Thus, as a company expands internationally, it must change its organizational structure and operating strategies to continually benefit from these alliances.

MNEs are interested in regional trade groups because they tend to be regional as well. Although we often think of MNEs as companies that do business in all of the **triad** regions of the world—Europe, North America, and Asia—current research demonstrates that most generate most of their revenues in their home regions. In a sample of the top 500

Case Review Note

companies in the world in terms of trade and FDI, it was found that 320 generate at least 50 percent of their revenues from their home region, 25 are biregional (at least 20 percent of their revenues from two regions but less than 50 percent from any single region), 11 are host-region oriented (more than half their revenue from a region outside their home region), and only 9 are truly global (at least 20 percent of their revenues from each of the three triad regions and with less than 50 percent of their sales from one region).[3]

However, companies that sell in their own region are also interested in trade agreements with other regions. For example, although U.S. furniture, electronics, and appliance store RC Willey does not generate any foreign sales, it imports products from all over the world. Managers of the company are very interested in trade agreements because of the potential impact on where they source their purchases to reduce costs and improve quality.

The World Trade Organization

Governments often actively cooperate with each other to remove trade barriers. The following discussion focuses on the **World Trade Organization (WTO)**, the successor to the **General Agreement on Tariffs and Trade (GATT)** and the major multilateral forum through which governments can come to agreements and settle disputes over trade.

GATT: PREDECESSOR TO THE WTO

In 1947, 23 countries formed GATT under the auspices of the United Nations to abolish quotas and reduce tariffs. By the time the WTO replaced GATT in 1995, 125 nations had become members. Many believe that GATT's contribution to trade liberalization enabled the expansion of world trade in the second half of the twentieth century.

Trade without Discrimination   The fundamental principle of GATT was that each member nation must open its markets equally to every other member nation. This principle of "trade without discrimination" was embodied in GATT's **most-favored-nation (MFN) clause**—once a country and its trading partners had agreed to reduce a tariff, that tariff cut was automatically extended to every other member country, irrespective of whether the country was a signatory to the agreement.

Over time, GATT grappled with the issue of nontariff barriers in terms of industrial standards, government procurement, subsidies and countervailing duties (duties in response to another country's protectionist measures), licensing, and customs valuation. In each area, GATT members agreed to apply the same product standards for imports as for domestically produced goods, treat bids by foreign companies on a nondiscriminatory basis for most large contracts, prohibit export subsidies except on agricultural products, simplify licensing procedures that permit the importation of foreign-made goods, and use a uniform procedure to value imports when assessing duties on them.

Then GATT slowly ran into problems. Its success led some governments to devise craftier methods of trade protection. World trade grew more complex, and trade in services—not covered by GATT rules—grew more important. Procedurally, GATT's institutional structure and its dispute-settlement system seemed increasingly overextended. Moreover, it could not enforce compliance with agreements. These market trends and organizational challenges made trade agreements harder to work out. Restoring an effective means for trade liberalization led officials to create the WTO in 1995.

WHAT DOES THE WTO DO?

The WTO adopted the principles and trade agreements reached under the auspices of GATT but expanded its mission to include trade in services, investment, intellectual property, sanitary measures, plant health, agriculture, and textiles, as well as technical

Concept Check

In Chapter 7, we explain that, in principle, no country allows an unregulated flow of goods and services across its borders; rather, governments routinely influence the flow of imports and exports. We also observe that governments directly or indirectly subsidize domestic industries to help them compete with foreign producers, whether at home or abroad. (In Chapter 1, we list the motivations for governments to engage in cross-national agreements—indeed, to cooperate at all.)

Concept Check

In Chapter 7, we define a **tariff** as the most common type of trade control and describe it as a "tax" that governments levy on goods shipped internationally. Here we emphasize the fact that tariff barriers affect the prices of goods that cross national borders.

Concept Check

In discussing "Nontariff Barriers" as instruments of trade control in Chapter 7, we include **subsidies,** which we describe as direct government payments made to domestic companies, either to compensate them for losses incurred from selling abroad or to make it more profitable for them to sell overseas.

The World Trade Organization is the major body for

- Reciprocal trade negotiations.
- Enforcement of trade agreements.

barriers to trade. The WTO has 153 members who collectively account for more than 97 percent of world trade. These include the BRIC countries of Brazil, India, and China, but not Russia, which was one of 30 countries in different stages of accession as of May 28, 2011. The organization also has 29 observer governments, many of which possess economic policies that are not aligned to WTO standards or who are preparing for full entry, as well as those that express interest in international business dealings, such as the Vatican. The entire membership makes significant decisions by consensus. However, there are provisions for a majority vote in the event of a nondecision by member countries. Agreements then must be ratified by the governments of the member nations.

Most Favored Nation   The WTO continued the MFN clause of GATT, which implies that member countries should trade without discrimination, basically giving foreign products "national treatment." Although the WTO restricts this privilege to official members, some exceptions are allowed, as follows:

1. Developing countries' manufactured products have been given preferential treatment over those from industrial countries.

2. Concessions granted to members within a regional trading alliance, such as the EU, have not been extended to countries outside the alliance. (Recall from our opening case, for instance, that although EU members can export and import cars from other EU nations without limitations, Japanese carmakers must comply with strict import tariffs.)

3. Countries can raise barriers against member countries who they feel are trading unfairly.

Exceptions are made in times of war or international tension.

Case Review Note

Dispute Settlement   One of the functions of the WTO that is garnering growing attention is the organization's dispute settlement mechanism, in which countries may bring charges of unfair trade practices to a WTO panel, and accused countries may appeal. There are time limits on all stages of deliberations, and the WTO's rulings are binding. If an offending country fails to comply with the panel's judgment, its trading partners have the right to compensation. If this penalty is ineffective, then the offending country's trading partners have the right to impose countervailing sanctions. However, the effectiveness of this system is under serious debate, given the ambiguity and time-consuming nature of certain cases.

One of the most interesting disputes brought before the WTO is between European company Airbus and its U.S. competitor, Boeing, two of the world's largest aerospace companies and defense contractors. Since late 2004, the companies have traded charges of unfair subsidies from their respective supporting governments, the EU and United States, with each initially preferring to resolve the dispute outside of WTO jurisdiction, but then resorting to WTO arbitration. Boeing accused Airbus of receiving advantageous loans to offset a portion of its "launch" costs for its family of civilian aircraft, and Airbus countered by accusing Boeing of gaining a competitive advantage from substantial U.S. government contracts and tax breaks in many of the regions of the United States in which the company operates. Negotiations to solve the dispute between the two companies and their representative governments outside of WTO arbitration broke down in 2004, and both parties elected to lodge formal complaints to the WTO in order to receive a binding resolution.[4]

The latest panel report did conclude that some of Boeing's tax breaks and a number of government contracts acted as specific subsidies in violation of WTO conventions, providing Airbus with a victory in the case. A final ruling on Boeing's subsidies was expected to be made by a WTO appeals court by the end of 2011. On the other hand, however, the panel also agreed with Boeing that Airbus was guilty of receiving favorable capital loans from its sponsor governments to pay for launch costs incurred in developing new aircraft, as well as specific subsidies in the form of infrastructural loans and aid representing serious violations of WTO regulations.[5] In May 2011, a WTO Appeals panel upheld the 2010 ruling that the European aid for the Airbus A380

Concept Check

In Chapter 7, we show how the imposition of import restrictions can be used as a means of persuading other countries to lower import barriers. Here we point out that the same practice can also be used to punish nations whose policies fail to comply with provisions of the WTO or other agreements.

caused Boeing to lose market share, but it also ruled that the aid was not tied specifically to exports and thus not prohibited.[6] Airbus will still have to make some changes in the way it does business, but the ruling by the WTO is not as severe as if it had ruled that the aid was specifically tied to exports.

The global economic crisis has made the grounds of the dispute even murkier, since governments on both sides of the Atlantic have tried to keep companies in various industries afloat using all kinds of subsidies and tax breaks. In addition, the Pentagon recently awarded a $30 billion refueling tanker contract to Boeing, which has already been criticized by officials from Airbus as being designed to favor the Boeing bid. This may lead to appeals to not only the U.S. government, but also provide more fuel to the fire of the ongoing dispute.[7]

Doha Round   Most of the agenda of the WTO was established by negotiations, or *rounds*, held by GATT—particularly the Uruguay Round, which took place from 1986 to 1994 and led up to the creation of the WTO. Perhaps the most complex issues the WTO currently faces, however, are those it is trying to address through the Doha Round, which commenced in Doha, Qatar, in 2001 and is focused on giving a boost to developing countries on the world scene. The largest of the disputes has essentially resulted in a split between developed members, such as the United States, Japan, and the EU, and developing countries, led by Brazil, China, and India, over the large agricultural subsidies maintained by the richer nations and the industrial subsidies enforced by developing countries.

The initial deadline for completing the Doha agenda was January 1, 2005, but that came and went when countries could not agree on key issues, as did the next three deadlines. By the third quarter of 2009, attempts to solve the problem of lowering tariffs on industrial goods (a demand by the United States and the EU) in return for reduced agricultural barriers (a demand of many developing countries) were not successful. In an interesting twist, Brazil sided with the United States and the EU, while India and China rejected the proposals because of their fear that imports would devastate their local economies in terms of both industrial and agricultural goods.[8] The sense of urgency seemed to stall as global trade increased by 70 percent to $14 trillion and FDI flows rose 25 percent to $1.5 trillion, even in the absence of the Doha Round.[9]

Then the global financial crisis got everyone's attention. Initially, it put the Doha agenda temporarily on hold as governments struggled to bring their economies back to life and reignite global trade, which collapsed in 2008. The World Bank estimated that the global economy shrunk by 1.9 percent in 2009 in terms of GDP and the WTO estimated that international trade in merchandise and services fell by 12 percent, respectively. This represents the steepest decline in trade since World War II.

The WTO set another deadline to complete negotiations on the Doha Round by the end of 2011. However, progress has not been easy. The WTO had hoped to scale back expectations on Doha by focusing on easier issues such as better coordinated exports rules and procedures and export incentive for developing countries. This new version, called "Doha Lite" or "Plan B" was approved by the WTO members in 2011 but not completely finalized.[10] The lighter version might be more likely than the full version of Doha given the focus on regional and bilateral agreements and the U.S. presidential election in 2012.[11]

CRITICISM

The WTO is not without its critics, who feel that its efforts are undermining global diversity and benefitting the rich at the expense of the poor. This has become such a big issue in recent years that the WTO published two brochures on its website called "10 Benefits of the WTO Trading System" and "10 Common Misunderstandings about the WTO."[12]

Some of the common criticisms of the WTO system include concerns about the ignorance of critical issues related to trade, such as labor and environmental conditions. Critics argue that the WTO does not do enough to protect against exploitive industrial development that threatens labor rights and the environment around the world.[13] In addition, the implementation of agreements by developed countries has been slow, thus denying many developing nations the incentives for which they joined the organization in the first place.[14]

The Rise of Bilateral Agreements

As the negotiations over the Doha Round broke down, Brazil and the EU announced a proposed strategic alliance between them that would give Brazil the same trading status that China and Russia have with the EU and would initiate discussions in other areas, such as energy, climate change, and human rights. Brazil also signed an important bilateral agreement with China, resulting in China's becoming Brazil's single biggest trading partner. In a similar fashion, South Korea signed a free trade pact with the United States, although it had not been ratified by the U.S. Congress as of May 2011, and India began negotiating a deal with the EU.[15] These examples highlight the increasing willingness of individual countries to circumvent the multilateral system and engage in bilateral agreements—also known as *preferential trade agreements* (PTAs) or *free trade agreements* (FTAs)—with each other to meet their global trade objectives.

Regional Economic Integration

Going beyond the bilateral approach is an approach known as *regional trade agreements*, or RTAs. It's hard to know exactly how many such agreements exist, since the WTO Database only includes those agreements that have been notified to the WTO or for which a public announcement has been made. But as of May 30, 2011, there were 209 RTAs in force. Some of the best known RTAs are the European Union, the European Free Trade Association, the North American Free Trade Agreement, the Southern Common Market (MERCOSUR), the Association of Southeast Asian Nations (ASEAN), the Asian Free Trade Area (AFTA), and the Common Market of Eastern and Southern Africa (COMESA).[16] These agreements, whether bilateral or regional, are also called *preferential trade agreements*, or *PTAs*. The rationale for the term *PTA* is that signatory countries give preferential treatment to those in the group.

Bilateral agreements can be between two individual countries or may involve one country dealing with a group of other countries.

Regional trade agreements—integration confined to a region and involving more than two countries.

Geographic proximity is an important reason for economic integration.

Concept Check

In discussing geographic distance in Chapter 6, we observe that because greater distances ordinarily mean higher transportation costs, geographic proximity usually encourages trade cooperation. In the same chapter, we explain **country-similarity theory** by showing that once a company has developed a new product in response to conditions in its home market, it will probably try to export it to those markets that it regards as most similar to its own.

FIGURE 8.1 Impact of Free Trade Agreements

When economic integration reduces or eliminates trade barriers, the effects on the nations involved may be either *static* or *dynamic*. *Static effects* apply primarily to trade barriers themselves—for member countries they go down, and for nonmembers they go up. Dynamic effects, on the other hand, apply to economic changes affecting the newly structured market—not only does the market expand, but so do local companies, which take advantage of the larger market.

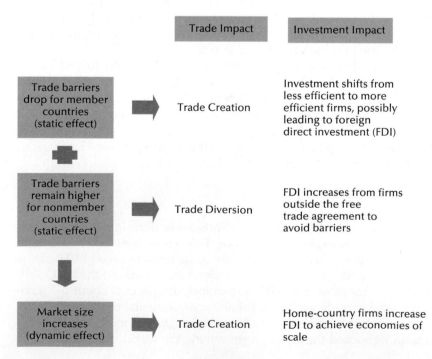

	Trade Impact	Investment Impact
Trade barriers drop for member countries (static effect)	Trade Creation	Investment shifts from less efficient to more efficient firms, possibly leading to foreign direct investment (FDI)
Trade barriers remain higher for nonmember countries (static effect)	Trade Diversion	FDI increases from firms outside the free trade agreement to avoid barriers
Market size increases (dynamic effect)	Trade Creation	Home-country firms increase FDI to achieve economies of scale

Does Ge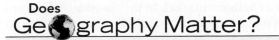graphy Matter?

It's logical that most trade groups contain countries in the same area of the world. Neighboring countries tend to ally for several reasons:

- The distances that goods need to travel between such countries are short.
- Consumers' tastes are likely to be similar, and distribution channels can easily be established in adjacent countries.
- Neighboring countries may have common histories and interests, and they may be more willing to coordinate their policies than non-neighbors.[17]

Even though geographic proximity is a major factor leading to regional trade agreements, that is not the case for all agreements. For example the Canada-Israel RTA is certainly not based on geographic proximity, but most others are. Armenia has RTAs in force with Kazahkstan, Moldova, the Russian Federation, Turkmenistan, and Ukraine. India has a number of trade agreements with most of the countries in its region. Germany, a member of the European Union, exports 62.9 percent of its merchandise exports to other EU members and imports 58.3 percent from them. Switzerland, which is not a member of the EU but which has a trade agreement with the EU, exports 59.7 percent of its merchandise exports to EU countries and imports 78 percent from them. NAFTA includes Canada, the United States, and Mexico.

There are a number of reasons why geography matters in the case of RTAs. Neighboring countries often, though not always, share a common history, language, culture, and currency. Unless the countries are at war with each other, they usually have already developed trading ties. Close proximity reduces transportation costs, thereby making traded products cheaper in general. Research has shown that as physical distance between two countries increases by 1 percent, international trade drops by 1.1 percent. On the other hand, trade is likely to rise by 80 percent between countries with a common border, 200 percent with a common language (such as English between Canada and the United States), and 340 percent with a common currency (such as the euro for countries in the EU that have adopted the euro). Another strong incentive for geographically close countries to establish an RTA is that trade among trading bloc members is likely to rise by 330 percent compared with not being in an agreement.[18] ●

As also noted earlier, the major reason to establish a regional trade group is to increase market size. There are two basic types of regional trade agreements from the standpoint of tariff policies:

- *Free Trade Agreement (FTA)* The goal of an FTA is to abolish all tariffs between member countries. It usually begins modestly by eliminating tariffs on goods that already have low tariffs, and there is usually an implementation period during which all tariffs are eliminated on all products. Moreover, each member country maintains its own external tariffs against non-FTA countries. About 90 percent of the RTAs identified by the WTO are free trade agreements.

- *Customs Union* In addition to eliminating internal tariffs, member countries levy a common external tariff on goods being imported from nonmembers. For example, the EU removed internal tariffs from 1959 to 1967, when it established a common external tariff. Now it negotiates as one region in the WTO rather than as separate countries. (Thus, as we observed in our opening case, when it came to import quotas on cars shipped to EU members, Japan had to negotiate with the EU as a whole, rather than with individual countries.) Customs unions account for less than 10 percent of the RTAs identified by the WTO. Most trade gains come from membership in an FTA, not a customs union, which is driven more by political than economic reasons.[19]

> Major types of economic integration:
>
> - Free trade area—no internal tariffs.
> - Customs union—no internal tariffs plus common external tariffs.
> - Common market—customs union plus factor mobility.

Case Review Note

COMMON MARKET (OR ECONOMIC INTEGRATION AGREEMENT)

Beyond the reduction of tariffs and nontariff barriers, countries can enhance their cooperation in a variety of other ways. The EU also allows free mobility of production factors such as labor and capital. This means that labor, for example, is free to work in any country in the common market without restriction. Adding free mobility of factors of production to a customs union results in a **common market.** In the absence of the common market arrangement, a worker from a member country would have to apply for an immigration visa, which can be difficult to come by.

In addition, the EU has harmonized its monetary policies through the creation of a common currency, complete with a central bank. This level of cooperation creates a degree of political integration among member countries, which means they lose a bit of their sovereignty. The EU is formally listed by the WTO as a customs union and economic integration agreement.

THE EFFECTS OF INTEGRATION

Regional economic integration can affect member countries in social, cultural, political, and economic ways. Initially, however, our focus is on its economic rationale. As we noted in Chapter 7, the imposition of tariff and nontariff barriers disrupts the free flow of goods, affecting resource allocation.

Static and Dynamic Effects   Regional economic integration reduces or eliminates those barriers for member countries, producing both *static effects* and *dynamic effects*. **Static effects** are the shifting of resources from inefficient to efficient companies as trade barriers fall. **Dynamic effects** are the overall growth in the market and the impact on a company caused by expanding production and by the company's ability to achieve greater economies of scale. Figure 8.1 shows how FTAs result in static and dynamic effects on trade and investment flows.

Static effects may develop when either of two conditions occurs:

1. *Trade Creation:* Production shifts to more efficient producers for reasons of comparative advantage, allowing consumers access to more goods at a lower price than would have been possible without integration. Companies protected in their domestic markets face real problems when the barriers are eliminated and they attempt to compete with more efficient producers. The strategic implication is that companies that were unable to export to another country—even though they might be more efficient than producers there—are now able to export when the barriers come down. Thus there will be more demand for their products and less for the protected ones. Investment also might shift to countries that are more efficient or that have a comparative advantage in one or more factors of production.

2. *Trade Diversion:* Trade shifts to countries in the group at the expense of trade with other countries, even though the nonmember companies might be more efficient in the absence of trade barriers.

Assume, for example, that U.S. companies are importing the same product from Mexico and Taiwan. If the United States enters into an FTA with Mexico but not with Taiwan, the companies might be more likely to import goods from Mexico than from Taiwan due to lower tariffs. Moreover, MNEs from countries outside the FTA might consider investing in the FTA countries to service the market more effectively. Trade diversion is a major criticism of RTAs, because the agreements result in greater trade among a few WTO members but not among all. This undermines the multilateral process of the WTO.

Economies of Scale   Dynamic effects of integration occur when trade barriers come down and markets grow. Because of that growth, companies can increase their production, which will result in lower costs per unit—a phenomenon we call **economies of scale.** Companies can produce more cheaply, which is good because they must become more efficient to survive. This could result in more trade between the member countries (trade creation) or an increase in FDI as the market grows and it becomes feasible for MNEs to invest in it.

Increased Competition   Another important effect of an FTA is greater efficiency due to increased competition. Many MNEs in Europe have attempted to grow through

---

Sidebar notes (left margin):

Regional integration has social, cultural, political, and economic effects.

Static effects of integration—the shifting of resources from inefficient to efficient companies as trade barriers fall.

Dynamic effects of integration—the overall growth in the market and the impact on a company caused by expanding production and by the company's ability to achieve greater economies of scale.

Concept Check

In Chapter 6, we define **comparative advantage** as the theory that global efficiency gains may result from trade if a country specializes in those products it can produce more efficiently than other products (regardless of whether other countries can produce the same products even more efficiently).

Trade creation—production shifts to more efficient producers for reasons of comparative advantage.

Trade diversion—trade shifts to countries in the group at the expense of trade with countries not in the group.

Economies of scale—the average cost per unit falls as the number of units produced rises; occurs in regional integration because of the growth in the market size.

mergers and acquisitions to achieve the size necessary to compete in the larger market. Companies in Mexico were forced to become more competitive with the passage of NAFTA due to competition from Canadian and U.S. companies. This could result in investment shifting from less efficient to more efficient companies, or it could result in existing companies becoming more efficient.

Major Regional Trading Groups

The two ways to look at different trading groups are by location and by type. Major trading groups exist in every region of the world, and it is impossible to cover every group in every region, so we'll discuss a few of the major groups. As noted above, most regional groups are free trade agreements, although a small percentage are also customs unions. Some, such as the EU, are common markets that are organized for political as well as economic reasons.

Companies are interested in regional trading groups for their markets, sources of raw materials, and production locations. The larger and richer the new market, the more likely it is to attract the attention of the major investor countries and companies.

THE EUROPEAN UNION

The largest and most comprehensive regional economic group is the **European Union (EU).** It began as a free trade agreement with the goal of becoming a customs union and to integrate in other ways. The formation of the European Parliament and the establishment of a common currency, the euro, makes the EU the most ambitious of all the regional trade groups.[20] Table 8.1 summarizes the EU's key milestones, while Map 8.1 identifies its members and other key European groups.

The European Union:

- Changed from the European Economic Community to the European Community to the European Union.
- Is the largest and most successful regional trade group.
- Provides free trade of goods, services, capital, and people.
- Uses common external tariff.
- Has common currency.

TABLE 8.1 European Union Milestones

From its inception in 1957, the EU has been moving toward complete economic integration. However, it is doubtful that its initial adherents ever dreamed that European cooperation would have achieved such integration as to move to a common currency.

1959	The first steps are taken in the progressive abolition of customs duties and quotas within the EEC (European Economic Community)
1960	The Stockholm Convention establishes the European Free Trade Association (EFTA) among seven European countries (Austria, Denmark, Norway, Portugal, Sweden, Switzerland, and the United Kingdom).
1961	The first regulation on free movement of workers within the EEC comes into force.
1962	The Common Agricultural Policy is adopted.
1966	Agreement is reached on a value-added tax (VAT) system; a treaty merging the Executives of the European Communities comes into force; and the EEC changes its name to European Community (EC).
1967	All remaining internal tariffs are eliminated, and a common external tariff is imposed.
1973	Denmark, Ireland, and the United Kingdom become members 7, 8, and 9 of the EC.
1981	Greece becomes the 10th member of the EC.
1986	Spain and Portugal become the 11th and the 12th members of the EC.
1990	East and West Germany unite.
1992	Agreement to change the EC to the European Union is adopted in 1992 and implemented in 1993
1995	Austria, Finland, and Sweden become the 13th, 14th, and 15th members of the EU.
1996	An EU summit names the 11 countries that will join the European single currency with all EU countries joining except Britain, Sweden, Denmark (by their choice), and Greece (not ready).
1999	The euro, the single European currency, comes into effect (January 1, 1999).
2001	Greece becomes the 12th country to adopt the euro (January 1, 2001).
2002	The euro coins and notes enter circulation (January 1, 2002).
	All 15 member states ratify the Kyoto Protocol.
2004	Admission of Cyprus, the Czech Republic, Estonia, Hungary, Latvia, Lithuania, Malta, Poland, Slovakia, and Slovenia, bringing number of member states to 25.
2007	Bulgaria and Romania join, bringing number of member states to 27. Candidate countries are Croatia, Former Yugoslav Republic of Macedonia, Turkey, and Iceland.

Source: Europa, "The History of the European Union," at http://europa.eu/abc/history (accessed May 31, 2011)

MAP 8.1   European Trade and Economic Integration

Although the 27-member EU is easily the dominant trading bloc in Europe, it's not the only one. Founded in 1960, the four-member European Free Trade Association (EFTA) also maintains joint free trade agreements with several other countries. The European Economic Area (EEA) includes three members of the EFTA and all members of the EU. The Central European Free Trade Agreement (CEFTA) was originally formed to integrate Western practices into the economies of former Soviet bloc nations, two of whom have already been admitted into the EU.

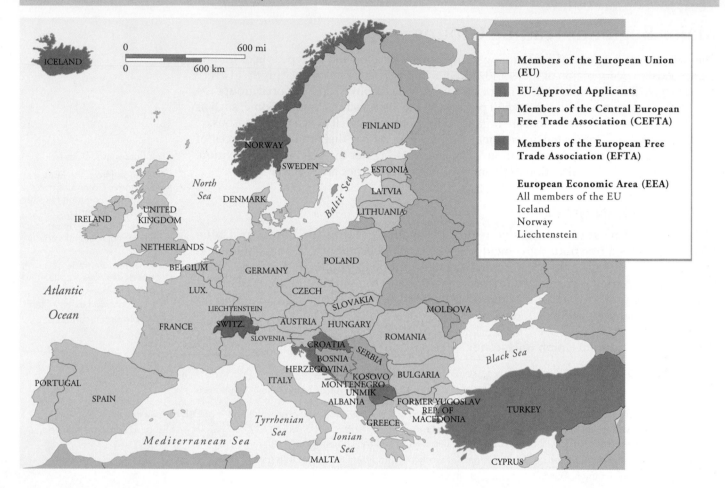

Legend:
- Members of the European Union (EU)
- EU-Approved Applicants
- Members of the Central European Free Trade Association (CEFTA)
- Members of the European Free Trade Association (EFTA)

European Economic Area (EEA)
All members of the EU
Iceland
Norway
Liechtenstein

Concept Check

In Chapter 6, we discuss the **theory of country size,** which holds that large countries usually depend less on trade than small countries. The same principle tends to be true of economic blocs, and here we point out that **regional integration** is one way to achieve the size necessary to reduce members' dependence on trade.

European Free Trade Association—FTA involving Iceland, Liechtenstein, Norway, and Switzerland, with close ties to the EU.

Predecessors   Because of the economic and human destruction left by World War II, European political leaders realized that greater cooperation among their countries would help speed up recovery. Many organizations were formed, including the European Economic Community (EEC), which eventually emerged as the organization that would bring together the countries of Europe into the most powerful trading bloc in the world. Several other countries, including the United Kingdom, formed the European Free Trade Association (EFTA) with the limited goal of eliminating internal tariffs. But most of those countries eventually became part of the EU, and those that have decided not to leave EFTA (Iceland, Liechtenstein, Norway, and Switzerland) are linked together with the EU as a customs union. Iceland has applied to be a member of the EU.

The EEC, later called the European Community (EC) and finally the EU, set about to abolish internal tariffs to integrate European markets more closely and, ideally, to allow economic cooperation to help avoid further political conflict.

Organizational Structure   The EU encompasses many governing bodies, among which are the European Commission, Council of the European Union, European Parliament, European Court of Justice, and European Central Bank.[21]

In Chapter 3, we noted how important it is for MNE management to understand the political environment of every country where it operates. The same is true for the EU. To be successful in Europe, MNEs need to understand the EU's governance process, just as they need to understand the governance process of each individual European country in which they invest or do business. These institutions set parameters within which companies must operate, so management needs to understand the institutions and how they make decisions that could affect corporate strategy. Recall from our opening case, for example, how EU policies shaped Toyota's corporate strategy in the region, inducing it to shift from limited exporting to the establishment of full design and manufacturing facilities.

Case Review Note

Key Governing Bodies The European Commission provides the EU's political leadership and direction. It is composed of commissioners nominated by each member government and approved by the European Parliament for a five-year term of office. The president of the commission is nominated by the member governments and approved by the European Parliament. The commissioners run the different programs of the EU on a day-to-day basis rather than serve as representatives of their respective governments. The commission drafts laws that it submits to the European Parliament and the Council of the European Union.

> The European Commission provides political leadership, drafts laws, and runs the various daily programs of the EU.

The Council of the European Union is composed of representatives of each member country whose interests it represents. Along with the European Parliament, the council is responsible for passing laws and making and enacting major policies, including those in the areas of security and foreign policy. The respective ministers of each country meet periodically to discuss the issues facing those ministries (ministers of agriculture meet to discuss issues facing agriculture, etc.). The presidents and/or prime ministers meet up to four times a year to set broad policy.

> The Council of the European Union, or European Summit, is composed of the heads of state of each member country.

The Parliament is composed of 736 members from all 27 member nations; they are elected every five years, and membership is based on country population. Its three major responsibilities are legislative power, control over the budget, and supervision of

> The three major responsibilities of the European Parliament are legislative power, control over the budget, and supervision of executive decisions.

◄ The European Parliament Building in Strasbourg, France, is the home to the 736-member Parliament representing the 27 member nations of the EU.
Source: AND Inc./Shutterstock.com

executive decisions. The commission presents community legislation to the Parliament, which must approve the legislation before it is submitted to the council for adoption.[22]

The Court of Justice ensures consistent interpretation and application of EU treaties. Member states, EC institutions, and individuals and companies may bring cases to the Court, which serves as an appeals court for individuals, firms, and organizations fined by the commission for infringing treaty law.[23]

> The European Court of Justice ensures consistent interpretation and application of EU treaties.

Antitrust Investigations

The EU has been very aggressive in enforcing antitrust laws in the area of high-tech where intellectual property is a very sensitive issue as countries move to protect their own industries from possible violations by foreign companies.

In 2009 Microsoft bowed to pressure from European antitrust regulators, agreeing to let European users of its Windows software have the option to choose which Web browsers they would like to use and be able to turn off Internet Explorer. Microsoft had already paid the equivalent of $2.4 billion in fines and penalties.[24] Antitrust investigations were also levied against IBM, SAP, Google, and Intel. Intel was fined €1 billion for their violations in constraining rival AMD.[25] Google, which is facing antitrust investigations in the United States, is being investigated in the EU for allegedly giving preferential placement to Google services and unfavorable treatment to competitors' services.[26]

The Single European Act and the Lisbon Treaty

> The Single European Act was designed to eliminate the remaining nontariff barriers to trade in Europe.

The passage of the Single European Act of 1987 was designed to eliminate the remaining barriers to a free market, such as customs posts and different certification procedures, rates of value-added tax, and excise duties. In addition, the Act resulted in closer cooperation in trade (the EU has one negotiator for the WTO who negotiates for all EU members), foreign policy, and the environment. However, there are still barriers, which is only natural given the diverse nature of the EU. One area has to do with labeling. The EU is considering country of origin labels for products sold in the EU, even though that is standard practice in many countries (the United States has required country-of-origin labels since the 1930s). One reason to encourage this policy is to protect companies that currently manufacture in Europe. However, exporters from China and other countries (including the United States) worry that this policy will discriminate against their products. As a Chinese official pointed out, "This will cause European investors to think twice about investing in China."[27]

The **Lisbon Treaty,** which went into effect on December 1, 2009, is a new treaty that amends the earlier treaties that led to the creation of the EU. Some of the major objectives of the Lisbon Treaty are to strengthen the governance process of the EU and improve the ability of the EU to make and implement decisions. However, some opponents view the new treaty as part of an agenda to create a stronger federalist union that reduces national sovereignty. It was difficult to pass, but finally all member countries voted to adopt the treaty.[28]

> The Treaty of Maastricht sought to foster political union and monetary union.

Monetary Union

In 1992, the members of the EU signed the Treaty of Maastricht in part to establish a monetary union. The decision to move to a common currency, the **euro,** in Europe has eliminated currency as a barrier to trade for member countries that have adopted it. As of June 7, 2011, 17 of the EU members had adopted the euro, with the late 2010 addition of Estonia. Others are preparing to adopt the euro as well, and only Denmark, Sweden, and the United Kingdom have opted out of the common currency. Other European countries also use the euro, even though they are not members of the EU. We'll discuss the euro in more detail in Chapter 10 as well as the debt crisis that began with Ireland, then spread to Greece, Spain, Italy, and Portugal. The inability of these countries to meet their external debt obligations has threatened the banking system and forced other European countries to come to the rescue. This could be the single biggest challenge to the EU and threatens the future of the euro.

> The euro
> - Is a common currency in Europe.
> - Is administered by the European Central Bank.
> - Was established on January 1, 1999.
> - Resulted in new bank notes in 2002.
> - Does not include the United Kingdom, Denmark, Sweden, or eight of the new entrants to the EU.

> The EU expanded from 15 to 25 countries in 2004 with countries from mostly Central and Eastern Europe. In 2007, it admitted Romania and Bulgaria, bringing the number to 27.

Expansion

One of the EU's major challenges is that of expansion. The May 2004 expansion has been its largest and included Cyprus, the Czech Republic, Estonia, Hungary, Latvia, Lithuania, Malta, Poland, the Slovak Republic, and Slovenia. Bulgaria and Romania were admitted at the beginning of 2007, and candidates for future membership currently include Iceland, Turkey, the former Yugoslav Republic of Macedonia, and Croatia. However, Turkey has been put on hold while it continues to improve its human rights record. Turkey offers many opportunities with its population of 78.8 million, second only to Germany with 82 million people. It has a strong manufacturing base and already strong trade ties with Europe. However, Turkey also is a Muslim country with 99.8 percent of population Sunni Muslim, although the government is a secular parliamentary representative democracy. Turkey has a unique history blending the Byzantine Empire and the Ottoman Empire. It straddles Europe and Asia and its progress toward future membership in the EU will be interesting to watch.

In July 2009, Iceland was put on a fast track to membership and began leapfrogging several countries that were in the queue to join. Despite the collapse of Iceland's currency and economy, the country is better poised to join the EU than some other candidates.

Old and New Members The acquisition of the 12 new countries increased the EU's population and added economic output, but the expansion brought in poor countries with fledgling democracies and high dependence on agriculture. Although the global financial crisis has exposed problems in all the EU member countries, the poorer countries of Eastern Europe have really suffered. When exports fell and capital inflows dried up, their currencies fell as well. The new members are becoming quite a challenge for the stability of the EU, despite the hope they initially brought as new, dynamic economies.

Despite the growth rates, many people from these countries are trying to emigrate to the higher-income nations, creating further challenges. The free movement of people is one of the "four freedoms" of movement of the EU (also including goods, services, and capital), allowing people to move freely within the EU without border controls once they enter one EU country. However, the financial crisis as well as the political crisis in North Africa has created a huge influx of people. Italy and France, for example, recommended that the rules be revised to allow for border controls in the case of exceptional difficulties. Even though Romania and Bulgaria are now members of the EU, they do not have open access to travel until 2014, and Germany and France are making sure they are not permitted to travel visa free until the last possible minute.[29]

Bilateral Agreements   In addition to reducing trade barriers for member countries, the EU has signed numerous bilateral free trade agreements with other countries outside the region. The EU signed a free-trade agreement with six Central American countries in May 2010, but for the treaty to go into effect, each member country must sign the agreement. It has also signed an agreement with Brazil.

Closer to home, the EU entered into an agreement with the EFTA members, excluding Switzerland, to form the European Economic Area (EEA). The three EFTA countries participate in the basic four freedoms with the EU as described above. The difference between the EEA and the expansion of the EU is that the EFTA members are not interested in complete membership in the EU; they just want to take advantage of the free flow of food, labor, services, and capital. However, with Iceland's application to join, EFTA will drop back to three countries. It will be interesting to see what happens to them in the future.

How to Do Business with the EU: Implications for Corporate Strategy   The EU is a tremendous market in terms of both population and income—one that companies cannot ignore. It is also a good example of how geographic proximity and the removal of trade barriers can influence trade. As noted earlier, more than half the merchandise exports and imports of EU countries are considered to be intrazonal trade.

Doing business in the EU can influence corporate strategy, especially for outside MNEs, in three ways:

1. *Determining where to produce.* One strategy is to produce in a central location in Europe to minimize transportation costs and the time it takes to move products from one country to another. However, the highest costs are in central Europe. As we saw in our opening case, for instance, manufacturing wages in the German auto industry

Concept Check

In Chapter 6, we point out that in countries where labor is abundant compared to capital, many workers (not surprisingly) tend to be either unemployed or poorly paid. If permitted, they will migrate to countries that enjoy full employment and higher wages—a form of **factor mobility** that governments in the latter group of countries often restrict.

Implications of the EU for corporate strategy:

- Companies need to determine where to produce products.
- Companies need to determine what their entry strategy will be.
- Companies need to balance the commonness of the EU with national differences.

Case Review Note

top $40 per hour, compared with much lower wages in Eastern European members. That's why Toyota opted to set up operations in lower-wage countries such as the Czech Republic and Poland.

2. *Determining whether to grow through new investments, through expanding existing investments, or through joint ventures and mergers.* As we've seen, Toyota has entered into a joint venture with PSA Peugeot-Citroën to build a new factory in the Czech Republic in order to take advantage of the European carmaker's supplier network. Mergers and acquisitions have really picked up in Europe. The market is still considered fragmented and inefficient compared with the United States, so most experts feel that mergers, takeovers, and spinoffs will continue in Europe for years to come. U.S. companies are buying European companies to gain a market presence and to get rid of competition.

3. *Balancing "common" denominators with national differences.* To quote the phrase "distance matters,"[30] there are wider national differences in the EU than in various U.S. states, mostly due to language and history. But there are also widely different growth rates. Many smaller nations, such as Ireland and Belgium, are experiencing unprecedented growth because their membership has increased their attractiveness for FDI, helped them develop global perspectives, and sheltered them from economic risks.

A good example of adapting business strategies to Europe is Toyota. In terms of products, Toyota is busy designing a European car, but for which Europe? Tastes and preferences—not to mention climate—vary greatly between northern and southern Europe. Toyota, however, is attempting to use production location and design to facilitate a pan-European strategy.

Companies will always struggle with the degree to which they develop a European strategy versus different national strategies inside Europe. In spite of the challenges, there are many opportunities for companies to expand their markets and sources of supply as the EU grows and encompasses more of Europe.

The North American Free Trade Agreement
• Includes Canada, the United States, and Mexico.
• Went into effect on January 1, 1994.
• Involves free trade in goods, services, and investment.
• Is a large trading bloc but includes countries of different sizes and wealth.

NAFTA rationale:

• U.S.-Canadian trade is the largest bilateral trade in the world.
• The United States is Mexico's and Canada's largest trading partner.

THE NORTH AMERICAN FREE TRADE AGREEMENT (NAFTA)

Various forms of mutual economic cooperation have historically existed between the United States and Canada, such as the Canada-U.S. Free Trade Agreement of 1989, which eliminated all tariffs on bilateral trade by 1998. In February 1991, Mexico approached the United States to establish a free trade agreement. Canada was included in the formal negotiations that began that summer and the resulting **North American Free Trade Agreement (NAFTA)** became effective on January 1, 1994.

Why NAFTA? NAFTA has a logical rationale in terms of both geographic location and trading importance. Although Canadian–Mexican trade was not significant when the agreement was signed, the U.S. had key trade relationships with each of them. In fact, the one between the United States and Canada is the largest in the world. As Table 8.2 indicates, NAFTA is a powerful trading bloc with a combined population and GDP slightly less than the 27-member EU. What is significant, especially when compared with the EU, is the tremendous size of the U.S. economy compared to those of its neighbors. In addition, Canada has a much richer economy than that of Mexico, even though its population is about a third of Mexico's. However, the EU has its own disparities. Germany, the largest country in the EU, has a population of 82 million people as noted above, whereas Malta, the smallest country, has a population of 408,000, and the average population in the EU is only 18 million people.

NAFTA is a free trade agreement in goods and services rather than a customs union or a common market. However, its cooperation extends far beyond reductions in tariff and nontariff barriers to include provisions for services, investment, and intellectual property. In addition, the agreement establishes a new dispute resolution process, but it does not include a common currency.

TABLE 8.2 Comparative Statistics by Trade Group

	Population in Millions (2009)	GDP Billions of $ (2009)	Per Capita GDP in $ (2009)
European Union (EU)	582.9	15,161.71	16,011
North American Free Trade Agreement (NAFTA)	461	17,557	38,085
Southern Common Market (MECOSUR)	254	2,102.2	8,276
ASEAN Free Trade Area (AFTA)*	559	3,017.45	5,394
Common Market of Eastern and Southern Africa (COMESA)	403.6	1,076.1	2,666
Pan Arab Free Trade Area (PAFTA) **	346.8	3,284.62	9,000

* The AFTA population and income numbers do not include Myanmar because that information is not available.

** Also known as the Greater Arab Free Trade Area (GAFTA). The population and income numbers do not include Palestine because that information is not available. Based on information from the CIA World Fact Book

Mexico made significant strides in tariff reduction after joining GATT in 1986, when its tariffs averaged 100 percent. As of January 1, 2008, all tariffs and quotas were eliminated on U.S. exports to Canada and Mexico.

Static and Dynamic Effects NAFTA provides the static and dynamic effects of economic integration discussed earlier in this chapter. For example, Canadian and U.S. consumers benefit from lower-cost agricultural products from Mexico, a *static* effect of economic liberalization. U.S. producers also benefit from the large and growing Mexican market, which has a huge appetite for U.S. products—a *dynamic* effect.

Trade Diversion NAFTA is also a good example of trade diversion. Prior to the agreement, many U.S. and Canadian companies had established manufacturing facilities in Asia to take advantage of low-cost labor. IBM, for example, was making computer parts in Singapore. After NAFTA, Mexico became a good option for those companies, and in five years IBM boosted exports from Mexico to the United States from $350 million to $2 billion.

Non-NAFTA companies are also investing in Mexico to take advantage of its FTA with Canada and the United States. Sony has huge manufacturing facilities there, especially in Tijuana, just over the border from Southern California. In 2009, Sony closed five factories worldwide and expanded its workforce in Tijuana, adding 1,500 new jobs to take up the slack.[31] The company is able to take advantage of NAFTA free trade provisions to ship products to the United States and save on time and transportation costs. Sony, Samsung, Sanyo, Panasonic, LG, and Sharp manufacture television sets in their facilities in Tijuana, most of which are exported to the United States, Europe, and elsewhere.

Rules of Origin and Regional Content An important component of NAFTA is the concept of rules of origin and regional content. Because it is a free trade agreement and not a customs union, each country sets its own tariffs to the rest of the world. That's why a product entering the United States from Canada must have a commercial or customs invoice that identifies the product's ultimate origin. Otherwise, an exporter from a third country could always ship the product to the NAFTA country with the lowest tariff and then re-export it to the other two countries duty-free. A major criticism of RTAs like NAFTA is that the rules of origin are complex and detract from the spirit of multilateral tariff reductions in the WTO.

Rules of Origin "Rules of origin" ensure that only goods that have been the subject of substantial economic activity within the free trade area are eligible for the more liberal tariff conditions created by NAFTA. This is a major contrast with the EU, which is a customs union rather than just an FTA. When a product enters France, for example, it can be shipped anywhere in the EU without worrying about rules of origin, because tariffs are the same for all member countries. If NAFTA were a customs union instead of a free trade agreement, a product entering Mexico from, say Japan and shipped to the United States would enter the U.S. duty-free because both countries would have the same duty on imports.[32]

NAFTA calls for the elimination of tariff and nontariff barriers, the harmonization of trade rules, the liberalization of restrictions on services and foreign investment, the enforcement of intellectual property rights, and a dispute settlement process.

NAFTA is a good example of trade diversion; Some U.S. trade with and investment in Asia have been diverted to Mexico.

Rules of origin—goods and services must originate in North America to get access to lower tariffs.

It is interesting to note that there are different rules-of-origin in the EU and NAFTA. In the EU, the country-of-origin depends on where the product becomes what is shipped to the EU. In the United States, the country-of-origin depends on where the product acquires most of its value. A chair made with wood from Indonesia and assembled in Thailand would have a label of "Made in Thailand" if it were shipped to the EU. However, if the value added in Thailand were less than the cost of the wood from Indonesia, the chair would have a label of "Made in Indonesia" if it were shipped to a NAFTA country. Imagine the labeling problems for a company like IKEA that assembles a product in one country, like Thailand in this case, and ships it all over the world to countries that have different points of view as to rules-of-origin.[33]

Regional content:

- The percentage of value that must be from North America for the product to be considered North American in terms of country of origin.
- 50 percent for most products; 62.5 percent for autos.

Rules of Regional Content   According to regional content rules, at least 50 percent of the net cost of most products must come from the NAFTA region. The exceptions are 55 percent for footwear, 62.5 percent for passenger automobiles and light trucks (plus their engines and transmissions), and 60 percent for other vehicles and automotive parts.[34] For example, a Ford car assembled in Mexico could use parts from Canada, the United States, and Mexico, as well as labor and other factors from Mexico. For the car to enter Canada and the United States according to the preferential NAFTA duty, at least 62.5 percent of its value must come from North America.

Additional NAFTA provisions:

- Workers' rights.
- The environment.
- Dispute resolution mechanism.

Special Provisions   Most FTAs in the world are based solely on one goal: to reduce tariffs. However, NAFTA is different. Because of labor unions' and environmentalists' strong objections, two auxiliary agreements covering their concerns were included in the agreement. In the first debates, opponents worried about the potential loss of jobs in Canada and the United States to Mexico as a result of its cheaper wages, poor working conditions, and lax environmental enforcement. U.S. union organizers, in particular, thought companies would close down factories in the north and set them up in Mexico. As a result, the labor lobby in the United States forced the inclusion of labor standards such as the right to unionize, while the environmental lobby pushed for an upgrade of environmental standards in Mexico and the strengthening of compliance.

This is a challenge internationally because not all countries care about labor and environmental standards. The United States often uses trade agreements to advance political and moral objectives. When China enters into a preferential trade agreement with other countries, it does not include such objectives in the agreements. Thus, it is easier for countries to enter into trade agreements with China than with the United States.

The Impact of NAFTA   There are pros and cons to any trade agreement, and NAFTA is no exception. It is obvious that trade and investment have increased significantly since the agreement was signed in 1994. U.S. goods and services trade with NAFTA totaled $1.6 trillion in 2009 (latest data available on goods and services trade).[35] Canada is the largest export market for U.S. goods, and Mexico is number two (the 27 members of the EU are number 1, but Canada and Mexico are more important trading partners than any individual member of the EU). China, Canada, and Mexico are the three largest exporter countries to the U.S. market.

Because of its size, the U.S. is very important to Canada and Mexico for both exports and imports. Canada exports 75 percent of its merchandise to the U.S. and receives 51.2 percent of its imports from there. For Mexico, the numbers are 80.7 percent and 48.1 percent, respectively. Although trade between Canada and Mexico has grown since the implementation of NAFTA, the United States is still the most significant market for their companies because of its size.

A major challenge to NAFTA is illegal immigration.

Immigration   A major challenge to NAFTA is immigration. As trade in agriculture increased with the advent of NAFTA, more than a million farm jobs disappeared in Mexico due to U.S. competition. Many of these farmers ended up as undocumented workers in the United States, sending home more money in wire transfers (see the opening case in

Chapter 9) than Mexico receives in FDI. This has become a major political issue in both countries, especially as the United States tries to figure out how to stop the flow of illegal immigrants and what to do with those already in the United States. As we have seen in the EU, immigration is not easy anywhere in the world, even in areas where free mobility of labor is supposed to exist. Obviously, illegal immigration is a big problem on both sides of the border, and politics plays a huge role in immigration policies.

How to Do Business with NAFTA: Implications for Corporate Strategy   Although NAFTA has not expanded beyond the original three countries due to political obstacles, each member has entered into bilateral agreements with other countries. However, when U.S. companies invest in Mexico, for example, they have an opportunity to penetrate markets in countries where Mexico has free trade agreements, as we will see in the case on Walmart at the end of the chapter. That allows them to add additional scale as the market broadens, even though countries with which Mexico has an FTA are not members of NAFTA.

Predictions and Outcomes   One of the predictions made when NAFTA was signed was that companies would look at it as one big regional market, allowing them to rationalize production, products, financing, and the like. That has largely happened in a number of industries, especially in automotive products and electronics. Each NAFTA member ships more automotive products, based on specialized production, to the other two countries than any other manufactured goods. Rationalization of automotive production has taken place for years in the United States and Canada, but Mexico is a recent entrant, attracting auto manufacturing from all over the world, not just the United States. NAFTA's rules of origin requiring 62.5 percent regional content have forced European and Asian automakers to bring in parts suppliers and set up assembly operations in Mexico. In one case, a Canadian entrepreneur established a metal-stamping plant in Puebla to supply Volkswagen, assembling the revitalized Beetle that is being supplied to the U.S. market.[36] When Daimler Benz purchased Chrysler, it began producing the PT Cruiser in Toluca for export to Canada, the United States, and Europe, using that one plant to manufacture one model for the entire world.

The story of DaimlerChrysler's production in the United States is similar. In 1993, it exported only 5,300 vehicles to Mexico. The following year, after the signing of NAFTA, it exported 17,500; in 2000, it was 60,000.[37] These examples indicate how production is intertwined among the member countries. Volkswagen AG opened a new manufacturing plant in Tennessee in 2011 to manufacture the Passat for the U.S. market, but it still assembles the Beetle in Mexico.[38] Auto assembly in the NAFTA environment is not an either-or situation. Some parts and models are produced and assembled in one country, whereas others are produced in others. And production is for local consumption as well as exported to all countries in NAFTA as well as other countries outside of NAFTA.

It is true that a lot of investment has expanded throughout the NAFTA region, and some investment may have resulted in jobs leaving Canada and the United States for lower-wage Mexico. U.S. FDI in Canada and Mexico has increased by 125 percent since 1993, and the stock of FDI exceeds the combined investments of Canadian and Mexican companies in the U.S. But some U.S. industries, such as automobiles, have moved from the higher-cost industrial heartland to the southern part of the United States where wages are lower and unions not as strong. Some of the "hollowing out" of industry has actually been a change in location inside the United States. A second prediction was that sophisticated U.S. companies would run Canadian and Mexican companies out of business once the markets opened up. That has not happened. In fact, U.S. firms along the Canadian border are finding that Canadian companies are generating more competition for them than low-wage Mexican companies. Also, many Mexican companies have restructured to compete with U.S. and Canadian firms. The lack of protection has resulted in much more competitive Mexican companies. However, as was discussed in the context of agriculture, some industries have been hard hit by U.S. competitors.

Concept Check

As you'll recall from Chapter 6, trade restrictions may diminish export capabilities and induce companies to locate some production in countries imposing the restrictions; the absence of trade barriers gives them more flexibility not only in deciding where to locate production but also in determining how to service different markets.

Case Review Note

And as we show in the Walmart case at the end of the chapter, Mexican retailers have had a difficult time adjusting to giant competitors like Walmart, Target, Costco, and Carrefour.

A final prediction had to do with looking at Mexico as a consumer market rather than just a production location. Initially, the excitement over Mexico for U.S. and Canadian companies was the low-wage environment. However, as Mexican income continues to rise—which it must do as more investment enters and more of its companies export production—demand is rising for foreign products.

However, the NAFTA agreement has not solved every problem. NAFTA was supposed to create a cross-border trucking program by 2000, but the International Brotherhood of Teamsters and its allies in the U.S. Congress blocked implementation on the grounds of safety concerns over Mexican trucks, so Mexico retaliated with tariffs on exports of some U.S. products to Mexico, which hurt unionized workers in the U.S.[39] Although the Obama administration proposed a three-year pilot program in April 2011 to see if some of the problems could be resolved, it is not clear how long it will take to finally implement this piece of NAFTA.[40]

REGIONAL ECONOMIC INTEGRATION IN THE AMERICAS

If you look at Maps 8.2 and 8.3, you'll see six major regional economic groups in the Americas, divided into Central American and South American. Central America (excluding Mexico) has the Caribbean Community (CARICOM), the Central American Common Market (CACM), and the Central American Free Trade Agreement (CAFTA-DR)—which includes the members of CACM but also Honduras and the Dominican Republic, along with the United States. The two major groups in South America are the Andean Community (CAN) and the Southern Common Market (MERCOSUR). The Andean Community is a customs union, whereas MERCOSUR is set up to be a common market.

MAP 8.2   Economic Integration in Central America and the Caribbean

Throughout Central America and the Caribbean, the focus on economic integration has shifted from the concept of the *free trade agreement* (whose goal is the abolition of trade barriers among members) to that of the *common market* (which calls for internal factor mobility as well as the abolition of internal trade barriers). The proposed structure of the Caribbean Community and Common Market (CARICOM) is modeled on that of the EU.

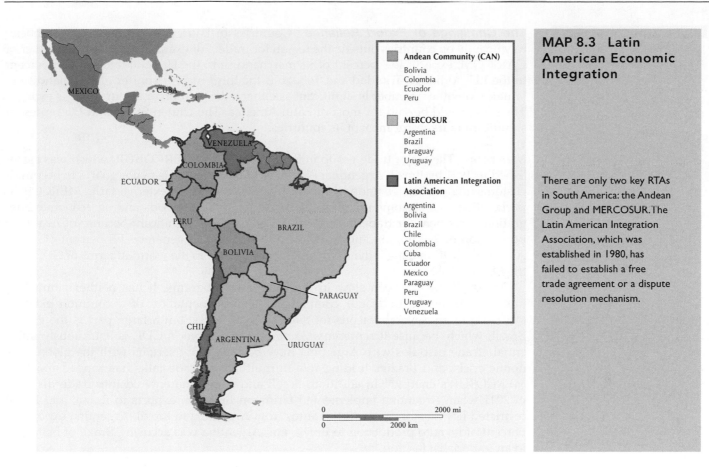

MAP 8.3 Latin American Economic Integration

Andean Community (CAN)
Bolivia
Colombia
Ecuador
Peru

MERCOSUR
Argentina
Brazil
Paraguay
Uruguay

Latin American Integration Association
Argentina
Bolivia
Brazil
Chile
Colombia
Cuba
Ecuador
Mexico
Paraguay
Peru
Uruguay
Venezuela

There are only two key RTAs in South America: the Andean Group and MERCOSUR. The Latin American Integration Association, which was established in 1980, has failed to establish a free trade agreement or a dispute resolution mechanism.

Other South American groups have popped up, but they are fairly new and limited in influence. One is UNASUR, the Union of South American Nations, which covers 12 countries and hopes to become like the EU at some point. Brazil helped initiate UNASUR to foster political cooperation and to replace a U.S. initiative to create a 34-nation Free Trade of the Americas. Mexico, Colombia, Peru, and Chile have engaged in talks to create a regional trade group as well. In reality, a string of bilateral treaties or regional treaties involving fewer countries that are close geographically have probably been more effective than the larger regional groups.

The major reason for these different collaborative groups was market size. The post–World War II strategy of import substitution to resolve balance-of-payments problems in much of Latin America was doomed because of the region's small national markets. Therefore, some form of economic cooperation was needed to enlarge the potential market size so that Latin American companies could achieve economies of scale and be more competitive worldwide.

Caricom: Benchmarking the EU Model The **Caribbean Community (CARICOM)** is working hard to establish an EU-style form of collaboration, complete with full movement of goods and services, the right of establishment, a common external tariff, free movement of capital and labor, a common trade policy, and so on. It is officially classified by the WTO as an economic integration agreement. Many of these initiatives have come about through an initiative called the CARICOM Single Market and Economy (CSME).

In some ways, the changes in the Caribbean Community mirror what has happened in the EU, though on a smaller scale. The entire population is only 6.5 million people, 60 percent of whom live in only two countries: Jamaica and Trinidad and Tobago. That would put it on the level of EU member Bulgaria in terms of population. However, it is important for CARICOM to succeed in order to expand market size and attract more investment and jobs.

MERCOSUR is a customs union among Argentina, Brazil, Paraguay, and Uruguay.

The Challenge of Export Reliance   Countries in Latin America and the Caribbean rely heavily on countries outside the region for trade. For example, Jamaica, a member of CARICOM, exports 49.3 percent of its merchandise to the United States and 18 percent to the EU. Although Trinidad and Tobago is the third major exporter of merchandise to Jamaica, no other member is significant as either a destination or a source for its exports. The same could be said for most of Latin America. The United States and EU represent significant markets for most of its countries.

Mercosur   The major trade group in South America is **MERCOSUR,** which was established in 1991 by Brazil, Argentina, Paraguay, and Uruguay. Its major goal is to become a customs union with free trade within the bloc and a common external tariff. MERCOSUR is classified as a customs union by the WTO for trade in goods and an economic integration agreement for trade in services. MERCOSUR is significant because of its size: a population of 242 million and a GDP of $1.95 trillion. It generates 75 percent of South America's GDP, making it the third largest trading bloc in the world in terms of GDP after the EU and NAFTA.

MERCOSUR has been slow in implementing programs. It has neither eliminated internal barriers to trade nor completed the implementation of a common external tariff. There are several reasons for such slow progress, but a large part is the role of Brazil, which, because it represents 70 percent of the bloc's GDP, is enormously influential. Trade disputes with Argentina have become more serious with the global economic crisis, and Brazil's leading role in multilateral trade talks has sapped much of MERCOSUR's energy.[41] In addition, Brazil and Argentina entered into trade disputes in 2011 when Argentina implemented tariffs on Brazilian exports to Brazil, and Brazil restricted licenses for the export of autos from Argentina to Brazil. Argentina exports 85 percent of its auto production to Brazil, and Argentina was accusing Brazil of behaving in an imperialist fashion.[42]

The Andean Community is one of the original regional economic groups but has not been successful in achieving its original goals.

Andean Community (CAN)   Although the **Andean Community (CAN)** is not as significant economically as MERCOSUR, it is the second most important regional group in South America. CAN has been around since 1969. However, its focus has shifted from one of isolationism and statism (placing economic control in the hands of the state—the central government) to being open to foreign trade and investment.

Latin American Integration Association (LAIA)   The LAIA includes members of MERCOSUR and CAN, as well as Chile, Cuba, and Mexico. Its predecessor was the Latin American Free Trade Association, which was signed into effect in 1960. However, the LAIA was signed in 1980 with the hope of going beyond an FTA to becoming a common market. In spite of being around for a long time, LAIA has not been able to achieve the status of a free trade agreement.

REGIONAL ECONOMIC INTEGRATION IN ASIA

Of the several RTAs in Asia recognized by the WTO, the most important is the Association of Southeast Asian Nations/ASEAN Free Trade Area. As is the case in Latin America, regional integration in Asia has not been as successful as in Europe or North America because most of the countries in the region have relied on U.S. and EU markets for as much as 20 to 30 percent of their exports—not as extensive as in Latin America but still significant. In addition, China and Japan, which are not members of ASEAN/AFTA, are significant players in the region in terms of trade and investment.

Association of Southeast Asian Nations (ASEAN)   Organized in 1967, the **Association of Southeast Asian Nations (ASEAN)** is a preferential trade agreement that comprises Brunei Darussalam, Cambodia, China, Indonesia, Laos, Malaysia, Myanmar, the

Is CAFTA-DR a Good Idea?

Point   **Yes** The Dominican Republic-Central America-United States Free Trade Agreement is a *great* idea. Linking the United States together with six other countries—Costa Rica, Dominican Republic, El Salvador, Guatemala, Honduras, and Nicaragua—the FTA holds enormous benefits for its signatories: opening the door for increased trade between the United States and the region; stimulating economic growth in the region by encouraging FDI and offering shorter international supply chains; and encouraging economic and political reform in an area historically plagued by Marxism, dictatorships, and civil wars.

The United States has 11 FTAs in force with 17 countries (as of June 1, 2011) and hopes to complete agreements with Korea, Panama, and Colombia. CAFTA-DR is an example of an FTA that is successful.

One of the biggest benefits for the United States is reciprocal tariff treatment from the other nations. Due to temporary trade-preference programs and other regional agreements, 80 percent of the products from at least five Central American nations already enter the United States duty-free. Prior to signing the agreement, U.S. manufactured exports were subject to tariffs that averaged 30 to 100 percent higher than those faced by Central American exports when entering the United States.[43] CAFTA-DR will allow the Central American nations to maintain these favorable gains, but it will also level the playing field for the United States to benefit similarly by reducing restrictions on 80 percent of U.S. consumer and industrial exports to the region, with the rest to be phased out over 10 years. Since the agreement is not a customs union, products eligible for the benefits must meet relevant rules of origin, similar to the provisions of NAFTA.

CAFTA-DR was the fifteenth largest U.S. export market in the world in 2010 and the third largest export market in Latin America after Mexico and Brazil.[44]

There's fear that the freer inflow of Central American agricultural products will undercut U.S. prices. But again, the United States is already largely open to these products, and although the heavily subsidized U.S. sugar industry adamantly opposed CAFTA-DR, the sugar deal will set a quota that will amount to only 1.7 percent of U.S. production in 15 years.

Although many critics argue that the benefits certain CAFTA-DR countries gain will come at the expense of other participating countries, in truth the gains will be mutual. For example, the growth that CAFTA-DR will foster in Central American industries, particularly its apparel industry, will also benefit exporters in the United States whose products are used in their manufacturing processes. Fifty-six percent of the apparel exports from the Central American region are produced from textiles exported from the United States; 40 percent of U.S. yarn exports and about 25 percent of its fabric exports are purchased by these nations. By working together through CAFTA-DR, the United States and Central America will prevent the loss of Central American apparel jobs to China, whose products contain little or no input from the United States. The National Council of Textile Organizations, which represents more than 75 textile companies, strongly supports CAFTA-DR. As the CAFTA-DR Free Trade Commission continues to adapt rules to strengthen the textile/apparel supply chain, U.S. textile and apparel exports increased, resulting in CAFTA-DR taking third place behind Mexico and Canada, whereas exports from the region to the United States trailed only China as a textile and apparel supplier to the United States.[45]

Another argument critics make is that CAFTA-DR will create job market shifts that will lead to thousands of job losses in the manufacturing and agricultural sectors. However, predictions from the U.S. Chamber of Commerce don't bear out this claim. For example, in North Carolina alone, CAFTA-DR should increase industrial output by $3.9 billion and create some 29,000 jobs over nine years. Other sources have stated that 250,000 jobs in Central America depend on CAFTA-DR being approved. And although labor organizations have decried the lack of worker-protection clauses in the agreement, a report from the International Labor Organization actually praises Central American labor laws and standards.[46]

Is CAFTA-DR a Good Idea?

Counterpoint   **No** CAFTA-DR is not a good idea at all—not for the United States or for the impoverished nations it is allegedly supposed to help. Much has been said about how the accord will boost trade between the two regions, support constructive economic and political reforms in Central America, create thousands of jobs, and demonstrate the benefits of free trade and open competition. However, there is neither the evidence to bear out these claims nor consideration for the consequences of the results. Besides, CAFTA-DR undermines the efforts of the WTO to liberalize trade worldwide rather than region by region.

The agreement will open the participating Central American countries to more duty-free exportation on behalf of U.S. manufacturers and farmers, but will this really translate into benefits for either side? The U.S. agricultural industry already can sell pretty much all the products it wants on the worldwide market; what it really needs is an increase in the worldwide market prices, but Central America's economies are too small to even affect world prices. Plus, the increased flow of U.S. corn and rice into Central America will devastate the region's own farm economies.

The idea that it will benefit the region by allowing increased imports to the United States is also faulty. Due to its giant deficit, the United States really cannot afford to tolerate many more imports, and their value to the United States is also expected to decrease, which means Central America will gain little economic advantage from them anyhow, especially given the concessions it must make in return.

In addition, CAFTA-DR will actually be increasing some barriers to free trade. For example, the accord may make it harder for countries such as Guatemala to obtain access to affordable lifesaving medicines because of stringent intellectual property clauses included in the agreement.

CAFTA-DR is also a bad move for labor and workers' rights. It will most likely trigger the loss of manufacturing jobs in the United States and agricultural jobs in Central America. Although proponents of the deal assert that it will stem illegal immigration from these poorer nations, the shift in jobs will most likely increase immigration, as it did with NAFTA.

Furthermore, it will trigger a "race to the bottom" when it comes to wages. The accord will open up U.S. labor markets to competition against a low-wage area, which will drive down the current wage level. NAFTA and other trade agreements currently in place have already stymied wage growth, which had been 9 percent over the last 30 years compared to an increase of 80 percent in worker productivity. And this depression of wages and shift of jobs created by current agreements has done little to improve the economic conditions of the developing Central American nations, where wages have grown only 12 percent since 1980, compared to 80 percent during the period between 1960 and 1979. Furthermore, no clauses in the agreement address the protection of workers or the banning of child labor.[47]

Because the accord involves developing countries with vastly different interests than the United States, it will be hard to please all parties. Costa Rica had a hard time ratifying the agreement and only came on board on January 1, 2009, long after the final agreement went into force in 2007 in the Dominican Republic. Costa Rica faced opposition from trade unions, farm groups, and even businesses, as well as fears about the accord's stringent intellectual-property clauses and the chance that it might force the country to privatize its free universal healthcare system. Costa Rica's hesitancy undermines the argument posed by Washington: that CAFTA-DR is something earnestly sought after by struggling Central American countries.[48]

In spite of the concerns, the agreement was implemented by all of the parties. U.S. exports to CAFTA-DR increased by 43 percent in the five years that the agreement has been in force, compared with an increase of only 25 percent in the five years prior to the agreement. It seems to have helped U.S. exports to the region, but have the CAFTA-DR countries benefited as well? Time will tell.

Philippines, Singapore, Thailand, and Vietnam (see Map 8.4). With a combined GDP of $1.5 trillion, total trade of $1.5 trillion, and an estimated population of 577 million people[49]—making it the fourth largest FTA in the world—ASEAN promotes cooperation in many areas, including industry and trade. Member countries are protected in terms of tariff and nontariff barriers, yet they hold promise for market and investment opportunities because of their large market size.

| The ASEAN Free Trade Area is a successful trade agreement among countries in Southeast Asia.

ASEAN Free Trade Area   On January 1, 1993, ASEAN officially formed the ASEAN Free Trade Area (AFTA) with the goal of cutting tariffs on all intrazonal trade to a maximum of 5 percent by January 1, 2008. The weaker ASEAN countries would be allowed to phase in their tariff reductions over a longer period. By 2005, most products traded among the AFTA countries were subject to duties from 0 to 5 percent, so AFTA has been successful in its objectives. Free trade is crucial to the member countries because their ratio of exports to GDP is almost 70 percent. The best achievement of AFTA is that is has reduced tariffs, attracted FDI, and turned the region into a huge network of production, leading to what some call "factory Asia."[50]

Although China is not a part of ASEAN, it is essential to ASEAN's future. China's working-age population is 798 million people, compared with 298 million for the ASEAN countries. Although the average monthly wages for manufacturing workers is much higher in Singapore ($2,832) and Malaysia ($666.10) than in China ($412.50),

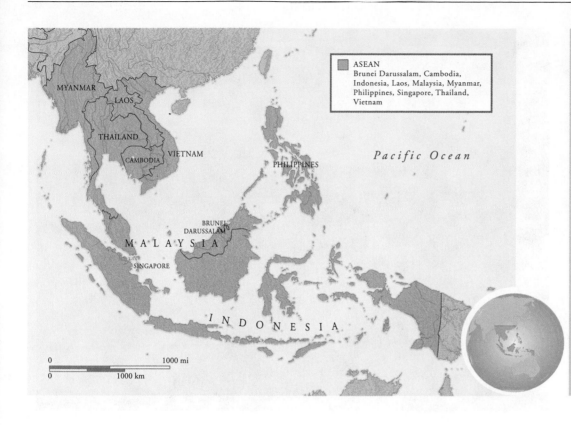

MAP 8.4 The Association of Southeast Asian Nations

Although the total population of ASEAN countries (as of 2004) is larger than that of either the EU or NAFTA, per capita GDP is considerably lower. Economic growth rates among ASEAN members, however, are among the highest in the world.

ASEAN
Brunei Darussalam, Cambodia, Indonesia, Laos, Malaysia, Myanmar, Philippines, Singapore, Thailand, Vietnam

wages are much lower in the other ASEAN countries. As wages continue to rise in China, there are opportunities for ASEAN countries to attract more FDI, but the ASEAN countries need to work hard to improve their infrastructure, especially supply chain and manufacturing infrastructure.[51] These opportunities combined with the competitive position of China are forcing ASEAN to work harder to strengthen the ties among member countries.

Asia Pacific Economic Cooperation (APEC) Formed in November 1989 to promote multilateral economic cooperation in trade and investment in the Pacific Rim,[52] **Asia Pacific Economic Cooperation (APEC)** is composed of 21 countries that border both Asia and the Americas. All but three members of AFTA are members of APEC, plus Canada, the United States, Mexico, Peru and Chile in the Americas; Australia and New Zealand; and China, Japan, Korea, Russia, and Chinese Taipei. It is a large and powerful organization that is focused on a wide range of activities related to trade and investment, security, energy, sustainability, and anti-corruption and transparency among other things. However, it is not an RTA as defined by the WTO and does not show up on that list of RTAs. The sheer size of APEC is what sets it apart—55 percent of global GDO and 43 percent of world trade. The United States hosted APEC in 2011 for the first time since 1993, and its meetings rotate among the 21 member nations.

APEC comprises 21 countries that border the Pacific Rim; progress toward free trade is hampered by size and geographic distance between member countries and the lack of a treaty.

The Goal of "Open Regionalism" APEC has the potential to become a significant economic bloc, especially because it generates such a large percentage of the world's output and merchandise trade. Its goal is to try to establish "open regionalism," whereby individual member countries can determine whether to apply trade liberalization to non-APEC countries on an unconditional, MFN basis or on a reciprocal, FTA basis. The United States prefers the latter approach. The key will be whether the liberalization process continues at a good pace.

REGIONAL ECONOMIC INTEGRATION IN AFRICA

There are several African trade groups, but they rely more on their former colonial powers and other developed markets for trade than they do on each other.

Africa is complicated because of the large number of countries on the continent and the fact that there are three regional monetary unions and five existing regional trade associations. On Map 8.5, we have selected only four of the RTAs to illustrate the situation in Africa. The problem is that African countries have been struggling to establish a political identity, and the different trade groups have political as well as economic underpinnings. Some African countries are members of more than one RTA. An example is Zambia, which is a member of both SADC and COMESA. That makes sense in one respect since Zambia borders COMESA on the North and SADC on the South. Another example is Egypt, which is a member of the Pan Arab Free Trade Area (also called the Greater Arab Free Trade Area) and COMESA. In addition, Egypt has access to Europe through free trade agreements with the EU and EFTA. Former colonial links are also important. Most but not all of the members of ECOWAS are former French colonies and thus still have economic ties with France.

The **Pan Arab Free Trade Area (PAFTA)** is an interesting group, because its members span North Africa (Egypt, Tunisia, Sudan, Libya, and Morroco) and the Middle East (UAE, Bahrain, Jordan, Saudi Arabia, Syria, Iraq, Oman, Palestine, Qatar, Kuwait, Lebanon, and Yemen). It is officially recognized by the WTO as an RTA, and its goal is to reduce trade barriers among its member countries. In addition to PAFTA, the **Arab League** represents more countries but with political rather than economic objectives. Subsets of Arab League countries, such as the **Gulf Cooperation Council (GCC)** are more effective than the larger Arab League and PAFTA because of the smaller number of countries involved. The GCC basically includes Bahrain, Saudi Arabia, Kuwait, Oman, Qatar, and the UAE. Whereas the African countries have large populations and a variety of natural resources in high demand, PAFTA and the GCC have smaller populations but huge oil and natural gas reserves. Political instability, especially a result of the Arab Spring of 2011, make economic collaboration a huge challenge, at least in the short run. Many of the members of PAFTA were embroiled in serious civil conflict in 2011 as a result of the Arab Spring, and many governments were overturned, complicating future trade deals.

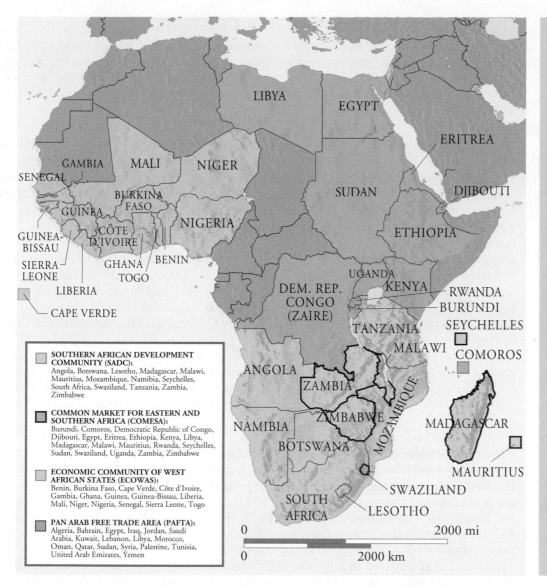

MAP 8.5 Regional Integration in Africa

Although African nations have joined to form several groups for the purpose of economic integration, total amount of trade among members remains relatively small. African nations tend to rely heavily on trading relationships with countries elsewhere in the world—notably with industrialized nations.

SOUTHERN AFRICAN DEVELOPMENT COMMUNITY (SADC):
Angola, Botswana, Lesotho, Madagascar, Malawi, Mauritius, Mozambique, Namibia, Seychelles, South Africa, Swaziland, Tanzania, Zambia, Zimbabwe

COMMON MARKET FOR EASTERN AND SOUTHERN AFRICA (COMESA):
Burundi, Comoros, Democratic Republic of Congo, Djibouti, Egypt, Eritrea, Ethiopia, Kenya, Libya, Madagascar, Malawi, Mauritius, Rwanda, Seychelles, Sudan, Swaziland, Uganda, Zambia, Zimbabwe

ECONOMIC COMMUNITY OF WEST AFRICAN STATES (ECOWAS):
Benin, Burkina Faso, Cape Verde, Côte d'Ivoire, Gambia, Ghana, Guinea, Guinea-Bissau, Liberia, Mali, Niger, Nigeria, Senegal, Sierra Leone, Togo

PAN ARAB FREE TRADE AREA (PAFTA):
Algeria, Bahrain, Egypt, Iraq, Jordan, Saudi Arabia, Kuwait, Lebanon, Libya, Morocco, Oman, Qatar, Sudan, Syria, Palestine, Tunisia, United Arab Emirates, Yemen

The African Union (AU)   One group not shown on Map 8.5 is the African Union, created by 53 countries in 2002 to focus on political issues in Africa, notably colonialism and racism. It has gotten involved in civilian conflicts throughout Africa and is not the organization that is pushing for trade liberalization. Civil war, corruption, diseases such as AIDS, and poor government infrastructures have hampered African countries and their ability to progress economically. The AU now includes every country in Africa except Morocco, and it is pushing aggressively to promote peace and security through openness and democracy. Eventually, the AU wants to push for economic integration, but it is not formally negotiating trade deals, letting the various regional trade groups to do that.[53]

Because most African countries rely more on trade links with former colonial powers than with each other, intrazonal trade is not significant. The markets, with the notable exception of South Africa, are relatively small and undeveloped, making trade liberalization a relatively minor contributor to economic growth in the region. However, any type of market expansion through regional integration will help these small countries.

OTHER FORMS OF INTERNATIONAL COOPERATION

Up to now, this chapter has focused on treaties between nations designed to reduce trade and investment barriers and increase trade and investment among member nations. We moved from the global—the WTO—to the bilateral and the regional. However, there are other forms of cooperation worth mentioning that could have an influence on MNE strategies.

The United Nations   The first form of cooperation worth exploring is the United Nations, which was established in 1945 in response to the devastation of World War II to promote international peace and security and to help solve global problems in such diverse areas as economic development, antiterrorism, and humanitarian actions. If the UN performs its responsibilities, it should improve the environment in which MNEs operate around the world, reducing risk and providing greater opportunities.

> The UN was established in 1945 following World War II to promote international peace and security. It deals with economic development, antiterrorism, and humanitarian movements.

Organization and Membership   The UN family of organizations is too large to list, but it includes the WTO, the International Monetary Fund, and the World Bank (the latter two discussed in subsequent chapters). These organizations are all part of the Economic and Social Council, one of six principal organs of the UN System, which also includes the General Assembly, the Security Council, and the International Court of Justice.

The UN has 192 member states represented in the General Assembly, including 15 member states that comprise the Security Council. There are five permanent members of the Security Council—China, France, the Russian Federation, the United Kingdom, and the United States—and 10 other members elected by the General Assembly to serve two-year terms.[54]

> UNCTAD was established to help developing countries participate in international trade.

Focus on Developing Nations: UNCTAD   As noted, the UN is involved in a variety of social, political, and economic activities. It also tends to focus on the problems of the developing countries in an attempt to resolve major issues facing them. One of the most important organizations in the UN that affects MNEs is the **UN Conference on Trade and Development,** or **UNCTAD,** a program authorized by the General Assembly and established in the 1960s to tackle the problems of those countries in international trade.

UNCTAD is involved in a variety of different activities: trade and commodities; investment, technology, and enterprise development; macroeconomic policies; and debt and development financing, to name just a few. It has also been active in conducting the so-called North-South dialogue (between the developed and the developing countries), formulating international commodities agreements, developing codes of conduct, working to resolve the debt crisis, and a variety of other projects.

> NGOs: Private nonprofit institutions that are independent of the government.

Nongovernmental Organizations (NGOs)   Nongovernmental, nonprofit voluntary organizations are all lumped under the category of NGOs: private institutions that are independent of any government. Some NGOs operate only within the confines of a specific country, whereas others are international in scope. An example of the latter is the International Red Cross, which is concerned with humanitarian issues around the world, not just in one country.

Many NGOs, such as Doctors without Borders, are like the Red Cross in that they are concerned about humanitarian issues. Other NGOs came about as a response to what is perceived as the negative side of globalization. Many of these were discussed in Chapter 5 with respect to environment and labor issues. One example was the U.K.-based Ethical Trading Initiative, or ETI.

Several NGOs concerned about workers' rights, such as Africa Now, Anti-Slavery International, Quaker Peace and Social Witness, Save the Children, and Working Women Worldwide, are members of ETI. NGOs perform an important role in bringing potential abuses to light and tend to be very narrowly focused, usually on a specific issue. There is a Committee on Non-Governmental Organizations that is a part of the Economic and Social Council (ECOSOC) of the UN that meets to discuss issues of importance to general and specific NGOs.

Global Compact As noted in Chapter 5, the United Nations Global Compact is a strategic policy initiative for businesses in the areas of human rights, labor, environment, and anticorruption. Although all of these areas are important, the issues of sustainability and anticorruption seem to be of great significance to the business community, especially in light of our discussions in Chapter 5 on global social responsibility. The Global Compact identifies 10 key principles that should govern the behavior of companies.[55] Its board includes high-profile members of the business community (such as the president and CEO of Petrobras, Brazil), international labor and business organizations (such as the general secretary of the International Trade Union Confederation and the secretary-general of the International Chamber of Commerce), and civil society (such as the Chair of Transparency International). The issues being discussed in the Global Compact and the commitment of the broad community in these efforts are quite important, especially given that the Global Compact has over 8700 corporate participants from over 130 countries.

Commodities and the World Economy

Commodities refer to raw materials or primary products that enter into trade, such as metals or agricultural products. Primary commodity exports—such as crude petroleum, natural gas, copper, tobacco, coffee, cocoa, tea, and sugar—are still important to the developing countries. Out of 143 developing countries, 96 countries, or 67 percent of the total, derive more than 50 percent of their export value from commodities.[56]

Both long-term trends and short-term fluctuations in commodity prices have important consequences for the world economy. On the demand side, commodity markets play an important role in industrial countries, transmitting business cycle disturbances to the rest of the economy and affecting the rate of growth of prices. On the supply side, as noted above, primary products account for a significant portion of the GDP and exports of many commodity-producing countries.

> The attempts of countries to stabilize commodity prices through producer alliances and commodity agreements have been largely unsuccessful.

CONSUMERS AND PRODUCERS

For many years, countries tried to band together as producer alliances or joint producer/consumer alliances to try to stabilize commodity prices. However, these efforts—with the exception of OPEC, which we discuss below—have not been very successful. UNCTAD established a Special Unit on Commodities to attempt to deal with the issues facing developing countries because of high dependence on commodities, especially agricultural commodities, for export revenues.

The most important international commodity organizations and bodies, such as the International Cocoa Organization and the International Copper Study Group, take part in UN-led discussions to help commodity-dependent countries establish effective policies and strategies. However, each one, such as the International Coffee Organization (ICO), has its own organizational structure independent of the UN. For example, the ICO is composed of 45 coffee exporting nations—all of them developing countries—and 32 importing nations, most of which are developed countries. ICO members are responsible for over 97 percent of the world's coffee exports and 80 percent of the world's coffee consumption. The latest agreement, which was signed in 2007, facilitates intergovernmental cooperation and improved transparency and sustainability.[57]

Whereas many of the original commodity agreements were designed to influence price through a variety of market-interfering mechanisms, most of the existing ones have

> **Concept Check**
>
> Commodities often represent natural advantages, which we define in Chapter 6 as advantages in producing products resulting from climatic conditions, access to certain natural resources, or availability of certain labor forces.

> **Concept Check**
>
> Remember from Chapter 6 the fact that lower-income countries depend much more on the production of primary products than do wealthier nations; consequently, they depend more heavily on **natural advantage** as opposed to the kinds of **acquired advantage** that involve more advanced technologies and processes.

Many commodity agreements now exist for the purpose of

- Discussing issues.
- Disseminating information.
- Improving product safety.

been established to discuss issues, disseminate information, improve product safety, and so on. Very little can be done outside of market forces to influence price.

Finally, because commodities are the raw materials used in the production process, it is important for managers of companies that use commodities to understand the factors that influence their prices. Investment and pricing decisions must be based on the cost of inputs, and it is difficult to forecast those costs when the commodities markets are highly volatile.

For many years, commodity prices fluctuated but did not increase dramatically. In the decade of the 2000s, however, global economic growth pulled up those prices. China, in particular, was growing so fast that it was pulling up most of them. This led to trade agreements between China and many commodity-producing countries, as well as substantial foreign investment. The global economic crisis, however, caused a significant contraction in commodity prices of nearly 17 percent in 2009, which had a very negative impact on the economies of the commodity-producing countries. Commodity prices increased by 23 percent from January 1, 2010 to January 2011 as the global economy began to recover.[58]

THE ORGANIZATION OF THE PETROLEUM EXPORTING COUNTRIES (OPEC)

OPEC is a producers' alliance in oil that has been successful in using quotas to keep oil prices high.

The **Organization of the Petroleum Exporting Countries (OPEC)** is an example of a producer cartel that relies on quotas to influence prices. It is a group of commodity-producing countries that have significant control over supply and band together to control output and price. OPEC is part of a larger category of energy commodities, which also includes coal and natural gas. Rather than being confined to the Middle East, its members are Algeria, Angola, Ecuador, Iran, Iraq, Kuwait, Libya, Nigeria, Qatar, Saudi Arabia, the United Arab Emirates, and Venezuela. Indonesia suspended its membership in January 2009.

Price Controls and Politics   OPEC controls prices by establishing production quotas on member countries. Saudi Arabia has historically performed the role of the dominant supplier in influencing supply and price. Periodically—at least annually—OPEC oil ministers gather together to determine the quota for each country based on estimates of supply and demand.

Politics is also an important dimension of the deliberations. OPEC member countries with large populations need large oil revenues to fund government programs. As a result, they are tempted to exceed their export quotas to generate more revenues.

Output and Exports   OPEC member countries produce about 42 percent of the world's crude oil and 18 percent of its natural gas. However, its oil exports represent about 580 percent of the oil traded internationally.[59] In addition, OPEC has 79.6 percent of the world's oil reserves, with the Middle East containing 70 percent of OPEC's total reserves. Therefore, OPEC can have a strong influence on the oil market, especially if it decides to reduce or increase its level of production. However, the biggest producer of crude oil is Russia, followed by Saudi Arabia, the United States, China, and Iran.

Sometimes OPEC policies work; sometimes they don't. In addition, events beyond its control can influence prices. The rapidly escalating price of crude oil in recent years is a mixture of rising demand worldwide (especially in China), political instability in the Middle East, and a shortage of refining capacity and environmental rules in some countries that preclude the building of new refineries. At the height of the global economic growth and strong demand for all commodities, oil prices spiked to $145 a barrel in July 2008 and then dropped to $33 a barrel that December, before rising again to about $68 a barrel in July 2009. During 2010, oil prices averaged $70 to 85 per barrel,

FIGURE 8.2

Source: Felipe Galindo/
www.CartoonStock.com

"The Arab world used to be known for its oil, now for its turmoil!"

and prices were expected to remain stable based on the assumption that the demand had recovered, especially in the emerging markets, and that the worst of the global financial crisis and economic downturn had ended. However, 2011 brought an increase in economic instability in Europe due to the debt problems in Greece as well as political stability across North Africa due to the Arab Spring. By June 13, 2011, prices had reached $113.33 a barrel, and the OPEC meetings ended without any decision about production quotas.

The Downside of High Prices Keeping oil prices high has some downside for OPEC. Competition from non-OPEC countries rises because the revenues accruing to the competitors are higher. Because some OPEC countries are putting up roadblocks to production, major producers like BP, ExxonMobil, and Shell are investing heavily in areas like the Caspian Basin, the Gulf of Mexico, and Angola and are trying to enter areas like the Russian Federation. Production in these areas is expected to grow significantly. High prices also attract competition to conventional oil, including nonconventional oil (such as oil shale and biofuels) and nuclear energy, although the damage to the nuclear reactors in Japan as a result of the earthquake and tsunami in 2011 had a chilling effect on nuclear energy.

Political and social forces also affect oil prices. The civil war in Libya impacted oil markets in 2011, causing oil prices to spike due to the fear that the unrest could spread to other big Middle East oil producers.

The downside of high oil prices for OPEC:

- Producers investing in countries outside of OPEC.
- Complication of balancing social, political, and economic objectives.

Looking to the

Future   Will the WTO Overcome Bilateral and Regional Integration Efforts?

Will regional integration be the wave of the future, or will the World Trade Organization become the focus of global economic integration? The WTO's objective is to reduce barriers to trade in goods, services, and investment. Regional groups attempt to do that and more. Although the EU has introduced a common currency and is increasing the degree of cooperation in areas such as security and foreign policy, the WTO will likely never engage in those issues. Regional integration deals with the specific problems facing member countries, whereas the WTO needs to be concerned about all countries in the world.

However, regional integration might actually help the WTO achieve its objectives in three major ways:

1. Regionalism can lead to liberalization of issues not covered by the WTO.

2. Regionalism is more flexible, given that it typically involves fewer countries with similar conditions and objectives.

3. Regional deals lock in liberalization, especially in developing countries.

As we have seen in the chapter, no trade agreement is easy or perfect. The WTO has serious challenges due to its size. Regional agreements like NAFTA, the EU, MERCOSUR, and others have many different challenges as well. In cases of NAFTA and MERCOSUR, one dominant country (the United States in the former and Brazil in the latter) implies that the balance of power among the member countries is not equal. The EU has its own challenges due to enlargement and the debt crisis of several member countries, especially Greece. In addition, the EU faces a real dilemma as it tries to figure out what to do with Turkey, which has applied for entrance into the EU. However, Turkey's population is larger than every country in the EU except for Germany and would be the only member with a predominantly Muslim population. Given the concerns with radical Islam and the fact that EU members have a common passport and full mobility of labor, it could be a security nightmare for the other members.

Regional integration in Africa will continue at a slow pace due to the existing political and economic problems there. However, Africa is flush with natural resources and will be a favorite trading partner of resource-hungry China for a long time to come.

That will help fill the foreign exchange coffers of the African countries and possibly help them resolve some of their long-standing problems. Asian integration, primarily in AFTA, will pick up steam as the economies of East and Southeast continue to open up and as they collaborate to meet the challenge of China. Since the beginning of the decade, Asian countries have signed over 70 trade agreements among themselves. Japan, which is not a member of AFTA, has signed a number of bilateral agreements with other countries in Asia including a free trade agreement in goods with the members of ASEAN and is in the process of implementing new agreements with Australia, the Gulf Cooperation Council, India, and Korea. However, the key to the growth of most countries in Southeast Asia may be China and its rapidly growing influence in Asia and the rest of the world.

The challenges to the WTO come not only from the growing strength of regional groups but also from the strong divisions between developed and developing countries within the organization. As we noted earlier in the chapter, the Doha agreement has been a disaster so far, and it doesn't look like the ambitious agenda of Doha will ever be adopted. Although bilateral agreements are likely to be the most effective in the future, even they have challenges. The United States, for example, has tried to adopt agreements with Korea, Panama, and Colombia, but the administration has not been able to get Congressional approval because of political issues from Democrats and unions. U.S. equipment manufacturer, Caterpillar, would love to see the Colombian agreement signed, because it would lead to a reduction of tariffs on mining equipment by 5 to 15 percent, significantly reducing the cost of equipment sales.[60] This would also lead to more union jobs to produce the equipment for export, but political and economic issues are difficult to resolve. Most bilateral agreements face similar challenges, depending on the countries involved. As noted earlier, China will always be able to sign bilateral agreements, because it is not concerned about labor and environmental issues, whereas some countries, such as the United States, face the prospect of being shut out of many potential bilateral agreements for political reasons. It will be interesting to see how the political side is resolved in the future. ∎

Walmart Goes South

Comercial Mexicana S.A. (Comerci), one of Mexico's largest retail chains, is faced with a serious dilemma.[61] Since Walmart's aggressive entry into the Mexican retail market, Comerci has found it increasingly difficult to remain competitive. Walmart's strong operating presence and low prices since NAFTA's lifting of tariffs have put pressure on Comerci, and now management must determine what Comerci needs to do to compete against Walmart.

What's caused this intense competitive pressure on Comerci, and what is likely to be its future? Mexico's retail sector has benefited greatly from the increasing trade liberalization the government has been pushing. After decades of protectionism, Mexico joined GATT in 1986 to help open its economy to new markets. In 1990, with Mexico's economy on the upswing and additional free trade negotiations with the United States and Canada taking place, the founder of Walmart, Sam Walton, met with the president of Cifra, Mexico's leading retail store. Their meeting resulted in a 50/50 joint venture in the opening of Mexico's first Sam's Club, a subsidiary of Walmart, in 1991 in Mexico City.

It only took several months after the opening to prove the store's success—it was breaking all the U.S. records for Sam's Club. The joint venture evolved to incorporate all new stores, and by 1997, Walmart purchased enough shares to have a controlling interest in Cifra. In 2000, the name changed to Walmart de México, S.A. de C.V., and the ticker symbol to WALMEX. After the consolidation of its operations in Central America, it became known as Walmart México y Centroamérica.

Prior to 1990, Walmart had never made moves to enter Mexico or any country other than the United States. Once Walmart started growing in Mexico, management created the Walmart International Division in 1993. By the first quarter of 2011, Walmart had expanded internationally to 15 countries outside the continental United States through new-store construction and acquisitions. It now operates in Argentina, Brazil, Canada, Chile, China, Costa Rica, El Salvador, Guatemala, Honduras, India, Japan, Mexico, Nicaragua, Puerto Rico, and the United Kingdom. Walmart serves customers and members more than 200 million times weekly through its international operations.

Walmart has successfully expanded into Mexico, and it's stores reflect the scale and quality of Walmart's best in the world. The familiar Walmart logo and color scheme are typical of the Walmart stores.

Source: Courtesy of Walmart de Mexico y Centroamerica files

With growth stalling in the United States, Walmart is looking to international expansion for growth. It currently has over 8,000 retail units worldwide, of which 4,557 are outside the continental United States, and it employs more than 730,000 people outside the United States. In fiscal year 2010, the international division increased sales over the previous year by 1.31 percent—to $100.1 billion. The international division accounts for approximately 24.7 percent of sales.

Nevertheless, Walmart's success internationally has varied by country. It has struggled to match consumer preferences and work successfully with suppliers in Japan, encountered trouble in the United Kingdom, and failed to turn profits in Germany and South Korea, forcing it to withdraw completely from both markets. However, it has flourished in Canada and, most notably, in Mexico. Walmart's operations in Canada began in 1994 with the acquisition of 122 Woolco stores. It now has more than 325 Walmart stores and enjoys strong partnerships with Canadian suppliers. In Mexico, Walmart operates 1,242 units, including Sam's Clubs, Bodegas (discount stores), Walmart Supercenters, Superamas (grocery stores), Suburbias (apparel stores), and VIPS restaurants, and it has become the largest retailer in the country.

Given its hit-and-miss success rate on the international scene, it is natural to wonder how much of Walmart's triumph in Canada and Mexico has stemmed from its internal processes, international strategies, and geographic proximity and how much can be attributed to the close economic ties shared by the United States with the two countries through NAFTA.

Walmart's Competitive Advantage

Much of Walmart's international success comes from the tested practices on which the U.S. division bases its success. Walmart is known for the slogan "Every Day Low Prices," which is the core of its value proposition. It has expanded that internally to "Every Day Low Costs" to inspire employees to spend company money wisely and work hard to lower costs. Because of its sheer size and volume of purchases, Walmart can negotiate with suppliers to drop prices to agreeable levels.

It also works closely with suppliers on inventory levels using an advanced information system that informs suppliers when purchases have been made and when Walmart will be ordering more merchandise. Suppliers can then plan production runs more accurately, thus reducing production costs, resulting in cost savings for Walmart, which then can pass on the savings to the consumer as lower prices.

Walmart also has a unique distribution system that reduces expenses. It builds super warehouses known as Distribution Centers (DCs) in central locations that receive the majority of merchandise sold in Walmart stores. It sorts and moves the merchandise via a complex system of bar codes, and its inventory information system then transports it to the various stores, using its company-owned fleet or a partner. The central distribution center helps Walmart negotiate lower prices with its suppliers because of the large purchasing volumes.

These strategies have resulted in great success for Walmart. And it even uses the second most powerful computer in the world—behind the Pentagon's—to run its logistics.

Walmart in Mexico

Prior to the passage of NAFTA, Walmart faced some challenges as it expanded into Mexico. One of the biggest challenges it faced was import charges on many of the goods sold in its stores, thus preventing Walmart from being able to offer its "Every Day Low Prices."

Unsure of local demand, Walmart stocked its shelves with items like ice skates, fishing tackle, and riding lawnmowers—all unpopular items in Mexico. Rather than informing headquarters that they wouldn't need those items, local managers heavily discounted the items, only to have the automatic inventory system reorder the products when the first batch sold. Walmart also encountered logistics problems due to poor roads and the scarcity of delivery trucks. Yet another problem was the culture clashes between the Arkansas executives and the local Mexican managers.

Some of these problems were solved by trial and error, but the emergence of NAFTA in 1994 helped solve most of the problems. Among other things, NAFTA reduced tariffs on American goods sold to Mexico from 10 to 3 percent. Prior to NAFTA, Walmart was not much of a threat to companies like Comerci, Gigante, and Soriana, Mexico's top retailers. But once the agreement was signed, the barriers fell and Walmart was on a level playing field with its competitors—all it needed to become number one. However, the retail sector in Mexico is the second most competitive sector of the economy behind auto parts, so Walmart has had its work cut out for it to remain competitive against local Mexican retail chains and other foreign retailers, such as U.S.-based Costco and French-based Carrefour.

Since NAFTA has gone into force, Mexico has invested significantly into public and private infrastructure, which has helped Walmart to improve the efficiencies in its distribution network. The signing of NAFTA also opened the gates wider to foreign investment in Mexico. Walmart was paying huge import fees on goods shipped to Mexico from areas like Europe and Asia. Foreign companies knew that if they built manufacturing plants in Mexico, they could keep costs low with Mexican labor and also ship to NAFTA's free trade zone—Mexico, the United States, or Canada.

As companies began to build manufacturing plants in Mexico, Walmart could buy these products without paying the high import tariffs. An example of this tactic is Sony's flat-screen television line, Wega. Sam's Clubs in Mexico imported Wega TVs from Japan with a 23 percent import tariff plus huge shipping costs, resulting in a $1,600 retail price at Sam's Club. In 1999, Sony built a manufacturing plant in Mexico, thus allowing Sam's Club to purchase the Wegas without import tariffs; this tactic also yields much lower shipping fees. Sam's Clubs passed on the savings to customers—with a retail price of only $600. As noted earlier in the chapter, Sony has expanded its manufacturing facility in Tijuana to produce flat-screen TVs that can be used to supply the local market or export to the United States.

NAFTA resulted in better suppliers due to an increase in competition, competitiveness and efficiency among companies in order to gain the trust of their clients. Suppliers have invested in being more productive in order to be more competitive, and at the same time, they have gained greater access to better materials and technologies in the region. Better suppliers also increased the variety of products available to consumer with wider price ranges, which allowed Walmart to offer customers better savings and thus increase their purchasing power. NAFTA also helped Mexico achieve greater economic growth a lower rates of inflation, which also added to the purchasing power of consumers.

Comerci and others have combated Walmart's tactics by lowering their own prices, but on many items, they can't get the prices as low. Walmart's negotiating power with its suppliers is large enough that it can get the better deal. Also, most of Mexico's retailers priced goods differently. They were used to putting certain items on sale or at deep discount, a strategy known as "high and low," rather than lowering all prices. They have been trying to adjust their pricing structure to match Walmart's, but they are still frustrated with Walmart's continued cost cutting.

Formation of Sinergia

Unable to compete with Walmart under the new conditions, Comerci, Soriana, and Gigante nearly faced extinction. Walmart is the largest retailer in Mexico and has become the largest private employer in Mexico with 219,700 employees. Fear over the giant retailer's predominance prompted the three supermarket chains to form a purchasing consortium that would allow them to negotiate better bulk prices from suppliers. The collaboration, known as Sinergia, ran into problems with Mexican regulators and the Consumer Product Council of Mexico over fear that Sinergia would use its purchasing power to force unreasonably low prices on suppliers. However, the consortium was at last approved, provided that it issue regular reports outlining the nature of its purchasing agreements and that it sign confidentiality agreements with the participating chains to prevent price-fixing and monopolistic behavior.

However, Walmart's continued expansion forced more drastic actions. Comerci had a bad year in 2010 where it had to restructure debt from losses resulting from foreign currency derivatives bets that resulted in heavy losses. In 2011, it announced that it was ready to expand by opening new stores. Comerci also entered into several strategic alliances, including one with U.S.-based Costco, a major competitor of Walmart, where Comerci owns 50 percent of Costco Mexico. In 2007, Gigante sold its supermarket chain to Soriana, allowing Soriana to expand by acquisition and gain greater purchasing efficiencies for its larger network of supermarkets.

Walmart's Expansion into Central America

Walmart also made two significant changes in its operations in Mexico. First, Walmart de Mexico purchased Walmart Centroamerica in 2009 and became known as Walmart de México y Centroamerica. One of the things that facilitated the acquisition was the fact that Mexico, in addition to being a member of NAFTA, signed free trade agreements with 49 countries around the world, including several in Central America. That meant that they could gain access to even more products and suppliers. In 2010, Walmart worked with over 26,200 suppliers throughout Mexico and Central America, with more than 60 percent of its suppliers based in Mexico composed of SMEs (small and medium-sized entities). They were also able to better coordinate the network of 14 distribution centers in Mexico and 11 in Central America, locating them strategically throughout the region.

Second, Walmart established a multiformat operations approach in the region to address different consumer segments. This occurred not only in Mexico but also in Central America through Bodegas and discount stores, hypermarkets, clubs and supermarkets. Two different store concepts it established are Bodega Aurrera and Superama, both supermarket stores aimed at different demographics. In addition, Walmart opened apparel stores and restaurants. Walmart also learned things in Mexico to help target the Hispanic community in the United States by opening at Latin-themed warehouse store in Houston, Texas, called Más. This is a spinoff of Sam's Club. In addition, Walmart imported products from Mexico for its stores in the United States for the Hispanic community. ■

Superama is a supermarket chain owned by Walmart in Mexico that caters to the tastes of more upscale Mexican consumers.

Source: Courtesy of Walmart de Mexico y Centroamerica files

QUESTIONS

1. How has the implementation of NAFTA affected Walmart's success in Mexico?

2. How much of Walmart's success is due to NAFTA, and how much is due to Walmart's inherent competitive strategy? In other words, could any other U.S. retailer have the same success in Mexico post-NAFTA, or is Walmart a special case?

3. What have Comerci and Soriana done to remain competitive? What else do you think they need to do to remain competitive in the future?

4. What do you think of Walmart's strategy in Mexico and Central America, and how have bilateral agreements and geographic proximity played a role in their success? What challenges do you think Walmart de Mexico e Centramérica will face as it continues to expand in Mexico and Central America?

Now that you have finished this chapter, go back to www.myiblab.com to continue practicing and applying the concepts you've learned.

MyIBLab

SUMMARY

- The General Agreement on Tariffs and Trade (GATT), begun in 1947, created a continuing means for countries to negotiate the reduction and elimination of trade barriers and to agree on simplified mechanisms for the conduct of international trade.

- The World Trade Organization (WTO) replaced GATT in 1995 as a continuing means of trade negotiations that aspires to foster the principle of trade without discrimination and to provide a better means of mediating trade disputes and of enforcing agreements.

- Efforts at regional economic integration began to emerge after World War II as countries saw benefits of cooperation and larger market sizes. The major types of economic integration are the free trade area and the customs union, followed by broader economic and political integration in the common market.

- Free trade agreements result in trade creation and trade diversion as barriers drop for member countries but remain higher for nonmember countries. There are static effects of the reduction of trade barriers. The static effects of economic integration improve the efficiency of resource allocation and affect both production and consumption. The dynamic effects are internal and external efficiencies that arise because of changes in market size.

- Once protection is eliminated among member countries, trade creation allows MNEs to specialize and trade based on comparative advantage.

- Trade diversion occurs when the supply of products shifts from countries that are not members of an economic bloc to those that are.

- Regional, as opposed to global, economic integration occurs because of the greater ease of promoting cooperation on a smaller scale.

- The European Union (EU) is an effective common market that has abolished most restrictions on factor mobility and is harmonizing national political, economic, and social policies. It is composed of 27 countries, including 12 countries from mostly Central and Eastern Europe that have joined since 2004. The EU has abolished trade barriers on intrazonal trade, instituted a common external tariff, and created a common currency, the euro.

- The North American Free Trade Agreement (NAFTA) is designed to eliminate tariff barriers and liberalize investment opportunities and trade in services. Key provisions in NAFTA are labor and environmental agreements.

- There are key trade groups in other parts of the world, including Latin America, Asia, and Africa.

- The United Nations is composed of representatives of most of the countries in the world and influences international trade and development in a number of significant ways.

- Many developing countries rely on commodity exports to supply the hard currency they need for economic development. Instability in commodity prices has resulted in fluctuations in export earnings. OPEC is an effective commodity agreement in terms of attempting to stabilize supply and price.

KEY TERMS

Andean Community (CAN) (p. 308)
Arab League (p. 312)
Asia Pacific Economic Cooperation (APEC) (p. 311)
Association of Southeast Asian Nations (ASEAN) (p. 308)
bilateral integration (p. 290)
Caribbean Community (CARICOM) (p. 307)
common market (p. 296)
dynamic effect (p. 296)
economic integration (p. 290)
economies of scale (p. 296)

euro (p. 300)
European Union (EU) (p. 297)
General Agreement on Tariffs and Trade (GATT) (p. 291)
global integration (p. 290)
Gulf Cooperation Council (GCC) (p. 312)
Lisbon Treaty (p. 300)
MERCOSUR (p. 308)
most-favored-nation (MFN) clause (p. 291)
North American Free Trade Agreement (NAFTA) (p. 302)

Organization of the Petroleum Exporting Countries (OPEC) (p. 316)
Pan Arab Free Trade Area (PAFTA) (p. 312)
regional integration (p. 290)
static effect (p. 296)
triad (p. 290)
UN Conference on Trade and Development (UNCTAD) (p. 314)
World Trade Organization (WTO) (p. 291)

ENDNOTES

1 *Sources include the following:* Stephen Power, "EU Auto Industry Faces Overhaul as Japanese Gain in Market Share," *Wall Street Journal* (October 14, 2004):A1; Jathon Sapsford, "Toyota Aims to Rival GM Production," *Wall Street Journal* (November 2, 2004): A3; Mari Koseki, "Quota on Auto Exports to EC Curbed at 1.089 Million in '93," *Japan Times* (April 12–18, 1993): 14; Nick Maling, "Japan Poised for EU Lift of Export Ceiling," *Marketing Week* (May 6, 1999): 26; Todd Zaun and Beth Demain, "Leading the News: Ambitious Toyota, Buoyed by Europe, Sets Global Goals," *Wall Street Journal* (October 22, 2002): A3; Mark M. Nelson, Thomas F. O'Boyle, and E. S. Browning, "International—The Road to European Unity—1992: EC's Auto Plan Would Keep Japan at Bay—1992 Unification Effort Smacks of Protectionism," *Wall Street Journal* (October 27, 1988): A1; Jathon Sapsford, "Toyota Posts 3.5% Profit Rise, Boosts Sales Forecast for Year," *Wall Street Journal* (February 4, 2005): A3; Gail Edmondson and Chester Dawson, "Revved Up for Battle," *Business Week* (January 10, 2005): 30; Joe Guy Collier, "Toyota Posts Record $14-Billion Profit," *Knight Ridder Tribune Business News* (May 9, 2007): 1; "ACEA Board of Directors Recommends Accepting Toyota Motor Europe Membership Application," *PR Newswire Europe Including UK Disclose* (May 4, 2007); Toyota home page, "Toyota—Joining Europe," retrieved May 10, 2007, from www.toyota-europe.com/experience/the _company/toyota-ineurope.aspx; Toyota home page, "Toyota: Company Company Profile," retrieved May 10, 2007, from www .toyota.co.jp/en/about_toyota/outline/index.html; Christoph Rauwald, "Leading the News: Toyota Sales in Europe Jump as Market Stalls," *Wall Street Journal* (March 16, 2007): 2; "World Business Briefing Europe: Germany: Sale of Unit Helps VW," *New York Times* (February 21, 2007): C10; Mark Milner, "Financial: Car Boss Calls on EU to Tackle Yen," *UK Guardian* (March 30, 2007): 32; Toyota Annual Report 2010: Toyota Motor Corporation, April 2010 (accessed March 23, 2011).

2 Peter J. Buckley, Jeremy Clagg, Nicolas Forsans, and Kevin T. Reilly, "Increasing the Size of the 'Country': Regional Economic Integration and Foreign Direct Investment in a Globalised World Economy," *Management International Review* 41:3 (2001): 251–75.

3 Alan M. Rugman and Alain Verbeke, "A Perspective on Regional and Global Strategies of Multinational Enterprises," *Journal of International Business Studies* 35 (2004): 7.

4 "Airbus wins WTO subsidy dispute, but Boeing says it's the winner" *New Europe* (March 28, 2010), retrieved April 15, 2011, from www.neurope.eu/articles/99919.php; John Miller and Daniel Michaels, "Boeing Set for Victory Over Airbus in Illegal Subsidy Case," *Wall Street Journal* (September 3, 2009): A1, A14.

5 World Trade Organization, Dispute Settlement; DS316 Panel Report (June 30, 2010): "European Communities — Measures Affecting Trade in Large Civil Aircraft (accessed April 8, 2011).

6 Nicola Clark, "W.T.O. Ruling on Airbus Subsidies Upheld on Appeal," *The New York Times* (May 19, 2011): B3; John W. Miller, "WTO Gives Airbus a Mixed Win," *The Wall Street Journal* (May 19, 2011): B3.

7 Nathan Hodge "Boeing Bid Beats Europe for Tanker," *Wall Street Journal* (February 25, 2011), retrieved April 15, 2011, from http://online.wsj.com/article/SB1000142405274870340860457616464 2983838266.html.

8 John W. Miller, "Global Trade Talks Fail as New Giants Flex Muscle," *Wall Street Journal* (July 30, 2008): A1.

9 Daniel Ikenson, "Greasing the World Economy without Doha," *Wall Street Journal* (July 30, 2008): A15.

10 John W. Miller, "Doha-Lite Trade Deal Clears Hurdle at WTO," *The Wall Street Journal* (June 1, 2011): A15.

11 Elizabeth Williamson, "APEC Ministers Discuss Future of Doha Trade Talks," *The Wall Street Journal (Online), May 20, 2011* (accessed June 7, 2011).

12 Retrieved October 1, 2009, from www.wto.org/english/thewto_e /whatis_e/10ben_e/ 10b00_e.htm and http://www.wto.org/english /thewto_e/ whatis_e/10mis_e/10m00_e.htm.

13 Steve Charnovitz "Addressing Environmental and Labor Issues in the World Trade Organization," Progressive Policy Institute, 1999, retrieved April 15, 2011, from www.ppionline.org/ppi_ci.cfm ?knlgAreaID=108&subsecID=128&contentID=649.

14 Martin Khor "Rethinking Liberalization and Reforming the WTO" (January 28, 2000); Third World Network, retrieved April 15, 2011, from www.twnside.org.sg/title/davos2-cn.htm.

15 John W. Miller, "Brazil and Others Push outside Doha for Trade Pacts," *Wall Street Journal* (July 5, 2007): A6; "EU Proposes 'Strategic Partner' Status for Brazil," CNN.com (accessed July 6, 2007).

16 "Regional Trade Agreements" World Trade Organization, retrieved May 30, 2011, from www.wto.org/english/tratop_e/region_e /region_e.htm#facts.

17 Bela Balassa, *The Theory of Economic Integration* (Homewood, IL: Richard D. Irwin, 1961): 40.

18 Panjak Ghemawat, "Distance Still Matters: The Hard Reality of Global Expansion," *Harvard Business Review* (September 2001): 3–11.

19 Buckley et al., "Increasing the Size of the 'Country.'"

20 For more information on the EU, check out its website at http://europa.eu.int/index_en.htm (accessed October 1, 2009).

21 "EU Institutions and Other Bodies," http://europa.eu/about-eu /institutions-bodies/index_en.htm.

22 "The European Parliament" (2005), retrieved October 1, 2009, from http://europa.eu.int/ institutions/parliament/index_en.htm.

23 "The European Court of Justice" (2002), retrieved October 1, 2009, from http://europa.eu.int/ inst/en/cj.htm.

24 Charles Forelle, "Microsoft Yields to EU on Browsers," *Wall Street Journal* (July 25/26, 2009): B1; Kevin J. Obrien, "Europe Drops Microsoft Antitrust Case," *The New York Times (online)*, December 16, 2009, accessed June 7, 2011.

25 Charles Forelle, "EU Adds IBM to Target List," *The Wall Street Journal* (July 27, 2010): B1.

26 James Canter, "Facing Antitrust Fights at Home, Google Tries to Avoid One in Europe," *The New York Times* (February 21, 2011): B1.

27 John W. Miller, "Country Labeling Sets off EU Debate," *The Wall Street Journal* (June 6, 2011): B1.

28 "Q&A: The Lisbon Treaty," *BBC News*, last updated on January 17, 2001 at http://news.bbc.co.uk/2/hi/europe/6901353.stm, and accessed online on June 7, 2011.

29 "Another Project in Trouble," *The Economist* (April 30, 2011): 57.

30 Pankaj Ghemawat, "Distance Still Matters: The Hard Reality of Global Expansion," *Harvard Business Review* 79:8 (September 2001): 137.

31 Sandra Dibble, "Sony Will Increase Work Force in Tijuana," *The San Diego Union-Tribune* (June 26, 2009): E1.

32 Text of the North American Free Trade Agreement, "Chapter 4: Rules of Origin," retrieved June 7, 2011, from www.ustr.gov/trade -agreements/free-trade-agreements/north-american-free-trade -agreement-nafta.

33 John W. Miller, "What Do You Mean By Made?" *The Wall Street Journal* (June 6, 2011): B1.

34 "Text of the North American Free Trade Agreement, Chapter 4: Rules of Origin/Regional Content."

35 Office of the United States Trade Representative, "North American Free Trade Agreement," retrieved June 7, 2011, from www.ustr.gov /trade-agreements/free-trade-agreements/north-american-free -trade-agreement-nafta.

36 Geri Smith and Elizabeth Malkin, "Mexican Makeover: NAFTA Creates the World's Newest Industrial Power," *Business* Week (December 21, 1998): 51.

37 Robert B. Zoellick, "Speech on NAFTA before the Foreign Trade Council," *USTR* (July 26, 2001): www.ustr.gov/speechtest/zoellick /zoellick_7.pdf.

38 Mike Ramsey, "VW Chops Labor Costs in U.S.," *The Wall Street Journal* (May 23, 2011): B1.

39 Gary Fields, "Trade Dispute Divides Workers," *The Wall Street Journal* (April 6, 2010): A5.

40 Chris Roberts, "Mexican Truckers to Drive Cargo into U.S. Interior," *El Paso Times* , (May 29, 2011), ProQuest document ID 2360820141.

41 Mario Osava, "South America: Brazil Outshines Regional Bloc," *Global Information Network* (July 27, 2009), Retrieved October 2, 2009, from www.proquest.com.

42 Matt Moffett and Paulo Prada, "Brazil, Argentina Drive to Settle Dispute Over Automobile Imports," *The Wall Street Journal* (May 21, 2011): A11.

43 Alan M. Field, "Showdown for CAFTA-DR," *Journal of Commerce* (April 11, 2005): 1.

44 Harold McGraw and Mark Weisbrot, "Is CAFTA-DR a Good Thing?" *Miami Herald* (April 16, 2005): 25A; "Dominican Republic-Central America-United States Free Trade Agreement," retrieved June 1, 2011, from http://export.gov/FTA/caftan-dr /index.asp.

45 "CAFTA-DR Partners Agree to Fix Technical Errors in Agreement," *Textile World* 161:2 (Mar/Apr 2011): 10.

46 Field, "Showdown for CAFTA-DR," 1.

47 McGraw and Weisbrot, "Is CAFTA-DR a Good Thing?" 25A.

48 John Lyons, "Costa Rica Balks at Free-Trade Pact," *Wall Street Journal* (May 3, 2005): A2.

49 The World Bank, "Countries - Data," retrieved June 2, 2011, from http://data.worldbank.org/country.

50 "AFTA Doha," *The Economist* (September 6, 2008): 85.

51 Patrick Barta and Alex Frangos, "Southeast Asia Linking Up to Compete with China," *The Wall Street Journal* (August 23, 2010): A2.

52 Asia-Pac Paul Cashin, Hong Liang, and C. John McDermott, "Do Commodity Price Shocks Last Too Long for Stabilization Schemes to Work?" *Finance & Development* 36:3 (Summer 1999); Asia-Pacific Economic Cooperation, "About APEC," retrieved October 1, 2009, from www.apecsec.org.sg.

53 "The African Union: Short of Cash and Teeth," *The Economist* (January 29, 2011): 46.

54 The United Nations, retrieved June 14, 2011, from www.un.org/en /mainbodies/ (accessed June 14, 2011).

55 United Nations, "United Nations Global Compact," retrieved June 14, 2011, from http://unglobalcompact.org/AboutTheGC /TheTenPrinciples/index.html.

56 United Nations Conference on Trade and Development, "Commodities at a Glance," March 2011, http://www.unctad.org /en/docs/suc20112_en.pdf, p. 17(accessed June 14, 2011).

57 International Coffee Organization, retrieved June 14, 2011, from www.ico.org (accessed June 14, 2011).

58 UNCTAD, Commodities at a Glance," 9.

59 OPEC, "Does OPEC Control the Oil Market?" retrieved June 14, 2011, from www.opec.org/opec_web/en/index.htm.

60 Mark Drajem and Eric Martin, "Why Caterpillar Digs a Colombian Trade Deal," *Business Week* (April 18-24, 2011): 32.

61 *Sources include the following:* Interview with Francisco Suarez Mogollon, Director Institutional Relations, Walmart de Mexico y Centroamérica, June 3, 2011; Dante Di Gregorio, Douglas E. Thomas, and Fernán González de Castilla, "Competition between Emerging Market and Multinational Firms: Walmart and Mexican Retailers," *International Journal of Management* 25:3 (September 2008): 532l; Gabriela Lopez, "Mexico Probes Retail Competition as Walmex Dominates," *Reuters Company News* (May 29, 2002); "Walmart around the World," *The Economist* (December 6, 2001), at www.economist.com/displayStory.cfm?Story_ID=895888; David Luhnow, "Crossover Success: How NAFTA Helped Walmart Reshape the Mexican Market," *Wall Street Journal* (August 31, 2001): A1; Alexander Hanrath, "Mexican Stores Wilt in the Face of US Group's Onslaught," *Financial Times* (August 14, 2002): 21; Richard C. Morais, "One Hot Tamale," *Forbes* (December 27, 2004): 134–47; Mike Troy, "Walmart International," *DSN Retailing Today* (December 13, 2004): 20–22; Ricardo Castillo Mireles, "Taking It to the Competition, Mexican Style," *Logistics Today* (December 2004): 10; Walmart Stores, "International Data Sheet," retrieved June 15, 2011, from http://walmartstores.com; *Walmart 2010 Annual Report*; Matthew Boyle, "Walmart v. the World," *CNNMoney* (December 19, 2007); "CATALYST: Walmart's Distribution Juggernaut," *Businessline* (June 14, 2007): 1. Jonathan Birchall, "Walmart Slims Down for China," *Financial Times* (December 2, 2010): 17; Miguel Bustillo, "After Early Errors, Wal-Mart Thinks Locally to Act Globally," *Wall Street Journal* (August 14, 2009): A1; Miguel Bustillo, "Sam's Club Tests the Big-Box Bodega," *Wall Street Journal* (August 10, 2009): B1; Karen Talley, "Wal-Mart Closes Moscow Office," *Wall Street Journal Online* (December 14, 2010) (accessed May 27, 2011); Comlay "Mexico's Comerci Boosts Investment, Store Openings," *Reuters* (May 24, 2011), retrieved May 27, 2011, from www.reuters.com/article/2011/05/24/comerci-idUKN2426789820110524.

chapter 9
Global Foreign-Exchange Markets

Another man's trade costs money.

—*Portuguese Proverb*

Source: © Alex Ramsay / Alamy

CASE

Going Down to the Wire in the Money-Transfer Market

Long known as "the fastest way to send money," U.S.-based Western Union controls nearly 80 percent of the money-transfer market and is widely acknowledged as the world leader in wire transfers—electronic transfers of funds from one financial institution to another.[1] In this case, it's a transfer from one Western Union office to another. However, Western Union is now facing stiff competition from banks threatening to encroach on its market share of the electronic money-transfer business.

Western Union was started in 1851 when a group of businessmen in Rochester, New York, formed a printing telegraph company. The company changed its name to Western Union in 1861 when it completed the first transcontinental telegraph line. Western Union introduced its money-transfer service in 1871 and started offering this service outside North America in 1989. Today, over 455,000 Western Union agent locations are found in over 200 countries and territories around the world. Money transfers account for 85 percent of Western Union's revenues, and about $50 billion is transferred annually through Western Union.

Customers have many different options when sending money through Western Union. Money can be sent in person at an agent location, over the phone, or online, and senders may use cash, debit cards, or credit cards. Customers can find Western Union offices in a variety of locations—an actual Western Union office, a grocery store, a post office—just about anywhere people go to transact business. To send money to India or Mexico using a Western Union agent location, the customer must fill out a "Send Money" form. He or she then receives a receipt, which includes a Money Transfer Control number. This number must be given to the person receiving the funds. The receiver fills out a "Receive Money" form and presents the Money Transfer Control number along with valid identification at a Western Union agent location to receive the money.

CONVERTING CURRENCY

The funds are converted into the foreign currency using an exchange rate set by Western Union. The transfer fees for sending money are determined based on how much money is sent, in what form it is sent (cash or debit/credit card), and where it is going. For example, sending $500 to Mexico from Utah costs $12. Part of Western Union's attractiveness is its speed and anonymity. Western Union can move cash from one location of the world to another in just minutes. Money can be sent through an agent by cash, debit card, credit card, or a Western Union Gold Card. People sending money are required to fill out a form and show a proper ID.

SOURCES AND DESTINATIONS OF MIGRATION

Migration is based on supply and demand. People work in other countries because of better economic opportunities. Countries accept migrant workers because they are short on labor. Each situation is different. The top five immigration countries in terms of the number of immigrants in 2010 were the United States (42.8 million), Russia (12.3 million), Germany (10.8 million), Saudi Arabia (7.3 million), and Canada (7.2 million). In terms of percentage of the total population, however, three of the top five destinations for migrant workers were from the Gulf Cooperation Council, with Qatar at number 1 (86.5 percent of the total population) and the United Arab Emirates, including Dubai, at number 3 (70 percent of the population). Of the top five emigration countries, Mexico was number 1 with 11.9 people working abroad, and India was number 2 with 11.4 million people. The top migration corridor in 2010 was from Mexico to the United States with 11.6 million workers. India sent 2.2 million workers to the UAE, which ranked as the number 9 migration corridor. Excluding the former Soviet Union, the India—UAE corridor ranked number 5 in the world.

The flow of money is also interesting. In 2010, the top remittance-receiving country was India at $55 billion, followed by China at $51 billion, and Mexico at $22.6 billion. The United States was by far the top remittance-sending country with $48.3 billion. It was estimated that there were more than 215 million international migrant workers in the world in 2010, generating $325 million dollars in remittances for the developing countries.

The Mexican Connection (I)

Most of the migrant workers in the United States come from Latin America and the Caribbean. Most of Western Union's wire transfer business in the United States comes from Mexican immigrants who send part of their paychecks home to support their families. Mexico has historically ranked as the largest host country in Latin America for remittances, followed by Brazil. Remittances already exceed foreign direct investment and overseas aid as sources of foreign exchange. Annual remittance income has passed tourism to become the second-largest source of foreign-exchange income in Mexico after oil revenues.

EXCHANGE RATES AND COMPETITION

A class-action lawsuit was filed against Western Union in 1997, charging that Western Union offered its customers lower exchange rates than the market exchange rates without informing them of the difference. The lawsuit was settled in 2000, and Western Union is now required to state on its receipts and advertisements that it uses its own exchange rate on transactions and that any difference between the company rate and the market rate is kept by the company. For example, the market exchange rate on June 10, 2011, for Mexican pesos was 11.87 pesos/US\$ (US\$500 = 5,935 pesos); Western Union's offered exchange rate was 11.56 pesos/US\$ (US\$500 = 5,780 pesos). One reason for the difference in rates is that the market rate is typically for very large commercial transactions, whereas the normal Western Union transaction is much smaller. The smaller the transaction, the less favorable the exchange rate. Compare that with buying products in bulk rather than a few items at a time.

Financial institutions such as banks have pressured Western Union to use better exchange rates. Profit margins in the money-transfer business can reach 30 percent, and many banks have started to offer their own money-transfer services in an attempt to take advantage of the continued expected growth of the foreign money-transfer industry. For example, in 2001, Wells Fargo agreed to accept consular identification cards from Mexican immigrants who want to open bank accounts but lack U.S. driver's licenses. These cards verify Mexicans' identities without revealing their immigration status. After Wells Fargo began accepting the consular identification card, the number of bank accounts opened with the consular ID jumped by over 500 percent within three years.

The Mexican Connection (II)

Wells Fargo and other U.S. banks, including Citibank and Bank of America, have established alliances with Mexican banks to offer remittance accounts to the immigrant workers in the United States. Workers can open U.S. bank accounts with their consular IDs and ask for two ATM cards, one for them and one for their families back home. They can then deposit remittance money in the U.S. account, and their family members at home can withdraw money from the Mexican bank.

In 2005, the Federal Reserve teamed up with Mexico's central bank to create a new program that facilitates remittances made from the United States to Mexico. This program allows U.S. commercial banks to make money transfers for Mexican workers through the Federal Reserve's own automated clearinghouse, which is linked to Banco de México, the Mexican central bank.

Even the wire transfer fees at banks are cheaper than Western Union's. For example, Wells Fargo charges a \$6 fee to send \$500 to Mexico, compared with Western Union's \$12 fee for the same transaction. Many banks are moving toward eliminating exchange-rate spreads (the difference between the market rate and the rate they use for the wire transfer) and transfer fees to Mexico to provide more attractive alternatives to immigrant workers.

This new onslaught of competition by banks has forced Western Union to cut its fees and offer new services, including a home-delivery service, where money is delivered directly to the recipient's door. Western Union is also moving into countries such as China and India to increase its market share. The increased competition has driven down remittance fees around the world. In Ukraine, for example, Western Union was forced to drop its fee from \$43 to \$20.

The Mexican Connection (III)

Immigrant workers complain about the high transfer fees and exchange-rate spread associated with Western Union, but many continue to use this service instead of the lower-cost method of remitting money through banks. Mexico has a history of unstable currencies and widespread inflation, resulting in a traditional mistrust of banks. Other immigrants base their choice on word of mouth or convenience and location. Many are simply unaware of the variety of choices available for sending money and do not know how to get the best deal.

Another reason why many continue to use Western Union is its worldwide availability. For thousands of tiny villages, Western Union is the main link to the outside world. For example, Coatetelco is a small

Mexican village south of Mexico City with no bank. A few people grow maize, chilies, and fruit, but remittances—mostly from agricultural or construction workers in Georgia and the Carolinas—account for 90 percent of the villagers' incomes. Patricio, 49, says that at the end of each month, he gets a call from his two sons, who are working illegally in Georgia. They give him a code number, and he drives or rides his horse 4 miles to the nearest Western Union office, located in a government telegraph office, to pick up the $600 they spent $40 to wire to him. Less expensive remittance services are available at the nearby Banamex bank in Mazatepec, but so far, Patricio and his neighbors are not willing to travel the 8 miles to get there. Besides, he says, "we do not trust the banks, and they make everything more difficult."

The Dubai Connection

Dubai is an interesting point of comparison with Mexico. Although workers from India and Pakistan go to Dubai to work because of higher wages, they are actually recruited by companies in Dubai. Because of Dubai's relatively small local Emirati population, there is no way the country could develop without foreign workers, including skilled, semi-skilled, and unskilled workers. India is the natural source of workers since it is only about 1200 miles (1900 km) from Mumbai, India, to Dubai, UAE. Workers must have a work permit to work in Dubai, typically for three years at a time, and they are not allowed to become citizens. In addition, there isn't any illegal immigration, and workers can be sent home whenever their employers decide they are no longer needed.

It was estimated that in 2009, about 25 million foreigners lived and worked in the GCC countries (which includes Dubai), making up an estimated 78 percent of total private and public sector workforce. The migrant workers increased the speed of urbanization, fast-tracked infrastructure and economic development, helped diversification from oil, and contributed to solid economic growth.

Given that the migrant workforce in Dubai cannot own property or invest in business ventures, workers need to send the money back home. Western Union has succeeded because it has developed a deep understanding of the remittance markets. Through this understanding, it has developed ethnic marketing expertise and diversified its presence to be closer to the customers. Because of its rapid growth in Dubai, Western Union has developed high and growing brand awareness and has worked hard to develop products and messages that appeal to the customers. Dubai and the United States are different in terms of size and the demand for labor, and India and Mexico are different in terms of how and why they are a supply of labor, but there is one constant: that people need to move money, and that is where Western Union comes in.

CRN
Case Review Note

Concept Check

When we introduced the idea of a **multinational enterprise (MNE)** in Chapter 1, we emphasized that MNEs are firms that take a global approach to production and markets. Here we add that the need to deal with **foreign exchange** is one of the important factors in the environment in which MNEs must conduct business.

Introduction

Changing money from one currency to another and moving it around to different parts of the world is serious business, on both a personal and a company level. To survive, MNEs and small import and export companies alike must understand foreign exchange and exchange rates. In a business setting, there is a fundamental difference between making a payment in the domestic market and making one abroad. In a domestic transaction, companies use only one currency. In a foreign transaction, they can use two or more. For example, a U.S. firm that exports skis to a French distributor may ask the French store to remit payment in dollars, unless the U.S. firm has some specific use for euros, such as paying a French supplier.

Assume you're a U.S. importer who has agreed to purchase a certain quantity of French perfume and pay the French exporter €4,000 for it. Assuming you had the money, how would you go about paying? First, you would go to the international department of your local bank to buy €4,000 at the going market rate. Let's assume the euro/dollar exchange rate is €0.6974 per dollar. Your bank would then charge your account $5,736 ($4,000/€0.6974) plus the transaction costs and give you a special check payable in euros made out to the exporter. The exporter would deposit it in a French bank, which would then credit the exporter's account with €4,000, and the foreign-exchange transaction would be complete.

What Is Foreign Exchange?

Foreign exchange is money denominated in the currency of another nation or group of nations.[2] The market in which such transactions take place is the **foreign-exchange market.** Foreign exchange can be in the form of cash, funds available on credit and debit cards, traveler's checks, bank deposits, or other short-term claims.[3] As an example, our opening case illustrates how Mexican immigrant workers in the United States often use Western Union to convert dollars to pesos and then wire the pesos to offices in Mexico where relatives can retrieve the cash.

An **exchange rate** is the price of a currency—specifically, the number of units of one currency that buy one unit of another currency. The number can change daily. On June 1, 2011, €1 could purchase US$1.4340 (or $1 could purchase €0.6974). Exchange rates make international price and cost comparisons possible.

Players on the Foreign-Exchange Market

The foreign-exchange market is made up of many different players. The **Bank for International Settlements (BIS),** a central banking institution in Basel, Switzerland, owned and controlled by 56 member central banks, divides the market into three major categories: *reporting dealers,* other *financial institutions,* and *nonfinancial institutions.*[4]

Reporting dealers, also known as *money center banks,* are financial institutions that actively participate in local and global foreign exchange and derivative markets. They are mainly the large commercial and investment banks and are widely assumed to include the 10 largest banks and financial institutions in terms of overall market share in foreign-exchange trading: Deutsche Bank, Barclays Capital, UBS, Citibank, JP Morgan, HSBC, RBS, Credit Suisse, Goldman Sachs, and Morgan Stanley. (In our closing case, we show how one money center bank, HSBC, was involved in the gradual internationalization of the Chinese yuan.) Because of the volume of transactions that the money center banks engage in, they influence price-setting and are the market makers.

The other financial institutions are financial institutions not classified as reporting dealers. They include smaller commercial banks, investment banks and securities houses, hedge funds, pension funds, money market funds, currency funds, mutual funds, specialized foreign-exchange trading companies, and so forth. Western Union, whose current activities are detailed in our opening case, is a good example of a nonbanking financial institution that deals in foreign exchange.

Nonfinancial customers are any counterparty other than those described above and include any nonfinancial end user, such governments and companies (MNEs as well as small- and medium-size corporations and firms). As illustrated in Figure 9.1, reporting dealers represent 39 percent of the counterparties in foreign currency transactions, other financial institutions were 48 percent of the counterparties, and nonfinancial customers were 13 percent of the counterparties.

How to Trade Foreign Exchange

Foreign exchange is traded using electronic methods (41.3 percent of all trades), customer direct (24.3 percent), interbank direct (18.5 percent), or voice broker (15.9 percent).[5] There are different kinds of electronic methods. One is an electronic broking system where trades are matched up for foreign exchange dealers using electronic systems such as EBS, Reuters, and Bloomberg. Another is an electronic trading system that is executed on a

Case Review Note

Foreign exchange—money denominated in the currency of another nation or group of nations.

Exchange rate—the price of a currency.

The Bank for International Settlements divides the foreign-exchange market into reporting dealers (also known as dealer banks or money center banks), other financial institutions, and nonfinancial institutions.

Case Review Note

Case Review Note

Dealers can trade foreign exchange

- Electronic methods.
- Directly with customers.
- Through the interbank market.
- Through voice brokers.

FIGURE 9.1   Foreign-Exchange Markets: Turnover by Counterparty, December 2010

Other financial institutions exceeded the number of transactions between reporting dealers for the first time in 2010. Turnover in other financial institutions actually grew by 42 percent to $1.9 trillion compared to $1.3 trillion in 2007.

Source: Based on Bank for International Settlements, *Central Bank Survey Report on Global Foreign Exchange Market Activity in 2010* (Basel, Switzerland: BIS, December 2010): 8.

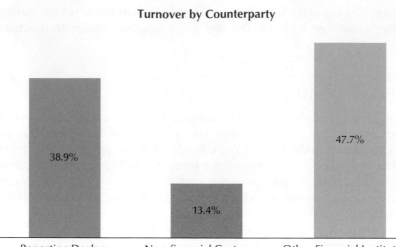

Turnover by Counterparty

Reporting Dealers 38.9%	Non-financial Customers 13.4%	Other Financial Institutions 47.7%

Concept Check

In discussing "The Political Environment" in Chapter 3, we observe that the relationships comprising a country's political system—relationships among its institutions, organizations, and interest groups—depend on the "political norms and rules" over which its government exercises control. As we'll see in Chapter 10, these include rules for trading currency; moreover, governments are active traders of foreign currency through money center banks.

single-bank proprietary system or a multibank dealing system. One example of this type of system is FXConnect, a Boston-based U.S. company that provides trading and settlement options for its clients. Customer direct refers to trades between a reporting dealer and either a non-reporting dealer or customer, without a third party being involved. Usually trades are executive by telephone or direct electronic trading. Interbank direct refers to trades between dealer banks via telephone or direct electronic trading. Voice broker is a trade via telephone communication with a foreign exchange voice broker.[6] Electronic methods are pretty evenly split among three options: broking systems, multibank trading systems, and single bank trading systems.

The electronic services provided for customers by EBS, Reuters, and Bloomberg also provide a great deal of market data, news, quotes, and statistics about different markets around the world. It is not uncommon for a trading room to have more than one electronic service and for traders to have different preferences within the same office. Bloomberg and Reuters provide market quotes from a large number of banks, so

Tourists changing currency at the foreign currency exchange counter at Central World in Bangkok, Thailand. Tourists have to pay a transactions fee to exchange currency and the traders use different rates to buy and sell foreign exchange.
Source: © nick cunard/Alamy

their quotes are close to the market consensus. EBS provides live trades through their system. Deutsche Bank, UBS, and Barclays Capital are moving to dominate e-trading of foreign exchange on their proprietary platforms. If you are accepted to trade on their platforms, you have to trade at the rates they quote. However, a quick check of the market consensus on Bloomberg or Reuters will let you know how good those quotes are.

Reuters, EBS, and Bloomberg provide electronic services for their customers. These services include market data, news, quotes, and statistics about different markets around the world.

Some Aspects of the Foreign-Exchange Market

The foreign-exchange market has two major segments: the over-the-counter market (OTC) and the exchange-traded market. The OTC market is composed of commercial banks as just described, investment banks, and other financial institutions. The exchange-traded market comprises securities exchanges, such as the CME Group (Chicago Mercantile Exchange), NASDAQ OMX, and NYSE Liffe, where certain types of foreign-exchange instruments, such as futures and options, are traded.

Foreign-exchange market:
- Over-the-counter (OTC) commercial and investment banks.
- Securities exchanges.

Global OTC foreign exchange instruments:
- Spot.
- Outright forward.
- FX swap.
- Currency swaps.
- Currency options.
- Other foreign exchange products.

GLOBAL OTC FOREIGN-EXCHANGE INSTRUMENTS

The phrase global OTC foreign-exchange instruments refers to *spot transactions, outright forwards, FX swaps, currency swaps, currency options, and other foreign-exchange products.* These instruments are all traded in the markets mentioned above. **Spot transactions** involve the exchange of currency at an agreed upon rate for delivery within two business days. The rate at which the transaction is settled is the **spot rate**. (Our opening case, which discusses Western Union's policies on currency conversion, gives a good idea of how individuals can trade foreign exchange on the spot market.)

Case Review Note

Outright forward transactions involve the exchange of currency on a future date beyond two business days. It is the single purchase or sale of a currency for future delivery. The rate at which the transaction is settled is the forward rate and is a contract rate between the two parties. The forward transaction will be settled at the forward rate no matter what the actual spot rate is at the time of settlement.

The spot rate is the exchange rate quoted for transactions that require delivery within two days.

In an **FX swap,** one currency is swapped for another on one date and then swapped back on a future date. Most often, the first or short leg of an FX swap is a spot transaction and the second or long leg a forward transaction. Let's say IBM receives a dividend in British pounds from its subsidiary in the United Kingdom but has no use for British pounds until it has to pay a U.K. supplier in 30 days. It would rather have dollars now than hold onto the pounds for a month. IBM could enter into an FX swap in which it sells the pounds for dollars to a dealer in the spot market at the spot rate and agrees to buy pounds for dollars from the dealer in 30 days at the forward rate. Although an FX swap is both a spot and a forward transaction, it is accounted for as a single transaction.

Outright forwards involve the exchange of currency beyond three days at a fixed exchange rate, known as the forward rate.

An FX swap is a simultaneous spot and forward transaction.

Currency swaps deal more with interest-bearing financial instruments (such as a bond) and involve the exchange of principal and interest payments. Western Union, the subject of our opening case, is more directly involved in spot transactions and in transferring funds from one country to another. **Options** are the right, but not the obligation, to trade foreign currency in the future.

Case Review Note

A **futures contract** is an agreement between two parties to buy or sell a particular currency at a particular price on a particular future date, as specified in a standardized contract to all participants in that currency futures exchange and is not traded OTC.

Figure 9.2 illustrates the turnover in foreign exchange by each of the instruments above (except for futures which are traded on an exchange instead of over the counter). Outright forwards and FX swaps remain the dominant category of instruments, although much of the gain from 2007–2010 was in the spot market, especially from trades by other financial institutions.

Currency swaps, options, and futures contracts are other forms of transactions in foreign exchange.

FIGURE 9.2   Foreign-Exchange Markets: Turnover by Instrument, December 2010

The spot market turnover increased by 8 percent since the 2007 survey. This is largely due to other financial institutions participating in more active trading. The rest of the markets grew as well but at more moderate paces.

Source: Based on Bank for International Settlements, *Central Bank Survey Report on Global Foreign Exchange Market Activity in 2010* (Basel, Switzerland: BIS, December 2010): 10.

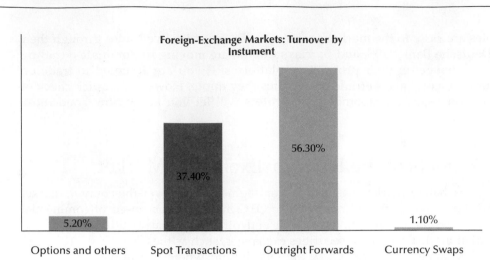

Foreign-Exchange Markets: Turnover by Instument

Options and others	Spot Transactions	Outright Forwards	Currency Swaps
5.20%	37.40%	56.30%	1.10%

Estimated daily foreign exchange turnover in 2010 was $4 trillion, up 20 percent from the 2007 survey

SIZE, COMPOSITION, AND LOCATION OF THE FOREIGN-EXCHANGE MARKET

Before we examine the market instruments in more detail, let's look at the size, composition, and geographic location of the market. Every three years, the BIS conducts a survey of foreign-exchange activity in the world. As noted in Figure 9.3, the BIS estimated daily foreign exchange turnover to be $4 trillion. This reflects an increase of 20 percent over the 2007 survey, driven largely by increases in spot market transactions as noted above. However, the rise in activity was much smaller than the 71 percent increase in trades from 2004 to 2007. The global economic crisis clearly slowed down the volume of foreign-exchange transactions, but global recovery from the crisis, although still a little slow, should cause foreign-exchange activity to pick up even more.

Some of the reasons for the increase in trading activity are the growing importance of foreign exchange as an alternative asset and a larger emphasis on **hedge funds**—funds typically used by wealthy individuals and institutions that are allowed to use aggressive strategies unavailable to mutual funds.

FIGURE 9.3   Foreign-Exchange Markets: Average Daily Volume, 1998–2010

The data compiled by the BIS include traditional foreign-exchange activity (such as spots, outright forwards, and FX swaps), as well as the volume of derivatives (such as hedge funds) traded in the OTC.

Source: Based on Bank for International Settlements, *Central Bank Survey Report on Global Foreign Exchange Market Activity in 2010* (Basel, Switzerland: BIS, December 2010): 7.

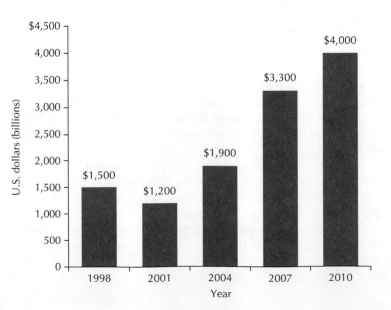

Year	U.S. dollars (billions)
1998	$1,500
2001	$1,200
2004	$1,900
2007	$3,300
2010	$4,000

Using the U.S. Dollar on the Foreign-Exchange Market The U.S. dollar is the most important currency on the foreign-exchange market; in 2010, it comprised one side (buy or sell) of 84.9 percent of all foreign currency transactions worldwide, as Table 9.1 shows. (Numbers in the table are percentages and add up to 200 percent because there are two sides to each transaction.) There are five major reasons why the dollar is so widely traded:[7]

1. It's an investment currency in many capital markets.
2. It's a reserve currency held by many central banks.
3. It's a transaction currency in many international commodity markets.
4. It's an invoice currency in many contracts.
5. It's an intervention currency employed by monetary authorities in market operations to influence their own exchange rates.

Because of the ready availability of U.S. dollars worldwide, this currency is important as a vehicle for foreign-exchange transactions between two countries other than the United States. Let's say a Mexican company importing products from a Japanese exporter converts Mexican pesos into dollars and sends them to the Japanese exporter, who converts them into yen. Thus, the dollar has one leg on both sides of the transaction—in Mexico and in Japan. Why? One reason is that the Japanese exporter might have no need for pesos but can use dollars for a variety of reasons. Or the Mexican importer might have trouble getting yen at a good exchange rate if the Mexican banks are not carrying yen balances. However, the banks undoubtedly carry dollar balances, so the importer might have easy access to the dollars. Thus, the dollar greatly simplifies life for a foreign bank because the bank doesn't have to carry balances in many different currencies. Note the rise in the euro and yen as a percentage of transactions and the slight fall in the U.S. dollar. The currencies of the BRIC countries do not show up on Table 9.1, because their trades are each less than 1 percent of the total. However, they are steadily rising in importance, and we'll explore the situation involving the Chinese yuan in the ending case.

Frequently Traded Currency Pairs Another way to consider foreign currency trades is to look at the most frequently traded currency pairs. The top seven pairs in the 2010 BIS Survey involved the U.S. dollar, with the top two being euro/dollar (EUR/USD)—28 percent of the total—and dollar/yen (USD/JPY).[8] Because of the importance of the dollar in foreign-exchange trade, the exchange rate between two currencies other than the U.S. dollar is known as a **cross rate.** For example, the exchange rate between the Swiss franc and the Brazilian real would be a cross rate.

Concept Check

It's interesting (though not necessarily surprising) to note that the most widely traded currencies in the world are those issued by countries that enjoy high levels of political freedom (see Chapter 3) and economic freedom (see Chapter 4).

The dollar is the most widely traded currency in the world:

- An investment currency in many capital markets.
- A reserve currency held by many central banks.
- A transaction currency in many international commodity markets.
- An invoice currency in many contracts.
- An intervention currency employed by monetary authorities in market operations to influence their own exchange rates.

The dollar is part of four of the top seven currency pairs traded:

- The dollar/euro is number one.
- The dollar/yen is number two.

TABLE 9.1 Global Foreign Exchange: Currency Distribution

The U.S. dollar is involved in 84.9 percent of all worldwide foreign-exchange transactions. Because it's so readily available, it's a popular choice for exchanges between two countries other than the United States, and it's involved in four of the seven most frequently traded currency pairs (the $/€ is number one, the $/¥ number two).

Currency	April 1998	April 2001	April 2004	April 2007	April 2010
U.S. dollar	86.8	89.9	88.0	85.6	84.9
Euro	—	37.9	37.4	37.0	39.1
Japanese yen	21.7	23.5	20.8	17.2	19.0
Pound sterling	11.0	13.0	16.5	14.9	12.9
Australian dollar	3.0	4.3	6.0	6.6	7.6
Swiss franc	7.1	6.0	6.0	6.8	6.4
All others	70.4	25.4	25.3	31.9	30.1

Source: Based on Bank for International Settlements, *Central Bank Survey Report on Global Foreign Exchange Market Activity in 2010* (Basel, Switzerland: BIS, December 2010): 12.

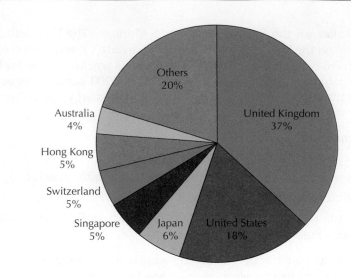

FIGURE 9.4 Foreign-Exchange Markets: Geographical Distribution, December 2010

The United Kingdom handles 37 percent of all world foreign-exchange activity (compared to just 18 percent by the United States). Location is a big factor in the United Kingdom's popularity: London is close to all the capital markets of Europe, and its time zone makes it convenient for making trades in both the U.S. and Asian markets.

Source: Based on Bank for International Settlements, *Central Bank Survey Report on Global Foreign Exchange Market Activity in 2010* (Basel, Switzerland: BIS, December 2010): 16.

The trade between the dollar and yen is very sensitive politically, because the exchange rate is often a function of trade negotiations between Japan and the United States.[9] The Japanese yen is an important currency in Asia because its value reflects the competitive positions of other countries in the region and because it is freely traded—unlike the Chinese yuan, which is more tightly controlled by the government but is moving to become more of a regional and eventually a global currency (as discussed in the ending case). The yen is also affected by what is called **carry trade.** With interest rates being so low in Japan, investors will borrow in yen and invest the proceeds in other countries, such as Brazil. However, at the slightest concern over a risky global economic environment, the investors will liquidate their investments in Brazil and "carry" the proceeds back to Japan. This also occurs at the end of the fiscal year in Japan (March 31) when companies may need Japanese yen. Other carry trades often followed by the market are the U.S. dollar against the South African rand and the Hong Kong dollar, the Australian dollar against the Japanese yen, and the New Zealand dollar against the Japanese yen.

The Euro   The euro is also in four of the top 10 currency pairs. Although the dollar is still more popular in most emerging markets, the euro is gaining ground, particularly in Eastern European countries. However, the euro is slowly increasing in importance as a trading currency, even outside of Europe. Given that the dollar is clearly the most widely traded currency in the world, you'd expect the biggest market for foreign-exchange trading would be in the United States. As Figure 9.4 illustrates, however, the biggest by far is in the United Kingdom. The four largest centers for foreign-exchange trading (the United Kingdom, the United States, Japan, and Singapore) account for 62.5 percent of the total average daily turnover. The U.K. market is so dominant that more dollars are traded in London than in New York.[10]

> The biggest market for foreign exchange is London, followed by New York, Tokyo, and Singapore.

Major Foreign-Exchange Markets

THE SPOT MARKET

Foreign-exchange dealers are the ones who quote the rates. The **bid (buy) rate** is the price at which the dealer is willing to buy foreign currency; the **offer (sell)** is the price at which the dealer is willing to sell foreign currency. In the spot market, the **spread** is the difference between the bid and offer rates, as well as the dealer's profit margin. In our opening case, we explain how Western Union quotes exchange rates for the purpose of trading dollars for pesos. Its rates are often different from those quoted by commercial banks, but some people prefer to use Western Union, pay higher fees, and get lower exchange rates. Why? In part, because of a lack of trust in the banking system.

Case Review Note

Does Ge🌐graphy Matter? Foreign-Exchange Trades

Given that the U.S. dollar is the most widely traded currency in the world, why is London so important as a trading center? There are two major reasons. First, London, which is close to the major capital markets in Europe, is a strong international financial center where many domestic and foreign financial institutions operate. Thus, its geographic location relative to significant global economic activity is key.

Second, London is positioned in a unique way because of its time zone. As Map 9.1 shows, noon in London is 7:00 a.m. in New York and evening in Asia. The London market opens toward the end of the trading day in Asia and is going strong as the New York foreign-exchange market opens up. Thus, the city straddles both of the other major world markets.

Another way to illustrate the importance of geography is to note the daily volume of market activity that takes place in different markets around the world, especially in North America and Europe. Figure 9.5 shows the average number of electronic conversations

MAP 9.1 International Time Zones and the Single World Market

The world's communication networks are now so good that we can talk of a single world market. It starts in a small way in New Zealand at around 9:00 a.m. (local time), just in time to catch the tail end of the previous night's market in New York (where it's about 4:00 p.m. local time). Two or three hours later, Tokyo opens, followed an hour later by Hong Kong and Manila, then half an hour later by Singapore. By now, with the Far East market in full swing, the focus moves to the Near and Middle East. Mumbai (formerly Bombay) opens two hours after Singapore, followed after an hour and a half by Abu Dhabi and Athens. At this stage, trading in the Far and Middle East is usually thin as dealers wait to see how Europe will trade. Paris and Frankfurt open an hour ahead of London, and by this time Tokyo is starting to close down, so the European market can judge the Japanese market. By lunchtime in London, New York is starting to open up, and as Europe closes down, positions can be passed westward. Midday in New York, trading tends to be quiet because there is nowhere to pass a position to. The San Francisco market, three hours behind New York, is effectively a satellite of the New York market, although very small positions can be passed on to New Zealand banks. (Note that in the former Soviet Union, standard time zones are advanced an hour. Also note that some countries and territories have adopted half-hour time zones, as shown by hatched lines.)

Source: Adapted from Julian Walmsley, *The Foreign Exchange Handbook* (New York: John Wiley, 1983): 7–8. Reprinted by permission of John Wiley & Sons, Inc. Some information taken from *The Cambridge Factfinders*, 3rd ed., David Crystal (ed.) (New York: Cambridge University Press, 1998): 440.

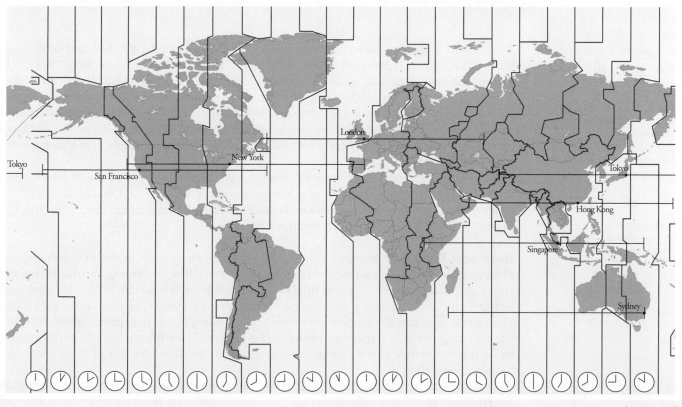

(continued)

FIGURE 9.5   The Circadian Rhythms of the Foreign-Exchange Market

Peak periods for foreign-exchange activity occur between about 0600 and 1200 hours (when both European and U.S. markets are open for business) and 1200 and 1800 hours (when both U.S. and Asian markets are active). Time (0100–2400) is Greenwich Mean Time.

Source: Zaheer, Srilata, "Circadian Rhythms: The Effects of Global Market Integration in the Currency Trading Industry, " *Journal of International Business Studies* 26:4 (1995): 699–728, Figure 1.

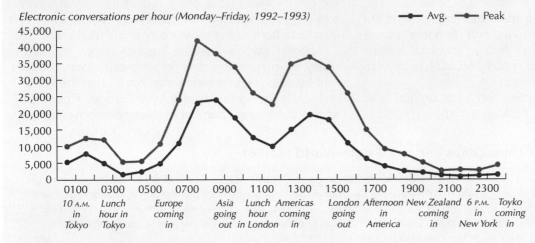

Electronic conversations per hour (Monday–Friday, 1992–1993)   ●— Avg.   ●— Peak

per hour as monitored by Reuters. It also shows how market activity is concentrated on the time period when both Asia and Europe are open, or when both Europe and the United States are open, even though the market is really open electronically 24 hours a day. Because the U.S. dollar is the world's most widely traded currency and London is the major market center for dollars traded outside the United States, it makes sense that most market activity would take place during the hours that the U.S. and London markets are open. A better price for currencies can be had when the markets are active and liquid. ●

Key foreign-exchange terms:

- Bid—the rate at which traders buy foreign exchange.
- Offer—the rate at which traders sell foreign exchange.
- Spread—the difference between bid and offer rates.
- American terms, or direct quote—the number of dollars per unit of foreign currency.
- European terms, or indirect quote—the number of units of foreign currency per dollar.

Direct and Indirect Quotes   Let's look at an example of how a bid and offer might work. The rate a U.S.-based dealer quotes for the British pound is $1.6339/41. This means the dealer is willing to buy pounds at $1.6339 each and sell them for $1.6341 each—i.e., buying low and selling high. In this example, the dealer quotes the foreign currency as the number of U.S. dollars for one unit of it. This method of quoting exchange rates is called the **direct quote,** which is the number of units of the domestic currency (the U.S. dollar in this case) for one unit of the foreign currency. It is also known as **American terms.**

The other convention for quoting foreign exchange is known as the **indirect quote,** which is the number of units of the foreign currency for one unit of the domestic currency. It is also known as **European terms.** In Table 9.2, the direct quote for the U.K. pound is $1.6339, and the indirect quote is £0.6120.

Base and Term Currencies   When dealers quote currencies to their customers, they always quote the **base currency** (the denominator) first, followed by the **terms currency** (the numerator). A quote for USD/JPY (also shown as USDJPY = X) means the dollar is the base currency and the yen is the terms currency. If you know the dollar/yen quote, you can divide that rate into 1 to get the yen/dollar quote. In other words, the exchange rate in American terms is the reciprocal or inverse of the exchange rate in European terms. For example, using the rates in Table 9.2 for the Japanese yen, 1/.012359 = ¥80.91.

In a dollar/yen quote, the dollar is the denominator and the yen is the numerator. By tracking changes in the exchange rate, managers can determine whether the base currency is strengthening or weakening. For example, on June 1, 2010, the dollar/yen rate

TABLE 9.2 Foreign-Exchange Markets, July 1, 2011

The *direct* quote—the price of the foreign currency in terms of the home-country currency—is given in the column headed "In US$"; the *indirect* quote—the price of the home-country currency in terms of the foreign currency—is given in the column headed "Per US$."

Country/currency	— Wed — In US$	per US$	US$ vs, YTDchg (%)	Country/currency	— Wed — In US$	per US$	US$ vs, YTDchg (%)
Americas				**Europe**			
Argentina peso*	.2449	4.0833	2.9	**Czech Rep.** koruna	.05851	17.091	−8.7
Brazil real	.6275	1.5936	−4.0	**Denmark** krone	.1923	5.2002	−6.7
Canada dollar	1.0253	.9753	−2.2	**Euro** area euro	1.4340	.6974	−6.8
1-mos forward	1.0245	.9761	−2.2	**Hungary** forint	.005375	186.05	−10.6
3-mos forward	1.0230	.9775	−2.2	**Norway** krone	.1839	5.4377	−6.7
6-mos forward	1.0204	.9800	−2.2	**Poland** zloty	.3612	2.7685	−6.6
Chile peso	.002135	468.38	0.1	**Russia** ruble‡	.03573	27.988	−8.5
Colombia peso	.0005580	1792.11	−6.7	**Sweden** krona	.1601	6.2461	−7.1
Ecuador US dollar	1	1	unch	**Switzerland** franc	1.1867	.8427	−9.8
Mexico peso*	.0855	11.6945	−5.2	1-mos forward	1.1869	.8425	−9.8
Peru new sol	.3593	2.783	−0.8	3-mos forward	1.1874	.8422	−9.8
Uruguay peso†	.05390	18.55	−6.7	6-mos forward	1.1882	.8416	−9.7
Venezuela b. fuerte	.232851	4.2946	unch	**Turkey** lira**	.6256	1.5985	3.7
				UK pound	1.6339	.6120	−4.5
Asia-Pacific				1-mos forward	1.6333	.6123	−4.5
				3-mos forward	1.6319	.6128	−4.5
Australian dollar	1.0617	.9419	−3.8	6-mos forward	1.6297	.6136	−4.5
China yuan	.1543	6.4790	−1.7				
Hong Kong dollar	.1285	7.7795	0.1	**Middle East/Africa**			
India rupee	.02227	44.904	−0.4				
Indonesia rupiah	.0001172	8532	−5.3	**Bahrain** dinar	2.6527	.3770	unch
Japan yen	.012359	80.91	−0.4	**Egypt** pound*	.1683	5.9404	2.3
1-mos forward	.012360	80.91	−0.3	**Israel** shekel	.2917	3.4282	−2.7
3-mos forward	.012364	80.88	−0.3	**Jordan** dinar	1.4106	.7089	0.1
6-mos forward	.012372	80.83	−0.3	**Kuwait** dinar	3.6298	.2755	−2.1
Malaysia ringgit	.3322	3.0102	−2.4	**Lebanon** pound	.0006618	1511.03	0.7
New Zealand dollar	.8162	1.2252	−4.6	**Saudi Arabia** riyal	.2667	3.7495	unch
Pakistan rupee	.01162	86.059	0.4	**South Africa** rand	.1463	6.8353	3.1
Philippines peso	.0232	43.048	−1.4	**UAE** dirham	.2723	3.6724	unch
Singapore dollar	.8072	1.2389	−3.5				
South Korea won	.0009273	1078.40	−3.8				
Taiwan dollar	.03499	28.580	−2.0				
Thailand baht	.03307	30.239	0.6				
Vietnam dong	.00004858	20585	5.6	SDR††	1.5998	.6251	−3.7

Source: Currencies and Commodities, *The Wall Street Journal* June 2, 2011:C4.

*Floating rate

†Financial

§Government rate

‡Russian Central Bank rate

**Rebased as of Jan 1, 2005

‡‡Special Drawing Rights (SDR); from the International Monetary Fund; based on exchange rates for U.S., British and Japanese currencies.

was ¥90.93/$1.00, and on June 1, 2011, it was ¥80.91/$1.00. As the numerator falls, the base currency (the dollar) is weakening or getting less expensive. Conversely, the terms currency (the yen) is strengthening or getting more expensive from a dollar perspective.

There are many ways to get exchange rate quotes, including online and print media. Because most currencies constantly fluctuate in value, many managers check

The foreign exchange trading floor of Deutsche Bank in the city of London shows terminals that provide information to the traders as they buy and sell the currencies for which they are responsible. Since current events are important in the psychology of the market, the overhead TV shows the Governor of the Bank of England addressing key economic forces.

Source: Edward Karaa/Dreamstime. com

the values daily. For example, the *Wall Street Journal* provides quotes in American terms (US$ equivalent) and European terms (currency per US$), as shown in Table 9.2. All quotes, except those noted as one-month, three-month, and six-month forwards, are spot quotes.

Interbank Transactions   The spot rates provided by the WSJ are the selling rates for **interbank transactions** of $1 million and more. Retail transactions—those between banks and companies or individuals—provide fewer foreign currency units per dollar than interbank transactions. Similar quotes can be found in other business publications and online. However, these are only approximations; exact quotes are available through the dealers.

THE FORWARD MARKET

The forward rate is the rate quoted for transactions that call for delivery after two business days.

As noted earlier, the spot market is for foreign-exchange transactions that occur within two business days. But in some transactions, a seller extends credit to the buyer for a period longer than that. For example, a Japanese exporter of consumer electronics might sell television sets to a U.S. importer with immediate delivery but payment due in 30 days. The U.S. importer is obligated to pay in yen in 30 days and may enter into a contract with a currency dealer to deliver the yen at a forward rate—the rate quoted today for future delivery.

In addition to the spot rates for each currency, Table 9.2 shows the forward rates for the British pound, Canadian dollar, Japanese yen, and Swiss franc—the most widely traded currencies in the forward market. However, forward contracts are available from dealers in many other currencies as well. Electronic services such as Bloomberg provide forward rates for most currencies for different maturity dates in the future. The more exotic the currency, the more difficult it is to get a forward quote out too far in the future, and the greater the difference is likely to be between the forward rate and the spot rate.

Forward Discounts and Premiums Building on what we said earlier, we now can say that the difference between the spot and forward rates is either the **forward discount** or the **forward premium.** An easy way to understand the difference between the forward and spot rates for U.S. companies is to use currency quotes in American terms. If the forward rate for a foreign currency is less than the spot rate, then the currency is selling at a forward discount. If the forward rate is greater than the spot rate, the currency is selling at a forward premium. Using the direct quotes in Table 9.2 for the Swiss franc for a six-month forward contract, the premium or discount would be computed as follows:

$$\frac{0.8416 - 0.8427}{0.8427} \times \frac{12}{6} = -0.0026107 \text{ or } -0.26\%$$

The discount percentage is annualized by multiplying the difference between the spot and forward rates by 12 months divided by the number of months forward—six months, in this example. Because the forward rate is less than the spot rate, the Swiss franc is selling at a discount in the forward market by .26 percent below the spot market.

A premium exists when the foreign currency is worth more in the forward market than in the spot market.

OPTIONS

An option is the *right*, but not the *obligation*, to buy or sell a foreign currency within a certain time period or on a specific date at a specific exchange rate. It can be purchased OTC from a commercial or investment bank or on an exchange. For example, a U.S. company purchases an OTC option from a commercial or investment bank to buy 1,000,000 Japanese yen at ¥85 per US$ ($0.011765 per yen)—or $11,765. The writer of the option will charge the company a fee for writing it. The more likely the option is to benefit the company, the higher the fee. The rate of ¥85 is called the *strike price* for the option; the fee or cost is called the *premium*. On the date when the option is set to expire, the company can look at the spot rate and compare it with the strike price to see what the better exchange rate is. If the spot rate were ¥90 per US$ ($0.01111 per yen)—or $11,000—it would not exercise the option because buying yen at the spot rate would cost less than buying them at the option rate. However, if the spot rate at that time were ¥80 per US$ ($0.0125 per yen)—or $12,500—the company would exercise the option because buying at the option rate would cost less than at the spot rate. The option gives the company flexibility because it can walk away from the option if the strike price is not a good price. In the case of a forward contract, the cost is usually cheaper than the cost for an option, but the company cannot walk away from the contract. So a forward contract is cheaper but less flexible than an option.

An option is the right, but not the obligation, to trade a foreign currency at a specific exchange rate.

The above example is for a simple, or *vanilla*, option. However, exotic or structured options are used more widely to hedge exposure, especially by European companies. The idea behind them is to provide an option product that meets a company's risk profile and tolerance and results in a premium that is as close to zero as possible. The writer of the option can still make money on the structured option, but if the option is set up effectively, the company buying it won't have to write out a big check for the premium. Exchange-traded options are more of the vanilla variety, whereas non-exchange traders have more flexibility to sell structured options.

FUTURES

A foreign currency futures contract resembles a forward contract insofar as it specifies an exchange rate some time in advance of the actual exchange of currency. However, a future is traded on an exchange, not OTC. Instead of working with a bank or other

A futures contract specifies an exchange rate in advance of the actual exchange of currency, but it is not as flexible as a forward contract.

financial institution, companies work with exchange brokers when purchasing futures contracts. A forward contract is tailored to the amount and time frame the company needs, whereas a futures contract is for a specific amount and maturity date. It is less valuable to a company than a forward contract. However, it may be useful to speculators and small companies that cannot enter into the latter.

The Foreign-Exchange Trading Process

When a company sells goods or services to a foreign customer and receives foreign currency, it needs to convert that currency into the domestic currency. When importing, the company needs to convert domestic to foreign currency to pay the foreign supplier. This conversion usually takes place between the company and its bank.

Originally, the commercial banks provided foreign-exchange services for their customers. Eventually, some of the commercial banks in New York and other U.S. money centers, such as Chicago and San Francisco, began to look at foreign-exchange trading as a major business activity instead of just a service. They became intermediaries for smaller banks by establishing correspondent relationships with them. They also became major dealers in foreign exchange.

The left side of Figure 9.6 shows what happens when U.S. Company A needs to sell euros for dollars. This situation could arise when A receives payment in euros from a German importer. The right side of the figure shows what happens when A needs to buy euros with dollars. This situation could arise when a company has to pay euros to a German supplier.

In either case, the U.S. company would contact its bank for help in converting the currency. If it is a large MNE, such as a Fortune 500 firm in the United States or a Global Fortune 500 company, it will probably deal directly with a money center bank (as shown on the top arrow in Figure 9.6) and not worry about another financial institution. Generally, because the MNE already has a strong banking relationship with its money center bank (or several different money center banks), the bank trades foreign exchange

FIGURE 9.6   The Foreign-Exchange Trading Process

Let's say that you're U.S. Company A, that you've received euros in payment for goods, and that you want to sell your euros in return for dollars. To make the exchange, you may contact your local bank or go directly to a money center bank.

On the other hand, perhaps you're U.S. Company B and you expect to receive euros as a future payment. To protect yourself against fluctuations in the exchange rate, you want to buy euros that you can subsequently trade back for dollars. You could choose, say, a forward or a swap, and your path would be essentially a mirror image of Company A's.

Finally, either Company A or Company B could choose to convert by such means as an option or a futures contract—in which case the trade could be made by an options and/or futures exchange, either directly or through a broker.

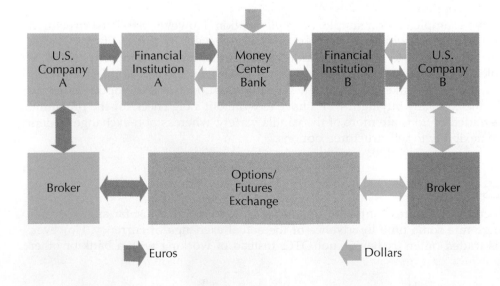

for the client as one of the services it offers. Companies below the Fortune 500 level operate through other financial institutions, such as local or regional banks or other banking institutions that can facilitate foreign-exchange trades. In that case, Financial Institution A and Financial Institution B still operate through a money center bank to make the trade, because they are too small to trade on their own. They typically have correspondent relationships with money center banks to allow them to make the trades.

Assume that U.S. Company B is going to receive euros in the future. Because it cannot convert in the spot market until it receives the euros, it can consider a forward, swap, options, or futures contract to protect itself until the currency is finally delivered. Financial Institution B can do a forward, swap, or options contract for Company B. However, Company B can also consider an options or futures contract on one of the exchanges, such as the CME Group. The same is true for Company A, which will need euros in the future.

BANKS AND EXCHANGES

At one time, only the big money center banks could deal directly in foreign exchange. Regional banks had to rely on them to execute trades on behalf of their clients. The emergence of electronic trading has changed that. Now even the regional banks can hook up to Bloomberg, Reuters, or EBS and deal directly in the interbank market or through brokers. Despite this, the greatest volume of foreign-exchange activity takes place with the big money center banks. Because of their reach and volume, they are the ones that set the prices in global trading of foreign exchange.

Top Foreign-Exchange Dealers There is more to servicing customers in the foreign-exchange market than size alone. Each year, *Euromoney* magazine surveys treasurers, traders, and investors worldwide to identify their favorite banks and the leading dealers in the interbank market. In addition to examining transaction volumes and quality of services, the criteria for selecting the top foreign-exchange dealers include the following:

- Ranking of banks by corporations and other banks in specific locations, such as London, Singapore, and New York
- Capability of handling major currencies, such as the U.S. dollar and the euro
- Capability of handling major cross-trades, such as those between the euro and pound or the euro and yen
- Capability of handling specific currencies
- Capability of handling **derivatives** (forwards, swaps, futures, and options)
- Capability of engaging in research and analytics.[11]

Given the differing capabilities, large companies may use several banks to deal in foreign exchange, selecting those that specialize in specific geographic areas, instruments, or currencies. In the past, for example, AT&T used Citibank for its broad geographic spread and wide coverage of different currencies, but it also used Deutsche Bank for euros, Swiss Bank Corporation for Swiss francs, NatWest Bank for British pounds, and Goldman Sachs for derivatives.

Table 9.3 identifies the top banks in the world in terms of foreign-exchange trading. They are the key players in the OTC market and include commercial banks (such as Deutsche Bank and Citibank) as well as investment banks (such as UBS, the London-based investment banking division of Union Bank of Switzerland and Swiss Bank Corporation). Whether one is looking at overall market share of foreign-exchange trading or the best banks in the trading of specific currency pairs, these top 10 banks are usually at or near the top in every category. It is also interesting to note that consolidation in the banking industry worldwide has resulted in a concentration of foreign exchange activity. For example, in 1998, 177 banks were responsible for 75 percent of the foreign-exchange turnover worldwide, whereas that number had dropped to only 93 banks in

TABLE 9.3   Foreign-Exchange Trades: Top Commercial and Investment Banks, 2011 as Ranked by Overall Market Share

Trading Bank	Estimated Market Share%	Market Share in Western Europe	Market Share in North America	Market Share in Asia	Market Share in Australasia
1. Deutsche Bank	15.64%	13.86%	14.95%	20.90%	26.26%
2. Barclays Capital	10.75%	10.30%	11.81%	10.79%	9.91%
3. UBS	10.59%	13.60%	9.32%	6.29%	7.17%
4. Citi	8.88%	7.34%	10.66%	10.18%	9.47%
5. JPMorgan	6.43%	5.36%	8.19%	5.38%	6.25%
6. HSBC	6.26%	6.93%	—	9.31%	4.12%
7. RBS	6.20%	6.90%	6.31%	5.87%	5.56%
8. Credit Suisse	4.80%	7.06%	—	—	—
9. Goldman Sachs	4.13%	3.07%	5.89%	—	5.74%
10. Morgan Stanley	3.64%	3.00%	6.75%	—	—

*Estimated Market Share source: "FX Poll 2001: Overall Market Share," *Euromoney* (May 2011) and Market Share by Region source: "FX Poll 2011: Market Share by Region," *Euromoney* (May 2011).

2010. In the United States, that number had dropped from 20 to 7, and in the United Kingdom, it had dropped from 24 to 9.[12]

Concept Check

In Chapter 11, we explain why companies work so hard to establish and maintain effective value chains—frameworks for dividing value-creating activities into separate processes. For one thing, a reliable value chain permits a firm to focus on its core competencies—the unique skills or knowledge that make it better at something than its competitors. Because managing currencies and cross-trades is typically not among a firm's core competencies, its bankers are key components of its value chain.

Major exchanges that deal in foreign currency derivatives are the CME Group, NASDAQ OMX, and NYSE Liffe.

TOP EXCHANGES FOR TRADING FOREIGN EXCHANGE

In addition to the OTC market, foreign-exchange instruments, mostly options and futures, are traded on commodities exchanges. Three of the best-known exchanges are the **Chicago Mercantile Exchange (CME) Group, NASDAQ OMX,** and **NYSE Liffe.**

CME Group   The CME Group was formed on July 9, 2007, as a merger between the Chicago Mercantile Exchange and the Chicago Board of Trade. The CME operates according to so-called open outcry: Traders stand in a pit and call out prices and quantities. The platform is also linked to an electronic trading platform, which is growing in popularity. The CME Group trades many different commodities. In terms of foreign exchange, it trades a suite of 54 futures and 31 options contacts, with a liquidity of over $100 billion daily. Futures and options are traded in G10 and emerging market currencies. Contracts are available for the dollar against a variety of currencies as well as cross-trades, such as the euro against the Australian dollar.

In 2005, CME entered into an agreement with Reuters to have its futures contracts quoted, which should increase the access of trades to futures contracts.[13] In 2007, CME and Reuters teamed up again to launch the world's first centrally cleared global foreign-exchange platform, *FXMarketSpace*. The basic idea behind the model is to establish a centrally cleared global platform that allows customers to buy and sell currencies anonymously. The new venture is targeting hedge funds that are using computer-driven trading models to trade foreign exchange.[14] CME uses two electronic trading platforms to trade different commodities, including currencies: CME Globex and CME Clearport. Technology is the key to opening access to trades and expanding their reach worldwide.

NASDAQ OMX   Prior to 2008, the Philadelphia Stock Exchange was one of the pioneers in trading currency options. In July 2008, PHLX merged with NASDAQ OMX and created the third-largest options market in the United States. They also formed a new hybrid of trading, which involves both traditional floor and online trading. Options were being offered by PHLX in the Australian dollar, the British pound, the Canadian dollar, the euro, the Japanese yen, and the Swiss franc. Futures were offered in British pounds and the euro.[15] These activities have now been absorbed by NASDAQ OMX.

NYSE Liffe   NYSE Liffe Futures and Options is the global derivatives business of the NYSE Euronext Group. Historically, the London International Financial Futures and Options Exchange (LIFFE) was founded in 1992 to trade a variety of futures contracts and options. It was subsequently bought in 2002 by Euronext, then a European stock exchange based in Paris but with subsidiaries in other European countries. Beginning in 2003, the electronic platform where its derivatives products traded on member exchanges was known as LIFFE CONNECT. In 2007, Euronext merged with the New York Stock Exchange to create NYSE Euronext. The international derivatives business of NYSE Euronext is now handled by NYSE Liffe, using the LIFFE CONNECT platform developed before the merger between NYSE and Euronext. Dollar/Euro and Euro/Dollar futures and options are traded on LIFFE CONNECT.

How Companies Use Foreign Exchange

Companies enter the foreign-exchange market to facilitate their regular business transactions and/or to speculate. Their treasury departments are responsible for establishing policies for trading currency and for managing banking relationships to make the trades. From a business standpoint, a company, first of all, trades foreign exchange for exports/ imports and the buying or selling of goods and services.

For example, when Boeing sells the new 787 Dreamliner commercial airplane to LAN, the largest airline in South America, it has to be concerned about the currency in which it will be paid and how it will receive payment. In this case, the sale is probably denominated in dollars, so Boeing will not have to worry about the foreign-exchange market (nor, in theory, will its employees—see the cartoon in Figure 9.7). However, LAN will have to worry about the market. Where will it come up with the dollars, and how will it pay Boeing?

> **Concept Check**
>
> In Chapter 19, we discuss the functions of a company's CFO, not only in managing its cash flows, but in managing its foreign-exchange exposure— the extent to which fluctuations in currencies can affect the costs of its international transactions.

FIGURE 9.7   Tourist Foreign Exchange

Source: Copyright John Morris, businesscartoons.co.uk.

BUSINESS PURPOSES (I): CASH FLOW ASPECTS OF IMPORTS AND EXPORTS

When a company must move money to pay for purchases, or receives money from sales, it has options as to the documents it can use, the currency of denomination, and the degree of protection it can ask for. Obviously, if Boeing wanted the greatest security possible, it could ask LAN to pay for the Dreamliner before LAN takes title to the aircraft. That is not very practical in this case, but sometimes it happens when the seller has all of the control in the transaction. More common is the use of commercial bills of exchange and letters of credit.

> With a draft or commercial bill of exchange, one party directs another party to make payment.

Commercial Bills of Exchange An individual or a company that pays a bill in a domestic setting can pay cash, but checks are typically used—often electronically transmitted. The check is also known as a **draft** or a **commercial bill of exchange.** A draft is an instrument in which one party (the *drawer*) directs another party (the *drawee*) to make a payment. The drawee can be either a company, like the importer, or a bank. In the latter case, the draft would be considered a bank draft.

> A sight draft requires payment to be made when it is presented. A time draft permits payment to be made after the date when it is presented.

Documentary drafts and documentary letters of credit are often used to protect both the buyer and the seller. They require that payment be made based on the presentation of documents conveying the title, and they leave an audit trail identifying the parties to the transactions. If the exporter requests payment to be made immediately, the draft is called a **sight draft.** If the payment is to be made later—say, 30 days after delivery—the instrument is called a **time draft.**

> A letter of credit obligates the buyer's bank to honor a draft presented to it and assume payment; a credit relationship exists between the importer and the importer's bank.

Letters of Credit With a bill of exchange, it is always possible that the importer will not be able to make payment to the exporter at the agreed-on time. A **letter of credit (L/C),** however, obligates the buyer's bank in the importing country to honor a draft presented to it, provided the draft is accompanied by the prescribed documents. Of course, the exporter still needs to be sure the bank's credit is valid as well, since the L/C could be a forgery issued by a "nonexistent bank." Even with the added security of the bank, the exporter still needs to rely on the importer's credit because of possible discrepancies that could arise in the transaction. The L/C could be denominated in the currency of either party. If it is in the importer's currency, the exporter will still have to convert the foreign exchange into its currency through its commercial bank.

Although a letter of credit is more secure than a documentary draft alone, there are still risks. For the L/C to be valid, all of the conditions described in the documents must be adhered to. For example, if the L/C states that the goods will be shipped in five packages, it will not be valid if they are shipped in four or six packages. It is important to understand the conditions of the documents, as well as counterparty risk. Although a forged L/C is an obvious danger, the global financial crisis has exposed counterparty risk when banks did not have sufficient capital to stand behind their L/Cs. Prior to 2008, the risk was not so significant; afterward, businesses were hesitant to trust their banks because they might not be able to deliver on an L/C. In addition, letters of credit are irrevocable, which means they cannot be canceled or changed in any way without the consent of all parties to the transaction.

A key issue related to this chapter is that the L/C needs to specify the currency of the contract. If the L/C is not in the exporter's currency, the exporter will have to convert the foreign exchange into that currency as soon as it is received.

Confirmed Letter of Credit A letter of credit transaction may include a confirming bank in addition to the parties mentioned previously. With a **confirmed letter of credit,** the exporter has the guarantee of an additional bank—sometimes in the exporter's home country, sometimes in a third country. It rarely happens that the exporter establishes the confirming relationship. Usually, the opening bank seeks the confirmation of the L/C with a bank with which it already has a credit relationship. For an irrevocable L/C, none of the conditions can be changed unless all four parties agree in advance.[16]

BUSINESS PURPOSES (II): OTHER FINANCIAL FLOWS

Companies may have to deal in foreign exchange for other reasons. For example, if a U.S. company has a subsidiary in the United Kingdom and the subsidiary sends a dividend to the parent company in British pounds, the parent company has to enter into the foreign-exchange market to convert pounds to dollars. If it lends dollars to the British subsidiary, the subsidiary has to convert the dollars into pounds. When paying principal and interest back to the parent company, it has to convert pounds into dollars.

> Companies also deal in foreign exchange for other transactions, such as the receipt or payment of dividends or the receipt or payment of loans and interest.

Speculation   Companies sometimes deal in foreign exchange for profit. This is especially true for some banks and all hedge funds. But sometimes corporate treasury departments see their foreign-exchange operations as profit centers and also buy and sell foreign exchange with the objective of earning profits.

Investors can use foreign-exchange transactions to speculate for profit or to protect against risk. **Speculation** is the buying or selling of a commodity—in this case, foreign currency—that has both an element of risk and a chance of great profit. Assume that a hedge fund buys euros in anticipation that the euro will strengthen against other currencies. If it does, the investor earns a profit; if it weakens, the investor incurs a loss. Speculators are important in the foreign-exchange market because they spot trends and try to take advantage of them. They can create demand for a currency by purchasing it in the market, or they can create a supply of it by selling it in the market. However, speculation is also a very risky business. In recent years, the advent of e-trading has attracted a lot of day traders in foreign exchange. The problem is that day traders rarely make money speculating in exchange rates. As we will show in Chapter 10, forecasting currency movements is indeed a risky business.

> Speculators take positions in foreign-exchange markets and other capital markets to earn a profit.

Arbitrage   One type of profit-seeking activity is **arbitrage,** which is the purchase of foreign currency on one market for immediate resale on another market (in a different country) to profit from a price discrepancy. For example, a dealer might sell U.S. dollars for Swiss francs in the United States, then Swiss francs for British pounds in Switzerland, then the British pounds for U.S. dollars back in the United States, with the goal of ending up with more dollars.

> Arbitrage is the buying and selling of foreign currencies at a profit due to price discrepancies.

Here's how the process might work. Assume the dealer converts 100 dollars into 150 Swiss francs when the exchange rate is 1.2 francs per dollar. The dealer then converts the 150 francs into 70 British pounds at an exchange rate of 0.467 pounds per franc and finally converts the pounds into 125 dollars at an exchange rate of 0.56 pounds per dollar. In this case, arbitrage yields $125 from the initial sale of $100. Given the transparency of exchange rate quotes globally, it is difficult to make a lot of money on arbitrage, but it is possible for an investor who has a lot of money and can move quickly.

Interest arbitrage is the investing in debt instruments, such as bonds, in different countries. A dealer might invest $1,000 in the United States for 90 days; or the dealer could convert $1,000 into British pounds, invest the money in the United Kingdom for 90 days, then convert the pounds back into dollars. The investor would try to pick the alternative that would yield the highest return at the end of 90 days.

> Interest arbitrage involves investing in interest-bearing instruments in foreign exchange in an effort to earn a profit due to interest rate differentials.

Point

Is It OK to Speculate on Currency?

Point

Yes People trade in foreign exchange for a number of reasons, and one of them is speculation, which is not illegal or necessarily bad. Just as stockbrokers invest people's money to try to earn a return higher than the market average, foreign currency traders invest people's money in foreign exchange to make a profit for the investors. Or individuals can become day traders and try to make a profit trading online on their own. Speculation is merely taking a position on a currency in order to profit from market trends.

Electronic trading has made it easier for a variety of investors to speculate in foreign exchange. Hedge funds are an important source of this foreign-exchange speculation. There is no one specific strategy that hedge fund managers follow. However, the transparency in trading has driven the smaller players out of the market and allowed the large institutions and traders to earn profits on small margins that require large volumes of transactions. Hedge funds generally deal in minimum investments that are quite large, so the hedge fund managers that trade in foreign exchange trade in very large volumes. They might make long-term bets on a currency based on macroeconomic conditions, or they might try to balance off buy-and-sell strategies in currencies so that one side offers protection against the other. In either case, the hedge fund manager is betting on the future position of a currency to earn money for the investors in the fund.

Speculation is not for the faint of heart. Political and economic conditions outside the speculators' control can quickly turn profits to losses—probably quicker than in the stock market. Currencies are inherently unstable. Consider the problems of the U.S. dollar in 2007 and 2008, when it was quite weak against the euro and the yen. What should hedge fund managers do? They might expect the dollar to continue to weaken. But what if it strengthens? Or they might think the dollar has reached its floor and is ready for a rise, which would argue that the managers should buy dollars. But when will it rise and by how much? By

mid-March 2008, the dollar had declined by 15 percent in the prior 12 months; two months later, many experts felt it had reached a low point and was expected to rise. This was based on the market expectations that interest cuts by the Fed were expected to stop and that the credit crisis was beginning to soften. Now the speculators have to decide what to do with those expectations. Similar trends occurred in 2010–2011 when the dollar fell from a mid-2010 high of $1.2187 per euro to a low of $1.4546 by early May 2011. However, uncertainty over the Greek debt crisis pushed the euro down, leaving speculators wondering what will happen next.

Sometimes speculators can buy a currency on the basis of good economic fundamentals, or they can buy or sell currency because they feel that governments are following poor economic policies. When they looked at the economic fundamentals behind the economy of Thailand in 1997, they felt the government was making poor choices and that the Thai baht could not continue to trade at its existing level. So they sold Thai baht on the assumption that the currency would have to fall. Is there anything wrong with that? Was the subsequent fall in the Thai baht because of evil speculators, or was it because the speculators profited on the inevitable? As long as markets are free and information is available, traders ought to be able to make some money on their predictions of the future. There is even a good argument that speculators help keep governments honest by betting in directions they feel reflect political and economic fundamentals. Either governments must adjust to reality or suffer the consequences.

The key is that currency speculation is a different way to invest money and allows investors to diversify their portfolios from traditional stocks and bonds. Just as foreign exchange can be traded for speculative purposes, trading in shares is also speculation. Even though we call such trades "investments," they are just another form of speculation hoping to gain a return that is higher than the market average and certainly higher than what a CD can yield.

Is It OK to Speculate on Currency?

Counterpoint

Counterpoint

No There are plenty of opportunities for a trader, whether in foreign exchange or securities, to make money illegally or contrary to company policy. The culture of individual traders trying to make money off trading foreign exchange or other securities, combined with lax controls in financial institutions, contributes greatly to these scandals.

One of the most publicized events in the derivatives markets in recent years involved 28-year-old Nicholas Leeson

and the 233-year-old British bank Barings PLC. Leeson, a dealer for Barings, went to Singapore in the early 1990s to help resolve some of the bank's problems. Within a year, he was promoted to chief dealer, with responsibility for trading securities and booking the settlements. This meant that there were no checks and balances on his trading actions, thus opening the door to fraud.

When two different people are assigned to trade securities and book settlements, the person booking the settlements can confirm independently whether the trades were accurate and legitimate. In 1994, Leeson bought stock index futures on the Singapore International Monetary Exchange, or SIMEX, on the assumption that the Tokyo stock market would rise. Most dealers watching his feverish trading activity assumed Barings had a large client that he was trading for. It turns out, however, that he was using the bank's money to speculate. Because the Japanese economy was recovering, it made sense to assume the market would continue to rise, thus generating more profits for Leeson and Barings. Unfortunately, something happened that nobody could predict—the January 17, 1995, earthquake that hit the port city of Kobe.

As a result of the devastation and uncertainty, the market fell, and Leeson had to come up with cash to cover the margin call on the futures contract. A margin is a deposit made as security for a financial transaction that is otherwise financed on credit. When the price of an instrument changes and the margin rises, the exchange "calls" the increased margin from the other party—in this case, Leeson.[17]

However, Leeson soon ran out of cash from Barings and had to come up with more. One approach he used was to write options contracts and use the premium he collected on the contracts to cover his margin call. Unfortunately, he was using Barings' funds to cover positions he was taking for himself, not for clients, and he also forged documents to cover his transactions.

As the Tokyo stock market continued to plunge, Leeson fell further and further behind and eventually fled the country, later to be caught and returned to Singapore for trial and prison. Barings estimated that Leeson generated losses in excess of $1 billion, and the bank eventually was purchased by Dutch bank ING.[18]

Since the collapse of Barings, measures have been put into place in banks to prohibit such consequences. However, negative outcomes of rogue trading continue to happen. Leeson's record losses were surpassed in 2008 by Jérôme Kerviel of French bank Société Générale. A onetime employee in the back office (the part of the bank that processes transactions), Kerviel became a trader in 2005 in the relatively unimportant Delta One trading unit. In his new position, he began trading futures on the bank's own account. His role was to take opposite positions on the direction of the market in order to earn money on the spread. However, he began to take one-way positions to earn even more money for the bank and hopefully a bigger bonus. The problem is that he bet the European markets would rise—and in early 2008 they fell rather sharply. Through a variety of actions that went against the internal controls of the banks as well as outright lies about what he was doing, he was able to fool bank insiders while hoping to cover his positions. The bank eventually found out what Kerviel was doing and discovered that he had exposed it to a €50 billion risk. By the time the bank had unwound all of its trading positions, it had lost €1.5 billion, or $2.22 billion. Unlike Leeson, Kerviel was not using his bank's money to trade on his own account, but like Leeson, he created serious problems for the bank, which lost a lot of money.[19]

Looking to the
Future Where Are Foreign-Exchange Markets Headed?

Significant strides have been made and will continue to be made in the development of foreign-exchange markets. The speed at which transactions are processed and information transmitted globally will certainly lead to greater efficiencies and more opportunities for foreign-exchange trading. The impact on companies is that trading costs should come down and companies should have faster access to more currencies.

In addition, exchange restrictions that hamper the free flow of goods and services should diminish as governments gain greater control over their economies and liberalize currency markets. Capital controls still affect foreign investment, but they will continue to become less of a factor for trade in goods and services. The introduction of the euro has allowed cross-border transactions in Europe to progress more smoothly. As the euro solidifies its position in Europe,

it will reduce exchange-rate volatility and should lead to the euro taking some of the pressure off the dollar, so that it is no longer the only major vehicle currency in the world. However, financial crisis in Europe is threatening the very existence of the euro and its role in global currency markets. In addition, the Chinese yuan is attempting to become more of an international currency, as will be discussed in the following case. A major trend for the future will clearly be the rise of the yuan. Even the Brazilian real, the currency of another BRIC country, is poised to make an impact on currency markets due to rising commodity prices. One trend that could be the wave of the future is currencies settling with each other rather than through the dollar. That is now occurring between the Chinese yuan and Brazilian real due to strong trading relationships between the two countries as Brazil exports

(continued)

commodities to China, and China exports manufactured goods to Brazil.

Technological Developments

Technological developments may not cause the foreign-exchange broker to disappear entirely, but they will certainly cause foreign-exchange trades to be executed more quickly and cheaply. The advent of technology clearly has caused the market to shift from phone trades to electronic trades.[20]

It is hard to know how extensive online trading will become. Numerous companies now advertise it for investors, but that is not where most of the trades take place. The growth of Internet trades in currency will take away some of the market share of dealers and allow more entrants into the foreign-exchange market. Internet trade will also increase currency price transparency and improve the ease of trading, thus allowing more investors into the market. It is interesting to note that Barclays Capital, the third largest bank in foreign-exchange trades, is trying to build its online trading portal by offering automated exchange tools to financial and nonfinancial clients. One idea is to offer the system to their correspondent banks, who can then offer it to their corporate clients. This is a response to the fact that foreign-exchange trading is shifting from telephone to online,[21] forcing the banks to offer more services to clients. Deutsche Bank and UBS, the top two foreign-exchange traders, are also expected to expand their proprietary platforms for e-trading. ∎

CASE   Do Yuan to Buy Some Renminbi?

In mid-2011, the Chinese government was trying to decide when was the right time to allow its currency, the renminbi, to float freely on global currency markets and permit the free flow of its currency from China to anywhere in the world as the final steps to allow the renminbi to take its place as one of the major currencies in the world. The renminbi (RMB), also known as the yuan, is the official name of the currency, and the yuan is the basic unit of account. In the currency markets, the sign for the currency is ¥ (the same symbol used for the Japanese yen) and the code is CNY. Since the terms are used interchangeably, we'll use "yuan" in the case. Although the yuan has been relatively fixed and controlled by the Chinese government, there are signs that the yuan is getting close to being unleashed. What does this mean for currency traders and the future balance of power in global currency markets currently dominated by the U.S. dollar, the euro, and the yen?

A Little History

On January 7, 1994, the Chinese government, after debating what to do with its currency, decided to fix the value of the yuan to the U.S. dollar at a rate of ¥8.690 per dollar.[22] Given that currency trading was controlled by the Chinese government with no trading allowed offshore, it was easy for them to fix the value of the currency against the U.S. dollar. In 2004, Hong Kong residents were allowed to exchange local Hong Kong dollars for yuan in a first move to allow some limited trading offshore. By early 2005, the yuan was trading at a fixed rate of ¥8.2665 per dollar. But pressure began to build in 2005 as both the European Union and the United States faced strong competition from imports from China as well as from Chinese exports to developing markets.

When China fixed the value of its currency in 1994, it was not considered a major economic powerhouse, but things began to change. In 1999, China was the largest country in the world in population and seventh largest in GNI. By 2003, it was the sixth largest country in the world in GNI, exceeded only by the United States, Japan, Germany, the United Kingdom, France, and Italy. It was also growing faster than any of the top six countries. In the decade of the 1990s, China grew by an annual average of 9.5 percent and was above 8 percent every year in the first half of the 2000s.

Because of China's low manufacturing wages, it was exporting far more to the United States than it was importing. In 2004, China had a trade surplus of $155 billion with the United States, compared with a surplus of only $86 billion with the EU. However, between 2002 and 2004, China's surplus with the EU doubled, whereas it grew by a little over a half with the United States. The major problem with the EU is that, during that time period, the euro had grown by 45 percent against the dollar, which meant it had also grown by 45 percent against the yuan, which was fixed against the dollar. In effect, Chinese exports had gotten cheaper against European products both in the euro zone as well as in Europe's export markets. Also during that time, there were capital controls on the flow of yuan in and out of China, so there was a tremendous inflow of yuan into the banking sector in China with no real way to move the money offshore. That meant that banks could lend money at very low interest rates, fueling a real estate boom. Also, China had to do something with its building reserves. Initially, it invested huge sums of money in U.S. treasury bills, helping to fund the growing U.S. budget deficit. Then it began encouraging foreign direct investment, especially in natural resources around the world.

However, the competitive pressure of China in Asia was not the same. Because most Asian currencies were also locked onto the dollar, the yuan traded in a narrow range against those currencies. Most of the Asian countries were using China as a new market for their products, and they were not anxious to have anything upset the Chinese economy and reduce demand for their products.

Critics from the United States and EU argued that the yuan was undervalued by 15 to 40 percent, and the Chinese government needed to free the currency and allow it to seek a market level. The pressures for and against change were both political and economic. The U.S. government had been working with the Chinese for an extended period of time to get them to revalue their currency, but the Chinese government had found plenty of excuses not to do that. Finally, many members of the U.S. Congress decided to force the issue, and they announced they would push to pass steep tariffs on Chinese exports if the Chinese didn't loosen their currency. The U.S. administration, concerned about possible protectionist threats by Congress, announced it would give the Chinese until October 2005 to revalue its currency, or it would consider that China's exchange-rate policy was, in fact, currency manipulation to improve its export position, forcing the government to negotiate sanctions against Chinese exports. The United States took the exchange-rate issue so seriously in 2005 that the U.S. treasury secretary named a special envoy to work with China on the issue.

Political Pressures in China

China had its own political pressures. For one thing, a lot of people had been moving currency into China in anticipation of a revaluation of the yuan, which was creating inflationary pressures in China. The Chinese government was forced to buy the dollars and issue yuan-denominated bonds as a way of "sterilizing" the currency—taking currency off the market to reduce inflationary pressures. The Chinese government was not very excited about revaluing the yuan and rewarding the speculators, so it kept saying it would not announce how much, if, or when it would revalue its currency. In addition, it did not want to revalue under pressure from foreign governments because it did not want to appear to be bowing under pressure from abroad.

Finally, China has serious problems with employment. Even though China's 1.3 billion in population is growing at only 1 percent a year, it adds the equivalent of a new country the size of Ecuador or Guatemala every year. China needs to add enough jobs to keep up with its population growth and displaced workers from its agricultural sector and state-owned firms. That means it needs to add 15 to 20 million new jobs per year or about 1.25 million jobs per month. In comparison, the United States created 275,000 new jobs in April 2005. If China slows down its economy to keep inflation in check, it needs to have a strong export sector to keep creating jobs. If the export sector cools because of a revalued currency, China could have political and social chaos.

The Advent of the Currency Basket

Given these pressures, China took a historic step on July 21, 2005 and de-linked the yuan from its decade-old peg to the U.S. dollar in favor of a currency basket. The basket was largely denominated by the dollar, the euro, the yen, and the won. These currencies were selected because of the impact they have on China's foreign trade, investment, and foreign debt. The yuan was also influenced by the currencies of several other countries, including Singapore, Britain, Malaysia, Russia, Australia, Thailand, and Canada.

The People's Bank of China (PBOC, the central bank of China) decides a central parity rate daily and then allows a trading band on either side of the decided point. The move to the currency basket increased the yuan-to-dollar rate by 2.1 percent. Before the peg was de-linked, the yuan was kept around ¥8.2665, and immediately following it rose to ¥8.1011, and increase of 2 percent. The United States, Europe, and Japan thought the change was too small and continued to assert that the yuan was undervalued.

By the end of 2006, the yuan had appreciated by 5.68 percent since the currency basket was instituted. This had little effect on the U.S. trade deficit because the first quarter 2007 trade deficit reached $56.9 billion, an increase of 35.8 percent over the $41.9 billion deficit in the first quarter of 2005. Pressures from the international community continued to be heaped on China.

The PBOC responded to the pressures by widening the trading band of the yuan on May 18, 2007 from 0.3 percent to 0.5 percent on either side of the fixed rate. Obviously, that small difference gave little room for traders to affect trades. The move came a week before the Chinese delegation was to meet for a second round of strategic economic talks with senior U.S. officials led by Treasury Secretary Henry Paulson and while the Treasury Department was preparing its semiannual report on the currency market. Many believed China would be cited as a currency manipulator in the Treasury Department report.

Baby Steps

Until the yuan began its ascent against the dollar, it was very easy to deal in foreign exchange in China because the rate was fixed against the U.S. dollar. It doesn't take a lot of judgment for a trader to operate in a fixed-rate world. The exchange rate is managed by the State Administration of Foreign Exchange (SAFE), which is closely linked to the PBOC. In fact, the Administrator of SAFE is also Deputy Governor of the PBOC. SAFE is responsible for establishing the new foreign-exchange trading guidelines as well as for managing China's foreign-exchange reserves. A major concern by the PBOC is that China's financial infrastructure might not have the capability to trade foreign exchange in a free market. In the Triennial Central Bank Survey on foreign-exchange market activity conducted by the Bank for International Statements in 2010, the Chinese yuan did not show up as an important currency in terms of turnover, and the Chinese banks were not represented in the 2011 *Euromoney* survey of top foreign exchange-trading banks. That is because most of the yuan was deposited in China, and Chinese banks were not permitted to set up operations in Hong Kong to trade their massive deposits in yuan in global capital markets.

SAFE was moving to change that. When the PBOC made the decision to loosen up the value of the yuan in 2005, it decided to allow banks in Shanghai to trade and quote prices in eight currency pairs, including the dollar-sterling and euro-yen. Prior to that, licensed banks were only allowed to trade the yuan against four currencies—the U.S. dollar, the Hong Kong dollar, the euro, and the yen. Shanghai was being positioned as the financial center of China, hopefully by 2020. However, all the trades were at fixed rates, and they did not involve trades in non-yuan currency pairs. SAFE also decided to open up trading to seven international banks (HSBC, Citigroup, Deutsche Bank, ABN AMRO, ING, Royal Bank of Scotland, and Bank of Montreal) and two domestic banks (Bank of China and CITIC Industrial Bank). Several of these international banks are among the most sophisticated foreign exchange traders in the world. For example, HSBC, which got its start in Hong Kong in 1865, has over 7500 offices in 87 countries, and its stock is listed on exchanges in London, Hong Kong,

HSBC is one of the most important non-Chinese traders of Chinese yuan in international capital markets, especially from their offices in Hong Kong. Hong Kong is important since it is the center of offshore trading in the Chinese yuan.
Source: © Mathias Beinling/Alamy

New York, and Bermuda. It has strong geographic reach that could easily expand the trading in yuan once controls are lifted.

Fast Forward

However, a major global challenge that affected China was the financial crisis of 2007–2008. Even though the yuan had been allowing its currency to rise gradually against a basket of currencies instead of just the U.S. dollar, the crisis brought that to a halt. The yuan returned to a peg against the U.S. dollar that lasted from July 2008 until June 2010. During that time, there was a war of words between the U.S. and China over the value of the currency. The U.S. wanted the Chinese to allow their currency to continue to rise to help solve the trade imbalance, and the Chinese wanted the U.S. to get its economy under control and stabilize the value of the dollar, which had been falling in value against most other currencies. China was even calling for the creation of a new reserve asset to take the place of the dollar in the global economy. Why was China so worried about the value of the dollar? China has the largest foreign exchange reserves in the world at more than $3 trillion, fed largely by its huge trade surplus. Most of the reserves are in U.S. dollars. The last thing China wanted was to have all of its dollar reserves losing value in the global economy.

China's Economic Challenges

By the end of 2010, not only had China replaced Japan as the number 2 country in the world in terms of GDP, it was closing fast on the United States. In addition, Japan surpassed Germany and the United States as the largest exporter in the world meaning that it was continuing to generate large foreign exchange assets which were exposed to losses in value as the dollar fell against other currencies in the world.

But China had its own set of problems, irrespective of what was going on in the United States. When China decided to let the yuan gradually rise against the dollar in June 2010, it resulted in a rise in the value of the yuan against the dollar of 3.6 percent by the end of 2010. However, inflation was rising in China faster than the United States, so Chinese exports were becoming increasingly expensive. The rise in the currency compounded the loss in competitive position brought on by the rise in inflation. Powerful Chinese exporters were very set against the government freeing up the currency and speeding up their competitive challenges. Because of inflation, Chinese workers were increasingly unhappy with their working conditions, and they began to demonstrate, sometimes violently, about the situation they found themselves in. As workers pushed for higher wages, manufacturers faced even greater cost pressures. With general inflation, higher wages, and the possibility of an even more expensive yuan, manufacturers were being forced to move further inland to find cheaper labor, or even move abroad.

Improvement of the Trading Infrastructure

In 2009, the PBOC announced that it was going to allow companies in Shanghai and four other major cities to settle foreign trade in yuan instead of dollars. Remember that 84.9 percent of all foreign exchange transactions worldwide take place in dollars. If Chinese companies can get more exporters and importers to settle their obligations in yuan instead of dollars, they can save a lot of transactions fees, and the yuan will gradually increase in importance.

Even though China wants to make Shanghai the future financial center of China, a lot of yuan transactions occur in Hong Kong, which generates 5 percent of the foreign exchange trades in the world. It is the only place outside of mainland China that is allowed to set up yuan bank accounts. Hong Kong is China's testing ground for the liberalization of currency trading. However, Singapore is also being considered as a place for yuan transactions, and Singapore also trades about the same in foreign exchange as Hong Kong.

As we will discuss in more detail in Chapter 19, the PBOC permitted HSBC and the Bank of East Asia to issue yuan-denominated bonds in Hong Kong in 2007. That is allowing Hong Kong to increase in importance as an offshore financial center for the trading of yuan. As banks and companies issue bonds and securities in yuan, the amount of yuan in circulation outside of China will steadily grow. From the standpoint of traditional foreign exchange trading, yuan trades in foreign currency swaps and forwards increased dramatically in 2010, by 60 percent and 235 percent respectively. Although still small, the trades are growing. And SAFE decided in April 2011 to allow option to be traded among banks and for banks to sell options to companies.

In October 2010, ICAP PLC and Thomson Reuters began to trade yuan on their electronic-trading platforms and announced that they were working with banks in the United States and Europe to use their platforms to trade yuan. Before this, banks in Hong Kong were trading yuan with each other OTC or through brokers. The use of the electronic platform promises to increase transparency and traffic. Banks such as Deutsche Bank AG can now use ICAP and Reuters platforms to trade yuan. In spite of these moves, the onshore market in mainland China still dwarfs the offshore trading, and the fixed exchange rate set by SAFE will be the most important rate. Even though Hong Kong is a special administrative region (SAR) with its own laws and administrative structure, it still works closely with China when it comes to things like currency trading in yuan.

In the second half of 2010, the Chinese government loosened some of the restrictions on how banks could use yuan in Hong Kong. They allowed banks and individuals to freely trade yuan outside of the mainland, and they expanded the number of Chinese companies that were allowed to settle trades in yuan, but they still controlled the inflow and outflow of capital between China and the rest of the world. A major fear of allowing the free flow of capital is that the government would lose control over inflation and interest rates. In addition, they still kept close control on the currency trades. In order for banks to participate in currency trades in Hong Kong, they need a clearing and settlement arrangement with a financial institution supervised by the Hong Kong Monetary Authority. Not every world currency is being traded against the yuan in Hong Kong. Initially, Thomson Reuters permitted trades against the dollar, euro and yen, whereas ICAP started only with trades against the dollar. However, both services are expected to expand the currencies available for trades. The dollar is essential since the Hong Kong dollar is fixed against the U.S. dollar, and most China trades have been going through U.S. dollars. Offshore yuan is quoted as CNH, whereas the standard symbol is CNY. As the rules changed in 2010, daily foreign exchange trading in yuan went from zero to $400 million in just a few months. Banks like HSBC and Citibank began to offer options and interest-rate derivatives in yuan.

The onshore market in mainland China is far more tightly controlled. Even though the major money center banks, such as HSBC are allowed to trade currency in China, their volume dwarfs that of the large Chinese banks. As the Chinese banks gain greater expertise in global trades, they will become even more significant outside of China. And as China and Singapore explore the possibility of Singapore becoming another location for yuan trades like Hong Kong, the international banks will ramp up their yuan trading competencies in Singapore as well as Hong Kong. As capital controls in China are loosened, the international banks will also have to ramp up their presence in China to compete with the huge Chinese banks that are now starting to get involved in the global forex trading game. ■

QUESTIONS

1. Why is it important for the Chinese yuan to become a major world currency?

2. What needs to take place for the yuan to be listed right along with the U.S. dollar and the euro as global currencies?

3. Why is the Chinese government so hesitant to open up the yuan to market forces to determine its value inside and outside of China?

4. What role do foreign banks like HSBC and electronic platforms like Thomson Reuters and ICAP play in helping the yuan move closer to becoming a global currency?

5. If you were to predict what the foreign exchange trading world will look like in 2014 when the Bank for International Settlements issues its next triennial survey on foreign exchange, what would you predict?

Now that you have finished this chapter, go back to www.myiblab.com to continue practicing and applying the concepts you've learned.

MyIBLab

SUMMARY

- Foreign exchange is money denominated in the currency of another nation or group of nations. The exchange rate is the price of a currency.

- The foreign-exchange market is dominated by the money center banks, but other financial institutions (such as local and regional banks) and nonfinancial institutions (such as corporations and governments) are also players in the foreign-exchange market.

- Dealers can trade currency by telephone or electronically, especially through Reuters, EBS, or Bloomberg.

- The foreign-exchange market is divided into the over-the-counter (OTC) market and the exchange-traded market.

- The traditional foreign-exchange market is composed of the spot, forward, and foreign-exchange swap markets. Other key foreign-exchange instruments are currency swaps, options, and futures.

- Spot transactions involve the exchange of currency on the second day after the date on which the two dealers agree to the transaction.

- Outright forward transactions involve the exchange of currency three or more days after the date on which the dealers agree to the transaction. A foreign-exchange swap is a simultaneous spot and forward transaction.

- Approximately $4.0 trillion in foreign exchange is traded every day. The dollar is the most widely traded currency in the world (on one side of 84.9 percent of all transactions), and London is the main foreign-exchange market in the world.

- Foreign-exchange dealers quote bid (buy) and offer (sell) rates on foreign exchange. If the quote is in American terms, the dealer quotes the foreign currency as the number of dollars and cents per unit of the foreign currency. If the quote is in European terms, the dealer quotes the number of units of the foreign currency per dollar. The numerator is called the *terms currency* and the denominator the *base currency*.

- If the foreign currency in a forward contract is expected to strengthen in the future (the dollar equivalent of the foreign currency is higher in the forward market than in the spot market), the currency is selling at a premium. If the opposite is true, it is selling at a discount.

- An option is the right, but not the obligation, to trade foreign currency in the future. Options can be traded OTC or on an exchange.

- A foreign currency future is an exchange-traded instrument that guarantees a future price for the trading of foreign exchange, but the contracts are for a specific amount and specific maturity date.

- Companies work with foreign-exchange dealers to trade currency. Dealers also work with each other and can trade currency through voice brokers, electronic brokerage services, or directly with other bank dealers. Internet trades of foreign exchange are becoming more significant.

- The major institutions that trade foreign exchange are the large commercial and investment banks and securities exchanges. Commercial and investment banks deal in a variety of different currencies all over the world. The CME Group and the Philadelphia Stock Exchange trade currency futures and options.

- Companies use foreign exchange to settle transactions involving the imports and exports of goods and services, for foreign investments, and to earn money through *arbitrage* or *speculation*.

KEY TERMS

American terms (p. 338)
arbitrage (p. 347)
Bank for International Settlements (BIS) (p. 331)
base currency (p. 338)
bid (buy) trade (p. 336)
carry trade (p. 336)
Chicago Mercantile Exchange (CME) Group (p. 344)
confirmed letter of credit (p. 346)
cross rate (p. 335)
currency swap (p. 333)
derivative (p. 343)
direct quote (p. 338)

draft (or commercial bill of exchange) (p. 346)
European terms (p. 338)
exchange rate (p. 331)
foreign exchange (p. 331)
foreign-exchange market (p. 331)
forward discount (p. 341)
forward premium (p. 341)
futures contract (p. 333)
FX swap (p. 333)
hedge fund (p. 334)
indirect quote (p. 338)
interbank transaction (p. 340)
interest arbitrage (p. 347)

letter of credit (L/C) (p. 346)
NASDAQ OMX (p. 344)
NYSE Liffe (p. 344)
offer (sell) (p. 336)
option (p. 333)
outright forward transactions (p. 333)
sight draft (p. 346)
speculation (p. 347)
spot rate (p. 333)
spot transaction (p. 333)
spread (p. 336)
terms currency (p. 338)
time draft (p. 346)

ENDNOTES

1 *Sources include the following:* World Bank, *Migration and Remittances Factbook 2011* (The International Bank for Reconstruction and Development/World Bank: Washington, DC, 2011); "Immigrants Sent 3.7 Billion Euros from Spain to Latin America in 2006, Says IDB Fund," press release, Inter-American Development Bank (June 5, 2007); "Remittances to Latin America and the Caribbean to Top $100 Billion a Year by 2010, IDB Fund Says," press release, Inter-American Development Bank (March 18, 2007); Marla Dickerson, "Cash Going to Mexico Likely to Start at a Bank," *Los Angeles Times* (February 14, 2007): 21; Miriam Jordan, "U.S. Banks Woo Migrants, Legal or Otherwise," *Wall Street Journal* (Eastern Edition) (October 11, 2006): B1; Ioan Grillo, "Wired Cash," *Business Mexico* 12:12/13:1 (2003): 44; Julie Rawe, "The Fastest Way to Make Money," *Time* (June 23, 2003): A6; Rosa Salter Rodriguez, "Money Transfers to Mexico Peak as Mother's Day Nears," *Fort*

Wayne (IN) *Journal Gazette* (May 1, 2005): 1D; Deborah Kong, "Mexicans Win Back Fee on Money They Wired," *Grand Rapids* (MI) *Press* (December 19, 2002): A9; Karen Krebsbach, "Following the Money," *USBanker* (September 2002): 62; Tyche Hendricks, "Wiring Cash Costly for Immigrants," *San Francisco Chronicle* (March 24, 2002): A23; Nancy Cleeland, "Firms Are Wired into Profits," *Los Angeles Times* (November 7, 1997): 1; David Fairlamb, Geri Smith, and Frederik Blafour, "Can Western Union Keep On Delivering?" *Business Week* (December 29, 2003): 57; Heather Timmons, "Western Union: Where the Money Is—In Small Bills," *Business Week* (November 26, 2001): 40.

2 Sam Y. Cross, *All about the Foreign Exchange Market in the United States* (New York: Federal Reserve Bank of New York, 1998): 9.

3 Ibid.

4 Bank for International Settlements, "Triennial Central Bank Survey: Report on Global Foreign Exchange Market Activity in 2010" (Basel: BIS, December 2010): 8–9.

5 Ibid., p. 16.

6 Ibid, p. 35.

7 Cross, *All about the Foreign Exchange Market*, 19.

8 Bank for International Settlements, "Triennial Central Bank Survey," 15.

9 Brian Dolan, "Tailoring Your Technical Approach to Currency Personalities," retrieved October 8, 2009, from www.forex.com /currency_pairs.html

10 Cross, *All about the Foreign Exchange Market*, 12.

11 See "Foreign Exchange Poll 2009: Methodology," *Euromoney* (May 2009): 76.

12 Bank for International Settlements, *op cit.*, p. 9.

13 Deborah Kimbell, "E-FX Takes Another Step Forward," *Euromoney* (February 2005): 1.

14 Peter Garnham, "Reuters Reveals Ambitions on Launch of FXMarketSpace," *Financial Times* (March 26, 2007): 21.

15 PHLX News Release, "The Philadelphia Stock Exchange and the Philadelphia Board of Trade to Expand World Currency Product Line with Launch of Options and Futures on Major Currencies," retrieved April 27, 2007, from http://phlx.com/news /pr2007/07pr042707.htm

16 A confirmed letter of credit adds the obligation of the exporter's bank to pay the exporter.

17 More specifically, Leeson did not actually buy the contracts outright but rather paid a certain percentage of the value of the contract, known as the *margin*. When the stock market fell, the index futures contract became riskier, and the broker who sold the contract required Leeson to increase the amount of the margin.

18 "The Collapse of Barings: A Fallen Star," *The Economist* (March 4, 1995): 19–21; Glen Whitney, "ING Puts Itself on the Map by Acquiring Barings," *Wall Street Journal* (March 8, 1995): B4; John S. Bowdidge and Kurt E. Chaloupecky, "Nicholas Leeson and Barings Bank Have Vividly Taught Some Internal Control Issues," *American Business Review* (January 1997): 71–77; "Trader in Barings Scandal Is Released from Prison," *Wall Street Journal* (July 6, 1999): A12; Ben Dolven, "Bearing Up," *Far Eastern Economic Review* (July 15, 1999): 47; "Nick Leeson and Barings Bank," bbc.co.uk, retrieved May 19, 2005, from www.bbc.co.uk/crime/caseclosed/nickleeson.shtml (accessed May 19, 2005); Nick Leeson and Edward Whitley, *Rogue Trader* (London: Little, Brown, 1996): 272.

19 David Gauthier-Villars and Carrick Mollenkamp, "Société Générale Blew Chances to Nab Trader," *Wall Street Journal* (January 29, 2008): 1; David Gauthier-Villars, Carrick Mollenkamp, and Alistair MacDonald, "French Bank Rocked by Rogue Trader," *Wall Street Journal* (January 25, 2008): A1; David Gauthier-Villars and Carrick Mollenkamp, "Portrait Emerges of Rogue Trader at French Bank," *Wall Street Journal* (February 2, 2008): A1.

20 Steve Bills, "State St.'s Forex Deal a Lure for Hedge Funds," *American Banker* (January 23, 2007): 10.

21 Steve Bills, "Barclays Seeking Forex Boost via Online Offerings," *American Banker* (October 10, 2006): 17.

22 *Sources include the following:* Tom Orlick, "Get Ready: Here Comes the Yuan," *The Wall Street Journal* (June 2, 2011): C7; Peter Stein, "The Chinese Test Kitchen," *The Wall Street Journal* (June 2, 2011): C8; Peter Stein and Shai Oster, "China Speeds Yuan Push," *The Wall Street Journal* (April 20, 2011); Lingling Wei, "Beijing Considers New Hub for Yuan," *The Wall Street Journal* (April 9–10, 2011): B1; Wynne Wang and Jean Yung, "China Allows More Options for Trading in Yuan," *The Wall Street Journal* (February 17, 2011): C2; "The Rise of the Redback," *The Economist* (January 22, 2011): 14; Shai Oster, Dinny McMahon, and Tom Lauricella, "Offshore Trading in Yuan Takes Off," *The Wall Street Journal* (December 14, 2010): A1; Dinny McMahon, "Yuan Goes Electronic in Global Market Bid, *The Wall Street Journal* (October 8, 2010): C1; Andrew Batson, "China's Currency Reserves Expand as Economy Continues to Surge," *Wall Street Journal* (July 12, 2007): A11; Natasha Brereton, "Revaluing the Yuan May Not Fix Imbalances," *Wall Street Journal* (July 17, 2007); Marcus Walker, "Euro Zone Suffers from China Syndrome," *Wall Street Journal* (May 17, 2005): A10; "What Do Yuant from Us?" *The Economist* (May 18, 2005); Edmund L. Andrews, "Toughening Its Line, U.S. Warns China on Currency," *New York Times* (May 18, 2005); Andrew Browne, "U.S., China Press Yuan Row," *Wall Street Journal* (May 19, 2005): A2; Greg Hitt, "U.S. Picks Envoy to Engage China on Exchange Rates," *Wall Street Journal* (May 20, 2005): C3.

chapter 10

The Determination of Exchange Rates

Source: © Philip Scalia / Alamy

Objectives

1. To describe the International Monetary Fund and its role in determining exchange rates

2. To discuss the major exchange-rate arrangements that countries use

3. To explain how the European Monetary System works and how the euro became the currency of the euro zone

4. To identify the major determinants of exchange rates

5. To show how managers try to forecast exchange-rate movements

6. To explain how exchange-rate movements influence business decisions

Access a host of interactive learning aids to help strengthen your understanding of the chapter concepts at www.myiblab.com.

MyIBLab

He that has no money has no friends.

—*Arabian proverb*

CASE

El Salvador Adopts the U.S. Dollar

El Salvador, a country of 7.2 million people, is the smallest and most densely populated country in Central America (see Atlas, M5—North America) and is about the size in area of the U.S. state of Massachusetts.[1] El Salvador has been a member of the Central American Common Market (CACM), which also includes Costa Rica, Guatemala, Honduras, and Nicaragua, since its inception in 1960. It was also the first of the Central American countries to sign on to the CAFTA-DR Agreement as of March 1, 2006, linking it closer to trade relations with the United States.

PEGGING THE COLÓN TO THE DOLLAR

In 1994, the government of El Salvador decided to peg the colón, the country's currency, to the U.S. dollar (US$). In 2001, the government decided to do away with the peg, do away with the colón and adopt the dollar as its currency, completing the transition to dollarization. It took several years to withdraw colones from circulation, but this eventually occurred. El Salvador is now one of 10 countries that have entered into an exchange arrangement in which they do not have their own currency, and seven of the 10 use the U.S. dollar.

Two other countries in Latin America have adopted the dollar as their currency—Panama, which adopted the dollar when it gained independence from Colombia over a century ago, and Ecuador, which dollarized its economy in 2000 as a means of eliminating hyperinflation.

Why the Dollar?

Why did El Salvador adopt the dollar? The economy of El Salvador is closely tied to the U.S. economy. At the time of the switch to the dollar, the United States imported over two-thirds of El Salvador's exports. In addition, over 2 million Salvadoreans lived in the United States and remitted earnings to their families back home, generating about the same amount of currency as they earned in exports. By switching to the dollar, companies and the government in El Salvador were able to get access to cheaper interest rates because dollarization eliminated, or at least reduced, the risk of devaluation, thereby infusing more confidence in foreign banks to lend to El Salvador. Corporate borrowing rates are among the lowest in Latin America, and consumer credit rose as lower interest rates made it more attractive to borrow. Research on the impact of dollarization showed that El Salvador reduced interest rates by 4 to 5 percent by reducing currency risk,

generating interest savings to both the public and private sectors. In addition, dollarization resulted in a significant positive association between dollarization and economic activity.

Ecuador: The Test Case

Ecuador's situation was a little different from that of El Salvador, but it tied its currency to the dollar in 2000. Ecuador has a population double the size of and a GNI a little less than twice that of El Salvador. In addition, it doesn't rely on the U.S. market as much as El Salvador does.

When Ecuador decided to dollarize its economy, the president was in the midst of a political crisis, and the announcement to dollarize was totally unexpected. In 1999, Ecuador's consumer price inflation was 52.2 percent, the highest in Latin America. Until February 1999, the central bank had maintained a crawling peg exchange-rate system. However, pressure on the currency forced the central bank to leave the peg and allow the currency to float freely. It promptly devalued by 65 percent in 1999.

At that time, Panama was the only country in Latin America that had dollarized, although Argentina had officially linked its currency to the dollar, so Ecuador was seen as a test case that many thought would spread to other countries in Latin America, especially El Salvador. A World Bank official, discussing the rationale for Ecuador's decision, noted that "most countries have a large amount of their debt in dollars, maintain a large percent of their reserves abroad in dollars, and write contracts indexed to the dollar."

In addition, Ecuador, a member of OPEC, generates most of its foreign-exchange earnings from oil, which is also priced in dollars. One difference between Ecuador and El Salvador is that Ecuador maintains its currency, the sucre (ESC), but it pegs the currency to the dollar at ESC 25,000 per US$. El Salvador no longer uses its currency but instead uses the dollar.

Test Results Ecuador's experiment with dollarization has been successful, but it has not been easy. When dollarization became official in 2000, inflation rose to 96.1 percent. But it dropped back to 29.2 percent in 2001, less than 20 percent in 2002, less than 7 percent in 2003, and an estimated 3.4 percent in 2006. However, with 70 percent of the population living below the poverty level, Ecuador still has political and economic problems that dollarization alone will not cure. In addition, the election of radical left-wing president Rafael Correa— who took office on January 1, 2007, and was reelected in

2009—have helped him solidify his power, even though tough economic times could create problems for him. In particular, the rise of the U.S. dollar against Ecuador's neighboring trading partners has created problems in Ecuador's trade balance. Added to those problems are the fall in oil prices and remittances from Ecuadorians working abroad.

THE DOWNSIDE OF DOLLARIZATION

As we noted, there are many advantages to dollarization, but what are the disadvantages? Consider El Salvador's neighbors. When El Salvador dollarized, over two-thirds of its exports went to the United States. By 2003, that had changed: 19.4 percent of El Salvador's exports went to the United States, putting the latter in the number-two spot after Guatemala. As of 2011, 46.6 percent of El Salvador's exports went to the United States, followed by 14.0 percent to Guatemala, 13.4 percent to Honduras, 5.8 percent to the 27-member EU, and 5.5 percent to Nicaragua. Thus four of the top five destinations for Salvadorean products were CACM countries. On the import side, the United States was the largest supplier to El Salvador, with 36.1 percent of the market, followed by Guatemala, Mexico, the EU, and Honduras.

Crawling Pegs and Crawling Bands

El Salvador's other neighbors in Central America had different exchange-rate regimes. Costa Rica and Nicaragua had crawling pegs, which means that their currencies were adjusted periodically in response to selected indicators. In their cases, the U.S. dollar was the key exchange-rate anchor on which they based the value of their currencies. However, their currencies were more flexible than those of El Salvador and Honduras, which had a currency pegged to the value of the dollar. Guatemala's currency was considered to be a managed floating currency, and it bases the value of its currency on inflation. During the global financial crisis in 2008, the value of the currencies did not stray very far from each other. That was much different than earlier in the decade, when the Costa Rican colón fell 43.9 percent against the dollar and the Nicaraguan cordoba fell 26.5 percent against the dollar. During that same period, the Honduran lempira fell about 15 percent against the dollar, but its currency regime is officially pegged to the dollar now. The Guatemalan quetzal has a managed floating currency, but its value remained relatively close to the U.S. dollar.

SURVIVING DOLLARIZATION

On one hand, the problem for Salvadorean companies is that their prices and competitiveness are closely tied to the value of the U.S. dollar. In the early part of the 2000s decade, companies from El Salvador were having a difficult time in export markets due to the strength of their currency against those of their Central American neighbors. How could they possibly compete against companies from Nicaragua and Honduras when those currencies had fallen against the dollar? That means Nicaraguan and Honduran companies were reaping a huge cost advantage in export markets. El Salvador has had to move into new sources of growth, such as shipping, tourism, and communications, to avoid having its economy hollowed out due to higher costs relative to its neighbors.

Case: Fresco Group S.A.

Many Salvadorean companies have had to change the way they do business. Fresco Group S.A., a family-owned textile company in El Salvador, has struggled to compete. Although the company was able to get low-cost loans to fund an expansion of facilities, it has had to move away from simple stitching of garments to creating designs, procuring materials, and manufacturing clothing based on a single sketch.

Basically, Fresco Group had to move upscale and leave the lower-end manufacturing to other Central American companies that benefited from weak currencies. In addition, Fresco Group was concerned about its ability to compete with textile companies from India and China, because textile and garment quotas were eliminated in 2005. Management wonders if they can move upscale fast enough and convince

Concept Check

In Chapter 8 we introduced the Central American Free Trade Agreement–Dominican Republic (CAFTA-DR) as a free trade agreement designed to reduce tariffs between the United States on the one hand and six Latin American countries on the other. We also note that, despite a membership of seven, it's actually a bilateral agreement.

Concept Check

In Chapter 4 we discuss the importance of the role of government in influencing the economic environment in which companies, both domestic and foreign, must operate. Here, we cite an instance of unforeseeable change in a country's economic environment: Although a government usually tries to build a consensus to support important political decisions, unexpected policy shifts are also a significant fact of life in the international business environment.

customers that their small size and better flexibility will overcome their cost disadvantage due to the strong dollar relative to other currencies in Central America.

Fresco Group may have disappeared in the onslaught of Chinese textile and garment exports since 2005, but Grupo Hilasal is an example of a vertically integrated textile company that has survived and thrived. Established in 1942 as a family-owned textile firm, Grupo Hilasal is currently one of the largest manufacturers of fiber-reactive printed beach towels in the world and the largest towel manufacturer in North America. Its new apparel division operates six plants with 2,000 workers and manufactures products for Polo, Champion, Sara Lee, and other companies.

The Future of Dollarization in El Salvador

Should El Salvador continue to use the dollar as its currency? Is it possible that the other members of CACM should move to dollar-based economies as they approach integration with and membership in CAFTA-DR? El Salvador is hoping that remittances by Salvadoreans living abroad, increased foreign direct investment, and the reduction of trade barriers with other countries will help stimulate the economy and offset any downsides to dollarization. As explained above, however, it does not appear that dollarization has had a negative affect on El Salvador's economy. Of course, the global financial crisis sharply reduced remittances from El Salvadoreans living abroad, and FDI dropped dramatically. But the currencies of its neighbors remained relatively close to the value of the dollar, thus reducing the impact of currency in El Salvador's ability to compete. The initial strengthening of the dollar in the fall of 2008 really hurt El Salvador's export competitiveness, but the subsequent weakening of the dollar has helped the country.

With the advent of CAFTA-DR, El Salvador's trade with the United States picked up again. Will this closer linkage with the United States be a good thing in the long run, or does it need to continue to diversify its trade as it did with the initial advent of the dollarization program? **CRN** Case Review Note

Introduction

As we learned in Chapter 9, an exchange rate represents the number of units of one currency needed to acquire one unit of another. Although this definition seems simple, managers must understand how governments set an exchange rate and what causes it to change. Such understanding can help them both anticipate exchange-rate changes and make decisions about business factors that are sensitive to those changes, such as the sourcing of raw materials and components, the placement of manufacturing and assembly, and the choice of final markets.

The International Monetary Fund

In 1944, toward the close of World War II, the major Allied governments met in Bretton Woods, New Hampshire, to determine what was needed to bring economic stability and growth to the postwar world. As a result of those meetings, the **International Monetary Fund (IMF)** came into official existence on December 27, 1945, with the goal of promoting exchange-rate stability and facilitating the international flow of currencies. The IMF began financial operations on March 1, 1947.[2]

ORIGIN AND OBJECTIVES

Twenty-nine countries initially signed the IMF agreement; there were 187 member countries as of July 1, 2011.[3] The fundamental mission of the IMF is to:

- Ensure stability in the international monetary system.
- Promote international monetary cooperation and exchange-rate stability.

- Facilitate the balanced growth of international trade.
- Provide resources to help members in balance-of-payments difficulties or to assist with poverty reduction.[4]

Through a process of surveillance, the IMF monitors the global economy as well as the economies of individual countries and advises on needed policy adjustments. In addition to surveillance, it provides technical assistance—mainly to low- and middle-income countries—and makes loans to countries with balance-of-payments problems. The processes of surveillance and technical assistance have been critical in the Greek debt crisis.

Bretton Woods and the Principle of Par Value The **Bretton Woods Agreement** established a system of fixed exchange rates under which each IMF member country set a **par value** for its currency based on gold and the U.S. dollar. Because the value of the dollar was fixed at $35 per ounce of gold, the par value would be the same whether gold or the dollar was used as the basis. This par value became a benchmark by which each country's currency was valued against others. Currencies were allowed to vary within 1 percent of their par value (extended to 2.25 percent in December 1971), depending on supply and demand. Additional moves from, and formal changes in, par value were possible with IMF approval. As we see later, par values were done away with when the IMF moved to greater exchange-rate flexibility.

Because of the U.S. dollar's strength during the 1940s and 1950s and its large reserves in monetary gold, currencies of IMF member countries were denominated in terms of gold and U.S. dollars. By 1947, the United States held 70 percent of the world's official gold reserves, so governments bought and sold dollars rather than gold. The understanding, though not set in stone, was that the United States would redeem dollars for gold. The dollar became the world benchmark for trading currency and has remained so, in spite of the move away from fixed rates to flexible exchange rates.

THE IMF TODAY

The Quota System When a country joins the IMF, it contributes a certain sum of money, called a **quota,** broadly based on its relative size in the global economy. The IMF can draw on this pool of money to lend to countries, and it uses the quota as the basis of how much a country can borrow from the Fund. It is also the basis on which the IMF allocates special drawing rights (SDRs), discussed later.

Moreover, the quota determines the voting rights of the individual members. On December 15, 2010, the Board of Governors of the IMF approved a package of reforms that would double the total quotas to SDR 476.8 (about $750 billion at current exchange rates at the time) and shift more of the quota shares to dynamic emerging market and developing countries (EMDCs). According to the realignment, the U.S. will still have the largest quota, but China would be number 3, and the four BRIC countries would be among the 10 largest shareholders in the Fund.[5] This realignment, where the top five countries used to be the United States, Japan, Germany, France, and the United Kingdom, addressed a major concern of the developing countries.

In 2011, the IMF went through a leadership crisis due to the scandal involving the Managing Director, Dominique Strauss-Kahn from France. Traditionally, a European holds the post of Managing Director, but many developing countries lobbied hard for someone from the developing countries to assume the post because that person would introduce a new perspective to the current crisis. However, the Executive Board of the IMF selected Christine Lagard, the Minister of Finance of France, to succeed Mr. Stauss-Kahn. It was felt that Ms. Lagard was in the best position to address the pressing issues of the debt crisis in Europe, because as the French finance minister, she was actively involved in trying to contain the European debt crisis.[6]

Concept Check

In Chapter 8, we report on the establishment of the United Nations and the subsequent creation of a number of UN satellite organizations, including the **IMF**. Today, the IMF is in a position to influence economic policy among UN-member nations.

The Bretton Woods Agreement established a par value, or benchmark value, for each currency initially quoted in terms of gold and the U.S. dollar.

The IMF quota—the sum of the total assessment to each country—becomes a pool of money that the IMF can draw on to lend to other countries. It is the basis for the voting power of each country—the higher its individual quota, the more votes a country has.

The IMF lends money to countries to help ease balance-of-payments difficulties.

Assistance Programs   In addition to identifying exchange-rate regimes, the IMF provides a great deal of assistance to member countries, negotiating with them to provide financial assistance if they agree to adopt certain economic stabilization policies. This arrangement is presented in a letter of intent to the executive board of the Fund, which, upon accepting it, releases the funds in phases so it can monitor progress.

The SDR is

- An international reserve asset given to each country to help increase its reserves.
- The unit of account in which the IMF keeps its financial records.

Special Drawing Rights (SDRs)   To help increase international reserves, the IMF created the **special drawing right (SDR)** in 1969 to help reinforce the fixed exchange-rate system that existed at that time. To support its currency in foreign-exchange markets, a country could use only U.S. dollars or gold to buy currency. However, because of the lack of sufficient gold and dollars, the SDR could provide member countries with instant reserve assets, thereby expanding global liquidity.[7] Thus, the SDR is an international reserve asset created to supplement members' official holdings of gold, foreign exchange, and IMF reserve positions. Serving as the IMF's *unit of account*—the unit in which the IMF keeps its records—SDRs are used for IMF transactions and operations.

Currencies making up the SDR basket are the U.S. dollar, the euro, the Japanese yen, and the British pound.

On January 1, 1981, the IMF began to use a simplified basket of four currencies for determining valuation. As of December 30, 2010, when the weights were last determined, the U.S. dollar made up 41.9 percent of the value of the SDR, the euro 37.4 percent, and the British pound sterling 11.3 percent, and the Japanese yen 9.4 percent.[8] These weights were chosen because they broadly reflect the importance of each particular currency in international trade and payments. Unless the executive board decides otherwise, the weights of each currency in the valuation basket will be in effect for the period 2011–2015.

In 2009 Russia announced that it supported expanding the currencies that make up the SDR to include the Russian ruble and the Chinese yuan. Russian leaders think that expanding the set of currencies in the SDR is logical; however, they do not believe that a new reserve currency will be accepted in the near future.[9]

THE GLOBAL FINANCIAL CRISIS AND THE IMF

Because of the global financial crisis, the G20 voted to significantly increase reserves available to the IMF to help countries in distress.

One of the fallouts of the global crisis in 2008–2009 was the concern over global liquidity, especially in the emerging markets. The G8 countries injected hundreds of billions of dollars into their financial systems and implemented large stimulus packages to get their economies moving. They also injected huge amounts of cash into the IMF. In April 2009, the G20 (the G8 expanded to include the central bank governors of 19 countries and the EU) voted to give approval to the IMF to raise $250 billion by issuing SDRs and to put another $500 billion into the IMF for it to use in case of a systemic crisis, thereby bringing the IMF's available resources to $1 trillion.

The IMF has played an important role in the Greek financial crisis that unfolded in 2010 and 2011. Greece, a member of the European Union, has adopted the euro as its currency and thus has no control over monetary policy. Interest rates are set by the European Central Bank. But Greece has piled up huge sovereign debt that exceeds 160 percent of GDP, largely to other banks in Europe. The Greek economy is in recession, the public sector generates 40 percent of the economy and 25 percent of the workforce, and the government keeps piling up budget deficits. In order to keep the government from defaulting on its debt, the IMF partnered with the European Union and the European Central Bank to provide loans to Greece on the condition that it would take severe austerity measures to solve its budget crisis, including raising taxes, cutting spending, and selling off state-owned assets. However, the recession has reduced tax revenues, and severe austerity measures will only increase unemployment, which has led to social unrest. Greece has few options. It can follow the austerity measures suggested by the ECB and IMF, it can try to restructure its debt, it could default on its debt like Argentina did in 2002, or it could leave the euro and bring back its own currency, the drachma, which would lead to severe devaluation relative to the euro. However, that would only make it even more impossible to pay back debt denominated in euro and dollars. It is interesting to note that whereas the IMF has traditionally taken the lead in providing technical assistance to countries in distress, the ECB has taken the lead in negotiating with Greece to help resolve the debt crisis.

On June 29, 2011, the bill that will cut spending and raise taxes was passed. That allowed the IMF and ECB to release funds to Greece to help meet some of its debt obligations. Some investors are happy because they feel that the debt crisis in Greece should be under more control now. However, Greeks continue to put forth a strong resistance in fear that the new bill will make their situation even worse, and many experts fear that Greece will not be able to meet the austerity conditions necessary to solve the crisis in the long run.[10]

EVOLUTION TO FLOATING EXCHANGE RATES

The IMF's system was initially one of fixed exchange rates. Because the U.S. dollar was the cornerstone of the international monetary system, its value remained constant with respect to the value of gold. Other countries could change the value of their currency against gold and the dollar, but the value of the dollar remained fixed.

On August 15, 1971, as the U.S. balance-of-trade deficit continued to worsen, U.S. president Richard Nixon announced that the United States would no longer trade dollars for gold unless other industrial countries agreed to support a restructuring of the international monetary system. He was afraid that the United States would lose its large gold reserves if countries, worried about holding so many dollars resulting from the large U.S. trade deficit, turned in their dollars to the U.S. government and demanded gold in return.

The Smithsonian Agreement The resulting **Smithsonian Agreement** of December 1971 had several important aspects:

- An 8 percent devaluation of the dollar (an official drop in the value of the dollar against gold)
- A revaluation of some other currencies (an official increase in the value of each currency against gold)
- A widening of exchange-rate flexibility (from 1 to 2.25 percent on either side of par value)

> Exchange-rate flexibility was widened in 1971 from 1 percent to 2.25 percent from par value.

This effort did not last, however. World currency markets remained unsteady during 1972, and the dollar was devalued again by 10 percent in early 1973 (the year of the Arab oil embargo and the start of fast-rising oil prices and global inflation). Major currencies began to float against each other, relying on the market to determine their value.

The Jamaica Agreement Because the Bretton Woods Agreement was based on a system of fixed exchange rates and par values, the IMF had to change its rules to accommodate floating exchange rates. The **Jamaica Agreement** of 1976 amended the original rules to eliminate the concept of par values and permit greater exchange-rate flexibility. The move toward greater flexibility can occur on an individual country basis as well as on an overall system basis. Let's see how this works.

> The Jamaica Agreement of 1976 resulted in greater exchange-rate flexibility and eliminated the use of par values.

Exchange-Rate Arrangements

The Jamaica Agreement formalized the break from fixed exchange rates. As part of this move, the IMF began to permit countries to select and maintain an exchange-rate arrangement of their choice, provided they communicate their decision to the IMF. The formal decision of a country to adopt a particular exchange-rate mechanism is called a *de jure* system. In addition, the IMF surveillance program determines the *de facto* exchange-rate system that a country uses.

> The IMF surveillance and consultation programs are designed to monitor exchange-rate policies of countries and to see if they are acting openly and responsibly in exchange-rate policies.

TABLE 10.1 Exchange-Rate Arrangements and Anchors

Exchange rate arrangement	Exchange rate anchor				Monetary Policy Framework			
	US dollar	Euro	Composite	Other	Monetary aggregate target	Inflation-targeting	Other	Total
Exchange rate arrangement with no separate legal tender	7	2		1				10
Currency board arrangement	8	4		1				13
Other conventional fixed-peg arrangement	36	20	7	5	4			72
Pegged exchange rate within horizontal bands		1	2					3
Crawling peg	6		2					8
Crawling band	1		1					2
Managed floating with no pre-determined path for the exchange rate	8		3		17	10	6	44
Independently floating					1	34	5	40
Total	66	27	15	7	22	44	11	192

Source: Adapted from the International Monetary Fund, "De Facto Classification of Exchange Rate Regimes and Monetary Policy Frameworks," http://www.imf.org/external/np/mfd/er/2008/eng/0408.htm (April 30, 2008).

The IMF also consults annually with countries to see if they are acting openly and responsibly in their exchange-rate policies. Each year, each country notifies the IMF of the arrangement it will use, and the IMF uses information provided by the country and evidence of how the country acts in the market to place it in a specific category. Table 10.1 identifies the different exchange-rate arrangements that countries have adopted. The arrangements are ranked primarily on their degree of flexibility, from least to most.

In addition, the IMF requires countries to identify how countries base their exchange rate mechanism, whether they use a specific anchor or a monetary framework. Some countries use an exchange rate such as the U.S. dollar as their anchor. Others use either monetary aggregate targets (such as M1 money supply) or inflation targets. Table 10.1 identifies the most recent exchange-rate arrangements and the monetary-policy framework used by each. The actual countries that fit in each cell can be found on the IMF website, as cited at the bottom of the table and in Map 10.1.

> The IMF requires countries to identify how they base their exchange rate mechanism.

THREE CHOICES: HARD PEG, SOFT PEG, OR FLOATING

The IMF classifies currencies into one of three broad categories, moving from the least to the most flexible. If they have adopted a hard peg (12.2 percent of the total), they lock their value onto something and don't change. If they have adopted a soft peg (45.7 percent), they are pretty rigid but not as rigid as the hard peg. If they have adopted a floating arrangement (42.1 percent), their value is based on supply and demand.[11]

Hard Peg There are two possibilities for countries that adopt a hard peg. One is like El Salvador, which has no separate legal tender but instead has adopted the U.S. dollar as their currency. Seven out of 10 currencies in that category use the U.S. dollar as their anchor. A few other European countries use the euro as their separate legal tender.

Using the dollar as an exchange arrangement with no separate legal tender is also called *dollarization* of the currency, as illustrated in our opening case. The idea would be for a country to take all of its currency out of circulation and replace it with dollars, allowing the U.S. Federal Reserve Bank (the Fed) greater control over

Case Review Note

> Countries can adopt another currency in place of their own, as is the case with El Salvador adopting the U.S. dollar, also called "dollarization."

monetary decisions instead of the governments of the countries so dollarizing. Prices and wages would be established in dollars rather than in the local currency, which would disappear.

The concern is that this would result in a loss of sovereignty and potentially lead to severe economic problems if the United States decided to tighten monetary policy when those countries needed to loosen policy to stimulate growth. Unfortunately, this is exactly what happened in Argentina in 2002. Although Argentina's exchange-rate regime did not go to the extreme of dollarization, its currency board regime was just a step away. The board tied the peso closely enough to the dollar and to the decisions made by the U.S. Fed that the government's ability to use monetary policy to strengthen its stalling economy was limited. As a result of the experiences in Argentina and the low popularity of the U.S. government, most countries in Latin America have decided not to go the route of dollarization.[12]

The second example of the hard peg is a *currency board*, which is what Argentina used to have. A currency board is an organization generally separate from a country's central bank that is responsible for issuing domestic currency typically anchored to a foreign currency. If it does not have deposits on hand in the foreign currency, it cannot issue more domestic currency. Thirteen countries now have currency boards. The Hong Kong currency board uses the U.S. dollar as its anchor currency. Even though the HK dollar is locked onto the U.S. dollar, it moves up and down against other currencies as the dollar changes in value. Thus it is both fixed (against the U.S. dollar) and flexible (because the U.S. dollar is an independently floating currency). However, the rising importance of the Chinese yuan is causing Hong Kong to rethink its link to the dollar.

> Another form of a hard peg is currency boards.

Soft Peg

There are several different types of soft pegs, but a majority of the countries in this category have adopted a *conventional fixed-peg arrangement*, a country pegs its currency to another currency or basket of currencies and allows the exchange rate to vary plus or minus 1 percent from that value. Most similar to the IMF's original fixed exchange-rate system, about an equal number of countries use the U.S. dollar and the euro as the anchor for their peg. In the other soft peg categories, the degree of flexibility increases, but the IMF determines that the currencies are not floating. The Chinese yuan fits in the soft peg category, more specifically in the stabilized arrangement, which means that the exchange rate remains within a margin of 2 percent against its anchor, which used to be the dollar and is now a basket of currency. However, the Chinese government is gradually increasing the margin of flexibility of the yuan. We note in our opening case that, whereas El Salvador has adopted a hard peg strategy by using the dollar as its currency, Costa Rica and Nicaragua, two of the countries with which it competes in CAFTA-DR, have adopted a soft peg strategy with greater flexibility than El Salvador but still linked to the U.S. dollar as an anchor.

> There are many different kinds of soft pegs but the most common is a conventional fixed-peg arrangement where a currency is pegged to another currency or basket of currencies with limited flexibility.

Case Review Note

Floating Arrangement

Currencies that are considered to be floating are either floating (46 countries) or free floating (33 countries). Floating currencies are those that generally change according to market forces but may be subject to market intervention. However, the intervention serves to moderate the rate of change or prevent undue fluctuations in the exchange rate, but the intention is not to deviate too far from market forces. Freely floating currencies are subject to intervention only in exception circumstances. The major trading currencies, including the U.S. dollar, the Japanese yen, the British pound, and the euro are freely floating currencies. Brazil and India, two of the BRIC countries, are considered to have floating currencies.

Anyone involved in international business needs to understand how the exchange rates of countries with which they do business are determined, because exchange rates affect marketing, production, and financial decisions, as we discuss at the end of the chapter. Note that countries sometimes change their approach to managing or not managing their currency, as Argentina did in 2002 when it moved from a currency board

> Floating exchange-rate regimes include floating and freely floating.

> Countries may change the exchange-rate regime they use, so managers need to monitor country policies carefully.

MAP 10.1
Exchange-Rate Arrangements, 2008

About half of the nations in the world have opted for floating exchange rates; the rest are either hard-peg or soft-peg arrangements.

Source: Data is from "De Facto Classification of Exchange Rate Regimes and Monetary Policy Frameworks" (April 30, 2008), International Monetary Fund, http://www.imf.org/external/np/mfd/er/2008/eng/0408.htm.

Note: Given that this is a Mercator projection, the scale approximates east-west distance at the equator; however, the farther you move from the equator, the more the east-west distance is distorted.

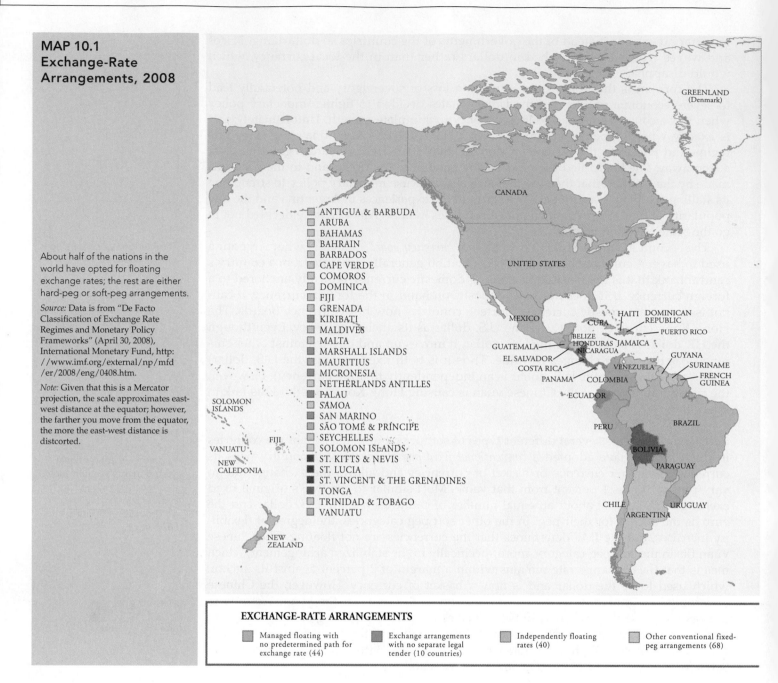

ANTIGUA & BARBUDA
ARUBA
BAHAMAS
BAHRAIN
BARBADOS
CAPE VERDE
COMOROS
DOMINICA
FIJI
GRENADA
KIRIBATI
MALDIVES
MALTA
MARSHALL ISLANDS
MAURITIUS
MICRONESIA
NETHERLANDS ANTILLES
PALAU
SAMOA
SAN MARINO
SÃO TOMÉ & PRÍNCIPE
SEYCHELLES
SOLOMON ISLANDS
ST. KITTS & NEVIS
ST. LUCIA
ST. VINCENT & THE GRENADINES
TONGA
TRINIDAD & TOBAGO
VANUATU

EXCHANGE-RATE ARRANGEMENTS

Managed floating with no predetermined path for exchange rate (44)

Exchange arrangements with no separate legal tender (10 countries)

Independently floating rates (40)

Other conventional fixed-peg arrangements (68)

to a floating currency. Chile was listed in a prior IMF survey as a country that kept its exchange rate within a crawling band, adjusting the exchange rate periodically according to inflation. But in late 1999, Chile suspended the trading bands it had established around the peso and moved to a floating-rate regime in an effort to stimulate export-led economic growth—and is now considered to have a freely floating currency. Likewise, in 2001 Iceland moved from a pegged regime, within a horizontal band, to a free-floating regime, as did Brazil in early 1999 and Turkey in 2001.[13]

It is important for MNEs to understand the exchange-rate arrangements for the currencies of countries where they are doing business so they can forecast trends more accurately. It is much easier to forecast a future exchange rate for a relatively stable currency pegged to the U.S. dollar, such as the Hong Kong dollar, than for a currency that is freely floating, such as the Japanese yen.

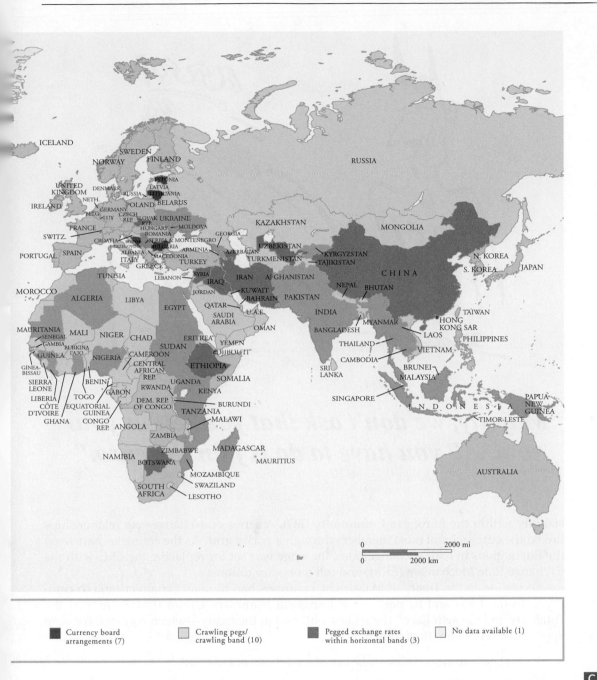

Currency board
arrangements (7)

Crawling pegs/
crawling band (10)

Pegged exchange rates
within horizontal bands (3)

No data available (1)

THE EURO

One of the most ambitious examples of a freely floating arrangement that resulted in countries giving up their own currency to create a new one is the euro. Not content with the economic integration envisaged in the Single European Act, the EU nations signed the Treaty of Maastricht in 1992, which set steps to accomplish two goals: political union and monetary union. The decision to move to a common currency in Europe has eliminated currency as a trade barrier. To replace each national currency with a single European currency called the *euro*, the countries first had to converge their economic policies.

The European Monetary System and the European Monetary Union   Monetary unity in Europe did not occur overnight. The roots of the system began in 1979, when the **European Monetary System (EMS)** was set up as a means of creating exchange-rate

FIGURE 10.1

Adopting the euro is not as easy as it seems. At first, all but a few members of the EU and as many of the new ones as possible wanted to join. With the huge debt challenges in Europe and pressures on countries that have adopted the euro, many are wondering if adopting the euro is almost as bad as selling your soul.

Source: BART/CartoonStock

"Majesty, we don't ask that you sell us your soul. All you have to do is join the euro."

stability within the European Community (EC). A series of exchange-rate relationships linked the currencies of most members through a parity grid. As the countries narrowed the fluctuations in their exchange rates, the stage was set for replacing the EMS with the Exchange Rate Mechanism (ERM) and full monetary union.

According to the Treaty of Maastricht, countries had to meet certain criteria to comply with the ERM and be part of the **European Monetary Union (EMU).** Termed the "Stability and Growth Pact," the criteria outlined in the treaty—which continue for euro applicants today—are the following:

> The criteria that are part of the Growth and Stability Pact include measures of deficits, debt, inflation, interest rates, and exchange rate stability.

- Annual government deficit must not exceed 3 percent of GDP.
- Total outstanding government debt must not exceed 60 percent of GDP.
- Rate of inflation must remain within 1.5 percent of the three best-performing EU countries.
- Average nominal long-term interest rate must be within 2 percent of the average rate in the three countries with the lowest inflation rates.
- Exchange-rate stability must be maintained, meaning that for at least two years the country concerned has kept within the "normal" fluctuation margins of the European Exchange Rate Mechanism.[14]

> The United Kingdom, Sweden, and Denmark are the only members of the original 15 EU countries that opted not to adopt the euro.

After a great deal of effort, 11 of the 15 countries in the EU joined the EMU on January 1, 1999, while Greece joined on January 1, 2001. Those of the original 15 countries not yet participating in the euro are the United Kingdom, Sweden, and Denmark. Sweden announced in July 2002 that it had met all the criteria for joining the EMU,[15] but voters' rejection of the euro in 2003 placed its entry on hold for the time being.[16] Denmark's currency is pegged to the euro as a conventional peg (soft peg category), whereas the currencies of the United Kingdom and Sweden are free-floating.

With the exception of those three countries, the other members of the EU that do not use the euro as their currency are new member states. Cyprus, Malta, Slovenia, and Slovakia had adopted the euro as of 2009, so 16 of the 27 EU countries have now done so. Table 10.1 notes that 27 countries use the euro as their exchange-rate anchor, four of which are non-adopting EU members with the rest being nations in Africa or Eastern Europe. Most of the remaining non-adopting EU countries have freely floating currencies and use inflation as the framework to target the value of their currencies. This is consistent with the role of the European Central Bank in closely monitoring inflation as a means of setting interest-rate policy.

The euro is administered by the **European Central Bank (ECB).** Established on July 1, 1998, the ECB has been responsible for setting monetary policy and for managing the exchange-rate system for all of Europe since January 1, 1999. The ERM is important in converging the EU economies. Because the ECB is an independent organization like the U.S. Fed, it can focus on its mandate of controlling inflation. Of course, different economies are growing at different rates in Europe, and it is difficult to have one monetary policy that fits all. Countries might be tempted to use an expansion fiscal policy to stimulate economic growth, but the deficit requirements of the ERM keep countries from stimulating too much.

> The European Central Bank sets monetary policy for the adopters of the euro.

Pluses and Minuses of the Conversion to the Euro   The initial move to the euro was smoother than predicted. Companies have been affected in a variety of ways. Banks have had to update their electronic networks to handle all aspects of monetary exchange, such as systems that trade global currencies, buy and sell stocks, transfer money between banks, manage customer accounts, or print out bank statements. Deutsche Bank estimates that the conversion process cost several hundred million dollars.[17]

However, many companies also believe the euro will increase price transparency (the ability to compare prices in different countries) and eliminate foreign-exchange costs and risks. Foreign-exchange costs are narrowing as companies operate in only one currency in Europe, while foreign-exchange risks between member states are also disappearing, although they still exist between the euro and nonmember currencies (the U.S. dollar, British pound, Swiss franc, and so on).

The Euro and the Global Financial Crisis   Since the initial introduction of the euro, the currency has steadily grown in strength and importance. In mid-2008, it was trading at around $1.59. However, after Lehman Brothers filed for bankruptcy in September 2008, the Dow Jones Industrial Average (DJIA) dropped over 500 points, followed by an even bigger loss on September 29, 2008. (The DJIA is a price-weighted average of 30 actively traded blue-chip stocks that is the most widely used indicator of the overall condition of the stock market in the United States.) An interesting thing happened in the exchange-rate relationship between the dollar and the euro. The collapse of the U.S. stock market at the end of September 2008 resulted in a drop in the value of the euro against the dollar, triggering two occurrences. First, the initial reaction by global investors was to put money into U.S. dollars—the flight to safety. Funds were pulled out of emerging markets and put into dollars as a safe-haven currency, thereby pushing down the euro. Second, the euro value began to track with the fortunes of the U.S. stock market. As the market collapsed, so did the euro; as the stock market began to recover somewhat, so did the euro. This is because the market sentiment shifted from safety to risk, and the risk appetite meant that investors were pulling money out of dollars and investing them in emerging markets and equities, making the euro more attractive than the dollar for investing. The relationship between the two has been volatile, with lots of peaks and valleys.

The role of the European Central Bank is to protect the euro against the ravages of inflation. Thus, interest rates in Europe, on average, are likely to be higher than they are in

> During the global financial crisis, investors fled to dollars as a safe-haven currency and returned to euros when their appetite for risk increased.

Concept Check

When we get to Chapter 11, we'll point out that when a country initiates a comprehensive policy change over which businesses (whether domestic or foreign) have no control, they should re-examine each link in their value chains—the collective activities required to move products from materials purchasing through operations to final distribution. Here we observe that a change in a nation's exchange-rate regime is just one of the changes in economic conditions that foreign firms can't control.

the United States, especially when the U.S. keeps interest rates low to stimulate economic growth, as in the crisis. This is why the spread in interest rates between the euro and dollar widened, favoring the euro as a place to invest funds. During the Greek debt crisis of 2011, the euro actually rose against the dollar, mainly because there was more pessimism over the state of the U.S. economy than over the European economy, and the U.S. Federal Reserve signaled that it was going to keep interest rates low to help stimulate the economy. The spread in interest rates favored the euro, helping to keep its value high against the dollar.

But there are still problems with the euro. One of the ongoing challenges for the euro is the lack of uniform standards of fiscal regulation among member nations, which allows nations like Greece or Portugal to spend well beyond their budgets to support their welfare systems with few actual checks from the European Central Bank. As we've seen from the worldwide financial crisis beginning in 2007, this has consequences for the entire euro zone, dragging down the currency's value and hurting countries relying on exports—namely the euro's primary benefactor—Germany. Without stronger regulations and the adoption of austerity measures in the bubble countries of Europe, the unequal distribution of the recession hinders the entire economy.

Another challenge to the euro zone's countries is the inability they have to adjust their own interest rates to counter inflation and stymie the depth of the recession. If interest rates are changed for the entire euro zone to help the few hardest-hit countries, this has the potential to harm some countries for whom the recession is not so profound. There are few ways to address the economic problems of the country without access to these levers of control, and fiscal responses in bankrupt countries require expensive bailouts.

In addition to these challenges, cultural differences within the euro zone itself create conflict on issues such as labor reform and social welfare systems, especially in light of the recent financial downturn. For example, the extremes of economic culture in Europe are perhaps best represented by the differences in policy on retirement in Greece and Germany. Prior to the financial crisis of 2008, Germany had already approved measures raising the age of receiving a state pension to 67. In Greece, however, workers can begin to collect a state pension at age 58, if they have worked for 35 years, despite the legal retirement age being 65.

These discrepancies in the internal workings of the various euro constituents can cause a great deal of instability, given the right circumstances. This not only decreases the currency's economic value to large, stable economies, such as Germany, but creates social inequalities that could be exploited by individual citizens within the euro zone.

Whether the euro survives depends on what happens with the debt crisis in Europe. If Greece defaults and pulls out of the euro, there could be a contagion effect on other countries such as Spain, Portugal and Italy. A default could also have a devastating impact on debt holders, many of whom are European banks. It will be interesting to see what happens.

Determining Exchange Rates

A lot of different factors cause exchange rates to adjust. The exchange-rate regimes described earlier in the chapter are either fixed (hard peg or soft peg) or floating, with fixed rates varying in terms of how fixed they are and floating rates varying in terms of how much they actually float. However, currencies change in different ways depending on the type of regime. Here we examine how supply and demand determine currency values in a floating world in the absence of government intervention, then show how governments can intervene in markets to help control the value of a currency.

NONINTERVENTION: CURRENCY IN A FLOATING-RATE WORLD

Currencies that float freely respond to supply and demand conditions uncontrolled by government intervention. This concept can be illustrated using a two-country model

Should Africa Develop a Common Currency?

Point **Yes** The success of the euro and the deep economic and political problems in Africa have caused many experts to wonder whether the continent should attempt to develop one common currency with a central bank to set monetary policy.[18] In 2003, the Association of African Central Bank Governors of the African Union (AU) announced it would work to create a common currency by 2021. This would benefit Africa by hastening economic integration in a continent that desperately needs to increase market size to achieve more trade and greater economies of scale. A common currency would lower transaction costs and make it easier to engage in intra-country trade.

Africa has several degrees of economic cooperation already, including two forms of currency cooperation that are classified by the IMF as conventional pegs tied to the euro:

1. The Economic and Monetary Community for Central Africa (CAEMC), including Cameroon, Central African Republic, Chad, Republic of Congo, Equatorial Guinea, and Gabon
2. The West African Economic and Monetary Union (WAEMU), including Benin, Burkina Faso, Côte d'Ivoire, Guinea-Bissau, Mali, Niger, Senegal, and Togo

Both monetary unions are part of the CFA franc zone, designated by the IMF as "other conventional fixed-peg arrangements" pegged to the euro,[19] and each has a central bank that monitors the value of the CFA franc.

Although successful in delivering low inflation, the CFA franc zone has not necessarily delivered high growth. The CMA is controlled by South Africa because of the size of its economy and the fact that its currency is the South African rand. Its members are also classified as "other conventional fixed-peg arrangement," with the exception of South Africa, which has an independently floating currency.

In addition to the three regional monetary unions, Africa has five existing regional economic communities: Arab Monetary Union, Common Market for Eastern and Southern Africa, Economic Community of Central African States, Economic Community of West African States, and Southern African Development Community. These groups are working hard to reduce trade barriers and increase trade among member countries, so all they would have to do is combine into one large African economic union, form a central bank, and establish a common monetary policy like the EU has.

A major advantage of establishing a central bank and common currency is that institutions in each African nation will have to improve, and the central bank may be able to insulate the monetary policy from political pressures, which often create inflationary pressures and subsequent devaluations.

Should Africa Develop a Common Currency?

Counterpoint **No** There is no way the countries of Africa will ever establish a common currency, even though the African Union hopes to do so by 2021. The institutional framework in the individual African nations is simply not ready. Few of the individual central banks are independent of the political process, so they often have to stimulate the economy to respond to political pressures. If the process is not managed properly and the currency is subject to frequent devaluation, there will be no pride in the region or clout on the international stage.

Further, each country will have to give up monetary sovereignty and rely on other measures, such as labor mobility, wage and price flexibility, and fiscal transfers, to weather the shocks. Even though there is good labor mobility in Africa, it is difficult to imagine that the African countries will be able to transfer tax revenues from country to country to help stimulate growth. In addition, it is difficult to transfer goods among the different countries in Africa because of transportation problems, which is not an issue in the EU.

The establishment of the euro in the EU was a monumental task that took years to establish, following a successful customs union and a gradual tightening of the ERM in Europe. For Africa to establish a common currency, there needs to be closer economic integration first. Thus, it is important to be patient and give Africa a chance to move forward. Maybe one way to move to a common currency is to strengthen the existing regional monetary unions, then gradually open them up to neighboring countries until there are a few huge monetary unions. These can then discuss ways to link together into a common African currency.

FIGURE 10.2 The Equilibrium Exchange Rate and How it Moves

Let's say that inflation in the United States is comparatively higher than in Japan. In that case (and assuming that Japanese consumers are buying U.S. goods and services), the demand for the Japanese yen will go up, but the supply will go down. What if Japan wants to keep the dollar-to-yen exchange rate at e_0? It can increase the supply of yen in the market—and therefore lower the exchange rate—by selling yen for dollars.

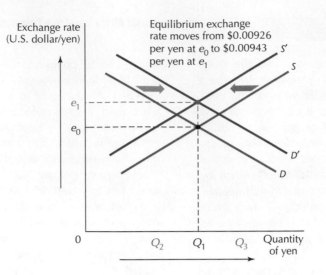

Demand for a country's currency is a function of the demand for that country's goods and services and financial assets.

involving the United States and Japan. Figure 10.2 shows the equilibrium exchange rate in the market and then a movement to a new equilibrium level as the market changes. The demand for yen in this example is a function of U.S. demand for Japanese goods and services, such as automobiles, and yen-denominated financial assets, such as securities.

The supply of yen is a function of Japanese demand for U.S. goods and services and dollar-denominated financial assets. Initially, this supply of and demand for yen meet at the equilibrium exchange rate e_0 (for example, 0.00926 dollar per yen, or 108 yen per dollar) and the quantity of yen Q_1.

Assume that Japanese consumers' demand for U.S. goods and services drops because of, say, high U.S. inflation. This lessening demand would result in a reduced supply of yen in the foreign-exchange market, causing the supply curve to shift to S'. Simultaneously, the rising prices of U.S. goods might lead to an increase in American consumers' demand for Japanese goods and services. This, in turn, would lead to an increase in demand for yen in the market, causing the demand curve to shift to D', and finally to an increase in the quantity of yen and in the exchange rate.

The new equilibrium exchange rate would be at e_1 (for example, 0.00943 dollar per yen, or 106 yen per dollar). From a dollar standpoint, the higher demand for Japanese goods would increase the supply of dollars as more consumers tried to trade their dollars for yen, and the reduced demand for U.S. goods would result in a drop in demand for dollars, causing a reduction in the dollar's value against the yen.

INTERVENTION: CURRENCY IN A FIXED-RATE OR MANAGED FLOATING-RATE WORLD

In the preceding example, Japanese and U.S. authorities allowed supply and demand to determine the values of the yen and dollar. That doesn't happen for currencies that fix their exchange rates and then don't allow them to move according to market forces. There can be times when one or both countries might not want exchange rates to change.

Assume, for example, that the United States and Japan decide to manage their exchange rates. Although both currencies are independently floating, their respective governments could intervene in the market. The U.S. government might not want its currency to weaken, because its companies and consumers would have to pay more for Japanese products, which would lead to more inflationary pressure in the United States. Or the Japanese government might not want the yen to strengthen, because it would mean unemployment in its export industries.

But how can the governments keep the values from changing when the United States is earning too few yen? Somehow the difference between yen supply and demand must be neutralized. To understand this process, let's first examine the role of central banks in foreign-exchange markets.

The Role of Central Banks   Each country has a central bank responsible for the policies affecting the value of its currency, although countries with currency boards independent from the central bank use them to control the currency value. The central bank in the United States is the Federal Reserve System (the "Fed"), a system of 12 regional banks. The New York Fed, in close coordination with and representing the Federal Reserve System and the U.S. Treasury, is responsible for intervening in foreign-exchange markets to achieve dollar exchange-rate policy objectives and counter disorderly conditions in foreign-exchange markets. The U.S. Treasury is responsible for setting exchange-rate policy, whereas the Fed is responsible for executing foreign-exchange intervention. Further, the New York Fed serves as a fiscal agent in the United States for foreign central banks and official international financial organizations.[20]

> Central banks control policies that affect the value of currencies; the Federal Reserve Bank of New York is the central bank in the United States.

In the European Union, the European Central Bank coordinates the activities of each member country's central bank to establish a common monetary policy in Europe, much as the Fed does in the United States. The ECB also is moving more aggressively to help contain the debt crisis in Europe instead of just managing interest rate policy. In China, the People's Bank of China (PBOC) is the Central Bank equivalent of the Fed and the ECB.

Central Bank Reserve Assets   Central bank reserve assets are kept in three major forms: foreign-exchange reserves, IMF-related assets (including SDRs), and gold. Foreign exchange comprises over 90 percent of total reserves worldwide. In fourth quarter 2010, the Composition of Official Foreign Exchange Reserves (COFER) reported that U.S. dollars represented about 61.4 percent of the total allocated foreign-exchange reserves (which includes only those reserves for which the currency is known), followed by the euro at about 26.3 percent of the total. Other currencies, such as the Japanese yen, British pound, and Swiss franc, are also reserve assets but at relatively small percentages. Clearly, the U.S. dollar and the euro are the two main reserve asset currencies. Their percentage of the total varies from year to year depending on their relative strengths; their relative position for different countries varies as well.[21]

> Central bank reserve assets are kept in three major forms: gold, foreign-exchange reserves, and IMF-related assets. Foreign exchange is 90 percent of reserve assets worldwide.

Some people believe that the dollar is going to lose its place as the number one reserve asset. Since the financial crisis in 2008, the United States has lost credibility, and in March 2009 China's central bank suggested a move away from the dollar as reserve currency. Instead, China has considered relying more on the SDR. This would not be an easy transition, and many are skeptical that the dollar will lose its number one status, but it is still something to watch out for.[22]

Having strong central bank reserve assets is essential to a country's fiscal strength. When the financial crises in Asia, Russia, and South America hit in the late 1990s, very few countries had strong central bank reserve assets. As a result, they had to borrow a lot of U.S. dollars, which turned out to be devastating when they finally had to devalue their currencies. Since 2000, however, the picture has changed. Due to strong commodity prices, expanding exports, and restraint in incurring dollar debt, many of those same countries have strengthened their financial position by increasing their reserves.

Take Brazil. Its foreign-exchange reserves were $192.9 billion at the end of 2008, leading the way for the rest of Latin America, where reserves have increased fourfold since 2000.[23] However, this is relatively small compared to China, which had nearly $2 trillion in reserves. The top countries in the world in terms of total reserves are China, Japan, Russia, Taiwan, India, Hong Kong, Brazil, and Singapore.

How Central Banks Intervene in the Market   A central bank can intervene in currency markets in several ways. The U.S. Fed, for example, usually uses foreign currencies to buy dollars when the dollar is weak, or sells dollars for foreign currency

> Central banks intervene in currency markets by buying and selling currency to affect its price.

when the dollar is strong. Depending on the market conditions, a central bank may do any of the following:

- Coordinate its action with other central banks or go it alone
- Enter the market aggressively to change attitudes about its views and policies
- Call for reassuring action to calm markets
- Intervene to reverse, resist, or support a market trend
- Announce or not announce its operations—be very visible or very discreet
- Operate openly or indirectly through brokers[24]

Case: The U.S. Dollar and the Japanese Yen   Although the U.S. dollar is an independently floating currency, let's continue with the example illustrated in Figure 10.2 and show how a central bank could intervene. In a managed fixed-exchange-rate system, the New York Fed would hold foreign-exchange reserves, which it would have built up through the years for this type of contingency. It could sell enough of its yen reserves (make up the difference between Q1 and Q3 in Figure 10.3) at the fixed exchange rate to maintain that rate. Or the Japanese central bank might be willing to accept dollars so that U.S. consumers can continue to buy Japanese goods. These dollars would then become part of Japan's foreign-exchange reserves. Although this is a two-country example, sometimes several central banks coordinate their intervention to support a currency.

The fixed rate could continue as long as the United States had reserves or as long as the Japanese were willing to add dollars to their holdings. Sometimes governments use monetary policy such as raising interest rates to create a demand for their currency and keep the value from falling. However, interest rate policy is usually a function of inflationary expectations and/or concerns about economic growth rather than just to influence exchange rates. Unless something changed the basic imbalance in the currency supply and demand, the New York Fed would run out of yen and the Japanese central bank would stop accepting dollars because it would fear amassing too many, similar to what happened to South Korea in early 2005 and Thailand in 2007. At this point, it would be necessary to change the exchange rate to lessen the demand for yen.

If a country determines that intervention will not work, it must adjust its currency's value. If the currency is freely floating, the exchange rate will seek the correct level according to the laws of supply and demand. However, a currency pegged to another

FIGURE 10.3   A snapshot of the five-year trend in the Japanese yen

This illustrates how the yen steadily strengthened against the dollar during the initial phases of the global financial crisis, the only major currency in the world to do so. However, it briefly weakened early in 2009 and then floated back and forth, creating problems for Sony and other large Japanese MNCs

Source: yahoo!inc. http://finance /yahoo.com

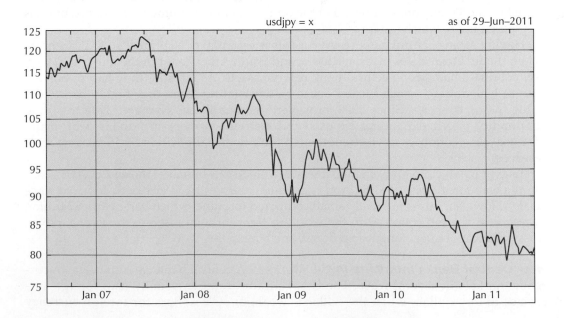

currency or to a basket of currencies usually is changed on a formal basis—in other words, through a devaluation (a weakening of the currency) or revaluation (a strengthening of the currency), depending on the direction of the change.

Different Attitudes toward Intervention   Government policies change over time, depending on economic conditions and the attitude of the prevailing administration in power, irrespective of whether the currency is considered to be freely floating.

Previously, however, the attitude toward intervention was a little different. In 1989 alone, the George H. W. Bush administration bought and sold dollars on 97 days and sold $19.5 billion. In the first two and a half years of the Clinton administration, the Fed intervened in the market by buying dollars on only 18 days, spending about $12.5 billion in the process.[25] But the U.S. government is hesitant to intervene directly in the foreign-exchange market, preferring to allow the market to determine the correct value. According to the New York Fed, the United States intervened in foreign-exchange markets on eight different days in 1995, but only twice from August 1995 through December 2010.[26] The Fed intervened in the foreign exchange markets on March 18, 2011, the first time since 2000, by purchasing $1 billion against the yen. The action was coordinated with the Central Bank of Japan, the European Central Bank, and the Central Banks of Canada and the United Kingdom.

The global financial crisis has roiled foreign-exchange markets and forced many central banks to intervene to support their currencies. Consider Hungary which is a member of the European Union, but which has not yet adopted the euro. However, the EU is its most important market, with 79 percent of its exports going to, and 70 percent of its imports coming from, EU members. The rising value of the euro against the U.S. dollar created serious economic problems for Hungary. Its forint fell 22 percent against the euro in the first few months of 2009, forcing the Hungarian central bank to intervene in foreign-exchange markets to support the forint.[27]

The Russian ruble is another currency affected by the global financial crisis. It is a pegged currency that uses a composite of currencies as its benchmark for determining its value. In late 2008, the Russian government was supporting the value of the ruble despite the fall in oil prices (its major source of foreign-exchange earnings) and capital flight from Russia by foreign investors who were taking their money from emerging markets and putting it into dollars. In order to keep the ruble from crashing in value, the government loosened the trading band for ruble trades and allowed the currency to weaken in a more orderly manner rather than exhibit the large swings seen in the dollar/euro exchange rate.

The global financial crisis basically destroyed the economy and currency of Iceland, which does not use the euro. In October 2008, its government raised interest rates to 18 percent in order to try to save the currency.[28] However, Iceland's government intervention did not work. Everyone from banks to individuals incurred huge foreign debts because foreign interest rates were so much lower than interest rates there. When the crisis hit, the currency fell in value and nobody could pay their debts. In July 2009, as the crisis escalated for Iceland, its parliament narrowly voted to join the EU and eventually adopt the euro.[29]

Besides the preceding illustrations, other countries were forced to intervene in the foreign-exchange markets to support their currencies during the global crisis. It was estimated that Brazil, Mexico, Russia, and India collectively drew down their foreign-exchange reserves by more than $75 billion in the fall of 2008 in an effort to protect their currencies, which had dropped dramatically against the dollar.[30] Achieving balance in the foreign-exchange markets seems to be a never-ending battle.

During the Greek debt crisis and battles in the United States over the budget deficit, the euro actually rose against the dollar, creating problems for non-euro countries. Poland, for example, was forced to intervene in foreign exchange markets in 2011 to strengthen its currency, the zyloty, because it was falling too much against the euro, raising fears that rising import prices would lead to higher inflation.[31]

Governments vary in their intervention policies by country and by administration.

Challenges with Intervention   As noted above, the United States disapproves of foreign-currency intervention because it is very difficult, if not impossible, for intervention to have a lasting impact on the value of a currency. Given the daily volume of foreign-exchange transactions, no one government can move the market unless its movements can change the market psychology. Intervention may temporarily halt a slide, but the country cannot force the market to move in a direction it doesn't want to go, at least for the long run. For that reason, it is important for countries to focus on correcting economic fundamentals instead of spending a lot of time and money on intervention. Nevertheless, countries still intervene, and the above examples illustrate different approaches to intervention, from raising interest rates to using foreign-exchange reserves to buy and sell currencies. When daily foreign-exchange trades are about $4 trillion, it is hard to intervene enough to move the markets very much. Any intervention can be construed as a central bank signal, but the long-term policies will eventually make the big difference.

Revisiting the BIS   Coordination of central bank intervention can take place bilaterally or multilaterally. The Bank for International Settlements (BIS) in Basel, Switzerland, links together the central banks of the world. As we noted in Chapter 9, the BIS was founded in 1930 and is owned and controlled by the major central banks of the world. Its major objective is to promote the cooperation of central banks to facilitate international financial stability. Although only 56 central banks or monetary authorities are shareholders in the BIS—11 of which are the founding banks and are from the major industrial countries—the BIS deals with some 140 central banks and other international financial institutions worldwide.[32]

The BIS acts as a central banker's bank. It gets involved in swaps and other currency transactions between the central banks in other countries. It is also a gathering place where central bankers can discuss monetary cooperation, and it is increasingly getting involved with other multilateral agencies, such as the IMF, in providing support during international financial crises. In addition, the BIS conducts the triennial central bank survey of foreign-exchange and derivatives market activity that is the basis for much of the trading data provided in Chapter 9.

BLACK MARKETS

In many of the countries that do not allow their currencies to float according to market forces, a **black market** can parallel the official market and be aligned more closely with the forces of supply and demand than the official market. The less flexible a country's exchange-rate arrangement, the more likely there will be a thriving black (or parallel) market. A black market exists when people are willing to pay more for dollars than the official rate. In order for such a market to work, the government must control access to foreign exchange so it can control the price of its currency.

One example of black market transactions occurred in Shenzhen, China, in 2009 when people who were worried about the future value of the Chinese yuan bought Hong Kong dollars on the black market. Some people even figured out that the demand for Hong Kong dollars was so high that they could buy them at state banks and make a tidy profit by selling them to others who could not get access to them.[33]

Zimbabwe's terrible financial problems are manifest in the currency markets. Its official currency regime is a soft-peg arrangement and used to be pegged to the U.S. dollar, but that didn't seem to have helped much. In 2007, with inflation hitting around 4,500 percent—the highest in the world—the currency was plunging. A loaf of bread cost 44,000 Zimbabwean dollars, which was only 18 cents at black-market rates but $176 at the official exchange rate.[34] By early 2009, the economy was still a disaster, and the country was suffering from a cholera epidemic and political turmoil. Hyperinflation was so bad that the central bank issued a $100 trillion banknote that was worth about US$33 on the black market. Prices were doubling every day, and food and fuel were in short

Inflation in Laos in 2002 made the local currency Kip (LAK) virtually useless and only used for small item purchases. At that time, USD1.00 was equal to LAK 13,000, filling up a shopping bag with stacks of notes. Larger purchases were therefore always made in USD or Thai Baht, keeping the black market alive and thriving. On November 15, 2010, a 100,000 kip banknote was issued to celebrate the 450th anniversary of the founding of the capital of Laos.

Source: Bjorn Svensson/Alamy

supply. In spite of an official exchange rate, most people were trading currency at the black-market rate.[35]

Even oil-rich Venezuela has black market problems. Sometimes the markets are illegal, and sometimes they are an essential part of the economy. Although Venezuela has an official ban against private firms buying and selling currency at black market rates, it relies on black-market trading houses to keep currency in the market. When oil prices fell in the latter part of 2008, a liquidity crisis hit Venezuela, and the finance ministry and state-owned oil company began selling dollars on the black market at three times the official rate, thus allowing them to continue operations.[36] For a while, the government maintained two official exchange rates, one for essential imports and one for other imports, as well as the unofficial floating black market rate. In 2011, however, the government moved to one exchange rate for the Bolivar fuerte for all imports and designated the exchange-rate regime as a conventional peg system with the U.S. dollar as the anchor currency. Through the first half of 2011, the exchange rate remained unchanged at 4.3500 per dollar, so it was maintaining its peg. However, the black market in 2011, though illegal, was still live and well with black market rates nearly double the official rate.

FOREIGN-EXCHANGE CONVERTIBILITY AND CONTROLS

Some countries with fixed exchange rates control access to their currencies. *Fully convertible currencies* are those that the government allows both residents and nonresidents to purchase in unlimited amounts.

Hard and Soft Currencies   **Hard currencies**—such as the U.S. dollar, euro, British pound, and Japanese yen—are those that are fully convertible. Highly liquid and relatively stable in value over a short period of time, they are generally accepted worldwide as payment for goods and services. They are also desirable assets. Currencies that are not fully convertible, or **soft currencies,** have just the opposite characteristics: They are very unstable in value, not very liquid, and not widely accepted as payment for goods and services. A major reason why countries restrict convertibility of their currencies is that they are short on foreign-exchange reserves and try to use those reserves for essential transactions. That's why soft currencies tend to be from developing countries, where

A hard currency is a currency that is usually fully convertible and strong or relatively stable in value in comparison with other currencies.

A soft currency is one that is usually not fully convertible and is also called a weak currency.

foreign-exchange reserves are low. The higher the reserves, the less a country has to resort to restricting convertibility. It is interesting to note that many developing countries dominate the list of nations with the highest foreign-exchange reserves. In spite of that, when paying for exports and imports they need to go through hard currencies such as the dollar, euro, and yen.

Most countries today have *nonresident* (or *external*) *convertibility*, meaning that foreigners can convert their currency into the local currency and convert back into theirs as well. Tourists generally have no problems doing this, although sometimes countries put restrictions or conditions on trade from the local currency back to the hard currency when tourists leave the country.

Controlling Convertibility   To conserve scarce foreign exchange, some governments impose exchange restrictions on companies or individuals who want to exchange money. The devices they use include *import licensing, multiple exchange rates, import deposit requirements,* and *quantity controls.*

In 2007, for instance, the value of the Thai baht—a managed floating currency that targets inflation in determining the currency value—was rising, approaching a 10-year high against the U.S. dollar. Given that the Thai government had limited the convertibility of the baht in some areas, it decided it might be best to loosen controls and encourage an outflow of currency to try to lower the value. On June 25, 2007, the government announced several measures to reduce controls:

> Among the measures, effective immediately, was approval for Thai-listed companies to purchase foreign exchange of up to $100 million a year for foreign investment. Institutional investors no longer need central bank approval to invest in deposits with foreign institutions, and individuals may now send up to $1 million a year overseas as transfers to expatriate relatives, as donations or to buy real estate.[37]

This quote serves to illustrate ways in which governments institute foreign-exchange controls to preserve a currency's value.

| Licensing occurs when a government requires that all foreign-exchange transactions be regulated and controlled by it. |

Licenses   Government licenses fix the exchange rate by requiring all recipients, exporters, and others who receive foreign currency to sell it to its central bank at the official buying rate. The bank then rations the foreign currency it acquires by selling it at fixed rates to those needing to make payment abroad for essential goods. An importer may purchase foreign exchange only if it has obtained an import license for the goods in question.

| In a multiple exchange-rate system, a government sets different exchange rates for different types of transactions. |

Multiple Exchange Rates   Another way governments control foreign-exchange convertibility is by establishing more than one exchange rate. This restrictive measure is called a **multiple exchange-rate system.** The government determines which kinds of transactions are to be conducted at which exchange rates. Countries with multiple rates often have a floating rate for luxury goods and financial flows, such as dividends, and a fixed, usually lower rate for other trade transactions such as imports of essential commodities and semi-manufactured goods. As noted above, Venezuela used a multiple exchange rate restriction until 2011. Under the system, essential imports, such as capital goods, food, and medicine converted at 2.6 bolivars to the dollar, whereas nonessential goods, such as cars, appliances, and alcohol were fixed at 4.3 bolivars to the dollar. At the time, the black market rate was nearly 8 bolivars to the dollar. However, under the system implemented in 2011, all imports used the official rate of 4.3500, significantly increasing the cost of essential imports.[38]

| Advance import deposit—a government requires deposit of money prior to the release of foreign exchange to pay for imports; varies to as long as a year in advance. |

Import Deposits   Another form of foreign-exchange convertibility control is the **advance import deposit.** In this case, the government tightens the issue of import licenses and requires importers to make a deposit with the central bank—often for as long as one year and interest-free—covering the full price of manufactured goods they would purchase from abroad.

Quantity Controls   Governments may also limit the amount of exchange through quantity controls, which often apply to tourism. A quantity control limits the amount of currency a local resident can purchase from the bank for foreign travel. The government sets a policy on how much money a tourist is allowed to take overseas, and the individual is allowed to convert only that amount of money.

In the past, currency controls have significantly added to the cost of doing business internationally, resulting in the overall reduction of trade. However, trade liberalization in recent years has eliminated a lot of these controls to the point that they are considered a minor impediment to trade.[39] In addition, the move from fixed to flexible exchange rates has also eliminated the need for controls in many countries.

> Quantity controls—the government limits the amount of foreign currency that can be used in a specific transaction.

EXCHANGE RATES AND PURCHASING POWER PARITY

The next three sections examine three interconnected issues: the relationship between inflation and exchange rates, the relationship between interest rates and exchange rates, and the factors you can use to forecast (or at least attempt to forecast) future exchange rates.

Purchasing power parity (PPP) is a well-known theory that, from the standpoint of exchange rates, seeks to define the relationships between currencies based on relative

◀ McDonald's is very successful in Brazil. This beautiful store in São Paulo is reminiscent of colonial times in Brazil. Because of the strong Brazilian real, a Big Mac costs the equivalent of $4.91 compared with $3.73 in the U.S. (See Table 10.2). At that cost difference, the real would be overvalued against the dollar by 31 percent.

Source: Jenny Matthews/Alamy

inflation. In essence, it claims that a change in relative inflation between two countries (meaning a comparison of the countries' rates of inflation) must cause a change in exchange rates to keep the prices of goods in the countries fairly similar. According to the PPP theory, if, say, Japanese inflation were 2 percent and U.S. inflation were 3.5 percent, the dollar would be expected to fall by the difference in inflation rates. The dollar would then be worth fewer yen than before the adjustment, and the yen would be worth more dollars than before the adjustment.

The "Big Mac Index"   An interesting illustration of the PPP theory for estimating exchange rates is the "Big Mac index" of currencies used by *The Economist* each year. Since 1986, the British periodical *The Economist* has used the price of a Big Mac to estimate the exchange rate between the dollar and another currency (see Table 10.2). Because the Big Mac is sold in more than 31,000 McDonald's restaurants serving more than 58 million people in 119 countries every day, it is easy to use it to compare prices. PPP would suggest that the exchange rate should leave hamburgers costing the same in the United States as abroad. However, the Big Mac sometimes costs more and sometimes less, demonstrating how far currencies are under- or overvalued against the dollar.

> If the domestic inflation rate is lower than that in the foreign country, the domestic currency should be stronger than that of the foreign country.

The Big Mac price in U.S. dollars is found by converting the price of a Big Mac in the local currency into dollars at the current exchange rate. For example, in Table 10.2, the dollar equivalent of a Big Mac in China is US$1.95, which is the price of the Big Mac in China (¥13.2) converted into dollars at the actual exchange rate (which was CNY6.7800). Column 3, the implied PPP of the dollar, shows what the exchange rate should be if the price in dollars equals the price in the local currency. Continuing with China as the example, if you divide ¥13.2 by U.S. $3.73 (the prices of the Big Mac in China and in the United States), you get ¥3.54 per dollar, which is what the exchange rate should be for a Big Mac to cost the same in the two countries. Column 4 shows the actual exchange rate, and column 5 shows how much the currency is under- or overvalued. For the Chinese yuan, you take $(3.54 - 6.78)/6.78 = -0.47788$; the yuan is undervalued against the dollar by 48 percent.

As you can see from Table 10.2, the euro and currencies of European countries tied to the euro, such as Switzerland, Denmark, and Sweden, were overvalued against the dollar, whereas those of many other countries in Latin America and Asia were undervalued. That makes it easier for U.S. companies to export to Europe and harder for European companies to export to the United States. Consider the challenge between the Chinese yuan and the euro. The euro is overvalued by 16 percent against the dollar, according to the Big Mac index, whereas the Chinese yuan is undervalued by 48 percent against the dollar. That means the euro is overvalued by 64 percent against the yuan, making their trade relationship even more complicated.[40]

The Big Mac index, also known as "McParity," has both supporters and detractors. Even though McParity may hold up in the long run, as some studies have shown, there are short-term problems that affect PPP:

- The theory of PPP falsely assumes there are no barriers to trade and that transportation costs are zero.

- Prices of the Big Mac in different countries are distorted by taxes. European countries with high value-added taxes are more likely to have higher prices than countries with low taxes.

- The Big Mac is not just a basket of commodities; its price also includes nontraded costs, such as rent, insurance, and so on, which tend to be lower in developing countries.

- Profit margins vary by the strength of competition: The higher the competition, the lower the profit margin and, therefore, the price.[41]

TABLE 10.2   The Big Mac Index

In order to estimate the exchange rate between the dollar and another currency, the index converts into U.S. $ the price of a Big Mac in the second currency. To appreciate the difference in price in U.S. $ made by differences in currency valuations, compare the data for the euro area with the data for Switzerland. Note that of the countries on the list, you can get the best deals on a Big Mac in Malaysia and South Africa.

	Big Mac prices		Implied PPP* of the dollar	Actual exchange rate: Jan 30, 2009	Under (−)/over (+) valuation against the dollar, %
	In local currency	In dollars			
United States†	$3.54	3.54	—	—	
Argentina	Peso 11.50	3.30	3.25	3.49	−7
Austria	A$3.45	2.19	0.97	1.57	−38
Brazil	Real 8.02	3.45	2.27	2.32	−2
Britain	£2.29	3.30	1.55‡	1.44†	−7
Canada	C$4.16	3.36	1.18	1.24	−5
Chile	Peso 1.550	2.51	438	617	−29
China	Yuan 12.5	1.83	3.53	5.84	−48
Czech Republic	Koruna 65.94	3.02	18.6	21.9	−15
Denmark	DK 29.5	5.07	8.33	6.82	43
Egypt	Pound 13.0	2.34	3.67	5.57	−34
Euro area §	€3.42	4.38	1.04**	1.28**	24
Hong Kong	HK$13.3	1.72	3.76	7.75	−52
Hungery	Forint 680	2.92	192	233	−18
Indonesia	Rupiah 19.800	1.74	5.593	11,380	−51
Israel	Shekel 15.0	3.69	4.24	4.07	4
Japan	¥290	3.23	81.9	89.8	−9
Malaysia	Ringgit 5.50	1.52	1.55	3.61	−57
Maxico	Peso 33.0	2.30	9.32	14.4	−35
New Zealand	NZ$4.90	2.48	1.38	1.97	−30
Norway	Kroner 40.0	5.79	11.3	6.91	63
Peru	Sol 8.06	2.54	2.28	3.18	−28
Philippines	Peso 98.0	2.07	27.7	47.4	−42
Poland	Zloty 7.00	2.01	1.98	3.48	−43
Russia	Ruble 62.0	1.73	17.5	35.7	−51
Saudi Arabia	Riyal 10.0	2.66	2.82	3.75	−25
Singapore	S$3.95	2.61	1.12	1.51	−26
South Africa	Rand 16.95	1.66	4.79	10.2	−53
South Korea	Won 3.300	2.39	932	1,380	−32
Sweden	SKR 38.0	4.58	10.7	8.30	29
Switzerland	CHF 6.50	5.60	1.84	1.16	58
Taiwan	NT$75.0	2.23	21.2	33.6	−37
Thailand	Baht 62.0	1.77	17.5	35.0	−50
Turkey	Lire 5.15	3.13	1.45	1.64	−12

*Purchasing power parity; local price divided by price in the United States
†Average of New York, Chicago, Atlanta, and San Francisco
‡Dollars per pound
§Weighted average of prices in euro area
**Dollars per euro
Source: McDonald's; The Economist

The value of the Big Mac index is in understanding that price differences are not sustainable in the long run. Exchange rates will eventually have to equalize price differences more closely, or the law of supply and demand will take over. Of course, nobody is going to import Big Macs from China to the United States because they are so cheap. But if Big Macs are cheap, so are other products, and trade flows could be influenced by price differences.

EXCHANGE RATES AND INTEREST RATES

Although inflation is the most important medium-term influence on exchange rates, interest rates are also important. Interest rate differentials, however, have both short-term and long-term components to them. In the short term, exchange rates are strongly influenced by interest rates. One factor keeping the euro strong against the dollar in late 2008 and early 2009 was that the European Central Bank was keeping interest rates relatively high compared to those in the United States. Once the appetite for risk returned to the market, investors looked at the euro as a good place to invest, so money flowed to the euro, increasing its value against the U.S. dollar. When the European Central Bank reduced interest rates to help stimulate economic growth, the difference between U.S. and European interest rates narrowed, so money stopped flowing to the euro and it fell in value.

In the long term, however, there is a strong relationship between inflation, interest rates, and exchange rates. To understand this, we need to examine two key finance theories: the *Fisher Effect* and the *International Fisher Effect*. The first links inflation and interest rates, while the second links interest rates and exchange rates.

The nominal interest rate is the real interest rate plus inflation. Because the real interest rate should be the same in every country, the country with the higher interest rate should have higher inflation.

The Fisher Effect   The **Fisher Effect** is the theory that the nominal interest rate in a country (r, the actual monetary interest rate earned on an investment) is determined by the real interest rate (R, the nominal rate less inflation) and the inflation rate (i) as follows:

$$(1 + r) = (1 + R)(1 + i) \text{ or } r = (1 + R)(1 + i) - 1$$

According to this theory, if the real interest rate is 5 percent, the U.S. inflation rate 2.9 percent, and the Japanese inflation rate 1.5 percent, then the nominal interest rates for the United States and Japan are computed as follows:

$$r_{US} = (1.05)(1.029) - 1 = 0.08045, \text{ or } 8.045\%$$
$$r_j = (1.05)(1.015) - 1 = 0.06575, \text{ or } 6.575\%$$

Thus, the difference between U.S. and Japanese interest rates is a function of the difference between their inflation rates. If those were the same (zero differential) but interest rates were 10 percent in the United States and 6.575 percent in Japan, investors would place their money in the United States, where they could get the higher real return.

The IFE implies that the currency of the country with the lower interest rate will strengthen in the future.

The International Fisher Effect   The bridge from interest rates to exchange rates can be explained by the **International Fisher Effect (IFE),** the theory that the interest-rate differential is an unbiased predictor of future changes in the spot exchange rate. For example, if the IFE predicts that nominal interest rates in the United States are higher than those in Japan, the dollar's value should fall in the future by that interest-rate differential, which would be an indication of a weakening, or depreciation, of the dollar. That is because the interest-rate differential is based on differences in inflation rates, as we discussed earlier. The previous discussion on PPP also demonstrates that the country with the higher inflation should have the weaker currency. Thus, the country with the higher interest rate (and the higher inflation) should have the weaker currency.

Of course, these issues cover the long run, but anything can happen in the short run. During periods of general price stability, a country that raises its interest rates is likely to attract capital and see its currency rise in value due to the increased demand. However, if the reason for the increase in interest rates is that inflation is higher than that of its major trading partners, and if the country's central bank is trying to reduce inflation, the currency will eventually weaken until inflation cools down.

Other key factors affecting exchange-rate movements are confidence and technical factors, such as the release of economic statistics.

OTHER FACTORS IN EXCHANGE-RATE DETERMINATION

Confidence   Various other factors can affect currency values. One factor not to be dismissed lightly is confidence: In times of turmoil, people prefer to hold currencies considered safe. During last quarter 2008, the dollar rose dramatically in value due to its status as a safe-haven currency. Even though the crisis started in the United States in 2007 with the subprime mortgage problems, the banking crisis in late 2008 resulted in capital being withdrawn from emerging markets and deposited in "safe" dollars. As long as the global economy continued on its downward spiral and the stock markets collapsed, the money continued to flow into dollars.

Appetite for Risk vs. Safe Haven Sometimes the appetite for risk is more important than safety. As soon as the markets began to recover and the restructuring of the banking system and auto industries took hold in the United States in 2008 and 2009, money began to flow into euros and back into the emerging markets, reducing the value of the dollar. As noted earlier in the chapter, the flight to safety was replaced by a flight to risk, where investors could earn a higher return. As noted earlier, during the Greek debt crisis, investors were putting money into euros because they felt like the economic problems in the United States were even worse than those in Europe.

Information It is interesting how the release of information can influence currency values. That is why services such as Bloomberg are so important, because they carry up-to-date financial news that traders can follow as they try to figure out what will happen to exchange rates. Two examples serve to illustrate that point. On December 29, 2008, an unemployed blogger, Park Dae-sung, wrote an anonymous blog accusing South Korean central bank officials of pushing bankers to buy won in order to bid up the price. When the blog was picked up by the news, the won plunged in value, forcing the government to intervene in the markets. Park was arrested a few weeks later and charged with spreading false rumors that led to a drop in the value of the currency.[42]

Even government officials have to be careful what they say. When U.S. treasury secretary Timothy Geithner mentioned in an interview that he was open to suggestions that SDRs be given a larger role in the IMF, the dollar fell. He subsequently had to state that the dollar was the world's dominant reserve currency and would continue to be so for a long time.[43]

Forecasting Exchange-Rate Movements

Because various factors influence exchange-rate movements, managers must be able to analyze them to formulate a general idea of the timing, magnitude, and direction of an exchange-rate movement. However, prediction is not a precise science, and many things can cause the best of predictions to differ significantly from reality.

Reasons vary widely as to why companies try to forecast exchange rates. A country manager establishing a budget for the coming year must estimate a variety of factors, including the exchange rate over the time horizon. Companies involved in buying or selling goods and services need to forecast future exchange rates as part of their pricing decisions, choice of currency, and hedging strategies. But forecasting is fraught with numerous difficulties. Others may try to forecast exchange rates as an investment strategy and hope that their forecasts can beat the market.

FUNDAMENTAL AND TECHNICAL FORECASTING

Managers can forecast exchange rates by using either of two approaches: fundamental and technical. **Fundamental forecasting** uses trends in economic variables to predict future rates. The data can be plugged into an econometric model or evaluated on a more subjective basis.

Technical forecasting uses past trends in exchange rates themselves to spot future rate trends. Technical forecasters, or *chartists*, assume that if current exchange rates reflect all facts in the market, then under similar circumstances future rates will follow the same patterns.[44] However, research has shown that except in the very short run, past exchange rates are not an accurate predictor of future ones. According to this theory, then, exchange rate movements are a random walk.[45] However, again, all forecasting is imprecise.

Fundamental forecasting uses trends in economic variables to predict future exchange rates. Technical forecasting uses past trends in exchange-rate movements to spot future trends.

Dealing with Biases   Some biases exist that can skew forecasts:

- Overreaction to unexpected and dramatic news events
- Illusory correlation—that is, the tendency to see correlations or associations in data that are not statistically present but are expected to occur on the basis of prior beliefs
- Focusing on a particular subset of information at the expense of the overall set of information
- Insufficient adjustment for subjective matters, such as market volatility
- The inability to learn from one's past mistakes, such as poor trading decisions
- Overconfidence in one's ability to forecast currencies accurately[46]

Good treasurers and bankers develop their own forecasts of what will happen to a particular currency and use fundamental or technical predictions of outside forecasters to corroborate them. Doing this helps them determine whether they are considering important factors and whether they need to revise their forecasts in light of outside analysis.

Managers need to be concerned with the timing, magnitude, and direction of an exchange-rate movement.

Timing, Direction, and Magnitude   Forecasting includes predicting the timing, direction, and magnitude of an exchange-rate change or movement. For countries whose currencies are not freely floating, the timing is often a political decision and not easy to predict. Although the direction of a change can probably be predicted, the magnitude is difficult to forecast.

It is hard to predict what will happen to currencies and to use those predictions to forecast profits and establish operating strategies. The problem with predicting the value of a freely floating currency like the euro is that you never know what could happen to its value. You might be tempted to think that a currency linked to, say, the Hong Kong dollar would be much easier to predict. But since political control of Hong Kong was handed over to China in 1997, numerous discussions have centered around Hong Kong's adoption of the Chinese yuan. Even rumors of this change spooked the region's financial markets. Hong Kong officials vowed to stick with the 19-year-old currency system, but many economists think it makes more sense for Hong Kong to change to the yuan.[47] Nevertheless, the Hong Kong dollar has continued to maintain its independence, while widening the trading range with the U.S. dollar. Again, experts predicted it was just a matter of time before Hong Kong switched to the yuan. Which prediction is correct? How should a company position itself in these two different scenarios?

FUNDAMENTAL FACTORS TO MONITOR

Key factors to monitor— the institutional setting, fundamental analysis, confidence factors, events, and technical analysis.

For freely fluctuating currencies, the law of supply and demand determines market value. Your ability to forecast exchange rates depends on your time horizon. In general, the best predictors of future exchange rates are interest rates for short-term movements, inflation for medium-term movements, and current account balances for long-term movements.[48] However, very few currencies in the world float freely without any government intervention. Most are managed to some extent, which implies that governments need to make political decisions about their currencies' value. Assuming governments use a rational basis for managing these values (an assumption that may not always be realistic), managers can monitor the same factors the governments follow to try to predict values:

- *Institutional Setting*
  - Does the currency float, or is it managed—and if so, is it pegged to another currency, to a basket, or to some other standard?
  - What are the intervention practices? Are they credible? Sustainable?
- *Fundamental Analyses*
  - Does the currency appear undervalued or overvalued in terms of PPP, balance of payments, foreign-exchange reserves, or other factors?

- ■ What is the cyclical situation in terms of employment, growth, savings, investment, and inflation?
- ■ What are the prospects for government monetary, fiscal, and debt policy?
- • *Confidence Factors*
  - ■ What are market views and expectations with respect to the political environment, as well as to the credibility of the government and central bank?
- • *Circumstances*
  - ■ Are there national or international incidents in the news, the possibility of crises or emergencies, or governmental or other important meetings coming up?
- • *Technical Analyses*
  - ■ What trends do the charts show? Are there signs of trend reversals?
  - ■ At what rates do there appear to be important buy and sell orders? Are they balanced? Is the market overbought? Oversold?
  - ■ What is the thinking and what are the expectations of other market players and analysts?[49]

We have already discussed interest rates and inflation, but what about current account balances? A current account surplus means that a country exports more than it imports and is building foreign-exchange reserves from the countries that are buying its goods and services. Long term, the expectation is that the currency of that country will strengthen vis-à-vis its trading partners. Conversely, a current account deficit means that a country imports more than it exports and is building up debt abroad as it struggles to find the foreign exchange to pay for its imports. In that case, the long-term expectation is that the currency will weaken vis-à-vis its trading partners.

Business Implications of Exchange-Rate Changes

Why do we need to bother with predicting exchange-rate changes? As we will see in the closing case, they can dramatically affect operating strategies as well as translated overseas profits. We now look briefly at how exchange-rate changes can affect companies' marketing, production, and financial decisions.

MARKETING DECISIONS

Marketing managers watch exchange rates because they can affect demand for a company's products at home and abroad. In early 2008, with the euro surging against the U.S. dollar, Italian companies struggled to export their products abroad, while U.S. companies were benefitting from a weak dollar. Task Force Tips, an Indiana-based company that makes fire-hose nozzles, doubled its exports in the three years prior to 2008, and exports represented one-third of its sales.[50] As long as the dollar was falling, U.S. companies were looking closely at export markets as a place to offset the slowdown in the domestic market. However, once the dollar began to rise late in the year, the situation reversed. Currency changes can create opportunities, and pull them back as well.

> Strengthening of a country's currency value could create problems for exporters as their products become more expensive in global markets.

PRODUCTION DECISIONS

Exchange-rate changes can also affect production decisions. A manufacturer in a country where wages and operating expenses are high might be tempted to relocate production to a country with a currency that is rapidly losing value. The company's currency would buy lots of the weak currency, making the company's initial investment cheap.

Further, goods manufactured in that country would be relatively low-cost in world markets. For example, BMW decided to invest in production facilities in South Carolina because of the unfavorable exchange rate between the Deutsche mark (now the euro)

> Companies might locate production in a weak-currency country because
>
> - Initial investment there is relatively cheap.
> - Such a country is a good base for inexpensive exportation.

and the dollar. However, the company announced plans to use the facilities not only to serve the U.S. market but also to export to Europe and other markets.[51] The issue worsened in 2004 when the euro rose significantly against the dollar. The devaluation of the Mexican peso came shortly after the introduction of NAFTA. Although companies had already begun to establish operations in Mexico to service North America, the cheaper peso certainly helped their manufacturing strategies.

FINANCIAL DECISIONS

Exchange rates can affect financial decisions primarily in sourcing financial resources, remitting funds across national borders, and reporting financial results. In the first area, a company might be tempted to borrow money in places where interest rates are lowest. However, recall that interest-rate differentials often are compensated for in money markets through exchange-rate changes.

In deciding about cross-border financial flows, a company would want to convert local currency into its own home-country currency when exchange rates are most favorable so it can maximize its return. However, countries with weak currencies often have currency controls, making it difficult for MNEs to do so.

Finally, exchange-rate changes can influence the reporting of financial results. A simple example illustrates their impact on income. If a U.S. company's Mexican subsidiary earns 2 million pesos when the exchange rate is 9.5 pesos per dollar, the dollar equivalent of its income is $210,526. If the peso depreciates to 10.2 pesos per dollar, the dollar equivalent of that income falls to $196,078. The opposite will occur if the local currency appreciates against that of the company's home country. United Technologies, a U.S.-based manufacturer of elevators, aerospace equipment, and other products, reported that for every penny the euro increases against the dollar, UT records an additional $10 million in extra profits.[52] It is important to learn about exchange rates and the forces that affect their change. Several years ago, a manager in a large U.S.-based telephone company was preparing a bid for a major telecommunications project in Turkey. Knowing nothing about the Turkish lira, and without consulting with the company's foreign-exchange specialists, he figured out the bid in dollars, then turned to the foreign-exchange table in the *Wall Street Journal* to see what rate he should use to convert the bid into lira. What he didn't realize was that the lira at that time was weakening against the dollar. By the time he was awarded the project, he had lost all of his profit to the change in the value of the lira against the dollar; by the time he finished the project, he had lost a lot of money. If he had talked to someone who knew anything about the lira, he could have forecast (or at least tried to forecast) the future value and maybe entered into a hedging strategy to protect his receivables in lira. Managers who don't understand how currency values are determined can make serious, costly mistakes.

Looking to the Future   Changes in the Relative Strength of the U.S. Dollar, the Euro, the Yen, and the Yuan

The international monetary system has undergone considerable change since the early 1970s, when the dollar was devalued the first time. New countries have been born with the breakup of the Soviet empire, and with them have come new currencies. As those countries have gone through transition to a market economy, the currencies have adjusted as well. The countries will continue to change over to a floating-rate system as they get their economies under control.

It will be interesting to see what happens to the currencies of Latin America. Since the collapse of the Argentine peso, economists across all ideologies have stepped up to predict what will happen with Argentina's exchange-rate regime. After the first election of President da Silva in Brazil, the real steadily strengthened against the dollar. Until the global financial crisis hit, the real was on an upward trajectory. In the latter part of 2008, however, it plummeted as investors pulled money out of Brazil and other emerging markets. Since then, the real has remained strong against the dollar, largely because of the high prices of commodities, a major export category in Brazil. As Brazil has continued to expand its commodities exports and stabilize its economy, it has attracted foreign direct and portfolio investment and increased its foreign exchange reserves. As long as commodity prices remain high and the Brazilians are able to keep inflation from igniting, their currency should remain strong.

The euro will continue to succeed as a currency and will eventually take away market share from the dollar as a prime reserve asset. Of course, this depends a great deal on how the Greek debt crisis is resolved. If Greece enters into a default and withdraws from the EU, there could be serious problems throughout Europe, especially in countries like Spain, Portugal, Ireland, and maybe even Italy. However, barring this doomsday scenario, the euro should continue to increase its influence throughout Europe as non–euro-zone countries adopt it or at least come into harmony with it.

No Asian currency can compare with the dollar in the Americas and the euro in Europe. The yen is too specific to Japan, and the inability of the Japanese economy to reform and open up will keep it from wielding the same kind of influence as the dollar and euro, even though the yen is one of the most widely traded currencies in the world. In fact, it is far more likely that the dollar will continue to be the benchmark in Asia insofar as Asian economies rely heavily on the U.S. market for a lot of their exports.

However, the real wild card in Asia is the Chinese yuan. As noted in the case in Chapter 9, the Chinese yuan is going through a significant liberalization process, even though isn't yet a floating currency. In addition, China is experimenting with offshore trading of the yuan in Hong Kong and is gradually loosening controls on the flow of yuan into and out of China. Clearly China is moving forward in its efforts to establish the CNY as one of the major currencies in the world. The U.S. dollar is being strongly influenced by budget crises, Europe is struggling to deal with debt crises in Greece and other countries, and China is trying to gradually liberalize the yuan. Japan must rebuild from the earthquake and tsunami of 2011, and it needs to find its place in Asia vis-à-vis China, but it is still strong currency. There is no way of predicting where we will be in five years. But it is clear that the yuan is the one currency that is likely to change the most. ■

Welcome to the World of Sony—Unless the Yen Keeps Rising[53]

CASE

2010 was a pretty tough year for Sony, and 2011 didn't seem to be getting much better. The global economic crisis not only resulted in a huge drop in demand worldwide, it also roiled the foreign currency markets. As if the global economic crisis were not enough, Japan was devastated on March 14, 2011, by the Pacific Coast of Tohoku 9.0 earthquake and tsunami. By the end of Sony's fiscal year 2010 and the release of its annual report (Sony, like most Japanese companies, has a fiscal year that ends on March 31), the yen was trading at ¥84.1184 per dollar. This is a significant increase in value from just five years earlier when the yen was trading at ¥110.5583 on August 15, 2008, shortly before the crash of the global economy. The crazy currency swings had a devastating impact on Sony and all other major MNCs in Japan. What will the future bring?

The Past

Before attacking the future, let's look at the past—especially from the perspective of the Japanese yen. In the post–World War II years, the yen was extremely weak against the dollar, trading at ¥357.65 in 1970. That hardly seems possible with today's high rates (remember that the lower the USD/JPY exchange rate, the higher the value of the yen against the dollar). Sony, founded in 1946 as Tokyo Tsushin Kogyo Corporation, officially became known as Sony Corporation in 1958, the year its stock was first listed on the Tokyo Stock Exchange. It also became the first Japanese company to list American Depositary Receipts (ADRs)

A model is using a Sony camera at a Japanese Cosplay festival in Bangkok, Thailand, bringing a unique aspect of Japanese youth culture to the costume convention where cosplayers dress up in their favorite costumes and wigs. As Sony says about its cameras, "believe that anything you imagine, you can make real.

Source: © dave stamboulis/Alamy

on the New York Stock Exchange in 1961 and finally listed its own shares on the NYSE in September 1970.

In those early years of operation, Sony had the luxury of operating in a currency that was not only weak against the dollar, but also highly controlled by the government. Japanese foreign-exchange policies favored companies and industries that the government wanted to succeed, especially in export markets. With a cheap yen, it was easy for companies to expand exports rapidly.

The First Endaka

From its 1970 high, the yen steadily strengthened until 1985, when it *really* shot up in value. Due to economic problems in the United States, the dollar began to fall during the latter part of 1985, and the yen ended at ¥200 per dollar by the end of 1985. By the latter part of 1986, the yen was trading at ¥150, a steep rise from its historical highs. The Japanese called this strengthening of the yen *endaka*, which literally translates "high yen." *Endaka* resulted in serious problems for Japanese exporters and potential pain for the entire Japanese economy, which was very dependent on international trade. However, one upside to *endaka* was that imports were cheaper, and Japan relied heavily on imports of virtually all commodities. Thus its input costs fell, even as it found its export prices rising.

The strong yen was due primarily to a strong Japanese economy, large trade surpluses, and the largest foreign-exchange reserves in the world. In addition, Japan had low unemployment, low interest rates, and low inflation. But cracks began to show in the Japanese economy. A combination of a drop in the stock market, a rise in inflation, and a real estate bubble hurt the Japanese economy and confidence in the yen. The governor of the Bank of Japan raised interest rates in December 1989, but the resulting furor forced him to stop raising rates. Since the interest rates in the United States were higher, investors pulled money out of Japan and put it into U.S. dollars to take advantage of higher returns. This drop in demand for yen and rise in demand for dollars pushed up the value of the dollar against the yen, and the yen closed out 1989 at ¥143.45, whereas it was ¥125.85 only a year earlier.

Both the United States and Japan were worried about inflation in the early 1990s, and they tried to coordinate exchange-rate policies, but the United States didn't want to push down the value of the dollar too much and lose its own fight against inflation. The United States and Japan tried to get the central banks of Germany, the United Kingdom, and other countries to intervene in the markets and sell their currencies for yen in order to strengthen the yen. But there wasn't much they could do to move the market given that interest rates were driving market psychology.

In the ensuing years, many factors influenced the yen/dollar exchange rate, including a weak U.S. economy (favoring a drop in interest rates), the Persian Gulf War (which favored the dollar as a safe-haven currency), a rise in Japanese interest rates relative to U.S. interest rates, and a lack of agreement among G8 countries in 1993 about whether the yen was too weak or about right.

A Second Endaka

As if one *endaka* were not enough, a second one hit in 1995, when the yen rose to ¥80.63 per dollar. Toyota announced that a one-point increase in the yen eliminated $111 million in dollar-denominated profits from its U.S. operations, and exporters were having a difficult time figuring out how to remain competitive in export markets. As they did with the first *endaka,* Japanese companies looked for ways to cut costs and remain competitive. During that period, the Japanese economy was in a recession, so the Bank of Japan dropped interest rates to stimulate demand, and the yen fell against the dollar, favoring exporters once again.

Competitive Pressures

During these decades of currency swings, Sony kept moving along as one of the premier companies in the world in consumer electronics, games, music, and movies. The wide array of product innovations earned Sony a premium in the market. However, competition began to step in. Korean companies, like Samsung and LG, began to produce cheaper products that rose in quality as each year went by. Samsung began to develop a reputation for innovation in electronics, which threatened Sony. In addition, Samsung and other competitors to Sony began setting up plants offshore, especially in China, to improve their cost advantage even more. Some of Sony's Japanese competitors, including Toshiba and Panasonic, responded by reducing their exposure to a strong yen by moving plants overseas, such as to Indonesia and the Philippines, and increasing the dollar-based imports of parts. By 2003, Toshiba was manufacturing 30 percent of its products outside Japan, compared with only 17 percent in 1995.

From the beginning of 2003 until the end of 2004, the dollar continued to weaken against both the euro and the yen. In an attempt to strengthen the dollar, the Japanese central bank spent a record 20 trillion yen in 2003 and 10 trillion yen in the first two months of 2004. Despite the efforts of the Japanese authorities, the yen rose 11 percent against the dollar in 2003 and continued to strengthen through 2004. The Japanese finance ministry stopped its foreign-exchange intervention in March 2004, but the dollar's continued weakening against both the euro and the yen at the end of 2004 sparked new threats of intervention by the Japanese and Europeans. A senior Japanese finance ministry official said, "It is natural for Japan and Europe to act when the dollar alone is falling. If the (dollar's) movement affects the European economy and the Japanese economy, we should defend ourselves."

Fast-Forward to 2008

The collapse in the housing market in the United States and the ensuing credit crisis that hit in 2007, followed by the bankruptcy of Lehman Brothers and the U.S. government takeover of global insurer AIG in September 2008, had a devastating impact on the global economy. The U.S. stock market crashed, followed by similar crashes around the world, and investors pulled funds out of risky emerging markets and placed them in safe-haven assets. Who were the major beneficiaries? The U.S. dollar and the Japanese yen! The euro dropped against both the dollar and the yen, and the Chinese yuan wasn't a factor because its currency is fixed against the dollar rather than flexible and subject to normal market forces. Although China is a good bet for foreign investment, the yuan is not an investment currency like the dollar and yen due to currency controls and lack of liquidity.

Why did this happen? In the case of the U.S. dollar, the market reaction was a standard flight to safety, which often happens when global events get scary, even when the U.S. markets started the collapse. The size of the U.S. economy and political stability, even in the face of a presidential election in November 2008, tend to make the United States an attractive place for investment. Thus, the fear factor seemed to be a critical vote for the dollar during the crisis. This is a short-term phenomenon, however, and will eventually be replaced by economic fundamentals. With the slowdown in the U.S. economy, export-dominated countries, especially emerging markets, were expected to suffer. Also, the credit crisis that the United States was going through was expected to expand to other countries. The euro is obviously a strong and important currency, but it lacks a strong central government that can coordinate a response to economic crisis. The European Central Bank can influence interest rates, but that's about all. Another thing that came out of the crisis is that the euro tends to be very sensitive to the U.S. stock market. When the market was falling, so was the euro. When the market began to recover, so did the euro. Thus, the dollar has been up and down depending on what news was most important. When the crisis was the news, the dollar was strong. When the news favored a recovery of the U.S. economy, money flowed into equity markets, both in the United States and abroad, seeking for higher returns and causing the dollar to drop in value.

What about the yen? Interestingly enough, the yen also became a safe-haven currency during the crisis, along with the dollar. Obviously, the yen is the most important currency in Asia, because Japan has the second-highest foreign-exchange reserves in the region and the world, just after China, but it is a freely convertible currency with high market liquidity and is also an important trading currency. Also, with Japanese interest rates so low, many investors were borrowing in yen and investing their proceeds abroad to get access to higher returns. When the crisis hit, the money quickly left the emerging markets and returned to Japan, a practice called *carry trade.* Whenever volatility in currency markets goes up, investors unwind (reverse) their trades, which gave strength to the yen.

The markets also demonstrated that the yen and U.S. stock market were inversely related. When markets are less risk-averse, stocks gain in value and the yen drops in value. When markets are more risk-averse, stock prices fall, and the yen trades higher. To illustrate that point, in July 2009 when the stock market started to climb, the yen fell against the dollar, although the fall was not dramatic or large.

2011—The Year of the Earthquake and Tsunami

The tragedy that struck Japan on March 11 and subsequent weeks was devastating in terms of lives lost and overall human tragedy. The estimated $300 billion price tag attached to the devastation will never compensate for the horror that individuals and families endured. In addition, there was a great deal of uncertainty over damage to nuclear reactors and disruption to the global supply chain. For example, Japanese factories produce about 25 percent of the world's semiconductors and 40 percent of electronic components. Sony makes 10 percent of the world's laptop computer batteries. Plants in affected areas were shut down due to property damage, power outages, and a transportation infrastructure that ground to a halt.

What happened to the Japanese yen? Conventional wisdom would say that the yen fell against the dollar, but it actually rose in value. After the quake, there was a massive inflow of capital from Japanese companies as part of what is called the "carry trade," where companies liquidate investments made with cheap Japanese money (low interest rates) and invested in emerging markets where returns are high. In addition, many Japanese companies often bring money back to Japan at the end of the fiscal year (March 31), so the need for capital resulted in a tremendous inflow of capital, causing the yen to rise in value. In fact, it rose so much that the U.S. government got involved with other countries to help push down the yen a little bit as discussed earlier in the chapter.

What Does All This Mean to Sony?

In 2010, Sony generated 29.1 percent of its sales in Japan, 22.1 percent in the United States, 22.8 percent in Europe, and 26.0 percent elsewhere. Thus, Sony was well diversified geographically, operating in some countries where the local currency was weaker and others where the local currency was stronger than the yen. Sony was also targeting the BRIC countries for future growth.

According to Sony's 2010 annual report, in addition to targeting global markets for sales, Sony was taking advantage of production outside of Japan. In the LCD televisions division, the factories in Tijuana, Mexico, and Nitra, Slovakia, are where the majority of LCD televisions are produced for the Americas and Europe. Also, in the digital imaging division Sony is moving some of its production of the DSLR camera from Japan to Thailand where the photo of the young woman taking the picture with the Sony camera was shot.

One major effect of the strong yen and the global slowdown was the sharp drop in exports from Japan. In January 2009, for example, exports dropped 49 percent compared with January 2008. As exporters found their sales falling, they cut orders from their suppliers, so there was a ripple effect in the Japanese economy, affecting both production and employment. These events caused a sharp contraction in the Japanese economy as GDP fell 12.1 percent in the fourth quarter of 2008 compared with the fourth quarter of 2007, and many experts felt that Japan was going through its worst recession since World War II. Deflation was also affecting the Japanese economy again, and consumers were delaying purchases hoping that prices would continue to fall, and companies were hesitant to invest more.

The strong yen was also hurting Sony's financial statements. As Sony translates U.S. dollar or euro financial statements into yen, net assets and earnings will be worth less in yen, dragging down Sony's consolidated results. The only way to offset this drop is to sell more and improve profit margins, both of which are hard to do in a slow global economy. From a cash-flow point of view, Sony's operations abroad are remitting dividends back to Japan, but they are worth less yen as the dollar and euro weaken against the yen. One silver lining is that the purchasing power of the yen rises as it strengthens compared with other currencies, so everything it imports into Japan for its manufacturing is cheaper. The same would be true for anything manufactured outside of Japan, thus reducing costs and hopefully increasing margins. As long as Sony is invoicing its exports in dollars to customers worldwide, it needs to match the dollar revenues with dollar expenses through investing more in the United States or in other countries in Asia, like Taiwan, where components such as flat panel displays are cheaper and where Sony can invoice its purchases in dollars.

One big challenge Sony faces is its competition from other Asian companies such as Samsung. Sony has to carefully watch the value of the yen against the Korean won to see what its competitive position is. If the yen rises against the won and other Asian currencies, Sony risks losing market share to other Asian companies because it will not be price competitive. This is forcing Sony to move offshore faster and localize production in other markets it hopes to penetrate. Sony has a lot of strengths, but it also has a lot of challenges that it will have to resolve in the future.

The 2011 earthquake and tsunami also affected Sony's results. Sony announced that the earthquake and tsunami probably helped push them to a $3.2 billion loss in the March 31 fiscal year, one of many Japanese manufacturers that reported substantial losses from the disaster. Nine of their plants in northeastern Japan where the most damage occurred were damaged, supply chains were disrupted, and a drop in domestic demand did not bode well for Sony in 2011. Coupled with the overall slowdown in the global economy, especially in the United States and debt-ridden Europe, demand for Sony products was not forecast to grow. If the euro collapses due to the debt crisis in Greece and possibly other EU countries and the dollar remains weak due to its own debt problems and low interest rates, the only major currency left is the yen. If the yen continues to rise in value, what will happen to Sony and other Japanese companies that rely on foreign markets, especially in Europe and the United States? ■

QUESTIONS

1. Why did the contraction of the U.S. and Japanese economies and the rise in the value of the yen hurt Sony's exports from Japan?
2. In what other ways has the strong yen affected Sony's bottom line? What would be the effect of a weak yen?
3. Given the instability in the currency markets, why do you think it is important for Sony to manufacture more products in the United States and Europe and to also buy more from suppliers in other countries in Asia?
4. What are the major forces that affected the Japanese yen prior to the global financial crisis in the fourth quarter of 2008? What has had the greatest impact on the yen since then, and where do you forecast the future value of the yen?

MyIBLab   Now that you have finished this chapter, go back to www.myiblab.com to continue practicing and applying the concepts you've learned.

SUMMARY

- The International Monetary Fund (IMF) was organized in 1945 to promote international monetary cooperation, facilitate the expansion and balanced growth of international trade, promote exchange-rate stability, establish a multilateral system of payments, and make its resources available to its members who are experiencing balance-of-payments difficulties.

- The special drawing right (SDR) is a special asset the IMF created to increase international reserves.

- The IMF started out with fixed exchange rates but now allows countries to choose how fixed or flexible they want their exchange rates to be.

- The euro is a common currency in Europe that has been adopted by 12 of the first 15 members of the EU, and was adopted by 16 total countries by the end of 2011, with other new EU members working to meet the convergence criteria.

- The Chinese yuan is poised to be one of the most influential currencies in the world as China strengthens its institutions and the regulatory structure and trading capacity of its banks and other financial institutions.

- African countries are committed to establishing a common currency by 2021, but many obstacles may prevent them from accomplishing this objective.

- Currencies that float freely respond to supply and demand conditions free from government intervention. The demand for a country's currency is a function of the demand for its goods and services and the demand for financial assets denominated in its currency.

- Fixed exchange rates do not automatically change in value due to supply and demand conditions, but are regulated by their central banks.

- Central banks are the key institutions in countries that intervene in foreign-exchange markets to influence currency values.

- The Bank for International Settlements (BIS) in Switzerland acts as a central banker's bank. It facilitates communication and transactions among the world's central banks.

- A central bank intervenes in money markets by increasing a supply of its country's currency when it wants to push down the value of the currency and by stimulating demand for the currency when it wants the currency's value to rise.

- Many countries that strictly control and regulate the convertibility of their currencies have a black market that maintains an exchange rate more indicative of supply and demand than the official rate.

- Fully convertible currencies, often called *hard currencies*, are those that the government allows both residents and nonresidents to purchase in unlimited amounts.

- Currencies that are not fully convertible are often called *soft* or *weak currencies*. They tend to be the currencies of developing countries.

- To conserve scarce foreign exchange, some governments impose exchange restrictions—such as import licensing, multiple exchange rates, import deposit requirements, and quantity controls—on companies or individuals who want to exchange money.

- Some factors that determine exchange rates are purchasing power parity (relative rates of inflation), differences in real interest rates (nominal interest rates reduced by the amount of inflation), confidence in the government's ability to manage the political and economic environment, and certain technical factors that result from trading.

KEY TERMS

advance import deposit (p. 380)
black market (p. 378)
Bretton Woods Agreement (p. 363)
European Central Bank (ECB) (p. 371)
European Monetary System (EMS) (p. 369)
European Monetary Union (EMU) (p. 370)

Fisher Effect (p. 384)
fundamental forecasting (p. 385)
hard currency (p. 379)
International Fisher Effect (IFE) (p. 384)
International Monetary Fund (IMF) (p. 362)
Jamaica Agreement (p. 365)
multiple exchange-rate system (p. 380)

par value (p. 363)
purchasing power parity (PPP) (p. 381)
quota (p. 363)
Smithsonian Agreement (p. 365)
soft (or weak) currency (p. 379)
special drawing right (SDR) (p. 364)
technical forecasting (p. 385)

ENDNOTES

1 *Sources include the following:* Andrew Swiston, "Official Dollarization as a Monetary as a Monetary Regime: Its Effects on El Salvador," *IMF Working Paper* (June 2011): 22–23; "El Salvador Learns to Love the Greenback," *The Economist* (September 26, 2002): 62; John Lyons, "Squeezed by Dollarization," *Wall Street Journal* (March 8, 2005): A18; Bureau of Economic and Business Affairs, U.S. Department of State, "2001 Country Reports on Economic Policy and Trade Practices" (February 2002), retrieved May 30, 2005, from www.state.gov/documents/ organization/8202.pdf; U.S. Department of State, "Background Note—El Salvador," retrieved May 30, 2005, from www .state.gov/r/pa/ei/bgn/2033.htm; U.S. Department of State, "Background Note—Ecuador," retrieved May 30, 2005, from www.state .gov/r/pa/ei/bgn/35761.htm; Juan Forero, "Ecuador's President Vows to Ride Out Crisis over Judges," *New York Times* (April 18, 2005): A12.

2 International Monetary Fund, "IMF Chronology," retrieved August 22, 2007, from http://imf .org/external/np/exr/chron/chron.asp

3 IMF, "The IMF at a Glance," *International Monetary Fund,* retrieved July 1, 2011, from http://imf .org/external/np/exr/facts /glance.htm

4 IMF, "About IMF," retrieved July 1, 2011, from http://imf.org /external/about/overview.htm

5 IMF, "International Monetary Fund Factsheet: IMF Quotas," retrieved July 1, 2011, from www.imf.org/external/np/exr/facts /pdf/quotas.pdf

6 Liz Alderman, "France's Finance Minister, Lagarde, Selected as I.M.F. Managing Director," *The New York Times* (June 29, 2011): B3.

7 IMF, "Special Drawing Rights (SDRs): A Factsheet," retrieved June 24, 2011, from http://imf. org/external/np/exr/facts/sdr .htm

8 IMF, "Currency Amounts in New Special Drawing Rights (SDR) Basket," retrieved July 1, 2011, from www.imf.org/external/np/tre /sdr/sdrbasket.htm

9 "Russian Wants Rouble, Yuan, Gold in SDR Basket," *Reuters News Service,* retrieved June 27, 2011, from www.reuters.com /article/2009/03/28/reserve-currency-russia-idUSLS37648120090328

10 "Greece OKs Austerity Plan as Riots Grip Athens," *Europe on MSNBC,* retrieved June 29, 2011, from www.msnbc.msn.com /id/43573232/ns/world_news-europe; Graham Bowley, "The Ripples of a Debt Crisis," *The New York Times* (June 29, 2011): B1.

11 International Monetary Fund. Annual Report on Exchange Arrangements and Exchange Restrictions (Washington, D.C., IMF, 2009): xi–xiii, l–lv.

12 See Mercedes Garcia-Escribano and Sebastián Sosa, "What Is Driving Financial De-dollarization in Latin America," *IMF Working Paper* (January 2011): 1–23; Guillermo A. Calvo and Carmen M.

Reinhart, "Capital Flow Reversals, the Exchange Rate Debate, and Dollarization," *Finance & Development* 36: 3 (1999): 13; "No More Peso?" *The Economist* (January 23, 1999): 69; Steve H. Hanke, "How to Make the Dollar Argentina's Currency," *Wall Street Journal* (February 19, 1999): A19; Michael M. Phillips, "U.S. Officials Urge Cautious Approach to Dollarization by Foreign Countries," *Wall Street Journal* (April 23, 1999): A4; "A Decline without Parallel," *The Economist* (February 28, 2002), www.economist.com

13 Craig Torres, "Chile Suspends Trading Band on Its Peso," *Wall Street Journal* (September 7, 1999): A21; "IMF Welcomes Flotation of Iceland's Krona," *IMF News Brief,* retrieved March 28, 2001, from www.imf.org/external/np/sec/nb/2001/nb0129.htm

14 "Convergence Criteria for European Monetary Union," *Bloomberg News,* retrieved August 9, 2002, from www.bloomberg.com

15 "Prime Minister Says Sweden Fulfills Criteria to Adopt Euro," *Dow Jones Newswires* (August 19, 2002), retrieved August 19, 2002, from www.wsj.com

16 Christopher Rhoads and G. Thomas Sims, "Rising Deficits in Europe Give Euro Its Toughest Challenge Yet," *Wall Street Journal* (September 15, 2003): A1.

17 Edmund L. Andrews, "On Euro Weekend, Financial Institutions in Vast Reprogramming," *New York Times* (January 2, 1999), retrieved October 12, 2009, from www.nytimes.com

18 Paul Masson and Catherine Patillo, "A Single Currency for Africa?" *Finance & Development* (December 2004): 9–15; "History of the CFA Franc," retrieved May 30, 2005, from www.bceao.int/internet /bcweb.nsf/pages/ umuse1); IMF, "The Fabric of Reform—An IMF Video," retrieved May 30, 2005, from www.imf.org/external/pubs /ft/fabric/ backgrnd.htm

19 Though initially pegged to the French franc, the peg shifted to the euro in 1999 when France adopted it as its currency. All of the countries in the CFA franc zone are former colonies of France and maintain French as the official language, except for Guinea-Bissau and Equatorial Guinea, which were ruled by Portugal and Spain, respectively.

20 "Operating Policy," retrieved July 1, 2011, from www.ny.frb.org /markets/foreignex.html

21 International Monetary Fund, "Currency Composition of Official Foreign Exchange Reserves (COFER)," retrieved October 8, 2009, from www.imf.org/ external/np/sta/cofer/eng/index.htm (last updated September 30, 2009).

22 Dennis Berman, "Inevitable End to Dollar's Reserve Role?," *Wall Street Journal* (September, 1 2009): C1.

23 Joanna Slater and John Lyons, "Emerging Markets Lose a Little of Their Resilience—Now Face Stress Test," *Wall Street Journal* (July 17, 2007): C1.

24 Sam Y. Cross, *All about the Foreign Exchange Market in the United States* (New York: Federal Bank of New York, 2002): 92–93.

25 David Wessel, "Intervention in Currency Shrinks under Clinton," *Wall Street Journal* (September 14, 1995): C1.

26 Federal Reserve Bank of New York, "U.S. Foreign Exchange Intervention," retrieved July 25, 2009, from www.ny.frb.org /aboutthefed/fedpoint/ fed44.html; "Treasury and Federal Reserve Foreign Exchange Operations: Quarterly Reports," retrieved July 1, 2011, from www.ny.frb.org/markets/quar_reports .html

27 Paul Evans, "Dollar Climbs Back on Rivals," *Wall Street Journal* (March 11, 2009): C14.

28 Charles Forelle and Bob Davis, "Iceland Raises Key Rate to 18% to Defend Currency," *Wall Street Journal* (October 29, 2008): A10.

29 Charles Forelle, "Iceland Votes to Try Joining EU," *Wall Street Journal* (July 17, 2009): A7.

30 Joanna Slater and Jon Hilsenrath, "Currency-Price Swings Disrupt Global Markets," *Wall Street Journal* (October 25–26, 2008): A10.

31 Andrew J. Johnson, "Dollar Tumbles; Poland Intervenes," *The Wall Street Journal* (May 22, 2011): C5.

32 Bank for International Settlements, "About BIS: Organisation and Governance," retrieved July 1, 2010, from www.bis.org/about /orggov.htm.

33 He Huifeng, "Shenzhen Traders Profit from Currency Uncertainty: Black Market Demand for HK Dollar Offers Opportunity," *South China Morning Post* (March 31, 2009): 4.

34 Sheridan Prasso, "Zimbabwe's Disposable Currency," *Fortune* (August 6, 2007), retrieved August 25, 2007, from CNNMoney.com

35 "Zimbabwe Unveils $1090-Trillion Banknote as Nation Battles Inflation," *National Post* (January 17, 2009): A11.

36 John Lyons and José Córdoba, "U.S. Seizure Slams Market for Dollars in Venezuela," *Wall Street Journal* (March 28–29, 2009): A1.

37 Phisanu Phromchanya, "Thai Currency Controls Eased in Bid to Cool Baht," *Wall Street Journal* (July 25, 2007): 2.

38 Benedict Mander, "Exchange Rate Irks Venezuela, *Financial Times* (April 30, 2010): 20.

39 Natalia T. Tamirisa, "Exchange and Capital Controls as Barriers to Trade," *IMF Staff Papers* 46: 1 (1999): 69.

40 "Burgernomics: When the Chips Are Down," *The Economist* (July 22, 2010): 72.

41 "The Big Mac Index: Food for Thought," *The Economist* (May 27, 2004): 75; quoting Michael Pakko and Patricia Polland, *For Here or to Go? Purchasing Power Parity and the Big Mac* (St. Louis, MO: Federal Reserve Bank of St. Louis, January 1996).

42 Evan Ramstad, "Blogger Arrested in Korea for Post That Led to Won's Decline," *Wall Street Journal* (January 13, 2009): A11.

43 Michael Phillips, "Geithner's Gaffe Briefly Hits Dollar," *Wall Street Journal* (March 26, 2009): A6.

44 "Forecasting Currencies: Technical or Fundamental?," *Business International Money Report* (October 15, 1990): 401–2.

45 See Ian H. Giddy and Gunter Dufey, "The Random Behavior of Flexible Exchange Rates: Implications for Forecasting," *Journal of International Business Studies* 6: 1 (1975): 1–32; Christopher J. Neely and Lucio Sarno, "How Well Do Monetary Fundamentals Forecast Exchange Rates?" St. Louis Fed (September/October 2002): 51–74, retrieved October 8, 2009, from www.research.stlouisfed.org/publications/review / 02/09/51-74Neely.pdf

46 Andrew C. Pollock and Mary E. Wilkie, "Briefing," *Euromoney* (June 1991): 123–24.

47 Dominic Lau, "Market Jitters Making HK Currency Peg Debate Taboo," *Reuters News Service*, retrieved September 24, 2002, from http://asia.news.yahoo.com

48 David A. Moss, *A Concise Guide to Macro Economics* (Boston: Harvard Business School Press, 2007): 131.

49 Cross, *All about the Foreign Exchange Market*, 114.

50 Timothy Aeppel and Joanna Slater, "Surging Exports Lighten the Gloom," *Wall Street Journal* (March 24, 2008): A2.

51 Oscar Suris, "BMW Expects U.S.-Made Cars to Have 80% Level of North American Content," *Wall Street Journal* (August 5, 1993): A2.

52 Ibid.

53 Thomas Black, "Now, a Weak Link in the Global Supply Chain," *Business* Week (March 21–27, 2011): 18; Hiroko Tabuchi, "Sony Warns of a Loss From Quake," *The Wall Street Journal* (May 24, 2011); Jamie McGeever, "Dollar Gets Battered across the Board," *Wall Street Journal* (December 9, 2003): C17; Sebastian Moffett, "Japan's Yen Strategy Offers Economic Relief," *Wall Street Journal* (January 12, 2004): A2; Miyako Takebe, "Japan Plans to Keep Intervening in Markets to Hold Down the Yen," *Wall Street Journal* (March 17, 2004): B4E; Alan Beattie, "Japan and ECB Consider Joint Currency Move as Dollar Falls," *Financial Times* (December 2, 2004): 11; Sony 2008 Annual Report; Robert Flint, "Yen Gains on Dollar, Europe in Flight from Risk," *Wall Street Journal* (January 13, 2009): C2; Joanna Slater, Yuka Hayashi, and Peter Stein, "Move to Stem Yen's Rise Is Likely," *Wall Street Journal* (October 28, 2008): C1; Stanley Reed, "What's Driving Up the Dollar," *Business Week* (December 8, 2008): 38; John Murphy and Hiroko Tabuchi, "Japan's Companies, Consumers, React to New Reality," *Wall Street Journal* (October 29, 2008): A13; John Murphy, "Toyota's Global Woes Start to Hit Home in Japan," *Wall Street Journal* (November 4, 2008): A10; Yumiko Ono and Andrew Monahan, "Japan Exports Fall 49% as U.S. Trade Plunges," *Wall Street Journal* (March 26, 2009): A7; John Murphy, Peter Stein, and Neil Shah, "Dollar Vexes Asian Central Banks," *Wall Street Journal* (May 26, 2009): C1.

PART FIVE

Global Strategy, Structure, and Implementation

chapter 11

The Strategy of International Business

Objectives

1. To evaluate industry structure, firm strategy, and value creation

2. To profile the features and functions of the value chain

3. To assess how managers configure and coordinate a value chain

4. To explain the ideas of global integration and local responsiveness

5. To profile the types of strategies used by MNEs

Access a host of interactive learning aids to help strengthen your understanding of the chapter concepts at www.myiblab.com.

MyIBLab

Source: Courtesy of Daniel Sullivan

Vision without action is a daydream. Action without vision is a nightmare.

—*Japanese proverb*

CASE

Value Creation in the Global Apparel Industry[1]

Traditionally, national retailers outsource apparel production, via global brokers, to thousands of small apparel makers. The typical apparel manufacturer, usually located in a low-wage country, is a small-scale operation that employs a few to a few dozen workers. In a labor-intensive process, workers make specific pieces of clothing, often in a narrow range of sizes and colors. These pieces are then integrated with the output of hundreds of other such companies spread across dozens of countries. As more companies in more countries make more specialized products—i.e., one factory makes zippers, one makes linings, one makes buttons, and so on—multinational trading companies perform as cross-border intermediaries and supervise the assembly of component pieces into finished goods.

Finished goods are shipped to apparel retailers. Responding to market shifts relentlessly pressures apparel retailers. In turn, they push multinational trading companies to improve coordination among themselves and apparel makers. Planning collections closer to the selling season, testing the market, placing smaller initial orders, and re-ordering more frequently let retailers reduce forecasting

errors and inventory risks. The final links are markets and customers. Although tastes overlap among countries, local customers' preferences traditionally varied. For example, the British seek stores based on class sensitivities, Germans are value conscious, Chinese shoppers are brand aware, and shoppers in the United States look for a mix of variety, quality, and price. Collectively, these conditions create a buyer-driven chain that links fragmented factories, global brokers, dispersed retailers, and local customers.

Industry wisdom spurred firms to choose a "sliver" of a particular activity—to make zippers, manage logistics, focus on store design, or cater to customer segments—instead of creating value across different slivers. Effectively, "do what you do best and outsource the rest" drove strategy in the global apparel industry. Globalization changes these relationships. Fewer barriers, better logistics, and improving communications create new industry standards and strategic choices.

A compelling example is the compression of cycle times in the apparel-buyer chain (see Figure 11.1). In the 1970s, getting a garment from the factory to the customer took nine

FIGURE 11.1 Cycle Time in the Global Apparel Industry

Globalization creates options for countries and companies in the apparel industry. Improving technology, sourcing, and production systems let innovative apparel makers compress cycle time. Shortening process time increases efficiencies and boosts profits. This chart highlights how Zara applied its innovative strategy to reset the standards of operational efficiency in the global apparel industry.

Source: Based on analysis Zara company documents.

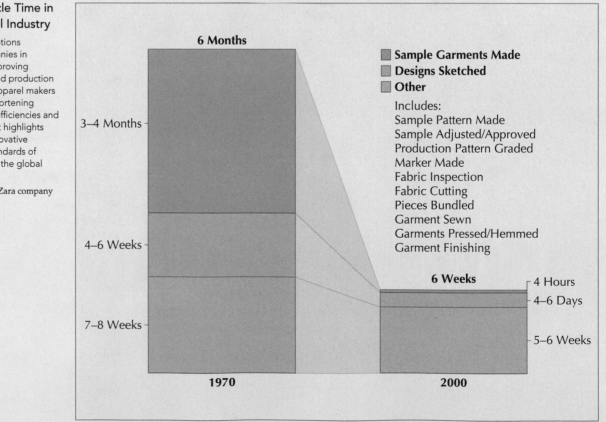

months—six months to design the collection and then another three months to make and ship it. In 2011, it takes the typical company from six months down to six weeks to run this cycle. However, for one firm, Zara, it takes between two to four weeks. By rejecting conventional standards, Zara had reset the relationship among industry structure, company strategy, and value creation.

ZARA WHO?

The Inditex Group, a Spanish apparel MNE, is the parent corporation of eight global retail chains, including Zara, Bershka, Massimo Dutti, Stradivarius, and Oysho. Zara is the crown jewel of Inditex, generating roughly two-thirds of total sales. Inditex runs operations from "The Cube," its gleaming, futuristic headquarters in Artexio, near La Coruña, a midsize city in northwest Spain (see Map 11.1). Inditex employs more than 90,000 people, half of them in Spain and the rest in the various countries where it operates. The company workforce is young (the average age is 26) and female (besides representing more than 80 percent of employees, women hold more than half of the executive, technical, and managerial positions).

Inditex's revenue pushed past $15 billion in 2010, just ahead of the long-time worldwide leader Gap's $14.7 billion. Spain, Inditex's home market, accounted for 28 percent of total sales in 2010, down from 32 percent in 2009. Asia and the Americas grew, accounting for 15 percent and 12 percent of sales, respectively. Nearly 90 percent of Inditex's total retail surface area of its more than 5,000 storefronts in 77 countries was outside Spain.

The first Zara shop opened its doors in 1975 in La Coruña. Today, Zara has 1,483 stores spread across 77 countries. It uses an innovative strategy to power its global performance, integrating fashion and infotech to make and move sophisticated clothing at appealing prices. One analyst called it, "Armani at moderate prices" while another characterized its fashions as more Banana Republic, but its prices as more Old Navy. No matter the description, all agreed that Zara applied a strategy that challenged historic ideas of creating value in the global apparel industry. Understanding its success requires understanding its competency in configuring and coordinating the activities it ran to create value.

MAP 11.1   Spain

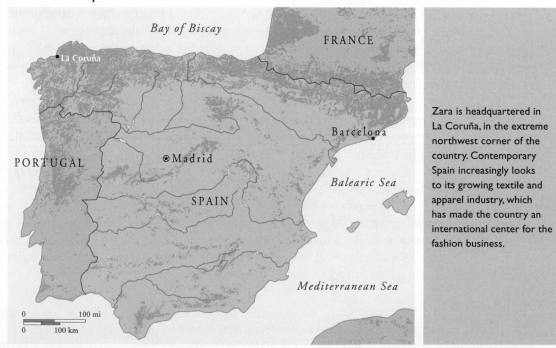

Zara is headquartered in La Coruña, in the extreme northwest corner of the country. Contemporary Spain increasingly looks to its growing textile and apparel industry, which has made the country an international center for the fashion business.

Design

Zara rejects the idea of conventional spring and autumn clothing collections in favor of "live collections" that are designed, manufactured, and sold almost as quickly as customers' fleeting tastes—no style lasts more than four weeks. Zara's 300 or so designers monitor market events, fashion trends, and customer preferences in designing about 11,000 distinct items per year compared with 2,000 to 4,000 items by rivals. Zara translates the latest fashion trend from a catwalk in Paris to its store shelves in Shanghai in as little as two weeks versus the industry standard of six months.

Designers get ideas from store managers, industry publications, TV, Internet, and films. Its trend spotters focused on university campuses and nightclubs. Zara's so-called slaves-to-fashion staff snapped shots at couture shows and posted them to designers who quickly reproduced the look for the mass market. For example, when Madonna played a series of concerts in Spain, teenage girls arrived to her final show sporting a Zara knock-off of the outfit she had worn during her first show.

Zara does not adapt products to a particular country's preferences. The convergence of fashion and taste across national boundaries endorses management's bias toward standardization. However, some product designs cater to physical, cultural, or climate differences—smaller sizes in Japan, special women's clothing in Arab countries, and different seasonal weights in South America. Still, Zara standardized about 85 percent of its designs for the global market.

Sourcing

Zara's headquarters staff and purchasing offices in Barcelona, Beijing, and Hong Kong acquire fabric, components, and finished products from suppliers in Spain, India, Turkey, Morocco, and the Far East. Linked into Zara's network, suppliers coordinate their production with its projections. Zara buys about half of its fabric "gray" (not yet dyed) in order to update designs quickly. José Maria Castellano, Inditex's CEO, explains, "We have the ability to scrap an entire production line if it is not selling. We can dye collections in new colors, and we can create a new fashion line in days."

Production

Like its rivals, notably the Gap of the United States and Hennes & Mauritz of Sweden, Zara sources finished garments from suppliers in Europe, North Africa, and Asia. Unlike its rivals, Zara employs nearly 20,000 people, distributed across 23 factories, to make about 50 percent of its finished garments. Zara makes its most time- and fashion-sensitive products in its 20 factories clustered in La Coruña. It outsources about a third of manufacturing to Asia and 14 percent to Europe; these suppliers made staple items with longer shelf lives, such as t-shirts and jeans. Zara's factories are highly automated, specialize by garment type, and focus on the capital-intensive parts of the production process— i.e., pattern design and cutting—as well as finishing and inspection.

Zara spent 20 to 40 percent more, mainly due to higher labor costs, to make garments in Spain and Portugal than rivals spent in Asia. Zara compensates for higher production costs by minimizing advertising, cutting inventory expenses, and quickly adjusting to fashion trends. Inditex's gross margins where 56.8 percent compared to 37.5 percent at Gap in 2010.

High-end garments require a human touch to make them. In response, Zara has built a network of some 500 workshops, located in Galicia, the home state of La Coruña as well as across the border in northern Portugal to hand-sew garment pieces that had been cut at its factories. These workshops are small operations, averaging about 20 to 30 workers that specialize by product type. Zara accounts for most, if not all, of their business and provides tools, technology, logistics, and working capital while paying them standard rates per finished garment. Many local cooperatives have worked with Inditex so long they no longer operate with written contracts.

Logistics

Almost all garments, both internally made and externally contracted, flow through Zara's massive distribution center in La Coruña—it is about the size of 90 football fields—or smaller satellite centers in Brazil and Mexico. A state-of-the-art mobile tracking system docks hanging garments in the appropriate bar-coded area, moves them along 125 miles of underground rails that link production sites, spins carousels capable of handling 45,000 folded garments per hour, and ships about two and a half-million items every week to stores.

Driving logistics process are the twice-weekly deliveries to Zara's stores, triggered by real-time inventory data and local customer feedback. Lorena Alba, Inditex's director of logistics, regards the warehouse as a place to move merchandise rather than store it. "The vast majority of clothes are in here only a few hours," and none stay at the distribution center for more than three days. Third-party delivery services manage the transfer of preprogrammed lots to stores. This fancy footwork has dropped Zara's inventory to 7 percent of annual revenues, compared with the mid- to high teens for its rivals.

Marketing

Zara's trailblazing challenges age-old retail marketing practices. Its product policy emphasizes reasonable-quality goods, adaptable product lines, and high fashionability. The company uses little advertising or promotion—the firm's founder regarded advertising as a "pointless distraction." Zara spends just 0.3 percent of sales on advertising, compared with 3 to 4 percent for most fashion retailers. It relies on word of mouth among its legions of loyal shoppers.

It specializes in lightning-quick turnarounds of the latest designer trends—many items you see in stores didn't exist three weeks earlier. Zara's pricing strategy, as noted above, is "Armani at moderate prices." Hence, Zara aggressively priced it products; explained Marcos Lopez of Inditex: "The key driver in our stores is the right fashion. Price is important, but it comes second." Zara adjusts pricing for the international market, making customers in foreign markets bear the costs of shipping products from Spain. On average, its prices are 10 percent higher in other European countries, 40 percent higher in northern European countries, 70 percent higher in the Americas, and 100 percent higher in Japan.

Store Operations

Zara's stores present the company's face to the world and function as grassroots marketing research agents. The stores command high-profile slots on premier shopping venues such as the Champs-Elysées in Paris, Regent Street in London, Fifth Avenue in New York, and Wafungjing Street in Beijing. Zara takes great care to put its best face forward. Traveling teams of window dressers and interior coordinators visit each store every three weeks, ensuring that window displays and interior presentations convey the targeted message.

Back at headquarters, designers wander the mock store space and test possible design themes, lighting schemes, and product presentation. Its "Fashion Street," in the basement of "The Cube," houses a Potemkin row of storefronts meant to mimic some of its locations. Store employees don Zara's fashions while working; store managers and staff suggest merchandise to order, discontinue, and recommend. Networked stores transfer data on merchandise sales, along with customer requests, to Zara's design teams, factories, and logistics center in La Coruña. Relaying color fabric preferences straight from its shoppers enables the retail staff to localize otherwise globally standardized products. Finding store managers capable of handling these responsibilities, according to CEO Castellano, constrains Zara's expansion.

Firm Infrastructure

A key competency is the infrastructure that Zara uses to coordinates its value chain. Two features stand out: managers' sense of customers and markets and their ability to coordinate worldwide activities. The allure of Zara is the freshness of its offerings, the creation of a sense of exclusiveness, attractive in-store ambience, and positive word of mouth. These ideas drive rapid product turnover, with new designs arriving in twice-weekly shipments. Zara's fans, by the way, learn which days of the week goods are delivered (so called "Z-days,") and shop accordingly. About three-quarters of merchandise on display changes every three to four weeks. This corresponds to the average time between customers' visits, given that the average Zara shopper visits 17 times a year—versus three to four visits per year for competitors.

Attractive stores, both inside and out, are vital. As Luis Blanc, a director at Inditex, explains, "We invest in prime locations. We place great care in the presentation of our storefronts. That is how we project our image. We want our clients to enter a beautiful store where they are offered the latest fashions. But most important, we want our customers to understand that if they like something, they must buy it now, because it won't be in the shops the following week. It is all about creating a climate of scarcity and opportunity."

Rapid turnover fans the "buy now because you won't see it later" phenomenon. Zara accentuates scarcity with small shipments, sparsely stocked shelves, and a display limit of one month. Rapid turnover means that even though consumers visit Zara frequently, when they do visit, things look different. The CEO of the National Retail Federation, reflecting on Z-Day and fast fashions, marveled that "It's like you walk into a new store every two weeks." Besides keeping its stores looking fresh, these policies reduced price markdowns: Zara books some 85 percent of its products at full price whereas the industry average markdown ratio is about 50 percent. The number of items that Zara puts on clearance sale is about half the industry average.

Not all was perfect in the land of Zara. Some wondered how long Zara could charge different prices in different countries. A bigger question is how much longer could it continue running global operations from its centralized base in Spain, especially given the rise of Asian markets. Did it still make sense to keep product design, manufacturing, and logistics activities in Spain now that Asia accounted for 15 percent of its sales and is slated to go higher? Given its concentrated value chain, some clothes Zara made in China are shipped to Spain and then sent to shops in China. Despite this quirk, the chief executive of Inditex, Pablo Isla, sees no need for a second product base: "We're not thinking of replicating the brain in Asia," but, he conceded, they may adjust logistics.

Ultimately, Zara's adept coordination of the overlapping activities among its designers, plants, storefronts, and salespeople testifies to the power of its strategy. No other company can design, make, ship, and sell fashion as speedily as Zara. Its strategy and business design leave rivals with less time to figure out how to better configure and coordinate operations. Some believe that firms have little option but to follow Zara's strategic lead. If they don't, warns a leading retail analyst, they "won't be in business in 10 years."

Introduction

The first half of our text explains that MNEs operate in environments shaped by cultural, political, legal, economic, trade, monetary, governmental, and institutional forces. Individually and combined, they influence managers' strategic decisions and operating actions (see Figure 11.2). What managers do to make their companies competitive, given conditions and trends in the international business environment, anchors this chapter. We focus on how they devise strategies to engage markets in order to boost current performance and sustain long-term growth.

Although commonalities across countries create opportunities, differences constrain MNEs. Therefore, this chapter profiles factors that influence managers' strategic analyses, including their evaluations of the idea of strategy, the tools that develop their choices, and the processes that put their vision into action. We apply the framework we build here in subsequent chapters, using it to assess a range of issues. How MNEs enter foreign markets, form alliances, and organize activities, to name just a few, follow from their choice of strategy. In the final section of the book, ideas from this chapter similarly anchor discussions of how MNEs design and implement their marketing, manufacturing, supply, accounting, finance, and human resource activities.

Our opening profile of Zara previews many of these issues. When Zara began its global expansion, strategy in the apparel business was dictated by the structure of the industry—a structure that was inefficient (it took too much time to design and deliver clothing) and ineffective (apparel makers and sellers were plagued by forecasting and inventory problems). Zara rejected the conventions dictated by this structure. Over the

Global integration standardizes worldwide activities to maximize efficiency whereas **national responsiveness** adapts local activities to optimize effectiveness.

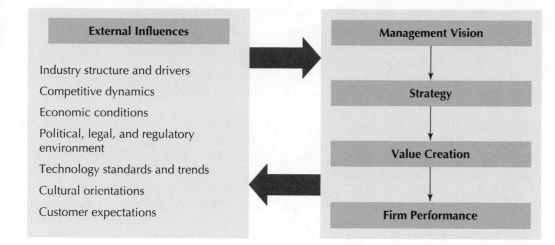

FIGURE 11.2   The Role of Strategy in International Business

Chapter 1 showed the MNEs' operating environment includes physical/social and competitive factors. Chapters 2 through 9 developed their key features. This chapter discusses these in relation to an MNE's strategy, showing how managers configure resources and coordinate operations. These ideas will guide ensuing discussions in Chapter 12 through 20.

next decade, it developed an innovative strategy that, as seen in figure 11.1, has set the standards of operational efficiency and market effectiveness. Zara's success disrupted the global apparel industry. It changed how a company creates value in design, manufacturing, logistics, and marketing. It changed standards for coordinating functions to support value creation. Ultimately, its decisions highlights the purpose of strategy in the MNE—create value by standardizing activities to maximize global efficiency while simultaneously adapting activities to optimize local effectiveness.

Industry Structure

Assessing strategy begins by assessing **industry structure** given that the forces in the MNE's immediate setting have the greatest impact on its strategy. For example, German carmaker BMW monitors how interest rate trends, political leadership changes, and technology developments affect the potential for profits in the auto industry. BMW is far more sensitive, however, to the actions of fellow industry members like Mercedes-Benz, Toyota, Michelin, Goodyear, and Bosch because they directly affect its performance.

Interpreting industry structure often relies on the concepts and tools represented in the **five-forces model**.[2] This model helps managers assess the dimension and their dynamics that determine the attractiveness of an industry. It maps the relationship among companies within an industry, highlighting how competitors, new entrants, suppliers, buyers, and substitute products affect potential profitability. It holds that firm performance is a function of its strategy, which is determined by industry factors that shape the corresponding pattern of competition.

For example, an industry with few entry barriers, lots of accessible buyers, and an expanding supply of low-cost, technologies tends to have many firms competing for profits. Think of, for example, cell phones, e-commerce, financial services, or entertainment. Conversely, an industry with high entry barriers, steep capital requirements, and tough research and development standards tends to have few firms competing for profits. Think of, for example, the pharmaceutical, aircraft, or automobile industries. In both types, the prevailing industry structure shapes an MNE's choices regarding research and innovation, product strategy, plant investment, and pricing behavior. These choices ultimately determine its performance.[3]

INDUSTRY CHANGE

Industry structure is dynamic. New products, new firms, new markets, and new managers trigger new developments in rivalry, pricing, substitutes, buyers, and suppliers. These developments often change a minor feature of the industry, such as the expansion of an

Concept Check

In Chapter 3, we used the dichotomy between **democracy** and **totalitarianism** to build a framework that integrates information about political freedom. In Chapter 4, we used the differences among **market, mixed,** and **command economies** and the notion of economic freedom to build a similar framework. A key framework in this chapter is the different ways managers think of **strategy** within the context of industry structure and the configuration and coordination of value activities.

An industry is composed of those companies engaged in a particular type of enterprise.

The idea of industry structure represents the relationships among

- Suppliers of inputs.
- Buyers of outputs.
- Substitute products.
- Potential new entrants.
- Rivalry among competing firms.

Firm conduct refers to the choices a company makes regarding research, manufacturing, marketing, distribution, and the like that influence its profitability.

existing distribution channel or availability of higher quality inputs. Minor changes leave managers the freedom to tweak their strategy.

Occasionally, an extraordinary change redefines one or more of the five forces, thereby disrupting the structure of the industry. Significant changes require MNEs assess their impact on industry structure and firm profitability. Often, big changes involve competitors, products, processes and politics. Let's take a closer look at each.

Competitive Disruptions   Big changes often follow big mergers, like that of Exxon and Mobil, or game-changing acquisitions, such as Aluminum Corporation of China aligning with Rio Tinto. For instance, Deutsche Telekom's choice to sell its American wireless unit, T-Mobile USA, to AT&T ended its decade-long expansion into the American market. Initially successful, its entry ultimately failed due to the advent of the iPhone. The iPhone, launched atop the expanding Apple technology platform, changed the relationship among buyers, sellers, and rivals. Initially sold exclusively by AT&T in the United States, it prompted the defection of many of T-Mobile USA's most lucrative customers. Explained an analyst, "The iPhone effect cannot be underestimated in this decision. Without being able to sell the iPhone, T-Mobile was in an unsustainable position and T-Mobile USA became a problem child."[4]

The structure of industries evolves. Disruptive innovations accelerate the rate of change.

Product Disruptions   More commonly, disruptive innovations drive industry change. New products make alternatives obsolete while new processes reset the way they are made, delivered, and serviced.[5] For example, out of nowhere, netbooks—small, cheap, light computers optimized for basic tasks such as Web browsing and email—disrupted the global PC industry in 2009. Traditional personal computers and the many companies that make their components, like Samsung, Intel, and Microsoft, faced the biggest upheaval in industry structure since the rise of the laptop. Noted an analyst, "A broad shift in the consumer market toward low-cost PCs clearly put pressure on the revenues of nearly every player in the value chain, from component suppliers to retailers."[6]

Then, once the netbook dust settled, the innovativeness of Apple's iPad disrupted the PC industry in 2010. Again, competitors had to adjust several elements of their strategies, rethinking chip architectures, performance to weight ratios, software platforms, and design ergonomics. By 2011, a slew of ever more powerful tablet devices decimated the traditional PC market far faster than forecast. Desktop PC sales dropped 1.1 percent while tablets grew 213 percent year over year. Some MNEs faced increasingly fearsome struggles.[7] HP, Dell, and Acer, the world's largest makers of desktop PCs and hailed as brilliant strategist just a few years earlier, scrambled to reposition in the face of falling sales and collapsing margins.

Concept Check

Fast-rising MNEs from emerging economies are disrupting industry structures with both their product and process innovation. In particular, their application of frugal engineering, a logical response given the prevalence of the Base of the Pyramid phenomenon in their home markets, pushes companies in the West to rethink strategies.

Process Disruptions   Innovations in management processes also drive industry change. For example, MNEs from emerging markets are reinventing systems of production and distribution, experimenting with new business models, and resetting the standards of innovation. Regarding the latter, companies are taking the needs of poor consumers at the Base of the Pyramid as a starting point and working backward to develop products that eliminate all but the most essential features in order to more economically fit existing needs. Frugal innovation pushes managers to rethink entire production processes and business models so that they can use existing technologies in imaginative new ways or apply mass production techniques to new and unexpected areas. Presently, Indians see frugal innovation as perhaps their distinctive contribution to management thinking. By no means though, is this competency found only there. Frugal innovation processes in Africa (i.e., Safaricom with mobile money) and Asia (i.e., reusable sutures from various Chinese suppliers) disrupt industry economics.[8]

Political Disruptions   Changes in the political arena continually concern managers. A powerful example is the recent global financial crisis. Consider that two of the five top-rated business environments in summer 2008—Ireland and the United Kingdom—saw shaky financial markets, spiraling unemployment, collapsing currencies, and shaken consumer confidence by that winter.[9] By mid-2009, similar, albeit less drastic, trends were evident in the United States, Taiwan, Japan, Spain, France, Germany, and Australia.

Fallout from the global financial crisis, for instance, continues resetting the structure of many industries. Dislocations in financial markets altered credit terms and financing options, thereby changing the cost of capital and return thresholds. Sovereign debt problems persist for many countries. Consequential falls in consumer, industrial, and public demand have changed the powers of buyers and suppliers. Pushback against economic freedom and growing state capitalism resets rivalry. The potential for profitability in industries is in flux. Managers react in kind, questioning their strategy, rethinking their value proposition, reorienting operations to faster growing product markets, and repositioning resources to preserve efficiencies.

Telltale Marks   Trends and disruptions play in all industry. Generally, no more than a few command the power to reset industry structure. Those that do include:

- Change in the long-term growth rate for an industry.
- New technologies, like containerization, wireless communications, or smart phones.
- New consumer purchase and usage patterns, such as streaming movies online or replacing land lines with VoIP systems.
- Manufacturing innovations that revise cost and efficiency frontiers, like *Six Sigma* or lean production programs.
- Diffusion of business, executive, and technical expertise across countries, such as the transfer of Eastern management approaches to Western companies.
- Change in government regulation, such as the privatization of state assets or escalating government involvement in capital markets.
- Entry or exit of firms, such as the emergence of state-owned companies.
- So-called black swan events that, although highly improbable, have radical impacts—as seen with the Internet or the global financial crisis.

> Industry structure changes because of events like
> - Competitors' moves.
> - Government policies.
> - Shifting preferences.
> - Technological developments.

Perspectives on Strategy

Understanding industries and how they change has led researchers to study how good companies achieved greatness. Related work studies how companies move from short-term enterprises to ones built to last.[10] Consistently, reports indicate that great companies apply a down-to-earth, pragmatic, committed-to-excellence framework that kept each company, its leaders, and its workers on track for the long haul. Net Implication? Managers' ability to develop and apply a "committed-to-excellence framework" separates short-term good performers from long-term great one. Easily said, this is difficult to do precisely because there are literally thousands of credible standards. Unquestionably, many are informative. Two prominent models of strategy—the **Industry Organization paradigm** and **Great by Choice**—help managers move from confusion to clarity. Let's take a closer look at each.

The Industry Organization Paradigm (IO)   The IO Paradigm emphasizes industry structure in the belief that it directly influences a company's profitability. It begins by presuming that markets demonstrate **perfect competition** in which there are many firms with small market shares, all firms are price takers, identical products are sold by all firms, companies can freely enter and exit the industry, and buyers know the features of the product being sold and the prices charged by other firms. In a perfectly competitive market, risk-adjusted rates of return should be constant. Put differently, over time, no firm or industry consistently outperforms others, no matter the innovativeness of a particular company or executive.[11] In situations of high profits, new companies enter,

> Perfect competition presumes
> - Many buyers and sellers such that no individual affects price or quantity.
> - Perfect information for both producers and consumers.
> - Few, if any, barriers to market entry and exit.
> - Full mobility of resources.
> - Perfect knowledge among firms and buyers.

thereby creating competition that lowers prices and profits. In situations of low profits, firms exit or markets close. As a general rule, an unattractive industry is one in which perfect competition drives down overall profitability.

In reality, many industries are far-from-perfectly competitive.[12] Different companies in different industries sustain different levels of profitability in ways that are shaped, but not determined, by the structure of the industry. Many industries exhibit situations in which entry barriers deter potential rivals or a few large sellers behave as oligarchs. Such "imperfect" industries include firms that consistently earn above-average, risk-adjusted returns, such as Intel in integrated circuits, Apple in technology, Infosys in business services, Safaricom in mobile money, LVMH in luxury products, Baidu in Internet search, Johnson & Johnson in healthcare, and Nestlé in food services. An attractive industry is one in which far-from-perfect competition lets companies consistently earn above-average profitability.

Great by Choice   If markets are not always perfectly competitive, industry structure does not entirely determine performance, and some firms consistently outperform rivals, then what explains performance? This question spotlights the power of bright, motivated managers and their keen sense of innovative products or processes to create value in ways that are not easily matched or cheaply copied. In doing so, they outperform their rivals. Essentially, industry structure matters, but some companies thrive on the basis of their executives' choice to be great and, we hasten to add, their distinctive competency in achieving their ambitions.[13]

For instance, Zara's strategy of making and moving sophisticated, moderately priced fashions demanded adept integration of design talent, customer responsiveness, and information technology. At the time, industry structure posed barriers to this strategy. Zara's managers developed a repertory of competencies spanning design, production, logistics, and retailing that converted an innovative strategy into action. Its standout performance highlights the idea that great managers make great strategies that make great companies that outperform their rivals over the long haul.

Case Review Note

Strategy's Hallmarks   The overlapping assumptions of the IO paradigm and Great by Choice perspective testify to the hallmarks of strategy. They define the perspectives and tools that an MNE applies to deal with industry structure, optimally allocate resources, and steadfastly progress toward objectives. Strategy builds and sustains the "committed to excellence framework" that separates great firms from the good. Difficult for all, these issues are especially tough for the MNE. Besides dealing with domestic issues, operating in different countries puts it in a challenging mix of consumers, industries, and institutions.

Managerial practices highlight a variety of tactical solutions. Common to all, however, is their contribution to an MNE's ability to generate value above industry benchmarks over the long-term. Essentially, they confirm the goal of strategy is to create value.[14] Technically, **value** is the measure of a firm's capability of selling what it makes for more than the costs incurred to make it. So defined, **strategy** is the committed to excellence framework that exploits industry conditions and leverages executive quality to create superior value. And, as we see in Figure 11.3, MNEs can create value here, or if need be, over there.

Approaches to Value Creation

Creating value requires an MNE develop a compelling value proposition (why a customer should buy its goods or use its services) that specifies its targeted markets (those customers for whom it creates goods or services). This analysis, whether done on a nation-by-nation, region-by-region, or worldwide basis, requires managers make and sell products that exceed customers' value expectations. MNEs translates this mandate into a committed to excellence framework that creates value by making products for a

"WE HAVE to GO GLOBAL SINCE NOBODY AROUND
HERE WILL BUY OUR PRODUCT."

FIGURE 11.3 The Global Option

The quest for value leads companies to many places. For some, international expansion is an intriguing option For others, it is their last resort.

Source: Harley Schwadron/ CartoonStock.com

lower cost than competitors (the strategy of cost leadership) or making products that consumers willingly pay a premium price (the strategy of differentiation).

COST LEADERSHIP

The MNE implementing the **cost leadership** strategy aims to be the low-cost producer in an industry for a given level of quality. It offers standardized products to the largest possible market at the lowest competitive price. It lowers its costs relative to rivals by streamlining product design, investing in state-of-the-art manufacturing technologies and processes, running efficient facilities, and applying rigorous controls.

No matter the program or proposal, the cost leadership strategy evaluates its usefulness in terms of its contribution to improving efficiency. Indisputably, costs converge across companies, particularly those producing a commodity such as gas, wheat, or memory chips. Still, companies incur different costs due to differences in executive quality, input prices, wage rates, employee productivity, production scale, and distribution expenses. Lower costs relative to rivals translates higher efficiency into superior value.

A cost-leadership strategy is a vital advantage in highly competitive industries, such as the airline, steel, mortgage, steel, white goods, or package delivery markets. It is practiced by companies such as Southwest Airlines, UPS, Haier, Hon Hai, Tata, Cemex, Virgin Mobile, and Foxconn. Competitive industries push MNEs to offset high capital requirements by exploiting the economies of large-scale standardization. In the brutal game of low-cost competition, increasing volume pressures less efficient competitors. In the event of a price war, for example, the low-cost leader can cut prices, thereby imposing losses on rivals yet still earning some profits. Even without a price war, as the industry matures and prices decline, the MNE that makes the lowest cost products outlast rivals.

Today, many Chinese companies apply the cost leadership strategy. They combine efficient manufacturing operations, inexpensive labor, global distribution, state support, and growing scientific and technological sophistication to undercut rivals on price.[15] For example, Chinese pearl farmers have begun flooding the world with low cost, high-quality pearls. By late 2011, A Chinese half-inch pearl sold for $4 to $8

Concept Check

In Chapter 2, we explain how **globalization** spurs a variety of managerial approaches. Similarly, in Chapters 3 and 4, we emphasize how companies operating internationally encounter a variety of **political, legal,** and **economic environments.** Here we engage the notion that globalization pressures in the face of local constraints bounds an MNE's strategy.

The cost leadership strategy reduces costs below those of competitors for a given level of quality.

at wholesale whereas a Tahitian pearl of similar size rang in at $25 to $35—a strand of perfectly round, blemish-free, half-inch pearls from China ran $1,800 whereas the same sort from Tahiti, although displaying a richer luster, cost $14,000. The influx of Chinese peals, noted one observer, "has made pearls affordable for the average working woman."[16] Not content to rest on their current price advantage, Chinese's pearl farmers are investing in automation and sequencing the genome of the mussels that produce freshwater pearls. If successful, the price of higher quality Chinese pearls will fall faster.

This situation is not unique to pearls; rather it spans the product gamut. Chinese companies' successful implementation of cost leadership strategies, consequently, leaves rivals worldwide a stark choice. Advised an analyst, "If you still make anything labor intensive, get out now rather than bleed to death. Shaving 5 percent here and there won't work. Chinese producers can make the same adjustments. You need an entirely new business model to compete."[17] The Director of Nalco China concurred, noting, "once you compete on price here, the game's over."[18]

DIFFERENTIATION

Industries marked by a continuous stream of branded product innovations—as we see in consumer electronics, software, entertainment, wealth management, or fashion markets—typically do not emphasize cost leadership. Instead, they opt for **differentiation,** creating value by generating customer insights, developing innovative products, designing high-profile marketing programs, and moving products to market quickly. Think for a moment of our opening profile of Zara, particularly its belief that "The key driver in our stores is the right fashion. Price is important, but it comes second." The matter of "right fashion," however, requires a range of creative design skills, built atop a tech intensive infrastructure that quickly turns cool ideas into hot fashions.

Differentiation dynamics play in many industries. For example, Sony began selling its first netbook computer in the fall of 2009, finally entering the only sector of the PC market then showing significant growth.[19] Its netbook used the same processor found in competing products and, like other netbooks, had a 10-inch screen. However, its display resolution was 1,366 × 768 pixels rather than the standard 1,024 × 600 pixels, meaning that more of a website would fit onto the screen. For scrolling, Sony's machine provided a touch panel same size as the larger one found on laptops. Hence, Sony used the higher resolution and larger touch pad as key differentiators between its product and competing netbooks. Granted, improving screen resolution or touchpad size are not revolutionary design innovations. However, they supported Sony's claim that its products are different, better, and therefore justifiably more expensive than those offered by rivals.

The differentiation strategy fixates on accelerating innovation, not relentlessly reducing costs, as the basis for sustainable value creation. Its goal is developing products that offer unique attributes to customers whose perception of them as superior to alternatives supports charging a premium price. Differentiation requires MNEs to develop competencies that rivals find hard, if not impossible, to match or copy. The sleek design of an Apple iPad, engineering of a Lexus sedan, customer service at a Ritz-Carlton, premium real estate slots for Zara shops, or efficiency of Google's search algorithm, besides generating profits, create high standards that rivals struggle to outdo.

The fact that today's innovation is often tomorrow's obsolescence is the key threat to the differentiation strategy. The presence of strong rivals worldwide, in both advanced and emerging economies, makes identifying the basis of differentiation an ongoing challenge. Innovations conceived in Germany quickly diffuse to rivals in Brazil, the United States, or China. Companies battling based on a superior product features must, as the CEO of IBM notes, tirelessly determine "what will cause work to move to me? On what basis will I differentiate and compete?"[20]

Case Review Note

Differentiation champions developing products that customers value and that rivals find hard, if not impossible, to match or copy.

The differentiation strategy accelerates innovation whereas cost leadership champions efficiency.

The Firm as Value Chain

In principle, an MNE can opt for cost leadership or differentiation—i.e., the asymmetric demands of each make it quite difficult to pursue both simultaneously. Whatever its choice, the potential profitability of a firm's strategy is a function of the value that customers see in its product relative to its corresponding costs. A firm earns higher profits than its rivals when it creates more value for its customers. Understanding this relationship and translating it into a "committed to excellence framework" is the hallmark of superior strategy.[21]

Cost leadership or differentiation ambitions reflect industry structure as well as executives' analytics. For example, Zara offers "Armani at moderate prices." Implementing this strategy triggers a series of questions: Where do we find design ideas? How should we set global standards? When does local responsiveness makes sense? Where should we make products? Can our suppliers support our plans? How do we distribute worldwide? What are the most effective marketing tools? What kind of people should we hire to staff retail outlets? How might rivals respond?

CRN
Case Review Note

These questions shape how an MNE organizes its operations to design, make, move, and sell products; how it finds efficiencies in various countries in doing so; and how it coordinates decisions in one part of the business with those made in others.[22] In isolation, these questions are tough. In totality, they separate the great companies from the good. The practices of successful MNEs advise managers to interpret the activities the firm performs as elements of a value chain.

The **value chain** follows from the principle that "every firm is a collection of discrete activities performed to do business that occur within the scope of the firm."[23] It specifies a clear-cut framework that lets managers deconstruct the abstraction of "create value" into a step-by-step system. Modeling its sequence requires MNEs configure functions and coordinate processes that move products from conception in R&D through sourcing materials, organizing manufacturing, supervising logistics, applying marketing, and setting up service options. Figure 11.4 maps this flow. It identifies the sequence of functions, called primary activities, which define a company's value chain.

> The value chain is the set of linked activities the company performs to design, produce, market, distribute, and support a product.

Primary activities define the core business functions: from developing a product, building the operations that make it, and onward through logistics, marketing, distributing, and servicing it (see Table 11.1). Because they reflect classic business activities and managerial orientations, primary activities carry functional labels. Figure 11.4 also identifies secondary processes called **support activities** that apply to each primary activity. Human resources, for example, are needed at each value activity, from supervising the arrival of raw materials, to running production processes, to shipping products and filling orders, to serving customers. These activities, besides defining the infrastructure of the firm, anchor the day-to-day implementation of the primary activities.

> A value chain disaggregates a firm into
> - Primary activities that design, make, sell, and deliver the product.
> - Support activities that implement primary activities.

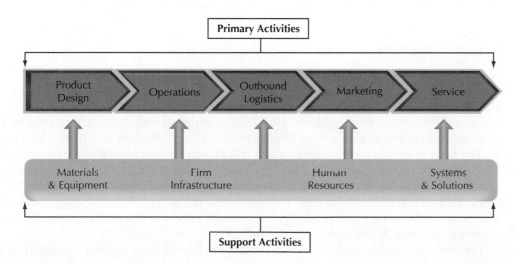

FIGURE 11.4 Primary and Support Activities of the Value Chain

Value chains are made up of primary that reflect classical business functions and managerial orientations. Value chains also rely on support activities that help carry out the day-to-day execution of the primary activities. Each support activity is relevant to all primary activities and runs along the entire value chain.

TABLE 11.1   Primary and Support Activities of the Value Chain

Value chains are made up of primary activities that reflect classical business functions and managerial orientations. Support activities represent the day-to-day tasks that help implement the primary activities.

The Value Chain			
Primary Activities	Product Design	Designing the functions, features, and aesthetics of the product or process.
	Operations	Converting inputs into finished product in terms of sourcing components, arranging supply chains, configuring plant location, and optimizing manufacturing processes.
	Outbound Logistics	Moving finished product from operations to wholesalers, retailers, or end-consumers. Deals with distribution channels, inventory management, warehousing, and transportation logistics.
	Marketing	Informing buyers and consumers about products and services, developing a sales force, devising packaging schemes, defining the brand, and devising promotions.
Support Activities	Service	Servicing customers with installation support, after-sales service, and training.
	Materials and Equipment	Managing the procurement, transportation, storage, and distribution of materials and equipment necessary to conduct the primary activities.
	Human Resource Management	Recruiting, developing, motivating, and rewarding the workforce.
	Systems and Solutions	Managing information processing, overseeing information systems, and integrating technologies platforms.
	Infrastructure	Classic overhead functions, like accounting, finance, legal, safety and security, and quality control, which all firms perform.

Managing the Value Chain

| A value chain identifies the format and interactions between its various activities.

| The worldwide distribution of value activities is the matter of configuration.

An MNE's competitiveness depends on efficiently distributing value activities and effectively linking them. Distributing value activities around the world is the matter of **configuration.** Linking them is the matter of **coordination.** Configuration and coordination, flip sides of the value chain coin, are intrinsically related. Still, each has unique characteristics.

CONFIGURATION

Concept Check

In discussing "Elements of the Economic Environment" in Chapter 4, we describe information on such factors as labor costs, wage rates, and productivity as key elements of a company's strategy for operating in foreign countries. In Chapter 6, we discuss methods of interpreting the relative economic performance of different countries. Here we underscore that location economics determine how MNEs configure value activities.

The option to go anywhere in the world to do any part of its business gives MNEs tremendous choice in configuring its value activities. No matter how big or small, every MNE looks to put value activities in the highest productivity spot in the world. In theory, configuration ranges from **concentrated** (performing all value-chain activities in one location) to **dispersed** (performing different value-chain activities in different locations).

The tension between concentration and dispersion follows from the fact that different activities have different costs in different countries. Recall that value creation is a function of an MNE selling what it makes for more than it costs to make it. Therefore, MNEs configure value activities to exploit **location economies,** specifically, the economies that arise from performing a value activity in the most productive location given prevailing economic, political, legal, and cultural conditions.

For example, say a single market provides the lowest cost, highest productivity environment for all activities. An MNE would concentrate its value chain there and serve its global market through exports. Conversely, when some activities cost less in country X, others cost less in country Y, and still others cost less than country Z, then a dispersed value chain make sense. So, if the best industrial designers are in Taiwan, the company bases design operations there. If the most productive labor force for assembly is in China, that's where it builds its plants. If the most imaginative minds are in Denmark, it develops its advertising campaign there.

Today, conflicting pressures for global integration and national responsiveness means few MNEs concentrate their value chain in a single location. Our opening case, for example, highlighted this dilemma as Zara's key challenge: should it continue concentrating its value chain in Spain, thereby maximizing global efficiencies, or disperse some value activities to its fastest-growing markets in Asia, thereby adapting activities to optimize local effectiveness. Hence, efficiently dispersing value activities among different countries to exploit location economics is the crux of value chain configuration in an MNE.

Where to Go   Location decisions are subject to the unpredictability of the prevailing economic, legal, political, and cultural conditions. This constraint frustrates configuration choices. Abrupt change can turn a low-cost location into one prohibitively expensive. Following yet another gyration in the business environment, Jack Welch, former chair and CEO of General Electric (GE), thought the best location for GE factories was a mobile platform, explaining, "Ideally, you'd have every plant you own on a barge, to move with currencies and changes in the economy."[24] The impracticality of an armada of barges ferrying factories through the seven seas requires managers monitor how market, legal, political, and cultural conditions moderate location economics. MNEs pay particular attention to *business environment quality, innovation context,* and *resource costs.* They then qualify analysis by considering aspects of *logistics, digitization, and economies of scale.*

Business Environment Quality   The impracticality of Jack Welch's factory-on-a-barge wish pushes MNEs to configure value chains to enter or, as the case may be, avoid a country given its business environment.[25] Countries recognize MNEs' sensitivity and take steps to improve their location economics. Techniques include reducing capital requirements for startups, streamlining property registration, expediting regulatory review, and liberalizing labor regulations. Often, opportunistic governments recruit foreign investors, promising business-friendly markets that offer flexible operating requirements, lower tax rates, cheap financing, and responsive public policies.[26] For example, Evergreen Solar was a leading manufacturer of solar panels in the United States in 2010. In 2011, it shut its Massachusetts factory, laid off 800 workers, and shifted production to a joint venture with a Chinese company in Wuhan, China. Evergreen Solar cited China's superior location economics given its low-cost loans, stronger government support, and cheaper labor.[27]

Presently, doing business remains easiest in high-income countries such as Singapore, Denmark, Hong Kong, New Zealand, Canada, Sweden, and the United States.[28] In contrast, some governments create risky environments. Countries whose governments condone the rule of man, for instance, often deters firms fearful of intellectual property theft. Presently, Venezuela, Zimbabwe, Chad, Burundi, Cameroon, Bolivia, and Tajikistan are rated among the worst business environments. Generally, circumstances are improving worldwide. The importance of business activity to economic growth spurs many countries to improve the economics of doing business there.

Innovation Context   The application of new ideas benefits consumers, companies, and countries.[29] Consumers enjoy rising living standards. Companies fortify competitiveness. Governments fuel economic growth. Looking forward, the dominant engine of innovation—technology—accelerates. The **singularity principle,** for instance, projects that in the next 30 years, the "pace of technological change will so rapid, its impact so deep...that technology appears to be expanding at infinite speed."[30] Developments in genetics, robotics, nanotechnology, and computing will overturn

---

Location economics influence the decision to concentrate or disperse value activities.

Case Review Note

Factors that influence the configuration of a value-chain include

- Business environment.
- Innovation context.
- Resource costs.
- Logistics.
- Digitization.
- Scale economies.

Concept Check

A consistent theme of our text thus far is the variability of business environments from country to country. Chapters 1 through 10 highlight the range of factors that vary, spanning the dimensions of people, product, process, and perspectives, that shape a country's business environment.

Doing business remains easiest in high-income countries.

many mainstream practices. Presently, predictions are that by 2013, a supercomputer will be built that exceeds the computational capability of the human brain. More radically, by 2050, a $1000 computer will exceed the capabilities of humanity. While these forecasts may overstate the scale of change, their implication to accelerating innovativeness is beyond debate.[31]

Standard-setting companies in these realms will generate vast wealth and many jobs. The rush to lead the race pushes MNEs to locate value activities in countries with rich innovation contexts. Whether the principle is singularity, duality, or plurality is still a matter of speculation. What is not, however, is the linkage between the innovation contexts across countries and how MNEs configure activities.

This race spurs governments to build knowledge-intensive, technology-enabled business environments. Promoting technologies, expanding human capacities, streamlining organizational capabilities, and improving institutional responsiveness determine those seen as best leveraging knowledge into market-changing innovation.[32] Presently, developed countries claim the top spots in the rankings, most notably, Denmark, Sweden, United States, Finland, and Hong Kong, Britain, Norway, Japan, Singapore, South Korea, Switzerland, and Canada.[33] Rising innovation in Asia is moving India, Turkey, and China up league tables. Collectively, Asian countries appear to be moving from practices that optimize production efficiencies to policies that improve the environment for innovation.[34] MNEs respond accordingly. Specifically, following openings in China and India, GE opened a research center in Brazil in 2010; each had taken steps to accelerate local innovation.

Resource Costs Cost differentials shape how MNEs configure value activities. Differences in wage rates, worker productivity, and government regulations mean that the cost of doing the same thing varies from country to country. MNEs scrutinize where it makes the most sense to locate activities, configuring and reconfiguring operations as situations change. For example, North American footwear makers once made shoes in the United States, but over a 30-year span, they moved production from subcontractors in Taiwan to the Philippines, Thailand, South Korea, Vietnam, and China in the quest for the low costs. Presently, average weekly wage rates vary dramatically from country to country. At the high end, Denmark mandates about $450 per week; at the low end, Uganda requires about $2.20 per week.[35]

Present and projected wage differences shape how MNEs configure their value chains. The quest for productive, low-cost labor has led thousands of MNEs to open operations in China. In 2003, the average hourly compensation for production workers in China was $0.80 versus $25.34 in the United States.[36] By 2007, average weekly wages in China were about 3 to 5 percent of those in the United States. Even after China raised minimum wages several times, by 2011 wages rates in China were 15 percent of the U.S. standard—Shanghai, for example, ranked first nationwide with a monthly minimum wage of ¥1,200 ($181) versus ¥7,656 ($1,160) in New York.[37]

Granted, high-wage workers could work harder, relying on higher productivity to offset wage disadvantages. Still, its difficult for relative productivity performances to neutralize these differences—excluding capital structures and technology differentials, a worker in the United States must be roughly seven times more productive than counterparts in China to equalize the per unit labor rate. For the record, 2010, productivity in China grew by 8.2 percent compared with a rise of 1 percent in the United States.[38]

Consider, for example, the implications of Wonder Auto of China. A maker of automobile parts, it cost US$4 million to set up an assembly line employing 20 workers in Jinzhou, a city of 800,000 in northeastern China. The combined wages of these 20 workers are a bit more than $40,000 a year—a sum that's roughly the annual base pay for one unionized auto-parts worker or two nonunion auto-parts workers in the United States.[39] Similarly, moving from Massachusetts to China let Evergreen Solar reduce weekly wages for its factory workers from $1,350 to $75.[40] Last, relocating service activities, such as call-center operations from United States to India, results in similarly striking cost differentials.[41]

Going forward, how might labor influence MNEs' configuration choices? Auguste Comte reasoned, "Demography is destiny." So it is, in large degree, with the configuration of value chains vis-à-vis labor. The demography of labor spurs MNEs whose activities are sensitive to labor cost differentials—such as those implementing a cost leadership strategy—to exploit favorable wage rates, labor supply, and worker productivity. Expectedly, many MNEs configure activities to maximize value creation by operating in lower-cost, higher-productivity locations.

For example, IBM grew its labor force in India from a few hundred in 1999 to nearly 74,000 in 2007, when it then became the MNE with the largest number of employees in India. IBM plans to recruit 24,000 more employees in 2011, boosting its Indian headcount to nearly 154,000.[42] Similarly, PWC China's headcount has gone from under a thousand in 2000, to 14,000 in 2011, and expects to hit 30,000 by 2020.

Given that higher supply results in lower wages, countries with the largest labor forces indicate where MNEs will seek inexpensive workers. Table 11.2 signals the likely direction of job migration as Western MNEs move operations to labor rich countries in Southeast Asia, Central and Eastern Europe, and South America. Already, we see powerful effects. Between 2000 and 2010, U.S. companies cut their workforces in the United States by nearly 3 million while concurrently increasing employment overseas by 2.4 million. In contrast, during the 1990s U.S. companies added 4.4 million workers in the United States but just 2.7 million workers abroad. Asked about the big shift, GE's CEO replied, "Today we go to Brazil, we go to China, we go to India because that's where the customers are."[43] As multinationals reconfigure activities, they redeploy labor.

Today, two countries—China and India—account for 38 percent of total labor in the world. In the longer term, many MNEs will look past China to opportunities in India. By 2050, China's population will rise about 79 million, the United States about 100 million, but India's more than 500 million. Over the next decade, the Indian workforce will increase by at least 80 million. This "demographic dividend" girds much of the optimism in India today.

Logistics Value chains, whether centralized or dispersed, generate transfers among primary and support activities. Consider the production of lithium ion batteries. First, an

TABLE 11.2   Global Distribution of Labor: Top 10 Countries

MNEs routinely configure value chains given the supply of resources such as, land, capital, technology, and labor. Regarding the latter, China and India are attractive sources of abundant, productive, low-cost labor. Expectedly, many MNEs from many countries configure their value chains to develop Chinese and Indian operations.

Rank	Country	Total Labor Force	Percent Share of Total World Labor Pool, 2010[1]
1	China	819,500,000	23.76
2	India	478,300,000	13.87
3	European Union	225,400,000	6.54
4	United States	154,900,000	4.49
5	Indonesia	116,500,000	3.38
6	Brazil	103,600,000	3.00
7	Russia	75,550,000	2.19
8	Bangladesh	73,870,000	2.14
9	Japan	65,700,000	1.90
10	Pakistan	55,770,000	1.62

[1] Global labor count: Approximately 3,449,094,753 workers.

Source: Based on Central Intelligence Agency, "Country Comparisons: Labor Force," *The World Factbook*, at www.cia.gov (accessed March 15, 2011).

Logistics involves how companies obtain, produce, and exchange material and services in the proper place and in proper quantities for the proper activity.

MNE mines lithium in Bolivia, moves it to a manufacturing plant in Guangzhou, ships batteries to its distributor in France, who supplies market channels in the European Union. Each transaction generates an exchange between different value activities. The management of these transactions is the matter of **logistics.** MNEs configure the location of value activities to minimize logistics expenses.

In some situations, the value-to-weight ratio of transactions shapes configuration decisions. The greater the value of a product to its weight, the less storage and transportation costs matter. Logistic costs are relevant, yet not decisive in this scenario. Consequently, the decision of where to make computer chips, software, or aircraft, unlike tractor axles or carpeting, need not pay attention to the distance between the factory and the consumer.

Digitization influences location economics by creating new sources of competencies.

Digitization   The process of **digitization** converts an analog product into a string of zeros and ones. Increasingly, MNEs digitize products such as software, music, and books and services like application processing, financial consolidation, and legal services. Plugged into the network, workers move goods and services anywhere in the world at negligible cost and complication. The potential to locate digital activities virtually anywhere, particularly as the Internet "cloud" expands, influences how an MNE configures its value chain. Digitization changes location economics, creating options that did not exist a decade ago—i.e. x-rays taken in Boston but read in Bangkok.

Ongoing digitization signals continuing disruption. Once, many activities could be done in a few, specialized places, such as due diligence processes in mergers and acquisitions that largely took place in New York City or London. Corresponding value activities were concentrated there. Digitization enables dispersing these activities. Indeed, digitization has created a new global model for financial services, unleashing disruptive innovations that change the rules of the game. Said an analyst, "there has never been an economic discontinuity of this magnitude in the history of the world.... These powerful forces are allowing companies to rethink their sourcing strategies across the entire value chain." [44]

Similar trends have begun to disrupt the legal field. India's legal outsourcing industry is growing from an experimental enterprise to a mainstream part of the global business of law. At Pangea3, a legal outsourcing firm in Noida, India, Indian lawyers do the routine work traditionally assigned to enterprising junior lawyers in the United

Future Customers, Colleagues, and Competitors

Schoolchildren with their newly arrived laptops at previously off-the-grid school in Ulaanbaatar, capital and largest city of Mongolia. The government is providing a laptop to every schoolchild with the goal of equipping the next generation of value creators with the tools to run globalization. Similar programs are unfolding in countries throughout the world. The implications of this program to the division of labor, the trade of products, and the performance of markets will shape MNEs' strategies.

Source: VAN CAKENBERGHE TO/ SIPA/Newscom

States at a fraction of the cost. Noted a director of Harvard Law School, "This is not a blip, this is a big historical movement."[45]

Going forward, the narrowing *digital divide*—the gap between those with regular access to digital technologies and those without—plugs more people into the global network. Accordingly, location economics change and configuration choices evolve. The adjacent photo of young children with new, low-priced laptops confirms that fewer and fewer spots in the world remain off the grid. As these children and their counterparts throughout the world—by early 2011, 2,100,000 children and teachers worldwide had such laptops—become proficient with information technologies, MNEs rethink configuration options in order to tap new sources of competencies. The consolidation of existing communication technologies, to say nothing of the construction of Internet bases with wireless transmissions in increasingly remote locations, supports "new business models to connect the poorest two billion people to the evolving nervous system of civilization."[46]

Economies of Scale The phenomenon whereby a firm doubles its cumulative output yet its total cost less than doubles due to corresponding gains in efficiency is the **economy of scale.** Put differently, the improved efficiency that comes with larger operations and increased usage of inputs systematically reduces per unit cost. The source of efficiency gains varies, including acquiring materials (bulk buying of materials through long-term contracts), production (distributing fixed costs across a large number of units), financial (access to a greater range of capital instruments in a wider range of countries), and advertising (spreading the expense of a promotion concept over more markets).

The power of these relationships explains many patterns of value chain configurations. Steep up-front capital costs create high potential for scale economies. Long production runs lower per unit costs as marginal production cost decreases while cumulative output increases. The MNE facing steep scale economies, particularly one following a cost leadership strategy, concentrates its value activities to capture the efficiencies provided by a few, large-scale plants.

> The high potential for scale economies encourages concentrated value chains.

For example, a minimum efficient-sized factory to make integrated circuits costs roughly US$3 to $5 billion. As a result, Intel, the world's largest semiconductor chipmaker, supplies the world from 12 fabrication plants located in four countries—7 in the United States, 3 in Ireland, and 1 in Israel and China. Certainly, Intel could opt for many smaller plants in more countries. The reduced efficiency of a dispersed value chain, however, would reduce Intel's competitiveness.

COORDINATION

Configuring activities arranges the architecture of the value chain. Making it perform require coordinating how activities transact with each other. One way to engage this idea is to think of the configuration process as placing pieces atop the global game board. Given location economics, an MNE moves its R&D piece to Brazil, factory piece to Vietnam, logistics piece to the United States, marketing piece to Italy, and the service piece to Japan. Once configured, executives must specify if and when the pieces move about the board as well as how they relate to other pieces. Against this backdrop, we define *coordination* as the means by which management links value activities.

Coordination ranges from not at all (each piece is independent) to extensive (each piece is dependent). Managing activities spanning the globe, as you would think, requires extensive coordination relationships. For example, consider the coordination demands imposed by Zara's strategy of rapid response to fashion trends. Headquarters coordinates reports from salespeople who, acting as grassroots market researchers, interpret buying trends, capture customers' comments, and propose improvements. Real-time data on customer preferences is uploaded to headquarters, which processes, summarizes, and relays it to product designers, materials managers, production supervisors, and logistics controllers. The task is brutal; managers coordinate information flows from a thousand-plus storefronts spanning the globe, oversee its translation

Case Review Note

> Coordination specifies how value activities transact with each other.

The Big Cluster ▶

Here we see a skyline vista of the financial district of New York City. This global financial cluster is home to the New York Stock Exchange, NASDAQ, New York Mercantile Exchange, and New York Board of Trade, as well as the headquarters or subsidiary of virtually every major financial firm in the world.

Source: Dobresum/Shutterstock.com

Concept Check

In discussing the worldwide "Increase and Expansion of Technology" in Chapter 1, we note that technology fosters new ways of communicating among worldwide operations. New technologies enable MNEs to experiment with options, many of them unprecedented, to coordinate dispersed value activities.

into innovative products, organize material flows from suppliers, forward orders to factories, and orchestrate delivery to the same storefronts—all within two weeks. Adding another level of complexity is the fact that linkages exist between primary and support activities. Executives must synchronize the company's infrastructure, developing human resources to staff operations, update technologies to expedite transactions, manage capital processes, and consolidate accounts.

Hence, coordinating activities requires adeptly moving ideas, materials, people, and capital. Done well, the MNE improves its performance. For example, IBM, GE, Microsoft, and Accenture opened R&D facilities in India, reasoning that the productivity of the local scientific community and its unique culture of frugal innovation offered new points of value creation. Breakthroughs at GE's Technology Center in Bengaluru, owing to adroit coordination processes, spread to GE's operations in Hungary, Brazil, China, the United States, and onward. For example, GE's Indian technology center helped develop a small, low-cost electrocardiograph machine for doctors and hospitals in rural communities. Its price and performance soon led to marketing units in Germany and the United States.[48]

Managers configure value chains with an eye to how they will coordinate activities. As did several factors moderate managers' decision on the former, so to with the latter. Specifically, managers coordinate activities mindful of *operational obstacles, core competency,* and *subsidiary networks.*

Factors that influence the coordination of a value-chain include:
- Operational obstacles.
- Core competency.
- Subsidiary networks.

Operational Obstacles   MNEs often struggle to get the links of their global value chain to engage each other. Granted, improving communications systems, made faster by cheaper voice, video, and data options, helps worker coordinate activities. Still, MNEs run into problems because of time zones, differing languages, and ambiguous meanings. Picture a company whose value chain spans the globe. Parts and products flow from Kenya and Chile to their ultimate destination in Malaysia, Germany, Canada, United States, and China. Each transfer, from mines to plants to ships to warehouses to storefronts, creates links that require coordination. Toss into the mix multiple time zones and multiple languages, and the potential for misalignment escalates.

Most MNEs apply browser-based communication tools to coordinate handoffs. Electronic transactions boost efficiency by streamlining exchanges among links in the

Does Geography Matter? Clusters and Configuring Value Chains

Geography shapes how MNEs configure their value chain. Of course, there are the obvious determinants such as where one finds raw materials or productive labor. Increasingly, MNEs configure value chains to tap **cluster effects**. Basically, just as birds of a feather flock together, so too with MNEs in particular industries—e.g., New York City for global finance, Baden-Württemberg for cars and electrical engineering, Dhahran Techno-Valley for energy, Holland for cut flowers, Silicon Valley for technology, Silicon Wadi for wireless telecom, Belluno for eyewear products, and Mumbai and Hollywood for entertainment.

The geographic mechanics of business clusters are straightforward. They emerge as companies in a particular industry group's more and more related value activities in a specific location. That is, competing, complementary, and interdependent firms and industries that do business with each other and share overlapping needs for talent, technology, and infrastructure increasingly operate in the same location. So, visiting any of the 800-plus clusters in the world finds companies in the same industry whose clustering has attracted related vendors, service providers, investors, analysts, skilled workers, trade association members, and consultants.[47]

The firms that comprise a cluster may be direct competitors or alliance partners. Typically, they purchase inputs from and rely on services provided by others in the cluster. Clustering related businesses and organizations in common locations creates systems with interdependent microeconomic capabilities that support collaboration. Too, clustering intensifies competition. Clustering also creates unique location economics that let's MNEs optimize the coordination of value chains.

Arguably, the key driver of business clusters is their reinforcing dynamic: As buyers and sellers of a product cluster Together, they induce others to relocate there as well. The expanding congregation creates a critical mass of companies, rivals, suppliers, and buyers. Their collective efforts improve the cluster's performance, thereby attracting more firms and repowering the cycle.

Countries actively promote clusters, hoping to influence MNEs' value-chain configurations. For instance, the Taiwanese government developed Hsinchu Science and Industrial Park, outside Taipei, into a high-tech cluster. Today, it is the hub of Taiwan's IT industry, home to about 400 high-tech companies who make more than 50 percent of all chips, nearly 70 percent of computer displays, and more than 90 percent of all portable computers used in the world. ●

---

chain. In larger markets, this interface is prevalent among manufacturers and their first-tier suppliers, such as the relationship between Costco and Procter & Gamble. Many MNEs set the open-source language protocol of the Internet—specifically, hypertext markup language (HTML) or XML—as the global standard. So far, though, there is slight consensus on interface standards, as evidenced in the proliferation of web service composition standards.[49] However, the increasing simplicity, generality, and usability of information exchange over the Internet spurs global standards.

Core Competency   The competitive imperative of necessity of leveraging core competencies throughout the value chain intensifies the importance of skillfully coordinating activities.[50] Like beauty, the idea of a core competency defies precise specification—it is an almost ethereal concept that many see as the basis of an MNE's distinctive success. Popular examples of core competencies include Apple's eye for design, Walmart's sophisticated information-management and product-distribution systems, Tata's legacy of product innovation, Honda's understanding of engine technology, and Nestlé's marketing finesse. Against this profile, a **core competency** is the special outlook, skill, capability, or technology that runs through the firm's operations, threading disconnected activities into an integrated value chain.[51]

An MNE's core competency gives everyone a principle that helps them coordinate transactions among value activities. Framing exchanges in the context of an MNE's core competency help managers see particular activities not as ends unto themselves but as

A core competency can emerge from various activities, including

- Product development.
- Employee productivity.
- Manufacturing expertise.
- Marketing imagination.
- Executive leadership.

parts of the larger, integrated scheme of creating value. Google, for instance, has configured its value chain to make information universally accessible; coordinating these activities follows Google's core competency in organizing the world's information. Put differently, Google's capability of associating its various activities, assets, costs, and revenues with its core competency helps its managers better coordinate its value chain.

Subsidiary Networks   Globalization and technology trends have built a world marked by real-time connectivity with anyone, anywhere. The Internet, some argue, is the most powerful force for globalization, democratization, economic growth, and education in history.[52] MNEs respond in kind, expanding operations to connect the poorest two billion people to the nervous system of civilization. Commensurately, the number of MNEs has grown from 30,000 in 1990 to more than 70,000 in 2010; these 70,000 operated approximately 900,000 subsidiaries worldwide. Hence, the average MNE has a subsidiary network of about 13 units, with a range of a few to a few hundred.[53] Growing connectivity among growing numbers of MNEs with expanding subsidiary networks influences how managers coordinate value activities.

Managers are keen to use their subsidiary networks to support efficient transactions and fortify core competencies. The advent of social networks, like LinkedIn, Orkut, or Facebook increasingly influences how managers achieve these goals.[54] Rather than transactions based on traditional business directives, social networking shows that information flows more efficiently in a collaborative, peer-to-peer format. Workers are more inclined to communicate and collaborate while simultaneously contributing and participating in coordinating the value chain.

Case Review Note

For example, in the case of Zara, interactions between store managers around the world and designers stationed in Spain helps localize what otherwise would be standardized global products. Retail input on particular colors or fabrics that sell better in certain locales versus others makes for easy product adaptations. Absent the real-time coordination between the field and headquarters, these adaptations would not take place.

Change and the Value Chain

Once configured, executives resist seeing the value chain set in stone. Product features and functions, as we see in computers, financial services, apparel, entertainment, and cell phones, continually change. Consequently, the basis of value creation in an industry evolves. Certainly, some firms, like Zara and Google, appear distinctively able to anticipate market situations and then keenly adapt activities. Far more common are those who struggle.

In the United States, for instance, the average time a company spends in the S&P 500 index, essentially the 500 premier public companies the United States, has declined from 75 years in the 1930s to about 15 years today. Up to 90 percent of start-ups fail shortly after being founded, venture-capital firms see more than 80 percent of their investments fail, more than 80 percent of equity mutual funds consistently underperform the S&P 500, and more than 75 percent of mergers and acquisitions never payoff.[56] Change and the value chain, therefore, alert managers that sometimes, rather than maximizing success, the task is sustaining the enterprise.

A CASE IN POINT

In 1997, Sony Corporation, Japan's premier electronics giant, took slight notice of the Samsung Electronics Company, a South Korean television maker then snared in a life-or-death struggle to survive the Asian currency crisis. A decade later, Samsung had nearly twice the market capitalization of Sony and commanded the role Sony had once claimed: the competitor with a portfolio of trend-setting products, world-class manufacturing, and premium brand appeal.

A back-of-the-store brand with bulky, low-quality televisions in 1997, Samsung powered its rise by radically rethinking its value chain. In terms of R&D, Samsung has been one of the world's "top 10" in U.S. patents for several years, relying on more than 13,000 researchers to invent tomorrow's products. Its quest to become "world's best" drives its massive capital spending in plants that make components for its many products, like memory chips and display panels, at some of the lowest costs in the world. Similarly, it has annually invested billions of dollars in advertising to burnish its image. By 2005, the change was complete. For the first time, Samsung's brand value exceeded that of Sony. It has since maintained this lead; by 2010, Samsung ranked 68th whereas Sony ranked 94th in the world for brand value.[57]

Interesting in its own right, the Sony–Samsung contest spotlights an intrinsic risk of strategy. The strategy literature holds that a decisive sense of purpose anchors short-term competitiveness and long-term sustainability. However, this outlook can also stifle creativity and erode the effectiveness of decision making.[58] As Samsung encroached on Sony's territory, Sony did not rest on its laurels. Its management improved products, served customers, anticipated new markets, and invested billions to improve its value chain. However, it saw little gain in market share and profits. Growing anxiety about its fading competitiveness led to shock therapy—it took the unprecedented step, for a major Japanese MNE, of naming an American as its chairperson.[59] It again reconfigured its value chain, reorganizing product and market divisions and invested in promising ventures. Ultimately, though, these efforts fell short of management's vision and problems persist. Sony reported fourth-quarter net income in 2010 of $885.6 million. Meanwhile Samsung reported profits of $3 billion.[60]

The upshot is that no matter how sensitive an MNE's strategic compass, executives' cognitive limitations, along with marketplace uncertainty, can turn a superbly configured and coordinated value chain into a liability.[61] Faced with such adversity, managers often return to basics, retry tired methods, and persuade themselves that "doing the same things, but better" will prevail. Compounding these limitations is large-scale change in the environment, whether owing to industry disruptions, or, as we see in our Point/Counterpoint feature, adjusting the value creation tools of the twentieth century to the opportunities and challenges of the twenty-first.

> Designing and delivering a strategy is an ongoing challenge. While some succeed, others fall short.

Point | **Building a Better Value Chain: Real or Virtual?**

Point Analysts conceived the value chain in the 1960s and 1970s to chart the step-by-step development strategy for mineral-exporting economies in developing countries—in essence, mapping an integrated system of production where none existed. It was then adopted in French planning literature as a *filière* (literally, a "thread") to describe the need for French industrial capability to build a competitive economic infrastructure based on a fully specified strategic framework. According to this reasoning, the idea of *filière*, or what we now call "core competency," argues that the full chain of activities that go into a product should take place within national boundaries. A country intent on developing capabilities in say, TVs, would set industry policies to create the infrastructure needed to develop expertise in display technology, to support circuit board design and manufacturing, and to enable design and production of electronic components and metal- and plastic-forming technologies. Specifying the optimal *filière*, the thinking

was, gave governments and companies a holistic view of developing the location economics to optimally configure and coordinate value chains.

A Foundation Tool Value chain analysis has since become a widespread management tool. It frames the evaluation of an MNE's strengths and weaknesses and interprets the determinants of its internal cost structure. It represents its core competency, emphasizing activities that support a cost leadership or differentiation strategy. In the case of cost leadership, it spurs management to understand costs and identify the potential for streamlining value activities. In the case of differentiation, it emphasizes activities that support out-innovating competitors on features for which customers willingly pay a premium. It links a rival's competencies to its marketplace strategy. Finally, it guides assessing industry structure. Value-chain analysis, in summary, helps managers leverage core competencies, set configuration and coordination policies, and stress-test scenarios against industry structure. This discipline boosts the effectiveness of strategic analysis in MNEs.

The Discipline of Boundaries The value chain, however, imposes analytical boundaries. It obliges managers to follow the model's template in data collection and interpretation. This template is defined by the activities, functions, and business processes that move a product through its design, production, marketing, and distribution stages. It imposes an analytical discipline that stipulates how managers assess markets. Acceptable for similar markets (say, the United States to Canada), this perspective struggles to adjust the analytics for markets that diverge (say, the United States to China).

In theory, anchoring analysis in terms of the orderly progression of value-chain activities lets managers formulate optimal strategies. Still, as with any systematic model, the template can reject data that fit poorly, distort the interpretation of disruptions, and misdirect strategic responses—as seen in MNEs struggling to improve performance.

Reality Trumps Virtuality What then of this notion, raised in the counterpoint, that virtuality trumps reality? Despite its limits, the traditionally defined value chain is best suited to deal with the realities of international operations. Expanding into familiar markets or heading to distant and different territories share commonalities that the value chain has proven it can manage. Granted, the idea of virtual companies operating in cyberspace, free of physical constraints, may come to pass. Too, we agree that the counterpoint does offer interesting points. However, the false promise of networked cyberspace ultimately mismaps global operations.

MNEs must not confuse hard analysis with wild conjecture. Unchecked, the dazzle of virtuality may lead some to underestimate the difficulties of configuring and coordinating value activities. Ultimately, international business takes place in the real world marked by real geographic borders, regulated by real national governments, and populated by real companies running real value chains. Good MNEs move toward great when their value chains reflects this reality.

Building a Better Value Chain: Real or Virtual?

Counterpoint

Counterpoint

The value chain has a beguiling yet flawed assumption: that management is a science with immutable laws that predictably configure and coordinate activities. In disruptive times, the static, sequential depiction of classic business functions no longer transcends time and place. The dynamism of the global marketplace signals the necessity of a different perspective that helps managers adapt their "committed to excellence framework." As reality gives way to virtuality in more facets of our lives, courtesy of the Internet and its many offshoots, so too must traditional principles of the value chain give way to emergent practices.

The Intersection Already, companies in agrochemical, business services, biotech, social networking, information, entertainment, and furniture industries see the intersection of Internet perspectives and management practices heralding the advent of the virtual value chain. MNEs in emerging markets are reinventing systems of production and distribution and experimenting with entirely new business models that move beyond the conventional formats found in Western MNEs. Products and processes once locked into traditional value chains evolve in unprecedented ways. The global financial crisis has ratcheted up the pressure on firms to accept this inevitability. Tough times require rethinking traditional cost cutting. Rebooting a company requires taking a hard look at business economics.

Virtuality Trumps Reality Insightful analysis, we argue, calls for abandoning reality for virtuality. Principles of virtuality

tap into the Internet's capacity to support new architectures that challenge the Industrial-Age view of the value chain as sequential steps organized by classic business functions. Managers must abandon static, internally focused "chains" commanded and controlled by analytically detached executives. Instead, the task is configuring activities as dynamic networks that apply principles of agent-based models. Such virtual value networks, as seen at Alibaba, Li & Fung, eBay, Facebook, and Cisco form open, interconnected systems that support dynamic configurations. By trumping the rigidities of conventional value chains, dynamic configurations support astute coordination methods.

Collecting and coordinating information flows among the members of an organization is the heart of virtuality. Leveraging ideas and insights lets companies generate new products to serve new markets, much the same way Google has evolved from a single-product search engine to a diversified information-management and media company that liberates information in whatever form it takes. Virtuality also pioneers paths for value creation, allowing managers to capture lower search, coordination, contracting, and collaboration costs. Streamlining information flows supports new methods of coordinating value activities, a competency that then supports new methods of configuring value activities.

Do What You Do Best Virtuality has provocative implications for how managers decide what to do and where to do it. Nike has limited production facilities; Reebok owns no plants. Many of Nike products, for example, are never touched by an employee, but built by a contract manufacturer, inspected remotely, and then shipped directly to the retailer or end customer. Nike, as do Apple, Cisco, and Qualcomm, outsource production to manufacturers in low-cost labor countries in order to do what each does best, maximizing value creation through research, development, and marketing. Although nominally independent, extensive coordination systems integrate agents into the network, thereby creating virtual production capabilities. Nike, for example, focuses efforts on increasing value creation by leveraging its core competencies in design and marketing, confident in manufacturers' expertise to change product mixes as consumer preferences evolve.

Granted, it is easy to overhype the virtues of virtuality. Prudent management acknowledges that the relative importance of a real versus virtual value chain depends on product features as well as dealing with the imperatives imposed by industry structure. As such, the potential of virtuality has transformational implications for Google's global expansion of its geography-free network but middling implications for Nestlé physical situations in different geographies. Therefore, while virtuality may be far-fetched for some MNEs, it is future defining for others. In any case, just asking the question "real or virtual?" sparks useful debate that improves configuration and coordination choices.

Global Integration versus Local Responsiveness

MNEs face asymmetric forces: pressures for **global integration** versus those for **local responsiveness.** This asymmetry puts contradictory demands on how managers configure and coordinate value chains. For instance, should an MNE concentrate activities or disperse them? Should it standardize value activities to simplify coordination or customize coordination to deal with particular market circumstances? Research suggests straightforward relationships: The higher the pressure for global integration, the greater the need to concentrate configuration and standardize coordination. Conversely, the higher the pressure for local responsiveness, the greater the need to disperse configuration and adapt coordination. Few companies operate in an industry where one perspective dominates. Rather, the common scenario is an industry where managers must reconcile competing imperatives.

> Global integration is the process of combining differentiated parts into a standardized whole. Local responsiveness is the process of disaggregating a standardized whole into differentiated parts.

PRESSURES FOR GLOBAL INTEGRATION

Global markets produce and consume more than 20 percent of world output and are projected to approach 80 percent by 2025. Similarly, more cross-national economic integration will take place in the next 30 years than occurred in the previous 10,000. Again, think of the agents promoting globalization: from 30,000 MNEs in 1990 to more than 70,000 today, operating 900,000 subsidiaries spread worldwide. Managers, companies, and industries react accordingly, as seen in the ongoing formation of global markets in chemicals, credit cards, financial services, accounting, food, healthcare, mass media, forest products, information technology, automobiles, telecommunications, and so on. Moreover, emerging economies intensify these processes. The United Nations estimates there are approximately 22,000 multinationals based in the emerging world; few of these existed 10 years ago. Earlier chapters identified many contributing factors. Here, we highlight two drivers of global integration, the *globalization of markets* and the *efficiency gains of standardization*.

> The convergence of national markets, standardization of business processes, and drives to maximize efficiency push MNEs to integrate activities.

Globalization of Markets   Global buying patterns indicate that consumers worldwide seek global products such as Apple iPhones, Starbucks lattes, Samsung LED screens, Huawei routers, Nokia cell phones, Caterpillar bulldozers, or Zara blouses.[62] Effectively, consumer behavior transcends geography, moving national markets to a global standard. Two conditions—one demand-pull, the other supply-push—drive this trend.

The intrinsic functions of money power demand-pull conditions. No matter the society, money exhibits three inalienable features: It is hard to acquire (one typically must work for it), difficult to save (on average, people spend more than they make), and scarce in supply (no matter how much one has, it often seems never enough). These functions push consumers worldwide to maximize their purchasing power by buying

> Money has three inalienable features:
> - Difficult to acquire.
> - Difficult to save.
> - Scarcity.

Source: Eric Fahrner/Shutterstock.com

Source: pcruciatti/Shutterstock.com

Different Dimensions, Similar Dynamics
Shoppers' quest to find the highest quality product for the lowest cost prevails from street markets in Tunisia to high-end retailers in Shanghai. The simple quest of discovering a deal powers the globalization of markets.

the highest-quality product for the lowest-possible price. Ultimately, goes this reasoning, economically rational consumers care little about the product's origin as long as it delivers superior value.

Assorted technologies standardize consumer preferences across countries. Improving communications promote and transportation logistics distribute standardized products worldwide. Shrinking the digital divide exposes more people to common media. Similarly, the expanding logistics network of globalization, designed by institutions, sanctioned by governments, and driven by companies, makes the same products available everywhere. The quest to maximize individual purchasing power, coupled with the growing exposure and access to higher-quality goods at lower prices, spurs the globalization of markets. In response, many MNE configure value chains to maximize standardization in the quest for global integration.

Our opening case chronicles one company's response to these imperatives. Zara realized that offering standardized fashion styles at reasonable prices neutralized stubborn local preferences. Its global network, supported by state-of-the-art logistics, gave customers worldwide real-time access to the newest, coolest fashion trends. Global markets let Zara leverage its global scale investment in design, manufacturing, distribution, and retail activities. The resulting efficiencies, in turn, supported making high-quality, low-cost products that, by offering compelling value, repowered the cycle. Similar circumstances in high-tech and high-touch products—seen most dramatically in worldwide releases of new goods and services—highlight the connection of global integration and value creation.

Standardization and Efficiency   Globalization, notes some, is the "process by which the experience of everyday life is becoming standardized around the world."[63] So put, it indicates that the handmaiden of globalization is standardization. It drives companies to produce low-cost, high-quality products that differ little, if any, in features and functionality but that appeal to consumers worldwide. Its logic is straightforward. Repeatedly doing the same task the same way, by capturing location, scale, and learning effects, translates efficiencies into lower prices without sacrificing quality standards. Standardization drives efficiency of effort, which, in turn, supports aggressive product development, lower-cost production, and lower retail prices.

For example, the MNE that standardizes the machinery used in the production stage of its value chain often negotiates quantity discounts on material purchases, streamlines materials management, and accelerates distribution logistics. It also realizes efficiencies in value activities such as R&D (leveraging a common design platform) and advertising (communicating a universal message). Therefore, an MNE mass-producing at optimal locations applies standardization to make higher-quality, lower-cost products.

Inevitably, this cause-effect link accelerates globalization, persuading more consumers to buy foreign-made products rather than the local substitutes given the former's higher quality and lower price. Whereas market globalization is the pull dynamic that unites consumer preferences, scale economies power the push dynamic that compels the mass production and mass distribution of standardized products.

Indisputably, MNEs prefer a seamless operating environment that enables the straightforward transfer of standardized practices, products, and processes. Globalization, taken to the ultimate degree, makes for a predictable, consistent market that enables absolute standardization. Several trends reinforce this scenario. Virtually every country in the world is a member of, or waiting to join, the WTO; membership requires replacing differentiated national regulations with global standards. Standardizing the rules of the globalization game, so to speak, supports standardizing the methods of play. Liberalizing trade permits configuring value activities in optimal locations without forsaking access to markets worldwide. Hence, business-process outsourcing firms in India, solar-panel makers in China, or chip designers in Taiwan can design value chains that maximize standardization without sacrificing access to consumers in other countries.

PRESSURES FOR LOCAL RESPONSIVENESS

Cultures, politics, laws, and economics differ across countries. Besides influencing the general business environment, they shape the product standards, financial regulations, distribution channels, and human resources, among others, that influence location economics. Consequently, MNEs face a diverse patchwork of principles and practices as they operate from country to country. Throw into the mix the variability of agents, rivals, and consumers and MNEs must adapt operations to particular conditions in particular

Technology, by shrinking the globe, powers the globalization of markets.

Case Review Note

Concept Check

Movements in national markets toward regional trade agreements along with the globalization of capital markets support the standardization of products and processes. Increasing standardization supports configuring concentrated value chains.

Standardization drives efficiency of effort, which, in turn, supports lower retail prices.

countries. Given that each adaptation requires reducing standardization, MNEs prefer deemphasizing local responsiveness. Pressure points, notably *consumer divergence* and *host-government policies*, limit the degree they do so.

Consumer Divergence

Contrary to the globalization of markets thesis, others argue that stubborn divergences in consumer preferences across countries necessitate locally responsive value chains. Certainly, money and technology standardize consumption, encouraging consumer behavior that emphasizes purchasing power over brand preferences or national allegiance. Nevertheless, differences in local consumers' preferences endure due to cultural predisposition, historical legacy, and latent nationalism (i.e., buy-local campaigns).[64] Consumers often prefer products that are sensitive to their distinctive, everyday idiosyncrasies. Often, they are willing to pay a premium for them. Thus, cross-national divergence presses MNEs to adapt value activities to local consumers' needs and wants.

Adapting to local preferences compels MNEs to sacrifice degrees of standardization. This response requires fine-tuning value chain configurations. Examples include designing and making products that local customers prefer (e.g., large cars in the United States, smaller cars in Europe, still smaller cars in emerging markets), tailoring channel structures to buyer preferences (e.g., Web-based and 4G-driven content in the United States, print and media promotion in France, personal selling in Brazil), and adapting marketing practices to consumption patterns (e.g., large package sizes in Australia, smaller sizes in Japan, single-unit sizes in poorer countries).

In some industries, local responsiveness is simply good business sense. For example, Nestlé has slight incentive to standardize many activities across countries. Local habits, cultural traditions, and social norms shape the standards of preferred, palatable food. Furthermore, food inputs are generally commodities, production has limited potential for scale economies, widespread distribution faces high costs given low value-to-weight ratios, and marketing is best done locally given differentiated tastes, competitors, and retail channels. Certainly, Nestlé can standardize some value activities such as brand names, as it does with Nestea or Perrier. Ultimately, though, many activities of Nestlé's value chain are intrinsically unsuitable for global standardization.

Host-Government Policies

A theme of our text is the variability of political, legal, cultural, and economic environments. The source of many variations is the policies, or the lack thereof, instituted by host-country governments. Prior to the global financial crisis, MNEs had steadily confronted fewer differences as free market principles shaped politics in more countries. Market fundamentalism encouraged countries to adopt freer trade, more privatization, and less regulation. Now, skepticism of capitalism spurs governments to tighten the rules of the game. Aggravating matters for MNEs is the fact that different countries have taken different paths to reset fiscal, monetary, and business regulations. Collectively, these trends push many MNEs to localize value activities.

A Case in Point   The pharmaceutical industry likely foreshadows this scenario. In theory, industry conditions in pharmaceuticals calls for hard economics to drive value chain configuration. Competitiveness hinges on achieving the cost advantages of global integration where and when possible. Many companies, for example, sell low-margin, standardized products such as aspirin; profitability demands efficient production. Alternatively, companies offering branded, proprietary products incur steep R&D costs; profitability demand selling to a global market.

Local responsiveness pressures, therefore, require the pharmaceutical MNE to trade efficiency for market access. Despite the lower efficiencies of a dispersed value chain, drug companies manufacture their products in several locations that are distributed among their key markets. Moreover, the criterion for "key" is not simply favorable

---

Differences in local consumers' preferences endure due to cultural predisposition, historical legacy, and endemic nationalism.

The great financial crisis spurred governments to make MNEs locally responsive.

location economics. Rather, MNEs disperse activities to meet government mandates regarding clinical testing, registration procedures, pricing restrictions, and marketing regulations.

Arguably, an enterprising pharmaceutical firm could reject industry practices, as Zara did in apparel, and concentrate its value chain to exploit location economics. Public regulation of the healthcare industry largely nullifies this option. Besides funding big chunks of the healthcare budget, governments regulate its delivery. Qualifying companies must show sensitivity to the national healthcare system, standards of care for citizens, and local stakeholders. Antagonizing political officials by deemphasizing local responsiveness is hazardous.

Concept Check

The unfolding consequences of the global financial crisis hit many facets of the business environment. Growing state intervention into the market reduces the freedom companies have to pursue the efficiencies of global integration. It also creates benefits for those who improve their responsiveness to national conditions.

A few years ago, the sweep of free markets and market fundamentalism meant fewer and fewer industries fell into this situation. The global financial crisis suggests that in a few years more and more will. Banks, energy providers, media, miners, insurance carriers, healthcare management, carmakers, and airlines, to name the most obvious, increasingly fall under the policy purview of national governments. Meeting growing demands for transparency will push MNEs to improve the local responsiveness of their value chains. Those that protest will likely face stern rebuke. Host governments have forceful tools to prod MNEs to adapt activities. Policies include protectionism to encourage local production, regulations to constrain market moves, or, ultimately, command to divest and depart.

WHEN PRESSURES INTERACT

No global industry exists in which complete standardization or full adaptation is an option. Rather, industries from commodities, such as oil, to high-tech, such as avionics, must deal with the interaction of global integration and local responsiveness pressures. The **Integration-Responsiveness (IR) grid** profiles industries in terms of this interaction, placing each in the quadrant that represents their sensitivity to each pressure (see Figure 11.5.)

The IR Grid relates the global and local pressures that influence and MNE's strategy.

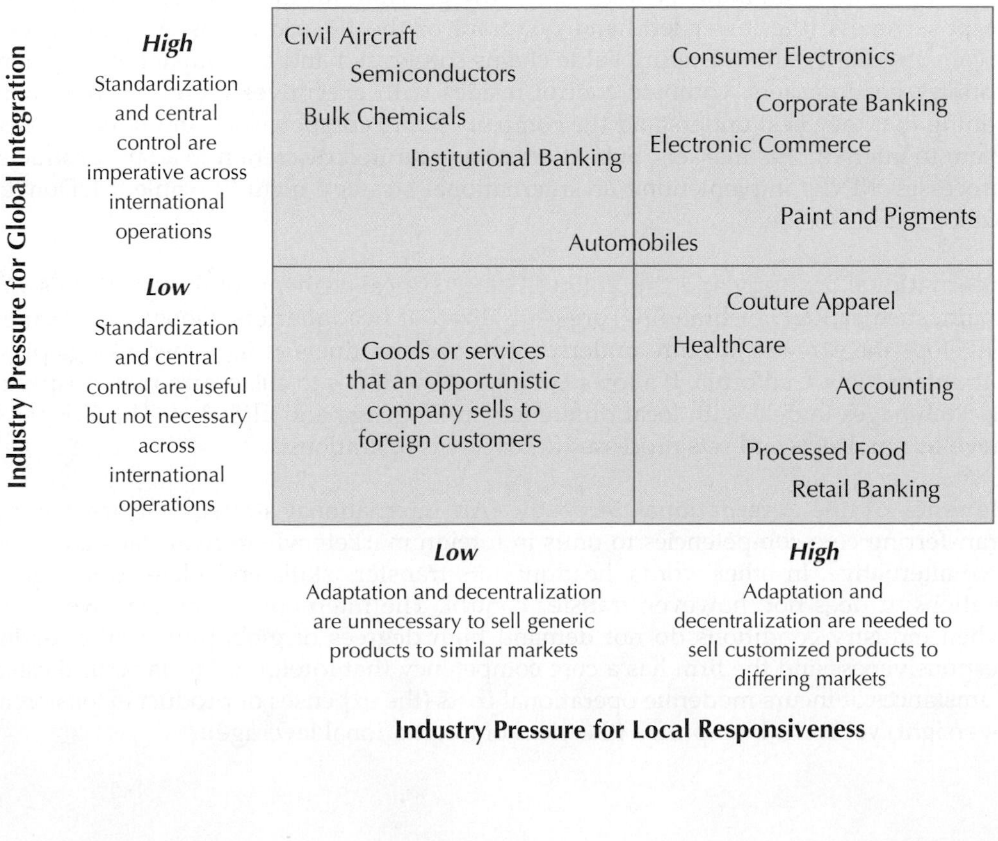
Industry Pressure for Global Integration
High
Standardization and central control are imperative across international operations
Low
Standardization and central control are useful but not necessary across international operations
Civil Aircraft
Semiconductors
Bulk Chemicals
Institutional Banking
Automobiles
Consumer Electronics
Corporate Banking
Electronic Commerce
Paint and Pigments
Goods or services that an opportunistic company sells to foreign customers
Couture Apparel
Healthcare
Accounting
Processed Food
Retail Banking
Low
Adaptation and decentralization are unnecessary to sell generic products to similar markets
High
Adaptation and decentralization are needed to sell customized products to differing markets
Industry Pressure for Local Responsiveness

FIGURE 11.5 The Integration-Responsiveness Grid: By Industry

Each type of strategy embodies a unique concept of value creation that reflects its resolution of the asymmetric pressure for global integration versus local responsiveness. The IR grid helps explain this response, highlighting the interaction between each pressure within a particular industry. As such, it helps managers map their strategy to reconcile the competing calls for standardization and adaptation.

The IR grid indicates that strong pressures for local responsiveness but low pressures to integrate globally encourage adapting value activities to host country conditions. In this scenario, MNEs like Procter & Gamble, Shiseido, or Unilever see few benefits from global integration but high returns from local responsiveness. Alternatively, high pressure to integrate globally along with slight pressure for local responsiveness encourages standardization. Thus, firms like Intel, Huawei, or ArcelorMittal meet cost and competitive pressures by concentrating value activities. Finally, a third class includes MNEs in industries such as telecommunications, information technology, automobiles, pharmaceuticals, and financial services.

These industries fall in the center zone of the IR grid, thereby indicating they deal with strong pressures for global integration while simultaneously facing powerful demands for local responsiveness. Configuring and coordinating value activities to resolve this dilemma pose enduring challenges. This situation, for companies like McKinsey, Citibank, Panasonic, or Infosys, requires more complex configuration formats and coordination systems.

In summary, the IR grid helps managers map strategy given prevailing pressures for standardization and adaptation in their particular industry.[65] In so doing, it helps us understand how industry structure sets the context, company strategy specifies the end, and the value chain defines the means.

Types of Strategy

The IR grid helps managers map strategy. Recurring patterns in the marketplace identify generic strategies among MNEs, namely the *international, multidomestic, global,* or *transnational strategies*. We now profile each type, emphasizing its implications to configuring and coordinating value chains. Table 11.3 summarizes these discussions.

INTERNATIONAL STRATEGY

Companies adopt an **international strategy** when they leverage core competencies internationally in an industry marked by low pressure for global integration and local responsiveness (the lower left-hand quadrant of the IR grid). This strategy relies on local subsidiaries administering value chains configured and coordinated by the home-country headquarters. Ultimate control resides with executives there, given their reasoning that they best understand the company's core competencies and how to transfer them to international markets. Subsidiaries have limited discretion to adapt products or processes. MNEs implementing an international strategy include Apple, McDonald's, Kellogg, and Google.

International Strategy and the Value Chain   Critical elements of the company's value chain, such as R&D or branding, are centralized at headquarters. Google, for example, develops the core architecture underlying its Web products at its famed Googleplex in Mountain View, California. It allows national subsidiaries to customize minor aspects of its Web pages to deal with local differences in language and alphabet. The Googleplex develops products and sets processes for overseas operations.

> The international strategy leverages a company's core competencies into foreign markets.

Benefits of the International Strategy   An international strategy creates value by transferring core competencies to units in foreign markets where rivals lack a competitive alternative. In other words, headquarters transfers skills and ideas to foreign operations; it does not, however, transfer control. The international strategy works well when industry conditions do not demand high degrees of global integration or local responsiveness and the firm has a core competency that foreign rivals lack. In these circumstances, it incurs moderate operational costs (the expenses of product extension and oversight) yet earns high profits (the yield of international leverage).

TABLE 11.3 Characteristics of the Strategy Types Used by MNEs

What factors enter into a firm's decisions about dealing the pressures spurring integration versus responsiveness? Managers, mindful of industry structure and drivers of value creation, trade-offs the characteristics of the four strategy archetypes in making their choice. This table summarizes key points of concern and comparison.

	International	**Multidomestic**	**Global**	**Transnational**
Orientation	Leverage core competencies and home country innovations into competitive positions abroad.	Differentiate products to respond to national differences in customer preferences, industry characteristics, or government regulation.	Target universal needs or wants that support selling standardized products worldwide. Emphasize volume, cost minimization, and efficiency.	Simultaneously manage the tensions of global integration and local differentiation in ways that leverage specialized knowledge and promote worldwide learning.
Value Chain Configuration	Concentrated; Value activities are centralized in the parent company.	Dispersed; Subsidiaries command discretion to adapt value activities to local conditions.	Concentrated; Value chain configuration exploits location economics.	Centralized production of major components given location economies and scale effects. Dispersed assembly and adaptation to local preferences.
Value Chain Coordination	Centralized coordination processes as parent retains control of value activities to apply, regulate, and protect core competencies.	Subsidiaries operate quasi-independently. Autonomy lets them adapt activity to local marketplace circumstances.	Industry pressures to maximize standardization and contain costs require coordinating value activities operations from a global perspective.	Resources are partly centralized and partly decentralized given simultaneous integration and responsiveness pressures. Coordination mechanisms support centralizing, either at headquarters or subsidiaries, value activities.
Key Advantage	Facilitates the transfer of skills and know-how from the parent company to international units.	Reduced need for central support to manage local activities. Greater sensitivity to local preferences.	Configures and coordinates value activities to make low-cost, high-quality products that differ little, but appeal to consumers worldwide.	Supports efficiency, compels effectiveness, and leverages learning that drive innovations to serve global and local markets.
Key Disadvantage	Centralizing the value chain in the home country often weakens configuration efficiency and coordination flexibility.	Encourages the "mini-me" phenomenon that results in management, design, production, and marketing activities inefficiently replicated from subsidiary to subsidiary.	Reduced learning opportunities given the dominance of global standard. Requires increased coordination to regulate global matrix of inputs and outputs.	Requires elaborate mechanisms to integrate dispersed operations. Difficult to configure, tough to coordinate, and prone to performance shortfalls.
IR Grid Positioning	Pressure for global integration: low. Pressure for national responsiveness: low.	Pressure for global integration: low. Pressure for national responsiveness: high.	Pressure for global integration: high. Pressure for national responsiveness: low.	Pressure for global integration: high Pressure for national responsiveness: high.
Examples	Kraft, Google, P&G, Nucor, Harley Davidson, Baidu, Apple, Carrefour, Infosys	Unilever, Nestle, Heinz, The Body Shop, McDonald's, Johnson & Johnson, Pfizer	Toyota, Canon, Haier, Texas Instruments, Caterpillar, Otis Elevator, Wal-Mart, and Huawei, Haier, LVMH, American Express, Nokia, Cisco	GE, Tata, Zara, IBM

Limitations of the International Strategy Headquarters' one-way view from the home office to the rest of the world may misread foreign markets. Leveraging the firm's core competency, as best understood by home-office executives, discourages local adaptation. The testing ground of new ideas, goes such thinking, is the home market, not foreign countries. This orientation proves successful as long as foreign rivals scramble futilely. Still, the odds are that one will find a way to compete. Unless aware, an unexpectedly innovative rival may disrupt industry structure. Google, for example, faces

An international strategy fits an MNE that (1) has a core competency that foreign rivals lack and (2) does not face strong demands for global integration or local responsiveness.

increasingly adept local rivals in South Korea and China—Naver and Baidu, respectively—whose native sensitivities to local search tendencies well-position them in fast-growing Asian markets.[66]

MULTIDOMESTIC STRATEGY

The **multidomestic strategy** holds that unique local conditions differentiate national markets, thereby thwarting headquarters' ambition to supervise foreign operations. Granted, headquarters may try to bridge the gap between markets; often it proves too wide. Simply put, the uniqueness of local conditions can create exceptions that exceed home country managers' competencies. So, managers based in Chicago, no matter how smart or motivated, inevitably hit cognitive limits when directing subordinates in markets that demand high degrees of local responsiveness.[67] Persistent signals that local managers command an intuitively better understanding of the local market than those at headquarters endorse a multidomestic strategy. Headquarters then delegates to foreign subsidiaries the authority to adapt value activities to local circumstances.

Johnson & Johnson (J&J) exemplifies this strategy. Philosophically, it reasons that inalienable differences among countries preclude universal direction from one. Company leaders reason it improves corporate performance by allowing its 250 business units worldwide to behave like small, innovative, entrepreneurial firms.[68] Headquarters' role is straightforward—provide world-class products, financial muscle, and marketing skills to support quasi-independent subsidiaries.

> The multidomestic strategy adjusts value activities to local circumstances.

Multidomestic Strategy and the Value Chain   Firms applying a multidomestic strategy maintain that unique conditions make value-chain design the prerogative of the local subsidiary, not a unilateral declaration by the home office. Thus, the managers of, say, a backpack factory in Singapore should decide what sort of backpack they want to make because they understand that their preferred design is more appealing to local customers. Consequently, the size, shape, and style may differ from those made by sister plants in the United States, Mexico, or Ukraine. Similarly, if the host government offers incentives for local manufacturing, the subsidiary can build its own plant; if local consumers prefer dealing directly with salespeople rather than relying on mass media, the subsidiary can build a sales force; if the country changes labor laws, the subsidiary can adjust human resource policies.

Benefits of the Multidomestic Strategy   A multidomestic strategy makes sense when an MNE faces high pressure for local responsiveness and a low need to reduce costs via global integration (the lower right-hand quadrant of the IR grid). This strategy also reduces political risk given the company's local standing, lowers exchange-rate risk given less calls to repatriate funds, improves prestige due to its national prominence, boost growth potential due to it's entrepreneurial zeal, and increases potential for innovative products from local R&D.

Procter & Gamble, for instance, follows a multidomestic strategy. The R&D unit at its Japanese subsidiary, responding to the scant storage space in the typical Japanese home, invented technology that reduced the thickness of an infant's diaper without reducing absorbency. This innovation created value for P&G in Japan and, eventually, P&G worldwide. Similarly, McDonald's began its worldwide pushback against coffee chains with an early test run in Russia. It opened its McCafés there in 2003, fine-tuned its espresso-style drinks, and moved the concept to the United States in 2009.[69] Success stories like these prompt MNEs implementing the multidomestic strategy to disperse their R&D centers around the world.

> The multidomestic strategy, by encouraging replication, often prove unacceptably costly.

Limitations of the Multidomestic Strategy   This strategy encourages replicating value activities from subsidiary to subsidiary. Essentially, the MNE operates "mini-me" units around the world. Customizing value activities to local markets is costly. Different product designs require different materials, production runs are shorter, marketing programs are specialized, distribution uses different channels, and information exchange follows different formats. Hence, the multidomestic strategy is impractical in cost-sensitive situations. Carrefour, for instance, ran into problems in the United States when, to deal with local preferences, it shifted from its successful international strategy to a multidomestic approach. Costly problems ultimately forced Carrefour to close its failing U.S. operations.

The multidomestic MNE often faces coordination complications. Local adaptation promotes management styles and value-chain designs that differ from unit to unit. Lacking sufficient authority, headquarters must resort to persuasion in lieu of command to coordinate activities; the difficulty of this task escalates as the number of subsidiaries rises. Ensuing power struggles blunt the company's competitiveness. For instance, J&J launched Tylenol in 1960 as an over-the-counter pain reliever in the United States. The product was available to worldwide units shortly thereafter. The quasi-independent Japanese unit, despite duress from headquarters, did not begin selling it until 2000.

GLOBAL STRATEGY

The **global strategy** drives worldwide performance by making and selling common products that vary little to none from country to country. Effectively, managers sense high pressures for global integration yet low pressures for local responsiveness—(the upper right-hand quadrant of the IR grid). MNEs in this situation follow absolute production and marketing standards as they battle for cost leadership.

In terms of production, they exploit location economies and capture scale economies, mindful that using resources for anything other than improving efficiency erodes competitiveness. In terms of marketing, the global strategy sells standardized products that require little to no adaptation. Global integration trumps calls for local responsiveness in setting operating parameters.

Although strident, the "China Price" phenomenon profiles the stakes of the global strategy. The China Price refers to situations where Chinese firms make something for significantly less than can be done in Western countries. In the worst cases, it means Chinese rivals sell products for less than the cost of materials in the West.[70] Many Chinese companies apply the China Price approach within the context of the global strategy. Rival MNEs implementing a global strategy must ingeniously configure and coordinate value activities. If not, the alternative is dire.[71]

> A global strategy unequivocally champions worldwide standardization.

For some products, notably **commodities,** the global strategy is essentially the only option. Commodities serve a universal need (think gasoline, steel, aspirin, memory chips, sugar, etc.). Consumer preferences in different countries, if not identical, are highly similar. The fact that consumers choose between essentially identical products (i.e., Company X gasoline versus Company Y gasoline) makes price the point of differentiation. The global strategy, by making and marketing a standardized product, converts global efficiency into price competitiveness.

The global strategy is not restricted to commodity markets. Market globalization encourages companies like Zara in apparel or LVMH in luxury goods to standardize historically differentiated products for the world market, manufacture them on a global scale, and market them through a few focused distribution channels. Unquestionably, cross-national differences in consumer preferences exist. The global strategy, however, presumes that local consumers will, if given the opportunity, buy a high-quality, low-priced product no matter its country of origin. Moreover, if the product offers comparatively higher quality at a lower price than the locally made substitute, consumers will discount nationalism to maximize purchasing power.

> Firms that choose the global strategy face strong pressure for cost reductions but weak pressure for local responsiveness.

Global Strategy and the Value Chain   The efficiency standards of the global strategy have stark imperatives to value chain configuration. Ideally, the MNE is the cost leader. If not, then it must be competitive with its industry's pacesetter. Cost leadership requires building global-scale factories in superior locations that support efficient operations—e.g., a shoe factory in Vietnam, an auto-parts maker in China, a service call center in India. Once configured, headquarters coordinates activities by standardizing practices and processes. Little, if any, strategic authority goes to the local level.

Benefits of the Global Strategy   The global strategy is suited to industries that (1) emphasize efficient operations and (2) where local responsiveness pressures are either nonexistent or can be neutralized by offering a higher-quality product for a lower price than the local substitute (essentially, the upper left-hand quadrant of the IR grid). These conditions prevail in many manufacturing and service industries.

The wireless industry, for example, endorses global standards that fuel demand for standardized products worldwide.[72] Similarly, the credit card industry has standardized electronic payment protocols that support customers using and merchants accepting this form of payment worldwide. In both industries, MNEs act accordingly: Nokia and American Express both pursue a global strategy.

Limitations of the Global Strategy   Standardization gives MNEs little latitude to adapt value activities to local conditions. Often, disruptive innovations turn a fine-tuned value chain into a misfiring machine. The fallout of the global financial crisis saw Citibank, Royal Bank of Scotland, and Fortis, among others, foiled by their global strategies. Despite global leadership in capital markets, the disruptive change of the crisis and ensuing demand for local responsiveness turned many of their strengths into liabilities.

TRANSNATIONAL STRATEGY

The **transnational strategy** holds that today's environment of interconnected consumers, industries, and markets requires an MNE configure a value chain that exploits location economies as well as coordinates value activities in order to leverage core competencies while simultaneously reconciling global and local pressures (the upper right-hand quadrant of the IR grid). Admittedly, a lot of ideas to process at once, it helps to think of the transnational strategy as a compromise between global integration and local responsiveness within a mindset of leveraging the MNE's specialized knowledge wherever and whenever possible.

In practical terms, the transnational strategy spurs an MNE to adapt, subject to minimum efficiency standards, its activities from country to country according to prevailing cultural, political, legal, and economic conditions. But, in a critical break from the multidomestic strategy, the transnational strategy applies coordination methods to diffuse insights gained from unique experiences in one subsidiary throughout its global operations. Diffusing innovations leverages newfound proprietary knowledge, thereby boosting competitiveness.

> The transnational strategy simultaneously reconciles global integration and local responsiveness in ways that leverage the firm's core competency throughout worldwide operations.

Transnational Strategy and the Value Chain   The transnational strategy endorses a sophisticated value chain that simultaneously promotes integration, responsiveness, and learning. It combines the market sensitivity standard of local responsiveness with the efficiency standard of global integration. It champions interactive "global learning," whereby as the MNE learns new ways to leverage its core competencies. It then diffuses these innovations throughout its global operations.

Rather than top-down (headquarters to a foreign subsidiary) or bottom-up (foreign subsidiary to the headquarters) coordination, this strategy promotes knowledge flows from the idea generator to idea adopters, no matter where one or the other resides. The transnational MNE strategy sees its subsidiary network as a competitive advantage—provided it finds ways to encourage workers to communicate and collaborate.

Transnational Strategy: A Case in Point   Can an MNE feasibly implement the transnational strategy? Though difficult, the record of GE indicates yes. In the 1980s, growing threats from low-cost competitors in Asia pushed GE to look to global markets to sell products. Managers reasoned that expanding sales globally would boost scale economies. At the time, CEO Jack Welch declared, "the idea of a company being global is nonsense. Businesses are global, not companies." As such, divisions, no matter where located, were held to a straightforward performance standard: "be either number 1 or 2" in its domestic industry or else face divestment.

In the late 1980s, GE's sense of globalization moved from finding new markets to finding new worldwide sources that supplied higher-quality inputs at lower cost. As integration linked more of its markets, GE redefined its outlook toward globalization, elevating it to a dominant strategic theme. Commensurately, Welch raised the performance standard for a business from its ranking in its domestic to its global industry.

Around this time, Welch articulated his vision of the *boundaryless company,* a term suggestive of the transnational organization. He reasoned that a boundaryless company was an "open, antiparochial environment, friendly toward the seeking and sharing of new ideas, regardless of their origins." Welch explained that the "boundaryless company we envision will remove the barriers among engineering, manufacturing, marketing, sales, and customer service; it will recognize no distinctions between domestic and foreign operations—we'll be as comfortable doing business in Budapest and Seoul as we are in Louisville and Schenectady."[73]

Success stories emerged from GE's value chain: increased efficiency in its appliance business, productivity solutions in lighting, improved transaction effectiveness in GE capital, cost reductions in aircraft engines, and better global account management in plastics. Lessons learned spread to other GE businesses. Indeed, careers ended if managers refused to share ideas with others; as Welch explained, "We take people who aren't boundaryless out of jobs. If you're turf-oriented, self-centered, don't share with people, and aren't searching for ideas, you don't belong here."

Soon thereafter, GE moved to phase three of its globalization evolution. Besides emphasizing global markets and global sources, Welch pushed his managers to "globalize the intellect of the company," seeking the best practices and compelling ideas from anyone, anywhere, then diffusing them throughout GE's global operations.

> The simultaneous goals of the transnational strategy: more efficient global integration, more effective local responsiveness, and more systematic diffusion of innovations.

By 1999, at the end of Welch's tenure, GE was named the most respected company in the world by the *Financial Times,* and Jack Welch was judged the CEO of the twentieth century. His successor, Jeffrey Immelt, has continued these efforts, explaining that success in international business is "truly about people, not about where the buildings are. You've got to develop people so they are prepared for leadership jobs and then promote. That's the most effective way to become more global."[74]

GE's performance speaks to principles of the transnational strategy. It made ideas—constantly tested, enhanced, and exchanged across units spanning the world—the basis of configuring and coordinating the value chain. As managers translated ideas into better designs, production methods, and programs, they made more profitable decisions. Ideas flowed from one unit in one part of the value chain to counterparts in far-flung units elsewhere. As a result, integration happened more efficiently, responsiveness happened more effectively, and innovations spread more systematically.

Benefits of the Transnational Strategy   The learning orientation of the transnational strategy helps balances the competing pressures for global integration versus local responsiveness. The vitality of learning prepares managers to respond to changing environments, reorienting activities without imposing additional bureaucracy. Ultimately, these capabilities permit standardizing some activities to generate the efficiencies required by global integration while also adapting other activities to local circumstances. The transnational MNE finds ways to do so without unduly sacrificing the benefits of standardization for the demands of responsiveness.

> The transnational strategy encourages sophisticated coordination methods to diffuse the lessons learned at one unit with all units.

Which sorts of MNEs, then, aspire to a transnational strategy? Generally, those facing pressures for global integration and local responsiveness yet seeing opportunities to leverage the unique knowledge that permeates their value chain. In the 1990s, this option attracted few companies. The impracticality of prevailing communication systems prevented efficiently diffusing ideas throughout subsidiary networks. Moreover, national differences, although shrinking, were substantial. The turn of the century saw industry conditions (more and more competitive MNEs from more and more countries) and environmental trends (the Internet, ancillary telecom systems, growing connections among countries) support the transnational strategy.

Today, surging calls for restoring MNEs' local responsiveness arguably accelerate the trend toward transnational strategies. Governments' mistrust of MNEs' global agendas and their agency conflicts has prompted aggressive local regulation. Preserving competitiveness in the face of intensifying rivalry requires MNEs configure sophisticated value chains that have the learning capacity to leverage the efficiencies of global integration while answering calls for local responsiveness.

> The transnational strategy, admittedly difficult to specify in theory, is difficult to implement in practice. Limitations arise from complicated agendas, high costs, and cognitive limits.

Limitations of the Transnational Strategy   The transnational strategy is difficult to configure, tough to coordinate, and prone to shortfalls. Reconciling integration and responsiveness pressures, further complicated by the need to manage knowledge worldwide, can overwhelm the best-intentioned MNEs. For every GE, there are ABBs, Philipses, Panasonics, and Acers that struggled to engage it. Furthermore, developing a network mind-set among employees, installing the requisite information systems, and navigating the ambiguity of multicriteria decision making is expensive. Such costs are difficult to justify when slowing economies require streamlining activities.

Looking to the
Future   What's New in the World of Strategy Types?

The strategy gamut of "international-multidomestic-global-transnational" has prevailed for several years in international business theory. Slowing globalization, growing host-country intervention, and fast-growing emerging economies pose a provocative issue: What types of strategies might MNEs follow in the future?

Evolution of the Multinational Corporation

Some see an evolutionary scenario whereby MNEs continue responding systematically to the steadily unfolding standards of globalization. One person with a provocative take on this thesis is Sam Palmisano, the CEO of IBM. Reflecting on IBM's evolution, he contends that the company passed through three strategic phases on its path to a global powerhouse.

First, there was the nineteenth-century "international model, whereby the company was headquartered both physically and mentally in its home country; it sold goods, when it was so inclined, through a scattering of overseas sales offices." IBM focused on its business dealings in its home country. Headquarters configured and coordinated the value chain with no input from overseas units. As such, MNEs implemented international strategies.

Phase two of the evolution ushered in the classic multinational firm of the late twentieth century. This model saw the parent company creating smaller versions of itself abroad. These "satellites" were run by home-nation executives sent from headquarters. They typically commanded technical expertise but little cultural fluency and minimal foreign-language competency. In a sense, the only thing multinational about these executives was their temporary overseas assignment. Steadily, the changing context of global competition eroded the economics of the "mini-me" option. The cost of redundancy—each country essentially operated its own value chain—became unacceptable.

The third phase, the "globally integrated enterprise," is one that puts investments, people, and work anywhere in the world "based on the right cost, the right skills and the right business environment [with] work flow[ing] to the places where it will be done...most efficiently and to the highest quality."[75] Previously, configuration and coordination barriers constrained knowledge flows, production opportunities, and organizational options. Now, like the Internet, the globally integrated enterprise designs its strategy, configures its activities, and coordinates its processes to connect everything, everywhere, 24/7.

The Metanational

A new type of global corporation, the metanational, thrives on seeking unique ideas, activities, and insights that complement its existing operations as well as creating new leverage points. It "builds a new kind of competitive advantage by discovering, accessing, mobilizing, and leveraging knowledge from many locations around the world."[76] Metanationals, goes the theory, conquer international markets by developing value chains with three competencies:

- The ability to prospect for and access untapped technologies and unidentified consumer trends.
- The ability to leverage globally the knowledge scattered throughout local subsidiaries.
- The ability to mobilize fragmented knowledge to generate innovations that produce, market, and deliver value on a global scale.

Some see MNEs like Shiseido and PolyGram as emergent metanationals, able to turn underutilized knowledge into global-dominant innovations.

The Micro-Multinational

The evolutionary frontier for MNEs is a matter of size, say others. Many assume that MNEs must be colossi that straddle the globe. However, the number of MNEs grows worldwide but their average size is falling—many of the 70,000 or so firms that operate internationally employ fewer than 250 people. This anomaly signals the era of so-called micro-multinationals: nimble, small firms that are born global, operating worldwide from day one.[77] Unlike their bigger counterparts that expanded internationally by gradually entering new markets, micro-multinationals go global immediately, entering countries with plentiful customers, productive labor, and attractive industries.

Glorecalization

Some advocate the power of regionalized thinking, expressed the awkward term "Glorecalization," to balance global and local imperatives.[78] Glorecalization champions consistent global values and customized local tactics. However, its calls for organizing the value chain with a bias toward regional environments. Doing so, goes the argument, enables the glorecalized MNE to leverage its regional network to gain necessary efficiencies while retaining the flexibility to adapt locally.

Three conditions support glorecalization. One, regional trade blocs (e.g., AU, ASEAN, CARICOM, EU, NAFTA) create markets with favorable location economics. Two, convenient flows of information, goods, and services enable efficient distribution and streamline trading mechanisms. Three, people within a region share similar outlooks and convergent interests.

The Cybercorp

Finally, there is the cybercorp, a form that was unimaginable a generation ago but plausible today.[79] National boundaries no longer organize consumers, markets, or industries to the cybercorp. Rather, evolving Internet technologies, not the physical geography of lines on a map, defines the boundaries of cyberspace. One example is Facebook, a company that exists physically in its California headquarters but whose workforce of 2,000 run a company that serves some 900 million "customers" in more than 150 nations through a website interface translated into more than 100 languages.

Cybercorps develop competencies that let them react in real time to changes in customers, industry, and environment. They engage perspectives and strategies that bias value chains toward virtuality in order to link competencies within dynamic networks. The cybercorp, built for speed and able to engage strategies that learn, evolve, and transform, will set the standards of the competitive MNE in a world defined by the Singularity Principle.

No Matter the Type ...

All things considered, the next global strategy is more speculation than stipulation. No matter the type that emerges, we expect it will exemplify the historic markers of a great strategy: an innovative value chain run by bright people who articulate insightful visions and practical goals that change the game.

CASE

Value Chains: Where, When, and Why[80]

The diffusion of work, technology, and companies outward from the United States and the West into emerging markets increasingly disrupts long running standards of globalization. MNEs in advanced and emerging markets respond in kind, rethinking their strategies and resetting their value chains to compete in the brave new world. For both cohorts, the improving sophistication of information technology opens new R&D options; keener supply-chain logistics enables dispersing production; and new frontiers open for products (solar cell panels made in Shanghai but sold in Stockholm) as well as previously non-tradable services (X-rays taken in Boston but read in Bangkok). These and similar trends change location economics. As a result, the standards of configuring and coordinating value activities evolve. Together, they spur companies in the wealthier markets as well as counterparts in emerging economies to identify the best way to do so. Let's take a look at current trends.

Advanced Economies: Realization, Adaptation, and Innovation

Many MNEs in advanced markets got hit hard by the global meltdown. In the aftermath, many reoriented their operations to still-growing emerging countries. Looking forward, wage patterns, debt structures, and population demography suggests slow growth is not a short-term problem for the richer countries.[81] In contrast, economic recovery has turbocharged growth in developing countries. Analysts expect nearly 70 percent of the world growth over the next few years to come from emerging markets, with 40 percent coming from China and India.[82] For many MNEs, just being in leading emerging economies, no matter the scale or scope of investment, takes precedence over prudently developing markets toeholds. Others are further along, some motivated by the opportunity, some motivated by the fear that "companies that don't take a vigorous approach to China and India will face threats to their very existence in as little as 10 years' time."[83]

For example, GM is going great guns in China, although it struggles in the United States. In 2009, China overtook the United States as the world's biggest auto market.[84] In 2010, GM's China sales surpassed those in the United States for the first time in the carmaker's 102-year-old history.[85] So, as GM streamlines its value-chain in the United States, it expands it throughout Asia.

More pointedly, consider McDonald's. Russia is its fastest growing market; it had 275 outlets in 2010, up from 128 in 2005. It plans to add hundreds more in the next few years, given the belief that "Russia remains the most dynamic, fastest-growing and profitable market for our system."[86] Successfully getting to 275 outlets required McDonald's to rethink its value chain. In the West, McDonald's buys ingredients from third parties, rather than producing its own. Upon entering Russia, it had to build a proprietary factory outside Moscow called the McComplex, given that there were no private businesses to supply the 300 needed ingredients. The fact that everything—from hamburger patties to fries to buns—was made from scratch at the McComplex required McDonald's rethink how to best configure and coordinate its activities.[87]

Walmart, in collaboration with Bharti Enterprises (one of India's leading business groups with interests in telecom, agri-business, insurance and retail), showcases other angles. Walmart and Bharti Enterprises are unfolding their pan-India strategy of cash-and-carry wholesale warehouses in line with ideas from the Base of the Pyramid. The stores, under the brand name BestPrice Modern Wholesale, are one-stop shops that meet the day-to-day needs of restaurant owners, fruit and vegetable resellers, kiranas, offices, hotels, and institutions. Walmart's retail expertise and supply chain skills configure value activities while Bharti contributes the local leadership needed to coordinate activities.

More dramatically, IBM is making India its center of gravity. IBM India's headcount has grown from a few hundred in 1999 to 110,000 today—or about one in four IBM workers. Symbolizing the growing primacy of its Indian operations was IBM's historic decision to hold its annual Investors Day in 2007 on the grounds of the Bangalore Palace; this event had never before been held outside of the United States. The change made perfect sense given that "India is at the epicenter of the flat world," explained its business development leader for India and China.[88] As IBM resets its axis of value creation, it accelerates as well as disrupts century-long trends in the evolution of its value chain. It is now revolutionizing its value chain to support a "globally integrated enterprise" that puts people, jobs, and investments anywhere in the world "based on the right cost, the right skills, and the right business environment."

Strategically, this means IBM's quest to find new ways to grow foreshadows new value-chain designs that move operations toward uncharted forms of virtuality. Operationally, IBM does state-of-the-art research and development, as well as compiles next-generation software in India, to say nothing of running low-cost call centers in locations that just a decade earlier were far off the global grid. Together, these trends mean that IBM now has more employees in India than in any other country except America. Straight-line projection of current trends shows that IBM will employ more in India than the United States within the next decade. Not surprisingly, some propose renaming IBM—officially International Business Machines—to "India-Beijing Machines."

Other examples amplify how emerging economies reset value chains. In 2005, Cisco combined all of its emerging-markets activities into a single unit—"Cisco East" in Bengaluru. In 2007, Cisco decided that 20 percent of its top talent should be in India within five years. To spearhead change, one of its highest-ranking executives moved to Cisco East with the title of chief globalization officer. Since then, the share of its revenues coming from emerging markets has grown from 8 to more than 20 percent. "We identify the country's most important industries and go to them with a blueprint for a strategy to improve them using our technology to beat global benchmarks; this is about revolutionary, not incremental change," explained the director of Cisco's emerging-markets business.

Emerging Economies: Opportunity, Expansion, and Innovation

It is easy to presume that large, established MNEs go where they wish, make their own rules, and inevitably triumph. Increasingly, though, Western MNEs face enterprising local rivals whose value chain choices strongly position them to disrupt industries throughout the West. Moreover, the global financial crisis accelerates their expansion. Growth in developing countries has slowed, but nowhere to the degree it has in advanced markets. While western rivals regroup in their faltering home markets, emerging giants power forth on the strength of theirs. For example, car sales and car companies have shrunk in the rich world but are growing in many developing countries—some forecast double-digit growth in Brazil, China, and India in 2012.

As competitors and consumers around the world economize, they look for lower costs and fewer features. The emerging giants' low-cost production models—configured given cheap, productive local labor and coordinated through efficient information technologies—bolsters their competitiveness. Furthermore, long-standing bias toward frugal engineering in emerging markets spurs designing value-chains that speak to the Base of the Pyramid. Companies in these markets, anchored in a culture of frugality and extreme resource constraints, are redesigning products to reduce costs up to 90 percent but without unduly sacrificing functionality.

Tata, maker of the Nano, the new "people's car" that sells for around $2,900 or so, did not merely leverage "cheap Indian engineers" or accept lower standards on safety or environmental emissions. Rather, Tata rethought the basic functionality of the car, applied state-of-the-art virtual design technology, made ingenious design breakthroughs, and configured the necessary value chain needed to exploit location economics. MNEs from emerging economies also redesign processes to do business better and faster than their rivals in the West. In addition, many have only recently begun operations, thereby liberating them from the legacy costs that hamper the flexibility of established MNEs.

Still, like their Western counterparts, emerging markets MNEs question how they should configure and coordinate value activities. For example, AirTel, the Indian market leader in mobile telephony, and Safaricom, the market leader in Kenya, charge some of the lowest prices in the world for calls yet still generate high returns. Increasing success spurs these and others to leverage innovations globally. Many emerging markets MNEs are dispersing their activities to fellow emerging markets, betting they will move more effectively between similar economies than trying to jump from developing to developed countries.

Traditionally, Western MNEs preferred to control value chains, taking a measured approach to concentrating some and dispersing others. Now, MNEs reason that going alone unacceptably slows expansion. Bharti Airtel, a global telecommunications company, is targeting fast-growing Africa. Rather than deliberately configure its African value chain, Bharti Airtel hired IBM to supply the computing technology and services needed to upgrade its cell phone network across 16 sub-Saharan countries. Besides coordinating customer service, IBM provides the hardware, software, and services to coordinate activities in billing, call-traffic management, and entertainment services. Both companies see a win-win: Bharti Airtel accelerates value chain configuration and IBM takes a "huge step forward in what we think is the next major emerging growth market."[89]

Desarrolladora Homex, a Mexican builder of low-cost housing, highlights another angle. It configured its value chain, explained its CEO, to serve communities "in highly populated and underserved areas where we believe our replicable business model will be most effective."[90] The company launched a joint venture in India and allied with an Egyptian company to build 50,000 low-cost new homes in Cairo.

Although perhaps obscure to many, MNEs like such as Haier, a Chinese white-goods firm; Asus, a Taiwanese computer manufacturer; Embraer, a Brazilian aircraft maker; CVRD, a Brazilian miner; MISC, a Malaysian shipping company; Infosys, an Indian software giant; Sasol, a South African energy producer; Tenaris, an Argentine steel maker; Cemex, a Mexican cement company; and Ranbaxy, an Indian drug company—steadily expand from local prominence to global distinction.

Going Forward

Unquestionably, as economic crises periodically show, circumstances can change far more than the most optimistic or dire forecasts. Therefore, situations and trends will likely look different in five years' time. Still, current market circumstances and location economics today compel MNEs from around the world to rethink and, more often than not, reset how they configure and coordinate value chains. As the CEO of IBM notes, the forces powering this trend "are irresistible.... The genie's out of the bottle and there's no stopping it."[91] Configuration standards and coordination protocols, always dynamic, will become more so going forward. ■

QUESTIONS

1. What sorts of conditions and motivations best explain how MNEs in the West traditionally develop value chains? Do these same principles apply to decisions made by emerging markets MNEs?

2. Dynamism creates opportunity as well as constraints. Identify the most promising opportunities for companies in advanced markets. Do the same for firms in developing markets. How are they similar? How do they differ?

3. Looking out over the next decade, estimate the likely standards of value creation. How would you advise a company like IBM or Cisco to configure and coordinate its value chain? Would you give the same advice to a company like Tata or Safaricom?

4. Given the option to work for a company in a particular market, would you choose to work for a Western MNE such as IBM, moving into a developing country, such as India? Alternatively, would you prefer to work for a company from an emerging economy, such as Bharti Airtel, moving into a Western market, such as France? Why?

5. What sorts of management skills and executive perspectives do you believe would make you an attractive candidate for a Western company expanding into emerging economies? Would they differ, and if so how, for a company expanding from its home base in an emerging economy into a Western economy?

SUMMARY

- Managers devise strategies to engage international markets in ways that boost the company's profitability and sustain its growth.

- Industry structure influences a company's profitability, especially in situations of perfect competition, less in situations of imperfect competition.

- Bright managers convert innovative strategies into above-average, risk-adjusted profitability, especially in situations of imperfect competition, less in situations of perfect competition.

- Managers anchor analysis of industry structure in the context of the five-forces model and its representation of competitive rivalry, threat of new entrants, substitutes, supplier power, and buyer power.

- Competitive rivalry refers to the moves of rivals battling for market share. Threat of new entrants refers to entry of new rivals seeking market share. A substitute refers to complementary products that give the consumer the option switch to less expensive choices. Supplier power refers to the push by input suppliers to charge more. Buyer power is the push by output buyers to pay less.

- Value measures a firm's ability to sell what it makes for more than the cost incurred to make it.

- MNEs create value through a cost leadership or a differentiation strategy. The former drives a firm to reduce its costs, for a given level of quality, below its competitors. The latter drives it to increase the perceived value of its products relative to that of rivals.

- The value chain lets managers deconstruct the general idea of "create value" into a series of discrete, sequential activities.

- Managers configure value activities to reflect location economics; factors that moderate it include cluster effects, logistics, degree of digitization, economies of scale, and business environments. Importantly, as location economics change, so too do configuration choices.

- Managers coordinate value activities to reflect core competencies, operational obstacles, and subsidiary networks.

- Global integration aims to standardize worldwide activities in order to maximize efficiency whereas national responsiveness adapts local activities in order to optimize effectiveness.

- Drivers of globalization include the integration of national markets and efficiency gains of standardization. Drivers of local-responsiveness include cross-national consumer divergences and host-government intervention.

- The higher the pressure for global integration, the greater the need to concentrate configuration and standardize coordination. Conversely, the higher the pressure for local responsiveness, the greater the need to disperse configuration and adapt coordination.

- The firm entering and competing in foreign markets can adopt an international, multidomestic, global, or transnational strategy.

- An international strategy transfers core competencies to foreign markets where local rivals lack an alternative and industry conditions impose low pressures for global integration and national responsiveness.

- A multidomestic strategy emphasizes responsiveness to the unique circumstances that prevail in a country's market.

- A global strategy drives performance by making standardized products that are marketed with minimum adaptation to local conditions.

- A transnational strategy simultaneously leverages core competencies worldwide, reduces costs by exploiting location economics, and adapts, subject to efficiency standards, to local conditions.

- The company implementing a transnational strategy aims not to work harder or work smarter than competitors but rather work differently based on diffusing the lessons it has learned and the knowledge it has earned throughout its worldwide operations

KEY TERMS

cluster effect (p. 417)
commodity (p. 429)
concentrated (p. 410)
configuration (p. 410)
coordination (p. 410)
core competency (p. 417)
cost leadership (p. 407)
differentiation (p. 408)
digitization (p. 414)
dispersed (p. 410)
economies of scale (p. 415)

five-forces model (p. 403)
global integration (p. 421)
global strategy (p. 429)
Great by Choice (p. 405)
industry organization (IO)
   paradigm (p. 405)
industry structure (p. 403)
Integration-Responsiveness (IR) grid
   (p. 425)
international strategy (p. 426)
local responsiveness (p. 421)

location economies (p. 410)
logistics (p. 414)
multidomestic strategy (p. 428)
perfect competition (p. 405)
primary activities (p. 409)
singularity principle (p. 411)
strategy (p. 406)
support activities (p. 409)
transnational strategy (p. 430)
value (p. 406)
value chain (p. 409)

ENDNOTES

1 *Sources include the following:* A. Bonnin, "The Fashion Industry in Galicia: Understanding the 'Zara' Phenomenon," *European Planning Studies* 10, (2002): 519; "Inditex: The Future of Fast Fashion" *The Economist*, retrieved May 31, 2011, from www.economist.com /node/4086117?story_id=4086117; "The Stars of Europe—Armancio Ortega, Chairman, Inditex," *Business Week,* (June 11, 2001): 65; "Rapid Response Retail," *Marketing* (April 3, 2003): 43; Richard Heller, "Galician Beauty," *Forbes* (May 28, 2001): 28; Patrick Byrne, "Closing the Gap between Strategy and Results," *Logistics Management* (March 2004): 13; Rachel Tiplady, "Zara: Taking the Lead in Fast-Fashion," *Business Week* (June 4, 2006): 19; "Shining Examples," *The Economist* (June 15, 2006): 54; "Zara Grows as Retail Rivals Struggle," *Wall Street Journal* (March 26, 2009): C-1; "Fashion for the Masses: Global Stretch," *The Economist* (March 10, 2011): 88. "Zara, the Lead in Fast Fashion," *Fashion Muse*, retrieved May 31, 2011, from www .fashionmuse.com/women-fashion/zara-lead-fast-fashion

2 Michael Porter, *Competitive Advantage* (New York: Free Press, 1985).

3 Research reports that industry effects explain 75 percent of the difference in average returns for companies in an industry. Jens Boyd, "Intra-Industry Structure and Performance: Strategic Groups and Strategic Blocks in the Worldwide Airline Industry," *European Management Review* 1 (2004): 132–45; Schmalensee, "Do Markets Differ Much?" *American Economic Review* 75: 3 (1985): 341–51.

4 "How the iPhone Led to the Sale of T-Mobile USA," NYTimes.com. Retrieved March 21, 2011, from: or dealbook.nytimes.com /2011/03/21/how-the-iphone-led-to-the-sale-of-t-mobile-usa/?hp

5 Joseph Bower and Clayton Christensen, "Disruptive Technologies: Catching the Wave" *Harvard Business Review* (January–February 1995).

6 Ashlee Vance and Matt Richtel, "Light and Cheap, Netbooks Are Poised to Reshape PC Industry," *New York Times* (April 1, 2009): C-1.

7 Chad Brooks, "PC Is Dead. Cloud Computing, Mobile Devices Taking Over," *CSMonitor.com*, retrieved June 9, 2011, from www .csmonitor.com/Business/Latest-News-Wires/2011/0608/PC-is -dead.-Cloud-computing-mobile-devices-taking-over

8 "A Special Report on Innovation in Emerging Markets: The World Turned Upside Down," *The Economist*, retrieved May 2, 2011, from www.economist.com/node/15879369

9 Jack Gage, "The Best Countries for Business," *Forbes* (June 26, 2008): 55.

10 Jim Collins, "Good to Great," retrieved April 26, 2011, from www .jimcollins.com/article_topics/articles/good-to-great.html

11 In general, the higher the risk, the higher the return. Therefore, riskier projects and investments must be evaluated differently from their riskless counterparts. By discounting risky cash flows against less-risky cash flows, risk-adjusted rates account for changes in the profile of the investment.

12 See B. Wernerfelt, "A Resource-Based View of the Firm," *Strategic Management Journal* (1984): 171–80; In addition, Rumelt found that corporate-parent effects contributed to the variance in firm performance (Richard Rumelt, "How Much Does Industry Matter?" *Strategic Management Journal* (1985): 167–86); McGahan and Porter (2002) found similar evidence of corporate-parent effects: see "What Do We Know about Variance in Accounting Profitability?" *Management Science* (2002): 834–51.

13 See Wyn Jenkins, "Competing in Times of Evolution and Revolution: An Essay on Long-Term Firm Survival," *Management Decisions* 43 (January 1, 2005): 26. Belen Villalonga, "Intangible Resources, Tobin's Q, and Sustainability of Performance Differences," *Journal of Economic Behavior & Organization* 54 (June 2004): 205. Determining whether a money manager outperforms a market index relies on separating the returns available from market movements (*beta* in the jargon) and managerial skill (*alpha*). Like great product managers,

great money managers find innovative ways to earn in excess of what would be predicted by an equilibrium model like the *capital asset pricing model* (CAPM). More specifically, we can compare the performance of investment managers by allowing for portfolio risk with the so-called Jensen index, also called Alpha. This measure uses the CAPM as its basis for determining whether a money manager outperformed a market index. The sum of the outperformance is known as alpha.

14 The idea of value can be defined in a variety of ways, including but by no means limited, to economic, market, pro forma, social, book, insurance, use, par, or replacement. We can also define value from different perspectives, such as those of customers, employees, stakeholders, or shareholders.

15 "Special Report: The China Price," *Business Week* (December 6, 2004), retrieved June 25, 2005, from www.businessweek.com/magazine /content/04_49/b3911401.htm

16 Keith Bradsher, "China's High-Quality Pearls Enter the Mass Market," NYTimes.com, retrieved August 16, 2011 from www .nytimes.com/2011/08/02/business/global/chinas-high-quality -pearls-enter-the-mass-market.html

17 Oded Shenkar, *The Chinese Century: The Rising Chinese Economy and Its Impact on the Global Economy, the Balance of Power, and Your Job* (Upper Saddle River, NJ: Pearson Prentice Hall, 2006).

18 Personal Conversation, Daniel Sullivan and Peter Leung, Director Nalco China, Beijing, March 1, 2011.

19 "Sony to Enter Netbook PC Market with New VAIO," *Reuters* (July 7, 2009): 3.

20 "Hungry Tiger, Dancing Elephant: How India Is Changing IBM's World," *The Economist* (April 4, 2007): 58–61.

21 Michael Porter, "What Is Strategy?" *Harvard Business Review* (November–December 1996): 61–79.

22 Managers may make decisions that they strongly reason support the firm's strategy but, in actuality, more often do not. Challenges emerge because often few managers understand the full demands of the company's strategy and its implications for international operations. More worrisome, managers are far more likely to make the wrong than right decision. See Dan Lovallo and Daniel Kahneman, "Delusions of Success: How Optimism Undermines Executives' Decisions," *Harvard Business Review* (July 2003): 56.

23 Michael Porter, "Competition in Global Industries: A Conceptual Framework," in M. Porter (ed.), *Competition in Global Industries*, (Boston: Harvard Business School Press, 1986).

24 Janet C. Lowe, *Welch: An American Icon* (New York: Wiley and Sons, 2002).

25 Shenkar, *The Chinese Century*, 16.

26 Keith Bradsher, "Solar Panel Maker Moves Work to China," NYTimes.com, retrieved March 9, 2011 from www.nytimes .com/2011/01/15/business/energy-environment/15solar.html ?pagewanted=2&_r=1&hpw

27 Personal Conversation, Daniel Sullivan and Peter Leung, Director Nalco China, Beijing, March 1, 2011.

28 Kurt Badenhausen, "Best Countries for Business,"Forbes.com, retrieved March 10, 2011, from www.forbes.com/lists/2010/6/best -countries-10_Best-Countries-for-Business_Rank.html

29 Christine Greenhalgh and Mark Rogers, *Innovation, Intellectual Property, and Economic Growth* (Princeton: Princeton University Press, 2010).

30 Jerome Glenn, Theodore Gordon, and Elizabeth Florescu "2009 State of the Future."The Millennium Project defines singularity as the "time in which technological change is so fast and significant that we today are incapable of conceiving what life might be like beyond

the year 2025" (p. 22), from http://www.millennium-project.org/millennium/sof2009.html.

31 "Futurology: The New Overlords," *The Economist* (May 12, 2011): 98.

32 Soumitra Dutta and Simon Caulki, "The World's Top Innovators," *The World Business/INSEAD Global Innovation Index* (2007), retrieved June 18, 2007, from www.worldbusinesslive.com/article/625441/the-worlds-topinnovators

33 Andrew Nusca, "Top 10 Innovative Countries: Denmark Leads World in 2010; Sweden, U.S. Follow," *SmartPlanet*, retrieved April 26, 2011, from www.smartplanet.com/business/blog/smart-takes/top-10-innovative-countries-denmark-leads-world-in-2010-sweden-us-follow/13487

34 Ibid.

35 The variation between these endpoints is similarly startling. The mean weekly wage is $136, while the standard deviation is $133. The mean is the statistical norm or average value, the standard deviation is the measure of the dispersion of a collection of values, and a high standard deviation indicates that the data are spread out over a large range of values.

36 See Arindam Bhattacharya et al., *Capturing Global Advantage: How Leading Industrial Companies Are Transforming Their Industries by Sourcing and Selling in China, India, and Other Low-Cost Countries* (Boston: Boston Consulting Group Publications, April 9, 2004), esp. Exhibit 7.

37 Currency conversions made March 15 at rate of ¥6.6 to $1; Paul Krugman, "Divided over Trade," *New York Times* (May 14, 2007): A-18; "Most of China Raises Minimum Wage," China.org.cn, retrieved March 11, 2011, from www.china.org.cn/business/2010-08/19/content 20744153.htm

38 Bower and Christensen, "Disruptive Technologies."

39 Keith Bradsher, "Chinese Auto Parts Enter the Global Market," *New York Times* (June 7, 2007): B-8.Calculated at the exchange rate of 7.65 yuan to the dollar, as of June 12, 2009.

40 Shenkar, *The Chinese Century*.

41 Diana Farrell, Noshi Kaka, and Sascha Sturze, "Ensuring India's Offshoring Future," *McKinsey Quarterly* (2005): 92–103.

42 *IBM India*, Wikipedia, retrieved May 18, 2011, from http://secure.wikimedia.org/wikipedia/en/wiki/IBM_India.

43 "Big US Firms Shift Hiring Abroad," *Wall Street Journal* (April 19, 2011): B1.

44 Quote from Bain's Mark Gottfredson, reported in "Financial Firms Hasten Their Move to Outsourcing," *New York Times* (August 18, 2004): C-1.

45 Heather Timmons, "Outsourcing to India Draws Western Lawyers," NYTimes.com, retrieved April 26, 2011, from www.nytimes.com/2010/08/05/business/global/05legal.html?_r=1. Presently, Pangea3 is "getting more résumés from United States lawyers than we know what to do with," said the managing director of its litigation services group.

46 "2009 State of the Future, The Millennium Project," 22.

47 See the Cluster Profiles Project of the Institute for Strategy and Competitiveness at Harvard Business School, data.isc.hbs.edu/cp/index.jsp.

48 "Innovations to Create New Streams of Profitable Growth," *Accenture Outlook*, retrieved June 9, 2011, from www.accenture.com/in-en/outlook/Pages/outlook-journal-2010-less-is-new-more-innovation.aspx

49 Platforms include ebXML Business Process Specification Schema, Web Services Business Process Execution Language, and so on. See lsdis.cs.uga.edu/proj/meteor/mwscf/standards.html for a fuller profile.

50 *Synergy* is defined as the combination of parts of a business such that the sum is worth more than the individual parts. It is often expressed in the equation $2 + 2 = 5$, with the additional unit of value the result of synergy. Research reports a relationship between a firm's performance and a manager's sophistication in diffusing core competencies throughout the value chain.

51 Technically, a core competence satisfies three conditions: It provides consumer benefits, it is difficult for competitors to imitate, and it is leveraged to different products and markets. The fact that rivals cannot easily match or replicate a firm's core competency serves as a powerful competitive advantage

52 Jerome Glenn, Theodore Gordon, and Elizabeth Florescu "2009 State of the Future."

53 Medard Gabel and Henry Bruner, *An Atlas of the Multinational Corporation Globalinc* (New York: The New Press, 2003).

54 Adam Bryant, "Google's 8-Point Plan to Help Managers Improve," NYTimes.com, retrieved March 13, 2011, from www.nytimes.com/2011/03/13/business/13hire.html?hp

55 Christopher A. Bartlett and Meg Wozny, "GE's Two-Decade Transformation: Jack Welch's Leadership," Harvard Business School Case 399-150 (Boston: HBSP, 2001).

56 "Schumpeter: Fail often, fail well," *The Economist*, retrieved April 28, 2011, from www.economist.com/node/18557776?story_id=18557776&fsrc=rss

57 "Top 100 Global Brands Scoreboard," *Business Week*, 208, retrieved May 19, 2007, from www.businessweek.com/brand/2005/ and bwnt.businessweek.com/ brand/2006; The Best Global Brands, retrieved April 8, 2009, from www.interbrand.com/best_global_brands.aspx; "The Top 100 Most Valuable Global Brands 2010," *Social Brand Value*, retrieved May 9, 2011, from www.social-brand-value.com/2010/04/28/the-top-100-most-valuable-global-brands-2010/

58 Lovallo and Kahneman, "Delusions of Success," 56.

59 James Brooke and Saul Hansel, "Samsung Is Now What Sony Once Was," *New York Times* (March 9, 2004): A-1.

60 Hiroko Tabuchi, "Sony's Profit Falls 8.6 percent in the 3rd Quarter," NYTimes.com, retrieved February 3, 2011, from www.nytimes.com/2011/02/04/business/global/04sony.html?ref=business

61 Lovallo and Kahneman, "Delusions of Success," 56. Often, analysis of these sorts of prescient management tends toward halo effects whereby a positive impression in one area, say the ease of Google's search algorithm, influences assessment of others, say, Google's executive leadership. Moreover, the often anecdotal "lessons learned" are not easily distilled into objective principles or useful to companies in dissimilar industries and countries.

62 Theodore Levitt, "The Globalization of Markets," *Harvard Business Review* 61 (1983): 92–102.

63 Encyclopedia Britannica, www.britannica.com/EBchecked/topic/1357503/cultural-globalization.

64 Regarding cultural predisposition, Japanese doctors disfavor the American-style, high-pressure sales force. Pharmaceutical sales representatives, therefore, adapt their marketing practices in that country. Regarding historical legacy, people drive on the left side of the road in England, thereby creating demand for right-hand drive cars, whereas people in Italy drive on the right side of the road, thereby creating demand for left-hand-drive cars. Similarly, consumer electrical systems are based on 110 volts in the United States, whereas many European countries use a 240-volt standard.

65 C. Prahalad and Y. Doz, *The Multinational Mission: Balancing Local Demands and Global Vision* (New York: Free Press, 1987).

66 "Google in Asia: Seeking success," *The Economist*, retrieved March 15, 2011, from www.economist.com/node/13185891?story_id=13185891

67 For example, the idea of just-in-time inventory management and lean production systems may have seemed extreme to Americans, but were critical to Japanese companies given the expense of land and raw materials.

68 "A Special Report on Entrepreneurship: Global Heroes," *The Economist*, retrieved March 15, 2011, from www.economist.com/node/13216025

69 Andrew Kramer, "The Evolution of Russia, as Seen From McDonald's," NYTimes.com, retrieved March 17, 2011, from http://www.nytimes.com/2010/02/02/business/global/02mcdonalds.html

70 Alexandra Harney, *The China Price: The True Cost of Chinese Competitive Advantage* (New York: Penguin, 2008); "The China Price," *Business Week*, retrieved March 30, 2011, from www.businessweek.com/magazine/content/04_49/b3911401.htm

71 Shenkar, *The Chinese Century.*

72 "A World of Connections," *The Economist* (April 26, 2007): 65.

73 Noel Tichy and Stratford Sherman, *Control Your Destiny or Someone Else Will* (New York: HarperCollins, 2005).

74 Quotations from the following: Jack Welch and John A. Byrne, *Jack: Straight from the Gut* (New York: Warner Business Books, 2001); Lovallo and Kahneman, "Delusions of Success," 56.

75 "Hungry Tiger, Dancing Elephant: How India Is Changing IBM's World," *The Economist* (April 4, 2007): 58–61.

76 Yves Doz, Jose Santos, and Peter Williamson, *Global to Metanational: How Companies Win in the Knowledge Economy* (Cambridge, MA: Harvard Business School Press, 2001).

77 Michael V. Copeland, "How Startups Go Global," *Business 2.0* (July 28, 2006): 424; Jim Hopkins, "The Rise of the Micro-Multinationals," *USA Today* (February 11, 2005): B-1.

78 Alan Rugman and Alain Verbeke, "A Perspective on Regional and Global Strategies of Multinational Enterprises," *Journal of International Business Studies* 35 (2004): 3–18; Pankaj Ghemawat, "Regional Strategies for Global Leadership," *Harvard Business Review* (2005, December).

79 Marc Singer, "Beyond the Unbundled Corporation," *The McKinsey Quarterly*, retrieved July 12, 2009, from www.mckinseyquarterly.com/Beyond_the_unbundled_corporation_1085; Remo Hacki and Julian Lighton, "The Future of the Networked Company," *McKinsey Quarterly*, retrieved July 12, 2009, from www.mckinseyquarterly.com/The_future_of_the_networked_company_1091; James Martin, "Only the Cyber-Fit Will Survive," *Datamation* (November 1996): 60.

80 "The New Champions," *The Economist* (September 18, 2008); Thomas Friedman, *The World Is Flat: A Brief History of the Twenty-First Century* (New York: Farrar, Straus and Giroux, 2005); Clyde V. Prestowitz, *Three Billion New Capitalists. The Great Shift of Wealth and Power to the East* (New York: Basic Books, 2006); "The Next Billions: Unleashing Business Potential in Untapped Markets," *World Economic Forum* (January 2009): 44; C. K. Prahalad and S. L. Hart, "The Fortune at the Bottom of the Pyramid," *Strategy+Business* 26 (2002): 54–67; C. K. Prahalad, *The Fortune at the Bottom of the Pyramid* (Philadelphia: Wharton School Publishing, 2004); Antoine van Agtmael, *The Emerging Markets Century: How a New Breed of World-Class Companies Is Overtaking the World* (Minneapolis, MN: Free Press, 2007).

81 Carmen Reinhart and Kenneth Rogoff, *This Time Is Different: Eight Centuries of Financial Folly* (Princeton, NJ: Princeton University Press, 2010).

82 "A Special Report on Innovation in Emerging Markets: The World Turned Upside Down," *The Economist,* retrieved April 21, 2011, from www.economist.com/node/15879369

83 Anil K. Gupta and Haiyan Wang, "How to Get China and India Right," *Wall Street Journal* (April 23, 2007): 1.

84 "GM Sales Up 22.3% in China," retrieved March 17, 2011, from www.industryweek.com/articles/gm_sales_up_22-3_in_china_23846.aspx

85 "GM's First-Half China Sales Surge Past the U.S," Businessweek.com, retrieved March 17, 2011, from www.businessweek.com/news/2010-07-02/gm-s-first-half-china-sales-surge-past-the-u-s-.html

86 "McDonald's Eyes Russia Growth with 40 New Stores," Reuters, retrieved February 26, 2009, from uk.reuters.com/article/idUKLQ86281720090226

87 "McDonald's to Invest More in Russia," Crain's Chicago Business, retrieved March 17, 2011, from www.chicagobusiness.com/article/20110302/NEWS0702/110309970/mcdonalds-to-invest-more-in-russia; Andrew Kramer, "The Evolution of Russia, as Seen from McDonald's," NYTimes.com, retrieved March 17, 2011, from www.nytimes.com/2010/02/02/business/global/02mcdonalds.html

88 "India Is Epicenter at the Flat World," BPO Tiger, retrieved May 10, 2011, from www.bpotiger.com/2007/04/india_is_epicenter_at_the_flat.html

89 Quote from Bruno Di Leo, general manager for growth markets for IBM, reported in Steve Lohr, "IBM: Africa Is the Next Growth Frontier," NYTimes.com, retrieved September 18, 2010, from bits.blogs.nytimes.com/2010/09/17/i-b-m-africa-is-the-next-growth-frontier/?hpw

90 Reported in "The New Champions," retrieved October 4, 2009, from www.financialexpress.com/ printer/news/365882

91 "Hungry Tiger, Dancing Elephant," 58–61.

chapter 12

Country Evaluation and Selection

Objectives

1. To grasp company strategies for sequencing the penetration of countries

2. To see how scanning techniques can help managers both limit geographic alternatives and consider otherwise overlooked areas

3. To discern the major opportunity and risk variables to consider when deciding whether and where to expand abroad

4. To know the methods and problems of collecting and comparing international information

5. To understand some simplifying tools for helping decide where to operate

6. To consider how companies allocate emphasis among the countries where they operate

7. To comprehend why location decisions do not necessarily compare different countries' possibilities

Access a host of interactive learning aids to help strengthen your understanding of the chapter concepts at www.myiblab.com.

MyIBLab

The place to get top speed out of a horse is not the place where you can get top speed out of a canoe.

—*African (Hausa) proverb*

Source: © Ucebistu | Dreamstime.com

441

CASE

Carrefour: Crossroads at a Crossroads

Carrefour, the largest retailer in Europe and Latin America and the second largest worldwide, means crossroads.[1] The name for this French giant that opened its first store in 1960 is apropos because it is facing tough choices for improving its future performance. Its recent results have been highly uneven by region, i.e., doing poorly in Southeast Asia, encountering fluctuating market share in France, but showing solid gains in Brazil and China. In 2011, it had more than 15,000 stores and about 475,000 employees, selling a combination of food and nonfood items. Apart from its hard discount division, which it reports separately, it derived 61 percent of its sales and 53 percent of its profits outside France. The Institute of Grocery Distribution ranks Carrefour as the world's most global retailer, based on foreign sales, number of countries with operations, and ratio of foreign sales to total sales. As of 2011, it had a presence in 34 countries. (The opening photo shows one of its Romanian stores.)

Carrefour must decide which countries to emphasize in its expansion and where in each country to locate new stores. Currently Carrefour's first priority is leadership in France. The second is to maintain growth or improve performance in three other European countries—Belgium, Italy, and Spain. And its third priority is to establish operations in countries with strong growth potential—mainly BRIC countries (Brazil, Russia, India, and China). Of these four, Carrefour entered Russia in 2009 and began Indian operations in 2010. Finally, the lowest priority is made up of other countries. Map 12.1 shows those countries.

Concomitantly, Carrefour must decide what to do with underperforming stores and countries. It sells stores and moves from countries that offer less potential profits than if capital is placed elsewhere. For instance, in 2006, it sold its operations in South Korea and Slovakia while expanding heavily in Poland. In 2010, it sold its stores in Thailand to put more emphasis on its domestic market. Carrefour sells in five types of stores: hypermarkets, supermarkets, hard discount stores, cash-and-carry stores, and convenience stores. Its hypermarkets account for the largest portion of its

MAP 12.1   Carrefour's Priority among Countries

In 2009, Carrefour published its priority among countries. Note that defense of present positions is most important; large growth markets are next in importance.

Source: The order of countries was taken from "Strategic Orientations March 2009," http://www.carrefour.com/cdc/group/our-strategy

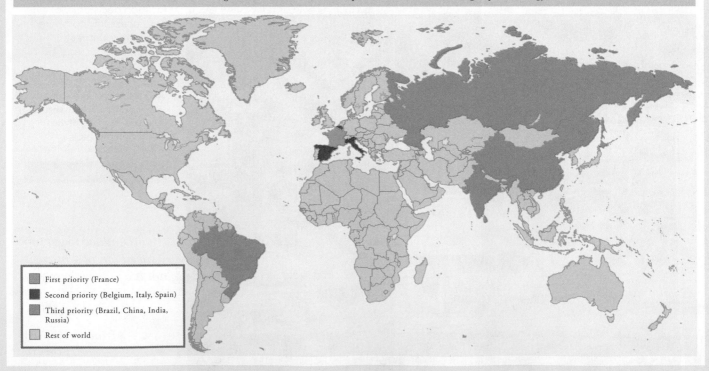

■ First priority (France)
■ Second priority (Belgium, Italy, Spain)
■ Third priority (Brazil, China, India, Russia)
□ Rest of world

sales (about 63 percent), retail space, and number of countries with retail operations. Carrefour invented and opened the first hypermarket—an enormous store combining a department store and a supermarket. Whereas a typical supermarket might have 40,000 square feet, a hypermarket might have 330,000.

As a general rule, a hypermarket requires 500,000 households within a 20-minute drive for sufficient business. Carrefour's supermarkets carry less variety than its hypermarkets, and its hard discount stores and cash-and-carry stores carry even less. The cash-and-carry stores cater strictly to the trade, such as to restaurant owners and hoteliers. Its convenience stores (more than 95 percent are franchise operations) are still smaller and carry fewer items. One of Carrefour's key contributions to franchisees is helping to select locations for their stores.

Carrefour's French hypermarket operation was an early success, due largely to the timing for introducing the concept. French supermarket operations were not yet well developed; consumers generally shopped for foods in different outlets—such as bread, meat, fish, cheese, and fresh vegetables in different specialty stores or markets. Moreover, few retailers had convenient or free parking, so customers made frequent and time-consuming trips to numerous stores. Carrefour came along when more French families had cars, refrigerators large enough to store a week's supply of fresh products, and higher disposable incomes to spend on nonfood items. Further, more women were working, and they wanted one-stop shopping. Thus French consumers flocked to Carrefour's suburban hypermarkets, which offered free parking and discounted prices on a very wide selection of merchandise.

However, French government authorities at times have restricted new hypermarket permits to safeguard town centers, protect small businesses, and prevent visual despoliation of the countryside. As a consequence, Carrefour decided to expand internationally. Figure 12.1 provides a chronology of Carrefour's expansion into foreign markets mainly via company-owned outlets. Its first foreign entry was a partnership in Belgium, and its first wholly owned foreign store was in Spain. Both are in neighboring countries, both entries were with hypermarkets, and both countries had consumers who were going through lifestyle changes similar to those we described for France.

Carrefour easily managed these ventures because its French suppliers provided much of the stores' stock and because its French managers could easily travel to oversee the operations. Since then, a guiding principle for Carrefour's international expansion has been countries' economic evolution. A former CEO said, "We can start with a developing country at the bottom of the economic curve and grow within the country to the top of the curve. To go global, you need to be early enough. Generally, in new countries you need to be the first in for the first win. When you arrive as number three or four, it is too late." When Carrefour has deviated from this principle, it has failed. It expanded unsuccessfully into the United States and the United Kingdom after both countries had gone through economic transitions and other distributors had satisfied the changed consumer needs. It also entered the Mexican, Japanese, Korean, and Chilean markets late and sold its operations there. Nevertheless, being first is not always enough. Carrefour was

FIGURE 12.1 Carrefour's Major Locations and Entry Dates

Data refer to mainly company-owned outlets and include a few franchises. Carrefour also entered and exited some foreign markets, including the United Kingdom, the United States, Japan, and Thailand.

Source: Based on data from Groupe Carrefour, "The Carrefour Group's Store Locations," at www.carrefour.com and updated via a variety of sources.

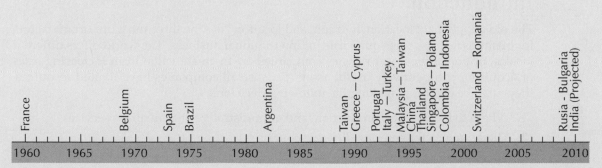

first in some Southeast Asian countries, but it lacked sufficient understanding of their different market needs, thus the later-entering competitors learned from Carrefour's mistakes.

Some additional factors have caused problems for Carrefour. In the United States, customers simply have not wanted to spend the time shopping in a hypermarket where they have to walk long distances before reaching even the first aisle. In the United Kingdom, Carrefour did well on food sales, but consumers preferred to shop for durables in city centers where they could compare different distributors' offerings. In Mexico, Carrefour was up against an established Walmart, which could integrate buying and distribution with its successful U.S. operations. In Japan, consumers were disappointed not to find a French shopping experience. In both Hong Kong and Chile, Carrefour was unable to build enough stores to gain the needed economies of distribution.

Another factor influencing Carrefour's choice of country has been the ability to find a viable partner familiar with local operating needs. It has found these in Switzerland, Taiwan, Turkey, and China. However, this was not the case in Mexico and Japan. Carrefour lasted only four years in Japan before selling out.

Why would another company want to partner with Carrefour? Aside from financial resources, Carrefour brings to a partnership expertise on store layout, clout in dealing with global suppliers (for example, it runs a global sales campaign, "Most Awaited Month," in which the largest manufacturers of global consumer goods provide its stores worldwide with lower prices for a one-month sale), direct e-mail links with suppliers that substantially reduce inventories and the need for Carrefour's buyers to visit suppliers, and the ability to export unique bargain items from one country to another.

Carrefour also considers whether a location can justify sufficient additional store expansion to gain distribution economies. To help gain these economies, Carrefour and some of its competitors have recently been expanding via acquisition. However, some analysts have felt that Carrefour may be expanding retail operations to too many countries and will not be able to build sufficient presence in each. In contrast, the British retailer Tesco is expanding to fewer countries but is building a large presence in each one.

Carrefour depends on locally produced goods for about 90 percent of its sales, using manufacturers' trademarks or no trademarks at all. This strategy contrasts with such retailers as Tesco, which depends heavily on own-label products. Thus consumers can easily compare prices of most Carrefour products with those of competitors because few of its products have unique labels.

Nevertheless, Carrefour has recently been pushing global purchasing. For example, when stores in one country find an exceptional supplier, the management passes on the information to Carrefour's merchandising group in Brussels, which then seeks markets within Carrefour stores in other countries. The Malaysian operation, for example, found a good local supplier of disposable gloves, and Carrefour now sells them in its stores worldwide.

Despite Carrefour's success in many markets, analysts feel that it will never become the world's largest retailer without a significant presence in the United States and the United Kingdom. Its only presence in either is a minority interest in Costco in the United States. However, whether Carrefour becomes the world's largest retailer or not, its choice of countries for operations will play a big role in its success.

CRN
Case Review Note

Introduction

The old adage that "location, location, and location" are the three most important factors for business success rings quite true for international business. The world offers different locales, opportunities, and risks as companies try to create value from increasing sales or acquiring competitively useful assets. Because all companies have limited resources, they must be careful in making the following decisions:

Companies lack resources to take advantage of all international opportunities.

1. Where to locate sales, production, and administrative and auxiliary services
2. The sequence for entering different countries
3. The portion of resources and efforts to allocate to each country where they operate

Committing human, technical, and financial resources to one locale may mean forgoing or delaying projects elsewhere. In our opening case, for instance, we saw that Carrefour, although the world's second largest retailer, has taken over 40 years to move into roughly 15 percent of the world's countries, and its presence in some of those is still quite small. In actuality, a company may first set a strategy of domestic versus international emphasis, after which it sequences entry by country. For instance, General Electric set an objective of having international operations account for 60 percent of its total sales.[2] Even after a firm is well established in most countries, it still needs to allocate resources by emphasizing some countries more than others. Thus, taking time and picking the right locations affects a firm's ability to gain and sustain competitive advantage.[3]

Figure 12.2 highlights the importance of MNEs' location decisions. By examining the external environment and comparing it with a company's objectives and capabilities, managers might ask: Where can we best leverage our existing competencies? And where can we go to best sustain, improve, or extend our competencies?

To answer those questions, managers need to answer two more: Which markets should we serve? and Where should we place production to serve them? On one hand, the answers to these questions can be the same, particularly if transport costs or government regulations mean that a firm must produce in the countries where it sells. Many service industries, such as hotels, construction, and retailing (like Carrefour), must locate facilities near their foreign customers.

On the other hand, large-scale production technology may favor producing in only a few countries and exporting to others, such as with companies in the capital-intensive automobile and steel industries. Finally, location decisions may be more complex, such as using multiple countries for sourcing raw materials and components that go into one finished product. Or a company may divide operating functions, such as having

CRN Case Review Note

Companies need to
- Determine the order of country entry.
- Set the rates of resource allocation among countries.

In choosing geographic sites, a company must decide
- Where to sell.
- Where to produce.

FIGURE 12.2 Location Decisions Affecting International Operations

In choosing locations for international operations, a company should begin by analyzing three factors; its *objectives*, its *contemporaries*, and its comparative *environmental* fit with conditions in the *countries* under *consideration*.

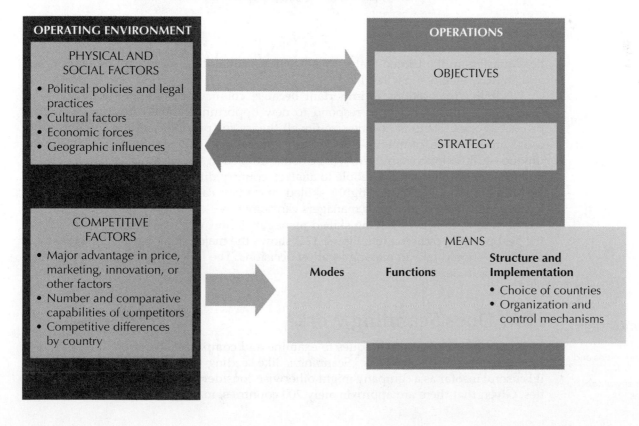

FIGURE 12.3   The Location-Decision Process

Location, location, location: Committing resources to an overseas location may entail a risky trade-off—say, deleting or abandoning projects elsewhere. The decision-making process is essentially twofold; examining the external environments of proposed locations and comparing each of them with the company's objectives and capabilities.

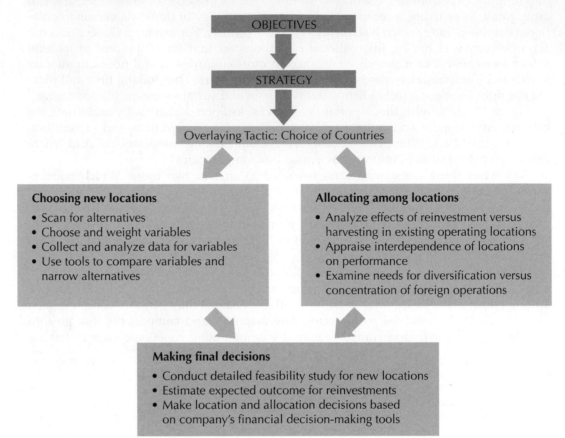

headquarters in the United States, a call center for handling service in the Philippines, and an R&D facility in Switzerland.

Flexibility in locations is important because country and competitive conditions change. A company needs to respond to new opportunities and withdraw from less profitable ones. There is no one-size-fits-all theory for picking operating locations because product lines, competitive positions, resources, and strategies make each company unique—a situation that, in turn, will be better utilized in some countries than in others.[4] In addition, hiring the right people to analyze country differences and implement company operations is critical. Highly skilled managers can sometimes compensate for location deficiencies, and poor managers can sometimes cause poor performance in the best locations. However, having skilled managers follow efficient location techniques is the best possible combination. Figure 12.3 shows the major steps international business managers should take in making location decisions. The following discussion examines those steps in depth.

How Does Scanning Work?

Without scanning, a company may
- Overlook opportunities and risks.
- Examine too many or too few possibilities.

Managers use scanning techniques to examine and compare countries on broad indicators of opportunities and risks.[5] Scanning is like seeding widely and then weeding out; it is useful insofar as a company might otherwise consider too few or too many possibilities. Given that there are approximately 200 countries, managers might easily overlook some good opportunities without first looking very broadly. Instead, they might zero in on those that come to mind first.

SCANNING VERSUS DETAILED ANALYSIS

Step 1: Scanning   Managers can examine most or all countries broadly and narrow them down to the most promising ones by **scanning.** That is, they compare country information that is readily available, inexpensive, and fairly comparable—usually without having to incur traveling expenses. They analyze publicly available information, such as from the Internet, and communicate with experienced people. They compare countries on a few conditions that could significantly affect the success or failure of their business and that fit with its resources and objectives. Because of using fairly easy-to-find information, they may consider a large group of countries at this point, such as all those within a global region.

Step 2: Detailed Analysis   Once managers narrow their consideration to the most promising countries, they need to compare the feasibility and desirability of each. At this point, unless they are satisfied enough to outsource all their production and sales, they almost always need to go on location to analyze and collect more specific information.

Take a situation in which managers need to decide where to place their sales efforts. They will likely need to visit the countries shortlisted through scanning in order to conduct market research and visit with distributors before making a final decision. Or let's say managers need to decide where to locate production of a finished product or component. If they plan to outsource the production, they may want to inspect potential contractors' facilities. If they plan to own facilities themselves, they will need to collect such specific on-site information as availability of land and suppliers before committing significant resources.

Intel's manufacturing expansion into Latin America illustrates an example. Intel used scanning techniques to limit visits to a few Latin American countries. The follow-up visits sought much more detailed information—even the availability of suitable housing, medical services, and food products for the personnel Intel would need to transfer. The visitors were also able to gain qualitative information, such as their impressions of the welcome they might get from local government officials and business leaders.

The more time and money companies invest in examining an alternative, the more likely they are to accept it, regardless of its merits—a situation known as an **escalation of commitment.** A feasibility study should have clear-cut decision points, whereby managers can cut the commitment before they invest too much time and money.

On-site visits follow scanning and are part of the final location decision process.

What Information Is Important in Scanning?

Managers should consider country conditions that could significantly affect their company's success or failure. These conditions should reveal both opportunities and risks, each of which is discussed below.

OPPORTUNITIES

Opportunities are divided here into sales expansion and resource acquisition, although some conditions affect both, given the relationship between the decisions of where to sell and where to produce.

Sales Expansion   Expansion of sales is probably the most important factor motivating companies to engage in international business, because of the assumption that more sales will lead to more profits. Thus, it is vital to decide where best to make those sales.

Concept Check

In Chapter 11, we focus on the importance of **value**— the measure of a company's ability to sell products for more than it costs to make them—in a firm's **strategy,** adding that "creating value" is primarily a matter of meeting (indeed, exceeding) customer expectations. Here we point out the importance of both factors—cost and customer needs—in taking advantage of foreign opportunities.

Expectation of a large market and sales growth is probably a potential location's major attraction.

FIGURE 12.4   Aluminum Consumption vs. GDP per Capita

By plotting a line based on GDP per capita, you can get a fairly good estimate of demand per capita for aluminum.

Source: From a presentation by Paul Thomas, North American Fabricated Products of Alcoa (April 20, 2004); "Globalization and the Aluminum Market—Opportunities and Challenges," The Aluminum Association Inc. (2004), at www .aluminum.org (accessed October 29, 2007).

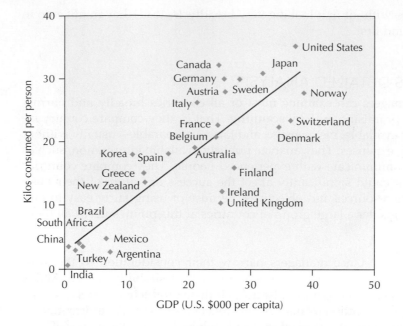

Of course, managers would like to have sales figures for the type of product they want to sell, but such information may not be available, especially if the product is a new one. In such instances, they could make rough estimates of sales potential by basing projections on what has happened to sales for a similar or complementary product. For instance, they might project the potential sales of flat-screen televisions based on figures for DVD equipment sales.

However, such complementary figures may not be available either. So what can they do? They can use economic and demographic data as sales potential—particularly historical data on other countries. Figure 12.4 shows an example of aluminum per capita consumption among a sample of countries. Management may make a rough estimate that aluminum demand for all countries will increase along the trend line as GDP per capita increases.

Of course, you should examine indicators related directly to your products. If you're trying to sell, say, luxury products, GDP per capita may tell you very little. Instead, you need to know how many people have income above a certain level. For instance, India's GDP per capita is low, but it has enough millionaires to support the sale of high-end luxury products.

Moreover, although your product or service may not appeal to the average customer, you may seek out niches within that market. Pollo Campero, a Guatemalan-based fast-food chain, and Gigante, a Mexican supermarket chain, have both successfully entered the United States by going to cities with large Central American and Mexican populations.[6]

Companies must consider variables other than income and population when estimating potential demand for their products in different countries.

Examining Economic and Demographic Variables   Some of the main things to consider when examining economic and demographic variables are listed below:

- *Obsolescence and leapfrogging of products.* Consumers in developing economies do not necessarily follow the same patterns as those in higher-income countries. In China, for example, consumers have leapfrogged the use of landline telephones by going from having no phones to using cellular phones almost exclusively.[7]

- *Prices.* If prices of essential products are high, consumers may spend more on them than what would be expected based on per capita GDP and thus have less to spend on discretionary purchases. The expenditures on food in Japan, for instance, are higher than would be predicted by either population or income level because food is expensive and work habits promote eating out.

- *Income elasticity.* A common tool for predicting total market potential is to divide the percentage of change in product demand by the percentage of change in income in a given country. The more demand shifts in relation to changes in income, the more elastic it is. Demand for necessities such as food is usually less elastic than for discretionary products such as flat-screen TVs.

- *Substitution.* Consumers in a given country may more conveniently substitute certain products or services than those in other countries. For example, there are fewer automobiles in Hong Kong than one would expect based on income and population, because the crowded conditions make the efficient mass transit system a desirable substitute for automobiles.

- *Income inequality.* Where income inequality is high, the per capita GDP figures are less meaningful. Many people have little to spend, while many others have substantial spending money, as noted by Mercedes-Benz sales in India.[8]

- *Cultural factors and taste.* Countries with similar per capita GDPs may have different preferences for products and services because of values or tastes. The same is true for consumer sub-segments within countries. The existence of a large Hindu population in India reduces per capita meat consumption there as compared with some countries with similar per capita GDPs, yet there is a large niche market of Indians who are neither Hindu nor vegetarian.

- *Existence of trading blocs.* Although a country may have a small population and GDP, its presence in a regional trading bloc gives its output access to a much larger market. For instance, Uruguay has a small domestic market, but its production has duty-free access to three other countries in MERCOSUR.[9]

Given all these factors, managers cannot project potential demand perfectly. However, by considering factors that may influence the sale of their products, they can make workable estimates that help them narrow detailed studies to a reasonable number.

Resource Acquisition   Companies undertake international business to secure resources that are either too expensive or not sufficiently available in their home countries. They may purchase these resources from another organization, or they may establish foreign investments to exploit them. In either case, they must prioritize where they can best secure what they're after.

If they want to acquire a scarce resource, they are obviously limited to those locales that have it, such as securing petroleum only in those countries that have reserves. However, even when the resource is limited to a few countries, there are better opportunities in some than in others. In the case of petroleum reserves, there are cost differences in extraction, transportation, and taxes. When considering cost differences, a particular resource may be overriding for specific industries or companies, such as sugar for candy companies or low-cost water power for aluminum companies.

Cost Considerations   A company's total cost is made up of numerous subcosts, many of which are industry- or company-specific. Nevertheless, several of the factors affecting these subcosts—*labor, infrastructure, ease of transportation and communications,* and *government incentives*—apply to a large-cross section of companies.

LABOR   Although capital intensity is growing in most industries, labor compensation remains an important cost for most companies. The scanning process allows examination of such factors as labor market size, labor compensation, minimum wages, customary and required fringe benefits, education levels, and unemployment rates in order to compare labor cost, skills, and availability.

Labor, however, is not homogeneous. Neither are companies' labor needs. For example, the desire to establish a low-cost call center has led many U.S. companies to locate in

Concept Check

Recall our discussion of "Regional Economic Integration" in Chapter 8, where we explain the **dynamic effects** of integration. As we point out, when trade barriers come down within a regional bloc, the size of the market available to small member nations typically increases quite dramatically.

Costs—especially labor costs—are an important factor in companies' production-location decisions.

the Philippines, with its many English speakers, but not in Senegal, where many French companies locate call centers to serve French-language markets. Or you may wish to establish an R&D facility where figures on the number of science and engineering graduates give you a rough idea that needed skills are available. In fact, many companies have recently set up R&D facilities in China, Hungary, India, and Israel because of the availability of technical talent at low cost.[10]

If a country's labor force lacks the specific skill levels required, an MNE might have to train, redesign production, or add supervision—all of which are expensive. Keep in mind also that there may be sector and geographic differences in wage rates within countries. In Mexico, tire wages are much higher than the average industrial wage, while wages in the capital and other large cities are higher than elsewhere.[11] In addition, you should look for conditions that can cause changes in labor availability and cost. For example, the HIV rate is very high in southern African countries, a problem that may drastically reduce their labor forces over the next 10 to 15 years.

When companies move into developing countries because of labor-cost differences, their advantages may be short-lived for one or more of three reasons:

- Competitors follow leaders into low-wage areas.
- There is little first-mover advantage for this type of production migration.
- The costs rise quickly as a result of pressure on wage or exchange rates.

| Infrastructure problems add to operating costs.

INFRASTRUCTURE   Poor internal infrastructure may easily negate cost differences in labor rates. In many developing countries, infrastructure is both substandard and unreliable, which adds to companies' costs of operating. Consider Cadbury Schweppes in Nigeria. Its workers spend extra hours getting to and from work on congested roads, which decreases their productivity. It uses its own power generators at two and a half times the cost of the unreliable publicly provided power to prevent assembly line stoppages that could cause food products to spoil. Because phone reception is often unreliable, Cadbury Schweppes must send people out to visit customers and suppliers. When goods are ready for delivery, they must again face the slow roads and congestion.[12] (The adjacent photo shows a congested street in India.)

This photo taken in Delhi, India shows a congested, narrow street where deliveries are slow because trucks must compete with pedestrians, pedaled vehicles, and even cows.

Source: JeremyRichards/ Shutterstock.com

Ease of Transportation and Communications   Related to infrastructure is the advantage of locating near customers and suppliers. However, firms with rapidly evolving technologies need to tightly coordinate product, process, and production technologies to speed the introduction of new products and diminish competitors' opportunity to copy them.[13] This tends to push more production into developed countries, where such firms conduct most of their R&D.

Other factors also affect the efficient flow of goods. One is distance, which roughly correlates with time and cost of shipments; thus, a geographically isolated country like New Zealand does not fit as easily into a company's global integration strategy because supplies to and production from there may be untimely and costly.[14] Second, there are advantages to locate in countries with few trade restrictions and efficient customs' operations in order to reduce tariff costs and administrative delays, thus, better assuring a continuous flow of components where they are needed.[15]

When entrepreneurs set up firms, they generally headquarter them where the founders reside because they can take advantage of personal networks that ease their operations; however, as companies become international, they may also find advantages in being near specialized private and public institutions handling international functions such as banks, financing firms, insurance groups, public accountants, freight forwarders, customs brokers, and consular offices. Once they shift the geographic center of their sales and operations, they may even move their headquarters to another country.[16] Halliburton relocated its CEO and corporate headquarters from the United States to Dubai to be closer to customers and employees. If a company is looking for a production location that will serve sales in more than one country, the ease of moving goods into and out of the country is very important, so managers should consider the efficiency of port facilities along with the country's trade liberalization agreements.[17]

> The need to coordinate product, process, production, and sales influences on location decisions.

Governmental Incentives and Disincentives   Most countries seek foreign investment because of the jobs it will create, the competitiveness it will enhance, and the impact it will have on their trade balance. It is common to see ads in business newspapers enticing foreign firms to consider a particular country as an investment location.

Because countries compete to attract investors, many offer incentives, through regulations or negotiations that cut operating costs. These include such things as lower taxes, training of employees, loan guarantees, low-interest loans, exemption of import duties, and subsidized energy and transportation. For example, the European structural funds program aimed at preventing European deindustrialization has helped fund projects by such companies as Coca-Cola, Fiat, and GlaxoSmithKline.[18] Differences in tax rates are particularly important when deciding where to produce within a regional trading bloc, inasmuch as companies can serve the entire region from any country within the bloc.[19]

At the same time, companies may begin operating more quickly and with fewer steps in some countries than in others. World Bank studies show that countries differ in terms of the ease or difficulty of starting a business, entering and enforcing contracts, hiring and firing workers, getting credit, and closing a business.[20] Government actions may delay or prevent companies from bringing in expatriate personnel and from timely clearing of needed imports through customs.

Countries also differ in both legal transparency and corruption. A disincentive occurs when managers must spend excessive time in satisfying government agencies on taxes, labor conditions, environmental compliance, and other matters when they are unsure of the legal consequences of their actions and competitive consequences of government corruption.[21] Nevertheless, there is some evidence that companies prefer operating in countries where both corporate social responsibility and environmental regulation are high, as long as rules and expectations are transparent.[22]

> Government practices may increase or decrease companies' costs.

A Caveat   The continuous development of new production technologies makes cost comparisons among countries more difficult. As the number of ways to make a product increases, a company might have to compare the cost of labor-intensive production in a

> **Concept Check**
>
> We show in Chapter 6 that, in applying **factor-proportions theory** to determine the best place to locate a manufacturing facility, a company may compare the amount (and cost) of machinery that it will need in one place to the number (and cost) of people that it will need in another.

low-wage country with that of capital-intensive production in a high-wage country. For instance, Volkswagen moved some production from Germany to Slovakia and switched from a highly automated, capital-intensive assembly line to a more labor-intensive plant because of cost reductions resulting from low Slovakian wages and high productivity.[23] A company should also compare the cost from large-scale production that reduces fixed costs per unit by serving multi-country markets with the cost from multiple smaller-scale production units that reduce transport and inventory costs.

RISKS

Any company decision involves weighing opportunity against risk. For example, a sales-seeking company may not necessarily go to the country showing the highest sales potential. Nor will an asset-seeking company necessarily go where the assets are cheapest. In both cases, this is because decision makers may perceive that the risks in those locales are too high.

Factors to Consider in Analyzing Risk   Keep in mind several factors as we discuss specific types of risk:

1. *Companies and their managers differ in their perceptions of what is risky,* how tolerant they are of taking risk, the returns they expect, and the portion of their assets they are willing to put at risk.[24]

2. *One company's risk may be another's opportunity.* For example, companies offering security solutions (e.g., alarm systems, guard services, insurance, weapons) may find their biggest sales opportunities where other companies find only operating risks.

3. *There are means by which companies may reduce their risks other than avoiding locations,* such as by insuring. But all these options incur costs that decision makers should take into account.

4. *There are trade-offs among risks.* For instance, avoiding a country where political risk is high may leave a company more vulnerable to competitive risk if another company earns good profits there. Finally, returns are usually higher where risk is higher.

Besides considering the individual nature of risk assessment, companies should consider a number of important factors. They are grouped into three categories: political, foreign exchange, and competitive.

Political Risk   Political risk may occur because of changes in political leaders' opinions and policies, civil disorder, and animosity between the host and other countries, particularly the firm's home country. It may be costly for companies because of the loss or damage of property, disrupted operations, and the need to adjust to changes in the rules governing business. Recently, Unilever encountered difficulty in attracting foreign executives to work in Pakistan because of security concerns; Chiquita Brands paid money to terrorists in Colombia to protect its employees there; Holcim had its cement investments nationalized in Venezuela; Marriott had a hotel bombed in Indonesia; and Coca-Cola has had interrupted services requiring police protection of its trucks and telephone connections in Angola.[25]

Managers use three approaches to predict political risk: *analyzing past patterns, analyzing opinions,* and *examining potentially risky social and economic conditions.*

Analyzing Past Patterns   Predicting foreign companies' risk on the basis of past political occurrences is problematic because situations may change for better or worse. Moreover, examining a country's overall situation masks political risk differences within countries and among MNEs. For example, unrest that leads to property damage and disruption of supplies or sales may be limited geographically. During the civil war that led to the breakup of Yugoslavia, companies in Slovenia escaped the damage that others incurred elsewhere there. With few exceptions, government takeovers of companies

Concept Check

Recall from Chapter 3 our definition of **political risk** as the possibility that political decisions, events, or conditions will affect a country's business environment in ways that will cost investors some or all of the value of their investment or force them to accept lower-than-projected rates of return.

have been highly selective, primarily affecting operations that have a visible widespread effect on the country because of their size or monopoly position.

When a company does incur property damage or asset takeover, it is not necessarily a full loss to investors. First, damage may be covered by insurance. Second, governments have preceded most takeovers with formal declarations of intent and have followed with legal processes to determine the foreign investor's compensation, such as the settlement between Venezuela and Holcim.[26] In addition to the investment's book value, other factors may determine the adequacy (or not) of compensation. On one hand, the compensation may earn a lower return elsewhere. On the other hand, other agreements (such as purchase and management contracts) may create additional benefits for the former investor. Past settlements may serve as indicators in predicting the likely loss if political problems occur.

Analyzing Opinions Because influential people may sway future political events affecting business, managers should access statements by political leaders both in and out of office to determine their private business philosophies, foreign business relations, the means of effecting economic changes, and their feelings toward given foreign countries. They should also access polls showing different leaders' likelihood of gaining political office. Modern technology has improved access to global media so that reports can be retrieved quickly. When considering a country for the first time, managers should visit to listen to a cross section of opinions, such as from embassy officials, foreign and local businesspeople, journalists, academicians, middle-level local government authorities, and labor leaders. These people usually reveal their own attitudes, which often reflect political conditions that may change and affect the business sector. If already operating within a country, the managers working therein can offer evaluations of changing situations.

A company also may rely on commercial risk-assessment services, of which there are many. In fact, companies have been relying more on these services rather than generating their own risk analyses because the services offer concise reports that managers view as credible. Nevertheless, determining what type of information goes into these reports, how it is collected, and what the track record has been for predictions is certainly useful.[27]

> Companies should
> - Examine views of government decision makers.
> - Get a cross section of opinions.
> - Use expert analysts.

Examining Social and Economic Conditions Countries' social and economic conditions may lead to unrest if population segments have unmet aspirations. Frustrated groups may disrupt business by calling general strikes and destroying property and supply lines, such as in the Niger Delta region of Nigeria, where groups have attacked foreign oil companies' property and kidnapped their employees. Frustrated groups might also replace government leaders, such as in response to the violent 2010–2011 demonstrations in Egypt and Tunisia. And political leaders sometimes harness support by blaming problems on foreigners and foreign companies, which could lead to boycotts or rule changes for MNEs or even expropriation of their properties. However, there is no general consensus as to what constitutes dangerous conditions or how such instability can be predicted. The lack of consensus is illustrated by the diverse reactions of companies to the same political situations.

Rather than political stability itself, the direction of change in government seems to be very important. But even if a company accurately predicts the change that will affect business, how long the government will take to enact new practices will still be uncertain.

Foreign Exchange Risk Changes in exchange rates or the ability to move funds out of a country may also affect an MNE. Let's examine these two types of risks.

Exchange-Rate Changes The change in foreign currency value is a two-edged sword, depending on whether you are going abroad to seek sales or resources. Let's say a U.S. company is doing business in India. If it is seeking export sales to India, then a deterioration in the value of the Indian rupee will make it less competitive because it will cost more rupees to buy the U.S. products or services. If it produces within India to serve the Indian market, its competitiveness in India will not change, but its rupee profits from India will buy fewer U.S. dollars when they are brought back to the United States. If,

> **Concept Check**
>
> As we explain in Chapter 9, an **exchange rate** is the price of a currency; in Chapter 10, we discuss some of the causes of exchange-rate changes (including floating rate regimes and interest rates) and explain various methods of forecasting exchange-rate movements (such as focusing on trends in economic variables or trends in the rates themselves).

however, it is seeking assets from India, such as Indian personnel to staff a call center, a fall in the rupee value lowers the U.S.-dollar cost of the personnel.

Companies may accept a lower return in order to move their financial resources more easily.

Mobility of Funds   If a company is to invest abroad, then the ability to get funds out of the country is a factor in country comparison. A theory that helps explain this is **liquidity preference,** which is much like option theory in that it relates to investors' desire for some of their holdings to be in highly liquid assets on which they are willing to take a lower return. They need liquidity to make near-term payments, such as paying out dividends; to cover unexpected contingencies, such as stockpiling materials if a strike threatens supply; and to be able to shift funds to even more profitable opportunities, such as purchasing materials at a discount during a temporary price depression.[28]

The comparative liquidity among countries varies because of capital market activity and government exchange control. An active capital market, particularly a stock market, helps a company sell its assets, especially if it wishes to sell shares on a local exchange or sell the entire operation. Thus, when comparing countries you may wish to include the existence of an active stock market as a favorable variable.

If the government restricts the conversion of funds (several countries have various degrees of exchange control), the foreign investor will be forced to spend some profits or

Does Ge🌐graphy Matter? Don't Fool with Mother Nature

In the past few years, major earthquakes hit Chile, Haiti, and New Zealand, torrential floods inundated parts of northeast Australia, and a deadly flu pandemic spread from Mexico. These events have publicized global vulnerability to natural disasters and communicable diseases. Each year, about 130 million people are exposed to earthquake risk, 119 million to tropical cyclone hazards, 196 million to catastrophic flooding, and 220 million to drought. Natural disasters, on average, claim 184 deaths per day and cause physical damage to industrial plants, crops, inventories, and infrastructure.

These natural disasters are spread unevenly around the world. For instance, some Asian countries are heavily exposed to earthquakes, while some African ones have the highest vulnerability to drought. The United Nations Development Programme has used 450 variables to analyze and publish a disaster risk index (DRI) that compares physical exposure to hazards by country.[29]

Although only 11 percent of the people exposed to these disasters are in the world's poorest nations, those nations account for 55 percent of the deaths because so much of their population lives in poor housing and lacks adequate medical assistance. Likewise, the rural-to-urban migration in developing countries is largely to dangerous mountainsides, ravines, and low-elevation areas ill-equipped to deal with earthquakes and cyclones.

Catastrophic events upset markets, infrastructure, and production while damaging companies' property and injuring their personnel. Who can forget the heartbreaking 2011 telecasts of Japanese houses, cars, and trains being tossed around like toys in a toddler's bath? The earthquake-induced tsunami caused an outbreak of global sympathy for the death and destruction. (See the following photo.) This disaster played havoc with global supplies as well, such as upsetting the world's auto industry production by creating auto parts shortages.[30]

Thus, natural events create additional operating risks and additional costs to insure against them. In turn, insurance companies are challenged to estimate the likelihood and cost of these events. The World Health Organization has developed global atlases of infectious diseases,[31] many of which occur where medical facilities are weakest because of the diseases' association with poverty. They are also associated with natural disaster, such as cholera and malaria outbreaks after flooding. Thus they tend to follow geographic patterns. For example, malaria kills about 2 million people a year, mainly in Africa.

The debilitating effects of disease have an impact on labor force participation and life expectancy and are costly to companies, such as Sasol Petroleum's need to set up a clinic in Mozambique to treat its workers for malaria.[32] Companies also hesitate to send their personnel to epidemic areas. During the Asian severe acute respiratory syndrome (SARS) outbreak, Walmart, Gap, Liz Claiborne, and other companies banned employee travel to affected countries, thus hindering their buying and quality-assurance programs.[33] ●

People all over the world sympathized with the Japanese in 2011 when a massive earthquake caused a tsunami, which then caused a nuclear reactor explosion. The photo shows an outpouring of condolences in the form of flowers and notes in Moscow, Russia.

Source: Anton Gvozdikov/Shutterstock.com

proceeds from share sale in the host country. Thus, it's not surprising that, if other things are equal, investors prefer projects in strong-currency countries with little likelihood of exchange controls.

Competitive Risk   The comparison of likely success among countries is largely contingent on competitors' actions. We now examine four competitive factors to be considered in choice of location: *making operations compatible, spreading risk, following competitors or customers,* and *heading off competitors.*

Making Operations Compatible   Because companies operating abroad encounter less familiar environments, they have more or different operating risks than local firms. Thus, managers initially prefer to operate where they perceive conditions to be more similar to their home country—provided, of course, that the location also offers sufficient opportunities in terms of sales or resource acquisition.[34] (The major types of attributes of similarity versus dissimilarity are shown in Table 12.1.) As they gain experience, they improve their assessments of consumer, competitor, and government actions, thereby reducing their uncertainty. In fact, MNEs have a lower survival rate than local companies for many years after they begin operations—a situation known as the **liability of foreignness.** However, those that learn about their new environments and manage to overcome their early problems eventually have survival rates comparable to those of local firms.[35]

This concept helps explain why, for instance, U.S. companies put earlier and greater emphasis on Canada and the United Kingdom than would be indicated by the opportunity and risk variables discussed so far. In short, managers feel more comfortable doing business in a similar language, culture, and legal system.[36] These similarities may also keep operating costs and risks low because of easier communications. Following early entries, companies also find it useful to create an expansion pattern that will allow management within a portfolio of countries to work interdependently with each other.[37] The ending case shows that Burger King has had a strong emphasis on Latin America and the Caribbean, largely because of distance and communications between that area and the headquarters in Miami.

Economic similarity is an important consideration. Both Canada and the United Kingdom have high per capita GDPs, similar to those in the United States, which

Companies are highly attracted to countries that

- Are located nearby.
- Share the same language.
- Have market conditions similar to those in their home countries.

Concept Check

In discussing "Cultural Distance" in Chapter 2, we observe that when two countries are culturally close, a company usually expects fewer differences—and must make fewer adjustments— when moving operations from one to the other. Here we point out that economic similarity often fosters the same conditions of compatibility.

CRN

Case Review Note

TABLE 12.1   The Distance Sensitivity of Industries: Indicators

Cultural distance	Administrative distance	Geographic distance	Economic distance
High linguistic content	Government involved in funding, procurement, regulating standard-setting, before international bodies, etc.	Low value-to-weight or bulk	High intensity of labor, other factors prone to absolute cost differences
Strong country of origin effects (vertical distance)	Strategic industry status (votes, money, staples, state control, national champions)	Hazards in transportation	Potential for international scale/ scope/experience economies
Significant differences in preferences/ standards (horizontal distance)	Specialized, durable sunk capital (and holdup potential)	Perishability/time-sensitivity	High income-related increases in willingness-to-pay
Entrenched tastes/ traditions	Restraints on trade/FDI (e.g., agriculture)	Need to perform key activities locally (favors FDI over trade)	Differences in customers/channels/ business systems

Source: Based on Pankaj Ghemawat, *World 3.0: World Prosperity and How to Achieve It*, (Boston: Harvard Business Review Press, 2011): 299, which is based on his earlier framework in "Distance Still Matters: The Hard Reality of Global Expansion," *Harvard Business Review*, 79:8 (September 2001): 140.

indicate a likely demand for products first created for the U.S. market. If you first develop products for your domestic market, you might consider other countries' similarity to yours in terms of economic level.

In addition, historical ties between pairs of countries help explain companies' geographic preferences for foreign operations.[38] While many of these ties relate to common culture and ethnicity, others occur because of a history of positive exchanges that reduce the perception of operating risk for companies in home countries and for stakeholders in host countries.

You should also try to ensure that a country's policies and norms are compatible with your company's competitive advantages. For example, Blockbuster failed in Germany because the laws prevented it from operating on evenings, Sundays, and holidays—popular times in the United States and for last-minute impulse decisions to rent videos anywhere. Further, Blockbuster had created a store environment to attract the whole family, but German consumers preferred to see family entertainment in a movie house and sought pornographic films from video stores.[39]

Companies may also prefer locales that will permit them to operate with product types, plant sizes, and operating practices familiar to their managers. When examining locales, teams that include personnel with backgrounds in each functional area—marketing, finance, human resources, engineering, and production—will more likely uncover the best fits with their companies' resources and objectives.

Finally, companies should consider local availability of resources in relation to their needs. Many foreign operations require local resources, which may severely restrict the feasibility of given locales. A company may need to find local personnel or a viable local partner with an understanding of its type of business and technology. Or it may need to add local capital to what it is willing to bring in.

Spreading Risk   By operating in diverse localities, companies may be able to smooth their sales and profits and gain a competitive advantage in raising funds.[40] They may further guard against the effects of currency value changes by locating in

Concept Check

Recall from Chapter 6 that a factor helping to explain trade patterns—why a country trades more with certain countries than with others—is the historical relationship between them, especially continued trade between a former colonizer with its former colonies.

countries whose exchange rates are not closely correlated with each other.[41] Such a strategy is in many ways opposite to what we just discussed about preferring countries similar to the home country. This is because the best smoothing of sales and profits will likely occur from operating in economies that are the least correlated; however, the downside of this is that operating in these dissimilar economies may give rise to greater competitive risk because management is less familiar with their operating conditions.

Following Competitors or Customers Managers may purposely crowd a market to prevent competitors from gaining advantages there that they can use to improve their competitive positions elsewhere—a situation known as **oligopolistic reaction**.[42] This helps explain why China now has more automobile producers than any other country, far more than market analysts believe it can sustain.[43]

At the same time, companies may gain advantages by locating where competitors are. To begin with, the competitors may have performed the costly task of evaluating locations and building market acceptance for a particular type of product, so followers may get a so-called free ride. Moreover, there are clusters of competitors (sometimes called agglomeration) in various locations—think of all the computer firms in California's Silicon Valley and in Dubai.[44] These clusters attract multiple suppliers and personnel with specialized skills, as well as buyers who want to compare potential sellers but don't want to travel great distances between them. A company gains better access to information about new developments by coming in frequent contact with personnel from the other firms.[45]

There are also advantages of following customers into a market. Bridgestone Tires was a major supplier to Japanese auto companies in Japan, and it followed them when they established U.S. manufacturing facilities. First, Bridgestone's track record with Japanese auto companies, such as Toyota, gave it an advantage over other tire manufacturers in the United States. Second, if another tire manufacturer were to develop a strong relationship with Toyota in the United States, it might use this experience as a successful springboard to undermine Bridgestone's position elsewhere.

Heading Off Competition A company may try to reduce competitive risk by getting a strong foothold in markets before competitors do, by avoiding strong competitors altogether, or, when its innovative advantage may be short-lived, by moving quickly into markets before competitors can copy the innovation. Of course, this strategy implies ample market where one locates. This is shown humorously in Figure 12.5.

Our opening case showed how Carrefour tries to enter growth markets before its major competitors, for fairly obvious reasons: By being first, it can more easily gain the best partners, best locations, and best suppliers—a strategy to gain **first-mover advantage.** However, in some cases this strategy disadvantaged Carrefour because competitors learned from its mistakes. Another first-mover advantage is the potential of gaining strong relations with the government, such as Volkswagen in China and Lockheed with Russia.[46]

Companies may also develop strategies to avoid significant competition, rather than going where it's located. PriceSmart, a discount operator, has all its warehouse stores outside its home country (the United States) and has had success by targeting locations in Central America, the Caribbean, and Asia that are considered too small to attract warehouse stores from competitors like Walmart and Carrefour.[47]

One strategy for exploiting temporary innovative advantages is known as the **imitation lag,** whereby a company moves first to those countries where local competitors are most likely to catch up to the innovative advantage.[48] The countries apt to catch up more rapidly are the ones whose companies invest a great deal in technology.

In terms of competition, some different strategies are to go

- First where other firms are most apt to enter the market as competitors.
- Into markets that competitors have not entered.
- Where there are clusters of competitors.

CRN
Case Review Note

FIGURE 12.5

Operating where there are no competitors may not be a good strategy if they have good reasons for avoiding the location.

Source: Frank Cotham/Cartoonbank .com

"I question your choice of locations."

Collecting and Analyzing Data

Information is needed at all levels of control.

• Companies should compare the cost of information with its value.

Companies undertake business research to reduce outcome uncertainties from their decisions and to assess their operating performance. The research includes finding answers to questions such as: Can we hire qualified personnel? Will the economic and political climate allow us to reasonably foresee our future? Are our distributors servicing sufficient accounts? What is our market share?

Clearly, information helps managers improve corporate performance. However, they can seldom get all the information they want, due to time and cost constraints. So managers should compare the estimated costs of information with the probable payoff it will generate in revenue gains or cost savings.

Information inaccuracies result from

• Inability to collect and analyze data.
• Purposefully misleading data.
• Exclusion of nonmarket and illegal activity.

SOME PROBLEMS WITH RESEARCH RESULTS AND DATA

Because of the lack, obsolescence, and inaccuracy of data on many countries, research can be difficult and expensive to undertake. Although there are problems everywhere, they are most acute in developing countries. Let's discuss the two basic problems: inaccurate information and noncomparability in information from different countries.

Inaccurate Information   For the most part, there are five basic reasons why reported information may be inaccurate:

1. Governmental resources may limit accurate data collection   Countries may have such limited resources that other projects necessarily receive budget priority, such as spending to improve the literacy rate rather than measuring it. Even if they emphasize data collection, funds may be short for buying the latest computer hardware and software and training the people to use them. The result may be gaps in reliable and timely information.

2. Governments may purposely publish misleading information Of equal concern to researchers is the publication of false or purposely deceptive information designed to mislead government superiors, the country's rank and file, or companies and institutions abroad. For instance, the European Commission rebuked Greece in 2010 for falsifying public finance data.[49]

3. Respondents may give false information to data collectors Mistrust of how the data will be used may lead respondents to answer questions incorrectly, particularly if they probe financial details or anything else that respondents may consider private. For example, many government figures are collected through questionnaires, such as those in the United States to estimate international travel and tourism expenditures. People may misstate their actual expenditures, particularly if they had not reported the true value of foreign purchases on incoming customs forms.

4. Official data may include only legal and reported market activities Further distortions may occur because nationally reported income figures include only legal and reported market activities. Thus, illegal income from such activities as the drug trade, theft, bribery, and prostitution is not included in national income figures, or it appears in other economic sectors because of money laundering. Contraband figures do not appear in official trade statistics and may be substantial, such as the smuggling of subsidized Bolivian oil into neighboring countries.[50] Finally, many economic activities, such as payments in cash to avoid tax payments on income, may also be substantial.

5. Poor methodology may be used Inaccuracies are also due to poor collection and analysis by researchers both within and outside the government. Too often, broad generalizations are drawn from too few observations on nonrepresentative samples and poorly designed questionnaires.

Noncomparable Information Countries do not necessarily publish reports such as censuses, output figures, and trade statistics for the same time periods or at the same time as each other. So a company must extrapolate in order to estimate how countries compare. Countries also differ in how they define items, such as family income, literacy, and FDI. Activities taking place outside the market economy, such as within the home, do not show up in income figures. Thus, the different extent among countries in terms of people producing for their own consumption (growing vegetables, preparing meals at home, sewing clothes, cutting hair, and so on) distorts country comparisons.

> Problems in information comparability arise from
> • Differences in definitions and base years.
> • Distortions in currency conversions.

Accounting rules such as depreciation also differ, resulting in noncomparable net national product figures. Another problem concerns exchange rates, which must be used to convert countries' financial data to some common currency. For instance, a 10 percent appreciation of the Japanese yen in relation to the U.S. dollar will result in a 10 percent increase in the per capita GDP of Japanese residents when figures are reported in dollars. Does this mean the Japanese are suddenly 10 percent richer? Obviously not, because they use about 85 percent of their yen income to make purchases in yen in their economy; thus, they have little additional purchasing power for 85 percent of what they buy.

EXTERNAL SOURCES OF INFORMATION

Although information is needed for making good location decisions, there are simply too many sources for us to include a comprehensive list. Chances are, at least for scanning purposes, that you will use the Internet to collect most of your information.

Some searches will lead you to free information, others to services for which you must pay. The following discussion highlights the major types of information sources in terms of their completeness, reliability, and cost.

Individualized Reports   Market research and business consulting companies conduct studies for a fee. They generally are the most costly information source because their individualized nature restricts prorating among a number of companies. However, the fact that a company can specify what information it wants often makes the expense worthwhile.

Specialized Studies   Research organizations prepare and sell fairly specific studies at costs much lower than those for individualized reports. These specialized studies are sometimes directories of companies that operate in a given locale, perhaps containing financial or other information about the companies. They may also be about business in certain locales, forms of business, or specific products.

Service Companies   Most companies providing services to international clients—such as banks, transportation agencies, and accounting firms—publish reports that are usually geared toward either the conduct of business in a given area or some specific subject of general interest, such as tax or trademark legislation. Because the service firms intend to reach a wide market of companies, their reports tend to be fairly general. Some also offer informal opinions about such things as the reputations of possible business associates and the names of people to contact in a company.

Government Agencies   When a government wants to stimulate foreign business activity, the amount and type of information it makes available may be substantial. The U.S. Department of Commerce compiles news about and regulations in individual foreign countries. It disseminates specific information on product sales location in the National Trade Data Bank, and its representatives also help set up appointments with businesspeople abroad.

International Organizations and Agencies   Numerous organizations and agencies are supported by more than one country, including the UN, the WTO, the IMF, the OECD, and the EU. All of them have large research staffs that compile basic statistics as well as prepare reports and recommendations concerning common trends and problems. Many of the international development banks even help finance investment-feasibility studies.

Trade Associations   Trade associations connected to various product lines collect, evaluate, and disseminate a wide variety of data dealing with technical and competitive factors in their industries. Many of these data are available in the trade journals published by such associations; others may or may not be available to nonmembers.

INTERNALLY GENERATED DATA

MNEs may have to collect much information themselves. Sometimes this may consist of no more than observing keenly and asking many questions. Investigators can see what kind of merchandise is available, determine who is buying and where, and uncover the hidden distribution points and competition. Hidden competition for ready-made clothing may be seamstresses working in private homes; for vacuum cleaners, it may be servants who clean with mops. Surreptitiously sold contraband may compete with locally produced goods. Traditional analysis methods would not reveal such facts.

Country Comparison Tools

Once companies scan for information, they need to analyze it. Two common tools for this are *grids* and *matrices*. In preparing either, it is useful to have a team made up of people from different functions so that production, marketing, finance, human

Should Companies Operate in and Send Employees to Violent Areas?

Point **Yes** Where there's risk, there are usually rewards. Companies should not shun areas with violence. Businesspeople have always taken risks, and employees have always gone to dangerous areas. As far back as the seventeenth century, immigrants to what are now the United States, India, and Australia encountered disease and hostile native populations. Had companies and immigrants not taken chances, the world would be far less developed today.

You can't look at the risk from violence apart from others. Although we don't have historical data, most situations are probably safer today. Disease is still a bigger danger than violence, but medical advances against a number of historical killers (polio, measles, smallpox, tuberculosis, etc.) have reduced that risk, while evacuation in case of a *real* emergency situation is much faster.

But let's assume for a moment that we decide to avoid countries with the potential for violence against our facilities and employees. Is there any such place? The opinions we get from so-called risk experts are certainly conflicting. One said, "It's an even playing field around the world. You can go to London, Caracas, Madrid, or New York, and from a terrorism standpoint, the risk is the same."[51] Another intelligence provider placed the United States as riskier for terrorism than Iraq, and Britain more dangerous than Nepal.[52] Although these analyses seem intuitively wrong, street riots in London, a bombing in

Oklahoma City, and U.S. school and university shootings certainly make one wonder. The deputy assistant director of the FBI said, "We are dealing every single day with a variety of domestic terrorism threats that are alive and well and in this country [United States]."[53] Until a protester went on a shooting rampage in 2011, Norway was considered a super-safe haven. Now about the only places that everyone agrees are low-risk are Greenland and Iceland.

Some industries don't have the luxury of avoiding violent countries. Take the petroleum industry. Oil companies have to go where there is a high likelihood of finding oil. It would be great to find it all in places like Iceland and Switzerland, but this is not the reality. Most of the credible alternatives are in areas that have had recent bombings, kidnappings, or organized crime—the Middle East, West Africa, the Central Asian former Soviet republics, Ecuador, and Venezuela.[54] If companies didn't go to these places, they'd be out of business.

In effect, we'll keep operating anywhere there are opportunities. If a place seems physically risky, we'll take whatever precautions we can. We'll share intelligence reports, put people through safety training courses (there are plenty of these available now), and take security actions abroad. And perhaps we won't transfer spouses and children to the "risky" areas so we don't have to be on top of what is happening with as many people.

Should Companies Operate in and Send Employees to Violent Areas?

Counterpoint **No** We're no longer concerned simply with being caught in the crossfire between opposing military factions. Antiglobalization groups want to harm our personnel and facilities so that we'll leave, or so that they gain international publicity. Groups see us as easy marks for extortion by threatening harm or kidnapping our personnel. Still others are against foreigners, regardless of their aims. Such a group in Afghanistan killed staff members from Médecins sans Frontières who were there to treat sick and injured people.

At the same time, getting caught in the crossfire has become a bigger risk. Arms trafficking has risen and has lowered prices not only to revolutionaries but also to drug and alien smugglers and money launderers.[55] As MNEs, we can't help being visible, and thus vulnerable.

In essence, if we operate where risk of violence is great, we put our personnel in danger. Although local personnel may be at a lesser risk of, say, kidnapping, experience shows that they

too are not immune. Furthermore, we have to send foreign personnel there. Some go as managers or technicians on long assignments; others must go on business trips, such as to audit books, ensure quality control, and offer staff advice that must involve on-site visits. The dangers are not inconsequential. There are thousands of reported kidnappings per year, many targeting foreign workers and their families. In Nigeria, for instance, there have been recent kidnappings of foreign oil workers, ship crew members, and even a visiting priest.[56]

It's simply unethical to put our employees in such situations. Of course, we don't force them to go to dangerous places, and we can get enough people to work there, especially during a global recession. However, our experience is that there are three types of people who want or are willing to work in such areas, and none are ideal. First are those who simply want the high compensation and big insurance policies, some of whom are experienced in military or undercover activities. They tend to be highly independent and hard to control. Second are the naïve who don't understand the danger and are difficult to safeguard through training and security activities. Third are the thrill seekers, who find that adrenaline is like an addictive drug; they are most at risk because of the thrill of danger and the reluctance to leave when situations worsen.[57]

High risk to individuals is indicative of a political situation out of control—a harbinger of additional risks that may occur through governmental changes, falls in consumer confidence, and a general malaise that damages revenues and operating regulations. This is not the kind of country in which to conduct operations.

resource, and legal factors are all considered. However, once companies commit to locations, they need continuous updates.

GRIDS

Grids are tools that
- May depict acceptable or unacceptable conditions.
- Rank countries by important variables.

Managers may use a grid to compare countries on whatever factors they deem important. Table 12.2 is an example of a grid with information placed into three categories. The managers may immediately eliminate certain countries from consideration because of characteristics they find unacceptable (companies vary in this). These factors are in the first category of variables, by which Country I is eliminated. The managers assign values and weights to other variables so that they rank each country according

TABLE 12.2   Simplified Market-Penetration Grid

This table is simply an example: In the real world, a company chooses the variables that it regards as most important and may weight some as more important than others. Here managers rate Country II the most attractive because it's regarded as high return–low risk. Country IV also promises a high return and Country III low risk. Note that Country I is eliminated immediately because the company will only go where 100 percent ownership is permitted.

Variable	Weight	I	II	III	IV	V
1. Acceptable (A), Unacceptable (U) factors						
a. Allows 100 percent ownership	—	U	A	A	A	A
b. Allows licensing to majority-owned subsidiary	—	A	A	A	A	A
2. Return (higher number = preferred rating)						
a. Size of investment needed	0–5	—	4	3	3	3
b. Direct costs	0–3	—	3	1	2	2
c. Tax rate	0–2	—	2	1	2	2
d. Market size, present	0–4	—	3	2	4	1
e. Market size, 3–10 years	0–3	—	2	1	3	1
f. Market share, immediate potential, 0–2 years	0–2	—	2	1	2	1
g. Market share, 3–10 years	0–2	—	2	1	2	0
Total			18	10	18	10
3. Risk (lower number = preferred rating)						
a. Market loss, 3–10 years (if no present penetration)	0–4	—	2	1	3	2
b. Exchange problems	0–3	—	0	0	3	3
c. Political-unrest potential	0–3	—	0	1	2	3
d. Business laws, present	0–4	—	1	0	4	3
e. Business laws, 3–10 years	0–2	—	0	1	2	2
Total			3	3	14	13

to attributes of relative importance to the company. In this hypothetical example, we've attached more weight to the size of investment needed than to the tax rate. For example, the table graphically pinpoints Country II as high return–low risk, Country III as low return–low risk, Country IV as high return–high risk, and Country V as low return–high risk.

Both the variables and the weights differ by product and company depending on the company's internal situation and its objectives. For instance, managers in a company selling a low-priced consumer product might weigh population size heavily as an indicator of market opportunity, whereas those in a company selling tires might weigh heavily the number of vehicles registered. The grid technique is useful even when a company does not compare countries, because it can set the minimum score needed for either investing additional resources or committing more funds to a more detailed feasibility study.

Grids do tend to get cumbersome, however, as the number of variables increases. Although they are useful in ranking countries, they often obscure interrelationships among them.

MATRICES

To more clearly show the opportunity/risk relationship, managers can plot values on a matrix such as the one shown in Figure 12.6. In this particular example, Countries E and F are high-opportunity and low-risk countries compared to Countries A, B, C, and D, making them better candidates for detailed analysis.

In reality, however, managers may sometimes have to choose between a country with high risk and high opportunity and another with low risk and low opportunity, thus making a decision based on their tolerance for risk and on the portfolio of countries where the company is already operating. Further, although A, B, C, and D are less appealing than E and F, the company may nevertheless find opportunities in A, B, C, and D—perhaps licensing or shared-ownership arrangements—without necessarily making a large commitment.

But how can managers plot values on such a matrix? They must determine which factors are good indicators of their companies' risk and opportunity and weight them to reflect their importance. For instance, on the risk axis they might give 20 percent (0.2) of

With an opportunity-risk matrix, a company can

- Decide on indicators and weight them.
- Evaluate each country on the weighted indicators.

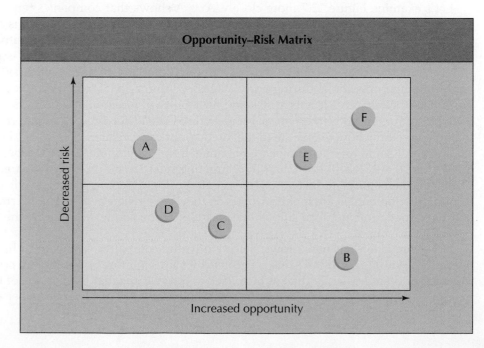

FIGURE 12.6
Opportunity–Risk Matrix

Countries E and F are the most desirable because they boast a combination of a high level of opportunity and a low level of risk. But what if the decision came down to Countries A and B? The level of opportunity in Country A may not be as high as a company would like, but the low level of risk may be attractive. Country B, on the other hand, promises a high level of opportunities but also threatens a high level of risk. A decision between Countries A and B will probably take the firm's *risk* tolerance into consideration.

the weight to expropriation risk, 25 percent (0.25) to foreign-exchange controls, 20 percent (0.2) to civil disturbances and terrorism, 20 percent (0.2) to natural disasters, and 15 percent (0.15) to exchange-rate change, for a total allocation of 100 percent. They would then rate each country on a scale, such as from 1 to 10 for each variable (with 10 indicating the best score), and multiply each variable by the weight they allocate to it. If they give Country A a rating of 8 on the expropriation-risk variable, they would multiply 8 by 0.2 (the weight they assign to expropriation) for a score of 1.6. They would then sum all of Country A's risk-variable scores to place it on the risk axis, and similarly plot the location of Country A on the opportunity axis.

A key element of this kind of matrix, and one that managers do not always include in practice, is the projection of where countries will be in the future, or at least the direction in which they *should* move. Such a projection is obviously useful, but the farther one forecasts into the future, the less certain is the projection.

Allocating among Locations

The scanning tools we have just discussed are useful for narrowing country alternatives and allocating operational emphasis among countries. We now discuss three complementary strategies for international expansion: alternative gradual commitments, geographic diversification versus concentration, and reinvestment versus harvesting.

ALTERNATIVE GRADUAL COMMITMENTS

Companies may reduce risks from the liability of foreignness by

- Going first to countries with characteristics similar to those of their home countries.
- Having experienced intermediaries handle operations for them.
- Operating in formats requiring commitment of fewer resources abroad.
- Moving initially to one or a few, rather than many, foreign countries.

As we've discussed, because of liability of foreignness, companies favor operations in areas similar to their home countries. Nevertheless, there are alternative means of risk-minimization expansion patterns they can undertake, as shown in Figure 12.7. As you examine this figure, note that the farther a company moves from the center on any axis, the deeper its international commitment becomes.

However, a company does not necessarily move at the same speed along each axis. In fact, it may jump over some of the steps. A slow movement along one axis may free up resources that allow faster expansion along another.

Let's examine Figure 12.7 more closely. Axis A shows that companies tend to move gradually from a purely domestic focus to one that encompasses operations in countries similar and then dissimilar to one's own country. However, an alternative when moving quickly along the A axis (and even jumping the intermediate step) is to move slowly along the B axis. The B axis shows that a company may use intermediaries to handle foreign operations during early stages of international expansion, because this minimizes the resources it puts at risk and its liability of foreignness. It can then commit fewer resources to both international endeavors, instead relying on the intermediaries that already know how to operate in the foreign market. A related example is the foreign expansion of some high technology companies from developing countries, particularly those from the BRICs. Rather than first targeting nearby countries with characteristics similar to their home markets, they have gone to high income countries where short-term market potentials are higher. However, they have relied heavily on intermediaries and have made foreign acquisitions that include the personnel who know the markets they are targeting.

However, if the business grows successfully, the company may want to handle the operations with its own staff. This is because by learning more about foreign operations it perceives them less risky than at the onset, and it realizes that the volume of business may justify the development of internal capabilities such as hiring trained personnel to maintain a department for foreign sales or purchases.

FIGURE 12.7 The Usual Pattern of Internationalization

The farther a company moves outward along any of the axes (A, B, C, D), the deeper its international commitment. Most companies move at different speeds along different axes.

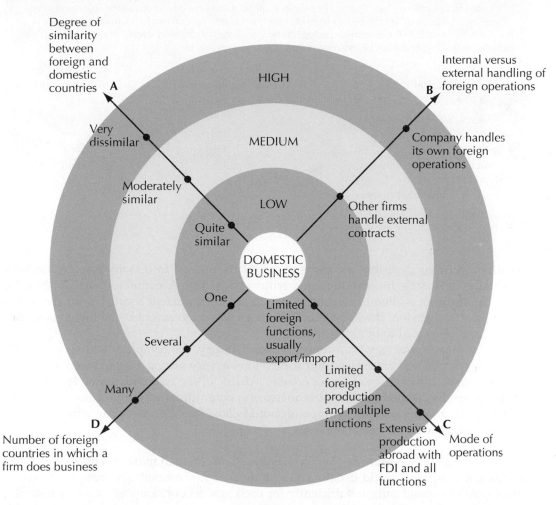

Axis C shows that importing or exporting is usually the first international mode a company undertakes. At an early stage of international involvement, importing and exporting require the placement of few company resources abroad. In fact, it may involve investing few additional resources if the company can use excess production capacity to produce more goods, which it would then export. Thus, moving along the C axis is a means to minimize the risk of the liability of foreignness because of forgoing such functions as managing a foreign workforce for production.

Later, the company might, in addition to exporting, make an even higher commitment through FDI to produce abroad. Its infusion of capital, personnel, and technology is highest for these operations. Axis D shows that companies can move internationally one country at a time, thus not having to become overwhelmed by learning about many countries all at once. However, as we discuss in the next section, there may be a competitive drive to move to a number of countries almost simultaneously.

GEOGRAPHIC DIVERSIFICATION VERSUS CONCENTRATION

Ultimately, a company may gain a sizable presence and commitment in most countries; however, there are different paths to that position. Although any move abroad means some geographic diversification, the term **diversification strategy** in the context of

Strategies for ultimately reaching a high level of commitment in many countries are

- Diversification—go to many fast and then build up slowly in each.
- Concentration—go to one or a few and build up fast before going to others.
- A hybrid of the two.

TABLE 12.3   To Diversify or to Concentrate: The Role of Product and Market Factors

If a company determines that "Product or Market Factors" satisfy the conditions in the column headed "Prefer Diversification," it may benefit from moving quickly into several markets simultaneously. If the same factors satisfy the conditions under "Prefer Concentration," it may decide to enter and work initially to develop a substantial presence in just one or a few markets.

Product or Market Factor	Prefer Diversification If:	Prefer Concentration If:
1. Growth rate of each market	Low	High
2. Sales stability in each market	Low	High
3. Competitive lead time	Short	Long
4. Spillover effects	High	Low
5. Need for product, communication, and distribution adaptation	Low	High
6. Program control requirements	Low	High

Source: "Marketing Expansion Strategies in Multinational Marketing," *Journal of Marketing* 43 (Spring 1979): 89. Reprinted by permission of the American Marketing Association © 1979.

location decisions describes a company's rapid movement into many foreign markets, gradually increasing its commitments within each one. A company can do this, for example, through a liberal licensing policy to ensure sufficient resources for the initial widespread expansion. It will eventually increase its involvement by taking on activities that it first contracted to other companies.

At the other extreme, with a **concentration strategy,** the company will move to only one or a few foreign countries until it develops a very strong involvement and competitive position there. There are, of course, hybrids of the two strategies—for example, moving rapidly to most markets but increasing commitment in only a few. Table 12.3 sums up the major variables a company should consider when deciding which strategy to use.[58] We now discuss each of these.

Case Review Note

Growth Rate in Each Market   When the growth rate in each market is high or needs to be high, a company should usually concentrate on a few markets, because it will cost a great deal to expand output sufficiently for each one. In our opening case, for instance, we point out that to be cost effective in an overseas market, Carrefour focuses on building a sufficient distribution presence in target countries. However, slower growth or the need for growth in each market may result in a company's having enough resources to build and maintain a market share in several different countries.[59]

Sales Stability in Each Market   As we have discussed, a company may smooth its earnings and sales because of operations in various parts of the world. The more stable the sales and profits within each market, the less advantage there is from a diversification strategy. Similarly, the more correlated the markets, the less smoothing is achieved by selling in each.

Competitive Lead Time   We have discussed Carrefour's plan to gain first-mover advantages. If a company determines that it has a long lead time over competitors, then it may be able to follow a concentration strategy and still beat competitors into other markets. Otherwise, it may need to either cede leadership in some countries to competitors or follow a diversification strategy.

Spillover Effects   Situations in which the marketing program in one country results in awareness of the product in other countries are known as **spillover effects.** These are advantageous because additional customers may be reached with little additional cost, which can happen if the product is advertised through media sent cross-nationally, such as U.S. television ads that reach Canadians. When marketing programs reach many countries, such as by satellite television or the Internet, a diversification strategy has advantages.

Need for Product, Communication, and Distribution Adaptation   Companies may have to alter products and methods of operating abroad—a process that, because of cost, favors a concentration strategy. The adaptation cost may limit the resources the company has for expanding in many different markets. Further, if the adaptations are unique to each country, the company cannot easily spread the costs over sales in more than one country to reduce total unit costs.

Program Control Requirements   The more a company needs to control its operations in a foreign country, the more favorable a concentration strategy is. This is because the company will need to use more of its resources to maintain that control, such as by taking a larger percentage of ownership in the operation. Its need for more control could result from various reasons, including the fear that collaboration with a partner will create a competitor.

REINVESTMENT AND HARVESTING

So far, we've discussed the sequencing of country entry. Then, once a company is operating abroad, it must evaluate how much effort to allocate to each location. With FDI, the company transfers financial capital and has physical and human capital in place. If the investment is successful, the company will earn money that it may remit back to headquarters or reinvest to increase the investment value. Over time, most of the value of a company's foreign investment, if successful, comes from reinvesting. If the investment is unsuccessful or its outlook less favorable than in other countries, the company may consider using the capital elsewhere or even discontinuing the investment.

Reinvestment Decisions   Companies treat decisions to replace depreciated assets or to add to the existing stock of capital from retained earnings abroad somewhat differently from original investment decisions. Once committed to a given locale, a company may find no option to move a substantial portion of the earnings elsewhere; to do so would endanger the continued successful operation of the given foreign facility. The failure to expand might result in a falling market share and a higher unit cost than that of competitors.

> A company may have to make new commitments to maintain competitiveness abroad.

Aside from competitive factors, a company may need several years of almost total reinvestment and allocation of new funds in one area to attain its objectives, such as to meet target growth. Another reason a company treats reinvestment decisions differently is that once experienced personnel are in a given country, they may be the best judges of what is needed there, so headquarters may delegate certain investment decisions to them.

Harvesting   Companies commonly reduce commitments in some countries because those countries have poorer performance prospects than do others—a process known as **harvesting (or divesting).** Carrefour, for example, sold off underperforming operations in Korea and Slovakia so as to have funds for more promising ventures into the Chinese, Indian, and Russian markets. There are other reasons as well. J. Sainsbury withdrew from the Egyptian market because its management did not expect a turnaround in its poorly performing operation there.[60] Dana sold its U.K. facility to use funds to concentrate on developing different automotive technologies.[61] Goodyear sold its Indonesian rubber plantation because of its decision to stop producing rubber.[62]

Case Review Note

> Companies must decide how to get out of operations if
> - They no longer fit the overall strategy.
> - There are better alternative opportunities.

Some indications suggest that companies might benefit by planning divestments better and by developing divestment specialists. Companies have tended to wait too long before divesting, instead trying expensive means of improving performance, such as those proposed by local managers, who fear losing their positions if the company abandons the operation.

Ideas for investment projects typically originate with middle managers or with managers in foreign subsidiaries who are enthusiastic about collecting information to accompany a proposal as it moves upward in the organization. After all, the evaluation and employment of these people depend on growth. They have no such incentive to propose divestments. These proposals typically originate at the top of the organization after upper management has tried most remedies for improving operational performance.[63]

Companies may divest by a sale or closure of facilities, usually preferring a sale because they receive some compensation. A company that considers divesting because of a country's well-publicized political or economic situation may find few potential buyers except at very low prices. In such situations, it may try to delay divestment, hoping that the situation will improve. If it does, the firm that waits out the situation generally is in a better position to regain markets and profits than one that forsakes its operation.

A company cannot always simply abandon an investment either. Governments frequently require performance contracts, such as substantial severance packages to employees that make a loss from divestment greater than the direct investment's net value. Further, the length of time to go through insolvency (up to 10 years in some countries) alters the percentage of value recovered from a divestment. For example, in Japan, Singapore, and Finland, investors recover an average of over 90 percent of the value, whereas in Brazil, Cambodia, and Madagascar they typically recover nothing.[64] Finally, many MNEs fear adverse international publicity and difficulty in reentering a market if they do not sever relations with a foreign government on amicable terms.

Noncomparative Decision Making

| Most companies examine proposals one at a time and accept them if they meet minimum-threshold criteria.

Because companies have limited resources at their disposal, it might seem that they maintain a storehouse of foreign operating proposals that they can rank by some predetermined criteria. If this were so, managers could simply start allocating resources to the top-ranked proposal and continue down the list until they could make no further commitments. This is often not the case, however. They make **go-no-go decisions** by examining one opportunity at a time and pursuing it if it meets some threshold criteria.

To begin with, companies sometimes need to respond quickly to prospects they had not anticipated. Many might need to respond to unsolicited proposals to sell abroad or sign joint venture or licensing contracts. Many might initiate export activity passively— that is, foreign companies or export intermediaries approach them to be suppliers. Similarly, undertakings may be onetime possibilities because a government or another company solicits requests. Or, a government may change rules to allow foreign acquisitions, such as Nigeria did for banking.[65] Further, there may be a chance to buy properties that another company divests. When Enron faced bankruptcy, it needed to sell many of its foreign facilities, so companies such as Tractebel from Belgium and Royal Dutch/ Shell bid on its Korean facilities.[66] In addition, having discussed the competitive advantages of following customers' and competitors' moves into foreign markets, we know we cannot always foresee when the customers and competitors will move.

Another factor inhibiting the comparison of country operations is that they may be so interdependent that one cannot meaningfully evaluate them separately. Profit figures from individual operations may obscure the real impact they have on overall company profits. For example, if a U.S. company were to establish an assembly operation in Australia, the operation could either increase or reduce exports from the United States, thus affecting U.S. profit figures. Moreover, headquarters may have to incur additional costs to oversee the Australian operation and coordinate the movement of components into Australia. These costs are difficult to estimate and will likely not show up in the Australian income figures.

Or perhaps by building a plant in Brazil to supply components to Volkswagen of Brazil, the company may increase the possibility of selling to Volkswagen in other countries. As a result of the Australian or Brazilian projects, management would have to make assumptions about the changed profits for the company's total global operations. Finally, interdependence occurs because much of the sales and purchases of foreign subsidiaries are among units of the same parent company. The prices the company charges on these transactions will affect the relative profitability of one unit compared to another.

Clearly, companies cannot afford to conduct very many feasibility studies simultaneously. Even if they can, the studies are apt to be in various stages of completion at any given time. Suppose a company completes its study for an Australian project while continuing studies on New Zealand, Japan, and Indonesia. Can the company afford to hold off on making a decision about Australia? Probably not. Waiting would likely invalidate much of the Australian study, thus necessitating added expense and further delays to update it. In sum, three factors inhibit companies from comparing investment opportunities: cost, time, and the interrelation of operations on global performance.

Looking to the
Future Will Prime Locations Change?

Future sales- and resource-seeking opportunities and risks may shift among countries because of a variety of demographic, sociocultural, political-legal, technological, and economic conditions. We will concentrate here on population changes and where populations can and will prefer to work. In Chapter 6, we discussed how demographers expect a slowing in the growth of global population through 2050, with some countries experiencing declining populations. At the same time, growth should remain robust in many developing economies, particularly those in sub-Saharan Africa. The projection is that the percentage of people living in currently developed countries is expected to fall to 13.7 percent from a 2000 figure of 19.7 percent. The least developed countries will have the biggest population increase.

Further, because the world's population will continue to age, the share of what we now consider the working-age population should fall for developed countries and increase in many developing ones. Because there is a positive relationship between the proportional size of the working-age population and per capita GDP, the growth in per capita GDP should be higher in today's developing economies than in today's developed countries unless we redefine working age.[67] These demographic changes, if they materialize, will have implications for the location of both markets and labor forces.

An intriguing possibility is the near-officeless headquarters for international companies. Technology may permit more people to work from anywhere as they email and teleconference with their colleagues, customers, and suppliers. In fact, they can live anywhere in the world and work from their homes, as is already occurring within some professions.[68]

However, if people can work from home, they may move those homes where they want to live rather than living where their employers are now located. Because we're talking here largely about highly creative and highly innovative self-motivated people, they can usually get permission to live in almost any country of the world.

A leading researcher on urbanization and planning has shown that beginning at least as early as the Roman Empire these types of people have been drawn to certain cities that were the centers of innovation. He maintains that this attraction is due to people's improvement through interchange with others like themselves—like "a very bright class in a school or a college. They all try to score off each other and do better." Thus, if he's correct, the brightest minds may work more at home but still need the face-to-face interaction with their colleagues.[69]

These arguments are provocative, particularly because we now have technology to allow people to communicate without traveling as much, yet the continued increase in business travel shows that there is still a need for face-to-face interaction. The researcher further suggests that these people will be drawn to the same places that attract tourists.

Concomitantly, another view is that in leading Western societies, the elite made up of intellectuals and highly educated people is increasingly using its capability to delay and block new technologies. If successful, their efforts will result in the emergence of different countries at the forefront of technological development and acceptance.[70] ■

Burger King® Beefs Up Global Operations

CASE

As of June 2011 Burger King, the world's largest flame-broiled and second largest hamburger fast food restaurant chain, operated 12,301 restaurants in 80 countries and territories.[71] It employed over 34,000 people directly, and franchises employed many more. Only Yum Brands (A&W, KFC, Long John Silver, Pizza Hut, and Taco Bell), McDonald's, and Subway, with 37,000, 32,400, and 32,000 restaurants respectively were larger, and Yum planned to divest two of its brands. Burger King Corporation plans to increase the number of operating units in the near future, with most of that increase coming in international operations.

Two major ways in which Burger King Corporation differentiates itself from competitors are the way it cooks hamburgers—by its flame-broiled method as opposed to grills that fry—and the options it offers customers as to how they want their burgers. Almost 60 percent of Burger King restaurants are in the United States. However, the company plans to up foreign operations to about 50 percent by 2015. The geographic distribution of Burger King restaurants is shown on Map 12.2. Although the company began in 1954 by offering just burgers, fries, milk shakes, and sodas, the menu has expanded to include breakfast as well as various chicken, fish, and salad offerings. Nevertheless, burgers remain the mainstay of the company, and 2007 marked the 50th anniversary of the Whopper® sandwich, which is considered the signature product for Burger King.

Burger King has also differentiated itself with some innovative advertising campaigns, such as its use of *HAVE IT YOUR WAY®* ads and the use of figure of a man who was the Burger "King" for many years. The Burger King logo has changed slightly through the years; for example, going from two buns separating a burger to two buns separating the company's

MAP 12.2 Burger King's Operations by Country

As of June 1, 2011, Burger King operated in 80 countries and territories. The number of countries by geographic area was: Americas (2), Latin America & Carribean (27), Europe (28), Middle East (10), and Asia Pacific (13).

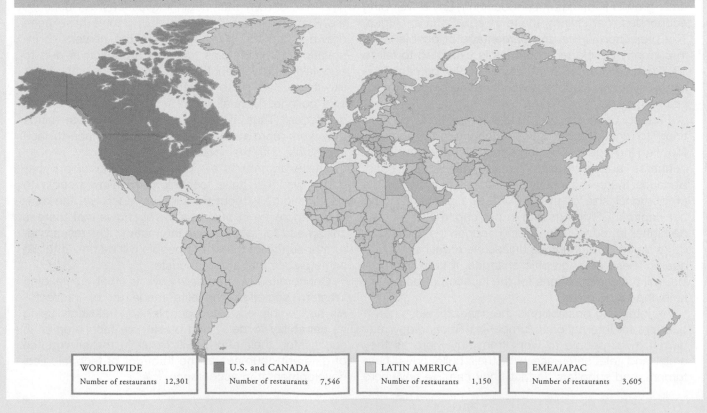

WORLDWIDE	U.S. and CANADA	LATIN AMERICA	EMEA/APAC
Number of restaurants 12,301	Number of restaurants 7,546	Number of restaurants 1,150	Number of restaurants 3,605

The photo shows a Burger King restaurant in Kuwait City, Kuwait. Note the use of both Arabic and English in the logos.
Source: © Kevpix/Alamy

name. Yet it has always been displayed and recognizable globally, as illustrated in the photo of a restaurant in Kuwait with Arabic lettering.

A Bit of History

Burger King can trace its roots to 1954, when it started as InstaBurger King. During its first five years, the private company grew to five restaurants, all in the Miami, Florida, area. In 1959, the name was changed to Burger King, and it began domestic franchising. In 1967, Pillsbury, which had several other retail food groups—such as Bennigan's, Steak and Ale, and Godfather's Pizza—bought Burger King, which by then had 274 restaurants. During the first few years of Pillsbury's ownership, franchising increased substantially. Then in 1989 Pillsbury got out of the restaurant business and sold Burger King to the British company Grand Metropolitan, which then converted most of its Wimpy restaurants in the United Kingdom to Burger King restaurants. Grand Metropolitan merged with Guinness in 1997 to form Diageo, and Diageo divested itself of restaurant operations in 2002 when it sold Burger King to a consortium of private equity firms controlled by TPG Capital, Bain Capital Partners, and the Goldman Sachs Funds. In May 2006, Burger King consummated its initial public offering, becoming a publicly traded company listed on the New York Stock Exchange. However, in 2010 3G Capital, backed by Brazilian investors, took the company private again with the prospect that management could concentrate on medium- and long-term operations, rather than being as subject to shareholder responses to short-term performance. The years of transformed ownership have caused changes in emphases for Burger King, and the company's interests have sometimes been secondary to those of its parent company.

Despite the evolving ownership, the company did expand internationally. In the early 1960s, it entered the Bahamas and Puerto Rico. In the 1970s, it entered markets in Europe, Asia, and Latin America. While some of these moves turned out to be highly successful, a few were not. It entered and then retreated from operations in such countries as Colombia, France, Israel, Japan, and Oman. (We will see in later discussion that Burger King has reentered some of these markets.) Much of Burger King's early international forays came about either because someone in another country approached Burger King or because someone in the company was familiar with a particular country and thought it would offer opportunities. Two reasons have been prevalent in the decision to leave a market: (1) The franchisee does not perform adequately, such as not investing sufficiently in the business or not making royalty payments; and (2) the market turned out to be too small to support the necessary infrastructure, such as being too small to develop slaughterhouse and beef grinding facilities.

Over time, Burger King has taken a more systematic approach toward restaurant expansion. While it still sees substantial growth opportunities within the United States, it sees the United States as a mature market for fast food, especially for hamburgers, in comparison with many foreign countries. In looking for new countries to enter, Burger King looks most favorably at those with large populations (especially of young people), high consumption of beef, availability of capital to franchisees for growth, a safe pro-business environment, growth in shopping centers, and availability of a potential franchisee with experience and resources.

Overall, Burger King has expanded internationally later than its primary rival competitor, McDonald's. This has resulted in both advantages and disadvantages. On the one hand, later entry is a disadvantage in very small markets because there may be few adequate suppliers. For instance, there may be only one slaughterhouse, and the owners may be unwilling to work with more than one customer. On the other hand, in larger markets, such as in the BRICs, being a later entrant may be advantageous because the earlier entrants have built demand for fast food and have created a supply infrastructure. In some later-entry markets, Burger King has been able to concentrate almost entirely on emphasizing its product (*HAVE IT YOUR WAY®*, good taste of flame-broiled burgers), without incurring the early developmental costs. For instance, in Latin America and the Caribbean, McDonald's and Burger King compete in 27 country or territory markets, with Burger King currently leading McDonald's in the number of restaurants in about half of those markets.

However, keep in mind that local companies also learn from the successes of foreign fast-food companies, and they sometimes alter their menus and flavorings to appeal to local tastes. Some notable examples are Bembos in Peru, Mr. Bigg's in Nigeria, Pollo Campero in Guatemala, and Quick in France.

Outside of its Americas group (United States and Canada), 35.0 percent of the Burger King countries and 24 percent of the restaurants are in the Latin American and Caribbean group, yet many of these countries have very small populations, such as the Cayman Islands, Aruba, and Saint Lucia. So why did Burger King develop a presence in these markets, even though at this writing it is not in countries with much bigger populations, such as India, Pakistan, Nigeria, and South Africa? The answer is largely due to a location factor. Burger King remains headquartered in Miami, which is often called the capital of Latin America. Because so many people from Latin America and the Caribbean come to or through Miami, the Burger King reputation spilled over to that area early on. This simplified gaining brand recognition and acceptance. Further, the nearness of the Latin American and Caribbean countries to Miami enhances the ability of Burger King's management to visit these countries and for franchisees to visit headquarters.

Although Burger King prefers to operate in markets through franchising, doing so is sometimes initially difficult because suppliers and prospective franchisees do not know the company well enough. If such a market looks sufficiently attractive, Burger King will enter with its owned operations. (Overall, Burger King owns about 10 percent of its restaurants and franchises the rest.) By owning, Burger King displays market commitment, and it can use an owned restaurant to demonstrate what it expects from franchisees. For instance, there may be only one meat-processing plant, and the owners may otherwise be reluctant to invest in added capacity or the processing of ground beef.

Throughout its long history, the company has consistently focused on expanding its global portfolio into new and existing markets. Very recently, it has entered a number of markets for the first time, including Morocco, Russia, and Slovenia. It has also re-entered several markets that it had earlier abandoned, including Colombia in 2008 and Oman in 2010. As an example of country evaluation, let's take a quick look at decisions regarding Colombia.

Re-Entering Colombia

Burger King entered the Colombian market in the early 1980s but pulled out after several years of operating in the market because of royalty expatriation restrictions. In addition, Colombia was going through a prolonged period of economic and political turmoil. These conditions combined to make Colombia a less attractive market for fast-food restaurants despite its being the third most populated country in Latin America, after Brazil and Mexico. By the time Burger King considered re-entering Colombia, Colombian cities were deemed safe for people to go out to eat, the Colombian peso was strong, and a rise in two-income families created more disposable income to spend on eating out. In 2005, about 77 percent of the population was classified as urban, and Colombia boasted some large cities such as Barranquilla, Bogotá, Cali, and Medellin—all with large and recently built shopping centers. About 31 percent of the population was under 15 years of age. Although incomes were very unevenly distributed, the richest 20 percent of the population (almost 9 million people) had a per capita expenditure in 2007 of over U.S. $17,000.

While all the above factors were favorable, there were some negative things to consider. From a political standpoint, there were potential problems with leftist-leaning governments in the neighboring countries of Ecuador and Venezuela, which could support a resurgence of political unrest. Economic problems in the United States from the global recession and in Venezuela from fluctuating oil prices could cause Colombia to lose sales because those two countries comprise half of the country's export earnings. Further, about 2 percent of Colombian GDP in 2007 came from remittances of Colombians working abroad, mainly in Spain. These were at risk because Spain was hard hit by the global recession. In effect, economic downturns could hit sales of fast foods. Burger King learned this lesson in Mexico and Germany, which in response caused the company to tactically develop a more relevant value proposition, including value meals.

Overall, though, the Colombian situation looked and has been bright. Burger King signed an agreement with KINCO, a well-established Colombian company with restaurant experience, for franchise rights to Medellin, Cali, and northern Colombia. Burger King signed a second franchise agreement with Alsea, a Mexican company, for rights to Bogotá. Alsea owned 75 percent of the Colombian operation of Domino's Pizza and operated Burger King restaurants in Mexico. Thus both of these companies seem very compatible with the Burger King criteria for selecting franchise operators with restaurant experience and capital.

The BRICs

In Chapter 4, we explored why so many companies have been putting emphasis on the BRIC countries of Brazil, Russia, India, and China. Burger King is no exception, and it has recently entered three of them. The BRIC possibilities are simply too great to ignore.

Burger King opened its first Brazilian and Chinese restaurants almost simultaneously, in November and June 2004 respectively. By then, many foreign fast-food franchisors had entered the markets, some with and some without success. For the most part, failure occurred because of underestimating what it would take to succeed in such large countries. While Burger King has had success in both of these countries, it has been able to expand much more rapidly in Brazil than in China. By 2011, it had 106 restaurants in the former and 40 in the latter.

Burger King expanded more rapidly into Brazil largely because of two factors. First, it has had much more of a recognition advantage in Brazil than in China because a half million Brazilians fly into Florida each year, where Burger King restaurants abound. In addition there are about 300,000 Brazilians living in the South Florida area, most of whom have relatives back in Brazil. Second, Burger King forged a strategy in Brazil that can be summarized in five parts: (1) Develop an infrastructure before putting in restaurants; (2) develop a local management team; (3) focus development on major cities and adjacent geographies with established shopping mall locations (they are prevalent in Brazil's largest cities), instead of the whole country; (4) establish a local office; and (5) support continuous development and the use of local suppliers that meet the Burger King global specifications.

For smaller markets or those where all the restaurants are franchised, Burger King does not set up a regional restaurant support center or local headquarters. However, management deemed a Brazilian office necessary because of Brazil's size (in both area and population), its language barrier (Portuguese), and the magnitude of investment that suppliers and franchisees would eventually need to make. At first, the office served to demonstrate the company's market commitment and to handle early supply-chain procurement and management. The result was that Burger King was able to initially secure about 80 percent of its supplies within Brazil and has since upped that figure to over 90 percent. By focusing initially on São Paulo, Brazil's largest city, Burger King has been able to develop economies in its marketing and distribution. Its subsequent expansion has focused on cities and states near São Paulo. Finally, by building a staff of Portuguese-speaking Brazilians, the company showed its commitment to the country and developed a competency to deal with external stakeholders.

The Burger King success in Brazil led its management to follow the same strategy for expansion into Russia, where it opened its first restaurants in 2010. Russia has been attractive for Burger King, not only because of the population and growth factors affecting all BRIC countries, but also because it can serve as a contiguous area for further expansion into Eastern Europe. Indeed, the entry into Slovenia in 2011 has benefitted from supply integration with the Russian operation.

Burger King set up offices in Moscow in advance of making its initial Russian penetration there. In fact, duplication of the successful Brazilian strategy is even more important for Russia because Burger King lacks the same pre-entry brand recognition that it had in Brazil. In addition, Burger King concluded that finding the right franchisee was essential for the Russian market, and its managers spent over a year getting to know well the eventual franchisee, Alex Kolobov, who owns Shokolanitsa, a chain of about 200 Russian coffee shops.

The Future

For the first quarter of 2011 same-store sales for Burger King fell 6 percent in North America. However, the drop in North American sales was largely offset by gains in the rest of the world so that the global decline was only 3.6 percent. To counter sales losses, Burger King management plans to update its restaurants so that they look more modern and to put extra emphasis on female customers by adding more menu options that are healthy. (Prior emphasis was largely on young males.) In addition, recent experience indicates that future expansion of international operations can be an integral alternative for improving performance. In terms of location emphasis Burger King has many options, such as stressing entry into new countries versus growing operations within markets where it is already operating. Despite its international growth, it is still in less than 40 percent of the world's countries. Thus, it faces the challenge of deciding where the best locations are for placing its future priorities. ∎

QUESTIONS

1. By mid-2011, Burger King was not in any of the following five countries: France, India, Nigeria, Pakistan, and South Africa. Compare these countries as possible future locations for Burger King.
2. When entering another country, discuss the advantages and disadvantages that an international restaurant company, specifically Burger King, would have in comparison with a local company in that market.
3. A bit over 60 percent of the Burger King restaurants are in its Americas region (United States and Canada) and a bit less than 40 percent elsewhere. Should this relationship change? If so, why and how?

4. The case mentions that Burger King prefers to enter countries with large numbers of youth and shopping centers. Why do you think these conditions would be advantageous?

5. How has the Burger King headquarters location influenced its international expansion? Has this location strengthened or weakened its global competitive position?

6. Evaluate the Burger King strategy of using the Brazilian experience to guide its entries into Russia, but not its entry into small markets.

Now that you have finished this chapter, go back to www.myiblab.com to continue practicing and applying the concepts you've learned.

MyIBLab

SUMMARY

- Because companies seldom have sufficient resources to exploit all opportunities, two major considerations facing managers are which markets to serve and where to locate the production to serve those markets.

- Companies' decisions on market and production location are highly interdependent, because companies often need to serve markets from local production and because they want to use existing production capacity.

- Scanning techniques aid managers in considering alternatives that might otherwise be overlooked. They also help limit the final detailed feasibility studies to a manageable number of those that appear most promising.

- Because each company has unique competitive capabilities and objectives, the factors affecting the choice of operating location will be different for each. Nevertheless, many consider similar-country comparative indicators when seeking advantages from foreign sales or foreign assets.

- Four broad categories of risk that companies may consider are political, foreign exchange, natural disaster, and competitive.

- The amount, accuracy, and timeliness of published data vary substantially among countries. Managers should be particularly aware of different definitions of terms, different collection methods, and different base years for reports, as well as misleading responses.

- Companies frequently use several tools to compare opportunities and risk in various countries, such as grids that rate country projects according to the number of separate dimensions and matrices on which companies plot opportunity on one axis and risk on another.

- When allocating resources among countries, companies need to consider how to treat reinvestments and divestments, the interdependence of operations in different countries, and whether they should follow diversification versus concentration strategies.

- Companies may reduce the risk of liability of foreignness by moving first to countries more similar to their home countries. Alternatively, they may contract with experienced companies to handle operations for them, limit the resources they commit to foreign operations, and delay entry to many countries until they are operating successfully in one or a few.

- Companies must develop location strategies for new investments and devise means of deemphasizing certain areas and divesting if necessary.

- Companies often evaluate entry to a country without comparing that country with other countries. This is because they may need to react quickly to proposals or respond to competitive threats, and because multiple feasibility studies seldom are finished simultaneously.

KEY TERMS

concentration strategy (p. 466)
diversification strategy (p. 465)
escalation of commitment (p. 447)
first-mover advantage (p. 457)

go-no-go decision (p. 468)
harvesting (or divesting) (p. 467)
imitation lag (p. 457)
liability of foreignness (p. 455)

liquidity preferences (p. 454)
oligopolistic reaction (p. 457)
scanning (p. 447)
spillover effect (p. 466)

ENDNOTES

1 *Sources include the following:* Carrefour, retrieved July 20, 2009, and May 16, 2011, from www.carrefour.com; Mimosa Spencer, "Carrefour Sells 42 Thai Stores to French Rival," *Wall Street Journal* (November 16, 2010): B4; Scheherazade Daneshkhu, "Carrefour's Upbeat Tone Brings Little Cheer," *Financial Times* (December 2, 2010): 20; "Business Crossroads: Carrefour," *The Economist* (March 17, 2007): 87; Elena Berton, "Carrefour Unveils Three-Year Growth Plan," *WWD* 198:1 (July 1, 2009): 7; Eirmalas are Bani, "Carrefour Gives Priority to Locally-Made Products," *Business Times* [Malaysia] (November 9, 1998): 3; *Business & Company News*, n.p.; Michiyo Nakamoto, "Carrefour Sounds Alarm for Japan's Ailing Retail Market," *Financial Times* (December 8, 2000): 36; Rosabeth Moss Kanter, "Global Competitiveness Revisited," *Washington Quarterly* (Spring 1999): 39–58; "Global Strategy—Why Tesco Will Beat Carrefour," *JRetail Week* (April 6, 2001): 14; "Carrefour Beats Wal-Mart to Global Crown," *JRetail Week* (December 15, 2000): 5; "Carrefour Aims to Win Global Retail Battle," *MMR* (June 26, 2000): 60; "Hypermarkets for Britain," *The Economist* (July 3, 1976): 77; "French Retailer Abandons 'Hypermarkets' in U.S.," *New York Times* (September 8, 1993): D4; "Strategies for Retail Globalisation," *Financial Times* (March 13, 1998): 4; Dexter Roberts, Wendy Zellner, and Carol Matlack, "Let China's Retail Wars Begin," *Business Week Online* (January 17, 2005), retrieved October 5, 2009, from www .businessweek.com/ magazine/content/05_03/b3916063_014 .htm; Luc Vandevelde, "Carrefour n'a besoin de personne pour se développer," *Les Echos* [France] (March 1, 2005): 32.

2 Paul Glader, "GE Is Reassigning Veteran Rice to Job Focusing on Overseas Sales," *Wall Street Journal* (November 9, 2010): B2.

3 Shige Makino, Takehiko Isobe, and Christine M. Chan, "Does Country Matter?" *Strategic Management Journal* 25 (2004): 1027–43.

4 Tony W. Tong, Todd M. Alessandri, Jeffrey J. Reuer, and Asda Chintakananda, "How Much Does Country Matter? An Analysis of Firms' Growth Options," *Journal of International Business Studies* 39: 3 (2008): 387–405.

5 Peter Enderwick, "The Imperative of Global Environmental Scanning," 11: 1 *AIB Insights* (2011): 12–15.

6 David Gonzalez, "Fried Chicken Takes Flight, Happily Nesting in U.S.," *New York Times* (September 20, 2002): A4; Joel Millman, "California City Fends Off Arrival of Mexican Supermarket," *Wall Street Journal* (August 7, 2002): B1+.

7 Don E. Schultz, "China May Leapfrog the West in Marketing," *Marketing News* (August 19, 2002): 8–9.

8 Anjjli Raval, "Mercedes-Benz Turns to India," *Financial Times* (July 19, 2010): 20.

9 Makino, Isobe, and Chan, "Does Country Matter?"

10 Anil Khurana, "Strategies for Global R&D," *Research Technology Management* (March/April 2006): 48–59.

11 David Luchnow, "Missing Piece of the Mexican Success Story," *Wall Street Journal* (March 4, 2002): A11+.

12 Michael Peel, "Bitter-Sweet Confections of Business in Nigeria," *Financial Times* (November 20, 2002): 10.

13 Andrew Bartmess and Keith Cerny, "Building Competitive Advantage through a Global Network of Capabilities," *California Management Review* 35: 2 (Winter 1993): 78–103.

14 G. Bruce Knecht, "Going the Wrong Way down a One-Way Street," *Wall Street Journal* (March 18, 2002): A1.

15 Alfredo J. Mauri and Arvind V. Phatak, "Global Integration as Inter-Area Product Flows: The Internationalization of Ownership and Location Factors Influencing Product Flows across MNC Units," *Management International Review* 41 (2001): 233–49.

16 Julian Birkinshaw, Pontus Braunerhjelm, and Ulf Holm, "Why Do Some Multinational Corporations Relocate Their Headquarters Overseas?" *Strategic Management Journal* 27 (2006): 681–700; Erik Stam, "Why Butterflies Don't Leave: Locational Behavior of Entrepreneurial Firms," 83: 1 *Economic Geography* (January 2007): 27–50.

17 Nagesh Kumar, "Multinational Enterprises, Regional Economic Integration, and Export-Platform Production in the Host Countries: An Empirical Analysis for the U.S. and Japanese Corporations," *Weltwirtschaftliches Archive* 134: 3 (1998): 450–83.

18 Cynthia O'Murchu and Jan Cienski, "Multinationals Reap the Rewards," *Financial Times* (December 2, 2010): 9.

19 C. Denbour, "Competition for Business Location: A Survey," *Journal of Industry, Competition and Trade,"* 8: 2 (June 2008): 89–111.

20 World Bank, International Finance Corporation, *Doing Business in 2005* (Washington, DC: The International Bank for Reconstruction and Development, 2005).

21 Hoon Park, "Determinants of Corruption: A Cross-National Analysis," *Multinational Business Review* 11: 2 (2003): 29–48.

22 Colin Kirkpatrick and Kenichi Shimamoto, "The Effect of Environmental Regulation on the Locational Choice of Japanese Direct Investment," 40: 11 *Applied Economics* (June 2008): 1399; and George Z. Peng and Paul W. Beamish, "The Effect of National Corporate Responsibility Environment on Japanese Foreign Direct Investment," 80: 4 (July 2008): 677-95.

23 "Volkswagen Switches Work to Low-Cost Unit in Slovakia," *Financial Times* (December 19, 1995): 4.

24 John D. Daniels and James A. Schweikart, "Political Risk, Assessment and Management of," in Rosalie L. Tung (ed.), *IEBM Handbook of International Business* (London: International Thomson Business Press, 1999): 502–14.

25 See Luciano Gremone and Ben Tsocanos, "Ongoing Political Risk in Venezuela Still Poses Challenges for Foreign Oil and Gas Companies," *Business News Americas* (February 14, 2007): 1; Farhan Bokhari, "Western Expatriates Give Way to Local Heroes," *Financial Times* (August 30, 2002): 8; Joseph T. Hallinan and Janet Adamy, "Chiquita Says It Paid Terrorists to Protect Workers in Colombia," *Wall Street Journal* (May 11, 2004): B10; Henri E. Cauvin, "Braving War and Graft, Coke Goes Back to Angola," *New York Times* (April 22, 2001): Sec. 3, 1+.

26 Haig Simonian, "Venezuela to Pay Holcim $650m Compensation for Seized Assets," *Financial Times* (September 14, 2010): 17.

27 Marvin Zonis and Sam Wilkin, "Driving Defensively through a Minefield of Political Risk," *Financial Times* (May 30, 2000): "Mastering Risk," 8–10.

28 Much like options theory, theory of liquidity preference is associated with the work of Robert C. Merton, Myron S. Scholes, and Fisher Black. For good, succinct coverage, see John Krainer, "The 1997 Nobel Prize in Economics," FRBSF Economic Letter No. 98–05 (February 13, 1998).

29 United Nations Environment Programme, *Reducing Disaster Risk: A Challenge for Development* (New York: United Nations, 2004).

30 Sharon Terlep and Mike Ramsey, "Disaster in Japan: Supply Shortages Stall Auto Makers," *Wall Street Journal* (March 19, 2011): 9.

31 WHO, Public Health Mapping and GIS, Map Library, retrieved June 11, 2007, from http://gamapserver.who.int/mapLibrary /default.aspx

32 "A Threat Deadlier than a Landmine," *Financial Times* (December 2, 2002): 10.

33 Amy Merrick and Ann Zimmerman, "Wal-Mart Bans Some Work Travel Due to SARS," *Wall Street Journal* (April 10, 2003): 36.

34 Paul D. Ellis, "Does Psychic Distance Moderate the Market Size-Entry Sequence Relationship?" *Journal of International Business Studies* 39: 3 (2008): 351–69.

35 See Srilata Zaheer and Elaine Mosakowski, "The Dynamics of the Liability of Foreignness: A Global Study of Survival in Financial Services," *Strategic Management Journal* 18 (1997): 439–64; Stewart R. Miller and Arvind Parkhe, "Is There a Liability of Foreignness in Global Banking? An Empirical Test of Banks' X-Efficiency," *Strategic Management Journal* 23 (2002): 55–75.

36 Mikhail V. Gratchev, "Making the Most of Cultural Differences," *Harvard Business Review* (October 2001): 28–30.

37 John Cantwell, "Location and the Multinational Company," 40: 1 *Journal of International Business Studies* January 2009): 35–41; Nandini Lahiri, "Geographic Distribution of R&D Activity: How Does It Affect Innovation Quality?" *Academy of Management Journal* 53: 5 (2010): 1194-1209; and Lilach Nachum and Sangyoung Song, ""The MNE as a Portfolio: Interdependencies in MNE Growth Trajectory," *Journal of International Business Studies* 42: 3 (April 2011): 381–405.

38 Shige Makino and Eric W.K. Tsang, "Historical Ties and Foreign Direct Investment: An Exploratory Study," *Journal of International Business Studies* 42: 4 (May 2011): 545–57.

39 Khanh T. L. Tran, "Blockbuster Finds Success in Japan," *Wall Street Journal* (August 19, 1998): A14; Cecile Rohwedder, "Blockbuster Hits Eject Button as Stores in Germany See Video-Rental Sales Sag," *Wall Street Journal* (January 16, 1998): B9A.

40 Jon A. Doukas and Ozgur B. Kan, "Does Global Diversification Destroy Firm Values?" *Journal of International Business Studies* 37 (2006): 352–71.

41 B. Kazaz, M. Dada, and H. Moskowitz, "Global Production Planning under Exchange-Rate Uncertainty," *Management Science* 51 (2005): 1101–9.

42 Edward B. Flowers, "Oligopolistic Reactions in European and Canadian Direct Investment in the United States," *Journal of International Business Studies* 7: 2 (Fall–Winter 1976): 43–55; Frederick Knickerbocker, *Oligopolistic Reaction and Multinational Enterprise* (Cambridge, MA: Harvard University, Graduate School of Business, Division of Research, 1973).

43 David Murphy and David Lague, "As China's Car Market Takes Off, the Party Grows a Bit Crowded," *Wall Street Journal* (July 3, 2002): A8; James Mackintosh and Richard McGregor, "Auto Industry," *Financial Times* (August 25, 2003): 13.

44 Hugh Pope, "Q: Why Are the World's IBMs Putting Down Roots in the Desert? A: Dubai," *Wall Street Journal* (January 23, 2001): A18; Lynn K. Mytelka and Lou Anne Barclay, "Using Foreign Investment Strategically for Innovation," paper presented at the Conference on Understanding FDI-Assisted Economic Development, University of Oslo, Norway (May 22–25, 2003).

45 See J. Myles Shaver and Fredrick Flyer, "Agglomeration Economies, Firm Heterogeneity, and Foreign Direct Investment in the United States," *Strategic Management Journal* 21 (2000): 1175–93; Philippe Martin and Gianmarco I. P. Ottaviano, "Growth and Agglomeration," *International Economic Review* 42 (2001): 947–68; Edward E. Leamer and Michael Storper, "The Economic Geography of the Internet Age," *Journal of International Business Studies* 32 (2001): 641–65.

46 Jedrzej George Frynas, Kamel Mellah, and Geoffrey Allen Pigman, "First Mover Advantages in International Business and Firm-Specific Political Resources," *Strategic Management Journal* 27 (2006): 321–45; Makino, Isobe, and Chan, "Does Country Matter?"

47 Joel Millman, "PriceSmart to Restate Results Due to an Accounting Error," *Wall Street Journal* (November 11, 2003): B9.

48 Philip Parker, "Choosing Where to Go Global: How to Prioritise Markets," *Financial Times* (November 16, 1998): Mastering Marketing, 7–8.

49 Tony Barber and Kerin Hope, "Brussels Attacks Greece over False Data," *Financial Times* (January 13, 2010): 8.

50 "Bolivia Economy: Border Law to Stop Contraband," *EIU ViewsWire* (2011) (accessed May 18, 2011).

51 Mary Kissel, "U.S. Expats Deal with Terror Threat," *Wall Street Journal* (May 12, 2004): B4a, quoting Frank Holder, of Kroll, Inc.

52 "Global Terrorism Index," *The Economist* (August 30, 2003): 74, using data from the World Markets Research Centre.

53 Andrew Ward, "Terror Threat from Within Keeps America on High Alert," *Financial Times* (April 19, 2005): 3, quoting John Lewis.

54 Harry Hurt III, "Making the World Safer, One Client at a Time," *New York Times* (May 11, 2004): C12.

55 Moisés Naím, "The Five Wars of Globalization," *Foreign Policy* (January–February 2003): 29–36.

56 A good history of violence and kidnapping in Nigeria appears in Soye Peniel Asawo, "Corporate Integrity and Company-Community Conflict Management in the Niger Delta Region of Nigeria," *Journal of Leadership, Accountability and Ethics* 8: 3 (March 2011): 77–88.

57 "Doing Business in Dangerous Places," *The Economist* (August 14, 2004): 11.

58 Igal Ayal and Jehiel Zif, "Marketing Expansion Strategies in Multinational Marketing," *Journal of Marketing* (Spring 1979): 84–94.

59 Makino, Isobe, and Chan, "Does Country Matter?"

60 Susanna Voyle and James Drummond, "J. Sainsbury to Withdraw from Egypt," *Financial Times* (April 10, 2001): 23.

61 Nikki Tait, "Dana Set to Sell UK-Based Components Arm," *Financial Times* (November 29, 2000): 22.

62 Makino, Isobe, and Chan, "Does Country Matter?"; Bernard Simon, "Goodyear Sells Its Last Plantation," *Financial Times* (December 1, 2004): 18.

63 See Jean J. Boddewyn, "Foreign and Domestic Divestment and Investment Decisions: Like or Unlike?" *Journal of International Business Studies* 14: 3 (Winter 1983): 28; Michelle Haynes, Steve Thompson, and Mike Wright, "The Determinants of Corporate Divestment in the U.K.," *Journal of Industrial Organization* 18 (2000): 1201–22; Jose Mata and Pedro Portugal, "Closure and Divestiture by Foreign Entrants: The Impact of Entry and Post-Entry Strategies," *Strategic Management Journal* 21 (2000): 549–62.

64 World Bank and International Finance Corporation, *Doing Business in 2005* (Washington, DC: The International Bank for Reconstruction and Development, 2005): 69.

65 Matthew Green, "Nigeria Set to Lift Decades-Old Ban on Foreign Takeovers of Its Banks," *Financial Times* (June 22, 2009): 1.

66 "Enron Assets Outside U.S. Go Up for Sale; Activity Seen in South Korea and India," *Wall Street Journal* (January 22, 2002): A6.

67 International Monetary Fund, *World Economic Outlook, September 2004* (Washington, DC: International Monetary Fund, 2004): 143–49.

68 Deborah Hargreaves, "'Virtual' Staff Make Themselves at Home in Offices of the Future," *Financial Times* (May 14, 1999): 8.

69 Peter Hall, *Cities in Civilization: Culture, Technology, and Urban Order* (London: Weidenfeld & Nicholson, 1998).

70 David Aviel, "The Causes and Consequences of Public Attitudes to Technology: A United States Analysis," *International Journal of Management* 18 (2001): 166.

71 *Sources include the following:* We'd like to acknowledge the invaluable assistance of Jonathan Fitzpatrick, Executive V.P. and Chief Brand Operations Officer; Julio A. Ramirez, former Executive Vice

President Global Operations; Arianne Cento, Senior Analyst, Global Communications; and Ana Miranda, Senior Manager Investor Relations, all with Burger King Corporation. Additional information came from Elaine Walker, "Burger King Goes for New Look," *Miami Herald* (May 31, 2011): 1A-2A; "Burger King," Wikipedia, retrieved April 14, 2009, and May 20, 2011, from http://en.wikipedia .org/wiki/Burger_King; "Burger King Plans to Double Restaurant Count in Russia in 2011," *Interfax; Ukraine Business Daily* (Kiev) (November 17, 2010); Helen Thomas, "Burger King Agrees $4 bn Sale to 3G Capital," *Financial Times* (September 1, 2010); "Negocio de Resaturantes Aumenta 8% en Colombia," *Noticieras Financieras* (December 22, 2010; Business Monitor International, *Colombia Food & Drink Report Q1 2009* (London: Business Monitor International, 2009); Elaine Walker, "Despite Spike in Profits, Burger King Lowers Annual Expectations," *McClatchy—Tribune Business News* (April 30, 2009): n.p.; Gemma Charles, "Burger King Adds First 'Value Meal' to Menu," *Marketing* (February 11, 2009): 3; "Burger King Corp. Opens Its 1,000th Restaurant in the Latin America & Caribbean Region," *Business Wire* (August 14, 2008): n.p.; "The Burger King's Brand Enters Colombia," *Business Wire* (December 13, 2007): n.p.

chapter 13
Export and Import

Objectives

1. To introduce the idea of exporting and profile its elements

2. To introduce the idea importing and profile its elements

3. To identify the problems and pitfalls that challenge international traders

4. To identify the resources and assistance that helps international traders

5. To discuss the idea of an export plan

6. To outline the practice of countertrade

Access a host of interactive learning aids to help strengthen your understanding of the chapter concepts at www.myiblab.com.

MyIBLab

When one is prepared, difficulties do not come.

—*Ethiopian proverb*

CASE

SpinCent: Starting-Up Export[1]

Big exporters, such as Boeing, Caterpillar, and General Electric, generate about 60 percent of total exports from the United States. Their smaller shipments are usually much larger than the largest shipments of smaller companies. Still, small and medium-size enterprises (SMEs), specifically, companies with fewer than 500 workers, account for 97 percent of all U.S. exporters. One such SME is SpinCent of Pennsylvania.

SpinCent manufactures laboratory and industrial centrifuges that provide separation solutions for firms in the chemical, pharmaceutical, food, environmental, and mining industries. In brief, a centrifuge is a piece of equipment that puts an object into highspeed rotation around a fixed axis. Centripetal acceleration causes substances to separate, moving heavy elements to the bottom and lighter objects toward the top of the container; in between is liquid. SpinCent's 54 employees—45 workers, four product engineers, and five managers—operates out of its 60,000-square-foot facility in suburban Philadelphia.

SpinCent began operations in 2000 with "one goal in mind…to create a line of centrifuges our customers had absolute confidence in." Its patented technology anchored a full line of automatic and manual centrifuges known for quality, high performance, and good value. It has always taken pride in offering complete custom-engineering design and tools that serve the most demanding industries. To this day, management believes it builds "centrifuges for which there simply are no equals."

To Export or Not to Export: That Is the Question

From its start, SpinCent had passively approached export. It international sales often resulted from orders from other U.S. companies that were destined for export, occasional sales leads received at trade shows, or an unsolicited order through the Web or mail. Export results had been mixed with sales generating somewhat reasonable returns; they would have been higher but for for unexpected problems and pitfalls.

Paul Knepper, CEO and founder, explained that a few concerns had dissuaded SpinCent from aggressively developing exports. First, he and his colleagues had general misgivings about the likelihood of international success. In previous efforts, they felt as if they spent more time on unfocused searching than on purposefully growing exports. Moreover, serving customers in the domestic market kept them quite busy. Stretching their thin management structure to develop

international operations would be tough. In addition, entering international markets would put SpinCent into direct competition with seasoned exporters from Germany and Japan.

Mr. Knepper knew SpinCent had to decide to export or not. Concerns about productivity, profitability, and diversification had been building for several years. The struggling U.S. economy, besides slowing SpinCent's growth, had led a few of its customers to import cheaper, lower-end centrifuges from foreign suppliers. If the trend continued, Mr. Knepper anticipated increasing price competition from both domestic and international rivals.

Add it all up and management realized it had a big decision: focus fully on the domestic market and wring out every possible efficiency or expand the company's frontier by aggressively escalating export. Ultimately, the decision was made for it. The slow-moving deindustrialization of the United States, forecasted to continue for years, would systematically reduce domestic demand. Concurrently, quickly industrializing emerging economies, particularly in Asia, signaled strong growth opportunities.

Asia's Calling

SpinCent identified key trends in Asia that signaled potential selling opportunities. "Industries were coming online everywhere and seemingly overnight," said Mr. Knepper. Pro-market reform, economic development, and globalization were industrializing activities in several countries. Increasingly, these emerging industries required the sophisticated sorts of centrifuges that SpinCent made. Unlike the United States, which was in the mature part of the product lifecycle, emerging economies were just starting and looked set to grow for years.

Getting Started

New to the idea of the Asian market, SpinCent sought help on how best to access the large, diverse region. It feared getting overstretched and wasting resources going solo. Moreover, Mr. Knepper was not looking to generate a burst of export sales. He aimed to develop relationships that would drive long-term export growth. Hence, his primary challenge was finding competent and trustworthy distributors who would take responsibility for local sales. Said Mr. Knepper, "We were looking for a long-term partner and not a quick export sale.… The right partner for SpinCent needed to be as confident and competent about the product as we are, and able to promote, educate, and serve consumers in the respective territories." To that end, he wanted background information on potential distributors beforehand, making sure possible agents were who they said they were. A few of the company's earlier export transactions, for instance, had run into problems with buyers who wouldn't pay or couldn't arrange letters of credit. Warned Mr. Knepper, "Getting paid is a huge part of running a business, and unless a company has the right payment policies in place, it will get scammed."

Mindful of these issues, Mr. Knepper attended a trade seminar sponsored by the U.S. Commercial Service's Export Assistance Center of Philadelphia. It featured market analysis and trade reports on the fast-growing, emerging economies of Asia. As he took his seat, his mind couldn't help but wonder about the opportunities. Sure, they sounded great. However, he had seen hype like this before come back to bite. Furthermore, he had heard various horror stories at trade shows about the inevitable problems and evolving pitfalls of exports. Indeed, he reflected, a key reason for attending the seminar was to reconcile his vague sense of the opportunities and threats.

Since exports promote economic growth, policymakers and government agencies offer extensive assistance. Trade seminars, market research, training programs, and financial planning are just some of the many services. Trade officials directed their energies toward SMEs, like SpinCent, seeing them as the major beneficiaries of initiatives to improve and accelerate international trade activity. U.S. trade officials, for instance, reasoned that since 60 percent of all SME exporters posted sales to only one foreign market, many could sharply boost exports by entering one or two new markets. Expanding SMEs' market horizons, through trade seminars and such, reduced their fear of the unfamiliar.

After a full morning of profiles and presentations, of the sort seen in our chapter's opening photo, Mr. Knepper increasingly believed the Asian markets held more opportunities than risk. While he learnt quite a bit about Asia, as well as general technicalities of exporting, his unfamiliarity with the region, compounded by the company's lack of local sales representatives, bothered him. He believed that grassroots research was necessary before committing. Before leaving that day, he spoke to Commercial Service agents. He arranged to tag along a 10-day trade mission that was heading to Hong Kong, Philippines, Vietnam, and Taiwan the next month.

Goal Setting

The goals of his trip were straightforward: assess market potential, identify competitors, get a sense of reasonable price points, and recruit local sales representatives. Although he had never traveled to Asia before, he believed he was well-prepared. His time with the trade experts in Philadelphia had educated him on the general characteristics and industry conditions in Asian markets. Also, in the past, SpinCent had received inquiries from Asian distributors asking to represent the company as well as the occasional request for product information. Depending on how busy the company had been with its domestic customers, which usually was quite, SpinCent tried to respond. Still, it saved all contacts; as such, he had a start on potential distributors and likely customers. In addition, Mr. Knepper tapped the Commercial Services Gold Key program to prescreen potential distributors. This service helps SMEs enlist Commercial Services agents overseas to scan local markets for qualified agents, distributors, and representatives.

Thinking back to his days as a Boy Scout, Mr. Knepper took comfort in the fact that he believed he had met the sacred command—Be Prepared. With a briefcase chock-full of brochures, a laptop loaded with profiles of his product line, and the sense of doing something potentially great, Mr. Knepper headed to Asia. Over the next 10 days, he interviewed potential agents, chatted with likely customers, scouted competitors' offerings, test called their service support, spoke to freight forwarders and logistics companies, and visited local government officials and customs agent.

SpinCent Answers

On the flight home, tired but charged, Mr. Knepper realized that despite all he had learned, he had been wrong about the whole thing. Yes, there were risks, but they were far more opportunities than he had imagined. Exporting was no longer an option for SpinCent. It was an imperative. Perhaps more importantly, he had a new sense of commitment. Too, he had a bit more confidence given that he had signed new distributorships in the Philippines and Taiwan as well as generated sales leads there and in Hong Kong.

Back in the office, he tested the Asian market a bit more. He sampled potential interest by advertising in trade publications as well as running banner ads on relevant trade sites in tandem with his newly signed distributors—he took care of the English ads, they managed the Mandarin versions. In addition, Mr. Knepper began working with an agent from Commercial Services on an export plan. This work helped SpinCent secure its largest overseas partner to date, a distributor in Hong Kong who served the booming Chinese market. Commercial Services also helped SpinCent set up meetings with others, eventually leading to signing a distributor in Singapore and getting leads in Australia.

Having found strong partners, SpinCent continues using the counseling and market intelligence provided by the various government agencies to improve its export plan. Indeed, the more he dealt with them, the more Mr. Knepper appreciated a friend's advice, "Let the government do it for you. This is their niche and they're the best at it."[2] Now, with the export plan in hand, Mr. Knepper had begun working with the Export-Import Bank to secure financing options for its overseas distributors and customers.[3]

Going Forward

Steadily, as SpinCent gained experience in Taiwan, Philippines, Hong Kong, and Singapore, it looks onward. Although exporting has created challenges, it helped SpinCent improve its performance. Indeed, overseas sales had provided SpinCent with a steady stream of business during the economic downturn in the United States; rivals who had not diversified via exports struggled. More importantly, exporting had given SpinCent a low-cost, high-return opportunity to leverage its core competency in centrifuge technology.

This experience, reflected Mr. Knepper, suggested straightforward lessons: "If you are thinking about exporting internationally, do it. Get going, do your homework, utilize low-cost resources, participate in trade missions, learn about cultures, and build international relationships.... Always check on your potential business partners. Gather as much information as you can. Don't assume; the wrong choice costs your business time and money.... Above all, no matter the problems you run into, stay committed to the goal. All of these seem tough, but they only cost pennies on the dollar and the returns can be substantial."

CRN
Case Review Note

Introduction

Exporting and importing is one of the fastest growing economic activities in the world.

International trade in the form of exports and imports has always been important for the global economy. As globalization, free trade agreements, and institutional development opened the economies of more and more countries, the importance of trade increased. In addition, the composition and direction of trade flows have changed significantly, given the ongoing transformation of developing economy into industrializing versions, emerging markets tapping developed countries for tools to continue doing so, and developed countries looking to their developing counterparts for competitively priced goods and services. For example, in mid-year 2011, China's exports were grown nearly 30 percent while its imports were up 20 percent.[4] Moreover, reflecting the changing composition of trade, firms trade a growing number of products among a larger set of countries—U.S. companies, as of 2010, exported products to 233 countries and territories.[5].

Companies worldwide respond accordingly, seeing exporting and importing as powerful means to engage international business. Granted, companies engage international business in a variety of modes. This chapter emphasizes the options of export and import. The choice a company makes, say, export versus licensing versus joint ventures versus FDI, follows its interpretation of external factors as well as internal competencies (See Figure 13.1).

Exporting sends products to another country; importing bring products in from another country.

Exporting and importing are the most common modes of international business. There has been steady and substantial growth in the number of firms that export and import. Popularity follows from the fact that both modes impose minimum business risk, require relatively low resource commitment, and improve marketplace flexibility. Moreover, whether large or small, international trade helps companies increase sales

FIGURE 13.1 Environmental Factors Influencing Export and Import Operations

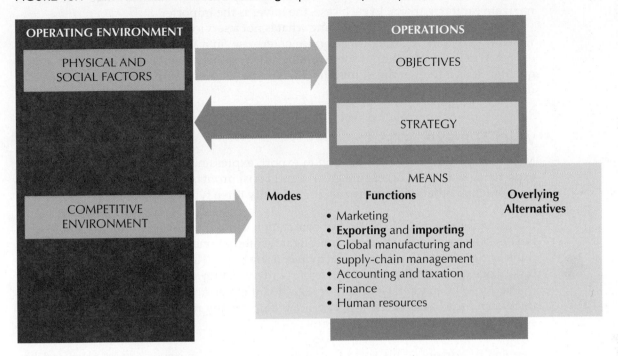

and profit, reduce dependence on the home market, and stabilize seasonal fluctuations. Lastly, there is the minor detail that most people live elsewhere in the world then in your country. From the view of the United States, for example, nearly 96 percent of consumers live in other countries who, by the way, command two-thirds of the world's purchasing power. Consequently, international trade has many opportunities. But, as this chapter also shows, it has problems and pitfalls.

Exporting

Exporting is the sale of goods or services produced by a firm based in one country to customers that reside in another country. The idea of exporting manufactured goods presents a clear situation, as in the case of Japanese carmaker Toyota shipping automobiles to customers in Russia. In this case, Toyota is the exporter while the buyers in Russia are the importers. Exports involve any good or service that is traded from sellers in one country to buyers in another country. Exportables include goods, services, or intellectual property.

Technically, a product does not need to physically leave a country to qualify as an export. Rather, it need only earn foreign currency. For example, one does not normally think of the foreign national students sitting alongside you in class as part of your country's export strategy. However, higher education ranks among the top 10 service exports of the United States. Tuition and living expenses paid by foreign students and their families brought nearly $20 billion to the U.S. economy during the 2009–2010 academic year.[6] Besides education, leading types of service exports include travel and tourism, transportation services, banking, financial insurance services, entertainment, and professional business services.

The trade of services, such as we see with higher education, makes it a bit tougher to define what qualifies as an export. Engineering contractors, such as Bechtel, Skanska AB, or Kajima, export services when they construct buildings, roads, utilities, airports, or seaports in a foreign country. Management consultants, such as McKinsey & Company, export when they perform advisory services for foreign clients. Investment banks, such

Concept Check

"Why Companies Engage in International Business" emphasized three operating objectives: expanding sales, acquiring resources, and minimizing risk. To achieve one or more of these objectives, companies choose from various "Modes of International Business." Among these modes, **exporting** and **importing** are the most prevalent, especially among small and medium-sized enterprises.

as Goldman Sachs and UBS, export when they help a foreign client arrange financing or navigate capital markets. In each case, the buyer is the importer.

Last, it clarifies matters by defining what is not a service export. Opening a Starbucks, which is generally regarded as a service enterprise, in a foreign market is not a service export. Foreign ownership of some or all of the productive assets of the local operation qualifies it as a foreign direct investment. No foreign ownership but a royalty fee qualifies it as a licensing agreement.

WHO ARE EXPORTERS?

Types of exporters include

- Non-exporter.
- Occasional exporter.
- Regular exporter.

Many companies claim the intention to export, expressing the motivation, outlook, and expectancy that it will accelerate growth and boost profits. In reality, not all do and some do more than others. Company practices identify three types of exporters.

Occasional Exporters   This sort of company has filled unsolicited orders from foreign buyers but it passively, if at all, investigates international trade options. For example, think of SpinCent's international activities prior to Mr. Knepper's realization of the necessity of export. It would try to fill export orders as they arrived, depending on activity in the domestic market. Generally, it regarded them as anomalies. Occasional exporters understand the basics of the export process. But, for any number of reasons, they do not see it as a vital aspect of their strategy.

Case Review Note

Regular Exporters   This sort of company aggressively pursues export sales and has extensive experience with its practicalities, complexities, and technicalities. It sees exporting as a productive, profitable, strategic activity. Again, think of SpinCent's activities following Mr. Knepper's realization, corroborated by his chats with Commercial Service agents and travels to Asia, of export's importance. Each step demystified aspects of exporting, thereby fortifying Mr. Knepper's interest and commitment. And, just as success feeds upon success, so to with exporting.

Case Review Note

Non-Exporters   This sort of company commands little to no knowledge about exporting. It often professes no intention, now or in the future, to engage international trade. Although this sounds as if it is a deficiency, many firms grow in their domestic market without exporting simply because they make goods or provide services that do not travel well to foreign markets. Still, there are many companies whose products would travel well. They simply prefer not to bother with exporting. This population is a primary target of public export promotion programs.

THE MATTER OF ADVANTAGES

Ownership advantages of the company, location advantages of the market, and internalization advantages from controlling transactions shape how firms enter foreign markets.

Understanding who is likely to begin and develop exporting directs us toward a broader conception of a company's choice of entry mode into foreign markets. Earlier materials profiled the influence of ownership, location, and internalization advantages on a firm's preferred entry mode into foreign markets.[7] Here we apply them to the export decision.

Ownership Advantages   A firm's core competencies, namely the special outlook, skill, capability, or technology that run through its operations, are the basis of its competitive advantage. These proprietary advantages directly support international expansion, through export, licensing, joint venture, or FDI. For instance, SpinCent capitalized on its ownership advantages by leveraging its core competency in designing, manufacturing, and servicing sophisticated centrifugal equipment. These advantages, "owned" by SpinCent due to its proprietary technology and expertise, support its international expansion. Companies that command weak ownership advantages, anticipating fierce struggles with foreign rivals, typically disregard export.

Case Review Note

Location Advantages   The combination of sales opportunity and investment risk in foreign markets creates favorable locations—more plainly, markets with many consumers that will likely buy your product. Expectedly, a favorable business environment, such as that found in Canada or Germany, attracts exporters. Increasingly, high-potential markets in far corners of the world attract aspiring and experienced traders. Again, SpinCent saw events and trends in Asia providing favorable locations marked by strong industrial demand, supportive business policies, and attractive industry structures. The industrialization of emerging economies spurs local companies to make the sorts of products that require high-performance centrifuges. Hence, targeting these fast developing markets taps location advantages that support SpinCent's international expansion.

Internalization Advantages   Companies often respond to market imperfections, namely the sorts of things that create uncertainties, by internalizing market processes. Directly controlling and managing market activities "inside" the company reduce risks and exploit gaps. Notably, internalizing activities enables executives to retain their core competency within the company rather than licensing or selling it. Again, SpinCent could have opted to license its technology to Asian manufacturers. This would likely prove cheap in the short-term but costly over the long haul as local licensees may evolve into local competitors. Indeed, earlier discussion of the rule of man as the basis of law, such as that found in several Asian markets, noted that it poorly protects intellectual property. This sort of market imperfection leads companies, such as we see with SpinCent, to retain control of their core competencies through internalization. Granted, SpinCent could have served its Asian customers by directly investing in a local manufacturing facility rather than exporting to local distributors. However, management reasoned that its resource constraints and risk outlook endorsed exports.

CHARACTERISTICS OF EXPORTERS

The effort to promote international trade has spurred identifying the characteristics of successful exporters. Pinpointing important attributes, the reasoning goes, will then help companies develop necessary competencies as well as help governments design better forms of assistance. Analysis often starts with firm size, comparing and contrasting the activities of big and small companies.

In exporting, company size matters in interesting ways. Naturally, large MNEs like Sony, Boeing, and Nokia are big exporters. Their ownership, location, internalization advantages help them identify markets, leverage organizational capabilities, and manage international risks. In this context, many presume that export is an option best left to large companies. There is some truth to this inference. The largest companies typically account for the lion share of exporting. In the United States, the 500 biggest companies accounted for more than 60 percent of total export value, the 250 biggest accounted for more than half, and the 100 biggest contributed nearly one-third.[8]

Nonetheless, there is considerable potential for export growth from so-called **small and medium-sized enterprises (SMEs).** These firms, by definition, have fewer than 500 employees.[9] In the United States, SMEs account for almost 97 percent of exporters and generate more than 30 percent of the total export value.[10] This situation is not unique to the United States. Worldwide, more than two-thirds of exporters have fewer than 20 employees. More than 98 percent of companies in the Asia-Pacific region are SMEs. China, for example, has around 42 million SMEs, defined as enterprises with annual revenues of less than $250 million. They accounted for about 99 percent of all companies and contributed approximately 60 percent of China's GDP, more than 70 percent of the country's employment, and more than 80 percent of its exports.[11]

Research confirms firm size matters in explaining who exports. Size does not, however, determine who exports. For example, SpinCent, a typical SME, marshaled the resources and made the commitment to grow exports. Its size moderated its decision to seek assistance from commercial services and the Ex-Im Bank. Its size, however, did not

Resource constrained or risk-averse companies that have strong ownership advantages often enter foreign markets through export.

Case Review Note

Case Review Note

Concept Check

The complexity posed by differing cultural, political, legal, economic environments, many of which were covered in the first half of the text, impose a so-called "liability of foreignness." This idea encompasses the economic and social costs of doing business in a local market that foreign companies, by virtue of their spotty familiarity, incur. Companies operating internationally offset this liability by capitalizing on advantages as well as selecting the mode of international business that best reflects their resource profile and risk outlook.

The largest companies are the biggest exporters. SMEs, however, are steadily expanding export activity.

Case Review Note

determine its decision to export. Instead, research directs our attention to the importance of other factors. Specifically, data shows that firm specific characteristics, such as core competencies, competitive prices, efficient production, executive leadership, and effective marketing techniques, better predict export activity.[12] Production efficiency, rather than firm size, predicted the export activity of Swedish companies—those with higher productivity targeted foreign markets while those with lower productivity focused on domestic customers.[13] Chinese SMEs' labor costs, R&D advantages, and state ownership better predicted their export activity than did their size.[14]

Likewise, firm competencies, not size, more significantly influenced Canadian companies' propensity to export, the number of countries they exported to, and their **export intensity** (the share of a firm's output that is exported). Similarly, top management's favorable perception of exports, based on the anticipated contribution of exports to growth and profits, fueled executives, commitment that powered exporting in British companies.[15]

In summary, firm size influences a company's inclination to initiate or escalate exporting. Often times, however, other features of the firm matter a bit more. More pointedly, Texas-based Coffee & More, a small company selling premium coffee, looked to boost growth through export. Its CEO reflected, "People thought we were cutting our throats by exporting, and I admit we had our own doubts. However, we knew the customer base for our product outside the United States was large, and so was the potential for success. Perseverance and commitment paid off. Now international exporting has become an integral part of the company," said the CEO. "Our international exports went from 2 percent of annual income in 2005 to 60 percent of annual income in 2009, and we've been able to add more jobs."[16]

A firm's characteristics moderate its export activity. Size matters, but often management commitment, efficiency, and cost structure matter more.

Why Export?

Several reasons motivate export. Companies that are capital- and research-intensive, such as pharmaceuticals or avionics, export to amortize the steep costs of product development and production. Many, such as advertisers, lawyers, and consultants, export their services to meet the needs of clients working abroad. Either they follow their clients abroad or risk losing them to the rival that does. Companies that are not leaders in their domestic markets may export as an indirect way to counter the volume advantage commanded by the industry leader. Finally, some companies export rather than invest abroad because of the higher risks of international operations. Serving foreign markets from the home office imposes far fewer operational requirements than other modes.

Although a diverse set of scenarios, essentially they reference the three dimensions that drive export:

Exporting helps companies

* *Increase profitability.*
* *Improve productivity.*
* *Diversify activities.*

Profitability   Point blank, the key advantage of exporting is the potential to increase profitability. Companies often sell their products for higher prices abroad than at home. Foreign markets may lack competitive alternatives or they may be in different stages of the product's life cycle. Mature products at home trigger price competition, whereas growth stages in foreign markets allow premium prices. Also, exports enable the firm to expand its sales frontier. Although not quite decisive to firms in big markets, such as the United States, accessing bigger markets is a make or break factor to firms in small markets, such as Switzerland. Said the Director of Business Development for Certified Worldwide, "by not exporting, we were not tapping our full sales potential—sort of like leaving money on the table."[17]

Productivity   Exporting helps companies improve productivity. Oftentimes, productivity is tied to increasing scale effects; by utilizing unused capacity or spreading research costs over more customers, companies improve their operational efficiency. Hence, selling more products in more markets drives productivity gains. In addition, the

Concept Check

The attractiveness of **trade** as a means of internationalization has been enhanced by the improving efficiencies of import and export. The liberalization of the cross-border movement of resources and the development of services that support trade make these modes more attractive to a broader range of companies.

knowledge flows between international buyers and foreign competitors spurs exporters to innovate. For example, Mississippi-based Domes International makes inexpensive housing. Deciding to expand internationally, it headed to India. Early experiences, although difficult, improved its productivity and fortified its competencies. Said its CEO, "There's no doubt that Domes International is a better company as a result of our experience in India. We are much more flexible and innovative. The client wanted a less expensive structure, so we went back to our labs and came up with an insulation solution that met their needs. Now we use these discoveries to improve core products and to offer more variations. We are much more confident going into new situations—listening, adapting, and finding the best solution."[18]

Diversification Exporting enables companies to diversify their activities, thereby fortifying their adaptability to changes in the marketplace. In the least, developing customers in different markets reduces vulnerability to the loss of a local buyer. It also improves bargaining power with existing suppliers. Furthermore, different growth rates in different markets enables a company to use strong sales in one country to offset weak sales in another. SpinCent, for example, looked to develop export markets in faster growing Asia to reduce its overreliance on the slowing U.S. economy.

Case Review Note

Going forward, more companies will look to diversify through export. The shift in economic power from the West to the East is often portrayed as a threat to developed countries. Alternatively, as SpinCent shows, it represents an opportunity for companies in the United States, Germany, and the like. They can diversify sales by exporting more advanced as well as luxury products to fast growing, increasingly wealthy emerging countries.[19]

Exporters: Initiation and Development

Research assesses how, when, and why companies initiate and develop exporting. Reports cover a lot of territory, evaluating the influence of managerial attitudes, product features, organizational resources, firm strategy, market trends, technology tools, public policy, and so on. Although there is some consensus, divergence persists. Indeed, as far back as 1991, research compiled more than 700 explanatory variables as plausible determinants of the internationalization of the firm.[20] Today, two perspectives anchor interpretation of the process that leads a firm to initiate and develop exporting.[21]

Two views of export shape interpretation: the deliberate, sequential dynamic of incremental internationalization and the instant internationalization of the born global.

SEQUENCES AND INCREMENTS

The first perspective, **incremental internationalization,** sees physical distance, cultural ties, and market similarities fundamentally shaping how companies approach export. Specifically, exporting follows a sequential process that leads a company to export initially from its home market to the most geographically and psychologically proximate countries. From there, it deliberately expands exports to increasingly dissimilar and distant countries.

Initially, companies find it easier as well as less risky to trade with customers in countries that share geographic, linguistic, political, and legal commonalities. As one would expect, trading with similar folks in similar markets who speak the same or similar languages and share historical legacies put less stress on managers' competencies. Trade data indicate strong effects: for example, countries will engage in 42 percent more trade if they share a common language than if they do not; 47 percent more if both countries belong to a trading bloc, such as the European Union or NAFTA; 114 percent more if they share a common currency; and 188 percent more if they have a common colonial past.[22]

Initial success trading with "similar" foreign customers, by developing managers' outlook and competencies, moderates ensuing export activity. That is, the firm's incremental export expansion follows a "learning process," in which managers' growing experience with and knowledge of foreign markets creates the confidence to export to countries that share fewer commonalities and are farther afield. In this scenario, companies in the United States would export first to Canada, then move on to Mexico, Europe, and eventually countries in South America, Asia, Africa, and the Middle East.[23]

BORN GLOBALS

The second perspective, derived from the international enterpreneurship literature, holds that some firms initiate exporting as a **born global** (also known as an "instant international" or "international new venture"). Rather than methodically engaging foreign markets, born globals immediately step onto the world stage, exporting from inception. International markets are not simply places it turns to when sales slow in the home market. The born global regards the domestic market as just one of many opportunities in the world.[24]

Born globals are found worldwide. No matter the location, a key characteristic is that their executives take a global focus from the outset and intentfully embark on rapid internationalization. This in itself is not a radical new development. Many companies following an incremental internationalization process are led by committed internationalists. What is "new," however, are managers' intent to adopt and apply a global focus from start-up. Perhaps most critically, managers can implement their vision quickly and cheaply given technological advances and the increasing openness of countries to international trade. Specifically, the born global phenomenon largely follows the ongoing globalization of markets, falling trade barriers, growing demand for specialized products, and improving communication technologies. Collectively, these changes create a powerful platform for a growing number of people with an international orientation, perhaps acquired as students studying abroad or as experienced managers, who aim to go global at the get-go.[25]

For example, Evertek Computer, a U.S. SME, started up in 1990 and quickly began exporting. By 2009, it exported to customers in 105 countries; 30 percent were in South America, 20 percent were in Europe, and 20 percent were in the Middle East and North Africa. Evertek's success comes from selling refurbished computers and parts. Worldwide, demand for "obsolete" computer equipment is large and growing because buyers, particular poorer ones, don't need the latest and most expensive equipment. Instead, said Evertek's international sales manager John Ortley, "They want cheap." Evertek's business model, he added, matches these folks with those who want to sell their used personal computer equipment.

Arguably, selling obsolete pieces and parts seems an unlikely basis of successful exporting. In the least, Evertek does not command the intimidating ownership advantage that usually supports exporting. However, the international orientation Evertek's top management creates a powerful driver. Mr. Oxley's enthusiasm for international business, for example, has helped the company realize that a big part of its business is going to be international: "For me it started with being curious about the world. I enjoy learning about other cultures and respecting people who have a different background than mine."[26] And, spoken like a true born global, he added "We're thriving. The world is shrinking, and it's getting easier and less expensive to do business on a global basis."[27]

INTERACTION EFFECTS

Neither the incremental nor born global perspective definitively represents how companies initiate and escalate exporting. Certainly, research as well as company practices

TABLE 13.1   Top Ten Trade Partners of the United States

While the United States trades with 233 different countries and territories, its top 10 trade partners dominate total volume. On the export side, the United States's top trade partner is Canada. On the import side, the United States' leading supplier of goods and services is China.

Total Export Value for Goods (millions $)		Total Import Value for Goods (millions $)	
Country	**Export**	**Country**	**Imports**
Canada	248,811	China	364,944
Mexico	163,321	Canada	276,478
China	91,878	Mexico	229,655
Japan	60,545	Japan	120,348
United Kingdom	48,497	Germany	82,680
Germany	48,201	United Kingdom	49,755
Korea	38,844	Korea	48,860
Brazil	35,357	France	38,551
Netherlands	34,998	Taiwan	35,907
Singapore	29,150	Ireland	33,898

Source: U.S. Census Bureau, Foreign Trade, U.S. International Trade Data, 2010.

confirm that each credibly interprets the export process. For instance, recall that U.S. exports travel to 233 countries and territories. Many reflect long-running trade relationships, such as that between the United States and Canada. Others reflect more recent relationships, such as the United States and Kyrgyzstan. The scale and scope of this export universe supports scenarios where companies have gradually developed the competencies to service these markets (the incremental internationalization perspective) as well as are able to reach faraway markets with greater ease and immediacy (the born global view).

Table 13.1, by indicating an interaction between the two perspectives, proposes a useful way to think about the export process. Between the top 10 countries that the United States exports to as well as imports from, the top seven overlap. The top three, Canada, China, and Mexico, account for more than 40 percent of the total export and import flows in the United States. Furthermore in the past two decades, trade with China and Mexico has grown significantly. So, on one hand we have the the acceleration of Mexico while on the other we have the emergence of China.

Mexico's role fits well with the incremental expansion thesis. Its geographic proximity, extensive cultural overlap, similar institutional context, and membership in NAFTA present few problems and pitfalls to the occasional or regular exporter in the United States. China, on the other hand, is politically, culturally, and economically dissimilar. However, Table 13.1 confirms China's consequence. Firm-level data elaborate this trade relationship. In 1992, 4,092 U.S. firms exported to China. By 2009, this number had increased more than 700 percent to 30,050 firms. This trend is particularly dramatic for SMEs in absolute terms as well as relative to large exporters. From 1992 to 2009, the number of SMEs exporting to China surged 776 percent versus 167 percent for large-company exporters. This effect is far more pronounced on the import side; SMEs accounted for 96 percent of the 87,910 U.S. firms that imported merchandise from China in 2009. The scale and scope of U.S.-China trade by a growing variety of SMEs speaks to the born global phenomenon.

Going forward, we anticipate stronger interaction effects between the incremental internationalization and born global perspectives. First, e-commerce continues turbo charging the born global trend. A generation ago, going global involved slow-acting trade officials directing slow-moving flows between tough-to-understand markets that differed on innumerable characteristics. Hence, incremental, market-by-market export expansion was not only practical, it was arguably the only feasible option.[28] Now,

Trade data suggest increasing interaction between the incremental international and born global perspectives.

Concept Check

The Internet influences political change, improves the operations of **foreign-exchange markets**, and changes the location economies that drive **value chain** configurations. Similarly, the Internet reshapes export and import activity by opening new markets, supporting new strategies, and providing new tools.

e-commerce immediately gives small startups global reach, providing a platform that efficiently overcomes historic barriers to internationalization. Our closing case profiles a leading intermediary, Alibaba.com, that facilitates this process. Second, for those exporters more inclined toward incremental expansion, the Internet provides cheap, easy, and effective means to analyze and access dissimilar markets. Hence, their expansion to far more dissimilar markets fits the incremental view whereas the acceleration of this process fits the born global perspective.

The Wildcard Role of Serendipity   It is appealing to depict export initiation and development, whether done incrementally or immediately, as a purposeful strategy designed and delivered by proactive executives. However, research tells of accidental exporters who, responding to happenstance or odd circumstances, successfully enter overseas markets. Essentially, some companies start exporting because of serendipity rather than design. Perhaps the most common trigger is the arrival of an unsolicited order in the mail. Others include a new hire that has connections to foreign buyers, an international contact made at an industry conference, personal travel abroad alerts one to new options, and so on. Thus, **serendipity**—making fortunate discoveries by accident—sometimes initiates the export process.

> Exporters are often proactive decision makers. Sometimes, however, serendipity—making fortunate discoveries by accident—initiates exports.

Edward Cutler is such a case. He is the owner and founder of Pennsylvania-based Squigle, a unique brand of toothpaste for people who cannot tolerate mass-produced varieties.[29] Upon launching Squigle Mr. Cutler focused on the U.S. market. Internet posters spread news of the product, and Squigle soon received inquiries from Taiwan, Turkey, and elsewhere. One customer, a canker-sore sufferer in Britain, was so enthusiastic about it that he began importing Squigle to England for sale. That was good news for Mr. Cutler because it let him expand abroad at little cost and low risk. Now he is eager to export more, explaining, "We're looking to sell overseas for the same reason the big companies do: Most of the world's population lies outside the United States."[30]

Similarly, Vellus, a small Ohio–based company that makes a line of high-end pet grooming products began its export odyssey when a Taiwanese businessperson, after trying its customized shampoos, bought $25,000 worth of the company's products to sell in Taiwan. Soon, word spread from show to show on the global canine circuit. Recounted Vellus's CEO, "I started receiving calls from people around the world who would hear of our products at dog shows and ask organizers how they could get in touch with me to buy our products. Today, Vellus exports products to about 30 countries."[31]

Approaches to Exporting

Granted, export sounds straightforward—make it, sell it, pack it, and ship it.[32] To some degree, this holds true for many trades. Generally, the ease of exporting follows from how a company approaches it. Companies, as we explain below, have a variety of options, namely:

Direct Exporting   In this scenario, the company directly sells its products to an independent intermediary, such as an agent, distributor, or retailer outside its home country, who then sells the product to the end consumer. **Direct exporting** is an ambitious approach. It requires the company manage the export process, minding the many aspects of making and marketing the product for foreign buyers. SpinCent highlights this process, showing how Mr. Knepper analyzed markets, assessed industries, prepped his company, traveled overseas, and sought, screened, and hired trustworthy distributors to supervise sales in Asian markets. Too, he took lead responsibility for developing an export plan and consulting with the Ex-Im Bank. Consequently, this approach requires executive commitment and company resources to get the show

Case Review Note

started and then to sustain activity. But with that said, once up and running, exporting directly through trustworthy distributors can prove straightforward. Explained Edward Cutler, maker of Squigle toothpaste, "It is just easier to deal with distributors. We prefer to deal in master shippers of 144 tubes. We don't have to do anything then but slap a label on it."[33]

Exporting directly involves independent representatives, distributors, or retailers outside of the exporter's home country.

Indirect Exporting   In this scenario, the company sells its products to an independent intermediary in the domestic market. The intermediary exports the product to its foreign agents who then sell it to the end consumer. **Indirect exporting** results because the exporter relies on the intermediary, say a global retailer, to supervise marketing, terms of sale, packaging, distribution, and credit and collection procedures. The intersection of retail and globalization trends makes indirect selling increasingly practical. Global retail chains such as Walmart, Carrefour, and Ahold facilitate the movement of products from exporters to storefronts. Think of, for example, a DVD manufacturer in China who supplies Walmart International with a product that Walmart then sells it in its retail locations worldwide. While not as lucrative as direct selling, indirect exporting makes far fewer demands. Indirect exporting is often a transition phase whereby the neophyte can gain familiarity about foreign consumers and competitors while still retaining some control over the product.

Indirect exports are products sold to an intermediary in the home market, which then exports them.

Passively Filling Orders from Domestic Buyers Who Then Export the Product   From the perspective of the seller, these sorts of international sales are indistinguishable from domestic sales. Essentially, a buyer contacts the company, submits an order, takes delivery, and exports the product. The company may be unaware that its products has been shipped abroad.

Selling to Domestic Buyers Who Represent Foreign End Users or Customers   MNEs, general contractors, foreign trading companies, foreign governments, and foreign distributors and retailers purchase goods for export. These buyers either need or see the need for a good in foreign markets. So, they buy it here and ship it there. Again, the company that makes the product may not know of its export.

WHICH APPROACH WHEN?

No one approach is superior in all situations. At the broadest level, the company's particular ownership, location, and internalization advantages moderate the optimal approach. Protecting ownership advantages endorses exporting directly. SpinCent, for example, saw direct selling as the best means to retain control of their core competency. Similarly, top management's outlook and company resources endorse some choices while discouraging others. A regular exporter is more likely to export directly. Firms new to exporting or those who are unable to commit staff and funds will likely prefer indirect or passive methods.

Case Review Note

Technology changes the relative merits of the different approaches The Internet increasingly supports exporting directly. It provides immediate, low-cost, access that lets regular exporters, particularly born globals, more easily access more markets.[34] In addition, e-commerce helps companies, both big and small, overcome capital and infrastructure limitations.[35] For example, exporters in Chile use extranets to communicate with importers around the world, while exporters in Costa Rica have used online shops to directly export.[36] Our closing case looks at how a little electronic magic at alibaba.com, the world's largest business-to-business online marketplace, helps SMEs engage their counterparts around the world. Twenty years ago, firm resources, communication channels, and trade logistics mattered immensely if you were a SME in Patagonia trying to reach markets in Europe. Today, due to alibaba.com and like-minded Internet platforms, they matter far less.

Internet marketing helps companies—both large and small—engage in international trade quickly, easily, and cheaply.

Case Review Note

The four approaches to exporting are not mutually exclusive; company and market circumstances moderate whether managers opt to apply one or use a mix.

Last, the four approaches to exporting are not mutually exclusive. A firm can engage different methods to serve different markets. For example, a U.S. firm may export directly to similar markets such as Canada, Mexico, and Britain while using indirect methods to handle exports to dissimilar markets in China, South Africa, or Japan. So while there are general rules, the ideal approach to export fits executives' commitment and the firm's competencies.

Importing

Importing is the purchase of a good or service by a buyer in one country from a seller in another. The foreign buyer is referred to as the importer whereas the seller, based in the other country, is referred to as the exporter. The import of goods is straightforward: Toyota's shipment of an automobile from Japan to a buyer in Bangkok registers as an import for Thailand. Service imports, given their intangibility, take various forms. Foreign banks, like Royal Bank of Canada, that provide financial services to U.S. customers qualify as service imports. Similarly, when Lloyd's of London writes an insurance policy for a client in Brazil, trade authorities in Brazil record an import.

A service import is all services that do not result in ownership and that are rendered by non-residents to local residents.

The import of services has subtle characteristics. For example, the installation of nuclear power equipment in Sweden by French firm Areva, even though it is a hard good, qualifies as a service import for Sweden. The standard to keep in mind is that an import of a service consists of any transaction that (1) does not result in ownership and (2) is rendered by nonresidents to residents.

Who Are Importers?

Our earlier classification of exporters—namely non-, occasional, and regular exporters—has broad analogues in the import sector. Although terminology sometimes differs, there are three types, namely:

There are three general types of importers:

• Input optimizers.
• Opportunistic.
• Arbitrageurs.

Input Optimizers   This sort of importer uses foreign sourcing to optimize, in terms of price or quality, the inputs fed into a supply chain. Essentially, a company scours the globe for optimal inputs. Once found, it directs them to various production points distributed among various countries. These factories assemble them into finished goods that are then imported by markets worldwide. Logically, the flow of inputs and finished goods from country to country, besides representing imports, also qualifies as exports.

Opportunistic   This sort of importer looks for products around the world that it can import and profitably sell to local citizens. These traders see a gap in the local marketplace—whether real (customers cannot find what they want) or perceived (the presumption that products from some countries are intrinsically superior to local substitutes). They exploit this opportunity by importing products available only from foreign suppliers.

For the opportunistic importer, the product is unimportant. Rather, the game is using imports to profitably fill gaps in the local marketplace. For example, the release of the iPad2 saw frenzied buying by a range of consumers, including scalpers intending to exploit a temporary market gap. Specifically, the iPad2, upon introduction, was only available in the United States for the first several weeks. Immense demand in other countries created compelling opportunities. For instance, buyers in China hired shoppers in New York to buy whatever quantity they could and overnight it to Shanghai. An iPad2 there sold for double to triple the price in the United States.[37] Eventually, as Apple stores begin selling it in China, the gap closed.

Arbitrageurs This sort of importer looks to foreign sourcing to get the highest-quality product at the lowest possible price. This motivation is timeless—an agent takes advantage of a price or quality difference between two or more markets, transacting deals that exploit the imbalance, and profiting from the difference. For instance, Utah-based SME ForEveryBody began making bath and body products locally. Eventually, discovering low-cost home decorations available from Asian manufacturers that were competitive with premium products in the United States, it became an importer.

CHARACTERISTICS OF IMPORTERS

Extensive research has investigated the characteristics of exporters. For any number of reasons, less research evaluates the features of importers. Presently, data indicates that importers are also likely to be exporters. Furthermore, these firms account for the bulk of exports and imports.[38] Specifically, of those U.S. companies that engaged in trade, 78,940 both exported and imported merchandise. Of these, 74,473 were SMEs, or 94.3 percent of all companies.[39] Therefore, in fundamental ways, our discussion of the characteristics of exporters applies to importers. Importers tailor international activity to reflect their ownership, localization, and internalization advantages, exhibit incremental and born global characteristics, and indicate that firm size, along with efficiency, innovation, and commitment explain their activity.

Several points qualify the degree of overlap. Historically, importers traded relatively few products with a relatively few developing countries.[40] Essentially, the bulk of imports tended toward opportunism or arbitrage—i.e., the cheap oil of Saudi Arabia became expensive oil in the United States. The emergence of fast-growing emerging economies accelerates and alters this relationship. They increasingly produce more goods and services that beat, in price and performance, local choices in advanced markets. Too, they increasingly provide higher-end products that once were the province of advanced markets—think, for example, of U.S. companies importing business process services from India-based firms. Last, globalization supports far more differentiated supply chains that have more links in longer chains that cross more markets. Their growth has commensurately increased the import of inputs.

Why Import?

Various factors spur a firm to begin importing as well as motivate ongoing activity. Research emphasizes high product quality, satisfactory order processing, delivery reliability, lower prices, and domestic shortages. These factors, singly and collectively, push importers to scan world markets, seeking lower-priced, better quality, or locally unavailable products. This supposition begs the question: Why do these market anomalies exist? Absent these gaps, there is little need for import or, for that matter, export. Others parts of the text, particularly Chapters 6 and 12, speak to this issue. For our purposes, we highlight the following import drivers.

Specialization of Labor Managers divide a production process into a sequence of stages. They assign workers to particular stages so that one worker does one task, another does another task, and so on. This specialization of labor enables organizing production to exploit location economics, most notably different wage rates, across countries. Improved efficiencies reduce costs that encourage companies to import cheaper products. For instance, Nike buys shoes manufactured by companies in several Asian countries. The latter make higher quality shoes for lower cost. Nike finds it impossible to manufacture the same products in its home market,, sell them at a reasonable price, and still make a profit. Consequently, Nike imports shoes.

Several reasons motivate importing:
- Specialization of labor.
- Global rivalry.
- Local unavailability.
- Diversification.
- Top management's outlook.

The same logic applies to the production of the iPad2. Specifically, Apple contracts with Foxconn to make the iPad2 in China that is then imported into the United States. Foxconn reportedly pays employees 1,200 yuan per month, or about $185.[41] If we generously assume an average 8-hour per day, 250-day per year schedule, that's works out to about $1.11/hour.[42] In contrast, the average U.S. manufacturing/mining/construction hourly compensation was officially $32.53 as of December 2010.[43] Reportedly, making the iPad2 requires about nine hours of direct labor. So, in this admittedly simple scenario, making the 32 GB Wi-Fi 3g iPad2 in China results in a retail price of $729 in the United States. Making it in the United States results in a retail price of $1,144.[44] Consequently, Apple imports iPad2s.

Global Rivalry   Industries with a high degree of global competitive rivalry, such as telecommunications, automobiles, and business services, impose relentless cost pressures. Many products, such as aircraft or cars, rely on thousands of parts produced in factories around the world. Companies use foreign suppliers in order to lower input costs or boost the quality of its finished products.

Local Unavailability   Companies import products they cannot obtain locally due to geographic, regulatory, or developmental reasons. For example, Canada imports bananas from tropical climates because of its own unsuitable climate. Absent imports, Canadians would not enjoy fresh bananas. The same goes for eating seasonal fruits and vegetables out-of-season; e.g., grapes from Chile grace Christmas dinner in Denmark.

Diversification   Importers, like exporters, diversify operating risks by tapping international markets. Developing alternative suppliers makes a company less vulnerable to the dictates or fortunes of a local supplier. For example, customers of U.S. steelmakers, such as companies in the automobile industry, have diversified their purchases to include European, Indian, and South Korean suppliers. This strategy reduces the risk of supply shortages or unilateral price hikes by U.S. steelmakers.

Concept Check

As straightforward as the concept of **exporting** may seem on the surface, whether you are a born-global entrepreneur or established **MNE**, it is fraught with challenges. *Behavioral barriers* complicate international operations. Political and legal codes pose pitfalls, *government regulation* impact trade relationships, and *foreign-exchange instruments* necessitate financial sophistication.

Importing and Exporting: Problems and Pitfalls

Companies, especially non- and occasional exporters, see a variety of problems and pitfalls that make international trade difficult. Moreover, trade veterans explain that selling and buying products internationally is fraught with ongoing complexities and evolving barriers. Presently, there is considerable variation regarding the type, characteristics, and impact of obstacles. Still, it is safe to say that exporters and importers face recurring difficulties that test the resolve of the most committed internationalist. Each routinely runs into problems and pitfalls that hinder their ability to initiate, to develop, or to sustain export or import.[45] Anecdotes and analysis indicate prominent types.

Financial Risks   Financial constraints are arguably the greatest impediment to international traders. A survey of 978 SMEs asked their perceptions of trade barriers; the top ranked factor was the "shortage of working capital to finance export."[46] Traders often reason that export or import offer low profitability given unexpected costs and unknown financial constraints, both of which are aggravated by fluctuating exchange rates. Managing these risks involves currency and credit processes that call for relatively sophisticated financial expertise. Moreover, completing international sales may require helping foreign customers obtain credit, whether in the form of trade credits, government-financed support, or bank guarantees.[47] Firms accustomed to offering financing in terms of the traditional 30- or 60-day trade-credit cycle at home regard the need for different arrangements abroad as excessively escalating risk.

SMEs regularly rate financial constraints as the most daunting barrier to international trade.

> ## Point

Exporting E-Waste: A Useful Solution?

Point **Yes** Exporting is a win-win situation: The more companies and countries export, the more they improve their performance. Exporting enables companies to increase sales, improve productivity, and diversify activities. Exporting enables countries to generate jobs, accelerate innovation, and improve living standards. Furthermore, exporting promotes connections among countries that improve foreign relations and stabilize market development.

Yes, a shady side of exporting is the trade of hazardous waste in the form of obsolete computer equipment. E-waste—trash composed of computers, monitors, electronics, game consoles, mobile phones, and other items—inexorably increases as the information era rolls on. In 2006, nearly 66 million used electronic components were collected for reuse or recycling in the United States; most were exported.[48] By 2011, e-waste was pushing 100 million pieces that clocked in at 3 million tonnes. Ongoing trends crank out newer, cooler, faster, smaller, fancier devices that will increase e-waste nearly 500 percent over the next decade.

Where Should E-waste Go? Where to put all the trash is a tough question. Many counties and municipalities in the United States, for example, ban outright dumping of e-waste in local landfills. This legislation means that disposing e-waste products, when possible, in any given industrialized country costs from $2500 to $4000 a ton. In contrast, selling untreated waste to countries in Africa and Asia, where it will be recycled and reused, reportedly goes as low as $50 a ton.[49] Low costs follow from cheap labor, different environmental regulations, and growing processing capacity in Asia and Africa. Too, the absence of public opposition and desperate folks seeking wages reduces processing expenses. Expectedly, major e-waste shipping routes show that the industrial nations export the bulk of their e-waste to developing countries, notably, China, Malaysia, India, Nigeria, and Bangladesh[50] (See Map 13.1).

Benefits for All Exporting e-waste to recycling centers throughout the world is a great way to solve a growing problem.

MAP 13.1 Where E-Waste Gets Shipped (or Dumped)

When computers, cell phones, and other electronic equipment become obsolete, they are no longer worth much in rich countries. E-waste, however, has some value in developing countries. That is exactly where, as exports, it usually ends up. Proponents note it promotes productive recycling as well as local economic development. Critics charge it viciously hazardous that callously exploits cheap labor and lax regulations.
Source: Basel Action Network; Silicon Valley Toxics Condition.

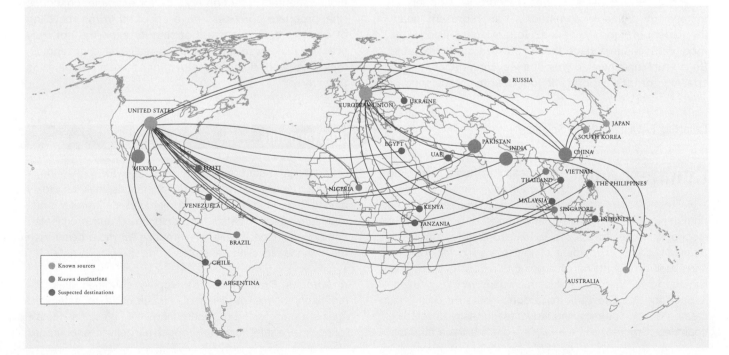

An enterprising Nigerian child running a grassroots recycling facility. Although ostensibly junk to many, scavenging and reselling these parts creates value.

Source: Enrique Soriano-Silverlens/ZUMA Press/Newscom

First and foremost, recycling sustains our resources and helps us to protect the environment. In developing countries, basic industries have sprung up to recycle old computers, monitors, circuit boards, scanners, printers, routers, cell phones, and network cards. While rudimentary, these industries create jobs in places where jobs are hard to find and difficult to sustain. To their credit, developing countries have converted their superior location economics into vital jobs, income, and markets.

Similarly, exporting e-waste helps entrepreneurs in developing countries create value by recovering, recycling, and reusing scarce resources. Copper, an increasingly valuable commodity, can represent nearly 20 percent of a mobile phone's total weight. Rising commodity prices have made these activities quite profitable. Says Atul Maheshwar, owner of a recycling depot in India, speaking of U.S. exports, "If your country keeps sending us the material, our business will be good."[51] In addition, much of the equipment shipped to Asia helps improve the local standard of living. Graham Wollaston of Scrap Computers, a recycler in Phoenix, claims that virtually every component of old electronic devices is reusable. Old televisions turn into fish tanks in Malaysia, while silicon shortage creates demand for old monitors. "There's no such thing as a third-world landfill," Mr. Wollaston explains. "If you were to put an old computer on the street, it would be taken apart for the parts." Similarly, Luc Lateille of the Canadian firm BMP Recycling says, "We don't send junk—we only send the materials that they are looking for."

Exporting hazardous waste also helps MNEs improve their social responsibility. Growing public concern pushes companies such as Samsung, Mitsubishi, and Nokia to assume cradle-to-grave responsibility for their products. Laggards, spurred by state regulation, grudgingly accept the virtue of green recycling. Since 2004, more than 20 U.S. states have required manufacturers recycle electronics. Likeminded laws are on deck in several other states and countries. Companies often comply by exporting their e-waste to countries that have an interest in recycling and the infrastructure to do it.

A Tough Solution   Certainly, callous companies dump useless e-waste around the world. And, yes, some of it pollutes landfills, poisons waterways, and contaminates the air. Overall, though, exporting e-waste works for citizens, consumers, companies, and countries. Ultimately, nations really don't have a choice. The U.S. Environmental Protection Agency, for example, concedes "inappropriate practices" have occurred in the recycling of e-waste but suggests stopping its export is not truly practical. Likewise, poor nations really have no choice; they must work doing something or condemn themselves to poverty.

Exporting E-Waste: A Useful Solution?

Counterpoint

Counterpoint   **No** Yes, in theory, recycling is beneficial. Recycling your e-waste, however, does not always mean you're doing the right thing. "The dirty little secret is that when you take [your electronic waste] to a recycler, instead of throwing it in a trashcan, about 80 percent of that material, very quickly, finds itself on a container ship going to a country like China, Nigeria, India, Vietnam, Pakistan—where very dirty things happen to it."[52] Growth in hazardous waste exporting has created dangerous recycling industries in many developing countries. Granted, some e-waste contains trace amounts of precious metals. However, most e-waste contains a mixture of more than a thousand chemicals, including toxic metals (e.g., lead, barium, and mercury), flame-retardants, cadmium, acids, plastics, and chlorinated and brominated compounds. Collectively, they impose far more costs than the pittance recycling generates.

A Witches Brew   Most developing countries lack the regulatory codes or disposal infrastructure to safeguard against such dangers. Extracting the precious metals found in e-waste, such as copper and silver, encourages

A frightful wasteland nearby Lagos, Nigeria. Notwithstanding the toxic waste, desperation spurs people to scavenge for anything of value.

Source: n86/ZUMA Press/Newscom

cash-strapped, loosly regulated recyclers to use unsafe, antiquated open-air incineration methods. Burning electronic parts to separate copper, solder, or other metals from plastic coatings releases dioxins and other hazardous chemicals. Local air quality suffers as "circuit boards are burned after acid washing, spewing deadly smoke, and exposing workers and people living around these facilities."[53] Once local scrap shops finish disassembling equipment, the trash typically goes into public landfills, the acid runoff flows into groundwater, and the noxious fumes follow air currents—all in all, a witches' brew of toxins that mercilessly contaminate the environment.

Casual Inhumanity Madhumita Dutta of Toxics-Link Delhi argues that these problems are less disturbing than the "appalling" working conditions in recycling facilities: "Everything from dismantling the computer to pulling out parts of the circuit boards to acid-washing boards to recover copper is done with bare hands without any protective gear or face protection." Rare is the worksite that uses proper disposal practices. Workers and society, to say nothing of environmental sustainability, suffer.

What, then, of the premise of charity—that is, sending computer equipment from countries where it has little use to countries where it can make a difference? Critics shred this strawman, asserting that wealthier countries and powerful companies conveniently donate obsolete equipment to dodge high recycling expenses. "Too often, justifications of 'building bridges over the digital divide' are used as excuses to obscure and ignore the fact that these bridges double as toxic waste pipelines," said one critic.[54] Moreover, most of the computer equipment sent is worthless trash—waste that that can be neither repaired nor resold.[55]

Institutional Gaps Some argue that manufacturers need to step up and take responsibility for the hazardous materials they used to build products that earned them profits.[56] Companies have moved in this direction, sponsoring green campaigns to recycle e-waste. Substantive progress has been slow, however. Environmentalists recommend that countries set tougher standards to monitor, control, and certify cross-border shipments of e-waste. That too has proven disappointing. Inspections of e-waste cargo at 18 European seaports awaiting export, for example, found that nearly half was illegal.[57]

Then again, presumed solutions can lead to unintended problems. The fact that many U.S. states require companies take responsibility for recycling electronic equipment has curtailed the export of e-waste to developing countries—but only of the more valuable components. Processors cherry-pick parts that can be refurbished for new use, then the machines are disassembled and their glass and precious metals recycled. The remaining trash, the worst of the worst, has no reuse market and is shipped to developing countries for disposal.[58]

Who to Turn To? Others endorse stronger enforcement of the Basel Convention on the Transboundary Movement of Hazardous Wastes and their Disposal, a United Nations treaty that regulates the generation, management, movements, and disposal of hazardous waste. It proposes aggressive measures, including an international ban on the export of all toxic waste, no matter whether for recovery, recycling, reuse, or final disposal. As of mid-2011, 172 countries had ratified the Basel Convention. The United States, which generates approximately 60 percent of the world's e-waste waste, has signed the treaty but not ratified it.[59]

Customer Management Historically, exports and imports were arm's-length, ship-it-and-forget-it transactions. Contact with customers relied on documents either faxed or posted overnight. This situation created useful time lags with which to deal with questions and complaints. Now, contacting vendors via e-mail or voice-over-Internet-protocol (VoIP) gives customers real-time access. By ratcheting up their service expectations, it reduces the appeal of international trade. "The new notch in the bar for us is the requests from our customers for additional services beyond the port of delivery," said the materials manager of Seco/Warwick Corp., a manufacturer of heat-treating equipment. "In

The problems and pitfalls of international trade consistently frustrate the occasional and regular exporter.

previous years, I would be responsible for cost, insurance, and freight (CIF) to the port of import, but now I'm often tasked with all aspects of the delivery to the customer's plant location. Now we're often involved in the installation and startup of the equipment, so we have service engineers and cranes waiting for the on-time delivery."[60]

Customer management concerns increasingly challenge SMEs. Their orientation toward specialized opportunities and narrow gaps in the market often prompt niche strategies. Recurring resource constraints as well as the preference to avoid competing head-on with larger companies reinforce these tendencies.[61] Targeting an export market niche usually push SMEs to customize services and marketing support beyond that offered in the home market.

An enduring barrier to exporting is misunderstanding the difficulty of profitably serving consumers in foreign market.

Case Review Note

Scant International Business Expertise   International traders note the difficulties of understanding foreign business practices. Ordinary as well as idiosyncratic problems include limited knowledge of foreign competitors, unfamiliarity with local custom regulations, uncertainty about the prevailing price to quality relationship, difficulty optimizing transportation and insurance options, and confusion about market channels and consumer behavior. Certainly, there are solutions, as we saw with our opening profile of SpinCent. Fear of misunderstanding local markets led it to hire local distributors. Firms that struggle interpreting export markets typically exit international trade.

Marketing Barriers   Traders regularly complain of high-shipment costs and logistic demands, difficulties matching foreign rivals' prices, effectively promoting products, establishing distribution networks, and weak foreign market connections. In addition, providing after-sales service imposes the aggravation of translating warranties as well as navigating ambiguous cultural differences. Non-exporters express greater anxiety about these marketing uncertainties, particularly when they benchmark them against the comparatively lower demands in their home market. The decidedly more complex demands of market structures and consumer behaviors in emerging markets amplify problems. Going from the United States to Canada is one thing; going from the United States to Turkmenistan is entirely another.

Persevering in the face of problems and pitfalls requires executives committed to internationalization.

Top Management Commitment   Management characteristics, most notably international outlook and risk orientation, influence import activity. Most companies, particularly SMEs, focus on domestic rather than foreign markets. In the United States for instance, SMEs comprise 97 percent of all exporters. However, less than 1 percent of all SMEs export. Furthermore, of SMEs that do export, nearly two-thirds export to just one foreign market.[62] Asked why they are export shy, managers cite familiarity with the home market along with equivocal top management commitment to venturing abroad. Even when top management acknowledges the benefit of international trade, its riskiness and resource demands dissuade most from steadfastly internationalizing operations.

Exporting and importing puts tough demands on management. Rare is the firm that has a surplus of resources to support and eagerness to adjust customary practices for foreign business standards. As a result, top management often emphasize the domestic market and note their intention to develop export down the road. For example, recall Mr. Knepper's original export outlook; at best, he was an occasional exporter who felt the risks outweighed rewards. Eventually, profitability and diversification concerns forced him to reconsider. From then on, his company's core competency, support from public agencies, and trustworthy distributors, fortified his export commitment.

Case Review Note

Trade Regulation   Export and import inefficiencies persist due to delays, documents, and administrative fees. The rules and regulations governing trade, not with standing the success of the WTO, endure. New Jersey–based Spectra Colors, manufacturer and distributor of high-quality customized dyes and colorants, runs into problems because import regulations differ from one country to the next. "In Europe, REACH regulations (Registration, Evaluation, and Authorization of Chemicals) have caused us lengthy delays and expense," said Spectra's business manager.[63] Occasionally, shipments to various markets require government clearance. Refusals come easily to officials facing product shortages at home or political tension abroad.

In the United States, homeland security issues constrain trade. For example, the logistics manager at Schott North America notes that the real danger to international trade these days isn't tariffs, it's "that your containers are stuck down at the terminal in New York [harbor] waiting for inspection" by radiation detection instruments before allowed to enter the United States.[64] Likewise, moving goods across borders takes far longer today than it did 10 years ago given homeland security procedures. Processing a truckload of goods across the Canadian–American border takes three times as long as it did pre-September 11, 2001.[65] Consequently, international traders must navigate complex national, regional, and global trade regulations.

Trade Documentation A battery of documents regulates international trade. Duty rates, customs clearance, and entry processes, though overlapping, invariably differ across countries. Tariff classifications, value declarations, and duty management spawn confusion and boost costs. Customs and security initiatives impose regulations on international traders. Navigating these obstacles requires traders manage the paper trail that documents, certifies, and legalizes transactions. Table 13.2 profiles key customs documents. For many companies, completing these and many others is unacceptably burdensome. A look at Figure 13.2 gives one a sense of this task—and keep in mind that this is just one of the many required forms.

Mistakes arise in any number of slots. For example, many loss-and-damage challenges stem in part from the sizable percentage of exporters that use incorrect International Commercial Terms (Incoterms).[66] The correct Incoterm help exporters avoid disputes

Concept Check

"Legal Issues in International Business," profiled in Chapter 3, note how a country's legal system influences the operating decisions in **international business**. Chapter 7 shows how governments influence import flows with instruments of trade control. Here we add revenue collection and homeland security to the list of moderators.

Governments require international traders thoroughly document transactions.

TABLE 13.2   Types of Export Documents

Type	Specification
Pro Forma Invoice	A document from the exporter to the importer that outlines the selling terms, price, and delivery as if the goods had actually shipped. If the importer accepts the terms and conditions, it sends a purchase order and arrange for payment, at which point the exporter issues a commercial invoice.
Shipper's Export Declaration	The most common of all export documents. It is used by the exporter's government to monitor exports and to compile trade statistics.
Bill of Lading	A receipt for goods delivered to the common carrier for transportation, a contract for services rendered by the carrier, and a document of title. The customer usually needs an original as proof of ownership before assuming title.
Consular Invoice	Sometimes required by countries to monitor imports. Used by governments to track import prices and generate revenue.
Certificate of Origin	Indicates the product's origination and is usually validated by an external source, such as the Chamber of Commerce. It helps countries determine the tariff schedule for imports.
Export-Packing List	Itemizes the material in each individual package, indicates the type of package, and is attached to the outside of the package. It is used by the shipper or freight forwarder, and sometimes customs officials, to verify the cargo.
Commercial Invoice	A bill for the goods from the buyer to the seller listing a description of the goods, addresses of buyer and seller, and delivery and payment terms. Governments use it to determine the value of goods when assessing customs duties. Figure 13.3 shows a sample of this form, identifying the various data an exporter must report to comply with current U.S. trade policy.

FIGURE 13.2 Sample Commercial Invoice

Here we see a sample of the sorts of forms that U.S. exporters routinely face. In this case, the form is a commercial invoice, basically a bill for the goods from the buyer to the seller. Completing this form correctly makes for efficient transfers. Completing it incorrectly results in costly delays and often higher duty charges.

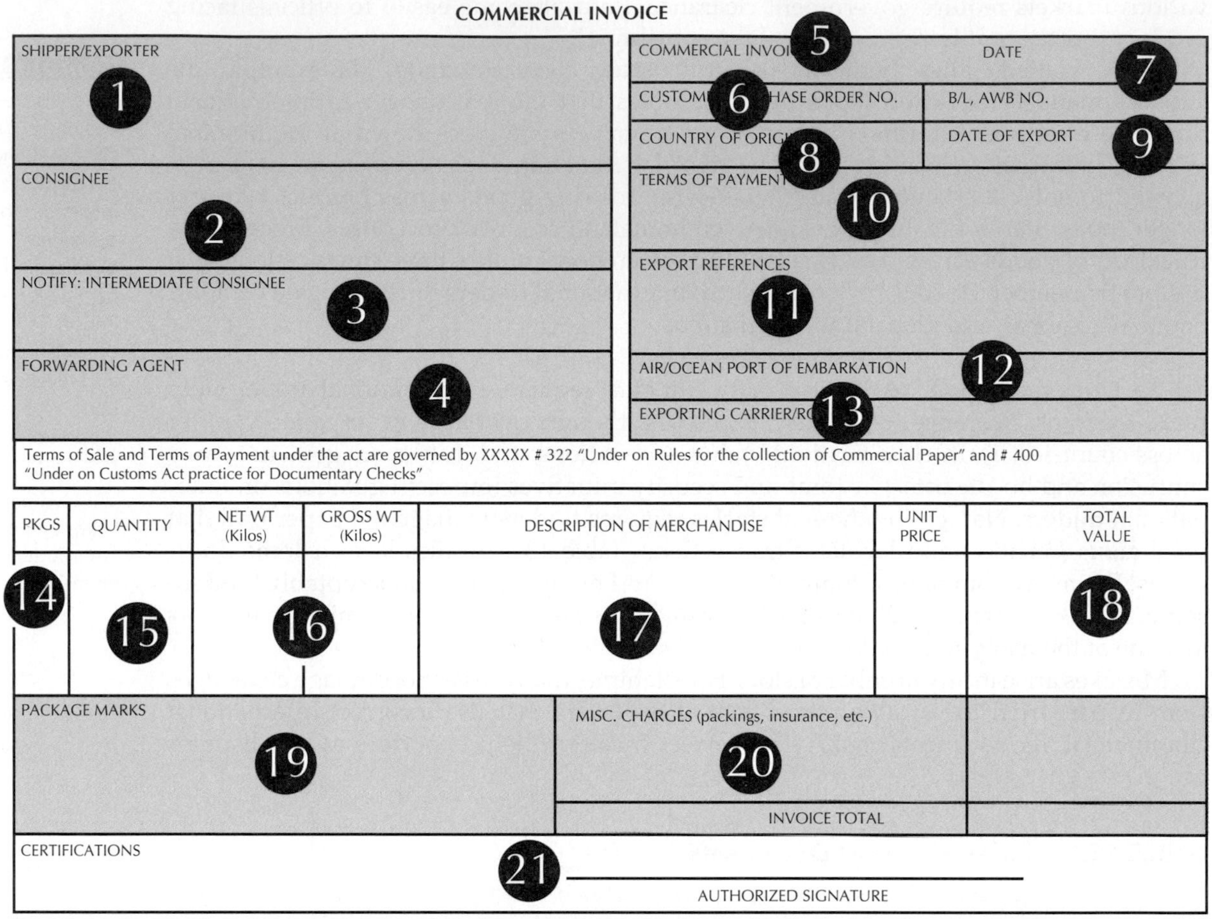

COMMERCIAL INVOICE

1.	**EXPORTER**	The name and address of the principal party responsible for effecting export from the United States. The exporter as named on the Export License.
2.	**CONSIGNEE**	The name and address of the person/company to whom the goods are shipped for the designated end use, or the party so designated on the Export License
3.	**INTERMEDIATE CONSIGNEE**	The name and address of the party who effects delivery of the merchandise to the ultimate consignee, or the party so named on the Export License.
4.	**FORWARDING AGENT**	The name and address of the duly authorized forwarder acting as agent for the exporter.
5.	**COMMERCIAL INVOICE NO.**	Commercial Invoice number assigned by the exporter
6.	**CUSTOMER PURCHASE ORDER NO**	Overseas customer's reference of order number
7.	**B/L, AWB NO.**	Bill of Lading, or Air Waybill number, if known
8.	**COUNTRY OF ORIGIN**	Country of origin of shipment
9.	**DATE OF EXPORT**	Actual date of export of merchandise
10.	**TERMS OF PAYMENT**	Describe the terms, conditions, and currency of settlement as agreed upon by the vendor and purchaser per the Pro Forma Invoice, customer Purchase Order, and/or Letter of Credit
11.	**EXPORT REFERENCES**	May be used to record other useful information, e.g. - other reference numbers, special handling requirements, routing requirements, etc.
12.	**AIR/OCEAN PORT OF EMBARKATION**	Ocean port/pier, or airport to be used for embarkation of merchandise
13.	**EXPORTING CARRIER/ROUTE**	Record airline carrier/flight number or vessel name/shipping line to be used for the shipment of merchandise
14.	**PACKAGES**	Record number of packages, cartons, or containers per description line
15.	**QUANTITY**	Record total number of units per description line.
16.	**NET WEIGHT/GROSS WEIGHT**	Record total net weight and total gross weight (includes weight of container) in kilograms per description line.
17.	**DESCRIPTION OF MERCHANDISE**	Provide a full description of items shipped, the type of container (carton, box, pack, etc.), the gross weight per container, and the quantity and unit of measure of the merchandise.
18.	**UNIT PRICE/TOTAL VALUE**	Record the unit price of the merchandise per the unit of measure, compute the extended total value of the line.
19.	**PACKAGE MARKS**	Record in this Field, as well as on each package, the package number (e.g. - 1 of 7, 3 of 7, etc.), shippers company name, country of origin (e.g. - made in USA), destination port of entry, package weight in kilograms, package size (length x width x height), and shipper's control number (e.g. - C/I number; optional).
20.	**MISC. CHARGES**	Record any miscellaneous charges which are to be paid for by the customer - export transportation, insurance, export packaging, inland freight to pier, etc.
21.	**CERTIFICATIONS**	Any certifications or declarations required of the shipper regarding any information recorded on the commercial invoice.

Source: http://www.unzco.com/basicguide/figure2.html Accessed March 19, 2009.

with customers by specifying each party's responsibilities. Sometimes, exporters fail to classify their products accurately in terms of the tariff schedule of the country of destination. Goods that arrive with commercial invoice descriptions that do not match those of the importing country's tariff classification are registered under a catchall description, such as "machinery, other." Besides slowing the transaction, imprecise descriptions often incur higher duty charges.

Importers typically receive products without purchasing them. That is, they take the title of ownership without laying out any money. The arrival of the shipment in country requires filing documents with various offices and agencies in order to pay up, take title, settle duty charges, and arrange delivery. Required documents vary by country. Typically, custom agencies require an entry manifest, commercial invoice, and packing list.[67]

Importing and Exporting: Resources and Assistance

The problems and pitfalls of international trade, besides discouraging potential exporters and importers, complicate the activities of committed internationalists and born globals. SMEs are particularly vulnerable. Many SMEs could boost profits and improve productivity by entering new markets.[68] In 2009, two thirds of SME exporters posted sales to only one foreign market. In contrast, more than half of big exporters recorded sales to five or more foreign markets. This trend is also evident on the import side. Sixty-two percent of all SMEs imported goods from one foreign market, while 57 percent of large firms imported from five or more foreign markets.[69]

Globalization, arguably, will push companies to expand their market frontiers. Liberalizing markets and opening borders inevitably increases trade. This is likely to apply to big and small companies. Many expect big companies will outperform. Their ownership and internalization advantages as well as superior resources position them to capture advances in moving goods, funds, and information. Most SMEs, unlike big companies, are removed from international business activities that promote helpful trade relationships. For example, in the United States, 92 percent of all SME exporters do business from a single location, and only 15 percent of SME exports go to related affiliates abroad. In contrast, 11 percent of large firms that export are single-location companies and 38 percent of their exports go to foreign affiliates.[70] Many SMEs find themselves in situations where public resources and assistance significantly influence their international activities.

Public agencies and private intermediaries provide non-, occasional, and regular exporters a wealth of resources. National, state, and local trade offices along with freight forwarders, custom brokers, trade intermediaries, international banks, and consultants are just a few of the many resources that help companies navigate the ins and outs of international trade. Our opening look at SpinCent highlighted the assistance provided by the U.S. Commercial Service's Export Assistance Center of Philadelphia; it helped Mr. Knepper assess the Asian markets, supported his tag along on the Asia trade mission, helped prescreen distributors, and arranged visits with local officials. Table 13.3 profiles leading sources of assistance.

GOVERNMENT AGENCIES

Public officials champion export given its macroeconomic and microeconomic benefits. From a macroeconomic perspective, export helps countries generate jobs, build foreign exchange reserves, improve the balance of trade, develop foreign relationships, and raise living standards. In the United States, for example, exports support more than 10 million jobs. In the manufacturing sector, export-related jobs accounted for 22 percent or more

Case Review Note

Concept Check

In Parts I and II of the text, we note that **international business** creates jobs, generates income, and raises living standards. Parts II and III show how governments shape trade relationships through pro-trade policies. Here we observe that governments devise a variety of programs to improve the ease and efficiency of **exporting** and **importing**.

TABLE 13.3   Trade Information by Type and Source

If your company is thinking about initiating or escalating international trade activity, the following organizations and agencies offer assistance.

Source	Nature of Assistance
Government Agencies	Market demographics, product demand, and competition
	Complying with domestic and foreign trade regulations
	Customs, regulatory, and tax issues
	Sales financing, credit, and insurance
	Trade data analysis
	Licenses and regulations
	International financing
	International sales and marketing
	Trade events, partners, and trade leads
	Shipping documentation and requirements
	Pricing, quotes, and negotiations
Trade Associations	Market demographics, product demand, and competition
	Export training seminars online and on-site
	Advertising and sales promotion alternatives
	Profile distribution channels and logistics networks
	Customs regulations and tax issues; compliance with global trade laws
	Navigating homeland security programs
	Standardize and streamline trade processes
Trade Intermediaries	Customs management system and tariff classification
	Online trade infrastructures and virtual trade shows
	Legal, accounting, security, and tax compliance
	Secure electronic procurement and automated supply chain processes
	Trade finance, credit-scoring, and insurance
	Exporting training and trade strategies
	Transport and logistics management

of total employment in ten U.S. manufacturing industries.[71] Overall, manufacturing exports support more than one of every five jobs in the United States. From a microeconomic perspective, exporting helps firms leverage core competencies, improve financial performance, fortify competitive positioning, and sustain the enterprise. New markets open paths to higher productivity and profitability. Consequently, governments in virtually every country assist potential and active exporters. To a lesser degree, they also protect the interests of their struggling importers.

In the margin: *In the United States, as in most countries, public agencies help firms initiate and develop exports and imports.*

In the United States, SMEs often start at the nearest Commercial Service office, the trade promotion arm of the U.S. Department of Commerce's International Trade Administration. It has representatives in over 100 U.S. cities and in more than 75 countries who help U.S. companies start exporting or increase sales in new markets. The U.S. government, through this and other resources, provides information and advice on the practicalities and technicalities of exporting. Its official gateway, www.export.gov, offers a variety of support services. Personal help is also available at export centers run by various branches of the Commerce Department, International Trade Administration, and the Small Business Administration. These and related agencies strengthen the competitiveness of U.S. industry, promote trade and investment, help U.S. companies compete at home and abroad, and ensure fair trade through the rigorous enforcement of trade laws and agreements.[72]

Similarly, most states and many cities run export financing programs, including pre- and post-shipment working-capital loans and guarantees, accounts receivable financing, and export insurance. The limited reserves of some agencies force them to make their assistance contingent on the exporter's proof that they do not risk losing much if the deal fails.

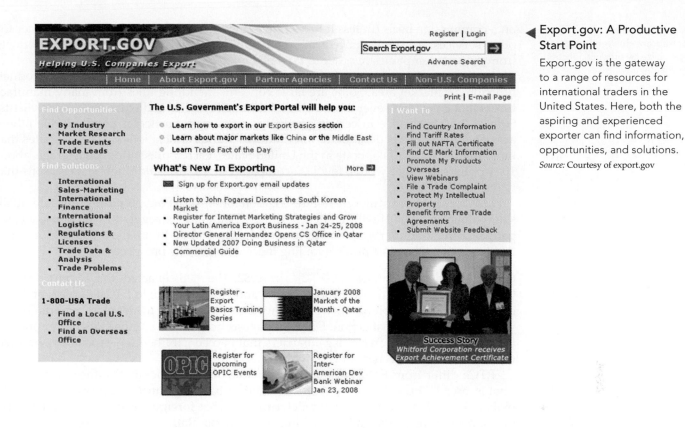

◀ **Export.gov: A Productive Start Point**

Export.gov is the gateway to a range of resources for international traders in the United States. Here, both the aspiring and experienced exporter can find information, opportunities, and solutions.

Source: Courtesy of export.gov

Authorities usually require a letter of credit or sufficient credit insurance. In some situations, states and cities require exporters to transact part of the deal within their jurisdiction.

EXPORT INTERMEDIARIES

Third-party firms that market products and services abroad on behalf of manufacturers, farm groups, and distributors qualify as **export intermediaries.** Many companies find they offer an operationally easier and relatively risk-free approach to manage the intricacies of international trade.[73] Their experience with regulations, taxes, duties, insurance, and transportation makes them productive resources. The major types of trade intermediaries are the export management company and the export trading company.

Export Management Companies (EMC) An EMC helps U.S. manufacturers establish an overseas market for their products. An EMC usually acts as the export arm of the company although it may also deal in imports. It maintains a close relationship with its clients, often acting as an unofficial marketing department. For instance, it may use their letterhead in communicating with foreign sales representatives and distributors. EMCs generate orders for their clients, organize distribution channels, develop promotions, collect, analyze, verify credit information, and advise on foreign accounts and payment terms. They can also oversee trade documents, arrange transportation, and arrange patent and trademark protection.[74] They expedite resolutions and, as needed, represent their clients at customs investigations.

EMCs operate on a contractual basis, providing exclusive representation in a formally defined market. Their contract with the company specifies pricing, credit, and financial policies, promotional services, and method of payment. An EMC might operate

> Trade intermediaries are third parties that provide international traders a variety of services.

Concept Check 10

In Chapter 1, we suggest **international business** is challenging for people who like to operate solo. Collecting information about foreign markets, navigating export regulations, mastering foreign-exchange procedures, or complying with homeland security policies can prove overwhelming. Consequently, some companies prefer to get help in finding information about potential markers. Intermediaries often command sophisticated knowledge of international trade.

Many EMCs are entrepreneurial ventures that specialize by product, function, or market area.

on a commission basis (unless it takes title to the merchandise) and charge a retainer for other services. It usually concentrates on complementary and noncompetitive products from various companies in order to market a full product line.

In the United States, most EMCs are entrepreneurial firms that specialize by product, function, or market area. Some are large concerns, handling lines from many manufacturers that cut across several industries. Others are smaller and work with fewer clients. Some EMCs specialize in certain products or focus on particular places, while others are generalists. The Federation of International Trade Associations (FITA) estimates that more than 1,000 EMCs operate in the United States, each representing, on average, about 10 suppliers. In other words, few U.S. companies use EMCs, although FITA reasons that many would benefit.[75]

EMCs, though versatile, are not the solution for all situations. Typically, they are small, stand-alone companies with limited resources. Some may struggle to warehouse a company's product or offer extended in-house financing. In addition, they focus on products that bring them the most profit, avoiding those with sketchy prospects.

Export Trading Companies (ETC) In 1982, the U.S. enacted the Export Trading Company Act, which removed some of the antitrust obstacles to ETCs. Groups of direct competitors, once prohibited, were allowed to form ETCs to develop exports jointly without fear of antitrust action. Dutch, Japanese, and British competitors had profitably long done so.[76] ETCs, free of legal barriers that had constrained their members, boosted the export competitiveness of U.S. companies.

The United States exempt ETCs from antitrust provisions so that competitors can collaborate in foreign markets.

ETCs differ from EMCs in that they operate based on demand rather than supply. That is, an ETC bring buyers and sellers together, basically functioning as a trade matchmaker. As such, it creates value by determining what foreign customers want, identifying domestic suppliers, and expediting transactions. Rather than representing a single manufacturer, an ETC works with many. ETCs, operating as independent distributors, generally avoid carrying inventory in their own name or performing post-sales service.

ETCs operate based on demand rather than supply. They identify suppliers who can fill orders in overseas markets.

Fees Trade intermediaries charge for their expertise and services. Commonly, they operate on (1) a commission rate ranging from 10 percent for consumer goods to 15 percent or more for industrial products, (2) a buy-sell basis that asks for a firm's best home country discount plus an extra discount for a product that is marked-up when sold abroad, and/or (3) a contributions for special events such as exhibiting products in a foreign trade show or an advance payement for advertising and promotion.

Besides payments, hiring a trade intermediary requires exporters relinquish some to considerable control. The matters of whom they sell to, the price they charge, quality of promotion materials, flexibility of delivery schedules, or standards of customer service are the calls of the intermediary. Some companies discover that if an intermediary feebly promotes their products, they struggle to generate international sales. To retain control, a company can employ them less comprehensively. As in any make-vs.-buy situation, companies trade off their preference for control versus the cost of directly managing export activity.[77]

CUSTOMS BROKERS

Years ago, loading a shipment onto a ship in one's home country essentially sealed one's part of the deal. Now, revenue, security, and trade regulations impose longer relationships. Furthermore, once cargo reaches its port of entry—say, going from Shanghai to Seattle—customs officials take nominal control of the product. **Customs agents** enforce the rules of trade for particular country. They control the flow of goods moving in and out of a country. In the United States, for example, the Bureau of Customs and Border Protection (CBP, formerly the U.S. Customs Service) of the Department of Homeland Security monitors imports and exports. The CBP assesses and collects duties, taxes, and fees on imported merchandise, enforces customs and related laws, and administers certain navigation laws and treaties. It also polices smuggling operations and is charged with protecting the United States from threatening imports.[78]

TABLE 13.4 Where the Trading Is Easy—and Where It Is Not

There is wide variability in the ease of exporting and importing among countries. Here we see those countries that lead and lag the world in increasing the ease of export and import. These rankings reflect the average of a country's performance in terms of the (1) number of documents it requires traders to complete and (2) the length of time and overall cost required to complete an import or export transaction.

Easiest	Rank	Hardest	Rank
Singapore	1	Angola	172
Hong Kong, China	2	Burkina Faso	173
Denmark	3	Azerbaijan	174
Finland	4	Central African Republic	175
Estonia	5	Congo, Republic	176
Sweden	6	Tajikistan	177
Norway	7	Iran	178
Panama	8	Afghanistan	179
Israel	9	Kazakhstan	180
Thailand	10	Kyrgyz Republic	181

Source: Based on The International Bank for Reconstruction and Development/The World Bank, "Doing Business in 2010."

Countries vary to the degree their customs agencies help or hinder international traders (see Table 13.4). Several of the top-10 countries on the ease-of-trading list are European. Trading across Europe has become increasingly seamless due to the ongoing market integration efforts of the European Union. Free trade pacts in other parts of the world have similar effects. Besides proximity, expediting trade among Canada, Mexico, and United States is their NAFTA relationship.

In contrast, irregular customs practices in African and South Asian markets routinely hamper exports and imports. Moving from port to port in these markets finds a hodgepodge of arbitrary and often contradictory regulations that can veer toward illegality. For example, a Zambian trader noted, "My cargo of copper wire was held up in Durban, South Africa, for a week. The port authorities required proof that the wooden pallets on which the wire was loaded were free of pests. After a few days, the Ministry of Agriculture's inspector checked that the wood was fumigated, for a $100 fee.[79] No matter the locale, importing requires understanding relevant customs regulations and policies, knowing how to clear goods through customs, assigning the appropriate customs duties, and complying with special procedures.

Finding Help In terms of procedures, when merchandise reaches its port of entry, the importer files documents with customs officials. These agents then assign a provisional value and tariff classification. The United States has nearly 10,000 classifications in its Harmonized Tariff Schedule. Approximately 60 percent of them are open to interpretation—that is, a particular product fits more than one classification. Often, it is a near art form to determine the tariff classification that minimizes duty assessment. Importing requires other points of expertise to manage the paperwork of trade. Not every company, especially SMEs, commands these proficiencies. Consequently, some hire a **customs broker** to help them:

> A customs broker helps an importer navigate the regulations imposed by customs agencies.

- *Qualify for duty refunds through drawback provisions.* Some exporters use imported inputs, for which they paid a custom duty, in their manufacturing process. In the United States, drawback provisions allow domestic exporters to apply for a 99 percent refund of the duty paid on the imported goods, as long as they inputs into the firm's exports.
- *Defer duties by using bonded warehouses and foreign trade zones (FTZ).* Companies need not pay duties on imports stored in bonded warehouses and FTZs until the goods are removed for sale or used in a manufacturing process. A broker oversees compliance with pertinent provisions.

> A customs broker helps importers in terms of
> - Valuation.
> - Qualification.
> - Deferment.
> - Liability.

A Torrent of TEUs

Like a Tetris game run amok, cargo must be sorted, stacked, and shipped in a correct order to keep the global trade game going. The logistic flow of the game is astounding–from 1990 through 2010, the global stock of 20 foot equivalent units (TEUs) containers, the most common means of shipping goods, grew from 28.7 million to about 190 million. In 2010, those containers made nearly 450 million "trips" among trading partners.

Source: Jorg Greuel/Getty Images

- *Value products so they qualify for favorable duty treatment.* Different products incur different duties, or assessed taxes, when crossing borders. For example, finished goods typically have a higher duty than components. Brokers' expertise helps determine the optimal classification.

- *Manage trade documentation.* Paperwork goes hand in hand with international trade, particularly that which falls under the auspices of homeland security. A broker obtains government permissions before forwarding paperwork to the carrier overseen delivery.

- *Limit liability by properly marking an import's country of origin.* Governments assess duties on imports based in part on the country of origin. A mistake in marking the country may increase the import duty. In the United States, if a product or its container is improperly marked when it enters the country, the product may be assigned a marking duty equal to 10 percent of the declared customs value. This charge is added to the normal tariff.[80]

FREIGHT FORWARDERS

A freight forwarder specializes in moving goods from sellers to buyers.

Freight forwarders are the largest export/import intermediary in terms of value and weight of products shipped internationally. Popularly known as the "travel agent of cargo," they move goods to foreign buyers.[81] Upon finalizing a foreign sale, an exporter hires a freight forwarder to arrange the fastest, cheapest transportation method. Balancing the constraints of space, speed, and cost, it identifies the optimal path to move products from the manufacturing facility to an air, land, or ocean terminal, clear customs, and deliver to the foreign buyer.

In the same process, the freight forwarder arranges storage prior to shipment, verifies letters of credit, obtains export licenses, pays consular fees, processes special documentation, and prepares shipping manifests. It may also advise on packing and labeling, transportation insurance, repacking of shipments damaged en route, and warehousing products. It does not take ownership title or act as a sales representative—that falls in the realm of an EMC or ETC. As a rule, freight forwarders offer fewer services than the latter two intermediaries.

Freight forwarders are particularly important when the cost or timing of freight can make or break a deal. One straightforward solution, advised the director of business development of Certified Worldwide, is to "Seek out your local Commercial Service office and find a freight forwarder, interview different freight forwarders, and remember that the company chosen will be responsible for shipping your product."[82]

The freight forwarder usually charges the exporter a percentage of the shipment value, plus a minimum charge depending on the number of services provided. It also receives a brokerage fee from the carrier. Most companies, especially SMEs, find it costly to deal with logistics. Forwarders' expertise enables them to secure shipping space at better rates and provides the flexibility to consolidate shipments.

THIRD-PARTY LOGISTICS

Third-party logistics (3PLs) are a growing force in international trade. Like freight forwarders, 3PLs move cargo and provide a range of logistic options. Unlike freight forwarders, 3PLs work in partnership with manufacturers, shippers, and retailers to relieve them of logistics responsibilities. They offer integration mechanisms, such as online shipping and tracking information, that help the company and customer track shipments. They also consolidate billing inclusive of all transportation, customs brokerage, duties, taxes, and package delivery services. Finally, they handle product returns, warranty claims, parts exchanges, and reverse logistics.

Expanding globalization and trade liberalization accelerate the growth of 3PLs. In 2010, 3PL, revenues grew, at 12 percent, faster than GDP growth in the United States.[83] 3PLs are particularly helpful to the born global company. Rather than building its own logistics operation, the born global need only tap the state-of-the-art sophistication of a 3PL. Big companies also benefit. Nearly 80 percent of Fortune 500 companies use 3PLs for logistics and supply chain functions. Procter & Gamble, Walmart, PepsiCo, and Ford, for example, use the services of 30 or more 3PLs. Overall, 3PLs have been growing their business at the expense of freight forwarders. In response, the latter are expanding their historic role as "travel agents of cargo" to offer some of the services provided by 3Pls.

> A 3PL is a trade intermediary that applies sophisticated technologies and systems to supervise trade logistics.

Reconciling Opportunity and Challenge: An Export Plan

Between the point at which they negotiate an international sale and the point at which the products has been shipped and received, the exporter and the importer manage an array of financial, logistic, and legal tasks. Each of these tasks represents a link in the **transaction chain** that shapes each firm's respective strategy (see Figure 13.3). Exporters and importers alike heed these activities when trading across nations. At times, some activities press more than others. Ultimately, all influence the process.

The decision to engage international trade, or, if already doing so, to escalate commitment, is one that few companies take lightly. The decision to go international influences resource allocation, executive effectiveness, and financial stability. Successful exporters report that developing an **export plan** is useful. Defining its current resources, specifying objectives, and formalizing commitment requires a company define objectives, sequence tactics, and set timelines. In addition, an export plan identifies useful resources, assigns responsibility, and stipulates controls. Collectively, it prevents losing track of the company's export strategy in the face of seemingly endless decisions. Table 13.5 provides a basic framework for an export plan. Remember, an export plan only need be just a few pages to start. It will steadily expand as it evolves.

FIGURE 13.3 The International Transaction Chain

Between the point at which they negotiate an international sale and the point at which products have been delivered, both the exporter and the importer manage a complex array of financial, logistics, and legal tasks. Each of these tasks defines a link in the *transaction chain* forged by each firm's respective strategy. Note, by the way, that financial transactions run along the chain.

Source: Export America 1 (November 1999): 17. Magazine published by the International Trade Administration of the U.S. Dept. of Commerce.

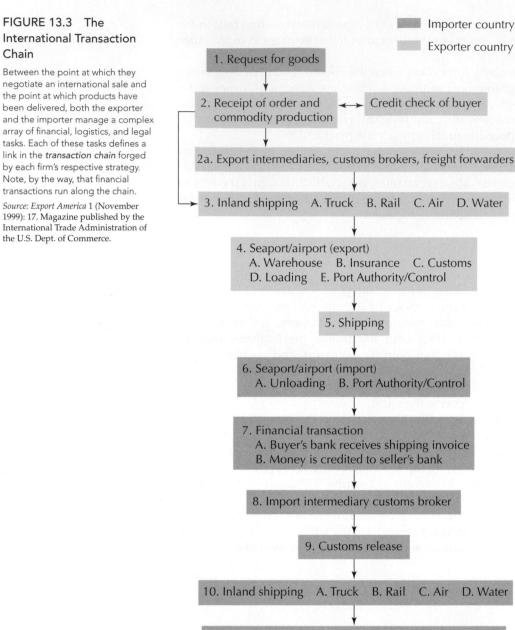

Importer country

Exporter country

1. Request for goods

2. Receipt of order and commodity production ←→ Credit check of buyer

2a. Export intermediaries, customs brokers, freight forwarders

3. Inland shipping   A. Truck   B. Rail   C. Air   D. Water

4. Seaport/airport (export)
   A. Warehouse   B. Insurance   C. Customs
   D. Loading   E. Port Authority/Control

5. Shipping

6. Seaport/airport (import)
   A. Unloading   B. Port Authority/Control

7. Financial transaction
   A. Buyer's bank receives shipping invoice
   B. Money is credited to seller's bank

8. Import intermediary customs broker

9. Customs release

10. Inland shipping   A. Truck   B. Rail   C. Air   D. Water

11. Receipt of goods by buyer
    A. Immediate sale   B. Warehousing
    C. Further refinement/incorporation into other goods

Importantly, managers develop an export plan in an open process. Successful exporters note that consulting government agencies and third-party intermediaries clarifies problems and avoids pitfalls. Noted the CEO of Coffee & More, "My advice to other companies considering exporting is to go for it, but be smart and do your homework first. Educate yourself and use your local U.S. Commercial Service office."[84] External validation goes a long way toward preempting blind spots as well as potential delusions about the likely success of export ventures. More practically, a well specified plan is a precondition for export financing assistance.

The element of an export plan that routinely stymies companies, particularly SMEs, is selecting the "right" foreign market. SMEs are often discouraged when their first forays fail. Instead of applying the standards of sound strategy that made them successful in the first place, many follow hunches about foreign markets—i.e., China is growing so fast that there must be a lot of people there who want my product.

An export plan defines a company's intent to leverage resources and manage constraints in initiating and developing export activity.

TABLE 13.5   An Export Plan

An export plan organizes analysis of issues that influence the initiation and escalation of export. The following list identifies key categories and issues

1. **Executive Summary**
   - Key elements of the export plan
   - Description of business and target markets
   - Specification of management team
   - Summary of projections
2. **Company Description**
   - History
   - Goals and objectives
   - Core competency
   - Management
   - The export team
   - Company finances
3. **Product/Service Description**
   - Export opportunity
   - Fit of company's products in export market
   - Growth potential
   - Product strategy
4. **Foreign Marketplace Analysis**
   - Rationale for exporting
   - Rationale for targeted foreign market
   - Country profile
   - Industry profile
   - Competitor analysis
   - Specification of key assumptions
5. **Market Entry Strategies**
   - Form of operation
   - Indirect/direct exporting
   - E-commerce options
   - Target customer profile
   - Pricing strategies
   - Sales and promotion strategies
   - Logistics and transportation
6. **International Law**
   - Dispute resolution
   - Language consideration
   - Contract terms and conditions

- Product liability considerations
- Intellectual property protection
- Sales agent and/or distributor agreements
- Export/import regulations

7. **Financial Analysis**
   - Facility and equipment requirements
   - Sales forecast
   - Cost of goods sold
   - Projected international income statement
   - Projected international cash flow
   - Breakdown analysis
   - Financing requirements
   - Current financing sources
   - Tax consequences
8. **Risk Management**
   - Country risk
   - Commercial risk
   - Credit Risk
   - Currency risk
   - Market risk
   - Political risk
9. **External Assistance**
   - Export America
   - U.S. Commerce Department
   - Census Bureau
   - Customs and Border Protection
   - www.export.gov
   - International Trade Administration
   - U.S. Export-Import Bank
   - National, regional, and local organizations
   - Cross-border trade consultancies
10. **Implementation Schedule**
    - Operational time line
    - Performance milestones
    - Contingency plans

Likewise, it is tough to try to conquer customers from Bonn to Beijing to Benares in a day. A useful rule is to look at a few markets where the odds favor success rather than trying to sell to the world.[85] Useful questions to debate during the development of an export plan include:

- Am I committed to exporting?
- Would our resources be better utilized developing our domestic businesses?
- What do we want to gain from exporting?
- Is exporting consistent with our long-term goals?
- What need does my product or service fill in the targeted foreign market?
- How much will it cost to get the product to the foreign market?
- Will exporting put undue demands on management, production, financing, and marketing?
- Does exporting leverage our core competency?

- Does exporting fit our value chain configuration?
- Do our coordination and control systems support exporting?
- Do the financial and strategic benefits of exporting exceed its direct and indirect costs?

Managers stress test an export plan by consulting trade specialists and public agencies.

Last, like yin and yang, import and export are complementary opposites within the greater whole of international trade. Strategic and practical aspects of the import process mirror those of the export process. So, just as the international transaction chain includes a sensitivity to those export and import issues, so too with the export plan. Changing the terminology from export to import plan does not require changing the contents of the plan. Rather, companies adjust their analytics, interpreting events from the analogous perspective of importing.

Countertrade

Currency or credit—easy, fast, and straightforward—are the preferred payment mediums for export or import transactions. Sometimes, though, companies face the reality that buyers cannot pay in cash because their home country's currency is nonconvertible or they have insufficient credit. Consequently, they resort to other means.

Concept Check

Recall our discussions of poverty in Chapters 4 and 5. Here we point out that shortages of resources impoverish nations as well as individuals. Some countries struggle to acquire the foreign reserves they need to purchase goods from other nations. If unsuccessful, they may resort to countertrade.

Consider, for instance, the following transactions. Coca-Cola has traded its syrup for cheese from a factory it built in the Soviet Union, for oranges from an orchard in planted in Egypt, for tomato paste from a plant it installed in Turkey, for Polish beer, and for soft drink bottles from Hungary. Malaysia swapped palm oil for fertilizer and machinery with North Korea, Cuba, and Russia and was negotiating similar trades with Morocco, Jordan, Syria, and Iran. Similarly, Thailand, the world's largest exporter of rice, has been negotiating rice for oil deals with Middle Eastern countries, whereas the Philippines, the world's largest importer of rice, secured rice supplies through an agreement with Vietnam.86 Boeing exchanged 10 747s for 34 million barrels of Saudi Arabian oil. Argentina awarded a fertilizer factory to Czechoslovakian firms with the stipulation that suppliers buy vegetables and other agricultural goods produced with fertilizer.[87]

Countertrade is an umbrella term for several sorts of trade, such as barter or offset, in which the seller accept goods or services, rather than currency or credit, as payment.

These sorts of trades fall under the umbrella term **countertrade.** Any one of several different arrangements that parties use to trade products via transactions that use limited or no currency or credit qualify as a countertrade. Table 13.6 identifies its principal forms.[88]

Inconsistent disclosure hinders estimating the volume of countertrade. Secretive government-to-government deals and disguised transactions are not unusual. The WTO

TABLE 13.6   Common Types of Countertrade

Barter	Transaction in which products are exchanged directly for products of equal value without the use of money as a means of purchase or payment.
Buyback	Transaction in which a supplier of capital or equipment agrees to accept future output generated by the investment as payment. For example: The exporter of equipment to a chemical plant may be repaid with output from the factory to whose owner it "sold" the equipment.
Offset	Transaction in which an exporter sells products for cash and then helps the importer find opportunities to earn hard currency for payment. Offsets are most common when big-ticket products (e.g., military equipment) are involved.
Switch or Swap Trading	Transaction in which one company sells to another its obligation to purchase something in a foreign country. They carry this label because the arrangement often involves switching the documentation and destination of merchandise while it's in transit.
Counter purchase	Transaction in which a company that sells products to a foreign country promises to make a future purchase of a specific product made in that country. In a supplier agrees to purchase products from a foreign buyer as a condition of getting the buyer's order.

estimates that countertrade accounts for around 5 percent of world trade, whereas the British Department of Trade and Industry has suggested as much as 15 percent. The general consensus is that countertrade, as a percent of world trade, falls somewhere in between.[89] It generally increases in economies that are experiencing economic problems. Since the latter is a seemingly inevitability, countertrade is likely an enduring feature of international trade.

COSTS

Countertrade is an inefficient way of doing business. Companies prefer the efficiency of cash or credit. With countertrade, rather than consulting foreign-exchange tables to set exchange rates, buyers and sellers negotiate a fair value for the exchange, such as how many tons of rice for how many farm tractors. In some situations, the goods sent as payment may be of poor quality, packaged unattractively, or difficult to sell and service. There is a lot of room for price and financial distortion in countertrade deals, given that nonmarket forces set the prices of these goods. Ultimately, countertrade and its variations threaten free market forces with protectionism and price-fixing. Unchecked, trade relations suffer.

> Countertrade is primarily used when a country or company trades with a counterpart whose currency or credit creates barriers to an efficient buy-sell exchange.

BENEFITS

The reality of international trade means that countertrade is often unavoidable for companies that want to do business with buyers who have limited or no access to cash or credit. Although some dislike it, companies and countries in tough binds use it to generate jobs, preserve foreign exchange holdings, and develop trade relationships. Countertrade helps countries reduce their need to borrow working capital and gives them access to MNEs' technological skills and marketing expertise. Companies also benefit. Countertrade may let them resolve bad debts, repatriate blocked funds, or build customer relationships. In addition, accepting countertrade signals a seller's good faith and flexibility. Such sensitivities can position a firm to gain preferential market access in the future.

> Countertrade has several disadvantages:
> - Inefficiency.
> - Risk.
> - Cumbersomeness.
>
> Companies and countries often use countertrade to build mutually beneficial relationships.

Looking to the Future   Technology and International Trade

The transaction costs of international trade steadily decrease. Advances in transportation and communications systems, by making it easier and cheaper to trade, accelerate export and import activity. The Internet helps individuals throughout the world engage each other easily and quickly. Online filing of cargo manifests, customs documents, and transit forms expedites shipments. Customs software that works in Hamburg or Sydney is used in Hong Kong and Long Beach. All in all, greater flexibility and improving efficiency lets companies engage an expanding range of export and import options.

Synchronizing import or export activities redefines the way companies, both big and small, connect with foreign buyers and sellers. Historically, big companies reaped the biggest rewards. Their superior resources positioned them to capture advances in moving goods, funds, and information. Now, the technology of trade seems to offer bigger benefits to smaller companies. Improving technologies create online, software, and logistics platforms that blur the distinction between the big, global giant and the small, neighborhood startup. In fact, it has become harder to tell the difference between an SME operating on a shoestring budget and its larger counterpart.

Online Platforms

Increasingly, companies look to online technologies to start or expand exporting. They rely on the Internet as their primary channel for getting information, sourcing products, finding suppliers, marketing products, and tapping new markets. In many cases, companies build a virtual value chain online, running export transactions from start to finish without ever leaving their hometown. The inexorable expansion of the Internet gives potential and practicing international traders nearly infinite resources. They can browse through

(continued)

catalog repositories, business-to-business exchanges, electronic trade boards, consumer surveys, online trade journals, and virtual trade shows to find a product to import or a market for their export.

Increasingly, as more SMEs throughout the world gain Internet access for the first time, they use online platforms to build an export business. Besides introducing mom-and-pop shops from around the world to each other, websites open a vast and largely uncharted small-business hinterland in markets from Tibet to Patagonia. Long the unseen production sites for many pieces of the global economy, these small companies had to trade within the context of global supply chains directed by large MNEs. Now, going online lets them go straight to buyers or sellers.

Software Platforms

A burst of business software in the past few years has "created a total revolution in what small businesses are able to accomplish overseas."[90] Collaborative software lets entrepreneurial exporters with single-digit head counts track foreign vendors without traveling the world. For example, U.S.-based Edgar Blazona used to log 100,000 miles of travel annually, visiting factories in the Far East. Now he uses two factories—one in Thailand and one in India—to manufacture his furniture designs that he then imports into the United States. A meeting and document-sharing program lets him work in real time with his overseas factories. Costing less than $100 per month, this software standardizes workflows, expedites exchanges, and eases communications.

Similarly, Evertek Computer Corporation, a U.S. SME, has capitalized on software innovations to build e-commerce Web sites and portals that expand its market frontier. In 1990, it began selling new and refurbished computers and parts. By 2008, Evertek had become the world's largest closeout computer wholesaler, clearance computer supplier, and closeout electronics wholesaler. Within a year of purchasing BuyUSA.com, an Internet-based program from the U.S. Commerce Department that helps find buyers around the world, Evertek began selling in 10 new countries, with single purchases reaching up to $75,000. In 2010, international sales zoomed to $34 million, an increase of 84 percent from the previous year, on exports to 105 countries.

Other companies use similarly innovative programs to manage overseas factories with tools that once were reserved for the big MNE. China Manufacturing Network, for instance, relies on its 10-person staff in California to coordinate production of industrial devices among more than 90 independent factories in China, Malaysia, and Singapore. It uses on-demand, scalable enterprise software to track activity orders, monitor build rates, and manage inventory across its manufacturing network.

Logistics Platforms

Improving logistics helps SMEs move products more cheaply and easily to more places. High-tech, low-cost shipping services rob big firms of a long-running competitive advantage. Now, the no-name, one-person exporter down the street from you, because of his big-name shipping partners spanning the globe, has many of the same logistics capabilities commanded by a large MNE but at a fraction of the cost. In fact, SMEs increasingly have as much, if not a bit more, logistic flexibility. Unlike big companies that rely on their in-house systems, SMEs can tap a range of sophisticated solutions from freight forwarders and 3PLs.

The small international trader can hire any of these sorts of intermediaries to warehouse, truck, sail, fly, and deliver goods from factories in Asia to customers in Europe—all the while never taking physical possession of the goods.

For example, South West Trading in Arizona, a family-owned startup, imports yarns made from bamboo, corn, and soy fibers by fabric plants in China. It suffered recurring logistics problems as it imported product from China. UPS provided a cheap, easy solution. Its Shanghai facility consolidated orders from various Chinese factories into one transport container, supervised customs paperwork, shipped it, and trucked the goods to the company's warehouse in Phoenix. South West Trading's bottom line immediately benefited. Where it once paid $9,400 to run four China-to-Arizona shipments per month, its once-a-month UPS shipment costs about $3,600 and reliably takes 21 days to travel.

The Great Leveling

Improving online, software, and logistics platforms, by improving the technology of trade, levels the playing field of international trade.[91] The combination of ubiquitous, fast Internet connections and cheap, plentiful, cloud-based computing power makes it easier to export and import. Big and small companies respond to these trends, confident that technology will create tools that let them jump hurdles and capture opportunities. SMEs, in particular, stand to prosper from the improving technology of trade. Perhaps most significantly, technology decouples the issues of size and capability. Observed the CEO of China Manufacturing, "Our customers can't really tell how big we are. In a way, it's irrelevant. What matters is that we can get the job done."[92] ■

A Little Electronic Magic at Alibaba.com

E-commerce, by changing the way companies around the world do business, makes trade easier and cheaper.[93] Before the Internet, tracking down a product to import, or finding foreign customers to export to, was daunting for the typical SME. Most relied on occasional trade shows and expensive, time-consuming foreign travels to identify possible products or assess potential suppliers. Certainly, traders could tap local embassies to support export promotion or provide import assistance. Although sounding straightforward, in practice they were cumbersome. Consequently, international trade was largely limited to big companies that could afford to attend trade shows, translate brochures, travel internationally, hire intermediaries, and supervise activities.

Today, the Internet gives SMEs cost-effective means to manage these demands. It makes information on any conceivable product from virtually any market readily and inexpensively accessible. Falling trade barriers, courtesy of the WTO, and more efficient logistics from 3PLs like FedEx, DHL, and UPS, offer an array of trade possibilities.[94]

The emergence of country-specific portals and Web exchanges accelerates this process. Replicating what eBay has done for consumer-to-consumer e-commerce, several sites offer online bazaars for international traders. Here, exporters can lay out their wares on the digital carpet and haggle with potential buyers from the far corners of the world. For instance, potential importers looking for products from South Korea can access www.koreatradeworld.com; those targeting India can check out www.trade-india.com; and those focusing on Europe need only visit www.bizeurope.com to tap into high-quality electronic trade boards. One can also ignore locking into one area and instead shop the world at or www.tradekey.com.

These and similar sites promote the commercial potential of a country or region. They provide direct services to large and small international traders, such as export training, cyber trade infrastructures, international special exhibitions, virtual trade shows, and trade strategies. Conceptually, they are straightforward: They help move products from sellers in one place to buyers in another. Operationally, they represent powerful business-to-business tools that improve the mechanics of trade, creating flexible and dynamic platforms that let buyers and sellers of everything from bamboo toothpicks to industrial equipment find each other, negotiate the terms of trade, and seal the deal.

Alibaba: Opening Global Markets

Spearheading these changes is Alibaba, a Chinese Internet company that specializes in introducing Chinese manufacturers to buyers worldwide. Founded in 1999 by Jack Ma, who has been dubbed "the Father of the Chinese Internet," it makes international trade cheaper, faster, and easier. Based in Hangzhou, about a two-hour drive south of Shanghai, Alibaba began operations with the goal of getting big by staying small. Jack Ma believes that his target customers are SMEs, not MNEs, or, in his words, "shrimps," not "whales."

The Framework

Making this happen is the world of www.alibaba.com, an English language global trade website that connects international buyers with Chinese sellers. Today, it is the world's largest online business-to-business marketplace, reaching Internet users in more than 240 countries and territories. The site supports an interactive community of millions of buyers and sellers who meet, chat, trade, and work online. Basically running an online global trade fair, Alibaba enables "shrimps" with import and export ambition but tight budgets to reach the global market. Alibaba also provides an array of business management software, Internet infrastructure services, payement processing, and export-related services.

Many Alibaba users are SMEs in developing countries around the world, from rural areas to large cities, in countries such as Kyrgyzstan, Sierra Leone, and Peru. Few are glamorous and high-tech; most are low-tech firms making labor-intensive, scale-insensitive products. However, Alibaba provides tools to expand their market reach and grow their businesses. An SME, working from even the smallest apartment anywhere in the world, can create a global business.

A New Face of
International Trade

This straightforward
screenshot of Alibaba's
web portal only hints at its
immense opportunities for
importers and exporters
to trade. Clicking through
to any of categories opens
many international trade
gateways.

Source: Courtesy of alibaba.com

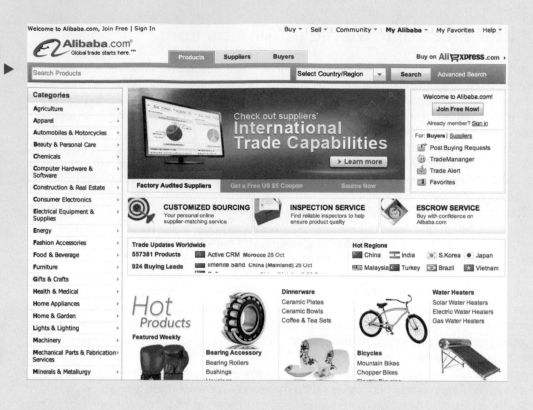

Operations

The mechanics of Alibaba are straightforward: Importers around the world request bids from suppliers for a mind-boggling array of goods—from cookware to poker chips, washing machines to MP3 players—as seen on the adjacent image of Alibaba's home page. Alibaba has organized more than a thousand product categories, each with many subcategories, and offers new channels to trade services. For example, the classic garage inventor in, say, Caracas or Chicago has the option to design a product and then use Alibaba to find Chinese factories to make, package, and ship it to customers worldwide.

Operationally, buyers use Alibaba to find potential suppliers, thereby eliminating the need to hire a local representative to negotiate with Chinese manufacturers. So, for example, an enterprising company in Argentina looking to buy 500 DVD players can visit Alibaba.com, search among the dozens of potential suppliers, learn their terms of trade, contact the preferred vendor, negotiate the specifics, and set the deal in motion. Said the cofounder of www.meetchina.com, a similar e-commerce site, "We want to make buying 1,000 bicycles from China as easy as buying a book from Amazon.com."

Trust and Transparency

As a rule, importers worry about being defrauded by unknown suppliers. More practically, how does an importer in Buenos Aires find a trustworthy supplier in Guangzhou? As sites like Alibaba inject more transparency into trade, buyers worry less about fraud. Alibaba users, like those on similar e-commerce sites, post information about their companies as well as review information about a vendor's reliability from other users. Buyers access Alibaba's profiles of its registered users, as well as the seller's posted references, to verify their status. These data let the importer in Argentina cross-check the credibility of potential trade partners.

This system of checks and balances is how Alibaba makes money. It offers a basic service of listing a company and its products on its Web site free of charge. It generates revenue from the 85,000 members who pay a few hundred to several thousand of dollars annually for services such as personalized Web pages, high-quality online introduction, and priority listing of products.

Crisis and Change

The global financial crisis, Jack Ma reasons, created an opportunity to transform Alibaba from a China-focused e-commerce provider into a global Web marketplace. "Before this financial crisis, we were helping China's products abroad. Now we are thinking about helping small and medium-sized enterprises in other parts of the world," says Ma. Too, he saw the chance to expand China's historic outward flow of products to the world to include flows throughout the world. "We want to help them sell across the nations, help them sell to China," explains Ma. "I believe in the next three years, China will be one of the world's largest buying markets. China needs to buy these things."

As the crisis diminished, Alibaba set its sights higher. It plans to build a network of warehouses across China to transform the country's logistics business. "Hopefully within 10 years' time, anyone placing an order online from anywhere in China will receive their goods within eight hours, allowing for the virtual urbanization of every village across China," said Ma. "In order to achieve this, we will need to establish a modern, 21st century logistics network." In addition, Alibaba expanded AliExpress to offer traders warehousing, shipping and logistics options. Essentially, noted an analyst, Alibaba "wants to be Amazon."[95] ■

QUESTIONS

1. Identify a product you would like to import. Visit www.alibaba.com, go to the advanced search field, and enter it. Select required criteria and click on "Search." Review the list of companies that qualify. Find a suitable seller. Analyze this process for ease, usefulness, and potential value.

2. List, in separate columns, the benefits and costs of using sites like Alibaba to trade internationally. What does your analysis say to companies like SpinCent (our opening case) as they develop an export plan?

3. Visit www.alibaba.com, www.trade-india.com, and www.europages.com. Compare and contrast these Web sites from the view of the seller to the buyer.

4. Do you think most trade between countries and companies might eventually take place through sites like Alibaba.com? If so, does that influence your interest in importing and exporting?

5. How transparent do sites like Alibaba.com make import-export transactions? Would you still worry about fraud?

Now that you have finished this chapter, go back to www.myiblab.com to continue practicing and applying the concepts you've learned.

MyIBLab

SUMMARY

- Exporting refers to the sale of goods or services produced by a company based in one country to customers that reside in another. Importing is the opposite: the purchase of products by a buyer in one country from a seller in another.

- A company's export activity is (1) related to but not determined by its size and (2) related to and often determined by a range of firm-specific characteristics, such as management interest, production efficiency, labor costs, and R&D advantages that are independent of its size.

- The incremental internationalization view holds that exporting begins as a sequential process of careful trial and

reasonable error that leads a company to expand from its home market to the most geographically and psychologically proximate markets. It then progressively sells to customers in increasingly distant and dissimilar countries.

- The born-global perspective holds that companies step straight onto the world stage, exporting from inception.

- The idea of serendipity refers to so-called accidental traders who, responding to happenstance or odd circumstances, successfully begin exporting or importing.

- A service import does not result in ownership and is rendered by nonresidents to the local residents in a country.

- The macro and micro benefits of international trade spur governments to help potential and active exporters.

- Exporters may deal directly with agents or distributors in a foreign country or indirectly through third-party intermediaries, such as export management firms or other types of trading companies.

- Trading companies perform many functions for which clients lack expertise but which regularly pose problems and pitfalls.

- A customs broker value a product to qualify for more favorable duty treatment, qualifies a product for duty refunds through drawback provisions, defers duties by using bonded

- warehouses, and limits liability by accurately marking an import's country of origin.

- Freight forwarders, the "travel agents of cargo," act as agents for international traders in supervising the movement of goods to foreign buyers.

- Third-party logistics (3PLs) provide state-of-the-art systems technology that helps traders understand their current practices, identify opportunities and risks, and shepherd shipments.

- Countertrade is any one of several different arrangements by which products are traded in transactions that do not involve cash or credit.

KEY TERMS

born global (p. 488)
countertrade (p. 510)
customs agents (p. 504)
customs broker (p. 505)
direct exporting (p. 490)
exporting (p. 483)
export intermediaries (p. 503)

export intensity (p. 486)
export plan (p. 507)
freight forwarder (p. 506)
importing (p. 492)
incremental internationalization (p. 487)
indirect exporting (p. 491)

serendipity (p. 490)
small and medium-sized enterprise (SME) (p. 485)
third-party logistics (p. 507)
transaction chain (p. 507)

ENDNOTES

1   *Sources include the following:* www.export.gov; United States International Trade Administration; United States Census Bureau, *Profile of U.S. Exporting Companies,* at www.census.gov/foreign-trade/aip/edbrel-0203.pdf; *Small & Medium-Sized Exporting Companies: Statistical Overview,* tse.export.gov/EDB/SelectReports.aspx?DATA=ExporterDB. SpinCent, while a fictitious company, represents the opinions and activitiesof real exporters.

2   See www.export.gov/articles/successstories/eg_success_story_021417.asp

3   The Ex-Im Bank is the official export-credit agency of the United States. The independent federal government agency helps to create and maintain U.S. jobs by financing the sales of U.S. exports, primarily to emerging markets throughout the world, providing loan guarantees, export-credit insurance and direct loans.

4   "China Reports Less-Than-Estimated $13 Billion Trade Surplus," Retrieved June 10, 2011, from http://billionaires.forbes.com/article/09o40vo9aX91d?q=Bloomberg+News

5   U.S. Trade Overview, October 13, 2010, International Trade Administration. Contact: Elizabeth Clark, Office of Trade and Industry Information, U.S. Census Bureau, Foreign Trade Division.

6   Francisco Sánchez, "No Better Export: Higher Education - Commentary - The Chronicle of Higher Education," retrieved May 3, 2011, from http://chronicle.com/article/No-Better-Export-Higher/126989

7   John H. Dunning, "The Eclectic Paradigm of International Production: Some Empirical Tests," *Journal of International Business Studies* (Spring 1988): 1–31.

8   "The Benefits of Exporting," retrieved May 15, 2011, from www.export.gov/about/eg_main_016807.asp

9   See, for example, http://secure.wikimedia.org/wikipedia/en/wiki/Small_and_medium_enterprises.

10 "The Benefits of Exporting."

11 Hernan Roxas, Vai Lindsay, Nicholas Ashill and Antong Victorio, "Institutional Analysis of Strategic Choice of Micro, Small, and Medium Enterprises: Development of a Conceptual Framework," *Singapore Management Review* 30.2 (July-Dec 2008): 47; Nancy Ku, "SMEs Look to Non-traditional Lenders," *China Brief,* American Chamber of Commerce in China (March 2009).

12 S. Cavusgil and S. Zou, "Marketing Strategic Performance Relationship," *Journal of Marketing* (1994); J. Meran and A. Moini, "Firm's Export Behavior," *American Business Review* (1999): 86.

13 David Greenway, Joakim Gullstrand, and Richard Kneller, "Exporting May Not Always Boost Firm Productivity," *Review of World Economics,* 4 (December 1, 2005): 561–82.

14 L. Yun, "Determinants of Export Intensity and FDI Presence: Case of Manufacturing Industries of Guangdong Province, the People's Republic of China," *International Journal of Logistics Systems and Management* (2006): 230–54.

15 D. Crick, "UK SMEs' Motives for Internationalizing: Differences between Firms Employing Particular Overseas Market Servicing Strategies," *Journal of International Entrepreneurship* (2007): 11–23 (Retrieved May 15, 2011).

16 Coffee & More, LLC, retrieved May 15, 2011, from www.export.gov/articles/successstories/eg_success_story_022775.asp

17 Certified Worldwide LLC, retrieved May 15, 2011, from www.export.gov/articles/successstories/eg_success_story_020902.asp

18 Domes International, retrieved May 15, 2011, from www.export.gov/articles/successstories/eg_success_story_021027.asp

19 "Global Development Horizons 2011—Multipolarity: The New Global Economy," *The World Bank,* retrieved May 30, 2011, from *http://web.worldbank.org/wbsite/external/extdec/extdecprospects /extgdh/0,,menupk:7933477~pagepk:64167702~pipk:64167676 ~thesitepk:7933464,00.html*

20 Hans Gemunden, "Success Factors of Export Marketing: A Meta-Analytic Critique of the Empirical Studies," in *New Perspectives on International Marketing*, (Ed.) S. Paliwoda (London: Routledge, 1991): 33–62.

21 Julia Armario, David Ruiz, and Enrique Armario. "Market Orientation and Internationalization in Small and Medium-Sized Enterprises," *Journal of Small Business Management* (October 2008): 485.

22 "Schumpeter: The Case Against Globaloney," *The Economist* (April 23, 2011): 72.

23 Paul Westhead, Mike Wright, and Deniz Ucbasaran, "International Market Selection Strategies Selected by 'Micro' and 'Small' Firms," *Omega* (February 2002): 51.

24 McKinsey & Co. (1993), "Emerging Exporters: Australia's High Value-added Manufacturing Exporters." Melbourne: Australian Manufacturing Council, retrieved May 17, 2011, from http://catalogue.nla.gov.au/Record/2621131

25 Oystein Moen, Roger Sorbeim, and Truls Erikson. "Born Global Firms and Informal Investors: Examining Investor Characteristics," *Journal of Small Business Management* (October, 2008): 536.

26 Evertek Computer Corp., retrieved May 15, 2011, from www.export.gov/articles/successstories/eg_success_story_021490.asp

27 Ibid.

28 Daniel Sullivan and Alan Bauerschmidt, "Incremental Internationalization: A Test of Johanson and Vahlne's Thesis," *Management International Review* (1990): 19–30.

29 Some folks object to the abrasives, flavors, tartar control agents, and bleaches found in mass-market product.

30 Mark Stein, "Export Opportunities Aren't Just for the Big Guys," *New York Times* (March 24, 2005): C-1.

31 Vellus Products, retrieved May 15, 2011, from www.export.gov/articles/successstories/eg_main_020763.asp

32 Adapted from *A Basic Guide to Exporting*, 10th edition, ISBN# 9780160792045.

33 Mark Stein, "Export Opportunities Aren't Just for the Big Guys," *New York Times* (March 24, 2005): C-1.

34 Jiang Jingjing, "Wal-Mart's China Inventory to Hit US $18B this Year," *China Business Weekly*, retrieved November 29, 2004, from www.chinadaily.com.cn/english/doc/2004–11/29/content_395728.htm

35 Anna Thomas and Susan Bridgewater, "Internet and Exporting: Determinants of Success in Virtual Export Channels," *International Marketing Review* 21:4 (2004): 393.

36 Merlin Bettina, "Internet Marketing in Exports—A Useful Tool for Small Businesses," *Small Enterprise Development* (December 2004): 38.

37 Pascal-Emmanuel Gobry, "Asian Scalpers Are Wiping Out Apple's Supply Of iPad 2s In New York," retrieved May 31, 2011, from www.businessinsider.com/ipad-scalpers-new-york-2011-3

38 Andrew Bernard, Bradford Jensen, and Peter Schott, "Importers, Exporters, and Multinationals: A Portrait of Firms in the U.S. that Trade Goods," NBER Working Paper No. 11404, June 2005.

39 Statistical Overview, 2009, U.S. International Trade Administration, retrieved May 12, 2011, from www.trade.gov/mas/ian/smeoutlook/tg_ian_001925.asp

40 Andrew Bernard, Bradford Jensen, and Peter Schott, "Importers, Exporters, and Multinationals: A Portrait of Firms in the U.S. that Trade Goods," NBER Working Paper No. 11404, June 2005.

41 Bases on exchange rates of yuan to dollar rate of 0.154/$1 as of May 6, 2011.

42 Arguably, an unrealistic assumption but one we make for the sake of convenience.

43 "Table 1. Civilian workers, by major occupational and industry group," *U.S. Bureau of Labor Statistics*, retrieved May 9, 2011, from www.bls.gov/news.release/ecec.t01.htm

44 "How Much Would The iPad 2 Cost If It Was Made in the U.S.A.?,[[[8239>]]]"Stone Street Advisors, retrieved May 9, 2011, from http://stonestreetadvisors.com/2011/05/06/how-much-would-the-ipad-2-cost-if-it-was-made-in-the-u-s-a; Andrew Rassweiler, "iPad 2 Carries Bill of Materials of $326.60, IHS iSuppli Teardown Analysis Shows," retrieved May 9, 2011, from www.isuppli.com/teardowns/news/pages/ipad-2-carries-bill-of-materials-of-$326-60-ihs-isuppli-teardown-analysis-shows.aspx

45 L. Leonidou, "An Analysis of the Export Barriers Hindering Small Business Export Development," *Journal of Small Business Management* (2004):279–-302; Martina Battisti and Martin Perry, "Creating Opportunity for Small-firm Exporters through Regional Free Trade Agreements: A Strategic Perspective from New Zealand," *Australasian Journal of Regional Studies* (2008): 275–86.

46 OECD, OECD-APEC paper on removing barriers to SME access to international market (2006). See also Alan Bauerschmidt, Daniel Sullivan, and Kate Gillespie "Common Factors Underlying Barriers to Export Studies in the U.S. Paper Industry," *Journal of International Business Studies*, 16:3 (1985): 111–23.

47 "Congress Pushes More Export Financing for Small Business," *Associated Press* (September 5, 2006).

48 J. Laurie Flynn, "Poor Nations Are Littered with Old PC's, Report Says," *New York Times* (October 24, 2005): C-2.

49 "Africa Waste Trade," retrieved May 4, 2011, from www1.american.edu/TED/oauwaste.htm; Estimates for developed taken from Hazardous Waste Disposal, www.uos.harvard.edu/ehs/environmental/hw_faq_answers.shtml; Leslie Kaufman, "A Green Way to Dump Low-Tech Electronics," *New York Times* (June 30, 2009).

50 Helen Baulch, "Error: Dumping Does Not Compute," *Alternatives Journal* (Summer 2002): 2.

51 Reported by Karl Schoenberger, "E-Waste Ignored in India," *Mercury News*, retrieved May 4, 2011, from www.ban.org/ban_news/ewaste_ignored_031228.html

52 "After Dump, What Happens to Electronic Waste?" *NPR*, retrieved April 19, 2011, from www.npr.org/2010/12/21/132204954/after-dump-what-happens-to-electronic-waste

53 Helen Baulch, "Error: Dumping Does Not Compute," *Alternatives Journal* (Summer 2002): 2.

54 "The Digital Dump: Exporting Reuse and Abuse to Africa," *Basel Action Network*, retrieved May 4, 2011, from www.ban.org/banreports/10-24-05/index.htm

55 Basel Action Network, retrieved May 5, 2007, from www.ban.org/index.html; Flynn, "Poor Nations Littered with Old PCs."

56 "E-Waste Importers," *Hazardous Waste Superfund Week* (December 23, 2002).

57 "Where Does E-Waste End Up?" retrieved May 4, 2011, from www.greenpeace.org/international/campaigns/toxics/electronics/where-does-e-waste-end-up

58 Kaufman, "A Green Way to Dump Low-Tech Electronics."

59 See "Secretariat of the Basel Convention, Competent Authorities," retrieved March 26, 2009, from www.basel.int. By definition, a "Competent Authority" means one governmental authority designated by a Party to be responsible within such geographic areas as the Party may think fit, for receiving the notification of a transboundary movement of hazardous wastes or other wastes, and any information related to it, and for responding to such a notification.

60 John Kerr, "Exporters Need to Connect with Customers," Logistics Management (March 1, 2006): 41.

61 O'Gorman, C. (2000), "Strategy and the Small Firm," In S. Carter and D. Jones-Evans (Eds.), *Enterprise and Small Business: Principles, Practice, and Policy* (Harlow: Prentice Hall, FT Pearson).

62 "The Benefits of Exporting."

63 Spectra Colors of NJ, retrieved May 15, 2011, from ww.export.gov /articles/successstories/eg_success_story_023038.asp

64 Kerr, "Exporters Need to Connect with Customers."

65 "Schumpeter: The Case against Globaloney," *The Economist* (April 20, 2011): 52.

66 Incoterms is short for International Commercial Terms, the rules for the division of cost and risk in international sales transactions.

67 The commercial invoice, for instance, contains information such as the country of origin, the port of entry to which the merchandise is destined, information on the importer and exporter, a detailed description of the merchandise, including its purchase price, and the currency used for the sale.

68 "The Benefits of Exporting."

69 Ibid.

70 Ibid.

71 Ibid.

72 Japan, for instance, relies on several offices, such as the Small and Medium Enterprise Agency, the Agency of Industrial Science and Technology, and the Ministry of International Trade and Industry. The latter, often referred to as MITI, develops policies and provides assistance to help Japanese companies trade.

73 Lee Li, "Joint Effects of Factors Affecting Exchanges Between Exporters and Their Foreign Intermediaries: An Exploratory Study," *Journal of Business & Industrial Marketing* (February–March 2003): 162–78. Trade intermediaries help navigate complex homeland security concerns. Increasing government regulation regarding what can be shipped where and to whom has prolonged border delays.

74 See U.S. Department of Commerce, *Guide to Exporting, 1998,* p. 20; Philip MacDonald, *Practical Exporting and Importing,* 2nd edition (New York: Ronald Press, 1959): 30–40.

75 Courtney Fingar, "ABCs of EMCs," The Federation of International Trade Associations (July 2001); Nelson T. Joyner, "How to Find and Use an Export Management Company," retrieved May 9, 2007, from www.fita.org/aotm/0499.html

76 Geoffrey G Jones, *The Multinational Trader* (Routledge International Studies in Business History, 1998).

77 "Basic Question: To Export Yourself or to Hire Someone to Do It for You?" *Business America* (April 27, 1987): 14–17.

78 Because a practical discussion of importing procedures in every trading country of the world is impossible within this chapter, we focus on the matter of importing to the United States. We note that although U.S. import requirements and procedures provide a sufficient base for judging situations in other countries, a company must assess the importing regulations applicable to those countries in which it plans to engage. For an organizational chart of the U.S. Customs Bureau, including a roster of specific responsibilities, go to the home page of the U.S. Bureau of Customs and Border Protection, www.customs.ustreas.gov.

79 International Bank/World Bank, "Doing Business in 2007."

80 U.S. Department of the Treasury, U.S. Customs Service, *Importing into the United States* (Washington, DC: U.S. Government Printing Office, September 1991).

81 U.S. Department of Commerce, *Guide to Exporting* (Washington, DC: U.S. Government Printing Office, 1998): 63.

82 Certified Worldwide LLC, retrieved May 4, 2011, from www.export .gov/articles/successstories/eg_success_story_020902.asp

83 Richard Armstrong, "The Top 40 3PLs 2010," *Logistics Quarterly Magazine* (2011).

84 Quote from CEO Robert Allen, Coffee & More, LLC, retrieved May 15, 2011, from www.export.gov/articles/successstories/eg_success _story_022775.asp

85 Benson Smith and Tony Rutigliano, *Discover Your Sales Strengths* (New York: Warner Business Books, 2003).

86 Javier Blas, "Nations Turn to Barter Deals to Secure Food," *Financial Times,* retrieved March 11, 2009, from www.ft.com /cms/s/0/3e5c633c-ebdc-11dd-8838-0000779fd2ac.html; Dan West, "Countertrade—An Innovative Approach to Marketing," retrieved May 15, 2007, from www.barternews.com/approach _ marketing.htm. On a more exotic note, Pepsi-Cola, which has the marketing rights for all Stolichnaya Vodka in the United States, delivers syrup that is paid for with Stolichnaya Vodka. In addition, early on, Pepsi took delivery of 17 submarines, a cruiser, a frigate, and a destroyer from the Russian government in payment for Pepsi products. In turn, Pepsi sold its "fleet" of 20 naval vessels for scrap steel, thereby paying for the Pepsi products sent to the Soviet Union.

87 V. S. Rama Rao, "Counter Trade," retrieved May 23, 2011, from www.citeman.com/2390-counter-trade

88 One can divide countertrade into two classes: barter, based on clearing arrangements used to avoid money-based exchange; and buybacks, offsets, and counter purchases, which are used to impose reciprocal commitments between the various parties.

89 Dan West, "Countertrade—An Innovative Approach to Marketing," retrieved March 12, 2009, from BarterNews.com

90 Julie Sloane, Justin Martin, and Alessandra Bianchi, "Small Companies That Play Big," *FSB Magazine* (November 1, 2006), quoting Ram Iyer.

91 Justin Lahart, "For Small Businesses, Big World Beckons," *WSJ.com,* retrieved January 27, 2011, from online.wsj.com/article/SB10001424 052748703951704576092010276714424.html?mod=WSJ_hp _MIDDLENexttoWhatsNewsFifth

92 Sloane, quoting Everette Phillips.

93 *Sources include the following:* Various sources at www.Alibaba .com; Forbes Global (April 25, 2005):30; TradeStats Express, retrieved July 1, 2009, from tse.export.gov; John Heilemann, "Jack Ma Aims to Unlock the Middle Kingdom," *Business 2.0 Magazin,* (July 31, 2006); Jack Ma, "China Discovers Its Future," *International Herald Tribune* (December 17, 2008); "Alibaba Prepares for Global Expansion," *Financial Times* (January 19, 2009).

94 The U.S. Small Business Administration estimates that the number of small companies exporting products tripled from 1994 through 2004. In terms of monetary flows, the value of exports from the United States grew from $731 billion in 2001 to $1.03 trillion in 2006, while imports grew from $1.14 trillion to $1.9 trillion.

95 "Alibaba wields its pricing power," *Asia Times Online,* retrieved February 17, 2011, from www.atimes.com/atimes/China_Business /MB18Cb01.html

chapter 14

Direct Investment and Collaborative Strategies

Source: Thor Jorgen Udvang / Shutterstock.com

Objectives

1. To clarify why companies may need to use modes other than exporting to operate effectively in international business

2. To comprehend why and how companies make foreign direct investments

3. To understand the major motives that guide managers in choosing a collaborative arrangement for international business

4. To define the major types of collaborative arrangements

5. To describe what to consider when entering into international arrangements with other companies

6. To grasp why collaborative arrangements succeed or fail

7. To see how companies can manage diverse collaborative arrangements

> Access a host of interactive learning aids to help strengthen your understanding of the chapter concepts at www.myiblab.com.
>
> **MyIBLab**

> *If you can't beat them, join them.*
>
> —*American proverb*

C A S E

The Fizz Biz: Coca-Cola

Sailin' 'round the world in a dirty gondola.
Oh, to be back in the land of Coca-Cola!
—**Bob Dylan, "When I Paint My Masterpiece"**

Although the United States is Dylan's "land of Coca-Cola," over half the firm's revenues are from the more than 200 other countries where it sells.[1] The Coca-Cola (Coke) brand is one of the world's most recognized; thus other companies, such as Coca-Cola Clothing in Brazil, pay Coke licensing fees to use the logo on their products and stores. As of 2011, the company had 15 brands selling over a billion U.S. dollars per year, and you are probably familiar with most of these. However, you probably can name few of the more than 400 other brand names the company uses globally within its five drink segments: juice drinks, energy drinks, water, soft drinks, and sports drinks. Here are just a few you might not recognize: Bonaqua Bonactive (Hong Kong), Novida (Kenya), Far Coast (Singapore), Mother (Australia), Multon (Russia), and Nanairo Acha (Japan). The company describes itself as a manufacturer, distributor, and marketer of nonalcoholic drinks. (The opening photo shows a hot air balloon in the shape of a Coke bottle flying in Pattaya, Thailand, during a balloon festival.)

A LITTLE HISTORY

Coca-Cola originated as a soda fountain drink in 1886, began bottling in 1894, commenced soda fountain sales in Canada and Mexico in 1897, and initiated its first foreign bottling plant in Panama in 1906. Coke continued to expand internationally during the 1920s and 1930s, even opening a foreign department in 1926. But its big international boost came during World War II. Recognizing that the war would bring a shortage of sugar, one of Coke's essential ingredients, its CEO announced on national radio that the company would ensure that all U.S. military personnel anywhere in the world could buy Coca-Cola. His propaganda message worked. Not only did Coca-Cola get all the sugar it wanted, even though U.S. households seldom found sugar in the grocery stores, it also got permission to build 64 bottling plants around the world during the war.

When the war ended, Coca-Cola was known almost everywhere, and returning service personnel had become loyal customers. Today, Coke's network of more than 1,000 plants operates a fleet of delivery trucks five times larger than that of UPS. It has the largest share of the soft-drink market, and more than 16,000 Coca-Cola beverages are consumed worldwide every second.

COLLABORATIVE ARRANGEMENTS

Suppliers

Although its product offerings and shrewd marketing are pillars of Coke's success, the company could not have reached its present position alone. Coke buys from over 84,000 suppliers, and it needs help in almost every aspect of its operations. For instance, in 1996, it formed a three-way joint venture for a facility in Kyrgyzstan. The joint venture hired a Turkish turnkey operator (Fintraco Insaat ve Taahhut), which used 400 trucks just to carry supplies from Turkey to build the plant.

In another example, Coca-Cola has paid to have a multipurpose exhibition and entertainment venue named the Coca-Cola Dome in Johannesburg, South Africa. The dome owner is the Sasol Pension Fund, which, in turn, pays Thebe Entertainment and Events a contractual fee for managing the facility. In sum, when operating both domestically and internationally, Coca-Cola uses a variety of collaborative operating forms, and it takes varying levels of ownership in operations that support its business.

The one area in which Coca-Cola maintains strict ownership control is in production of the concentrate, thus ensuring that its "secret formula" does not fall into the hands of competitors.

Franchises: Bottlers

Coca-Cola sees its bottlers worldwide as the backbone of the company. These bottlers operate under franchise agreements in which each has exclusive rights to sell within a given territory. They not only bottle Coke beverages, but they also deliver them to such outlets as grocery stores and vending machines. They put up ad displays in stores and even make sure bottles are aligned correctly on supermarket shelves. In short, they know and respond well to their local markets. By turning activities over to the franchised bottlers, Coca-Cola can concentrate its efforts on what it feels it can do best. And these efforts help the profitability of bottlers. However, by turning activities over, Coke loses some control, such as in distribution and in budget allocations as consumers' tastes change. This is why Coke upped its ownership from 34 percent to 100 percent in the North American operations of bottler Coca-Cola Enterprises in 2010.

What's in It for Bottlers?

So what do the bottlers get in return from Coca-Cola?

1. They get the results of Coca-Cola's innovation in developing new products, such as Coca-Cola Zero, and

in developing ad campaigns that help sell Coca-Cola products worldwide. These have included such themes as "Coke side of life," "It's the real thing," "Things go better with Coca-Cola," and "I'd like to teach the world to sing."

2. They benefit from Coca-Cola's strict quality control, which includes procedures for and inspection of water purification and the mixing of syrup, concentrate, and carbonation. Quality control is important in that a slipup in one bottling plant can adversely affect sales in many countries.

3. They get help in instituting work processes to increase their efficiency. Coca-Cola studies and compares bottlers, and because they are not in competition with each other, Coca-Cola shares information among them. Finally, last but not least, Coca-Cola makes the concentrate that all its bottlers must buy.

The Franchise as Big Business

Some of the franchisees are quite large and are themselves traded publicly. For example, Coca-Cola HBC is headquartered in Greece, has operating rights in 28 countries with a combined population of 550 million, and is traded on stock exchanges in Greece, the United Kingdom, Australia, and the United States. When franchise rights cover a large territory, the franchisees generally subfranchise to bottlers throughout their region.

A few large franchisees account for a large percent of Coca-Cola's worldwide sales. In these, Coca-Cola has taken a significant minority ownership stake, which is sufficient to gain considerable influence in the operations.

OWNERSHIP OPTIONS

Coca-Cola's ownership abroad varies substantially. For example, within China, it wholly owns its concentrate plant but has joint ventures with various bottling plants. Coca-Cola's ownership in foreign bottling operations has become sufficiently significant that it has set up a Bottle Investment Group within the company. It has sometimes taken an equity position abroad, even a wholly owned one, to sustain production where it would like to sell. For instance, in the Philippines, Coca-Cola bought some poorly performing bottlers that might otherwise have ceased production and merged them with successful bottling operations there. When entering the Vietnamese market, it did so with a local joint-venture bottling partner that needed Coke's financial and marketing help. After the operation became viable, Coke sold its interest.

Further, Coca-Cola has sometimes had to settle for a joint venture when it might have preferred full ownership. One case in point is India. Coca-Cola once left the market because of the Indian government's insistence on knowing Coke's concentrate formula. To return about 15 years later, the Indian government required Coca-Cola (and PepsiCo as well) to share ownership with an Indian company. Another case in point was when Coca-Cola wished to acquire Inca Kola, the largest soft-drink brand in Peru. The family owners of Inca Kola refused to sell the whole company, and Coke settled for a half ownership.

RED COUNTRIES VERSUS BLUE COUNTRIES

Whereas the two major U.S. political parties talk about red states and blue states, the two major soft-drink competitors refer to red countries (Coca-Cola) and blue countries (Pepsi) where each has the larger market share. These are shown on Map 14.1.

Coca-Cola not only leads PepsiCo in most foreign markets—it depends much more on foreign sales than PepsiCo does. This is positive for Coke's future inasmuch as soft-drink sales in the United States have been declining.

Competitive Markets and Product Lines

Much of the future competitive relationship between Coke and Pepsi will depend on what happens in the two markets with the fastest growth potential: China and India. Not only are these the two most populated countries, but their annual soft-drink per capita consumption is also low (e.g., 1.2 liters in China

MAP 14.1   We'd Like to Sell the World a Cola

In the countries shown in red, Coke leads Pepsi in market share; Pepsi leads Coke in the blue countries. Of course, the two soft-drink giants compete in a lot of other places as well, but market-share data are unavailable for some areas. Note that although red countries outnumber blue countries, the world's two most populous nations—China and India—are in the blue column. Data reflect sales of Coke/Diet Coke and Pepsi/Diet Pepsi only.

Source: Based on "I'd Like to Sell the World a Coke," *New York Times* (May 27, 2007), at www.nytimes.com (accessed November 5, 2007). Data from Euromonitor International and the Coca-Cola Co.

■ Coke/Diet Coke
■ Pepsi/Diet Pepsi
■ Data Unavailable

and 0.1 liters in India as compared with 31.3 liters in the United States and 20.2 liters in Brazil); thus, there seems to be great potential for growth in those markets as the economies grow. The growth potential in these two markets undoubtedly affected both companies' acceptance of operating terms in India that they may not have accepted elsewhere. Map 14.1 shows Pepsi leading in both of these markets; however, the map is only for the regular and diet versions of colas. In China, Coca-Cola leads in total carbonated soft drink sales, largely because Sprite is the top selling brand there. Additionally, Coca-Cola's Minute Maid Pulpy, a drink for the Chinese market, is one of its billion-dollar-a-year brands.

Coca-Cola has learned that it must widen its product line and that doing so by simply adding cherry or vanilla flavoring to Coca-Cola is not enough. If Coca-Cola does not offer a larger variety of nonalcoholic drinks, it might lose exclusive sales to large customers, such as food franchisors and airlines. Coke's bottlers have also added production and distribution of products not available from Coke, such as Cadbury Schweppes' coffee latte drink, Cinnabon.

Collaboration as Expansion Strategy

Because of changes in the market for nonalcoholic drinks, Coca-Cola has been expanding its product offerings in four ways:

* Developing new products
* Acquiring companies that have complementary products
* Gaining licenses to use brand names of other companies
* Distributing soft drinks from other companies

Coke has been doing some of this broadening on its own, some in partnership with other companies, and some through acquisitions. Its acquisitions have been widespread, including juice companies in Brazil and Russia and specialty water companies in Denmark, Germany, and the United States. It has a joint venture with Nestlé for tea products outside the United States and a joint venture with Cargill to develop a new sweetener to put into drinks. It is spending heavily on licensing for the production and sale of products using different trademarks. One of the most important license agreements is with Danone for various water brands including Sparkletts. It also distributes the Seagram's nonalcoholic beverages, such as ginger ale, tonic, and soda water.

CRN Case Review Note

Introduction

As Figure 14.1 shows, companies must choose an international operating mode to fulfill their objectives and carry out their strategies. The preceding chapter examined exporting and importing—the preferred and most common modes of international business. Nevertheless, compelling factors can make these choices impractical. When companies depend, instead, on foreign production, they may own it in whole or in part, develop or acquire it, and/or use some type of collaborative agreement with another company.

Figure 14.2 shows the types of operating modes associated with each of these options, categorized by whether the company has foreign ownership, whether collaboration is involved, and whether production is located at home or abroad. The truly experienced MNE with a fully global orientation commonly uses most of the operational modes available, selecting them according to company capabilities, specific product, and foreign operating characteristics. The modes may also be combined, as with Coca-Cola's wholly owned concentrate plant in China in addition to its partially owned and franchised bottling plants there.

In this chapter, we will examine exporting/importing versus other options, the associated operating modes, and the advantages and problems with each, then conclude by discussing the management of these modes, particularly as foreign operations evolve over time.

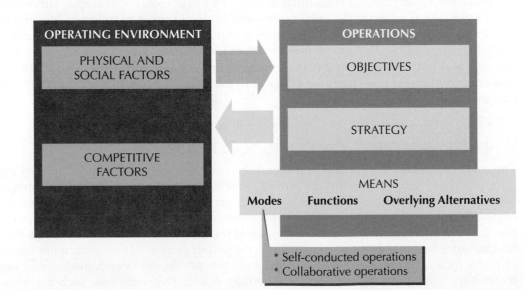

FIGURE 14.1 Factors Affecting Operating Modes in International Business

Companies may conduct international business operations independently or in collaboration with other companies. The choice will be determined both by external factors in the firm's operating environment and by internal factors that include its objectives, strategies, and means of operation (e.g., such modes of international business as exporting, franchising, etc.).

FIGURE 14.2 Foreign
Expansion: Alternative
Operating Modes

A firm may choose to operate
globally either through equity
arrangements (e.g., joint venture)
or through nonequity arrangements
(e.g., licensing). Exporting
operations are conducted in the
home country, while all other
modes entail production in foreign
locations. The modes listed in the
purple shaded area are collaborative
arrangements. Note that, in any
given location, a firm can conduct
operations in multiple modes.

PRODUCTION OWNERSHIP	PRODUCTION LOCATION	
	Home country	Foreign country
Equity arrangements	a. Exporting	a. Wholly owned operations b. Partially owned with remainder widely held c. Joint ventures d. Equity alliances
Nonequity arrangements		a. Licensing b. Franchising c. Management contracts d. Turnkey operations

Why Exporting May Not Be Feasible

Companies may find more advantages by producing in foreign countries than by exporting to them. The advantages occur under six conditions:

1. When production abroad is cheaper than at home
2. When transportation costs to move goods or services internationally are too expensive
3. When companies lack domestic capacity
4. When products and services need to be altered substantially to gain sufficient consumer demand abroad
5. When governments inhibit the import of foreign products
6. When buyers prefer products originating from a particular country

WHEN IT'S CHEAPER TO PRODUCE ABROAD

Although companies may offer products or services desired by consumers abroad, producing them in their home markets may be too expensive, especially if other companies
can make reasonably similar substitutes abroad at a lower cost. For example, Turkey has
been a growing market for the sale of automobiles. However, it is generally less expensive to produce the vehicles in Turkey than to export them there, because the country's
skilled laborers and sophisticated engineers cost less and are willing to work more days
per year and longer hours per day than workers in the home countries. Thus, the automakers and many of their parts suppliers have established Turkish production to serve
that market.[2]

WHEN TRANSPORTATION COSTS TOO MUCH

Transportation raises costs
so much that it becomes
impractical to export some
products.

The cost of transportation added to production costs makes some products and services
impractical to export. Generally, the farther away the market, the higher the transportation costs, and the higher those are relative to production costs, the more difficult for
companies to develop viable export markets. For instance, the international transportation cost for a soft drink is a high percentage of the manufacturing cost, so a sales price
that includes both would be so high through exporting that soft-drink companies would
sell very little of the product. This drawback, as we saw in our opening case, is among
the reasons Coca-Cola depends on local bottling plants. (Nevertheless, such brands as

CRN
Case Review Note

Perrier successfully serve niche markets for exported bottled water that sells at high prices relative to production costs.)

However, products such as watches have low transportation costs relative to production costs, thus watch manufacturers lose few sales through exporting. The result is that companies such as Universal Genève and Seiko export watches from Switzerland and Japan, respectively, into the markets where they sell them.

Keep in mind that transport costs are dynamic—depending on fuel prices, new infrastructure (e.g., a widened Panama Canal will cut many export distances), risk factors (e.g., ship piracy increases security costs), and climate changes (e.g., warming makes the Northwest Passage a viable option).

WHEN DOMESTIC CAPACITY ISN'T ENOUGH

As long as a company has excess capacity, it may compete effectively in export markets despite high transport costs. This ability occurs when domestic sales cover fixed operating expenses, enabling the company to set foreign prices on the basis of variable rather than full (variable + fixed) costs. In fact, its average cost of production per unit usually goes down as foreign sales increase, but the cost decrease continues only as long as there is unused capacity.

Thus, companies typically produce in one location, from which they export before establishing plants in more than one country. Volkswagen located its first plant to build the new Beetle at its facilities in Mexico, which served global markets. However, when demand pushed that plant toward capacity, Volkswagen built a second plant in Europe to serve the markets there, thus freeing Mexican capacity to serve nearby markets while reducing transport costs for European sales.[3]

> **Excess capacity**
> - usually leads to exporting rather than new direct investment.
> - may lead to competitive exports because of variable cost pricing.

WHEN PRODUCTS AND SERVICES NEED ALTERING

Altering products to gain sufficient sales in a foreign market affects production costs in two ways. First, firms must make an additional investment, such as an automobile company adding an assembly line to put steering wheels on the right as well as on the left. Second, they lose some of the economies from large-scale production. As long as they must run an added assembly line anyway, they may place this line near the market they wish to serve.

The more a product must be altered for foreign markets, the more likely some production will shift abroad. Appliance maker Whirlpool, for example, finds that most U.S. demand is for top-loading washing machines with large capacity using 110 electrical voltage, whereas most European demand is for front-loading washers (more efficient in using energy and water) with smaller capacity using 220 voltage.[4] Given the differences in product preferences, Whirlpool produces in both the United States and Europe.

> Product alterations for foreign markets may lead to foreign production of the products.

WHEN TRADE RESTRICTIONS HINDER IMPORTS

Although governments have been reducing import barriers, they still restrict many imports. As a result, companies may find that they must produce in a foreign country if they are to sell there. This has been the case with many auto companies—Volkswagen, Mercedes Benz, BMW, Renault, and Fiat—which decided to manufacture in India because India charged over 100 percent duty on fully built imported cars.[5]

Managers must view import barriers along with other factors, such as the market size of the country imposing the barriers and the scale of technology used in production. For example, import trade restrictions have been highly influential in enticing automobile producers to locate in Brazil because of its large market. Similar restrictions by Central American countries have been ineffective because of their small markets. However,

> **Concept Check**
>
> In Chapter 8, we explain why governments are currently reducing trade restrictions, whether through **bilateral integration** (in which two countries agree to cooperate), **regional integration** (in which a group of geographically related countries agrees to cooperate), or agreements reached by the **WTO,** which serves as a multilateral forum. Here we observe that importers still face certain regulatory restrictions, some of which are designed to encourage forms of direct investment.

Central American import barriers on products requiring lower amounts of capital investment for production, such as pharmaceuticals, have been highly effective in enticing direct investment because these industries can be efficient with smaller-scale technologies and markets.

Regional or bilateral trade agreements may also attract direct investment, possibly because they create an expanded market that may justify scale economies and an ability to export part of the production. EU entry was a factor affecting FDI increases in Bulgaria, Greece, Romania, and Slovenia. Further, the prospect of EU entry spurred an influx of FDI to Albania, Bosnia and Herzegovina, Macedonia, and Turkey.[6]

WHEN COUNTRY OF ORIGIN BECOMES AN ISSUE

Consumers sometimes prefer domestically produced goods because of

- nationalism.
- a belief that these products are better.
- a fear that foreign-made goods may not be delivered on time.

If consumers prefer to buy goods produced in their own country rather than another (perhaps because of nationalism), exporting to them will be difficult.[7] They may push for identification labels showing that goods are domestically produced, such as those for Australian-made products.[8] They may require labels showing where products are made, as with U.S. labeling of agricultural products. Or they may require governments to purchase domestic products or services, such as those under The American Disaster Relief Act of 2010.

Consumers may prefer goods from certain countries, believing them to be superior, like German cars and Italian fashion.[9] They may also fear that service and replacement parts for imported products will be more difficult to obtain. Finally, companies using just-in-time manufacturing systems favor nearby suppliers who can deliver quickly and reliably. In any of these cases, companies may find advantages in placing production where their output will best be accepted.

Noncollaborative Foreign Equity Arrangements

In situations where exporting is not feasible, a company may choose to contract with another company to produce or provide services on its behalf—a transaction across the market between unrelated entities. Given liability of foreignness and the extra costs of investing abroad, contracting another company is appealing, but only if management can find a foreign provider at acceptable terms. The extent to which companies take controlling ownership equity (FDI) in foreign operations—such as in warehousing, sales offices, or production facilities—indicates market failure in finding such foreign providers. In these instances, companies must control foreign production within their own management structures (internal hierarchies) rather than depending on the external market to do it for them.[10] Recall the four types of equity arrangements in Figure 14.2. In this section, we discuss the two not involving collaboration: wholly owned operations and partially owned with the remainder widely held. We also discuss the resources and methods for making FDI.

Concept Check

Recall that in discussing **global strategy** as a type of international strategy in Chapter 11, we explain why some companies treat the world as a single market, preferring to integrate and measure performance on a global basis rather than on a country-by-country basis. Here we observe that the strategy of having wholly owned subsidiaries supports a global international strategy.

TAKING CONTROL: FOREIGN DIRECT INVESTMENT

Generally, the more ownership a company has, the greater its control over decisions. However, governments often protect minority owners so that majority owners do not act against their interests, thus companies may opt for 100 percent ownership if they want control. There are three primary explanations for companies to want a controlling interest: *internalization theory, appropriability theory,* and *freedom to pursue global objectives.*

Internalization   Control through self-handling of operations is known as **internalization.**[11] The concept comes from *transactions cost theory,* which holds that companies should seek the lower cost between conducting operations internally and contracting another party to do so for them. In actuality, a company may not easily find a firm to handle its operations because of, say, a unique or hard-to-grasp technology. In other cases, self-handling may reduce costs for a number of reasons:

1. *Different operating units within the same company are likely to share a common corporate culture, which expedites communications.* Executives participating in a Thought Leadership Summit on Digital Strategies concluded that a lack of trust, common terminology, and knowledge are major obstacles to successful collaboration.[12]

2. *The company can use its own managers, who understand and are committed to carrying out its objectives.* When GE acquired a controlling interest in the Hungarian company Tungsram, it was able to expedite control and changes because it put GE managers in key positions.[13]

3. *The company can avoid protracted negotiations with another company on such matters as how each will be compensated for contributions.* The U.S. and Russian automakers GM and AvtoVAZ shut down production in their Russian joint venture while negotiating a higher price for critical components supplied by AvtoVAZ.[14]

4. *The company can avoid possible enforcement problems.* Tommy Hilfiger sued Mountain High Hosiery, manufacturer of its socks, for selling cheaply to unauthorized distributors, who cheapened the brand image.[15]

Appropriability   The idea of denying rivals access to resources is called the **appropriability theory**.[16] Companies are reluctant to transfer vital resources—capital, patents, trademarks, and management know-how—to another organization for fear of their competitive position being undermined. In fact, Chinese automakers, such as SAIV, Dongfeng, and Changan, that have collaborative arrangements with major global auto competitors, such as GM, Volkswagen, Nissan, and Ford, make no secret of their desire to learn from their partners so as to become global competitors in their own right.[17] Nevertheless, companies are less concerned about appropriability in countries they perceive as having a strong rule of law.[18] On the other hand, as the opening case points out, Coca-Cola, which is committed to a variety of collaborative operating forms with partners all over the world, steadfastly refuses to share ownership in the production of its concentrate. The formula is simply too critical to the company's competitive viability.

> Companies may want to operate through FDI to lessen the chance of developing competitors.

Case Review Note

Freedom to Pursue a Global Strategy   A company that has a wholly owned foreign operation may find it easier to allow the operation to participate in a global strategy. For instance, a U.S. company that owns 100 percent of its Brazilian operation might be able to take actions that, although suboptimizing Brazilian performance, could deal more effectively with actual or potential competitors and customers globally, such as by decreasing prices to an industrial customer in Brazil to gain that customer's business in Germany. Or it might standardize its product to gain global cost savings even though this might result in some lost sales in Brazil. But if the company shared ownership in Brazil, either action might be detrimental to the Brazilian owners, who would balk at such practices.

HOW TO MAKE FDI

FDI ownership takes place by transferring abroad financial and/or other tangible or intangible assets. Firms have two ways to use these assets to invest in a foreign country: They can either acquire an interest in an existing operation or construct new facilities—an option known as a *greenfield investment*. The reasons for each are below.

Acquisition   Whether a company makes a direct investment by acquisition or start-up depends, of course, on which companies are available for purchase. The recent global economic crisis and bankruptcy situations have put many firms on the market, and other firms, including those from other countries, have exploited this opportunity to buy them.[19]

The advantages of acquiring an existing operation include

- adding no further capacity to the market.
- avoiding start-up problems.
- easier financing at times.

Why Buy?   There are many reasons for seeking acquisitions. One is to obtain some vital resource that may otherwise be slow or difficult for the investor to secure.[20] Let's say a company has knowledgeable personnel that the investor cannot easily hire at a good price on its own.[21] Or, perhaps, an investor could acquire the personnel, but lacks experience in managing them effectively. For instance, many Russian companies have recently expanded internationally through acquisition. They have had good scientific inventions and innovative products, but they have lacked experience in managing the transformation from R&D to market success.[22] By buying a company, the buyer gets not only labor and management but also an existing organization with experience in coordinating such functions as the development of products and their subsequent sales.

In addition, a company may gain the goodwill, brand identification, and access to distribution that are important to marketing its products, especially if the cost and risk of breaking in a new brand are high. Recently, much Chinese investment in the United States has been by acquisition, seemingly because of Chinese companies' desire to secure well-known brand names that will help them sell.[23]

There are also financial considerations. A company depending substantially on local financing rather than on transferring capital may find local capital suppliers more willing to put money into a known ongoing operation than to invest in a less familiar foreign enterprise. A foreign firm also may merge with an existing company through an exchange of stock.

In other ways, acquisitions may reduce costs and risks—and save time. A company may be able to buy facilities, particularly those of a poorly performing operation, for less than the cost of new construction. If an investor fears that a market does not justify added capacity, acquisition enables it to avoid the risk of depressed prices through overcapacity. Finally, by buying a company, an investor avoids start-up inefficiencies and gets an immediate cash flow rather than tying up funds during construction.

Companies may choose to build if

- no desired company is available for acquisition.
- acquisition will lead to carryover problems.
- acquisition is harder to finance.

Making Greenfield Investments   Although acquisitions offer advantages, companies frequently invest in sectors where there are few, if any, companies operating, so finding a company to buy may be difficult. Moreover, local governments may prevent acquisitions because they want more competitors in the market and fear market dominance by a single foreign enterprise.

Even if acquisitions are available, they often don't succeed.[24] First, turning around a poorly performing operation is difficult because of potential personnel and labor relations problems, ill will toward its products and brands, and inefficient or poorly located facilities. Second, managers in the acquiring and acquired companies may not work well together because of different management styles and organizational cultures or because of conflicts over decision-making authority.[25] Nevertheless, there is some evidence that acquiring firms' success increases with more international acquisition experience.[26] Intuition tells us that acquisitions in more culturally distant countries would perform less well than those in more culturally similar countries; however, evidence shows the contrary, likely due to a combination of factors: organizational gains from added diversity, greater care in selection in dissimilar countries (particularly to get a better match between organizational cultures), and less attempt to integrate these operations into the corporate culture.[27] Finally, a foreign company may find local financing easier to obtain from development banks if it builds facilities because of being able to show that it is creating employment.

Why Companies Collaborate

Companies collaborate (use alliances that are often called *strategic alliances*) abroad for much the same reasons they do domestically. In our opening case, we saw that Coca-Cola franchises most of its bottling operations in both the United States and foreign countries. However, there are other reasons for collaborating abroad. For example, one of the reasons Coke established a joint venture in India was because Indian law prohibited its gaining 100 percent ownership. Figure 14.3 shows both the general and internationally specific reasons for collaborative arrangements.

CRN
Case Review Note

FIGURE 14.3 Collaborative Arrangements and International Objectives

A company may enter into an international collaborative arrangement for the same general reason that it may enter into a domestic arrangement (e.g., to spread costs). In other cases, it may enter into a collaborative arrangement to meet objectives that are specific to its foreign-expansion strategies (e.g., to diversify geographically).

OBJECTIVES OF INTERNATIONAL BUSINESS
- Sales expansion
- Resource acquisition
- Risk minimization

MOTIVES FOR COLLABORATIVE ARRANGEMENTS
General
- Spread and reduce costs
- Specialize in competencies
- Avoid or counter competition
- Secure vertical and horizontal links
- Learn from other companies

MOTIVES FOR COLLABORATIVE ARRANGEMENTS
Specific to International Business
- Gain location-specific assets
- Overcome legal constraints
- Diversify geographically
- Minimize exposure in risky environments

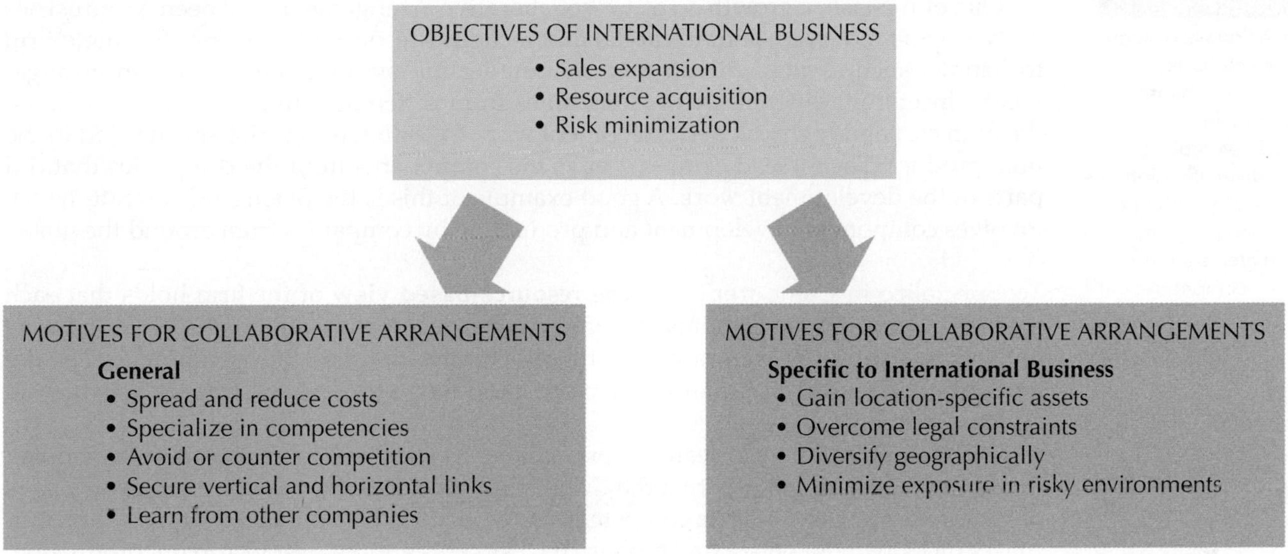

ALLIANCE TYPES

Different terms are used to describe alliances based on their objectives and where they fit in a firm's value chain. In terms of objectives, *scale alliances* aim to provide efficiency by pooling similar assets so that partners can carry out business activities in which they already have experience. Coca-Cola and Procter & Gamble allied to gain distribution economies by combining grocery sales of Coke's juices and P&G's snacks.

Link alliances use complementary resources so that participating companies can expand into new business areas.[28] While we're on the subject, let's take a quick look back at our opening case. In terms of its value chain, Coke's typical franchising arrangement with bottlers calls for a type of *vertical alliance*, because each partner functions on a different level of the value chain. Its partnership with Inca Kola, in contrast, calls for a *horizontal alliance*, because it extends Coke's operations on the same level of the value chain.

GENERAL MOTIVES FOR COLLABORATIVE ARRANGEMENTS

Why do companies collaborate in either domestic or foreign operations? As explained in this section, reasons include spreading and reducing costs, the ability to specialize in their competencies, avoiding competition, securing vertical and horizontal links, and gaining knowledge.

To Spread and Reduce Costs To produce or sell abroad, a company must incur certain fixed costs. At a small volume of business, contract to a specialist rather than self-handling may be cheaper because a specialist can spread the fixed costs to more than one company. If business increases enough, the contracting company may then be able to handle the business more cheaply itself.

A company with excess production or sales capacity can use that excess to handle the activities for a client company. This may lower its average costs by covering its fixed costs more fully, and it will prevent the client from having to incur fixed costs and longer delays for start-up and receipt of cash flows.

Individual companies may lack the resources to "go it alone"—especially small and young ones.[29] By pooling their efforts, they may be able to undertake activities that

Case Review Note

Sometimes it's cheaper to get another company to handle work, especially

- at small volume.
- when the other company has excess capacity.

otherwise would be beyond their means. But large companies may also benefit when the cost of development and/or investment is very high. For instance, the development cost of Disney's theme park in Hong Kong was so high that Disney and the Hong Kong government share ownership and expenses.[30]

One of the fastest growth areas for collaborative arrangements has been in industries with projects too large, both in capital and technical-resource needs, for any single firm to handle, such as new aircraft and communication systems. From such an arrangement's inception, different firms (sometimes from different countries) agree to take on the high cost and high risk of development work for different components needed in the final product. Then a lead company buys the components from the companies that did parts of the development work. A good example of this is the Boeing 787 aircraft, which involves component development and production by companies from around the globe.

To Specialize in Competencies   The **resource-based view** of the firm holds that each company has a unique combination of competencies. A company may seek to improve its performance by concentrating on those activities that best fit its competencies, depending on other firms to supply it with products, services, or support activities in which it was less competent.

This concentration may lead to horizontal or vertical collaboration. Take horizontal. In our opening case, we saw that the Coca-Cola logo can be valuable for selling a variety of products, but Coke sees its competence as being in nonalcoholic beverages, thus it licenses its logo to use on apparel because it lacks skills and interest in apparel production. Now consider vertical. Coca-Cola prefers to franchise its bottling so it can focus on innovative product and advertising development. However, a collaborative arrangement has a limited time frame, which may allow a company to exploit a particular product, asset, or technology itself at a later date if its core competencies change.

To Avoid or Counter Competition   When markets are not large enough to accommodate many competitors, companies may band together so as not to compete. Companies may also combine resources to fight a market leader, such as Coca-Cola and Danone joining efforts to challenge PepsiCo and Nestlé in U.S. bottled water sales.[31] Or they may simply collude to raise everyone's profits. For example, Canpotex is made up of a group of Canadian companies that join together to sell potash outside the United States and Canada and account for more than a quarter of the product's world market.[32] Only a few countries take substantial actions against the collusion of competitors.[33]

To Secure Vertical and Horizontal Links   Potential cost savings and supply assurances can be attained through vertical integration. However, both small and large companies may lack the competence or resources necessary to own and manage the full value chain of activities. A study of small and medium-sized Argentine furniture manufacturers showed that they gained not only manufacturing efficiencies and better access to global markets through vertical alliances, but also better access to support and supplies, such as through governmental agencies and private companies, by pooling resources through horizontal alliances.[34]

Horizontal links may provide economies of scope in distribution, such as by having a full line of products to sell, thereby increasing the sales per fixed cost of a visit to potential customers. For example, Duracell and Gillette combine their sales forces to market batteries and razor blades in many parts of the world to gain economies of scope.[35]

To Gain Knowledge   Many companies pursue collaborative arrangements to learn about a partner's technology, operating methods, or home market so that their own competencies will broaden or deepen, making them more competitive in the future.[36] An example is Chinese authorities allowing foreign companies to tap the Chinese market in exchange for their transference of technology. Sometimes each partner can learn from the other, a motive driving joint ventures between U.S. and European winemakers—such as

the Opus One Winery owned by Constellation Brands' Robert Mondavi from the United States and Baron Philippe de Rothschild from France.[37]

INTERNATIONAL MOTIVES FOR COLLABORATIVE ARRANGEMENTS

In this section, we continue discussing why companies enter into collaborative arrangements, covering those reasons that apply only to international operations. Specifically, the reasons are to gain location-specific assets, overcome legal constraints, diversify geographically, and minimize risk exposure.

To Gain Location-Specific Assets Cultural, political, competitive, and economic differences among countries create barriers for firms abroad. Those ill-equipped to handle these differences may seek collaboration with local firms that will help them. When Walmart first tried to enter the Japanese market on its own, it gave up after having disappointing sales. It has since returned with a Japanese partner, Seiyu, which is more familiar with Japanese tastes and rules for opening new stores.[38] In fact, most foreign companies in Japan need to collaborate with Japanese firms that can help in securing distribution and a competent workforce—two assets that are difficult for MNEs to gain on their own there.

To Overcome Governmental Constraints Virtually all countries limit foreign ownership in some sectors. India and Russia exemplify countries that are particularly restrictive in that they set maximum foreign percentage ownership in an array of industries.[39] They also usually require lengthy negotiations with governments to determine the operating terms; a savvy local partner can help in this regard. Thus, companies may have to collaborate if they are to serve certain foreign markets. In the airline passenger industry, international collaboration has become very important, partly because, with few exceptions, governments allow only domestically owned airlines to carry passengers on domestic routes. Our ending case demonstrates collaborative motives among companies in the oneworld airline alliance.

Government procurement is another area that may encourage companies to collaborate, because preference is often given to bids that include national companies or evidence that the foreign company is transferring technology to a local company so that it becomes more internationally competitive in the future. For example, Taiwan does this with purchases by the state enterprise monopoly, Taiwan Power (Tai Power).[40]

Protecting Assets Many countries provide little de facto protection for intellectual property rights such as trademarks, patents, and copyrights unless authorities are prodded consistently. To prevent pirating of these proprietary assets, companies sometimes make collaborative agreements with local companies, which then monitor so that no one else uses the asset locally.

In addition, some countries provide protection only if the internationally registered asset is exploited locally within a specified period. If a company does not use the asset within the country during that time, then whatever entity first does so gains the right to it. Because Burger King did not use its name in time in the Australian market, another company now uses it there, and Burger King sells its fare in Hungry Jack restaurants.[41]

In other cases, local citizens, known as *trademark squatters*, register rights to the unused trademarks, then negotiate sales to the original owners when they do try to enter the market. One Russian company registered over 300 foreign trademarks, including Starbucks's trademark. Foreign companies then had to pay to regain their rights or go through lengthy court proceedings that could be even more expensive.[42]

To Diversify Geographically For a company wishing to pursue a geographic diversification strategy, collaborative arrangements offer a faster initial means of entering

Legal factors may be

- direct prohibitions against certain operating forms.
- indirect (e.g., regulations affecting profitability).

Case Review Note

Collaboration hinders nonassociated companies from pirating the asset.

multiple markets because other companies contribute resources. However, the arrangements will be less appealing for companies whose activities are already widely extended or for those that have ample resources for such extension.

To Minimize Risk Exposure   Companies worry that political or economic changes will affect the safety of assets and earnings in their foreign operations. One way to minimize loss from foreign political occurrences is to minimize the base of assets located abroad—or share them. A government may be less willing to move against a shared operation for fear of encountering opposition from multiple companies, especially if they are from different countries and can potentially elicit support from their home governments. Another way to spread risk is to place operations in a number of different countries, which firms may be unable to afford alone. This strategy reduces the chance that all foreign assets will encounter adversity at the same time.

Collaborative arrangements allow for greater spreading of assets among countries.

Types of Collaborative Arrangements

The forms of foreign operations differ in the amount of resources a company commits and the proportion of the resources located abroad. Licensing, for instance, may result in a lower additional capital commitment than a foreign joint venture will. Exporting commits fewer resources abroad than does FDI.

The higher managers perceive the risk to be in a foreign market, the greater their desire to form collaborative arrangements in that market.

Throughout this discussion, keep in mind that there are *trade-offs*. A decision, let's say, to take no ownership in foreign production, such as by licensing to a foreign company, may reduce exposure to political risk. However, learning about that environment will be slow, delaying (perhaps permanently) the ability to reap the full profits from producing and selling the product abroad.

Furthermore, when a company has a desired, unique, difficult-to-duplicate resource, it is in a good position to choose the operating form it would most like to use. When it lacks this bargaining strength, competition or governmental actions may force it to settle on a form that is lower on its priority list.

Companies have a wider choice of operating form when there is less likelihood of competition.

A further constraint is finding a desirable collaboration partner. For example, if the collaboration includes a transfer of technology, it may be impossible to find a local company familiar enough with the technology or having sufficiently similar values and priorities as the company making the transfer.[43] In effect, costs are associated with transferring technology to another entity, which include the time spent in cooperating to ensure that partners are trustworthy and cognizant of technologies and that they agree on objectives and means of implementing practices.[44]

SOME CONSIDERATIONS IN COLLABORATIVE ARRANGEMENTS

Two factors influence managers' choice of arrangement type: their desire for control over foreign operations and their companies' prior foreign expansion.

Control   The more a company depends on collaboration, the more likely it is to lose decision-making control, such as on quality, new-product directions, and expansion. This is because each partner favors its own performance over that of the company network involved, which necessitates compromises.

Internal handling of foreign operations usually means more control and no sharing of profits.

Collaboration also implies sharing revenues and knowledge—an important consideration when profit potentials are high and when information sharing might increase potential competition. Thus, loss of control over flexibility, revenues, and competition is an important consideration guiding a company's selection of the type of foreign operation.

Prior Company Expansion   When a company already has operations (especially wholly owned ones) in place in a foreign country, some of the advantages of collaboration are no

Should Countries Limit Foreign Control of Key Industries?

Point **Yes** I believe they should, because a *key industry* affects a very large segment of the economy by virtue of its size or influence on other sectors. Thus, I'm talking neither about foreign control of small investments nor about noncontrolling interest in large investments. If countries need foreign firms' resources—technology, capital, export markets, branded products, and so on—they can get them through collaborations without ceding control to foreigners. In turn, the foreign companies can still achieve their objectives, such as gaining access to markets.

Of course, each country should—and does—determine for itself what a key industry is. Mexico limits foreign control in its oil industry because it is such a dominant part of the Mexican economy. The United States is primarily concerned about security, so the president can halt any foreign investment that endangers national security.

The United States also prohibits foreign control of television and radio stations, because they could be used as foreign propaganda instruments. It protects domestic transportation, a vital sector for national security, by prohibiting foreign control of domestic airlines and by preventing foreign airlines and ships from transporting passengers and cargo directly from one U.S. city to another.

The rationale for protecting key industries is supported by history, which shows that home governments have used powerful foreign companies to influence policies in the countries where they operate. During colonial periods, firms such as Levant and the British East India Company often acted as the political arm of their home governments.

More recently, governments, especially the United States, have pressured their companies to leave certain areas (e.g., Libya, Nicaragua), not to pay taxes to a regime (Angola, Panama), and to prohibit their subsidiaries from doing business with certain countries (Cuba, North Korea), even though the prohibition is counter to the interests of the countries where the subsidiaries were located.

At the same time, some companies are so powerful that they can influence their home-country governments to intercede on their behalf. Probably the most notorious example was United Fruit Company (UFC) in so-called banana republics, which persuaded the United States to overthrow governments to protect its investments. Miguel Angel Asturias, a Nobel laureate in literature, referred to UFC's head as the "Green Pope" who "lifts a finger and a ship starts or stops. He says a word and a republic is bought. He sneezes and a president...falls....He rubs his behind on a chair and a revolution breaks out."[45]

Whenever a company is controlled from abroad, its decisions can be made there. Such control means that corporate management abroad can decide such factors as personnel staffing, export prices, and the retention and payout of profits. These decisions might cause different rates of expansion in different countries as well as possible plant closings, sometimes with subsequent employment disruption.

Finally, by withholding resources or allowing strikes, MNEs may affect other local industries adversely. In essence, the MNE looks after its global interests, which may not coincide with what is best for an operation in a given country.

Should Countries Limit Foreign Control of Key Industries?

Counterpoint **No** The passionate arguments against foreign control of key industries don't convince me that such control leads to corporate decisions that are any different from what local companies would make. Nor do they convince me that limits on foreign ownership are in the best interests of people in host countries.

Certainly, companies make strategic global decisions at headquarters, but typically they depend on a good deal of local advice beforehand. Further, MNEs staff their foreign subsidiaries mainly with nationals of the countries where they operate, and these nationals make most routine decisions.

Regardless of the decision makers' or companies' nationalities, managers decide based on what they think is best for their firms' business, rather than based on some

home-country or local socioeconomic agenda. At the same time, their decisions have to adhere to local laws and consider the views of their local stakeholders. Of course, MNEs sometimes make locally unpopular decisions, but so do local companies. In the meantime, governments can and do enact laws that apply to both local and international companies, and these laws can ensure that companies act in the so-called local interest.

Although preventing foreign control of key industries may be well intentioned, the resultant local control may lead to the protection of inefficient performance. Further, the key-industry argument appeals to emotions rather than reason. That's why the arguments in the United States for security make little sense on close examination. Although foreign propaganda through foreign ownership of radio and television stations is the rationale for ownership restrictions, there are no such restrictions on foreign ownership of U.S. newspapers. (Is this because people who read the news are presumed to be less swayed by propaganda?) In fact, Thompson (Canadian) owns many U.S. newspapers.

The protection of U.S. domestic transportation for security reasons is a sham, just to protect the shipbuilding industry and maritime employees. For instance, U.S. merchant flagships must employ only U.S. citizens as crews because of the vulnerability to bombs on ships in U.S. waters, but foreign flag carriers regularly use U.S. ports, and foreigners can join the U.S. Navy.

The banana-republic arguments are outdated and go back to *dependencia* **theory**, which holds that emerging economies have practically no power in their dealings with MNEs.[46] More recent *bargaining school* **theory** states that

the terms of a foreign investor's operations depend on how much the investor and host country need each other.[47] In effect, companies need countries because of their markets and resources, while countries need MNEs because of their technology, capital, access to foreign markets, and expertise. Through a bargaining process, they come to an agreement or contract that stipulates what the MNE can and cannot do.

I completely disagree that either countries or companies can necessarily gain the same through collaborative agreements as through FDI. Although collaborative agreements are often preferable, there are company and country advantages from foreign-controlled operations. For example, with wholly owned operations, companies are less concerned about developing competitors, thus they are more willing to transfer essential and valuable technology abroad.

longer as important. It knows how to operate within that country and may have excess plant or human resource capacity it can use for new production or sales.

However, much depends on the compatibility between existing foreign operations and the new ones the company is planning abroad. If there is similarity, as with production of a new type of office equipment already made there, the new production will likely be handled internally. If product, function, or location is dissimilar, collaborating with an experienced company may be more advantageous.

LICENSING

| Licensing agreements may be
| • exclusive or nonexclusive.
| • used for patents, copyrights, trademarks, and other intangible property.

Under a licensing agreement, a company (the licensor) grants intangible property rights to another company (the licensee) to use in a specified geographic area for a specified period. In exchange, the licensee ordinarily pays a royalty to the licensor. The rights may be for an *exclusive license* (the licensor can give rights to no other company for the specified geographic area for a specified period of time) or a nonexclusive one.

The U.S. Internal Revenue Service classifies intangible property into five categories:

1. Patents, inventions, formulas, processes, designs, patterns
2. Copyrights for literary, musical, or artistic compositions
3. Trademarks, trade names, brand names
4. Franchises, licenses, contracts
5. Methods, programs, procedures, systems

Usually, the licensor is obliged to furnish sufficient information and assistance, and the licensee is obliged to exploit the rights effectively and pay compensation to the licensor.

| Licensing often has an economic motive, such as the desire for faster start-up, lower costs, or access to additional resources.

Major Motives for Licensing   Frequently, a new product or process may affect only part of a company's total output, and then only for a limited time. In such a situation, the company may foresee insufficient sales volume to warrant establishing its own foreign manufacturing and sales facilities. Meanwhile, it may find a licensee that can produce and sell at a low cost and within a short start-up time. In turn, the licensee's cost may be less than if it developed the new product or process on its own.

For industries in which technological changes are frequent and affect many products, companies in various countries often exchange technology or other intangible property rather than compete with each other on every product in every market—an arrangement known as **cross-licensing.** An example is Kodak (U.S.) and NEC Technology (Japan) entering a cross-licensing agreement for access to each other's patent portfolio.[48]

Payment Considerations   The amount and type of payment for licensing arrangements vary, as each contract is negotiated on its own merits. For instance, the value to the licensee will be greater if potential sales are high. Potential sales depend, in turn, on such factors as the geographic scope of the sales territory, the length of time the asset will have market value, and the market experience of using the asset elsewhere.

Putting a Price on Technology and Knowledge   Valuing partners' contributions and rewards is complex and always subject to negotiation, as shown humorously in Figure 14.4. Companies commonly negotiate a "front-end" payment to cover technology transfer costs. Licensors of technology do this because there is usually more involved than simply transferring *explicit* knowledge, such as through publications and reports. The move requires the transfer of *tacit* knowledge, such as through engineering, consultation, and adaptation. The licensee usually bears the incurred transfer costs so that the licensor is motivated to ensure a smooth adaptation. Of course, the license of some assets, such as copyrights or brand names, has much lower transfer costs.

Technology may be old or new, obsolete or still in use at home when a company licenses it. Many companies transfer technology at an early or even a developmental stage so products hit different markets simultaneously. This is important when selling to the same industrial customers in different countries and when global advertising campaigns can be effective. On one hand, a licensee may be willing to pay more for a new technology because it may have a longer useful life. On the other hand, a licensee may be willing to pay less for a newer technology, particularly one in the development phase, because of its uncertain market value.

Selling to Subsidiaries   Although we think of licensing agreements as collaborative arrangements among unassociated companies, licensing is also common between parents and their foreign subsidiaries. One reason is that operations in a foreign country, even if 100 percent owned by the parent, are usually subsidiaries, which are legally separate companies. When a company owns less than 100 percent, a separate licensing arrangement may

"*As you know, Ed, my pockets are considerably deeper than yours. Therefore, in addition to my share I'll be needing a percentage of yours.*"

FIGURE 14.4   Negotiations on the terms for responsibilities and remuneration within collaboratve arrangements may be long and complex, with each party seeking to maximize its position. However, unless the objectives of all partners are achieved, the alliance is likely to fail.

Source: Jack Ziegler/Cartoonbank.com

be a means of compensating the licensor for contributions beyond the mere investment in capital and managerial resources. (We noted in our opening case, for example, that Danone licensed its brand names to the joint venture that it established with Coca-Cola.)

FRANCHISING

| Franchising includes providing an intangible asset (usually a trademark) and continually infusing necessary assets.

Franchising is a specialized form of licensing in which the franchisor not only grants a franchisee the use of the intangible property (usually a trademark), but also operationally assists the business on a continuing basis, such as through sales promotion and training. In many cases, the franchisor provides supplies, such as the concentrate Coca-Cola sells to its bottlers. In a sense, the two parties act almost like a vertically integrated company, because they are interdependent and each creates part of the product or service that ultimately reaches the consumer.

| Many types of products and many countries participate in franchising.

Today, franchising is mostly associated with U.S. fast-food operations, although many international franchisors are from other countries and in many other sectors. A Danish company, Cryos International, even franchises sperm banks in about 40 countries. It initially supplied the frozen sperm from donors in Denmark, but it now uses local donors, such as in India.[49]

Franchisors once depended on trade shows a few times a year and costly visits to foreign countries to promote their expansion. While such trade shows are still important, especially for young franchising operations that are not well known, the Internet allows companies to send and receive e-mailed information around the clock, seven days a week.

Franchise Organization A franchisor may penetrate a foreign country by dealing directly with individual franchisees or by setting up a *master franchise* and giving that organization the rights to open outlets on its own or develop subfranchisees in the country or region. In the latter case, subfranchisees pay royalties to the master franchisee, which then remits some predetermined percentage to the franchisor. Coke handles most of its bottling franchising this way. Companies are most apt to use a master franchise system when they are not confident about evaluating potential individual franchisees and when overseeing and controlling them directly would be expensive.[50]

If the franchisor is not well known to many local people, or if local people are unsure about its market commitment, convincing them to make investments may be difficult. In effect, people are usually willing to invest only in known franchises, because the name is a guarantee of quality that can attract customers. Therefore, lesser-known franchisors commonly enter foreign markets with some company-owned outlets that serve as a showcase to attract franchisees.

Operational Modifications Finding suppliers can add difficulties and expense for food franchisors. McDonald's, for instance, had to build a plant to make hamburger buns in the United Kingdom, while in Thailand it had to help farmers develop potato production.[51]

| Franchisors face a dilemma:
| • The more global standardization, the less acceptance in the foreign country.
| • The more adjustment to the foreign country, the less the franchisor is needed.

Franchisors' success generally depends on three factors: product and service standardization, high identification through promotion, and effective cost controls. A dilemma when operating abroad is that the first of these may be difficult to transfer. In food franchising, for example, standardization is important so that consumers know what to expect. But when a company enters a foreign country, taste preferences may differ—even within regions of large countries. In response to such differences in China, Yum! Brands offers regionally different food in its KFC and Pizza Hut outlets.[52]

At the same time, the more adjustments made for the host consumers' different tastes, the less a franchisor has to offer a potential franchisee. U.S. food franchisors' success in Japan is mostly due to Japan's enthusiastic assimilation of Western products. Even so, food franchisors have had to make adjustments there as well. Pizza Hut has squid, oysters, and duck breast as pizza toppings.[53]

MANAGEMENT CONTRACTS

In a foreign management contract, a company is paid a fee to transfer management personnel and administrative know-how abroad to assist a company. Contracts usually cover three to five years, and fixed fees or fees based on volume rather than profits are most common.

A company may pay for managerial assistance when it believes another organization can manage its operation more efficiently than it can. This ability is most apt to occur because of industry-specific capabilities. An illustration is the British Airport Authority (BAA), which has contracts to manage some airports in the United States, Italy, and Australia because it has developed successful airport management skills.[54]

With management contracts, the owners and host country get the assistance they want without foreign companies' control of the operations. In turn, the management company receives income without having to make a capital outlay. This pattern has been important in hotel operations where hotel chains have been shying away from property ownership abroad because of risk and where some host-country property owners know more about real estate than about managing a hotel. These were the motives for the Canadian-based Four Seasons Hotels and Resorts' management contract with Three C Universal Developers in India.[55]

> Foreign management contracts are used primarily when the foreign company can manage better than the owners.

TURNKEY OPERATIONS

Turnkey operations are a type of collaborative arrangement in which one company, usually an industrial-equipment manufacturer, a construction company, or a consulting firm, contracts with another to build complete, ready-to-operate facilities. Manufacturers also sometimes decide to construct facilities for others if they believe an investment on their own behalf is infeasible. The customer for a turnkey operation is often a governmental agency. Recently, most large projects have been in those developing countries that are moving rapidly toward infrastructure development and industrialization.

> Turnkey operations are
> - most commonly performed by industrial-equipment, construction, and consulting companies.
> - often performed for a governmental agency.

Contracting to Scale   One characteristic that sets the turnkey business apart from most other international business operations is the size of many of the contracts, frequently for hundreds of millions of dollars and into the billions. This means that a few very large companies—such as Bechtel (U.S.), Fluor (U.S.), Skanska (Sweden), and Hochtief (Germany)—account for a significant share of the international market. Often, smaller firms either serve as subcontractors for primary turnkey suppliers or specialize in a particular sector, such as the handling of hazardous waste. The following photos illustrate both the existing Panama Canal and a current large turnkey project, the building of an additional and wider Panama Canal channel, to accommodate larger ships that now must go around South America for routes between the Atlantic and Pacific Oceans. This project is being handled by a consortium of turnkey operators, led by Spain's Sacyr Vallehermoso.

Making Contacts   The nature of these contracts places importance on hiring executives with top-level governmental contacts abroad, as well as on ceremony and building goodwill, such as opening a facility on a country's independence day or getting a head of state to inaugurate a facility. Although public relations is important to gaining turnkey contracts, other factors—price, export financing, managerial and technological quality, experience, reputation, and so on—are necessary to sell contracts of such magnitude.

Marshaling Resources   Many turnkey contracts are for construction in remote areas, necessitating massive housing construction and importation of personnel. Projects may involve building an entire infrastructure under the most adverse conditions, such as Bechtel's complex for Minera Escondida, which is high in the Andes. So, turnkey operators must have expertise in hiring people willing to work in remote areas for extended periods and in transporting and using supplies under very adverse conditions.

▲The first photo shows ships passing through the Panama Canal. Note there are two channels, thus ships can pass simultaneously in both directions. The second photo shows currect construction by a consortium of turnkey operations, led by Spain's Sacyr Vallehermoso SA, that will increase capacity and allow larger ships to pass through instead of having to sail around South America.

If a company holds a monopoly on certain assets or resources, such as the latest refining technology, other companies will find difficulty in competing to secure a turnkey contract. As the production process becomes known, however, the number of competitors for such contracts increases. Companies from developed countries have moved largely toward projects involving high technology, whereas those from such countries as China, India, Korea, and Turkey can compete better for conventional projects requiring low labor costs. For example, the Chinese companies China State Construction Engineering and Shanghai Construction Group have worked on a subway system in Iran, a railway line in Nigeria, an oil pipeline in Sudan, and office buildings in the United States.

Arranging Payment   Payment for a turnkey operation usually occurs in stages as a project develops, with final payment once the facility is operating in accordance with the contract. Because currency fluctuations can occur during the long time frame between conception and completion, contracts commonly include price escalation clauses or cost-plus pricing.

Because the final payment is usually made only if the facility is operating satisfactorily, disagreements sometimes arise on what constitutes "satisfactorily." For this reason, many turnkey operators insist on performing a feasibility study as part of the contract so they don't build something that, although desired by a local government, may be too large or inefficient.

JOINT VENTURES

Joint ventures may have various combinations of participants and ownership.

A type of operational sharing popular among MNEs is the joint venture (JV). While they are sometimes non-equity arrangements, they usually involve equity ownership by more than one organization. We emphasize this latter type in our discussion. Although joint ventures are usually formed to achieve particular objectives, they may continue to operate indefinitely as objectives are redefined. Thought of as 50/50 companies, JVs may nonetheless involve more than two companies, one of which may own more than 50 percent. For instance, Global Alumina, a joint venture in Guinea for bauxite extraction and processing has four partners—two from Dubai and one each from Australia and Canada.[56] When more than two organizations participate, the venture is sometimes called a **consortium.**

Possible Combinations   An international joint venture may contain any combination of partners, as long as at least one partner is foreign. Examples include:

- Two companies from the same country joining together in a foreign market, e.g., NEC and Mitsubishi (Japan) in the United Kingdom
- A foreign company joining with a local company, e.g., Great Lakes Chemical (U.S.) and A. H. Al Zamil in Saudi Arabia
- Companies from two or more countries establishing a joint venture in a third country, e.g., Tata Motors (India) and Fiat (Italy) in Argentina
- A private company and a local government forming a joint venture, or *mixed venture*, e.g., that of Gazprom (Russia) with the Bulgarian government
- A private company joining a government-owned company in a third country, e.g., BP Amoco (private British-U.S.) and Eni (government-owned Italian) in Egypt

The more companies in the joint venture, the more complex its management becomes. Development of the long-delayed Boeing 787 (the Dreamliner) is a joint effort among numerous companies from eight countries.[57] In essence, the project is hard to control, and a delay by any one of the participating companies delays the others. Figure 14.5 shows that as a company increases the number of partners and decreases the amount of equity it owns in a foreign operation, its ability to control that operation decreases.

Certain types of companies favor joint ventures more than others, such as those new at foreign operations or having decentralized domestic decision making. Because they are accustomed to extending control downward in their organizations, it is easier for them to do the same thing in a joint venture.

EQUITY ALLIANCES

An **equity alliance** is a collaborative arrangement in which at least one of the companies takes an ownership position (almost always minority) in the other(s). Recall from our opening case that Coke maintains significant ownership positions in most master franchise bottlers that account for a significant part of its foreign sales. In some cases, each party takes an ownership, such as by buying part of each other's shares or by swapping some shares with each other. Panama-based Copa and Colombia-based AeroRepublic (airlines) took equity in each other.[58]

Equity alliances help solidify collaboration.

Case Review Note

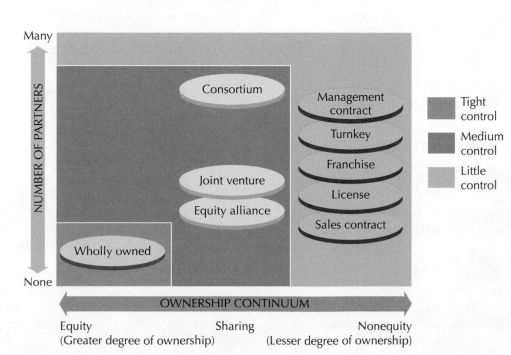

FIGURE 14.5
Collaborative Strategy and Complexity of Control

The more equity a firm puts into a collaborative arrangement, coupled with the fewer partners it takes on, the more control it will have over the foreign operations conducted under the arrangement. Note that nonequity arrangements typically entail at least one and often several partners.

Source: Adapted from Shaker Zahra and Galal Elhagrasey, "Strategic Management of International Joint Ventures," *European Management Journal* 12:1 (March 1994): 83–93. Reprinted with permission of Elsevier.

The purpose of the equity ownership is to solidify a collaborating contract, such as a supplier-buyer contract, so that it is more difficult to break—particularly if the ownership is large enough to secure a board membership for the investing company.

Problems with Collaborative Arrangements

Keep in mind that all parties to a collaborative arrangement must be satisfied with performance. Otherwise, the arrangement may fail. Problems can develop that lead partners to renegotiate in terms of responsibilities, ownership, or management structure. Despite new relationships, many agreements break down or are not renewed at the end of an initial contract period, often because at least one partner becomes dissatisfied with the venture. Frequently, a partner buys out the other's interest and the operation continues as a wholly owned foreign subsidiary. In other breakups, companies agree to dissolve the arrangement or they restructure their alliance.

Figure 14.6 shows that joint venture divorce (and divorce from other collaborative arrangements) can be planned or unplanned, friendly or unfriendly, mutual or nonmutual. The major strains on the arrangements are due to five factors:

- Relative importance to partners
- Divergent objectives
- Control problems
- Comparative contributions and appropriations
- Differences in culture[59]

In spite of our focus on these problems, we do not mean to imply that there are no success stories. There are. The joint venture between Xerox (U.S.) and Rank (U.K.) is a case in point: not only has it performed well for a long period of time, it even has a joint venture in Japan with Fuji Photo, which has also performed well.

FIGURE 14.6   How to Dissolve a Joint Venture

There's more than one way to dissolve a joint venture—and to influence the future of its erstwhile operations.

Source: Adapted from Manuel G. Serapio Jr. and Wayne F. Cascio, "End Games in International Alliances," *Academy of Management Executive* (May 1996): 67.

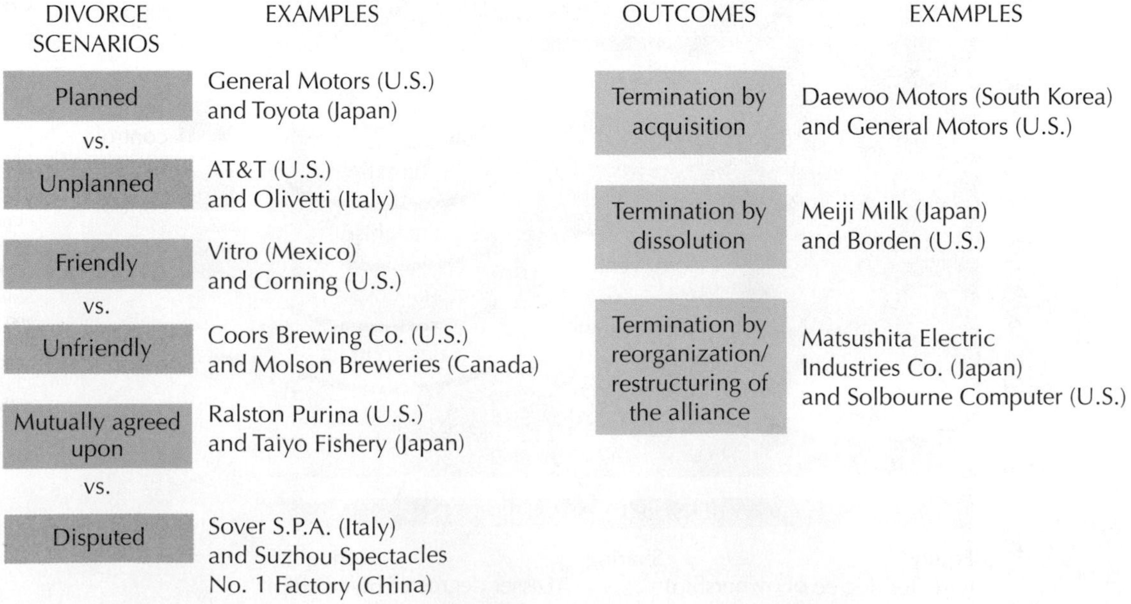

DIVORCE SCENARIOS	EXAMPLES	OUTCOMES	EXAMPLES
Planned	General Motors (U.S.) and Toyota (Japan)	Termination by acquisition	Daewoo Motors (South Korea) and General Motors (U.S.)
vs.			
Unplanned	AT&T (U.S.) and Olivetti (Italy)	Termination by dissolution	Meiji Milk (Japan) and Borden (U.S.)
Friendly	Vitro (Mexico) and Corning (U.S.)		
vs.		Termination by reorganization/ restructuring of the alliance	Matsushita Electric Industries Co. (Japan) and Solbourne Computer (U.S.)
Unfriendly	Coors Brewing Co. (U.S.) and Molson Breweries (Canada)		
Mutually agreed upon	Ralston Purina (U.S.) and Taiyo Fishery (Japan)		
vs.			
Disputed	Sover S.P.A. (Italy) and Suzhou Spectacles No. 1 Factory (China)		

RELATIVE IMPORTANCE

One partner may give more management attention than the other to a collaborative arrangement. If things go wrong, the active partner blames the less active partner for its lack of attention, while the latter blames the former for making poor decisions. The difference in attention may be due to the partners' different sizes. For example, a JV between a large and a small company comprises a larger portion of operations for the small company than for the large one, so the small company may take more interest in the venture.

In addition, if disagreements need to be settled legally, the smaller firm may be at a disadvantage because it lacks the resources to fight its bigger partner. After Igen, a small U.S. firm, licensed its technology to Boehringer Mannheim of Germany, a company with sales of more than 100 times those of Igen, the two companies began to disagree over royalty payments. Igen fought for four years and spent $40 million in legal fees (about the amount of one year of its sales) to win a settlement of over a half billion dollars.[60] This example is unusual, however, because most small firms cannot or will not fight a larger company so effectively.

DIVERGENT OBJECTIVES

Although companies enter into collaborative arrangements because they have complementary goals and capabilities, these may evolve differently over time. One partner may want to reinvest earnings for growth while the other wants to receive dividends. Or one partner may want to expand the product line and sales territory while the other may see this as competition with its wholly owned operations (a point of disagreement between BP and its Russian partner, TNK.)[61] If one partner wants to sell or buy from the venture, the other may disagree with the price.

Partners also may differ over performance standards. In GM's joint venture in Thailand with Fuji Heavy Industries, the companies' disagreements over quality have led to both of them performing inspections, which is time-consuming and expensive. They've even argued over standards for paint jobs.[62]

QUESTIONS OF CONTROL

Sharing assets with another company may generate confusion over control, as happened when the Israeli company Remedia partnered with the German firm Humana Milchunion to make baby formula. Humana Milchunion removed Vitamin B1 from the formula concentrate without notifying its partners, which led to the deaths of three infants.[63] Moreover, when companies license their logos and trademarks for use on products they do not produce, they may lack the ability to discern and control quality, with a detrimental effect on sales of all products in various countries using the brand name and logo. Pierre Cardin's licensing of its label for hundreds of products—from clothing to clocks to toilets—led to poor-quality goods that hurt the image of the high-quality ones.[64]

In collaborative arrangements, even though control is ceded to one of the partners, both may be held responsible for problems. Further, the question of control is rife with gray areas and may cause anxiety among employees. In a proposed joint venture between Merrill Lynch and UFJ, a Japanese senior manager queried, "Who is going to be in charge—a Japanese, an American, or both?"[65] When no single company has control of a collaborative arrangement, the operation may lack direction. At the same time, if one partner dominates, it must still consider the other's interests.

COMPARATIVE CONTRIBUTIONS AND APPROPRIATIONS

Partners' relative capabilities of contributing technology, capital, or some other asset may change over time. Relative contributions may also change when partners alter their strategy. In addition, Partner A may suspect that Partner B is taking more from the operation (particularly knowledge-based assets) than Partner A is, which would enable Partner B to become a competitor. In the face of such suspicions, information may be withheld, eventually weakening the operation. There are many examples of companies "going it alone" after they no longer needed their partner—particularly if the purpose of the collaboration was to gain knowledge.

CULTURE CLASHES

Differences in Country Cultures   Managers and companies alike are affected by their national cultures, and collaborative arrangements bring them directly together. For instance, they may vary in preferences in the method, timing, and frequency they report on project management progress.[66] Further, there are national differences in whether they evaluate primarily on the operations' effect on shareholders versus stakeholders in general.[67] These differences may mean that one partner is satisfied while the other is not. Such a clash led to the dissolution of a joint venture between Danone and its Chinese government-owned partner because the latter put employment maximization ahead of efficiencies and profits.[68]

Finally, some companies don't like to collaborate with those of very different cultures. Nevertheless, joint ventures from culturally distant countries can thrive as partners learn to deal with each other's differences.[69]

Differences in Corporate Cultures   Similar corporate cultures aid companies' ability to communicate and transfer knowledge to each other, whereas collaborations can nevertheless experience problems when the corporate cultures differ.[70] One partner may be accustomed to internal managerial promotions while the other opens its searches to outsiders. One may use a participatory management style and the other an authoritarian style. One may be entrepreneurial, the other risk-averse. This is why many companies that develop joint ventures collaborate only after they have had long-term positive experiences with each other, such as through distributorship or licensing arrangements. In fact, there is evidence that a gradual increase in commitment, such as developing an alliance with a company before acquiring it, is a means of improving performance.[71] Of course, as with marriage, a good prior relationship between two companies does not guarantee a good match in a joint venture.[72]

Managing International Collaborations

If collaboration can achieve strategic objectives better than "going it alone," a company should give little consideration to taking on duties itself. However, as an arrangement evolves, partners need to reassess certain decisions. For example, changes in a company's resource base may render collaboration either more or less advantageous.

The external environment can also change. Perhaps a certain location becomes economically risky, or a host government forbids or eases foreign ownership in areas where firms would like to do future business. Because of such changes, a company needs to continually reexamine the fit between collaboration and its strategy, using various modes of operations simultaneously because of its own capabilities (including experience), the specific products involved, and the market characteristics.

We now discuss how companies change their operating forms, how they may find potential partners and negotiate with them, and how they need to assess the performance of collaborative arrangements.

> The evolution to a different operating mode may
> - be the result of experience.
> - necessitate costly termination fees.
> - create organizational tensions.

DYNAMICS OF COLLABORATIVE ARRANGEMENTS

Companies' capabilities may change over time and influence the form of operations undertaken. Collaboration may allow a company to learn from its partner, enabling it to

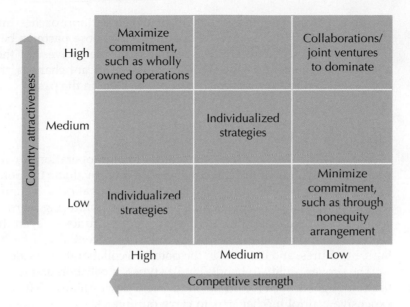

FIGURE 14.7   Country Attractiveness/Company Strength Matrix

In a given scenario, a country in the upper left-hand corner may be the most attractive place for a company to locate operations. Why? Because its market is well suited to the company's greatest competitive strength and thus to its highest level of commitment (e.g., establishing a wholly owned subsidiary). A country in the upper right-hand corner also boasts an attractive market but poses a problem for a company whose competitive strengths don't quite match the opportunity (perhaps it has no experience in this particular market). It needn't forgo the opportunity, but it will probably prefer a joint venture or some other form of collaborative operation. Finally, note that because everything is subject to change—both a company's capabilities and the features of a country's market—firms try to be dynamic in their approach to potential operating modes.

make a deeper commitment confidently. However, switching from one form to another, such as from licensing to wholly owned facilities, may incur contractual termination fees and other high costs.

Country Attractiveness and Operational Options   Figure 14.7 illustrates a type of matrix that relates country attractiveness with operating forms. A company should ordinarily make a higher level of commitment, such as wholly owned operations, in the countries that appear in the top left corner, which are very attractive and fit best with its capabilities.

Country attractiveness is also high in the top right corner, but a company has weak competitive strength for those markets if, say, it lacks the knowledge of operating therein. If the cost is not too high, the company might attempt to gain greater domination in those markets by partnering with another whose assets are complementary.

A company might divest in countries in the bottom right corner or "harvest" by pulling out all possible cash it can generate while not replacing depreciated facilities. It could also engage in nonequity arrangements, thereby generating some income without the need for investment outlays. In other areas, it must analyze situations individually to decide which approach to take. These are marginal areas that do not fit as neatly in the analysis.

Although such a matrix may serve to guide decision making, managers must use it with caution. First, separating the attractiveness of a country from a company's position is often difficult; the country may seem attractive because it fits with the company. Second, some of the recommended actions take a defeatist attitude toward competitive position. Many companies have built competitive strength in markets previously dominated by competitors or built profitable positions without being the competitive leader.

Changing Conditions   Tension may develop internally as the form of international operations changes and individuals gain or lose responsibilities. For example, moving from exporting to foreign production may reduce the size of domestic marketing and manufacturing divisions. The people who then end up with less responsibility may be at a disadvantage if bonuses and promotions are based largely on the size of their sales or profits. Given that lower performance is due to decisions outside their control, companies should largely evaluate those things that personnel in different divisions can control.

Some evidence indicates that as companies gain experience by entering more collaborative arrangements, they perform better within them. However, improved performance is most associated with similar types of collaborations, such as joint ventures,

from one place to another and with management approaches that are similar in a series of alliances.[73] In essence, companies may choose partners better and learn how to improve synergies between their partners and themselves. At the same time, effective alliance management has been undergoing significant changes, thus companies cannot necessarily replicate what has succeeded for them in the past.[74]

FINDING COMPATIBLE PARTNERS

A company can seek out a partner for its foreign operations or react to a collaboration proposal from another firm. In either case, it must evaluate the potential partner not only for the resources it can supply but also for its motivation and compatibility.

Managers can identify potential partners by monitoring journals, attending technical conferences, developing links with academic institutions—even through social acquaintances.[75] Company visibility and partnership potential can be boosted through trade fairs, brochures, and contacts in the potential collaboration locale.

The proven ability to handle similar types of collaboration is a key professional qualification. A good track record may indicate trustworthiness that could negate the need for expensive control mechanisms to carry out interests. Once into a collaboration, partners can also build trust through actions.[76] But every company has to start somewhere. Without a proven track record, a firm may have to negotiate harder and make more concessions.

NEGOTIATING THE ARRANGEMENT

In technology agreements,

- a seller does not want to give information without assurance of payment.
- a buyer does not want to pay without evaluating information.

The value of many technologies would diminish if they were widely used or understood. Contracts historically have included provisions that the recipient will not divulge such information, while some sellers have held onto the ownership and production of specific components so recipients would not have full knowledge of the product or the capability to produce an exact copy. Often companies want to sell techniques they have not yet used commercially. A buyer is reluctant to buy what it has not seen, but a seller that shows the work in process to the potential buyer risks divulging the technology. For these and other reasons, it is common to set up pre-agreements that protect all parties.

A controversial negotiation area is the secrecy surrounding the financial terms of arrangements. In some countries, for example, licensing contracts must be approved by governmental agencies, which consult their counterparts in other countries about similar agreements in order to improve their negotiating position. Many MNEs object to this procedure, because they believe that contract terms between two companies are proprietary information with competitive importance, and market conditions usually dictate the need for very different terms in different countries.

Concept Check

In discussing "Behavioral Factors" with regard to international business in Chapter 2, we observe that there are substantial differences in the degrees of trust that people in different **cultures** extend to others. We go on to explain that when trust is high, managers tend to spend more time focusing on operational issues and less fussing over every little detail. Not surprisingly, the cost of doing business tends to be lower in this scenario.

DRAWING UP THE CONTRACT

Contracts with other companies cause some loss of control over the asset or intangible property being transferred. This creates a host of potential problems that must be settled as well as possible by setting mutual goals and spelling out all expectations in the contract. Of course, not everything can be included in a contract. The parties need to develop sufficient rapport so that common sense also plays a part in running the collaboration.[77] Partnering with a firm that highly values its reputation is probably a plus as well, inasmuch as it may prefer to settle differences quietly rather than having them exposed in the press. Frank communications may help determine potential partners' underlying expectations, which may otherwise come as a surprise. One study of local firms in China and Russia discovered that they had expected their foreign partners to deal much more with the Chinese and Russian governments (such as to alleviate bribery payments) than the foreign partners actually did.[78]

A Few Specific Issues Although contracts have limits, their provisions should at least address the following issues:

- Will the agreement be terminated if the parties don't adhere to the directives?
- What methods will be used to test for quality?
- What geographic limitations should be placed on an asset's use?
- Which company will manage which parts of the operation outlined in the agreement?
- What will be each company's future commitments?
- How will each company buy from, sell to, or otherwise use intangible assets that result from the collaborative arrangement?

In addition to contract terms, trust in the management of another company is an important consideration in choosing a partner. At the same time, trust is affected by national culture and, in turn, influences how much a partner wants to cover in a contract. Thus, if parties from cultures with similar levels of trust come together, they are more likely able to agree on what must be incorporated in detailed contractual arrangements and what must be left to trust.[79]

IMPROVING PERFORMANCE

When collaborating with another company, managers must

- Continue to monitor performance
- Assess whether to change the form of operations
- Develop competency in managing a portfolio of arrangements

Contracting with a capable and compatible partner is necessary but insufficient to ensure success. An agreement, once operational, must be run effectively. Management should estimate potential sales and costs, determine whether the arrangement is meeting quality standards, and assess servicing requirements to check whether goals are being met and whether each partner is doing an adequate job.

In addition to continually assessing partners' performance, a company also must periodically assess the need for change in the type of collaboration, such as whether to replace a licensing agreement with a joint venture. At the same time, as its number of collaborations grows, it should consider developing competency in managing the portfolio of arrangements so that it applies what it learns in one situation to others.[80]

Looking to the

Future Why Innovation Breeds Collaboration

More than a half century ago, John Kenneth Galbraith wrote that the era of cheap invention was over, noting that "because development is costly, it follows that it can be carried out only by a firm that has the resources associated with considerable size."[81] The statement seems prophetic in terms of the estimated billions of investment dollars needed to bring a new commercial aircraft to market, eliminate death from diseases, develop defenses against unfriendly countries and terrorists, guard against cyberspace intrusions, and commercialize energy substitutes for petroleum. However, it overlooks the ability of companies to pool resources through collaboration—and that such collaboration will likely continue to grow.

Markets must be truly global if high development costs are to be recouped. The sums needed to develop and market these new inventions are out of reach of most companies acting alone. Even if the companies become ever larger through internal growth or mergers and acquisitions, governments nevertheless place limits because of antitrust concerns.

(continued)

Moreover, with the realization that the costs of integrating a merged or acquired company can be very high, collaborative arrangements will likely become even more important in the future, involving both horizontal and vertical linkages among firms from many industries in many countries. However, some evidence indicates that collaborations slow the speed of innovation because of internalization and appropriation factors.[82] Thus, large companies that have the resources to go it alone may have advantages over small companies that do not.

Although some product development requires huge sums, most is much more modest. Nevertheless, companies lack all the product- and market-specific resources to go it alone everywhere in the world, especially if national differences dictate operating changes on a country-to-country basis. Such situations present opportunities for alliances that employ complementary resources from different companies.

Collaborative arrangements will bring both opportunities and problems as MNEs move simultaneously to new countries and to contractual arrangements with new companies. Differences must be overcome in a number of areas:

- Country cultures that may cause partners to obtain and evaluate information differently
- National disparities in governmental policies, institutions, and industry structures that constrain companies from using operating forms they would prefer
- Distinct underlying ideologies and values affecting corporate cultures and practices that strain relationships
- Different strategic directions resulting from partners' interests that cause disagreement over objectives and contributions
- Diverse management styles and organizational structures that cause partners to interact ineffectively[83]

The more partners in an alliance, the more cumbersome the decision-making and control processes. ■

CASE

Connecting within oneworld

Following 2010 approval by U.S. and Japanese authorities for antitrust immunity, American Airlines (AA) and Japan Airlines (JAL) began sharing routes in 2011 that connect mainland North America with East Asia through a nonequity joint venture.[84] Map 14.2 shows these routes and also illustrates that flights between Honolulu and Japan are not included in the agreement. This joint venture is similar to one forged among AA, British Airways, and Iberia for trans-Atlantic travel that began operating in 2010. In both cases, the agreements allow representatives from each airline to jointly manage capacity, sell and promote space on flights operated by each other, divide revenues, and schedule connecting flights. The major thrusts for these ventures are to cut operating costs by better controlling capacity, avoid disruptive price competition among them, and schedule so that there are more and better departure times and connections for passengers.

The proposals are merely extensions to a historical series of alliances linking international airlines. In fact, the airline industry is unique in that its need to form collaborative arrangements has been important almost from the start of international air travel because of regulatory, cost, and competitive factors. In recent years, this need has accelerated because of airlines' difficult profit performance.

In effect, the airlines have been squeezed. First, costs have been rising, particularly because of oil prices and the requirement for greater security since 9/11. For instance, the International Air Transport Association (IATA), which represents most global carriers, predicted a three-quarter decrease in profits from 2010 to 2011 because of crude oil prices. While pre-departure airport passenger-security checks are well publicized, some other costly airline security processes are not. These include, for example, providing governmental agencies with advance passenger information and working with freight forwarders and supply-chain operators to ensure the safety of cargo shipments carried on passenger aircraft. Second, there has been a long-term trend toward greater price competition, which hinders airlines' ability to pass on increased costs to passengers. This situation has

MAP 14.2 American Airlines and Japan Airlines: Trans-Pacific Routes

Note that the joint activity involves only flights from mainland North America into East Asia as of July 1, 2011. The Boston-Narita joint activity starts April 22, 2012.

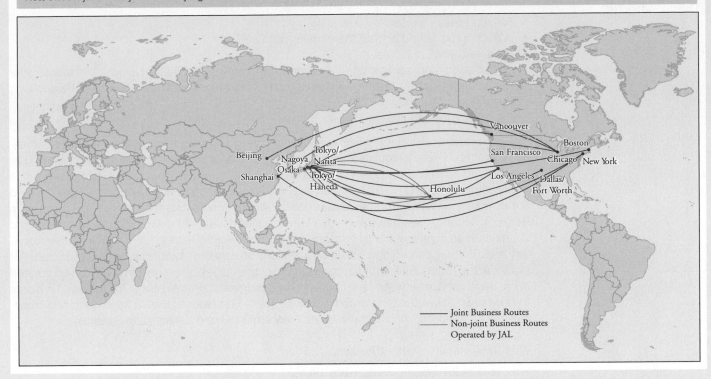

Joint Business Routes
Non-joint Business Routes
Operated by JAL

been exacerbated by the emergence of discount airlines and customers' ability to search the Internet for lower fares. Third, the global recession has affected passenger demand negatively, and the airline industry has responded by adding capacity sparingly. Fourth, the Japanese nuclear disaster along with North African and Middle Eastern political turmoil have softened air passage demand to these areas.

Although the growth in international passenger jet travel has been a major factor spurring globalization, no airline has sufficient finances or aircraft to serve the whole world. Yet passengers are traveling the whole world and perceive advantage in booking on airline connections that will minimize both distances and connecting times at airports, while offering them reasonable assurance of reaching their destinations with their checked bags more or less on schedule. Thus, airlines have increasingly worked together to provide more seamless experiences for passengers and to cut costs.

The above discussion, however, should not imply that all cost cuts necessitate collaboration. For example, in recent years, airlines have implemented a number of cost-saving changes that cover the gamut from passengers' ticket purchase to their arrival at destination. Online purchases of electronic tickets have largely replaced airlines' need to pay hefty commissions to travel agencies and to issue and maintain costly inventories of paper tickets. Self-service check-in at airports reduces the need for agents. On board, especially on short flights, less is included in the price of the ticket, such as food, pillows, and headphones. In fact, the trip may be on one of the airlines' discount subsidiaries.

A Bit of History: Changing Government Regulations

Historically, governments played a major role in airline ownership. Many government-owned airlines were monopolies within their domestic markets, money losers, and recipients of government subsidies. However, there has been a subsequent move toward privatization.

What Governments Can Regulate

Despite the move toward privatization, governments still regulate airlines and agree on restrictions and rights largely through reciprocal agreements. Specifically, they control:

- Which foreign carriers have landing rights.
- Which airports and aircraft the carriers can use.
- The frequency of flights.
- Whether foreign carriers can fly beyond the country—for instance, whether Iberia, after flying from Spain to the United States, can then fly from the United States to Panama.
- Overflight privileges.
- Fares airlines can charge.

There have been several notable regulatory changes in recent years. First, the U.S. domestic market has been deregulated, which means that any approved U.S. carrier can fly any U.S. domestic route in any frequency while charging what the market will bear. Once deregulation was instituted, many U.S. airlines (such as Braniff, Eastern, and TWA) were competitively forced out of business. Within Europe, similar deregulation helped cause the demise of Sabena from Belgium. Second, there have been several open-skies agreements, which permit any airline from countries in an agreement to fly from any city in one signatory area to any city in the other signatory area. Further, these flights have no restrictions on capacity, frequency, or type of aircraft. For instance, the United States and Japan signed an open-skies agreement in 2010, which spurred AA to begin service between New York and Haneda International Airport in Tokyo, which is closer to downtown Tokyo than the airport at Narita. Third, European countries have permitted cross-national acquisitions, such as those by Air France of KLM and Lufthansa of Swissair.

Why Governments Protect Airlines

Four factors influence governments' protection of their airlines:

1. Countries believe they can save money by maintaining small air forces and relying on domestic airlines in times of unusual air transport needs. For example, the U.S. government used U.S. commercial carriers to help carry troops to and from Iraq.

2. Public opinion favors spending "at home"—especially for government-paid travel. The public sees the maintenance of national airlines and the requirement that government employees fly on those airlines as foreign-exchange savings.

3. Airlines are a source of national pride, and aircraft (sporting their national flags) symbolize a country's sovereignty and technical competence. This national identification is less important than it used to be, but it is still important in some developing countries.

4. Countries have worried about protecting their airspace for security reasons. This is less of a concern today, because foreign carriers routinely overfly a country's territory to reach inland gateways, such as JAL's flights between Tokyo and Chicago. Further, overflight treaties are quite common, even among unfriendly nations. For example, Cubana overflies the United States en route to Canada, and AA overflies Cuba en route to South America.

Regulatory Obstacles to Expansion

Even if airlines had the financial capacity to expand everywhere in the world, national regulations would limit this expansion. With few exceptions, airlines cannot fly on lucrative domestic routes in foreign countries. For example, JAL cannot compete on the New York to Los Angeles route, nor can AA fly between Tokyo and Nagoya. Further, the U.S. government limits foreign ownership in a U.S. airline to 25 percent of voting stock.

Thus, airlines cannot easily control a flight network abroad that will feed passengers into their international flights. For example, JAL has no U.S. domestic flights to take passengers into Chicago for connections to Tokyo, but AA has scores of such flights. However, JAL has an advantage within Japan.

Finally, airlines usually cannot service pairs of foreign countries. AA cannot fly between Brazil and South Africa, because the Brazilian and South African governments give landing rights on these routes only to Brazilian and South African airlines. To avoid these restrictions, airlines must ally themselves with carriers from other countries.

Collaboration Examples Related to Motives

Cost Factors

Certain airlines have always dominated certain international airports. They have amassed critical capabilities in those airports, such as baggage handlers and aircraft-handling equipment. Sharing these capabilities with other airlines may spread costs. For example, BA has long handled passenger check-in, baggage loading, and maintenance for a number of other airlines in London's Heathrow Airport.

The high cost of maintenance and reservations systems has led to joint ventures involving multiple airlines from multiple countries, such as ownership in the Apollo and Galileo reservation systems. Actually, the reservations systems are motivated by more than cost savings, inasmuch as the pooling of resources allows customers to get better service.

Connecting Flights

Given that governments restrict domestic or regional routes to their own carriers, airlines have long had agreements whereby passengers can transfer from one airline to another with a through ticket. However, there is a tendency for people to select from among the first routings that show up on computer screens, and routings from one airline to another often appear on screens after those involving only one airline. Further, when passengers see that they must change airlines, they worry more about making those connections across great distances within ever-larger airports. To help avoid this worry, airlines have agreed to code sharing—a procedure whereby the same flight may have a designation for more than one carrier. For instance, the same flight operated by BA from New York-JFK to London Heathrow is listed as AA 6143, BA 178, and Iberia 4618. Hence, AA passengers originating in, say Tampa, and connecting at JFK to Heathrow, may worry less about the JFK connection because they see themselves on the same airline all the way. However, these passengers may still need to go from one terminal to another to make the plane-change. In such a situation, airlines must adhere to a longer minimum connecting time when showing a through/connecting flight.

The oneworld Alliance

The oneworld Alliance comprises 12 airlines (AA, BA, Cathay Pacific, Finnair, Iberia, JAL, LAN, Malév, Mexicana, Qantas, Royal Jordanian, and S7). The picture on page 550 shows the tail fins of these 12 airlines in alphabetical order going from the right to the left. Three other airlines (Air Berlin, Kingfisher, and Malaysian Airlines) are in process of becoming members. oneworld competes largely with two other alliances, Star and SkyTeam. Airlines in these alliances cooperate on various programs, such as allowing passengers to earn credits for free or upgraded travel on any one of them. In the case of oneworld, all members flying into Narita Airport in Tokyo have moved into terminal 2, which shortens legal connecting times among them. They also advertise their affiliation, and you may have seen aircraft painted with the airline's name and logo along with the oneworld name. These alliances allow for considerable cooperation, such as code-sharing; however, antitrust regulations prohibit their members from coordinating routes, schedules, and prices. Thus, anti-trust immunity allows the advantage of performing this coordination.

The Trans-Atlantic Joint Venture

The three airlines—AA, BA, and Iberia—have a combined network of over 400 destinations in over 100 countries and account for more than 6,000 daily departures. When their joint venture and anti-trust immunity were approved, they had collectively 48 different routes

The photo shows the tailfins of 12 oneworld member airlines as of July 1, 2011. However, Mexicana (fourth from left) was not operating at the time because of bankruptcy proceedings. Three other airlines will soon be added to the list.

Source: Courtesy oneworld

between Europe and North America that included 22 North American and 13 European cities. Of these 48 routes, they competed directly on only nine.

In the short time since the airlines entered this joint venture, they have been able to co-ordinate schedules better for the convenience of passengers. For instance, AA and BA used to have flights leaving between New York-JKF and London-Heathrow within minutes of each other. They now operate 16 flights per day between those two airports and have been able to coordinate departure times so that the flights leave approximately one hour apart. This gives passengers more options in finding a departure time convenient to them, and it allows for more connecting flight alternatives in either direction. Further, the participating airlines can now designate their own flight numbers on domestic connections when they connect to trans-Atlantic destinations. For instance, Iberia shows one of its routes as San Diego to Madrid, even though both the San Diego–Chicago and Chicago–Madrid flights are operated by AA.

Because of dual or multiple designations and the sharing of revenue, more than one airline's sales force is trying to fill seats on the same route. The result is boosted sales, which allows the joint venture members to offer new routes, such as non-stop service between Chicago and Helsinki and between New York and Budapest that have come about since the joint venture's formation.

The AA–JAL Joint Venture

JAL is also a large airline, serving 85 cities in 20 countries and territories. Its joint venture with AA has the same advantages and objectives as the joint venture across the Atlantic. Although at this writing, it is still in a fledgling stage, some changes are already quite notable. By altering each company's flight times between Chicago O'Hare and Tokyo Narita and tweaking schedules of connecting flights in both cities, many more passengers can make connections within two hours. For instance, 22 more flights from 20 more departure cities can make such connections for travel from O'Hare to Narita.

JAL has moved its Chicago O'Hare flights from the international terminal to be adjacent to AA. Meanwhile, AA has moved its Japanese offices to JAL's headquarters building, a move that will ease communications between the two airlines. For example, the two airlines are helping each other with cultural questions such as JAL's help with AA's public address announcements in Japanese to make them more meaningful to Japanese passengers.

Meanwhile, plans are afoot for greatly increasing code sharing between the two airlines, especially to points beyond gateway cities, such as showing a JAL flight as Tokyo–Salt Lake City and as an AA flight beyond Tokyo to JAL-served cities such as Hanoi.

Why Not a Merger or an Acquisition?

To begin with, governmental regulations, such as the ownership requirements we have discussed, would prevent a merger or acquisition. However, even if they did not, there are daunting problems in fusing companies together, especially airlines from different countries. For example, the respective pilots' unions are strong and operate under different operating and compensation systems. The proposed joint venture, however, allows each company to keep its own identity and to operate independently except for the coordination of the transoceanic routes.

In addition, each of the airlines in the joint ventures as well as the other airlines within oneworld has developed its own culture and brand to appeal to its own nationality. For instance, BA is still strongest with British passengers as is JAL with Japanese passengers. By keeping separate identities, despite sharing flights, the member airlines can capitalize on the differences.

Nevertheless, there are natural extensions that are possible by strengthening collaboration, such as having check-in counters worldwide that handle all oneworld passengers and combining more airport lounges as a cost saving measure. It is probably safe to say that future cooperation will strengthen rather than weaken among oneworld members. ∎

QUESTIONS

1. Both the Star and Sky Team alliances have depended more on mergers and acquisitions (M&A) than has the oneworld alliance. For instance, Delta and Northwest (Sky Team) have merged, as have Continental and United (Star). What are the advantages and disadvantages of M&A versus non-equity alliances in this industry?

2. Some airlines, such as Southwest, have survived as niche players without extensive international connections. Can they continue this strategy?

3. Why should an airline not be able to establish service anywhere in the world simply by demonstrating that it can and will comply with the local labor and business laws of the host country?

4. The U.S. law limiting foreign ownership of U.S. airlines to no more than 25 percent of voting shares was enacted in 1938. Is this law an anachronism, or are there valid reasons for having it today?

5. What will be the consequences if a few large airlines or networks dominate global air service?

6. Many airlines have recently been no more than marginally profitable. Is this such a vital industry that governments should intervene to guarantee their survival? If so, how?

7. What methods could JAL and AA use to divide revenue and expenses on code-shared routes?

Now that you have finished this chapter, go back to www.myiblab.com to continue practicing and applying the concepts you've learned.

MyIBLab

SUMMARY

- Selling abroad by exporting home-country production may not be advantageous because of lower production costs abroad, high transport costs, the need to alter products substantially, protectionist barriers, lack of domestic capacity, and consumer preferences to buy from specific countries.

- Companies often prefer to operate with FDI, especially wholly owned, because such operations may lower operating costs, lessen the possibility of developing competitors, and free them to follow global strategies.

- Some advantages of collaborative arrangements, whether a company is operating domestically or internationally, are to

spread and reduce costs, allow a company to specialize in its primary competencies, avoid certain competition, secure vertical and horizontal links, and learn from other companies.

- Some motivations for collaborative arrangements that are specific to international operations are to gain location-specific assets, overcome legal constraints, diversify among countries, and minimize exposure in risky environments.

- The forms of foreign operations differ in how many resources a company commits and the proportion of resources committed at home rather than abroad. Collaborative arrangements reduce such commitment.

- Although the type of collaborative arrangement a company chooses should match its strategic objectives, the choice often means a trade-off among objectives.

- Licensing is granting another company the use of some rights (such as patents, copyrights, or trademarks), usually for a fee. It is a means of establishing foreign production and reaching foreign markets that may minimize the licensor's capital outlays, prevent the free use of assets by other companies, allow the receipt of assets from other companies in return, and allow for income in some markets in which exportation or investment is not feasible.

- Franchising differs from licensing in that granting the use of intangible property (usually a trademark) requires the franchisor to assist in operations on a continuing basis.

- An international management contract is a means to secure income by managing a foreign operation while providing little of the capital outlay.

- Turnkey projects are contracts for construction of another company's operating facilities. Historically large and diverse, they necessitate specialized skills and abilities to deal with top-level government authorities.

- Joint ventures are a special type of collaborative arrangement in which two or more organizations share an operation or project, usually with each taking equity in it.

- There are various combinations of joint venture participants, including governments and private companies and two or more participants from the same or different countries.

- Equity alliances occur when a company takes an equity position in the company with which it has a collaborative arrangement so as to solidify the collaborating contract.

- A common motive for collaboration is to take advantage of different companies' complementary resources.

- Problems occur in collaborative arrangements when partners place different levels of importance on them, have different objectives, encounter control problems, worry that their partner is putting in too little or taking out too much from the operation, and misunderstand each other as a result of their different country or company cultures.

- Contracting performance by another company does not negate management's responsibility to develop objectives and assess performance.

- Companies may use different types of collaborative arrangements for their foreign operations in different countries or for different products. As diversity increases, coordinating and managing the foreign operations becomes more complex.

KEY TERMS

appropriability theory (p. 527)
consortium (p. 538)
bargaining school theory (p. 534)

cross-licensing (p. 534)
dependencia theory (p. 534)
equity alliance (p. 539)

internalization (p. 526)
resource-based view (of the firm) (p. 530)

ENDNOTES

1   *Sources include the following:* Coca-Cola Annual Report, 2010; Dana Cimilluca, and Jeffrey McCracken, "Coke Near Deal for Bottler," *Wall Street Journal* (February 25, 2010): A1+; "Coca-Cola Intros Seagram's Sparkle across the U.S." *Food and Beverage Close–Up* (March 3, 2011); "Brazil: Coca-Cola Clothing Getting Dressed for Debut," *Valor Economico* (March 23, 2011); "Coca-Cola Adds 15th," *Beverage Industry* 102: 5 (May 2011); "Coca-Cola May Boost China Investment, Chief Executive Kent Says," *Bloomberg News* (October 31, 2010); The Coca-Cola Company, "Around the World" (2007), retrieved July 3, 2007, from www.thecoca-colacompany .com/ourcompany/ aroundworld.html; Valerie Bauerlein, "Coca-Cola CEO Defends Bottling System," *Wall Street Journal* (April 22, 2009): B3; Bernardette S. Santo Domingo, "Coca-Cola Pledges $1-B Investment to Expand RP Operations," *Business World* (August 3, 2009), retrieved October 9, 2009, from http://iiiprxy.library.miami .edu: 3122/ us/Inacademic/frame.do?reloadEntirePage=true&ran; Leo Paul Dana, "Turkish Coca-Cola," *British Food Journal* 101: 5/6 (1999): 468; "Coca-Cola Dome-Sasol Management Contract Renewed," retrieved July 3, 2007, from www .thebeexhibitions .co.za/press5.htm; Sara Yin, "Coca-Cola Opens Concept Store," *Media* (December 1, 2006): 2; "Coca-Cola, Danone Create Joint Venture to Sell Bottled Water," *Wall Street Journal* (June 18, 2002): C18; "Coca-Cola, Nestlé Narrow Joint Venture," *Beverage Industry*

98: 4 (2007): 6; Kevin Parker, "ERP and SOA at the Coca-Cola Company," *Manufacturing Business Technology* 25: 5 (2007): 2; Betsy McKay, "Smaller Brands Hitch Brands with Coke Distributors," *Wall Street Journal* (January 29, 2007): B1; Betsy McKay, "More Fizz," *Wall Street Journal* (June 1, 2007): A1+; *Coca-Cola 2008 Annual Report.*

2   "Looking to the Future," *Business Europe* 50: 18 (October 1, 2010): 7.

3   John Griffiths, "VW May Build Beetle in Europe to Meet Demand," *Financial Times* (November 11, 1998): 17.

4   Peter Marsh, "The World's Wash Day," *Financial Times* (April 29, 2002): 6.

5   "India-EU FTA to Include Tariff Reduction on Import of Vehicles," *Accord Fintech* [Mumbai] (May 20, 2011).

6   Vildan Serin and Ahmet Çalişkan, "Economic Liberalization Policies and Foreign Direct Investment in Southeastern Europe," *Journal of Economic and Social Research* 12: 2 (2010): 81–100.

7   Jill Gabrielle Klein, "Us versus Them, or Us versus Everyone? Delineating Consumer Aversion to Foreign Goods," *Journal of International Business Studies* 33: 2 (2002): 34563.

8   "'Made in Australia' Label Confuses Shoppers: Choice Survey," *Asia Pulse* (May 18, 2011).

9   John S. Hulland, "The Effects of Country-of-Brand and Brand Name on Product Evaluation and Consideration: A Cross-Country

Comparison," *Journal of International Consumer Marketing* 11 (1999): 23–39; Ali Riza Apil and Erdener Kaynak, "Georgian Consumers' Evaluation of Products Sourced from European Union Member Countries," *International Journal of Commerce and Management* 20: 2 (2010): 167–87.

10 An excellent overview of the literature is Jean-François Hennart, "Transaction Cost Theory and International Business," *Journal of Retailing* 86: 3 (September 2010): 257–69.

11 *Internalization theory,* or holding a monopoly control over certain information or other proprietary assets, builds on earlier market-imperfections work by Ronald H. Coase, "The Nature of the Firm," *Economica* 4 (1937): 386–405. It has been noted by such writers as M. Casson, "The Theory of Foreign Direct Investment," Discussion Paper No. 50 (Reading, UK: University of Reading International Investment and Business Studies, November 1980); Alan M. Rugman, *Inside the Multinationals: The Economics of Internal Markets* (New York: Columbia University Press, 1981); David J. Teece, "Transactions Cost Economics and the Multinational Enterprise," Berkeley Business School International Business Working Paper Series No. IB-3 (1985); B. Kogut and U. Zander, "Knowledge of the Firm and the Evolutionary Theory of the Multinational Corporation," *Journal of International Business Studies* 24: 4 (1993): 625–45; Peter W. Liesch and Gary A. Knight, "Information Internalization and Hurdle Rates in Small and Medium Enterprise Internationalization," *Journal of International Business Studies* 30: 2 (1999): 383–96.

12 Eric M. Johnson, "Harnessing the Power of Partnerships," *Financial Times* (October 8, 2004): Mastering Innovation Section, 4.

13 Paul Marer and Vincent Mabert, "GE Acquires and Restructures Tungsram: The First Six Years (1990–1995)," *OECD, Trends and Policies in Privatization* III: 1 (Paris: OECD, 1996): 149–85; and their unpublished 1999 revision, "GE's Acquisition of Hungary's Tungsram."

14 James Mackintosh and Arkady Ostrovsky, "Partners Settle Lada Parts Dispute," *Financial Times* (February 21, 2006): 16.

15 Matthew Lynch, "Hilfiger Sues Former Sock Licensee," *WWD* 198: 73 (October 7, 2009): 18.

16 Stephen Magee, "Information and the MNC: An Appropriability Theory of Direct Foreign Investment," in Jagdish N. Bhagwati (ed.), *The New International Economic Order* (Cambridge, MA: MIT Press, 1977): 317–40; C. W. Hill, L. P. Hwang, and W. C. Kim, "An Eclectic Theory of the Choice on International Entry Mode," *Strategic Management Journal* 11 (1990): 117–18; Ashish Arora and Andrea Fosfuri, "Wholly Owned Subsidiary versus Technology Licensing in the Worldwide Chemical Industry," *Journal of International Business Studies* 31: 4 (2000): 555–72.

17 Peter Wonacott, "Global Aims of China's Car Makers Put Existing Ties at Risk," *Wall Street Journal* (August 24, 2004): B1+; Norihiko Shirouzu and Peter Wonacott, "People's Republic of Autos," *Wall Street Journal* (April 18, 2005): B1+.

18 Jean-Paul Roy and Christine Oliver, "International Joint Venture Partner Selection: The Role of the Host-Country Legal Environment," *Journal of International Business Studies* 40: 5 (2009): 779–801.

19 Andrew Taylor, "Overseas Groups Get on the UK Utility Map," *Financial Times* (June 17, 2002): 4.

20 Anne-Wil Harzing, "Acquisitions versus Greenfield Investments: International Strategy and Management of Entry Modes," *Strategic Management Journal* 23: 3 (2002): 211–27.

21 Jaideep Anand and Andrew Delios, "Absolute and Relative Resources as Determinants of International Acquisitions," *Strategic Management Journal* 23: 2 (2002): 119–34.

22 Sergery Filippov, "Innovation and R&D in Emerging Russian Multiantionals," *Economics, Management and Financial Markets,* 6: 1 (March 2011): 182–206.

23 Geoff Dyer, Francesco Guerrera, and Alexandra Harney, "Chinese Companies Make Plans to Join the Multinational Club," *Financial Times* (June 23, 2005): 19.

24 Two such indications are from studies by Alan Gregory, which is cited in Kate Burgess, "Acquisitions in U.S. 'Disastrous' for British Companies," *Financial Times* (October 11, 2004): 18; and Ping Deng, "Absorptive Capacity and a Failed Cross Border M&A," *Management Research Review* 33: 7 (2010): 673–82.

25 John Child, David Faulkner, and Robert Pitethly, *The Management of International Acquisitions* (Oxford: Oxford University Press, 2001); Peter Martin, "A Clash of Corporate Cultures," *Financial Times* (June 2–3, 2001): Weekend section, xxiv.

26 Vlatka Bilas and Vedran Baci, "Utjecaj Akvizicijskog Iskustva Na Uspjesnost Mcdunarodnih Spajanja I Preuzimanja U Farmaceutskoj Industriji 2001–2009," *Ekonomska Misao* 19: 2 (2010): 187–209.

27 Rajesh Chakrabarti, Swasti Gupta-Mukherjee, and Narayanan Jayaraman, "Mars-Venus Marriages: Culture and Cross-Border M&A," *Journal of International Business Studies* 40: 2 (2009): 216–36; See also Mary Yoki Brannen and Mark F. Peterson, "Merging Without Alienating: Interventions Promoting Cross-Cultural Organization and Their Limitations," *Journal of International Business Studies* 40: 3 (2009): 468–89.

28 Pierre Dussauge, Bernard Garrette, and Will Mitchell, "Asymmetric Performance: The Market Share Impact of Scale and Link Alliances in the Global Auto Industry," *Strategic Management Journal* 25 (2004): 701–11; and Candace E. Ybarra and Thomas A. Turk, "Strategic Alliances with Competing firms and Shareholder Value," *Journal of Management and Marketing Research* 6 (January 2011): 1–10.

29 Gabriel Baffour Awuah, Amal Mohamed, "Impact of Globalization: The Ability of Less Developed Countries' (LDCs') Firms to Cope with Opportunities and Challenges," *European Business Review* 23: 1 (2011): 120–32; Rodney C. Shrader, "Collaboration and Performance in Foreign Markets: The Case of Young High-Technology Manufacturing Firms," *Academy of Management Journal* 44: 1 (2001): 45–60.

30 Rahul Jacob, "Hong Kong Banks on New Disney Park for Boost," *Financial Times* (August 31, 2001): 6.

31 Betsy McKay and Robert Frank, "Coke, Danone Discuss Joint Venture," *Wall Street Journal* (June 17, 2002): B5.

32 Phred Dvorak and Scott Kilman, "BHP Roils Potash Cartel," *Wall Street Journal* (August 25, 2010): 1.

33 John M. Connor, "Global Antitrust Prosecutions of Modern International Cartels," *Journal of Industry, Competition and Trade* 4: 3 (2004): 239.

34 Luiz F. Mesquita and Sergio G. Lazzarini, "Horizontal and Vertical Relationships in Developing Economies: Implications for SMEs' Access to Global Markets," *Academy of Management Journal* 51: 2 (2008): 359–80.

35 Peter Marsh, "Profile Duracell," *Financial Times* (May 10, 1999): 27.

36 Destan Kandemir and G. Tomas Hult, "A Conceptualization of an Organizational Learning Culture in International Joint Ventures," *Industrial Marketing Management* 34: 5 (2005): 440.

37 Robert F. Howe, "The Fall of the House of Mondavi," *Business 2.0* 6: 3 (2005): 98.

38 Yumiko Ono and Ann Zimmerman, "Wal-Mart Enters Japan with Seiyu Stake," *Wall Street Journal* (March 15, 2002): B5.

39 Peter Wonacott and Eric Bellman, "Foreign Firms Find Rough Passage to India," *Wall Street Journal* (February 1, 2007): A6; Neil Buckly, "Russia Sets New Rules for Investors in Key Sectors," *Financial Times* (May 6, 2009): 3; Amy Kazmin, "Ikea Ditches Plans for India after New Delhi Refuses to Change Law," *Financial Times* (June 12, 2009): 13.

40 Jia-Ruey Ou, "An Analytical Model for Innovating Localization Policy," *International Journal of Electronic Business Management* 8: 2 (2010): 110–19.

41 Julie Bennett, "Road to Foreign Franchises Is Paved with New Problems," *Wall Street Journal* (May 14, 2001): B10.

42 "H&M Wins Back Name in Russia," *Managing Intellectual Property* (April 2007): 1; and Steven Seidenberg, "Trademark Squatting on the Rise in U.S." *Inside Counsel* (May 2010): n.p.

43 Peter J. Lane, Jane E. Salk, and Marjorie A. Lyles, "Absorptive Capacity, Learning, and Performance in International Joint Ventures," *Strategic Management Journal* 22 (2001): 1139–61.

44 Steven White and Steven Siu-Yun Lui, "Distinguishing Costs of Cooperation and Control in Alliances," *Strategic Management Journal* 26 (2005): 913–32.

45 Miguel Angel Asturias, *Strong Wind*, trans. Gregory Rabassa (New York: Delacorte Press, 1968): 112.

46 For an extensive treatise on the theory, see Robert A. Packenham, *The Dependency Movement: Scholarship and Politics in Development Studies* (Cambridge, MA: Harvard University Press, 1992). For some different national views of its validity, see Ndiva Kofele-Kale, "The Political Economy of Foreign Direct Investment: A Framework for Analyzing Investment Laws and Regulations in Developing Countries," *Law & Policy in International Business* 23: 2/3 (1992): 619–71; and Stanley K. Sheinbaum, "Very Recent History Has Absolved Socialism," *New Perspectives Quarterly* 13: 1 (1996).

47 Ravi Ramamurti, "The Obsolescing 'Bargaining Model'? MNC-Host Developing Country Relations Revisited," *Journal of International Business Studies* 32 (2001): 23; Yadong Luo, "Toward a Cooperative View of MNC-Host Government Relations: Building Blocks and Performance Implication," *Journal of International Business Studies* 32 (2001): 401.

48 "Kodak Enters into Technology Cross-Licensing Agreement with NEC," *Asia Pulse* (December 28, 2010).

49 Lizette Alvarez, "Spreading Scandinavian Genes, without Viking Boats," *New York Times* (September 30, 2004): A4; and "Cryos Sets Up Sperm Banks in Mumbai," *Businessline* (September 25, 2008).

50 Fred Burton, Adam R. Cross, and Mark Rhodes, "Foreign Market Servicing Strategies of UK Franchisors: An Empirical Enquiry from a Transactions Cost Perspective," *Management International Review* 40: 4 (2000): 373–400.

51 John K. Ryans, Jr., Sherry Lotz, and Robert Krampf, "Do Master Franchisors Drive Global Franchising?" *Marketing Management* 8: 2 (1999): 33–38.

52 Janet Adamy, "Chinese Food the KFC Way," *Wall Street Journal Asian Edition* (October 20–22, 2006): 14–15.

53 Julie Bennett, "Product Pitfalls Proliferate in a Global Cultural Maze," *Wall Street Journal* (May 14, 2001): B11; Jane Wooldridge, "Fast Food Universe," *Miami Herald* (November 28, 2004): J1.

54 British Airport Authority, "International Airports" (2007), retrieved July 6, 2007, from www.baa.com/portal/page/Corporate%5EAbout+BAA%5EWho+does+what%5EInternational+airports/b0ccadc5c5c72010V gnVCM100000147e120a__/448c6a4c7f1b0010VgnVCM200000 357e1 20a__/

55 "Four Seasons Signs Management Contract with Three C Universal Developers," *Mint* [New Delhi] (April 21, 2011).

56 "Global Alumina Releases Third Quarter 2010 Results," *PR Newswire* (November 2010).

57 Peter Sanders, Daniel Michaels, and August Cole, "Boeing Delays New Jet Again," *Wall Street Journal* (June 24, 2009): A1+; Peter Sanders, "Boeing Settles In for a Bumpy Ride," *Wall Street Journal* (October 7, 2009): B1+.

58 Luis Zalamea, "AeroRepublica, Copa Offer Details of New Alliance," *Aviation Daily* (March 11, 2005): 5.

59 There are many different ways of classifying the problems. Two useful ways are found in Manuel G. Serapio Jr. and Wayne F. Cascio, "End Games in International Alliances," *Academy of Management Executive* 10: 1 (1996): 62–73; and Joel Bleeke and David Ernst, "Is Your Strategic Alliance Really a Sale?" *Harvard Business Review* (January–February 1995): 97–105.

60 Terrence Chea, "No Perfect Partnership," *Washington Post* (June 3, 2002): E1.

61 Mikhail Fridman, "BP Has Been Treating Russians as Subjects," *Financial Times* (July 7, 2008): 9.

62 Gregory L. White, "In Asia, GM Pins Hope on a Delicate Web of Alliances," *Wall Street Journal* (October 23, 2002): A23.

63 Ramit Plushnick-Masti, "German Firm Faulted for Taking Vitamin out of Baby Formula," *Miami Herald* (November 12, 2003): 19A.

64 William H. Meyers, "Maxim's Name Is the Game," *New York Times Magazine* (May 3, 1987): 33–35; Cristina Passariello, "Pierre Cardin Ready to Sell His Overstretched Label," *Wall Street Journal* (May 3, 2011): 1.

65 David Ibison, "Culture Clashes Prove Biggest Hurdle to International Links," *Financial Times* (January 24, 2002): 17.

66 Diana Elena Ranf, "Cultural Differences in Project Management," *Annales Universitatis Apulensis Series Oeconomica* 12: 2 (2010): 657–62.

67 Marshall Geiger and Joyce van der Laan Smith, "The Effect of Institutional and Cultural Factors on the Perceptions of Earnings Management," *Journal of International Accounting Research* 9: 2 (2010): 21–43.

68 James T. Areddy, "Danone Pulls Out of Disputed China Venture," *Wall Street Journal* (October 1, 2009): B1.

69 Seung Ho Park and Gerardo R. Ungson, "The Effect of National Culture, Organizational Complementarity, and Economic Motivation on Joint Venture Dissolution," *Academy of Management Journal* 40: 2 (April 1997): 279–307; Harry G. Barkema, Oded Shenkar, Freek Vermeulen, and John H. J. Bell, "Working Abroad, Working with Others: How Firms Learn to Operate International Joint Ventures," *Academy of Management Journal* 40: 2 (April 1997): 426–42, found survival differences only for differences in uncertainty avoidance.

70 Rikka M. Sarala and Eero Vaara, "Cultural Differences, Convergence, and Crossvergence as Explanations of Knowledge Transfer in International Acquisitions," *Journal of International Business Studies* 41: 8 (October-November 2010): 1365–90.

71 Akbar Zaheer, Exequiel Hernandez, and Sanjay Banerjee, "Prior Alliances with Targets and Acquisition Performance in Knowledge-Intensive Industries," *Organization Science* 21: 5 (September-October 2010): 1072–91+.

72 Mike W. Peng and Oded Shenkar, "Joint Venture Dissolution as Corporate Divorce," *Academy of Management Executive* 16: 2 (May 2002): 92–105.

73 Bharat Anand and Tarun Khanna, "Do Firms Learn to Create Value? The Case of Alliances," *Strategic Management Journal* 21: 3 (March 2000): 295–315; Anthony Goerzen and Paul W. Beamish, "The Effect of Alliance Network Diversity on Multinational Enterprise Performance," *Strategic Management Journal* 26 (2005): 333–54; and Maurizio Zollo and Jeffrey J. Reuer, "Experience Spillovers Across Corporate Development Activities," *Organization Science* 21: 6 (November-December 2010): 1195–1212.

74 Rachelle C. Sampson, "Experience Effects and Collaborative Returns in R&D Alliances," *Strategic Management Journal* 26 (2005): 1009–31.

75 Anne Smith and Marie-Claude Reney, "The Mating Dance: A Case Study of Local Partnering Processes in Developing Countries," *European Management Journal* 15: 2 (1997): 174–82.

76 Sanjiv Kumar and Anju Seth, "The Design of Coordination and Control Mechanisms for Managing Joint Venture–Parent Relationships," *Strategic Management Journal* 19: 6 (June 1998): 579–99; T. K. Das and Bing-Sheng Teng, "Between Trust and Control: Developing Confidence in Partner Cooperation in Alliances," *Academy of Management Journal* 23: 3 (July 1998): 491–512; Arvind Parkhe, "Building Trust in International Alliances," *Journal of World Business* 33: 4 (1998): 417–37; Prashant Kale, Harbir Singh,

and Howard Perlmutter, "Learning and Protection of Proprietary Assets in Strategic Alliances: Building Relational Capital," *Strategic Management Journal* 21: 3 (March 2000): 217–37; and Dina Preston-Ortiz, "The Effects of Trust in Virtual Strategic-Alliance Performance Outcomes," unpublished doctoral dissertation (Phoenix: University of Phoenix, 2010).

77 Africa Ariño and Jeffrey J. Reuer, "Designing and Renegotiating Strategic Alliance Contracts," *Academy of Management Executive* 18: 3 (2004): 37–48.

78 Gary D. Burton, David Ahlstrom, Michael N. Young, and Yuri Rubanik, "In Emerging Markets, Know What Your Partners Expect," *Wall Street Journal* (December 15, 2008): R5.

79 Srilata Zaheer and Akbar Zaheer, "Trust across Borders," *Journal of International Business Studies* 37: 1 (2006): 21.

80 Prashant Kale and Harbir Singh, "Managing Strategic Alliances: What Do We Know Now and Where Do We Go from Here?" *Academy of Management Perspectives* 23: 3 (August 2009): 45–62.

81 John Kenneth Galbraith, *American Capitalism* (Boston: Houghton Mifflin, 1952): 91–92.

82 Eric H. Kessler, Paul E. Bierly, and Shanthi Gopalakrishnan, "Internal vs. External Learning in New Product Development: Effects of Speed, Costs and Competitive Advantage," *R & D Management* 30: 3 (2000): 213–23.

83 These are adapted from Arvind Parkhe, "Interfirm Diversity, Organizational Learning, and Longevity in Global Strategic Alliances," *Journal of International Business Studies* 22: 4 (1991): 579–601.

84 We wish to acknowledge the assistance of several American Airlines and oneworld executives, who, although wishing to remain anonymous, supplied useful information for and feedback on this case. Additional information came from "American Airlines to Operate Only Service between New York and Japan's Tokyo International Airport at Haneda After Historic Open Skies Agreement," *Entertainment Newsweekly* (March 4, 2011): 172; Andrea Ahles, "American Airlines, Japan Airlines Announce Joint Venture," *McClatchy–Tribune Business News* (January 12, 2011): n.p.; Julie Johnsson, "American Airlines Combining Pacific Flights with Japan Airlines," *McClatchy–Tribune Business News* (January 12, 2011): n.p.; "American to Move Its Asia-Pacific Regional Office to the Japan Airlines Building in Tokyo," *Journal of Transportation* (September 18, 2010): 26; "Japan Airlines and American Airlines Announce Joint Business Benefits for Trans-Pacific Consumers," *The Pak Banker* (January 11, 2011): n.p.; "Airline Profits to Tumble in 2011: IATA," *The Pak Banker* (June 8, 2011): n.p.; "Europe: Trans-Atlantic Alliances Are Set to Tighten," *Oxford Analytica Daily Brief Service* (January 3, 2008): 1; Alfred Kahn and Dorothy Robyn, "The Sky Must Be No Limit to Global Competition," *Financial Times* (February 15, 2006): 17; Bruce Bernard, "American Airlines Seeks OK for Trans-Atlantic Tie-up," *Journal of Commerce Online* (August 15, 2008); International Air Transport Association, *Annual Report* (2008).

chapter 15

The Organization of International Business

Objectives

1. To profile the evolving process of organizing a company for international business

2. To describe the features of classical structures

3. To describe the features of neoclassical structures

4. To discuss the systems used to coordinate and control international activities

5. To profile the role and characteristics of organizational culture

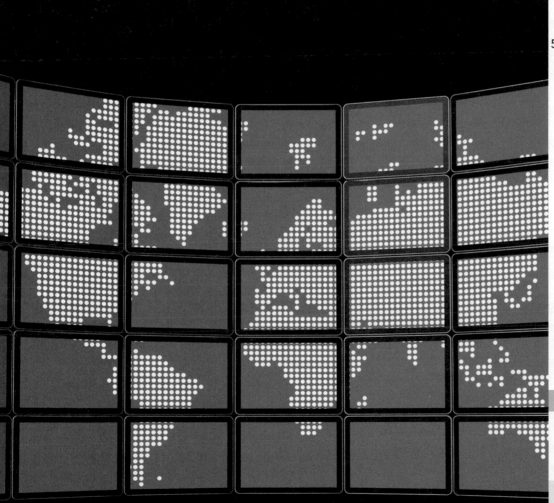

Source: Daboost/Shutterstock.com

Access a host of interactive learning aids to help strengthen your understanding of the chapter concepts at www.myiblab.com.

MyIBLab

Laws control the lesser man. Right conduct controls the greater one.

—Chinese proverb

CASE

Building an Organization at Johnson & Johnson

The typical pharmaceutical company relies on global integration, given its steep product development costs and potential scale economies.[1] Meanwhile, it must respond to local market conditions, obtaining government approval for each product in each country and establishing local sales and distribution systems. Consequently, headquarters and subsidiaries jointly implement the company's strategy. Building an organization that can meet this mission is tough. One standout that does is Johnson & Johnson (J&J).

Since the start of its U.S. operations in 1886, J&J has evolved into the most broadly based healthcare company in the world. International activity began in 1919 with J&J Canada. Headquartered in New Brunswick, New Jersey, J&J now lists 250 operating companies across the world, holds more than 54,000 U.S. and foreign patents, sells products in more than 175 countries, and employs about 115,000 people worldwide, with nearly 70,000 working in 57 countries outside the United States. Its steady success is renowned. Sales in 2010 were $61.6 billion and it increased its dividend for the forty-ninth consecutive year. J&J is generally regarded as the most admired pharmaceutical company in the world. The quality of J&J's portfolio of anti-infective, cardiovascular, dermatology, immunology, and oncology products is legendary. Some, though, believed the intricacy of the company's organization, in terms of its decentralized structure, sophisticated coordination and control systems, and Credo-based culture, anchored its superior performance.

THE "MAGIC" OF DECENTRALIZATION

Decentralized management is the heart of J&J's organization. It allows managers who are closest to customers and competitors to make decisions. As the company says, it aims to be big and small all at once, building a global profile based on the conglomeration of many small units. By design, each of its 250 units operates with substantial autonomy, commanding the authority to act as it believes best given local conditions. Each is its own business, entrepreneurial in character, and aware that success depends on anticipating local customers' needs and delivering solutions.

Decentralization, explains Ralph Larsen, former CEO, "gives people a sense of ownership and control—and the freedom to act more rapidly." His successor, William Weldon, concurs, adding, "The magic around J&J is decentralization." Expanding these ideas, he explains:

> The decentralized manner in which we operate our businesses marries the best qualities of smaller companies with entrepreneurial drive for growth and

close proximity to customers with the resources, know-how, and investment capital of a Fortune 500 company. This strategic approach gives us many advantages over a centralized operation. One is a strong sense of ownership, entrepreneurship, agility, and accountability seldom seen in large multinational corporations. The leadership and employees of our 250 operating companies around the world are intensely competitive. We look to the leaders of our decentralized businesses to grow their businesses faster than their competitors. They are driven to innovate…[and] to bring greater value to the marketplace through internal discoveries, application of new science, technology, licensing, and acquisition. We believe our decentralized approach to running the business yields better decisions—in the long run—for patients, health professionals and other customers, because the decision makers are close to the customers and are in a better position to understand their needs. Finally, our decentralized approach to managing the business is a tremendous magnet for talent, because it gives people room to grow and room to explore new ideas, thus developing their own skills and careers.

The entrepreneurial ethos of decentralization powered J&J's units worldwide. Backstopping their performance was the deep pools of products, processes, and people found in a large, successful MNE. Combined, J&J's local effectiveness and global efficiencies made for a commanding competitive advantage.

THE DILEMMA OF DECENTRALIZATION

J&J entered new markets by adding subsidiaries through investment, alliance, or acquisition. New units did not fear being overrun by legions of expatriates directed by headquarters-based generals. With few exceptions, citizens of the host country direct local subsidiaries. Granted, headquarters would install some systems to coordinate and control activities as well as negotiate financial targets. It would then support subsidiaries as needed, patiently awaiting superior results. Its philosophy is that people who understand how the company creates value, are familiar with the company's competencies, and are culturally and physically close to the market ought to run the local business. Thus, baby oil managers in Italy decide how big a bottle to use, even if that bottle differs from the one sold in Germany, Japan, or Mexico.

Autonomy inevitably created dilemmas for local management. Early on, the heads of J&J's foreign subsidiaries had once enjoyed so much autonomy that they were seen as "kings of their own countries." This situation no longer existed. Still, decentralization gave locals considerable authority. Inevitably, questions arose about their primary allegiance. How should they, for example, optimize local activities while maximizing global performance? Moreover, when push came to shove, which perspective should take precedence? So, while decentralization enabled J&J to respond quickly to local needs, it slowed the global diffusion of products and programs. For example, J&J launched Tylenol in 1960 as an over-the-counter pain reliever in the United States. Although it was available to local operating units shortly thereafter, the Japanese unit did not begin local sales until 2000.[2] Inconsistent market development and duplication of efforts fanned friction between headquarters and subsidiaries. Furthermore, growing pressures to integrate international operations, due to market trends, competitors' moves, and changing technologies, tested J&J's commitment to decentralization.

COORDINATION AND CONTROL SYSTEMS

Preserving the magic of decentralization, in the face of the contest between local autonomy and global integration, led headquarters to tighten coordination and control systems. They installed channels of communication that cut across the organization, thereby helping far-flung units share ideas. Self-directed councils—for research, engineering, and operations, among others—met regularly to swap ideas. Planning formats were negotiated, reports were scheduled, and budgets framed interactions. Successful employees rotated among operating units, spreading their insights and expertise. Global perspectives bore down on local decision making. Likewise, local concerns influenced global discussions.

Significantly, J&J began recentralizing some activities from operating units. Senior executives deal with issues common to all operating units, such as finance, science and technology, government affairs, and quality management. Managing these sorts of support activities at headquarters, senior executives reasoned, freed operating units to concentrate on their day-to-day performance. J&J installed an Executive Committee and Group Operating Committees to systematize this change.

In many situations, headquarters' efforts, while understood, were unwelcome by local units. Some local units resisted integration, arguing that global standards poorly fit their circumstances. Senior management acknowledged these concerns and reiterated their commitment to decentralization. But, they argued, the imperatives of the company's strategy coupled with the tough standards of the global market meant that when J&J rolls out a product, all country operations roll with it.

CULTURE AND THE CREDO

Encouraging employees to act as local entrepreneurs while ensuring they act with a global awareness takes us to the role of culture in J&J. Fundamentally, from the CEO to the director of the smallest unit, management believes that the people and their values are J&J greatest assets. As they often note, employees have powered every invention, every product, and every breakthrough. This is not terribly unusual. Many companies, perhaps even some that you have worked for, likely expressed similar sentiment. Separating J&J from the pack is its organization culture, embodied in "Our Credo." Crafted in 1943 by Robert Wood Johnson, company chair from 1932 to 1963, this one-page ethical code of conduct states how J&J fulfills its responsibilities. Indeed, former CEO Ralph Larsen referred to it as the "glue that binds this company together."

The Credo specifies who and what to care about and in what order. J&J's "first responsibility is to the doctors, nurses, patients, mothers and fathers who use our products and services." It addresses the communities where J&J operates and the roles and duties of employees. Notably, shareholders come last, long after suppliers and distributors. It declares that shareholders will get a fair return if other constituents get first priority. Essentially, J&J holds that the business is well served by putting customers first. Collectively, the "Credo underscores J&J's personal responsibility to put the needs...of the people we serve first. It liberates our passion and deepens our commitment to delivering meaningful health innovations." The company maintains that the Credo is more than just a moral compass; it is the basis of success. The proof,

Johnson & Johnson: The Credo

Originally spelled out in 1943, the Johnson & Johnson Credo has been updated several times over the years to further define the responsibilities outlined in the document. The Credo is available in more than 36 languages across Johnson & Johnson's global enterprise. The values codified in the Credo, says the company, challenge every employee to put the needs and well-being of stakeholders first. This 'ethics oath' communicates the mission, vision, and accountability that every employee holds to each other and the communities they serve.

Source: Johnson & Johnson, "Our Company: Our Credo" (November 14, 2005), at http://www.jnj.com

says J&J, is in the fact that it is one of a handful of companies that have flourished through more than a century of change.

The Credo is available in more than 36 languages across their global enterprise. Despite its direct message, executives worried that differing outlooks might blur understandings. Consequently, the company periodically surveys employees on how well they meet their Credo responsibilities. Where there are shortcomings, senior management steps in. For example, J&J updated some of the language of the Credo given the rising visibility of the environment and work/family balance. Despite revisions, management believes the founding spirit of the Credo endures.

THE POWER OF AN ORGANIZATION

J&J believed the basis of continued success was building an organization that is flexible enough to exploit the knowledge and skills of each employee. They have, by developing, adjusting, and improving their structure, systems, and culture, built an organization that confidently leverages bright ideas, no matter if they are championed by global executives or local subsidiary leaders. Ultimately, the magic of decentralization, the balance of coordination and control systems, and the clarity of the Credo has developed an organization that lets employees capitalize on their initiative, develop their capabilities, enrich their perspectives, and, quite possibly, change the game.

CRN
Case Review Note

Introduction

Artfully engineering an organization that adeptly runs global activities is a frontier of international business operations. Superior performance has a clear mandate. MNEs create value by standardizing activities to maximize global efficiency while simultaneously adapting activities to optimize local effectiveness. Therefore, managers construct, piece by piece, the requisite organization that makes the intricacies of this task straight-forward.[3] This chapter examines how MNEs do so.

If formulating strategy is the first step of a long march, the second step is implementing it. This task directs managers' attention to the issue of organizing international operations. J&J exemplifies this situation. Its strategy of delivering superior healthcare required building a network of decentralized subsidiaries, tailoring technology, human resources, and information systems to coordinate and control activities, and relying on its Credo to sustain a meaningful culture. Each and all aspects of its organization helps J&J convert ambition into accomplishment.

J&J, as well as many others we profile in this chapter, shows how an MNE sets its structure, specifies its systems, and shapes its culture to implement its strategy. Organizing operations for international business, therefore, is not merely fine-tuning an MNE's strategy. Rather, it is the process of organizing how employees contribute to its mission, minding how to coordinate interdependent activities, applying controls when situations go awry, and sponsoring values that create a common cause. This task, as we see in Figure 15.1, requires specifying a structure that arranges the workplace, installing the systems to get it moving, and promoting the culture that sustains it.[4]

Case Review Note

Changing Situations, Changing Organizations

In the early 20th century, MNEs responded to the emerging technologies of railroads, telephone, and telegraph by engaging then heretical ideas.[5] Then global titans, such as General Motors, Ford, DuPont, and Sears, developed hierarchical structures, reasoning they would best implement their strategy. Succeeding generations of managers refined these designs, evaluating the changing scale and scope of their operations, continually engaging the issues of who did what job, who worked in which unit, who reported to whom, who could make which decisions, and who told whom what to do. The output—codified in the MNE's formal structure—instituted a system of constraints and contracts that spurred the compliance of workers worldwide.[6] This outlook has routinely organized the international expansion and operation of MNEs.

Environmental trends, industry conditions, and market opportunities prod managers to rethink this approach. Specifically:

Environmental differences, technology trends, executive practices, and labor markets challenge organizing the MNE.

Expansion of International Business The growth and diffusion of global business has changed MNEs' opportunity set and efficiency frontier. Markets, once predominant,

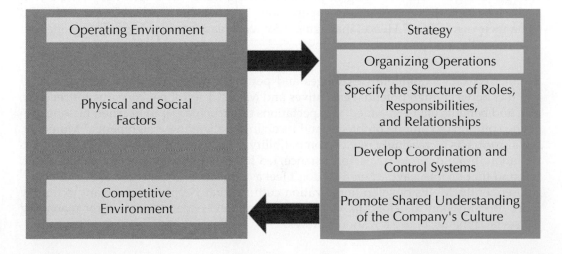

FIGURE 15.1 Factors Affecting Organizing Operations

The idea of an organization refers to the activities through which the MNE builds the structures, systems, and culture needed to implement its strategy.

like the United States, Japan, and Germany, transition to new positions. Markets once on the periphery, such as Brazil, Russia, China, and India, move toward center stage. MNEs, by choice or by force, respond. They engage unprecedented strategies that demand far more sophisticated organizations than any used in the past. For example, IBM, which celebrated its centennial in 2011, is boldly moving into its third organizational phase. It is building a "globally integrated enterprise" that puts investments, people, and work anywhere in the world "based on the right cost, the right skills and the right business environment [with] work flow[ing] to the places where it will be done...most efficiently and to the highest quality."[7] Managing an increasingly sophisticated strategy calls for managing a commensurately sophisticated organization.

Implementing increasingly sophisticated strategies require increasingly sophisticated organizations.

The Internet as a Design Standard   The invention of the telephone and telegraph, by improving global communication, reset the standards of organizing activities. MNEs at the time responded with formats that reflected the organizing logic of these then contemporary technologies. We see the same today. The Internet as an organization metaphor pushes managers to rethink their assumptions of how they arrange work, roles, and responsibilities. The Internet is a supremely efficient and effective organization of knowledge, resources, and people. In the height of irony, however, it has no formal structure, no board of directors, and no central administrator. Its self-organizing and self-regulating capabilities prompt questioning conventional notions of design, coordination, and control. For example, Facebook, Red Hat, Yandex, PayPal, Naver, Baidu, and Alibaba exist today. They could not have 20 years ago. Therefore, as did changing designs calls for changing structures in 1900, so too do we see the same in 2012. Hence, managing new workplace arrangements call for managing new structural formats.

Managerial Standards   The evolving nature of work changes the conduct and context of employees' jobs, whether done at the biggest headquarters or the smallest subsidiary. Change in the nature of work changes the nature of management. Historically, the higher one's level in the hierarchy, the more one knew about the various jobs in the company. That is no longer the case. Similarly, frontline employees at the subsidiary level were masters of their local marketplace but far removed from the global drama. That too no longer holds. Real-time access to information, facilitated by cheap, powerful telecommunications, eliminates knowledge gaps. As a result, there are far fewer jobs that senior managers can standardize or subsidiary managers cannot do. Furthermore, employees working with information technologies create value of astonishing variability, problem solving, and intellectual content. It is difficult and usually counterproductive to control workers charged with reasoning or problem-solving tasks; the bright people who staff such slots typically oppose direct supervision. "Knowledge workers" effectively aim to be their own CEOs.[8] Hence, managing new workplace standards calls for managing novel coordination and control systems.

Changes in the market environment and nature of work push managers to question how they organize activities.

Social Contract   Competitive changes and performance expectations alter the social contract between high potential executives and MNEs. Traditional concerns for security, pay, and benefits have expanded to expectations of participating in decision making, devising solutions to unique problems, and receiving challenging assignments.[9] Moreover, social contracts increasingly rely on compatibility of values and outlooks. Google's worries about brain drain to rivals, for instance, led it to identify why people typically quit. It found that people leave when they don't feel a connection to the company's mission.[10] Consequently, MNEs develop organization cultures that people do not want to merely work for, but want to belong to. Hence, managing new expectations call for managing the social dynamic of organization cultures.

BUILDING A "MAGICAL" ORGANIZATION

These trends push MNEs to rethink the best mix of structure, systems, and values in building, as J&J called it, a "magical" organization. The payoff is clear: doing so helps employees perform creatively, responsibly, and entrepreneurially. Some, like Nestlé in Switzerland, Cemex in Mexico, Toyota in Japan, Infosys in India, and DuPont in the United States apply and improve classical formats. They fine-tune their organizations, clarify the work environment, improve systems, and process map activities. Reengineering workflows, streamlining information technology, tightening planning sequences, and minimizing duplication are some of their tools of change.

Others, like Oticon in Sweden, Cisco in the United States, Grupo Empresarial Antioqueño of Colombia, Mitsui of Japan, and Li & Fung in Hong Kong, engage unprecedented formats. They design flexible models that replace the command and control ethos of the classical hierarchy with the goal to coordinate and cultivate in the context of neoclassical formats. Cross-functional task forces, network designs, web-based collaboration services, and social networking methods are some of their tools of change.

We examine the intricacies of each approach, as well as their respective tools, throughout this chapter. More precisely we study how an MNE builds an **organization** by its choices on the structure it specifies to arrange work, the systems it installs to coordinate and control what gets done, and the culture it promotes to sustain worldwide effort.

Organization Structure

The formal arrangement of roles, responsibilities, and relationships in the MNE represents its **organization structure.** It configures the elements of the company, identifying the lines of authority and communication, assigning rights and duties, stipulating flows between and among units, and indicating how the company aims to utilizes its resources. It can spell the difference between success and failure for a company, as well as for the individuals who work there.[11] In the case of J&J, for example, managers believe their decentralized structure was the bedrock of their "magical" organization. Similarly, recall the profile of Zara in Chapter 11 and its CEO's view, "Our structure gives us tremendous advantages over our competition." Innovatively combining vertical integration, technology-orchestrated coordination, just-in-time manufacturing, finely tuned logistics, and state of the art merchandising pose tough challenges. Zara's structure, by arranging jobs, roles, rules, and responsibilities, imposed clarity upon what otherwise would trend toward chaos.

Step one in building an organization is determining the best structure for arranging individuals and units to implement the firm's strategy. Generally, an MNE's choice depends on many factors. The environmental and workplace trends discussed earlier highlight general conditions. Then there are the constraints that affect MNEs. That is, the parameters of the optimal structure for an international operation are more complex than those of a domestic enterprise. Designing a structure for the latter permits one to treat economic development, cultural orientation, and workplace practices as constants. Organizing internationally converts these to variables.

In addition, there are conditions that specifically influence an MNE's situation. Has it configured its value chain, for instance, to emphasize integration or adaptation? Alternatively, do location economics lead it to concentrate or disperse activities? These and similar questions uniquely influence the structure that best supports an MNE's strategy. Managers sort through them by working through two issues: **vertical differentiation** (the balance between the centralization and decentralization of authority) and **horizontal differentiation** (the matter of specifying which people do which jobs in which units).

Organizing is the process of building the structure, systems, and culture needed to implement a strategy.

Case Review Note

Structure is the formal arrangement of jobs that specifies roles, responsibilities, and relationships.

Differentiation means that the company is composed of different units that work on different kinds of tasks with different degrees of authority.

VERTICAL DIFFERENTIATION

No matter the particular mix of markets, types of products, or executive ambitions, MNEs face competing calls for global integration and local responsiveness. They reconcile these pressures by specifying who has the authority to make what decisions. Questions run the operational gamut. Who should decide to close a factory in Switzerland or open one in Malaysia? Who is responsible for new product development? Who determines advertising and promotion campaigns? Does only headquarters decide whom to hire and whom to fire, both at home and overseas? How often and in what format do foreign subsidiaries report to headquarters?

Managers resolve these issues by vertically differentiating the company's structure in terms of **centralization** (how high up) versus **decentralization** (how low down) of decision making. Centralization and decentralization, as we see in Table 15.1, endorse different principles, advocate different practices, and emphasize different objectives. Perhaps the key issue of vertical differentiation is that of the locus of power.

TABLE 15.1   The Principles and Practice of Centralization and Decentralization

Centralization	Decentralization
Premise	**Premise**
Decisions should be made by senior managers who have the experience, expertise, and judgment to find the best course of action for the company.	Decisions should be made by the employees who are closest to and, arguably, most familiar with the situation.
The effective configuration and coordination of the value chain depend on headquarters retaining authority over what happens.	The effective configuration and coordination of the value chain depend on local managers adapting it to local conditions.
Centralized decision making ensures that operations in different countries help achieve global objectives.	Decentralized decision making ensures that operations in different countries work toward achieving global objectives by meeting national goals.
Advantages	**Advantages**
Facilitates coordination of the value chain.	Decisions are made by managers who directly deal with customers, competitors, and markets.
Ensures that decisions are consistent with strategic objectives.	Encourages lower-level managers to exercise initiative.
Gives senior executives the authority to direct major change.	Motivates greater effort to do a better job by lower-level employees.
Preempts duplicating activities across various subsidiaries.	
Reduces the risk that lower-level employees make mistakes.	Enables more flexible response to rapid environmental changes.
Ensures consistent dealing with stakeholders—government officials, employees, suppliers, consumers, and the general public.	Permits holding subsidiary managers more accountable for their unit's performance.
Disadvantages	**Disadvantages**
Discourages initiative among lower-level employees.	Puts the organization at risk if many bad decisions are made at lower levels.
Demoralized lower-level employees simply wait to be told what to do.	Impedes cross-unit coordination.
Information flows from the top down, thereby preempting the possible innovations from bottom-up information flow.	Subsidiaries may favor local interests at the expense of global performance.
Factors Encouraging More Centralization	**Factors Encouraging More Decentralization**
General environment and specific industry conditions push for global integration and worldwide uniformity of products, purchases, methods, and policies.	General environment and specific industry conditions push for local responsiveness.
Interdependent subsidiaries that share value activities or deal with common competitors and customers.	Products, methods, and policies are suitable for local adaptation.
Need for company to move resources—capital, personnel, or technology—efficiently from one value activity to another.	Economies of scale can be achieved via national production.
Lower-level managers are not as capable or experienced at making decisions as upper-level managers.	Lower-level managers are capable and experienced at making decisions.
Decisions are important and the risk of loss is great.	Decisions are relatively minor but must be made quickly.
	Low need for foreign nationals to reach senior-level headquarters positions.

Centralized structure concentrates decision-making power in the top layer of management. Tight control is the rule of order. In MNEs implementing an international or global strategy, for instance, centralization is the standard as headquarters makes decisions and subsidiaries follow orders. A decentralized structure distributes decision-making power among departments and divisions.

Strategic circumstances determine the appropriate degrees of autonomy. An MNE implementing a multidomestic strategy, for instance, decentralizes authority to those closest to the action. As a general rule, decisions made above the subsidiary level are considered centralized, whereas those made at or below that level are decentralized.

The Internet changes the calculus of who should have the authority to make which decision. Technology makes it easier for executives at headquarters and subsidiaries to track global conditions and local performance in real time. Collectively, email, VoIP, teleconferencing, social networks, and related technologies help MNEs respond to the state of **globality** in which "Business flows in every direction. Companies have no centers. The idea of foreignness is foreign. Commerce swirls and market dominance shifts."[12] Competing with everyone, from everywhere, for everything diminishes the need to centralize this activity or decentralize that activity.

The interdependency of activities requires the executives running headquarters understand the subtleties of country operations and the executives running subsidiaries respect global imperatives. Recall, for instance, our opening profile of J&J showed that headquarters reasoned local managers' improving real-time access to global and local information supported decentralizing decision making. Besides tracking local developments, subsidiary managers efficiently monitor global trends and conditions.

Centralization is the degree to which high-level managers, usually above the country level, make strategic decisions and delegate them to lower levels for implementation.

Decentralization is the degree to which lower-level managers, usually at or below the country level, make and implement strategic decisions.

Case Review Note

DYNAMIC BALANCE

The centralized-versus-decentralized choice is often represented as an either-or proposition. In reality, an MNE is never entirely one or the other. The erratic evolution of the global market along with occasional disruptions makes for a continual balancing of authority between headquarters and subsidiaries. Arguably, a generation ago, MNEs could function effectively if all decisions were made solely by a select group of senior executives or local managers. Today, few, if any, can. Much like the swings of a pendulum, centralization and decentralization tend toward dynamic balance.[13]

In principle, decision making should occur at the level of those who (1) are most directly affected by the outcome and (2) have the most direct knowledge of the situation.

Horizontal Differentiation

Vertical differentiation deals with the chain of command from the top to the bottom of the organization. Companies also run sideways, say, from function to function. The task of horizontal differentiation turns managers' attention to how they divide themselves into discrete units that are responsible for specialized tasks—who, for example, directs manufacturing, finance, marketing, and all the various jobs that go with each function.

Deciding these issues makes manageable the otherwise immense scale and scope of international operations. Therefore, an MNE horizontally differentiates its structure to (1) specify the set of tasks that must be done, (2) divide those tasks among SBUs, divisions, subsidiaries, departments, committees, teams, jobs, and individuals, and (3) stipulates superior and subordinate relationships.

Managers horizontally differentiate a structure in terms of the business function, type of business, geographic area, or some combination. The long-running use of these formats designates them as classical structures. The first standard anchors a *functional* structure, the second installs an *area* or *divisional* structure, and the combination results in a *matrix* or *mixed* structure.

Vertical differentiation deals with the chain of command that runs from the 'top to the bottom'. Horizontal differentiation deals with the separate tasks or skills that run 'sideways' in the company in the organization.

FIGURE 15.2　Classical Organizational Structures for International Business

Although shown here in simplified forms, these types of classical structures have been adopted by many MNEs. A useful perspective is to compare the nature of differentiation—both vertical and horizontal—represented in each diagram.

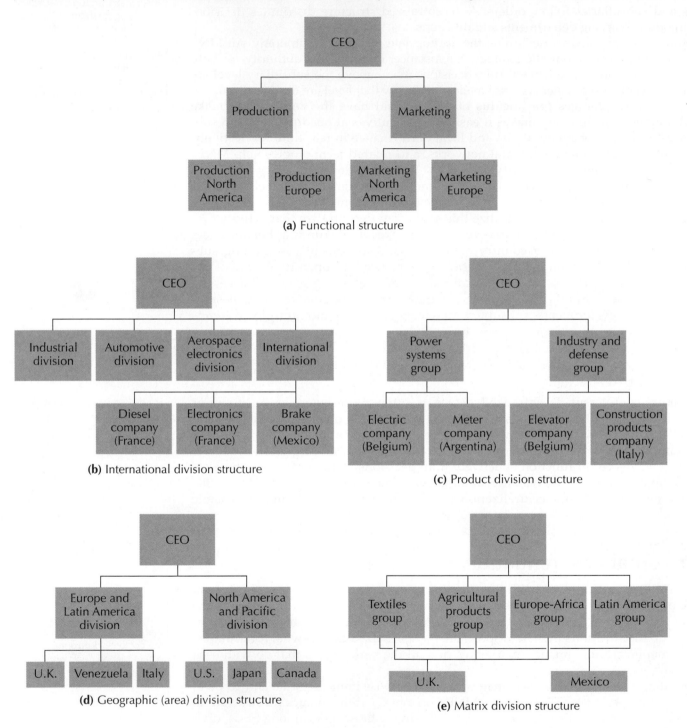

(a) Functional structure

(b) International division structure

(c) Product division structure

(d) Geographic (area) division structure

(e) Matrix division structure

FUNCTIONAL STRUCTURE

A **functional structure,** as depicted in Figure 15.2 (a), is the ideal way to organize work when global integration trumps local responsiveness, industry structure encourages cost leadership, and companies have anchored their value chains in the global or international strategy. The functional structure helps managers maximize scale economies by efficiently arranging responsibilities and relationships. It creates specific departments that arrange work by business functions—i.e., production people work with production people, marketing people work with marketing people, and so on. Functional structures are popular among MNEs with a narrow range of products, particularly those whose capital-intensity creates economies of scale. Energy and extraction MNEs, such as ExxonMobil, Vale, or Rio Tinto, commonly use this structure.

A functional structure has drawbacks. The goal to maximize efficiency encourages standardized activities that may miss local opportunities. Differentiating people and processes by business function also slows the development of broader knowledge-generating and decision-making relationships. As a result, coordinating activities between departments, say in response to an environmental change or market disruption, is difficult. The often-extreme vertical differentiation of a functional structure, represented by a long chain of command that spans many levels of the hierarchy, adds a deliberate pace to activity. Often, as the volume of data expands faster than the processing capacity of the multi-layered hierarchy, decision-making progressively slows.

Functional structures:

- Group people based on common expertise and resources.
- Are popular among companies that have narrow product lines.

DIVISIONAL STRUCTURES

Whereas executives specify roles and relationships in a functional structure in terms of inputs, they use a **divisional structure** to specify them according to outputs. Each division has responsibility for a different set of products or markets. Depending on its strategy, an MNE can opt for an international division, global product, or worldwide area structure.

Divisional structures:

- Divide employees based on the product, customer segment, or geographical location.
- Duplicate functions and resources across divisions.

International Division   This format installs a separate operating group that has responsibility for international activities. Domestic units supervise the home market, leaving the international division to manage the typically less strategic foreign sector (Figure 15.2[b]). Clustering international personnel supports responding quickly to foreign events; all the people needed to act are division mates. This format also limits costly country-to-country duplication. It is best suited for strategies that demand modest integration between domestic and foreign operations. Historically, it has been popular among U.S. MNEs, given the immense scale of their home market. It has been less used by European and Asian MNEs.

An international division:

- Creates a critical mass of international expertise.
- Competes with powerful domestic divisions for resources.

Segregating an MNE into discrete divisions, by blocking relationships, can fan "domestic vs. international" tension. Domestic managers, evaluated based on their home market performance, may withhold resources from the international division in order to boost their relative performance. Corporate performance generally suffers when domestic and international counterparts receive little credit for the other's successes.

Product Division   Product divisions are the most popular type of structure among MNEs. Usefulness follows from the fact that most MNEs make and sell a broad portfolio of products.[14] Effectively, the broader the portfolio, the more likely an MNE looks to arrange its structure in terms of product divisions.

For example, the merger of Moët Hennessy and Louis Vuitton created the world's largest luxury goods group. It also created a wide portfolio of brands that included Christian Dior perfume, Tag Heuer watches, Louis Vuitton bags, and Moët & Chandon champagne. Although each product targets the same high-end market niche, the dissimilarity from fragrances to watches to luggage to liquor led managers to split LVMH into five divisions: wines and spirits; fashion and leather goods; perfumes and cosmetics; watches and jewelry; and selective retailing. Despite overlapping markets, distribution channels, and supply chains, divisions independently run their product portfolio.

Independence means that different subsidiaries from different product divisions within the same foreign country often report to different executives at headquarters. Figure 15.2 (c) indicate, for example, that the Belgian electric and elevator subsidiaries report to different units at headquarters. Unless safeguarded, coordination suffers. For example, at one point, a Westinghouse subsidiary paid a premium to borrow funds while a nother unit in the same country, but housed in a different product division, held excess cash. Similarly, at one point Nestlé had more than 500 factories in nearly 90 countries manufacturing its 8,000 brands. Headquarters in Switzerland struggled to determine the costs of the raw materials its subsidiaries bought from suppliers. In an extreme case, each of Nestlé's more than 40 U.S. factories purchased raw materials independently. Lack of coordination, compounded by the fact that Nestlé then used five different e-mail systems, meant that its U.S. factories paid more than 20 different prices for vanilla to the same supplier.[15]

Geographic (Area) Division   An MNE uses geographic divisions, as depicted in Figure 15.2 (d), when it has large foreign operations that are not dominated by a single country or region (including the home country). Therefore, it groups activities on the basis of geography; i.e, Division A is responsible for Europe, Division B tends to North America, and Division C manages Asia. Historically, the area structure has been more common among European MNEs than among U.S. MNEs. European firms based in small countries inevitably expanded into bigger markets worldwide. Geographic proximity, such as Canada, United States, and Mexico comprising North America, supported demarcating the world by regions.

The emergence of fast-growing developing markets pushes MNEs to tweak the geographic structure. For example, the rising strategic profile of China and Eastern Europe led Nike to reset its four-region structure into six areas—North America, Western Europe, Eastern/Central Europe, Japan, Greater China, and Emerging Markets. Furthermore, Nike announced that China and Eastern Europe would operate separately from the other divisions. Their growing share of the company's total sales, coupled with their faster growth rates, led Nike to adjust its structure accordingly.[16]

> Geographic divisions are popular when foreign operations are large and no single country or region dominates sales.

The geographic division structure has been commonly associated with companies pursuing multidomestic strategies on a country or regional basis—as seen in Nike's decision to differentiate Eastern Europe and China. The decentralization of the area structure gives local managers more authority to adapt value activities. As Nike explained about its new structure, "We are confident these changes will best position us for future growth.... This model allows our global categories to connect directly with consumers at the local level."

Similar moves by other MNEs highlight the trend afoot for traditionally West-centric companies to rethink their structures given the emergence of larger, faster-growing markets. For example, Panasonic adjusted its structure given sales trends in emerging versus developed economies. Historically, Panasonic maintained a conventional geographic format—e.g., North America, Europe, and Asia. Now, given the equatorial proximity of many emerging economies, it thinks about organizing by temperature and tropical climate zones. Longitude, not latitude, matters more. Operationally, executives from Brazil, who previously conferred with colleagues in South America, now swap ideas with in Malaysia, who previously conferred with colleagues in Asia.[17]

The key limitation of the geographic structure is duplication due to configuring similar activities in several places. Each area essentially builds its own operation. Replication can prove unwieldy and expensive. However, one should note that this inefficiency is the price some MNEs, such as J&J, pay to build a locally responsive organization. Rather than a structural deficiency, strategic requirements may necessitate duplication.

MATRIX STRUCTURE

Some MNEs pursue strategies that simultaneously face high pressures for global integration and local responsiveness. This choice often leads to a **matrix structure,** as depicted in Figure 15.2 (e). Simultaneously targeting the strengths of the functional and divisional structures, it horizontally differentiates the organization such that a subsidiary reports to two different executives.

Arguably, this approach best position's MNEs to reconcile opposing pressures for integration and adaptation. Bringing to bear both perspectives, through blending units that are sensitive to different pressure points, improves the odds of decision-making dealing with both. Operationally, a subsidiary now has two bosses: one representing the interests of, say, a business function like manufacturing, the other representing the interests of a sales region. The matrix structure requires the two units extensively coordinate resources and fairly share rewards.[18] Indeed, both managers must sign off on key decisions. As such, the matrix installs the basis for communication and collaboration to reconcile global imperatives and local standards.

Collaboration also fans competition. That is, a matrix structure requires quasi-independent groups compete for resources and rewards. Disputes among lower-level managers often head-up the hierarchy. Besides delaying decisions, upper management involvement may favor a group, such as manufacturing and their call to standardize activities, to the annoyance of their matrix counterpart, such as the Asian sales group, who champion adapting product features to local preferences. Others in the firm may conclude that the true locus of power lies with the victor. Unchecked, gamesmanship threatens collaboration, thereby short-circuiting the knowledge-generating and decision-making relationships that were the original promise of the matrix.

A matrix structure also institutes a dual hierarchy that violates the **unity-of-command principle.** This notion holds that an unbroken chain of command should flow from the CEO to the entry-level worker. Giving one worker two bosses, by blurring lines of responsibility, creates conflicting lines of command and nebulous accountability. The CEO of Dow Chemical, an early adopter of the matrix structure, explained, "We were an organization that was matrixed and depended on teamwork, but there was no one in charge. When things went well, we didn't know whom to reward; and when things went poorly, we didn't know whom to blame."[19] Persistent problems coordinating responsibilities and resources have led many MNEs to forsake the matrix structure.[20]

MIXED STRUCTURE

In reality, few MNEs have a structure that neatly mimics a functional, divisional, or matrix format. Different growth rates and market conditions, as we saw in Nike's dilemma with its various regions, usually prevent all of a firm's activities from corresponding to a single organizing logic. Thus, some MNEs combine features of the functional, geographic, and product structures into a **mixed structure.** Again, we saw this happen as Nike installed vertical and horizontal arrangements for China and Eastern Europe that were unsuitable for the others regions.

Similarly, changes in industry conditions and company capabilities can unevenly change a structure. For instance, IBM reorganized its European operations to "have decision-making staff closer to customers." This redesign necessitated reducing the scale of its EMEA (Europe, Middle East, and Africa) headquarters in Paris, a major unit in place since the end of World War II. Many of its responsibilities gradually moved to smaller hubs in Madrid and Zurich.[21] Meanwhile, IBM's North American and Asian operations, implementing different programs given different pressures, adopted different structures. Hence, although MNEs prefers structural consistency worldwide, adapting to market conditions often result in mixed structures.

A matrix organization:

- Institutes overlaps among functional and divisional forms.
- Gives functional, product, and geographic groups a common focus.
- Has dual-reporting relationships rather than a single line of command.

Concept Check

Discussion of the "Types of Economic Systems" in Chapter 4 noted that a mixed economy combines some of the benefits of a free market with certain features of command systems. A mixed organizational structure reflects a similar imperative to sacrifice purity to practicality. Managers customize "model" organizational configurations to accommodate their mix of businesses and countries.

Each MNE's structure reflects its particular:

- Executive preferences.
- Value chain configuration.
- Market circumstances.

Neoclassical Structures

Some MNEs find that the hierarchical architecture of classical structures poorly implements their increasingly sophisticated strategies.[22] Burgeoning international activities, expanding internal relationships, and differentiated foreign operations strain their versatility. However, various environmental, organizational, and workplace trends, discussed earlier, suggest different structural formats. These trends move MNEs from the classical formats organized by function, product, or area to radically different structural configurations. These formats, regarded as **neoclassical structures**, still configure the elements of the company, stipulate how its utilizes resources, install communication platforms, and indicate authority, rights, and responsibilities. However, they apply different devices to resovlve the shortcomings, such as conformity, rigidity, bureaucracy, and authoritarism, that limit the versatility of classical functional and divisional formats.

IBM symbolizes this transition as it moves into its third organizational phase. Its read of market circumstances spurs it to build a "globally integrated enterprise" that puts investments, people, and work anywhere in the world based on the optimal mix of costs, skills, and environment.[23] The competitive necessity to rearrange workflow pushes IBM to rethink the functionality of vertical and horizontal differentiation. Increasingly intricate workflow patterns calls for new approaches to coordination, collaboration, and control. Thanks to ever-improving telecom capabilities, from 4G to VoIP to teleconferencing and beyond, globally dispersed executives can manage activities as effectively as those at headquarters did a generation ago. So, as IBM, like innumerable other MNEs, pursues increasingly sophisticated strategies, it applies increasingly ambitious structures to organize its activities.[24]

IBM's earlier activities in Europe elaborate the ins and outs of this evolution.[25] As had many MNEs operating in Europe in the post-WWII era, IBM implemented a multidomestic strategy through a geographic structure that was overlaid atop quasi-autonomous country operations. IBM relied on a regional office in Paris, staffed by thousands, to consolidate operations, coordinate policies, and control irregularities. Integration within the European Union in the 1990s pushed IBM to move more decision making from local subsidiaries to the regional office, seeing regional centralization as the means to implement its pan-European strategy. Performance, however, steadily fell short of ambition. Eventually, IBM began dismantling national and regional fiefdoms in Europe, ultimately firing thousands there and hiring thousands elsewhere, most notably in India.

Changing Times, Changing Strategies, Changing Structures   A generation ago, technology, costs, and skills meant people in a particular country served local customers. Hence IBM's multidomestic strategy and geographic structure. Now, new markets and new technologies enable moving work to "places where it will be done. . . most efficiently and to the highest quality."[26] Today, Indian software engineers, for instance, work on projects that arise in markets around the world without missing a beat. Customers, meanwhile, care less where work is done as long as the results meet contract specifications. Within this context, IBM's decision to reset its structure to organize its changing workflow speaks to the simple fact that markets and technologies meant it now could build a globally integrated enterprise. This opportunity, intensified by competitors such as SAP, Infosys, Wipro, Cognizant, and others traveling the same path, spurs IBM to champion the coordination, collaboration, control features of a neoclassical structure.

Likewise, consider the choices made by Cisco. Changing markets along with enterprising rivals put it at a structural crossroad. Rather than reinstall a traditional divisional hierarchy, Cisco developed an elaborate system of cross-functional, cross-market, and cross-business committees. Some committees do without a formal leader and behave more like a sports team, relying on a culture of collaboration. Indeed, Cisco has fired so-called lone rangers, whereas those who work well with others have been promoted. Asked why he led Cisco into unchartered organizational territory, CEO John Chambers replied because he had no choice. He needed a structure that reacts quickly to new opportunities, develops entire solutions rather than stand-alone products, and "helps Cisco to become a globally integrated company by making it easier for executives from all around the world to weigh in." Going forward, he adds, as technology makes communication much cheaper, executives must migrate from the static command and control approach to the flexibility of coordinate and cultivate.[27]

BOUNDARY BUSTING

The transition from a classical to a neoclassical structure directs MNEs, such as IBM and Cisco, to the issue of boundaries. Classical structures vertically and horizontally differentiate activities to arrange rules, responsibilities, and relationships. Inevitably, differentiation imposes boundaries. Think of, for example, the schematic of boxes and lines shown in Figure 15.2; each demarcates boundaries that segregate functions, markets, and businesses. In practical terms, **boundaries** are (1) vertical constraints that separate employees into specific slots in the hierarchy and the (2) horizontal constraints that follow from having specific employees do only specific jobs in specific units.[28]

Increasingly sophisticated strategies require improving collaboration, sharing, and engagement across the MNE. The boundaries of vertically and horizontally differentiated structures, by hampering these activities, constrain performance. For example, Sony's CEO blames his company's poor turnaround performance on divisions and rivalries between its "silos" that prevent integrating activites.[29] The globally integrated enterprise depends on breaching silos. Failure, as Sony shows, prolongs poor performance.[30]

Difficulties Posed by Boundaries   The intrinsic boundaries of classical structures impede knowledge flows and interrupt coordination. Resolving those rests upon busting the boundaries between vertical ranks and roles, between horizontal units in different functions, products, and areas, and between the firm and its suppliers, distributors, joint-venture partners, strategic allies, and customers.

These mandates if possible, insert a new paragraph break were initially advocated by Jack Welch. Directing GE's far-flung global operations led Welsh to experiment with organizational formats. Reflecting on his nearly 20-year run as CEO, he explained that his goal had been to build an organization that eliminated the vertical and horizontal boundaries that put barriers between the company and managers and their customers, suppliers, and stakeholders. As Welch explained, "The simplest definition of what we are trying to create—what our objective is—is a **boundaryless** company, a company where the artificial barriers and walls people are forever building around themselves or each other—for status, security, or to keep change away—are demolished and everyone has access to the same information, everyone pulls in the same direction, and everyone shares in the rewards of winning—in the soul as well as in the wallet."[31]

Neoclassical structures move the MNE toward these outcomes. They promote loosely connected networks of self-organizing and self-governing agents. They develop less rigid structural forms that are marked by fewer rules, regulations, and processes, and expectedly, better coordination of knowledge and cultivation of relationships. Unlike classical structures, in which the formal attributes of managers (i.e., title, location, reports) matter most, in neoclassical formats the managers' relationships with other agents in the network matter more. Neoclassical structures, in theory, spurs people to share, not control, information; collaborate, not compete, on projects; promote,

> Boundarylessness refers to eliminating vertical, horizontal, and external boundaries that hinder the flow of information and formation of relationships.

not suppress, innovation; cultivate, not command, relationships, and engage, not resist, change. Leading examples of neoclassical structures include the network structure and virtual organization.

NETWORK STRUCTURE

The **network structure** provides an efficient and dynamic format to manage interdependent value activities. It brings to bear bear multidimensional perspectives in a flexible, integrative process. It arranges differentiated elements in a patterned flows of activity that allocates people and resources to problems and projects in a decentralized manner.[32] Figure 15.2, in profiling the connectivity of the the Internet, provides a visual representation of a network. Figure 15.3 depicts a simplified application.

The network structure is anchored by a core organization that outsources activities in which it has no core competency to firms that do—or, as the saying goes, "Do what you do best and outsource the rest." For example, MNEs like Nike, Apple, Qualcomm, and Cisco concentrates on research and development, product design, and marketing, their core competencies, and hire other companies, like Yue Yuen Industrial, Foxconn, Hon Hai, or Flextronics, who excel in manufacturing, to make their products. Relationships in the network are not solely designed to improve transactional efficiency. Rather, companies in the network cultivate specialized decision-making relationships, based on long-term common interests that improve coordination and collaboration.

Again, consider the activities of Qualcomm, Nike, and Cisco. Essentially, each is a research, development, and marketing MNE that uses outside suppliers and independent manufacturers to assemble its products. Operationally, each enters joint ownership arrangements with other companies to share production, distribution, and technology-development facilities. Each contracts with other companies to produce and distribute goods and components. Each organizes its many alliances with the latest and greatest communication technology, using the Internet, e-mail, file sharing, and conferencing to link partners in its network.

FIGURE 15.3   A simplified Network Structure

A network is an interconnected system of people, products, and processes. At the center of the network structure is a core unit. Its function is to outsource value-adding activities for which it does not possess core competencies. The network itself consists of partner organizations that focus on areas in which they can deliver maximum value. Finally, there are the channels through which units communicate with other units. To manage the network, the core unit uses these channels to coordinate and integrate activities carried on throughout the system.

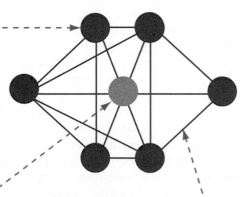

Differentiated units to which headquarters delegates decision-making authority. These units, whether they are local marketing subsidiaries, international production centers, or cross-functional teams, are the front line of the network with responsibility for sensing, processing, and acting upon specialized and generalized information in an entrepreneurial fashion.

The formal center of the network that coordinates strategic objectives and operational policies across the differentiated units. This unit ensures the efficient flow of resources, supplies, components, and funds throughout the network. It aims to, and effectively collects, sorts, and distributes the organization's accumulated wisdom, knowledge, and experiences.

The channels of exchange that manage and fine-tune the volume, content, and flow of hard and soft information. These linkages animate the network by setting paths of interaction, coordination, and integration between differentiated yet interdependent functional, area, and product units.

Networks Aren't New   Although a novel format for some, the network structure is not unprecedented. Japanese MNEs have long-used the so-called *keiretsu* format, an integrated collective of nominally independent companies in which each owns a share of the others.[33] *Keiretsus* rely on long-term personal relationships among the companies' executives. Sometimes they are vertical, notably the *seisan keiretsu*, a manufacturing network, or the *ryūtsū keiretsu*, a distribution network. In the former, managers connect the factors of production of a certain product (such as the network between Toyota and its parts suppliers). Another type is horizontal, namely, a *kigyō shūdan*. This format, essentially a diversified business groups, links companies across related and different industries. At the center of this type of network is a *sogo shosha* (trading company), like Mitsubishi, or financial institution, like Sumitomo. In both vertical and horizontal *keiretsus*, the network center coordinates marketing and controls financing among the allied units.

> A network structure anchors a small core organization that outsources value activities to firms whose core competency supports greater innovation at lower cost.

Worldwide, companies exhibiting a *keiretsu* form of the network structure include the Virgin Group, Cisco, Grupo Empresarial Antioqueño. South Korean companies, like Samsung, share some of the characteristics of a *keiretsu* in their *chaebol* format. German companies, such as Deutsche Bank, are similarly intertwined, but there is no formal term to describe them.[34] Like their Japanse counterparts, these groups have extensive, self-sustaining connections. Unlike the Japanse, they rely more on centralized controls.

> Forms of the network structures are used by MNEs worldwide.

VIRTUAL ORGANIZATION

A **virtual organization** represents a temporary arrangement among independent companies, suppliers, customers, and even rivals that "works across space, time, and organizational boundaries with links strengthened by webs of communication technologies."[35] Deemphasizing formal rules, responsibilities, procedures, and relationships within the group promotes informal communication that usually moves laterally and has little regard for traditional hierarchy. Improving technologies, by supporting coordination among people working from different locations, ease cultivating relationships, acquiring resources, and developing strategic capabilities.[36]

> A virtual organization is a dynamic arrangement among partners that efficiently adapts to market change.

The film industry provides a popular mode. People from around the world are essentially "free agents" who move from project to project applying their skills (i.e., directing, talent search, costuming, and set design) as needed. Temporary arrangements mean virtual organizations organize and reorganize as opportunities evolve.[37] Market mechanisms, such as contracts, anchor it. Strong performers replace poor performers.

A virtual organization consists of a core of full-time employees that rely on outside specialists to work on opportunities. The international advertising agency StrawberryFrog is one example. Its peculiar name was inspired by a rare amphibian with a red body and blue legs, a nimble creature that, as its CEO explains, represents the opposite of the existing "dinosaur agencies, established in the industrial age as monoliths, which have the greatest difficulty in adapting to the new era."[38] Competing with advertising MNEs employing thousands, StrawberryFrog has a small staff, known as "frogs," based in New York, Sao Paulo, Amsterdam, and Mumbai. It bulks up as needed by hiring freelancers from around the world.[39] Free of the overhead, constraints, and complexity of hierarchies, it offers clients the agility and cost-effectiveness of a high-powered, loosely coupled organization.[40]

> The flexibility of virtual organizations enables easily replacing poor performers.

PITFALLS OF NEOCLASSICAL STRUCTURES

Like its classical counterparts, neoclassical structures have limits. First is the difficulty of formatting something that, by definition, is ever changing. The fact that networks are dynamic structures makes adaptive reconfiguration, responsive coordination, and reasonable control challenging.[41] Cisco, for example, worries that the internal workings of its many management committees may prove too socially complex as well as physically tiring. Also, Cisco has struggled to assemble and disassemble teams given its acquisitions, divestures, and evolving business strategies.

Then there are executives who champion self-organization yet intrude in decision-making. When push comes to shove, they intervene in workers' creative independence and self-direction. Managers' intrusion into the workflow fans motivational problems. In addition, neoclassical structures can develop hidden hierarchies that arise as workers organize around rules, rewards, and punishments.[42] Said one observer, "I've been inside a lot of companies that espouse flat organizational structures and self-management. But when you really start looking at how things actually work, you find that there is in fact a hierarchy—just one that is not explicit."[43]

Coordination Systems

> The MNE uses coordination and control systems to synchronize, integrate, and regulate value activities.

Changing pressures for global integration and local responsiveness, along with dynamic industry structures and evolving market conditions, push MNEs to devise sophisticated strategies. These path-breaking plans require coordination methods and control measures. The importance of **coordination** follows from the reality of life in the MNE. Designing innovative products in Taiwan, sourcing inputs from Australia, transporting them to production facilities in China, and distributing them to consumers worldwide creates interdependencies. Coordination systems synchronize rules, responsibilities, and relationships so that the MNE uses its resources efficiently and makes decisions effectively.

Without the means to coordinate activities, the competitiveness of a strategy, no matter how brightly conceived, erodes. Therefore, designing an organization, whether the format is classical or neoclassical, requires managers apply coordination methods. Prevalent approaches include coordination by *standardization*, *plan*, and *mutual adjustment*.

COORDINATION BY STANDARDIZATION

Operational consistency, by applying absolute rules and precise procedures, helps an MNE leverage its core competency as well as minimize inefficiencies. This assumption endorses coordination by standardization. This approach specifies the way employees do their jobs, work with one another, and deal with customers. Aspects range from the mundane (i.e., dress and decorum requirements stipulated in employee manuals) to the strategic (i.e., protocols to enter new markets, dealing with joint-venture partners). Asked why Starbucks standardizes its products, processes, and procedures for worldwide markets, its CEO notes the need to replicate the look, operations, and feel of the elusive atmosphere of its U.S. coffee shop concept to the thousands of Starbucks shops around the world. Starbucks in Seattle must be operationally interchangeable with Starbucks in Sydney. Coordination by standardization, by stipulating the scripts that tell people how to do their jobs, supports this goal.

> Coordination by standardization
> - Sets universal rules and procedures that apply to units worldwide.
> - Enforces consistency of activities among dispersed units.

Coordination by standardization is ideally suited for the MNEs implementing international or global strategies. Their imperative of worldwide consistency perfectly fits standardization's specification of the one, right way. In the case of the international strategy, transferring, applying, and protecting core competencies necessitates specifying rules and regulations. In the case of the global strategy, integrating densely linked activities tolerates no deviations. Resources and components, for instance, are needed at specific plants at specific times. Standardizing coordination methods—such as the format for processing information and supervising logistics—preempts irregularities.

Standardizing activities controls the influence of national cultures on coordination systems. For example, the performance of a value chain depends on links between activities meeting timetables. Units in monochronic cultures may see deadlines as hard

The Superior Structure: Hierarchy or Hyperarchy?

Point **Yes** Proponents of the classical hierarchy argue that it is the enduring foundation for how MNEs optimally arrange roles, responsibilities, and relationships. The hierarchy supports a clear unity of command, functional span of control, allocation of authority, and assignment of tasks. It offers the ideal degree of rules, regulations, policies, and procedures. Hierarchies impose clarity on otherwise confusing situations. Vertical and horizontal differentiations as suggested in Figure 15.5, precisely specify roles and relationships. This, in turn, supports sophisticated planning, information, and control systems. One of the strongest advocates of the hierarchy, Harold Geneen of ITT, believed it helped "make people as predictable and controllable as the capital resources that they're responsible for."[44] The hierarchy's strengths make it the *sine qua non* of the professional management model.

Ongoing Refinements The implication of contemporary technological, regulatory, and competitive trends to organizational standards is interesting. In addition, we realize that as environments change, so too must companies' strategies and structures. However, calls to discard the classical principles of the hierarchy are reckless. Rather, one needs only reengineer processes, through programs like total quality management, supply chain management, and Six Sigma, to fortify it. These efforts effectively reset the division of work and differentiation of authority for changing market circumstances.[45]

What then, you ask, do we think of the neoclassical alternative of a hyperarchy that is championed in the Counterpoint? In our view, such radical tinkering with the day-to-day reality of organizing international operations is a leap into the unknown. Avoiding a costly fall calls for thoughtful adjustment to the way organizations run, not the wistfulness of a brave, new cyberworld.

Leading Indicator Arguably, Google foreshadows building an organization that respects the past but engages the future. It organizes its senior executives and business groups by function, with the largest functions engineering, product management, and product marketing. Despite the founders' description of Google as "engineering-centric," they see virtue in chaos by design. Insiders' tales of of orderly disorder, purposeful disarray, and certain uncertainty signal Google's plans to thrive on the edge of controlled chaos.[46]

Rather than retreat to the hierarchical conventions commonly found in engineering-centric companies, like DuPont and General Motors in earlier times, Google stretches its hierarchy as much as possible. Asked why, Larry Page, Google's co-founder, CEO, and unofficial thought leader, explained, "I want to run a company where we are moving too quickly and doing too much, not being too cautious and doing too little. If we don't have any of these mistakes, we're just not taking enough risk."

FIGURE 15.4 A Classical Hierarchy

Admittedly quite simple, this depiction effectively communicates the organizing logic of a hierarchy—different people of different ranks at different levels doing different jobs. As such, the various shades speak to matters of horizontal differentiation while the top-down flow highlights ideas of vertical differentiation.

Source: Paperboat/Shutterstock.com

The Superior Structure: Hierarchy or Hyperarchy?

Counterpoint   **No** The state of the world heralds the dawn of a new structural format that positions confident MNEs to jump ahead of their competitors. As had emerging technologies in the early 1900s supported the then-heretical hierarchy, emerging technologies in the twenty-first century enable new types of organization. Quite simply, "digital infrastructures allow companies to organize and manage their activities in new ways."[47] Now, just as then, bright executives question convention, finding ways that leverage the information flowing in, through, and out of the MNE.

The Crux of Change   Unquestionably, the hierarchy has virtues. Nevertheless, it is marked by flaws. It organizes information flows in ways that work against integrating pieces. Hierarchies, even with matrix overlays and mixed adjustments, slow relationships and make work more complex.[48] It leashes the intrinsic motivation of employees, stifles adaptation, and squelches enterprise. Responding to the expanding data of today business world, we argue, requires an organization that diffuses information and coordinates its flows.

The Hyperarchy   This neoclassical format, sometimes referred to as a as a *flat hierarchy, social network*, or *peer-to-peer format*, exhibits the properties of a *hyperarchy*. Technically, a hyperarchy is "a large-scale, self-organizing community that sets free unusually high degrees of energy and engagement—despite the lack of clear or direct economic payoff for participants."[49] Much like a network, a hyperarchy is a constellation of actors and relationships that follow from the interactions of technology, knowledge, social relations, administrative routines, and legal ties—as we see to some degree in Figure 15.6.

Actors are connected to other actors through direct and indirect relationships . As a result, the hyperarchy is "infinitely large, never balanced, never optimal and has unique perspectives for all members."[50] Now, "information flows along multiple and intermediate paths; this allows for multiple and overlapping points at which information can be sorted and interpreted. It makes it possible to process an abundance of information effectively."[51] The hyperarchy, by remedying the hierarchy's bias toward boundaries, provides managers the tools to build a globally integrated enterprise.

Perhaps the best-known hyperarchy is the open source model, a software movement in which program source code is given away to volunteers who help fix bugs and design new features with no direct compensation. Operationally, it applies basic rules to increase transparency, coordinate efforts, and control performance. Programmers' ability to monitor peers' production encourages bartering and collaboration. Similar situations unfold with the intriguing ecosystems that power the Apple and Android "app" phenomena.

The Test   We are witnessing a fundamental shift in our idea of organization. The precision of vertical and horizontal differentiation gives way to formats that are less bounded by vertical and horizontal differentiation.[52] Andy Grove, CEO of Intel for many years, foreshadows how the contest between the order of the hierarchy and chaos of the hyperarchy might shake out. He believes that a structure must encourage and energize constructive confrontation in ways that let people agree and disagree but, ultimately, commit to the same goals. The challenge is developing a structure that, Grove reasons, enables them to "let chaos reign and then rein in chaos."[53] The hyperarchy, not hierarchy, we submit, meets this mission.

FIGURE 15.5
A Neoclassical Hyperarchy

This depiction of a hyperarchy, again quite simplified, highlights key features. Rather than the ranks and divisions found in a classical hierarchy, we see patterns of relationships, aided and abetted by technologies, that outline lines of communication, coordination, and collaboration among equivalent "blue" managers.

Source: Paperboat/Shutterstock.com

promises while counterparts in polychronic cultures regard them as loose guidelines. Standardization synchronizes responsibilities. Similarly, say an MNE has factories in Japan and Mexico that manufacture the same product but, due to cultural legacies and location economics, apply different production philosophies. The Mexican factory uses a traditional assembly-line operation given the local conditions of inexpensive labor, patchy transportation infrastructure, and high marginal cost of technology. The Japanese factory, in contrast, uses a lean production system, given local labor competency, manufacturing expertise, efficient logistics, and high warehouse expense. Coordination by standardization synchronizes different manufacturing orientations.

Differences in industry conduct and host-government attitudes complicate coordination by standardization. MNEs that adapt activities to local conditions, like those implementing a multidomestic strategy, are sensitive to this pressure. The fact that rules and procedures do not apply to every situation in every unit in every country creates exceptions that disrupt routines. Ongoing exceptions undermine the authority of standardization. Hence, MNEs following a multidomestic strategy, such as J&J, reason that standardization is unsuitable given the different conditions they face in different markets.

Concept Check

In Chapter 2, we note that managers deal with differences in the ways in which colleagues and subordinates, especially those from foreign cultures, respond when it comes to issues like work motivation, relationship preferences, and other factors in workplace behavior. Here we observe that, to accommodate these differences, MNEs mind cultural orientations when setting coordination systems.

COORDINATION BY PLAN

Often market circumstance, strategic goals, or workflow patterns prevent specifying exact rules and procedures. Making effective decisions requires manager have the authority to adjust to situations. Optimizing, as oppose to maximizing, objectives leads an MNE to use **coordination by plan.** This mode gives managers of interdependent units the latitude to mutually adjust goals and schedules—provided they still meet deadlines and hit targets.

Coordination by plan requires interdependent units meet common deadlines and objectives.

General objectives and detailed schedules are the basis for coordination by plan. They define critical success factors, specify expectations, and set hard deadlines. Systems create the means for units to accept, adopt, and, where legitimate, adapt plans. They also identify participating managers and programs, establish timing and format, and set communication methods.

No matter how insightful the plan, the unexpected is ever-present; or, more poetically, "The best-laid plans of mice and men often go awry." Market disruptions, government intervention, and conflict with local partners spur adjusting objectives and schedules. These complicate coordination by plan. Managing objectives and schedules depends on extensive communication and exchange between superiors, equals, and subordinates. Geographic distance and cultural divergence increase the time, expense, and errors in cross-national communications. Improving communication platforms steadily diminishes problems. Teleconferencing, most notably, easily lets those that prefer dealing with counterparts through face-to-face contact still capture the non-verbal nuances of body language.

Management methods bolster coordination by plan. Six Sigma, a rigorous and disciplined planning process, uses data and statistical analysis to coordinate practices and systems. Credit Suisse, Siemens, GE, Korea Telecom, Wipro, but then it wouldn't Nortel Networks, Air Canada, and DuPont, for instance, have used it to improve their planning process. The parameters and analytics of similar programs, such as the Balanced Scorecard or TQM, are used worldwide.

Coordinating planning activities requires "synchronizing" people across countries and cultures.[54] Hence, national cultures pose complications. Many differ in their orientations toward trust, exchange, and collaboration.[55] Units anchored in individualistic versus collectivist cultures may disagree over information sharing or collaboration responsibilities; conflicts muddle coordination. These differences are less disruptive in standardized situations, yet they shape the effectiveness of coordination by plan.

Generally, their challenge is proportional to the importance of sharing specialized knowledge among personnel. if personnel.

MNEs report that a useful tool is building teams with members from different countries with different responsibilities to imagine future market scenarios.[56] Similarly, some MNEs locate international and domestic personnel in proximity to each other—say, by placing the international division in the same building as product divisions—to promote networks that facilitate coordination by plan.

COORDINATION BY MUTUAL ADJUSTMENT

Some MNEs coordinate value activities through less formal mechanisms than standards or plans. They opt for the personal touch, socially engineering systems to cultivate relationships among employees, that, in turn, support coordination. Rather than rules and regulations or objectives and schedules, they rely on social networking tools, web-based collaboration, social interactions, and extensive communications. Managers reason that aggressively promoting collaboration among coworkers helps implements their strategy. This outlook leads to **coordination by mutual adjustment.**

For example, consider 3M's technology experts in more than 100 laboratories around the world. Success, 3M believes, depends on these folks developing robust knowledge-generating and decision-making relationships that support exchanging ideas, coordinating programs, and integrating results. The abstraction and complexity of lab activities prevents standardizing or scripting coordination. Hence, 3M used coordination by mutual adjustment. Tools included a Technical Council, comprised of the heads of the major labs, who meet monthly and have a three-day annual retreat to discuss ways to improve cross-unit exchange. A broader-based Technical Forum, composed of scientists and technical experts chosen as representatives, facilitates grassroots communication.[57] Both methods support the flexible exchange of ideas, a key precondition of coordinating activities by mutual adjustment.

Here, There, and Everywhere

The bane of international business has been the necessity of visiting far-away colleagues, partners, and customers, often at a moment's notice, high expense, and considerable personal effort. Now, teleconferencing—the magical ability to be two places at once—changes the nature of control and coordination in organizations.

Source: © Asia Images Group Pte Ltd/Alamy

3M's profile suggests a straightforward process. In practice, coordination by mutual adjustment imposes tough demands. Collaboration among associates in different parts of the world is a key part of coordination by adjustment. The scale of global operations makes simple activities, such as teleconferencing, tricky. Typically, geographic constraints means that teams must alternate meetings between early morning and late evening to accommodate various time zones. It is not usual, over the course of the day, for a manager in the United States to teleconference with folks in Asia at 2 AM, colleagues in Western Europe at 9 AM, and coworkers and South America at 3 PM. For example, Cisco averages nearly 6,000 teleconferences a week. Senior executives working on three to five coordination groups, and often many more, may have teleconferencing meetings literally around the clock.

> Coordination by mutual adjustment depends on managers interacting extensively with counterparts.

Besides geographies, various processes of coordination by mutual adjustment can prove difficult. Decision making often slows as views evolve. Managers' commitment may waver as they tire of ongoing negotiation. Personal relationship challenge roles, status, and power. Whereas standardizing and planning processes reinforce vertical and horizontal differentiation, processes of mutual adjustment blur authority. Collaboration requires cooperation, not control.

Also, the fact that that innovations, knowledge, and skills can arise anywhere within the firm's global network, not just at the center, changes the role of headquarters.[58] Coordination by mutual adjustment requires senior managers break down boundaries, reselling their role from telling people what to do to facilitating their success. Hence, coordination by mutual adjustment is philosophically and practically compatible with forms of neoclassical structures.

Coordination by mutual adjustment uses a range of management methods. Commonly, MNEs select managers from different units to resolve cross-national questions. Assembled and charged with collaborating, these teams share viewpoints and champion cooperative efforts. They also establish liaisons among subsidiaries to integrate actions among different groups. Similarly, MNEs rotate managers between domestic and international positions, reasoning that personal familiarity cultivates relationships that promote collaboration. Too, rotation across divisional, business, or functional lines promotes relationships that weaken insular thinking and reinforces idea sharing.

A Case in Point Although difficult, coordination by mutual adjustment processes can productively moves an MNE's strategy forward. For example, Red Hat's Global Support Services solves complex technical problems facing its customers. Its technical support engineers, technical account managers, and software maintenance engineers work from 16 countries, support 58 offices in 28 countries, and provide round the clock customer service in nine languages.

Many questions from customers are consultative in nature given the intricate technical architecture of its software. Improving performance, management realized, depended on taking advantage of the organization's collective knowledge by fostering collaboration on a global scale. The fact that solutions were often unique to a particular technical problem ruled out standardization and mitigated the effectiveness of planning scripts. Still, even though many answers were unique to a client, overlapping aspects meant that Red Hat's consultants frequently reinvented parts of the software wheel. Improving the ability of its globally diverse technical support associates, it found, depended on improving collaboration within the context of coordination by adjustment.

Over the course of a year or so, cross-geo teams eliminated structural, cultural, and procedural boundaries that separated colleagues. Eventually, Red Hat installed coordination by mutual adjustment systems that connected people from several different functional roles, across 16 countries, through nine languages, and dozens of areas of domain knowledge. The eventual creation of Knowledge Centered Support and its "intelligent swarming model" let Red Hat more quickly resolve complicated problems as well as

> **Concept Check**
>
> No matter the coordination approach adopted by an MNE, none is immune to the complications posed by national cultures. Different national cultures differently influence the social, workplace, political, legal, and economic contexts. Differences in cultural conditions also influence a company's strategic options, shaping its choices regarding coordination by standardization, planning, or adjustment.

handle greater call volumes without increasing staff. Improved accuracy, consistency, and responsiveness boosted customer satisfaction.[59]

Control Systems

MNEs monitor performance to make sure that employees do what needs to be done. If plants are performing poorly, responses are slowing, schedules are slipping, or resources are wasted, then managers take forceful steps. **Control systems,** the means of forceful change, are part of a well-designed organization.[60] They define how managers compare performance to plans, identify differences, and, where found, assess the basis for the gap and impose corrections. Control systems regulate executive efforts, resource allocation, and self-interest. They directly complement coordination processes and structural designs. Prominent systems of control include:

BUREAUCRATIC CONTROL

> Bureaucratic control emphasizes organizational authority and relies on rules and regulations.

Situations whereby an MNE uses centralized authority to install rules and procedures to govern activities imposes bureaucratic control. This system of control supports operations that lend themselves to absolute rules and exact scripts. It is highly effective in some situations, such as Six Sigma efforts or quality management, which rely on precise directions to process map an activity. Regimenting and regulating, however, requires a good deal of resources. Bureaucratic control shares organizing principles with coordination by standardization and the classical forms of structure.

MARKET CONTROL

> Market control uses external market mechanisms to establish objective standards.

Situations whereby an MNE uses external market mechanisms, like profitability or market share, to establish performance benchmarks imposes market control. Controls, ever present, escalate when a unit deviates from benchmarks. Relying on market standards creates universal metrics that work in all countries—e.g., profitability and market share are measured the same everywhere. everywhere.

Case Review Note

For example, J&J decentralizes considerable authority to the local subsidiaries, preferring that citizens of the host country run local operations. Headquarters then supports subsidiaries and waits for superior results. If not forthcoming, control systems activate, and senior executives step in. The fact that J&J operates 250 units worldwide means, absent objective indicators such as market share, senior executives would struggle to assess a unit's performance. Market control shares organizing principles with coordination by plan as well as the classical and neoclassical structures.

CLAN CONTROL

Situations whereby an MNE relies on shared values among employees to idealize and enforce its preferred way of doing business imposes clan control. Operationally, it relies on values, beliefs, and norms to regulate employee behaviors and facilitate goal achievement. Hence, the key is encouraging employees to identify with the MNEs' vision and strategy how they do their job.[61]

Clan control is difficult in any context but particularly in the MNE. Its' presumed commonality of vision is more than likely to conflict with the values and norms held by subsidiary-level managers. Certainly, there are notable successes, like the control aspects of J&J's Credo or the "Toyota Way" of Toyota. Still, executives are often wary of its organizational and managerial demands. Clan control shares organizing principles with coordination by mutual adjustment and the neoclassical structures.

> Clan control uses shared values and ideals to moderate employee behavior.

CONTROL MECHANISMS

The objectivity of control encourages engineering precise mechanisms. A generation ago, the comparatively costly economics of prevailing travel, data exchange, and communication technologies endorsed certain mechanisms. Improving economics, courtesy of falling communication costs, make them cheaper, faster, and easier. This process has reduced the usefulness of some, boosted the usefulness of others and created the possibility for new mechanisms. MNEs often support their control system with the following tools.

Reports The intricacies of international business make reports a vital control method. Managers rely on frequent, accurate, and real-time reports to allocate resources, monitor performance, and reward successes. Reports also function as early warning systems, alerting managers to plan deviations. Often, MNEs use report formats and schedules for foreign operations that resemble those uses domestically. They reason that if report methods have worked for the home office, they will also work internationally. The global diffusion of standardized software packages from SAP, Oracle, IBM, Microsoft, and Red Hat, for instance, supports this outlook. Standardizing the format of reports worldwide, by leveraging corporate management's familiarity, lessens the need for new types of reporting mechanisms. Reports that share the same format also ease comparing units.

Timely reports allow managers to respond effectively.

Visits to Subsidiaries Formal reports only go so far. Many senior managers, especially those MNEs applying coordination by adjustment and clan control, often visit subsidiaries. Face-to-face meetings, budget reviews, and planning seminars fortify control systems. Old-school subsidiary visits promote direct, credible communication between headquarters and local managers.[62] Increasingly, technologies like teleconferencing expands managers' social options. Ongoing innovation in teleconferencing, supported by wikis, social networking, and web-based collaboration services, help MNEs reduce travel, save time, boost productivity, and tighten controls. For instance, recall that Cisco averages about 6,000 teleconferences a week; this has cut its annual travel budget by more than half.[63]

Evaluative Metrics Headquarters evaluate subsidiaries and their managers on many measures. Financial metrics dominate evaluations, particularly when an MNE relies on coordination by plan and control by bureaucracy. Perhaps the most important internal metrics are performance on "budget compared with profit" and "budget compared with sales value." They affect consolidated corporate figures so headquarters is sensitive to their status. Nonfinancial criteria include market-share, quality control, and turnover ratios. MNEs adjust evaluation metrics to avoid penalizing or rewarding managers or subsidiaries for conditions beyond their control. For example, headquarters may decide not to expand further in a country because of its slow growth and risky environment. Punishing managers for the country's adverse situation, independent of their performance, is demotivating. Balance requires qualifying evaluation for local conditions and global trends.

Concept Check

Chapter 11 explains that MNEs face "Operational Obstacles" in building communication channels among the links in their **value chains.** Chapter 12 explains that in deciding where to locate production operations, MNEs consider the costs of moving information, materials, and products to and from product-development, supply, and distribution facilities. Not long ago, inefficient transportation and expensive communications hindered efforts to coordinate global activities. Today, dramatic cost reductions make clan control an increasingly practical option.

Information Systems Information technology platforms provide useful control tools. Most MNEs use enterprise resource planning to monitor activities, such as product planning, parts purchasing, maintaining inventories, customer service, and order fulfillment.[64] MNEs, as do you, face constraints in acquiring information, notably the cost of the information compared to its value, identifying redundancies, and excluding the irrelevant. Useful information for a subsidiary, such as which customs official clears goods, need not be reported to headquarters. MNEs periodically reevaluate the information sources they use to preempt overload. Their centralization, coordination, and control policies guide triage.

A system that relies on a combination of measurements is more reliable than one that does not.

WHICH CONTROL SYSTEM WHEN?

An MNE tailors its control system to support its strategy. MNEs following a global strategy prefer market controls, given that they can use objective benchmarks to evaluate performance in any market. Transnational companies find value in clan control. The vitality of open exchange among geographically diffuse people fits the idea that common values, beliefs, and norms facilitate collaboration.

With all that said, there are no hard and fast rules. Complications posed by the competing pressures of integration and responsiveness, along with evolving industry structures, lead to dynamic value chain configurations. To support increasingly sophisticated strategies. Managers act in kind, thinking and tinkering with various control methods. Like the circumstances spurring a mixed structure, few MNEs rely on a single method. J&J, for instance, used market and clan control to regulate performance. It, like other astute MNEs, designs its control systems to reinforce its structure as well as fit its methods of coordination.

Case Review Note

Organization culture is the shared meaning and beliefs that shape how employees interpret information, make decisions, and implement actions.

Organization Culture

Having examined the roles played by structure and systems in organizing an MNE, we now turn to the final element of design: its organization culture. In theory, one could profile this idea from an applied perspective, specifying it as the way things are done in an MNE and evaluating how workers organize around rules, rewards, and punishments. Alternatively, we could follow the suggestion of Chapter 2 and adopt a philosophical view, regarding it as an embedded set of shared normative principles that guides actions and sanctions acceptable behaviors. behaviors.

We opt to integrate these perspectives and define **organization culture** as the coherent set of assumptions about an MNE and its goals and practices shared by its members. This system of shared values about what is important and beliefs about how the world works shapes how managers make decisions, take actions, and sustain a common cause.

A KEY PIECE OF THE PUZZLE

Multinational operations involve a difficult balancing act: giving people around the world the freedom to develop new ideas but ensuing that they implement them ever-mindful of global objectives. Few MNEs get this right in the long term by relying on their struture and systems. To this point, Jack Welch of GE cautioned, "Objectives don't get you there. Values do." Therefore, MNEs look to a resourceful organization culture to complete the trick.

Executives have long understood that their organization culture influenced performance. They now take an expansive view, seeing it as a powerful tool to implement their strategy. To that effect, studies confirm a significant link between an MNE's organization culture and its success. Facets of organization culture, such as the values and principles of management, nature of the work climate and atmosphere, and traditions and ethical standards, influence firm performance.[65]

Successful MNEs develop an organization culture that instills in their employees the enthusiasm beyond that justified solely by economic rewards. Organization culture stimulates people to engage the company's vision, do their jobs well, and collaborate with others while lessening the need to regulate their behaviors with elaborate structures and systems. Culture's capacity to power high performance puts the onus on managers to build a company that people do not want to merely work for, but want to belong to. The shared values that enact organization culture, goes the reasoning, influence what employees perceive, how they interpret, and what they do to respond to their world.

J&J, for example, anchors its strategic purpose and ideas of value creation in the principles of its Credo. This ethics manifesto unequivocally champions the values that embody the company's responsibilities to its stakeholders worldwide. When employees are confronted with opportunities or threats anywhere in the world, the Credo helps them define, analyze, and resolve them in ways that respect and reinforce J&J's culture and, by extension, its strategy.

Case Review Note

Organization culture is a critical component of an MNE's transition from "good" to "great" status. Unquestionably, technology, product development, marketing ingenuity, and financial stewardship play key roles. Greatness, however, depends on a culture of unwavering faith and passion, rigorous discipline and focus, clearly communicated and practiced core values and timeless principles, strong work ethics, and finding and promoting people with the right outlook.[66]

Great companies develop overarching overarching values, perspectives, and practices, much as J&J does with its Credo or Toyota with its Toyota Way, in order to give employees a consistent way to relate to their job, to each other, to customers, to shareholders, and to business partners. Fundamentally, the organization culture supports the strategy and legitimates the company's mission in the eyes of employees.

CULTURE'S INCREASING IMPORTANCE

The importance of organization culture will grow in coming years. Earlier chapters highlight pressures to improve global competitiveness, whereas later chapters discuss the novel approaches that MNEs apply. The rise in emerging economies and maturing growth in the West push managers to question strategies and reposition operations. Both ultimately require MNEs to rethink their strategy. For example, GE continues reconfiguring its value chain to reflect market trends. Notably, this has led it to adjust its West-centric orientation for the accelerating rise in emerging economies. Asked about GE's future, its CEO replied, "we've globalized around markets, not cheap labor. The era of globalization around cheap labor is over. Today we go to Brazil, we go to China, we go to India because that's where the customers are."[67]

New competitors from fast-growing economies devise strategies to navigate bustling markets that run the gamut from the Base of the Pyramid to surging affluence. Companies from both the East and the West pursue new, often astounding opportunities. Capturing them involves reinventing systems of production and distribution as well as experimenting with entirely new business models.

Increasingly sophisticated value chain configurations escalate demands on the organization. These demands have lower odds of success without a supportive organization culture. Certainly, MNEs could develop elaborate constraints, controls, and contracts that compel employees to do their best. And, granted, the notion that "beatings will continue until morale improves" may boost short-term performance. This approach inevitably proves counterproductive. Improving compatibility between an MNE's culture and its strategy has proven a more effective approach to superior performance.[68]

> MNEs proactively develop their organization culture, just as they design their structure and systems.

BUILDING AN ORGANIZATION CULTURE

Despite its pivotal function, few MNEs have been able to parlay their organization culture into consistently high performance. A survey of 1,200 international executives found that "fewer than 10 percent of their companies currently succeed at building high-performance cultures."[69] This shortfall stands in sharp contrast to the report that nine of 10 CEOs acknowledge that "corporate culture is as important as a strategy for business success."[70] Navigating the expectations-performance gap makes culture a key aspect of an MNE's organization design.

Historically, uncertainty about the dynamic of social engineering led managers to adopt a benign perspective, letting culture naturally emerge and evolve. Information and advice on "how things work around here" spread by word of mouth on factory floors and conversations around lunch tables. Today, MNEs proactively manage their emergence and evolution.[71] Organizing a globally integrated enterprise requires extensive coordination and collaboration among workers. Convergent values ease the exchange of ideas and best practices between people.

Techniques and Tools   In reality, the values and outlooks of managers, especially those from culturally dissimilar countries, often differ.[72] Furthermore, many workers have slight exposure to the values held by senior managers. Different values impose boundaries that undercut coordination and control systems. Therefore, managers use a variety of techniques to preempt these threats. Many advocates arranging closer contact among managers from different countries to unify values. Cross-national teams are a prevalent tool.[73] Developing a consensus depends on members' engaging common values, rather than mechanical compliance with coordination routines or control codes.

Others take a more comprehensive approach whereby they rotate high-performing executives from headquarters and subsidiaries throughout global units. For example, Wipro, an Indian technology company, employs 54,000 people in 35 countries, more than 11,000 of whom work for units outside of India and more than 90 percent of whom are Indian. Explained the chief executive of global programs, "We sprinkle Indians in new markets to help seed and set up the culture and intensity."[74] Some take a less direct approach. GE's Leadership Development Center pulls managers from different businesses and different parts of the world to share best practices and improve understanding of the company's culture.

Similarly, Mattel has 25,000 employees in 36 countries and sells its toys in 150 nations. Although you would think selling the fun of toys would converge cultural ideals, transcending different values has proven problematic. As a result, Mattel runs executive development programs via a global e-learning system. Improving managers' understanding, both at headquarters and subsidiaries, of Mattel's world means, "global management is more closely aligned with the corporate strategies and goals. This, in turn, produces innovative and creative products, reduces costs, and improves employee satisfaction." Employees are becoming "one Mattel company," rather than workers of various subsidiaries operating separately.[75]

MNEs from other cultures share parallel outlooks and apply similar practices. Toyota, for example, relies on its Technical Skills Academy, its corporate university in Toyota City, to fortify is culture as well as firmly anchor its next generation of leadership in it. Some sessions teach factory controls and assembly procedure, others teach management skills, but all inculcate the principles of the esteemed "Toyota Way."[76] Socializing employee with some of the most prized management secrets in corporate Japan enables everyone in the company to base decisions on a "philosophical sense of purpose, to think long term, to have a process for solving problems, to add value to the organization by developing its people, and to recognize that continuously solving root problems drives organizational learning."[77] High-profile graduates then travel to offices around the world, acting as missionaries who share the Toyota Way. This task steadily has beome increasingly importance given senior management's concern that the organization culture is "getting more and more diluted as Toyota grows overseas."[78]

Instead of simply letting an organization's culture emerge naturally, many managers do as they do with structure and systems. They purposefully and proactively develop the system of shared values they reason girds strategic success. As we just reviewed, they use a variety of approaches to socialize employees. An intriguing development, showcased in our *Looking to the Future* insert, is the rising prominence of corporate universities.

ORGANIZATION CULTURE AND STRATEGY

Strategy imposes organization requirements that call for certain configuration of structures and systems. Likewise, the preferred principles and practices of organization culture vary with the requirements of the MNE's strategy (See Figure 15.4). An MNE implementing a global strategy, for example, engineers a forceful culture that insists on universal goals, priorities, and practices. Standardizing value activities calls for standardizing employees' views regarding the specification of tasks, the arrangement of work, and the stipulation of rules, rewards, and punishments. Competing interpretations are not an option. The imperative of consistency calls for socially engineering an organization culture that spurs employees worldwide to accept and adopt the MNE's standards. This, in turn, endorses coordinating through standardization and controlling through bureaucracy as well as a tighter set of common values and a lower tolerance for different perspectives.

Alternatively, companies implementing a multidomestic strategy encourage greater variety in the local interpretation of global goals. Adapting value activities to local standards requires decentralization. This, in turn, necessitates looser values and higher tolerance for different perspectives in order to sustain the vitality of local outlooks. Consequently, people in different units share fewer common values.

Differentiation is not necessarily a deficiency provided the MNE has an integrative perspective. J&J's multidomestic strategy led it to organize a decentralized area structure, install coordination by planning, and apply control through market metrics. However, J&J relied on its Credo to integrate this mix. Recall that its Credo specifies who and what to care about and in what order. Without it, J&J would likely see its organization fracture into autonomous fiefdoms that increasingly overlapped less. With it, J&J reinforces the ability of its structure and system to unify its 250 quasi-independent business units into a globally integrated enterprise.

> An organization's culture shapes its strategic moves.

> Organization culture varies with the strategy the MNE pursues.

Case Review Note

GLOBAL	**TRANSNATIONAL**
Strategic Objectives: Productivity and efficiency,	Strategic Objectives: Integration, responsiveness, learning,
Strategic Emphasis: Integration and consistency,	Strategic Emphasis: Innovation, ideas, and growth,
Dominant Attribute: Standardized goal achievement, global competitiveness,	Dominant Attribute: Innovation, creativity, dynamism, flexibility,
Leadership Style: Production and achievement-oriented, decisive control orientation,	Leadership Style: Innovator, risk affinitive, congruence between individual values and company goals,
Collaboration Standard: Goal orientation, production,competition,	Collaboration Standard: Flexibility, risk, entrepreneurship,
INTERNATIONAL	**MULTIDOMESTIC**
Strategic Objectives: Leverage core competencies,	Strategic Objectives: Local responsiveness,
Strategic Emphasis: Control, stability, predictability,	Strategic Emphasis: Esprit de corps, commitment, consensus,
Dominant Attribute: Formal order, rules and regulations, uniformity,	Dominant Attributes: Cohesiveness, trust, affiliation,
Leadership style: Director, administrator, enforcer,	Leadership Satyle: Mentor, facilitator, coach, adaptability,
Collaboration Standard: Rules, policies and procedures, clear expectations,	Collaboration Standard: Loyalty and tradition,

Pressure for Global Integration: High / Low

Pressure for Local Responsiveness: Low / High

Pressure for Local Responsiveness

FIGURE 15.6   Strategy and Organizational Culture in International Business

The four strategies charted here correspond to the four types of strategies covered in Chapter 11. Each type has specific indications for the features and forms of the company's organization.

Creating a Vision
Infosys claims the largest corporate university in the world. Headquartered on its world renowned campus in Mysore, India, it aligns corporate learning to support the company's global strategy.
Source: © Belinda Lawley/Alamy

Looking to the
Future   The Rise of Corporate Universities

An intriguing development is the rise of corporate universities as a vector of organization culture. Physical and virtual institutions lead training efforts, facilitate learning, and upgrade competencies with an eye toward advocating the philosophical ideals that anchor the practices of the company's culture. Worldwide, more than a thousand new ones have recently opened. By region, they are steadily expanding in the United States, thriving in Europe, and accelerating in Asia. The number of U.S. corporate universities grew from around 400 in 1993, to 2,000 in 2001, to nearly 4,000 today. Many of the *Fortune* 500, including Walt Disney, Boeing, Motorola, General Electric, J.P. Morgan Chase, and Southwest Airlines, run one.[79]

The first big one, McDonald's Hamburger University, began operating in 1961. By 2011, it had trained 80,000 managers and owner/operators in 28 languages from 119 countries. In 2010, McDonald's opened a Hamburger University in Shanghai, China, with its eye to supporting its goal of 5,000 Chinese outlets. Likewise, Infosys's 35-acre campus houses the world's largest corporate university. It 250 faculty members annually train thousands of new hires and provide advanced instruction for tens of thousands of existing employees.

Whereas some attach their universities to headquarters, others sprinkle them at various offices. Unisys, for example, has campuses in its key market regions.

Last, others opt to break free of geography. They run virtual, online universities where employees e-learn via live webcasts, online chat and discussion groups, webinars, videoconferences, and interactive sessions.

An Expanding Mission

Originally, corporate universities aimed to teach practical skills and workplace systems. The founding goal of McDonald's Hamburger University, for instance, was preparing people to run the day-to-day operations of a franchise. Today, "training isn't just a nice thing to do anymore," reports the American Society for Training and Development. "Companies are now thinking of training as a strategic imperative."[80] They use their corporate university to embed new hires with a strategic understanding of operations as well as fortify the commitment of current workers. Others amplify this theme, declaring their corporate university "inculcates everyone, from the clerical assistant to the top executive, in the culture and values that make the organization unique and special and to define behaviors that enable employees to 'live the values.'"[81]

Linking executive learning with the company's strategy drives the recent and projected growth of the corporate university model. The CEO of Unipart, a British auto parts maker, notes that his company's university "is at the very heart of the business" and a "key enabler for future growth of the business."[82] Like many other CEOs, he runs a monthly course on the philosophy and principles of Unipart's approach to business. Jack Welch of General Electric probably set the standard. Over his 20-year role as CEO, he appeared more than 300 times at GE's training center at Croton-on-Hudson. Holding forth in "the Pit," he taught and socialized some 20,000 GE managers.[83]

Senior executives who take on the hat of teacher generate great benefits. The director of LVMH's university believes that putting top people into the pit "gives them access to people they would never get access to.... It is the role of our top senior executives to get a feel for what is going on."[84] Benefits accrue to attendees too. Activities, seminars, and training sessions build skills and promote social networks. They also improve their analytics and return to their divisions with new ideas. Finally, they leave with a better sense of how their professional development stacks up to global counterparts.

Last, sophisticated strategies push MNEs to involve more employees, both those staying home and those heading abroad, in general international development. The need to generate, transfer, and adopt ideas from wherever they originate to wherever they add value, particularly compelling for MNEs building a globally integrated enterprise, calls for preparing all employees to do so.

In addition, MNEs implementing an international, multidomestic, or global strategy face pressures, given growing globalization, to help employees understand worldwide operations, opportunities, and constraints. Hence, MNEs add international business content once reserved for expatriates to the curriculum irrespective of whether attendees plan to work abroad. Examples include Mattel's and Infosys's regional training centers, where managers from several countries convene to examine specific topics; Procter & Gamble's training on globalization issues; and programs at Honda of America to improve cultural awareness.

Integrating Diversity

Unquestionably, a mandate for corporate universities is integrating diverse workforces. Hiring people from around the world expands the mix of nationalities and ethnicities. Hiring engineers in Mumbai or Sophia to collaborate with folks in Redmond makes compelling economic sense. Preempting a Tower of Babel requires helping a diversity of people work in proliferating global groups.

Tempting as it is to rely upon happenstance to manage the process, benign neglect is risky. Corporate universities provide a robust platform to manage the process in a controlled, purposeful setting. Explained the vice president of Unisys University, it provides continual learning for employees in ways that align it with the strategy of the business and have a strong impact on the organization culture.[85]

Moreover, expanding global operations challenges sustaining common values. Toyota, for example, saw the globalization of its business steadily diluting the principles of the "Toyota Way." When Toyota was primarily Japan-centric, it relied upon chats on the factory floor and in executive suites to sustain the organization culture. "Before, when everyone was Japanese, we didn't have to make these things explicit," said the director of Toyota Institute, its corporate university. "Now we have to set the Toyota Way down on paper and teach it." To that end, Toyota opened the Toyota Institute in Toyota City, Japan and was building satellite centers in the United States and Thailand.

The Crucible of Change

A recent change in the corporate university model is finding new ways to prepare future leaders. Current performance and future growth drive the search for global leaders. Corporate universities run programs that engage high-potential executives on key topics. They push executives to develop the insights and cultivate the personal relationships that organize the globally integrated enterprise. Its rise as the agent of ideas may make it the crucible of company strategy. Some foresee a future where an MNE's university its becomes its thought center, formulating, rather than following, strategy.

Filling Gaps

The recent global economic crisis boosts the role of corporate universities—but for less than charitable reasons. Analysts and educators debate whether the manner of teaching business students in traditional university settings may have aggravated the global financial crisis.[86] Critics hold that conventionally designed MBA programs grew too scientific, too detached from real-world issues, and too isolated from the moral implications of choice and action. The orthodoxy of MBA programs, arguably, distorted students' view of the moral, ethical, and social considerations of business leadership. These shortcomings poorly prepared graduates to do the right thing for their company and for society. Consequently, more companies increasingly look to their universities to develop socially responsible outlooks. ∎

Infosys: The Search for the Best and the Brightest

India produces more than 300,000 engineering graduates each year, offering a fresh pool of talented, hard-working, and ambitious candidates eager to work at a fraction of the cost of their Western counterparts.[87] This advantage has catapulted India from a slow-moving economy to the forefront of the global offshore market. More specifically, its offshoring sector, the world's largest and fastest growing, is dominated by its information technology (IT) services. Leading the charge is Infosys Technologies Limited.

Who Is Infosys?

Founded in Pune, India, in 1981, Infosys is headquartered in Bangalura, ground zero of the Indian business process outsourcing (BPO) industry. It is a global technology services firm that defines, designs, and delivers IT-enabled, end-to-end business solutions that leverage technology. It provides clients in financial services, manufacturing, telecommunications, retail, utilities, logistics, and several other industries an expanding array IT infrastructure and BPO services. Its global footprint includes 50 overseas business offices and development centers in India, China, Australia, the Czech Republic, Poland, the UK, Canada, and Japan.

The "Global Delivery Model"

Historically, Indian software companies had, at high cost, executed most of their software projects end-to-end on-site at clients' facilities. Infosys turned this concept upside down, presuming that it could provide the same service much more cost-efficiently if it could do the work in talent-rich India. Infosys translated this ambition into its pioneering "Global Delivery Model" (GDM), which now distributes work and integrates components across global locations to provide maximum value. The GDM took outsourcing to the next level—modular global sourcing enabled by technology, driven by a global talent pool, and spurred by new business models to accelerate innovation. The GDM moves work to the most productive location, makes the best economic sense to do the job, and poses the least amount of risk. So, operationally Infosys accepts a software design job, breaks it down into its logical components, and distributes them to the optimal locations.

The economics of this simple yet compelling innovation were indisputable—application-development costs in India, for example, are a fraction of those in the United States. Implementing this innovation, however, is easier said than done. It required building and sustaining an organization that, explained Narayana Murthy, the company's founder, can "source capital from where it is cheapest, produce where it is most cost-effective, and sell where it is most profitable, all without being constrained by national boundaries."

Two Decades of Growth

Infosys began in 1981 with a capitalization of U.S. $250. The company grew modestly during its first decade, finishing 1991 with revenues of US$3.89 million. The liberalization of the Indian economy in 1991, fueled by the growing adoption of free market principles, accelerated its growth. Executives began to focus on global markets, supported by sophisticated and inexpensive communication technologies. Revenues increased to U.S. $121 million by 1998–1999; by 2012, they approached US$6.4 billion, with net income move past U.S. $1.5 billion. Along the way, employee head count grew from the "founding seven" to 132,000 in 2011.

Stating (and Restating) a Mission

Although a global juggernaut today, Infosys began with humble goals. Murthy, along with six friends, met in his small apartment to debate the company's mission. They resolved that their mission was not, he says, "to be the best, the biggest or the most profitable company, but to earn the respect of all our stakeholders.... My view was if we sought respect, we'd automatically do the right thing by each of them. We'd satisfy our customers, be fair to our employees, and follow the finest principles with respect to investors.... We would not violate laws, and, finally, we'd make a difference to society.... [A]utomatically, you'll get revenues and profits and all that." Murthy adds, "We started out as seven people in 1981, with $250. We had just one customer.... We never imagined we would come this far."

Although many successful companies share similar goals, the founding vision of Infosys is a legacy that its leaders fervently work to imbue throughout the company. It begins in its mission statement: "To achieve our objectives in an environment of fairness, honesty, and courtesy towards our clients, employees, vendors, and society at large." It translates these ideals into the philosophical pillars of the organization culture. More poetically, it declares, "We believe that the softest pillow is a clear conscience. The values that drive us underscore our commitment to:

- *Customer Delight* To surpass customer expectations consistently
- *Leadership by Example* To set standards in our business and transactions and be an exemplar for the industry and ourselves
- *Integrity and Transparency* To be ethical, sincere and open in all our transactions
- *Fairness* To be objective and transaction-oriented, and thereby earn trust and respect
- *Pursuit of Excellence* To strive relentlessly, constantly improve ourselves, our teams, our services and products to become the best

The Science of Being Smart

Senior executives at Infosys emphasize the importance of objectively developing rigorous knowledge through a process of observation, data collection, analysis, and conclusion. Able management, they reason, enables translating newfound knowledge into pioneering software solutions. Nevertheless, as the saying goes, even the grandest vision depends on the success of the smallest details. The evolution and success of Infosys—it took the company 23 years to become a U.S. $1 billion company but only 23 months to double that—depends on its smallest components.

Infosys holds firm that this knowledge cannot be archived in a static database. Rather, its knowledge is encapsulated in the people it hires. Explains Murthy, "Our respect for our professionals can be summed up by our belief that the market capitalization of Infosys becomes zero after working hours end at 5 P.M., no matter what it was during the day.... It's our belief that the first duty of a corporation is to uphold respect and dignity for the individual."

Recruiting: Looking for "Learnability"

Fast-growing companies often struggle to communicate their core values to new employees. Infosys was no exception. However, its approach to socializing employees to the philosophy and practices of the company is noteworthy. In 2010, the company staffed about 25,000 slots. Although entry-level jobs carried annual salaries under US$10,000, more than 4 million people applied. Around 77,000 applicants took a rigorous examination composed of math equations and logic puzzles designed to assess their aptitude for "learnability" (Infosys-speak for being a quick study). Then, approximately 61,000 were interviewed and 26,200 received job offers.

Those who cleared these hurdles shared similar characteristics. First, they were extremely smart. They had also shown the ability to learn quickly—a critical competency given the dynamic nature of the company and its markets. Indeed, learnability was a key criterion in selection, promotion, and retention precisely because the rapid evolution of IT demanded workers who could learn as technology advanced, customers emerged, and market circumstances changed. In addition, Infosys screened people for their overall attitude, looking for those individuals with positive outlooks on life.

Transferring an understanding of the company to new employees demands more than simply escorting new hires to their personal workstation on their first day and setting them loose. The importance of values and visions to practices and performance put a premium on purposefully transferring the corporation's culture. Infosys CEO Nandan Nilekani summed it up this way: "There aren't many companies growing like this....Companies haven't been investing enough in people. Rather than train them, they let them go. Our people are our capital. The more we invest in them, the more they can be effective." To that end, Infosys invests $65 of every $1,000 in revenue to training programs and educational initiatives. No competitor matches this sum; most fall far short.

Training: Preaching "Technical Evangelism"

Training and development begins right off the bat at "Infosys U." Even though the new hires excel academically, all go through a 14-week brain-busting boot camp. Each attends a rigorous training program, taking classes from more than 250 instructors—or in the world of Infosys, so-called "technical evangelists." Course work includes analytical thinking and problem-solving skills, principles of operating database-management systems, and information networks. Over time, as Infosys expanded operations in to overseas markets, it expanded the curriculum to include social networking perspectives and instruction in team building, customer facing, business etiquette, and negotiation skills.

The curriculum communicates the company's values, systems, and processes. In particular, it addresses an intriguing aspect of the Indian psyche. As Murthy explains, "We have realized that our challenge is to take the reactive mind-set of Indian youngsters and change them into proactive problem-solving ones. By and large, because of our culture, family background, etc., we are reactive. To change that, we have to understand problem-solving as a science and an art. We have to understand algorithmic thinking."

For the average hardworking, stressed-out student, surviving the training program is no guarantee that he or she will "graduate," despite the training costs of $5,000 per student. Completing the program earns a slot to take two three-hour comprehensive exams. Passing changes one's status from a "fresher" to an "Infoscion."

Tapping a Global Labor Pool

The geographic distribution of Infosys's clients—firms in 18 countries account for 98 percent of its business—pushed it to diversify its labor pool and ensure its capacity to deliver superb service. Karthik Sarman, associate vice president of human resources, reasons, "a Japanese worker will tend to do better in Japan. It is a matter of being able to connect with clients on more than just the technical level." Hence, Infosys launched its Global Talent Program to recruit job candidates from around the world. The goal was to hire individuals with specialized understanding of the clients' cultural orientation.

Cautious about hiring people unfamiliar with its approaches spurred Infosys to bring employees from other countries to Bangalura for technical education and executive socialization. New recruits visit India for a six-month training and orientation program, and then return to their home countries as local agents. The first cohorts of this program included "Infoscions" from China, Mauritius, and the United States. The pursuit of talent beyond its home country's borders has proven successful—Infosys's employees represent 75 nationalities who speak more than 40 languages. Nevertheless, Sarman notes "[t]he need for qualified talent will become more pressing as we continue to mature."

"No Past, No Creed, Only Merit."

Thus far, evolution from a start-up to a global juggernaut has gone well. Performance suggests that Infosys commands a keen sense of how a company builds to succeed in global markets. Indeed, as its 30th anniversary dawned, Infosys continues to inspire trust and

◀ **Communicating a Vision**
An auditorium on the Bengalura campus of Infosys. Blazoned on the screen is the message, "Powered By Intellect, Driven By Values," that anchors the company's organizational culture.
Source: © Belinda Lawley / Alamy

confidence among customers, investors and other constituents.Once again, it was ranked India's Most Admired Company in 2010 for the ninth year in a row. Too, its ranked among the top ten global technology companies in annual total shareholder return.[88]

Three Challenges

Meeting the test of markets and the challenge of rivals is within Infosys's realm, Murthy notes, as long as the company continues progressing. This task set clear imperatives:

> *Our biggest challenge is to become proactive problem-definers rather than be re-active problem-solvers. Right now, we solve problems our customers define. We need to be able to go to customers and say, "These are the problems we believe you will face, and here are some solutions." Our focus is on providing solutions leveraging IT. We need to help shape the design of the technology solutions and then implement those solutions. This is the biggest challenge we face—there's no doubt about that.*
>
> *The second challenge is to become more and more and more multicultural. We have efforts under way to integrate people across various cultures. For instance, on large deals we make sure that people from different parts of the world contribute, on a collaborative basis, to prepare a proposal, to defend the proposal, and to execute the proposal. We also lay great emphasis on integrating leadership. We rotate selected managers from our operations everywhere in the world through our Infosys Leadership Institute. But there is much more that we need to do. For instance, it has not been easy for us to transfer somebody from the United States to India. We are able to transfer people from the United States to Europe and from one function to another—from software development to sales and marketing, for instance. But transferring an employee from the United States to India is not easy.*
>
> *Finally, the third challenge is to continue to retain the soul of a small organization in the body of a large organization. It will be tricky to balance the tension between scaling the organization as quickly as we have been doing against the need to maintain disciplined processes as well as an integrated multicultural organization.*

Infosys, ever humble but sincerely confident, believes it has built an organization that can successfully meet these challenges and, its CEO declares, "win in a flat world." ∎

QUESTIONS

1. How might Infosys retain its founding values as it grows and globalizes?
2. What organizational problems do you think will prove troublesome? How would you use the strengths of the current organization to manage them?
3. Consider the options presented in the chapter regarding structural design, coordination and control, and corporate culture. Map the interplay among these dimensions at Infosys.
4. What do you think were the two or three key events that powered the evolution of Infosys's organization? What do you think the Infosys organization will look like in 2015?
5. How do you think classes at Infosys's corporate university differ from those in a traditional Bachelor of Business Administration or MBA program?

MyIBLab   Now that you have finished this chapter, go back to www.myiblab.com to continue practicing and applying the concepts you've learned.

SUMMARY

- Organization in the MNE is a function of how the company defines the structure that specifies the framework for work, develops the systems that coordinate and control what gets done, and cultivates shared values among employees.

- Environmental and workplace trends, along with the fallout of the global financial crisis, push managers to refine their customary approaches to organizing their companies. Managers compare the classical command-and-control model versus the potential of the coordinate and cultivate approach of neoclassical formats.

- Vertical differentiation is the matter of how the company balances centralization versus decentralization in decision making. Horizontal differentiation is the matter of how the company opts to divide itself into specific units to do specific jobs.

- Centralization in a company is influenced by the pressures for global integration versus local responsiveness, the competence of headquarters versus subsidiary personnel, and the importance, expediency, and quality expectations of the decision at hand.

- Classical structures, like the functional, divisional, and matrix formats, rely on the hierarchy to arrange roles, responsibilities, and relationships.

- Neoclassical structures, like the network or virtual format, arrange work roles, responsibilities, and relationships in ways that bypass the horizontal, vertical, or external boundaries that block the development of knowledge-generating and decision-making relationships.

- Firms engaging different strategies build different organizations. Firms engaging international, multidomestic, global, or transnational strategies tailor their structure, systems, and cultures to their respective demands.

- Coordination can take place via standardization, plans, and mutual adjustment. Standardization relies on specifying standard operating procedures; planning relies on general goals and detailed objectives; and mutual adjustment relies on frequent interaction among related parties.

- Control systems help managers compare performance to plans, identify differences, and, where found, assess the gap and implement corrective action.

- Companies exercise control through market, bureaucratic, and clan mechanisms. Market control relies on external market mechanisms, bureaucratic control relies on extensive rules and procedures, and clan control relies on shared values among all employees.

- Organization culture refers to the set of values shared among employees. Values express themselves as the behavior patterns or style of an organization that workers encourage new hires to follow.

KEY TERMS

boundaries (p. 571)
boundaryless (p. 571)
centralization (p. 564)
control systems (p. 580)
coordination (p. 574)
coordination by mutual adjustment (p. 578)
coordination by plan (p. 577)

decentralization (p. 564)
divisional structure (p. 567)
functional structure (p. 566)
globality (p. 565)
horizontal differentiation (p. 563)
matrix structure (p. 569)
mixed structure (p. 569)
neoclassical structure (p. 570)

network structure (p. 572)
organization (p. 563)
organization culture (p. 582)
organization structure (p. 563)
unity-of-command principle (p. 569)
vertical differentiation (p. 563)
virtual organization (p. 573)

ENDNOTES

1 Sources include the following: www.jnj.com; J&J 2007, 2008, 2009, 2010 Annual Reports; "J&J shares climb after upbeat update on its drugs" *BusinessWeek*, www.businessweek.com/ap/financialnews /D9NFV7U00.htm, (Retrieved June 1, 2011); Avi Salzman, "J&J Now the 'Best Biotech Play', Says Goldman," *Barrons.com,* blogs.barrons .com/stockstowatchtoday/2011/05/27/jj-now-the-best-biotech -play-says-goldman/, (Retrieved June 1, 2011); Margaret Cronin Fisk and Beth Hawkins, "Johnson & Johnson Hid Antibiotic Levaquin Risk, Lawyer Says - Bloomberg." www.bloomberg.com/news /2011-06-01/johnson-johnson-hid-risks-of-antibiotic-levaquin-la wyer-says-at-trial.html, (Retrieved June 1, 2011).

2 "Tylenol (Acetaminophen) To Be Available In Japan In Early Fall, 2000," retrieved June 15, 2011, from www.pslgroup.com/dg/1d9dfa .htm

3 "The Organization Man, Dead at 76," *Journal of Business Strategy* 18 (1997): 6.

4 Lowell Bryan and Claudia Joyce, "Better Strategy through Organizational Design," *The McKinsey Quarterly* (May 2007).

5 Alfred P. Sloan, , John McDonald, ed., *My Years with General Motors* (New York: Doubleday, 1964).

6 Chris Bartlett, "MNCs: Get Off the Reorganization Merry-Go-Round," *Harvard Business Review* (March–April 1983): 88–101.

7 "Hungry Tiger, Dancing Elephant: How India Is Changing IBM's World," *The Economist* (April 4, 2007): 58–61. "A Survey of Globalisation: The Empire Strikes Back," *The Economist*, retrieved June 5, 2011, from www.economist.com/node/12080723: 72.

8 Peter Drucker, "Managing Oneself," *Harvard Business Review* (1999).

9 As some have suggested: Before: "Thanks for letting me work here." Today: "Improve my professional mobility or I will find a company that will."

10 Adam Bryant, "Google's 8-Point Plan to Help Managers Improve," NYTimes.com, retrieved March 12, 2011, from www.nytimes .com/2011/03/13/business/13hire.html?hp

11 Craig W. Fontaine, "Organization structure," human resource management knowledge base Northeastern University (August 2007).

12 Harold Sirkin, James Hemerling, Arindam Bhattacharya, *Globality: Competing with Everyone from Everywhere for Everything* (New York: Business Plus, 2008).

13 The Tao offers insight on this standard: The second principle of Taoism is that of Dynamic Balance. There are always two basic distinctions in nature, symbolized by the yin and yang (sun and moon, heaven and earth, dark and light, chaos and order, etc.), but Taoism sees balance as the basic characteristic underlying these distinctions.

14 Julian Birkinshaw, "The Structures behind Global Companies," *Financial Times* (December 4, 2000): 2–4.

15 "Nestlé Is Starting to Slim Down at Last," *Business Week* (October 27, 2003): 56–58; "Daring, Defying, to Grow," *The Economist* (August 7, 2004): 55–57.

16 Andria Cheng, "Nike Reorganizes into Six Geographic Regions: Faster-Growing China, Eastern Europe regions to be Managed Separately," *MarketWatch* (March 20, 2009).

17 "Japanese Firms Push into Emerging Markets: The New Frontier for Corporate Japan," *The Economist*, retrieved April 19, 2011, from www.economist.com/node/16743435

18 John W. Hunt, "Is Matrix Management a Recipe for Chaos?" *Financial Times* (January 12, 1998): 10.

19 Richard Hodgetts, "Dow Chemical CEO William Stavropoulos on Structure," *Academy of Management Executive* (May 30, 1999): 30.

20 John Gapper and Nicholas Denton, "The Barings Report," *Financial Times* (October 18, 1995): 8.

21 "Axe to Fall Heavily at IBM, Unions Fear," *New York Times* (May 6, 2005): A-1.

22 The *strategy-structure-systems model* was first adopted by General Motors, DuPont, Sears, and Standard Oil in the 1920s. Not until the post–World War II era did many companies began to develop divisional structures that then led to the rapid adoption of diversification strategies. Some reason that the network structure and its variants will follow the same pattern, moving from the few in the early 2000s to the many over the ensuing decades.

23 "Hungry Tiger, Dancing Elephant: How India Is Changing IBM's World," *The Economist* (April 4, 2007): 58–61.

24 Just as these demands trigger the emergence of the transnational strategy, they likewise spur what some broadly call the *transnational organization.*

25 Others pointed to W. L. Gore and its egalitarian workforce philosophy—no titles, workers collaborating in small teams, and no hierarchy fuels creativity and innovation: "We work hard at maximizing individual potential, maintaining an emphasis on product integrity and cultivating an environment where creativity can flourish," says CEO Terri Kelly. "A fundamental belief in our people and their abilities continues to be the key to our success, even as we expand globally." "It isn't a company for everyone," Brinton says. "It takes a special kind of person to be effective here—someone who is really passionate about sharing information, as opposed to controlling it."

26 "Hungry Tiger, Dancing Elephant: How India Is Changing IBM's World.

27 "The World According to Chambers," *The Economist* (August 27, 2009): 81–84.

28 For example, in the case of the latter, people see that the more senior executives have specialized knowledge that gives them personal respect as well as positional power. Hence, the more power their knowledge gives them, the less incentive they have to share with others. This develops boundaries between different levels of hierachy.

29 Hiroko Tabuchi and Brooks Barnes, "Sony Chief Is Still in Search of a Turnaround," *New York Time,* (May 26, 2011): A-1.

30 Sony adds another angle of analysis. In Chapter 11, we described how Sony ran big losses as markets, weakened by the global crisis, exposed weaknesses in its system. Fighting to rescue the company, CEO Sir Howard Stringer felt the need to revitalize the company's culture in order to jump-start new relationships and trigger new ways of thinking. Reorganization began in spring 2009.Senior executives opposed to restructuring efforts were replaced by four young, loyal lieutenants—dubbed "the Four Musketeers"—to lead Sony's redesigned businesses. Ironically, explained Sir Howard, "When this crisis came along, for me it was a godsend, because I could reorganize the company without having to battle the forces of the status quo"; "Game on: Sir Howard Stringer Believes He Is Finally in a Position to Fix Sony," *The Economist* (March 5, 2009): 73.

31 Statement from Jack Welch's Letter to Shareholders, "Boundarylessness Company in a Decade of Change," reported in GE's 1990 *Annual Report*.

32 W. Baker, the Network Organization in Theory and Practice. In N. Nohria and R. Eccles (Eds.), *Networks and Organizations*, (Cambridge, MA: Harvard Business School Press, 1992), 327–429.

33 The keiretsu appeared in Japan during the "economic miracle" following World War II. Before Japan's surrender, Japanese industry was controlled by large family-controlled vertical monopolies called zaibatsu.

34 "A Tangled Web," *Financial Times* (June 12, 2001): 7.

35 J. Lipnack and J. Stamps, *Virtual Teams: Researching across Space, Time, and Organizations with Technology* (New York: John Wiley and Sons, 1997); Sonny Ariss, Nick Nykodym, and Aimee Cole-Laramore, "Trust and Technology in the Virtual Organization," *SAM Advanced Management Journal* 67 (Autumn 2002): 22–26; William M. Fitzpatrick

and Donald R. Burke, "Competitive Intelligence, Corporate Security and the Virtual Organization," *Advances in Competitiveness Research* 11 (2003): 20–46.

36 Manju Ahuja and Kathleen Carley "Network Structure in Virtual Organizations," retrieved June 10, 2011, from http://jcmc.indiana .edu/vol3/issue4/ahuja.html

37 Alf Crossman and Liz Lee-Kelley, "Trust, Commitment and Team Working: The Paradox of Virtual Organizations," *Global Networks: A Journal of Transnational Affairs* 4 (October 2004): 375–91; Philip J. Holt and James E. Lodge, "Merging Collaboration and Technology: The Virtual Research Organization," *Applied Clinical Trials* 12 (October 2003): 38–42.

38 Scott Goodson, StrawberryFrog, "Special Report: Global Players," *Advertising Age* (January 26, 2004): S4; Juliana Koranteng, "Virtual Agency Goes Global via the Web," *AdAgeGlobal* 1 (2000): 46.

39 Theresa Howard, "StrawberryFrog Hops to a Different Drummer," *USA Today* (October 10, 2005): C-1.

40 Similar trend are afoot in other industries. The legal field, for example, increasingly rewards efficiency. "Clearspire, a virtual origination, relies on some 20 or so lawyers work who mostly from home, collaborating on a multi-million-dollar platform that mimics a virtual office. A lawyer checking in on a colleague automatically sees a picture of her on the phone when she is, in fact, on the phone. Clients use the platform too, commenting on and even changing their own documents as they are being drawn up. Conventional lawyers are far less open; "Bargain Briefs," *The Economist* (August 13, 2011): 64.

41 Dmitry Ivanov, Boris Sokolov, and Joachim Kaeschel, "Structure Dynamics Control-Based Framework for Adaptive Reconfiguration of Collaborative Enterprise Networks," *International Journal of Manufacturing Technology and Management*, 17 (2009): 23.

42 Nicolai J. Foss. "Selective Intervention and Internal Hybrids: Interpreting and Learning from the Rise and Decline of the Oticon Spaghetti Organization," *Organization Science* 14 (May–June 2003): 331–50.

43 Patrick Kiger, "Hidden Hierarchies," *Workforce Management* (February 27, 2006): 24.

44 Beaman, Karen, "An Interview with Christopher Bartlett," *Boundaryless HR: Human Capital Management in the Global Economy* (San Francisco: IHRIM Press, June 2002).

45 Darrell Rigby, "Bain & Company's 2005 Management Tools & Trends," retrieved August 2, 2005, from www.bain.com /management_tools

46 Adam Lashinsky, "Chaos by Design," *Fortune* (October 2, 2006); Geoffrey Colvin, "Managing in Chaos," *Fortune* (October 2, 2006).

47 Steve Lohr, "How Crisis Shapes the Corporate Model," *The New York Times* (March 28, 2009).

48 Lowell Bryan and Claudia Joyce, "The 21st-Century Organization," *The McKinsey Quarterly* 3 (2005).

49 Loren Cary, "The Rise of Hyperarchies," *Harvard Business Review* (March 2004).

50 Karl-Heinrich Grote and Erik K. Antonsson (Eds.), *Springer Handbook of Mechanical Engineering* (New York: Springer, 2009): 1344.

51 The Boston Consulting Group, "Reorganized Information Processing Vital to Improving U.S. Intelligence Capabilities," *BCG Media Releases*, retrieved May 6, 2007, from www.bcg.com/news_media /news_media_releases.jsp?id=928

52 In contrast, one could precisely design a structure that looks great on paper but struggles in the stress test of reality.

53 More specifically, Grove reasoned: "Let chaos reign, then rein in chaos. Does that mean that you shouldn't plan? Not at all. You need to plan the way a fire department plans. It cannot anticipate fires, so it has to shape a flexible organization that is capable of responding to unpredictable events"; Michael E. Rock, "Case Example: Intel's

Andy Grove," *CanadaOne*, retrieved October 31, 2007, from www .canadaone.com/magazine/mr2060198.html

54 Michel Domsch & Elena Hristozova, (Eds.), *Human Resource Management in Consulting* (New York: Springer, 2006).

55 Anoop Madhok, "Revisiting Multinational Firms' Tolerance for Joint Ventures: A Trust-Based Approach." *Journal of International Business Studies* (2006): 30–43.

56 Daniel Erasmus, "A Common Language for Strategy," *Financial Times* (April 5, 1999): 7–8.

57 Sumantra Ghoshal and Christopher Bartlett, "Changing the Role of Top Management: Beyond Structure to Process," *Harvard Business Review* 73 (January–February 1995): 93–94.

58 Jennifer Spencer, "Firms' Knowledge-Sharing Strategies in the Global Innovation System: Empirical Evidence from the Flat Panel Display Industry," *Strategic Management Journal* 23 (March 2003): 217–33.

59 Sam Folk-Williams, "Designing Open Collaboration in Red Hat Global Support Services," Management Innovation eXchange, retrieved June 2, 2011, from www.managementexchange.com/ story-36

60 Ultimately, every MNE regulates what people do. If they don't, the consequences can be grave. Failure, as we saw in the global credit crisis, permits opportunistic managers to take actions that crash the MNE. Experiences at several companies, such as Citibank, UBS, Siemens, Merrill Lynch, Lehman, Royal Bank of Scotland, AIG, and Société Générale, dramatize how weak controls enable destructive opportunism.

61 Clan control represents humanist values that contrast with the scientific norms of bureaucratic control.

62 If conducted poorly, visits fan tension. Experience suggests "rules" for optimizing such visits. If subsidiary managers overload social activities and underplay hard business reviews, corporate personnel will see the trip as wasteful. If corporate personnel visit warm-weather subsidiaries during their home's cold-weather seasons, locals may perceive the trips as diversions. Further, if visitors arrive only when upset about local performance, subsidiary folks may be defensive.

63 "The World According to Chambers."

64 For instance, the Japanese retailer Ito-Yokado, which owns and operates the 7-Eleven convenience store franchise in Japan, links stores' cash registers into an ERP system. It records sales and monitors inventory as well as schedules daily and weekly tasks. It also benchmarks managers' use of analytical tools, graphs, and forecasts; N. Shirouzu and J. Bigness, "7-Eleven Operators Resist System to Monitor Managers," *Wall Street Journal* (June 16, 1997): B1.

65 Eric Flamholtz and Rangapriya Kannan-Narasimhan, "Differential Impact of Cultural Elements in Financial Performance," *European Management Journal* (February 2005): 50–65; Ursula Fairbairn, "HR as a Strategic Partner: Culture Change as an American Express Case Study," *Human Resource Management* 44 (Spring 2005): 79–84.

66 Jim Collins, *Good to Great: Why Some Companies Make the Leap…and Others Don't* (New York: HarperCollins, 2001). For example, on the importance of technology, Collins reports "80 percent of the good-to-great executives—from more than 1400 companies over a 15 year span—we interviewed didn't even mention technology as one of the top five factors in the transition."

67 Big US Firms Shift Hiring Abroad, *Wall Street Journal* (April 19, 2011): B1.

68 H. Schwartz, "Matching Corporate Culture and Business Strategy," *Organizational Dynamics* (1981). Andrew Klein, "Corporate Culture: Its Value as a Resource for Competitive Advantage," *Journal of Business Strategy*, (2011): 21–28.

69 Bain & Company, "Executives Are Taking a Hard Look at Soft Issues" (March 27, 2007), retrieved October 31, 2007, from www .bain.com/bainweb/publications/printer_ready.asp?id=25728

70 Ibid.

71 Dinker Raval and Bala Subramanian, "Effective Transfer of Best Practices across Cultures," *Competitiveness Review* (Summer–Fall 2000): 183.

72 The severity of this problem is proportional to the importance of knowledge-generating and decision-making relationships to the MNE's organization; Alison Maitland, "Bridging the Culture Gap," *Financial Times* (January 28, 2002): 8.

73 Tatiana Kostova, "Transnational Transfer of Strategic Organizational Practices: A Contextual Perspective," *Academy of Management Review* 24 (1999): 308–24; Nitin Nohria and Sumantra Ghoshal, "Differentiated Fit and Shared Values: Alternatives for Managing Headquarters-Subsidiary Relations," *Strategic Management Journal* 15 (July 1994): 491–502. For a discussion of how capabilities improve with experience, see Andrew Delios and Paul Beamish, "Survival and Profitability: The Roles of Experience and Intangible Assets in Foreign Subsidiary Performance," *Academy of Management Journal* 44 (2001): 1028–38.

74 "Staffing Globalisation: Travelling More Lightly," *The Economist* (June 23, 2006): 55.

75 Leslie Gross Klaff, "Many People, One Mattel," *Workforce Management* (March 2004): 42–44.

76 Martin Fackler, "The 'Toyota Way' Is Translated for a New Generation of Foreign Managers," *New York Times*, retrieved August 5, 2010, from www.nytimes.com/2007/02/15/business/worldbusiness/15toyota.html

77 *The Toyota Way*, retrieved May 25, 2011, from http://secure.wikimedia.org/wikipedia/en/wiki/The_Toyota_Way

78 Ibid.

79 Rebecca Knight, "Corporate Universities: Move to a Collaborative Effort," *Financial Times* (March 19, 2007).

80 Donna Fenn, "Corporate Universities for Small Companies," *Inc.com*, retrieved May 6, 2007, from www.inc.com/magazine/19990201/730.html

81 Jeanne C. Meister, *Corporate Universities: Lessons in Building a World-Class Work Force* (New York: McGraw-Hill, 1998).

82 John Griffiths, "Unipart University," *Financial Times* (March 21, 2002).

83 The Pit is the well of a bright, multitier lecture hall.

84 Della Bradshaw, "LVMH," *Financial Times* (March 21, 2002).

85 Steve Trehern, "More Than Just Learning Process," *Financial Times* (March 21, 2002).

86 Kelley Holland, "Is It Time to Retrain B-Schools? *New York Times* (March 14, 2009): A-1.

87 ***Sources include the following***: Edward Luce, *In Spite of the Gods: The Strange Rise of Modern India* (New York: Doubleday, 2007); Julie Schlosser, "Harder Than Harvard," *Fortune* (March 17, 2006); "Virtual Champions," Survey: Business in India, *The Economist* (June 1, 2006); Anand Giridharadas, "India's Edge Goes Beyond Outsourcing," *New York Times* (April 4, 2007); Steve Hamm, "Passing the Baton at Infosys," *Business Week* (June 16, 2006); "Infosys' Murthy: Sharing a Simple Yet Powerful Vision," *Knowledge@Wharton* (May 23, 2001); Gautam Kumra and Jayant Sinha, "The Next Hurdle for Indian IT," *McKinsey Quarterly* (2003), Special edition: Global Directions; Life lessons from Narayana Murthy, Rediff, retrieved June 16, 2009, from www.rediff.com/money/2007/may/28bspec.htm. The amazing Infosys story, *Rediff*, retrieved June 16, 2009, from http://specials.rediff.com/money/2006/jul/11sld1.htm. "Infosys Rejects 94% Job Applicants, also Gets Rejected by Many, "*Economic Times*, retrieved May 24, 2011, from articles.economictimes.indiatimes.com/2010-05-31/news/27624027_1_net-addition-gross-addition-applicants; "Infosys Technologies Toughs Out Global Storm to Win Asia 200 in India," *WSJ.com*, retrieved May 19, 2011, from online.wsj.com/article/SB10001424052702304173704575577683613256368.html

88 "2010 Value Creators," Report of the Boston Consulting Group, retrieved May 19, 2011, from www.infosys.com/Links/redirectlink.aspx?id=bcg-file59590.aspx

chapter 16
Marketing Globally

Objectives

1. To understand a variety of international product policies and their appropriate circumstances

2. To be aware of product alterations when deciding between standardized and differentiated marketing programs among countries

3. To appreciate the pricing complexities when selling in foreign markets

4. To be familiar with country differences that may necessitate alterations in promotional practices

5. To comprehend the different branding strategies companies may employ internationally

6. To discern effective practices and complications of international distribution

7. To perceive why and how emphasis within the marketing mix may vary among countries

Access a host of interactive learning aids to help strengthen your understanding of the chapter concepts at www.myiblab.com.

MyIBLab

TOMMY ■ HILFIGER

Source: © Ralukattudor (Raluka Tudor) | Dreamstime.com

Markets have customs and communes have traditions.

—*Vietnamese proverb*

597

CASE

Tommy Hilfiger

For it's Tommy this, an' Tommy that

-Rudyard Kipling, "Tommy"

Mark Twain said, "The finest clothing is a person's skin, but, of course, society demands more than this."[1] Tommy Hilfiger, one of the notable international brands within the highly competitive clothing industry, exemplifies efforts to develop and respond to these demands. Hilfiger has added such lines as fragrances, bedding, bath products, eye wear, and luggage. It also acquired the Karl Lagerfeld label, but our discussion centers on the clothing brands using the Hilfiger name. Before we examine its international marketing practices, let's look for a moment at the company's description and history.

A BRIEF HISTORY

The early success of the Hilfiger brand was largely due to two men: U.S. designer Tommy Hilfiger and Indian textile magnate Mohan Murjani. Hilfiger designed blue jeans for Jordache, but in 1984 when he was 33, Murjani sought him out to be a designer for Murjani International. As one of the instrumental people in bringing about the designer blue-jeans craze of the 1970s, Murjani wanted to develop a new brand of clothing by offering a line of slightly less preppy and less expensive clothes than those offered by Ralph Lauren that he thought would appeal to a young mass-appeal audience.

Sales success came quickly for the Hilfiger brand, but Murjani International faced financial problems along with difficulty in separating its attention among its different brands, which it sold to the same department stores. Hilfiger, Murjani, and two other investors bought out Murjani International in 1988 and changed the name to Tommy Hilfiger. In 2009, Phillips-Van Heusen (now PVH) bought the company.

Hilfiger began with only a men's line, but it has added women's and children's wear as well. There are over 1000 Tommy Hilfiger stores globally, and sales outside the United States now account for more than half of total sales. Europe accounts for the largest portion of Hilfiger's international sales, although it also has stores in Asia, South America, and the Middle East. The opening photo shows a Tommy Hilfiger window display in Florence, Italy.

PROMOTION AND BRANDING

Hilfiger's promotion and branding have been so intertwined that it is almost impossible to separate them. At the beginning, Murjani saw two primary needs: to convince stores to stock a new brand and to convince customers to want it. Although his ad budget for the first year (1985) was U.S. $1.4 million—quite small for selling in a mass consumer market, especially for an unknown brand—the ads were aimed strictly at getting Tommy Hilfiger's name known. He placed two-page ads in leading magazines and newspapers, along with a billboard in New York's Times Square without showing any clothes or any models. The ads included Hilfiger's face, the logo for the clothes, and words describing him as being on a par with such well-known designers as Ralph Lauren, Perry Ellis, and Calvin Klein.

The ads were so unusual that the brand received free publicity through newspaper write-ups. Even Johnny Carson quipped about Hilfiger on his popular evening TV show. Within a short time, surveys in New York revealed that people thought of Hilfiger as one of the four or five most important U.S. designers. Department and specialty stores were willing to sell the clothes, and the logo-loving public was rushing to buy them. There was also some fortunate timing inasmuch as many young managers were eager to be seen in upscale sportswear during the newly popular "casual Friday" workdays.

Early on, Hilfiger received much publicity in newspaper and magazine columns globally that mentioned or showed celebrities wearing its clothes. These celebrities were certainly an eclectic group and included Bill Clinton, the Prince of Wales, Michael Jackson, Elton John, and Snoop Dogg. This fed into the image that Hilfiger clothes had cachet; thus the company's image was fairly well established internationally before the company expanded there.

Hilfiger has used celebrity advertising, including Sheryl Crow, Jewel, Beyonce and the husband-wife team of entertainer David Bowie and supermodel Iman. To help sell a limited edition bag to support Breast Health International, the company has used film actresses Renee Zellweger and Claudia Gerini and France's first lady Carla Bruni. To promote Indian sales, it used Bollywood actor Shah Rukh Khan. More recently, Hilfiger has also turned to "delebs" (dead celebrities), such as Grace Kelly and James Dean. However, aside from celebrities, Hilfiger learned that the type of models it uses to sell its merchandise successfully in the United States may not work well in Europe. For example, its models for men's underwear in Europe, including those on point-of-purchase package displays, must be thinner and less muscular than those it uses in the United States. But it augments these thinner models by adding scantily clad, seductive-looking women who stand behind the male models in the photos. Hilfiger also found that its average consumer in Germany was older than its average consumer in the United States, so it has dropped the Tommy Jeans name because it sounded too much like a teenage name.

PRODUCT AND PRICE

Although early promotion with the brand name has been instrumental in Hilfiger's success, logo and image are not enough. From the start, Hilfiger clothes have been casual and of good quality. They are distinctive enough in color and shape so the public can usually distinguish a Hilfiger from clothing made by competitors. (The little red, white, and blue logo is, nevertheless, visibly displayed on most merchandise.) Nevertheless, this is an industry in which product lines must evolve. Hilfiger said, "Fashion brands have to reinvent themselves, just like Madonna does." Hilfiger has gone from preppy to urban and back again.

Hilfiger initially encountered some negative reactions abroad to its image of being a U.S. brand. Although some U.S. clothing products have been well received abroad (such as jeans), many U.S. clothing brands have encountered problems in Europe because Europeans tend to see France and Italy as the centers of upscale fashions. Thus, clothing brands from other countries find this opinion difficult to overcome. However, Hilfiger has since played up its Americanism, and the perception that the brand and price are a step below the pure luxury brands have successfully helped Hilfiger's European sales find a niche.

In addition, Hilfiger has encountered some differing national preferences. For example, in Germany, Hilfiger's largest European market, men don't mind paying $50 more than the highest-priced Hilfiger shirts in the United States, but they want them in a higher-quality cotton. Hilfiger has found throughout Europe that there is hardly any demand for the cotton sweaters so popular in the United States, so it has switched to wool sweaters. Hilfiger has adjusted to the European preference for slimmer-looking jeans and smaller logos on shirts. It has also created a line of added-luxury items, such as leather jackets and cashmere sweaters for the Italian market.

To make these changes, Hilfiger set up a design staff in Amsterdam that includes almost 30 different nationalities. It has adapted the Hilfiger look to the European demands. The success in Europe has led to more harmonization in the products offered in the United States and Europe, a move more upmarket in the United States, and a greater dependence on the European design team.

DISTRIBUTION

In the United States, Hilfiger traditionally relied mainly on wholesaling to about 1,800 department stores, of which many had stand-alone Hilfiger departments within. It has stayed away from chains that are viewed as more lower end, such as JCPenney and Sears, but it does sell its outdated stock to discount chains T.J. Maxx and Marshalls. However, in 2007, Hilfiger gave Macy's exclusive rights to sell its sportswear lines. Although Macy's has about 800 stores, the move required Hilfiger to pull sales from other department stores, such as Dillard's.

Distribution is perhaps the biggest difference that Hilfiger found when entering Europe. Because the company succeeded in the United States by first going into department stores, it put an early European emphasis on department stores as well. This led to its entry into such leading chains as Galeries Lafayette in France and El Corte Inglés in Spain. Hilfiger's CEO has described the U.S. market as one of concentration (sending a lot to department stores) and the European market as one of fragmentation (sending small amounts to small stores that carry select pieces). European operational costs are about three times those in the United States because of its more fragmented retail and wholesale system. Hilfiger now has about 5,000 wholesale accounts in Europe—much more than in the United States. On top of that, the margins at the final consumer level in Europe run from 50 to 100 percent higher than in the United States. The result is that prices for Hilfiger merchandise are much higher in Europe than in the United States.

Hilfiger entered most Asian countries through licensing agreements; however, as sales grew substantially in China and Japan, it turned to self-ownership within those markets.

In recent years, Hilfiger has been inaugurating large flagship stores in prime locations within large markets, such as on Fifth Avenue in New York City and the Champs-Élysées in Paris. It will open a flagship store in Tokyo in 2012. These stores serve not only to make sales, but also to demonstrate the variety of merchandise under the Hilfiger label. The foreign stores are decorated to emphasize an American image, while simultaneously connecting the United States to the host country. For instance, the Paris store has a poster of a U.S. magazine with the Eiffel Tower on the cover. By locating in prestige areas, Hilfiger promotes an aura of having luxury products.

There is an old adage that clothes make the man. Hilfiger, while making and selling clothes, has succeeded in convincing customers that its merchandise will help boost (or make) their positions. CRN

Case Review Note

Introduction

As the Hilfiger case points out, similar marketing principles in domestic and foreign markets hold that regardless of where a company operates, it must have desirable products and services, tell people about them, and offer them at acceptable prices and accessible locations favored by consumers. However, country differences may cause companies to apply these principles differently abroad, such as by offering product variations to correspond with local preferences—as Hilfiger has done by offering higher-quality cotton for shirts in Germany. Hilfiger's experience also emphasizes the need to find the right balance between the benefits of local responsiveness and the efficiency gains of standardization.

Whatever marketing approach a company takes abroad should be compatible with its overall aims and strategies. This does not imply that it must follow the same strategy for every product or every country. Such factors as cost leadership or differentiation may matter more in some markets than in others. Choosing to follow the same tactics globally may lead to, say, a mass-market orientation in one country and a focused strategy in another. Finally, the degree of global standardization versus national responsiveness may vary within elements of the marketing mix, such as standardizing the product as much as possible while promoting it differently among countries.

Figure 16.1 shows marketing's place in international business. Here, we discuss the application of different marketing strategies to international operations, examine the marketing mix elements of product, pricing, promotion, branding, and distribution, and explain the major factors to consider for each element when operating internationally. Finally, we consider the need to vary the emphasis within the marketing mix to fit the conditions of each country.

FIGURE 16.1   Marketing as a Means of Pursuing an International Strategy

Recall that we used Figure 14.1 to introduce the various *means* by which a company can pursue its international objectives and strategy. Among those means we included *functions*, and here we focus on one of the most important of those functions: *marketing*.

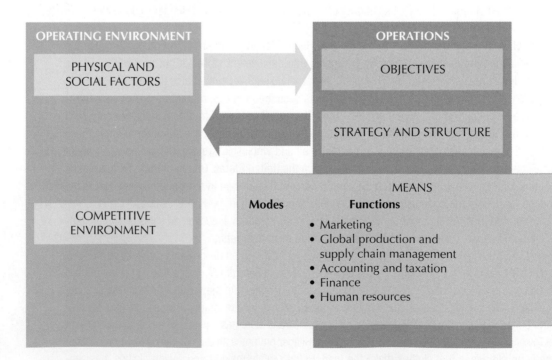

Marketing Strategies

We first discuss the worldwide application of the marketing orientations commonly found in marketing texts, then conclude by examining market segmentation and targeting and how they relate both to the orientations and to the marketing mix elements.

Overall international marketing strategies should depend on the company's

* Marketing orientation.
* Target market.

MARKETING ORIENTATIONS

Five common marketing orientations can be applied around the world: *production, sales, customer, strategic marketing,* and *social marketing.* Each is discussed below.

Production Orientation A company may focus primarily on production—either efficiency or high-quality—with little emphasis on marketing. Rather than analyzing consumer needs to a high degree, managers assume that customers simply want lower prices or higher quality. Although this approach has largely gone out of vogue, it is used internationally for certain cases:

Price is the most important factor in selling many commodities.

* *Commodity sales,* especially those for which there is little need or possibility of product differentiation
* *Passive exports,* particularly those that serve to reduce surpluses within the domestic market
* *Foreign-market segments or niches* that may resemble segments targeted domestically

Commodity Sales Companies sell many undifferentiated raw materials and agricultural commodities primarily on the basis of price, because of universal demand. However, even for commodities, companies have sometimes had positive international sales results through differentiation, such as with the Chiquita brand on bananas.

In addition, oil producers, such as PDVSA, LUKoil, and Aramco, have bought branded gasoline-distribution operations abroad to help them sell an otherwise undifferentiated product. Commodity producers also put effort into business-to-business marketing by providing innovative financing and ensuring timely, high-quality supplies.

Concept Check

In explaining "Commodity Agreements" in Chapter 8, we define commodities as raw materials or primary products (e.g., crude petroleum, copper, coffee). Commodities account for a significant portion of global merchandise trade.

Passive Exports Many companies begin exporting very passively by filling unsolicited requests from abroad. At this point, they adapt their products very little, if at all, to foreign consumers' preferences. This suffices for many companies that view foreign sales simply as a means to dispose of excess inventory they can't reasonably sell domestically. In fact, if fixed costs are covered from domestic sales, they can quote lower export prices to liquidate inventories without disrupting their domestic markets.

Passive sales occur when foreign buyers seek new products.

Foreign Niches A company may aim a product at a large share of the domestic market and then find a few consumers abroad who are also willing to buy it. Inca Kola, the largest-selling soft drink in Peru, has only small niche markets abroad, primarily among people who consumed it in Peru. However, a niche market abroad may become a mass market, as is the case with Mexico's Corona beer.

A company may also use a production orientation when selling in countries with only a small market potential, particularly in small developing nations. In effect, the market size does not justify the alteration expense—for instance, not even changing electrical plugs to fit local sockets, which local purchasers must convert themselves.

The unaltered product may have appeal at home and abroad

* Because of spillover in product information from its home country.
* Through a simultaneous multicountry launch.
* Because of foreign and domestic input in development.

Sales Orientation Internationally, a sales orientation means a company tries to sell abroad what it can sell domestically, with the same approach, on the assumption that consumers are sufficiently similar globally. Whirlpool successfully launched its high-capacity front-loading washing machines almost simultaneously in multiple countries this way.[2] Once operating abroad, a strong information exchange between the foreign subsidiary and headquarters can help develop products that can be sufficiently standardized and still fit the needs of consumers in different countries.[3]

This orientation differs from the production orientation because of its active rather than passive approach to promoting sales. However, there is much anecdotal evidence of foreign-marketing failures because managers assume without sufficient research that products will be accepted the same as at home, or that heavy sales efforts abroad can overcome negative foreign attitudes toward the product, price, or distribution method. Even so, there are successful examples of marketing abroad with little or no research on what foreign consumers want.

Of course, some products other than commodities need no international adaptation, such as razor blades, aircraft, cat food, and cameras. For others, however, a company may succeed best with a sales orientation by selling to culturally similar countries with a great deal of spillover in product information, such as between the United States and Canada.[4]

Customer Orientation   In a company that operates according to a sales orientation, management is usually guided by answers to such questions as: Should the company send some exports abroad? Where can it sell more of product X? That is, the product is held constant and the sales location is varied.

In contrast, a customer orientation asks: What and how can the company sell in country A or to a particular type of consumer? In this case, the country or type of consumer is held constant and the product and marketing method vary. An MNE may most likely take this approach because it finds the country's size and growth potential or the particular type of consumer attractive. In an extreme case, it would move to completely different products—an uncommon strategy that some MNEs nonetheless have adopted. Compañía Chilena de Fósforos, a Chilean match producer, wanted to tap the Japanese market because of its growth and size. However, because the company's matches were not price competitive in Japan, it successfully entered the market by making chopsticks, a product that would use its poplar forest resources and wood-processing capabilities.[5]

Business-to-business suppliers may be primarily concerned with promoting their production capabilities, prices, and delivery reliability rather than determining what will sell in foreign markets. Instead, they depend on other companies' purchasing agents to give them product specifications. For example, Hong Kong's Yue Yuen Industrial is the world's largest branded-footwear manufacturer, making athletic shoes to the specifications of companies such as Nike, New Balance, and Adidas.

Strategic Marketing Orientation   Most companies committed to continual rather than sporadic foreign sales adopt a strategy that combines production, sales, and customer orientations. Companies that don't make changes to accommodate foreign customers' needs may lose too many sales, especially if aggressive competitors are willing to do so. At the same time, they must consider their competencies, lest they deviate too much from what they do well. Thus, they rely on marketing variations. When breweries such as Heineken and Stroh faced alcoholic beverage restrictions in Saudi Arabia, they turned to sales of nonalcoholic beer (marketed as malt), which was closely related to their managers' areas of expertise. To enter the Argentine home-building market, Pulte Homes kept the same floor plans and exterior look of its U.S. homes to gain economies of standardization, but added large rear patios and bathroom bidets to fit Argentine preferences.[6]

Social Marketing Orientation   Companies with social marketing orientations pay close attention to the potential environmental, health, social, and work-related problems that may arise when selling or making their products abroad. For instance, Tesco is building "green" stores and has introduced carbon labeling on its products.[7] Such groups as consumer associations, political parties, labor unions, and NGOs are becoming more

---

A customer orientation takes geographic areas as given.

The most common product strategy is to adapt by degree.

Companies consider the effects on all stakeholders when selling or making their products.

globally aware—and vocal. They can quell demand when they believe a product somehow violates their concept of social responsibility.

Companies must increasingly consider not only how a product is purchased but also how it is made and disposed of and how it might be changed to be more socially desirable. Such considerations have led Coca-Cola to develop a vitamin-enriched beverage for Botswana, distribute rehydration salts in its packing crates in several countries, and use returnable glass containers for Argentina and Brazil.[8] Our ending case deals with a joint venture that aims to use social responsibility as a competitive advantage.

Case Review Note

SEGMENTING AND TARGETING MARKETS

Although population and income may give a rough estimate of market size, seldom can the same marketing mix be used to convince virtually an entire population to consume a product. Thus, based on the orientations just discussed, companies must segment markets for their products and services and then decide which to target and how. The most common way to do this is through demographics, such as by income, age, gender, ethnicity, religion, or a combination of factors (such as a segment that consists of women age 20 to 30 earning $20,000–$30,000 per year). Companies may further refine these segments by adding psychographics (attitudes, values, and lifestyles). Internationally, there are three basic approaches to segmentation.[9]

> Companies must decide on their target markets, which may include segments that exist in more than one country.

By Country Let's say a company decides to go only to the Japanese market for the time being because of its population size and purchasing power. It will then need to decide whether to target one or multiple segments there, whether to use the same marketing mix to sell to all segments, whether to tailor the products separately to each segment, and whether to vary the promotion and distribution separately as well. However, although this approach may lead to success in Japan, it overlooks the possible similarities of various Japanese market segments with those in other countries, leaving little opportunity to gain economies through standardization in order to serve market segments that cut across countries.

By Global Segment An MNE may identify some segments around the world, such as those based primarily on income or on cultural attributes that transcend countries.[10] Thus, each country may have some people within this same segment, but the proportional size of each segment will vary by country. Although this may bring about economies of standardization, the company may still need to prioritize by country of entry, delay tapping bigger markets in some countries, and face high entry costs in other countries where the targeted segment is small.

By Multiple Criteria MNEs can combine these choices by looking at countries as segments, identifying segments within each country, and comparing them with those in other countries. They can then determine similarities for targeting the most promising cross-country segments, gain efficiencies through standardization, and still tailor other marketing mix aspects—product offerings, promotion, branding, and distribution—to be compatible with the needs of each country's market.

In effect, a company may hold one or more elements of these marketing functions constant while altering the others. For instance, Chanel aims its cosmetics sales to a segment that transcends national boundaries. It uses branding, promotion, pricing, and distribution globally, but adapts the cosmetics to local ethnic and climatic norms.[11]

Mass Markets versus Niche Markets At the same time, most companies have multiple products and product variations that appeal to different segments; thus, they must decide which to introduce abroad and whether to target them to mass markets or niche segments. Sales to a mass market may be necessary to gain sufficient economies

> **Concept Check**
>
> In Chapter 12, we describe the importance of economic demographic variables in the process whereby companies evaluate and select countries as locations for international operations. Many of the demographic data considered in international marketing decisions are the same. In addressing the question "Will Prime Locations Change?" for example, we point out that while populations in such high-income countries as Japan are declining, those in many developing countries are growing.

FIGURE 16.2

Products and the percentage of people wanting them are not the same everywhere.

Source: Paul Noth/Cartoonbank.com

"I hear he's huge in Japan."

in production and distribution. As an example, foreign beer companies entering China with a focus on the premium sector found that, although the Chinese premium beer market is large, it is so dispersed that high distribution costs (transport costs are high relative to product cost) made the strategy unprofitable.[12] In contrast, General Motors entered China with its Buick models aimed at a high-income segment and found not only a large enough market, but also reasonable distribution economies because the cost of transport is low compared to the cost of production.

Because the percentage of people who fall into any segment may vary substantially among countries, a niche market in one country may be a mass market in another. (Figure 16.2 shows this humorously.) An MNE may be content to accept a combination of mass and niche markets; however, if it wishes to appeal to mass markets everywhere, it may need to change elements in its marketing program. U.S.-based Bell South successfully managed to reach a much larger Venezuelan market by selling fewer minutes on phone cards—it added $4 phone cards to the $10 and $20 cards it customarily sold.[13]

Product Policies

Cost is a compelling reason to standardize marketing globally. Companies that change any part of their marketing mix to serve foreign markets incur additional costs to develop the change, plus the resulting costs of coordinating and controlling added diversity. Within the marketing mix, MNEs emphazise product standardization because changes generally incur the biggest expense.[14] Nevertheless, product adaptations are common. We now consider the reasons for making them for foreign markets, their costs, the extent and mix of product lines, and product life-cycle considerations.

WHY FIRMS ALTER PRODUCTS

Companies have legal, cultural, and economic reasons for altering their products to fit the needs of customers in different countries. Each is examined in turn below.

Legal Considerations   Explicit legal requirements, usually meant to protect consumers, are the most obvious reason to alter products for foreign markets. If you don't comply with the law, you won't be allowed to sell.[15] Pharmaceuticals and foods are particularly subject to regulations concerning purity, testing, and labeling, while automobiles must conform to diverse safety, pollution, and fuel-economy standards.

> Legal factors are usually related to safety or health protection.

When standards (such as for safety) differ among countries, MNEs may either conform to the minimum standards of each country or make and sell products fabricated to the highest global standard everywhere. Managers must consider cost along with any ill will that may result by having lower standards in some countries. Critics have complained, for example, about companies' sales abroad—especially in developing countries—of such products as toys, automobiles, contraceptives, and pharmaceuticals that did not meet safety or quality standards elsewhere.

> **Point** | Should Home Governments Regulate Their Companies' Marketing in Developing Countries?

Point **Yes** MNEs advertise, promote, and sell products in developing markets that their home countries have banned. If we've made a decision not to sell these products domestically because of their dangers or ethical implications, we have a moral obligation to prevent the same consequences abroad. This statement may smack of extraterritoriality, but let's face it: Too many consumers in developing countries lack the education and reliable information to make intelligent decisions, and/or they are saddled with corrupt political leaders who don't look after their interests. We must ensure that they spend on needs rather than on wants engendered by MNEs' clever promotion programs. If developed countries don't regulate to protect consumers in developing countries, who will?

Companies also export products that don't meet quality standards at home or are potentially dangerous. Take DDT: It's so dangerous to the environment that all developed countries have banned its use—but not its production. Or battery recycling. We've pretty much abandoned that business because of strict antipollution requirements to prevent lead poisoning, which shows up only after slow, cumulative ingestion through the years. So now companies export the batteries to developing countries that have either weak or weakly enforced pollution laws.[16]

With the World Health Organization (WHO) estimating that tobacco is the leading cause of preventable death in the world, we have also attempted to limit tobacco use through warning labels and advertisements, restrictions on sales to minors, and smoking bans in certain public areas.

Just 5 percent of the global population is protected by anti-smoking programs, and that is centered almost entirely in developed countries.[17] With such a rise in anti-smoking actions, tobacco companies have increased their promotions in developing countries.

There are also examples of products suitable for most customers in the developed world but not for poorer countries. The most famous case involves infant-formula sales, in which infant mortality rates rose in developing countries when bottle-feeding supplanted breast-feeding. Because of low incomes and poor education, mothers frequently overdiluted formula and gave it to their babies in unsanitary conditions. And the governments did little to stop the sales. Global publicity about the situation led WHO to pass a voluntary code to restrict formula promotion—but not sales—in such areas. Critics hit Nestlé hardest, because it had the largest share of infant-formula sales in developing countries and because its name-identified products facilitated the organization of a boycott. Nestlé ceased advertising that could discourage breast-feeding, limited free formula supplies at hospitals, and banned personal gifts to health officials.[18]

MNEs also pay too little attention to the needs of consumers in developing markets. Instead, they primarily create products suitable to the needs of wealthier consumers who can afford them, but superfluous for low-income consumers, to whom MNEs introduce and promote them heavily. Thus, the poor end up buying products they don't need instead of spending their money on nutritional and health items. Bottled water, sold mainly in plastic bottles by such companies as Nestlé, Danone, Coca-Cola, and PepsiCo, is an example. It is often no better than tap water (in fact, it often *is* tap water), but it sells for 10,000 times more in bottles that are thrown out and take 1,000 years to biodegrade. The crude oil used to make such bottles just for the United States could fuel 100,000 cars per year.[19]

Finally, MNEs spend little to make products to fit the needs of developing countries. Consider that only 10 percent of the global health research budget is spent on diseases that account for 90 percent of the global disease burden—mainly those that largely bypass developed countries.[20] Instead of

spending heavily on life-threatening illnesses like malaria, Chagas disease, and sleeping sickness, they spend on lifestyle treatments, such as penile erectile dysfunction and baldness. The U.S. Food and Drug Administration (FDA) did institute an incentive in 2008—faster approval of potential "blockbuster drugs"—for pharmaceutical companies that research previously neglected diseases. However, there is skepticism about whether faster approval is enough of an incentive.[21] Surely we can find the regulatory means to force companies to meet real needs in the developing world rather than concentrating on selling dangerous and superfluous products there.

Should Home Governments Regulate Their Companies' Marketing in Developing Countries?

Counterpoint

No The answer here is education rather than limiting people's choices by regulating MNEs. In fact, there are many examples of behavior change in both consumers and governments when they learn the facts. Thailand, for instance, has restricted tobacco smoking in response to statistics linking it with death.[22]

Your argument that products banned at home should not be sold abroad assumes that the home government knows best. This may reflect a difference in morals rather than a problem of creating physical danger. For instance, some countries have banned the sale of the morning-after pill RU-486 on moral grounds. But to ban sales in other countries that accept a different morality would smack of cultural imperialism.

Conditions between rich and poor countries are sometimes so different that they need different regulations. Take your example of DDT exports. Developing countries are aware of DDT's adverse long-term effect on the environment, but in the short term many of them face a malaria crisis. When South Africa was persuaded to ban the use of DDT and turned instead to a different pesticide, the number of new malaria cases tripled in four years; renewing DDT spraying brought that number down again.[23] Until there is a better solution for malaria, DDT bans will do more harm than good. Certainly, if one government has found a product dangerous, it should pass on this information to other governments; in terms of DDT and toxic materials exports, this is already being done.

Yes, tobacco companies are promoting more heavily in developing countries. Keep in mind, though, that a good part of that promotion is for smokeless tobacco products, which are safer than cigarettes and can help smokers stop.[24] However, if other governments were to limit their companies' sales or promotion of tobacco, their citizens would still be able to buy it. Many developing countries have indigenous tobacco companies, some of which are even government-owned, such as the China National Tobacco Company.

The infant formula situation truly shows the complexity of this issue. Other factors also influenced the rise in bottle-feeding—specifically, more working mothers and fewer

Counterpoint

products and services originating in the home. Together, they led to feeding babies "home brews" that, sadly, were also often unsanitary. Promoting infant formula may simply have persuaded them to give up the home brews in favor of the most nutritious breast-milk substitute available. Moreover, well-intentioned anti-formula groups succeeded in replacing bottle-feeding with breast-feeding. However, the HIV virus is transmitted through breast milk—a particular problem in HIV/AIDS-plagued southern Africa.[25] Now there are campaigns to get mothers not to breast-feed! This starkly shows the futility of trying to legislate what is good for people.

How far can we go to try to protect people? Obesity, considered a growing health problem in the developed world, is being attacked through education—the same way we should attack problems in developing countries. I can't imagine us rationing or banning sugars, fats, and carbohydrates. Certainly, products such as soft drinks seem superfluous when people are ill-nourished and in poor health. But there is no clear-cut means of drawing a line between people who can and can't afford these products. Moreover, Coca-Cola has experimented with adding nutrition to products, but critics complain that soft drinks should not be sold at all.

Companies *do* alter products to fit the needs of poor people—everything from less expensive packages to less expensive products. The pharmaceutical firms you criticized for not attacking low-income health needs spend heavily to find solutions to diseases that attack all people, such as cancer and diabetes. In fact, they have seen, and expect to see, huge prescription drug growth in emerging markets.[26] However, they must recoup their expenses if they are to survive, so they concentrate on drugs for which they can be paid. Governmental research centers and nonprofit foundations are better candidates for solving the developing countries' health problems. Some are working jointly with pharmaceutical firms to find solutions, while the National Institutes of Health (NIH) in the United States has instituted a program to find treatments for some of the 6,800 diseases for which there is likely insufficient revenue to recoup research expenditures.[27]

Labeling Requirements   One of the more cumbersome product alterations for companies concerns laws on labeling, such as for origin, ingredients, and warnings. The difference between the EU and the United States on label requirements for bioengineered foods, for example, has induced Unilever to use different types of oil in its Hellmann's mayonnaise.[28]

Environmental-Protection Regulations   Another problem concerns laws that protect the environment, such as Denmark's onetime ban on aluminum cans and current refundable deposit on them. Other countries restrict the volume of packaging materials to save resources and decrease trash. There are also differences in national requirements as to whether containers must be reusable and whether companies use packaging materials that must be recycled, incinerated, or composted.

Indirect Legal Considerations   Indirect legal requirements also affect product content or demand. In some nations, companies cannot easily import certain raw materials or components, forcing them to construct an end product with local substitutes that may substantially alter the final result. Legal requirements such as high taxes on heavy automobiles also shift companies' sales to smaller models, thus indirectly altering demand for tire sizes and grades of gasoline.

Issues of Standardization   A recurring issue is the need to arrive at international product standards and eliminate some of the wasteful product requirements for alterations among countries. Although governments have reached agreements on some products (technical standards on mobile phones, bar codes to identify products), other products (railroad gauges, power supplies) continue to vary. A global standard has usually resulted from companies wanting to emulate a dominant producer, such as making personal computers that are IBM-compatible.

> Although some standardization of products would eliminate wasteful alterations, there is resistance because
>
> - A changeover would be costly.
> - People are familiar with the "old."

In reality, there is both consumer and economic resistance to standardization—such as the reluctance to adapt to the metric system in the United States. Economically, a complete changeover would be more costly than simply educating people and relabeling. Containers would have to be redesigned and production retooled so that sizes would be in even numbers. (Would U.S. football have a first down with 9.144 meters to go?) Even for new products or those still under development, companies and countries are slow to reach agreement, because they want to protect the investments they've already made. At best, international standards will come very slowly.

Cultural Considerations   Religious differences obviously limit the standardization of product offerings globally, such as food franchises limiting sales of pork products in Islamic countries and meat of any kind in India. However, cultural differences affecting product demand are often not always so easily discerned. Toyota initially failed to sell enough pickup trucks in the United States until it redesigned the interior with enough headroom for drivers to wear cowboy hats, while Volkswagen and Audi have extended the wheelbase for China to accommodate more passengers for weekend outings.[29] International food marketers substantially alter ingredients (especially fat, sodium, and sugar) to fit local tastes and requirements, such as Kellogg's All-Bran bar having three times as much salt in the United States as in Mexico.

> Examination of cultural differences may pinpoint possible problem areas.

Economic Considerations

Income Level and Distribution   If a country's average consumers have low incomes, few of them may be able to buy products that MNEs sell domestically. But this creates an opportunity to sell to those with sufficient income while designing cheaper alternatives for those with lower incomes. For instance in Peru, Unilever sells deodorants in aerosol cans to more affluent consumers, and it sells small containers of cream sachet to those with lower incomes. Often, consumers have so little extra cash that they buy personal items in small quantities as they use them. In another Peruvian example, Kimberley Clarke sells Huggies (disposable diapers) in regular boxes along

> Personal incomes and infrastructures affect product demand.

High frequency stores in developing countries, including this one in Kuala Lumpur, Malaysia, often crowd small packages into a small area to serve customers who shop frequently because they cannot afford to buy in large quantities.

Source: CHEN WEI SENG/ Shutterstock.com

with a single Huggies in a small package.[30] When segmenting sales to different economic levels, a company may need to differentiate its products with different brand names, such as what Gillette does in China with both a Duracell and Nanfu brand of batteries.[31] The adjacent photo shows a high-frequency store catering to this type of consumer.

Infrastructure   Poor infrastructure may also require product alterations, such as the ability to withstand rough terrain and utility outages. The washing machine models Whirlpool sells in remote areas of India have rat guards to protect hoses, extra-strong parts to survive transportation on potholed roads, and heavy-duty wiring to cope with electrical ebbs and surges.[32] Japan, despite having an excellent infrastructure, is characterized by crowded conditions and high land prices. Some large foreign automobile models are too wide to fit into elevators that carry cars to upper floors to be parked, or to make narrow turns on back streets.

ALTERATION COSTS

Companies usually can substantially cut production and inventory costs through product standardization. Nevertheless, as you've just seen, there can be compelling reasons to alter products for different national markets. Some alterations, such as package labeling, are cheaper to make than others, such as designing a different car model. However, even packaging changes may necessitate costly research if the aim is to convey a particular product perception to a target market with different characteristics than those at home. For example, there is evidence that packaging can partially sway consumers in buying decisions, but the image needed to do this may differ by target market.[33] Thus, companies should always compare the cost of an alteration to the likely cost of lost sales without it.

MNEs can compromise between uniformity and diversity by standardizing products a great deal while altering some components. Whirlpool does this by putting the same basic compressor, casing, evaporator, and sealant system in all its refrigerators while changing such features as doors and shelves for different countries.[34]

Concept Check

In Chapter 12, we list the factors that companies consider when "scanning" potential overseas locations to determine what conditions in the host country's environment are likely to affect the success of international operations. Under "Cost Considerations," we point out that poor internal infrastructure inflates operating costs and can in fact negate cost savings afforded by low labor rates.

Some alterations cost less than others.

THE PRODUCT LINE: EXTENT AND MIX

It is doubtful that all of an MNE's multiple products could generate sufficient sales to justify the cost of penetrating each market with each product. Even if they could, the company might offer only a portion of its product line, perhaps as an entry strategy.

Broadening the product line may gain distribution economies.

Sales and Cost Considerations   In reaching product-line decisions, managers should consider the possible effects on sales and the cost of having a large versus small family of products. Sometimes a firm must produce and sell a wide variety of products to gain distribution with large retailers. In contrast, if the foreign sales per customer are small, selling costs per unit may be high because of the associated fixed distribution costs. In such a case, the company can broaden the product line it handles, either by introducing a larger family of products or by grouping sales of several manufacturers.

Product Life-Cycle Considerations   Countries may differ in either the shape or the length of a product's life cycle. Thus, a product facing declining sales in one country may have growing or sustained sales in another. Consider cars. They are a mature product in Western Europe, the United States, and Japan, in the late growth stage in South Korea, and in the early growth stage in India. At the mature stage, automobile companies must emphasize characteristics that encourage people to replace their still-functional cars, such as lifestyle, speed, and accessories. In the early growth stage, they need to appeal to first-time buyers who worry about cost, so they emphasize fuel consumption and price.[35]

Pricing Strategies

Within the marketing mix, a price must be low enough to gain sales but high enough to guarantee the flow of funds required to cover such expenses as R&D, production, and distribution. A competitive strategy, such as cost leadership versus product differentiation, also affects pricing decisions. The proper price not only ensures short-term profits but also provides the resources necessary to achieve long-term competitive viability.

POTENTIAL OBSTACLES IN INTERNATIONAL PRICING

Pricing is more complex internationally than domestically because of various factors that we'll now examine.

Government Intervention   Every country has laws that affect the prices of goods, such as price controls. Minimum prices are usually set to prevent companies from eliminating competitors to gain monopoly positions. Maximum prices are usually set so that poor consumers can buy products and services.

Governmental price controls may
- Set minimum or maximum prices.
- Prohibit certain competitive pricing practices.

The WTO, under its antidumping regulations, permits countries to establish restrictions against any import entering at a price below cost. Why would a company wish to sell below its cost? First, it may want to induce customers to try a product, such as by offering a low price or even free samples. Second, it may be testing the market. Nestlé did this when it exported Lean Cuisine products from Canada to the United Kingdom at a price below cost, then sold them temporarily at the consumer price it would charge if it produced them in the United Kingdom. The loss was small compared to the value of the information gained and the amount of Nestlé's eventual commitment. However, antidumping regulations may prevent companies from fully utilizing the advantages from such temporary below-cost selling.

Market Diversity   Although a company can segment the domestic market and charge different prices in each segment, country-to-country variations create even more natural segments. A seafood company would sell few sea urchins or tuna eyeballs in the United States at any price, but it can export them to Japan, where they are delicacies.

Consumers in some countries simply like certain products more and are willing to pay more for them.

Pricing Tactics In some places, a company may have many competitors and thus little discretion in setting its prices. Elsewhere, a near-monopoly situation may allow it to exercise considerable pricing discretion by using any of the following tactics:

- A **skimming strategy**—charging a high price for a new product by aiming first at consumers willing to pay that much, then progressively lowering the price to sell to other consumers

- A **penetration strategy**—introducing a product at a low price to induce a maximum number of consumers to try it

- A **cost-plus strategy**—pricing at a desired margin over cost

Country-of-origin stereotypes also limit pricing possibilities. For example, exporters in developing economies must often compete primarily through low prices because of negative perceptions about their products' quality. The danger is that a lower price may reduce the product image even further.

Diversity in buying on credit affects sales. Credit buying raises costs, which consumers in some countries are less willing to pay than consumers elsewhere. For instance, in Japan it is harder to use credit payments as a means of inducing the sale of goods than it is in the United States.

Cash versus credit buying affects demand.

Price generally goes up by more than transport and duty costs.

Concept Check

In discussing "Export Strategy" in Chapter 13, we discuss the importance of **export intermediaries** in the international business **transaction chain** and explain their place in a carefully considered export business plan. In turning to "The Export Process," we describe the process of indirect selling and explain the central role of home-country intermediaries—independent companies that facilitate the international trade of goods.

Export Price Escalation If standard markups occur within distribution channels, lengthening the channels or adding expenses somewhere in the system will further raise the price to the consumer—a situation known as *export price escalation*. If a product's markup is 50 percent and its production cost is $1.00, the price to the consumer would be $1.50. However, if expenses in the system were to raise costs to $1.20, the 50 percent markup would make the price $1.80, not $1.70 as might be expected.

Figure 16.3 shows price escalation in export sales, which occurs for two reasons:

1. Channels of distribution usually include additional intermediaries because exporters need to contract with organizations that know how to sell in foreign markets.

2. Tariffs and transport are added costs that may be passed on to consumers.

There are two main implications of price escalation. Seemingly exportable products may turn out to be noncompetitive abroad if companies use cost-plus pricing—which many do. To become competitive in exporting, a company may have to sell its product to intermediaries at a lower price to lessen the amount of escalation.

FIGURE 16.3   Why Cost-Plus Pricing Pushes Up Prices

Let's say that a product is being exported from Country A and imported into Country B for purchase by consumers there. Let's also say that both the producer/exporter and the importer/distributor tack on 50 percent markups to the prices they pay for the product. If you add in the costs of transport and tariffs, the product is substantially more expensive in Country B than in Country A—perhaps too expensive to be sold competitively.

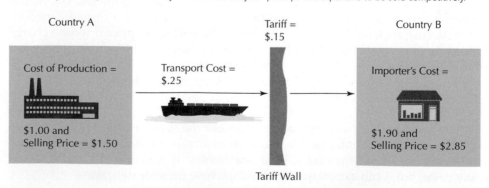

Fluctuations in Currency Value   For companies accustomed to operating with one (relatively) stable currency, pricing in highly volatile currencies can be extremely troublesome. Managers should price to ensure the company enough funds to replenish its inventory and still make a profit. Otherwise, it may be making a "paper profit" while liquidating itself—that is, what shows on paper as a profit may result from the failure to adjust for inflation while the merchandise is in stock.[36]

Two other pricing problems occur because of inflationary conditions:

1. The receipt of funds in a foreign currency that, when converted, buy less of the company's own currency than had been expected

2. The frequent readjustment of prices necessary to compensate for continual cost increases

In the first case, the company sometimes (depending on competitive factors and governmental regulations) can specify an equivalency in some hard currency in sales contracts. For example, a U.S. firm's sale to a company in Uruguay may specify that payment be made in dollars or in pesos at an equivalent price in terms of dollars at the time payment is made.

In the second case, frequent price increases may hamper the ability to quote prices in letters or catalogs, or even what the company would otherwise prefer for distribution. For instance, price increases in vending-machine sales are often difficult because of the need to recalibrate machines and come up with coins or tokens that correspond to the new prices. Another alternative is to change the product's size, which is what Coca-Cola did to its soft-drink cans in Hong Kong when aluminum prices rose.[37]

Currency-value changes also affect pricing decisions for any product that has potential foreign competition. For example, when the U.S. dollar is strong, companies can sell non-U.S.-made goods more cheaply in the U.S. market because their price in dollars decreases. In such a situation, U.S. producers may have to accept a lower profit margin to be competitive. When the dollar is weak, however, foreign producers may have to adjust their margins downward.

When companies sell similar goods in multiple countries, price differences among them must not exceed by much the cost of bringing the goods in from a lower-priced country, or spillover in buying will occur. Ice cream manufacturers, for example, can vary their prices by a large percentage from country to country because the transportation costs compared to the product's price render large-scale movements across borders impractical. However, if the transportation costs compared to the product's price are low, consumers can feasibly buy abroad and import when prices vary substantially from country to country.

The Gray Market

The Gray Market   The **gray market,** or **product diversion,** is the selling and handling of goods through unofficial distributors. Such unauthorized selling can undermine the longer-term viability of the distributorship system, induce a company's operations in different countries to compete with each other, and prevent companies from charging what the market will bear in each country. Let's say a firm's product is sold in Asia at a lower price than in the United States because of different market conditions. If an unauthorized distributor buys the product in Asia and resells it at a lower price than the authorized retailer in the United States, the authorized U.S. retailer either loses sales or can no longer sell at the price the market will bear. One consulting firm estimates that U.S. companies lose $63 billion a year because of the gray market.[38] In essence, it has become more difficult to maintain price differences among countries because consumers have more global information, such as through the Internet, and more access to buying abroad, such as because of lower trade barriers and more foreign travel.

Fixed versus Variable Pricing   MNEs often negotiate their export prices with importers. Small firms, especially those from developing countries, frequently give price

Concept Check

We define **foreign exchange** in Chapter 9 as the currency of one country denominated in the currency of another country or group of countries. We point out that most foreign-exchange transactions stem from the activities of commercial banks, but we also observe that exporters and importers are players on the **foreign-exchange market** and explain how such factors as **exchange rates** affect certain international business activities, especially the process of making overseas payments.

There are country-to-country differences in

- Whether manufacturers set prices.
- Whether prices are fixed or bargained in stores.
- Where bargaining occurs.

concessions too quickly, limiting their ability to negotiate on a range of marketing factors that affect their costs:

- Discounts for quantity or repeat orders
- Deadlines that increase production or transportation costs
- Credit and payment terms
- Service
- Supply of promotional materials
- Training of sales personnel or customers

Table 16.1 shows ways in which an exporter (or other marketers as well) may deal more effectively in price negotiations.

Custom influences price negotiations, such as the reluctance of most German managers to take the time to bargain. Rather, they tend simply to say thanks and look for another provider.[39] Custom also causes substantial variation in whether, where, and for what products consumers bargain in order to settle on an agreed price. In the United

TABLE 16.1　Negotiating Import-Export Prices

Exporters export because they want to sell their products in foreign markets, and pricing is a key factor in selling products profitably. MNEs and other veteran exporters have learned that negotiating prices—both their own and those of their import partners—is an effective way of considering all the factors that should go into pricing decisions.

The goal is to delay a pricing commitment while discussing a whole package of other commitments.

Importer's Reaction to Price Offer	Exporter's Response
1. Your offer is too expensive.	- Ask what is meant by too expensive. - Find out what is considered acceptable and on what basis. - Respond by providing justification. - Avoid lowering your price until you learn more about what the other party is looking for. - Find out if the objection is due to your price offer or if it reflects other factors. - Ask yourself, "If I'm too expensive, why are they negotiating with me?"
2. We don't have that kind of budget.	- Find out how large the budget is and for what time frame. - Explore whether your offer can fit within the overall budget by combining several budget lines. - Propose deferred-payment schedules. - Confirm the order and postpone deliveries until a new budget is allocated. - Split your order into smaller units or miniorders to meet current budget limitations.
3. That's not what we are looking for.	- Ask what they are looking for, and insist on specifics. - Keep questioning until you understand the real needs. - Repackage your offer in light of the new information received.
4. Your offer is not competitive.	- Ask what "not competitive" means. - Find out if competitors' offers are comparable to yours. - Find weaknesses in other offers and emphasize your strengths. - Reformulate your offer by avoiding direct comparison with competition. Stress the unique features of your products/services.

Source: Claude Cellich, "Business Negotiations: Making the First Offer," *International Trade Journal* 2 (2000): 12–16. Reprinted by permission of Taylor and Francis Group LLC www.taylorandfrancis.com.

States, consumers commonly bargain for automobiles, real estate, and large orders of industrial supplies but not for grocery items. However, some auto dealerships sell only on a fixed-price basis, while bargaining for smaller items is growing, as the Internet allows consumers to confront distributors with alternative prices they have easily obtained. In contrast, consumers in most developing countries commonly bargain for both large and small items, but more routinely in traditional markets than in retail stores.[40]

Supplier Relations   Dominant companies with clout can get suppliers to offer them lower prices, in turn enabling them to gain cost advantages over competitors. But they may lack this clout in foreign markets because of not having the dominance there. Take dominant retailers. Walmart, Marks & Spencer, and Carrefour have such clout in their respective domestic United States, United Kingdom, and French markets. However, they have been hard pressed to gain the same advantage when entering the others' home markets.

The Internet is also causing more companies to compete for the same business, especially for sales of largely undifferentiated materials. Thus, many industrial buyers are claiming large price decreases through Internet buying. However, sellers can improve their positions by negotiating and by combining the Internet with face-to-face interaction.[41]

Promotion Strategies

Promotion is the presentation of messages intended to help sell a product or service. The types and direction of messages and the methods of presentation may be extremely diverse, depending on the company, product, and country of operation.

THE PUSH-PULL MIX

Promotion may be categorized as **push**, which uses direct selling techniques, or **pull**, which relies on mass media. Most companies use combinations of both. For each product in each country, a company must determine its total promotional budget as well as the mix between push and pull. The photo of London's Piccadilly Circus shows pull ads by a number of international companies.

◀ The advertisements at Piccadilly Circus in London represent logos from several countries, such as Coca-Cola, McDonald's, Budweiser, and Burger King (United States), TDK and Sanyo (Japan), and Samsung (Korea).

Source: Kaspars Grinvalds / Shutterstock.com

Factors in Push-Pull Decisions   Several factors help determine the mix of push and pull among countries:

- Type of distribution system
- Cost and availability of media to reach target markets
- Consumer attitudes toward sources of information
- Price of the product compared to incomes

Generally, the more tightly controlled the distribution system, the more likely a company is to emphasize a push strategy to distributors, because it requires a greater effort to get them to handle a product. This is true in Belgium, where most distributors can carry few brands because they are small and highly fragmented, thus companies are forced to concentrate on making their goods available.

Also affecting the push-pull mix is the amount of contact between salespeople and consumers. In a self-service situation in which there are no or few salespeople to whom customers can turn for opinions on products, it is more important for the company to use a pull strategy by advertising through mass media or at the point of purchase.

Finally, consumers react to word of mouth opinions, especially where uncertainty avoidance is high.[42] Thus companies need to establish appropriate means to persuade existing customers that their purchases have been of high quality and at reasonable prices, such as by providing after-sales support and service.

SOME PROBLEMS IN INTERNATIONAL PROMOTION

Because of diverse national environments, promotional problems are extremely varied and often problematic. For example, over 50 percent of China's population is rural, most are poor, and many lack access to traditional media to view advertisements. Thus, PC Makers such as Lenova and Hewlett Packard promote in rural areas by providing variety shows and films where they demonstrate their products. They also demonstrate at rural markets where customers visit a few times per month.[43] In rural Nigeria, Kuwait's Mobile Telecommunications Company found that its billboards were stolen to use in construction and that its direct marketers faced too many dangers. The company then turned successfully to small shop owners—tailors, retailers, etc.—and established a mini-franchise system with them.[44]

In many countries, government regulations pose an even greater barrier, such as television refusing to accept commercials in Scandinavia. Other countries may put legal constraints on what a company says. For instance, the United States and New Zealand allow pharmaceutical firms to advertise prescription drugs directly to consumers, but European countries and Australia do not. Thus, in the former countries, pharmaceutical companies describe physical symptoms, such as erectile dysfunction, in television ads and tell viewers to ask their physicians about a particular brand, such as Viagra or Cialis. Since European countries are more restrictive about mentioning the name of a drug, Pfizer's and Eli Lilly's European ads tell TV viewers to talk with their physicians about erectile dysfunction, but they never mention the name of the drugs.[45]

Finally, when a product's price compared to consumer income is high, consumers will usually want more time and information before making a decision. Information is best conveyed in a personal selling situation that fosters two-way communication. In developing economies, MNEs usually have to use push strategies for more products because of the lower incomes.

Standardization: Pro and Con   The savings from using the same advertising programs, such as on a global basis or among countries with shared consumer attributes, are significant, although not as great as those from product standardization. In addition to reducing costs, advertising standardization may improve the quality of ads at the local level (because local agencies may lack expertise), prevent internationally mobile consumers from being confused by different images, and speed the entry of products into different countries.

However, globally standardized advertising usually refers to a program that is *similar* from market to market rather than one that is *identical* in each. An example is Apple using the same theme in its "Mac versus PC" ad series in the United States and the United Kingdom, but with TV personalities from each respective country.[46]

Standardization usually implies using the same ad agency globally. By using the same agency, MNEs such as IBM, Colgate, and Tambrands have found that they can take good ideas from one market and quickly introduce them into others without worrying about legal and ethical problems over agency copying. However, Procter & Gamble and other companies prefer to use more than one agency to keep them in a state of perpetual competition and to cover one's weak spots by drawing on the ideas of another.

A Few Related Issues   Finally, the issue of standardization in advertising raises problems in a few other areas—namely, *translation, legality,* and *message needs.*

Translation   When media reach audiences in multiple countries, the ads cannot be translated because viewers watch the same transmission. An additional problem is that the product may not be available everywhere it is advertised.

When a company is going to sell in a country with a different language, translation is usually necessary unless the advertiser is trying to communicate an aura of foreignness. The most audible problem in commercial translation is dubbing, because words on an added sound track never quite correspond to lip movements. Companies can avoid this problem by creating commercials in which actors do not speak and add a voice or print overlay in the appropriate language.

A growing type of dubbing in advertising involves product placement in books, movies, and television shows. Because these shows are widely distributed internationally, a large audience sees the placement. Again, however, the product may not be available everywhere. So technology now permits the products to be removed and replaced for given markets. *Spider-Man 2* had Cadbury Schweppes's Dr. Pepper logo on a refrigerator for U.S. screenings and PepsiCo's Mirinda logo in Europe.[47]

On the surface, translating a message would seem to be easy. However, some messages, particularly plays on words, simply don't translate—even between countries that have the same language. Sometimes an acceptable word or direct translation in one place is offensive, misleading, or meaningless in another. In the Apple commercial referred to earlier, the U.S. version used the word "doozy" and the U.K. version used the word "humdinger." Another issue lies in choosing the language when a country has more than one, such as using Creole in Haiti to reach the general population but French to reach the upper class.

Legality   What is legal advertising in one country may be illegal elsewhere. The differences result mainly from varying national views on consumer protection, competitive protection, civil rights promotion, standards of morality and behavior, and nationalism. For example, there are many products that some societies view as being in sufficiently bad taste that they restrict advertisement of them, such as whether they can be advertised on television and, if so, at what time.[48]

In terms of consumer protection, policies differ on the amount of deception permitted and what can be advertised to children. The United Kingdom and the United States allow direct comparisons with competitive brands, while the Philippines prohibits them. Only a few countries regulate sexism in advertising. Elsewhere, governments restrict ads that might prompt misbehavior or law-breaking (such as promoting automobile speeds that exceed the speed limit), as well as those that show barely clad women.[49]

Message Needs   An advertising theme may not be appropriate everywhere because of country differences in consumers' product awareness and perception, the people who

Concept Check

In Chapter 2, we emphasize that the effort to apply language practices across cultures can have an entirely different effect. In discussing "Spoken and Written Language," we identify several reasons why internationally minded companies should be careful in translating a message conceived in one language into a message to be delivered in another. We also emphasize that words may have different meanings even among countries using the same language, e.g., about 4000 words have a different meaning in American and British English. As for advertising in visual media, we also discuss a variety of potential pitfalls in "Silent Language"—nonverbal communication ranging from body language to the use of colors.

make the purchasing decision, and what appeals are most important. For example, fewer Italians own dishwashers than you would expect from Italian income levels because the housewives feel that buying for the sake of convenience reduces cleanliness; hence, a group of dishwasher manufacturers have teamed up to advertise that dishwashers clean better because they use hotter water.[50] Because of economic differences, Home Depot promotes its U.S. stores by appealing to hobbyists, whereas in Mexico it promotes the cost savings for do-it-yourselfers.[51]

The reaction to how messages are presented may also vary. For example, Leo Burnett Worldwide produced a public service ad to promote breast exams that showed an attractive woman being admired in a low-cut sundress, with a voice-over message saying, "If only women paid as much attention to their breasts as men do…" Japanese viewers found this a humorous way to draw attention to breast cancer, but French viewers found it offensive because cancer should not be viewed humorously.[52] Given the increase in television transmissions that reach audiences in multiple countries, advertisers must find common themes and messages that will appeal to potential consumers everywhere their ads are viewed.

Branding Strategies

A *brand* is an identifying mark for products or services. A legally registered brand is a trademark. A brand gives a product or service instant recognition and may save promotional costs. From a consumer standpoint, it conveys a perception of whether firms will deliver what they promise; however, the importance is more crucial in countries with strong cultural characteristics of uncertainty avoidance.[53]

Case Review Note

The importance of brand can be illustrated by comparing examples of two companies. Our opening case illustrates how Tommy Hilfiger built a following for its brand even before consumers were familiar with its product offerings. In contrast, Chinese appliance maker Haier has had trouble with U.S. sales because its brand name is not well known in the United States.[54]

Keep in mind though that a company may use the same brand globally while altering the brand image for different markets. For example, in more individualistic cultures, there are greater advantages in creating an image of innovativeness than there is in collectivist cultures. However, within collectivist cultures, images of social responsibility apparently contribute more to brand commitment than in individualist cultures.[55]

Because companies have spent heavily in the past to create brand awareness, *Business Week* estimates that 67 global brands in 2011 were worth at least $5 billion. U.S. companies dominate the ownership of these brands, accounting for 52 of the top 100. Further, the companies with top brands have fared better than other companies during the global economic recession.[56]

WORLDWIDE BRAND VERSUS LOCAL BRANDS

In addition to the same branding decisions every producer has to make, international marketers must decide whether to adopt a worldwide brand or use different brands for a variety of country markets. In this section, we discuss some of the ways in which the international environment affects this decision.

Advantages of a Worldwide Brand   Some companies, such as Sony, have opted to use the same brand and logo for most of their products around the world. This helps develop a global image, especially for customers who travel internationally. In addition, there is evidence that the use of global brands helps identify companies as global players. Within the United States, consumers (especially ethnic minorities) view products of global players more favorably.[57] Other companies, such as Nestlé, associate many of their products under the same family of brands, such as Nestea and Nescafé, to share the positive perception of the Nestlé name.

Some Problems with Uniform Brands   Nevertheless, a number of problems are inherent in trying to use uniform brands internationally.

Language   One problem is that brand names may carry a different association in another language. GM renamed its Buick LaCrosse in Canada after it discovered that the word was slang in Quebec for masturbation.[58] Coca-Cola tries to use global branding wherever possible but discovered that the word *diet* in Diet Coke had a connotation of illness in Germany and Italy. The brand is now called Coca-Cola Light outside the United States.

Pronunciation presents other problems, since a foreign language may lack some of the sounds of a brand name, or give it a different meaning. Marcel Bich dropped the *h* from his name when branding Bic pens because of the fear of mispronunciation in English. Some locally popular soft drinks have unappetizing meanings when pronounced in English: Mucos (Japan), Pipi (Croatia), Pshitt (France), and Zit (Greece).

Different alphabets present still other problems. For example, consumers judge brand names by whether they sound appealing; those in Chinese need to have visual appeal as well, because the Chinese alphabet consists of pictograms. Such MNEs as Coca-Cola, Mercedes-Benz, and Boeing have taken great pains to ensure not only that the translation of their names is pronounced roughly the same in Mandarin or Cantonese Chinese as elsewhere but also that the brand name is meaningful in pictograms. Coca-Cola is pronounced *Ke-kou-ke-le* in Mandarin Chinese and means "tasty" and "happy." Google became Gu Ge in Mandarin because it means "harvest song" instead of "doggy" or "old hound," as the original name was being pronounced.[59] Companies seek names considered lucky in China, such as one with eight strokes in it and displayed in red rather than blue. Similarly, the digit 8 is overrepresented in product prices.[60]

Brand Acquisition   Much international expansion takes place by acquiring foreign companies with branded products. Sara Lee, for instance, acquired various Brazilian coffee roasters and is trying to consolidate them into a national brand. Stretching the promotional budget over many brands leads to promotions that are less effective than they might be.[61] Overall, the proportion of local to international brands is decreasing; however, there are many examples of strong local brands that companies cannot easily displace.[62] Similarly, there are sometimes advantages of having a combination of global and local brands, such as those used by the beer company Anheuser-Busch InBev, that appeal to different segments.[63]

Country-of-Origin Image   MNE managers should consider whether to create a local or foreign image for their products and, if foreign what country image, because of both quality perceptions and the emotional affinity potential consumers have toward certain countries.[64] Because many Japanese believe that clothing made abroad is superior to that made in Japan, Burberry has created separate labels for its products made there and those made in the United Kingdom (Burberry London brand). The British have a positive image of Australian wine; thus, a young Australian winery sought a very Australian name, Barramundi, for its wine exports to the United Kingdom.[65] Keep in mind, though, that both the country of origin and the brand have positive and negative images that interact. Evidence suggests that a positive brand image can help overcome negative perceptions of the country where the product is made.[66]

Still, images can change. Consider that for many years various Korean firms sold abroad under private labels or under contract with well-known companies. Some, such as Samsung, now emphasize their own trade names and Korean product quality. At the same time, the Korean LG Group, best known for its Gold Star brand, has introduced a line of high-end appliances with a European-sounding name, LG Tromm.[67]

Using the same brand name globally is hampered by

- Language differences.
- Acquisitions.

Images of products are affected by where they are made.

- The brand image may help overcome the country image.
- Images can change.

Nevertheless, there is evidence that consumers have limited knowledge of the country of origin of most brands and that they often mis-classify the origins.[68]

One ongoing international legal debate concerns product names associated with location. The EU protects the names of many European products based on location names, such as Roquefort and Gorgonzola cheeses, Parma ham, and Chianti wine. More recently, it has pushed for protection against the foreign use of regulated names associated with wines, such as *clos, chateau, tawny, noble, ruby,* and *vintage.*[69]

> If a brand name is used for a class of product, the company may lose the trademark.

Generic and Near-Generic Names
Companies want their product names to become household words, but not so much that competitors can use trademarks to describe their similar products. In the United States, the brand names Xerox and Kleenex are nearly synonymous with copiers and facial tissue, but they have nevertheless remained proprietary brands. Some other names that were once proprietary—such as cellophane, linoleum, and Cornish hens—have become **generic** and available for anyone to use.

In this context, companies sometimes face differences among countries that may either stimulate or frustrate their sales. For example, *aspirin* and *Swiss Army knives* are proprietary names in Europe but generic in the United States—a situation that impairs European export sales of those products to the United States, since U.S. companies can produce them.

Distribution Strategies

A company may accurately assess market potential, design goods or services for that market, price them appropriately, and promote them to probable consumers. However, it will have little likelihood of reaching its sales potential if it doesn't make the goods or services conveniently available to customers. Goods need to be placed where people want to buy them. At the same time, a company's system of distribution may give it strategic advantages not easily copied by competitors, such as Avon's strategy of selling directly through independent reps and Amazon.com's Internet sales. **Distribution** is the course—physical path or legal title—that goods take between production and consumption. In international marketing, managers must decide on the method of distribution among countries as well as the method within the country where final sale occurs.

> A company may enter a market gradually by limiting geographic coverage.

Companies may limit early distribution in given foreign countries by selling regionally before moving nationally. Many products and markets lend themselves to this sort of gradual development. Often, geographic barriers and poor internal transportation systems divide countries into very distinct markets. In some countries, very little wealth or few potential sales may lie outside the large metropolitan areas. In others, advertising and distribution may be handled effectively on a regional basis.

We've already discussed operating forms for foreign-market penetration. Chapter 13 discussed distribution channels: moving goods among countries and transferring titles. Rather than reviewing these aspects of distribution, this section discusses distributional differences and conditions within foreign countries that an international marketer should understand.

DECIDING WHETHER TO STANDARDIZE

> Distribution reflects different country environments:
> - It may vary substantially among countries.
> - It is difficult to change.

Within the marketing mix, MNEs find distribution one of the most difficult functions to standardize internationally, for several reasons. Each country has its own distribution system, which an MNE finds difficult to modify because it is entwined with the country's cultural, economic, and legal environments. Nevertheless, many retailers are successfully moving internationally.

Some of the factors that influence the distribution of goods in a given country are citizens' attitudes toward owning their own store, the cost of paying retail workers, legislation restricting store sizes and operating hours, different effects of laws on chain

Geography Matter? Is Necessity the Mother of Invention?

You've probably heard the saying that it is as "difficult as selling a refrigerator to Eskimos." Climate is a great influence on the demand for many products—clothes, sporting equipment, snow tires, air conditioners, and sunscreen, to name a few—and is a variable when identifying market segments. Seasonal changes that occur at opposite times in the Northern and Southern Hemispheres allow you to spread your sales more evenly throughout the year, such as by focusing ski sales in Switzerland from December through March and in Chile from June through September. This hemispheric difference may also lead to your making adjustments. Films aimed at young audiences sometimes debut months apart between the Northern and Southern Hemispheres so as to be viewed during school vacation periods that usually correspond to the hot months.

Natural conditions, such as mountains, waterways, and deserts, create both barriers and expediencies to distribution. For example, countries can more easily build infrastructure where there are flat areas without obstructions; thus, other things being equal, these areas provide better internal distribution possibilities.

Immigration is largely clustered, because people move where others of their ethnic group have gone before, thus forming subcultures. Understanding where these groups exist can help identify potential markets.[70]

Because transportation cost roughly correlates with distance, it is usually higher when the distance between production and market is greater. This extra cost must either be passed on to consumers or be absorbed by the selling company. Moreover, if markets are close to each other, it is more difficult to maintain different price schedules between them, because promotion likely reaches both markets. In turn, consumers will buy from the less expensive location. In fact, the closeness of most Canadians to the U.S. border has influenced Canadian stores to stay open longer and operate on more days, lest Canadians cross the border to buy in the United States.

Although geography does play a role in product demand, higher disposable income and technology help overcome many geographic constraints. Thus people in hot climates do buy winter clothes and skis, because they travel to snowy areas for recreation. People in Dubai even enjoy an indoor ski resort complex. And there's even a market for refrigerators among the Eskimos. ●

stores and individually owned stores, the trust owners have in their employees, the efficacy of the postal system, the quality of the infrastructure system, and the financial ability to carry large inventories. Compare Hong Kong with the United States: Hong Kong supermarkets carry a higher proportion of fresh goods, are smaller, sell less per customer, and are closer to each other, which means that companies selling canned, boxed, or frozen foods there encounter less demand per store, have to make smaller deliveries, and have a harder time fighting for shelf space. Elsewhere, Finland has few stores per capita because general-line retailers predominate there, whereas Italian distribution has a fragmented retail and wholesale structure. In the Netherlands, buyers' cooperatives deal directly with manufacturers. Japan has cash-and-carry wholesalers for retailers that do not need financing or delivery services. Mail-order sales are very important in Germany, but not in many developing countries with less reliable delivery systems.

How do such differences affect marketing activities? One beverage company, for example, has targeted most of its European sales through grocery stores. However, the method for getting its products to those stores varies. In the United Kingdom, one national distributor has gained sufficient coverage and shelf space so that the company can concentrate on other aspects of its marketing mix. In France, a single distributor has good coverage in the larger supermarkets but not in smaller retailers, so the company has had to explore how to get secondary distribution without upsetting its relationship with the primary distributor. In Norway, regional distributors predominate, so the company has found it difficult to effect national promotion campaigns. In Belgium, the company could find no acceptable distributor, so it has had to assume that function itself.

CHOOSING DISTRIBUTORS AND CHANNELS

Should companies handle their own distribution? Or should they contract other companies to do it for them? How should they choose outside distributors? These and other concerns are discussed below.

Distribution may be handled internally

- When volume is high.
- When companies have sufficient resources.
- When there is a need to deal directly with the customer because of the nature of the product.
- When the customer is global.
- When the distribution form is a competitive advantage.

Is Internal Handling Feasible?   When sales volume is low, a company usually finds reliance on external distributors to be more economical. As sales grow, it may handle distribution itself to gain more control. However, such self-handling may still be difficult for small firms that lack necessary resources. Circumstances conducive to the internal handling of distribution include not only high sales volume but also the following factors:

- When a product has the characteristic of high price, high technology, or the need for complex after-sales servicing (such as aircraft), the company will probably have to deal directly with the buyer. It may simultaneously use a distributor within the foreign country to identify sales leads.

- When the company deals with global customers, especially business-to-business (such as an auto-parts manufacturer selling original equipment to the same automakers in multiple countries), sales may go directly to the global customer.

- When the company's main competitive advantage is its distribution methods, it may control distribution abroad, such as Avon's direct selling through independent representatives. In addition, food franchisors typically maintain some restaurants of their own to serve as "flagships."

Some evaluation criteria for distributors include their

- Financial capability.
- Connections with customers.
- Fit with a company's product.
- Other resources.
- Trustworthiness.
- Compatibility with product image.

Which Distributors Are Qualified?   A company can usually choose from a number of potential foreign distributors, using these common criteria to help make its choice:

- The distributor's financial strength
- Its good connections
- Extent of its other business commitments
- Current status of its personnel, facilities, and equipment
- Its reliability as an honest performer
- Its image in relation to the product or service being sold

The distributor's financial strength is important because of the potential long-term relationship involved and because of the assurance that money will be available for such things as maintaining sufficient inventory. Good connections are particularly important if sales must be directed to certain types of buyers, such as governmental procurement agencies. They are also important in societies like China, where connections and mutual loyalty are often more important than product and price for making sales.[71]

The number of business commitments can indicate whether the distributor has time for the company's product and whether it currently handles competitive or complementary products. The current status of its personnel, facilities, and equipment indicates not only its ability to deal with the product but also how quickly start-up can occur and how likely the distributorship will stay in business. A distributor's history and image as a responsible business entity help create trust as a means of enforcing performance.[72] This is especially important in some parts of the Middle East and Latin America, where manufacturers cannot easily terminate agreements simply because distributors have performed poorly.

Replacement parts and service are important for sales.

How Reliable Is After-Sales Service?   Consumers are reluctant to buy products that may require replacement parts and service in the future unless they feel sure that these will be readily available in good quality and at reasonable prices. For fairly mature products, there are usually multiple service companies to which consumers can turn in case of problems. However, for products encompassing new technology, especially complex and expensive products, it is more important for producers to develop after-sales servicing. Thus, companies may need to invest in service centers for groups of distributors that serve as intermediaries between producers and consumers. Earnings from sales of parts and after-sales service may sometimes exceed that of the original product.

The question of after-sales service is especially important for technologically oriented entrepreneurial companies from developing countries. These companies have been growing in importance, especially those from the BRICs. They face multiple problems in selling abroad because they are young, small, fairly unknown, likely suffering negative country-of-origin effects, and often assumed to be laggards in technological development.[73]

DISTRIBUTION CHALLENGES

Companies must evaluate potential distributors, but distributors must choose which companies and products to represent and emphasize. Wholesalers and retailers alike have limited storage facilities, display space, money for inventories, and transportation and personnel to move and sell merchandise, so they try to carry only those products that have the greatest profit potential.

In many cases, distributors are tied into exclusive arrangements with manufacturers that impede new competitive entries. This happened when breweries owned U.K. pubs, where for years they sold only their own beer, thus forcing Anheuser-Busch to enter the market strictly with supermarket sales. In Japan, many manufacturers have arrangements with thousands of distributors to sell only their products.

Any company that is new to a country and wants to introduce products that competitors are already selling may meet difficulty in finding distributors to handle its brands. Even established companies can find distribution difficult for new products, although they have the dual advantage of being known and of being able to offer existing profitable lines only if distributors accept the new unproven goods. Managers wanting to use existing distribution channels may need to analyze competitive conditions carefully to offer effective handling incentives (higher profit margins, after-sales servicing, promotional support, and so on), or identify distributors' problems so as to gain their loyalty by offering assistance. In the end, however, incentives will be of little use unless the distributors believe the company is reliable and its products viable.

> Distributors choose which companies and products to handle. Companies
> - May need to give incentives.
> - May use successful products as bait for new ones.
> - Must convince distributors that product and company are viable.

HIDDEN DISTRIBUTION COSTS AND GAINS

A company considering launching products in foreign markets must approximate final consumer prices to estimate sales potential. Five factors that often contribute to distribution cost differences among countries are *infrastructure conditions, the number of levels in the distribution system, retail inefficiencies, size and operating-hour restrictions,* and *inventory stock-outs.*

Many countries' roads and warehousing facilities are in such bad condition that getting goods to consumers quickly, cheaply, and with minimum damage or loss en route is problematic. For example, poor roads and theft en route to and from warehouses in China make transporting products hazardous, thus compromising the country's market potential.[74]

Some countries also have multi-tiered wholesalers that sell to each other before the product reaches the retail level. National wholesalers sell to regional ones, which sell to local ones, and so on. Japan, although changing rapidly, has had many more levels of distribution than, say, France and the United States. Because as each intermediary adds a markup, prices escalate.

In some countries, particularly developing ones, low labor costs and owners' basic distrust of nonfamily members cause many retailers to engage in practices that result in diminished productivity in serving customers. This distrust is evident in retailers' preference for counter service rather than self-service. A customer who decides to purchase something gets an invoice to take to a cashier's line to pay, then goes to another line to pick up the merchandise after presenting the stamped invoice. In some countries, counter service is common for purchases as small as a pencil. On the one hand, the additional personnel add to retailing costs, and the added time people must be in the store means fewer people being served in the given space. On the other hand, because the retailers tend to be small and highly dispersed, they reduce the time, cost, and effort for customers to shop.[75] In contrast, most retailers in some (mainly economically developed) countries have equipment that improves the efficiency of handling customers and reports, such as electronic scanners, cash registers linked to inventory-control records, and machines connecting purchases to credit-card companies.

France, Germany, Japan, and many other nations have laws protecting small retailers, effectively limiting the number of large retail establishments and the efficiencies they bring to sales. Most countries have patchwork systems that limit days or hours of operations for religious purposes or to protect employees from having to work late at night or on weekends.[76] At the same time, the limits keep retailers from covering the fixed cost of their space over more hours, so these costs are usually passed on to consumers.

Where most retail establishments are small, particularly in developing countries, there is little space to store inventory. Wholesalers must incur the cost of making small deliveries to many more establishments, sometimes visiting each retailer more frequently because of stock outages. However, these latter costs may be overcome through labor and transport cost savings resulting from low-paid delivery personnel who may carry small quantities of merchandise on bicycles. Further, the retailers themselves incur lower costs because their inventory-carrying costs are low compared to sales.[77]

E-COMMERCE AND THE INTERNET

The growth in online availability creates new distributional opportunities and challenges in selling globally over the Internet.

Estimates vary widely on the current and future number of worldwide online households and the electronic commerce generated through online sales. Nevertheless, they all indicate substantial growth. Further, the adjacent photo shows that people may generally access the Internet through publicly available facilities even though they have no online connections in their households. As e-commerce grows, customers worldwide can quickly compare prices from different distributors, which should drive prices down. There is evidence that online shoppers universally have some similar characteristics: They want convenience, use e-mail and the Internet heavily, and have favorable attitudes toward direct marketing and advertising.[78]

Opportunities E-commerce offers firms an opportunity to promote products globally. It does not, however, relieve them of the need to develop the marketing tools discussed throughout the chapter. For some products and services, such as airline tickets and hotel space, the Internet has largely replaced traditional sales methods. But even here, companies may need to adapt to country differences, such as providing access through various languages.[79] There are certainly many success stories. One is the New Zealand prefab housing company Tristyle International, for which about 95 percent of sales are export and 40 percent are through the Internet.[80]

The Internet also permits suppliers to deal more quickly with their customers. Lee Hung Fat Garment Factory of Hong Kong and Bangladesh produces for apparel companies abroad and flashes pictures of merchandise samples to them over the Web. Customers can tinker with the samples and transmit new versions so that Lee Hung Fat produces exactly what the apparel companies want.

Problems Global Internet sales are not without glitches. A company that wants to reach global markets may need to supplement its Internet sales with other means of promotion

Where Internet connectivity is low, entrepreneurs have opened internet cafes to serve clientele. This one is in Dahab, Egypt.

Source: © Masr | Dreamstime.com

and distribution, which can be very expensive. Further, a switch to Internet sales may upset existing distribution and, if unsuccessful, make future sales more difficult.[81]

An MNE cannot easily differentiate its marketing program for each country in which it operates. The same Web ads and prices reach customers everywhere, even though different appeals and prices for different countries might yield more sales and profits. If the MNE makes international sales over the Internet, it must expeditiously deliver what it sells, which may necessitate having warehouses and service facilities abroad.

Finally, the MNE's Internet ads and prices must comply with the laws of each country of sales. This is a challenge, because of the global reach of websites. Clearly, although the Internet creates opportunities for companies to sell internationally, it also creates challenges for them.

Managing the Marketing Mix

Although every element in the marketing mix—product, price, promotion, brand, and distribution—is important, the relative importance of one versus another may vary from place to place and over time. Thus, management must monitor and adjust its marketing programs accordingly.

GAP ANALYSIS

Once a company is operating in a country and estimates that market potential, it must calculate how well it is doing there and how it might do better. A useful tool in this respect is **gap analysis,** a method for estimating a company's potential sales by identifying prospective customers it is not serving adequately.[82] When sales are lower than the estimated market potential for a given type of product, the company has the possibility for increased sales.

FIGURE 16.4   Gap Analysis

Why aren't sales as much as they could be? That's the question asked by a company's managers when they undertake *gap analysis*. The arrow at the top represents *total sales potential* for all competitors during a given period. The arrow at A indicates *actual sales*. Notice that there's a gap between the product's potential and actual sales—the socalled *usage gap*. But there are other gaps as well. The arrow bracketing points A and B, for example, designates all sales lost by the company to its competitors— the *gap*, that is, between what the company did sell and what it could have sold if, for a variety of reasons, it hadn't lost so many sales to competitors. Finally, remember that in the real world, gap sizes will fluctuate.

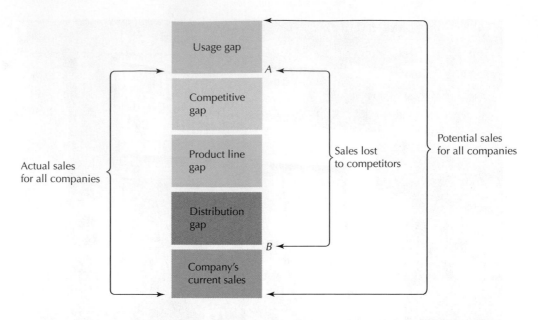

The difference between total market potential and a company's sales is due to gaps:

- Usage—collectively, all competitors sell less than the market potential
- Product line—company lacks some product variations
- Distribution—company misses geographic or intensity coverage
- Competitive—competitors' sales not explained by product line and distribution gaps

Figure 16.4 is a bar showing four types of gaps: *usage, competitive, product line,* and *distribution.* To construct such a bar, a company first needs to estimate the potential demand for all competitors in the country for a relevant period—say, for the next year, or the next five years. This figure gives the height of the bar. Second, a company needs to estimate current sales by all competitors, which is point A. The space between point A and the top of the bar is a *usage gap,* meaning that this is the growth potential for all competitors in the market for the relevant period. Third, a company needs to plot its own current sales of the product, point B.

Finally, the company divides the difference between point A and point B into types of gaps based on its estimate of sales lost to competitors. The *distribution gap* represents losses to competitors who distribute where the company does not, such as to additional geographic areas or types of outlets. The *product line gap* represents losses to competitors who have product variations the company lacks. The *competitive gap* is the remaining unexplained sales lost to competitors who may have a better image or lower prices.

Usage Gaps   Companies may have different-sized gaps in different markets. Large chocolate companies, for instance, have altered their marketing programs among countries because of their different gaps. In some markets, they have found substantial usage gaps—less chocolate being consumed than expected on the basis of population and income levels. Industry specialists estimate that in many countries, much of the population has never tasted chocolate, leading companies to promote sales in those areas for chocolate in general.

The U.S. market shows another type of usage gap. Nearly everyone in this market has tried most chocolate products, but per capita consumption has fallen because of growing concern about weight. To boost chocolate consumption in general, for a short time Nestlé promoted chocolate as an energy source for the sports-minded. Note, however, that building general consumption is most useful to the market leader. Nestlé, with U.S. chocolate sales below those of Mars and Hershey, actually benefited its competitors during the short-lived campaign.

Product Line and Distribution Gaps Chocolate companies have also found that they have product-line gaps. Some lack sugar-free chocolate products, which boosts competitors' sales. Or their products may be sold in too few places. Ferrero Rocher has recently emphasized product placement in more mainstream outlets.

Competitive Gaps Finally, there are competitive gaps—sales by competitors that cannot be explained by differences between product lines and distribution. That is, competitors are selling more because of their prices, advertising campaigns, goodwill, or any of a host of other factors. In markets where per capita chocolate consumption is high, companies exert most of their efforts in gaining sales at the expense of competitors. For instance, Switzerland has the world's highest per capita chocolate consumption. In that market, such competitors as Migros, Lindt, and Nestlé's Cailler go head to head in creating images of better quality.[83]

Although gap analysis is primarily a means of prioritizing elements in the marketing mix within given countries, it is also possible to use the tool by aggregating needs among countries. Let's say the product-line gap is too small in a single country to justify the expense of developing a specific new product, such as a heat-resistant chocolate bar. Nevertheless, the combined market potential among several countries for this product may justify the product- and promotional-development costs. Thus, gap analysis may help managers improve country-level performance along with enhancing synergies among the countries where they operate.

Looking to the Future — Evolving Challenges to Segment Markets

Recall the discussion earlier in the chapter on three approaches to segmentation. While all of these involve the geographic unit of the nation as one of the key components, such segmentation also involves both demographics and psychographics. How both of these will unfold in future years will likely affect international marketing. The following discussion highlights a key area of both.

Income Demographics

Most projections are that disparities between the "haves" and "have-nots" will grow in the foreseeable future, both within and among countries. Furthermore, because haves will be more educated and more connected to the Internet, they will be better able to search globally for lower product prices. Therefore, around the world, the affluent segment will have even more purchasing power than their incomes indicate.

As their discretionary income increases, some luxury products will become more commonplace (partly because it will take fewer hours of work to purchase them), and seemingly dissimilar products and services (such as cars, travel, jewelry, and furniture) will compete with each other for the same discretionary spending.

For example, Japan was the premier importer of luxury goods during the 1980s and early 1990s, but competition from an array of other luxury products and services, such as spas and expensive restaurants, have eroded those imports.[84] In addition, there is evidence that many Japanese consumers have moved down-market during the global economic crisis, and there is speculation that they may not move up-market again when the economy improves. Nevertheless, because of better communications and rising educational levels of the haves, they will want more choices. However, market segments may not fall primarily along national lines. Rather, companies will identify consumer niches that cut across country lines.

At the other extreme, because of growing numbers of poor people with little disposable income, companies will have opportunities to develop low-cost standardized products to fit the needs of the have-nots. In reality, low-income households collectively have considerable purchasing power as we discussed in Chapter 4. They will likely spend mainly on housing, food, healthcare, education, communications, finance charges, and consumer goods.[85] Thus, companies will have conflicting opportunities: develop luxury to serve the haves and cut costs to serve the have-nots.

(continued)

Despite the growing proportions of haves and have-nots, demographers project that the actual numbers of people moving out of poverty levels and into middle-income levels will increase. This is largely because of population and income growth in some low-income countries, especially in Asia. Such a shift will likely mean that companies' sales growth in poorer countries will mainly be for products that are mature in industrial countries, such as many consumer electronics and household appliances.

Will National Markets Become Passé?

In addition to demographic differences, especially those concerning incomes, attitudinal differences affect demand in general as well as for particular types of products and services. Although global communications are reaching far-flung populations, different people react differently to them. At least three types of personality traits interact and affect how potential consumers react.[86] These are not mutually exclusive traits. They exist in all countries (thus creating a segment that cuts across the globe), but the portion of people who are strongly influenced by one versus the other presently varies by country. How these factors evolve in the future will likely have a profound influence on the future of international marketing.

The first of the traits is materialism, which refers to the importance of acquiring possessions as a means of self-satisfaction and happiness, as well as for the appearance of success. There is evidence of a growing and spreading global materialistic culture. However, there is also some evidence that people who have always been affluent may exhibit lower materialistic behaviors than those who have recently become affluent. The second of these traits is cosmopolitanism, which refers to openness to the world. While there is debate on whether this is a learned or an inborn trait, some of the characteristics include comparing oneself with the world rather than with the local situation. Cosmopolitanists may actually seek out foreign products and services. The third of these traits is consumer ethnocentrism, which refers to preference of local to global, such as seeking out local alternatives when buying products and services. ■

CASE   Marketing to the Base of the Pyramid (BoP) in Bangladesh: Grameen Danone Foods

Professors John D. Daniels and Jon Jungbien Moon

In 1932, Franklin D. Roosevelt referred to an impoverished person as "the forgotten man at the bottom [base] of the economic pyramid." Few places have more impoverished persons than Bangladesh.[87] With 158 million people, the average daily income for the bottom 40 percent of its income pyramid is less than $2.66. That group is below the poverty line, defined as the income needed to buy life's basic necessities—food, clothing, housing — and the most important sociocultural needs. Thus, Bangladesh has many conditions that correlate closely with poverty. It has an adult illiteracy rate of over 50 percent, a high incidence of infectious diseases, a poor infrastructure, and high underemployment. In addition, crowded conditions (imagine half the U.S. population squeezed into the state of Iowa) and more than its share of natural disasters, especially periodic flooding, which impede development. Despite these ominous conditions, two companies—the Grameen Foundation from Bangladesh and Groupe Danone from France—formed a joint venture (JV) social business to serve Bangladesh's BoP. Map 16.1 shows Bangladesh.

What Is a Social Business?

Mohammad Yunus founded the Grameen Bank (GB) in 1974 and won the Nobel Peace Prize in 2006. He originated concepts for two types of social business, both of which aim to help needy people by achieving some social goal. The Grameen Danone Foods JV operates as the type that, although established to make a profit, pays no dividends. All earnings are

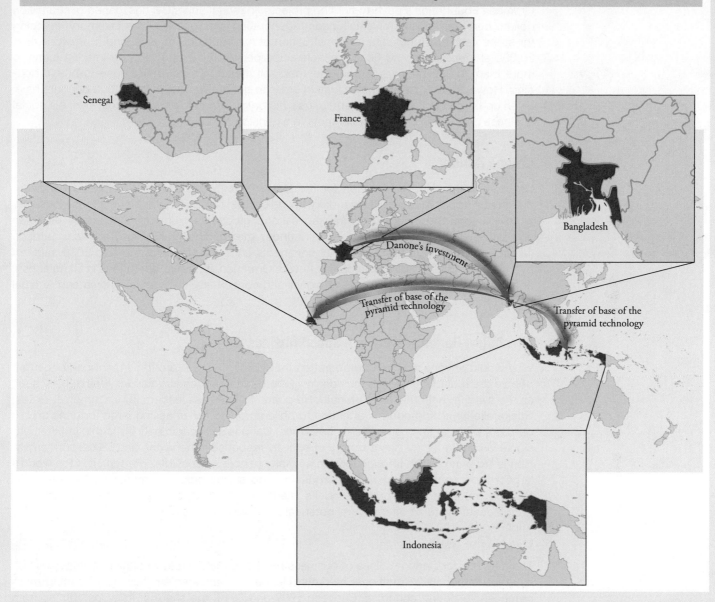

MAP 16.1   Grameen Danone Foods Joint Venture

Groupe Dannon joined the Grameen Foundation to form a social business joint venture in Bangladesh. Subsequently, Group Dannone learned about serving the base of the pyramid and has transformed this knowledge to help it operate in Indonesia and Senegal

reinvested, except that investors may recoup their original capital input. Unlike NGOs, charities, and not-for-profit organizations, a social business must sustain itself by earning profits competitively rather than receiving continual new contributions to carry on.

The Grameen Bank and Foundation

GB began when Yunus lent $27 to a group of indigent villagers who repaid the money even though he had required no collateral from them. This small beginning, which was contrary to Bangladeshi bank practices, led to GB's microfinancing program. It has competed primarily with usurious money lenders who charge as much as 10 percent per day. GB's typical rate of 20 percent per year may sound high, but Bangladesh has had an inflation rate of about 8 percent, and GB supports many non-interest loans as well. Some banks outside Bangladesh, such as Citigroup and Deutsche Bank, have since used GB's example as a model.

Before GB, hardly any Bangladeshi loans went to women, and Yunus had to convince religious opposition that the Prophet Mohammad would have supported what he was doing. About 97 percent of GB's loans go to women, and audits show a repayment rate of 98 percent. GB uses repayments and interest to make additional loans and to support the Grameen Foundation's poverty-fighting projects. In recent years GB has loaned over a billion dollars per year, mostly for small income-generating activities such as inventory financing for street vendors. It has lent for construction of over 600,000 houses, and it provides over 20,000 student loans and 50,000 scholarships per year. It has given non-interest loans to more than 70,000 beggars so that they can sell trinkets during their house-to-house begging. However, they must repay a loan in order to get a new one. About 2,000 beggars have given up begging altogether. Given Yunus's history of altruistic aims and activities, his social business concept is certainly a compatible extension for the Foundation.

Groupe Danone

Groupe Danone (spelled Dannon for the U.S. market), the largest French food company, operates in four product divisions: dairy (world's largest with Danone being almost a generic word for yogurt); bottled water (ranked second globally, including such brands as Evian and Volvic); baby food (second globally under the Blédine brand); and medical nutrition (largest in Europe). It operates on all continents except Antarctica and had 2010 sales of over €17 billion ($22 billion). Before its JV with Grameen, it had no operations in Bangladesh, and it aimed most of its products at higher-end consumers, such as its Activia and Actimel brands of yogurt.

Why Might Danone Invest in a Social Business?

Why would anyone invest in an operation that yields them no profits? Yunus contends that people are multidimensional, thus desiring more than economic gains for themselves, such as a craving to help the less fortunate. He points to business leaders (e.g., Carnegie, Gates, Rockefeller) who turned their attention to philanthropy after amassing large fortunes and to people's willingness to give to charities. Thus, Danone's JV participation fits this multidimensional vision. In fact, it has a history of socially responsible behavior, and its corporate mission is "to bring health through food to as many people as possible." Further, it is the world's largest food company devoted to producing and selling only healthy foods. Nevertheless, Danone must generate profits, and its management must answer to shareholders. The Bangladeshi JV could offer several potential profit advantages to Danone.

Maturing of Traditional Markets

The demand for Danone's lines of business has been maturing in wealthier countries, which have been Danone's traditional markets. Hence, its management has been shifting more emphasis to poorer countries. Between 1999 and 2010, the share of its sales coming from LDCs increased from 6 percent to 49 percent. Yet, even in LDCs, its sales have centered on affluent segments about which its chairman, Frank Riboud said, "it would be crazy to think only about the peak of the pyramid." Thus, Bangladesh could serve as a laboratory for learning about customers and ways of operating at the BoP.

Promoting LDC Growth

Critics complain that MNEs' sale of superfluous products in developing countries contributes to economic underdevelopment because poor consumers then lack the means to purchase nutritious food to make them more physically productive. Danone's products are all healthy and sanitary. Although one company's successful marketing of such products is not likely to have any significant impact on development, it is nevertheless a potential catalyst, which might also lead to favorable publicity. Further, as BoP consumers move upward economically, they will have more to spend on other Danone products and may favor them because of their earlier experience. Riboud said, "When poverty is on the rise, my own growth prospects shrink. [This] means that combating poverty is good for my business."

Building Sales and Loyalty Abroad

Being perceived as socially responsible, such as helping needy causes, may help business performance in various ways. However, there are an almost infinite number of competing needy causes to which Danone can contribute. The amount that Danone needed to invest in the JV was $500,000, a small outlay for a company of Danone's size; and it would get this money back if the operation became sufficiently profitable. In addition, if Danone could invest in the first social business company, it might receive more free publicity than otherwise. In retrospect, after establishing the JV, Riboud said, "Even the people in Paris who book our travel to Bangladesh feel they are part of this project; they have pictures of villages on their walls. This small initiative has revitalized our culture."

Preceding the Bangladeshi JV

At a 2005 lunch in Paris, Riboud asked Yunus what Danone might do to help the poor. Yunus explained the social business concept. Riboud immediately said "Let's do it," and the two shook hands on setting up a JV. The following photo shows Yunus and Riboud together at a later date.

Although this JV is probably the first social business, it does not imply that Roosevelt's "the forgotten man" expression was accurate. Many organizations have marketed to the BoP before and after his pronouncement, and many have developed products specific to the base's needs (most notably in the 1970s' heyday of the appropriate technology movement), such as crank-operated cash registers, dung-powered stoves, and bicycle-propelled water pumps. Nor is this JV the first effort aimed at nourishing the poor. A notable example is the protein powder (Incaparina) that was developed in Central America and is more nutritious and less expensive than milk. Despite its being introduced in some countries for profit and in others as a not-for-profit, the results have been quite mixed. From this and other experiences, there are some conditions and lessons for companies wishing to tap the BoP with a nutritious product:

◀ Franc Riboud, CEO of Danone, and Mohammad Yunus, Nobel Peace Prize laureat, participated in a discussion about social business.
Source: Sipa via AP Images

- **Price** Low and stable prices help create and sustain sales, so companies are advantaged by finding new means to cut and stabilize their own costs, which they then pass on to customers.
- **Product compatibility** No matter how high the nutrition or low the price, many customers shy away from products that fit poorly with their accustomed consumption and are visually and flavorfully distasteful to them. Therefore, picking the right products and adapting them to local market are vital.
- **Education** Within some countries this segment is largely illiterate, has low access to popular media, and is unconvinced about cause-effect scientific relationships. Hence, reaching them by nontraditional means, explaining that changes from nutrition take time, and making arguments that they believe are important.
- **Promotion** Publicity prior to the start of sales is valuable. Use of opinion leaders (those that this group accepts) is essential in developing credibility.
- **Competition** Given efforts to help the poor, competition within this segment may come from government programs, not-for-profit organizations, and charities. Thus, companies need to out-perform this competition or find means of working cooperatively with it.

The JV and Its Marketing Program

After the 2005 Paris handshake, Grameen and Danone managed to begin production in less than two years, during which time they planned and carried out preliminary work.

Strategic Thrust and Orientation

The partners started with a small rural factory (poverty is higher in rural areas) to serve only its surrounding area. Given the JV's social responsibility objective, they agreed that product and production would be as green as possible. The factory covers 7,500 square feet with a capacity of only one percent of Danone's standard factories elsewhere. It has the latest equipment, treatment of both incoming and outgoing water, and solar panels to generate renewable energy.

Product Policies

The introductory plant makes only yogurt, a product of high nutritional value for children. It relies on efficient small-scale production and nearby supplies of the main ingredient (milk).

Through market testing, Danone decided to sweeten its yogurt recipe slightly with sugar and molasses and to sell a thin version, drinkable directly from the container. (Later market feedback led the JV to sell spoons as well.) It also fortifies the yogurt with 30 percent of the daily need for vitamin A, zinc, and iodine. The JV acquired Chinese biodegradable technology so that containers can be converted to fertilizer.

Pricing

To keep prices low and still be profitable, the JV must keep its costs low. First, the plant obtains all ingredients locally, mainly from small suppliers such as farmers with only one or two cows, who collect and deliver milk in jugs. This process saves refrigeration and transport costs. Second, all sales are by commission (about 20 percent of commissions to individual sales ladies and 80 percent to small local stores), thus fixed sales costs are held low. Third, all personnel (after the start-up phase) are from Bangladesh, hence, the JV avoids high expatriate compensation. Although the yogurt plant lacks scale economies, its unit costs are equivalent to Danone's larger plants elsewhere.

Two factors created temporary cost problems. First, initial plans called for buying milk at 14–16 takas per liter, but milk prices increased to 20–22 by the time the plant opened. Management subsequently negotiated longer term contracts with farmers to stabilize prices more; hence the JV pays higher than market price sometimes and less at other times. Second, sales ladies expected to sell more than what materialized. Rather than raising commissions, the company successfully suggested they sell additional products during their house-to-house visits.

Promotion

Most promotion is word of mouth; however, one promotional event was noteworthy. Riboud arranged for the visit of the best known French person in Bangladesh, the soccer star Zinédine Zidane (Zizou), to visit for the plant's opening. This event made large headlines in newspapers throughout the country. While in Bangladesh, he played with youth in the national stadium, signed the cornerstone of the plant, and provided instant national recognition for the new JV and its yogurt.

Branding

The joint venture name puts Grameen before Danone because the former name was already well recognized in Bangladesh. The yogurt brand is Shoki Doi, which means yogurt for power. The symbol of the brand is a muscled lion, appearing on the product and in other ads. In addition, the company dresses a person as a mascot to look like the symbol. The mascot visits youth areas to describe the value of eating yogurt.

Distribution

Bangladesh's high underemployment attracted more than enough women to work part-time selling yogurt. These were mainly poor mothers who resembled very much the JV's target sales market. However, the JV had to contend (successfully) with a backlash, similar to the one GB faced when lending to women; the complaint this time was about the impropriety of women going house-to-house. The next task, and one of the most essential for marketing efforts, was to train the saleswomen on (1) why, other than the commission, was it important to sell the yogurt, and (2) the importance of and how to maintain the quality of the yogurt.

Nourishment was the prime reason given for selling. For this, the company brought in doctors, who expressed the ongoing theme that children's consumption of only two cups of yogurt per week enables them to regain within nine to 10 months any physical loss from previously deprived nutrition. The second reason for selling was to improve the economy, such as helping suppliers who would then hire more people and spend within the community.

Maintaining yogurt quality was important because of a lack of refrigeration in homes and the negative consequences if customers became ill from eating a spoiled product. The company demonstrated how it makes yogurt. It provided saleswomen with insulated bags, and it instilled upon them the need to use the bags properly and to carry a minimum inventory so as to prevent the chance of spoilage.

Evaluation

Financial performance evaluation of the JV is straightforward; however, evaluating the social effects of the JV activities is something new. For this, the JV has hired a Swiss-based nutrition organization (GAIN) to develop, test, and validate the JV's performance in terms of meeting the objectives for poor people.

The Future

The JV's sales have increased steadily. Further, Danone has learned much in Bangladesh about running small-scale production efficiently, and it is transferring this knowledge to help with its operations in Indonesia and Senegal. However, to expand to more affluent market segments, Danone will need to evaluate how brand recognition and good-will at the BoP can be harnessed for sales farther up the pyramid. ∎

QUESTIONS

1. How much do you think Danone's decision to set up a social business was motivated by wanting to be socially responsible versus believing the move would help its performance? Does the answer to this make any difference?

2. What marketing pitfalls might Danone face if it tries to duplicate its Bangladesh experience to serve BoP customers in other countries?

3. Assume a company, such as Danone, wishes eventually to serve all income segments within a country. What advantages and disadvantages might it encounter by first serving the BoP? How might it later deal with any disadvantages?

4. If Danone were to add products to sell to the BoP, which of its products would be the best candidates? Why?

5. Since establishment of the Grameen Danone Food social business, the number of social businesses worldwide has grown so much that there is now an annual global summit in Wolfsburg, Germany. Are there types of companies that might not be good candidates to establish social businesses? If so, what are they and why?

6. In 2010, Bangladeshi Prime Minister Sheikh Hasina said that Grameen had been "sucking money out of the people after giving them loans. There has been no improvement in the lifestyle of the poor so far. They were just used as pawns to get more aid." In response, Yunus resigned from the bank, saying that he did not want to distract from its activities. Evaluate the Prime Minister's statement. How might Yunus's resignation affect the future of the Grameen Danone Food's JV?

MyIBLab   Now that you have finished this chapter, go back to www.myiblab.com to continue practicing and applying the concepts you've learned.

SUMMARY

- Although the principles for selling abroad are the same as those for selling domestically, the international manager must deal with a less familiar environment.

- International marketing strategies depend on companies' orientations, which include production, sales, customer, strategic, and social.

- Companies need to decide which market segments to target, including different or similar groups from different countries. Once they make this determination, their product, branding, promotion, pricing, and distribution decisions should be compatible with the needs of their target markets.

- A standardized approach to marketing means maximum uniformity in products and programs among the countries in which sales occur. Although this approach minimizes expenses, most companies make marketing adaptations to fit country needs to increase sales volume.

- A variety of legal, cultural, and economic conditions may call for altering products to capture foreign demand, but the cost of alteration relative to additional sales potential should be considered. In addition to determining when to alter products, companies also must decide how many and which products to sell abroad.

- Government regulations may directly or indirectly affect the prices that companies charge. International pricing is further complicated because of currency value fluctuations, differences in product preferences, price escalation in exporting, and variations in fixed versus variable pricing practices.

- For each product in each country, a company must determine not only its promotional budget but also the mix between push and pull strategies and promotions. The relationship between push and pull should depend on the distribution system, the cost and availability of media, consumer attitudes, and the product's price compared with incomes.

- Major problems for standardizing advertising among countries are translation, legality, and message needs.

- Global branding is hampered by language differences, expansion by acquisition, nationality images, and laws concerning generic names. Nevertheless, global brands help develop a global image.

- Distribution channels vary substantially among countries. The differences may affect not only the relative costs of operating but also the ease of making initial sales.

- Companies need to choose distributors carefully, both on the basis of their abilities and on their trustworthiness. At the same time, companies have to sell themselves to get distributors to handle their products and services.

- Although the Internet offers opportunities to sell internationally, using it does not negate companies' needs to develop sound programs within their marketing mix.

- Gap analysis is a tool that helps companies determine why they have not met their market potentials for given countries and decide what part of the marketing mix to emphasize.

KEY TERMS

cost-plus strategy (p. 610)
distribution (p. 618)
gap analysis (p. 623)
generic (p. 618)

gray market (p. 611)
penetration strategy (p. 610)
product diversion (p. 611)
pull (p. 613)

push (p. 613)
skimming strategy (p. 610)

ENDNOTES

1 *Sources include the following:* "Apax Partners Reaches Definitive Agreement to Sell Tommy Hilfiger Group to Phillips-Van Heusen for Euro 2.2 Billion," *PR Newswire* (March 15, 2010): n.p.; Lisa Lockwood, "Tommy Hilfiger," *Women's Wear Daily* 200:94 (November 3, 2010): n.p.; "Tommy Hilfiger Announces Its Largest Flagship store in Asia," *Asia Pulse* (November 11, 2010): n.p.; Ray A. Smith, ""A Designer Changes His Stripes," *Wall Street Journal* (June 2, 2011): D1+; Drew Fitzgerald, "Phillips Van Heusen Swings to Profit," *Wall Street Journal* (May 31, 2011): n.p.; Rachel Dodes, "Macy's Buying Clout Drives Supplier Consolidation, *Wall Street Journal* (March 22, 2010): n.p.; "Tommy Hilfiger Group," *Entertainment News Weekly* (October 2, 2009): 105; "Tommy Hilfiger to Assume Direct Control of Distribution in China," *PR Newswire* (March 31, 2010): n.p.; Joe Fernandez, "Fashion: Hilfiger to Use 'Delebs' for Silver Anniversary," *Marketing Week* (June 10, 2010): 4; Miles Socha and Joelle Diderich, "Hilfiger: American in Paris," *Women's Wear Daily*, 200: 107 (November 18, 2010): n.p.; "Tommy Hilfiger," *Investment Weekly News* (April 23, 2011): 898; Neha Dewan, "We Will Expand in Smaller Cities," *The Economic Times*, October 12, 2010): n.p.; Michael Barbaro, "Macy's and Hilfiger Strike Exclusive Deal," *New York Times* (October 27, 2007): 1; Cathy Horyn, "Still Tommy after All These Years," *New York Times* (December 7, 2008): Section M3, 182; Teri Agins, "Costume Change," *Wall Street Journal* (February 2, 2007): A1+; Miles Socha, "Tommy Takes Paris," *DNR* (October 23, 2006): 26; Miles Socha, "Tommy's Latest Take," *WWD* (October 20, 2006): 1; Julie Naughton, "Hilfiger and Lauder Aim for Perfect 10," *WWD* (June 23, 2006): 4; Lisa Lockwood, "CEO Says Tommy to Now Trade Up," *WWD* (May 11, 2006): 3.

2 "The World's Wash Day," *Financial Times* (April 29, 2002): 6.

3 Ruby P. Lee, Qimei Chen, Daekwan Kim, and Jean L. Johnson, "Knowledge Transfer between Multinational Corporations' Headquarters and Their Subsidiaries: Influences on and Implications for New Product Outcomes," *Journal of International Marketing* 16:2 (2008): 1–31.

4 Constantine S. Katsikeas, Saeed Damiee, and Marios Theodosiou, "Strategy Fit and Performance Consequences of International Marketing Standardization," *Strategic Management Journal* 27 (2006): 867–90.

5 Matt Moffett, "Learning to Adapt to a Tough Market, Chilean Firms Pry Open Door to Japan," *Wall Street Journal* (June 7, 1994): A10.

6 Evan Pérez, "A Bit of America Rises near Old-World Buenos Aires," *Wall Street Journal* (January 16, 2002): B1.

7 Andrea Felsted, "Tesco," *Financial Times* (December 3, 2009): 39.

8 Betsy McKay, "Drinks for Developing Countries," *Wall Street Journal* (November 27, 2001): B1+; McKay, "Coke's Heyer Finds Test in Latin America," *Wall Street Journal* (October 15, 2002): B4; and "Vitamin Angels," retrieved July 1, 2011, from www.vitaminangels.org /blogs/results/taxonomy%3A84?page=5

9 Manoj K. Agarwal, "Developing Global Segments and Forecasting Market Shares: A Simultaneous Approach Using Survey Data," *Journal of International Marketing* 11:4 (2003): 56.

10 Rosalie L. Tung, ""The Cross-Cultural Research Imperative: The Need to Balance Cross-National and Intra-National Diversity," *Journal of International Business Studies* 39:1 (2008): 41–46; James

Agarwal, Naresh Malhotra, and Ruth N. Bolton, "A Cross-National and Cross-Cultural Approach to Global Market Segmentation: An Application Using Consumers' Perceived Service Quality," *Journal of International Marketing* 18:3 (2010): 18-40.

11 Rebecca Rose, "Global Diversity Gets All Cosmetic," *Financial Times* (April 10–11, 2004): W11.

12 Leslie T. Chang, "Nestlé Stumbles in China's Evolving Market," *Wall Street Journal* (December 8, 2004): A10.

13 Allen L. Hammond and C. K. Prahalad, "Selling to the Poor," *Foreign Policy* (May–June 2004): 30–37.

14 Katsikeas et al., "Strategy Fit."

15 "Music for the Masses," *Financial Times* (December 14, 2004): 9.

16 Bernardo V. Lopez, "Upshot," *Business World* (September 18, 2003): 1.

17 Andrew Jack, "WHO Says Smoking Fight Is Being Lost," *Financial Times* (February 8, 2008): 5.

18 "Cause for Concern with Nestlé in the Spotlight Again over Its Advertising Tactics," *Marketing Week* (February 11, 1999): 28–31.

19 Andrew Ward, "Global Thirst for Bottled Water Attacked," *Financial Times* (February 13, 2006): 3, referring to data from the Earth Policy Institute.

20 Sarah Houlton, "Drugs for Neglected Diseases," *Pharmaceutical Executive* 23:8 (2003): 28.

21 Andrew Jack, "FDA to Stimulate Tropical Disease Research," *Financial Times* (May 1, 2008): 6.

22 Garrett Mehl, Heather Wipfli, and Peter Winch, "Controlling Tobacco," *Harvard International Review* 27:1 (Spring 2005): 54–58.

23 Michael Finkel, "Bedlam in the Blood: Malaria," *National Geographic* (July 2007): 63.

24 Kevin Helliker, "Smokeless Tobacco to Get Push by Venture Overseas," *Wall Street Journal* (February 4, 2009): B1+.

25 Michael Waldholz, "Sparks Fly at AIDS Meeting over Breast-Feeding," *Wall Street Journal* (July 12, 2000): B2; Jolene Skordis and Nicoli Nattrass, "Paying to Waste Lives: The Affordability of Reducing Mother-to-Child Transmission of HIV in South Africa," *Journal of Health Economics* 21:3 (May 2002): 405.

26 Avery Johnson, "Drug Firms See Poorer Nations as Sales Cure," *Wall Street Journal* (July 7, 2009): A1+.

27 Andrew Jack, "Anti-Malaria Drug to Sell at Cost Price," *Financial Times* (March 2, 2007): 3; Jennifer Corbett Dooren, "Research to Target Neglected Diseases," *Wall Street Journal* (May 21, 2009): 16.

28 Scott Miller, "EU's New Rules Will Shake Up Market for Bioengineered Food," *Wall Street Journal* (April 16, 2004): A1; Deborah Ball, Sarah Ellison, Janet Adamy, and Geoffrey A. Fowler, "Recipes without Borders?" *Wall Street Journal* (August 18, 2004): B1+.

29 Norihiko Shirouzu, "Tailoring World's Cars to U.S. Taste," *Wall Street Journal* (January 15, 2001):B1; Norihiko Shirouzu and Peter Wonacott, "People's Republic of Autos," *Wall Street Journal* (April 18, 2005): B1+.

30 Louise Lucas, "Multinationals Try to Make the Most of their Local Credentials," *Financial Times* (September 22, 2010): Peru section 10.

31 Orit Gadiesh and Till Vestring, "The Consequences of China's Rising Global Heavyweights," *MIT Sloan Management Review* 49:3 (Spring 2008): 10–11.

32 Keith Bradsher, "India Gains on China among Multinationals," *International Herald Tribune* (June 12–13, 2004): 13.

33 Yonca Limon, Lynn R. Kahle, and Ulrich R. Orth, "Package Design as a Communications Vehicle in Cross-Cultural Values Shopping," *Journal of International Marketing* 17:1 (2009): 30–57.

34 "The World's Wash Day," *Financial Times*, 6.

35 Arvind Sahay, "Finding the Right International Mix," *Financial Times* (November 16, 1998): Mastering Marketing section, 2–3.

36 Peter Rosenwald, "Surveying the Latin American Landscape," *Catalog Age* 18:2 (February 2001): 67–69.

37 Jenny Wiggins and Chris Flood, "Coke to Shrink Size of Cans in Hong Kong," *Financial Times* (July 25, 2008): 18.

38 Carol Wolf, "Losing $63 Billion in Diverted U.S. Goods Is Sleuth Obsession," Bloomberg.com (accessed April 9, 2009), referring to a study by Deloitte & Touche.

39 Ana Campoy, "Think Locally," *Wall Street Journal* (September 27, 2004): R8.

40 C. Gopinath, "Fixed Price and Bargaining," *Business Line* (July 15, 2002): 1.

41 Claude Cellich, "FAQ…about Business Negotiations on the Internet," *International Trade Forum* 1 (2001): 10–11.

42 Jan H. Schumann, Florian v. Wagenheim, Anne Stringfellow, Zhilin Yang, Vera Blazevic, Sandra Praxmarer, G. Shainesh, Marcin Komor, Randall M. Shannon, and Fernando R. Jiménez, "Cross-Cultural Differences in the Effect of Received Word-of-Mouth Referral in Relational service Exchange," *Journal of International Marketing* 18:3 (2010): 62–80.

43 Loretta Chao, "PC Makers Cultivate Buyers in Rural China," *Wall Street Journal* (September 23, 2009): B1.

44 Jamie Anderson, Martin Kupp, and Ronan Moaligou, "Lessons from the Developing World," *Wall Street Journal* (August 17, 2009): R6.

45 Owen M. Bradfield, Caroline Parker, and Leonie Goodwin, "Sustaining Performance: Learning from Buyers' Experience," *Journal of Medical Marketing* 9:4 (October 2009): 343–53.

46 Miho Inada, "Mac and PC's Overseas Adventures," *Wall Street Journal* (March 1, 2007): B1.

47 Charles Goldsmith, "Dubbing in Product Plugs," *Wall Street Journal* (December 6, 2004): B1+.

48 Ouidade Sabri, Delphine Manceau, and Bernard Pras, "Taboo: An Underexplored Concept in Marketing: RAM," false *Recherche et Applications en Marketing* 25:1 (2010): 59–85.

49 Gemma Charles, "Don't Be a Code Breaker," *Marketing* (March 17, 2010): 17; Ernest Cyril De Run, "Attitudes Towards Offensive Advertising: Malaysian Muslims' Views," *Journal of Islamic Marketing* 1:1 (2010): 25–36.

50 Deborah Ball, "Women in Italy Like to Clean but Shun the Quick and Easy," *Wall Street Journal* (April 25, 2006): A1+.

51 Andrew Ward, "Home Improvements Abroad," *Financial Times* (April 6, 2006): 8.

52 Sarah Ellison, "Sex-Themed Ads Often Don't Travel Well," *Wall Street Journal* (March 31, 2000): B7.

53 Tulin Erdem, Joffre Swait, and Ana Valenzuela, "Brands as Signals: A Cross-Country Validation Study," *Journal of Marketing* 70:1 (2006): 34; Desmond Lam, "Cultural Influence on Proneness to Brand Loyalty," *Journal of International Consumer Marketing* 19:3 (2006): 7.

54 Mei Fong, "Chinese Refrigerator Maker Finds U.S. Chilly," *Wall Street Journal* (March 18, 2008): B1+.

55 Andreas B. Eisingerich and Gale Rubera, "Drivers of Brand Commitment: A Cross-National Investigation," 18:2 (2010): 64–79.

56 "Top 100 Global Brands Scoreboard," *Bloomberg Businessweek*, retrieved July 1, 2011, from www.businessweek.com/interactive_reports/top_brands.html; and John Gapper, "Big Names Prove Worth in Crisis," *Financial Times* (April 28, 2010): Global Brands section 1.

57 Claudiu V. Dimofte, Johny K. Johansson, and Richard P. Bagozzi, "Global Brands in the United States: How Consumer Ethnicity Mediates the Global Brand Effect," *Journal of International Marketing* 18:1 (2010): 81–106.

58 Laura Bogomolny, "The Name Game," *Canadian Business* 78:18 (September 25, 2005): 134–35.

59 Mure Dickie, "Google Becomes Gu Ge in China," *Financial Times* (April 13, 2006): 19.

60 Lee Simmons and Robert M. Schindler, "Cultural Superstitions and the Price Endings Used in Chinese Advertising," *Journal of International Marketing* 11:2 (2003): 101.

61 Miriam Jordan, "Sara Lee Wants to Percolate through All of Brazil," *Wall Street Journal* (May 8, 2002): A14+.

62 Isabelle Schuiling and Jean-Noël Kapferer, "Executive Insights: Real Differences between Local and International Brands: Strategic Implications for International Marketers," *Journal of International Marketing* 12:4 (2004): 197.

63 Jan-Benedict, E.M. Steenkamp, and Martijn G. de Jong, "A Global Investigation into the Constellation of Consumer Attitudes Toward Global and Local Products," *Journal of Marketing* 74 (November 2010): 18–40.

64 Eva M. Oberecker and Adamantios Diamantopoulos, "Consumers' Emotional Bonds with Foreign Countries: Does Consumer Affinity Affect behavioral Intentions?" *Journal of International Marketing* 19:2 (2011): 45–72.

65 Gideon Rachman, "Christmas Survey: The Brand's the Thing," *The Economist* (December 18, 1999): 97–99.

66 Daniel Laufer, Kate Gillespie, and David H. Silvera, "The Role of Country of Manufacture in Consumers' Attributions of Blame in an Ambiguous Product-Harm Crisis," *Journal of International Consumer Marketing* 21 (2009): 189–201.

67 Seah Park, "LG's Kitchen Makeover," *Wall Street Journal* (September 22, 2004): A19.

68 Saeed Samiee, Terrence A. Shimp, and Subash Sharma, "Brand Origin Recognition Accuracy: Its Antecedents and Consumers' Cognitive Limitations," *Journal of International Business Studies* 36 (2005): 379–97; George Balabanis and Adamantios, "Gains and Losses from the Misperception of Brand Origin: The Role of Brand Strength and Country-of Origin Image," *Journal of International Marketing* 19:2 (2011): 95–116.

69 Kevin McCallum, "Grape Debate," *Miami Herald* (March 27, 2009): 1C+.

70 "Opportunities in Sub-Culture," *Business Line* (February 12, 2004): 1.

71 Gary F. Keller and Creig R. Kronstedt, "Connecting Confucianism, Communism, and the Chinese Culture of Commerce," *Journal of Language for International Business* 16:1 (2005): 60–75.

72 S. Tamer Cavusgil, Seyda Deligonul, and Chun Zhang, "Curbing Foreign Distributor Opportunism: An Examination of Trust, Contracts, and the Legal Environment in International Channel Relationships," *Journal of International Marketing* 12:2 (2004).

73 Susanna Khavul, Mark Peterson, Drake Mullens, and Abdul A. Rasheed, "Going Global with Innovations from Emerging Economies: Investment in Customer Support Capabilities Pays Off," *Journal of International Marketing* 18:4 (2010): 22–42.

74 James T. Areddy, "Solving China's Logistics Riddle," *Wall Street Journal* (October 15, 2003): A18+.

75 Tomasz Lenartowicz and Sridhar Balasubramanian, "Practices and Performance of Small Retail Stores in Developing Economies," *Journal of International Marketing* 17:1 (2009): 58–90.

76 Marko Grunhagen, Stephen J. Grove, and James W. Gentry, "The Dynamics of Store Hour Changes and Consumption Behavior: Results of a Longitudinal Study of Consumer Attitudes toward Saturday Shopping in Germany," *European Journal of Marketing* 37:11/12 (2003): 1801–19.

77 Lenartowicz and Balasubramanian, "Practices and Performance of Small Retail Stores in Developing Economies."

78 Thomas G. Brashear, Vishal Kashyap, Michael D. Musante, and Naveen Donthu, "A Profile of the Internet Shopper: Evidence from Six Countries," *Journal of Marketing Theory and Practice* 17:3 (Summer 2009): 267–81.

79 Rita Marcella and Sylvie Davies, "The Use of Customer Language in International Marketing Communication in the Scottish Food and Drink Industry," *European Journal of Marketing* 38:11/12 (2004): 1382.

80 *New Zealand Business* 18:11 (2004): 21–27.

81 Moen Øystein, Iver Endresen, and Morten Gavlen, "Executive Insights: Use of the Internet in International Marketing: A Case Study of Small Computer Software Firms," *Journal of International Marketing* 11:4 (2003): 129–44.

82 J. A. Weber, "Comparing Growth Opportunities in the International Marketplace," *Management International Review* 1 (1979): 47–54; Van R. Wood, John R. Darling, and Mark Siders, "Consumer Desire to Buy and Use Products in International Markets: How to Capture It, How to Sustain It," *International Marketing Review* 16:3 (1999): 231–42.

83 Haig Simonian, "Nestlé Enriches Its Choc Value," *Financial Times* (March 24, 2006): 9.

84 Michiyo Nakamoto, "Japanese Fall out of Love with Luxury," *Financial Times* (June 3, 2009): 15.

85 Allen L. Hammond and C. K. Prahalad, "Selling to the Poor," *Foreign Policy* (May/June 2004): 30–37.

86 For an excellent discussion of these traits and their interactions, see Mark Cleveland, Michel Laroche, and Nicolas Papadopoulos, "Cosmopolitanism, Consumer Ethnocentrism, and Materialism: An Eight-Country Study of Antecedents and Outcomes," *Journal of International Marketing* 17:1 (2009): 116–46.

87 Information for the case was taken from Muhammad Yunus, *Creating a World Without Poverty* (New York: PublicAffairs, 2007); Sheridan Prasso, "Saving the World With a Cup of Yogurt," *Fortune* 155:2 (March 15, 2007): 44; John F. Jones, "Social Finance: Commerce and Community in Developing Countries," *International Journal of Social Economics* 37:6 (2010): 415–28; Nevin S. Scrimshaw, "History and Early Development of INCAP1, 2," *The Journal of Nutrition* 140:2 (February 2010): 394-96; Sarah Murray, "Yogurt Maker's Recipe for funding Social Businesses," *Financial Times* (July 7, 2008): 16; Christina Passariello, "Danone Expands Its Pantry to Woo the World's Poor," *Wall Street Journal* (June 29, 2010): A1; Paul Bennet, "The Biggest Idea Might Be Learning to Think Small," *Financial Times* (December 31, 2009): 10; Michael Fitzgerald, "As the World Turns," 133 *Fast Company* (March 2009): 33–34; Scheherazade Daneshkhu, "The Off-the-Wall Executive," *Financial Times* (November 22, 2010): 12; "Top CEOs Talk on Global Social Business in Germany," *The Global Express* [Dhaka] (November 12, 2010): n.p.; and Dean Nelson, "Pioneer Bank in Turmoil," *The Sunday Telegraph* [London] (February 13, 2011): 3.

chapter 17

Global Manufacturing and Supply-Chain Management

Objectives

1. To describe the different dimensions of a global manufacturing strategy

2. To examine the elements of global supply-chain management

3. To show how quality affects the global supply chain

4. To illustrate how supplier networks function

5. To explain how inventory management is a key dimension of the global supply chain

6. To present different alternatives for transporting products along the supply chain

Access a host of interactive learning aids to help strengthen your understanding of the chapter concepts at www.myiblab.com.

MyIBLab

A cheap thing doesn't lack defect, nor an expensive thing quality.

—*Afghan proverb*

637

CASE

Samsonite's Global Supply Chain

Samsonite, the world's biggest luggage maker, which was founded in the United States and is headquartered in Luxembourg, manufactures and distributes luggage all over the world.[1] By the end of 2010, Samsonite products (under the Samsonite and American Tourister brand names) were sold in more than 37,000 points of sale in over 100 countries through a variety of wholesale and retail distribution channels. The company was founded in 1910 in Denver, Colorado, and it took many years for it to become a global company. In 1963, Samsonite set up its first European operation in the Netherlands and later, in 1965, began production in Belgium. Shortly thereafter, it erected a joint-venture plant in Mexico to service the growing but highly protected Mexican market. By the end of the 1960s, Samsonite was manufacturing luggage in Spain and Japan as well. In addition to its manufacturing operations, Samsonite was selling luggage worldwide through a variety of distributors.

In the 1970s, business began to take off in Europe. In 1974, Samsonite developed its first real European product, called the Prestige Attaché, and business began to expand in Italy, causing the country to rival Germany as Samsonite's biggest market in Europe. Although the U.S. market began to turn to soft-side luggage in the 1980s, the European market still demanded hard-side luggage, so Samsonite developed a new hard-side suitcase for Europe called the Oyster case. At that point, soft-side luggage began to increase in importance, although Europe was still considered a hard-side market. In the 1980s, Samsonite opened a new plant in France to manufacture the Prestige Attaché and other key products.

With the fall of the Iron Curtain in the early 1990s, Samsonite purchased a Hungarian luggage manufacturer and began to expand throughout Eastern Europe. During this same time period, Samsonite established several joint-venture companies throughout Asia, including China, to extend its reach there.

STRATEGIES FOR THE 1990s

The Quality Initiative

To establish products of high quality, Samsonite embarked on two different programs. The first was an internal program in which Samsonite conducted drop, tumble, wheel, and handle tests to determine if its products were strong enough and of sufficient quality for customers. The second was composed of two different, independent quality-assurance tests:

- The European-based ISO 9002 certification
- The GS Mark, which is the number-one government-regulated third-party product test mark (similar to brand) of Germany

The GS Mark, *Gepruefte Sicherheit* (translated "Tested for Safety"), is designed to help companies comply with European product liability laws as well as other areas of quality and safety. To enhance quality, Samsonite introduced state-of-the-art CAD-CAM machinery in its plants. Samsonite also introduced a manufacturing technique in which autonomous cells of about a dozen employees assembled a product from start to finish.

As you can see in Map 17.1, Samsonite had three company-owned production facilities and two headquarters offices in Europe by the late 1990s. In addition, it had subsidiaries, joint ventures, retail franchises, distributors, and agents set up to service the European market. Although Samsonite initially serviced the European markets through exports, the transportation costs were high, and the demand for luggage soared in Europe, so Samsonite decided to begin production in Belgium in 1965.

SUPPLY-CHAIN DECENTRALIZATION

In the early years, Samsonite had a decentralized supply chain, as illustrated in Figure 17.1, whereby it operated through different wholesale layers before it finally got the product to the retailers.

As Samsonite's business grew, management decided to centralize its supply chain so that products were manufactured and shipped to a central European warehouse, which then directly supplied retailers upon request (see Figure 17.2). This centralized structure was put into place to eliminate the need to rely on wholesalers.

Samsonite had to worry about transporting manufactured products to the warehouse, storing them, and transporting them to the retailers in the different European markets. The company invested heavily in information technology to link the retailers to the warehouse and thereby manage its European distribution system more effectively. Retailers would place an order with a salesperson or the local Samsonite office in their area, and the order would be transmitted to the warehouse and shipping company by modem.

The retail market in Europe began shifting at the turn of the new century, so Samsonite responded by opening franchised retail outlets in October 2002, beginning in Antwerp and spreading to other areas. As the vice president of marketing and sales put it, "We are anticipating a shift in the market, in which the traditional luggage channel will no longer be at the forefront and a wide new retail opportunity will emerge."

MAP 17.1 Where Samsonite Operates in Europe

The products that Samsonite sells in Europe are made at production facilities located in Europe. Six of these facilities are company owned, and one is a joint venture. In order to serve its European market, the company also maintains subsidiaries and retail outlets and deals with distributors and agents.

R&D AND PRODUCT INNOVATION

As noted earlier, Samsonite sold two basic types of suitcases: hard-side and soft-side. Most of the R&D was initially done in the United States, but the need to develop products for the European market led the company to establish R&D facilities in Europe. Samsonite invested heavily in R&D and in the manufacture of specialized machinery to help keep a competitive edge. To facilitate the transportation and storage of suitcases, Samsonite located its production facilities close to the centralized warehouse.

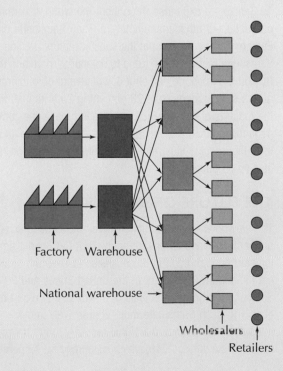

FIGURE 17.1 The Samsonite European Supply Chain (I): Decentralized, 1965–1974

For about a decade after it had first penetrated the European market, Samsonite shipped products from *factories* to *factory warehouses* and then to *national warehouses*. From there, products went to *wholesalers* and, at long last, to *retailers*. Needless to say, the system was cumbersome, lengthening the factory-to-retailer process and bumping up costs at every step of the way.

Source: F. De Beule and D. Van Den Bulcke, "The International Supply Chain Management of Samsonite Europe," Discussion Paper No. 1998/E/34 (Centre for International Management and Development, University of Antwerp, 1998):13.

FIGURE 17.2 The Samsonite European Supply Chain (II): Centralized, 1975–Mid-1980s

In the mid-1970s, Samsonite decided to streamline the cumbersome supply chain illustrated in Figure 17.1. For the next decade or so, the company shipped products from *factories* to a *central European warehouse*, which then shipped them, upon request, to *retailers* located across the continent.

Source: F. De Beule and D. Van Den Bulcke, "The International Supply Chain Management of Samsonite Europe." Discussion Paper No. 1998/E/34 (Centre for International Management and Development, University of Antwerp, 1998):14.

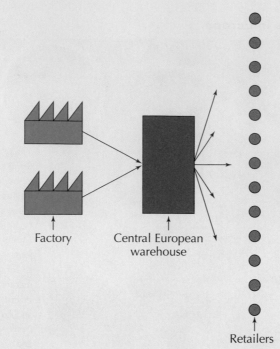

Factory   Central European warehouse

Retailers

Soft-side luggage is less complex technologically than hard-side, and Samsonite purchased Oda, the Belgium soft-side luggage company, to enter that market. Then it licensed its technology to other European companies. By the mid-1990s, 48 percent of Samsonite's sales came from hard-side luggage, 22 percent from soft-side, and 30 percent from attaché cases and travel bags, some of which were hard-side and some soft-side. However, by fiscal 2000, soft-side luggage comprised 51 percent of European sales. In 2001 and 2002, sales of soft-side luggage continued to increase as a percentage, and hard-side luggage sales declined.

OUTSOURCING

As Samsonite expanded throughout the world, it continued to manufacture its own products and license production to other manufacturers. Then Samsonite entered into subcontract arrangements in Asia and Eastern Europe. In Europe, the subcontractors provide final goods as well as the subassemblies used in Samsonite factories. The trend to outsource more and more of its production has been steadily increasing. By 2007, Samsonite had shut down several of its plants in Europe and decreased internal manufacturing of soft-side luggage from 23 percent in 2004 to just under 10 percent in 2007. Although it still produces the majority of its hard-side luggage internally, the company now sources 90 percent of its soft-side luggage from third-party manufacturers to consolidate its manufacturing capacities and to achieve cost savings. Figure 17.3 illustrates Samsonite's coordination of outsourced parts and finished goods, along with its own production.

THE FUTURE OF SAMSONITE

The slowdown in international travel and consumer spending in 2008 to 2009 nearly drove Samsonite under. It is owned by private equity firm CVC, and a deal between CVC and Royal Bank of Scotland (RBS) injected enough cash in the business to save the company. In addition, top management was forced to cut headcount 50 percent in the United States and 30 percent in Europe, closing 115 shops. In addition, Samsonite cut out some lines of business that didn't make much sense in a falling travel market. CVC's goal is to push Samsonite more aggressively into Asia, where a growing middle class loves to travel. As a result of this push and a global recovery in the travel industry, Samsonite saw a 45 percent increase in sales in Asia during 2010, which accounted for 42 percent of its group profits.

FIGURE 17.3   The Samsonite European Supply Chain (III): Globalized, 1996–Present

As it expanded production throughout Europe, Samsonite was soon obliged to establish arrangements with subcontractors (who provided both final products and subassemblies). Because the company now had to coordinate outsourced goods and parts in addition to production from its own factories, it reconfigured its supply chain once again: Today, all products and parts, whether company produced or outsourced, go to a central European warehouse and, from there, straight to retailers.

Source: F. De Beule and D. Van Den Bulcke. "The International Supply Chain Management of Samsonite Europe," Discussion Paper No. 1998/E/34 (Centre for International Management and Development, University of Antwerp, 1998):21.

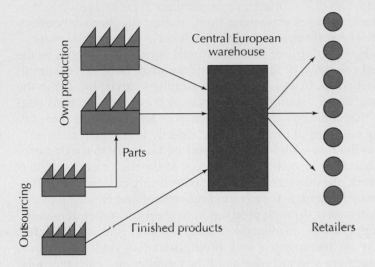

Consistent with its focus on Asia, Samsonite also decided to list its shares as an IPO (Initial Public Offering) on the Hong Kong exchange in June 2011. This move resulted in Samsonite raising $1.3 billion in cash, which it could use to reduce its debt. CVS Capital reduced its ownership stake in Samsonite to 28.7 percent from 29.8 percent, and RBS reduced its stake to 15.2 percent from 15.8 percent. As Samsonite expands more to Asia from its original base in the United States and Europe, it will have to figure out how to organize its supply chain, as it did in Europe, but in a larger, more complex international environment. However, the experience in Europe should help the company as it establishes its supply chain worldwide.

Introduction

The case of Samsonite illustrates dimensions of the supply-chain networks that link suppliers with manufacturers and customers. Most companies agree that effective supply-chain management is one of their most important tools in reducing costs and increasing revenue.[2] This chapter examines these different networks and explores how to manage the links most effectively to reach customers. The discussion covers the major issues: an effective global manufacturing strategy; the role of information technology in global supply-chain management; quality; supplier networks; and inventory management, including the importance of effective transportation networks.

Let's note here that effective supply-chain management is as important for services as for manufacturing. While our opening case traces developments in the supply-chain strategy of a traditional manufacturer, the closing case on Nokero involves the manufacturing of a low-cost product, the heart of the case is how to provide a service—light—on a global basis in a cost-effective and environmentally friendly way. As we discuss different aspects of outsourcing, we'll discuss the benefits of outsourcing services on a global basis. Even in the section on global manufacturing strategy, the same issues apply to an effective global *services* strategy: cost minimization, dependability, quality, innovation, flexibility, and service locations.

What Is Supply-Chain Management?

Supply chain—the coordination of materials, information, and funds from the initial raw-material supplier to the ultimate customer.

The **supply chain** is the network that links together the different aspects of the value chain (defined in Chapter 11), coordinating materials, information, and funds from the initial raw-material supplier to the ultimate customer.[3] *Supply-chain management*, also called operations and supply-chain management or OSM, is defined as "the design, operation, and improvement of the systems that create and deliver the firm's primary products and services."[4] In its broadest definition, OSM encompasses everything from creating supplier relationships to getting the product to the final consumer, with logistics included as an important aspect.

Suppliers can be part of the manufacturer's organizational structure, as would be the case in a vertically integrated company, or they can be independent of it. Direct suppliers, in fact, have their own networks. In a global context, suppliers can be located in the country where the manufacturing or assembly takes place, or they can be located elsewhere and ship materials to that country, either to the factory or to an intermediate storage point. Manufacturing process output can be shipped directly to the customers or to a warehouse network, as was the case with Samsonite, and sold directly to the end consumer or to a distributor, wholesaler, or retailer, and then on to the final consumer. As is the case in the supplier network, the output can be sold domestically or internationally.

Logistics (also called materials management)—that part of the supply-chain process that plans, implements, and controls the efficient, effective flow and storage of goods, services, and related information from the point of origin to the point of consumption in order to meet customers' requirements.

Logistics, or **materials management,** is the inbound movement and handling of materials and products from purchasing through production to meet consumer demands.[5] The difference between supply-chain management and logistics is one of degree. Logistics focuses much more on transporting and storing materials and final goods, whereas supply-chain management also includes handling supplier and customer relations. However, firms often have their own interpretation of how the two differ.

Many MNEs that have excelled in their ability to manage their supply-chain networks, such as Apple in the United States, Tesco in the United Kingdom, Samsung in Korea, Nokia in Finland, Toyota in Japan, and Zara in Spain. The companies we study in this chapter are considered part of a global network that links together designers, suppliers, subcontractors, manufacturers, and customers. The supply-chain network is quite broad, and its coordination takes place through interactions between firms in the network.[6]

Global Manufacturing Strategies

Case Review Note

Concept Check

In Chapter 1, we explain **value** as the underlying principle of strategy, defining it as "the measure of a firm's capability to sell what it makes for more than the costs incurred to make it." Here, while further refining our discussion of strategy to enumerate factors contributing to a successful strategy, we hasten to repeat our definition of **strategy** as the effort of managers to build and sustain the company's competitive position within its industry to create value.

Recall from our opening case that Samsonite initially exported to Europe but eventually set up manufacturing facilities in several countries there because of *location-specific advantages* (notably, hefty demand), choosing to enter the market through FDI in order to take advantage of its own *firm-specific assets* (especially an excellent product line and a solid manufacturing process). The emphasis here is on Samsonite's strategic decision to internalize those advantages rather than sell them to an outside manufacturer.[7] Thus, although the company entered into some licensing agreements and subcontracted some manufacturing, it initially kept most of its production—especially in high-end hard-side luggage—under its own control.

Although Samsonite engaged in its own manufacturing for the most part, it eventually outsourced it to other firms, as have other MNEs. Nike subcontracts manufacturing to other companies, remaining basically a design and marketing company. Mattel does not own facilities in China to manufacture Barbie dolls; it outsources the manufacturing to a Hong Kong–based company that has investments in China. Some of the toys in McDonald's Happy Meals or Burger King's meals are also subcontracted to a Hong Kong–based manufacturer.

FACTORS IN MANUFACTURING STRATEGY

Manufacturing is just one piece in supply-chain strategy. It is preceded by sourcing inputs from suppliers and followed by distribution of the final product to consumers. The success of a global manufacturing strategy depends on four key factors: *compatibility, configuration, coordination,* and *control.*[8]

Compatibility   Compatibility in this context is the degree of consistency between the foreign investment decision and the company's competitive strategy. Direct manufacturing, for instance, made sense in Samsonite's case but not in Nike's. Here are some company strategies that managers must consider:

- *Efficiency/cost*—reduction of manufacturing costs
- *Dependability*—degree of trust in a company's products, its delivery, and its price promises
- *Quality*—performance reliability, good service, speed of delivery, and reliable product maintenance
- *Innovation*—ability to develop new products and ideas
- *Flexibility*—ability of the production process to make different kinds of products and adjust the volume of output[9]

Efficiency/Cost Strategies   *Cost-minimization strategies* and the drive for global efficiencies force MNEs to establish economies of scale in manufacturing, often by producing in areas with low-cost labor. This is one of the major reasons why many MNEs have established manufacturing facilities in Asia, Mexico, and Eastern Europe—a type of FDI known as **offshore manufacturing.**

Offshore Manufacturing   The 1960s and 1970s saw a sharp escalation in offshore manufacturing as one electronics company after another set up production facilities in the Far East, mostly in Taiwan and Singapore. Those locations were attractive because of low labor costs, the availability of cheap materials and components, and the proximity to markets. Even the athletic-shoe market left the United States for Korea and Taiwan. As wages rose in Korea, however, manufacturing began to shift to other low-cost countries, such as Indonesia, Malaysia, Thailand, and Vietnam. Piaggio, for instance, could have manufactured Vespa motorbikes in Italy and exported them to Vietnam, but

Concept Check

In discussing the process of "Creating Value" in Chapter 11, we explain that a firm that aspires to a position of "Cost Leadership" strives to be the low-cost producer in an industry for a given level of quality. This strategy, we observe, means that the firm adopts one of two tactics, both of which must be compatible with the structure of its value chain: (1) earning a profit higher than industry rivals by selling products at average industry prices or (2) capturing market share by selling products at prices below the industry average.

Compatibility—the degree of consistency between FDI decisions and a company's competitive strategy.

Offshore manufacturing—any investment that takes place in a country other than the home country.

A worker at the Delphi Automotive maquiladora in Ciudad Juarez, Chihuahua, Mexico assembles a dashboard harness for GM cars.
Source: Keith Dannemiller/Alamy

it made more sense to manufacture them in Vietnam, with its cheaper costs, manageable transportation and tariffs, and a good market for the product.

China in particular has become the hot spot for manufacturing and has even been termed by the *Wall Street Journal* "the world's factory floor." Its output is so large and wide-ranging that it exerts deflationary pressure around the world on products such as textiles, TVs, furniture, auto parts, and mobile phones. China is now the world's fourth-largest industrial base behind the United States, Japan, and Germany. Many MNEs set up operations there in the 1980s to capitalize on its huge population and growing demand.

Samsonite is among the companies that have found it more cost-effective to manufacture products in China—and not just for the Chinese market, but for export to the rest of the world as well. Meanwhile, Dutch company Philips Electronics produces some of its products solely in China and plans to make the country its global supply base for exporting its products around the world.[10] As will be explained in the closing case, Nokero manufactures its solar light bulbs in Shenzhen, China. Still other companies, such as Hewlett-Packard, Microsoft, and Motorola, have looked beyond simply outsourcing manufacturing to China and have established R&D centers within the country. IBM and General Motors are even using China as a global center for their companies' procurement operations.[11]

Case Review Note

Total cost analysis—an in-depth assessment of the complete cost of a transaction that takes into account acquisition, ownership, and disposal costs.

Total Cost Analysis   When employing a cost-minimization strategy, companies tend to overlook important elements—and extra costs—of offshore manufacturing, such as shipping distances, extra inventory, political and security risks, and the availability of skilled and educated workers. In other words, when making decisions to source abroad, companies should consider the total cost of facilitating the strategy, as opposed to merely the acquisition cost.

A *total cost analysis* takes into account the costs of ownership, such as storing and transporting inventory as well as disposal. In some instances, wages may be such a small percentage of overall costs that employing cheap labor abroad does not effectively save the company money. For example, Nike decided to employ a small contractor in San Francisco to produce some of its made-to-order goods—despite the $15-per-hour rates that were 20 times those of contractors in China—because the overhead costs, such as management of the flow of goods from halfway around the world and the risk of stockouts and high inventories, were so much higher.[12]

Dependability Strategies   Many factors besides cost must also be taken into consideration. The growing customer demand for *dependability* and prompt deliveries has caused companies such as Dell Computer to locate plants closer to customers rather than in low-wage areas. When a longer supply chain risks late deliveries of components or finished goods, shortening the distance can improve dependability.

Innovation and Quality Strategies   Many companies are also responding to the importance of *innovation* and *quality*. One example of innovation is a new technology known as 3D printing. Instead of ink cartridges, 3D printers are filled with materials such as plastic and titanium. After you create a blueprint on your computer, you press print, and the printer builds up your object one layer at a time. These printers are able to do the job of a manufacturing machine in about the same time, with less waste, and with more opportunities to customize the product.[13] However, when first investing abroad to take advantage of low-cost labor, companies are not as concerned about innovation. But as more and more establish R&D facilities abroad, they are able to move beyond low-end manufacturing.

Quality is a major issue, however—one discussed later in more detail. As long as foreign operations ensure high quality and contribute to innovation, companies will keep setting up operations abroad. However, after a decade-long trend of sourcing in low-cost countries like China, Japanese firms such as Honda, Canon, and Sharp are now relocating production back in their home country. In 2003, Japanese companies registered to build 844 factories in Japan and 434 abroad; in 2006, the numbers were 1,782 and 182, respectively. These MNEs have been responding to the need for access to Japan's pool of skilled workers, as well as its proximity to engineers, parts suppliers, and decision makers. They believe that to ensure innovation and quality, close communication between product development and manufacturing is essential.[14] However, the strong yen has forced many Japanese companies to rethink their investment strategies and invest more offshore to take advantage of weaker-currency countries in the Asia region.

Flexibility Strategies   The need for responsiveness or *flexibility* in the face of national market differences may result in regional manufacturing to service local markets. It may not be possible to produce all products in one location and ship them around the world. Wall's Unilever, for example, produces ice cream in China, so it is able to develop products that are unique to the Chinese market as well as produce such global brands as the Magnum Bar and the Cornetto. However, Wall's Unilever has found that it can produce some of its global brands during the winter when demand is down and ship them to South Africa and Australia during their summer, enabling the use of excess production facilities and cost reductions in markets outside China.[15] Still, despite such flexibility, differences in measurement systems, time zones, and problem-solving approaches can also add unnecessary complexity to the supply chain.

Changes in Strategy   As a company's competitive strategies change, so do its manufacturing strategies. In fact, it may adopt different strategies for different product lines, depending on their competitive priorities. For example, to reduce the cost and complexity of its products, Finnish mobile-phone maker Nokia designs phones that contain fewer parts and bases its different models on the same basic components. This has allowed Nokia to maintain 17 percent profit margins on its low-end phones and 19 percent on its higher-end models—substantial numbers in the highly competitive market for cellular phones.[16]

Priding itself on high quality, Toyota has traditionally relied on manufacturing in Toyota City, Japan, where it is close to suppliers and can ensure high quality and adherence to its manufacturing strategy. However, it has developed a family of vehicles based on a single low-cost platform that is targeted to emerging markets. To keep the prices low enough to compete in the developing world, Toyota has abandoned its traditional practice of sourcing key components from its Japanese plants and is locating factories for these parts in low-wage areas such as South America, Africa, and Southeast Asia. This has helped reduce the costs by 20 to 25 percent (although managers are concerned that they may lose control over quality).[17] This became a real concern when Toyota faced significant recalls due to safety concerns. Many suggested that the drive for global market share caused Toyota to sacrifice quality and safety.

Manufacturing Configuration   There are three basic configurations that MNEs must consider in establishing a global manufacturing strategy:

- *Centralized Manufacturing:* Basically a manufacture-and-export strategy that offers a selection of standard, lower-priced products to different markets, this is common for companies new to exporting, typically through their home-country facilities. It is also important for expensive items for which economies of scale in manufacturing are key and there is little need to localize them for consumption in different markets, such as aircraft. Nokero, as will be described in more detail in the ending case, is a U.S.-based company that manufactures solar light bulbs in one factory in China and exports them around the world.

- *Regional Manufacturing:* These facilities serve customers within a specific region, as Samsonite initially did in Europe with its production facilities in Belgium, and as

Concept Check

In Chapter 11, in discussing "Configuration" as a factor in creating a **value chain,** we explain the importance of identifying the best location economies—those in which operations can be most effective given prevailing economic, political, and cultural conditions. We also analyze several factors that may influence a company's decisions in configuring its value chain (e.g., cost, logistics, economies of scale, buyers' needs).

Concept Check

Recall from Chapter 11 our extended discussion of "Global Integration versus Local Responsiveness" as an issue in configuring and coordinating a firm's value chain. We then proceed to explain how efforts to resolve this issue may contribute to the formulation of a **global** strategy or a **multidomestic** strategy for international operations. Here we analyze ways in which this same issue can put pressure on specific strategic decisions about the configuration of manufacturing facilities.

Manufacturing configuration:
- Centralized manufacturing in one country.
- Manufacturing facilities in specific regions to service those regions.
- Multidomestic facilities in each country.

Case Review Note

Toyota is doing in developing countries. Dell assembles computers in Brazil and exports them to different markets in South America, which is another example of a regional strategy since it doesn't assemble computers in every country where it sells them.

- *Multidomestic Manufacturing:* Market expansion in individual countries, especially when the demand there becomes significant, might entail this approach in which a firm manufactures products close to its customers, using country-specific manufacturing facilities to meet local needs.[18] This is the approach that Philips, the Dutch electronics company, used after World War II, because there were barriers to entry in European countries. To maintain market share in the individual countries, Philips had to manufacture on a country-by-country basis. The reduction of trade barriers reduces the need to have manufacturing facilities in every country, but country size may result in companies establishing manufacturing facilities to supply the local market. Unless an MNE has such facilities in every country it operates in, it must combine exporting with manufacturing. In reality, MNEs choose a combination of these approaches depending on their product strategies.

Countries often also specialize in the production of parts or final goods—a process known as *rationalization*. A good example can be borrowed from our opening case. In the 1980s, Samsonite opened a new factory in Hénin-Beaumont, France, to manufacture Prestige Attaché and a few other products. Thus, it was able to remove their production from its facility in Oudenaarde, Belgium, where it could then focus on its new Oyster product line. This strategy of specializing the manufacture of certain products in certain plants eventually made it feasible to export all production to a centralized European warehouse, from which Samsonite could then distribute its whole product line to retailers all over Europe.

Coordination and Control   Coordination and control fit well together. *Coordination* is the linking or integrating of activities into a unified system.[19] The activities include everything along the global supply chain, from purchasing to warehousing to shipment. It is hard to coordinate supplier relations and logistics activities if those issues are not considered when the manufacturing configuration is set up.

Once the company determines the manufacturing configuration it will use, it must adopt a control system to ensure that company strategies are carried out. *Control* can be the measuring of performance so companies can respond appropriately to changing conditions. Another aspect of a control structure is the organizational structure, discussed in more detail in Chapter 15. Samsonite established its European headquarters in Belgium (in Oudenaarde) for the basic purpose of controlling all of its European activities—a strategy also designed to maximize the company's ability to respond to local and/or regional differences in a very large market.

Case Review Note

Information Technology and Global Supply-Chain Management

A comprehensive supply-chain strategy is most effective with a strong commitment to information technology (IT), which aids in quick and efficient production, proficient inventory management, effective supplier communication, and customer satisfaction. In *The World Is Flat*, Thomas Friedman discusses 10 "flatteners" that are changing the world, and Flattener number 3 is Work Flow Software.[20] This is his third base or foundation in the technology platform that is helping to flatten the world. The work flow software, basically the standard protocols, such as HTTP that allow computers to work with each other and business processes such as SAP, are critical for the supply-chain management process. We'll discuss some of them below and then examine how some of the other "flatteners" that build on the technology platform are important in global supply chain management.

ELECTRONIC DATA INTERCHANGE (EDI)

The key to making a global information system work is getting the relevant information in a timely manner, as Samsonite did by investing heavily in IT that enabled retailers or salespeople to trigger orders directly by contacting a central warehouse. Many companies use an **electronic data interchange (EDI)** to link suppliers, manufacturers, customers, and intermediaries, especially in the food-manufacturing and car-making industries, in which suppliers replenish in high volumes.

In a global context, EDI has been used to link exporters with customs to facilitate the quick processing of customs forms, thus speeding up cross-border deliveries. Walmart is known for its revolutionary use of EDI to connect its global suppliers to its inventory ordering system.[21]

> EDI (electronic data interchange)—the electronic linkage of suppliers, customers, and third-party intermediaries to expedite documents and financial flows.

ENTERPRISE RESOURCE PLANNING/MATERIAL REQUIREMENTS PLANNING

The next wave of technology affecting the global supply chain was the implementation of IT packages known as **enterprise resource planning (ERP).** Companies such as Oracle, Baan, PeopleSoft, and German software giant SAP introduced software to integrate everything in the back office (the part of the business dealing with internal matters, as opposed to the front office, which deals with the customer). ERP is essential for bringing together the information inside the firm and from different geographic areas, but its inability to tie in to the customer and take advantage of e-commerce has been a problem.

An extension of ERP is *material requirements planning* (MRP), a computerized information system that addresses complex inventory situations and calculates the demand for parts from the production schedules of the companies that use them. DENSO, the Japanese auto parts supplier for Toyota, uses MRP extensively to calculate the demand for parts from the production schedules of the non-Toyota companies it supplies.

> ERP (enterprise resource planning)—software that can link information flows from different parts of a business and from different geographic areas.

> Material requirements planning (MRP)—computerized information system that addresses complex inventory situations and calculates the demand for parts from the production schedules of the companies that use the parts.

RADIO FREQUENCY ID (RFID)

A newer wave has recently swept the technology scene in the form of *radio frequency ID (RFID)*, a system that labels a product with an electronic tag that stores and transmits information on the product's origin, destination, and quantity. When electronic readers scan the tags by means of radio waves, the data can be rewritten or captured and sent to a computer-network database, which collects, organizes, stores, and moves the data— often in conjunction with an ERP system.

Such real-time information allows manufacturers, suppliers, and distributors to keep track of products and components throughout their manufacturing processes and transportation networks, resulting in greater efficiency and more visibility along the supply chain. In June 2003, Walmart mandated that its top suppliers use RFID tags at the pallet level, predicting that it could save billions of dollars for the entire retail industry through supply-chain efficiencies.[22] The use of RFID in the Las Vegas airport to track luggage has resulted in more accurate sorting, better tracking, and fewer lost bags.[23] Walmart announced in 2010 that it would experiment with placing removable "smart tags" on individual garments such as jeans and underwear that would allow workers to use hand-held scanners to identify exact inventory on the shelves or in the backroom. There are concerns over privacy, but RFID tags placed on removable labels or packaging is not as invasive as imbedding them in the clothing, which could then be tracked anywhere.[24]

> Radio frequency ID (RFID)—a system that labels products with an electronic tag, which stores and transmits information regarding the product's origin, destination, and quantity.

E-COMMERCE

E-commerce—the use of the Internet to join together suppliers with companies and companies with customers.

The next technological wave linking together the parts of the global supply chain is **e-commerce.** To illustrate, Dell's factory in Ireland supplies custom-built PCs all over Europe. Customers transmit orders to Dell via call centers or its website, and the company relays the demand for components to its suppliers. Trucks deliver the components to the factory and haul off the completed computers within a few hours. All of this activity, of course, is made possible by the Internet. Since Walmart moved its EDI-based infrastructure from traditional but expensive value-added networks (VANs) to the Internet, it was been good news for thousands of worldwide vendors. All of their transactions with Walmart are now on the Web—a substantial cost savings for the MNE and its vendors.[25]

Most experts agree that the Internet is revolutionizing communications across all levels of the global supply chain, although at different speeds in different areas. The number of worldwide Internet users rose from 420 million in 2000 to more than a 1.83 billion in 2009, growing at an average rate of 160 million users per year.[26]

Concept Check

In discussing "Contemporary Approaches to Organizational Change" in Chapter 15, we observe that the Internet, which accelerates the spread of ideas throughout an organization, has become a "metaphor" for organization structure. In other words, as a supremely efficient and effective means of organizing global knowledge, resources, and people, the Internet has inspired many people to imagine new ways of effectively organizing a company's resources (especially its people). We also point out the ironic attractiveness of a self-regulating organizational model that features no formal organizational hierarchy.

Private technology exchange (PTX)—an online collaboration model that brings manufacturers, distributors, value-added resellers, and customers together to execute trading transactions.

Extranets and Intranets   Dell has established an **extranet** for its suppliers—a linkage to its information system via the Internet—so they can organize production and delivery of parts. Plugged into Dell's customer database, they can keep track of changes in demand; plugged into the ordering process, they can track the progress of their orders from factory to doorstep.[27]

The real attraction of the Internet in global supply-chain management is that it not only helps automate and speed up internal processes in a company through an **intranet,** but it also spreads efficiency gains to the business systems of its customers and suppliers.[28] The new technology wave is **private technology exchange (PTX),** an online collaboration model that brings manufacturers, distributors, value-added resellers, and customers together through the Internet to execute trading transactions and share information about demand, production, availability, and more.

"The Digital Divide"   The challenge in global supply-chain management is that although some networks can be managed through the Internet, others—particularly in emerging markets—cannot because of the lack of technology or low Internet speeds. The use of the Internet varies by location and by industry. North America is at least five years ahead of some countries in Europe, especially Eastern Europe, but it is behind Asia, especially in some key infrastructures. Industries such as computing and electronics, aerospace and defense, and motor vehicles are blasting ahead; industrial equipment, food and agriculture, heavy industries, and consumer goods are lagging.

This so-called digital divide has created difficulties for companies such as U.S.-based Newmont Mining Corporation. Newmont has struggled to implement its ordering and inventory management information system with its suppliers in Indonesia, who have to rent computers in different towns to even access the Internet and whose managers are typically former farmers who likely have never even used e-mail.[29] It is no coincidence that the leaders in e-commerce are those who have invested significant amounts of money over the years in IT—notably in the defense and motor-vehicle industries.

The preceding discussion shows that IT can help companies manage their global supply chains but must carefully integrate it into their overall strategy. Because IT is highly technical as well as a support to a company's lines of business, it is often difficult to align it with company strategy. This is especially true in the international arena, where personnel in different countries may be accustomed to their own IT systems and may have difficulty adopting a global IT format that will allow them to achieve some economies of scale as well as fully integrate it in the overall strategy.

Quality

An important aspect of all levels of the global supply chain is quality management, for service firms as well as manufacturers. **Quality** can be defined as meeting or exceeding customer expectations. More specifically, it is conformance to specifications, value, fitness for use, support (provided by the company), and psychological impressions (image).[30] Quality involves careful design of a product or service and ensuring that the organizations' systems can consistently produce the design.[31] For example, no one wants to buy computer software that has a lot of bugs. However, the need to get software to market quickly may mean speeding it there as soon as possible and correcting errors later. In the airline industry, service is key. Some airlines, such as Singapore Air, have developed a worldwide reputation for excellence in service—a distinct competitive advantage, especially when trying to attract the business traveler.

> Quality—meeting or exceeding the expectations of a customer.

A Case in Point: Car Quality Quality—or the lack thereof—can have serious ramifications for a company. Ford lost around $1 billion in 2001 because of faulty Firestone tires on its Explorers. Because of this and other quality problems, many car manufacturers began to look at the way Japanese carmakers, especially Toyota, manufactured their cars with higher efficiency and fewer defects. However, accidents resulting from the sudden acceleration of Toyota automobiles in the mid-2000s called into question the reliability of supposedly defect-free Toyotas. Although no final source of the problem was found, including possibly driver error, this was the first of many defects that Toyota admitted to. In spite of that, Toyota set off a flight to quality by all auto manufactures trying to emulate Toyota's success in manufacturing autos that were relatively defect-free. In 2011, J.D. Power & Associates named three assembly plants that received its highest award for producing models yielding the fewest defects and malfunctions: two are Toyota plants in Canada and Japan, which produced the Lexus, and the third is a Honda's plant in Greensburg, Indiana (U.S.), which produces the Civic. Although all three plants are Japanese plants, it is interesting that two of the three are outside of Japan.[32]

Each year, J.D. Power & Associates releases two different quality rankings on automobiles: the Initial Quality Study (IQS) and the Vehicle Dependability Study (VDS), which measures quality after three years of ownership. In the 2011 Dependability Ratings, Lincoln (Ford) was the highest-rated nameplate in the survey for the first time ever, followed by Lexus, Jaguar, Porsche, and Toyota. Toyota won seven awards across the different categories, although Ford/Lincoln was in second place. As a whole, Japanese companies walked away with ten awards compared to seven for U.S. companies. Although the Japanese automakers have long dominated the rankings, the 2011 results exhibited marked improvements for American carmakers, although they are still behind the Japanese models. However, the initial quality ratings for U.S. automakers have been steadily improving, and that should be translated into higher dependability rates three years later, so it appears that the focus on quality is narrowing the gap among the top auto manufacturers worldwide.[33]

ZERO DEFECTS VERSUS ACCEPTABLE QUALITY LEVEL

Quality has begun to mean **zero defects,** an idea perfected by Japanese manufacturers who refuse to tolerate flaws of any kind. Before this strong emphasis on zero defects, many companies operated according to the premise of **acceptable quality level (AQL),** which held that a few unacceptable products would be dealt with through repair facilities and service warranties. This type of manufacturing/operating environment required buffer inventories, rework stations, and expediting, with the goal of pushing through products as fast as possible and then dealing with the mistakes later. Now, it is increasingly evident that AQL is inferior to zero defects and that global companies that take quality more seriously will beat the competition.[34]

> Zero defects—the refusal to tolerate defects of any kind.

> Acceptable quality level (AQL)—a tolerable level of defects that can be corrected through repair and service warranties.

THE DEMING APPROACH TO QUALITY MANAGEMENT

Deming's approach to quality encompasses the idea that the responsibility for quality resides within the policies and practices of managers.

In the late 1970s, when Japanese companies began to seriously outpace those in the United States in achieving high-quality products and processes, a new emphasis was placed on actively managing the operations that affect quality. One contributor to this focus on *quality management*, and one of the people who trained the Japanese in quality was W. Edwards Deming. To espouse the idea that the responsibility for quality resides within the policies and practices of managers, Deming developed several suggestions, which have come to be known as **Deming's 14 Points**. Deming's focus on quality was designed to reduce the variance in the manufacturing process through statistical control, design, and training and through the policies and practices of managers. His feeling was that higher quality would lead to lower costs and better acceptance by the consumer. The Deming approach is highly prized by Japanese manufacturers and has gained significant traction in other countries as well.[35]

The emphasis on quality management has continued to provide a major source of competitive advantage and play a major role for companies across the globe. However, just as different countries possess various cultures, product preferences, and business practices, various regions of the world have approached the concept of quality management in different ways. The Japanese have long focused on lean production processes that eliminate waste and boost visibility, whereas the American approach has historically been more statistically based, and the Europeans have opted to concentrate more on standards of quality.[36] These different attitudes toward quality create a high level of complexity for MNEs with global operations. As we will see, however, many of the best practices concerning quality have been perfected in Japan and are being used worldwide.

TOTAL QUALITY MANAGEMENT (TQM)

Concept Check

Compare the concept of employee involvement as it's characterized here with the idea of coordination by mutual adjustment, which we discuss in Chapter 15. Both approaches to coordination signal a willingness to coordinate value activities through a range of informal mechanisms, including means by which employees are encouraged to engage one another in decisions about matters of mutual importance.

Total quality management (TQM)—a process that stresses customer satisfaction, employee involvement, and continuous improvement of quality. Its goal is to eliminate all defects.

The Japanese approach to quality is **total quality management (TQM),** a process that stresses three principles: *customer satisfaction, continuous improvement,* and *employee involvement.*[37] Its goal is to eliminate all defects. TQM often focuses on benchmarking world-class standards, product and service design, process design, and purchasing.[38]

The center of the entire process, however, is customer satisfaction, the achievement of which may raise production costs. The difference between AQL and TQM centers on attitude toward quality. In AQL, quality is a characteristic of a product that meets or exceeds engineering standards. In TQM, quality means the product is so good that the customer wouldn't think of buying from anyone else.

TQM is a process of continuous improvement at every organizational level—from the mailroom to the boardroom. It implies that the company is doing everything it can to achieve quality at every stage of the process. For example, if management accounting systems are focused strictly on cost, they will preclude measures that could lead to higher quality. The key is to understand the company's overall strategy.

TQM does not use any specific production philosophy or require the use of other techniques, such as a just-in-time system for inventory delivery. It is a proactive strategy. Although benchmarking—determining the best processes used by the best companies—is an important part of TQM, it is not intended to be a goal. In essence, TQM means that a company will try to be better than the best.

Executives who have adopted the zero-defects philosophy of TQM claim that long-run production costs decline as defects decline. The continuous improvement process is also known as *kaizen*, which means identifying problems and enlisting employees at all levels to help eliminate problems. The key is to make continuous improvement a part of every employee's daily work.

TQM in a global setting is challenging because of cultural and environmental differences. When Samsonite entered into an agreement with a Hungarian manufacturer to supply low-end soft-side luggage, a lack of advanced technology prevented the Hungarian firm from delivering products that satisfied Samsonite's world-class quality

CRN

Case Review Note

standards. As a result, Samsonite was forced to invest heavily in the partner to get a supply of products that would satisfy even the low end of its European market.

SIX SIGMA

Six Sigma is an effective statistical approach to quality management developed by Motorola and popularized by General Electric. As a highly focused system of quality control that scrutinizes a company's entire production system, it aims to eliminate defects, slash product cycle times, and cut costs across the board. The Six Sigma process uses data and rigorous statistical analysis to identify "defects" in a process or product, reduce variability, and achieve as close to zero defects as possible.[39] General Electric has operationalized six sigma on a project basis using the acronym DMAIC. This refers to define (especially customers and their priorities), measure (the process and its performance), analyze (determine the most likely cause of defects), improve (determine how to remove the causes of the defects), and control (how to maintain the improvements).[40]

Since Motorola introduced Six Sigma in the 1980s, it's been adopted by many MNEs, including GE, GlaxoSmithKline, and Lockheed Martin. Although some have accused the Six Sigma program of diverting attention away from customers and squashing innovation, most of the 100 largest companies in the United States have embraced it.[41] Its main goal is defect reduction. Fewer defects should cause an improvement in yields, which should improve customer satisfaction, which should lead to enhanced income. Given that Six Sigma is a metric designed to measure defects, some argue that it is most effective when used in conjunction with the Baldrige Criteria for Excellence or the European Quality Award.[42]

Six Sigma—a quality control system aimed at eliminating defects, slashing product cycle times, and cutting costs across the board.

QUALITY STANDARDS

There are three different levels of quality standards: *general, industry-specific,* and *company-specific.* The first is a general standard, such as the Deming Award, which is presented to firms that demonstrate excellence in quality, or the Malcolm Baldrige National Quality Award, which is presented annually to companies that demonstrate quality strategies and achievements. However, even more important than awards is certification of quality.

General-Level Standards The **International Organization for Standardization (ISO)** in Geneva was formed in 1947 to facilitate the international coordination and unification of industrial standards. From the beginning, it has partnered with the IEC (International Electrotechnical Commission), which is the originator of global technical standards. It also collaborates with the International Telecommunications Union and the World Trade Organization. As an NGO, the ISO represents a network of standard setters in 163 countries and has established over 18,500 international quality standards.[43]

Levels of quality standards:

- General level—ISO 9000, Malcolm Baldrige National Quality Award.
- Industry-specific level.
- Company level.

ISO 9000 and ISO 14000 In addition to the 118,536 standards (as of December 31, 2010), there are some 1100 new standards being published every year. Two main families of standards are ISO 9000, which describes the fundamentals of quality management systems, and ISO 14000, which addresses what the company does to improve its environmental performance.

ISO 9000 is a set of universal standards for a quality assurance system that is accepted around the world. Applying uniformly to companies in any industry and of any size, it is intended to promote the idea of quality at every organizational level. Initially, it was designed to harmonize technical norms within the EU. Now it is an important part of business operations throughout Europe. Under the ISO 9000 family of standards, companies must document how workers perform every function affecting quality and install mechanisms to ensure that they follow through on the documented routine. The

ISO 9000—a global set of quality standards intended to promote quality at every level of an organization.

ISO 14000—a quality standard concerned with environmental management.

documentation is generic and applicable to any organization that produces products or services. A major advantage of the ISO 9000 process is the documentation process since it not only requires workers to examine what they do to improve quality but also ensures continuity as workers change positions.

ISO certification entails a complex analysis of management systems and procedures, not just quality-control standards. Rather than judging the quality of a particular product, ISO evaluates the management of the manufacturing or service process according to the standards it has created in 20 domains, from purchasing to design to training. The operation principles of its management-system standards are plan, do, check, and act (correct and improve plans). A company that wants to be ISO certified must fill out a report and submit to certification by a team of independent auditors.[44] The process can be expensive and time-consuming, as each site of a company must be separately certified. The ISO 14000 family of standards is designed to help companies establish high-quality environmental standards in terms of air, water, and soil; how the companies will ensure that environmental standards are followed; and how they will develop products and services that are environmentally friendly.

Most MNEs claim ISO certification, but ISO is not the solution to all quality issues. One estimate holds that in some places, including China, as much as 40 percent of ISO certifications are falsified.[45] However, being certified will help suppliers obtain more business, especially with European companies.

Non-European companies operating in Europe need to become ISO certified in order to maintain access to that market.

U.S. companies that operate in Europe are seeking ISO certification to maintain access to the European market. When DuPont lost a major European contract to an ISO-certified European company, it decided to become certified. By doing so, not only was it able to position itself better in the European market, it also benefited from the experience of going through the certification process and focusing on quality within itself. Some European companies are so committed to ISO that they will not do business with a certified company if its suppliers are not also ISO certified. They want to be sure that quality flows back to every level of the supply chain.

Industry-Specific Standards   In addition to the general standards described earlier, there are industry-specific standards for quality, especially for suppliers to follow. Since ISO standards are relatively generic, some industries, such as the auto industry, have developed more specific standards to fit the industry. One such example is QS9000, which was initially required for any supplier of Ford and General Motors. However, it was eventually replaced by ISO/TS 16949:2009, which was more applicable to the auto industry. It is supposed to be used in conjunction with ISO 9001, and it defines the quality management system requirements for the design and development, production, installation, and service of automotive-related products.[46]

Case Review Note

Company-Specific Standards   Individual companies also set their own standards for suppliers to meet if they are going to continue to supply them. A good example is Samsonite's efforts to bring the output of its Eastern European suppliers up to its own quality standards. Toyota is another company that works aggressively with its suppliers to ensure delivery of high-quality parts based on what it deems acceptable. In the service sector, global public accounting firms, such as KPMG and PWC, have set high audit practices that they expect their affiliates around the world to use. This is always complicated since public accounting firms are an association of individual national partnerships operating under one name, but the audit of a multinational client must be performed to high standards.

Supplier Networks

Sourcing—the process of a firm having inputs supplied to it from outside suppliers (both domestic and foreign) for the production process.

Global sourcing and production strategies can be better understood by taking a look at Figure 17.4. **Sourcing** is a firm's process of obtaining a supply of inputs (raw materials and parts) for production. Figure 17.4 illustrates the basic operating-environment

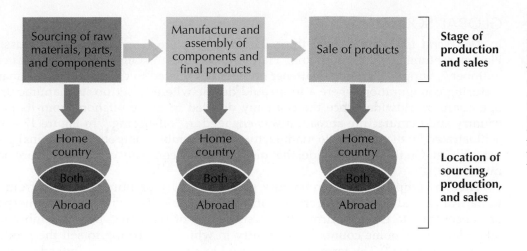

FIGURE 17.4 Global Sourcing and Production Strategy

When a company wants to *source* raw materials, parts, or components as a function of its global strategy, it's faced with some key decisions. It may, for example, decide to source components at home, assemble them abroad, and then export the final product to the home market, to foreign markets, or to both.

choices (home country or any foreign country) by stage in the production process (sourcing of raw materials and parts, manufacture and assembly of final products). Global sourcing is the first step in the process of materials management, which includes sourcing, inventory management, and transportation between suppliers, manufacturers, and customers.

From a supplier network perspective, auto companies are good examples. Ford assembles some of its models in Hermosillo, Mexico, and ships them into the United States for end-use consumers. Some of these models are designed by Mazda, a Japanese company, and use some Japanese parts. Ford can purchase parts manufactured in Japan and ship them to the United States for final assembly and sale in the U.S. market, or it can have Japanese- and U.S.-made parts shipped to Mexico for final assembly and sale in the United States and Mexico. For Mexican assembly, some of the parts come from the United States, some from Japan, and a small percentage from Mexico.

A Case in Point: A Loaf of Whole-Grain White Bread Although global sourcing is often linked with high-tech and complex products, the process affects even the low-cost products we use and consume every day. Take U.S.-based Sara Lee's whole-grain white bread. To make this bread, Sara Lee acquires ingredients from a variety of suppliers, nearly a third of whom are located in foreign countries. Its guar gum, used to keep the bread moist, is a powder that comes from the guar-plant seedpods grown in India. Calcium propionate, a powdery mold inhibitor that is manufactured in several countries, is sourced in the Netherlands. Honey, used as a natural sweetener, is purchased from suppliers in the United States, China, Vietnam, Brazil, Uruguay, India, Canada, Mexico, and Argentina. Sara Lee sources from several different countries besides the United States because the U.S. supply can often run short. Flour enrichments to replenish the vitamins lost in the milling process come from China. Due to industry consolidation, suppliers of flour enrichments are limited. Beta-carotene, an artificial coloring used to provide color to the bread and crust, is sourced from Switzerland, although it is available in many countries. Vitamin D3 is sourced from China, while wheat gluten comes from several countries, including France, Poland, Russia, the Netherlands, and Australia.[47]

With its ingredient sources spread all over the globe, Sara Lee must manage its supply chain carefully to ensure timeliness, safety, and quality. So it has centralized its global ingredients purchasing by consolidating its previously scattered procurement operations into a single division known as the "nerve center" located at company headquarters. Purchasing specialists monitor weather patterns, commodity trends, and energy prices. They also communicate and work closely with Sara Lee's diverse base of suppliers—in some cases even investing money in suppliers' operations to ensure that they are complying with U.S. food safety standards.[48]

GLOBAL SOURCING

In *The World Is Flat*, there are three flatteners that are relevant to this discussion: Flattener Number 5, Outsourcing; Flattener Number 6, Offshoring; and Flattener Number 7, Supply-Chaining. Flattener number 6 is related to the discussion on manufacturing configuration where a firm could decide where to set up its manufacturing operations worldwide. Once the company decided to move offshore from its home country and manufacture abroad, it was engaged in "offshoring." In Figure 17.4, that is illustrated by the decision to manufacture and assemble components and final products abroad. On the sourcing side, that means that the company can manufacture parts internally.

Companies can manufacture parts internally or purchase them from external manufacturers.

Thus, a company can manufacture parts internally or purchase them from external (unrelated) manufacturers. It can also assemble its own products internally or subcontract to external firms; the manufacture of parts and final assembly may take place in its home country, the country in which it is trying to sell the product, or a third country.[49] The term *sourcing* is used in a variety of ways. **Outsourcing,** for instance, refers to a situation in which one company externalizes a process or function to another business. This most often occurs with the IT function but is also being used in other areas, such as research, service centers, and even accounting and tax functions. In addition to *offshore manufacturing*, another type of offshoring occurs when a company moves part of its business processes outside its home country but internalizes the function rather than outsourcing it to another firm, such as setting up its own R&D facilities in another country or where a U.S.-based public accounting firm sets up a branch of its tax practice in India. Outsourcing can be domestic or offshore.

Another way to look at outsourcing is Flattener number 7, **supply-chaining.** This is where a company decides to outsource its parts, or components, or products or even its manufacturing to an external company. One example is Walmart, which purchases

FIGURE 17.5   Outsourcing

Source: Aaron Bacall/Cartoon Stock

"I think the only reason my job hasn't been outsourced is because nobody knows what I do around here."

its products from external suppliers, both domestic and international. Another example is where an auto company, such as Toyota, purchases its parts from external companies, such as DENSO. Supply-chaining is slightly different from traditional outsourcing, which focuses more on a business process. Supply-chaining is far more extensive and complicated since it relates more directly to the final product the company sells to customers.

Sourcing in the home country enables companies to avoid numerous problems, such as language differences, long distances and lengthy supply lines, exchange-rate fluctuations, wars and insurrections, strikes, politics, tariffs, and complex transportation channels. However, for many companies, domestic sources may be unavailable or may be more expensive than foreign sources. In Japan, foreign procurement is critical because nearly all of the country's uranium, bauxite, nickel, crude oil, iron ore, copper, and coking coal are imported, as well as about 30 percent of its agricultural products. Japanese trading companies came into being expressly to acquire the raw materials needed to fuel Japan's manufacturing.

Procter & Gamble has also found that sourcing chemicals from a variety of suppliers abroad is necessary to provide flexibility in a global environment of volatile energy prices. By diversifying its chemical supplier base, P&G plans on being able to switch procurement between different suppliers as energy prices shift in different regions.[50]

> Using domestic sources for raw materials and components allows a company to avoid problems with language differences, distance, currency, politics, and tariffs, as well as other problems.

Why Global Sourcing?   Companies pursue global sourcing strategies for a number of reasons:

> Companies outsource abroad to lower costs and improve quality, among other reasons.

- To reduce costs through cheaper labor, laxer work rules, and lower land and facilities costs
- To improve quality
- To increase exposure to worldwide technology
- To improve the delivery-of-supplies process
- To strengthen the reliability of supply by supplementing domestic suppliers with foreign ones
- To gain access to materials that are only available abroad, possibly because of technical specifications or product capabilities
- To establish a presence in a foreign market
- To satisfy offset requirements
- To react to competitors' offshore sourcing practices[51]

The reasons given here to engage in global sourcing are similar to the benefits to FDI discussed in Chapter 14. Whether the suppliers are company-owned or independent firms, MNEs can take advantage of the location-specific advantages in foreign countries.

In some ways, however, global sourcing is more expensive than domestic sourcing. For example, transportation and communications cost more, and companies may have to pay broker and agent fees. Given the longer length of supply lines, it often takes more time to get components from abroad, and lead times are less certain. This problem increases inventory carrying costs and makes it more difficult to get parts to the production site in time. If imported components come in with errors and need to be reworked, the cost per unit will rise, and some components may have to be shipped back to the supplier.

Concerns in Global Sourcing   One concern with global sourcing is quality and safety. In 2008, more than 20 countries banned Chinese dairy products because of contaminated milk that killed four infants and left over 50,000 people sick.[52] Witness also the highly publicized recalls of tainted pet food and toothpaste, defective tires, and toys with traces of lead in their paint that were produced in China. Regulators and inspectors closed 180 food plants and uncovered more than 23,000 food safety violations,[53] forcing the government to admit that 20 percent of China's consumer goods have failed safety inspections.

A major challenge with these issues is finding the problem. Supply chains have become so long and complex that buyers can't be sure who the original producer is.[54] In Chapter 5, we mentioned about the problem IKEA faced when it was accused of exploiting child labor by purchasing carpets in India and Pakistan from suppliers who were using child labor. IKEA had to make a more concerted effort to find out what suppliers were doing and require them to live up to high hiring standards to eliminate the abuse of child labor.

Companies must also pay attention to natural disasters that can affect countries where they get their goods. The earthquake and tsunami that hit Japan in 2011 was not only disastrous for those who live there, but it also affected those who relied on goods from factories that were destroyed. The auto industry was particularly hit hard. Many automakers relied on Hitachi to supply airflow sensors. Unfortunately, the Hitachi factory in Japan incurred a lot of damage during the disaster. General Motors halted some of its production and Peugeot-Citroën reduced production because of the airflow sensor shortage. Ford was keeping an hourly watch on its supply so that it could keep tabs on its airflow sensor inventory. Other parts, such as LCD chips that are used to monitor the fuel, were also hard to come by after the tsunami and earthquake. One estimate claimed that "about one-third of vehicle production globally [was] expected to grind to a halt." Automakers soon realized how quickly their supply chain could be disrupted due to forces that were outside of their control.[55]

MAJOR SOURCING CONFIGURATIONS

Vertical Integration   **Vertical integration** occurs when a company owns the entire supplier network or at least a significant part of it. The company may have to purchase raw materials from outside suppliers, but it produces the most expensive parts itself. Integrating vertically can reduce transaction costs (finding suppliers, selling output, negotiating contracts, monitoring contracts, settling disputes with unrelated companies) by internalizing the different levels in the value chain.[56]

Industrial Clusters   Outsourcing through **industrial clusters** is an alternative way to reduce transportation and transaction costs. Under clustering, buyers and suppliers locate close to each other to facilitate doing business. For example, Dell established an assembly operation in the Multimedia Supercorridor in Malaysia, where it is close to its key suppliers.

Japanese Keiretsus   Japanese *keiretsus* are groups of independent companies that work together to manage the flow of goods and services along the entire value chain.[57] Toyota's highly coordinated supplier network is among the most successful and well known of the Japanese *keiretsus* and a good example of industrial clustering. It borders on vertical integration, because parts suppliers tend to set up shop close to Toyota's assembly operations, and Toyota usually has an ownership interest in them. However, recent changes in its global markets and price pressures resulting from the high cost of steel and the strong yen have caused the company to start looking beyond its closely knit supplier base in Japan. To meet its goal of cutting costs for buying car parts by 30 percent—an objective outlined in its "Construction of Cost Competitiveness for the 21st Century" program—Toyota is pressuring its *keiretsu* suppliers by benchmarking them to China's cheaper suppliers and by courting suppliers outside Japan. These outside suppliers are leaping at the chance of breaking into the supplier network of the world's second-largest automaker.[58]

Concept Check

In discussing "Taking Control: Foreign Direct Investment" in Chapter 14, we define internalization as the self-handling of operations (that is, by keeping them internal to the company). We point out the genesis of this concept in transactions cost theory, which holds that when there's a decision to be made between handling something internally and contracting with someone else to handle it, companies should opt for the lower-cost alternative. As we suggest later in this chapter, make-or-buy decisions invite the application of this principle.

Major outsourcing configurations

- Vertical integration.
- Outsourcing through industrial clusters.
- Other outsourcing.

THE MAKE-OR-BUY DECISION

MNE managers struggle with a dilemma: Which production activities should be performed internally and which ones could be subcontracted to independent companies? This is the *make-or-buy decision*. In the case of subcontracting, they must also decide whether the activities should be carried out in the home market or abroad. It's like developing a strategy that involves the three flatteners: outsourcing, offshoring, and supply-chaining.

In deciding whether to make or buy, MNEs can focus on those parts that are critical to the product and that they are particularly good at making. They can outsource parts when suppliers have a distinct comparative advantage, such as greater scale, lower cost structure, or stronger performance incentives. They can also use outsourcing as an implied threat to underperforming employees: Improve, or we move the business elsewhere.[59]

In determining whether to make or buy, the MNE needs to determine the design and manufacturing capabilities of potential suppliers compared to its own capabilities. If the supplier has a clear advantage, management needs to decide what it would cost to catch up to the best suppliers and whether it would make sense to do so.

SUPPLIER RELATIONS

Supplier relationships are very important but sometimes complicated, especially for MNEs trying to manage them around the world. The CEO of U.S.-based MNE John Deere stated,

Point ▷ **Should Firms Outsource Innovation?**

Point **Yes** Firms should outsource innovative processes if it will allow them to maintain their focus and position themselves effectively in the roiling high-tech and electronics industries. More and more companies are coming to realize the advantages of doing so. Suppliers are taking on such responsibilities as designing and manufacturing prototypes, converting them into workable products, upgrading mature products, conducting quality tests, putting together user manuals, and selecting parts vendors. The designs of 65 percent of PC notebooks and those of 70 percent of PDAs are outsourced. Companies such as Dell, Motorola, and Philips are buying complete designs from Asian developers. Even Boeing has collaborated with an Indian company to develop software for its 787 Dreamliner jet.

Companies willing to outsource some R&D and technological designs can experience enormous cost savings. Although innovation is key to remaining competitive, more and more firms find that their internal R&D teams aren't producing results that justify the large amount of investments in them. Thus, in the face of demanding customers and relentless competition that pressures margins, managers must find a way to reduce costs or increase R&D productivity.

Outsourcing is a viable solution. Companies can save millions by simply buying designs rather than developing them in-house. For instance, using a predesigned platform for cell phones can reduce the costs of developing them from scratch—which takes approximately $10 million and 150 engineers—by 70 percent. Furthermore, demands by retailers and customers as well as uncertain future market trends require developing a costly range of product models. Third-party developers are better equipped to handle such costs, spreading them over many buyers and possessing the expertise to develop a variety of models from a single basic design.

Outsourcing also helps get products to market faster, which is crucial where products become commodities in a matter of months. Hewlett-Packard claims that by working with partners and suppliers on designs, it now gets a new concept to the market in 60 percent less time. Critics worry that by outsourcing technology, companies are outsourcing their fonts of competitive advantage; still, outsourcing certain design and development processes allows firms to focus more on their true core competencies. Few, if any, companies plan on completely eliminating their own R&D forces, and most insist they will continue with the more proprietary R&D work.

No one company can manage everything in-house. Even the Chief Technology Officer of Nokia—a company that once prided itself on developing almost everything on its own—has stated, "Nobody can master it all." In fact, a recent survey of MNEs found that almost three-quarters of respondents believed they could boost innovation dramatically by collaborating with outsiders, even competitors.[60] The companies that will survive in the future are those able to control, efficiently and effectively, a network of partners and suppliers around the world.

Should Firms Outsource Innovation?

Counterpoint

No When it comes to outsourcing R&D, design, and development work, how does a firm know where to draw the line? How does it determine what is core intellectual property and what is commodity technology? The truth is, outsourcing turns the former into the latter, which becomes available to most anyone. Look at Toshiba. By working with South Korean chipmakers to develop its DRAM memory chips, it allowed the technology behind these components to become commoditized and is now struggling to stay ahead.[61]

Competitive advantage often depends on trade secrets that set a firm apart from its rivals. Outsourcing innovation enhances the risk that it will pass on these proprietary technologies to suppliers and partners, thereby fostering new competitors. Because suppliers rarely cooperate solely with one customer, the R&D they do for one can easily be transferred to another. Such was the case for Japanese company Sharp, which worked closely with suppliers to develop a "sixth-generation" plant for making larger flat panels for televisions. Unfortunately, its suppliers also work closely with Sharp's rivals, many of them Taiwanese companies, and not long after the completion of the plant, these competitors were constructing their own "Gen-6" facilities. Sharp now takes extra precautions, such as secretly rewriting software on some equipment and fixing machinery in-house rather than having suppliers do it.[62]

Suppliers and partners might also take what information and technology have been shared with them and become competitors themselves. After Motorola hired Taiwanese

Counterpoint

company BenQ Corp. to design and manufacture its mobile phones, BenQ began selling the phones under its own brand name in the highly competitive Chinese market, causing Motorola to terminate the contract.

Perhaps more important than giving rise to new competitors is losing competitive edge and investment incentive. Although some assert that outsourcing certain development and design work allows companies to focus more on new innovative technologies, in actuality it more often prompts companies to decrease internal R&D investments and become lazy in their pursuit of future breakthroughs, relying too much on suppliers to do their work. Jim Andrew, senior vice president of Boston Consulting Group, warns, "If the innovation starts residing in the suppliers, you could incrementalize yourself to the point where there isn't much left."

High-tech and electronics firms that outsource their innovative processes risk losing the essence of their actual business, becoming mere marketing fronts for others. It also sends a bad message to investors, who might have difficulty finding intrinsic value in a company that owns little true intellectual property and whose profits from successful products are most likely being paid out in licensing fees to the companies that actually developed them.

Much has been made of manufacturing outsourcing in the past few decades, but outsourcing innovation poses a potentially greater threat to high-tech firms that see it as a shortcut to cost savings. Looking to immediate savings is shortsighted, and firms that do so will ultimately damage their competitive positions and lose viability as true industry players.[63]

Our supplier partners have been at the heart of [our] effort to put superior value into our products...around the world and throughout the enterprise. Together with our suppliers and dealers, we are enriching the word "value" to include the very best design, quality, delivery, process and...cost, all at the same time. We know it has not been easy for suppliers and it still isn't! Following our example, suppliers have had to make major adjustments in how they do business. We've been pretty demanding on ourselves and others, but...by working together to aggressively reduce costs, increase quality, and improve delivery time, they've become stronger businesses, as well as stronger Deere suppliers. Like us, they too need a great business in order to sustain long-term success.[64]

A Case in Point: Toyota   If an MNE decides it must outsource rather than integrate vertically, it must determine how to work with suppliers. Toyota pioneered the Toyota Production System to do this. It sends a team of manufacturing experts to each key supplier to observe how the factory is organized and parts are made, then advise the firm on how to cut costs and boost quality. Toyota also commonly identifies two suppliers for each part and has them compete aggressively with each other, rewarding the best performer with the most business. However, both suppliers know they will have an ongoing relationship with Toyota and will not be dumped easily.[65]

This is a good example of the close relationships Japanese companies develop with their suppliers. It is very different from the arm's-length relationship U.S. firms and suppliers tend to have. Moreover, Toyota has been able to reduce the number of supplier relationships it develops, allowing it to focus on a few key ones and promising to give them a lot of business if they perform up to Toyota standards.

In fact, the relationship between Toyota and its suppliers is often so close that when Toyota opens up production in foreign locations, its suppliers do so as well. One major Toyota supplier, DENSO, invested $1 million to establish a new plant in Tianjin, China, to produce car navigation systems for the Toyota plant located there. It did so partly to follow Toyota there, but also because Toyota made it clear that DENSO had to match Chinese prices or lose its business. The best way for DENSO to protect its market was to move some production to China.

A Case in Point: JCPenney   The decision to work closely with suppliers requires a great deal of trust and often involves making drastic—and sometimes risky—changes. However, such changes can provide sizable strategic advantages, as happened for JCPenney and its Hong Kong–based shirt supplier, TAL Apparel Ltd. JCPenny literally allows TAL to take over some of its own processes. Rather than simply responding to orders the retailer sends, TAL tracks its sales data directly through its personally designed computer program to determine the number, sizes, colors, and styles of shirts to make, then ships the shirts directly to individual JCPenney stores, completely bypassing the retailer's warehouses.

This cooperation has resulted in quicker merchandise turnovers and an inventory level of virtually zero—a significant improvement over the eight months' worth of inventory JCPenney used to keep. TAL has also been allowed to handle market testing and style designs, which has given it the ability to respond more quickly and effectively to customer demands. With the leverage given it, TAL can roll out a new style in just four months.[66]

Of course, not all customer-supplier relationships are as collaborative as those of Toyota and JCPenney. Sometimes large customers can use their strong market presence and buying power to place additional demands on suppliers. For many years, GM has pressured its U.S. suppliers to lower costs by certain set percentages each year and then to pass those cost savings on to GM via lower prices. As it moved to increase production in China, some suppliers felt pressured to set up facilities in China to accommodate GM.[67]

The relationships MNEs establish with their suppliers are based largely on their individual competitive strategies, the nature of their products, the competitive environment they are facing, supplier capabilities, and the level of experience and trust they share with them. MNEs must consider these factors as they determine what kind of supplier relationship will best meet their needs.

THE PURCHASING FUNCTION

The purchasing agent is the link between the company's outsourcing decision and its supplier relationships. Just as companies go through stages of globalization, so does the purchasing agent's scope of responsibilities. Typically, purchasing goes through four phases before becoming "global":

1. Domestic purchasing only
2. Foreign buying based on need
3. Foreign buying as part of procurement strategy
4. Integration of global procurement strategy[68]

Phase 4 occurs when the company realizes the benefits that result from the integration and coordination of purchasing on a global basis and are most applicable to the MNE—as opposed to, say, the exporter.

Global progression in the purchasing function:

- Domestic purchasing only.
- Foreign buying based on need.
- Foreign buying as part of a procurement strategy.
- Integration of global procurement strategy.

When purchasing becomes this global, MNEs often face the centralize/decentralize dilemma. Should they allow each subsidiary to make every purchasing decision, or should they centralize all or some of them? The primary benefits of decentralization include increased production-facility control over purchases, better responsiveness to facility needs, and more effective use of local suppliers. The primary benefits of centralization are increased leverage with suppliers, better prices, eliminating administrative duplication, allowing purchasers to develop specialized knowledge in purchasing techniques, reducing the number of orders processed, and enabling purchasing to build solid supplier relationships.[69]

A Case in Point: Electrolux   Swedish appliance manufacturer Electrolux has adopted a global purchasing strategy. Despite the worldwide downturn in 2009, Electrolux had a good second quarter due largely to its cost-reduction efforts. One aspect of the strategy was offshoring production to low-cost countries. Another was the reduction of personnel costs. Still another was lowered purchasing and product costs through efficient global purchasing, which cut the cost of buying raw materials and components.[70]

Sourcing strategies in the global context:

- Assign domestic buyers for foreign purchasing.
- Use foreign subsidiaries or business agents.
- Establish international purchasing offices.
- Assign the responsibility for global sourcing to a specific business unit or units.
- Integrate and coordinate worldwide sourcing.

Major Sourcing Strategies   Companies pursue five major sourcing strategies as they move into phases 3 and 4 in the preceding list. Moving from the simple to the complex (where there is no difference between domestic and foreign sources), they are:

1. Assigning domestic buyer(s) for international purchasing
2. Using foreign subsidiaries or business agents
3. Establishing international purchasing offices
4. Assigning responsibility for global sourcing to a specific business unit or units
5. Integrating and coordinating global sourcing[71]

Some companies go even further than the last step and coordinate worldwide purchasing with competitor companies. Two automakers, Nissan and Renault, have saved millions of dollars in production costs by entering into joint purchasing agreements with each other. Approximately 40 percent of the parts they use in their vehicles are the same, and the two are looking to increase this amount to 70 percent to achieve further cost reductions.[72] The key is for managers to select the best supplier, establish a solid relationship, and continuously evaluate the supplier's performance to ensure the best price, highest quality, and on-time delivery.

Inventory Management

Distance, time, and uncertainty in foreign environments cause foreign sourcing to complicate inventory management.

Whether a company decides to source parts internally or externally or from domestic or foreign sources, it needs to manage the flow and storage of inventory. This is true of raw materials and parts sourced from suppliers, work-in-process and finished-goods inventory inside the manufacturing plant, and finished goods stored at a distribution center (such as the centralized European warehouse for Samsonite).

LEAN MANUFACTURING AND JUST-IN-TIME SYSTEMS

Lean manufacturing—a productive system whose focus is on optimizing processes through the philosophy of continual improvement.

One reason why companies might hesitate when considering whether to source parts from foreign suppliers is because of *lean manufacturing*, "a productive system whose focus is on optimizing processes through the philosophy of continual improvement." It embodies the ideas of waste reduction and optimizing quality processes.[73] Because it relies on the efficiencies gained by reducing waste and defects, lean manufacturing is also closely tied to quality management.

Just-in-time approach to inventory management—a system that sources raw materials and parts just as they are needed in the manufacturing process.

An important element of lean manufacturing is just-in-time (JIT) inventory management, which focuses on "reducing inefficiency and unproductive time in the production process to improve continuously the process and the quality of the product or service."[74]

The JIT system gets raw materials, parts, and components to the buyer "just in time" for use, sparing companies the cost of storing large inventories.

That is what Dell hoped to accomplish in its Irish plant by having parts delivered just as they were to enter the production process and then go out the door to consumers as soon as the computers were built. However, the use of JIT means that parts must have few defects and must arrive on time. That is why companies need to develop solid supplier relationships to ensure good quality and delivery times if JIT is to work—and why industrial clustering is a popular way of linking more closely with suppliers.

Risks in Foreign Sourcing   Foreign sourcing can create big risks for companies that use lean manufacturing and JIT, because interruptions in the supply line can cause havoc. MNEs are becoming experts at meeting the requirements of JIT: ships that take two weeks to cross the Pacific dock within an hour of scheduled arrival, factories that are able to more easily fill small orders, and so on. However, because of distances alone, the supply chain is open to more problems and delays.[75]

> It is hard to combine foreign sourcing and JIT production without having safety stocks of inventory on hand—which defeats the concept of JIT.

As mentioned earlier in the chapter, companies such as Toyota that have set up manufacturing and assembly facilities overseas to service local markets have practically forced their domestic parts suppliers to move overseas as well to allow the companies to continue with JIT manufacturing. That is why so many Japanese parts suppliers have moved to the United States and Mexico to be near their major customers.

A company's inventory management strategy—especially in terms of stock sizes and whether JIT will be used—determines the frequency of needed shipments. The less frequent the delivery, the more likely the need to store inventory somewhere. Because JIT requires delivery just as the inventory is to be used, some concession must be made for inventory arriving from foreign suppliers. Sometimes that means adjusting the arrival time to a few days before use rather than a few hours. Kawasaki Motors Corp., U.S.A., carries a minimum of three days' inventory on parts coming from Japan, with an average inventory of five days.[76]

U.S. Synthetics, a company based in Utah, used to ship some of its parts from Eastern Africa. However, these shipments became unreliable because of the pirates in Somalia. These pirates hold ships carrying goods hostage; they then demand a ransom in return for what they have stolen. U.S. Synthetics now makes these parts in house so they don't have to worry about when the shipments will arrive.

The _Kanban_ System   One system pioneered by Toyota to facilitate its JIT strategies is the _kanban system. Kanban_ is Japanese for "card" or "visible record." Kanban cards are used to control the flow of production through a factory. In the system used by Toyota, components are shipped to a plant just before they need to go into production, where they are kept in a bin with an attached card identifying the quantity of items in the bin. When the assembly process begins, a production-order card signifies that a bin needs to be moved to the assembly line. When the bin is emptied, it is moved to a storage area and replaced with a full bin. The kanban card is then removed from the empty bin and is used to order a replacement from the supplier.

> A _kanban_ system facilitates JIT by using cards to control the flow of production through a factory.

FOREIGN TRADE ZONES

In recent years, **foreign trade zones** have become more popular as an intermediate step in the process between import and final use. FTZs are areas in which domestic and imported merchandise can be stored, inspected, and manufactured free from formal customs procedures until the goods leave the zones. They are intended to encourage companies to locate in the country by allowing them to defer duties, pay fewer duties, or avoid certain duties completely. Sometimes inventory is stored in an FTZ until it needs to be used for domestic manufacture. As noted earlier, one of the problems with JIT is the length of the supply line when relying on global sourcing, possibly causing either the

> Foreign trade zones (FTZs)—special locations for storing domestic and imported inventory in order to avoid paying duties until the inventory is used in production or sold.

FIGURE 17.6

Source: Kjell Nilsson-Maki/Cartoon
Stock

buyer or the supplier to stockpile inventory somewhere until it is needed in the manufacturing process. One place to stockpile inventory is in a warehouse in an FTZ.

General-Purpose Zones and Subzones   A general-purpose FTZ is usually established near a port of entry, such as a shipping port, a border crossing, or an airport, and usually consists of a distribution facility or an industrial park used primarily for warehousing and distribution. A subzone is usually physically separate from a general-purpose zone but under the same administrative structure, commonly located at a manufacturing facility. Since 1982, the major growth in FTZs has been in subzones rather than in general-purpose zones, because companies have sought to defer duties on parts that are foreign-sourced until they need to be used in the production process.

Dubai in the United Arab Emirates has established 18 different free zones, including Jebel Ali Free Zone Authority, Dubai Healthcare City, Dubai International Financial Center, Dubai Media City, and Dubai Internet City. The advantage of these free zones is that they allow 100 percent ownership of your enterprise, 100 percent repatriation of capital and profits, no minimum capital investment, no corporate or personal tax, and no need for a local partner. Different zones focus on different industries. For example, the major banks, financial, and law firms are in the DIFC; CNN, BBC, CNBC, and Dow Jones Thomson Reuters are in the Media Center; and Cox Internet, Hughes Satellite and Internet, and ATT Internet are in Internet City. Jebel Ali Free Zone includes standard assembly operations that one would find in any similar free zone. For example, Unilever has a major tea factory in the Free Zone that is one of their largest in the world. It receives raw materials from different countries, packages them in the Free Zone, and ships them around the world.[77]

The major growth in subzones in the United States has been in the automobile industry, especially in the Midwest. Subzone activity is spreading to other industries, especially shipbuilding, pharmaceuticals, and home appliances, and is becoming more heavily oriented to manufacturing and assembly than was originally envisioned. Merchandise in U.S. FTZs may be assembled, exhibited, cleaned, manipulated, manufactured, mixed, processed, relabeled, repackaged, repaired, salvaged, sampled, stored, tested, displayed, and destroyed.[78]

The United States has about 250 general-purpose zones and more than 450 subzones in all 50 states and Puerto Rico. Over $300 billion a year in merchandise is handled in the FTZs, and $19 billion is exported from them each year.[79] FTZs in the United States have been used primarily as a means of providing greater flexibility as to when and how customs duties are paid. However, their use in the export business has been expanding.

The benefits to a zone user are:

- No duties or quota charges on goods imported into a zone and re-exported

- Customs duties and federal excise tax deferred on imports until taken from the zone and used in the domestic market

- Duties reduced if foreign inputs that enter the zone at one duty are higher than the duty would have been on the finished product leaving the zone for domestic sales (called an inverted tariff)

- Streamlined customs procedures

- Elimination of state and local inventory taxes if the goods are held in the zone for export[80]

TRANSPORTATION NETWORKS

For a firm, the transportation of goods in an international context is extremely complicated in terms of documentation, choice of carrier (air or ocean), and the decision of whether to establish its own transportation department or outsource to a third-party intermediary. Transportation is a crucial element of a logistics system. The key is to link together suppliers and manufacturers on the one hand and manufacturers and final consumers on the other. Along the way, the company has to determine its warehouse configuration. For example, in providing food items to its franchises around the world, McDonald's has warehouses in different countries to service different geographic areas.

Transportation links together suppliers, companies, and customers.

A Case in Point: Panalpina   As outsourcing of both manufacturing and other supply-chain functions grows ever more popular, third-party intermediaries are essential in storing and transporting goods. They constitute an important dimension of transportation networks. Panalpina is a Swiss forwarding and logistics services provider that focuses on intercontinental airfreight and sea freight, as well as other aspects of supply-chain management. Using its main hub in Luxembourg to connect to 500 branches in 80 countries throughout the world and partners in another 60 countries, Panalpina seeks to simplify the complexity of its customers' supply chains by handling their transportation, distribution, customs brokerage, warehousing, and inventory control, as well as providing door-to-door transport insurance and real-time track-and-trace systems.[81]

One company Panalpina provides such services to is IBM and its operations in Latin America. Through its selected airfreight services provider, ASB-Air, and through the management of its local branches, Panalpina coordinates vehicles to pick up IBM products in Europe and transport them to Luxembourg. From there, the goods travel by air to the cargo center in Miami, where products destined for various locations in South America are split and reconsolidated into pallets that are then loaded directly into Panalpina's space-controlled aircraft and transferred to its own company warehouses operated by its own staff. The warehouse personnel complete all customs details, taking advantage of the on-site offices of customs authorities, and update the company's information systems with current status messages.

Looking to the

Future   Uncertainty and the Global Supply Chain

Two competing ideas have been emphasized in this chapter: first, globalization has pushed companies to establish operations abroad or to outsource to foreign suppliers to reduce costs and be closer to markets; second, the longer the supply line, the greater the risk. Since September 11, 2001, the risks of longer supply lines have increased dramatically. At any time, global political events could completely disrupt a well-organized supply chain and put a company at risk. This was demonstrated more recently in 2011 with the earthquake and tsunami in Japan.

Because some of Sara Lee's suppliers have consolidated, there are fewer options for purchasing key ingredients for Sara Lee products. What if no supplier could deliver because of political events or safety/quality concerns? Ford Motor Company's announcement that the economic slowdown was forcing it to cut its suppliers by 50 percent created a ripple effect throughout the auto industry, since suppliers tend to supply many different companies.

As a supply chain stretches and uncertainty grows, companies have to become much better at scenario building so that viable contingencies are available.

Maybe this means they will pursue more multidomestic strategies to insulate their foreign operations from other countries and allow them to be more responsive to local consumers. However, as MNEs in the developed countries respond to competitive pressures to reduce costs, they will be forced to continue sourcing abroad, either in company-owned facilities or from third parties—at least until nobody can source abroad.

That's probably a little extreme, but the important thing is to continue to look at the "what-ifs." What if there is no secure air or ocean transportation available to move goods? What if the goods can move, but there are delays? What if terrorists begin to use the global supply chain of legitimate companies to contaminate products or move hazardous materials? Clearly, the future appears much more complicated than current or past conditions, so let the manager beware. These uncertainties as well as high oil and other transportation costs as well as escalating costs in China, the manufacturing floor of the world, are causing many firms to look closer to home for their sourcing decisions. ■

Once customs has been cleared, an electronic data transfer is sent to IBM while the goods are shipped to IBM warehouses. Panalpina maintains control of the goods throughout the entire process, using electronic documentation and tracking to maintain real-time data and keep IBM informed. In this example, you can see all of the elements of transportation networks that are so essential in international logistics.[82]

The logistics management that companies like Panalpina engage in is very detail oriented, requiring the ability to gather, track, and process large quantities of information. To be effective, logistics companies need to implement key technologies, including communication systems, satellite tracking systems, bar-coding applications, and automated materials-handling systems.[83] It is interesting to note how important the Flatteners are in this part of the supply chain network and how critical the third-party logistics companies are to ensure the smooth flow of products around the world.

 CASE   Nokero: Lighting The World

Professor Manuel Serapio
Business School and Institute for International Business,
University of Colorado Denver prepared this case.

In June 2011, Steve Katsaros, founder and CEO of Nokero, was contemplating how to build on his company's accomplishments during the last 12 months. Nokero, a marketer of solar light bulbs, has emerged as a successful born-global social enterprise.[84] During

Boys at an orphanage in Kisii, Kenya, use the Nokera solar light to read at night. While the brightness of the N200 light is not the same as traditional LED lighting, it's brightness is five times brighter than that of a kerosene lantern, which is commonly used in developing countries where electricity is scarce or nonexistent.

Source: Institute for International Business

the past year, Nokero had sold more than 150,000 solar light bulbs to over 90 countries. The company has also started to attract significant media attention. *CNN, The New York Times* (online), *The Washington Post, Fast Company, Popular Mechanics, Popular Science, The Denver Post*, and *Engadget,* to name just a few, have featured Nokero's story of doing well by doing good as a provider of environmentally friendly solar lighting to the world's poor.

While Katsaros was very pleased with his company's overall performance during the past year, he was concerned with three fundamental questions. First, what market segments should the company focus on for profitable growth? Several opportunities had propelled Nokero's sales in recent months. The company has made tens of thousands of dollars in small and sample order sales through the company's website from thousands of customers in North America and abroad. Additionally, Nokero has entered into or is in the process of signing distributorship agreements in about a dozen countries. For example, Nokero has engaged Westinghouse Lighting Corporation to distribute its solar lights in selected markets in Latin America. Finally, governments, international agencies, and non-governmental organizations have partnered with or approached Nokero on collaborative social programs relating to environmental sustainability, renewable energy, poverty alleviation, and disaster and relief projects. Katsaros wanted to make sure that Nokero explores the best pathways for growth in both the social enterprise sector and commercial channels.

Second, where should the company grow? Currently, Nokero has pursued an opportunistic sales approach. The company's major customers are in diverse and dispersed locations in Ghana, South Africa, Fiji, Mexico, India, Nigeria, Vanuatu, Haiti, Kenya, and other markets. Although practical business sense may dictate that international new ventures like Nokero focus on a few markets at a time, Katsaros was hesitant to pursue this approach since it contradicted the company's social mission of reaching out to as many people as possible that could benefit from Nokero's solar light bulbs.

Third, how should Nokero manage its supply chain to support the company's growth? Katsaros understood that the company's future success hinges on its ability to reach its customers. In turn, this requires Nokero to address critical global supply chain issues effectively. How can the company serve different market and customer segments that are dispersed in many countries? How can Nokero bring down distribution costs to make the product more affordable to its customers? What should the company do to address the "last mile issue" of reaching customers in the most remote locations?

The Nokero Story

Identifying the Opportunity

Nokero (short for "No Kerosene") was established by Steve Katsaros in order to develop safe and environmentally friendly solar products that eliminated the need for harmful and polluting fuels used for light and heat around the world and are affordable to the customers that need them. Katsaros saw a significant opportunity in developing a solar light product to replace kerosene and diesel lanterns. Katsaros described the opportunity as follows:

> *In many parts of the world, non-electrified dwellings and workplaces are illuminated by kerosene or diesel lamps, candles or wood. There are electric options but most are expensive, or fragile, or don't have replaceable, rechargeable batteries.*

More than 1.6 billion people live without electricity. Of these, 704 million people are in South Asia, 550 million in sub-Saharan Africa, and 225 million in Southeast Asia. Many of these people live in remote areas and rely on kerosene and diesel-fueled lanterns for their lighting. By substituting solar light bulbs for kerosene lanterns, these people are able to re-coup their purchase price within a period of 12 days to two months, depending on market forces. Moreover, the replacement of kerosene lanterns with solar light bulbs generates significant environmental and health benefits. Every solar light that replaces a kerosene lantern saves three-quarters of a ton of CO_2 emissions over the five-year lifetime of the product. According to the World Bank, daily exposure to emissions from kerosene lanterns is like smoking two packs of cigarettes per day

Inventing the Solution: The N100 and N200

Katsaros invented the first Nokero light bulb (the Nokero N100) on January 24, 2010, drawing a sketch of the idea on a notepad. Four days later, he filed a U.S. patent on the N100 that was eventually granted in February 2011. Production on the light bulb commenced in June 2010 and a new model, the N200, was introduced in November 2010.

The Nokero solar light bulb is a small, lightweight, portable light, shaped like a light bulb for easy identification. The bulb hangs in the sun to charge and can be hung or laid on its side at night. A "pivot" feature allows users to swivel the solar panel toward the sun to maximize charge capability. The bulb can be swiveled at night to direct light where needed. The LED lights are enclosed in the shatter-resistant bulb, do not get hot, and produce an even light.

The Nokero solar light bulb is a small, lightweight, portable light, shaped like a light bulb for easy identification. The bulb hangs in the sun to charge and can be hung or laid on its side at night. A "pivot" feature allows users to swivel the solar panel toward the sun to maximize charge capability.

Source: Institute for International Business

The N200's brightness is 13.5 lumens on high illumination and 8 lumens on low illumination. The duration of light is 6 to 8 hours on one day's charge or 12 to 16 hours on two days' charge on the low light setting. For the high light setting, the light duration is 2.5 hours on one day's charge and 5 hours on two days' charge. While the brightness is not the same as traditional LED lighting, the N200's brightness is five times brighter than that of a kerosene lantern. The N200 is shatter- and rain-proof and built to last for five years.

Nokero sells the N200 in large quantity orders (e.g., over 1,000 light bulbs) for about $6.00 (FOB China). Sample sales are priced between $15 and $20 (depending on shipping costs).

Building a Born-Global Company

A few weeks after developing the N100, Katsaros worked on Nokero's business model, package design, pricing, and manufacturing and distribution processes. In April 2010, he formed Nokero International Ltd., the operating company of Nokero.

The speed by which Nokero developed and manufactured the N100 and formed the business entity could be attributed to Katsaros' experience as an inventor and entrepreneur. He had previously licensed inventions to sports companies, such as Dynastar Skis, K2, and HaberVision, and built RevoPower, a motorized wheel for bicycles that gets 200 miles per gallon at 20 miles per hour. A BS Mechanical Engineering graduate from Purdue University, a Bard Center for Entrepreneurship certificate graduate recipient at the University of Colorado Denver, and a B.F. Goodrich Collegiate Inventors awardee, Katsaros is a patent agent registered with the U.S. Patent Office and Trademark Office, which has issued him several patents for his previous inventions.

From the start, Nokero was a born-global company with customers in different parts of the world, and co-owners and supplier partners in Hong Kong and China. Katsaros partnered with three Hong Kong–based entrepreneurs to form Nokero International Ltd. in Hong Kong. These partners, associates of Katsaros in previous businesses, provided start-up capital that represented a minority equity interest in Nokero and helped Katsaros find a strong and reliable factory supplier in China. Nokero also leveraged the HK partners' connections with the factory supplier to secure a trade financing line from the supplier. The HK partners manage Nokero's operations, including overseeing the supplier factory in China, filling large orders directly from the factory, maintaining an outsourced fulfillment center in Shenzhen, China, to supply small and sample sales from all over the world, and managing the company's supply chain.

Nokero's Chinese supplier is an established factory that has significant experience and scale in consumer electronics. In solar-powered consumer electronic products alone, the supplier produces more than 30 million pieces of solar products every year. The supplier's clients include Walmart, Home Depot, Lowes, and other major retail customers in the United States and Europe.

Nokero maintains its headquarters in Denver, Colorado, where the company oversees sales and marketing, business development, web-based sales, and overall administration of the business. To help him start and grow the business, Katsaros brought two of his closest associates, Evan Husney, who serves as General Counsel and the person responsible for business development, large orders, and the establishment of Nokero's dealer network, as well as Tom Boyd, who manages the company's corporate and marketing communications.

Creating Groundswell Support

Widespread and favorable coverage by traditional and social media outlets has been instrumental in getting the Nokero story out to as many people as possible. A key moment came with a six-minute daytime television segment featuring Katsaros and Nokero with Ali Velshi on the CNN show *The Big Eye*. Not only did the coverage reach a global audience, it helped legitimize Nokero to those who were interested in solar lighting in general and Nokero's products in particular.

In 2010–2011, Nokero has benefited from dozens of stories by traditional print media and TV networks and hundreds of stories from news and social media, including sources from abroad such as O Globo (Brazil), *Sydney Times* (Australia), Air France, and Sudwestrundfunk (Germany). In a story titled "A Solar Light Bulb May Light the Way," *The New York Time*s noted that "Where Nokero's bulb appears to break ground is in its design; it is small enough to carry, self-contained, highly durable and features a replaceable battery." In another article, "The Power of Light," *The Denver Post* lauded the environmental, health, and safety benefits of Nokero's products and the social entrepreneurial aspects of the company's business model.

Social media, particularly blogs, have been a powerful way for the company to create community groundswell support. In July 2010, an influential London businessman offered support to the company, an offer that led to an endorsement of Nokero's products by popular soccer star Didier Drogba of Cote D' Ivoire. Social media have also been instrumental in creating awareness and mobilizing community participation in social initiatives championed by Nokero and other partners. For example, Nokero has partnered with Project C.U.R.E on a buy-give program. Under this program, customers who buy a solar light bulb from Nokero can give a second light bulb to Project C.U.R.E. that the latter will distribute to people in need throughout the world.

Similarly, filmmaker Kurt Mann's organization, American Green, brought light bulbs to Haiti to help victims who have been devastated by the country's earthquake. Nokero and America Green have jointly set up a program, "The Gift of Light," for people to donate light bulbs to Haiti. Most recently, Nokero responded to the earthquake in Japan by instituting a program that led to the donation of over 2,000 light bulbs within a few weeks after the catastrophe.

Growing the Business

Opportunities in Working with Governments and International Organizations

Several governments, international non-governmental organizations, and international agencies have approached Katsaros and Nokero on a number of potential large-scale partnerships and projects. A group out of France is exploring the sales and distribution of solar light bulbs to Africa by leveraging a carbon-credit-based financing program. The same group successfully executed a similar program with fluorescent bulbs. Likewise, the governments of Mexico and Congo are pursuing the idea of buying Nokero's products for distribution to people in their respective countries who are earning less than $2 per day (i.e., bottom of the pyramid consumers) and do not have access to electricity.

Katsaros and his team have also initiated discussions with international agencies, such as the United Nations, USAID, and various international foundations. While governments and international organization sales represent attractive opportunities for Nokero, they have posed three major challenges. First, the sales cycle in these organizations tends to be long and requires specialized skills and major business development resources. To address this challenge, Nokero has brought on board a consultant who is knowledgeable and networked with these kinds of entities.

Second, the company would have to significantly scale production to fill larger orders from these governments. The governments that Nokero has been dealing with have talked about buying not thousands but *millions* of light bulbs. In addition, these governments are also likely to pressure Nokero to lower its price. Third, selling to these governments portends production and supply chain challenges.

Can Nokero continue to supply all of its light bulb orders from a single factory location in China? Should the company maintain a fulfillment warehouse in Africa, Asia, and Latin America? And how should the company help these governments address the last mile issue of accessing people in the most remote locations?

Opportunities in the Social Enterprise Sector

As previously mentioned, Nokero has been engaged in partnership programs with various social enterprises, such as Project C.U.R.E. and American Green. Social enterprises have actively sought out Nokero for possible partnerships. Katsaros validated this strong interest when he attended his first international trade show for Nokero, The AID and International Development Forum, in May 2011 in Washington, DC. Nokero's booth was one of the most popular in the trade show and Katsaros received dozens of inquiries and sales leads from social enterprise attendees during the Forum.

In contrast to working with governments and international organizations, partnerships with social enterprises entail a different set of challenges for Nokero. The programs championed by these partners are quite diverse, the customers that they serve are widely dispersed, and their order amounts tend to be smaller—although purchases are made more frequently. All of these considerations require different order and fulfillment mechanisms in Nokero's supply chain. While these processes may be more demanding, Katsaros is committed to working with micro-business and the social enterprise sector since serving the people that these enterprises reach out to is at the core of Nokero's mission.

Opportunities in Commercial Channels

Nokero has driven sales through the commercial channel in two ways: through direct, web-based sales and through licensed distributors. Customers order directly through Nokero's website (Nokero.com) and pay using a credit card or an account through PayPal. Once an order is placed and payment is verified, the order is added to a sales spreadsheet and is exported nightly to Nokero's fulfillment center, which handles the order deliveries. Nokero fills orders using Hong Kong Post or Singapore Post. The customer can then log on to Nokero's website to track the shipment of its package and order history by entering the email address that it used to place the order.

In its first year, Nokero was successful in selling tens of thousands of dollars worth of light bulbs to more than 90 countries through its website. Accordingly, one major opportunity that Katsaros sees in this channel is sales conversion—i.e., converting people who have placed sample orders to sign up as distributors. To date, Nokero has no strategy or process in place for such sales conversion other than a form on its website that invites people to apply to become distributors.

The company's largest customers are distributors, associations, and individuals that have ordered thousands of light bulbs, including Anzocare (South African Alternative Energy Association), Westinghouse Lighting Corporation, and three major individual distributors from Zambia, Ghana, and Fiji. Additional distributors are in place in Nigeria, Cote D' Ivoire, Mali, Burkina Faso, Vietnam, Tanzania, Vanuatu, and other countries. Large commercial orders are filled directly from Nokero's factory in China via the port of Shenzhen, China. Nokero's outsourced fulfillment partner in Shenzhen, China, serves smaller orders.

How should Nokero build its distribution footprint in international markets? Should the company focus its expansion in one or a few regions at a time? If so, what regions should the company emphasize? What performance standards or metrics should Nokero put in place for distributors? A number of potential distributors have asked Nokero for exclusive rights in key geographic markets. Should Nokero grant exclusive country distribution rights?

Addressing Supply Chain Issues

As previously mentioned, Katsaros understands that the success of Nokero's business hinges on its ability to address critical supply chain issues. Katsaros and his Hong Kong partners must ensure that the company is ready to fill both large and concentrated orders from government and international organizations as well as sample and small order sales from hundreds of customers that are geographically dispersed. At this point, Nokero needs to evaluate whether it should bring on board a second or third supplier that will support its major supplier partner in China. Moreover, it needs to evaluate the locations of the company's fulfillment centers. Will it be more desirable to have distributed fulfillment centers in closer proximity to its customers in Africa and Latin America to support its fulfillment center in Shenzhen, China?

In addition, Katsaros needs to address some operational issues related to supply chain management. These include the following:

1. *Payments and Pricing of Shipping Charges.* Currently, customers who order through the Web site pay by credit card or PayPal. However, PayPal is not accepted in all countries, particularly in some markets that represent attractive markets for Nokero in Asia and Africa. In addition, determining the correct amount to charge for shipping has been a challenge since Nokero's fulfillment center does not provide a live feed with updated international pricing of shipping charges, and in general it is extremely difficult to reliably estimate the cost of shipping small orders to all the regions of the world.

2. *Order Tracking.* Tracking information usually stops once the package has left China (i.e., the Chinese factory location or fulfillment center in Shenzhen) making the tracking information limited and less useful.

3. *Timely Delivery.* Orders are filled and shipped in a timely manner from Nokero's factory and fulfillment center. However, the delivery process relies heavily on the timeliness and reliability of the postal system in the receiving country. In some instances, it has taken months for a sample or small order to be delivered to the customer.

4. *Last Mile Issue.* Often Nokero's customers are in remote locations that cannot be accessed by regular postal delivery. Even social enterprises and government organizations that partner with Nokero find it challenging to reach users in remote locations.

Katsaros knows that the *growth* strategy that Nokero chooses to pursue will have important implications for the company's supply-chain strategy, processes, and probable results. In turn, generating greater efficiencies in distribution and the supply chain will be critical to Nokero's ability to lower its price and make its products more affordable to its customers. Katsaros wants to ensure that Nokero effectively addresses the key strategic and tactical issues related to the management of the company's supply chain, which will in turn help the company in anticipating and capitalizing on further and faster growth in the coming years. ■

QUESTIONS

1. What market segments should the company focus on for profitable growth?
2. Where should the company grow?
3. What type of manufacturing strategy should Nokero pursue?
4. How should Nokero manage its supply chain to support the company's growth?

MyIBLab   Now that you have finished this chapter, go back to www.myiblab.com to continue practicing and applying the concepts you've learned.

SUMMARY

- A company's supply chain encompasses the coordination of materials, information, and funds from the initial raw- materials supplier to the ultimate customer.

- Logistics, or materials management, is the part of the supply-chain process that plans, implements, and controls the efficient, effective flow and storage of goods, services, and related information from the point of origin to the point of consumption to meet customers' requirements.

- The success of a global manufacturing strategy depends on compatibility, configuration, coordination, and control.

- Cost-minimization strategies and the drive for global efficiencies often force MNEs offshore to low-cost manufacturing areas, especially in Asia and Eastern Europe.

- Three broad categories of manufacturing configuration are one centralized facility, regional facilities, and multidomestic facilities. Offshoring is where the facilities are moved from the home country to another country.

- The key to making a global supply-chain system work is information. Companies are rapidly turning to the Internet as a way to link suppliers with manufacturing and eventually with end-use customers.

- Quality is defined as meeting or exceeding the expectations of customers. Quality standards can be general level (ISO 9000), industry-specific, or company-specific (AQL, zero defects, TQM, and Six Sigma).

- Total quality management (TQM) is a process that stresses customer satisfaction, employee involvement, and continuous improvements in quality while aiming for zero defects.

- Global sourcing is the process of a firm having raw materials and parts supplied to it from domestic and foreign sources. Outsourcing involves having another company do a limited function that you were doing in-house, such as payroll. That could be done domestic or offshore. Supply-chaining involves having another company make the stuff you sell—such as Walmart purchasing goods from suppliers that it sells in its stores. Suppliers can be domestic or offshore.

- Domestic sourcing allows the company to avoid problems related to language, culture, currency, tariffs, and so forth. Foreign sourcing allows the company to reduce costs and improve quality, among other things.

- Under the make-or-buy decision, companies have to decide whether to make their own parts or buy them from an independent company.

- Companies go through different purchasing phases as they become more committed to global sourcing.

- When a company sources parts from suppliers around the world, distance, time, and the uncertainty of political and economic environments can make it difficult to manage inventory flows accurately.

- Lean manufacturing and just-in-time systems focus on reducing inefficiency and unproductive time in the production process to continuously improve the process and quality of the product or service.

- The transportation system links together suppliers with manufacturers and manufacturers with customers.

KEY TERMS

acceptable quality level (AQL) (p. 649)
Deming's 14 Points (p. 650)
e-commerce (p. 648)
electronic data interchange (EDI) (p. 647)
enterprise resource planning (ERP) (p. 647)
extranet (p. 648)
foreign trade zones (FTZs) (p. 661)
industrial clusters (p. 656)

International Organization for Standardization (ISO) (p. 651)
intranet (p. 648)
logistics (or materials management) (p. 642)
offshore manufacturing (p. 643)
outsourcing (p. 654)
private technology exchange (PTX) (p. 648)

quality (p. 649)
Six Sigma (p. 651)
sourcing (p. 652)
supply chain (p. 642)
supply-chaining (p. 654)
total quality management (TQM) (p. 650)
vertical integration (p. 656)
zero defects (p. 649)

ENDNOTES

1 *Sources include the following:* Nikhil Kumar, "Samsonite IPO Size Rises to $1.3 bn," *The Independent* (London) (July 11, 2011): 34; James Ashton, "The Pounds 90 Million Man in a Suitcase," *Sunday Times* (London) (June 19, 2011): 6; F. De Beule and D. Van Den Bulcke, "The International Supply Chain Management of Samsonite Europe," Discussion Paper No. 1998/E/34, Centre for International Management and Development, University of Antwerp (1998); "About Samsonite: History," retrieved October 15, 2009, from www.corporate.samsonite.com/samsonite/about/history; "Company Briefing Book," *Wall Street Journal*, retrieved January 27, 2000, from www.wsj.com; *Samsonite Quarterly Report*, SEC Form 10-Q, 2002; "Samsonite to Be Sold," *New York Times* (July 6, 2007): C4; "Samsonite Fiscal Year 2007 Annual 10-K," Samsonite (January 31, 2007); "Samsonite Introduces POINT A Franchise Concept," *Samsonite: Life's a Journey* (October 1, 2002), retrieved from www.samsonite.com/samsonite/?404= http://www.samsonite.com/global/globl_pressrelease_europ5.jsp; Helia Ebrahimi, "Samsonite Bags Debt-for-Equity Rescue Deal," *Sunday Telegraph* (May 31, 2009); Godfrey Deeny, "Y-3 Seals Luggage License with Samsonite," *Fashion Wire Daily* (May 7, 2009); Samsonite Corporation, *Hoover's Company Records,* 40046, retrieved July 30, 2009, from *Entrepreneurship* (Document ID 168172041); Chris V. Nicholson, "IPO Values Samsonite at $1.5 Billion," *The New York Times* (June 1, 2011): B9.

2 "The Fourth Annual Global Survey of Supply Chain Progress," Computer Sciences Corporation (CSC) and *Supply Chain Management Review* (2006); Darrell Rigby, "Management Tools 2005," *Bain & Company* (2005): 58.

3 Deloitte & Touche, "Energizing the Supply Chain," *The Review* (January 17, 2000): 1.

4 F. Robert Jacobs and Richard B. Chase, *Operations and Supply Management: The Core*, 2nd edition (New York: McGraw Hill, 2010): 6.

5 Council of Supply Chain Management Professionals, "Supply Chain Management/Logistics Management Definitions" (2007), retrieved August 28, 2007, from www.cscmp.org/AboutCSCMP/Definitions/Definitions.asp

6 Homin Chen and Tain-Jy Chen, "Network Linkages and Location Choice in Foreign Direct Investment," *Journal of International Business Studies* 29:3 (1998): 447.

7   For a discussion of firm-specific advantages, location-specific advantages, and internalization, see John H. Dunning, *International Production and the Multinational Enterprise* (London: Allen & Unwin, 1981); Peter Buckley and Mark Casson, *The Future of the Multinational Enterprise* (London: Macmillan Press, 1976); Peter Caves, "International Corporations: The Industrial Economics of Foreign Investment," *Economica* 56 (1971): 279–93.

8   Stanley E. Fawcett and Anthony S. Roath, "The Viability of Mexican Production Sharing: Assessing the Four Cs of Strategic Fit," *Urbana* 3:1 (1996): 29.

9   See S. C. Wheelwright, "Reflecting Corporate Strategy in Manufacturing Decisions," *Business Horizons* (1978): 21; S. C. Wheelwright, "Manufacturing Strategy: Defining the Missing Link," *Strategic Management Journal* 5 (1984): 77–91; Frank DuBois, Brian Toyne, and Michael D. Oliff, "International Manufacturing Strategies of U.S. Multinationals: A Conceptual Framework Based on a Four-Industry Study," *Journal of International Business Studies* 24:2 (1993): 313–14; Robert H. Hayes, Steven C. Wheelwright, and Kim B. Clark, *Dynamic Manufacturing* (New York: Free Press, 1988): 10–11.

10 Karby Leggett and Peter Wonacott, "Surge in Exports from China Gives a Jolt to Global Industry," *Wall Street Journal*, retrieved October 10, 2002, from www.wsj.com

11 Jim Hemerling, "China: Ready for the Next Sourcing Wave?" *Business Week* (April 4, 2007): 1.

12 See James P. Womack and Daniel T. Jones, "Lean Consumption: Locating for Lean Provision," *Harvard Business Review* (March 2005): 66–67.

13 "Print Me a Stradivarius," *The Economist* (February 12, 2011): 11.

14 Yuka Hayashi, "Japan Adds Factories at Home," *Wall Street Journal* (June 12, 2007): A8.

15 Interview by author of Wall's Unilever personnel in Beijing, China (June 2006).

16 Jack Ewing, "Why Nokia Is Leaving Moto in the Dust," *Business Week* (July 19, 2007), retrieved November 9, 2007, from www .businessweek.com/globalbiz/content/jul2007/gb20070719_088898 .htm, 1.

17 Norihiko Shirouzu and Jathon Sapsford, "Heavy Load—For Toyota, a New Small Truck Carries Hopes for Topping GM," *Wall Street Journal* (May 12, 2005): A1.

18 Michael E. McGrath and Richard W. Hoole, "Manufacturing's New Economies of Scale," *Harvard Business Review* (May–June 1992): 94.

19 Fawcett and Roath, "The Viability of Mexican Production Sharing," 29.

20 Thomas L. Friedman, *The World is Flat: a Brief History of the Twenty-First Century*, Release 3.0 (New York: Picador, 2007): 77.

21 Richard Karpinski, "Wal-Mart Mandates Secure, Internet-Based EDI for Suppliers," Internetweek.com (September 12, 2002), retrieved October 1, 2002, from www.internetweek.com/supplyChain /INW20020912S0011; R. Sridharan and Shamni Pande, "Surviving Wal-Mart," *Business Today* (July 29, 2007): 166.

22 Vlad Krotov and Iris Junglas, "RFID as a Disruptive Innovation," *Journal of Theoretical and Applied Electronic Commerce Research* 3:2 (August 2008): 44.

23 Scott McCartney, "A New Way to Prevent Lost Luggage," *Wall Street Journal* (February 27, 2007): D1.

24 Miguel Bustillo, "Wal-Mart Radio Tags to Track Clothing," *The Wall Street Journal* (July 22, 2010), accessed online July 25, 2011.

25 Karpinski, "Wal-Mart Mandates Secure, Internet-Based EDI for Suppliers."

26 "Worldwide Internet Users Top 1.8 Billion in 2009," in Press Releases in *Computer Industry Almanac Inc.* (July 12, 2010), retrieved July 25, 2011, from www.c-i-a.com

27 Check the Dell *Annual Report* for 2002 at www.dell.com (retrieved April 20, 2002) and as updated in subsequent *Reports* (retrieved

October 15, 2009). Go to "About Dell" at the bottom of the Web page, select "Investors," and search under "Year" to access annual reports.

28 "You'll Never Walk Alone," 17.

29 Jeremy Wagstaff, "Digital Deliverance; Asia's Technology Conundrum," *Asian Wall Street Journal* (July 27, 2007): W8.

30 Lee J. Krajewski and Larry P. Ritzman, *Operations Management: Strategy and Analysis*, 4th ed. (Reading, MA: Addison-Wesley, 1996): 141–42.

31 Jacobs and Chase, *Operations and Supply Managment*, 134.

32 J.S. Power, "2011 U.S. Initial Quality Study," retrieved July 25, 2011, from www.jdpower.com/news/pressrelease.aspx?ID=2011089

33 J.D. Power & Associates Press Releases, "2011 Vehicle Dependability Study," retrieved July 26, 2011, from www.jdpower.com/autos /car-ratings

34 Hayes, Wheelwright, and Clark, *Dynamic Manufacturing*, 17.

35 S. Thomas Foster, *Managing Quality: Integrating the Supply Chain*, 3rd ed. (Upper Saddle River, NJ: Prentice Hall, 2007): 36–38.

36 Foster, *Managing Quality*, 70–90.

37 Krajewski and Ritzman, *Operations Management*, 140.

38 Ibid, 156.

39 "Six Sigma Definition," retrieved November 9, 2007, from www .sixsigmasurvival.com/SixSigmaDefinition.html

40 Jacobs and Chase, *Operations and Supply Managment*, 142.

41 Brian Hindo and Brian Grow, "Six Sigma: So Yesterday?" *Business Week* (June 11, 2007): 11.

42 Robert McClusky, "The Rise, Fall and Revival of Six Sigma Quality," *Quality Focus* 4:2 (2000): 6.

43 International Organization for Standardization, "ISO Standards," retrieved July 26, 2011, from www.iso.org

44 See Jonathan B. Levine, "Want EC Business? You Have Two Choices," *Business Week* (October 19, 1992): 58; International Organization for Standardization, "ISO 9000:2000" (2007), retrieved November 9, 2007, from www.iso.org/iso/catalogue _detail?csnumber=21823

45 Foster, *Managing Quality*.

46 International Organization for Standardization, "ISO/TS 16949:2009," retrieved July 30, 2009, from www.iso.org/iso /catalogue_detail?csnumber=36155

47 Amy Schoenfeld, "A Multinational Loaf," *New York Times* (June 20, 2007), retrieved November 9, 2007, from www.nytimes.com /imagepages/2007/06/15/business/20070616_FOOD_GRAPHIC.html

48 Alexei Barrionuevo, "Globalization in Every Loaf," *New York Times* (June 16, 2007), retrieved November 9, 2007, from www .nytimes.com/2007/06/16/business/worldbusiness/16food .html?partner=rssnyt&emc=rss

49 Masaaki Kotabe and Glen S. Omura, "Sourcing Strategies of European and Japanese Multinationals: A Comparison," *Journal of International Business Studies* (Spring 1989): 120–22.

50 David Hannon, "Procter & Gamble Puts a New Spin on Global Chemicals Sourcing," *Purchasing* (February 15, 2007): 32C5.

51 Robert M. Monczka and Robert J. Trent, "Global Sourcing: A Development Approach," *International Journal of Purchasing and Materials Management* (Spring 1991): 3.

52 Chi-Chu Tschang, "How China's Farmers Spoiled the Milk," *Business Week* (October 13, 2008): 84.

53 David Barboza, "Food-Safety Crackdown in China," *New York Times* (June 28, 2007): C1.

54 Nicholas Zamiska and David Kesmodel, "Tainted Ginger's Long Trip from China to U.S. Stores," *Wall Street Journal* (November 19, 2007): A1.

55 Mike Ramsey and Sebastian Moffett, "Japan Parts Shortage Hits Auto Makers," *The Wall Street Journal* (March 24, 2011):B1; Andrew

Pollack and Steve Lohr, "The Chip that Powers Cars," *The Walls Street Journal* (April 28, 2011): B1.

56 R. D'Aveni and D. Ravenscraft, "Economies of Integration versus Bureaucracy Costs: Does Vertical Integration Improve Performance?" *Academy of Management Journal* 37:5 (1994): 1167–1206; O. Williamson, "Vertical Integration and Related Variations on a Transaction-Cost Theme," in J. Stiglitz and G. Mathewson (eds.), *New Developments in the Analysis of Market Structure* (Cambridge, MA: MIT Press, 1986); O. Williamson, *The Economic Institutions of Capitalism* (New York: The Free Press, 1985).

57 Russell Johnston and Paul R. Lawrence, "Beyond Vertical Integration—The Rise of the Value-Adding Partnership," *Harvard Business Review* (July–August 1988): 98.

58 Chester Dawson, "A 'China Price' for Toyota," *Business Week* (February 21, 2005): 50–51.

59 John McMillan, "Managing Suppliers: Incentive Systems in Japanese and U.S. Industry," *California Management Review* (Summer 1990): 38.

60 Rigby, "Management Tools 2005."

61 "Still Made in Japan," Economist.com (April 7, 2004), retrieved November 9, 2007, from www.economist.com/printedition /displayStory. cfm?Story_ id=2571689

62 Ibid.

63 Adapted from Pete Engardio and Bruce Einhorn, "Outsourcing Innovation," *Business Week* (March 21, 2005): 84–94.

64 Robert W. Lane, "Competing Globally, Winning Locally," speech to the Waterloo Chamber of Commerce, retrieved August 19, 2004, from www.deere.com/en_US/compinfo/speeches/2004/040819 _lane.html

65 Joseph B. White, "Japanese Auto Makers Help Parts Suppliers Become More Efficient," *Wall Street Journal* (September 10, 1991): 1.

66 Gabriel Kahn, "Invisible Supplier Has Penney's Shirts All Buttoned Up," *Wall Street Journal* (September 11, 2003): A1.

67 Lee Hawkins Jr., "GM Is Pushing Its U.S. Suppliers to Reduce Prices," *Wall Street Journal* (April 7, 2005): A2.

68 Monczka and Trent, "Global Sourcing: A Development Approach," 4–5.

69 Stanley E. Fawcett, "The Globalization of the Supply Environment," *The Supply Environment 2* (Tempe, AZ: NAPM, 2000).

70 "Electrolux Delivers Strong Results in a Very Tough Market," *National Post* (June 25, 2009): FP 9.

71 Monczka and Trent, "Worldwide Sourcing," 17–18.

72 Guy Anderson, "Nissan Gearing Up for a Partnership," *Wall Street Journal* (December 8, 2004): 42.

73 Foster, *Managing Quality,* 87.

74 Krajewski and Ritzman, *Operations Management,* 732.

75 Gabriel Kahn, Trish Saywell, and Quenna Sook Kim, "Backlog at West Coast Docks Keeps Christmas Toys at Sea," *Wall Street Journal* (October 21, 2002), retrieved October 25, 2002, from www.wsj.com

76 Shawnee K. Vickery, "International Sourcing: Implications for Just-in-Time Manufacturing," *Production and Inventory Management Journal* (1989): 67.

77 Government of Dubai, www.dubai.ae. See "free zones."

78 International Trade Administration, "What Activity Is Permitted in Zones?" retrieved July 26, 2011, from http://ia.ita.doc.gov

79 Foreign-Trade Zones Board, "How Many Zones Exist Now?" under FAQ, retrieved July 26, 2011, from http://ia.ita.doc.gov/ftzpage /info/zonestats.html

80 Foreign-Trade Zones Board, "What Are the Benefits to a Zone User," under FAQ, retrieved July 26, 2011, from http://ia.ita.doc.gov /ftzpage/info/ftzstart.html

81 Panalpina, retrieved July 27, 2011, from www.panalpina.com, various pages

82 Panalpina, "Transporting IBM Products to Latin America" (2005), retrieved June 15, 2007, from www.panalpina.com/press/casestudies

83 Fawcett, "The Globalization of the Supply Environment," 11.

84 The information on Nokero is from the author's personal interviews with Steve Katsaros, Founder and CEO, Nokero, and Tom Boyd, Director of Communications and Marketing, Nokero. Nokero's Steve Katsaros, Evan Husney, Tom Boyd, and Beth Polizzotto, University of Colorado Denver provided research materials for the case; John Collins Rudolf, "A Solar Bulb May Light The Way," *The New York Times* (June 25, 2010); Jason Blevins, "The Power of Light," *The Denver Post* (July 10, 2010); Tom Boyd, "A Year after Quake, Nokero and American Green Light up Orphanage, Tent City in Haiti," (January 14, 2010). Nokero.com, and Nokero blog, Nokero: Solar Empowerment.

chapter 18

International Accounting Issues

Objectives

1. To examine the major factors influencing the development of accounting practices in different countries

2. To examine the global convergence of accounting standards

3. To explain how companies account for foreign-currency transactions and translate foreign-currency financial statements

4. To discuss different forms of performance evaluation of foreign operations and how foreign exchange can complicate the budget process

5. To explain how arbitrary transfer pricing can complicate performance evaluation and control

6. To introduce the balanced scorecard as an approach to evaluating performance

Access a host of interactive learning aids to help strengthen your understanding of the chapter concepts at www.myiblab.com.

MyIBLab

Even between parents and children, money matters make strangers.

—*Japanese proverb*

Source: Trinity Mirror/Mirrorpix/Alamy

CASE

Parmalat: Europe's Enron

In January 2002, a European magazine published an article titled "Enron: Could It Happen Here?" At the time the article was published, perhaps most people outside the United States would have answered "no" to that question.[1] In the wake of massive corporate frauds at Enron and WorldCom, there was a feeling outside the United States that such scandals were "an American problem" caused by the more aggressive business environment and practices there. However, a family-owned Italian firm was about to show the world that massive corporate scandals can happen anywhere.

A BRIEF BACKGROUND CHECK

After Calisto Tanzi inherited his father's company at age 22, he directed it into the production of dairy products in 1961 and created the Parmalat brand in 1963. Parmalat was the first Italian manufacturer of branded milk. In 1966, using packaging technology from Tetra Pak, Parmalat created its signature product: milk pasteurized at ultra high temperatures (UHT), giving milk a shelf life of over six months. UHT milk provided Parmalat with a technological competitiveness in the milk industry, placing Parmalat ahead of its competition. In 1970, the law permitted the sale of whole milk in grocery stores, removing the limitation of specialty milk shops. Parmalat quickly became the dominant milk supplier of Italy.

The "Champion's Milk"

Parmalat became known as the "champion's milk" after sponsoring the Ski World Cup and world-champion Formula One race-car driver Nicki Lauda in the 1970s as shown in the photo on p. 675. The company moved into new markets with the production of cheese, butter, and a variety of desserts near the end of the decade. As it increased in popularity, Parmalat also began international expansion through acquisitions in Germany and France, which marked the beginning of a global dairy empire.

The Pious Pioneer Sports Marketer

Calisto Tanzi, an almost legendary figure in Italy, was the author of such growth. It was he who discovered the power of sports marketing to make Parmalat a famous brand. He had friends in important government positions that helped pass laws favoring Parmalat. A pious Catholic, Tanzi was a generous benefactor who sponsored the restoration of Parma's eleventh-century basilica and funded its professional soccer team. And he seemed modest about his achievements. He didn't smoke, drank little, and drove his own Lexus.

Throughout Parmalat's expansion, Tanzi maintained a paternalistic approach to the business. "He would stand, for example, at the plant, spoon in hand, ready to taste the first sample each time a new yoghurt [flavor] was launched."

Going Public and Going Global

In 1989, the firm was acquired by a holding company and changed its name to Parmalat Finanziaria SpA. The milk giant showed healthy profits every year, and its balance sheet appeared strong, with large amounts of cash on hand. This allowed Parmalat to go public in Italy and raise capital in the United States and other countries by selling shares and issuing bonds. The company used this new capital to expand into Latin America, where it dominated the dairy markets in Brazil, Argentina, Venezuela, and several other countries.

By the early 1990s, Parmalat was popular not only among grocery shoppers, but investors and creditors deemed the firm a profitable business partner. Large international banks collected hefty fees by helping the company issue bonds, list stock in foreign markets, and raise capital to fund international acquisitions. As CFO Alberto Ferraris put it, "Outside my office, there was always a line of bankers, asking about new business." There was only one problem: The profits that Parmalat reported were only an illusion created by a set of accounting manipulations.

ACCOUNTING ISSUES

One of the most interesting aspects of Parmalat's case is the simplicity of its fraudulent accounting (which was not *quite* as simple as the scheme suggested in Figure 18.1). The purpose of the fraud was straightforward: to hide operating losses so as not to disappoint investors and creditors. The core of the scheme was double billing to Italian supermarkets and other retailers. By standard accounting procedures, every time product is shipped to a customer, a company records a receivable that it later expects to collect as cash. Because receivables count as sales revenue, Parmalat billed customers twice for each shipment, thus greatly enlarging its sales. The company used these inflated revenues as a means of securing loans from several international banks.

"Off-Balance-Sheet Financing"

By 1995, Parmalat was losing more than $300 million annually in Latin America alone. These continued operating losses caused company executives to search for more complex ways of masking the firm's true performance. Using a trick

FIGURE 18.1

Cooking the books is sometimes more complicated than it seems.

Source: David Brown/Cartoon Stock

called "off-balance-sheet financing," executives set up three shell companies based in the Caribbean. These firms pretended to sell Parmalat products, and Parmalat would send them fake invoices and charge costs and fees to make the "sales" look legitimate. Then Parmalat would write out a credit note for the amount the subsidiaries supposedly owed it and take that to banks to raise money.

Off-balance-sheet financing was also used to hide debts. The company transferred over half of its liabilities to the books of small subsidiaries based in offshore tax havens such as the Cayman Islands. This allowed Parmalat to present a "healthy" balance sheet and a profitable income statement to investors and creditors by hiding large amounts of debt and overstating sales revenue. In 2002, Parmalat reported liabilities of close to $8 billion on its consolidated balance sheet. In reality, the company had roughly $14 billion in debt.

The Art of Milking Growth

Taking advantage of its image, Parmalat issued bonds in the United States and Europe, which were backed up by falsified assets, especially cash. "It was a reversal of logic," said the chief investigating magistrate after the scheme was discovered. Usually, companies take on debt to grow. But in Parmalat's case, "they had to grow to hide the debt." In other words, the company would obtain loans to pay off previous loans (this sounds a little like Greek sovereign debt). Investigators report that without the accounting manipulations, the company would have reported operating losses every year between 1990 and 2003.

The circle of hiding operating losses by incurring increasingly larger amounts of debt eventually became hard to sustain. To perpetuate the fraud, Parmalat needed to continue incurring debt, paying interest on old debts with no real cash of its own and finding new ways to create false sales. Alberto Ferraris, who was appointed CFO in March 2003, mentioned that "he couldn't understand why the company was paying so much to service its debt; the interest payments seemed far higher than warranted for the €5.4 billion in debt on the books."

By the late 1990s, auditors in Argentina and Brazil raised several red flags that pointed to problems with Parmalat's accounting. In early December 2003, the company failed to make a €150 million bond payment. This puzzled those familiar with the company because, according to the 2002 financial statements, Parmalat had plenty of cash on hand.

The fraud became public on December 19, 2003, when Grant Thornton, the company's auditor, made a startling discovery. While auditing Bonlat, a fully owned subsidiary of Parmalat based in the Cayman Islands, the auditors contacted Bank of America to confirm a letter held by Bonlat in which Bank of America allegedly certified that the company had €3.95 billion in cash. Bank of America responded that such an account didn't exist. This resulted in investigators swooping into Parmalat's headquarters to confiscate documents and computer hard drives, which uncovered the accounting tricks. On one computer hard drive, prosecutors found clues to the deception: They found "Account 999," which contained details of secret transactions amounting to more than €8 billion.

THE CONSEQUENCES

Parmalat filed for bankruptcy protection on December 24, 2003. CEO Calisto Tanzi resigned and was detained by Italian authorities three days later and sent to prison. He was subsequently confined to house arrest until September 27, 2004. Also accused of wrongdoing were Fausto Tonna, CFO during most of the period under investigation; Giovanni, Stefano, and Francesca Tanzi, brother, son, and daughter of Calisto Tanzi; and other key employees believed to have been involved in the scheme.

Convicted

Initially, it was thought that misstatements were created only to hide operating losses; however, prosecutors demonstrated that the Tanzi family financially benefited from the fraud. For example, Calisto Tanzi revealed that $638 million was moved to "a family-owned tourism business." In December 2008, Calisto was finally sentenced to 10 years in jail for market rigging in a Milan court. In 2010 Calisto was sentenced another 18 years in prison by a judge in Parma for contributing to the company's demise. Others have served or are serving jail time, and Stefano, Calisto's son, is being tried in Switzerland on fraud and money-laundering charges.

Enrico Bondi was appointed by the government as CEO of Parmalat to direct recovery efforts. As part of his campaign, he brought lawsuits against Grant Thornton and Deloitte, the auditors, for not performing the audit with proper care and not bringing their suspicions to the attention of management. In 2009 a judge in New York dismissed the case against Grant Thornton, but in early 2011 the case was revived. It is still unclear how this case will end. Grant Thornton cut ties with its Italian practice after Parmalat's problems surfaced. In addition, Bondi is suing major international banks, such as Bank of America, Credit Suisse First Boston, Citigroup, and Deutsche Bank. Although these cases are still active in Parma, in 2011 a judge in Milan cleared the charges facing the banks.

Lawsuits, Rounds I and II

The lawsuits accuse the banks of ignoring the fraud to obtain fees from doing business with Parmalat. As mentioned earlier, these banks were instrumental in helping the company raise capital to fund its international expansion. The banks and the auditors deny any wrongdoing and claim they were victims of the scheme. Citigroup Inc., UBS AG, Deutsche Bank AG, and Morgan Stanley were involved in the Milan trial for "failing to have procedures that would have prevented crimes that contributed to" Parmalat's failure. As of mid-June 2007, Bondi has collected almost $900 million in settlements in Italy and the United States, but Parmalat lost its case against Citigroup and actually had to pay them damages.

Parmalat, in turn, has been sued by investors, banks, and other organizations. In the United States, the SEC filed a complaint against Parmalat on December 29, 2003, alleging that the company fraudulently raised money through bonds in the United States by overstating assets and understating liabilities. On July 30, 2004, Parmalat agreed to settle with the SEC without admitting or denying the claims. Parmalat won't be fined but has agreed to make changes to strengthen its board of directors and improve governance.

Restructuring

Besides the legal battles that have resulted from the fraud, Bondi's restructuring campaign calls for aggressive changes in Parmalat's organization. On March 29, 2004, the company announced it would narrow its focus in markets in Italy, Canada, Australia, South Africa, Spain, Portugal, Russia, and Romania and would pull out of other regions. However, in May 2007, "Parmalat…agreed to sell its Spanish assets to Lacteos Siglo XXI." Latin American countries "with strong and profitable positions," such as Colombia, Nicaragua, and Venezuela, would be retained. In addition, Parmalat would cut its workforce from 32,000 to less than 17,000, slash the number of brands from 120 to 30, and concentrate on "healthy lifestyle" products.

By 2010 Parmalat had moved into Botswana, Cuba, Ecuador, Mozambique, Paraguay, Swaziland, and Zambia. It also has a presence through licensees in a number of countries. Recently, Parmalat has been focusing on higher value-added products. Along with this focus, it has scheduled market testing to take place in 2011 that will help determine how much potential new products have in different geographic locations.

SO, WHAT'S THE BOTTOM LINE?

In Europe, the Parmalat scandal created deep concern among authorities. The European Commission suggested that it would like to strengthen auditing standards by insisting that member countries introduce accounting-oversight boards similar to those in the United States. Many organizations have proposed reforms to prevent another scandal of such magnitude. One of the areas of reform considered was more transparency in the bond market in Europe; in other words, bond-price disclosure. However, "the [European Commission] has indicated that it will allow traders to police themselves instead of requiring the same data about bonds as for stocks."

From an accounting perspective, Parmalat joined the ranks of other European companies by adopting International Financial Reporting Standards published by the International Accounting Standards Board and adopted by the European Commission for its consolidated financial statements. In addition, Parmalat's independent auditors are now global auditing firm PricewaterhouseCoopers. The hope is that these two moves will help convince investors that Parmalat is moving in the right direction on the accounting side. After the restructuring, Parmalat has risen from the ashes, is now listed again on the Milan stock exchange, and is Italy's biggest listed food company. At least it didn't suffer Enron's fate.

Plus a Little Corporate Misgovernance

However, even though these accounting moves were taken to help Parmalat recover, they are not enough. Although the fraud was perpetrated through a set of accounting tricks, several issues converged to allow such manipulations to happen. One of the clearest deficiencies at Parmalat was its corporate governance system. As a family-owned business, the company was tightly controlled by insiders, especially Calisto Tanzi, who held the positions of CEO and chairman of the board of directors.

Most of the other board members were family members or managers of Parmalat. This prevented the company from having a strong, independent voice to stop the actions taken by management. In addition, Italian law allowed Parmalat to have two auditors instead of one. Grant Thornton was the main auditor, but Deloitte audited some of the subsidiaries, including Bonlat, where the fraud was uncovered. This arrangement made it more difficult for the auditors to have one clear, coherent picture of Parmalat's financial condition. As noted, neither of these auditors is used by Parmalat now. Finally, and perhaps most importantly, management integrity failed. In the end, a manager determined to commit fraud will most likely succeed even in a very good governance system.

Parmalat is now taking the necessary steps to provide better corporate governance. It is working hard to comply with the Italian Corporate Governance Code along with other general principles. Parmalat has also created its own Code of Ethics, Code of Conduct, and Internal Dealing Code of Conduct. All employees at Parmalat are required to abide by the codes set in place.

The 2010 Annual Report was audited by global accounting firm PricewaterhouseCoopers SpA according to the rules set down by CONSOB, the Italian regulatory body that supervises companies and stock exchanges. Financial statements were prepared according to Italian accounting standards and IFRS as adopted by the European Union. The report was originally prepared in Italian, signed by Italian partner Elena Cogliate, and translated into English for convenience of international readers.

In the aftermath of Parmalat's fraud, investigators were left wondering how a few accounting numbers could fool so many people. One thing, however, was clear: Europe now had its very own Enron.

Introduction

International business managers cannot make good decisions without relevant and reliable information about **accounting**—one of the functional areas critical for an MNE's operations. Accounting and Information System (IS) specialists provide such information, but managers must understand which data they need as well as the problems specialists face in gathering the data from different accounting systems around the world.

The Crossroads of Accounting and Finance

> The accountant is essential in providing information to financial decision makers.

The accounting and finance functions are closely related. Each relies on the other to fulfill its own responsibilities. The chief financial officer (CFO) of any company is responsible for procuring and managing the company's financial resources. Usually a member of the company's top management team, the CFO relies on the controller, or chief accountant, to provide the right information for making decisions. In addition, the internal audit staff ensures that corporate policies and procedures are followed. They and the CFO and controller work closely with the external auditor to try to safeguard the assets of the business. (As you can see from our opening case on the Parmalat scandal, however, things can go wrong, especially when topmost management is willing to shirk its fiduciary responsibility and the external auditor may see a different sort of value in the company's assets.)

The actual and potential flow of assets across national boundaries complicates the finance and accounting functions. So MNEs must learn to cope with differing inflation rates, exchange-rate changes, currency controls, expropriation risks, customs duties, tax rates and methods of determining taxable income, levels of sophistication of local accounting personnel, and local as well as home-country reporting requirements.

WHAT DOES THE CONTROLLER CONTROL?

> **Concept Check**
>
> We discuss **foreign currency exchange rates** and the ways in which they affect the operations of an MNE in Chapter 9. Here we explain the responsibilities of the CFO in overseeing a company's closely related financial and **accounting** functions. As we'll see, financial management deals with the effects of exchange rates on such financial-statement items as *receivables* and *payables*.

The role of the company controller has expanded beyond the traditional tasks of management accounting. As Figure 18.2 indicates, the controller is part of the financial function of the firm. Some of the typical responsibilities are shown in Figure 18.2, although the exact duties and allocation among the finance staff, the controller, and the treasurer vary from company to company.

Today's controller is engaged in a variety of activities outside the typical accounting and reporting functions that support the firm's general strategy, such as managing the supply chain, evaluating potential acquisitions abroad, disposing of a subsidiary or a division, managing cash flow, hedging currency and interest-rate risks, tax planning, internal auditing, and helping to plan corporate strategy. In fact, today's accountants

FIGURE 18.2   What the Controller Controls

We have our controller reporting to either a VP of finance or a chief financial officer. Note that our controller's area of responsibility, like that of many contemporary controllers, is twofold: He or she oversees not only activities in accounting but those in financial management as well.

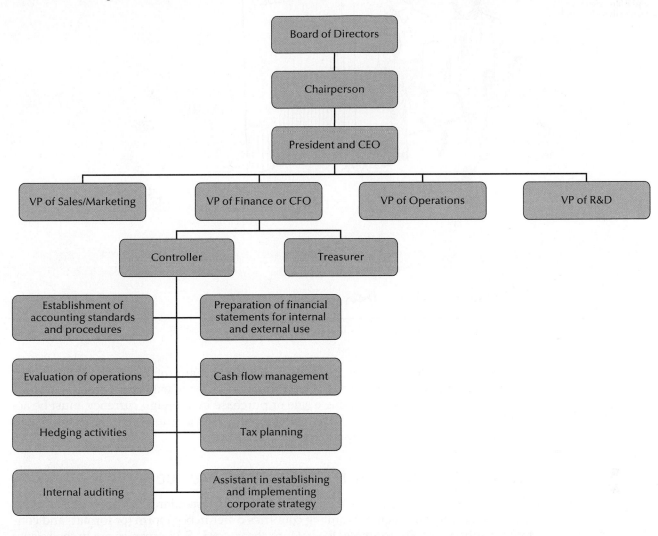

overall must have a much broader perspective of business in general—and international business in particular, for our purposes—than the old stereotypes of accountants (see Figure 18.3).

As noted in Chapter 15 and elaborated on here, foreign managers and subsidiaries are usually evaluated at headquarters on the basis of data generated in the company's reporting system set up and coordinated by the controller's office. The controller generates reports for internal consideration, local government needs, creditors, employees, suppliers, stockholders, and prospective investors, while handling the impact of many different currencies and inflation rates on the statements and becoming familiar with different countries' accounting systems.

In discussing some key accounting issues facing MNEs, this chapter initially examines how accounting differs around the world and how global capital markets are forcing countries to consider converging their accounting and reporting standards as we attempt to move to one set of globally accepted standards. It then examines some unique issues facing MNEs, such as accounting for foreign-currency transactions, translating foreign-currency financial statements, reporting on foreign operations to shareholders and potential investors, and evaluating the performance of foreign operations and managers.

> The controller of an international company must be concerned about a range of issues dealing with corporate strategy broader than just accounting issues.

FIGURE 18.3   Accountants
Get a Little Semantic
Respect.

Source: From the Wall Street Journal/
Permission Cartoon Features Syndicate

"Remember when they used to be called 'bean counters'?"

Although the focus here is on MNEs' problems, many of these issues affect any company doing business overseas, even a small importer or exporter. Foreign-currency transactions, such as denominating a sale or purchase in a foreign currency, must be accounted for in the currency of the parent company. This is true of both large and small companies, as well as service and manufacturing firms.

Accounting for International Differences

Both the form and the content of financial statements are different in different countries.

One problem an MNE faces is the varying accounting standards and practices around the world. Financial statements among countries differ in both form (or format) and content (or substance). For example, the balance sheets for U.S. companies are in the *balance format:*

$$\text{Assets} - \text{Liabilities} = \text{Shareholders' equity}$$

The balance sheet varies in the order of liquidity of the accounts presented. Some companies start with the least liquid assets (those that are harder to convert into cash quickly) and go to those that are most liquid (such as cash), whereas other companies go from the most to the least liquid assets (such as property, plants, and equipment). The former practice is very common among European companies; the latter is used by U.S.-based companies. Parmalat, for example, has a very similar balance sheet approach to U.S. companies except that it starts out with the least liquid assets:

$$\text{Noncurrent assets} + \text{Current assets} = \text{Shareholders' equity} + \text{Noncurrent liabilities} + \text{Current liabilities}$$

The balance sheets for many other European (especially British) companies including Marks and Spencer are prepared in a different form known as the *analytical format:*

$$\text{Noncurrent assets} + \text{Current assets} - \text{Current liabilities} - \text{Noncurrent liabilities} = \text{Shareholders' equity}$$

Marks & Spencer, the British retail firm, has operations worldwide, including Dubai in the United Arab Emirates. Their financial statements in Dubai must eventually conform to the format that M&S uses for investors and creditors worldwide.

Source: Peter Bowater/Alamy

Some of the terminology used in presenting financial statements varies for companies around the world. What is referred to by U.S. companies as *inventories* is called *stocks* in other English-speaking countries, whereas *stocks* in the United States are called *shares* elsewhere. U.S. firms, for example, present only a set of consolidated financial statements (also called group statements), whereas European firms present both parent company and group financial statements.

ACCOUNTING OBJECTIVES

It is important in the accounting process to identify, record, and interpret economic events. Every country needs to determine the objectives of the accounting system it has put into place. According to the **Financial Accounting Standards Board (FASB)**, the private-sector body that establishes accounting standards in the United States, and the **International Accounting Standards Board (IASB)**, a London-based organization that sets accounting standards for the broader global community, general purpose financial reporting should "provide financial information about the reporting entity that is useful for potential investors, lenders, and other creditors in making decisions about providing resources to the entity." As noted in Figure 18.4, there are many users of general financial information, but the primary users are existing and potential investors, lenders, and other creditors.[2]

It's important to identify primary users, because a focus on different users might result in different financial information being reported. For example, because Germany's major users have historically been banks, accounting has focused more on the balance sheet, which contains a description of the company's assets. In the United States, however, the major users are investors, so accounting has focused more on the income statement. Investors see the income statement as an indication of the future success of the company, affecting the company's stock price (or share price) and its flow of dividends.

> The accounting process identifies, records, and interprets economic events.

> The Financial Accounting Standards Board (FASB) sets accounting standards in the United States.

> Critical users of accounting information are investors, employees, lenders, suppliers, and other trade creditors, customers, governments and their agencies, and the public.

FIGURE 18.4   Who Uses Accounting Information?

Although there are many important users of accounting information as illustrated in this figure, the key users as identified by FASB and the IASB are current and potential investors, lenders, and other creditors. In some countries, such as the United States, investors might be more important than lenders, and in other countries such as Germany, lenders (primarily the banks) have historically been the most important source of funding.

Source: Financial Accounting Standards Board, "Conceptual Framework: Statement of Financial Accounting Concepts No. 8, Chapter 1, The Objective of General Purpose Financial Reporting, paragraphs OB2 – OB11.

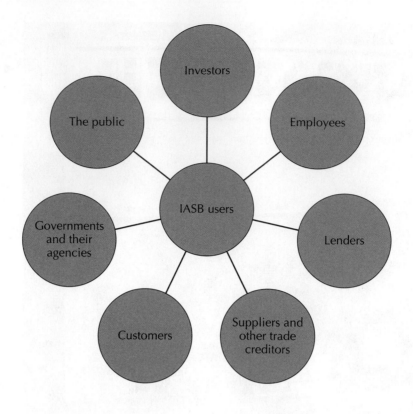

Concept Check

In discussing "Legal Issues in International Business" in Chapter 3, we survey the various ways in which local legal standards can affect foreign firms in *operational concerns*—in the ways in which they function on a day-to-day basis. Naturally, these standards include **accounting** standards, and here we emphasize that attitudes toward—and, more importantly, regulations concerning—accounting practices vary widely from country to country. Remember, too, that although standard-setting bodies may be public or private organizations, policies such as those pertaining to **FASB** and **GAAP** are strongly influenced by local governments.

Case Review Note

Culture influences measurement and disclosure practices:

• Measurement—how to value assets.
• Disclosure—the presentation of information and discussion of results.

FACTORS IN INTERNATIONAL ACCOUNTING PRACTICES

Figure 18.5 identifies some of the forces leading to the development of international accounting standards and practices. Although all the factors shown are significant, their importance varies by country. For example, investors are influential in the United States and the United Kingdom, but creditors—primarily banks—have traditionally had more influence in Germany and Switzerland. Figure 18.5 is comprehensive, because it focuses on *all* elements of the accounting process: national and international influences, users, regulators, auditors, and educators.

Cultural issues cut across all countries and strongly influence the development of accounting. Institutional factors such as legal and tax systems have a big influence on accounting standards and practices in most of the world, including India, Japan, France, and other countries in southern Europe, but is less important in the United States. Certain international factors also have weight, such as former colonial influence and foreign investment. For example, most countries that are current or former members of the British Commonwealth have accounting systems similar to the United Kingdom's, former French colonies use the French model, and so forth. As shown later, however, the **convergence** of accounting standards being led by the IASB will eventually reduce many of these differences.

International public accounting firms, such as Deloitte, E&Y, KPMG, and PricewaterhouseCoopers, are also important sources of influence because they transfer high levels of accounting and auditing practices worldwide. As we observe in our opening case on the Parmalat matter, public accounting firms are also responsible for ensuring that proper accounting practices are followed and that publicly released financial statements accurately represent a firm's financial position.

CULTURAL DIFFERENCES IN ACCOUNTING

The differences in measurement and disclosure practices among countries are of special interest to international investors—*measurement* meaning how companies value assets, including inventory and fixed assets, and *disclosure* referring to how and what

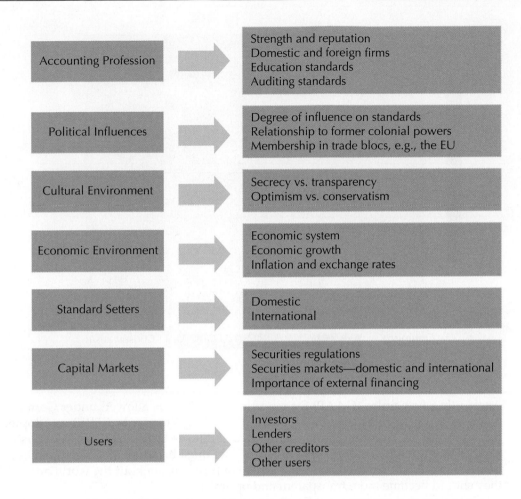

FIGURE 18.5 Sources of Influence on Accounting

Every aspect of the accounting process is influenced by a variety of internal and external factors, and they're all potentially important. Degree of importance will vary by country.

Source: Based on The International Journal of Accounting, Vol. 10, No. 3, Lee H. Radebaugh, Environmental Factors Influencing the Development of Accounting, Objectives, Standards and Practices', p. 41, 1975.

information companies provide and discuss in their annual and interim reports for external financial data users.

Much of the work on culture and accounting is initially based on Hofstede's research on the structural elements of culture, particularly those that most strongly affect behavior in the work situations of organizations and institutions.[3] Hofstede's work was extended into the accounting area by Gray,[4] which resulted in country classifications according to disclosure and measurement principles, specifically, secrecy/transparency and optimism/conservatism.

The Secrecy–Transparency/Optimism–Conservatism Matrix Figure 18.6 depicts the accounting practices of various groupings of countries within a matrix of the cultural values of secrecy–transparency and optimism–conservatism. With respect to accounting, secrecy and transparency indicate the degree to which companies disclose information to the public. Countries such as Germany, Switzerland, and Japan tend to have less disclosure (illustrating the cultural value of secrecy) than do the United States and the United Kingdom (Anglo-American countries, which are more transparent or open with respect to disclosure). Our opening case on the Parmalat scandal demonstrates that even companies that list on global exchanges, borrow money from the largest banks in the world, and turn their financial statements over to the best auditing firms in the world can have secretive corporate cultures.

Generally Accepted Accounting Principles In addition, as companies from the upper-right quadrant of secrecy and conservatism use capital markets more extensively, they move closer to the Anglo-American mode. This is especially true of companies like Deutsche Bank and DaimlerChrysler, which adopted U.S. **Generally Accepted**

Concept Check

Chapter 2 is devoted to illustrating the many ways in which local culture shapes the environment in which international business is conducted from country to country. Here we point out that culture also affects differences in approaches to **accounting** systems and policies. In Chapter 2, we cite Geert Hofstede among the researchers who've studied national differences in managerial attitudes and preferences, and here we use applications of Hofstede's findings to studies of work-situation behavior as a means of shedding light on the effect of cultural differences on accounting standards and practices.

Case Review Note

FIGURE 18.6

A Disclosure/Assessment Matrix for National Accounting Systems

The vertical axis reflects practices according to transparency-secrecy (the extent to which companies in a country disclose information to the public). The horizontal axis reflects practices accounting to optimism-conservatism (the degree of caution taken by companies when it comes to valuing assets and recognizing income). Note that, not surprisingly, transparency and optimism tend to go hand in hand, as do secrecy and conservatism.

Source: Lee H. Radebaugh and Sidney J. Gray, International Accounting and Multinational Enterprises, 5th ed. (New York: John Wiley & Sons, 2002) 2002. Reprinted by permission of John Wiley & Sons.

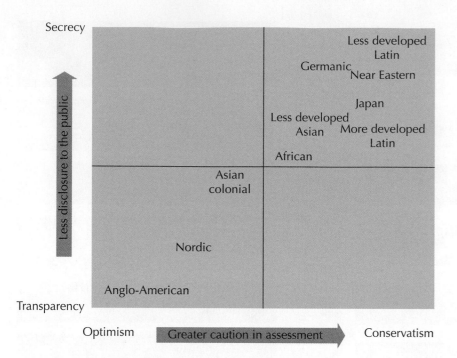

Secrecy and transparency refer to the degree to which corporations disclose information to the public. Optimism and conservatism refer to the degree of caution companies display in valuing assets and recognizing income.

British companies are optimistic when recognizing income. U.S. companies are slightly less optimistic. Japanese and continental European companies are even less optimistic than U.S. companies.

Accounting Principles (GAAP) for reporting purposes, as allowed under German law, before moving to **International Financial Reporting Standards (IFRS)** as adopted by the International Accounting Standards Board. IFRS is to the IASB as GAAP is to the FASB. They refer to standards and practices that must be adopted. As companies headquartered in the European Union and other countries throughout the world adopt IFRS, they should become more transparent and optimistic.

Optimism and conservatism (in an accounting, not a political, sense) are the degree of caution companies exhibit in valuing assets and recognizing income—an illustration of the measurement issues mentioned earlier. The more conservative countries tend to understate assets and income, whereas optimistic countries tend to be more liberal in their recognition of income. Banks primarily fund French companies, as they do in Germany and Japan, and banks are concerned with liquidity. So French companies tend to be very conservative both when recording profits that keep them from paying taxes and when declaring dividends to pile up cash reserves to service their bank debts.

In contrast, U.S. companies want to show earning power to impress and attract investors. British companies tend to be more optimistic in earnings recognition than their U.S. counterparts, but the latter are much more optimistic than continental European and Japanese companies.

Classifying Accounting Systems

Although accounting standards and practices differ significantly worldwide, we can still group systems used in various countries according to common characteristics. Figure 18.7 illustrates one approach to doing this. Countries that have small or weak equity markets tend to rely more on banks, government, and internally-generated wealth to fund operations. Accounting standards are usually based on tax law, and they are often included in legal statutes.

Countries that have strong equity markets, such as the United States, tend to rely on accounting standards issued by an independent accounting profession and often reflect pragmatic business practices rather than detailed legal and tax requirements. Accounting standards in those countries rely more on global reporting standards, such

FIGURE 18.7 Weak vs. Strong Equity Markets and the Influence on Accounting Standards

As a class, macro-uniform accounting systems have developed in countries with strong, codified legal systems. They're also shaped more heavily by government influences than are micro-based accounting system, which, as a class, prevail in countries where accounting practices have developed in response to pragmatic business needs.

Source: Based on Christopher Nobes and Robert Parker, Comparative International Accounting, 7th ed. (Harlow, England: FT Prentice Hall, 2002), 67; and C. W. Nobes, "A Judgmental International Classification of Financial Reporting Practices," *Journal of Business Finance and Accounting* (Spring 1963).

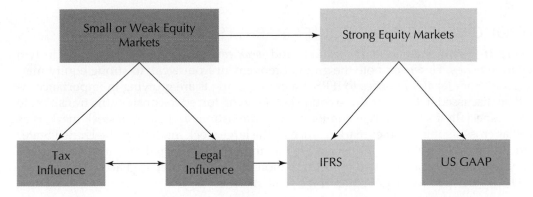

as IFRS or U.S. GAAP. Notice that IFRS is closer to the legal and tax influence than is U.S. GAAP. The reason for this proximity is that countries in small equity markets that are moving to upgrade their financial reporting are moving to adopt IFRS due to its more flexible and less detailed nature. However, they often cling to their own reporting requirements as well. Thus India, which has announced that it has adopted IFRS has not completely moved to IFRS due to unique tax considerations in India. On the other hand, if they had tried to adopt U.S. GAAP, they would be required to adopt it completely. As we will discuss later in the chapter, IFRS and U.S. GAAP are attempting to move closer together, but there are still a number of issues that need to be resolved.

FROM MACRO-UNIFORM TO MICRO-BASED SYSTEMS

Figure 18.7 reflects the difference between macro-uniform and micro-based systems in generating accounting standards. Macro-uniform systems, which are often most typical of weak equity markets, are shaped more by government influence than are micro-based systems. The major accounting influences on countries that fit into the macro-uniform category are a strong legal system—especially codified rather than common law—and tax law. For example, Brazil is a country that has a strong legal tradition, and accounting standards that are adopted in the law in Brazil must be followed Another aspect of the influence of law is tax law. When tax law dominates, which is the tradition in most southern European countries, tax authorities use the statutory financial statements prepared according to local accounting standards to determine tax liability. Thus, accounting standards are tax-based, and law requires that they be followed. Macro-uniform-based systems also tend to be more conservative and secretive about disclosure. Japan and Germany are legal-based systems, even their equity markets have grown dramatically in the last decade, while Spain and France are tax-based systems. The former Soviet-bloc countries and China would also fit in the macro category, as would most countries in the Middle East, Africa, and Latin America.

Micro-based systems include features that support pragmatic business practice and have evolved from the British system. The United States is an example of a country that fits in the micro category. It exhibits more optimism and transparency than countries in the macro category and relies less on legal and tax requirements than macro-uniform countries like Germany, France, and Japan. The focus tends to be more on capital markets and less on banks and tax authorities. That's not to say that banks and taxes are unimportant, but there is a separation in most cases between tax income and income provided to the capital markets, and banks tend to be less important than investors.

Macro-uniform accounting systems are shaped more by government influence, whereas micro-based systems rely on pragmatic business practice.

Other countries that closely model the United States are Mexico and Canada, two members of NAFTA, although Mexico also comes from a strong legal and tax tradition inherited from its Spanish roots. The British model is also a micro-based model, but it relies even less on legal and tax influences than the United States. Current and former members of the British Commonwealth, such as the Bahamas, Australia, and New Zealand, also fit into this category.[5]

STRONG VERSUS WEAK EQUITY MARKETS

Concept Check

In discussing "Regional Economic Integration" in Chapter 8, we observe that the momentum toward cooperation in such blocs as the EU and NAFTA has spilled over into areas of international business that lie beyond the originally targeted terrain of trade and tariffs. Here we cite developments in such areas as accounting **convergence**—especially in the case of the EU—as particularly good examples of this phenomenon.

Countries can be distinguished between those with strong and weak equity-market and shareholder orientations.

Major reporting issues:

- Language.
- Currency.
- Type of statements.
- Financial statement format.
- Extent of footnote disclosures.
- Underlying GAAP on which the financial statements are based.

Figure 18.7 shows *strong equity* markets and *weak equity* markets as if they are in two separate boxes. However, note the gradual movement from weak to strong equity markets and from legal influences to IFRS. Emerging markets are growing in importance, as will be discussed in Chapter 19, so countries are being forced to consider the transition to IFRS, especially for their larger companies that are listing on their own stock markets as well as cross-listing on other markets such as the large stock markets in the United States and Europe. Legal and tax influences are still important, especially for individual company reports, but consolidated reports are more likely to be prepared according to IFRS or U.S. GAAP due to the demands of the stock markets.[6]

DIFFERENCES IN FINANCIAL STATEMENTS

The bottom line is that MNEs need to adjust to different accounting systems around the world, thus making the accounting function more complex and costly. A company's financial statements, for example, include not only the statements themselves but also the accompanying footnotes. Companies that list on stock exchanges usually provide an income statement, a balance sheet (also known as a statement of financial position, a statement of shareowners equity, a cash-flow statement), and detailed footnotes as an important part of their annual report. The financial statements of one country differ from those in another country in four major ways:

1. Language
2. Currency
3. Statement type (including format and extent of footnote disclosure)
4. Underlying GAAP on which the statements are based

Language Differences   English tends to be the first choice of companies choosing to raise capital abroad. For example, German company Daimler issues financial statements in both German and English, while Swedish telecom firm Ericsson provides its annual reports in Swedish and English.

Many companies also provide a significant amount of information on their Internet home pages. Managers can just click on the desired language button, and all the information is provided in that language. Ericsson's home page is full of information for people all over the world. It even has a link that gives financial as well as general information in Portuguese for Brazilian readers. However, on its Brazilian link, it provides links to its annual report only in English and Swedish.

Currency Differences   Companies around the world prepare their financial statements in different currencies. Daimler's are in euros; Ericsson's are in Swedish kronor; Coca-Cola uses U.S. dollars; and so on. In its 2010 annual report, Adidas provided its financial information in euros and disclosed information on the firm's currency-translation policies as well as gave average exchange rates for the U.S. dollar, the British pound, the Japanese yen, the Russian ruble, and the Chinese yuan to allow investors to make convenience translations from euros into the above currencies.[7]

Differences in Types of Statements As noted earlier in the chapter, financial-statement format is not a big issue, but it can be confusing to read a balance sheet prepared in an analytical format when one is used to seeing it in the balance format. A major area of difference is the use of footnotes. Footnote disclosures in countries with strong equity markets, such as the United States, tend to be very comprehensive. Greater transparency is synonymous with more extensive footnote disclosures. Companies that list on multiple stock exchanges, such as Daimler AG, have extensive footnotes as well, because they have to comply with the reporting requirements of a global investing community.

GAAP Usage Differences A major hurdle in raising capital in different countries is dealing with widely varying accounting and disclosure requirements. Although this problem is decreasing as more stock exchanges and countries allow the use of IFRS, some countries care more about those differences than others. In addition, most countries may apply one set of accounting standards for consolidated groups while using another set for the individual companies in the group. In this situation, individual companies in a group must use local accounting standards that are usually tied to legal requirements and are the basis for tax accounting. Consolidated financial statements, which are used for capital markets and not for tax purposes, are prepared by a different set of standards, such as IFRS. U.S. companies do not have the same situation. They disclose only consolidated financial statements, not individual company financial statements. There are some differences for tax accounting, but those differences are reconciled in the financial statements rather than as separate statements for each company in a group.

Mutual Recognition versus Reconciliation Before the rise in importance of global capital markets, it was common for most countries to apply the principle of **mutual recognition**, whereby a regulator, such as the German stock exchange, would accept financial statements provided in U.S. GAAP of a U.S. company wanting to list securities in Germany. Prior to the requirement in 2005 that EU companies provide financial statements prepared according to IFRS, some German companies such as Daimler and Deutsche Bank prepared their consolidated financial statements according to U.S. GAAP, as permitted at the time by German law. This made it easier for them to list on the New York Stock Exchange. However, they dropped this practice and moved to IFRS in 2007. In Daimler's 2010 annual report, it stated that "the consolidated financial statements of Daimler AG and its subsidiaries have been prepared in accordance with Section 315a of the German Commercial Code (HGB) and International Financial Reporting Standards (IFRS) and related interpretations as issued by the International Accounting Standards Board (IASB) and as adopted by the European Union."

> Major approaches to dealing with accounting and reporting differences:
>
> - Mutual recognition.
> - Reconciliation to local GAAP.
> - Recasting of financial statements in terms of local GAAP.

The United States uses two approaches: adoption of U.S. standards or **reconciliation,** whereby a company can list American Depositary Receipts on a U.S. exchange and then reconcile its home-country GAAP with U.S. GAAP in a special statement called Form 20-F on net income and shareholders' equity. This is the approach Daimler used before it adopted U.S. GAAP for its consolidated financial statements. Since 2007, however, the SEC permits foreign issuers to list without a reconciliation statement as long as their financial statements are prepared in accordance with full IFRS. The EU was going to require U.S. firms that want to list on European exchanges to list in accordance with IFRS. However, it announced in 2008 that it would allow U.S. firms to continue to list on EU markets using U.S. GAAP, given the progress of convergence and the fact that U.S. GAAP and IFRS are essentially equivalent. In addition, the SEC's dropping the 20-F reconciliation for European firms using IFRS was a contributing factor.[8]

International Standards and Global Convergence

Convergence is the process of bringing different national Generally Accepted Accounting Principles (GAAP) into line with International Financial Reporting Standards (IFRS) issued by the IASB.

Major forces leading to convergence.

- Investor orientation.
- Global integration of capital markets.
- MNEs' need for foreign capital.
- Regional political and economic harmonization.
- MNEs' desire to reduce accounting and reporting costs.
- Convergence efforts of standards-setting bodies.

Historically, U.S. GAAP has been the international standard because of the size of the major capital markets in the United States and the need for companies in locations all over the world to list on these exchanges to raise capital. That forced foreign issuers to either adopt U.S. GAAP or reconcile their financial statements to it on Form 20-F.

Despite the many differences in accounting standards and practices around the world, a number of forces are leading to convergence:

- A movement to provide information compatible with the needs of investors
- The global integration of capital markets, which means easier and faster access to investment opportunities around the world and, therefore, the need for more comparable financial information
- The need of MNEs to raise capital outside their home-country capital markets while generating as few different financial statements as possible
- Regional political and economic harmonization, such as the efforts of the EU, which affect accounting as well as trade and investment issues
- Pressure from MNEs for more uniform standards to allow greater ease and reduced costs in general reporting in each country

THE FIRST STEPS IN CONVERGENCE

Established in 1973, the International Accounting Standards Committee (IASC), the forerunner of the IASB, began working toward harmonizing accounting standards by issuing a set of International Accounting Standards (IAS) that they hoped anyone in the world could use. Its original standards had a strong capital-markets focus so that they

FIGURE 18.8
Development of Accounting Systems in the West

Financial results depend on which accounting standards a company follows. The greater the difference between home country and local GAAP, the greater the room to adjust financial information. However, the move to IFRS for group reporting on stock markets should reduce the differences.

Source: Theresa McCracken/ Cartoon Stock.

"But under a different accounting convention ..."

could be used worldwide to facilitate the free flow of capital. With such a goal, the IASC tended to lean more toward the traditions of the United States and the United Kingdom rather than the legal- and tax-based systems of Germany and France, where funding was more the domain of banks than broadly based capital markets. This engendered some hostility in other countries, which disliked the similarity to U.S. standards. In addition, these were often very light, with too many options to capture the support of everyone.

The turning point in the significance of IAS came in 1995, when the **International Organization of Securities Commissions (IOSCO)** announced publicly it would endorse IAS if the IASC developed a set of core standards acceptable to it. IOSCO is significant because it comprises the regulators of most of the world's stock markets, including the SEC in the United States. In May 2000, the IASC completed a core set of standards acceptable to IOSCO, and securities market regulators began the process of convincing their standards setters to adopt IFRS.

> The International Organization of Securities Commissions accepted a core set of accounting standards issued by the IASB in which securities regulators can be confident.

THE INTERNATIONAL ACCOUNTING STANDARDS BOARD

In March 2001, the IASC was reorganized into the International Accounting Standards Committee Foundation (now called the IFRS Foundation) and the International Accounting Standards Board (IASB). The IFRS Foundation is the parent entity of the IASB, which assumed the major standard-setting functions of the old IASC.[9] The IASB is responsible for setting the standards, and the Trustees of the IFES Foundation are responsible to oversee the activities of the IASB, as well as review its effectiveness, appoint members to the Board, and provide funding for the Board's activities. Trustees of the Foundation search for and appoint members of the IASB. They serve for three years and come from different regions of the world. Six must be selected from the Asia/Oceania region, six from Europe, six from North America, one from Africa, one from South America, and two from the rest of the world.[10] The Trustees also appoint members to the IFRS Advisory Council which provides strategic advice to the IASB. The Trustees also members of the IFRS Interpretations Committee which is responsible for reviewing accounting issues not covered in existing IFRS and for issuing interpretations of IFRS for which unsatisfactory or conflicting interpretations might exist. Thus the new structure of the IFRS standard-setting process includes lots of guidance and influence from around the world and from different sectors of the global economy.

International Financial Reporting Standards (IFRS) When the IASB was organized, all of the old standards from the IASC were adopted, and the board began to go through each standard to upgrade them. Then the board began to issue the new International Financial Reporting Standards; thus, when we use the term *IFRS*, we refer to the new standards as well as the old IAS. The objectives of the IFRS Foundation and the IASB are to generate high quality standards that can be used worldwide and that can also be used by national standard setters to achieve the ultimate goal of converging standards internationally.

> The IASB is attempting to harmonize accounting standards through issuing International Financial Reporting Standards (IFRS).

The Relationship Between the FASB and the IASB The FASB and IASB have been working closely to achieve a convergence of accounting standards. In the past, the two have not exactly competed with each other, but they maintained a professional distance. That's no longer the case—in 2002, they reached the Norwalk Agreement, pledging their best efforts to:

> FASB and IASB are trying to converge their standards through a variety of different activities.

a. undertake a short-term project aimed at removing a variety of individual differences between U.S. GAAP and International Financial Reporting Standards (IFRSs, which include International Accounting Standards, IASs);

b. remove other differences between IFRSs and U.S. GAAP that will remain at January 1, 2005, through coordination of their future work programs; that is, through the mutual undertaking of discrete, substantial projects which both Boards would address concurrently;

c. continue progress on the joint projects that they are currently undertaking; and,

d. encourage their respective interpretative bodies to coordinate their activities.[11]

Convergence implies a goal and a path to achieve the goal. The goal is to eliminate differences in accounting standards between FASB and the IASB. The convergence process (or path) takes several forms. Initially, the two boards identified standards that could easily be converged. Now that they have joint projects to establish new standards, they are trying to eliminate existing differences in a short-term convergence project for standards that should be easy to converge, and the FASB is explicitly considering the impact of IFRS on every standard it sets. Some more complicated standards are part of a long-term convergence process.[12]

However, standard-setting in the United States depends on the cooperation of the SEC, whose mission is to "protect investors, maintain fair, orderly, and efficient markets, and facilitate capital formation."[13] Although the SEC does not set accounting standards, it empowers the FASB to do so, because companies—both foreign and domestic—that want to raise capital in the United States must follow the SEC guidelines. As mentioned above, the SEC permitted foreign private issuers that follow IFRS to eliminate providing information in Form 20-F to reconcile IFRS GAAP to U.S. GAAP. It also proposed the establishment of a Roadmap that could result in U.S. firms being allowed to list in the United States according to IFRS. In the proposal, which was *not* a rule, the SEC identified several milestones that had to be met, including improvements in IFRS and accountability and funding of the IFRS Foundation. In the Roadmap, the SEC has not identified a "date certain" for IFRS adoption.

According to the proposed Roadmap, companies could be permitted to issue financial statements in the United States using IFRS as early as 2014 for the largest U.S. companies, followed by another group in 2015, and the final group of smaller companies by 2016.[14] The SEC also proposed a rule for certain U.S. companies meeting certain criteria to adopt IFRS in 2009. However, as of mid-2011, no final decisions have been made on the final convergence process.

The European Response to Convergence   The main body of financial reporting requirements for limited liability companies in the EU consists of two directives issued by the European Council. Thus, it is important to understand that IFRS and interpretations must be approved by the European Parliament and the European Council and adopted as an official regulation by the European Commission to have legal standing in the EU.[15] This illustrates the importance of the political process in IFRS adoption. Prior to the development of the IASB, the European Union was working to harmonize reporting practices to better coordinate financial markets. To enhance that process, it supported the efforts of the IASB and, in the spring of 2002, directed its member countries to adopt IFRS by 2005. In the case of the EU, this meant that 7,000 publicly listed companies started using IFRS for their consolidated financial statements in 2005.[16] The two main reasons for the EU to push IFRS were to allow it to influence IASB standards and to avoid funding and developing a competing standard-setting body.[17] By working with the IASB, the EU would avoid relying on standards developed in the United States for capital market reporting.

The EU has adopted most of the standards as written, but has "carved out" or suspended the standard on financial instruments due largely to political pressure from French banks, which has been a problem. The fear is that the EU could end up with its own version of IFRS, resulting from political pressures rather than sound accounting judgment. So the EU ruled that any IFRS must be officially approved by the EU before it would have the force of law. It set up its own advisory process to review IFRS and recommend whether the standard would be acceptable to the EU. As a result, European companies, such as noted earlier in the chapter in the example of Daimler AG, must state that they adopt IFRS "as adopted by the EU." That means that upon recommendation of the EU, EU member companies can "opt out" or "carve out" certain standards, meaning that they could end up with their own version of IFRS. The convergence process has been very unsettling to some Europeans, because they feel the close cooperation of the

IASB and FASB is making the new IFRS suspiciously similar to standards issued by FASB. However, six of the IFRS trustees are from Europe and six from North America, including Canada, so the United States certainly does not dominate the Foundation.

Initial reactions of various parties to the adoption of IFRS by European firms have been interesting. Although companies in EU countries adopted IFRS in 2005, various interpretations and applications exist. Some companies use wide judgment in applying IFRS, while others use an adapted form with changes or alternative interpretations based on individual country accounting treatments. Moreover, the EU's versions of IFRS are not the full IFRS as approved by the EU. Our closing case will examine the process by which the Swedish company Ericsson has configured an EU version of IFRS as a means of responding to its particular needs in generating financial statements.

Differences in opinion exist on how IFRS should be applied across borders, even within the European Union. The Accounting Regulatory Committee of the European Commission must "recommend endorsement" of the new standards and interpretations, which must then be followed by an adoption of the new standards and interpretations by the Commission itself.[18] Concerns have also arisen as to how the new rules will be enforced. If companies disclose that their financial statements have been issued according to IFRS, it is up to the independent external auditors to verify that companies are complying with IFRS. That principle implies that the quality of the auditing profession is the same worldwide—a dubious assumption.

There are differences in Europe as to the relative power of government regulatory bodies and private sector approaches to setting accounting standards. France has the most restrictive/powerful regulatory government body. Differences in regulatory powers and structures may yield differences in the application of the accounting rules. It will be interesting to observe just how IFRS is applied and enforced in countries where these standards have been adopted. Also, IFRS adoption in the EU is applicable only to companies that are publicly traded. Private firms must still use local GAAP, although the IASB issued a set of standards in 2009 for SMEs.[19]

Convergence and Mutual Recognition   The move to convergence adds an interesting twist to mutual recognition. Today's version of mutual recognition in the United States is that foreign issuers are allowed to list securities using full IFRS without reconciliation to U.S. GAAP. EU members can use the EU form of IFRS and still be exempted from the reconciliation to U.S. GAAP. However, mutual recognition does not extend to companies that generate financial statements in their home-country GAAP. They are still required to issue Form 20-F. In early 2007, when there was a lot of support for IFRS convergence, representatives of the SEC and the U.S. Treasury made statements that supported the mutual recognition of IFRS in the United States.

Two things have now changed the landscape for convergence. The first is the world economic crisis, which diverted attention away from convergence to trying to resolve the credit crisis and global recession. The second was the appointment of a new SEC Chairman, who was less inclined to pursue the proposed Roadmap to convergence than her predecessor. In 2011, the path to convergence became even more complicated as the governments in Europe and the United States seemed to be more concerned about financial regulation and budget crises than convergence. However, the G20 met in 2009 and strongly recommend the adoption of IFRS worldwide, which lent even stronger support to the work of the IASB. In December 2010, the Chief Accountant of the SEC came up with the idea of "condorsement" as the approach the SEC might follow in the future, which is a combination of convergence and endorsement. The convergence part would refer to the completion of the Memorandum of Understanding (MOU) outlined in the Norwalk Agreement, and the endorsement part would involve having FASB endorse future IFRS as deemed appropriate in the context of U.S. capital markets.[20] However, an SEC Commissioner commented in June 2011 that the SEC must decide to incorporate IFRS for U.S. issuers.[21] The SEC hopes to make a decision by the end of 2011, so we'll see what happens.

Point

Yes A major issue for investors around the world is obtaining reliable, comparable financial-statement information for company evaluation and comparison. Creditors and other users also need this information for making well-informed decisions on a global basis. As the composition of the business world has shifted from domestic economies to a global economy, the need for a single set of financial reporting standards has never been greater. IFRS are required for listed entities in many countries, such as all countries in the European Union, Canada, Australia, Korea, and Turkey. Other countries have established implementation dates beyond 2011, and many others are considering how and when to adopt IFRS.

U.S. GAAP and IFRS are the two most recognized sets of standards today, and they are steadily becoming nearly identical to each other. The combined efforts of the IASB and the FASB in their convergence project have brought IFRS and U.S. GAAP closer than ever before. The SEC currently allows foreign firms that list on U.S. exchanges to use IFRS for financial reporting and should allow U.S. firms as well. Not only would this make the United States more a part of the global economy, U.S. firms could also raise more

Should U.S. Companies Be Allowed to Close the GAAP?

capital, because investors in countries that use it would be more familiar and able to keep up with the single international set of standards.

U.S. investors would also benefit. They would become more familiar with the international standards and would feel more apt to invest in international companies. As the IFRS/U.S. GAAP gap shrinks, the quality of the financial information presented under IFRS will not be lower than it has been under GAAP.

The "principles-based" approach of IFRS may actually enhance the quality of financial information and help the economy avoid some of the scandals that have occurred due to manipulation of loopholes in the more "rules-based" system that is U.S. GAAP. Principles-based accounting means that the standard-setters identify key principles in a conceptual framework used to set standards and then try to establish rules that are simple but conform to the principles. A rules-based system is very legalistic, with lots of detail and difficulty. Finally, if the United States does not adopt IFRS, it runs the risk of being left out of the debate for setting new standards. The rest of the world will be responsible for those.

Should U.S. Companies Be Allowed to Close the GAAP?

Counterpoint

No It is unrealistic to assume that IFRS would be appropriate for the unique U.S. economic environment. As the largest economy in the world, with the largest and most sophisticated capital market, the United States should have the most stringent and transparent financial reporting standards in the world. Many companies around the globe continue to prepare their financial information in accordance with U.S. GAAP, because it has historically been the world's most reliable set of standards, designed to present information that is both relevant and reliable. GAAP is set out in over 25,000 pages, compared to 2,500 of IFRS, so there is no way IFRS is as thorough, broad, or responsive to issues in the U.S. economy.

Allowing American companies to use IFRS would impose tremendous costs on the U.S. economy. Publicly traded firms would need trained employees proficient in IFRS application. U.S. accounting firms would be responsible for training their existing auditors in IFRS, hiring new employees and training them or hiring existing IFRS experts. This training and/or hiring would impose tremendous burdens in

both time and money on these important firms, which would still be held responsible for meeting all the rigorous standards of the Public Company Accounting Oversight Board (PCAOB) and the Sarbanes-Oxley Act of 2002.

The differences between IFRS and U.S. GAAP, although growing more insignificant, still exist. The standards are not directly comparable, which could mean trouble for investors who may have difficulty seeing the differences. In addition, more than one set of IFRS seems to exist: (1) IFRS as issued by the IASB, (2) IFRS as adopted by the EU, and (3) IFRS as applied/adopted on an individual-country basis. How will investors ascertain which set is being used by various companies, and how will this information be comparable?

Valuable invested money may leave the United States and be invested in foreign corporations not even listed in the country as U.S. investors become more expert in analyzing financial statements prepared in accordance with IFRS. And with more room for interpretation and discretion when applying IFRS, more accounting scandals could result when U.S. companies use the more "principles-based" IFRS instead of the more "rules-based" U.S. GAAP.

Transactions in Foreign Currencies

When a company operates outside the domestic market, it must concern itself with the proper recording and subsequent accounting of assets, liabilities, revenues, and expenses that are measured or denominated in foreign currencies. These transactions can result from the purchase and sale of goods and services as well as the borrowing and lending of foreign currency.

RECORDING TRANSACTIONS

Any time an importer has to pay for equipment or merchandise in a foreign currency, it must trade its own currency for that of the exporter to make the payment. Assume that Sundance Ski Lodge, a U.S. company, imports skis from a French supplier for €5,000 and agrees to pay in euros when the exchange rate is $1.4500/euro. Sundance records the following in its books:

Purchases	7,250	
Accounts payable		7,250
€5,000 @ 1.4500		

If Sundance pays immediately, there's no problem. But what happens if the exporter extends 30 days' credit to Sundance? If the rate changed to, say, $1.5000/euro by the time the payment was due, Sundance would record a final settlement as:

Accounts payable	7,250	
Foreign-exchange loss	250	
Cash		7,500

The merchandise stays at the original value of $7,250, but there is a difference between the dollar value of the account payable to the exporter ($7,250) and the actual number of dollars the importer must come up with to purchase the euros to pay the exporter ($7,500). The difference between the two accounts ($250) is the loss on foreign exchange and is always recognized in the income statement.

The company that denominates the sale or purchase in the foreign currency (in this case, the importer) must recognize the gains and losses arising from foreign-currency transactions at the end of each accounting period—usually quarterly. In the example here, assume that the end of the quarter has arrived and Sundance has still not paid the French exporter. The skis continue to be valued at $7,250, but the payable has to be updated to the new exchange rate of $1.5000/euro. The journal entry would be:

> Foreign-currency receivables and payables give rise to gains and losses whenever the exchange rate changes. Transaction gains and losses must be included in the income statement in the accounting period in which they arise.

Foreign-exchange loss	250	
Accounts payable		250

The payable would now be worth $7,500. If settlement were made in the month following the end of the quarter and the exchange rate remained the same, the final entry would be:

Accounts payable	7,500	
Cash		7,500

If the U.S. company were an exporter and anticipated receiving foreign currency, the corresponding entries (using the same information as in the example here) would be:

Accounts receivable	7,250	
Sales		7,250
Cash	7,500	
Foreign-exchange gain		250
Accounts receivable		7,250

In this case, a gain results because the company received more cash than if it had collected its money immediately.

CORRECT PROCEDURES FOR U.S. COMPANIES

The procedures U.S. companies must follow to account for foreign-currency transactions are found in FASB Statement No. 52, "Foreign Currency Translation," which requires them to record the initial transaction at the spot exchange rate in effect on the transaction date and to record receivables and payables on subsequent balance-sheet dates at the spot exchange rate on those dates. Any foreign-exchange gains and losses that arise from carrying receivables or payables during a period in which the exchange rate changes are recognized in the income statement in that period.[22] This is basically the same procedure required by the IASB as well as in IAS 21.

> The FASB requires that U.S. companies report foreign-currency transactions at the original spot exchange rate and that subsequent gains and losses on foreign-currency receivables or payables be put on the income statement. The same procedure must be followed according to IFRS.

Translating Foreign-Currency Financial Statements

> Translation—the process of restating foreign-currency financial statements.

> Consolidation—the process of combining the translated financial statements of a parent and its subsidiaries into one set of financial statements.

Even though U.S.-based MNEs receive reports originally developed in a variety of different currencies, they eventually must end up with one set of financial statements in U.S. dollars to help management and investors understand their worldwide activities in a common currency. The process of restating foreign-currency financial statements into U.S. dollars is called **translation.** The combination of all of these translated financial statements into one is **consolidation.** The same concept exists for other countries, such as a British-based MNE that has to come up with a set of financial statements in British pounds. For the sake of illustration, we use a U.S.-based MNE.

Translation in the United States is a two-step process:

1. *Companies recast foreign-currency financial statements into statements consistent with U.S. GAAP.* This occurs because a U.S. company with a subsidiary in Brazil, for example, must keep the books and records in Brazil according to Brazilian GAAP. For consolidation purposes, however, the resulting financial statements have to be issued according to U.S. GAAP in format as well as content. As an example of content, Brazil might require that inventories be valued a certain way. For the U.S. consolidated financial statements, however, inventories must be valued according to U.S., not Brazilian, standards. This is a big issue when local GAAP is very different from U.S. GAAP. As more foreign countries adopt IFRS, the differences between IFRS financial statements and U.S. GAAP financial statements will be less significant.

2. *Companies translate all foreign-currency amounts into U.S. dollars.* FASB Statement No. 52 describes how companies must translate their foreign-currency financial statements into dollars. All U.S. companies, as well as foreign firms that list on a U.S. exchange, must use Statement No. 52.

TRANSLATION METHODS

Statement No. 52 and IAS 21, the relevant translation standards issued by the FASB and the IASB, respectively, are basically the same in how they require MNEs to translate their foreign-currency financial statements into the currency of the parent's country. For simplicity's sake, we continue to use the example of a U.S.-based MNE that must translate its foreign-currency financial statements into dollars. It would use FASB Statement 52, while a British-based MNE would use IAS 21. The two standards yield the same result.

> The functional currency is the currency of the primary economic environment in which the entity operates.

Two Methods: Current-Rate and Temporal   Both standards allow companies to use either of two methods in the translation process: the **current-rate method** (called the *closing rate method* under IFRS) or the **temporal method**. The one the company chooses depends on the **functional currency** of the foreign operation, which is the currency of the primary economic environment in which that entity operates. Whichever method a company uses, it has to determine the proper exchange rate to translate the foreign-currency balances into U.S. dollars.

For example, one of Coca-Cola's largest operations outside the United States is in Japan. Its primary economic environment is Japan, and its functional currency is the Japanese yen. The FASB identifies several factors that can help management determine the functional currency: cash flows, sales prices, sales market data, expenses, financing, and transactions with other entities within the corporate group. So if, say, the cash flows and expenses are primarily in the foreign operation's currency, that is the functional currency; if they are in the parent's currency, that is the functional currency.

If the functional currency is that of the local operating environment, the company must use the current-rate method, which provides that it translates all assets and liabilities at the current exchange rate, which is the spot exchange rate on the balance-sheet date. All income-statement items are translated at the average exchange rate, and owners' equity is translated at the rates in effect when the company issued capital stock and accumulated retained earnings.

> The current-rate method applies when the local currency is the functional currency.

If the functional currency is the parent's currency, the MNE must use the temporal method, which provides that only monetary assets (cash, marketable securities, and receivables) and liabilities are translated at the current exchange rate. The company translates inventory, property, plants, and equipment at the historical exchange rates (the transaction rate in IASB terminology), which are the exchange rates in effect when the assets were acquired. In general, the company translates most income-statement accounts at the average exchange rate, but it translates cost of goods sold and depreciation expense, as well as owners' equity, at the appropriate historical exchange rates.

> The temporal method applies when the parent's reporting currency is the functional currency.

Because companies can choose the translation method—current-rate or temporal—that's most appropriate for a particular foreign subsidiary, they don't have to use one or the other for all subsidiaries. Coca-Cola sells its products in over 200 countries and uses 75 different functional currencies.[23] This practice is typical of many MNEs.

Figure 18.9 summarizes the selection of translation method, depending on the choice of functional currency. As in the preceding explanation, if the functional currency is the currency of the country where the foreign subsidiary is located, the current-rate method applies. If it is the reporting currency of the parent company, the temporal method applies.

The Translation Process Tables 18.1 and 18.2 show a balance sheet and income statement developed under both approaches to compare the differences in translation methodologies. The beginning balance in retained earnings for both methods is assumed to be $40,000. Using the explanation above, the following exchange rates are used to perform the translation process in Tables 18.1 and 18.2:

- $1.5000—Historical exchange rate when fixed assets were acquired and capital stock issued
- $1.6980—Current exchange rate on December 31, 2009

FIGURE 18.9 Selecting a Translation Method

When an MNE receives reports from subsidiaries or branched located in different countries, the accounting department is faces with financial figures stated in different currencies. Accountants must translate these foreign-currency figures into amounts stated in the currency of the parent's home country. The functional currency may be either the currency of the economic environment in which the subsidiary or branch operates or the parent firm's currency, and the choice of functional currency will determine the translation method that the company will use.

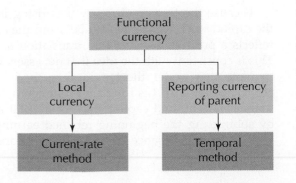

TABLE 18.1   Translating Foreign Currency: The Balance Sheet

	Foreign Currency	Temporal Method Rate	Temporal Method Dollars	Current-Rate Method Rate	Current-Rate Method Dollars
Cash	20,000	1.6980	33,960	1.6980	33,960
Accounts receivable	40,000	1.6980	67,920	1.6980	67,920
Inventories	40,000	1.5606	62,424	1.6980	67,920
Fixed assets	100,000	1.5000	150,000	1.6980	169,800
Accumulated depreciation	(20,000)	1.5000	(30,000)	1.6980	(33,960)
Total Assets	**180,000**		**284,304**		**305,960**
Accounts payable	30,000	1.6980	50,940	1.6980	50,940
Long-term debt	44,000	1.6980	74,712	1.6980	74,712
Capital stock	60,000	1.5000	90,000	1.5000	90,000
Retained earnings	46,000	*	68,652	*	77,481
Accumulated translation adjustment					12,507
Total Liabilities and Owners' Equity	**180,000**		**284,304**		**305,640**

Retained earnings is the U.S. dollar equivalent of all income earned in prior years retained in the business rather than distributed to shareholders plus this year's income. There is no single exchange rate used to translate retained earnings into dollars.

TABLE 18.2   Translating Foreign Currency: The Income Statement

	Foreign Currency	Temporal Method Rate	Temporal Method Dollars	Current-Rate Method Rate	Current-Rate Method Dollars
Sales	230,000	1.5617	359,191	1.5617	359,191
Expenses:					
Cost of goods sold	(110,000)	1.5600	(171,600)	1.5617	(171,787)
Depreciation	(10,000)	1.5000	(15,000)	1.5617	(15,617)
Other	(80,000)	1.5617	(124,936)	1.5617	(124,936)
Taxes	(6,000)	1.5617	(9,370)	1.5617	(9,370)
Translation gain (loss)	24,000		(9,633)		
Net Income	**24,000**		**28,652**		**37,481**

- $1.5617—Average exchange rate during 2009
- $1.5606—Exchange rate during which the ending inventory was acquired
- $1.5600—Historical exchange rate for cost of goods sold

With the current-rate method, the translation gain or loss is recognized in comprehensive income rather than net income, and therefore it goes to owners' equity. With the temporal method, the translation gain or loss is recognized on the income statement.

Because the foreign currency was rising in value (strengthening) between the time the capital stock was issued ($1.500) and the end of the year ($1.6980), the balance sheet reflects a positive accumulated translation adjustment under the current-rate method. This is consistent with the idea that net assets were gaining value in a strong currency.

Note that under the temporal method, the ending retained earnings balance of $68,652 in Table 18.1 is found by subtracting the translated values of accounts payable, long-term debt, and capital stock from total assets. In Table 18.2, net income is found by subtracting the beginning retained earnings balance ($40,000) from the ending retained earnings balance ($68,652). When translating the income-statement accounts in

Table 18.2, however, it is necessary to plug in the translation loss of $9,633 to get the net-income figure of $28,652. In the case of the current-rate method, net income is found in Table 18.2 by subtracting translated expenses from revenues. There is no translation gain or loss on the income statement, as will be explained below. On the balance sheet in Table 18.1, the retained earnings balance of $77,841 is found by adding net income ($37,481) to the beginning retained earnings balance ($40,000). However, total assets must equal total liabilities and owners' equity, so the accumulated translation adjustment of $12,507 must be plugged in to get the right total balance.

Disclosing Foreign-Exchange Gains and Losses A major difference between the two translation methods is in the recognition of foreign-exchange gains and losses. Under the current-rate method, the gain or loss is called an *accumulated translation adjustment* and is taken to comprehensive income rather than net income, so it appears as a separate line item in owners' equity. This is important, because the accumulated translation adjustment does not affect earnings per share, a key figure that financial analysts monitor. From a cultural perspective, this points out how important net income is to U.S.-based companies, which rely on the stock market as a major source of funding. Under the temporal method, the gain or loss is taken directly to net income and thus affects earnings per share.

Management Accounting Issues

We have discussed some important financial accounting issues that relate to preparing financial statements for external users, especially the stock markets. Now we turn to some important management accounting issues MNEs must deal with, including *performance evaluation and control*, the *impact of transfer pricing on performance evaluation*, and the use of the *balanced scorecard* as a means of broadly evaluating performance.

PERFORMANCE EVALUATION AND CONTROL

Chapter 15 addressed the importance of using reports as part of the control mechanism. Setting strategic objectives usually requires managers to focus on choosing a suitable business metric or metrics. Metrics can be quantified in terms of a particular budget number or financial ratio, and they seem to vary considerably from country to country. Possible metrics include return on investment, sales, cost reduction, quality targets, market share, profitability, and a comparison of budget (such as the sales revenue budget) to actual results (such as actual sales revenues). There may also be environmental targets companies are trying to reach, especially given that many companies must meet Kyoto Protocol goals for reducing greenhouse gas emissions.

The choice of metric depends on the company, the home country, and the strategic intent—global versus multidomestic, sales versus cost minimization, and so forth. Sales or market share is particularly relevant for a unit that has no control over its input costs and whose primary purpose is to sell the goods of some other unit. Profitability, measured as a ratio or some other measure, is most appropriate for a fully fledged SBU.

U.S.-based MNEs are more likely to use return on investment (ROI) as the most important metric.[24] In a study of British MNEs, companies tended to use budget versus actual comparisons, followed by some form of ROI.[25] A study of Japanese MNEs, with a significantly different culture, found that sales was the most important metric.[26] Thus, you can see some major differences in selecting metrics, and most MNEs use a variety of metrics, not just one.

> Different measures are used to evaluate performance of foreign operations, including ROI, sales, cost reduction, quality targets, market share, profitability, and budget to actual.

When using a budget, management must select a currency to set the budget and a currency to evaluate performance.

The most widely used approaches to translate budgets and compare with performance use forecasts of the exchange rate.

Performance Evaluation in the Budgeting Process   A complicating factor for MNEs is setting targets or budgets in different currencies. The budget will be set either at headquarters in dollars (for a U.S.-based MNE) and then translated into local currency or at the foreign location in the local currency and translated into dollars for use at headquarters. Either way, the MNE must deal with currency in the budgeting process.

There are many different ways firms can translate the budget from the local currency into the parent currency and then monitor actual performance.[27] Three different exchange rates are used in Table 18.3:

1. The actual rate in effect when the budget was established (A-1)
2. The rate projected at the time the budget was established in the local currency (P-1)
3. The actual rate in effect when the budgeted period took place (E-1)

The attractiveness of the first rate is that it is an objective spot rate that actually exists on a given day. It is a reasonable rate to use in a stable environment, but it may be meaningless in an unstable foreign-exchange environment. The projected rate is an attempt on the part of management to forecast what it thinks the rate will be for the budgeted time period. For example, management might project in November 2011 that the exchange rate between the U.S. dollar and the British pound will be $1.680000 during the first six months of 2012, so that would be the projected exchange rate used in the budgeting process. The actual exchange rate found in cell E-3 is an update of the exchange rate in effect when the budget was established, and provides the actual rate in effect when the time period takes place.

These three exchange rates need to be considered for establishing the budget as well as monitoring performance. In cells A-1, P-2, and E-3, the exchange rate used to establish the budget and monitor performance is the same, so any variances will be due to price and volume, not the rate. The value of P-2 over A-1 and E-3 is that it forces management to think initially of what its performance will be if the forecast is reasonably accurate. A-1 never takes into account what the exchange rate will be, and it does not attempt to reconcile the difference in the budget comparing the original rate with the actual rate. Given the instability in exchange rates, however, some would argue that a forecast rate is no more accurate than any other. E-3 does take into consideration what performance is at the actual exchange rate, but it does not force management to be forward-thinking during the budget process.

A-3 and P-3 result in a variance that is a function of operating results and exchange-rate changes. Under A-3, the budget is established at the initial rate, but actual performance is translated at the actual rate. Thus, there is an exchange-rate variance that is the difference between the original and actual rates. P-3 results in a variance that is the difference between what management thought the exchange rate would be and what it actually was at the end of the operating period. If management's forecast was reasonably accurate, P-3 should result in a very small foreign-exchange variance.

If the exchange rate between the parent and local currency is relatively stable, A-3 should also result in a relatively small variance. However, it is important to realize that the use of A-3 and P-3 means that someone (usually local management) will be held accountable for the variances.

Forecast Rates   As you can see in Table 18.3 the most widely used approaches for considering foreign exchange when comparing budget with actual performance for a sample of British MNEs are A-1, P-2, and P-3. The use of a *forecast rate* for setting budgets is by far the preferred approach. A forecast is usually made by the economists in the corporate treasury or in consultation with banks.

TABLE 18.3 Exchange Rates and the British MNE Budget

Note that among British MNEs, using *forecast* rates for setting budgets (P-2 and P-3) is the preferred method. Both methods are also conducive to the use of *hedging strategies*—strategies, such as *forward contracts* and *options,* that allow companies to transfer risk to other parties.

| | Rate Used for Performance Evaluation | | | |
Rate Used to Determine Budget	Actual Rate at Time of Budget	Projected Rate at Time of Budget	Actual Rate at End of Budget Period	Total
Actual Rate at Time of Budget	A-1 10 Firms	A-2 0 Firms	A-3 4 Firms	**14 Firms**
Projected Rate at Time of Budget	P-1 0 Firms	P-2 16 Firms	P-3 11 Firms	**27 Firms**
Actual Rate at End of Budget Period	E-1 0 Firms	E-2 0 Firms	E-3 0 Firms	**0 Firms**
Total	**10 Firms**	**16 Firms**	**15 Firms**	

Source: Based on S. Demirag and Cristina De Fuentes, "Exchange Rate Fluctuations and Management Control in UK-Based MNCs: An Examination of the Theory and Practice," *European Journal of Finance* 5:3 (1999): 3–28.

If the budget process is centralized, corporate treasury probably consults its lead money center bank or a couple of banks to get a consensus forecast of exchange rates. If the process is decentralized, the local operations probably consult one or more local banks. Given that most money center banks have operations worldwide, corporate treasury will receive forecasts from the money center bank's subsidiaries in countries where they have operations.

Notice also in Table 18.3 that the largest number of entities compared their initial budget prepared with a projected exchange rate with actual results using the projected exchange rate. In essence, those entities held exchange rates constant. However, the next largest number of companies used a projected rate to establish the budget but compared the budget with actual results translated at the actual exchange rate at the end of the period. The reason to follow that approach is because investors and creditors want to know what actual results are, so by comparing the budget with actual results, management can align the needs of investors and creditors with their internal measurement of results. Adidas illustrates how companies try to separate the impact of foreign exchange from their operating performance. In its 2010 annual report, Adidas provided information comparing its 2009 and 2010 results, but it also reported that "in 2010, Group revenues grew 9 percent on a currency-neutral basis, as a result of sales increases in Wholesale, Retail, and Other businesses." It also stated that currency-neutral sales grew in all segments and in all regions except for Greater China.[28]

Hedging Strategies Another interesting twist to using P-2 and P-3 is for companies that extensively use *hedging strategies*. In that case, they may use a hedge rate instead of a forecast rate for setting budgets. Assume, for example, that a U.S.-based MNE decides to hedge its future balance sheet and income statement in Brazil by entering into forward contracts. Because management knows the forward rate, it could set its budget at that rate instead of a forecast rate from a bank. The variance would be the difference between the forward rate and the future spot rate.

TRANSFER PRICING AND PERFORMANCE EVALUATION

An additional element of MNE management is **transfer pricing**, which refers to the pricing of goods and services that are transferred (bought and sold) between members of

Transfer pricing refers to prices on intracompany transfers of goods, services, and capital.

a corporate family—parent to subsidiaries, between subsidiaries, from subsidiaries to parent, and so on. As such, internal transfers include raw materials, semifinished and finished goods, allocation of fixed costs, loans, fees, royalties for use of trademarks, copyrights, and other factors. In theory, such prices should be based on production costs, but in reality they often are not.

There are conflicting reasons for setting transfer prices that make it difficult for top management to select the correct price.

An important reason for arbitrarily establishing transfer prices is taxation. However, it is only one of a number of reasons why internal transfers may be priced with little consideration for market prices or production costs. Companies may underprice goods sold to foreign affiliates so the affiliates can then sell them at prices their local competitors cannot match. If tough antidumping laws exist on final products in the affiliate country, a company could underprice components and semifinished products to its affiliates. The affiliates could then assemble or finish the final product at prices that would have been classified as dumping prices had they been imported directly into the country rather than produced domestically.

High transfer prices might be used to circumvent or significantly lessen the impact of national controls. A government prohibition on dividend remittances could restrict a firm's ability to maneuver income out of a country. However, overpricing the goods shipped to a subsidiary in such a country would enable funds to be taken out. High transfer prices would also be of considerable value to a firm when it is paid a subsidy or earns a tax credit on the value of goods it exports. The higher the transfer prices on exported goods, the greater the subsidies earned or tax credit received.

High transfer prices on goods shipped to subsidiaries might be desirable when a parent wishes to lower the apparent profitability of its subsidiary. This is because of the subsidiary workers' demands for higher wages or greater participation in company profits, political pressures to expropriate high-profit, foreign-owned operations, or new competitors being lured into the industry by high profits. There might also be inducements for channeling high-priced transfers to the subsidiary when a local partner is involved, the inducement being that the increase in the parent-company profits will not have to be split with the local partner. High transfer prices may also be desired when increases from existing price controls in the subsidiary's country are based on product costs (including high transfer prices for purchases).

Table 18.4 identifies the conditions in a subsidiary's country inducing either a high or a low transfer price on flows between affiliates and the parent. The challenge in setting an optimal transfer price is that there could be conflicting conditions in the local country. For example, a subsidiary could be in a country with a low corporate income tax rate (which calls for low transfer prices on goods shipped from parent to subsidiary to maximize profits at the subsidiary level) but with high political instability (which calls for high transfer prices to get money out of the country as quickly as possible).

THE BALANCED SCORECARD

The concept of the **balanced scorecard (BSC)** is another approach to performance measurement increasingly being used by companies, especially in the United States and Europe. At one time, approximately 50 percent of *Fortune* 1000 companies in North America and about 40 percent in Europe used a version of it, according to a survey by Bain & Co.[29] This approach endeavors to link more closely the strategic and financial perspectives of a firm and takes a broad view of business performance.[30]

The BSC provides a framework for looking at the strategies giving rise to value creation from the following perspectives:

The balanced scorecard is an approach to performance measurement that closely links the strategic and financial perspectives of a business.

1. *Financial*—growth, profitability, and risk from a shareholder perspective
2. *Customer*—value and differentiation from a customer perspective

TABLE 18.4 Factors Influencing High and Low Transfer Prices

Members of corporate families are constantly selling goods and services among themselves, and they can sometimes create competitive or financial advantages when determining the prices that they set on internally transferred goods and services. A wide range of factors can influence a parent company's decision to raise or lower prices charged to a subsidiary.

Conditions Conducive to *Low* Transfer Prices *from* Parent Company and *High* Transfer Prices *to* Parent Company	Conditions Conducive to *High* Transfer Prices *from* Parent Company and *Low* Transfer Prices *to* Parent Company
High ad valorem tariffs	Local partners
Corporate income tax rate lower than in parent's country	Pressure from workers to obtain greater share of company profit
Significant competition	Political pressure to nationalize or expropriate high-profit foreign firms
Local loans based on financial appearance of subsidiary	Restrictions on profit or dividend remittances
Export subsidy or tax credit on value of exports	Political instability
Lower inflation rate than in parent's country	Substantial tie-in sales agreements
Restrictions (ceilings) in subsidiary's country on the *value* of products that can be imported	Price of final product controlled by government but based on production cost
	Desire to mask profitability of subsidiary operations to keep competitors out

Source: Jeffrey S. Arpan, *Intracorporate Pricing: Non-American Systems and Views* (New York: Praeger, 1972).

3. *Internal business processes*—the priorities for various business processes that create customer and shareholder satisfaction

4. *Learning and growth*—the priorities to create a climate supporting organizational change, innovation, and growth

Although the focus is still ultimately on financial performance, the BSC approach reveals the drivers of long-term competitive performance. In simple terms, learning and growth help create more efficient business processes, which create value for customers, who then reward the firm financially. The challenge is to clearly identify these drivers, agree on relevant measures, and implement the new system at all organization levels. The significant aspect about this measurement approach, however, is that it also creates a focus for the future, because the measures used communicate to managers what is important.

> Using the balanced scorecard helps management avoid using only one measure of performance.

A Case in Point: Internal Learning and Growth at IKEA Although a firm's BSC is a proprietary strategic tool and generally not available to the general public, its principles are evident in the strategic decisions made by MNEs. IKEA, the Swedish firm, is a case in point. With strong roots in the Swedish culture and a centralized operating style, IKEA has grown to become the world's largest furniture retailer. The company uses a global strategy to spread a simple concept: Offer the broadest range of furniture at the lowest price possible.

IKEA's success begins with internal learning and growth by ensuring that all employees are trained in the cost-saving, hands-on, customer-focused mentality, enabling them to focus on creating efficient processes that keep costs down. As an example, the design team is constantly looking for new materials and suppliers to lower the cost of furniture without sacrificing quality.

Since its founding, IKEA has identified a customer base that would find value in low-cost, innovative furniture: young couples looking to furnish their first apartment. This strategic cohesiveness has rewarded the company with phenomenal growth. By the end of August 2010 (the close of IKEA's fiscal year), IKEA was operating 316 stores in more than 35 countries, with sales of €23.8 billion.[31]

Although the BSC offers the advantages of logically connecting financial performance with its nonfinancial drivers, establishing a coherent scorecard for an MNE has its challenges. As IKEA grows, it faces different customer bases in different countries and must ensure that its streamlined product line has appeal in its several markets of operation.

The cultural, geographic, and financial complexity of an MNE makes it challenging to establish a set of interrelated cause-and-effect performance measures. This task appears simpler for MNEs with global strategies like IKEA. However, multidomestic MNEs, such as Philips, have successfully implemented the BSC concept.

Perhaps the BSC helps solve many of the control and evaluation dilemmas presented throughout this chapter. Adequate use of it helps managers avoid using only one metric (such as ROI or sales growth) and forces them to link financial measures with the nonfinancial factors that drive them. In addition, subsidiaries are evaluated based on a coherent set of performance bases instead of just one base that may or may not be directly controlled by that subsidiary. Thus, the BSC concept has been refined into a strategic management system, which replaces the traditional focus on the budget as the center of the management process.[32]

The crucial consideration is to identify the most essential drivers for success and to look broadly, as recommended in the BSC, rather than focusing on a narrow financial measure. Management must then identify the most important metrics, or set of measurements, to identify how the company is performing.[33] This could be ROI, or it could also be the number of times a company is criticized for using call-center employees who are not fluent in the target language of customers.

Corporate Governance

The work of the controller is an important dimension in the overall corporate governance program a company puts into place. **Corporate governance** refers to the combination of external and internal mechanisms implemented to safeguard the assets of a company and protect the rights of the shareholders. Though not a new concept, corporate scandals in recent years have resulted in increased attention being given to corporate governance. A major problem at Parmalat, for example, was management collusion in diverting corporate resources into private family businesses and defrauding investors and creditors by means of improper accounting and reporting. In short, there was very little oversight of Parmalat's operations (and certainly none at the top).

Case Review Note

Corporate governance is the external and internal factors designed to safeguard the assets of a company and protect the rights of shareholders.

EXTERNAL CONTROL MECHANISMS: THE LEGAL SYSTEM

An important external mechanism in corporate governance is the legal system. Countries like the United States have a very litigious environment that allows people to sue company management. Countries with a strong legal tradition, such as in many Latin American countries, must have corporate governance practices put into law to ensure that companies follow the best practices.

Much of the world, especially developing countries, has an underdeveloped and poorly functioning legal system that pays scant attention to corporate governance. Other countries have moved forward to institute needed legislation. Mexico passed a law on corporate governance in 2000 to encourage more accurate financial reporting and more transparent disclosure practices by management.[34] Brazil has increased its corporate governance through the opening of the Novo Mercado (New Market) on BM and F BOVESPA, the Brazilian stock exchange. A firm wanting to list on the Novo Mercado must adhere to the highest possible standards of corporate governance required by the Exchange. Because of this, some listed Brazilian companies are rated as having the highest levels of corporate governance in Latin America.[35]

The Sarbanes-Oxley Act in the United States As a result of U.S. corporate scandals, especially Enron, the U.S. government passed the Sarbanes-Oxley Act of 2002 (SOX), which resulted in strict reporting requirements for public firms in the United States and for foreign firms listing there. SOX also required stronger internal controls and tougher oversight on the part of external auditors.

Satisfying this requirement has proved quite expensive for MNEs, especially those from other countries that list on the New York Stock Exchange. However, it also required foreign firms to adopt higher levels of internal control than were required in their home countries, hoping to avoid the types of problems that occurred with Enron and similar corporate scandals. As a result, many foreign MNEs have decided to exit the NYSE as a place to raise capital, and others have decided against listing on the NYSE for the first time. However, some have argued that these decisions were part of an overall cost-benefit analysis of whether to list on the NYSE or NASDAQ, given that other stock markets, especially in Europe, are becoming important places to raise capital, and that firms didn't want to go through the rigorous process of registering with the SEC.

> Corporate governance practices worldwide are partly a function of the legal environment in the countries where companies operate.

> The Sarbanes-Oxley Act of 2002 was passed in the United States to improve financial reporting and strengthen internal controls.

INTERNAL CONTROL MECHANISMS

Internal mechanisms refer to the management and ownership structure of the firm as well as the role of the board of directors in overseeing its operations.[36] Large U.S.-based MNEs rely on the stock market as a major source of financing. Thus, a firm's corporate governance system has to take into account how it protects investors and discloses information to the public.

Firms in developing countries tend to be family-controlled, with family members in key management positions and occupying important seats on the boards of directors. This is a major problem that led to Parmalat's fraud. Voting rights for stocks also tend to be in the hands of family members instead of outside investors. Thus, the rights of minority owners are not protected very much in the absence of legal requirements. Firms from developing countries that list on foreign stock exchanges, however, have to conform more to corporate governance practices in the developed countries.

CRN
Case Review Note

Boards of directors are now taking a stronger role worldwide, especially in the audit area. It is more common to have an outside member of the board be responsible for the audit function, which is designed to improve the integrity of financial reporting. The implementation of IFRS worldwide is important, but if companies don't implement strong corporate governance practices, investors will still not be safeguarded as much as they need to be.

Looking to the
Future   Will IFRS Become the Global Accounting Standard?

With the adoption of IFRS by the EU, Australia, Brazil, New Zealand, and others, more than 100 countries on six continents will be requiring or permitting its use for some or all domestic listed companies. The adoption of IFRS has been a steady process, and the key will be how the United States responds to the call to adopt them. From an accounting standpoint, the key question is this: What will become the Coca-Cola of accounting standards: U.S. GAAP or IFRS? In other words, which will have the most recognized "brand name"?

IFRS has a lot going for it, and its proponents are working hard to ensure that it is accepted around the world. The IASB reaches through its board members and committees to various regions of the world by assignment to help them with adopting or converging with IFRS. The SEC simply sets guidelines and expects companies that wish to list in the United States to abide by these guidelines and laws.

IFRS is being set by collaboration with many of the major countries in the world, so it is the product of a great deal of negotiation, compromise, and broad-

(continued)

based input. It's appealing to Europeans because they have a lot of influence in the development of the standards and it's free of regulation by the SEC. It also has EU backing, as noted earlier. Initially, it appeared that by 2009, non-European companies (including U.S. firms) would have to list on European exchanges using IFRS. If they also wanted to list in the United States, they would have to list according to U.S. GAAP unless they were fully compliant with IFRS. However, at least the new IFRS have a strong capital market orientation. At some point, the United States may simply adopt IFRS, but timing is everything. There is just too much inertia behind the adoption of IFRS. Even the G20 is strongly pushing the adoption of IFRS as one way to strengthen the regulation of securities markets worldwide.

The major vote in favor of U.S. GAAP is that half the world's stock market capitalization is located in the United States, and companies that want access to U.S. capital must play by U.S. rules. Americans have always felt that their standards were the best in the world and that it would be unfair for U.S. companies competing for cash in the U.S. market to allow foreign companies to list using IFRS, which is perceived as more flexible and less comprehensive than U.S. GAAP. Foreign companies that want to list outside their national markets typically look to the United States first and thus have to adopt U.S. reporting requirements. However, the decision by the SEC to allow foreign firms to list in the U.S. if they use IFRS is a major game changer. As European stock markets continue to grow in importance, more European companies are choosing to list in Europe instead of the United States. An additional complication to combining or converging IFRS and U.S. GAAP is the Sarbanes-Oxley Act of 2002. Requiring companies to establish solid internal controls over financial reporting, this legislation limits the types of services that may be performed by primary auditors in addition to the financial-statement audit and requires the managers of publicly traded companies to assess internal controls and make a statement on this assessment, which must be examined and opined on by external auditors.

All of these requirements add additional costs to those already related to complying with U.S. GAAP. Although perhaps good for companies in the long term, as they must establish effective controls over financial reporting, the initial costs of complying with the Sarbanes-Oxley Act of 2002 may be too great for some firms to consider listing on U.S. exchanges. In addition, the United States has strict laws on granting stock options to managers, while the U.S. market has a heightened sensitivity to wrongdoing because of recent major accounting scandals.

The convergence project between the FASB and IASB may solve some of these problems in the long run. To its credit, the IASB has expanded coverage of key topics and has narrowed the alternatives available to companies. It has sold itself as based on *principles* rather than *rules,* although it is more accurate to say that the standards are simpler and less comprehensive. Anytime you have a standard, you have to have a rule. It's just that U.S. GAAP is very rule-based and complicated and covers far more topics and industries. However, the FASB and IASB are narrowing the differences in existing standards and developing new ones together. Now they jointly write new standards so that even the wording is the same. In addition, public accounting firms and publicly traded companies have five years of experience in adopting the requirements of Sarbanes-Oxley. Maybe the future of accounting standards will be like a merger of Coca-Cola and Pepsi—although accounting is a lot more complicated than soft drinks. ∎

CASE   Ericsson: The Challenges of Listing on Global Capital Markets and the Move to Adopt International Financial Reporting Standards

In 2002, the European Union mandated that its member countries adopt International Financial Reporting Standards (IFRS) as the basis for preparing and issuing consolidated financial statements beginning in 2005.[37] Ericsson, the Swedish MNE that supplies products and services to the world's largest mobile- and fixed-network operators, is a public limited-liability company that must follow the Swedish Companies Act and the listing requirements of the Swedish Stock Exchange. In addition, it must comply with the listing requirements of NASDAQ in the United States, because it lists securities on that stock exchange. Given that Sweden is a member of the EU, Ericsson was required to adopt IFRS as of 2005, which is a change from its past practices. However, there are currently two sets of IFRS: (1) EU-approved IFRS and (2) full IFRS as issued by the International Accounting Standards Board (IASB).

Should Ericsson adopt the full IFRS or just the more limited EU-approved IFRS? What are the implications of its decision to list on NASDAQ, and what are some of the other issues Ericsson has to face as a result of its decision to raise capital outside of its home market of Sweden?

A Little More about Ericsson

L. M. Ericsson was founded in Sweden in 1876 and is best known to the casual consumer through a Sony Ericsson joint venture that sells cellular handsets worldwide. However, it fits in the broader network of the communications equipment industry. Although Ericsson is known as one of Sweden's premier MNEs, it generates 24 percent of its sales in North America; 21 percent in the EU countries; 13 percent in China and Northeast Asia; 10 percent in Western and Central Europe—but only 6 percent in Northern Europe and Central Asia.

It issues stock (shares) in two major stock markets: Stockholm and NASDAQ. Thus it raises capital from investors internationally and generates most of its sales outside its native Sweden. In fact, only 2 percent of its sales are generated in Sweden, even though 63.1 percent of its fixed assets and 19 percent of its employees are located there. Ericsson's major competitors are Nokia, Motorola, Cisco Systems, and Alcatel-Lucent.

Before the Changeover to IFRS

Prior to the move to IFRS in 2005, Ericsson reported its financial results in compliance with Swedish GAAP—a bit of a mixture between Anglo-American accounting, which is driven by the capital markets, and Germanic accounting, which is driven by bank financing and taxation. Swedish reporting tends to be a little more transparent than German accounting but less transparent than Anglo-American accounting.

Issues of Transparency

One of the reasons why Swedish accounting has been less transparent is its orientation to creditors, government, and tax authorities. However, companies like Ericsson have had to become more transparent because of their desire to raise capital on foreign stock exchanges. In addition, because the Swedish Stock Exchange has become a focal point for listings by Nordic companies, the influential Swedish accounting profession has pushed for consolidated accounts to represent the needs of shareholders, whereas the parent-company accounts have reflected Swedish legal requirements. Swedish accounting tends to be very conservative due to the importance of taxes to fund extensive social welfare programs and the tendency of the Swedish government to use tax policies to influence investment in areas deemed important to the government and its social objectives.

Sweden and the EU

Since Sweden entered the EU, Swedish accounting has evolved to incorporate EU accounting directives and philosophies. The Swedish government established an Accounting Standards Board (BFN) in 1976 to recommend accounting principles that fit within the framework of the Company Law. The Swedish Financial Accounting Council (RR) was established in 1991 to take over the role of the accounting profession in making recommendations on accounting practices, especially with respect to how to prepare an annual report according to the Annual Accounts Act.

The Swedish Stock Exchange has supported the efforts of the Accounting Council and the BFN, even though the recommendations of both bodies are voluntary and subject to the Company Law. However, the decision by the EU to require firms to use IFRS for consolidated financial statements takes precedence over everything for consolidated financial statements.

The Gap between U.S. GAAP and Swedish GAAP

In its 2004 annual report, Ericsson still disclosed information according to the Swedish Company Law, although it knew by then that it would have to adopt IFRS the following year. Because so many IFRS were still being finalized in 2004, it did not "early adopt" the new standards. In its Note on Accounting Policies, Ericsson stated that it prepared its consolidated and parent-company financial statements "in accordance with accounting principles generally accepted in Sweden." However, it also mentioned that "these accounting principles differ in certain respects from generally accepted accounting principles in the United States (US GAAP)" and it gave a description of those differences in a later footnote in the report.

Even though it was trading shares on the London Stock Exchange at the time, it did not make any reference to differences between Swedish GAAP and U.K. GAAP. This is because the London Stock Exchange does not require a reconciliation like the U.S. exchanges do.

Applying the Conservatism Index   In its Note to the Financial Statements detailing the differences between Swedish GAAP and U.S. GAAP, Ericsson mentions that the major differences are the treatment of capitalization of development expenses, provisions for restructuring, pension costs, hedge accounting, and goodwill. The overall difference in income is fairly significant. Using *Gray's conservatism index,* we can calculate the degree to which Ericsson's net income in 2004 was more or less conservative compared to U.S. income. We gain this information from Ericsson's Form 20-F, which provides a reconciliation from foreign GAAP to U.S. GAAP required by the SEC for U.S.-listed companies (see Table 18.5).

TABLE 18.5   Ericsson's Form 20-F: Net Income Reconciliation, 2004

Adjustment of Net Income	2004	2003	2002
Net income as reported per Swedish GAAP	19,024	−10,844	−19,013
U.S. GAAP adjustments before taxes:			
Pensions	−245	−840	412
Pension premium refund	—	—	47
Capital discount on convertible debentures	—	179	124
Goodwill amortization	475	1,636	1,064
Sale-leaseback	352	682	113
Hedging	−2,915	1,603	2,884
Capitalization of development costs for products to be sold	−2,606	−4,798	−4,018
for internal use	−131	−355	−922
Restructuring costs	−1,354	1,225	−1,240
Unrealized gains and losses on available-for-sale securities	−82	370	−370
Other	37	12	35
Tax effect of U.S. GAAP adjustments	1,831	533	966
Net income in accordance with U.S. GAAP	**14,386**	**−10,597**	**−19,918**
Earnings per share in accordance with U.S. GAAP			
Earnings per share per U.S. GAAP, basic	0.91	−0.68	−1.58
Earnings per share per U.S. GAAP, diluted	0.91	−0.68[*]	−1.58[*]
Average number of shares, basic, per U.S. GAAP (million)	15,829	15,823	12,573
Average number of shares, diluted, per U.S. GAAP (million)	15,855	15,831	12,684

[*]Potential ordinary shares are not considered when their conversion to ordinary shares would increase earnings per share.

Source: Telefonaktiebolaget LM Ericsson, *Ericsson Annual Report on Form 20-F 2004,* www.ericsson.com (accessed May 31, 2007).

Given that Sweden is more driven by conservatism and tax issues, one would expect Swedish GAAP income to be more conservative than U.S. GAAP income. Gray's index of conservatism for 2004 is computed as follows:

$$\text{Index} = 1 - \frac{\text{U.S. GAAP earnings} - \text{Swedish GAAP earnings}}{\text{U.S. GAAP earnings}}$$

or

$$\text{Index} = 1 - \frac{(14{,}386 - 19{,}024)}{14{,}386} = 1.3224$$

The result implies that Swedish GAAP income for Ericsson was less conservative than U.S. GAAP income. For example, under U.S. GAAP, the cost of developing new products must be expensed in the period in which it occurs, which lowers net income. In Sweden, development costs can be capitalized, which means they don't show up as expenses for the period, thus resulting in higher income. That was one of the largest adjustments for 2004, so Swedish net income had to be reduced by the amount of development costs amortized to get U.S. GAAP net income.

In addition to these differences, Ericsson mentioned in its report that in 2004 it had adopted a new U.S. accounting standard issued by the FASB and that it planned to adopt two other U.S. standards and pronouncements in 2005. This is interesting, because Ericsson already knew it was going to adopt IFRS the next year. Why, then, did it continue to adopt U.S. standards?

Impact of IFRS on Ericsson's Results

In the Note on Accounting Policies in its 2004 annual report, Ericsson disclosed that from 2005 it would prepare its financial statements according to IFRS. It also mentioned that the IFRS that were likely to have the greatest impact on income and shareholder equity were standards regarding capitalization of development costs, business combinations, share-based payments, and financial instruments.

◀ Swedish multinational Ericsson has operations worldwide. In Duesseldorf, the headquarters of Ericsson in Germany, financial statements are prepared in euros according to German accounting standards and then have to be restated in IFRS to conform with Ericsson's reporting requirements for an EU multinational. Even though Germany also has to use IFRS for group reports, it issues individual company reports according to German law.
Source: vario images GmbH & Co.KG/ Alamy

Conversion Costs

Ericsson estimated that the conversion to IFRS in 2005 would result in a difference of about 1.5 billion Swedish kronor for 2004 net income and a difference of 5.7 billion kronor for equity as of January 1, 2005. Net income under Swedish GAAP would have been 17,539 million kronor under IFRS, compared with 19,024 million kronor under Swedish GAAP. In addition, the recognition of cash on the balance sheet appears to be quite different under IFRS than it is under Swedish GAAP, with cash under IFRS being SEK46.1 billion less than cash under Swedish GAAP. From Ericsson's Form 20-F report, one can also see that cash at the end of 2004 was the same under U.S. GAAP and IFRS.

Costs of implementing IFRS are difficult to gauge. Many countries implemented national regulations that attempted alignment with IFRS (e.g., Sweden). Thus costs of implementation may have been spread out over several years because companies knew that full IFRS implementation was drawing near. Ericsson's management notes the following in the 2004 annual report:

> Because Swedish GAAP, in recent years, has been adapted to IFRS to a high degree and as the rules for first time adopters allows certain exemptions from full retrospective restatements, the transition from Swedish GAAP to IFRS is expected to have a relatively limited effect on our financial statements. Furthermore, we believe the conversion to IFRS will align our reporting more closely with US GAAP.

After the Changeover to IFRS

As Ericsson studied the transition to IFRS, it had to decide if it wanted to adopt full IFRS or the EU-mandated IFRS. Ericsson stated the following in its 2006 annual report:

> The consolidated financial reports as at and for the year ended December 31, 2006, have been prepared in accordance with International Financial Reporting Standards as endorsed by the EU, RR 30:05 Additional rules for Group Accounting and related interpretations by the Swedish Financial Accounting Standards Council (Redovisningsrådet) and the Swedish Annual Accounts Act. For the Company there is no difference between IFRS and IFRS endorsed by the EU, nor is RR 30:05 or the Swedish Annual Accounts Act in conflict with IFRS.

Note P1 to the Parent Company Financial Statements of Ericsson indicates that the parent company generally follows Swedish GAAP, with the following stipulation:

> The Parent Company, Telefonaktiebolaget LM Ericsson, adopted RR32 'Reporting in separate financial statements' from January 1, 2005. The adoption of RR32 has not had any effect on reported profit or loss for 2004 and 2005. The amended RR32:05 (from 2006) requires the Parent Company to use the same accounting principles as for the Group, i.e. IFRS to the extent allowed by RR32:05.

The Swedish MNE Electrolux, which lists on the Swedish Stock Exchange and trades in the United States through an American Depositary Receipt, states the following in its 2006 annual report:

> The consolidated financial statements are prepared in accordance with International Financial Reporting Standards (IFRS) as adopted by the European Union. Some additional information is disclosed based on the standard RR 30:05 from the Swedish Financial Accounting Standards Council. As required by IAS 1, Electrolux companies apply uniform accounting rules, irrespective of national legislation, as defined in the Electrolux Accounting Manual, which is fully compliant with IFRS.... The Parent Company's financial statements are prepared in accordance with the Swedish Annual Accounts Act and the standard RR 32:05 from the Swedish Financial Accounting Standards Council.

Future Reconciliation to U.S. GAAP

As we noted in the chapter, companies will not have to file reconciliations to U.S. GAAP in their 20-F reports with the SEC in the future if the companies are in compliance with IFRS.

So far, the SEC allows European companies to list according to the EU version of IFRS, but what if the EU identifies several carve-outs in the future? Will the SEC sill allow registrants to use the EU version or the version endorsed and issued by the IASB? For a while, it looked like the EU was not going to allow U.S. companies to list on European exchanges while preparing financial statements solely in conformance with U.S. GAAP. Thus, if firms wanted to disclose results in U.S. GAAP and list on European exchanges, they would have to report financial results in both U.S. GAAP and IFRS. The cost of using two reporting systems can be large for firms but may not be any larger than the cost currently incurred by firms that reconcile from IFRS to U.S. GAAP and from U.S. GAAP to IFRS today. Although that requirement has been relaxed since the SEC has relaxed it's reconciliation requirement, who knows what will happen if the U.S. begins to distance itself from IFRS.

Ericsson's shares trade as "pink sheets" (securities traded over the counter (OTC) rather than on an exchange) and on NASDAQ. Because it lists in the United States, Ericsson has to prepare Form 20-F reports with the SEC. Interestingly, however, in its 2006 annual report, no reconciliation to U.S. GAAP is presented, whereas reconciliations were presented in the 2004 annual report. This change in presentation shows that the transition to IFRS is real and that companies in Europe, as well as shareholders, may consider IFRS to be at least as valid as U.S. GAAP.

Even though the reconciliation was not included in the 2006 annual report, Ericsson filed Form 20-F separately with the SEC for 2006. Table 18.6 illustrates that the difference

TABLE 18.6 Ericsson's Form 20-F: Net Income Reconciliation, 2006

Adjustment of Net Income	2006	2005	2004
Net income attributable to stockholders of the parent company per IFRSs	26,251	24,315	17,539
U.S. GAAP adjustments before taxes:			
Pensions	−439	−64	−245
Sale-leaseback	93	191	352
Hedging	0	408	−2,915
Capitalization of development costs	−37	−78	−76
Restructuring costs	−4	120	−1,354
Unrealized gains and losses on available-for-sale securities	0	0	−82
Reversals of impairment losses	−31	−380	0
Other	93	56	82
Tax effect of U.S. GAAP adjustments	154	−73	1,085
Net income in accordance with U.S. GAAP	**26,080**	**24,495**	**14,386**
Earnings per share in accordance with U.S. GAAP			
Earnings per share per U.S. GAAP, basic	1.64	1.55	0.91
Earnings per share per U.S. GAAP, diluted	1.64	1.54	0.91
Average number of shares, basic, per U.S. GAAP (million)	15,871	15,843	15,829
Average number of shares, diluted, per U.S. GAAP (million)	15,943	15,907	15,855
Net income for the period from continuing operations according to U.S. GAAP	23,260	24,312	14,228
Net income for the period from discontinued operations according to U.S. GAAP	2,820	183	158
Total income for the period according to U.S. GAAP	**26,080**	**24,495**	**14,386**
Earnings per share from continuing operations, basic	1.47	1.53	0.90
Earning per share from discontinued operations, basic	0.17	0.02	0.01
Total earnings per share, basic	**1.64**	**1.55**	**0.91**

Source: Telefonaktiebolaget LM Ericsson, *Ericsson Annual Report on Form 20-F 2006,* www.ericsson.com (accessed July 31, 2007).

between IFRS net income and U.S. GAAP net income was much less than that between Swedish GAAP net income and U.S. GAAP net income in 2004.

Fast Forward to 2010

Because Ericsson now registers with the SEC using IFRS, it doesn't have to provide a reconciliation report to U.S. GAAP. In the statement on accounting policy, Ericsson discloses the following:

The consolidated financial statements for the year ended December 31, 2010, have been prepared in accordance with International Financial Reporting Standards (IFRS) as endorsed by the EU and RFR 1 "Additional Rules for Group Accounting," related interpretations issued by the Swedish Financial Reporting Board (Rådet för Finansiell Rapportering), and the Swedish Annual Accounts Act. For the financial reporting of 2010, the Company has applied IFRS as issued by the IASB (IFRS effective as per December 31, 2010) and without any early application. There is no difference between IFRS effective as per December 31, 2010, and IFRS as endorsed by the EU, nor is RFR 1 related interpretations issued by the Swedish Financial Reporting Board or the or the Swedish Annual Accounts Act in conflict with IFRS. ∎

QUESTIONS

1. What are the major sources of influence on Ericsson's accounting standards and practices?
2. What has been the impact on Ericsson's reporting of its listing on the London Stock Exchange? On NASDAQ?
3. What type of IFRS did Ericsson decide to disclose in its financial statements in 2006? In 2010?
4. How has the gradual change from Swedish GAAP to IFRS affected the difference in Ericsson's net income compared with what it would be under U.S. GAAP?
5. Why does Ericsson use IFRS as endorsed by the EU instead of full IFRS? What difference does it make?

My|B Lab   Now that you have finished this chapter, go back to www.myiblab.com to continue practicing and applying the concepts you've learned.

SUMMARY

- The MNE must learn to cope with differing inflation rates, exchange-rate changes, currency controls, expropriation risks, customs duties, tax rates and methods of determining taxable income, levels of sophistication of local accounting personnel, and local as well as home-country reporting requirements.

- A company's accounting or controllership function is responsible for collecting and analyzing data for internal and external users.

- Culture can have a strong influence on the accounting dimensions of measurement and disclosure. The cultural values of secrecy and transparency refer to the degree of information disclosure. The cultural values of optimism and conservatism refer to the valuation of assets and the recognition of income. Conservatism results in the undervaluation of both assets and income.

- Financial statements differ in terms of language, currency, type of statements (income statement, balance sheet, etc.), financial-

statement format, extent of footnote disclosures, and the underlying GAAP on which the financial statements are based.

- Important users of financial statements that must be considered in determining accounting standards are investors, employees, lenders, suppliers and other trade creditors, customers, governments and their agencies, and the public.

- Some of the most important sources of influence on the development of accounting standards and practices are culture, capital markets, regional and global standard-setting groups, management, and accountants.

- The International Accounting Standards Board is charged with developing a single set of high-quality, understandable, and enforceable global accounting standards. Standards developed by the IASB require transparent and comparable information in general-purpose financial statements.

- In cooperation with national standard-setters around the world, especially the Financial Accounting Standards Board

(FASB) in the United States, the IASB hopes to achieve convergence in accounting standards.

- The elimination of reconciliation information in the Form 20-F requirement for foreign companies listing in the United States and different methods of adopting IFRS are major issues that could affect the global convergence of accounting standards.

- When transactions denominated in a foreign currency are translated into dollars, all accounts are recorded initially at the exchange rate in effect at the time of the transaction. At each subsequent balance-sheet date, recorded dollar balances representing amounts owed by or to the company that are denominated in a foreign currency are adjusted to reflect the current rate.

- Companies enter foreign-exchange gains and losses arising from foreign-currency transactions on the income statement during the period in which they occur. Companies enter gains and losses arising from translating financial statements by the current-rate method as a separate component of owners' equity. Companies enter gains and losses arising from translating according to the temporal method directly on the income statement.

- Many different metrics are used for global operations, especially return on investment (ROI) and budget compared with actual performance.

- In comparing budget with actual performance, MNEs need to decide which rate to use to translate the budget into the parent currency and in which currency to monitor results. They must then decide who is responsible for exchange-rate variances.

- MNEs may set arbitrary transfer prices to take advantage of tax differences between countries or to accomplish other corporate objectives, such as performance evaluation, profit manipulation, and so on.

- The balanced scorecard provides a framework for looking at the strategies giving rise to value creation from the following perspectives: financial, customer, internal business processes, and learning and growth.

- Corporate governance refers to the combination of external and internal mechanisms implemented to safeguard the assets of a company and protect the rights of the shareholders. It involves improved financial disclosures and stronger internal controls, with oversight by an independent board of directors.

KEY TERMS

accounting (p. 680)
balanced scorecard (BSC) (p. 702)
consolidation (p. 696)
convergence (p. 684)
corporate governance (p. 704)
current-rate method (p. 696)
Financial Accounting Standards Board (FASB) (p. 683)
functional currency (p. 697)

Generally Accepted Accounting Principles (GAAP) (p. 685)
International Accounting Standards Board (IASB) (p. 683)
International Financial Reporting Standards (IFRS) (p. 686)
International Organization of Securities Commissions (IOSCO) (p. 691)

mutual recognition (p. 689)
reconciliation (p. 689)
temporal method (p. 697)
transfer pricing (p. 701)
translation (p. 696)

ENDNOTES

1 *Sources include the following:* Vincent Boland, "The Saga of Parmalat's Collapse," FT.com (December 19, 2008); Catherine Boyle, "Parmalat's Founder Is Sentenced to Ten Years' Jail for Market-Rigging," *The Times* (December 19, 2008): 64; Judith Burns, "Parmalat to Settle SEC Charges of Fraud for U.S. Bond Offering," *Wall Street Journal* (Europe) (July 30, 2004): A6; "The Pause after Parmalat," *The Economist* (January 17, 2004): 13; Alessandra Galloni and Yaroslav Trofimov, "Tanzi's Power Games Helped Parmalat Rise, but Didn't Cushion Fall," *Wall Street Journal* (Europe) (March 8, 2004): A1; Mark Tran, "The Milk Sheikh Whose Dream Curdled," *The Guardian* (December 31, 2003), retrieved October 19, 2009, from www .guardian.co.uk/business/2003/dec/31/italy.parmalat1; Peter Gumbel, "How It All Went So Sour," *Time* (Europe) (November 29, 2004): 44; Hoover's Online, "Parmalat," retrieved April 19, 2005, from www.hoovers.com; Michelle Perry, "Enron: Could It Happen Here?" *Accountancy Age* (January 25, 2004), retrieved October 19, 2009, from www.accountancyage.com/accountancyage/analysis/2040660 /enron-happen-here; David Reilly and Alessandra Galloni, "Spilling Over: Banks Come under Scrutiny for Role in Parmalat Scandal," *Wall Street Journal* (September 28, 2004): A1; David Reilly and Matt Moffett, "Parmalat Inquiry Is Joined by Brazil," *Wall Street Journal* (Europe) (January 7, 2004): A1; Susannah Rodgers and Kenneth Maxwell,

"Parmalat Fallout Hits Farmers; Dairies Worry about Their Future as Milk Seller Misses Payments," *Wall Street Journal* (Europe) (January 15, 2004): B6; Securities and Exchange Commission (SEC): Complaint #18527 (December 29, 2003); "Parmalat to Trim Key Operations in 10 Countries," *Wall Street Journal* (Europe) (March 29, 2004): A4; "How Parmalat Differs from U.S. Scandals," Knowledge@Wharton (January 28, 2004), retrieved November 15, 2007, frrom http://knowledge .wharton.upenn.edu; Adrian Michaels, "Parmalat Case Leads to First Jail Sentences," *Financial Times* (June 29, 2005): 28; Bruce Johnston and Caroline Muspratt, "Court Frees Daughter of Parmalat Founder," *The* [London] *Daily Telegraph* (March 9, 2004): 29; "Daughter of Founder of Parmalat Is Freed," *Wall Street Journal* (Eastern Edition) (March 9, 2004): 1; Eric Sylvers, "In First Trial, Parmalat's Founder Charges That Banks Led Him Astray," *International Herald Tribune* (March 9, 2006): 13; John Hooper, "Parmalat Fraudsters to Avoid Prison," *The Guardian* (June 29, 2005): 18; Giada Zampano and Sabrina Cohen, "Parmalat Trial to Focus on Banks," *Wall Street Journal* (Eastern Edition) (June 14, 2007): C3; "Parmalat Settles Suits with Three Financial Firms," *International Herald Tribune* (June 19, 2007): 16; "Parmalat SpA," *Wall Street Journal* (Europe) (May 18, 2007): 6; Steve Rothwell and Sebastian Boyd, "EU Backing Off Effort on Bond Transparency," *International Herald Tribune* (November 22, 2006): 13; Eric Sylvers, "Judge Clears

Banks in Parmalat Case,"*New York Times* (April 18, 2011), retrieved July 5, 2005, from http://dealbook.nytimes.com/2011/04/18/judge-clears-banks-in-parmalat-case; Bob Van Voris, "Parmalats Suits Against Grant Thornton Revivd by Court," *Bloomberg,* (January 18, 2011), retrieved July 6, 2011, from www.bloomberg.com/news/2011-01-18/parmalat-claim-against-grant-thornton-revived-by-court-update1-.html; Parmalat (2011), *Annual Report 2010,* (accessed July 6, 2011).

2 Financial Accounting Standards Board, "Chapter 1: The Objective of General Purpose Financial Reporting," *Statement of Financial Accounting Concepts No. 8* (Stamford, CT: FASB, September 2010): paragraph OB2.

3 Geert Hofstede, *Culture's Consequences: International Differences in Work-Related Values* (Beverly Hills: Sage, 1980); Hofstede and Michael H. Bond, "The Confucius Connection: From Cultural Roots to Economic Growth," *Organizational Dynamics* 16: 4 (1988): 4; Hofstede, *Cultures and Organizations* (Maidenhead, England: McGraw-Hill, 1991).

4 Sidney J. Gray, "Towards a Theory of Cultural Influence on the Development of Accounting Systems Internationally," *Abacus* (March 1988): 1.

5 C. W. Nobes and R. H. Parker (eds.), *Comparative International Accounting,* 6th ed. (Upper Saddle River, NJ: Prentice Hall, 2000).

6 Christopher Nobes and Robert Parker, *Comparative International Accounting,* 7th ed. (England: FT Prentice Hall, 2002).

7 Adidas Group, *Annual Report 2010,* retrieved July 5, 2005, from http://adidas-group.corporate-publications.com/2010/gb/files/pdf/en/ADS_GB_2010_En.pdf

8 European Union, "Third Countries/Convergence," retrieved July 11, 2011, from http://ec.europa.eu/internal_market/accounting/third_countries/index_en.htm

9 "IFRS: About the Organzation," retrieved July 11, 2011, from www.ifrs.org/The+organisation/IASCF+and+IASB.htm

10 IFRS Foundation, The Organization, Trustees, retrieved July 11, 2011, from www.ifrs.org/The+organisation/Trustees/Trustees.htm

11 Financial Accounting Standards Board, "Memorandum of Understanding, - The Norwalk Agreement," in International Convergence of Accounting Standards – Overview," retrieved July 11, 2011, from www.fasb.org/jsp/FASB/Page/SectionPage&cid=1176156245663

12 FASB, "Convergence with the International Accounting Standards Board."

13 Securities and Exchange Commission, "About the SEC: What We Do," retrieved October 21, 2009, from www.sec.gov/about/whatwedo.shtml (accessed October 21, 2009).

14 Floyd Norris, "U.S. Moves Toward International Accounting Rules," *New York Times* (August 28, 2008), retrieved October 21, 2009, from www.nytimes.com

15 European Union, "Regulations Adopting IAS," retrieved October 21, 2009, from http://ec.europa .eu/internal_market/accounting/legal_framework/regulations_adopting_ias_en.htm

16 "Finance and Economics: Speaking in Tongues," *The Economist* (May 19, 2007): 77–78.

17 "Uniform Rules for International Accounting Standards from 2005 Onwards," *European Parliament Daily Notebook*, Report on the Proposal for a European Parliament and Council Regulation on the Application of International Accounting Standards, (COM(2001) 80-C5-0061/2001-2001/004 (COD), Doc.: A5-0070/2002, retrieved OCtober 21, 2009, from www.europarl.europa.eu/sides/getDoc.do?pubRef=-//EP//TEXT+PRESS+DN-20020312-1+0+DOC+XML+V0//EN&language=EN#SECTION5

18 International Accounting Standards Board, "IASB Publishes IFRS for SMEs" (July 9, 2009), retrieved OCtober 21, 2009, from www.iasb.org/News/Press+Releases/IASB+publishes+IFRS+for+SMEs.htm

19 Deloitte Touche Tohmatsu, "IASB Agenda Project" (2007), retrieved May 29, 2007, from www.iasplus.com/agenda/sme.htm

20 Paul A. Beswick, "Remarks Before the 2010 AICPA National Conference on Current SEC and PCAOB Developments, " December 8, 2010, retrieved June 15, 2011, from www.sec.gov/news/speech/eo10/spch120610pab.htm

21 Kathleen L. Casey, "Keynote Address at the Society of Corporate Secretaries and Governance Professionals 65th Annual Conference," June 29, 2011, retrieved June 15, 2011, from www.sec.gov/news/speech/2011/spch062411klc.htm

22 FASB, "Foreign Currency Translation," Statement of Financial Accounting Standards No. 52 (Stamford, CT: FASB, December 1981): 6–7.

23 The Coca-Cola Company, 2010 Form 10-K (February 28, 2011): 34, 81.

24 S. Robbins and R. Stobaugh, "The Bent Measuring Stick for Foreign Subsidiaries," *Harvard Business Review* (September– October 1973): 80.

25 A. Appleyard, N. Strong, and P. Walton, "Budgetary Control of Foreign Subsidiaries," *Management Accounting* (U.K.) (September 1990): 44–45.

26 M. Shields, C. Chow, Y. Kato, and Y. Nakagawa, "Management Accounting Practices in the U.S. and Japan: Comparative Survey Findings and Research Implications," *Journal of International Financial Management and Accounting* 3: 1 (1991): 61–77.

27 Donald Lessard and Peter Lorange, "Currency Changes and Management Control: Resolving the Centralization/Decentralization Dilemma," *Accounting Review* (July 1977): 628.

28 Addidas Group Annual Report 2010, p. 133.

29 A. Gumbus and B. Lyons, "The Balanced Scorecard at Phillips Electronics," *Strategic Finance* 84: 5 (2002): 45–50.

30 R. Kaplan and D. P. Norton, "The Balanced Scorecard—Measures That Drive Performance," *Harvard Business Review* (January–February 1992): 71–79.

31 "About the IKEA Concept and IKEA Franchising," retrieved July 12, 2011, from www.ikea.com

32 R. Kaplan and D. P. Norton, *The Strategy-Focused Organization* (Cambridge, MA: Harvard Business School Press, 2001).

33 Mark Hammer, "The 7 Deadly Sins of Performance Measurement and How to Avoid Them," *MIT Sloan Management Review* 40: 3 (2007): 19–28.

34 Susan Machuga and Karen Teitel, "The Effects of the Mexican Corporate Governance Code on Quality of Earnings and Its Components," *Journal of International Accounting Research* 6: 1 (Spring 2007).

35 Jason Mitchell, "Best Latam Companies 2009: Petrobras Makes the Most of a Special Situation," *Euromoney* (March 2009): 70; "Brazil Extends Governance Lead," *LatinFinance* (June 2008), retrieved October 23, 2009, from www.latinfinance.com/ArticleTop100.aspx?ArticleID= 1938037

36 D. K. Denis and J. J. McConnell, "International Corporate Governance," *Journal of Financial and Quantitative Analysis* 38: 1 (2003): 1–36.

37 **Sources include the following:** Telefonaktiebolaget LM Ericsson, *Annual Report 2004* (2005), retrieved May 31, 2007, from www.ericsson.com/ericsson/investors/financial_reports/2004/annual04/ericsson_ar2004_complete_en.pdf; Ericsson, Form 20-F (March 23, 2005), retrieved May 31, 2007, from www.ericsson.com/ericsson/investors/financial_reports/2004/20f.pdf; Electrolux, "Corporate Information," retrieved May 31, 2007, from www.electrolux.com/node60.aspx?year=2004; BMW Group, "Investor relations," retrieved June 1, 2007, from www.bmwgroup.com/e/nav/index.html?../0_0_www_bmwgroup_com/home/home.html& source=overview; "Finance and Economics: Speaking in Tongues," *The Economist* (May 19, 2007): 77–78; Ericsson, Form 20-F (June 7, 2007), retrieved July 24, 2007, from www.sec.gov/Archives/ edgar/data/717826/000119312507131377/ d20f.htm; Ericsson, Form 20-F (June 7, 2007), retrieved July 31, 2007, from www.ericsson .com/ericsson/investors/financial_reports/2006/20f.pdf; Telefonaktiebolaget LM Ericsson, *Annual Report 2010* (2011), retrieved July 8, 2011, from www.ericsson.com/res/investors/docs/2010/ericsson_ar_2010_en.pdf

chapter 19

The Multinational
Finance Function

To have money is a good thing; to have a say over the money is even better.

—*Yiddish proverb*

CASE

GPS: In the Market for an Effective Hedging Strategy?

On April 10, 2000, U.S.-based Wells Fargo & Company and First Security Corporation announced that they had signed a merger agreement of their banks in San Francisco and Salt Lake City, Utah, respectively.[1] Both banks, located in the West, were clearly positioning themselves to compete with each other, especially in the Utah market, which is composed of individuals, small businesses, middle-market businesses, farmers and ranchers, and a few large corporate customers. Wells Fargo was operating in 22 states, whereas First Security was operating in seven states. Given the overlapping markets and client demographics, it was clear that services would be consolidated over the next several months.

Three key First Security personnel in the international banking area were Ali Manbeian, Jason Langston, and Ryan Gibbons, VP and manager of the Foreign Exchange Department at First Security. On January 31, 2000, Manbeian had been promoted to VP and trade products manager in the International Banking Division, and Langston had been promoted to VP and foreign-exchange trader. All three had significant experience in international banking, and First Security Bank had a trading room where they could provide foreign-exchange services and trade-related collections and payments for clients. With the merger, however, many of the more interesting businesses shifted to San Francisco, and the three could see the writing on the wall.

THE START-UP OF GPS

In 2002, with the help of some key investors, the three entrepreneurs formed GPS Capital Markets Inc. (GPS—see the window to their offices on p. 715). They realized that there was a niche market in foreign exchange that was no longer being served in the Intermountain West, and they decided to strike out on their own with a business model they believed could be successful.

Bringing investors on board was essential to their success, because they needed the necessary credit backing and reputation to enter the wholesale market. Without that financial backing, they wouldn't be able to access large clients and brokers. Jason Langston noted that "90 percent of the transactions [we've] done in the past wouldn't have happened without these credible investors." However, GPS has been able to move beyond the help of their initial investors due to a strong working capital position.

TARGET MARKET AND CLIENT STRATEGY

To compete effectively in the market, GPS initially decided to target small and medium-sized companies (SMEs). They focused on serving companies that had significant foreign-exchange needs but not their own foreign-exchange team. With this in mind, they started out by providing the regular services that commercial banks offer. Their feeling was that with their expertise and low overhead, they would be able to outbid the larger banks for their business.

At first, they offered traditional inbound and outbound payments, areas in which they excelled at First Security Bank. These payments are the basic needs of companies that are going to receive or are required to pay invoices in a different currency.

But GPS was finding it difficult to obtain clients. The first choice for most companies when it comes to foreign exchange is to use their commercial bank with which they already have a good relationship and which provides traditional banking services, including inbound and outbound payments. GPS financial advisers have overcome this obstacle with their competitors by visiting potential clients personally and building an open and transparent relationship. It is more expensive, as they travel to New York, Los Angeles, and other cities outside of the Rocky Mountain region, but it has paid off because they have developed relationships and obtained new clients. Some competitive advantages that GPS has over the commercial banks are lower transaction costs, 100 percent transparency, and customizing solutions to satisfy customer needs.

Commercial banks have so many different departments and services that the foreign-exchange transactions tend to be more expensive to meet the overhead. Also, the banks look at foreign exchange as a potential area to earn a lot of money, so they price aggressively to build their profits. GPS is more specialized in the foreign-exchange market and smaller, so it can keep its costs low and pass on lower prices to companies.

Until the Internet brought more transparency to foreign-exchange markets, companies often didn't know how much banks or brokers were making on foreign-exchange transactions. GPS adopted 100 percent transparency with its clients: GPS shows clients how much it will make on the deal, something the commercial banks hesitate to do. By showing clients the value-added services it is providing, GPS can justify its profits and not hesitate to disclose its model.

GPS has tried to focus on satisfying the foreign-exchange needs of its clients individually, whereas big banks tend to want to sell standardized services—one size fits all. GPS managers sit down with clients and discuss needs and strategies, and they come up with innovative solutions that result in more satisfactory foreign-exchange transactions. These strategies appear to be working, because GPS has grown significantly since its inception.

Reuters and Bloomberg play an important role in the business of GPS. The company uses them because they have the most powerful analytical tools and real-time pricing. In spite of the high cost of subscribing to Reuters's and Bloomberg's services, GPS decided to go with both. In fact, the three partners have different preferences as to which service they like the best. This has generated a friendly rivalry over the merits of Reuters versus Bloomberg. The two services provide real-time market information, analytics, and a trading platform. In addition, the services are essential for trying to price more complex foreign-exchange products such as options.

FUTURE CHALLENGES

Although GPS has never lost a client to another competitor, the future holds a number of challenges. The first challenge it faces is services. If GPS had stuck with its initial goal of providing traditional foreign-exchange services, it would have opened itself up to significant competition with the banks and other market entrants, such as boutique firms that can focus only on the payments side in the SME market. So the key was to find ways to move its clientele upstream with other value-added services. The problem was to decide what areas it should enter and where to find the expertise. What areas of corporate finance could GPS choose that would leverage its expertise in trading? All three of the founding members had banking backgrounds. Would that be enough as the company moved into new areas?

A second challenge has to do with its target market. Given the merger and acquisition activity in the United States, could GPS continue to maintain its client base, or would its clients get bought out by larger firms, just as Wells Fargo snapped up First Security? If that were to happen, GPS would have to figure out how to sell its expertise to larger clients who had no experience or track record with it. A third challenge is the potential of unfavorable new regulations. The regulatory environment of the foreign-exchange trade is intense and changes frequently. The regulatory environment is changing in the United States, as well as in foreign markets. The Dodd-Frank Wall Street Reform and Consumer Protection Act was signed into law in the United States on July 21, 2010, with potentially significant ramifications to GPS's business in the foreign currency derivatives market. Among other things, the Dodds-Frank Act established a Financial Stability Oversight Council with the power to regulate non-bank financial companies in areas such improved transparency and accountability for trading in derivatives. However, there is uncertainty about the rules and regulations that need to be followed and the impact on derivatives, which have an important business purpose for GPS's clients. There is a battle in the U.S. Congress to dismantle the FSOC before it even gets a chance to get organized and implement regulations, so the next few years will be very uncertain and will require GPS to monitor developments closely and develop alternative strategies depending on which way the regulations go.

THE GLOBAL FINANCIAL CRISIS: CHALLENGES AND OPPORTUNITIES

When the global financial crisis hit in 2008, it became obvious that *counterparty risk* was a real issue. Counterparty risk is the risk that the other party to an agreement—in this case a money center bank entering into a foreign-exchange agreement—might default. Many of GPS's clients or potential clients became nervous as one major money center bank after another ran into problems in late 2008. Because GPS was on sound financial footing, many companies flocked to them to handle their foreign-exchange transactions. This caused a large spike in activity. In addition, GPS's lower rates were also more attractive. As the global economy began to contract, they realized how important it was to squeeze out any savings they could, and this played right into the hands of GPS.

Just as the crisis dropped a lot of business in GPS's lap, the government bailout pulled it right back. As soon as the U.S. Fed decided to bail out the banks and reduce the counterparty risk, many of GPS's new

Concept Check

We're concerned in this chapter with the *financial* aspects of MNE operations—in particular, with the ways in which MNEs gain access to *capital* in both local and global markets. Recall, however, our introduction of such global information providers as Reuters and Bloomberg in Chapter 9, where we refer to their role in furnishing *money center banks* with the data about **foreign exchange** that the banks pass on to client MNEs. Here, we hasten to reaffirm the importance of information and information flows in making not only **exchange-rate** transactions but a vast range of other decisions as well.

clients went right back to their banks. Although GPS was able to retain some clients, it lost others. Given how tight credit was, companies realized that they needed to go back to the banks.

EXPANDED SERVICES: A KEY TO FUTURE GROWTH

As Manbeian, Langston, and Gibbons looked at their business, they realized that the key to their future was to develop a broader base of services to their clients. As a result, they decided to focus on their strength—corporate foreign exchange—and to provide expanded services in global business risk management. The general idea of trading currencies to satisfy their initial core business of import and export transactions was simple. Some transactions went beyond exports and imports and involved derivatives to protect against future risks. With their connection to Bloomberg and Reuters, they had the capabilities necessary to enter into any transaction that the client needed.

But as they began to work with SME companies with operations around the world, they realized that many of these companies were spending a lot of money making trades. As they analyzed the cash flows in different currencies, it was easy to see that as their clients' markets and the currencies in which they operated increased, they had to enter into more and more foreign-exchange transactions.

One of their clients, a large technology firm, was expanding internationally so rapidly that the growth was straining the capabilities of its finances to keep up with it. With hundreds of currency pairs and financial statements being generated in many different currencies and using several different functional currencies, the client was having a difficult time keeping on top of the complexities. GPS realized that it could save its client a lot of money by netting its transactions. Instead of having each entity around the world settle its transactions with every other entity, GPS helped the firm set up a system that could reduce the number of times they had to exchange currency. As it did that, it reduced the costs of each transaction—an important source of revenue to the client's bank.

FXpert

GPS developed proprietary software called FXpert to help its clients monitor foreign-exchange flows and determine how to save money on transactions. After identifying the timing and nature of the cash flows through a specialized audit, a GPS financial adviser proposes an effective hedging solution that GPS can provide. The solution might be as simple as reducing the number of foreign-currency transactions or as complex as hedging some of the exposures using forwards, options, or futures contracts.

The global risk-management business also offers foreign accounts receivable review, global business consultation on global finance methods, dispute resolution in solving payment disputes, international loan packaging, and letters of credit. As it has developed these services, GPS has had to expand its expertise base to include an understanding of complex accounting rules on derivatives, complex financial hedging strategies, and software development.

ADDITIONAL STRATEGIC MOVES

Given the risky foreign-exchange environment, GPS has shifted some of its efforts to work as an agent or broker with its clients' banks instead of being the direct counterparty in foreign-exchange transactions. That allows the company to do what it does best—utilize its proprietary software to find business solutions for clients to reduce foreign-exchange risks and lower the costs of trading foreign exchange. With its knowledge of the markets, GPS is able to negotiate with its clients' banks to get the best possible exchange rate on a transaction and earn a little in the process.

In addition to its technical expertise, GPS has developed a solid marketing strategy. It has continued to focus on SMEs and it has expanded its client base by setting up regional offices in Los Angeles, Phoenix, Dallas, and Boston.

As GPS expands, the partners need to constantly refine their message. From a sales point of view, what do the CFO and treasurer need to know about GPS and what it has to offer? What is the best way to tell its story, and what materials does it need to provide to potential clients?

Finally, a key aspect of GPS's success is its proprietary software. Given the rapidly changing market and the need to constantly upgrade the quality of what it has to offer, GPS needs to bring its software development in-house. That involves higher costs, but it also results in a better product, and it is essential to control the speed and quality of innovation. Foreign-exchange exposure has provided lots of opportunities, and now GPS needs to keep pushing ahead with its competitive advantage in global capital markets.

Introduction

Why do you need to understand capital markets, cash management, and financial risk? Having a good product idea is not sufficient for success. MNEs need to get access to capital markets in different countries to finance expansion. Indeed, finance is integral to firms' international strategies. The small company involved in international business only tangentially may not be concerned about global capital markets, but it will probably still have to deal in foreign exchange through its commercial bank to settle payments for exports and imports. However, the MNE investing and operating abroad is usually concerned about access to capital in local markets as well as in large global markets.

This chapter examines external sources of debt and equity capital available to companies operating abroad as well as internal sources of funds that arise from intercompany links. It also explores the international dimensions of the capital-investment decision, global cash management, foreign-exchange risk-management strategies, and international tax issues.

The Finance Function

One of the key people on the management team is the chief financial officer (CFO)—the manager with the most important global finance-related responsibilities. Figure 19.1 illustrates how the responsibilities of the CFO, controller, and treasurer fit into the organizational structure of the firm and especially how global financial management fits into the overall finance function, which focuses on short- and long-term cash flows. The role of financial management is to maintain and create economic value or wealth by maximizing shareholder wealth—the market value of existing shareholders' common stock.[2] The management activities related to cash flows can be divided into four major areas:

- *Capital structure*—determining the proper mix of debt and equity
- *Long-term financing*—selecting, issuing, and managing long-term debt and equity capital, including location (home country or elsewhere) and currency (home or foreign)
- *Capital budgeting*—analyzing investment opportunities
- *Working capital management*—managing the company's currency assets and liabilities (cash, receivables, marketable securities, inventory, trade receivables and payables, short-term bank debt)

The following sections discuss these areas as well as the impact of taxation on each of these decisions.[3]

THE ROLE OF THE CFO

The CFO acquires financial resources–that is, generates funds either internally or from external sources at the lowest possible cost—and allocates them among the company's activities and projects. For instance, when GPS began, the founders needed outside investors with significant resources to fund the start-up as well as lend credibility to potential clients. Then it shifted to internally generated cash to fund operations. Allocating

Case Review Note

FIGURE 19.1   The Role of the Treasurer in the Financial Function

As a firm's chief accounting officer, the *controller* evaluates the financial results of business operations. The *treasurer* writes the checks—or, more precisely, controls the company's cash payments. The treasurer's department handles both domestic and foreign financial functions, including cash and exposure management, capital expenditure, and foreign-currency processing.

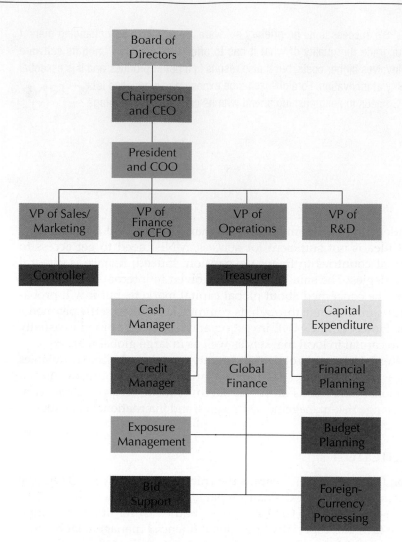

resources (investing) means increasing stockholders' wealth through the allocation of funds to different projects and investment opportunities.[4]

The CFO's Global Perspective   The CFO's job is more complex in a global environment than in the domestic setting because of forces such as foreign-exchange risk, currency flows and restrictions, political risk, different tax rates and laws on determining taxable income, and regulations on access to capital in different markets. In the remainder of the chapter, we examine the following areas:

1. Overall capital structure
2. Global capital markets
3. Offshore financial centers
4. Capital budgeting in a global context
5. Internal sources of funds
6. Foreign-exchange risk management
7. Taxation of foreign-source income

Capital Structure

The CFO must determine the company's proper mix between long-term debt and equity—in other words, its *capital structure*. Many companies start off with an initial investment and then grow through internally generated funds. However, when those sources are inadequate to fund continued growth into new markets, the CFO's office must decide the proper debt/equity mix.

LEVERAGING DEBT FINANCING

The degree to which a firm funds the growth of business by debt is known as **leverage.** The weighted average cost of capital of a company is found as follows:

Leverage—the degree to which a firm funds the growth of business by debt.

$$
\begin{array}{l}
\text{Weighted} \\
\text{average cost} \\
\text{of capital}
\end{array} =
\begin{bmatrix}
\text{After-tax} & & \text{Proportion} \\
\text{cost of} & \times & \text{of debt} \\
\text{debt} & & \text{financing}
\end{bmatrix} +
\begin{bmatrix}
\text{Cost} & & \text{Proportion} \\
\text{of} & \times & \text{of equity} \\
\text{equity} & & \text{financing}
\end{bmatrix}
$$

The degree to which companies use leverage instead of *equity capital*—known as stocks or shares—varies throughout the world. Country-specific factors are a more important determinant of a firm's capital structure than any other factor, because a firm tends to follow the financing trends in its own country and within its particular industry there. Japanese companies, for example, are more likely to follow the capital structure of other Japanese companies than of those in the United States or Europe. Leveraging is often perceived as the most cost-effective route to capitalization, because the interest that companies pay on debt is a tax-deductible expense in most countries, whereas the dividends paid to investors are not.

When Is Leveraging Not the Best Option?   Leveraging is not always the best approach in all countries, for two major reasons. First, excessive reliance on long-term debt raises financial risk and thus requires a higher return for investors. Second, foreign subsidiaries of an MNE may have limited access to local capital markets, making it difficult for the MNE to rely on debt to fund asset acquisition.[5]

Table 19.1 shows the debt-to-asset and equity-to-asset ratios for a large sample of companies in a selected group of countries. We have included data for 2007 and 2010 for the purposes of comparison. Note the relatively higher reliance on equity capital of Russia, Mexico, Brazil, and Japan for 2007. In many emerging markets, wealth is usually concentrated in families, so even though there appears to be a heavy reliance on equity, there may only be a few shareholders. In contrast, shares of stock are broadly held in countries such as the United States and United Kingdom. However, notice the changes from 2007–2010. Russian firms began to rely more on debt than in the 2007 survey, which is evident from the number of Russian firms that have issued Eurobonds to raise funds.

TABLE 19.1   Selected Capital Structures, FY 2007

Because companies tend to follow financing practices that predominate in their own countries, country-specific factors are important in a firm's capital structure. Taxation is among such factors. If in a given country, for example, interest paid on debt is tax deductible and interest paid to shareholders is not, then *leveraging*—funding growth by debt—may be regarded as more cost-effective than *equity financing*.

	2007		2010	
Country	**Debt-Asset(%)**	**Equity-Asset(%)**	**Debt-Asset(%)**	**Equity-Asset(%)**
Russia	26.2	73.8	47.1	52.9
Mexico	51.3	48.7	51.7	48.3
Brazil	54.3	45.7	58.3	41.7
Japan	55.4	44.6	42.4	57.6
UK	62.0	38.0	49.9	50.1
USA	63.9	36.1	57.4	42.6
France	70.9	29.1	58.6	41.4
Germany	71.8	28.2	54.5	45.5

Source: Data collected by Compustat Global; available at www.wrds.wharton.upenn.edu (accessed July 9, 2011).

On the other hand, the debt/asset ratio dropped and equity/asset ratio rose for firms in Japan, the United Kingdom, United States, France, and Germany. The differences across the samples narrowed in the 2010 survey compared with 2007. In part, that may have been due to the debt crisis that began in 2008, which forced companies to rely more on equity than debt. Although research has confirmed that country-specific factors are important determinants of firms' capital structure,[6] we can also see that broader macroeconomic forces can influence the mix of debt to equity in funding the business.

FACTORS AFFECTING THE CHOICE OF CAPITAL STRUCTURE

Choice of capital structure depends on tax rates, degree of development of local equity markets, and creditor rights.

Many factors influence the choice of MNEs' capital structure, both within a country and with affiliates in different countries. They include local tax rates, the degree of development of local equity markets, and creditor rights. One study of the capital structure of foreign affiliates of U.S.-based MNEs found that local tax rates influenced the debt-to-equity ratios. Although there might be a debt-to-equity ratio for the firm as a whole that is based on U.S. capital-market expectations, its foreign affiliates have to be sensitive to local conditions. The study noted:

> Ten percent higher local tax rates are associated with 2.8 percent higher debt/asset ratios, with internal borrowing particularly sensitive to taxes. Multinational affiliates are financed with less external debt in countries with underdeveloped capital markets or weak creditor rights, reflecting significantly higher local borrowing costs. Instrumental variable analysis indicates that greater borrowing from parent companies substitutes for three-quarters of reduced external borrowing induced by capital market conditions. Multinational firms appear to employ internal capital markets opportunistically to overcome imperfections in external capital markets.[7]

In addition, different tax rates, dividend remission policies, and exchange controls may cause a company to rely more on debt in some situations and more on equity in others. Understand that the different debt and equity markets discussed in this chapter have different levels of importance for companies worldwide.

A major cause of the Asian financial crisis of 1997 was excessive dollar bank debt. The crisis of 2010 and 2011 was due more to sovereign liquidity than exchange rate risk.

Debt and Exchange Rates   As with the Asian financial crisis of 1997, the global financial crisis of 2007–2009 highlighted foreign-exchange risk. Many individuals, banks, and companies borrowed in dollars or euros leading up to the crisis because of the relatively lower interest rates in the United States and Europe. Although this phenomenon happened around the world, it was especially problematic in Eastern Europe and Iceland.

In Iceland, a country with its own currency (the krona), the Central Bank kept interest rates high, attracting lots of foreign investment and keeping the krona strong. People's standards of living, among the highest in the world, were supported by the strong currency and the ability to import products. They sustained their high consumption by financing houses and other purchases through borrowing in cheaper currencies. When the crisis hit, however, the krona plunged in value, the banks failed, and consumers could not afford to service their debts. The lower foreign interest rates were replaced by exchange-rate risk.[8]

One of the major causes of the Asian financial crisis in 1997 was that Asian companies relied too much on debt to fund their growth, especially bank debt. The lack of development of bond and equity markets in those countries forced firms to rely on bank debt for growth. Many of the Asian banks borrowed dollars from international banks and lent the money to local companies in local currencies, not dollars. At the time, many Asian countries pegged their currencies to the U.S. dollar, so the assumption was that if you borrow in dollars, it is the same as borrowing in the local currency. When the Asian currencies fell against the dollar, many of the banks could not service their loans and went into bankruptcy. Asian companies that borrowed directly in dollars suffered the same fate. History does tend to repeat itself.

The economic crisis in Europe in 2010–2011 occurred for different reasons. The slowdown in the global economy meant that many countries in Europe, especially Ireland and Greece (with potential problems in Italy, Spain, and Portugal), could not generate enough revenues to service their sovereign debt. However, the European Central Bank kept interest rates relatively higher than U.S. rates due to fears of inflation, so the euro did not fall in value. Since much of the debt was denominated in euros, the banks and countries did not necessarily have exchange rate risk as was the case with Iceland in 2008, but there was simply not enough cash being generated to pay off loan obligations. As noted in Chapter 10, that forced the European Central Bank and the IMF to work out an agreement that was a mix of rescheduling some debt, providing loans to help cover existing debt payments, and working with the countries to reduce their budget deficits and hopefully generate more funds to meet future debt obligations. The impact on European companies is that the general stress in the financial system could impair their ability to borrow from banks or issue bonds.

SOURCES OF CAPITAL

The following sections of the chapter will discuss debt and equity markets in greater detail, but in addition to understanding the markets, it is important to understand the suppliers of capital. As companies raise capital through debt and equity markets, who do they go to? The easiest way to raise capital, especially in debt markets, is through banks. This could be an individual bank or a syndicate of banks where a lead bank works with other banks to take on a large loan. Retail investors (individuals) are more apt to get involved in the equity markets, although wealthy retail investors can also take positions in the bond markets. However, most retail investors utilize investment opportunities provided by other financial institutions, such as mutual funds, hedge funds and pension funds that are the major investors in both debt and equity markets. They invest in companies and bundle together investment opportunities for their clients. They often provide a portfolio of opportunities with increasing levels of risk for investors to choose from.

An important source of wealth is **sovereign wealth funds.** A sovereign wealth fund is defined as "pools of money derived from a country's reserves, which are set aside for investment purposes that will benefit the country's economy and citizens. The funding for a sovereign wealth fund (SWF) comes from central bank reserves that accumulate as a result of budget and trade surpluses, and even from revenue generated from the exports of natural resources."[9] The Middle East is home to some of the largest SWFs in the world. The largest is the Abu Dhabi Investment Authority (ADIA) with approximately U.S. $627 billion in assets under management in 2009. It was followed by the Saudi Arabia Monetary Agency and SWFs in Kuwait, Libya, and Qatar. Obviously, these SWFs derived their funding from oil and natural gas. Outside of the Middle East, there are huge SWFs in Norway, China, and Russia, among other countries, and some countries have multiple SWFs. These funds can invest in massive government infrastructure projects or invest on their own account outside of the region. For example, Invest AD (a SWF in Abu Dhabi) is involved in asset management projects inside and outside of the UAE and also has a private equity division that has established a private equity fund that provides growth capital to late-stage companies in the Middle East North Africa (MENA) region and Turkey. Thus SWFs are a type of institutional investor that can enter stock markets and take positions in stocks sold on those markets (such as Prada in the ending case in the chapter).

DEBT MARKETS AS MEANS OF EXPANSION

An MNE that needs to raise capital through debt markets has a number of options. The local domestic debt market is the first source to tap. This means Japan for Japanese companies, but it could also mean Japan for the Japanese subsidiary of a U.S. company. Nissan is a good example of domestic and foreign borrowing. In its FY 2010 annual report, it listed bonds issued in Japanese yen by domestic and international subsidiaries, and U.S. dollars and Mexican pesos by foreign subsidiaries.[10] A significant amount of the bonds payable are in yen because of low interest rates compared to bond interest rates in other countries.

Here's another example. In the early 1990s, Nu Skin, a direct seller of skin-treatment and personal-care products, embarked on a program of expansion into Japan and borrowed capital in yen in order to fund a portion of that expansion. As a result, its long-term debt ultimately included the long-term portion of Japanese yen-denominated 10-year notes issued to the Prudential Insurance Company of America in 2000. The notes bore interest at an effective rate of 3 percent per annum and were due October 2010, with annual principal payments that began in October 2004.[11] Since then, Nu Skin has issued more debt in U.S. dollars and Japanese yen. The yen debt has much lower interest rates—ranging from 1.7 to 3.3 percent, compared with U.S. dollar debt which is at 6.2 percent. The lower-cost Japanese debt is okay as long as the yen remains stable against the dollar. When the yen strengthens against the dollar, however, the dollar equivalent of the debt rises and may wipe out any gains on the lower interest rates. For example, in January 2008 Nu Skin converted $20 million in debt from dollars to yen at an exchange rate of ¥108.5 (an equivalent of ¥2.17 billion). The interest rate dropped from 6.2 to 3.3 percent. By December 31, 2010, the yen had strengthened to 81.1274, and the debt was now worth over $26 million.

MNEs have an advantage because they can tap local debt and equity markets, foreign debt and equity markets (such as the Eurodollar, Eurobond, and Euroequity markets, discussed later), and internal funds from the corporate family. Most local companies are locked into local debt markets or possibly foreign debt markets, but they may not have the ability to raise funds as extensively as the local affiliates of MNEs do, unless they are MNEs themselves, such as Toyota or Nissan.

> Companies can use local and international debt markets to raise funds.

Global Capital Markets

> Two major sources of funds external to the MNE's normal operations are debt markets and equity markets.

Companies have many ways of raising capital to fund operations, and their home countries have debt and equity markets. However, this section takes a look at the role of foreign debt and equity markets as sources of funds for MNEs.

EUROCURRENCIES AND THE EUROCURRENCY MARKET

> A Eurocurrency is any currency banked outside its country of origin, but it is primarily dollars banked outside the United States.

The **Eurocurrency market** is an important source of debt financing to complement what MNEs can find in their domestic markets. A **Eurocurrency** is any currency banked outside its country of origin. Currencies banked outside their country of origin are also known as *offshore currencies.*

The Eurodollar market is the most significant eurocurrency market. A **Eurodollar** is a certificate of deposit in dollars in a bank outside of the United States. Most Eurodollar CDs are held in London, but they could be held anywhere outside of the United States, including the Bahamas, the Cayman Islands, Hong Kong, Japan, the Netherlands Antilles, etc. A major advantage of the Eurodollar market is that it is not regulated by the U.S. Federal Reserve Bank. The same is true for other Eurocurrencies and their major regulators. The Eurodollar market started with the deposit of U.S. dollars in London banks during the Cold War by the Soviet Union to avoid the possibility that their accounts could be frozen in the United States. As other currencies entered the offshore market, the broader "Eurocurrency" name was adopted for market use, although the market tends to use the name of the specific currency, such as *Euroyen* or *Eurosterling* for offshore Japanese yen and British pounds sterling. Eurodollars constitute a fairly consistent 65 to 80 percent of the Eurocurrency market. Dollars held by foreigners on deposit in the United States are not Eurodollars, but dollars held at branches of U.S. or other banks outside the United States are.

Major Sources of Eurocurrencies   There are four major sources of Eurocurrencies:

- Foreign governments or individuals who want to hold dollars outside the United States
- Multinational enterprises that have cash in excess of current needs
- European banks with foreign currency in excess of current needs
- Countries such as China, Germany, Japan, and Taiwan that have large balance-of-trade surpluses held as reserves

The demand for Eurocurrencies comes from sovereign governments, supranational agencies such as the World Bank, companies, and individuals. Eurocurrencies exist partly for the convenience and security of the user and partly because of cheaper lending rates for the borrower and better yield for the lender.

Characteristics of the Eurocurrency Market   Because the Eurocurrency market is a wholesale (companies and other institutions) rather than a retail (individuals) market, transactions are very large. Public borrowers such as governments, central banks, and public-sector corporations are the major players. Although MNEs are involved in the Eurodollar market, the Eurodollar market has historically been an interbank market. Since the late 1990s, however, London banks have shifted to using nonbank customers for Eurodollar transactions, partly because of the introduction of the euro, the subsequent fall in foreign transactions, and consolidation in the banking sector.[12]

The Eurocurrency market is both short- and medium-term. Short-term borrowing is composed of maturities of less than one year. Anything from one to five years is considered a **Eurocredit,** which may be a loan, a line of credit, or another form of medium- and long-term credit. This would include **syndication,** in which several banks pool resources to extend credit to a borrower and spread the risk. Short-term borrowings are called eurocommercial paper and are unsecured loans issued by a bank or corporation in the offshore money market. Maturities are less than one year.

Interest Rates in the Eurocurrency Market   A major attraction of the Eurocurrency market is the difference in interest rates compared to those in domestic markets. Domestic interest rates are a function of the monetary policies adopted by the Central Banks of each country. In July 2011, for example, the European Central Bank raised its key benchmark interest rate to 1.5 percent because of concern over inflation in the Eurozone. In the United States, however, interest rates remained lower due to concerns over slow economic growth and high unemployment. The interest rate differential contributed to a relative weakness of the dollar against the euro. The interest rate companies have to pay to get loans or issue bonds depends not only on benchmark interest rates but also their credit worthiness. The better the credit worthiness, the lower the interest rate companies have to pay compared to other borrowers.

London Inter-Bank Offered Rate   Because of the large transactions and the lack of controls and their attendant costs, Eurocurrency deposits tend to yield more than domestic deposits do, and loans tend to be cheaper than in domestic markets. Traditionally, loans are made at a certain percentage above the **London Inter-Bank Offered Rate (LIBOR),** which is a short-term interest rate for U.S. dollar loans in London. The LIBOR rates quoted on July 12, 2011, for Eurodollars were 0.18650 percent for one month, 0.249005 percent for three months, 0.40975 percent for six months, and 0.74050 percent for one year. The rate for three-month Euro LIBOR was 1.544, which is higher than the three-month Eurodollar LIBOR rate. That is consistent with the discussion above about the ECB benchmark interest rate being higher than the comparable rate set by the Federal Reserve Bank in the United States. The amount of the interest rate above LIBOR that a borrower is charged depends on the creditworthiness of the customer and must be large enough to cover expenses and build reserves against

LIBOR is a short-term interest rate for dollars held in the Eurodollar market.

possible losses. Most loans are variable rate, and the rate-fixing period is generally six months, although it may be one or three months.

INTERNATIONAL BONDS

Many countries have active bond markets available to domestic and foreign investors. The United States is the largest market in the world for domestic bonds, accounting for 38 percent of all those issued in 2010. Bonds are used by governments, financial institutions, and corporations, with corporate issues being the smallest segment.[13] Just to give you an idea of the size of the global bond market, amounts outstanding on the global bond market were $95 trillion in 2010, of which domestic bonds were 70 percent and international bonds were 30 percent. Following the United States as the second largest market for issuing bonds was Japan, driven largely by the size of the Japanese economies as well as the high levels of borrowing by the U.S. and Japanese governments.[14] However, 2009 saw a significant rise in the issuance of global corporate bonds due to the lack of bank credit, and this continued in 2010 as well, especially from U.S. companies.[15]

One reason the bond (and stock) markets in the United States are so influential is because the companies of continental Europe still rely disproportionately on banks for finance. As noted, however, that began to change in 2009 due to the economic crisis and its impact on the banks. Emerging markets are increasingly turning to the bond market for funding and now constitute about 10 percent of the market worldwide.[16]

There are two types of international bonds: foreign bonds and Eurobonds, both described below. The international bond market is primarily a wholesale market where holders of the bonds are usually institutional investors and where issuers are large companies, governments, and international organizations. Government bond issues aren't necessarily bad, unless the governments don't have the financial resources to pay principal and interest as illustrated by the Greek debt crisis in 2011.

> A foreign bond is one sold outside the country of the borrower but denominated in the currency of the country of issue. A Eurobond is a bond issue sold in a currency other than that of the country of issue.

Foreign Bonds   **Foreign bonds** are sold outside the borrower's country but denominated in the currency of the country of issue. A French company floating a bond issue in the United States in U.S. dollars, say, would be issuing a foreign bond. They also have creative names, such as Yankee bond (issued in the United States), Samurai bond (Japan), Bulldog bond (England), and Panda bond (China).

Eurobonds   A **Eurobond** is usually underwritten (placed in the market for the borrower) by a syndicate of banks from different countries and sold in a currency other than that of the country of issue. A bond issue floated by a U.S. company in dollars in London, Luxembourg, or Switzerland is a Eurobond. In 2010, 71 percent of the international bonds issued (both foreign and Eurobond) were in U.S. dollars, followed by euros denominated sales at 22 percent. However, these amounts fluctuate a lot from one year to the next. In 2008, for example, the leading currency in the Eurobond market was the euro, which made up 48 percent of the market, followed by the dollar, which accounted for 36 percent. London and New York are the two largest centers for the issuance of international bonds. Rising in importance are "dim sum" bonds, which are offshore bonds that are denominated in Chinese yuan. They are growing in popularity as China looks for a way to capitalize on its immense foreign exchange reserves. Foreign investors who want to buy debt denominated in Chinese yuan usually face strict capital controls. However, these obstacles do not exist when it comes to dim sum bonds, which are typically issued in Hong Kong.[17] Companies like McDonald's and Unilever have started taking advantage of this new offshore bond.[18] A slight variation of the Eurobond is a **Global Bond**, which is a Eurobond issued in more than one country at the same time to take advantage of investors in different markets.

What's So Attractive about the International Bond Market?   The international bond market is a desirable place to borrow money. For one thing, it allows a company to diversify its funding sources from the local banks and the domestic bond market and borrow in maturities that might not be available in the domestic markets. It also tends to be less expensive than local bond markets. However, not all companies are interested in global bonds or Eurobonds. Before the Asian financial crisis hit, Asian companies relied on their domestic banks more because of the ready availability of cheap loans, as well as the cozier relationship than that between Western companies and banks.[19] However, the crisis demonstrated the fundamental flaws in this strategy as banks went bankrupt and companies were forced to face the fact that they couldn't generate enough funds to pay back the loans. The same story was repeated with the global financial crisis in the late 2000s.

Although the Eurobond market is centered in Europe, it has no national boundaries. In contrast to most conventional bonds, Eurobonds are sold simultaneously in several financial centers through multinational underwriting syndicates and are purchased by an international investing public that extends far beyond the confines of the countries of issue.

U.S. companies first issued Eurobonds in 1963 as a means of avoiding U.S. tax and disclosure regulations. They are typically issued in denominations of $5,000 or $10,000, pay interest annually, are held in bearer form, and are traded over the counter (OTC), most frequently in London.[20] Any investor who holds a bearer bond is entitled to receive the principal and interest payments. In contrast, for a registered bond, which is more typical in the United States, the investor is required to be registered as the bond's owner to receive payments. An OTC bond is traded with or through an investment bank rather than on a securities exchange, such as the London Stock Exchange.

How Corporations Use Eurobonds to Fund Expansion Eurobond issues are very popular with companies in Russia and the former Soviet Union as a way to get access to international capital, contributing to the change in debt/equity mix discussed above. For example, in 2010, Gazprom, the Russian-based company that is the largest extractor of natural gas in the world and Russia's largest company, raised about $1 billion in Eurobonds, with JP Morgan and Calyon (which became the Crédit Agricole Corporate and Investment Bank) as the organizers of the issue. The same is true for state-owned enterprises from the Middle East, notably Dubai, that ran into serious cash-flow problems due to Dubai's financial crisis in 2010. However, private sector corporations use Eurobonds as well. In 2011, Amcor, the large Australian packaging solutions company, announced a €550 million Eurobond issue with a maturity of April 16, 2019. The Eurobond will be listed on the Singapore Stock Exchange with BNP Paribas and Deutsche Bank as the lead banks. The proceeds will be in euro rather than swapped into another currency and will be used to refinance maturing bond and existing floating rate debt.[21] This is a good example of a Eurobond, because it is issued in euros, outside of Australia and in Singapore where the currency is not the euro.

Occasionally, Eurobonds may provide currency options, which enable the creditor to demand repayment in one of several currencies, thus reducing the exchange risk inherent in single-currency foreign bonds. More often, however, both interest and principal on Eurobonds are payable to the creditor in U.S. dollars (or in the currency of issue, such as euros in the example of Amcor). It is also possible to issue a Eurobond in one currency—say, the U.S. dollar—and then swap the obligation to another. For example, a U.S. company with a subsidiary in Britain would generate large quantities of British pounds through normal operations, then use them to pay off a British-pound bond. If the U.S. company had issued Eurobonds in dollars in London, it could enter into a swap agreement through an investment bank to exchange its future dollar obligations with a British-pound obligation and use the pound revenues to pay off the swapped obligation.

EQUITY SECURITIES AND THE EUROEQUITY MARKET

Another source of financing is *equity securities*, whereby an investor takes an ownership position in return for shares of stock in the company and the promises of capital gains—an appreciation in the value of the stock—and maybe dividends.

Access to Equity Capital   One way a company can easily and cheaply get access to capital is through a private placement with a venture capitalist (or perhaps a venture-capital firm investing the money of one or several wealthy individuals), who invests money in a new venture in exchange for stock.

In addition to private placements, companies can access the *equity-capital market*, more commonly known as the *stock market*. They can raise new capital by listing their shares on a stock exchange, home-country or foreign. For example, Beijing-based China Techfaith Wireless Communication Technology Ltd., a designer and manufacturer of mobile handsets, offered 8.73 million shares on an initial public offering (IPO) on NASDAQ on May 5, 2005. Its underwriters were Merrill Lynch, Lehman Brothers, and CIBC World Markets Corporation. Its shares listed at $16.27, and it raised $141.8 million.

Another example of an international IPO was the listing of Prada on the Hong Kong Stock Exchange in 2011, which will be discussed in more detail in the ending case for the chapter. Samsonite, which we discussed in the opening case in Chapter 17, also issued an IPO on the Hong Kong Stock Exchange in 2011. Sistema, the largest private-sector consumer-services company in Russia, issued a U.S. $1.56 billion offering on the London Stock Exchange in 2004, the largest-ever Russian IPO on a public market anywhere. Sistema's offering comprised 1.8 million common shares in the form of 91.6 million Global Depositary Receipts (GDRs), with 50 GDRs representing one common share. (A GDR is listed in several different markets simultaneously.) Sistema needed access to equity dollars, which it was not able to raise inside Russia, so the Euroequity market in London was an obvious choice for it. The growth in globalization has forced companies to look at equity markets as an alternative to debt markets and banks as a source of funds.

THE SIZE OF GLOBAL STOCK MARKETS

Map 19.1 identifies the 10 largest high income stock markets in the world and 10 largest emerging economy stock markets in terms of **market capitalization**—the total number of shares of stock listed times the market price per share. Although, stock market capitalization worldwide dropped by 46.5 percent between the end of 2007 and the end of 2008, it began to recover. However, the markets have been extremely volatile due to various crises, such as the Greek debt crisis and the U.S. budget crisis, as will be illustrated in the Prada case at the end of the chapter. Debt markets are even more uncertain, so the equity markets are still an important source of funding for companies.

The three largest stock markets in the world are in New York, Tokyo, and London, with the U.S. markets controlling nearly half of the world's stock market capitalization.

The numbers in Map 19.1 represent each specific stock market rather than all of the markets in the country. For example, New York-based NYSE Euronext Group as a whole is listed as number one, but that does not include NASDAQ OMX, the second largest stock market in the world and also based in the United States. One interesting trend is the rise in importance of the stock markets in emerging economies, especially China. The Shanghai Stock Exchange was largest emerging stock market in the world in 2010, and its market capitalization would have ranked it just slightly above Hong Kong as the sixth largest stock market in the world.

Trends in Global Stock Market   With the introduction of electronic platforms and high-frequency trading, the major stock exchanges have seen a drop in their trading volume. For example, in 2001 80 percent of trading volume was held by NYSE and NASDAQ. However, in 2011 that had dropped to 27 percent. Because of this change, global stock markets are talking about merging.[22] For example, the shareholders of Deutsche Börse (Germany) announced on July 15, 2011, that they approved a proposed combination with NYSE Euronext, subject to approval by regulators in both markets. If approval is received, the combined exchange would be a powerful venue for raising capital as well as becoming a world leader in derivatives and risk management.[23]

Emerging Stock Markets   It has been interesting to track the development of the emerging stock markets. For many years, they were growing fairly rapidly. By 1998,

MAP 19.1   Global Markets: Market Capitalization, 2008

Data reflects domestic market capitalization—total number of shares of stock listed multiplied by market price per share.

Source: World Federation of Exchanges (http://www.world-exchanges.org/statistics/annual/2010/equity-markets/domestic-market-capitalization) accessed July 14, 2011.

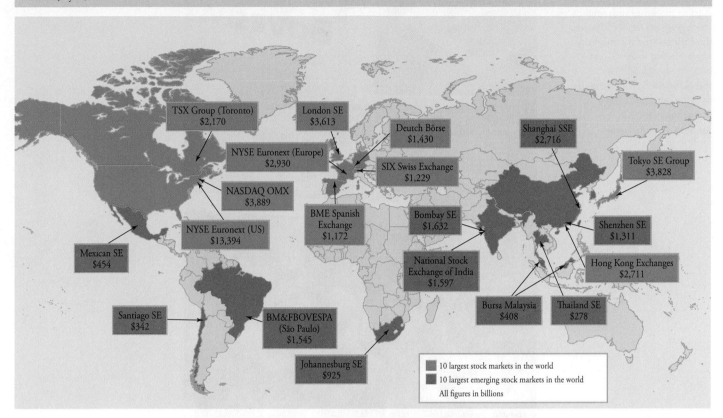

however, the Asian financial crisis had clobbered them, and they plunged to only 6.9 percent of total. That was followed by crises in Russia and Latin America. However, as the global economy recovered after the Asian financial crisis, the emerging markets rose in importance as investors were looking for higher returns. The flight to safety in 2008 pulled money out of the markets, but the funds began flowing back in as the markets began to recover. The emerging markets benefit from the flight to risk and the rise in commodities prices but fall if there is a flight to safety. However, the trajectory seems to be steadily upward in light of problems in the United States and Europe. Again, broad macroeconomic factors will determine how those markets fare in the future. As noted in Map 19.1, four of the 10 largest emerging stock markets in 2010 are actually bigger than the markets in Switzerland and Spain, number 9 and 10 on the list of the biggest high-income stock markets.

The Rise of the Euroequity Market   Another significant event in the past decade is the creation of the **Euroequity market,** the market for shares sold outside the boundaries of the issuing firm's home country. Prior to 1980, few companies thought about offering stock outside the national boundaries of their headquarters country. Since then, hundreds of firms worldwide have issued stock simultaneously in two or more countries to attract more capital from a wider variety of shareholders. For example, when Daimler and Chrysler merged, the company issued global shares on 21 different markets in eight different countries: Germany, the United States, Austria, Canada, France, Britain, Japan, and Switzerland.

> Euroequities are shares listed on stock exchanges in countries other than the home country of the issuing company.

BOVESPA, the Brazilian Stock market, is one of the rising stars in the emerging market stock markets. BOVESPA was the fourth largest emerging stock market in 2010, just behind Shanghai, Bombay, and the National Stock Exchange of India, and just above Shenzhen.

Source: Julio Etchart/Alamy

The Trend Toward Delisting   The trend of listing on more than one exchange, which was popular in the 1990s, has begun to reverse as more and more companies reduce the number of exchanges on which their stocks are listed. An example is IBM, which announced in March 2005 that it would remove its shares from the Tokyo Stock Exchange, after already having removed them from exchanges in Vienna, Frankfurt, and Zurich. Investors are finding that the best price for stocks is usually in the home market of the company in which they are investing.

Furthermore, companies pay annual fees to list on exchanges, so if trading is light on a certain exchange, they can save money by listing on an exchange with heavier trading volume. Other reasons for delisting shares include weak market returns (fewer investors are putting their money into stocks) and increased regulation (such as the U.S. Sarbanes-Oxley Act). DaimlerChrysler used to list on 15 different stock exchanges in Germany, the United States, France, Japan, and Switzerland, but in 2008, Daimler (no longer DaimlerChrysler) listed only on stock exchanges in Frankfurt, New York, and Stuttgart.

The merger movement is one way to try to blunt the trend to delist. NYSE Euronext, for example, was created in 2007 by combining the NYSE Group, Inc. and Euronext N.V. It is comprised of a family of stock exchanges located in six countries, including the NYSE, which is the world's largest cash equities market, NYSE Euronext which is the

Eurozone's largest cash equities market, and NYSE Alternext, a pan-European market designed for emerging companies. If the proposed combination with Deutsche Börse is approved, it will expand the global reach of NYSE Euronext. The U.S. market is important for American and foreign companies looking for equity capital and is popular for Euroequity issues, partly because of the market size and the speed with which offerings are completed. The large pension funds in the United States can buy big blocks of stock at low transaction costs. Pension fund managers regard foreign stocks as a good form of portfolio diversification.

American Depositary Receipt The most popular way for a Euroequity to get a listing in the United States is to issue an **American Depositary Receipt (ADR),** a negotiable certificate issued by a U.S. bank in the United States to represent the underlying shares of a foreign corporation's stock held in trust at a custodian bank in the foreign country. ADRs are traded like shares of stock, with each one representing some number of shares of the underlying stock. For example, Toyota has listed ADRs on the NYSE since 1999 at a rate of two per common Toyota share. They issue through a sponsored ADR facility operated by the Bank of New York as ADRs.

> Most foreign companies that list on the U.S. stock exchanges do so through American Depositary Receipts, which are financial documents that represent a share or part of a share of stock in the foreign company.

The United States is not the only market for Euroequities; there are also Global Depositary Receipts and European Depositary Receipts, as illustrated in the earlier Sistema example. The U.S. market does dominate the depositary receipt market, but compared to the NYSE, a much larger percentage of the total shares traded on the London Stock Exchange belongs to foreign companies, even though the total trading volume in the United States is quite large. The creation of NYSE Euronext has complicated the comparisons, because now the merger brings together six cash equities exchanges from five countries.

Many foreign corporations try to raise capital in the United States but don't want to list on an exchange because they don't want to comply with the onerous reporting requirements of the SEC. Still, those that do gain access to a large percentage of the world's market capitalization, a fact that is a significant advantage to those with a U.S. listing. Companies generally list on their home country's exchange first and then venture into the international exchanges with depositary receipts. One important change in ADR regulations is that non-U.S. companies that have adopted IFRS can list in the United States without having to reconcile their financial statements to U.S. GAAP, which eliminates a major reporting requirement.

Offshore Financing and Offshore Financial Centers

Offshore financing is the provision of financial services by banks and other agents to nonresidents. In its simplest form, this involves borrowing money from and lending to the nonresidents.[24] A good example of legitimate offshore financing is the use of the Eurodollar market. A U.S. company can raise Eurodollars in London by working with a bank to issue bonds or syndicate a loan.

> **Concept Check**
>
> We introduce the *OECD* in discussing the OECD Anti-Bribery Convention in Chapter 5. In addition, the OECD is concerned about a broader range of activities that involve cross-border operations. We also mention the OECD's earlier Guidelines for MNEs, which came out in 1976 and includes a code of conduct for MNEs engaged in cross-border operations. Here we observe that, because **offshore financing** has proved conducive to such misbehavior as tax avoidance, the OECD and several other multilateral organizations have made efforts to strengthen ethical practices in offshore transactions.

> Offshore financing—the provision of financial services by banks and other agents to nonresidents.

WHAT'S AN OFC?

Offshore financial centers (OFCs) are cities or countries that provide large amounts of funds in currencies other than their own and are used as locations in which to raise and accumulate cash. Usually, the financial transactions are conducted in currencies other than that of the country and are thus the centers for the Eurocurrency market. An OFC could be defined as any financial center where offshore activity takes place, but a more practical definition is a center where the bulk of financial activity is offshore on both sides of the balance sheet, the transactions are initiated elsewhere, and the majority of the institutions involved are controlled by nonresidents.[25]

> Offshore financial centers (OFCs)—cities or countries that provide large amounts of funds in currencies other than their own.

> OFCs offer low or zero taxation, moderate or light financial regulation, and banking secrecy and anonymity.

Characteristics of OFCs   Generally, the markets in these centers are regulated differently—and usually more flexibly—than domestic markets. The centers provide an alternative, (usually) a cheaper source of funding for MNEs so that they don't have to rely strictly on their own national markets. Offshore financial centers have one or more of the following characteristics:

- A large foreign-currency (Eurocurrency) market for deposits and loans (in London, say)
- A market that functions as a large net supplier of funds to the world financial markets (such as in Switzerland)
- A market that functions as an intermediary or pass-through for international loan funds (e.g., the Bahamas and the Cayman Islands)
- Economic and political stability
- An efficient and experienced financial community
- Good communications and support services
- An official regulatory climate favorable to the financial industry, in the sense that it protects investors without unduly restricting financial institutions[26]

However, the OECD prefers to differentiate between well and poorly regulated financial centers rather than offshore and onshore.[27]

Operational versus Booking Centers   *Operational centers* have extensive banking activities involving short-term financial transactions; *booking centers* have little actual banking activity taking place but transactions are recorded to take advantage of secrecy and low (or no) tax rates. In the latter case, individuals may deposit money offshore to hide it from their home-country tax authorities, either because the money is earned and/or to be used illegally—such as in the drug trade or to finance terrorist activities—or because the individual or company does not want to pay tax. London is an example of an operational center; the Cayman Islands is an example of a booking center.

OFCs as "Tax Havens"   A major concern with OFCs is the tax avoidance dimension of their activities. The OECD has been working closely with the major OFCs to ensure that they are engaged in legal activity. It uses the following key factors in identifying tax havens: (1) no or only nominal taxes, (2) lack of effective exchange of information (especially bank secrecy), (3) lack of transparency, and (4) no substantial activities.[28] Although not trying to tell the sovereign countries what their tax rates should be, the OECD is trying to eliminate harmful tax practices in these four areas:

1. The regime imposes low or no taxes on the relevant income (from geographically mobile financial and other service activities).
2. The regime is ring fenced (i.e., separated) from the domestic economy.
3. The regime lacks transparency; for example, the details of it or its application are not apparent or there is inadequate regulatory supervision or financial disclosure.
4. There is no effective exchange of information with respect to the regime.[29]

Obviously, there is a lot of overlap in these definitions. In a 2009 report, the OECD identified 28 tax-haven countries and 10 other financial centers that were moving to adopt their standards for good tax behavior, while no national jurisdictions were reported that had not committed to the internationally accepted tax standard. That is pretty significant progress.[30] The OECD is trying to reduce harmful tax practices through improved translation and disclosure. Putting the spotlight on countries seems to be the best approach.

Should Offshore Financial Centers and Aggressive Tax Practices Be Eliminated?

Point **Yes** The problem with OFCs is that they operate in a shroud of secrecy that allows companies to establish operations there for illegal and unethical behavior. In December 2001, U.S. energy giant Enron filed for bankruptcy—one of the largest in corporate history. Contributing to Enron's problems was the creation of hundreds of subsidiaries in tax havens, including 662 in the Cayman Islands, 119 in Turks and Caicos, 43 in Mauritius, and 8 in Bermuda, that were used to pass off corporate debts, losses, and executive compensation.[31] The fondness of unscrupulous MNEs for OFCs only serves to underscore the unqualified truth voiced in Figure 19.2.

As pointed out in Chapter 18, Parmalat set up three shell companies based in the Caribbean to capture cash. The companies allegedly sold Parmalat products, and Parmalat sent them fake invoices and charged costs and fees to make the sales look legitimate. It would then write out a credit note for the amount the subsidiaries supposedly owed and take that to banks to raise money. Given

the location of the subsidiaries, you would think the banks would have been suspicious, but Parmalat got away with these activities.

Off-balance-sheet financing was also used to hide debts. The company transferred over half of its liabilities to the books of small subsidiaries based in offshore tax havens such as the Cayman Islands. This allowed Parmalat to present a healthy balance sheet and a profitable income statement to investors and creditors by hiding large amounts of debt, understating interest expenses (thus overstating income), and overstating revenues for false bookings. Parmalat's actual debt was nearly double the amount disclosed to outsiders.

Terrorists and drug dealers also use OFCs to launder money. When the U.S. government went after the money of Osama bin Laden, it went after OFCs notorious for their secrecy. When a bank in the Bahamas refused to open its books to U.S. government investigators, the United States cut off the bank from the world's wire transfer systems. Within two hours, the bank changed policies.[32]

"It's snappy, it's today -- I like it."

FIGURE 19.2   The Classic Lure of Offshore Tax Laxity

Source: David Brown/Cartoon Stock

Counterpoint   **No** OFCs are an efficient way for companies to use their financial resources more effectively. They are good locations for establishing finance subsidiaries that can raise capital for the parent company or its subsidiaries. And they allow the finance subsidiaries to take advantage of lower borrowing costs and tax rates.

This type of activity is not illegal, because the companies are still subject to home- and host-country laws and tax regulations. It is true that some transactions may be illegal, but most are not. The key to policing truly illegal activities, such as hiding drug money or engaging in corporate fraud like the Parmalat case, is to improve transparency and reporting.

Why shouldn't countries have the opportunity to attract business by offering tax-haven status to MNEs? Many don't have other visible means of generating resources. They are too small to set up manufacturing operations, have too small a population base to offer low-cost labor, and don't have natural resources they can sell. So what can they do? Companies and individuals need places to bank their wealth

or raise capital, so the OFCs have decided to use the theory of factor proportions (discussed in Chapter 6) and develop the banking and financial infrastructure necessary to attract wealth. As long as they establish banking, privacy, and taxation laws that attract money, they should be allowed to do so. The Cayman Islands attracts a lot of tourism, but it is also the world's fifth-biggest financial center and has worked hard to crack down on money laundering so that it can use its financial expertise in legal ways to help companies and individuals.[33]

OFCs don't rely on taxation to fund huge government expenditures, because they don't have a large military budget or significant welfare costs. Is there anything wrong with not collecting large amounts of taxes? Some countries are upset that they offer a tax-free environment for revenues generated offshore, but that's the countries' business. Nobody should force them to collect higher taxes just because the high-tax countries are at a disadvantage in attracting banking and finance. If countries want to charge high taxes on financial transactions, let them do so, but don't force the OFCs to play their game.

Capital Budgeting in a Global Context

Capital budgeting—the process whereby MNEs determine which projects and countries will receive capital investment funds.

The next international dimension of the financial function is the capital budgeting decision, whereby the MNE determines which projects and countries will receive its capital investment funds. The parent company must compare the net present value or internal rate of return of a potential foreign project with that of its other projects around the world to determine the best place to invest resources. The technique used to compare different projects is called *capital budgeting*.

METHODS OF CAPITAL BUDGETING

Capital budgeting techniques:

- Payback period
- Net present value of a project
- Internal rate of return

Payback Period   One approach to capital budgeting is to determine the **payback period** of a project, or the number of years required to recover the initial investment made. This is typically done by estimating the annual after-tax free cash flow from the investment, determining the present value of the future cash flow for each year, and then determining how many years it will take to recoup the initial investment.

Net Present Value   A second approach is to determine the **net present value (NPV)** of a project, which is defined as follows:

$$NPV = \sum_{t=1}^{n} \frac{FCF_t}{(1+k)^t} - IO$$

where FCF_t = the annual free cash flow in time period t

k = the appropriate discount rate; that is, the required rate of return or cost of capital

IO = the initial cash outlay

n = the project's expected life

The required rate of return is the rate the company must get from the project to justify the cost of raising the initial investment or at least maintaining the value of its common stock. If the NPV is positive, the project is also considered positive. If the NPV is negative, the company should not enter into the project.

Internal Rate of Return A third approach is to compute the internal rate of return (IRR) of the project—the rate that equates the present value of future cash flows with the present value of the initial investment—and compare it with the required rate of return. If it is greater than the required rate of return, the investment is considered positive. However, the company then needs to compare the IRR with that of competing projects in other countries.

> MNEs need to determine free cash flows based on cash flow estimates and tax rates in different countries and an appropriate required rate of return adjusted for risk.

Several things are common about each of the methods. First, the firm needs to determine the free cash flows, which involves estimating cash flows as well as bringing into the equation different tax rates from different countries. Second, in the case of both NPV and IRR, the company needs to determine what the required rate of return is.

COMPLICATIONS IN CAPITAL BUDGETING

Several aspects of capital budgeting are unique to foreign-project assessment:

- Parent cash flows (those from the project back to the parent in the parent's currency) must be distinguished from project cash flows (those in local currency from the sale of goods and services). Will the decision be based on one, the other, or both?

- Remittance of funds to the parent, such as dividends, interest on loans, and payment of intracompany receivables and payables, is affected by differing tax systems, legal and political constraints on the movement of funds, local business norms, and differences in how financial markets and institutions function. In addition, tax systems affect free cash flows on the project, irrespective of the remittance issue.

- Differing rates of inflation must be anticipated by both the parent and the subsidiary because of their importance in causing changes in competitive position and cash flows over time.

- The parent must consider the possibility of unanticipated exchange-rate changes because of their direct effects on the value of cash flows and their indirect effects on the foreign subsidiary's competitive position.

- The parent company must evaluate political risk in a target market, because political events can drastically reduce the value or availability of expected cash flows.

- The terminal value (the value of the project at the end of the budgeting period) is difficult to estimate, because potential purchasers from host, home, or third countries—or from the private or public sector—may have widely divergent perspectives on the project's value. The terminal value is critical in determining the total cash flows from the project. The total cash outlay is partially offset by the terminal value—the amount of cash the parent company can get from the subsidiary or project if it eventually sells.[34]

Because of all the forces listed here, it's very difficult to estimate future cash flows, both to the subsidiary and to the parent company. There are two ways to deal with the variations in future cash flows. One is to set out several different scenarios and then determine the payback period, net present value, or internal rate of return of the project under each scenario. The other is to adjust the hurdle rate, which is the minimum required rate of return the project must achieve for it to receive capital. The adjustment is usually made by increasing the hurdle rate above its minimal level.

> Determine different cash flow scenarios or adjust the hurdle rate (the minimum required rate of return for a project).

Once the budget is complete, the MNE must examine both the return in local currency and the return to the parent in dollars from cash flows. Examining the return in local currency will give management a chance to compare the project with other investment alternatives in the country. However, cash flows to the parent are important, since dividends are paid to shareholders from those flows. If the MNE cannot generate a sufficient return to the parent in the parent's currency, it will eventually fall behind in its ability to pay shareholders and pay off corporate debt. Finally, the decision must be made in the strategic context of the investment, not just the financial context.

Internal Sources of Funds

Funds are working capital, or current assets minus current liabilities.

Although the term *funds* usually means "cash," it is used in a much broader sense in business and generally refers to working capital—that is, the difference between current assets and current liabilities. From a general perspective, funds come from the normal operations of a business (selling merchandise or services) as well as from financing activities, such as borrowing money, issuing bonds, or issuing shares. They are used to purchase fixed assets, pay employees, buy materials and supplies, and invest in marketable securities or long-term investments.

CASH FLOWS AND THE MNE

Cash flows in an MNE are significantly more complex than for a company that operates in a strictly domestic environment. An MNE that wants to expand operations or needs additional capital can look not only to the domestic and international debt and equity markets but also to sources within itself. The complexity of its internal sources is magnified because of the number of its subsidiaries and the diverse environments in which they operate.

Sources of internal funds are

• Loans.
• Investments through equity capital.
• Intercompany receivables and payables.
• Dividends.

Figure 19.3 shows a parent company that has two foreign subsidiaries. Parent and subsidiaries may be increasing funds through normal operations that may be used on a company-wide basis, perhaps through loans. The parent can lend funds directly to one subsidiary or guarantee an outside loan to the other. Equity capital from the parent is another source of funds for the subsidiary.

Funds can also go from subsidiary to parent. The subsidiary could declare a dividend to the parent as a return on capital, or lend cash directly to it. If the subsidiary declared a dividend, the parent could lend the funds back. The dividend would not be tax deductible to the subsidiary, but it would be included as income to the parent, so the parent would have to pay tax on the dividend. If the subsidiary lent money to the parent, the interest paid by the parent would be tax-deductible to the parent and taxable income for the subsidiary.

Merchandise, people (in service firms), and financial flows can travel between subsidiaries, giving rise to receivables and payables. Companies can move money between

FIGURE 19.3   How the MNE Handles Its Funds (I): Internal Funds

Funds consist of *working capital* that comes from normal business operations and that may be used to purchase assets and materials, to pay employees, and to make investments. If the company is an MNE, funds may come from either parent or subsidiary operations, or both, and can be used by the parent to support either its own operations or those of its subsidiaries.

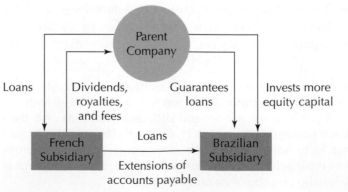

and among related entities by paying quickly, or they can accumulate funds by deferring payment. They can also adjust the size of the payment by arbitrarily raising or lowering the price of intercompany transactions in comparison with the market price—a transfer pricing strategy.

GLOBAL CASH MANAGEMENT

Managing cash effectively is a chief concern of the CFO, who must answer the following three questions:

1. What are the local and corporate system needs for cash?
2. How can the cash be withdrawn from subsidiaries and centralized?
3. Once the cash has been centralized, what should be done with it?

The cash manager, who reports to the treasurer (see Figure 19.1), must collect and pay cash in the company's normal operational cycle and then deal with financial institutions, such as commercial and investment banks, when generating and investing it. Before remitting any cash into the MNE's control center—whether at regional or headquarters level—the cash manager must first assess local cash needs through cash budgets and forecasts. Because the forecast projects the excess cash that will be available, the cash manager will know how much can be invested for short-term profits.

> Cash budgets and forecasts are essential in assessing a company's cash needs.

Once local cash needs are met, the cash manager must decide whether to allow the local manager to invest any excess cash or have it remitted to a central cash pool. If the cash is centralized, the manager must find a way to make the transfer. A cash dividend is the easiest way to distribute cash, but government restrictions may interfere. For example, foreign-exchange controls may prevent the company from remitting as large a dividend as it would like. Cash can also be remitted through royalties, management fees, and repayment of principal and interest on loans.

> Dividends are a good source of intercompany transfers, but governments often restrict their free movement.

Multilateral Netting An important cash-management strategy is **netting** cash flows internationally. For example, an MNE with operations in four European countries could have several different intercompany cash transfers resulting from loans, the sale of goods, licensing agreements, and so forth. In the illustration in Figure 19.4, for example, there are no fewer than seven different transfers among four subsidiaries. Among its special services, GPS Capital Inc., the foreign-exchange company profiled in our opening case, helps clients determine their foreign-currency cash flows and assists them in developing strategies to net cash flows by minimizing the number of their foreign-currency transactions.

> Multilateral netting—the process of coordinating cash inflows and outflows among subsidiaries so that only net cash is transferred, reducing transaction costs.

Case Review Note

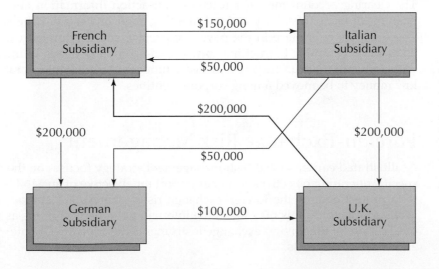

FIGURE 19.4 How the MNE Handles Its Funds (II): Multilateral Cash Flows

As the various subsidiaries of the MNE go about their business, cash can be transferred among them for a variety of reasons (e.g., in the form of loans or as proceeds from the sale of goods). Cash, of course, can flow in any direction, and if the MNE doesn't maintain some kind of cash-management center, each subsidiary must settle its accounts (receivables, payables, etc.) independently.

TABLE 19.2   How the MNE Handles Its Funds (III): Net Positions

Assume that these data are from the same MNE as the one introduced in Figure 19.4. Because the company has no cash-management center, *net positions*—the difference between *total receivables* and *total payables*—must be determined on a subsidiary-by-subsidiary basis.

Subsidiary	Total Receivables	Total Payables	Net Position
French	250,000	350,000	(100,000)
German	250,000	100,000	150,000
Italian	150,000	300,000	(150,000)
U.K.	300,000	200,000	100,000

FIGURE 19.5   How the MNE Handles Its Funds (IV): Multilateral Netting

Dissatisfied with the process represented in Figure 19.4, our MNE has now established a cash-management center—a *clearing account*—into which each subsidiary transfers its net cash. Naturally, the MNE may in turn distribute the total to support subsidiary operations.

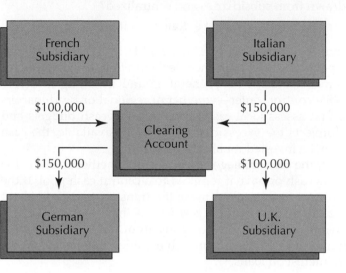

Netting requires sophisticated software and good banking relationships in different countries.

Concept Check

In Chapter 10, we explain why it's important for MNEs to anticipate exchange-rate changes and make decisions about business activities that may be sensitive to those changes—decisions, for instance, about the sourcing of raw materials and components or the location of manufacturing and assembly facilities. We take up the same theme in Chapter 12, where we cite exchange-rate movement as just one factor that can affect wages in a particular country—and thus any advantage in labor-cost differences that a company might hope to gain from locating operations in that country.

Table 19.2 identifies the total receivables, payables, and net position for each subsidiary. Rather than have each subsidiary settle its accounts independently with subsidiaries in other countries, many MNEs are establishing cash-management centers in one city (such as Brussels) to coordinate cash flows among subsidiaries from several countries.

Figure 19.5 illustrates how each subsidiary in a net payable position transfers funds to the central clearing account. The account manager then transfers funds to the accounts of the net receiver subsidiaries. In this example, only four transfers need to take place. The clearing account manager receives transaction information and computes the net position of each subsidiary at least monthly, then orchestrates the settlement process. The transfers take place in the payer's currency, and the foreign-exchange conversion takes place centrally. For netting to work, the company needs to match its cash needs with software that can track and transfer funds and with banking relationships that allow money to be moved among corporate entities.

Foreign-Exchange Risk Management

As illustrated earlier, global cash-management strategy focuses on the flow of money for specific operating objectives. Another important objective of an MNE's financial strategy is to protect against the foreign-exchange risks of investing abroad. The strategies an MNE adopts to do this may mean the internal movement of funds as well as the use of one or more of the foreign-exchange instruments described in Chapter 9, such as options and forward contracts.

TYPES OF EXPOSURE

If all exchange rates were fixed in relation to one another, there would be no foreign-exchange risk. However, rates are not fixed, and currency values change frequently. Instead of infrequent, one-way changes, currencies fluctuate often and both up and down. A change in the exchange rate can result in three different exposures for a company: *translation exposure, transaction exposure,* and *economic* or *operational exposure.*

Translation Exposure Foreign-currency financial statements are translated into the reporting currency of the parent company (assumed to be USD for U.S. companies) so they can be combined with financial statements of other companies in the corporate group to form the consolidated financial statements. **Translation exposure** occurs because exposed accounts—those translated at the balance-sheet rate or current exchange rate—either gain or lose value in dollars when the exchange rate changes.

Consider the translation exposure example in Table 19.3 (Panel A) of a U.S. company with a subsidiary in Mexico. The subsidiary has 900,000 pesos in the bank. So what is the value of the cash *after* the exchange rate changes? The subsidiary still has pesos in the bank account; it's just that the dollar equivalent of the pesos has fallen, resulting in a loss. The gain or loss does not represent an actual cash flow effect because the pesos are only translated, not converted, into dollars. In addition, reported earnings can either rise or fall against the dollar because of the translation effect, which can affect earnings per share and stock prices.

Transaction Exposure Denominating a transaction in a foreign currency gives rise to **transaction exposure,** because the company has accounts receivable or payable in foreign currency that must be settled eventually. Consider the transaction-exposure example in Table 19.3 (Panel B) of a U.S. exporter delivering merchandise to a British importer. If the exporter were to receive payment in dollars, there would be no immediate impact on the exporter if the dollar/pound exchange rate changed. If payment were to be received in pounds, however, the exporter might incur a foreign-exchange gain or loss. In this case, because the pound is falling in value, the exporter would receive fewer dollars from the sale after the change in the exchange rate. This would be an actual cash flow gain or loss to the exporter.

Economic (or Operating) Exposure **Economic exposure,** also known as **operating exposure,** is the potential for change in expected cash flows that arises from the pricing of products, the sourcing and cost of inputs, and the location of investments. Pricing strategies have both an immediate and a long-term impact on cash flows. Consider the economic exposure example from Table 19.3 (Panel C) of the U.S. exporter and the British importer. The first part of Panel C shows what happens if the importer has to pay the exporter $500,000 for the merchandise. Because the pound is falling in value, the importer must convert more pounds into dollars to pay the exporter. Now, the *importer* can either sell the product at the original price and not earn as much profit, or it can raise the price and hope that consumers will be willing to pay it. The *exporter,* however, also has two choices. It can continue to sell the merchandise at the same price, or it can lower it. If it lowers the price, it will incur a lower profit margin. If it continues to sell at the same price, the importer will have to pay more for the merchandise, then decide what to do.

Another economic-exposure decision involves how to make investment decisions. In 2011, Volkswagen AG decided to open a factory in the United States to take advantage of the strong euro vs. the dollar. Because of the strength of the euro, it had not been cost-competitive in the United States, and it realized that by opening a factory in Tennessee, the southern part of the U.S., it could take advantage of the strong euro as well as lower labor costs. Following BMW's example of investing in the United States in 2005, VW hopes to not only be competitive in the United States but also use the United States as an export platform to other countries. Both VW and BMW found that

Three types of foreign-exchange exposure: translation, transaction, economic or operational.

Translation exposure arises because the dollar value of the exposed asset or liability changes as the exchange rate changes.

Transaction exposure arises when a transaction is denominated in a foreign currency and where the settlement gives rises to a cash flow gain or loss.

Economic, or operating, exposure arises from the effects of exchange-rate changes on

- *Future cash flows.*
- *The sourcing of parts and components.*
- *The location of investments.*
- *The competitive position of the company in different markets.*

TABLE 19.3   The Effects of Foreign-Exchange Exposure

Panel A—Translation Exposure

A Mexican subsidiary reports cash in the bank of 900,000 pesos at a time when 9.5 pesos will buy U.S. $1; thus its U.S. parent translates the net in pesos into U.S. $94,737. When the exchange rate changes, however, and 10 pesos are required to buy U.S. $1, the total of 900,000 pesos must be retranslated from U.S. $94,737 into U.S. $90,000.

U.S. Company Bank Account in Mexico	900,000 pesos
Initial Exchange Rate	9.5 pesos/$
Initial Bank Account Worth	$94,737
Calculation: 900,000/9.5 = $94,737	
Subsequent Exchange Rate	10 pesos/$
Subsequent Bank Account Worth	$90,000
Calculation: 900,000/10 = $90,000	

Panel B—Transaction Exposure

If a U.S. company denominates its sales in dollars, it has no transaction exposure. If it denominates the sale in British pounds, the dollar value of the receivable rises or falls as the exchange rate changes, as illustrated below.

Total Price of Merchandise on Exporter's Books	$500,000
Initial Exchange Rate	1.9000 $/£
Initial Underlying Value of Sale	£263,158
Calculation: $500,000/1.9000 = £263,158	
Amount Received by Exporter	£263,158
Subsequent Exchange Rate	1.8800 $/£
Subsequent Payment Value of Collected Receivable	$494,737
Calculation: £263,158 × 1.8800 = $494,737	
Loss to the Exporter	$5,263
Calculation: $500,000 − $494,737 = $5,263	

PANEL B—Transaction Exposure When a U.S. company exports books worth U.S. $500,000 to an importer in the U.K., it's paid with £263,158—the equivalent in U.K. pounds of U.S. $500,000 at an exchange rate of 1.9000 $/£. Subsequently, however, when the value of the U.K. pound falls to a rate of 1.8800 $/£, the value of the U.S. firm's holding in pounds declines from U.S. $500,000 to U.S. $494,737.

Panel C—Economic (or Operating) Exposure

The transaction is the same as in Panel B, but this time the British importer must pay the U.S. exporter in dollars. The first calculation shows how many British pounds the importer must come up with to convert to dollars to pay the exporter. That amount is then marked up 10 percent for sale in the United Kingdom. The next calculation assumes that the British pound weakens to $1.8800 per pound, meaning that the importer has to come up with more pounds to convert to dollars to pay the exporter. The higher amount is then marked up by 10 percent, and we show how much more the importer would have to charge in the market and how much the importer's profit margin would be at the higher price. However, the economic exposure is that the importer may not be able to sell the products at a higher price, so there are two options. One is for the importer to sell the product for the same price as before and accept a lower profit margin (£23,517). The second is for the exporter to charge only $494,737, which would allow the importer to pay the same amount in British pounds as before the exchange-rate change and still be able to keep the price the same in the United Kingdom and earn the same profit margin as before. The difference between the last two calculations is that the importer suffers a drop in profits in the first case and the exporter suffers a drop in profits in the second case.

Total Price of Merchandise on Exporter's Books	$500,000
Initial Exchange Rate	1.9000 $/£
Initial Underlying Value of Sale	£263,158
Calculation: $500,000/1.9000 = £263,158	
Amount Charged by Importer after 10% Markup	£289,474
Subsequent Exchange Rate	1.8800 $/£
Subsequent Underlying Value of Sale	£265,957
Calculation: $500,000/1.8800 = £265,957	
Amount Charged by Importer after 10% Markup	£292,553
Difference in Sales Price before and after Rate Change	£3,079
Profit to Importer If Importer Charges Higher Price	£26,596
Calculation: £292,553 − £265,957 = £26,596	
Profit to Importer If Importer Absorbs Cost Increase	£23,517
Calculation: £289,474 − £265,957 = £23,517	
Price Charged by Exporter for Constant Cost to Importer	$494,737
Calculation: £263,158 × 1.8800 = $494,737	

exporting to the United States was complicated because costs were generated in euros (most of its manufacturing facilities were in Europe) while revenues in the United States were in dollars. Thus they was generating revenues in a weak currency and costs in a strong currency, severely affecting earnings. One of the economic solutions was to expand manufacturing operations in the United States to balance revenues and expenses in the same currency.[35]

EXPOSURE-MANAGEMENT STRATEGY

To adequately protect assets against the risks from translation, transaction, and economic exposure to exchange-rate fluctuations, management must do the following:

- Define and measure exposure
- Organize and implement a reporting system that monitors exposure and exchange-rate movements
- Adopt a policy assigning responsibility for minimizing—or hedging—exposure
- Formulate strategies for hedging exposure

Defining and Measuring Exposure   Most MNEs see all three types of exposure: translation, transaction, and economic. To develop a viable hedging strategy, an MNE must forecast the degree of exposure in each major currency in which it operates. Because the types differ, the actual exposure by currency must be tracked separately. For example, the translation exposure in Brazilian reals should be kept track of separately from the transaction exposure because it will result in an actual cash flow, whereas the translation exposure may not. Thus, the company generates one report for each type of exposure. It may also adopt different hedging strategies for the different types. Recall from our opening case that GPS developed proprietary software, called FXpert, which not only conducts specialized audits of clients' foreign-exchange cash flows but proposes effective hedging strategies for improving them. Solutions may include such well-known hedging strategies as forwards, options, and futures contracts, but GPS has designed FXpert to tailor strategies to clients' specific needs.

A key aspect of measuring exposure is forecasting exchange rates. A company should estimate and use ranges within which it expects a currency to vary over the forecasting period by developing in-house capabilities to monitor exchange rates or using economists who also try to obtain a consensus of exchange-rate movements from the banks they deal with. Their concern is to forecast the direction, magnitude, and timing of an exchange-rate change. As we note in Chapter 10, however, forecasting is imprecise.

Creating a Reporting System   Once the company has decided how to define and measure exposure and estimate future exchange rates, it must create a reporting system that will assist in protecting it against risk. To achieve this goal, substantial participation from foreign operations must be combined with effective central control. Foreign input is important to ensure that the information the company uses in forecasting is effective. U.S.-based Dell Computer has developed a system whereby hedging strategies are developed jointly by financial management at corporate headquarters and local management at its subsidiaries around the world.

Because exchange rates move frequently, the company must obtain input from those who are attuned to the foreign country's economy. Central control of exposure protects resources more efficiently than letting each subsidiary and branch manage its own. Each organizational unit may be able to define its own exposure, but the company also has an overall exposure. To set hedging policies on a separate-entity basis might not take into account the fact that exposures of several entities (that is, branches, subsidiaries, affiliates, and so on) could offset one another.

Once each basic reporting unit has identified its exposure, the data should be sent to the next organizational level for preliminary consolidation, which enables the region or division to determine exposure by account and by currency for each time period. The resulting reports should be routine, periodic, and standardized to ensure comparability and timeliness in formulating strategies. Final reporting should be at the corporate level, where top management can see the amount of foreign-exchange exposure. Specific hedging strategies can be taken at any level, but each level of management must be aware of the size of the exposure and the potential impact on the company.

Formulating Hedging Strategies   Once a company has identified its level of exposure and determined which exposure is critical, it can hedge its position by adopting operational and/or financial strategies, each with cost-benefit as well as operational implications. The safest position is a balanced one in which exposed assets equal exposed liabilities.

| Hedging strategies can be operational or financial. |

Operational Hedging Strategies   The use of debt to balance exposure is an interesting strategy. Many companies "borrow locally," especially in weak-currency countries, because that helps them avoid foreign-exchange risk from borrowing in a foreign currency and balances off their exposed position in assets and earnings. One problem with this strategy is that, because interest rates in weak-currency countries tend to be high, there must be a trade-off between the cost of borrowing and the potential loss from exchange-rate variations.

| Operational strategies include
- Using local debt to balance local assets.
- Taking advantage of leads and lags for intercompany payments. |

Protecting against loss from transaction exposure becomes complex. In dealing with foreign customers, it is always safest for the company to denominate the transaction in its own currency to avoid any foreign-exchange exposure. The risk shifts to the foreign customer that has to come up with the company's currency. Or the company could denominate purchases in a weaker currency and sales in a stronger one. If forced to make purchases in a strong currency and sales in a weak one, it could resort to contractual measures such as forward contracts or options, or it could try to balance its inflows and outflows through astute sales and purchasing strategies.

Leads and Lags   Other operational strategies protect cash flows among related entities, such as a parent and subsidiaries. A **lead strategy** means either collecting foreign-currency receivables before they are due when the foreign currency is expected to weaken, or paying foreign-currency payables before they are due when the foreign currency is expected to strengthen. With a **lag strategy**, a company either delays collection of foreign-currency receivables if that currency is expected to strengthen, or delays payables when the currency is expected to weaken. In other words, a company usually leads into and lags out of a hard currency and leads out of and lags into a weak one.

| A lead strategy means collecting or paying early. A lag strategy means collecting or paying late. |

Sometimes an operational strategy means shifting assets overseas to take advantage of currency changes. As mentioned earlier, when the euro strengthened against the U.S. dollar, BMW shifted some of its manufacturing to the United States.

Using Derivatives to Hedge Foreign-Exchange Risk   In addition to the operational strategies just mentioned, a company may hedge exposure through *derivative* financial contracts such as forward contracts and options, with the most common hedge being a forward contract.

| Forward contracts can establish a fixed exchange rate for future transactions. Currency options can ensure access to foreign currency at a fixed exchange rate for a specific period of time. |

Consider a U.S. exporter selling goods to a British manufacturer for £1 million when the exchange rate is $1.9000/£. If the exporter could collect the money right away and convert it into dollars, it would receive $1.9 million. However, if the exporter were not expected to receive payment for 90 days, it would be exposed to an exchange-rate change. One way to protect against this is to enter into a forward contract with a bank to deliver pounds and receive dollars at the forward rate of, say, $1.8500. In 90 days, the exporter would convert the pounds into dollars at $1.8500 and receive $1,850,000, which is less than it would have received at the initial spot rate. But if the pound had deteriorated even more in value, the exporter would still receive the $1.85 million, which is not a bad deal.

A foreign-currency option is more flexible than a forward contract because it gives its purchaser the right, though not the obligation, to buy or sell a certain amount of foreign currency at a set exchange rate within a specified amount of time. In the same situation described above, the exporter would enter into an option contract with a trader to convert pounds into dollars at a certain exchange rate. For the cost of protection, the exporter pays a premium to the trader, which is like insurance. When the exporter receives the cash from the importer, it can decide whether to exercise the option. If the option gives it more money than the spot rate, the exporter will exercise the option. If not, it won't.

Taxation of Foreign-Source Income

Tax planning is a crucial responsibility for the CFO, because taxes can profoundly affect profitability and cash flow. This is especially true in international business. As complex as domestic taxation seems, it is child's play compared to the intricacies of international taxation. The international tax specialist must be familiar with both the home country's tax policy on foreign operations and the tax laws of each country in which the MNE operates.

Tax planning influences profitability and cash flow.

Taxation has a strong impact on several choices:

- Location of operations
- Choice of operating form, such as export or import, licensing agreement, or overseas investment
- Legal form of the new enterprise, such as branch or subsidiary
- Possible facilities in tax-haven countries to raise capital and manage cash
- Method of financing, such as internal or external sourcing and debt or equity
- Capital budgeting decisions
- Method of setting transfer prices

◄ As is the case with GPS in the opening case, a foreign exchange trader on the trading floor of Moneycorp in London is watching rates to help clients manage financial risk and provide cash management advice.

Source: Alex Segre/Alamy

INTERNATIONAL TAX PRACTICES

Problems with different countries' tax practices arise from
- Lack of familiarity with laws.
- Loose enforcement.

Differences in tax practices around the world often cause problems for MNEs. Lack of familiarity with laws and customs can create confusion. In some countries, tax laws are loosely enforced. In others, taxes may generally be negotiated between the tax collector and the taxpayer—if they are ever paid at all. In still others, they have to be rigidly followed.

With a value-added tax, each company pays a percentage of the value added to a product at each stage of the business process.

Differences in Types of Taxes   Countries differ in terms of the types of taxes they have (income versus excise), the tax rates applied to income, the determination of taxable income, and the treatment of foreign-source income. Although we focus in this section on corporate income tax, excise taxes are another important source of income to governments. The value-added tax is an example of an excise tax used in Europe. It is a percentage levied on products at the point of sale in every stage of the value chain, and it is included in the final price of the product rather than added to the price, as is the case with the sales tax in the United States. There are many other excise taxes, and the large number of taxes in some countries, like Brazil, is very confusing to both local and foreign investors.

Differences in GAAP   Variations among countries in GAAP can lead to differences in determining taxable income. In countries where tax laws allow companies to depreciate assets faster than accounting standards allow but where companies must use the same standards for tax and book accounting, higher depreciation expenses result in lower income and therefore lower taxes. Revenue recognition is also an important issue. Some countries tax income from worldwide revenues of MNEs, whereas others only recognize income from revenues generated in the domestic environment.

Corporate tax rates vary from country to country.

Differences in Tax Rates   Corporate tax rates also vary from country to country. The OECD publishes the corporate tax rates of 33 member countries, where central-government corporate income-tax rates range from a low of 8.5 percent in Switzerland to a high of 35 percent in the United States. However, the total corporate income tax burden includes subcentral government taxes (such as provincial or state and local taxes) as well as the central-government corporate income tax. In this case, the combined rate ranges from a low of 12.5 percent in Ireland to a high of 39.54 percent in Japan and 39.2 percent in the United States.[36]

Two Approaches to Corporate Taxation   Taxation of corporate income is accomplished through one of two approaches in most countries: the *separate entity approach* (also known as the *classical approach*) or the *integrated system approach*.

In the separate entity approach, governments tax each taxable entity when it earns income.

Separate Entity Approach   In the separate entity approach, which the United States uses, each separate unit—company or individual—is taxed when it earns income. For example, a corporation is taxed on its earnings, while stockholders are taxed on the distribution of earnings (dividends). The result can be double taxation.

An integrated system tries to avoid double taxation of corporate income through split tax rates or tax credits.

Integrated System Approach   Many other developed countries use an integrated system to eliminate double taxation. Australia and New Zealand, for example, give a dividend credit to shareholders to shelter them from double taxation. This means that when shareholders report the dividends in their taxable income, they also get a credit for taxes paid on that income by the company that issued the dividend. That keeps the shareholders from paying tax on the dividend, because the company has already done so.

Germany used to have a split-rate system with two different tax rates on corporate earnings: one on retained earnings and one on distributed earnings. However, they abolished the split-rate system in 2001 and adopted a classical system with an overall lower corporate tax rate on earnings of 15 percent plus a 5.5 percent solidarity surcharge (to help in the reunification with East Germany), resulting in a combined rate of 15.8

percent.[37] Taxation of foreign-source income depends on the country where the parent company is domiciled. It is common for most developed countries to tax MNEs on their worldwide income and give them a credit for foreign corporate income taxes paid. That is not true everywhere, however. Hong Kong companies, for example, pay tax only on Hong Kong-source income, even if remitted to Hong Kong, and their corporate tax rate is only 16.5 percent.[38]

TAXING BRANCHES AND SUBSIDIARIES

To illustrate the complexities of taxing foreign-source income, let's look at how U.S.-based companies tax earnings from a *foreign branch* and a *foreign subsidiary*.

The Foreign Branch   A foreign branch is an extension of the parent company rather than an enterprise incorporated in a foreign country. Any income the branch generates is taxable immediately to the parent, whether or not cash is remitted by the branch to the parent as a distribution of earnings. However, if the branch suffers a loss, the parent is allowed to deduct that loss from its taxable income, reducing its overall tax liability.

> Foreign branch income (or loss) is directly included in the parent's taxable income.

The Foreign Subsidiary   Whereas a branch is a legal extension of a parent company, a foreign corporation is an independent legal entity set up in a country (incorporated) according to the laws of incorporation of that country. When an MNE purchases a foreign corporation or sets up a new one in a foreign country, it is called a *subsidiary* of the parent. Income earned by the subsidiary is either reinvested in the subsidiary or remitted as a dividend to the parent company.

Subsidiary income is either taxable to the parent or tax-deferred—that is, it is not taxed until it is remitted as a dividend to the parent. Which tax status applies depends on whether the foreign subsidiary is a *controlled foreign corporation (CFC)*—a technical term in the U.S. tax code—and on whether the income is active or passive.

> Tax deferral means that income is not taxed until it is remitted to the parent company as a dividend.

The Controlled Foreign Corporation   A **controlled foreign corporation (CFC),** from the standpoint of the U.S. tax code, is any foreign corporation that meets the following condition: More than 50 percent of its voting stock is held by "U.S. shareholders." A U.S. shareholder is any U.S. person or company that holds 10 percent or more of the CFC's voting stock. Any foreign subsidiary of an MNE would automatically be considered a CFC from the standpoint of the tax code. However, a joint-venture company abroad that is partly owned by the U.S.-based MNE and partly by local investors might not be a CFC if the U.S. MNE does not own more than 50 percent of the JV's stock.

> In a CFC, U.S. shareholders hold more than 50 percent of the voting stock.

Table 19.4 shows how this might work. Foreign Corporation A is a CFC, because it is a wholly owned subsidiary of a U.S. parent company (U.S. Person V). Foreign Corporation B also is a CFC, because U.S. Persons V, W, and X each own 10 percent or more of the voting stock, which means they qualify as U.S. shareholders and their combined voting stock is more than 50 percent of the total. This situation might exist if three U.S. companies partnered together with a foreign partner to establish a joint venture overseas.

Such collaborative arrangements are not uncommon, especially in telecommunications and high-tech industries. Foreign Corporation C is not a CFC, because even though U.S. Persons V and W qualify as U.S. shareholders, their combined stock ownership is only 40 percent. U.S. Persons X and Y do not qualify as U.S. shareholders, because their individual ownership shares are only 8 percent each. When Enron set up its shell companies in tax-haven countries, it was careful not to own more than 50 percent of the stock so that it could avoid having to include the debt in those operations in its consolidated income.[39]

Active versus Passive Income   If a foreign subsidiary qualifies as a CFC, the U.S. tax law requires the U.S. investor to classify the foreign-source income as *active* or *Subpart F*

> Active income is derived from the direct conduct of a trade or business. Passive income (also called Subpart F income) is usually derived from operations in a tax-haven country.

TABLE 19.4   Controlled Foreign Corporations

To qualify as a *controlled foreign corporation (CFC)*, more than 50 percent of a company's voting shares must be held by U.S. shareholders. A *U.S. shareholder* must be a U.S. person or company holding at least 10 percent of the corporation's voting shares. Foreign Corporation B qualifies as a CFC, because the combined shares of U.S. Persons V, W, and X (each consisting of at least 10 percent) add up to 75 percent of the total.

	Percentages of the Voting Stock		
Shareholder	Foreign Corporation A	Foreign Corporation B	Foreign Corporation C
U.S. Person V	100%	45%	30%
U.S. Person W		10	10
U.S. Person X		20	8
U.S. Person Y		25	8
Foreign Person Z			44
Total	**100%**	**100%**	**100%**

(or *passive*) *income*. **Active income** is derived from the direct conduct of a trade or business, such as from sales of products manufactured in the foreign country. **Subpart F** or **passive income,** which is specifically defined in Subpart F of the U.S. Internal Revenue Code, comes from sources other than those connected with the direct conduct of a trade or business, generally in tax-haven countries, and includes the following:

- *Holding company income*—income primarily from dividends, interest, rents, royalties, and gains on sale of stocks.

- *Sales income*—income from foreign sales corporations that are separately incorporated from their manufacturing operations. The product of such entities is manufactured outside and sold for use outside the CFC's country of incorporation, and the CFC has not performed significant operations on the product.

- *Service income*—income from the performance of technical, managerial, or similar services for a company in the same corporate family as the CFC and outside the country in which the CFC resides.

Subpart F income usually derives from the activities of subsidiaries in tax-haven countries such as the Bahamas, the Netherlands Antilles, Panama, and Switzerland. The tax-haven subsidiary may act as an investment company, a sales agent or distributor, an agent for the parent in licensing agreements, or a holding company of stock in other foreign subsidiaries that are called *grandchild—or second-tier—subsidiaries.* This setup is illustrated in Figure 19.6. In the role of a holding company, its purpose is to concentrate cash from the parent's foreign operations into the low-tax country and use the cash for global expansion.

FIGURE 19.6   The Tax-Haven Subsidiary as Holding Company

A U.S. company has established a *tax-haven subsidiary* as a *holding company* in an offshore location. As such, the offshore subsidiary owns shares in three foreign subsidiaries called *grandchild subsidiaries.* The offshore holding company generates *holding company income,* which is recorded by the U.S. parent company as *Subpart F income.*

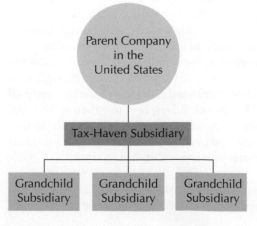

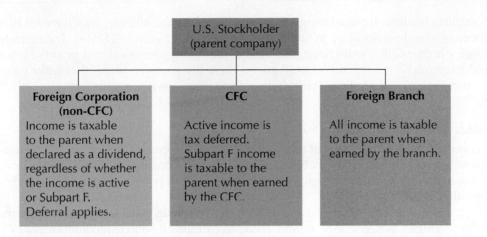

FIGURE 19.7 The Tax Status of U.S.-Owned Foreign Subsidiaries

Both CFC and Subpart F provisions are designed to prevent U.S. firms from establishing tax-haven subsidiaries for the purpose of investing *passive income* indefinitely—and thus earning tax-free income. Basically, these provisions treat tax income just as if it had been remitted to the U.S. parent at the time when it was earned.

Determining a Subsidiary's Income Figure 19.7 illustrates how the tax status of a subsidiary's income is determined. All non-CFC income—active and Subpart F—earned by the foreign corporation is deferred until remitted as a dividend to the U.S. shareholder (the parent company in this example). In contrast, a CFC's active income is tax deferred to the parent, but its Subpart F income is taxable immediately to the parent as soon as the CFC earns it, subject to some limitations and exceptions. If a foreign branch earns income, it is immediately taxable to the parent company, whether it is active or Subpart F income.

> Different rules regarding the tax status and deferability of income are in effect for non-CFCs, CFCs, and foreign branches.

TRANSFER PRICES

As noted in Chapter 18, a major tax challenge as well as an impediment to performance evaluation is the extensive use of transfer pricing in international operations. Because the price is between related entities, it is not necessarily an **arm's-length price**—that is, a price between two companies that do not have an ownership interest in each other. The assumption is that an arm's-length price is more likely than a transfer price to reflect the market accurately.

> A transfer price is a price on goods and services one member of a corporate family sells to another.

Transfer Prices and Taxation Companies establish arbitrary transfer prices primarily because of differences in taxation between countries. For example, if the corporate tax rate is higher in the parent company's country than in the subsidiary's country, the parent could set a low transfer price on products it sells the subsidiary to keep taxable profits low in its country and high in the subsidiary's country. The parent also could set a high transfer price on products sold to it by the subsidiary.

The OECD is very concerned about the ways in which companies manipulate transfer prices to minimize their tax liability worldwide. Its recommendation is that to determine the tax liability in each country, an arm's-length price should be applied, and it has issued guidelines on the matter. The OECD Centre for Tax Policy and Administration meets periodically to discuss a wide range of tax issues, including the adoption of sound transfer pricing policies. The OECD issued guidelines on transfer pricing in 1979 and updated the policies in 1995 to give guidance on how to tell if a transfer between independent firms is similar to a transfer within a group and on different transfer pricing methods that could be used. Additional revisions have been published since 1995 and are published periodically.[40]

Companies can get into disputes with different tax jurisdictions over transfer pricing policies. GlaxoSmithKline (GSK), the British pharmaceutical company, settled a transfer pricing dispute with the U.S. Internal Revenue Service in 2006 by paying $3.1 billion in federal, state, and local taxes and interest—slightly less than the $5 billion the IRS was seeking and nearly half of GSK's operating cash flow. The IRS contends that GSK charged its U.S. affiliate too little for marketing services provided by the affiliate, which meant that U.S. earnings were low, resulting in lower taxes collected in the United States. The dispute arose over whether GSK should have paid for the marketing services at cost or at the price it would have paid an independent third party. These are complex issues that leave companies open to significant financial risks if they don't price services or products correctly.[41]

DOUBLE TAXATION AND TAX CREDIT

Every country has a sovereign right to levy taxes on all income generated within its borders. However, MNEs run into problems when they earn income taxed in the country where it was earned and where it might also be taxed in the parent country as well. This could result in double taxation.

The IRS allows a tax credit for corporate income tax U.S. companies pay to another country. A tax credit is a dollar-for-dollar reduction of tax liability and must coincide with the recognition of income.

In U.S. tax law, a U.S. MNE gets a credit for income taxes paid to a foreign government. For example, when a U.S. parent recognizes foreign-source income (such as a dividend from a foreign subsidiary) in its taxable income, it must pay U.S. tax on that income. However, the IRS allows the parent company to reduce its tax liability by the amount of foreign income tax already paid. It is limited by the amount it would have had to pay in the United States on that income.

Assume, for example, that U.S. MNE A earns $100,000 of foreign-source income on which it paid $40,000 (40 percent tax rate) on that income in the foreign jurisdiction. If that income is considered taxable in the United States, Company A would have to pay $35,000 in income taxes (35 percent tax rate). In the absence of a tax credit, Company A would have paid a total of $75,000 in income tax on the $100,000 of income, a 75 percent tax rate.

The IRS, however, allows Company A to reduce its U.S. tax liability by a maximum of $35,000—what it would have paid in the United States if the income had been earned there. If Company A's subsidiary had paid $20,000 in foreign income tax (a 20 percent tax rate), it would be able to claim the entire $20,000 as a credit because it was less than the U.S. liability of $35,000. Company A will pay a total of $35,000 in corporate income tax on its foreign-source income—$20,000 to the foreign government and $15,000 to the U.S. government.

The purpose of tax treaties is to prevent double taxation or to provide remedies when it occurs.

Tax Treaties: Eliminating Double Taxation   The primary purpose of tax treaties is to prevent international double taxation or to provide remedies when it occurs. The United States is an active participant in 65 different tax treaties.[42] The general pattern between two treaty countries is to grant reciprocal deductions on dividend withholding and to exempt royalties—and sometimes interest payments—from any withholding tax.

The United States has a withholding tax of 30 percent for owners (individuals and corporations) of U.S. securities issued in countries with which it has no tax treaty. However, interest on portfolio obligations and on bank deposits is normally exempted from withholding. When a tax treaty is in effect, the U.S. rate on dividends is generally reduced to 5 to 15 percent, and the tax on interest and royalties is either eliminated or reduced to 5 to 10 percent.

Looking to the
 Future   Technology and Cash Flows

As companies drive down costs to boost their profitability and market value, they will need to reduce borrowing costs. Greater emphasis will be placed on moving corporate cash worldwide to take advantage of differing rates of return. In addition, they will need to perfect their strategies for issuing bonds at the cheapest price possible and minimizing their tax bills worldwide.

However, the United States has been clamping down on tax minimization schemes and attacking the providers of such schemes (such as law firms and public accounting firms), as well as going after the corporate clients that are adopting them. In addition, they and other OECD countries are going after tax-haven countries and trying to break down the barriers to bank secrecy so they can get access to the records of individuals and companies who they suspect are illegally avoiding taxes. As companies establish strategies to take advantage of tax havens, they must be very careful to avoid strategies that will turn them into the next Enron or Parmalat. The move to drive down costs can't come at the expense of the future viability of the company.

The explosion of information and technology and the growing number and sophistication of hedging instruments (financial derivatives such as options and forwards) will significantly influence the cash-management and hedging strategies of MNEs in the future. Advances in information systems will continue to enable companies to get information more quickly and cheaply.

In addition, electronic data interchange (EDI) will allow them to transfer information and money instantaneously worldwide. Companies will significantly reduce paper flow and increase the speed of delivery of information and funds, enabling them to manage cash and use intercompany resources much more effectively than before. Consequently, companies will reduce not only the cost of producing information but also interest and other borrowing costs.

Investment and commercial banks will continue to develop new derivative instruments that will help companies hedge their currency and interest-rate exposures in the short and long term. However, new standards in accounting for derivative financial instruments by the FASB and IASB will force companies to mark most derivatives to market (recognize them at market values rather than what they cost when they were entered into) and recognize gains and losses in income. Despite the tightening of accounting standards, derivatives will be a big help to companies as they attempt to hedge their cash flows and protect against the erosion of earnings in an unstable financial environment.

The OECD, the IMF, and the EU are three institutions that will help countries narrow their tax differences and crack down on the transfer of money for illegal purposes. Although illegal financial transfers have occurred for years, especially due to drug trafficking, the attacks on 9/11 and subsequent moves to track down money laundering by terrorists have created a more urgent need to reform the global financial system. This will continue to narrow the options of companies to move funds, but that isn't a bad idea. ∎

Does The Devil Really Wear Prada?

CASE

Probably not, but the Italian Prada Group is clearly one of the top luxury businesses in the world, designing, producing, and distributing luxury handbags, leather goods, footwear, ready-to-wear apparel, accessories, eyewear and fragrances all over the world.[43] They operate in 70 countries through 319 directly operated stores, 35 franchise stores and high-end multi-brand stores and luxury department stores. Prada is a closely held firm where the Prada family, led by Miuccia Prada, President and head designer and her husband, CEO Patrizio Bertelli, hold 95 percent of the shares with Italian bank Intesa SanPaolo holding the rest. As Bertelli and Prada realized that the future of luxury consumption would be in Asia, they had to decide how they were going to fund their expansion. Due to a string of debt-financed acquisitions in the early 2000's, Prada ran into liquidity problems and had to turn to Intesa for funding. Intesa purchased the 5 percent interest in Prada in 2006 for €100 million, which put a valuation on Prada of €2 billion at the time. They had considered an Initial Public Offering (IPO) in 2001 and 2008, but the collapse in global stock markets both times forced them to pull back. However, 2011 seemed like a good time. Issuing stock to outside investors would bring in new money, but it would also force Prada to deal with non-family shareholders and the financial discipline of the market. Also, they had to figure out where to issue the IPO and how much of the company they should sell. Should they list on the Milan Stock Exchange, as they were being advised by nearly everyone in Italy, or should they become the first Italian company to list in Hong Kong, where they could be closer to the future growth markets in China?

Who Is Prada?

Prada began in 1913 when Mario Prada opened a luxury store in the Galleria Vittorio Emanuele II in Milan. Prada quickly built a strong reputation in luxury goods due to its exclusive designs, superior manufacturing techniques, and high-quality materials. By 1919, Prada became an official supplier to the Italian Royal Family and a benchmark for fashion throughout Europe. At the end of the 1970s, Mario's great-granddaughter, Miuccia Prada entered into a partnership with Patrizio Bertelli, a Tuscan businessman who was involved in high-quality leather goods. Initially, Bertelli's company, I.P.I. SpA had an exclusive license to produce and distribute leather goods using the Prada name, but by 2003, I.P.I. SpA and Prada merged into Prada SpA. (Spa or SpA—Società per anzioni is the same as "corporation" in the United States or plc in the United Kingdom).

In the 1990s and early 2000s, Prada began to expand by launching new brands (such as Miu Miu) and acquiring new businesses (such as Church's Group and Car Shoe) and entering into licensing and joint venture agreements with Italian eyewear manufacturer Luxottica and Spanish cosmetic manufacturer PUIG Beauty & Fashion Group. With these acquisitions, Prada expanded its product lines and opened new stores. It even launched a new phone by LG of South Korea.

In 2010, Prada was basically a European company, generating nearly half of its revenues from Europe, including 19.5 percent from Italy. However, the importance of Asia was expanding. Revenues in the Asia-Pacific region, not counting Japan, rose from 25.9 percent to 32 percent of total revenues. In spite of its acquisitions, the Prada brand still counted for nearly 80 percent of Prada's global revenues. The Asia–Pacific area had the highest growth rate of all geographic areas in which Prada was operating, benefitting from organic growth rather than acquisitions. Prada opened 17 new stores in the region and did a lot of work upgrading existing stores.

Why China?

The luxury goods market, of which Prada is a member, is hard to define. It is typically comprised of goods that are high priced, high quality, and high status. Some of the other largest luxury goods firm in the world are French-based LVMH (Louis Vuittan, Moët Hennessy), Christian Dior (which holds 42 percent of LVMH), PPR (which includes Gucci and Yves Saint Laurent), and Richemont (which includes Cartier, Chloé, Alfred Dunhil, and has a joint venture with Polo Ralph Lauren). Of course, there are also luxury goods firms in many industries, such as fashion, automobiles, watches and jewelry, and drinks. It is clear, however, that Asia, especially China, is rapidly becoming the future of the luxury goods industry.

In addition to having the largest population in the world, China is now the world's second largest economy, growing at a faster rate than any of the advanced countries and the rest of the BRIC countries. There are several reasons why China is becoming the target of the luxury goods markets. China is expected to be the largest luxury market in the world by 2020, catering to both men and women. Until recently, the market was driven by men, but women are becoming increasingly important. Maserati SpA and Bulgari SpA have been successful in China because they have positioned themselves as the ultimate male status symbols. Much of the luxury goods purchases were by men for women, but now women are starting to assert themselves as consumers. In 2009, for example, 30 percent of Maserati's sales were to women, up from 7 percent in 2005. This compares with the European and U.S. markets where women drivers are only 2 percent to 5 percent. In the broader luxury market sales, women accounted for over half of the $15 billion in sales, compared with 45 percent in 2008. Also, the average female luxury consumer spent 22 percent more in 2010 than in 2008.

The upshot to the emerging female luxury goods consumer is that brands that have catered more to women are putting even greater emphasis on China. Chloé, for example, predicts that China will be its biggest market by 2013. Female luxury consumers in China are a result of more women achieving success in business. It is estimated that 11 of the world's 20 richest self-made women are in China, with 153 women multimillionaires.

PRADA is moving aggressively in Asia to take advantage of the strong demand for luxury goods, as illustrated by this poster in Aberdeen Harbor in Hong Kong.
Source: Prisma Bildagentur AG/Alamy

This is not lost on Prada, but it is interested in China for other reasons as well. As the head designer for Prada, Ms. Prada is especially drawn to Chinese influences on fashion, which she feels is more contemporary than conservative Europe. Prada has a design team of 60 designers that Prada feels are curious, excited, fresh, and innovative. To take advantage of this talent, Prada is opening a design center in Hong Kong and hopes to expand its stores by 10 to 12 per year from 14 stores in 2011. Not only is China the market of the future for Prada, as it is for many other luxury goods companies, but it is also the location of ideas. It makes sense that Prada would need to set up a team to design products for the Chinese market, as well as get innovative ideas that it can use for its products worldwide.

Where to Issue the IPO?

If Prada wants to expand, where will it get the funds? It could borrow from banks, issue bonds in the domestic and international bond markets, and bring in outside investors. In 2010, 51 percent of Prada's assets were funded by equity and 49 percent by debt. This compares with a sample of Italian companies whose average debt/asset ratio in 2009/2010 was much higher at 57.4 percent. Of the debt, 57 percent was in current liabilities and 43 percent in long-term debt. Prada's long-term debt is primarily bank debt, sometimes to a syndicate of banks. Although Prada's largest exposure in long-term debt is in euro, it also has long-term debt in U.S. dollars, Chinese Renminbi, Japanese yen, and British pounds. It appears that Prada's strategy in debt markets has been to work with banks instead of relying on the Eurobond or Foreign Bond markets. Although Prada was a privately held company in 2010, it issued financial statements on its website. The statements dated January 31, 2011, were prepared in euro and according to IFRS as issued by the International Accounting Standards Board, approved by the European Union, and in accordance with the Italian commercial code. Their auditor was Deloitte & Touche SpA, a global public accounting firm, and signed by one of their Italian partners. After issuing the IPO, Prada will have to adopt the reporting requirements of the jurisdiction where the stock is issued, and its financial disclosures will have to meet the reporting requirements of a sophisticated investing public. The use of Deloitte as their auditor will be a big help since Deloitte is recognized in all major capital markets in the world as a competent auditing firm.

The decision to raise capital in the form of equity is complicated. As noted earlier, Prada is a closely held family company, so raising capital through an IPO is a major departure from the past. Would the Prada family be willing to give up a say in the future of the company? If so, where would be the best place to list the IPO? As an Italian company based in Milan, it would seem logical to list on the Milan stock exchange. But being the rebel she is, Ms. Prada had other ideas. Her feeling was that Hong Kong would be a better choice for several reasons. First, brand name companies feel that having an important presence in the region is the best to get your brand out to the consumer. Road shows attract a lot of press and attention from consumers as well as the financial community. Given the projected growth of China, Hong Kong makes sense. Second, Hong Kong was the world's biggest IPO market in 2010 with U.S. $57.7 billion raised from 87 listings.

Timing is everything, of course. Prada has tried to raise capital before, but the timing just wasn't right, mostly because of factors out of their control. After the Japanese earthquake on March 11, 2011, there was a lull in market activity, but that began to pick up again once markets quieted down. Galaxy Resources Ltd. of Australia was ready to raise significant capital in Hong Kong but was a victim of bad timing when the markets deteriorated after the Japan earthquake. However, the IPO market in general seemed promising, especially after Glencore International PLC raised more than $10 billion in a London–Hong Kong listing, which was the largest in 2011. Finally, the rapid influx of capital into Hong Kong from China coincided with Prada's decision to go to the markets.

The IPO

Finally, Prada decided to move forward with the IPO in Hong Kong, not Milan. The feeling was that since the proceeds would be used to fund expansion in China, why not bring in investors from Hong Kong, the gateway to China? Prada decided to sell a 20 percent stake in the company, significantly changing its ownership structure. But Ms. Prada was convinced that it was the right move. Friends and advisors convinced her that in some respects, the stock market and the discipline it imposes will help ensure the future of Prada and help with the succession. Prada hoped to raise 20 billion HK$ in the offering (about U.S. $2.6 billion), a significant amount of money. The goal was to sell about 423 million shares at HK$36.50 to HK$48.00. If the demand were strong, Prada could sell an additional 63 million shares, or 15 percent of the offer on an overallotment option. The goal was to list on the stock exchange on June 24, 2011, after beginning the process with institutional investors and then the wider investing public. As Prada got closer to the listing date, prices began to move down a little due to uncertainty in global markets, especially because of the European debt crisis, the U.S. debt crisis, and inflation in China. Prada adjusted its target price to consumers to a range of HK$39.50 to HK$42.25 per share, or U.S. $5.07 to U.S. $5.42 per share. This would put the value of Prada as 22.8 to 24.4 times 2011 expected earnings, which is still higher than LVMH, which trades at 20.1 times earnings. Pricing is clearly better in Hong Kong than elsewhere.

When the stock finally hit the exchange, retail investors didn't come into the market as much as anticipated, and Prada wasn't able to sell all of the shares allotted to investors. In addition, prices didn't really jump all that much initially. Within about two weeks, however, prices were up 13 percent over their HK$39.50 IPO price, or HK$44.64. Now we'll see how this move will affect Prada in the future, as well as other companies preparing to jump into

Hong Kong to take advantage of rising expectations in China. If this is a successful move, will Prada issue more stock in the future and further dilute the ownership of the Prada family? Only time will tell. ∎

QUESTIONS

1. Why does Prada need to raise additional funds?

2. Do you agree with the decision to list an IPO, or should Prada have borrowed more money, possibly floating a dim sum bond or a Eurobond in London or elsewhere?

3. What do you feel are the best justifications for Prada to issue the IPO in Hong Kong? Are there any downsides to their decision to list in Hong Kong?

4. Many of the other luxury fashion companies are also largely family owned. What is the impact to Prada of diluting the family ownership, and is this a model that other companies can be expected to follow?

5. What types of foreign exchange risk does Prada face, and what advice would you give them to hedge against their risks?

Now that you have finished this chapter, go back to www.myiblab.com to continue practicing and applying the concepts you've learned.

MyIBLab

SUMMARY

- The corporate finance function deals with the acquisition of financial resources and their allocation among the company's present and potential activities and projects.

- CFOs need to be concerned with the international dimensions of the company's capital structure, capital budgeting decisions, long-term financing, and working capital management.

- Country-specific factors are the most important determination of a company's capital structure.

- Two major sources of funds external to the MNE's normal operations are debt markets and equity markets.

- A Eurocurrency is any currency banked outside its country of origin, but it is primarily dollars banked outside the United States.

- A foreign bond is one sold outside the country of the borrower but denominated in the currency of the country of issue. A Eurobond is a bond issue sold in a currency other than that of the country of issue.

- Euroequities are shares listed on stock exchanges in countries other than the home country of the issuing company. Most foreign companies that list on the U.S. stock exchanges do so through American Depositary Receipts (ADRs), which are financial documents that represent a share or part of a share of stock in the foreign company. ADRs are easier to trade on the U.S. exchanges than are foreign shares.

- Offshore financial centers such as Bahrain, the Caribbean, Hong Kong, London, New York, Singapore, and Switzerland deal in large amounts of foreign currency and enable companies to take advantage of favorable tax rates.

- When deciding to invest abroad, MNE management must evaluate the cash flows from the local operation as well as the cash flows from the project to the parent. The former allows management to determine how the project stacks up with other opportunities in the foreign country, and the latter allows management to compare projects from different countries.

- The major sources of internal funds for an MNE are dividends, royalties, management fees, loans from parent to subsidiaries and vice versa, purchases and sales of inventory, and equity flows from parent to subsidiaries.

- Global cash management is complicated by differing inflation rates, changes in exchange rates, and government restrictions on the flow of funds. A sound cash-management system for an MNE requires timely reports from affiliates worldwide.

- Management must protect corporate assets from losses due to exchange-rate changes. Exchange rates can influence the dollar equivalent of foreign-currency financial statements, the amount of cash that can be earned from foreign-currency transactions, and a company's production and marketing decisions.

- Foreign-exchange risk management involves defining and measuring exposure, setting up a good monitoring and reporting system, adopting a policy to assign responsibility for exposure management, and formulating strategies for hedging exposure.

- Companies can enter into operational or financial strategies for hedging exposures. Operational strategies include balancing exposed assets with exposed liabilities, using leads and lags in cash flows, and balancing revenues in one currency with expenses in the same currency. Financial strategies involve using forward contracts, options, or other financial instruments to hedge an exposed position.

- International tax planning has a strong impact on the choice of location for the initial investment, the legal form of the new enterprise, the method of financing, and the method of setting transfer prices.

- Countries differ in terms of the types of taxes they have (income versus excise), the tax rates applied to income, the determination of taxable income, and the treatment of foreign-source income.

- Tax deferral means that the income a foreign subsidiary earns is taxed only when it is remitted to the parent as a dividend, not when it is earned.

- A controlled foreign corporation (CFC) must declare its Subpart F income as taxable to the parent in the year it is earned, regardless of whether it is remitted as a dividend.

- A tax credit allows a parent company to reduce its tax liability by the direct amount its subsidiary pays a foreign government on income that must be taxed by the parent company's government.

- The purpose of tax treaties is to prevent international double taxation or to provide remedies when it occurs.

KEY TERMS

active income (p. 746)
American Depositary Receipt
 (ADR) (p. 731)
arm's-length price (p. 747)
controlled foreign corporation
 (CFC) (p. 745)
economic (or operating) exposure
 (p. 739)
Eurobond (p. 726)
Eurocredit (p. 725)
Eurocurrency (p. 724)

Eurocurrency market (p. 724)
Eurodollar (p. 724)
Euroequity market (p. 729)
foreign bonds (p. 726)
Global Bond (p. 726)
lag strategy (p. 742)
lead strategy (p. 742)
leverage (p. 721)
London Inter-Bank Offered Rate
 (LIBOR) (p. 725)
market capitalization (p. 728)

net present value (NPV) (p. 734)
netting (p. 737)
offshore financial centers (OFCs)
 (p. 731)
offshore financing (p. 731)
payback period (p. 734)
sovereign wealth funds (p. 723)
Subpart F or passive income (p. 746)
syndication (p. 725)
transaction exposure (p. 739)
translation exposure (p. 739)

ENDNOTES

1 *Sources include the following:* "People on the Move," *Deseret News* (January 31, 1999): M02; Wells Fargo News Release, "Wells Fargo & Company and First Security Corporation Agree to Merge" (April 10, 2000), retrieved November 20, 2007, from www.wellsfargo.com /press/firstsec20000410?year= 2000; interviews with Ali Manbeian and Jason Langston; Wells Fargo company literature.

2 Arthur J. Keown, John D. Martin, J. William Petty, and David F. Scott Jr., *Financial Management*, 10th ed. (Upper Saddle River, NJ: Pearson Prentice Hall, 2005): 5.

3 Based on David K. Eiteman, Arthur I. Stonehill, and Michael H. Moffett, *Multinational Business Finance*, 12th ed. (Reading, MA: Addison-Wesley, 2010): 3.

4 Keown et al., *Financial Management*, 290.

5 "Theory versus the Real World," *Finance & Treasury* (April 26, 1993): 1.

6 Abe de Jong, Rezaul Kabir, and Thuy Thu Nguyen, "Capital Structure around the World: The Roles of Firm- and Country-Specific Determinants" (November 2006); EFA 2006 Zurich Meetings, at SSRN, retrieved November 20, 2007, from http://ssrn.com/abstract=890525

7 Ibid.

8 Charles Forelle, "The Isle That Rattled the World—Tiny Iceland Created a Vast Bubble, Leaving Wreckage Everywhere When It Popped," *Wall Street Journal* (December 27, 2008): A1.

9 "Sovereign Wealth Fund – SWF," from Investopedia, retrieved July 21, 2011, from www.investopedia.com/terms/s/sovereign_wealth _fund.asp

10 Nissan, "Schedule of Bonds Payable," *Nissan Annual Report* (2010): 127, retrieved July 13, 2011, from www.nissan-global.com/EN /DOCUMENT/PDF/FR/2010/fr2010.pdf

11 Nu Skin Enterprises Inc., *Nu Skin Annual Report* (2010): 62.

12 Patrick McGuire, "A Shift in London's Eurodollar Market," *BIS Quarterly Review* (September 2004): 67.

13 Financial Market Series, *Bond Markets July 2011*, retrieved July 11, 2011, from www.thecityuk.com

14 TheCityUK, "Bond Markets: July 2011," retrieved July 18, 2011, from www.thecityuk.com/assets/Reports/Financial-Markets-Series /BondMarkets2011.pdf

15 International Monetary Fund, "IMF Global Financial Stability Report, 2009," 28 (April 2009), retrieved July 11, 2011, from www .imf.org/external/pubs/ft/gfsr/2009/01

16 "IMF Global Stability Report, 2009," 177.

17 Peter Stein, "'Dim Sum Bonds' on the Menu for Foreign Investors," *The Wall Street Journal* (October 31, 2010), retrieved July 13, 2011, from http:// wsj.com

18 Shai Oster and Natasha Brereton, "Unilever Issues Dim Sum Bonds," *The Wall Street Journal* (March 26, 2011), retrieved July 13, 2011, from http://online.wsj.com/article/SB10001424052748703739204576228303769941410.html

19 "An Offer They Can Refuse," *Euromoney* (February 1995): 76.

20 Anant Sundaram, "International Financial Markets," in Dennis E. Logue (ed.), *Handbook of Modern Finance* (New York: Warren, Gorham, Lamont, 1994): F3–F4.

21 "Amcor Announces Successful €550 Million Benchmarkt Bond Issue," AMCOR News Release, retrieved July 18, 2011, from www.amcor.com/about_us/media_centre/news/117550924.html

22 Maggie Lake, "Stock Marker Merger Mania: Marriage of Necessity?" *CNN* (February 10, 2011), retrieved July 14, 2011, from http://business.blogs.cnn.com/2011/02/10/stock-market-merger-mania

23 Simon Goodley and Dominic Rushe, "Stock Exchange Merger Frenzy Shocks Markets," *The Guardian* (February 9, 2011), retrieved July 14, 2011, from www.guardian.co.uk/business/2011/feb/09/stock-exchange-merger-frenzy-shocks-markets; NYSE Euronext, "Deutsche Boerse Shareholders Approve Combined Combination with NYSE Euronext," in News Releases, July 15, 2011, www.nyse.com/press.html

24 IMF Monetary and Exchange Affairs Department, "IMF Background Paper: Offshore Financial Centers" (June 23, 2000).

25 Ibid.

26 "How the Heavyweights Shape Up," *Euromoney* (May 1990): 56.

27 "On or Off? It's a Matter of Degree," in "Places in the Sun: A Special Report on Offshore Finance," *The Economist* (February 24, 2007): 7.

28 OECD, *Harmful Tax Competition: An Emerging Global Issue* (Paris: OECD, 1998): 23.

29 Ibid., 27.

30 OECD, *Overview or the OECD's Work on Countering International Tax Evasion* (Paris: OECD, August 11, 2009): 8, retrieved October 23, 2009, from www.oecd.org/dataoecd/32/45/42356522.pdf

31 David Cay Johnston, "Enron Avoided Income Taxes in 4 of 5 Years," *New York Times (Late Edition (East Coast))* (January 17, 2002): A1.

32 Lucy Komisar, "Funny Money," *Metroactive News & Issues* (January 24, 2002), retrieved June 7, 2005, from www.metroactive.com/papers/sonoma/01.24.02/offshorebanking-0204.html

33 Nick Davis, "Tax Spotlight Worries Cayman Islands," *BBC News* (March 31, 2009), retrieved October 23, 2009, from http://news.bbc.co.uk/go/pr/fr/-/2/hi/americas/7972695.stm

34 Eiteman et al., *Multinational Business Finance.*

35 Mike Ramsey, "VW Chops Labor Costs in U.S.," *The Wqll Street Journal* (May 23, 2011):B1, Stephen Power, "BMW's Profit Softened in Quarter," *Wall Street Journal* (May 4, 2005): A12.

36 OECD, "Taxation of Corporate and Capital Income, Table II.1," *OECD Tax Database* (2011), retrieved October 28, 2011, from www.oecd.org/ctp/taxdatabase

37 Deloitte, "International Tax and Business Guide: Germany" (2009), retrieved October 23, 2009, from www.deloitte.com/view/en_GX/global/services/tax/international-tax/international-tax-and-business-guides/article/d7c2a6c82b10e110VgnVCM100000ba42f00aRCRD.htm

38 Deloitte, "International Tax and Business Guide: Hong Kong" (2009), retrieved October 23, 2009, from www.deloitte.com/view/en_GX/global/services/tax/international-tax/international-tax-and-business-guides/article/3872a9fd91ffd110VgnVCM100000ba42f00aRCRD.htm

39 Johnston, "Enron Avoided Income Taxes in 4 of 5 Years."

40 OECD, *Transfer Pricing Guidelines for Multinational Enterprises and Tax Administrations* (Paris: OECD Publishing, August 11, 2009), retrieved October 23, 2009, from www.oecd.org/document/34/0,3343,en_2649_33753_1915490_1_1_1_1,00.html

41 Ronald Fink, "Haven or Hell," *CFO Magazine* (March 2004), retrieved October 23, 2009, from www.cfo.com/article.cfm/3012017; Helen Shaw, "Transfer Students," *CFO Magazine* (April 2007), retrieved August 30, 2007, from www.cfo.com/article.cfm/8885626/c_8910395?f=insidecfo

42 Deloitte, "International Tax and Business Guide: United States" (2009), retrieved October 23, 2009, from www.deloitte.com/view/en_GX/global/services/tax/international-tax/international-tax-and-business-guides/article/1ad803082e10e110VgnVCM100000ba42f00aRCRD.htm, 7–9.

43 PRADA Group 2010 Annual Report, retrieved July 21, 2011, from www.pradagroup.com/en.html ; "Hong Kong's Fickle IPO Investors," *The Wall Street Journal* (July 11, 2011); Kelvin Chan, "Prada Says Hong Kong IPO Roadshow Going Well," *Bloomberg Business Week* (June 12, 2011); George Stalk and David Michael, "What the West Doesn't Get About China," *Harvard Business Review* (June 2011): 25–27; Prudence Ho, "Hong Kong's IPO Engine Sputters," *The Wall Street Journal* (June) ; Nisha Gopolan and Prudence Ho, "Prada's Promising IPO," *The Wall Street Journal* (June 7, 2011): C3; Laurie Burkett, "In China, Women Begin Splurging," *The Wall Street Journal* (June 13, 2011): B11; Prudence Ho and Yvonne Lee, "Hong Kong IPOs Back in Fashion," *The Wall Street Journal* (May 23, 2011): B2; Alison Tudor, "Prada Sees Future in Asia," *The Wall Street Journal* (June 13, 2011): C3.

chapter 20

International Human Resources

Access a host of interactive learning aids to help strengthen your understanding of the chapter concepts at www.myiblab.com.

MyIBLab

If you are planning for a year, plant grain. If you are planning for a decade, plant trees. If you are planning for a century, plant people.

—Chinese proverb

Source: ARENA Creative/Shutterstock.com

CASE

Globalizing Your Career

MNEs have been moving people around for centuries, capturing the benefits of putting the right person into the right job at the right place at the right time at the right pay. Now, it's more important than ever that they do so. In a borderless marketplace, market patterns and strategic actions in one country can determine the fate of a company on the far side of the world.

Globalization, by spurring trade, capital, and investment flows, has expanded the hundreds of thousands of existing subsidiaries and added tens of thousands of new units in fast-emerging markets. Each unit requires executives that navigate economic complexities, cultural ambiguities, and political challenges, all the while improving the MNE's global efficiency and optimizing its local responsiveness. Declared GE's Jeffrey Immelt, "A good global company does three things: It's a global sales company—meaning it's number one with customers all over the world, whether in Chicago or Paris or Tokyo. It's a global products company, with technologies, factories, and products made for the world, not just for a single region. And, most important, it's a global people company—a company that keeps getting better by capturing global markets and brains."[1]

Changing career standards push you to globalize your career track. Market trends, company strategies, and executive performance collectively indicate that success requires you go global. From Afghanistan to Zimbabwe and all countries in between, leadership demands a global mindset. "You have to have an intuitive sense of how the world works and how people behave," says Paul Laudicina, vice president of A. T. Kearney. Observed Daniel Meiland of Egon Zehender International, an executive search firm:

> ...the world is getting smaller, and markets are getting bigger. In my more than 25 years in the executive search profession, we've always talked about the global executive, but the need to find managers who can be effective in many different settings is growing ever more urgent. In addition to looking for intelligence, specific skills, and technical insights, MNEs are also looking for executives who are comfortable on the world stage.

THE EXPATRIATE

MNEs use *expatriates*—people sent to live and work in another country—to run their foreign operations. Some MNEs, such as FedEx and J&J, use only a few; others, like Royal Dutch Shell and Wipro Technologies, use many.

Unfortunately, few standards advise MNEs on why, when, and where they should use "expats," to say nothing of selecting the right one, developing the right predeparture program, designing the right compensation package, and determining the right way to reintegrate them into the home company when they complete their tour of duty.

The benefits of success and costs of failure press MNEs to manage their human resources. Honeywell, for example, begins developing potential expatriates years before they might head abroad. It briefs candidates on their cross-cultural skills and prescribes training paths that deal with likely points of culture shock. Says its vice president of HR, "We give them a horizon, a perspective, and, gradually, we tell them they are potentially on an international path.... We want them to develop a cross-cultural intellect, what we call 'strategic accountability.'" To this end, Honeywell might advise an employee to network with experienced expatriates, study another language, or explore areas where he or she might struggle while living abroad.

The pace of globalization, particularly for MNEs in emerging economies like India, China, and Brazil, accelerates this process. Some managers even begin identifying people before they hire them. Sanjay Joshi, chief executive of global programmes at India's Wipro Technologies, notes, "A big part of our recruiting is telling people that they will get a chance to work abroad." This appoach, he believes, improves the quality of new hires while fortifying the company's growing cadre of expatriates.[2]

NEW PLACES AND NEW WAYS

Figure 20.1 lists the top benefits of working abroad. Reaping these rewards does not come easily. Successful expatriates testify to the merits of the quest, describing how the experience changed their perception of business. Many note that working abroad pushed them, sometimes reluctantly, sometimes eagerly, to look at situations differently. Explained Galina Naumenko, of PwC Russia, an international assignment "spurs global networking among employees, gives them an understanding of different cultures, and gets them thinking about alternative ways of approaching problems and solving them." Added Michael Cannon-Brookes, head of strategy for IBM's Growth Markets, "You get very different thinking if you sit in Shanghai or São Paulo or Dubai than if you sit in New York."[3]

Working internationally compels employees to develop richer management repertoires. Consider Joan Pattle, a

FIGURE 20.1   Top Benefits of Becoming an Expatriate

Executives speak of many benefits that result from their international assignment. Here we see leading personal and professional motivations to working abroad.

Source: HSBC Bank, International

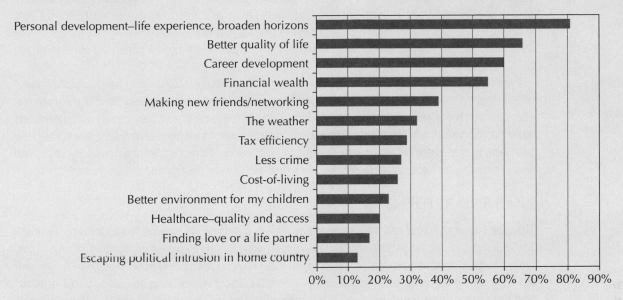

Microsoft marketing manager who worked at headquarters in Seattle before accepting a post as product leader in Great Britain. Her U.K. job came with much wider responsibilities: "At home, my job was very strictly defined. I basically had to know everything about managing a database. But when I got to London, I was also in charge of direct marketing and press relations. I was exposed to a much broader set of experiences." Similarly, Laura Anderson, a spokesperson for Intel, explained that an assignment in Hong Kong improved her sense of the company's business. In fact, several Asian media relations encounters opened her eyes. "For me," she said, "it was a tremendous growth experience."

NEW PROBLEMS AND NEW STRESSES

Notwithstanding the glamour and riches, expatriate living is not for everyone. The inability to adapt, no matter the intent to do so, is the primary cause of nearly half of failed foreign assignments. Simply put, living and working abroad can be risky. Cultural clashes, language difficulties, murky business practices, and harsh environments rule out anything beyond a short-term visit for many executives. Other problems arise when a company asks an executive to transfer to second- or third-tier cities in less preferred countries.

The gap between life at home versus "over there" often fans professional, family, and personal problems. Many expats struggle with the foreign culture. Difficulty understanding and respecting differences, no matter how mundane, spiritual, or philosophical, lead to expensive failures. To top it off, international business travel "is perhaps the most dangerous form of travel. Tourists wouldn't consider flying into a Colombian war zone for a week, yet folks from oil, computer, pharmaceutical, agricultural and telecom MNEs do it regularly."[4] Once there, merely frequenting high-profile hotels and restaurants with colleagues makes them prime targets.

COMING HOME

Floating around the world today are so-called "expat lifers." Moving from assignment to assignment, whether with the same company or others, they plan never to return home. The vast majority, however, eventually do—pack the bags, bid farewell to colleagues, board the plane, and return to a hero's welcome. A snap, right? Not so. In many cases, everything but the hero's welcome happens. As Tom Schiro of Deloitte & Touche observed, "Some MNEs just send somebody overseas and forget about them for two years."

Communication with the home unit helps preempt problems. Likewise, careful career planning makes a big difference when it's time to return home. Following a four-year assignment in Tokyo, Bryan Krueger returned to a promotion to president of Baxter Fenwal North America. When he had left for Tokyo, his company had not guaranteed him a promotion upon his return. While away, he kept up-to-date with the goings-on at headquarters. Krueger credited his smooth return to his intensive networking. During his stint in Tokyo, he returned to the United States four to five times a year to see colleagues. As he explains, "I was definitely proactive. Anyone who is not is doing himself a disservice. I made a conscious effort to stay in touch, and it paid off."

Not all expats share such success stories. A survey of repatriated executives who had successfully completed their overseas assignment found that more than a third held temporary assignments three months after returning home, nearly 80 percent felt their new job was a demotion from their foreign assignment, and more than 60 percent felt they did not have opportunities to transfer their international expertise to their new job. Some tolerate these outcomes. Others don't. In 2010, nearly 40 percent left their company within one year of returning from abroad, while another 25 percent left between the first and second years.[5]

RISKS AND RETURNS

The choice to work abroad has a high upside and a steep downside. On balance, the former tips the scale. The allure of such an assignment has become so compelling that we see growing numbers of expat-lifers. While overseas, an expatriate can be well-paid, have big responsibilities, and achieve prestige. A penchant for living abroad makes an international career irresistible, effectively creating so-called "global nomads" who travel from one country to the next. For example, after stints in Singapore and London, a Morgan Stanley expat in India muses, "I still don't want to go back to the United States. It's a big world—lots of things to see."

Then again, there are the career implications. MNEs regularly tout a foreign assignment as a meaningful development experience that prepares managers for broader responsibilities. As the reasoning goes, it improves skills and expertise, fosters cultural awareness, increases confidence in overcoming challenges, and enhances creativity through exposure to new ways of doing things. Until recently, however, the odds were on a neutral or negative career outcome. MNEs were typically slow to reward a manager's successful international experience with an expanded leadership role.

EMERGING STANDARDS

Globalization changes this outlook. Already, it has led to supply shortages of talented executives. MNEs worldwide report difficulty finding skillful candidates, investing more time interviewing and hiring, and worrying more about rivals poaching their high performers. By changing the game, globalization changes performance standards, with more MNEs regarding international experience as the cornerstone of a high-profile career.

At Procter & Gamble, 39 of the company's top 44 global officers have had a foreign assignment, and 22 were born outside the United States. Said P&G's HR director, global awareness and experience are "ingredient[s] you must have if you aspire to be a global player in the long term." P&G expects its leaders to be both innovative and worldly; they cannot rise to the top without running operations in a foreign market and managing a product around the world.[6]

Globalization spurs MNEs like Samsung, Infosys, AstraZeneca, and Dow Chemical to see multinational experience as essential as multifunctional and multiproduct experiences in developing high-performance executives targeting the upper echelons. Data confirm this trend. Nearly 33 percent of *FTSE 100* companies have a foreign national as CEO, and just under 70 percent of them have had a foreign assignment. Among the *Fortune 100*, the figures clock in at 10 percent and 33 percent, respectively.[7]

In summary, environmental trends, market conditions, and workplace standards urge aspiring executives to heed Daniel Meiland's caution: "If you look ahead five to ten years, the people with the top jobs in large corporations, even in the United States, will be those who have lived in several cultures and who can converse in at least two languages. Most CEOs will have had true global exposure, and their MNEs will be all the stronger for it."

CRN
Case Review Note

Introduction

Indisputably, successful MNEs have insightful strategies, great supply chains, sharp financial systems, and the like. Ultimately, though, success is a function of the people who start and sustain the company. The challenge of putting the right person into the right job in the right place at the right time for the right compensation takes us to the front lines of international business. From opening markets to returning home, international business careers take any number of directions. At the center is the individual facing challenges that often lead to surprising opportunities. The contest between challenges and opportunities is the spirit of a career in international business.[8]

What is HRM?

Human resource management (HRM) shepherds an organization's most valued assets—its people. Opening and operating a business, whether a small-scale micronational or vast multinational, requires finding people to implement the strategy, motivating them to perform well, upgrading their skills so they can move on to more challenging tasks, and, ultimately, retaining them.[9] HRM directs these functions.

Here we elaborate these issues, building on themes introduced in Chapter 11 and applied since to principal business functions and operating activities. We evaluate HRM from the perspective that successful MNEs staff their operations with people who leverage core competencies while reconciling pressures for local responsiveness and global integration. This perspective emphasizes that HRM activities, like discrete activities in the company's value chain, perform best when managers link them to the strategy of the firm (see Figure 20.2).

Concept Check

Recall our discussion in Chapter 1 of "The Forces Driving Globalization," in which we identify several factors that power "interdependent relationships" among people worldwide. The convergence of cultures, politics, and markets diminish the physical and psychic distances between countries. Here we suggest that this trend has begun to make the prospect of moving from one country to another a more attractive career plan.

HRM refers to activities that staff the MNE.

FIGURE 20.2 Factors Influencing HRM in International Business

Successful MNEs consistently show that managing human resources, like managing finances, marketing efforts, and supply chains, is best set by the requirements of the chosen strategy. In the case of HRM, the task centers on putting the right person in the right job in the right place at the right time for the right compensation—with the standard of "right" determined by the MNE's strategy.

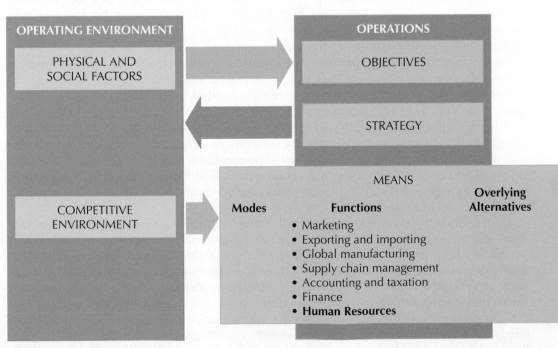

HRM AND THE GLOBAL COMPANY

HRM is far more difficult for the MNE than its domestic counterpart. Besides dealing with situations in the home market, an MNE adjusts its HRM practices for the political, cultural, legal, and economic differences in foreign markets. For example, leadership styles and management practices vary from country to country, causing difficulties between people at different units—say, headquarters and a local subsidiary.[10] The differences can turn great managers at home into ineffective ones overseas, as their personal struggle to adapt erodes company performance.

Similarly, labor markets vary in the mix of workers, costs, productivity, and regulations. Regarding the latter, local labor laws often require that MNEs change their workplace standards. Adjusting labor management practices complicates decision making. Finally, dual career and family obligations make it tough to convince executives to take a foreign assignment. Consequently, MNEs continually evaluate how to staff international operations, fine-tuning the mix of recruitment, training, compensation, transfer, and retention programs that persuade and prepare executives to work abroad.

One may wonder why MNEs and executives put up with these aggravations. The short answer is that the megatrend of globalization demands doing so. The long answer is that in the face of globalization, navigating these challenges creates competitive advantages and sustains the MNE's profitability. Both answers highlight HRM's mandate: Develop the methods to build, develop, and retain the cadre of managers that will lead the company.[11] Below we discuss ways of doing so. We now profile how HRM organizes the selection, development, compensation, and retention of international managers.[12]

Strategizing HRM

Anecdotes suggest and research confirms a powerful relationship between HRM processes, management productivity, and strategic performance.[13] Chapter 11 reported that GE's CEO believes success in becoming global is "truly about people, not about where the buildings are. You've got to develop people so they are prepared for leadership jobs and then promote them. That's the most effective way to become more global." As we saw in our opening case, he adds that "a good global company" is "a global people company," one that is as interested in world-class brainpower as it is in world markets.

No matter the scale or scope of international operations, superior human resources sustain high productivity, competitive advantage, and value creation. The Human Capital Index, synthesized from the practices of 2,000 MNEs in Asia, Europe, and the United States, found that superior HRM positively correlated with a firm's financial returns. It was also a leading indicator of increased shareholder value.[14] MNEs with superior human capital practices, on average, created more shareholder value than those with run-of-the-mill practices.

The default thesis had been that superior financial outcomes lead MNEs to develop superior HRM practices. In actuality, the analysis revealed the reverse: Superior HRM was a key determinant of corporate financial performance and a more powerful driver of financial performance. Others report similar effects, finding that the interaction between a firm's strategy and its HRM practices accounts for more variation in strategic performance than HRM in isolation.[15]

The relationship between superior HRM and high productivity, competitive advantage, and value creation confirms the significance of people to performance. The power of this relationship transforms HRM. No longer is it a glorified term for personnel management, concerned with administering routine employee processes and setting short-term employment policies. Now it is a performance driver, developing the executive talent that steers an MNE into the brave, new world.

Our earlier look at the strategies MNEs follow elaborates this view. Chapter 11 profiled those that are commonly implemented: the international strategy and its quest

---

HRM is more difficult for the MNE than its domestic counterpart due to

- Environmental differences.
- Strategic contingencies.
- Organizational challenges.

HRM policies that support the MNE's strategy generate high productivity and competitive advantage.

Concept Check

A recurring theme of ours is the usefulness of adopting a strategic perspective. No matter if the topic involves political, legal, economic, cultural dimensions of the marketplace, superior performance compels the MNE to link these trends, circumstances, and conditions to its long-term goals.

to leverage core competencies abroad; the multidomestic strategy and its quest to maximize the local responsiveness of foreign operations; the global strategy and its quest to maximize worldwide integration; and the transnational strategy and its quest to optimize all three tasks simultaneously. Each imposes unique standards for configuring and coordinating value activities. Hence, each calls on HRM to find, staff, compensate, and retain the executives that command the requisite skills and outlooks. Struggling to do so, irrespective of the brilliance of its strategy, undercuts an MNE's performance. Getting it right requires integrating strategy and HRM.

A Case In Point   Looking at the role of HRM in the context of GE's evolution elaborates these ideas. Beginning in the 1980s, GE focused on globalizing its markets by selling existing products abroad (the international strategy). In the late 1980s, it began globalizing its material sources to get higher-quality inputs for lower prices in the quest to minimize costs (the global strategy). In the mid-1990s, it began globalizing its intellect, seeking, learning, and transferring ideas throughout operations (the transnational strategy).

Each stop along its evolution saw GE reset its HRM philosophy and practices to make sure it developed the requisite human capital. The key to its international strategy was staffing people who could develop foreign markets based on its core competencies. The key to its global strategy was staffing people who could optimize location economics and manage global supply chains. The key to its transnational strategy has been staffing people around the world who can develop, transfer, and engage ideas no matter the business function or market source. At each stage in GE's evolution, HRM aligned executive selection, development, and compensation policies with the demands of its strategy.

As GE's strategy evolved, so did its understanding of the role of expatriates. Jeffrey Immelt explains, "When I first joined General Electric [in 1982], globalization meant training the Americans to be global thinkers. So, Americans got the expat assignments. We still have many Americans living around the world, and that's good, but we shifted our emphasis in the late 1990s to getting overseas assignments for non-Americans. Now you see non-Americans doing new jobs, big jobs, important jobs at every level and in every country." Today, GE has a cadre of international managers with the expertise to leverage its core competencies in developing and diffusing ideas around the world.

GE's success in international business, like that of many other MNEs profiled throughout this chapter, reemphasizes HRM's mission: find, staff, compensate, and retain executives with the qualifications needed to support and sustain company strategy. Done well, HRM supports higher productivity, stronger competitiveness, and improving profitability. Done poorly, people problems fan frustrations that undermine performance and ruin careers.

The Perspective of the Expatriate

One can evaluate HRM from many perspectives. Two reasons motivate an executive perspective. First, in the MNE, the tip of the operational spear is the executive running international operations. Expatriates drive critical tasks of the company's strategy; they launch new ventures, build local management expertise, fill local skills gaps, transfer core competencies, erect technology platforms, and diffuse the organization culture. Second, an executive perspective speaks to your likely interest in working internationally. Students routinely ask teachers about the why, how, when, where, and what of careers in international business. This chapter provides some guidelines, suggestions, and insights on your career ambitions. Thus, an executive perspective directs our attention to the principles and practices HRM applies to specify the selection, role, responsibility, development, compensation, and retention of expatriates.

An executive perspective directs attention to the tasks required to run an international business operations.

WHO IS WHO

First, though, some definitions of who is who. There are two broad types of MNE executives: *locals* or *expatriates*. A local is hired by the MNE in his or her home country to staff the local operations; no special provisions apply to the work contract. An **expatriate** (or "expat") is sent to work temporarily in a country other than his or her legal residence. There are two types of expatriates. One is a **home-country national** who is a citizen of the country where the firm is headquartered, such as a Brazilian national running the German operations of his Brazilian company. The other type is a **third-country national**, a citizen of another country altogether, such as an Estonian national running the German subsidiary of an Australian company.

TRENDS IN EXPATRIATE ASSIGNMENTS

We are witnessing a burst in worldwide demand for expatriates.[16] The emergence of fast-growing economies has led to opening many new subsidiaries. Western MNEs, besides running their existing operations, struggle to staff many startup operations in many new markets. Emerging MNEs similarly build operations in foreign markets. There are approximately 22,000 multinationals based in the emerging world; few of these existed 10 years ago.[17] Each unit of each MNE requires executive talent.

Staffing the latest wave of globalization also refines the idea of who is an expatriate. Unquestionably, the long-running standard of an expat as someone who leaves the country to work abroad endures. The precise classification is no longer quite so static. Historically, an expatriate was posted to a particular host country for a three- to five-year assignment, with the ultimate plan of returning to the home country. Now, most international assignments are much shorter. A decade ago, 10 percent or so of international assignments were scheduled for one year or less; today, 80 percent or more run that short.[18] Short-term assignments, besides being more economical than long-term tours, quickly transfer skills and resources to local subsidiaries.[19]

The Young, Old, and Restless   Traditionally, expatriates were mid-level executives being groomed for higher levels of responsibility. Essentially, international assignments were midcareer stepping-stones for the MNE's future leaders. Now HRM expands its search criteria to include older employees whose children have grown and whose spouses regard an international assignment positively. In addition, HRM looks to younger employees who are single, more mobile, and eager to experience life in foreign places.

In term of posting younger managers to international assignments, MNEs increasingly trade performance track records for long-term potential. For example, PricewaterhouseCoopers offers its Early PwC International Challenge program (EPIC) to accelerate international assignments for its younger employees. EPIC identifies promising workers who are interested in living abroad and have established a promising track record. Operationally, candidates jump-start the process by completing an online assessment and consulting PwC's career pages. EPIC encouarges them to choose their preferred destination, then posts them abroad for two-year assigments with the goal of developing them for senior leadership roles.[20] Thus, candidates can skip a rung or two on the career ladder as well as escape slow-growth job markets. Likewise, HRM identifies high performers who command leadership, entrepreneurial zest, and a tolerance for uncertainty.

Rising Role of Women   The gender dimension is similarly evolving. In absolute terms, females comprise roughly 20 percent of expatriates.[21] Since 2001, MNEs in the Asia-Pacific region have seen a sixteen-fold increase in women on international assignment, MNEs in North America have seen nearly a four-fold rise, and Europe

◀ **Go East, Young Man**
One of the many who heed the call of opportunity in emerging economies, Mick Xomir, a junior at a U.S. university, is on the way to his summer internship in Beijing.
Source: SHIHO FUKADA/Redux Pictures.

has doubled its count. Surveys indicate that more than half of MNEs expect the number of female assignees to increase, about a third believe the number will hold steady, and a handful see it declining. Reasoned an observer, "Going on expatriate placements can be an important step on the career ladder, and women are increasingly interested in taking these assignments."[22]

Growing Scope of Third-Country Nationals The changing workplace of globalization elevates the role of third-country nationals.[23] MNEs often establish operations abroad in increasingly dissimilar markets—say, from the United States to Canada to England to India to Singapore to China to Vietnam. Third-country nationals often have the particular outlook and versatile competencies that are needed to adeptly implement this sort of market sequence.

The move toward short-term assignments boosts the logistical appeal of third-country nationals—an executive living in London yet working for a U.S. MNE, for instance, may spend Monday through Friday working in Zurich, then return home for the weekend. Then, as the need arises for help in the MNE's Stockholm office, she can reset her commute. Such mobility lets an MNE more easily adapt its strategy, confident it has executives who are well-positioned to implement it.

Reverse Expatriates The rising importance of emerging markets adds a new twist to our evolving ideas of expatriates. Historically, MNEs selected them from the pool of executives in richer countries and sent them to staff operations in developing countries. Now, well-educated executives from emerging economies, so called "reverse-expats," are sent straight to the richer countries to accelerate their development, spending anywhere from a month to a year in some of the MNE's operations.[24] Once they learn the ropes, they return home, often replacing a traditionally defined, usually much higher-priced expatriate.

Some tweak this option further. Goldman Sachs relies on its Growth Markets Opportunity Program to hire high-potential Asians and Latin Americans with MBAs from leading Western universities. It then posts them to its New York or London offices for up to a year before assigning them to leaderhip positions in local operations in Singapore, Hong Kong, China, Brazil, India, and other emerging economies.[25]

PRESSURES TO ECONOMIZE

Economic pressures and cost concerns spur companies to emphasize more business travel in lieu of a longer-term international assignment.

The global financial crisis pushes MNEs to rethink the economics of expatriates. Sending workers abroad, as we discuss later, is quite expensive. More MNEs design short-term assignments, cross-border commuter assignments, and extended business travel in lieu of traditional "permanent assigments." Rather than moving to foreign markets, executives travel far more often to far more places that lie farther from their homebase.

The compelling economics of commuter expats resets historic standards; some 35 percent of expats report living in their host country for more than five years, compared to 58 percent in 2009. [26] On related fronts, cost concerns accelerate deploying third-country nationals in place of executives from the home office. The latter often demand richer compensation packages and impose higher relocation costs.

Cost concerns also drive MNEs to "localize" assignments. **Localization** is the the process whereby an expatriate retains the foreign assignment by accepting the status of a local hire and the corresponding, typically lower, host-location salary. Effectively, one accepts lower compensation in order to work abroad. IBM's "Project Match" adds an interesting twist to localization. It offers terminated employees in the United States the option to move to a local unit in India, China, Brazil, Nigeria, Russia, or other developing countries provided the candidate had been a "satisfactory performer" and is "willing to work on local terms and conditions."[27] In other words, you have the option to move abroad and preserve your job but your compensation will be set by pay scales in the particular local market.

THE ONE CONSTANT

Change in the global environment—whether due to market opportunities or cost pressures—influences ideas on staffing international operations. Hence, the types and mechanics of expat assignments evolving. Nevertheless, there is a fundamental constant: Running the hundreds of thousands of subsidiaries throughout the world requires talented, enterprising locals as well as home-country and third-country expatriates. So keen is the demand that MNEs report historic shortages of expatriate talent and, correspondingly, the increasing consideration of the young, old, and restless for overseas slots.[28]

While the global financial crisis may have relieved some immediate pressure, the accelerating growth in emerging economies will likely pick up the slack. Therefore, no matter how costly or complex, MNEs face the increasingly vital task of staffing the right person in the right job in the right place at the right time for the right compensation. Success drives strategy. Failure ruins careers and jeopardizes profitablity.

Staffing Frameworks in the MNE

Three perspectives anchor an MNE's staffing policy:
- Ethnocentrism
- Polycentricism
- Geocentricism

MNEs apply staffing frameworks—basic conceptual structures that help solve complex issues—to guide HRM decisions. First, these frameworks identify the optimal mix of local workers from the host nation, expatriates sent from the home country, and third-country nationals. Second, they set selection, training, compensation, and repatriation guidelines. In broad terms, these frameworks reintroduce our earlier discussion of the notions of ethnocentrism, polycentrism, and geocentrism.

THE ETHNOCENTRIC FRAMEWORK

Ethnocentrism results when one group places itself at the top of an imagined hierarchy of relevant groups, thereby regarding others as inferior. Hence, the **ethnocentric framework** signifies the belief that the management principles and business practices used by headquarters are superior to those used by rivals in other countries. The proven success of the company's way of doing things, goes this thinking, means there is little call to adapt it to foreign markets.[29] Thus, MNEs tend to staff expatriate slots with executives from its home market.

Advantages of the Ethnocentric Framework Table 20.1 lists the benefits of an ethnocentric framework. Notably, MNEs that link performance to transferring core competencies abroad find value in it. Consider that a firm earns success in its home market doing something exceptional—what we earlier defined as a core competency. A legacy of success leads an MNE to see its way of doing business as the superior means of creating value. Logically, an MNE sees its international success dependent on controlling the transfer and regulating the use of its core competencies.

For instance, India's Wipro Technology employs 54,000 people in 35 countries, more than 11,000 of whom are expatriates, and more than 90 percent of those being Indian. Wipro posts Indian executives internationally who then run business development and train local staff in order to spread the Wipro Way throughout the world. "We sprinkle Indians in new markets to help seed and set up the culture and intensity," says Sanjay Joshi, chief executive of global programs.[30]

Staffing overseas operations with people from the home country helps an MNE regulate the transfer of its core competency.[31] This is particularly vital when a core competency is difficult to articulate, specify, or standardize, such as Apple's product-design and media expertise, Walmart's information-management and product-distribution systems, or Honda's understanding of engine technology. Posting a home-country manager with direct experience in developing, applying, and protecting the company's core competency to the foreign subsidiary puts it under the direction of a seasoned, trustworthy manager. The HSBC Group long epitomized this outlook. For generations, most top executives came from a tight-knit cadre of elite expatriates who, in going from one foreign position to another, disperse "the DNA of the organization."[32]

The mounting importance of protecting ownership advantages spurs an MNE to safeguard its core competency. With it, the firm prospers; without it, the firm struggles. This stark reality leads headquarters to entrust control of the company's "crown jewels" to those who will best protect them: namely, colleagues from the home country. Earlier discussion of intellectual property explained that safeguards deter but by no means prevent theft. The ethnocentric framework fortifies defenses, posting home country executives who vigilantly protect corporate assets.

Drawbacks of the Ethnocentric Framework As the adage goes, "Vices are simply virtues taken to extreme." The same applies to the ethnocentric framework. Force-fitting foreign operations with a standardized staffing policy risks pounding circular pegs into

Concept Check

"Company and Management Orientations" in Chapter 2 introduced the idea of polycentrism, ethnocentrism, and geocentrism to describe how MNE's and their managers approach foreign cultures. Here, we reintroduce these terms, highlighting the ways these "attitudes or orientations" influence a MNE's staffing framework.

An ethnocentric framework fills key management positions with home-country nationals.

TABLE 20.1 The Ethnocentric Framework: Key Benefits

Several factors encourage an MNE to adopt an ethnocentric staffing framework. As we see below, these factors tap competitive, personnel, economic, and leadership concerns. The criterion of evaluation for the ethnocentric framework, we note, is the presumption that the means, methods, and managers of the home office work well anywhere in the world.

Command and control	Familiarity with the way decisions are made and things get done at headquarters means that expatriates can be counted on to transfer home-country procedures to foreign operations.
Local talent gaps	Shortage of qualified local candidates makes expatriates a direct and immediate solution to staffing shortfalls.
Social integration	Posting expatriates symbolically and operationally diffuses corporate policies and practices. Spreading the faith fortifies the organization's culture.
Local implementation	Expatriates offset the tendency for policies and practices to break down when transferred from the home to the host country.
High turnover among locals	Expatriates' lower likelihood of defecting to a local rival reduces the information leaks and competitive disruption.
Management development	Expatriates' hard-earned experience boosts a company's knowledge and promotes executive leadership.

square slots. Certainly, an MNE can make its foreign operations mirror the outward appearance of the home office. Moreover, MNEs have compelling rationales when asked why they rely on home-country nationals to run foreign operations. Often, they note there is no shortage of brainpower in a particular country, just a shortage of people with the right mix of technical skills, experience with the particular business methods, and professional standards. However, assigning home office executives to foreign operations does not automatically create a successful "mini-me" subsidiary. Consequently, an ethnocentric framework can prove detrimental, blinding the MNE to different, possibly better, business methods.

Ethnocentric staffing policies often demotivate local executives. Its implicit assumption—all the smart, capable people live within a 25-mile radius of headquarters—sends the message that the home office does not value subsidiary personnel. Unless a foreign assignment is intended to develop unique skills, local employees may resent the expat who they see as no more qualified than themselves. Unchecked, resentment can lower productivity and increase turnover as locals see an upper limit on their rise.

Finally, an ethnocentric staffing policy can prove impractical. Host governments, alert to the importance of developing and employing their nation's workforce, prefer that subsidiaries hire locals. MNEs' plea that the unique nature of their operations prevents their doing so often falls on deaf ears. Governments, as they deem necessary, impose immigration laws or workplace regulations that prod MNEs to hire locals.

THE POLYCENTRIC FRAMEWORK

Polycentrism is the principle of organizing around different political, social, or economic centers. Hence, a **polycentric framework** sees the effectiveness of the business practices of foreign "centers" as philosophically and practically equivalent to those in the home "center." Given that the circumstances of the home office differ from those of local subsidiaries, and anchored in the larger thesis that neither is intrinsically superior, an MNE accordingly adjusts its HRM policies. Thus, staffing operating units, from headquarters to foreign subsidiaries, draws from the local environment—Chinese run the China operations, Mexicans run the Mexico operations, Austrians run the Austria operations, and so on.

A polycentric framework uses host-country nationals to manage local subsidiaries.

Advantages of the Polycentric Framework   Staffing foreign operations with locals has economic, political, and cultural advantages (see Table 20.2). Johnson & Johnson, a MNE that applies the polycentric framework, highlights some of them. With few exceptions, home-country nationals run J&J's subsidiaries. Each unit operates with

TABLE 20.2   The Polycentric Framework: Key Benefits

Several factors encourage a polycentric staffing framework. As we see below, these factors tap country, personnel, economic, and leadership concerns. The criterion of evaluation, we note, is the presumption that the means and methods of the home office must be adjusted to reflect national circumstances.

Economical	A local hire, given prevailing workplace standards and wage conditions, requires less compensation than an expatriate.
Nationalism	Host countries—especially those suspicious of foreign-controlled operations—prefer local managers who champion local objectives.
Management Development	Awarding top jobs to local managers helps attract, motivate, and retain local employees.
Employee Morale	Local workers, for numerous social and cultural reasons, prefer to work for local managers.
Expatriate Failure	Expatriate failure is expensive, corrosive, and demoralizing. *Ceteris paribus*, locals are less likely to fail, given their familiarity with the local environment.
Local Innovation	Better understanding of local markets gives local managers a keen sense of innovation opportunities.

substantial autonomy, commanding the freedom to act as it sees best given local market conditions. Thus liberated, each foreign unit acts as a small business, entrepreneurial in character and aware that success depends on its comparatively superior sense in anticipating local customers' needs and delivering meaningful solutions. More formally, J&J's CEO explained that relying on locals to staff local operations "is a tremendous magnet for talent, because it gives people room to grow and room to explore new ideas, thus developing their own skills and careers."[33]

Benefits   A compelling motivation of the polycentric approach is its implications for the economics of staffing international operations. Hiring local managers eliminates the exorbitant expense of posting expatriates to local slots. By and large, it is difficult to pinpoint the total cost or an expat assignment due to the range of relevant variables. A general rule is that the total annual cost of an expat on assignment is three times his or her annual salary. Indirect administrative expenses boost this sum. For example, an expat slot generates far more documentation than a comparable domestic executive slot. Consequently, on average, supporting expatriates requires twice as many HR professionals (1 HR professional to 37 expats) versus home-country executives (1 HR professional to 70 managers).[34]

These costs are far more dramatic when qualified by the corresponding expense of a local hire. Typically, an expat costs the employer three to five times as much as an equivalent local worker, after taking into account financial incentives, relocation costs, cost-of-living allowances, local tax differentials, and so on. The stark economics of expatriate-versus-home-country-national encourages MNEs to staff operations with the latter. Five years ago, HSBC Group had more than 1,000 expats out of 312,000 worldwide employees, but its concern for rising costs spurred local hires; it now has about 380 expatriates, drawn from 33 nations.

Host governments typically see local managers as "better citizens" than expatriates, given the belief that locals will champion national interests over global objectives. Besides politically astute choices, hiring local managers boosts employee morale.[35] There are also impediments to using expats, such as licensing requirements that prevent MNEs from using expatriate accountants and lawyers or visa regulations that put a hard cap on the number of foreigners who can staff a local subsidiary. Hiring locals neutralizes these constraints.

> Using host-country managers boosts local motivation and morale. Still, likely costs include gaps with global operations due to of problems of accountability and allegiance.

Finally, proponents of polycentrism reason that local managers are stronger performers given their keener understanding of local customers, markets, and institutions. When operating outside the United States, for example, Microsoft tries to hire home-country nationals. As its former COO explains, "You want people who know the local situation, its value system, the way work gets done, the way people use technology in that particular country, and who the key competitors are.... If you send someone in fresh from a different region or country, they don't know those things."[36] More philosophically, Bill Gates, Microsoft's chairperson, reasons that a polycentric policy is a moral obligation of international business, declaring that when staffing an international office, "It sends the wrong message to have a foreigner come over to run things."[37]

Drawbacks to the Polycentric Framework   A polycentric policy requires that an MNE decentralize authority to locals to run operations. This can create accountability and allegiance difficulties. Accountability issues emerge when local units depend less and less on the home office for resources. Moreover, as local managers develop skills and outlooks, they often build thriving local operations. Success supports growing resource independence from the home office and often powers the transition of the local subsidiary into a quasi-autonomous unit. Unchecked, local subsidiaries, regarding the global company as a federation of loosely connected and largely autonomous national operations, pay increasingly less mind to headquarters. For instance, when J&J launched Tylenol in 1960 as an over-the-counter pain reliever in the United States, the product was available to worldwide units shortly thereafter. However, the quasi-independent Japanese unit, despite duress from headquarters, did not begin selling it until 2000.[38]

> The polycentric staffing framework can fan murky accountability and promote conflicting allegiances.

Likewise, allegiance issues emerge when host-country nationals in charge of a subsidiary prefer loyalty to local colleagues instead of to the foreigners running the faraway headquarters. In theory, local managers balance the competing demands of making sense of events from a local and home office view. In practice, however, national concerns typically take precedence given the tyranny of immediacy.[39]

Compounding this situation is a subtle drawback of polycentric staffing—namely, the potential disengagement of local staff from the parent company. By definition and design, there are a few slots for expatriates in the polycentric framework; locals have scant opportunities to work outside the home country. This outcome constrains the international mobility of host-country nationals. As a result, there may be little incentive for local managers to study business and cultural practices in other markets. Unaddressed, these differences isolate national subsidiaries.

THE GEOCENTRIC FRAMEWORK

Geocentrism is a world-oriented set of attitudes and values that regards humanity as a single entity. Hence, the **geocentric framework** does not heed national boundaries, seeing the blunt division of home-, host-, and third-country managers as needless. Rather, HRM's task is developing the best people for key jobs throughout the organization, regardless of their nationality. As GE's CEO notes, "It's more important to find the best people, wherever they may be, and develop them so that they can lead big businesses, wherever those may be."

> A geocentric framework seeks the best people for key jobs throughout the organization, regardless of nationality.

Advantages of the Geocentric Framework   A geocentric policy develops international executives who move between countries and cultures without forfeiting their personal effectiveness.[40] This helps MNEs pursue global and, especially, transnational strategies, both of which rely on exploiting learning opportunities around the world to generate and leverage ideas. As the CEO of Schering-Plough explains, "Good ideas can come from anywhere...the more places you are, the more ideas you will get. And the more ideas you get, the more places you can sell them and the more competitive you will be. Managing in many places requires a willingness to accept good ideas no matter where they come from—which means having a global attitude."[41]

> Economic factors, decision-making routines, and legal contingencies complicate a geocentric framework.

Drawbacks to the Geocentric Framework   A geocentric policy is tough to develop and costly to maintain. Certainly, the notion of a world-oriented set of attitudes and values is intellectually engaging. Too, the resulting multinational composition of senior management reduces cultural myopia and enhances local responsiveness. Difficulty plagues adoption, however, given the need for executives to retain a sense of identity in the face of extreme diversity. At one point, for instance, J. P. Morgan housed managers of more than 50 nationalities in its London office, reasoning that putting the best people together, regardless of nationality, powered strategic insights.[42]

Research reports that working with groups marked by cultural diversity takes on a different vibe than with groups made up of people of similar ethnicities and nationalities. Often, the mix of different perspectives generates creative breakthroughs. However, the task of making sense of the various outlooks that potentially bear on a decision can prove overwhelming. Akin to the Tower of Babel, geocentrism can erode the sense of common purpose as the clarity of the task is lost in a hodgepodge of competing perspectives.

The logistics of the geocentric framework are costly. Exposing people to different ideas in diverse places is expensive. Compensation and relocation costs quickly escalate when transferring high-priced executives from country to country. Often the higher pay and prestige enjoyed by those in the executive vanguard triggers resentment from those not. Current cost sensitivities, aggravated by the global financial crisis, pressure MNEs to economize. In recourse, they experiment with short-term engagements, commuter relationships, and extended business travel in lieu of multi-year assignments.

WHICH FRAMEWORK WHEN?

Table 20.3 summarizes the merits and constraints of the three frameworks. It suggests there is no theoretically superior approach. Rather, HRM's task is to optimize staffing policies in terms of the demands of the MNE's strategy. Earlier we noted that expatriates drive the critical tasks of the company's strategy; they launch new ventures, build management expertise, fill local skills gaps, transfer technology, and diffuse organization culture. Each strategy, whether international, multidomestic, global, or transnational, imposes different requirements to run these activities. Therefore, HRM's job is devising the staffing framework that develops the executive resources required by the MNE's strategy.[43] More to the point, a survey of MNEs noted that nearly 90 percent prepared for global expansion by determining strategic goals and needs. They then assess their pool of potential expatriates, looking for the requisite outlooks and skills and filling gaps as needed.[44]

Concept Check

Table 20.3 demonstrates a principle that we develop throughout this book: Although most of us are prone to look for the "one best way" of doing things, it's seldom a promising approach in any area. This outlook applies to formulating a staffing strategy for international operations.

TABLE 20.3 Frameworks to Staff International Operations: Principles and Practices

The assumptions, advantages, drawbacks, and strategic fit of the leading staffing frameworks run the gamut. HRM, keen to the requirements of the MNE's strategy, applies the most appropriate staffing framework.

Staffing Framework	General Assumptions	Advantages	Drawbacks	Strategic Fit
Ethnocentric	• The leadership ideals, management values, and workplace practices of one's company are superior to those in foreign markets. • Headquarters makes key decisions and foreign subsidiaries follow orders.	• Leverages a company's core competence. • Gives people a strong point of perspective. Develops the senior management team.	• Can inspire belief that one's company is intrinsically better at everything. • Can promote cultural arrogance and illiteracy. • May blind managers to innovations in other countries.	International
Polycentric	• Adapts to differences, real or imaginary, between home and host countries. • Headquarters makes broad strategic decisions that local units adapt to their marketplace.	• Acknowledges the unique merits of a country. • The least expensive staffing approach. Eases adapting to the local market's workplace norms. • Placates host governments and promotes local executive development.	• Complicates coordinating and controlling value activities. • Isolates country operations. • Reduces incentive among locals to engage a global perspective. • Creates agency dilemmas for quasi-autonomous country operations.	Multidomestic
Geocentric	• All nations are created equal and possess inalienable characteristics that are neither superior nor inferior but simply there. • Headquarters and subsidiaries collaborate to identify, transfer, and diffuse best practices.	• Adept way to deal with different people in different counties. • Leverages powerful ideas worldwide. • Promotes learning dynamics.	• Tough to develop, costly to run, hard to maintain. • Contrary to many countries' market development plans. • Difficult to find qualified expatriates that effectively move from country to country.	Global and Transnational

Does Geography Matter? Expatriate Assignments and Activities

A generation ago, the bulk of expatriates worked in the developed markets of Japan, United States, and Europe. Certainly, there were many scattered throughout Africa, Asia, South America, and the Middle East. Generally, though, these folks worked in primary or extractive industries, such as a petroleum engineer posted to Saudi Arabia to assist ExxonMobil's drilling operation. Expatriates, by and large, flocked to business centers in Europe, America, and Japan.

Changing Company Strategies

Today, trends indicate that the geography of assignments is changing. First and foremost, Western MNEs are increasingly reorienting their strategies toward markets that were once far off the beaten path. The rising importance of emerging economies, particularly in rapidly growing Asia, leads Western MNEs to relocate a larger share of operations there.

In Europe, we see companies such as HSBC, Nokia, and Volkswagen downscaling their European activities as they ramp up those in Asia. In the United States, companies such as GE, Microsoft, Walmart, and Caterpillar do the same. In the 2000s, for example, U.S. companies cut their workforces in the United States by nearly 3 million while concurrently increasing employment overseas by 2.4 million. In contrast, during the 1990s they added 4.4 million workers in the United States versus 2.7 million workers abroad. Asked about the shift, GE's chief executive replied, "Today we go to Brazil, we go to China, we go to India, because that's where the customers are."[45]

As multinationals redeploy their operations, they reset their labor force. Correspondingly, MNEs reorganize their executives, moving those that had worked in the West to the business centers in the East.

Changing Career Strategies

The allure of emerging markets appeals not only to companies. Graduates face slow-growing markets and executive saturation in mature Western economies. Many see a better chance of getting promoted, to say nothing of just getting a job, in São Paulo, Shanghai, or Mumbai than in New York, Tokyo, or London. "A lot of my friends are going to Asia and Latin America to do their internships," said a student at a leading U.S. business school. "It may be outside their comfort zone, but they see getting some experience there as helpful, since that's where many of the jobs will be."[46]

So, rather than patiently waiting for opportunities, students jump-start the process and head straight to markets they see representing the future. Expectedly, this is particularly true for of graduates with cultural links to those countries and of Westerners with relevant language fluency. Still, the siren call attracts even those with limited cultural experience and linguistic skills.[47] The allure of surging economies, lower costs of living, higher after-tax compensation, and the chance to bypass years of dues-paying entry jobs prove irresistible.

Damn the Torpedoes

Therefore, as sales, growth, labor, and executive opportunity migrate from the West to faster growing emerging economies, we anticipate a radical reset of the geography of expatriate assignments and activities. Data already confirm the trend is underway: China, Brazil, India, and Singapore are the leading destinations for expatriates.[48] ●

Managing Expatriates

Developing a cadre of high-performance expatriates requires that MNEs find people who are prepared for an international assignment, devise ways to motivate them, post them to the appropriate job, and capitalize on their new skills and refined outlook when they are ready for their next position. Therefore, we turn now to the matters of expatriate selection, preparation, compensation, and repatriation.

EXPATRIATE SELECTION

Case Review Note

Some people enjoy the thrill of living and working abroad. Our opening case profiled a Morgan Stanley expatriate who has worked in Britain, Singapore, and India and remains excited about the prospect of seeing the "big world." Others, however, prefer not to work abroad. Consequently, few MNEs command a cadre of mobile, economical, and experienced expatriates. Again, recall how Honeywell screens candidates years before they might go abroad in order to maximize the probability of success and, more often than not, minimize the odds of failure.

Screening executives to find those with the greatest inclination and highest potential for a foreign assignment is the process of **expatriate selection.** Always difficult, it grows increasingly so given talent shortages and rising expenses of international assignments.[49] Indisputably, there are many potential candidates for an overseas assignment, particularly as slowing economies make jobs less secure. The problem, however, is not the supply of candidates but the selection of those that will succeed abroad. HR executives, try as they might, cannot consult a battery of technical indicators that consistently predict the likely performance of a potential expatriate. In extreme situations, selection is a matter of arbitrary convenience—or, as one executive notes, "There's not a lot of science there at all...people may just get sent because they're willing to go."[50]

The growing need for expats to run expanding international operations, along with the rising cost of failure, spurs systematizing selection processes. IHRM evaluates career, cultural, and psychological measures, anchored in the company's staffing framework, to organize expatriate selection. These measures, applied through objective evaluations and in-depth interviews, screen candidates on many dimensions. Anecdotes and analysis emphasize *technical competence*, *adaptiveness*, and *leadership*.

Technical Competence Asked to rank the important objectives of an international assignment, HR directors commonly identify the goal to fill a skills gap in foreign operations. They reason that a high-performance executive can quickly transfer management methods, improve operational efficiency, or fine-tune marketing campaigns when posted abroad. A precondition of selection, therefore, is the executive's functional expertise and understanding of how to apply it in the foreign operation.[51] Consequently, managers often have several years' of work experience before working abroad. The fact that expatriate selections are usually made by line managers based on a candidate's operational track record reinforces this tendency. Moreover, many see outstanding technical competence as an indicator of the self-confidence needed to work well abroad.

Overall, HR executives, expats, and local staff agree that technical competence, usually indicated by past job performance, has been and continues to be the leading determinant of success in foreign assignments.[52] However, this predisposition is changing; recall that some MNEs are seeking younger employees to staff international slots, trading trade performance records for long-term potential. Figure 20.3 gives a somewhat extreme take of this outlook.

Adaptiveness Success in one's home country is a necessary but by no means sufficient basis for success abroad. Effective expatriates are adaptive; thrust into new, unusual situations, they develop the outlook, skills, and poise needed to thrive. Therefore, MNEs evaluate a possible expatriate in terms of various adaptive characteristics, most notably:

Self-Maintenance These qualities, such as personal resourcefulness, are useful when things do not go as planned—which is not an unlikely situation in the zone of international business. The difficulty specifying reliable indicators of resourcefulness show in MNEs' struggles to identify candidates who command it. Like many MNEs, the selection process at HSBC uses tests, interviews, and exercises to get a sense of a candidate's potential. Still, HSBC evaluates several intrinsically intangible indicators. Its CEO explains, "We don't look so much at what or where people have studied but rather at their drive, initiative, cultural sensitivity, and readiness to see the world as their oyster. Whether they've studied classics, economics, history, or languages is irrelevant. What matters are the skills and qualities necessary to be good, well-rounded executives in a highly international institution operating in a diverse set of communities."[53]

Satisfactory Relationships with Host Nationals Living and working in different cultures demands flexibility and tolerance. Whether referred to *cultural empathy* or *others-orientation* , this outlook enhances an expat's interactions with different people in different places and, importantly, to understand why some go well and others do not. Two factors

Concept Check

In Chapters 2, 3, and 4, we analyze the environments—cultural, political, legal, and economic—that frame international business operations. The variability in each context prevents setting absolute "standards" for running international operations. Here, we observe that implication of variability to selecting expatriates. General guidelines more often than not take the place of absolute standards.

Technical competence, adaptiveness, and leadership ability are leading determinants of who is selected for an international assignment.

Adaptiveness refers to a person's potential for

- Self-maintenance and personal resourcefulness.
- Developing meaningful relationships.
- Interpreting the immediate environment.

FIGURE 20.3   The Promise and Problem of Potential

Changing circumstances in staffing international slots directs attention to younger employees. But, notwithstanding its suggestion, rarely this youthful.

Source: Peter C. Vey/Cartoon Bank

"You'll be perfect for heading up our new push into the global market place but what's this about you still living at home with your mother?"

play vital roles: the ability to develop sincere, honest friendships with foreign nationals and the willingness to use, no matter how rudimentarily, the host-country language.

Sensitivity to Host Environments   As anyone who has traveled abroad understands, new situations in new settings challenge one's values and outlooks. Interpreting how colleagues, customers, and competitors in the local market see events, rather than unduly criticizing them for dissimilarities, supports strong performance. Interpreting events in ways that reject stereotypes, preconceptions, and unrealistic expectations help one go far in international business.[54]

For example, fast-growing markets have attracted many foreign firms and, by extension, their expatriates. More than a few of the firms hail from a rule of law environment, such as Germany, and move into a rule of man setting, like China. In the former, the rules governing business are straightforward directives; in the latter, they are often seen as flexible guidelines. Said one expat, in "the West, everything is transparent. If you want to obtain a license to do something, you don't need to spend money bribing an official or hiring a go-between: You just download the form from the Internet and apply."[55] Moving from the transparency of Germany to the opacity of China can prove daunting for those accustomed to following the straight and narrow. The ability to adapt to the ways of the host country, whether it involves cultures, laws, or simply getting around town, shapes an expatriate's effectiveness.

Leadership   The precise job descriptions found in the job bank of the home office inevitably give way to far broader responsibilities in foreign subsidiaries. Typically, the expat director of a foreign subsidiary lacks the battery of resources he commanded at the home office. The call to do many jobs simultaneously requires finding ways to interpret how locals approach the workplace in terms of problem solving, tolerance for uncertainty, use of power, and consensus building. In addition, the expat will confront different trade rules, investment regulations, and business practices. Microsoft's Joan Pattle found that working abroad imposed new demands. At home, her job in marketing meant

Senior executives in subsidiaries usually assume a greater range of leadership roles and broader duties than do managers of similar-size home-country operations.

Case Review Note

FIGURE 20.4 Key Competencies of Expartiates

Survey of the preferred competencies of expatriates consistently emphasize facets of an executive outlook. Effectively, survey data indicates that technical skills open the door to an international assignment, but leadership skills and attitudes move you through it. *Source:* Jeitosa Group International

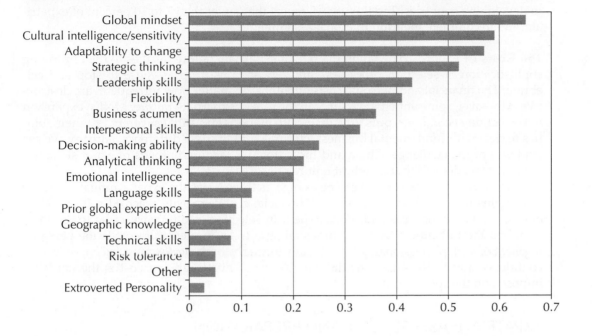

working in her department with little responsibility for other business functions. Her expatriate assignment in the United Kingdom pushed her beyond the customary tasks of marketing. The scale and scope of foreign assignments therefore, push executives to move from managing an activity to leading a company. Posting a specialist, such as an engineer or finance officer, gurantees he or she will face a range of technical and behavioral situations. The efficient adminitration of matters will likely fall short. Effective resolution, HRM reasons, depends on the expat's leadership ability and aptitude. Figure 20.4 elaborates this perspective, highlighting the importance of a global mindset and cultural intelligence/sensitivity to succeeding abroad.

MNEs increasingly see leadership as a key to expatriate selection and success. To that end, testing and improving the leadership ability of high-potential executives is a common objective of an international assignment.[56] Experience testifies to the usefulness of a foreign assignment in doing so. The records of successful expats indicate that they did not recoil from the differences they encountered. Rather, they developed the communication, motivation, self-reliance, risk-taking, and diplomacy qualities we commonly attribute to executive leadership. Specifically, McKinsey & Co. concluded that whereas technical competence is a given, today's expatriates "must have a particular mind-set.... When you look behind the success stories of leading globalizers, you find MNEs that have learned how to think differently from the herd. They seek out different information, process it in a different way, come to different conclusions, and make different decisions. Where others see threats and complexity, they see opportunity. Where others see a barren landscape, they see a cornucopia of choices."[57] Consequently, MNEs post high potential executives overseas, giving them the opportunity to step up to the challenge, battle test their skills, and improve their global mindset.

Studies indicate that successful expatriates see not a barren landscape but rather a cornucopia of choices upon entering foreign markets.

EXPATRIATE FAILURE

Best-laid plans, as we all know, often go awry. MNEs experience this situation when they select their best and brightest executives, send them to a foreign market, pay them well, and watch them fail. **Expatriate failure,** narrowly defined, is a manager's

Expatriate failure is operationally costly and professionally detrimental.

premature return home due to poor performance. Broadly defined, it is the breakdown of the MNE's expatriate selection process. In both cases, it is an enduring concern among MNEs. In the 1980s, research reported that nearly a third of American managers assigned to advanced countries returned early; the failure rate was twice that for those sent to developing countries. Today, surveys report that fewer than 7 to 10 percent of expatriates fail to complete their international assignments.[58]

The Costs of Failure   The fall in the rate of expatriate failure testifies to the improving sophistication of selection processes. Still, few see this drop as cause to stop and celebrate. The financial and personal costs of failure, no matter how infrequent, are destructive. Moreover, some anticipate a surge in the rate of expatriate failure. MNEs' expansion into emerging economies puts executives into markets spots that severely test their abilities to deal with fundamental business, cultural, and lifestyle difference. Already, we see evidence of the challenge. China and India, today's leading hotbeds of expat slots, top the list of locations with the highest failure rates.[59]

The average cost per failure can be as high as three times the expat's annual domestic salary plus the cost of relocation.[60] The financial cost can easily reach $1 million when one accounts for the time and money spent in selection, preliminary visits to the location, and the lost productivity as things fall apart. An incalculable cost is the personal implications of professional failure to the formerly high-performing executive's self-confidence and leadership potential. Finally, a potentially greater cost is the hardship imposed on the spouse and family.[61]

EXPATRIATE ASSESSMENT AND PREPARATION

Sometimes failure is the consequence of poor assignment planning putting the wrong person in the wrong job at the wrong time with the wrong expectations. Other times it comes as a surprise, as personal circumstances disrupt what many saw as a sure thing. Both situations spur MNEs to improve their assessment and predeparture preparation programs.

Assessment typically focus on the expatriate's technical expertise, ability to cope with challenging new environments, resolve personal or emotional difficulties, and adjust family life to the foreign environment. HRM's growing sophistication has reduced the rate of expatriate failure due to inadequate technical expertise. Indeed, rare is the foreign assignment that fails because HRM misjudged a candidate's technical qualifications.

Improving understanding shifts HRM's attention toward preparing the expatriate. Figure 20.5 ranks the top stress points prior to departure. Reestablishing a social life, feeling lonely, and missing friends and family top the list. HRM extrapolates from these long-running concerns that improving cultural sensitivities and skills improves the odd of successful adjustment and, by extension, a successful expat assignment.[62]

Today, most MNEs provide predeparture preparation in the form of cross-cultural training, destination familiarization, and language lessons. They encourage individuals to understand their own culture and the way it influences their behavior, rather than focusing on the differences they are likely to encounter. Increasingly, MNEs use CD-based or Web-based programs to ease preparation. In fact, 35 percent of companies said they provided media-based or Web-based training in 2010—an all-time high.[63] The convenience, efficiency, and cost provide excellent predeparture preparation as well as in-country reinforcement. Not matter the tools uses, HRM follows a clear-cut rule: Helping an expat prepare in any or all ways helps her thrive abroad.

A Fundamental Challenge   Generally, a foreign assignment is more stressful for the family than for the expatriate. Consistently, the leading cause of expatriate failure is the inability of a spouse and children to adapt to the host nation. Challenges include the children's education, family adjustment, and the spouse's resistance to and regret from moving abroad. Increasingly, the struggle of a previously employed spouse to find local employment poses severe difficulties.[64]

FIGURE 20.5 Leadings Concerns of Expatriates Ahead of Moving to Their Foreign Assignment

A foreign assignment is rich with opportunity yet fraught with challenges. Prior to heading abroad, executives worry about various issues–as reported in this chart. Anticipating these and making early adjustments improves the odds of a successful experience.

Source: HSBC Bank, International

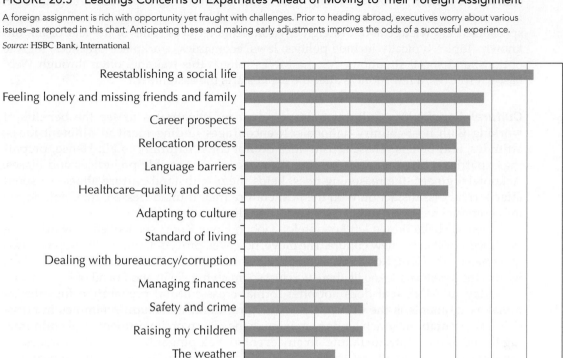

Expats commonly speak of a recurring dynamic. Abrupt separation from friends, family, and career isolate the spouse and children. It leads many to look to the expatriate for companionship and reassurance. Job demands, however, result in little time to provide extra support. Sometimes slowly, sometimes quickly, but almost always, family harmony suffers as stress escalates. Unchecked, the expat's work performance declines because, "If the family starts to unravel, the employee will at some time start to unravel too."[65]

As a result, HRM takes a proactive approach in preparing the expat, spouse, and family. It monitors families' adjustment process and experiments with ways to minimize family disruption. Executives may be sent on short-term or "commuter" assignments where they need not uproot their families. Moves to send younger or older expats speak to this threat; the younger are more likely single whereas the older have grown children and more agreeable partners.[66] In fact, only 47 percent of expatriates had children accompanying them in 2010—an all-time low.[67]

Preparation Programs Greater concern for functional performance traditionally led HRM to tailor predeparture programs toward improving technical skills and administrative competencies. The matter of developing adaptiveness was largely left up to the individual. A manager interested in an international career would, through her own devices, find ways to travel abroad, monitor world events, and socialize with people of different ethnicities, cultures, and nationalities.[68] When eventually posted to a foreign assignment, these sorts of managers often performed well.

The variability in performance among expatriates, by consistently highlighting gaps in predeparture training, encourages MNEs to expand preparation beyond technical capabilities. HRM assesses adaptive capabilities, international orientation and outlook, geographic preferences, or foreign-language qualifications.[69] It then tailors preparation to improve an expat's understanding of a country, raise cultural awareness, and devise practical skills. Honeywell, for instance, begins training potential expatriates early and focuses on cross-cultural skills, including those necessary for dealing with culture shock. Let's take a closer look at each.

Training and predeparture preparations can lower the probability of expatriate failure. Increasingly, preparation activities include the spouse and family members.

Concept Check

In Chapter 11, we explain the concept of "The Firm as Value Chain" and discuss strategies by which an MNE strengthens its competitive position. Here we observe that successful MNEs boost performance by linking the expatriate selection process to the requirements of their strategy.

Case Review Note

General Country Understanding

The most common predeparture training is an informational briefing about the way things work in the host country. Transferring specialized knowledge about foreign environments reduces some of the fear of the unknown. Topics typically include politics, laws, economics, workplace practices, logistic options, and social situations.[70] Some MNEs refresh this training, often through Web-based resources, a few months after the expat starts the assignment.

Cultural Sensitivity

Cultural training sensitizes expatriates to see the benefits of working with host-country nationals. It encourages finding merit in different ideas, attitudes, and beliefs. These sensitivities do not come naturally to all. Hence, preparing expatriates often requires helping them recognize possible prejudices and biases. Acknowledgment, the reasoning goes, helps them withstand **culture shock**—a soon-after-arrival dissatisfaction with the host culture that, if unaddressed, may deteriorate into homesickness, irritability, arrogance, and disdain.

When Michelle Brown left London for a job in Hong Kong, she looked forward to immersing herself in the new culture. The move, however, proved daunting. "I suppose I was quite naive, but Hong Kong was a complete culture shock," she says. "The humidity was insane, the smells made me ill, there was just so much to take in and not all of it pleasant."

Today, an MNE that does not offer formal cross-cultural preparation for international assignments is the outlier.[71] An emerging trend is including families in cross-cultural orientation, which tends to maximize the return on investment while minimizing the odds of expatriate failure. In any event, developing interpersonal awareness in the context of cross-cultural sensitivity training tends to make people more receptive to and tolerant of foreign environments.

Practical Skills

Practical training aims to familiarize expatriates and their families with the routines of life in the host country. The sooner they develop a useful pattern of schooling, socializing, and shopping, the higher the odds of withstanding culture shock. This is easier said than done for many countries. Expatriates report that India, Qatar, the Russian Federation, and Saudi Arabia top the list in terms of the difficulty of setting up finances, health care, accommodations, and utilities. South Africa, Canada, Thailand, and Australia are notably easier.[72] Expatriates improve adjustment by consulting former expats on their successes and struggles and, once abroad, socializing with local community groups.

Exceptions and Anomalies

All things held equal, MNEs tend to under—rather than over—prepare executives for international responsibilities. In some circumstances, managers receive cursory predeparture training, often scanning reports and reviewing resources on the flight to their new home. Usually an MNE will blame this circumstance on the urgency of the situation, noting there is insufficient time for the expat to take a familiarization trip to the host country, let alone a comprehensive profile of its history, culture, politics, economy, religion, and business environment. Typically, the home office fears rapid deterioration in the performance of the foreign subsidiary or the rapid fade of a key opportunity. Hence, it quickly dispatches help, worrying more about technical competency than cultural IQ.

Ultimately, it is important to note that some causes of expatriate failure are intractable simply because some people do not adjust well to working abroad. The awareness of differences, as one might hear from an executive about to depart Boston for Bangkok, does not necessarily signify the willingness to adapt to them.

Changes in socializing, logistics, and safety often push people far beyond their comfort zone. Culture shock follows and emotional distress esclates. Put simply, notwithstanding the glamour and riches or the comprehensiveness of predeparture training, the expatriate lifestyle is not for everyone. For some, a sought-after adventure devolves into a stressful sentence.

MNEs usually anchor training programs to transfer specific information about the host country as well as improve the executive's cultural sensitivity.

Key to successfully transitioning to a foreign assignment is mastering the new ways of schooling, socializing, and shopping.

Point

Yes When asked about the importance of employees' foreign-language needs, many respond that such competency adds professional and personal value.[73] Surveys report that managers who learn one or more foreign languages find new ways to make innovative contributions. Even if they are far from fluent, their willingness to communicate in the language of the locals builds rapport with colleagues, thereby improving their effectiveness. Proponents point out that countries have different cultural and business expectations that can only be deciphered through the local language.

New Networks Foreign language aversion, which many see as signifying cross-cultural illiteracy, excludes one from influential business networks, complicates relations with local officials, and slows socializing with workmates.[74] Working abroad is itself a challenge; language limitations make it further isolating.[75] Microsoft's Joan Pattle noted that her inability to speak Turkish made her seven-month stint in Istanbul very lonely, explaining, "You can't really mix with the locals...[or] use local transportation because you can't read any of the signs."[76]

Symbolically, the effort to speak the local language, no matter how poorly, sends a subtle but essential cultural message. Just making an effort to say a few words in the native tongue can make a good impression, sending a subliminal message that "We are equal."[77] Moreover, as anyone who has struggled to learn a foreign language can attest, unexpected benefits include a good dose of humility and respect for others.

New Ways of Thinking Proponents of foreign language competency maintain that learning another language is a personally enriching experience. Studying another culture illuminates one's values and outlooks. Understanding local language and, in the course, local culture, clarifies the consequences of globalization. International cooperation and exchange depend on people who possess foreign-language proficiency.

Learning a Foreign Language: Is It Still Useful?

Perhaps most significantly, learning a foreign language teaches you that there are several ways to express a concept, interpret an abstraction, and make sense of a situation. Learning a new way of thinking, besides improving exchanges with supplies, buyers, officials, and stakeholders, sharpens your business skills and refines your global mindset.

New Requirements Even if not for enrichment, some say learning a foreign language will soon be a competitive necessity. The expanding international links and intercultural connections of a globalizing world make linguistic skills crucial for getting many jobs and accelerating careers. In the context of the widespread unemployment resulting from the global financial crisis, any means to differentiate one's competencies, such as that demonstrated by linguistic skills, creates opportunities.

Inevitably, some respond that the spread of English competency worldwide means those who already speak it need not worry. Critics note, however, that marketplace trends will punish, not privilege, English-only speakers. Eventually, they will lose the advantages that once came with being among the small number of native Anglophones who could speak the most useful language of the business world. Bilinguals or multilinguals will offer the same as English monoglots but with richer language skills and broader international perspectives.

In some parts of the world, officials have institutionalized incentives to support this movement. For instance, the EU's official language policy is "mother tongue plus two," whereby citizens are encouraged to learn two additional languages. The majority choose English.

Which One? Ultimately, one wonders, which foreign language should I study? Presently, growth in expatriate positions is moving rapidly from Western Europe and North America to the booming emerging economies. As MNEs struggle to place expatriates in these high-growth markets, proficiency in languages like Mandarin, Portuguese, or Hindi will translate into job opportunities and salary premiums. Finally, entrepreneurs may look around their hometown and go for fast-spreading languages such as Spanish, Mandarin, or Arabic.

Learning a Foreign Language: Is It Still Useful?

Counterpoint

No The prevalence of English throughout the world indicates that learning a foreign is nice but unnecessary. Like it or not, English ably performs in world business, supported by growing numbers who regard it as a practical alternative to their native language. Indeed, about a quarter of the world's population speaks some English, including the 400 million who speak it as their mother tongue and about the same number for whom it is a second language.

When you get down to hard dollars, however, English predominates. It accounts for a much larger share of world output than that represented by the proportion of native speakers in the world. Though the first language of only 6 percent of the world's population, its speakers generate more than 40 percent of world output. Inexorably, English becomes the world's *lingua franca.*

The Preferred Choice   Situations in the EU, where more than half the population claims to be reasonably conversant in English, highlight this trend. Among Europeans born before WWII, English, French, and German are almost equally common. But 15- to-24-year-olds are five times more likely to speak English as a foreign language than either German or French. Add native speakers to those who have learned it, and some 60 percent of young Europeans speak English "well or very well."[78] Many envision developing it further; more than 70 percent in a survey of 16,000 people living in the EU agreed, "Everybody should speak English."

We see similar trends elsewhere. In 2005, India claims the world's largest English-speaking and understanding population. It now has the second-largest "fluent" English-speaking population, after the United States, and expects to have the world's largest number of fluent English speakers within a decade. Even today, Hindi films, most advertising billboards, and higher education are in English. Virtually every well-paying job in India require an understanding of English.[79]

The Default Choice   Although English is not an official language in many countries, it is most often taught as the second language. In the EU, English is studied by schoolchildren (89 percent), followed by French (32 percent), German (18 percent), and Spanish (8 percent).[80] Nearly 200 million students in China are learning English in school, and more than a fifth of Japanese 5-year-olds attend classes in English conversation. Countries from Chile to Mongolia aim to become bilingual in English in the next decade or two. Collectively, with 2 billion people speaking or studying it today, we are on the verge of a massive diffusion of English competency.[81]

The Online Choice   The prevalence of English is best seen in its predominance on the Internet, where one can conduct business worldwide using the English interface of one's preferred browser.[82] More than 80 percent of home pages on the Web are in English. Heavyweight publications around the world, like *Der Spiegel* and *China Daily*, offer English-language websites that list translated news stories and opinion pieces. On a related front, the growing sophistication of translation software makes foreign language competency a moot point for those who prefer using their local language on the Internet.

The Only Choice   Many companies respond in kind. *The Economist* reports that just under half of employers rate language skills as important—a tendency linked to the laborious struggle to master a foreign language. Language competency ranked well behind technical competencies, leadership skills, and career development when evaluating a potential expatriate; it just edged motivation for working abroad.[83]

Finally, some say language proficiency is an easy but ultimately misleading proxy of an expatriate's potential. As the CEO of Schering-Plough notes, "I've met many people who speak three or four languages yet still have a very narrow view of the world. At the same time, I've come across people who speak only English but have a real passion and curiosity about the world and who are very effective in different cultures."[84]

COMPENSATING EXPATRIATES

If a U.S. company transfers its finance manager who makes $325,000 a year in Miami to Shanghai, where the going rate is $175,000, what should the manager's salary be? Alternatively, if a Chinese finance manager is transferred to the United States, what pay should the company offer? Should it compensate in dollars or yuans? Which set of fringe benefits should apply? How should it resolve tax policies?

These are a few of the many compensation questions a company faces when it posts expatriates. Managing an international workforce requires that HRM resolve differing pay levels, benefits, tax programs, and prerequisites. On the one hand, HRM must prevent the already high costs of an expatriate assignment from spiraling—MNEs in the United States spend nearly $1.3 million per expatriate during the course of a typical three-year foreign assignment.[85] On the other hand, HRM must pay people enough to motivate them as well as incent the family to move abroad.

Ceteris paribus, compensation can make or break an expatriate's motivation.

All things being equal, compensation can determine the likelihood and success of expatriate assignments. Pay too little, and people decline to go; if they do go, they may likely regret it. Pay them too much, and costs escalate, returns fall short, and pay inequities fan dissension. Further complicating the pay-performance link is the weak to nonexistent correlation between higher pay and improved performance. More often than not, the higher the pay, the longer an expatriate assignment tends to last. Some managers, quite content to prolong a munificent lifestyle, are less than eager to return home.[86]

A surprisingly common situation in Beijing : A street sign with Mandarin and English indications. Indeed, throughout Beijing there are plenty of signs with English translations. To those traveling elsewhere: good luck finding similarly helpful signs in New York, São Paulo, or Mumbai.
Source: Courtesy of Daniel Sullivan

The task facing HRM, then, is straightforward: Devise a compensation package that gets people to go abroad, lets them maintain their standard of living, reflects the responsibility of the foreign assignment, and ensures that after-tax income will not fall because of the foreign assignment. Developing a solution, however, is not quite so straightforward. HRM must balance the company's financial needs with the need for an attractive salary and benefits package, while ensuring that the package preserves pay equity among peers, promotes parity among expatriates, competes with packages offered by industry rivals, and can be easily administered. Finally, HRM has to balance its responsibility to company goals and individual needs with a win-win compensation plan.

> Compensation must neither overly reward nor unduly punish a person for accepting a foreign assignment.

Types of Compensation Plans   Many MNEs, especially in the United States, apply the **balance sheet approach** to manage expatriate compensation.[87] This approach develops a salary structure that equalizes purchasing power across countries so expatriates have the same living standard in their foreign posting that they had at home, no matter where their assignment takes them.[88] Its fundamental principle is equalization: Expatriates should neither overly prosper nor unduly suffer from working abroad. It also outlines how the company provides financial incentives that offset qualitative differences between assignment locations.

> The most common approach to expatriate pay is the balance sheet approach.

Three common methods of implementing a balance sheet compensation plan are the home-based, headquarters-based, and host-based. Let's take a closer look at each.

Home-Based Method   This method bases expatriates' compensation on the salary of a comparable job in their home city, thereby preserving equity with home-country colleagues and simplifying the eventual return. The evolving dynamics of globalization challenges the home-country balance sheet approach. Initially designed to compensate employees and families transferred from Western-headquartered MNEs out to the world, it based its cost of living indices and support allowances on moves from high-cost countries, such as England and the United States, to countries like Argentina or Saudi Arabia. Today's global environment is marked by expatriates of many different nationalities, different home and host combinations, varying salary levels and transfers to or from headquarters, and a growing number of transfers between subsidiaries. Hence, MNEs applying the balance sheet struggle to maintain pay equity and benefit consistency among their evolving expatriate populations.

The home-based method is the most prevalent compensation plan, particularly for expatriates sent abroad from emerging markets. For example, Chinese expatriates tend not to enjoy lavish pay and perks. China Unicom's managing director in Europe received his modest Chinese salary plus a small cost-of-living allowance during his foreign assignment. All combined, they totaled to 30 percent of the local entry-level salary for his firm.[89]

The changing demography of expatriates increasingly complicates efficiently administering the home-based method.

Headquarters-Based Method   A useful way to tweak the home-based method is to set the expatriate's salary in terms of that of a comparable job in the city where the MNE has its headquarters. For example, if a Boston-headquartered MNE posts expats to its offices in London, Santiago, and Jakarta, it would give each a salary structured in terms of the going wage in Boston. This plan recognizes the disruption of a foreign assignment and helps expatriates live as they had in their home country.

Host-Based Method   Sometimes called *destination pricing* or *localization*, this method fine-tunes expatriate compensation by basing it on the prevailing pay scales of the foreign locale. Basically, an expatriate starts with a salary equivalent to that of a local executive with similar responsibilities, then adds whatever foreign-service premiums, extra allowances, home-country benefits, and taxation compensation that have been negotiated. Operationally, the host-based method pays expats less in order to reduce tension between them and their host-country colleagues. This plan also improves the company's return on its investment. It is, however, not as lucrative for the expat as the other compensation plans. PwC, for example, uses the host-based method for expats involved in its EPIC program. PwC improves its offers by assisting with immigration, relocation, and language and intercultural training.

Key Aspects of Expatriate Compensation   Table 20.4 illustrates a typical compensation package. Expatriates negotiate their package in terms of a base salary, a foreign-service premium, various allowances, fringe benefits, tax differentials, and benefits. Let's review each.[90]

TABLE 20.4   Compensating an Expatriate: A Common Wage and Benefits Package

Estimates reflect the following scenario: A Denver-based MNE assigns an US-based executive to run its local subsidiary in Tokyo. In the United States, the executive, who has a working spouse and two children, earns an annual income of $150,000. This balance sheet profiles how HRM organizes his compensation for the foreign assignment.

Direct Compensation Costs	
Base salary	$150,000
Foreign-service premium	25,000
Goods and services differential	120,000
Housing	97,000
U.S. (hypothetical) taxes	(38,000)
Company-Paid Costs	
Education (schooling for two children)	30,000
Japanese income taxes	115,000
Transfer moving costs	47,000
Miscellaneous costs (i.e., shipping and storage; home sale or property management fees; cultural, practical, and language training; preassignment orientation trip, destination assistance)	85,000
Working spouse allowance	75,000
Annual home leave (airfare for four, hotel, and meals)	15,000
Additional health insurance, pension supplements, evacuation coverage	20,000

Base Salary   An expatriate's base salary normally falls in the same range as that for a comparable job in the home country. It is paid either in the home-country currency or in the local currency.

Foreign Service Premium   A *foreign service premium*, often called a *mobility premium*, is a cash incentive to compensate individuals for the inconvenience of moving to a new country, living away from family and friends, dealing with the day-to-day challenges of the new culture, language, and workplace practices, and the reality that they will ultimately have to disrupt their lives upon return. Long-term assignments usually qualify for a mobility premium; short-term assignments rarely do. Typically, the premium is expressed as a percentage of annual base salary (between 5 and 15 percent) and varies depending on whether it is an intra-regional transfer or an intercontinental transfer.

Tax Differentials   Varying tax polices require that MNEs adjust compensation so that expatriates' after-tax income does not suffer from taxes imposed by a foreign assignment. Tax equalization is a costly component of expatriate compensation. If there is no reciprocal tax treaty between the home and host countries, the expat may be legally obligated to pay income tax to both governments. In such situations, the MNE ordinarily pays the tax bill in the host country. Practically, companies monitor tax code variations. Commonly, tax authorities regulate issues regarding filing procedures, financial information, and penalties for noncompliance.

An important part of long-term assignments, tax policy is crucial in administering commuter and short-term assignments. For example, Chinese tax authorities stipulate that an expatriate who has spent less than 30 continuous days inside or more than 90 cumulative days outside China per tax year will not be considered as having been in China for that tax year. Consequently, executives monitor their time there, tracking arrival and departure dates.

Fringe Benefits   Firms provide expatriates the same level of medical and retirement benefits abroad that they received at home rather than those customarily granted in the host country. However, most MNEs expand these benefits to deal with local contingencies, such as bearing the cost of transferring ill expatriates or family members to suitable medical facilities.

Allowances   Sending an executive on an international assignment imposes expensive logistics and considerable stress. MNEs adjust the total compensation package with a variety of allowances, described below, that help reduce the difficulties facing the expatriate and family.

Cost-of-Living Allowance   Expatriates receive a cost-of-living allowance (sometimes called a "goods-and-services differential") so they don't suffer a decline in their standard of living due to the steep expense of a particular city (London or Lagos) or nation (Switzerland).[91] Some companies reduce the cost-of-living differential over time, reasoning that as expatriates adapt to their environment they should adopt local purchasing practices, such as substituting items from a neighborhood market in place of imported packaged goods.[92]

A fair, consistent compensation package reflects the cost of living in the assigned foreign city. HRM designs it given the prevailing cost of goods and services, including housing, transportation, food, clothing, household goods, and entertainment in a particular location.[93] Setting New York as the benchmark, cost-of-living estimates for 214 cities around the world indicate Luanda, Angola, is the world's most expensive city for expatriates, followed by Tokyo, Ndjamena (Chad), Moscow, and Geneva. The least expensive are Pakistan's Karachi and Islamabad, Nicaragua's Managua, Bolivia's La Paz, and Addis Ababa in Ethiopia.[94] Table 20.5 reports regional data.

Housing Allowance   Moving from, say, mid-price Salt Lake City to high-price Singapore is a tough sell to potential expatriates. A housing allowance ensures they will

Designing compensation packages for expatriates leads HRM to considers a variety of issues such as

- Base salary.
- Foreign service allowances.
- Fringe benefits.
- Tax differentials.

Allowances give HRM the flexibility to tailor compensation plan to deal with special situations. Allowances often involve

- Cost-of-living.
- Housing.
- Spouse support.
- Hardships.

TABLE 20.5   Top Five Most Expensive Cities for Expatriates by Region

Executives moving from spot to spot often run into different living costs. Those assigned to the following cities, organized by market regions, report the local cost of living ranks among the highest in the world.

Americas	Asia Pacific	Europe	Middle East & Africa
São Paolo, Brazil	Tokyo, Japan	Moscow, Russia	Luanda, Angola
New York, United States	Osaka, Japan	Geneva, Switzerland	N'Djamena, Chad
Rio de Janeiro, Brazil	Hong Kong, Hong Kong	Zurich, Switzerland	Libreville, Gabon
Havana, Cuba	Singapore, Singapore	Copenhagen, Denmark	Victoria, Seychelles
Los Angeles, United States	Seoul, South Korea	Oslo, Norway	Tel Aviv, Israel

duplicate their accustomed quality of housing. Housing costs vary because of crowded conditions that raise land prices as well as shortages of homes that are acceptable to expatriates.[95] Westerners pay steep premiums is some parts of Asia to rent accommodations with Western-style bathrooms and kitchens.[96]

Spouse Allowance   A spouse allowance supports the spouse's job search and cross-cultural training. In some cases, it helps offset lost income due to the spouse's employment loss or separation.[97] About a quarter of MNEs provide trailing spouses with job-search assistance, often through networks with other MNEs. It is becoming increasingly difficult for previously employed partners to find jobs during foreign assignments. Hitting an all-time low, only 9 percent of spouses, compared to a historical average of 14 percent, were employed both before and during assignments.[98] Difficulties arise due to economic conditions, locations, and language and cultural differences. Immigration and visa complications further discourage potential employers.

Hardship Allowances   Expatriates assigned to difficult environments or dangerous locations typically qualify for a hardship allowance. Living in certain settings poses severe hardships, such as harsh climatic or health conditions, or exposes the expatriate to security threats.[99] For instance, expat personnel of many MNEs, given their high profiles, have been targeted for kidnapping and assault. Hardship allowances or as some call it, combat pay, include ransom insurance, safety training programs, and alarm systems and security guards.[100] Sometimes, expats encounter living conditions that are substandard to those at home, thus qualifying for a hardship allowance. They may also receive miscellaneous allowances. Popular options include travel allowances that let an expatriate and family come home periodically, or education allowances to finance higher-quality schools.

Trends in Allowances   Spurred by cost pressures and unstable job markets, MNEs have begun reducing the range and extent of expatriate allowances. Foreign service premiums, for example, have been phased out by many companies. Globalization moves many employees to sustain their careers by working abroad, while more individuals see international assignments as a chance to develop business skills and leadership qualities. These folks are more willing to go abroad for less compensation; in fact, one survey found that 81 percent believe that broadening their horizons and gaining life experience, not financial gain, is the most important benefit of a foreign assignment.[101] Consequently, expatiate assignments have "gone from being special and unique, with piles of money thrown at them, to being an everyday part of the company."[102]

Cost-reduction techniques include dropping benefits and allowances (many MNEs with operations in Europe now treat the continent as if it were one country) and cutting "hardship" allowances for locales that are not as difficult as they once were, such as an assignment to Prague or Shanghai. Calls to reduce pay and perquisites will continue, driven by pressures to economize as well as a growing supply of executives from developing countries eager to work worldwide.

MNEs often provide additional compensation or fringe benefits to employees who work in remote or dangerous locations.

Concept Check

The expanding scale and scope of globalization, driven by the increasing physical and cybernetic connectivity of countries discussed throughout this text, increasingly blurs the idea of expatriates. Where once foreigners seemed foreign, today they seem almost commonplace in many hometowns. Consequently, there is less and less need to pay people premiums to go to places that are more and more similar.

Compensation Complications In addition to more than 1,700 expatriates stationed in more than 50 countries, Unilever has 20,000-plus managers spread over 90 countries.[103] Should it pay executives in different countries according to the prevailing standards in each? Alternatively, should it equalize pay for each position on a global basis? Legal, cultural, and regulatory factors complicate compensating managers abroad. Ideally, systematizing pay and benefit programs while removing inconsistencies makes for fair and equitable compensation plans. Considerable progress has been made in the past decade; salaries for similar jobs vary less substantially among countries.

Still, regulatory and cultural differences require tailoring performance-based pay by country and region. In particular, these situations challenge companies applying a geocentric staffing policy. Global and transnational strategies depend on developing a cadre of international managers, which more than likely includes different nationalities. At issue is whether all managers who perform the same job but in different locations are paid the same salary. For Finland's Nokia, say, this would require compensating its foreign nationals, no matter where they worked, in terms of Finnish salary levels. If Nokia opts not to develop an equitable arrangement, it will likely result in underpaid expatriates resenting their higher-paid counterparts.

> MNEs struggle to determine the proper degree to which they should equalize pay for the same type of job that is done in different countries.

Firms applying ethnocentric or polycentric staffing policies, though largely immune to these distortions, also adjust their compensation programs for national differences. If not, then they may pay someone more than necessary to persuade him or her to go abroad. Pay disparities for people doing the same jobs weaken the motivation of home- or host-country managers. Although the company with an ethnocentric or polycentric staffing policy may have few expatriates today, likely growth in its international activities will make it increasingly cumbersome to administer foreign compensation packages on a case-by-case basis.

Compensating CEOs Pay practices at the top set standards throughout the company. CEOs in the United States enjoy the largest and most comprehensive pay packages, both in terms of base compensation and total remuneration. CEOs in France, Germany, Italy, Switzerland, and the United Kingdom also command higher levels of total compensation than their peers elsewhere. This model inspires emulation; Asian and Latin American MNEs are instituting similar pay practices, particularly the use of performance-based pay that ties compensation to business results.

> Total, as well as forms of, compensation vary substantially among countries.

Differences persist. Long-term incentives, such as options on restricted stock, are popular in the United States but not in Germany. However, German managers often receive compensation that U.S. managers do not, such as housing allowances and partial payment of salary outside Germany, neither of which is taxable. Similarly, countries with aggressive personal income tax rates spur employees to ask for pay plans that reduce taxable base salaries in favor of tax-exempt fringe benefits. Ultimately, as MNEs from more countries become more multinational, they compete globally for executive talent. Likewise, local firms must tailor compensation to retain executives. Therefore, convergence in compensation practices is the order of the day.

REPATRIATING EXPATRIATES

MNEs apply staffing frameworks that create a cycle of events: expatriate selection, pre-departure preparation, a motivating compensation package design, and a plan to bring the executive back home intact and in good spirits. The latter task, **repatriation,** defines the process of reintegrating an expatriate into the home company upon completion of the foreign assignment. Success at each stage in the cycle, not just early on, is vital. Consistent success supports a self-sustaining cycle whereby returning employees share their knowledge, experiences, and enthusiasm with colleagues. High-performing executives, seeing the virtues of an international assignment, are then more receptive to the prospect of working abroad.

> The repatriation process is an often unexpected challenge for expatriates and their families.

The repatriation system works for many. Between a quarter to a third of returning expatriates believe their international experience boosted their career trajectory. Faster promotions and obtaining new positions more easily are commonly cited benefits. Indeed, nearly one in four expatriates who returns home is promoted in his or her first year of repatriation.

For others, the repatriation system falls short. Promotions are rare and wasted effort is common. A survey of repatriated executives who had successfully completed their overseas assignment found that more than a third held temporary assignments three months after returning home, nearly 80 percent believed their new job was a demotion from their foreign assignment, and more than 60 percent felt they did not have opportunities to transfer their international expertise to their new job. A surprising share of these former high flyers move on to other companies. In 2010, nearly 40 percent left their firm within one year of returning from abroad (the 15-year average is 22 percent), whereas another 25 percent left between the first and second year.[104]

Explanations for these anomalies commonly cite MNEs' greater concern for preparing and paying workers for the foreign assignment than for supporting them upon their return.[105] Anticipation, opportunity, and preparation prior to departure receive attention from a host of support functions. The backside of the cycle is far less prominent and promising. Returning home can deteriorate into a disappointing part of the assignment. Ironically, companies are well aware of this shortfall. Most MNEs see repatriation as important, yet just 20 percent conclude they manage it effectively for the executive or for the company.[106]

Unquestionably, job placement dominates repatriation concerns. Stress also arises in fitting back in with the home-country organization, changes in personal finances, and readjusting to life at home. Let's take a closer look at each.

Readjustment to Home-Country Organization   Going back to one's previous office poses problems for expats on several levels. Returnees may find that their former peers have been promoted above them; they may enjoy less autonomy as they return to being a "little fish in a big pond." Colleagues may question whether they've maintained cutting-edge market knowledge and technical skills during their "vacation" abroad. They may struggle to rejoin an office network that might not know quite what to do with them. In such situations, resentment often builds as executives reason that they have worked hard to progress professionally, sacrificed much for the company, and rightfully deserve a promotion.

A key cause of tension is the suspicion that "out of sight overseas" turns out to be "out of mind back home." This fear leads led many fast-tracking executives to decline an expatriate assignment. Effectively, going abroad means leaving the power center. Explains one executive, "MNEs station people abroad and then forget about them. If anything, advancement is even more difficult for the expat when he returns to headquarters, having missed out on opportunities to network with top management."[107]

This situation plays havoc in cultures, particularly collectivist types, where face time with the right people is critical to winning promotions. Some may actually interpret a foreign assignment as pushing them off the fast track by dumping them into a slow, periphery market—say, from booming Australia to mature Belgium.

More than half of returning expatriates report that their company had been vague about the repatriation process, their pending jobs, and future career progression. MNEs reply that repatriation puts them between a rock and a hard place. The expatriate's office cannot just sit vacant. Cost-cutting measures, mergers, or acquisitions changes company's plans and, by extension, its plans for the expatriate. Likewise, permitting repatriated employees to bump their "replacements" on return is unfair.

Still, expatriates are likely to stay if the company gives them chances to apply their expertise.[108] Increasingly, headquarters pushes expatriates them to short take more responsibility for their return, often encouraging them to spend a stint at the home office before completing their foreign assignment.

Changes in Personal Finances   Changes in personal finances can be dramatic upon returning home. Most expatriates enjoy rich benefits during their foreign assignment. Many live in exclusive neighborhoods, send their children to prestigious schools, employ domestic help, socialize with elites, and still save a good amount. Returning home to a reasonable compensation plan with far fewer perks and privileges can prove demoralizing.

Personal Readjustment   Readjusting to life at home is stressful.[109] Troubles emerge as returning expatriates and their families experience "reverse culture shock." Both need to relearn some of what they once took for granted. Meantime, children may struggle to fit into the local school system while spouses may feel isolated or out of touch with the career or friends they had, once again, left behind.

MANAGING REPATRIATION

MNEs are not blind to repatriation problems. Ignoring them is not an option. The greater the difficulties that confront returning expatriates, the greater the difficulty of convincing others to accept international assignments. Surveys report that three of four MNEs have written repatriation policies, whereas 95 percent have identified new jobs within the company for returning expats.[110]

Some companies, like Dow Chemical, pledge that repatriated employees will return to jobs at least as good as those they left behind. Others integrate foreign assignments into career planning and develop mentoring programs to look after the expats' domestic interests. PwC's EPIC program relies on several safety nets, promising participants that "unrivaled support mechanisms" safeguard their careers.[111] Prior to an international assignment, EPIC participants are linked to a mentor at home and a colleague awaiting their arrival overseas to help smooth the transition. Both share responsibly for supporting the expat's career development. Similarly, Avaya charges the manager who originally sponsored an expatriate with the job of helping that protégé find a job upon repatriation. Certainly, Avaya worries about the expat's career plan. Cold economics also play a part, given Avaya's stand that it has "invested in this person. To leave him overseas or to lose him to another company is a waste of money."[112]

Nevertheless, statistics show that many expatriates are unhappy upon return. Pressed to pinpoint where repatriation breakdown begins, they target the difficulty of returning to the right job. One report concludes, "People who have spent two years working in different ways across varied markets and cultures are not always happy to return to the same desk and the same prospects. In this vacuum of direction, many have a career 'wobble,' then leave via a recruitment market in which their experience is seen as increasingly valuable."[113]

Personal career management, therefore, is as vital to being selected for a foreign assignment as triumphantly returning home. Recall from our opening case the experience of Bryan Krueger, who accepted a four-year assignment in Tokyo without guarantee of a promotion when he got home. Krueger was conscientiously "proactive," networking avidly, keeping up with events at headquarters, and visiting the home office. Passivity is hazardous; navigating repatriation requires a keen sense of its positive and negative aspects—before departure, while abroad, and particularly before coming home.[114]

Looking to the

uture   Brainpower: Drains, Circulation, or Returns?

As capital, technology, and information grow more mobile among countries and companies, executive development increasingly explains competitive differences. Consequently, companies' access to and retention of more qualified personnel grows more important as they face the challenge of recruiting and retaining highly skilled workers.

Worker populations will grow much faster in emerging economies than in the wealthier countries through 2030 (China being the notable exception). Concurrently, the number of retirees in the wealthier countries will grow as people live longer and retire earlier. People will also require more education to qualify for better jobs. These trends indicate that there will be fewer people to do productive work in the wealthier countries. The countries are already trying to adjust, engaging in a range of education and training programs.[115] Still, these programs pose social and economic consequences to which MNEs must adapt.

Brain Drain

One adjustment might be for wealthier countries to encourage emigration from emerging economies that struggle to generate enough jobs for their swelling workforce. In Canada, the United States, and parts of Western Europe, there has been a long-term inward migration, both legally and illegally, of foreign workers from emerging economies. These movements generate assimilation costs within wealthier countries and, for developing economies, a brain drain as their highly qualified people migrate to other countries. Some, however, suggest that emigration benefits everyone by encouraging brain circulation among wealthier and developing economies.[116]

As fallout from the global financial crisis has spread, growing unemployment in advanced markets has altered migration patterns. Concern about creating jobs for locals often devolves into excluding foreigners who aspire to those positions.

This situation is particularly glaring in the American high-tech industry, which has relied extensively on foreign workers to staff operations in the United States. The industry maintains that the United States does not produce enough scientists and engineers to meet its demand; evidence suggests this is true, given that more than 60 percent of computer science Ph.D. students in the United States are internationals. Nevertheless, facing outcry from constituents seeking employment as well as nationalistic calls to put Americans to work in America, Congress imposed rules on immigration of foreign workers into the United States. Most notably, it reset the rules governing H-1B visas, the necessary visa permission that allows U.S. firms to employ highly qualified foreign workers temporarily.[117]

Times of economic downturns typically see unemployed workers blame foreign workers for their plight. Under this scenario, companies will have to spend more time getting work permits and integrating different nationalities into their workforces.

Labor-Saving Threats

Another potential adjustment in wealthier countries is the continued push toward adopting robotics and other laborsaving processes.[118] Although this may help solve some of the worker shortages, it escalates companies' need for workers who command higher skill levels. Less educated workers will likely face few prospects for "good jobs," thereby pushing them to compete with immigrants for lower-paying, less appealing jobs.

Gaps between haves and have-nots may widen within wealthier countries as well as between those countries and emerging economies. In this scenario, the growing ranks of the have-nots will likely lobby governments to push companies to shift technological development away from laborsaving priorities.

Brain Circulation

A third possible adjustment is accelerating business migration to emerging economies to tap rich supplies of inexpensive, productive labor. Concurrently, emerging economies may devise ways to support brain circulation or, if unsuccessful, to halt brain drain. Either approach will shift more entry-level production jobs from wealthier countries to their emerging counterparts.[119]

If successful, managers who return to their countries will likely shift many low-skilled jobs to their home market. Governments in wealthier countries will then face the problem of underqualified workers facing deteriorating job prospects.[120] ∎

Tel-Comm-Tek (TCT)[121]

In May 2011, Mark Hopkins of Tel-Comm-Tek (TCT) India, a US-headquartered MNE, announced his retirement. At the time, he was the managing director of the Indian subsidiary of TCT. During his tenure, Hopkins had led the dramatic increase in growth, market share, and profitability of the Indian operation. Upon his announcement, TCT began searching for his replacement.

TCT: A Brief Introduction

TCT manufactures a variety of small office equipment in 12 countries. It distributes and sells products such as copying machines, dictation units, laser printers, and paper shredders worldwide. Most recently, it reported sales in more than 85 countries. TCT has been in India since the early 1990s. Originally, it lacked its own in-country operation, relying on local agents to sell and services its products. Increasing sales led TCT India to open a marketing subsidiary in New Delhi in 1998 (see Map 20.1). Since then, the booming Indian IT industry has boosted its sales. Forecasts saw this accelerating over the next decade. Headquarters forecast TCT India becoming the center point of its expanding Asian operations. Collectively, these trends led TCT to expand its Indian operations with the addition of a manufacturing facility.

India: An Emerging Juggernaut

Fast Growth Some see India developing into the world's next big industrial power. This view has led many MNEs to increase their Indian operations. For example, IBM, a longtime customer of TCT, increased its Indian staff from a handful in 1998 to nearly 120,000 employees in 2012. TCT expects India's growth will push its total sales past those of the United States by 2020.

Improved Infrastructure Reinforcing TCT India's expansion plan is the evolving Indian transportation infrastructure. Improvement in highways, railways, and seaports boost the efficiency of product movement both in and out of the country. Management saw TCT India becoming a vital link in its global supply chain. Presently, it integrates input suppliers, production, and wholesalers in the United States and Europe. Long-term plans emphasize building supply points throughout Asia. TCT India was slated to function as the hub of this network.

Democratic Traditions India's independence in 1947 institutionalized a democratic tradition of accountability, transparency, and freedom. From 1947 through 1990, India's centrally planned economy had led to the infamous "License Raj," a situation marked by elaborate licenses and regulations that were administered by an entrenched, elaborate bureaucracy. In 1991, India began moving toward a free market marked by rising investment, trade, and operating freedom. Its transition, an ongoing process, has stabilized the economy and boosted India's attractiveness as a manufacturing site.

India: Laws and Legacies

Outmoded Labor Laws India's labor laws have been only slightly revised since its independence in 1947. They still impose many obstacles. For instance, it is difficult to fire workers even if a company hits hard times; India's Industrial Disputes Act, for example, requires any company employing 100 or more workers to get the state's permission before firing anyone.[122] Permission, often requires extensive negotiations and settlements. Consequently, "companies think twice, 10 times, before they hire new people,"

MAP 20.1 India

U.S.-based Tel-Comm-Tek (TCT), which makes small office equipment in 12 countries and sells in more than 85, opened an Indian sales office in the capital of New Delhi in 1998 and broke ground on a manufacturing plant in Bengaluru in 2012. India is a competitive location from which TCT can supply its markets throughout Asia. Headquarters expects that total sales through its Indian subsidiary will eventually surpass those in the United States.

Source: Central Intelligence Agency, "India," *The World Factbook 2009,* www.cia.gov (accessed October 23, 2009).

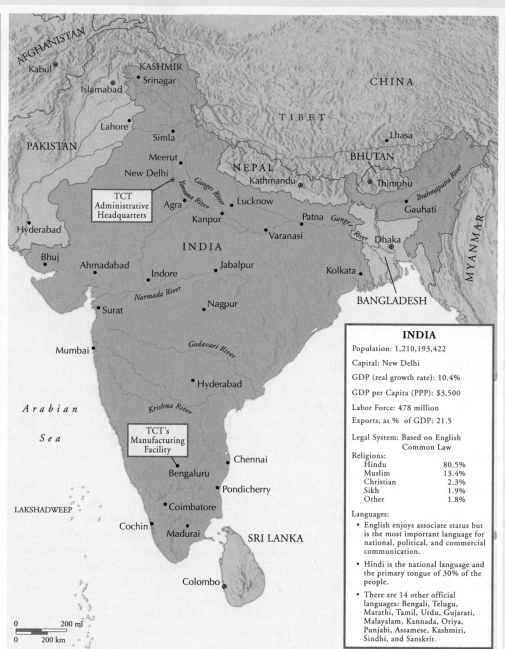

INDIA

Population: 1,210,193,422

Capital: New Delhi

GDP (real growth rate): 10.4%

GDP per Capita (PPP): $3,500

Labor Force: 478 million

Exports, as % of GDP: 21.5

Legal System: Based on English Common Law

Religions:
Hindu	80.5%
Muslim	13.4%
Christian	2.3%
Sikh	1.9%
Other	1.8%

Languages:
- English enjoys associate status but is the most important language for national, political, and commercial communication.
- Hindi is the national language and the primary tongue of 30% of the people.
- There are 14 other official languages: Bengali, Telugu, Marathi, Tamil, Urdu, Gujarati, Malayalam, Kannada, Oriya, Punjabi, Assamese, Kashmiri, Sindhi, and Sanskrit.

said the CEO of India's Hero Group.[123] Finally, some of India's labor laws discourage flexibility. MNEs, for example, are prohibited from allowing manufacturing workers to clock more than 54 hours of overtime in any three-month period, even if workers are willing to do so.

Anticompetitive Legislation   Although fading, a battery of laws restricts MNEs from competing in many Indian industries. These laws protect the millions of small enterprises operating in scattered villages throughout India. Another challenge is high tariffs. Put in place long ago to promote domestic production, they still apply to many imports, including a few that are inputs into products TCT India plans to manufacture.

Corruption India's business environment poses challenges. Its legal system, although endorsing the rule of law, struggles with corruption that is driven by its vast bureaucracy—a legacy of its centrally planned economy. Partial success dismantling the License Raj apparatus has promoted more regulatory transparency. Still, legacies of its inefficient past endure. High-tech MNEs, in particular, often struggled to enforce their intellectual property rights.

Moving Forward

In late 2011, TCT began building its first factory in Bengaluru, the center of India's Silicon Valley. The plant will make entry-level to high-end laser printers. The first production run was set for May 2012. TCT plans initially to supply the factory with components from its manufacturing facilities in Europe and the United States—at this point, it could import all with reasonable duties. Eventually, the company plans to make or buy the parts locally.

TCT India initially planned to hire 75 to 90 workers to run its assembly line. TCT anticipates no problems in hiring a skilled labor force given other MNEs' success stories. For example, the South Korean conglomerate LG looked to staff 458 assembly-line jobs at its new Indian factory. It required each applicant to have at least 15 years of education—a condition that translates into having both high school and technical college certification. Seeking a young workforce, LG also decided that no more than 1 percent of the workers have work experience. Ultimately, some 55,000 people qualified for interviews. Likewise, as a point of elaboration, some 4 million applied for 25,000 slots at Infosys in 2010, a prominent Indian IT MNE.[124]

TCT enlisted a U.S. engineering firm to supervise construction of its Bengaluru plant. Upon completion, TCT will "turn over the key" to the on-site factory director, Gary Kent, a technically experienced U.S. expatriate sent to run it. Mr. Kent will rely on translators as needed. He will report to TCT's U.S. headquarters on production, quality control, and supply chain logistics. He will also report to TCT India's managing director in New Delhi (the position made vacant by Hopkins' retirement) on support activities like accounting, finance, and labor relations. The managing director of TCT India, in turn, will report to Michael Stephens, direction of TCT's Asian Regional Office in Singapore. It is anticipated that in the next 12 to 18 months Mr. Kent will return to United States, at which time the managing director of TCT India will assume his duties.

Selecting the Managing Director

TCT fills executive vacancies by internal promotion. It uses a mix of home-, host-, and third-country nationals to staff slots in foreign countries. It rotates managers among its foreign and U.S. locations, believing international experience is a key facet of leadership.

Tom Wallace
Source: Andresr/Shutterstock.com

The Candidates

The Asian Regional Office charged a selection committee to nominate the new managing director for TCT India. The committee identified six candidates:

- **Tom Wallace** A 30-year TCT veteran, Wallace is knowledgeable and experienced in the technical and sales aspects of the job. He has worked with Mr. Kent on several projects in developing supply chain initiatives in the United States. Although he has never worked abroad, he has toured the company's foreign operations and recently expressed interest in an expatriate slot. His superiors typically rate his performance as excellent.

  Wallace is due to retire in about seven years; he and his wife speak only English. They have three grown children who live with their own families in the United States. Presently, Wallace manages a U.S.-based operation that is a little larger than the present size of TCT India. The merger of his unit with another TCT division will eliminate his current position in six months.

- **Brett Harrison** Harrison, 44, has spent 15 years with TCT running both line activities as well as supervising staff. His superiors consider him highly competent and poised to move into upper-level management within the next few years. For the past three

Brett Harrison
Source: EDHAR/Shutterstock.com

years, he has worked in the Asian Regional Office and has regularly toured TCT's Asian operations.

Both he and his wife have traveled to India a few times and are somewhat familiar with its geography, politics, customs, and outlooks. The Harrisons know other expatriates in the Bengaluru region. Their children, ages 14 and 16, have vacationed in India with their parents. Mrs. Harrison is a midlevel executive with a multinational pharmaceuticals company. It presently does not have an Indian operation.

Atasi Das
Source: Amy Dunn/Shutterstock.com

- **Atasi Das** Born in the United States, Das joined TCT 16 years ago after earning her MBA from a university in New England. At 45, she has successfully moved between staff and line positions and assumed broader responsibilities in strategic planning. For two years, she was the assistant director of a product group that was about half the size of TCT India. Her performance regularly earns excellent ratings. Currently, she works on a planning team based at TCT headquarters.

  Upon joining TCT, she stated her goal was to work around the world, noting an undergraduate major in international management as evidence of her long-term interest. She recently reiterated her interest in international responsibilities, seeing it as an essential career step. She speaks Hindi and is unmarried. Her parents, who now live in the United States, are first-generation immigrants from India. A few relatives live in India's northern states, Kashmir and Punjab.

Ravi Desai
Source: C Samford/Shutterstock.com

- **Ravi Desai** Desai, 35, is currently an assistant managing director in TCT Asia who oversees production and sales for Singapore and Malaysia. A citizen of India, he has spent his 10 years with TCT working in various operational slots throughout Asia. He holds an MBA from the prestigious Indian Institute of Management. Some see him as a likely candidate to direct the Indian operation eventually. He is married, has two children (ages 2 and 7), and speaks English and Hindi well. His wife, also a native of India, neither works outside the home nor speaks English.

- **Jalan Bukit Seng** Seng, 52, is the managing director of TCT's assembly operation in Malaysia. A citizen of Singapore, he has primarily worked in Singapore or Malaysia. He has regularly commuted to various TCT factories, helping to reset production systems and supervising equipment refits. He earned an undergraduate and M.B.A. degrees from the National University of Singapore. Seng is fluent in Singapore's four official languages: Malay, English, Mandarin, and Tamil. His performance reviews are consistently positive, with a periodic ranking of excellent. Seng is unmarried but has family members in Singapore and Malaysia.

Jalan Bukit Seng
Source: Ajay Bhaskar/Shutterstock.com

- **Saumitra Chakraborty** At 33, Chakraborty is the assistant to the departing managing director in India. He has held that position since joining TCT India upon graduating from a small private university in Europe six years earlier. Unmarried, he consistently earns a job performance rating of competent in operational matters and exceptional in customer relationship management. Presently, he lacks line experience. He has successfully increased TCT India's sales, somewhat owing to his personal connections with prominent Indian families and government officials, along with his skillfulness in the ways of the Indian business environment. Besides speaking India's main languages of English and Hindi fluently, Chakraborty speaks Kannada (the local language of Bengaluru).

QUESTIONS

1. Identify the advantages of each candidate. Identify their liabilities. Rank order the candidates, from high to low.
2. What challenges might the person you recommend encounter if named the managing director?
3. How might your recommended candidates minimize those challenges?
4. What guidelines do you advise TCT to follow in designing the compensation package?
5. Returning to material covered in Chapter 15—specifically that dealing with the idea of a matrix organization. Do you see any benefit to appointing two individuals to the same post? For example, one individual would direct internal affairs, while the other would manage external affairs. What might be the likely benefits and problems with this arrangement?

Saumitra Chakraborty
Source: Kharidehal Abhirama Ashwin/Shutterstock.com

Now that you have finished this chapter, go back to www.myiblab.com to continue practicing and applying the concepts you've learned.

SUMMARY

- The task of HRM is putting the right person into the right job at the right place at the right time at the right pay. Effective HRM policies support the MNE's strategy to create value.

- Market developments, workforce demographics, globalization, and technology are converging to create an unprecedented demand for expatriate talent.

- Market trends and competitive challenges push MNEs to use short-term assignments, cross-border commuter assignments, and extended business travel in lieu of traditional longer-term "permanent assignments."

- The ethnocentric framework approach fills foreign management positions with home-country nationals. The polycentric framework uses host-country nationals to manage local subsidiaries. The geocentric framework seeks the best people for key jobs throughout the organization, regardless of nationality.

- Executives transferred from headquarters to local operations are more likely to understand the company's core competencies. However, an ethnocentric framework can impose a narrow perspective.

- MNEs often employ more locals than expatriate managers because the former understand local circumstances and require less compensation. In addition, they demonstrate that opportunities are open to hard-working people as well as respond to national interests.

- Selecting an individual for an expatriate position is influenced by the candidate's technical competence, adaptiveness, and leadership ability.

- MNEs use expatriates to transfer technical competence and home-country business practices, control foreign operations, develop leadership skills, and diffuse the organization culture.

- Training and predeparture preparations include general country orientation, cultural sensitivity, and practical training. They reduce the odds of expatriate failure. Increasingly, preparations include the expatriate's spouse and family.

- Expatriate failure, narrowly defined, is the manager's premature return home due to poor performance. Broadly defined, it is the failure of the MNE's selection policies to find individuals who succeed abroad.

- The primary causes of expatriate failure are difficulty adjusting to new environment and a spouse and/or family who struggle with the foreign assignment.

- Hardships and cost-of-living differences, among other aspects, moderate an expatriate's compensation.

- Compensation must neither overly reward nor unduly punish the expatriate. Most MNEs use the balance sheet approach to manage this dilemma. Compensation practices by emerging market MNEs, given their typically lower salary scales, complicate application.

- Repatriation, the act of returning home from a foreign assignment, is difficult. Finding the right job for the expatriate to return to is a consistent challenge.

KEY TERMS

balance sheet approach (p. 781)
culture shock (p. 778)
ethnocentric framework (p. 766)
expatriate (p. 764)
expatriate selection (p. 773)

expatriate failure (p. 775)
geocentric framework (p. 770)
home-country national (p. 764)
human resource management (HRM)
  (p. 761)

localization (p. 766)
polycentric framework (p. 768)
repatriation (p. 785)
third-country national (p. 764)

ENDNOTES

1 *Sources include the following:* "In Search of Global Leaders: View of Jeffery Immelt, Chairman and CEO, General Electric," *Harvard Business Review* (August 1, 2003); B. Ettorre, "A Brave New World," *Management Review* (1993):10–16; M. Larson, "More Employees Go Abroad as International Operations Grow," *Workforce Management* (June 1, 2006); J. Fraser and J. Oppenheim, "What's New About Globalization?" *The McKinsey Quarterly* (1997):168–179; "Go East, My Son," *The Economist* (August 10, 2006):78; "China's Recruitment Market Is Booming," *The Economist* (September 21, 2006):46; S. Jones, "Going Stateside: Once the Overseas Hitch Is Over, Homeward-Bound Expats Hit Turbulence," *Crain's Chicago Business* (July 24, 2000); B. Newman, "Expat Archipelago," *Wall Street Journal* (Retrieved December 12, 1995):A1; R. Pelton, "The World's Most Dangerous Places," *Harper Resource* (2003); Joe Sharkey, "Global Economy Is Leading to More Dangerous Places," *New York Times* (April 19, 2005); M. Schoeff, "P&G Places a Premium on International Experience," *Workforce Management* (April 10, 2006):28; E. Marx, "Route to the Top, 2006," Cranfield University School of Management, (2007); Robert Half Global Financial Employment Monitor, retrieved April 29, 2009, from www.rhi.com/OurServices; Global Relocation Trends 2010, *GMAC Global Relocations Services*, www.gmac.com; Early PwC International Challenge, (EPIC), retrieved May 21, 2009, from www.pwc.com/extweb/career.nsf/docid/9204374F898F3E5A8525748F00741E9D.

2 "Staffing Globalisation: Travelling More Lightly," *The Economist* (June 23, 2006).

3 "Globalisation: The Empire Strikes Back," *The Economist* (September 18, 2008):51.

4 Joe Sharkey, "Global Economy Is Leading To More Dangerous Places," *New York Times* (April 19, 2005):C-3.

5 "Globalisation: The Empire Strikes Back."

6 "Schumpeter: The Tussle for Talent," *The Economist* (January 6, 2011).

7 "Routes to the Top: How CEOs embrace Global Mobility," Global Mobility Articles and Studies, retrieved June 6, 2011, from www. articles.totallyexpat.com/routes-to-the-top-how-ceos-embrace-global-mobility,

8 Paula Caligiuri and Victoria Di Santo, "Global Competence: What Is it, and Can It Be Developed through Global Assignments?" *Human Resource Planning* (September 2001):27–36; Mark Morgan, "Career-Building Strategies: It's Time to Do a Job Assessment: Are Your Skills Helping You up the Corporate Ladder?" *Strategic Finance* (June 2002):38–44.

9 Hoon Park, "Global Human Resource Management: A Synthetic Approach." *The Journal of International Business and Economics* (2002):28–51.

10 William Judge, "Is a Leader's Character Culture-Bound or Culture-Free? An Empirical Comparison of the Character Traits of American and Taiwanese CEOs," *Journal of Leadership Studies* 8 (Fall 2001):63–79.

11 Keith Brouthers, "Institutional, Cultural and Transaction Cost Influences on Entry Mode Choice and Performance," *Journal of International Business Studies* 33 (Summer 2002):203–222.

12 Ben Kedia, Richard Nordtvedt, and Liliana M. Perez, "International Business Strategies, Decision-Making Theories, and Leadership Styles: An Integrated Framework," *Competitiveness Review* 12 (Winter–Spring 2002):38–53.

13 Sully Taylor, Schon Beechler, and Nancy Napier, "Toward an Integrative Model of Strategic International Resource Management," *Academy of Management Review* 21 (1996):959–985, discuss these models in the context of multidomestic and a combination of global and transnational strategies.

14 Watson Wyatt Worldwide, "Human Capital Index: Human Capital as a Lead Indicator of Shareholder Value," retrieved November 27, 2007, from www.watsonwyatt.com/research/resrender.asp?id=w-488&page=1

15 See, for example, N. Khatri, "Managing Human Resource for Competitive Advantage: A Study of MNEs in Singapore," *International Journal of Human Resource Management* 11:2 (2000):336.

16 "Travelling More Lightly," *The Economist* (June 22, 2006).

17 "A Special Report on Innovation in Emerging Markets: The World Turned Upside Down," *The Economist*, retrieved 21, 2011, from www.economist.com/node/15879369

18 Leslie Klaff, "Thinning the Ranks of the Career Expats," *Workforce Management* (October 2004):84–87.

19 Yvonne Sonsino, reported in "Travelling More Lightly." See also Mercer LLC, "International Assignments Increasing."

20 PwC International Challenge (EPIC), retrieved May 4, 2009, from www.pwc.com/extweb/career.nsf/docid/9204374F898F3E5A85257 48F00741E9D

21 Global Relocation Trends, *GMAC Global Relocations Services*, retrieved April 21, 2011, from www.gmac.com, .

22 "More Females Sent on International Assignment than ever Before, Survey Finds," retrieved April 25, 2009, from www.mercer.com/pressrelease/details.htm?idContent=1246090

23 Calvin Reynolds, "Strategic Employment of Third Country Nationals: Keys to Sustaining the Transformation of HR Functions," *Human Resource Planning* 20 (March 1997):33–50.

24 Jeffrey Joerres, "Beyond Expats: Better Managers for Emerging Markets," *McKinsey Quarterly* (May 2011).

25 "Financial Careers: Go East, Young Moneyman," *The Economist* (April 16, 2011):79–80.

26 *Global Relocation Trends: 2011 Survey Report*, Brookfield Global Relocation Services, retrieved June 15, 2011, from www.brookfieldgrs.com/insights_ideas/grts

27 Karina Frayter, "IBM to Laid-off: Want a Job in India?, retrieved April 29, 2009, from http://money.cnn.com/2009/02/05/news/MNEs/ibm_jobs

28 Adrian Wooldridge, "The Battle for the Best," *The Economist: The World in 2007*.

29 Chi-fai Chan and Neil Holbert, "Marketing Home and Away: Perceptions of Managers in Headquarters and Subsidiaries," *Journal of World Business* 36 (Summer 2001):205.

30 "Staffing Globalisation."

31 Tsun-yan Hsieh, Johanne Lavoie, and Robert Samek, "Are You Taking Your Expatriate Talent Seriously?" *The McKinsey Quarterly* (Summer 1999):71.

32 "Staffing Globalisation."

33 William C. Weldon, "Chairman's Letter: To Our Shareholders," *Annual Report 2006* (Johnson & Johnson, 2007), retrieved November 27, 2007, from http://jnj.v1.papiervirtuel.com/report/2007030901

34 PricewaterhouseCoopers LLP and Cranfield School of Management, "Measuring the Value of International Assignments" (November 9, 2006), at www.som.cranfield.ac.uk/som/news/story.asp?id=329

35 Vijay Pothukuchi, Fariborz Damanpour, Jaepil Choi, Chao C. Chen, and Seung Ho Park, "National and Organizational Culture Differences and International Joint Venture Performance," *Journal of International Business Studies* 33 (Summer 2002):243–266.

36 J. Kahn, "The World's Most Admired MNEs," *Fortune* (October 11, 1999):267.

37 Kahn, "The World's Most Admired MNEs."

38 "Tylenol (Acetaminophen) to Be Available in Japan in Early Fall, 2000," *Doctor's Guide*, retrieved June 15, 2011, from www.pslgroup.com/dg/1d9dfa.htm

39 David Ahlstrom, Garry Bruton, and Eunice S. Chan, "HRM of Foreign Firms in China: The Challenge of Managing Host Country Personnel," *Business Horizons* 44 (May 2001):59.

40 "High-Tech Nomads: These Engineers Work as Temps on Wireless Projects All over the World," *Time* (November 26, 2001):B20; B. Kedia and A. Mukherji, "Global Managers: Developing a Mindset for Global Competitiveness," *Journal of World Business* 34 (Fall 1999):30.

41 "In Search of Global Leaders: View of Fred Hassan, Chairman and CEO, Schering-Plough," *Harvard Business Review* (August 1, 2003).

42 A. Wendlandt, "The Name Game Is a Puzzle for Expats at Work," *Financial Times* (August 15, 2000):3.

43 The type of ownership of its foreign operations influences an MNE's staffing policy. Expatriates transferred abroad to a foreign joint venture, for example, may find themselves in ambiguous situations, unsure of whom they represent and uncertain of whether they report to both partners or to the partner that transferred them. Typically, MNEs insist on using their own executives when they're concerned that local personnel may make decisions in their own interest rather than that of the joint venture.

44 Global Relocation Trends, *GMAC Global Relocations Services*, retrieved April 21, 2011, from www.gmac.com

45 "Big US Firms Shift Hiring Abroad," *Wall Street Journal* (April 19, 2011):B1.

46 "Financial Careers: Go East, Young Moneyman."

47 H. Seligson, "Shut Out at Home, Americans Seek Opportunity in China," NYTimes.com, retrieved May 4, 2011, from www.nytimes.com/2009/08/11/business/economy/11expats.html

48 *Global Relocation Trends: 2011 Survey Report.*

49 Wooldridge, "The Battle for the Best."

50 View of Y. Sonsino, a partner at Mercer, reported in "Staffing Globalisation: Travelling More Lightly," *Economist Intelligence Unit* (June 23, 2006).

51 Caligiuri and Di Santo, "Global Competence"; Hsieh et al., "Are You Taking Your Expatriate Talent Seriously?"

52 Susan Schneider and Rosalie Tung, "Introduction to the International Human Resource Management Special Issue," *Journal of World Business* 36 (Winter 2001):341–346.

53 "In Search of Global Leaders: View of Stephen Green, Group CEO, HSBC," *Harvard Business Review* (August 1, 2003). At the company level, Google's decision to reroute its servers to Hong Kong after refusing China's calls to censor e-mails highlights adaptiveness.

54 S. Jun, J. Gentry, and Y. Hyun, "Cultural Adaptation of Business Expatriates in the Host Marketplace," *Journal of International Business Studies* 32 (Summer 2001):369.

55 "Business in China and the West: A Tale of Two Expats," *The Economist* (December 29, 2010).

56 *The New International Executive Business Leadership for the 21st Century* (Harvard Business School and Amrop International, 1995); Reported in Andrew Crisp, "International Careers Made Easy," *The European* (March 24, 1995):27.

57 Wooldridge, "The Battle for the Best."

58 John. Daniels and Gary Insch, "Why Are Early Departure Rates from Foreign Assignments Lower Than Historically Reported?" *Multinational Business Review* 6:1 (1998):13–23.

59 "Global Relocation Trends Survey 2010 | Global Mobility Articles and Studies." retrieved April 4, 2011, from www.articles.totallyexpat.com/global-relocation-trends-survey-2010; Global Relocation Trends 2010, *GMAC Global Relocations Services*, retrieved April 21, 2011, from www.gmac.com

60 Data provided by National Foreign Trade Council. Maria L. Kraimer, Sandy Wayne, and Renata Jaworski, "Sources of Support and Expatriate Performance: The Mediating Role of Expatriate Adjustment," *Personnel Psychology* 54 (Spring 2001):71.

61 *Global Relocation Trends*, GMAC Global Relocations Services, retrieved April 21, 2011, from www.gmac.com

62 M. Shaffer, D. Harrison, M. Gilley, and D. Luk, "Struggling for Balance amid Turbulence on International Assignments: Work-Family Conflict, Support and Commitment," *Journal of Management* 27 (January–February 2001):99; Chris Moss, "Expats: Thinking of Living and Working Abroad?" *The Guardian* (October 19, 2000):4.

63 "In Search of Global Leaders."

64 Ibid.

65 Diane E. Lewis, "Families Make, Break Overseas Moves," *Boston Globe* (October 4, 1998):5D. "Expat Spouses: It Takes Two," *Financial Times* (March 1, 2002):C-1; Klaff, "Thinning the Ranks of the Career Expats."

66 "Expat Spouses: It Takes Two."

67 *Global Relocation Trends: 2011 Survey Report*; *The Expat Explorer Survey 2010*, HSBC Bank International, survey of 4,127 expatriates form more than 100 countries.

68 Chris Brewster, "Making Their Own Way: International Experience Through Self-Initiated Foreign Assignments," *Journal of World Business* 35 (Winter 2000):417; Vesa Suutari, Kerr Inkson, Judith Pringle, Michael B. Arthur, and Sean Barry, "Expatriate Assignment versus Overseas Experience: Contrasting Models of International Human Resource Development," *Journal of World Business* 32 (1997):351–368.

69 D. Ones and C. Viswesvaran, "Relative Importance of Personality Dimensions for Expatriate Selection: A Policy Capturing Study," *Human Performance* 12 (1999):275–294.

70 Valerie Frazee, "Send Your Expats Prepared for Success," *Workforce* 78 (March 1999):S6.

71 S. Larson, "More Employees Go Abroad as International Operations Grow," Workforce.com, retrieved April 27, 2009, from www.workforce.com/index.html

72 *Global Relocation Trends: 2011 Survey Report.*

73 C. Panella, "Meeting the Needs of International Business: A Customer Service-Oriented Business Language Course," *The Journal of Language for International Business* 9 (1998):65–75; M. Inman, "How Foreign Language Study Can Enhance Career Possibilities" (Washington DC: ERIC Clearinghouse on Languages and Linguistics, 1987), retrieved November 27, 2007, from www.ericdigests.org/pre-927/career.htm; C. Randlesome and A. Myers, "Cultural Fluency: Results from a UK and Irish Survey," *Business Communication Quarterly* 60:3 (1997):9–22.

74 S. Baker, "Catching the Continental Drift: These Days, English Will Suffice for Americans Working in Europe," *Business Week* (August 14, 2001).

75 C. Cole, "Bridging the Language Gap: Expatriates Find Learning Korean Key to Enjoying a More Satisfying Life," *The Korea Herald* (August 16, 2002).

76 M. Ligos, "The Foreign Assignment: An Incubator, or Exile?" *New York Times* (October 22, 2000):A-1.

77 View of the American Council on the Teaching of Foreign Languages, reported in Tanya Mohn, "All Aboard the Foreign Language Express," *New York Times* (October 11, 2000):A-1.

78 "English Is Coming: The Adverse Side-Effects of the Growing Dominance of English," *The Economist* (February 14, 2009):85.

79 M. Joseph, "India Faces a Linguistic Truth - English Spoken Here," *New York Times* (February 16, 2011):B-1.

80 European Commission, "Languages of Europe," *Education and Training*, retrieved July 18, 2007, from http://europa.eu. int/comm/education/policies/lang/languages/index_en.html

81 "Global Spread of English Poses Problems for UK," *People's Daily Online* (February 18, 2006).

82 A. Sitze, "Language of Business: Can E-Learning Help International MNEs Speak a Common Language?" *Online Learning* (March 2002):19–23.

83 PricewaterhouseCoopers, *International Assignments: European Policy and Practice* (1997), www.pwcglobal.com/extweb/ncsurvres.nsf

84 "In Search of Global Leaders: View of Fred Hassan, Chairman and CEO, Schering-Plough," *Harvard Business Review* (August 1, 2003).

85 Estimate reported in the second annual study of expatriate issues, conducted from January through March 2002, sponsored by CIGNA International Expatriate Benefits; the National Foreign Trade Council, an association of multinational MNEs that supports open international trade and investment; and WorldatWork, retrieved September 2, 2005, from www.prnewswire.com/micro/CI9

86 "Measuring the Value of International Assignments."

87 C. Gould, "What's the Latest in Global Compensation?" *Global Workforce* (July 1997):28.

88 G. Latta, "Expatriate Policy and Practice: A Ten-Year Comparison of Trends," *Compensation and Benefits Review* 31:4 (1999):35–39, quoting studies reported by Organization Resources Counselors.

89 "Business in China and the West: A Tale of Two Expats," *The Economist* (December 29, 2010):65.

90 "Designing Competitive Expatriate Compensation Packages," Mercer, retrieved May 3, 2009, from www.mercer.com/referencecontent.htm?idContent=1303865

91 This practice, however, appears to be disappearing, especially for assignments in so-called world capitals like New York, London, and Tokyo, in which many executives are interested and where there is (relatively) little "deprivation." In addition, the number and nature of "hardships" resulting from foreign assignments are in decline, particularly as advances in transportation and communications enable expatriates to keep in closer contact with home countries;

the openness of economies allows them to buy familiar goods and services; and the general level of housing, schooling, and medical services increasingly meets their needs.

92 A U.S. family based in China, for example, commonly spends more money to get the same goods than they would buy back home. Why? Because they prefer Western items that must be imported and have thus been subjected to high tariffs. Expatriates often obtain food and housing at rates higher than going local rates because they don't know the language well, where to buy, or how to bargain.

93 Towers Perrin and CIGNA, for example, specialize in international compensation. In addition, MNEs rely on estimates of cost-of-living differences—even if they are imperfect. MNEs commonly use such sources as the U.S. State Department's cost-of-living index, published yearly in *Labor Developments Abroad,* the UN *Monthly Bulletin of Statistics,* and surveys by the *Financial Times,* P-E International, Business International, and the Staff Papers of the International Monetary Fund.

94 Adapted from "Cost of Living survey 2010—City rankings," retrieved April 5, 2011, from www.mercer.com/press-releases/13111 45?siteLanguage=100

95 "Home Away from Home: Expatriate Housing in Asia," *The Korea Herald* (May 2, 2002).

96 "Tokyo Tops in H.K. Survey on Living Cost for Expatriates," *Japan Economic Newswire* (January 24, 2002).

97 A. Maitland, "A Hard Balancing Act: Management of Dual Careers," *Financial Times* (May 10, 1999):11.

98 V. Frazee, "Expert Help for Dual-Career Spouses," *Workforce* 78 (March 1999):S18.

99 J. Clark, "Added Global Risks Impact Security Planning for Oil, Gas Expat Workers," *The Oil and Gas Journal* (April 2002):32–37.

100 R. Ceniceros, "Precautions, Training Can Lessen Risk of Kidnapping," *Business Insurance* 35 (May 14, 2001):26.

101 "The Expat Explorer Survey 2010," HSBC Bank International, retrieved April 4, 2011, from www.expatexplorer.hsbc.com/files/pdfs/overall-reports/2010/experience.pdf

102 Mercer, "International Assignments Increasing."

103 Gould, "What's the Latest in Global Compensation?"

104 "In Search of Global Leaders."

105 "New Survey Suggests Ways to Maximize Expatriate Performance and Loyalty," *Internet Wire* (March 27, 2001). Estimates reported at 2001 National Foreign Trade Council's International HR Management Symposium. Klaff, "Thinning the Ranks of the Career Expats"; J. Barbian, "Return to Sender: MNEs That Fail to Effectively Manage Employees Returning from a Foreign Assignment May Find Their Investments Permanently Hitting the Road," *Training* 39 (January 2002):40–43.

106 PricewaterhouseCoopers LLP and Cranfield School of Management, "Understanding and Avoiding Barriers to International Mobility," *Geodesy,* (October 2005), retrieved November 27, 2007, from www.pwc.extweb/pwcpublications.nfs/docid/7ACA93FA424E80E88525121E006E82C/$file/geodesy.pdf

107 "In Search of Global Leaders: View of Daniel Meiland, Executive Chairman, Egon Zehender International," *Harvard Business Review* (August 1, 2003).

108 "Global Relocation Trends 2008," GMAC Global Relocations Services, www.gmac.com

109 M. Lazarova and P. Caligiuri, "Retaining Repatriates: The Role of Organizational Support Practices," *Journal of World Business* 36 (Winter 2001):389–402.

110 "In Search of Global Leaders."

111 PwC International Challenge, retrieved May 4, 2009, from www.pwc.com/extweb/career.nsf/docid/9204374F898F3E5A8525748F00 741E9D

112 Klaff, "Thinning the Ranks of the Career Expats."

113 "Abroad but Not Forgotten: Improving the Career Management of Employees on International Assignments," *Human Resource Management International Digest* 15 (2007):29–31.

114 I. Varner and T. Palmer, "Successful Expatriation and Organizational Strategies," *Review of Business* 23 (Spring 2002):8–12; J. Selmer, "Practice Makes Perfect? International Experience and Expatriate Adjustment," *Management International Review* 42 (January 2002):71–88.

115 The Annecy Symposium, "The Future of Work, Employment and Social Protection," *International Labour Review* 140 (Winter 2001):453–475.

116 A. Saxenian, "Brain Circulation: How High-Skill Immigration Makes Everyone Better Off," *Brookings Review* 20 (Winter 2002):28–32; M. Naim, "The New Diaspora," *Foreign Policy* (July–August 2002):96–98.

117 "H-1B Visas Applications to Decline, Target Existing Workers," *Workforce Management* (Winter 2009).

118 M. Poster, "Workers as Cyborgs: Labor and Networked Computers," *Journal of Labor Research* 23 (Summer 2002):339–354.

119 "We Must Halt the Brain-Drain," *Africa News Service* (December 17, 2001).

120 "The Poorest Are Again Losing Ground," *Business Week* (April 23, 2001):130.

121 Sources include the following: Central Intelligence Agency, "India"; *The World Factbook,* at www.cia.gov/cia/publications/factbook/geos/in.html; Library of Congress, "A Country Study: India," *Country Studies*), at http://memory.loc.gov/frd/cs/intoc.html; "Hungry Tiger, Dancing Elephant," *The Economist* (April 4, 2007); "Virtual Champions, Survey: Business in India," *The Economist* (June 1, 2006); Manu Joseph, "India Faces a Linguistic Truth—English Spoken Here," *New York Times* (February 16, 2011).

121 "Economics Focus: The Himalayas of Hiring," *The Economist* (August 7, 2010):76.

121 K. Bradsher, "A Younger India Is Flexing Its Industrial Brawn," *New York Times* (September 1, 2006):A-1

122 "Economics Focus: The Himalayas of Hiring.

123 K. Bradsher, "A Younger India Is Flexing Its Industrial Brawn.

124 "Infosys Rejects 94% Job Applicants, also Gets Rejected by Many," *Economic Times,* retrieved May 24, 2011, from articles.economictimes.indiatimes.com/2010-05-31/news/27624027_1_net-addition-gross-addition-applicants.

glossary

Absolute advantage: A theory first presented by Adam Smith, which holds that because certain countries can produce some goods more efficiently than other countries, they should specialize in and export those things they can produce more efficiently and trade for other things they need.

Acceptable quality level (AQL): A concept of quality control whereby managers are willing to accept a certain level of production defects, which are dealt with through repair facilities and service centers.

Accounting: The process of collecting and analyzing data for internal and external users of information.

Acquired advantage: A form of trade advantage due to technology rather than due to the availability of natural resources, climate, etc.

Acquired group membership: Affiliation not determined by birth, such as religions, political affiliations, and professional and other associations.

Active income: Income of a CFC that is derived from the active conduct of a trade or business, as specified by the U.S. Internal Revenue Code.

Ad valorem duty: A duty (tariff) assessed as a percentage of the value of the item.

ADR: *See* American Depositary Receipt.

Advance import deposit: A form of foreign-exchange convertibility control where the government tightens control of import licenses and requires importers to make a deposit with the central bank.

AFTA: *See* ASEAN Free Trade Area.

Agglomeration: A theory that competitive companies may gain efficiencies by locating near each other.

American Depositary Receipt (ADR): A negotiable certificate issued by a U.S. bank in the United States to represent the underlying shares of a foreign corporation's stock held in trust at a custodian bank in the foreign country.

American terms: The practice of using the direct quote for exchange rates.

Andean Community (CAN): A South American form of economic integration involving Bolivia, Colombia, Ecuador, Peru, and Venezuela.

APEC: *See* Asia Pacific Economic Cooperation.

Appropriability theory: The theory that companies will favor foreign direct investment over such nonequity operating forms as licensing arrangements so that potential competitors will be less likely to gain access to proprietary information.

Arab League: A group similar to PAFTA but with more representative countries and political rather than economic objectives.

Arbitrage: The process of buying and selling foreign currency at a profit that results from price discrepancies between or among markets.

Arm's-length price: A price between two companies that do not have an ownership interest in each other.

Ascribed group membership: Affiliation determined by birth, such as those based on gender, family, age, caste, and ethnic, racial, or national origin.

ASEAN: *See* Association of South East Asian Nations.

ASEAN Free Trade Area (AFTA): A free trade area formed by the ASEAN countries on January 1, 1993, with the goal of cutting tariffs on all intrazonal trade to a maximum of 5 percent by January 1, 2008.

Asia Pacific Economic Cooperation (APEC): A cooperation formed by 21 countries that border the Pacific Rim to promote multilateral economic cooperation in trade and investment in the Pacific Rim.

Association of South East Asian Nations (ASEAN): A free trade area involving the Asian countries of Brunei, Indonesia, Malaysia, the Philippines, Singapore, and Thailand.

Authoritarianism: A system of government in which leaders are not subjected to the test of free elections and who suppress individual freedoms.

Back translation: A method to check the validity of translations by having one person translate to another language and a second person translate it back to the original.

Balance of payments: Statement that summarizes all economic transactions between a country and the rest of the world during a given period of time.

Balance-of-payments deficit: An imbalance of some specific component within the balance of payments, such as merchandise trade or current account, that implies that a country is importing more than it exports.

Balance-of-payments effects: The impact of a foreign direct investment on imports, exports and capital flows.

Balance-of-payments surplus: An imbalance in the balance of payments that exists when a country exports more than it imports.

Balance of trade: The value of a country's exports less the value of its imports ("trade" can be defined as merchandise trade, services, unilateral transfers, or some combination of these three).

Balanced scorecard: An approach to performance measurement that endeavors to more closely link the strategic and financial perspectives of a business and take a broad view of business performance.

Balance sheet approach: Compensation plan that sets expatriate salaries to equalize purchashing power across countries.

Bank for International Settlements (BIS): A bank in Basel, Switzerland, that facilitates transactions among central banks; it is effectively the central banks' central bank.

Bargaining school theory: A theory holding that the negotiated terms for foreign investors depend on how much investors and host countries need each other's assets.

Barriers to entry: Factors that make it difficult or costly for firms to enter an industry or market.

Barter: The exchange of goods for goods or services instead of for money.

Base currency: The currency whose value is implicitly 1 when a quote is made between two currencies; for example, if the Brazilian real is trading at 1.9 reals (reais) per dollar, the dollar is the base currency and the real is the quoted currency.

Bid (buy) rate: The amount a trader is willing to pay for foreign exchange.

Bilateral agreement: An agreement between two countries.

Bilateral integration: A form of integration between two countries in which they decide to cooperate more closely together, usually in the form of tariff reductions.

BIS: *See* Bank for International Settlements.

Black market: The foreign-exchange market that lies outside the official market.

Booking center: An offshore financial center whose main function is to act as an accounting center in order to minimize the payment of taxes.

Born-global company: A company that adopts a global orientation from inception.

Base of the Pyramid: The billions of people living on less than a few dollars per day yet who some see as the next market frontier of the global economy.

Boundaries: In terms of political environments, an official or perceived point of separation that defines the boundary of a nation. In terms of organization structure, horizontal constraints that follow from having specific employees only do specific jobs in specific units as well as the vertical constraints that separate employees into specific levels of a precisely stipulated command-and-control hierarchy.

Boundarylessness: State whereby companies build organizations that eliminate the vertical, horizontal, and external boundaries that impede information flows and hinder developing relationship.

Brain drain: A condition whereby countries lose potentially productive resources when its bright people migrate to other countries.

Bretton Woods Agreement: An agreement among IMF countries to promote exchange-rate stability and to facilitate the international flow of currencies.

Broker (in foreign exchange): Specialists who facilitate transactions in the interbank market.

Bureaucratic control: System whereby an organization uses centralized authority to install rules and procedures to govern activities.

Business environment: The economic, political, legal, and cultural context of business activity.

Buy local legislation: Laws that are intended to favor the purchase of domestically sourced goods or services over imported ones, even though the imports may be a better buy.

CACM: *See* Central American Common Market.

Canada-U.S. Free Trade Agreement: An agreement, enacted in 1989, establishing a free trade area involving the United States and Canada.

Capital accounts: component of the Balance of Payments that tracks both loans given to foreigners and loans received by citizens.

Capitalism: An economic system characterized by private ownership, pricing, production, and distribution of goods.

Caribbean Community (CARICOM): A customs union in the Caribbean region.

Caribbean Free Trade Association (CARIFTA): *See* Caribbean Community and Common Market.

CARICOM: *See* Caribbean Community.

Carry trade: Borrow a currency at a low interest rate and invest it in a currency with a higher interest rate.

Central American Common Market (CACM): A customs union in Central America.

Central American Free Trade Association-DR (CAFTA-DR): A free trade association between the United States and the CACM countries plus the Dominican Republic.

Central bank: A government institution responsible for setting a country's monetary policy. In the United States, the Federal Reserve Bank is the Central Bank.

Centralization: The degree to which high-level managers, usually above the country level, make strategic dicisions and delegate them to lower levels for implementation.

Centrally planned economy (CPE): *See* Command economy.

Certificate of origin: A shipping document that determines the origin of products and is usually validated by an external source, such as a chamber of commerce; it helps countries determine the specific tariff schedule for imports.

Chaebol: Korean business groups that are similar to *keiretsu* and also contain a trading company as part of the group.

Chicago Mercantile Exchange (CME) Group: The CME Group is the world's largest derivatives marketplace, dealing in future and options products for a wide variety of asset classes, including foreign exchange.

Choice of law clause: Provision in a contract that specifies the jurisdiction whose laws will govern legal disputes.

Civil law system: A legal system based on a detailed set of laws that are organized into a code; countries with a civil law system, also called a codified legal system, include Germany, France, and Japan.

Civil liberties: The freedom to develop one's own views and attitudes.

Clan control: System whereby an MNE relies on shared values among employees to idealize and enforce preferred behaviors.

Cluster effects: Follows from the congregation of buyers and sellers of a particular good or service in a certain locale; they, in turn, induce other buyers and sellers to relocate there.

Clustering: The location of companies where there are many competitors and suppliers.

Code of conduct: A set of principles guiding the actions of MNEs in their contacts with societies.

Codetermination: A process by which both labor and management participate in the management of a company.

Collaborative arrangement: A formal, long-term contractual agreement among companies.

Collective bargaining: The process of negotiation between employers (or their representatives) and a union on wages and other employment conditions.

Collectivism: Perspective that the needs of the group take precedence over the needs of the individual; Encourages dependence on the organization.

Command economy: An economic system in which the political authorities make major decisions regarding the production and distribution of goods and services.

Commercial bill of exchange: An instrument of payment in international business that instructs the importer to forward payment to the exporter.

Commodity: A product that is difficult to differentiate from those of competitors, such as raw materials or agricultural output.

Common law system: A legal system based on tradition, precedent, and custom and usage, in which the courts interpret the law based on those conventions; found in the United Kingdom and former British colonies.

Common market: A form of regional economic integration in which countries abolish internal tariffs, use a common external tariff, and abolish restrictions on factor mobility.

Communism: A form of totalitarianism initially theorized by Karl Marx in which the political and economic systems are virtually inseparable.

Comparable access argument: Companies and industries often argue that they are entitled to the same access to foreign markets as foreign industries and companies have to their markets.

Comparative advantage: The theory that there is global efficiency gains from trade if a country specializes in those products that it can produce more efficiently than other products regardless of whether other countries can produce those products even more efficiently.

Competitive advantage: The strategies, skills, knowledge, resources or competencies that differentiate a business from its competitors.

Compound duty: A tax placed on goods traded internationally, based on value plus units.

Concentrated value chain: Performing all value-chain activities in one location.

Concentration strategy: A strategy by which an international company builds up operations quickly in one or a few countries before going to another.

Configuration: To set up, arrange, and disperse value activities to the ideal locations around the world so that the company can start and sustain operations.

Confirmed letter of credit: A letter of credit to which a bank in the exporter's country adds its guarantee of payment.

Conservatism: A characteristic of accounting systems that implies that companies are hesitant to disclose high profits or profits that are consistent with their actual operating results; more common in Germanic countries.

Consolidation: An accounting process in which financial statements of related entities, such as a parent and its subsidiaries, are combined to yield a unified set of financial statements; in the process, transactions among the related enterprises are eliminated so that the statements reflect transactions with outside parties.

Consortium: The joining together of several entities, such as companies or governments, in order to strengthen the possibility of achieving some objective.

Constitutional law: Law that is created and changed by the people.

Consumer price index (CPI): A measure of the cost of typical wage-earner purchases of goods and services expressed as a percentage of the cost of these same goods and services in some base period.

Consumer sovereignty: The freedom of consumers to influence production through the choices they make.

Control: The planning, implementation, evaluation, and correction of performance to ensure that organizational objectives are achieved.

Control systems: Process by which managers compare performance to plans, identify differences, and, where found, assess the basis for the gap and implement corrective action; ensure that activities are completed in ways that support the company's strategy.

Contemporary structure: Vertical and horizontal differentiation creates boundaries that constrain how managers coordinate interdependent value activities; contemporary structures eliminate these boundaries.

Controlled foreign corporation (CFC): A foreign corporation of which more than 50 percent of the voting stock is owned by U.S. shareholders (taxable entities that own at least 10 percent of the voting stock of the corporation).

Convergence: Efforts by the FASB and IASC to move toward a common global set of accounting standards.

Coordination: Systems that synchronize the work responsibilities of the value chain so that the company uses its resources efficiently and makes decisions effectively.

Coordination by mutual adjustment: System whereby managers interact extensively with counterparts in setting common goals.

Coordination by plan: System that relies on general goals and detailed objectives to coordinate activities.

Coordination by standardization: System whereby universal rules and procedures that apply to units worldwide, thereby enforcing consistency in the performance of activities in geographically dispersed units.

Core competency: A special outlook, skill, capability, or technology that runs through the firm's operations, weaving together disparate value activities into an integrated value chain.

Corporate culture: The common values shared by employees in a corporation, which form a control mechanism that is implicit and helps enforce other explicit control mechanisms.

Corporate governance: The combination of external and internal mechanisms implemented to safeguard the assets of a company and protect the rights of the shareholders.

Corporate social responsibility: An expression used to describe what some see as a company's obligation to be sensitive to the needs of "all" of its stakeholders in its business operations and produce an overall positive impact on society.

Correspondent (bank): A bank in which funds are kept by another, usually foreign, bank to facilitate check clearing and other business relationships.

Cost-of-living adjustment: An increase in compensation given to an expatriate employee when foreign living costs are more expensive than those in the home country.

Cost leadership: Strategy whereby a firm sells its products at the average industry price to earn a profit higher than that of rivals or below the average industry prices to capture market share.

Cost-plus strategy: The strategy of pricing at a desired margin over cost.

Council of the European Union: One of the five major institutions of the European Union; made up of the heads of state of each of the EU members.

Counterfeiting: The unauthorized copying or imitating of an item which is later passed on as an original.

Countertrade: A requirement that an exporter create value in the importing country, such as by transferring technology or receiving payment in the importing country's merchandise. An umbrella term for several sorts of trade, such as barter or offset, in which the seller accepts goods or services, rather than currency or credit, as payment.

Country of origin: Where products or services are created, which affects trade in that consumers may prefer to buy goods produced in one country rather than another usually because of quality perceptions or because of nationalism.

Country-similarity theory: The theory that a company will seek to exploit opportunities in those countries most similar to its home country because of the perceived need to make fewer operating adjustments.

Country size theory: The theory that larger countries are generally more self-sufficient than smaller countries.

Creolization: The process by which some, but not all, elements of an outside culture are introduced.

Criminal law: Body of laws dealing with crimes against the public and members of the public.

Cross-licensing: The exchange of technology by different companies.

Cross rate: An exchange rate between two currencies used in the spot market and computed from the exchange rate of each currency in relation to the U.S. dollar.

Cultural collision: A condition that occurs when divergent cultures come in contact with each other.

Cultural diffusion: The cultural changes that occur when different cultures come in contact with each other.

Cultural distance: The degree to which countries differ from each other as measured by different cultural factors; the greater the difference, the greater the distance.

Cultural friction: The result of changes in power relationships and sovereignty when cultures come into contact with each other.

Cultural imperialism: Cultural change by imposition.

Culture: The specific learned norms of a group's attitudes, values, and beliefs.

Culture shock: A generalized trauma one experiences in a new and different culture because of having to learn and cope with a vast array of new cues and expectations.

Currency swap: The exchange of principal and interest payments.

Current-rate method: A method of translating foreign-currency financial statements that is used when the functional currency is that of the local operating environment.

Customs agent: Enforce the rules of trade for particular country. They control the flow of goods moving in and out of a country.

Customary law system: A legal system anchored in the wisdom of daily experience or great spiritual or philosophical traditions.

Customer orientation: A customer orientation asks: What and how can the company sell in country A? In this case, the country is held constant and the product and method of marketing it is varied.

Customs union: A form of regional economic integration that eliminates internal tariffs among member nations and establishes common external tariffs.

Customs valuation: The value of goods on which customs authorities charge tariffs.

Debt: The total of a government's financial obligations, measures what the state borrows from its citizens, foreign organizations, foreign governments, and international institutions.

Decentralization: The degree to which lower-level managers, usually at or below the country level, make and implement strategic decisions.

Deflation: A decrease in the general price level of goods and services; often caused by a reduction in the supply of money or credit.

Democracy: A political system that relies on citizens' participation in the decision-making process.

Deontological approach: An approach which asserts that moral reasoning occurs independent of consequences.

Derivative: A foreign-exchange instrument such as an option or futures contract that derives its value from the underlying currency.

Derivatives market: Market in which forward contracts, futures, options, and swaps are traded in order to hedge or protect foreign-exchange transactions.

Devaluation: A formal reduction in the value of a currency in relation to another currency; the foreign-currency equivalent of the devalued currency falls.

Developed country: High-income country. Also called industrial country.

Developing country: A low-income country, also known as an emerging economy less developed country.

Diamond of national advantage theory: A theory that says countries usually need four conditions (demand; factors; related and supporting industries; and strategy, structure and rivalry) to develop and sustain a product's competitive advantage.

Differentiation: A business strategy in which a company tries to gain a competitive advantage by providing a unique product or service, or providing a unique brand of customer service.

Digitization: The conversion of paper and other media in existing collections to digital form.

Direct exports: Products sold to an independent party outside of the exporter's home country.

Direct investment: *See* Foreign Direct Investment.

Direct quote: A quote expressed in terms of the number of units of the domestic currency given for one unit of a foreign currency.

Direct selling: A sale of goods by an exporter directly to distributors or final consumers rather than to trading companies or other intermediaries in order to achieve greater control over the marketing function and to earn higher profits.

Disclosure: The presentation of financial information and discussion of results.

Discount: The difference between the spot and forward exchange rates in the forward market; a foreign currency sells at a discount when the forward rate is less than the spot rate and when the domestic currency is quoted on a direct basis.

Dispersed value chain: Performing different value-chain activities in different locations

Distribution: The physical path or legal title that goods take from production to consumption.

Diversification strategy: A term used in international business to describe a strategy whereby a company moves rapidly into many markets and gradually increases its commitments within each one.

Divesting: Reduction in the amount of investment.

Divisional structures: An organization that contains separate divisions based around individual product lines or based on the geographic areas of the markets served.

Draft: An instrument of payment in international business that instructs the importer to forward payment to the exporter.

Dumping: The underpricing of exports, usually below cost or below the home-country price.

Duty: A government tax (tariff) levied on goods shipped internationally. Also called tariff.

Dynamic effects: The overall growth in the market and the impact on a company of expanding production and achieving greater economies of scale.

EC: *See* European Community.

E-commerce: The use of the Internet to join together suppliers with companies and companies with customers.

Economic Community of West African States (ECOWAS): A form of economic integration among certain countries in West Africa.

Economic exposure (operational exposure): The foreign-exchange risk that international businesses face in the pricing of products, the source and cost of inputs, and the location of investments.

Economic freedom: The absence of government coercion or constraint on the production, distribution, or consumption of goods and services beyond the extent necessary for citizens to protect and maintain liberty.

Economic Freedom Index: The systematic measurement of economic freedom in countries throughout the world. The survey is sponsored by the Heritage Foundation and the *Wall Street Journal*.

Economic integration: The abolition of economic discrimination between national economies, such as within the EU.

Economic system: The system concerned with the allocation of scarce resources.

Economic geography: The study of the location, distribution, and spatial organization of economic activities across the earth.

Economics: A social science concerned chiefly with the description and analysis of the production, distribution, and consumption of goods and services.

Economies of scale: The lowering of cost per unit as output increases because of allocation of fixed costs over more units produced.

Economies of scope: Decreases in average total cost made possible by increasing the range of goods produced or sold.

Effective tariff: The real tariff on the manufactured portion of developing countries' exports, which is higher than indicated by the published rates because the ad valorem tariff is based on the total value of the products, which includes raw materials that would have had duty-free entry.

EFTA: *See* European Free Trade Association.

Electronic data interchange (EDI): The electronic movement of money and information via computers and telecommunications equipment.

Embargo: A specific type of quota that prohibits all trade.

Emerging economy: Countries with developing economies, often experiencing rapid growth and offering lucrative investment opportunities, but also characterized by political instability and high risk.

EMS: *See* European Monetary System.

Enterprise resource planning (ERP): Software that can link information flows from different parts of a business and from different geographic areas.

Equity alliance: A situation in which a cooperating company takes an equity position (almost always a minority) in the company with which it has a collaborative arrangement.

ERP: *See* Enterprise resource planning.

Escalation of commitment: The more time and money companies invest in examining an alternative, the more likely they are to accept it regardless of its merits.

Essential-industry argument: The argument holding that certain domestic industries need protection for national security purposes.

Ethnocentric framework: A staffing approach in which all key management positions, whether in the home country or abroad, are filled by home country nationals.

Ethnocentrism: A belief that one's own group is superior to others; also used to describe a company's belief that what worked at home should work abroad.

Euro: The common currency of the European Union; as of 12/31/09, 16 EU members had adopted the euro, and others were in the process of qualifying for adoption.

Eurobond: A bond sold in a country other than the one in whose currency it is denominated.

Eurocredit: A loan, line of credit, or other form of medium- or long-term credit on the Eurocurrency market that has a maturity of more than one year.

Eurocurrency: Any currency that is banked outside of its country of origin.

Eurocurrency market: An international wholesale market that deals in Eurocurrencies.

Eurodollars: Dollars banked outside of the United States.

Euroequity market: The market for shares sold outside the boundaries of the issuing company's home country.

European Central Bank (ECB): Established July 1, 1998, the ECB is responsible for setting the monetary policy and for managing the exchange-rate system for all of Europe since January 1, 1999.

European Commission: One of the five major institutions of the EU; composed of 27 women and men, one from each EU country. The president is chosen by EU governments and endorsed by the European Parliament. The commissioners do not represent their home country governments, and they serve as an executive branch for the EU.

European Community (EC): The predecessor of the European Union.

European Court of Justice: The court of the European Union. The Court is an appeals court and ensures interpretation and application of EU treaties. One of the five major institutions of the EU; composed of one member from each country in the EU and serves as a supreme appeals court for EU law.

European Economic Community (EEC): The predecessor of the European Community.

European Free Trade Association (EFTA): A free trade area among a group of European countries that are not members of the EU.

European Monetary System (EMS): A cooperative foreign-exchange agreement involving many members of the EU and designed to promote exchange-rate stability within the EU.

European Monetary Union: An agreement by participating European Union member countries that consists of three stages coordinating economic policy and culminating with the adoption of the euro.

European Parliament: One of the five major institutions of the EU; its representatives are elected directly in each member country.

European terms: The practice of using the indirect quote for exchange rates.

European Union (EU): A form of regional economic integration among countries in Europe that involves a free trade area, a customs union, and the free mobility of factors of production that is working toward political and economic union.

Exchange rate: The price of one currency in terms of another currency.

Expatriate compensation: The process of setting the appropriate level of direct and indirect benefits to motivate someone to accept and perform an international assignment.

Expatriate failure: The premature return of an expatriate manager.

Expatriates: Noncitizens of the country in which they are working.

Expatriate selection: The process of screening executives to find those with the greatest inclination and highest potential for a foreign assignment.

Experience curve: The relationship of production cost reductions to increases in output.

Exporting: The sale of goods or services produced by a company based in one country to customers that reside in a different country.

Export intermediaries: Individuals or companies that assume responsibility for different combinations of finding overseas buyers, sourcing and shipping products, and getting paid on the behalf of a manufacturer. The export intermediary may be a commissioned agent, an export management company (EMC), an export trading company (ETC), an export agent, or a re-marketer.

Export intensity: The fraction of the total output of a firm, or sometimes an industry within a country, that is exported.

Export-led development: An industrialization policy emphasizing industries that will have export capabilities.

Export license: A government document that grants permission to ship certain products to a specific country.

Export management company (EMC): A company that buys merchandise from manufacturers for international distribution or sometimes acts as an agent for manufacturers.

Export plan: Specification of the key issues that shape the success of exporting.

Export tariff: A tax on goods leaving a country.

Export trading company (ETC): A form of trading company sanctioned by U.S. law to become involved in international commerce as independent distributors to match up foreign buyers with domestic sellers.

Exports: Goods or services leaving a country for another.

Exposure: A situation in which a foreign-exchange account is subject to a gain or loss if the exchange rate changes.

Expropriation: The taking over of ownership of private property by a country's government.

Extended family: A family situation which includes family members of several generations or family members which stretches out horizontally, including aunts, uncles, cousins, etc.

External debt: Debt owed by a country to non-residents repayable in foreign currency, goods or service.

External environment: The physical, social, and competitive factors in a country that influence a company's international strategy.

Externalities: The impact of an economic activity on someone external to the specific activity, such as the impact of pollution on those not involved in the economic activity that created pollution; the externalities may be positive or negative.

Extranet: The use of the Internet to link a company with outsiders.

Extraterritoriality: The extension by a government of the application of its laws to foreign operations of companies.

Factor-mobility theory: The movement of factors of production such as labor and capital from one location to another.

Factor-proportions theory: The theory that differences in a country's proportionate holdings of factors of production (land, labor, and capital) explain differences in the costs of the factors and that export advantages lie in the production of goods that use the most abundant factors.

Fairness argument: Like the comparable access argument, domestic companies contend that they should have the same access to foreign markets as foreign companies have to their markets.

FASB: *See* Financial Accounting Standards Board.

Fascism: A system of government that promotes extreme nationalism, repression, and anticommunism that is commonly ruled by a dictator.

Fatalism: A belief that events are fixed in advance and that human beings are powerless to change them.

Favorable balance of trade: An indication that a country is exporting more than it imports.

FCPA: *See* Foreign Corrupt Practices Act.

FDI: *See* Foreign direct investment.

Fees: Payments for services.

Financial Accounting Standards Board (FASB): The private-sector organization that sets financial accounting standards in the United States.

Firm-specific advantage or assets: Advantages or assets that a company can exploit to be effective in global markets.

First-mover advantage: A cost-reduction advantage attained through moving into a foreign market ahead of competitors.

Fisher Effect: The theory about the relationship between inflation and interest rates; for example, if the nominal interest rate in one country is lower than that in another, the first country's inflation should be lower so that the real interest rates will be equal.

Five-forces model: A framework used to assess industry structure and business strategy in estimating the potential for profitability.

Floating currency: A currency whose value responds to the supply of and demand for that currency.

Floating exchange rate: An exchange rate determined by the laws of supply and demand and with minimal government interference.

Focus strategy: An attempt to sell to a target- rather than a mass-market.

Foreign bond: A bond sold outside of the borrower's country but denominated in the currency of the country of issue.

Foreign Corrupt Practices Act (FCPA): A law that criminalizes certain types of payments by U.S. companies, suchas bribes to foreign government officials.

Foreign direct investment (FDI): An investment that gives the investor a controlling interest in a foreign company.

Foreign exchange: Checks and other instruments for making payments in another country's currency.

Foreign-exchange control: A requirement that an individual or company must apply to government authorities for permission to buy foreign currency above some determined threshold amount.

Foreign-exchange market: The market where foreign exchange is traded; usually banks, non-bank financial institutions, and exchanges, such as the CME.

Foreign investment: Direct or portfolio ownership of assets in another country.

Foreign service premium: A cash allowance given to an employee who agrees to transfer to a foreign location. Also called International Adjustment Allowance or International Assignment Premium.

Foreign trade zone (FTZ): A government-designated area in which goods can be stored, inspected, or manufactured without being subject to formal customs procedures until they leave the zone.

Forward contract: A contract between a company or individual and a bank to deliver foreign currency at a specific exchange rate on a future date.

Forward discount: *See* Discount.

Forward premium: *See* Premium.

Forward rate: A contractually established exchange rate between a foreign-exchange trader and the trader's client for delivery of foreign currency on a specific date.

Franchising: A specialized form of licensing in which one party (the franchisor) gives permission to an independent party (the franchisee) the use of a trademark that is an essential asset for the franchisee's business and also gives continual assistance in the operation of the business.

Freedom: The condition of being free; the power to act, speak, and think without externally imposed restraints.

Freedom House: Organization that attempts to classify countries according to political and economic freedom.

Freely convertible currency: *See* Hard currency.

Free trade agreement: An agreement between countries that has the goal of abolishing all tariffs between member countries.

Free trade area (FTA): A form of regional economic integration in which internal tariffs are abolished, but member countries set their own external tariffs.

Freight forwarder: A company that facilitates the movement of goods from one country to another.

FTZ: *See* Foreign trade zone.

Functional currency: The currency of the primary economic environment in which an entity operates; useful in helping a firm determine how to translate its foreign currency financial statements into the current of the parent company.

Functional structure: An organization that is structured according to functional areas of business.

Fundamental forecasting: A forecasting tool that uses trends in economic variables to predict future exchange rates.

Future orientation: An orientation where people invest for the future and delay instant gratification.

Futures contract: An agreement between two parties to buy or sell a particular currency at a particular price on a particular future date, as specified in a standardized contract to all participants in that currency futures exchange.

FX swap: A simultaneous spot and forward transaction in foreign exchange.

GAAP: *See* Generally Accepted Accounting Principles.

Gap analysis: A tool used to discover why a company's sales of a given product are less than the market potential in a country; the reason may be a usage, competition, product line, or distribution gap.

GATT: *See* General Agreement on Tariffs and Trade.

General Agreement on Tariffs and Trade (GATT): A multilateral arrangement aimed at reducing barriers to trade, both tariff and nontariff ones; at the signing of the Uruguay round, the GATT was designated to become the World Trade Organization (WTO).

Generally Accepted Accounting Principles (GAAP): The accounting standards accepted by the accounting profession in each country as required for the preparation of financial statements for external users.

Generic: Any of a class of products, rather than the brand of a particular company; also relates to pharmaceutical products which have lost patent protection and can be sold by any company under a name that is different from the original branded name.

Generic names: Formerly trademarked names that have become part of the public domain.

Geocentric: Operations based on an informed knowledge of both home and host country needs.

Geocentric framework: Staffing perspective that seeks the best people for key jobs throughout the organization, regardless of nationality.

Geographic division structure: A structure in which a company's operations are separated for reporting purposes into regional areas.

Gini coefficient: A measure of the extent to which the distribution of income deviates from a perfectly equal distribution.

Globality: The state of affairs where one competes with everyone, from everywhere, for everything.

Global bond: A combination of domestic bond and Eurobond that is issued simultaneously in several markets and that must be registered in each national market according to that market's registration requirements.

Global company: A company that integrates operations located in different countries.

Global integration: The unification of distinct national economic systems into a global market.

Globalization: The broadening set of interdependent relationships among people from different parts of a world that happens to be divided into nations. The term sometimes refers to the integration of world economies through the reduction of barriers to the movement of trade, capital, technology, and people.

Global sourcing: The acquisition on a worldwide basis of raw materials, parts, and subassemblies for the manufacturing process.

Global strategy: A strategy that increases profitability by achieving cost reductions from experience curves and location economies.

Globalization of markets: Thesis that consumers worldwide seek low-cost, high-quality products regardless of country of origin.

Go-no-go decision: A decision is based on a proposal's meeting a specific threshold rather than comparing it with other alternatives.

Gray market: The handling of goods through unofficial distributors.

Green economics: Transdisciplinary field that studies the interdependence and coevolution of human economies and natural ecosystems.

Green GNP: The measurement of national output that attempts to take into account various effects on the environment and natural resources.

Gross domestic product (GDP): The total of all economic activity in a country, regardless of who owns the productive assets.

Gross national income (GNI): Formerly referred to as Gross national product.

Gross national product (GNP): The total of incomes earned by residents of a country, regardless of where the productive assets are located.

Group of 7 (G7): A group of developed countries that periodically meets to make economic decisions; this group consists of Canada, France, Germany, Italy, Japan, the United Kingdom, and the United States.

Group of 8 (G8): The Group of 7 (G7) plus Russia.

Group of 20 (G20): Group of finance ministers and central bank governors from 19 countries plus the European Union.

Gulf Cooperation Council: A subset of the Arab League countries that basically includes Bahrain, Saudi Arabia, Kuwait, Oman, Qatar, and the UAE.

Happynomics: Evaluating a country's performance and potential by directly considering peoples' life satisfaction.

Hard currency: A currency that is freely traded without many restrictions and for which there is usually strong external demand; often called a freely convertible currency.

Hardship allowance: A supplement to compensate expatriates for working in dangerous or adverse conditions.

Harvesting: Reduction in the amount of investment. Also known as divestment.

Hedge: To attempt to protect foreign-currency holdings against an adverse movement of an exchange rate.

Hedge fund: An investment fund available to a limited number of investors that is managed more aggressively than mutual funds.

Heterarchy: An organizational structure in which management of an alliance of companies is shared by so-called equals rather than being set up in a superior-subordinate relationship.

Hierarchy-of-needs theory: A well-known motivation theory stating that there is a hierarchy of needs and that people must fulfill the lower-order needs sufficiently before they will be motivated by the higher-order ones.

High-context culture: A culture in which most people consider that peripheral and indirect information is necessary for decision making because such information bears on the context of the situation.

Home country: The country in which an international company is headquartered.

Home-country nationals: Expatriate employees who are citizens of the country in which the company is headquartered.

Horizontal alliance: An alliance of companies that produce similar products, as opposed to a vertical alliance which links together different elements of the value chain from raw materials to final consumption.

Horizontal differentiation: The process of specifying, dividing, and assigning organizational tasks.

Horizontally extended family: Includes aunts, uncles, and cousins.

Host country: Any foreign country in which an international company operates.

Host government policies: The programs put into place by the national government to regulate business activity.

Human development index: A measurement of human progress used by the United Nations Development Programme that combines indicators of purchasing power, education, and health.

Human resource management: The staffing function of the organization; includes the activities of human resources planning, recruitment, selection, performance appraisal, compensation, retention, and labor relations.

Hyperinflation: A rapid increase (at least 1 percent per day) in general price levels for a sustained period of time.

IASB: *See* International Accounting Standards Board.

Idealism: Trying to determine principles before settling small issues.

Ideology: The systematic and integrated body of constructs, theories, and aims that constitute a society.

IFE: *See* International Fisher Effect.

IMF: *See* International Monetary Fund.

Imitation lag: A strategy for exploiting temporary monopoly advantages by moving first to those countries most likely to develop local production.

Import broker: An individual who obtains various government permissions and other clearances before forwarding necessary paperwork to the carrier who delivers the goods to the importer.

Import documentation: The various documents required in international trade transactions.

Importing: The purchase of products by a company based in one country from sellers that reside in another.

Import (or export) license: A method of government control of the exchange rate whereby all recipients, exporters, and others who receive foreign exchange are required to sell to the central bank at the official buying rate.

Import plan: Specification of the key issues that shape successful importing.

Import substitution: An industrialization policy whereby new industrial development emphasizes products that would otherwise be imported.

Imports: Goods or services that enter a country from another.

Import tariff: A tax on goods entering a country.

Income distribution: The distribution of national income among groups of individuals, households, social classes, or factors of production.

Incremental internalization: The view that as a company gains experience, resources, and confidence, it progressively exports to increasingly distant and dissimilar countries.

Indirect exports: Exports that are not handled directly by the manufacturer or producer but through an export agent, freight forwarder, or 3PL.

Indirect quote: An exchange rate given in terms of the number of units of the foreign currency for one unit of the domestic currency.

Indirect selling: A sale of goods by an exporter through another domestic company as an intermediary.

Individualism: An emphasis on the importance of guaranteeing individual freedom and self-expression. Encourages fulfilling leisure time and improving skills outside the organization.

Individualistic paradigm: A view that endorses minimal government intervention in the economy.

Industrial clusters: When buyers and sellers locate close to each other to facilitate doing business.

Industrialization argument: A rationale for protectionism that argues that the development of industrial output should come about even though domestic prices may not become competitive on the world market.

Industry organization paradigm: Field of economics that studies the strategic behavior of firms, the structure of markets, and their interactions.

Industry structure: The makeup of an industry: its number of sellers and their size distribution, the nature of the product, and the extent of barriers to entry.

Infant-industry argument: The position that holds that an emerging industry should be guaranteed a large share of the domestic market until it becomes efficient enough to compete against imports.

Inflation: A general and progressive increase in prices.

Innovation: A new idea, method, or device that, in creating a new product or process, creates competitive advantage.

Integration-responsiveness (IR) grid: Schema that helps managers measure the global and local pressures that influence the configuration and coordination of value chains.

Intellectual property: Property in the form of patents, trademarks, service marks, trade names, trade secrets, and copyrights.

Intellectual property rights: Ownership rights to intangible assets, such as patents, trademarks, copyrights, and know-how.

Interbank market: The market for foreign-exchange transactions among commercial banks.

Interbank transactions: Foreign-exchange transactions that take place between commercial banks.

Interest arbitage: Investing in debt instruments in different countries to take advantage of interest differentials. The investment is "covered" if the investor converts money into foreign exchange at the spot rate, invests it in the foreign market at a higher interest rate, and enters into a forward contract so that it can convert principle and interest back into the home currency and earn more than if that money had been invested in the home currency.

Intermodal transportation: The transportation of freight in a container or vehicle, using multiple modes of transportation (rail, ocean vessel, and truck), without any handling of the freight itself when changing modes.

Internal debt: Part of a country's debts that is owed to creditors who are citizens of that country.

Internalization: Control through self-handling of foreign operations, primarily because such control is less expensive to deal with in the same corporate family than to contract with an external organization.

International Accounting Standards Board (IASB): The international private-sector organization that sets financial accounting standards for worldwide use.

International business: All commercial transactions involving of two or more countries.

International division structure: A structure whereby the company creates a stand-alone division that is responsible for its international activities.

International Financial Reporting Standards (IFRS): A set of accounting standards often known by the older name of International Accounting Standards (IAS). They are issued by the International Accounting Standards Board (IASB).

International Fisher Effect (IFE): The theory that the relationship between interest rates and exchange rates implies that the currency of the country with the lower interest rate will strengthen in the future.

Internationalization: The process by which companies gradually increase their commitments to international business.

International law: The regulations resulting from treaties among countries.

International Monetary Fund (IMF): A multi-governmental association organized in 1945 to promote exchange-rate stability and to facilitate the international flow of currencies.

International Organization of Securities Commissions (IOSCO): An international organization of securities regulators that supports the efforts of the IASB to establish comprehensive accounting standards.

International Organization for Standardization (ISO): An international non-governmental organization headquartered in Geneva that publishes industrial and commercial standards.

International strategy: The effort of managers to create value by transferring core competencies from the home market to foreign markets in which local competitors lack those competencies.

Intranet: The use of the Internet to link together the different divisions and functions inside a company.

Invisible hand: Market forces independent of government policies that guide the efficient allocation of resources.

IOSCO: *See* International Organization of Securities Commissions.

Irrevocable letter of credit (L/C): A letter of credit that cannot be canceled or changed without the consent of all parties involved.

ISO 9000: A quality standard developed by the International Organization for Standardization in Geneva that requires companies to document their commitment to quality at all levels of the organization.

Jamaica Agreement: A 1976 agreement among countries that permitted greater flexibility of exchange rates, basically formalizing the break from fixed exchange rates.

JIT: *See* Just-in-time manufacturing.

Joint venture: An investment in which two or more companies share the ownership.

Just-in-time (JIT) manufacturing system: A system that reduces inventory costs by having components and parts delivered as they are needed in production.

Kaizen: The Japanese process of continuous improvement, the cornerstone of TQM.

Keiretsu: A corporate relationship linking certain Japanese companies, usually involving a noncontrolling interest in each other, strong high-level personal relationships among managers in the different companies, and interlocking directorships.

Kyoto Protocol: The international agreement among countries to reduce the emission of green house gasses.

LAFTA: *See* Latin American Free Trade Association.

Lag strategy: An operational strategy that involves either delaying collection of foreign-currency receivables if the currency is expected to strengthen or delaying payment of foreign-currency payables when the currency is expected to weaken; the opposite of a lead strategy.

Laissez-faire: The concept of minimal government intervention in a society's economic activity.

Latin American Free Trade Association (LAFTA): A free trade area formed by Mexico and the South American countries in 1960; it was replaced by ALADI in 1980.

Latin American Integration Association (ALADI): A form of regional economic integration involving 12 Latin American countries.

Law: A binding custom or practice of a community.

Lead strategy: An operational strategy that involves either collecting foreign-currency receivables before they are due when the currency is expected to weaken or paying foreign-currency payables before they are due when the currency is expected to strengthen; the opposite of a lag strategy.

Lean manufacturing: A production system whose focus is on optimizing processes through the philosophy of continual improvement.

Learning curve: A concept used to support the infant-industry argument for protection; it assumes that costs will decline as workers and managers gain more experience.

Legal system: The rules that regulate behavior, the processes that enforce the laws of a country, and the procedures used to resolve grievances.

Letter of credit (L/C): A precise document by which the importer's bank extends credit to the importer and agrees to pay the exporter.

Leverage: The amount of debt used to finance a firm's assets.

Liability of foreignness: Foreign companies' lower survival rate in comparison to local companies for many years after they begin operations.

LIBOR: *See* London Inter-Bank Offered Rate.

License (import or export): Formal or legal permission to do some specified action; a government method of fixing the exchange rate by requiring all recipients, exporters, and others that receive foreign exchange to sell it to the central bank at the official buying rate.

Licensing agreement: Agreement whereby one company gives rights to another for the use, usually for a fee, of such assets as trademarks, patents, copyrights, or other know-how.

Liquidity preferences: A theory that helps explain capital budgeting and, when applied to international operations, means that investors are willing to take less return in order to be able to shift the resources to alternative uses.

Local content: A term used in trade agreements which refers to the percentage of a product which is produced in the member countries to the agreement. Preferential tariff provisions often depend on the amount of local or regional content included in a product.

Localization: Process whereby an expatriate retains a foreign assignment provided she accept the status, and corresponding compensation, of a local hire.

Local responsiveness: The process of adapting globally standardized operations to improve responsiveness to local market circumstances.

Locals: Citizens of the country in which they are working.

Location economies: Cost advantages arising from performing a value activity in the optimal location.

Location-specific advantage: A combination of factor and demand conditions, along with other qualities, that a country has to offer domestic and foreign investors.

Logistics (materials management): That part of the supply chain process that plans, implements, and controls the efficient, effective flow and storage of goods, services, and related information from the point of origin to the point of consumption, to meet customers' requirements; sometimes called materials management.

London Inter-Bank Offered Rate (LIBOR): The interest rate for large interbank loans of Eurocurrencies.

London International Financial Futures Exchange (LIFFE): An exchange dealing in futures contracts for several major currencies. Now part of NYSE Euronext.

London Stock Exchange (LSE): A stock exchange located in London and dealing in Euroequities.

Low-context culture: A culture in which most people consider relevant only information that they receive firsthand and that bears very directly on the decision they need to make.

Maastricht (Treaty of): The treaty approved in December 1991 that was designed to bring the EU to a higher level of integration and is divided into the Economic Monetary Union (EMU) and a political union.

Management contract: An arrangement whereby one company provides management personnel, who perform general or specialized management functions, to another company for a fee.

Maquiladora: An industrial operation, originally developed between the United States and Mexico but now used in other geographic areas, in which components may be shipped duty free, assembled, and then re-exported.

Market capitalization: A common measure of the size of a stock market, which is computed by multiplying the total number of shares of stock listed on the exchange by the market price per share.

Market control: System whereby an MNE uses external market mechanisms to establish internal performance benchmarks and standards.

Market economy: An economic system in which resources are allocated and controlled by consumers who "vote" by buying goods; emphasizes minimal government involvement.

Market environment: The environment that involves the interactions between households (or individuals) and companies in the allocation of resources, free from government ownership or control.

Masculinity-femininity index: An index comparing countries' norms on empathy for successful achievers versus the unfortunate, preference for being better than others versus being on a par with them, belief that it's better "to live to work" versus "to work to live," preference for performance and growth versus quality of life and the environment, and belief that gender roles should be different versus similar.

Master franchise: A franchise agreement that is given to one franchisee in a country to establish franchises in many different areas, possibly the entire country.

Materials management: *See* Logistics.

Matrix structure: A structure in which foreign units report (by product, function, or area) to more than one group, each of which shares responsibility over the foreign unit.

Mercantilism: An economic philosophy based on the beliefs that a country's wealth is dependent on its holdings of treasure, usually in the form of gold, and that countries should export more than they import in order to increase wealth.

Merchandise export: A good sent out of a country.

Merchandise imports: A good brought into a country.

Merchandise trade balance: The part of a country's current account that measures the trade deficit or surplus; its balance is the net of merchandise imports and exports.

MERCOSUR: A major subregional group established by Argentina, Brazil, Paraguay, and Uruguay, which spun off from ALADI in 1991 with the goal of setting up a customs union and common market. Venezuela has applied for membership.

MFN: *See* Most-favored-nation clause.

Misery index: The sum of a country's inflation and unemployment rate.

Mixed economy: An economic system characterized by some mixture of market and command economies; balances public and private ownership of factors of production.

Mixed legal system: A legal system that emerges when two or more legal systems function in a country.

Mixed structure: A structure that integrates various aspects of classical structures.

MNC: See multinational corporation or classical company.

MNE: *See* Multinational enterprise.

Monochronic (approach to tasking): A culture in which most people prefer to deal with situations sequentially (especially those involving other people), such as finishing with one customer before dealing with another.

Most-favored-nation (MFN) clause: A GATT (and now a WTO) requirement that a trade concession that is given to one country must be given to all other countries.

Multidomestic strategy: An approach that emphasizes responsiveness to the unique conditions prevailing in different national markets.

Multilateral agreement: An agreement among three or more countries.

Multinational corporation or company (MNC): A company that has operations in more than one country; sometimes used simultaneously with multinational corporation or company or transnational corporation.

Multinational enterprise (MNE): A company that has operations in more than one

country; sometimes used simultaneously with multinational corporation or company or transnational corporation.

Multiparty democracy: Multiparty system in which three or more political parties have the capacity to gain control of government separately or in coalition.

Multiple exchange-rate system: A means of foreign-exchange control whereby the government sets different exchange rates for different transactions.

Mutual recognition: The principle that a foreign registrant that wants to list and have its securities traded on a foreign stock exchange need only provide information prepared according to the GAAP of the home country.

NASDAQ OMX: The third-largest options market in the United States which pioneered a hybrid from of trading involving both traditional floor and online trading.

National responsiveness: Readiness to implement operating adjustments in foreign countries in order to reach a satisfactory level of performance.

Natural advantage: Climatic conditions, access to certain natural resources, or availability of labor, which gives a country an advantage in producing some product.

Neoclassical structure: Applies different devices to resovlve the shortcomings, such as conformity, rigidity, bureaucracy, and authoritarism, often found in the classical formats of functional and divisional structures.

Neomercantilism: The approach of countries that apparently try to run favorable balances of trade in an attempt to achieve some social or political objective.

Net present value: The sum of the present values of the annual cash flows minus the initial investment.

Netting: The transfer of funds from subsidiaries in a net payable position to a central clearing account and from there to the accounts of the net receiver subsidiaries.

Network structure: Neoclassical structure whereby a small core organization outsources value activities to linked firms whose core competencies support greater innovation.

Network organization: A situation in which an interrelated group of companies integrate activities.

Nontariff barriers: Barriers to imports that are not tariffs; examples include administrative controls, "Buy America" policies, and so forth.

Nontradable goods: Products and services that are seldom practical to export, primarily because of high transportation costs.

Normativism: A theory stating that universal standards of behavior (based on people's own values) exist that all cultures should follow, making nonintervention unethical.

North American Free Trade Agreement (NAFTA): A free trade agreement involving the United States, Canada, and Mexico that went into effect on January 1, 1994, and will be phased in over a period of 15 years.

NYSE Liffe: The global derivatives business of the NYSE Euronext Group.

Nuclear family: A family consisting of parents and children.

OAU: *See* Organization of African Unity.

OECD: *See* Organization for Economic Cooperation and Development.

Offer (sell): The amount for which a foreign-exchange trader is willing to sell a currency.

Official reserves: A country's holdings of monetary gold, Special Drawing Rights, and internationally acceptable currencies.

Offsets: A form of countertrade in which an exporter sells goods for cash but then helps businesses in the importing country to find opportunities to earn hard currency.

Offshore financial centers: Cities or countries that provide large amounts of funds in currencies other than their own and are used as locations in which to raise and accumulate cash.

Offshore financing: The provision of financial services by banks and other agents to non-residents.

Offshoring: The process of shifting production to a foreign country.

Oligopolistic reaction: The process in oligopoly industries for competitors to emulate each other, such as going to the same locations.

OPEC: *See* Organization of Petroleum Exporting Countries.

Operational centers: Offshore financial centers that perform specific functions, such as the sale and servicing of goods.

Opinion leader: One whose acceptance of some concept is apt to be emulated by others.

Opportunity-risk matrix: An investment matrix that compares the opportunities of investing in a country with the risks and is a tool that companies can use to help determine where to invest.

Optimum-tariff theory: The argument that a foreign producer will lower its prices if an import tax is placed on its products.

Option: A foreign-exchange instrument that gives the purchaser the right, but not the obligation, to buy or sell a certain amount of foreign currency at a set exchange rate within a specified amount of time.

Organization: The specification of the framework for work, development of the systems that coordinate and control what work is done, and the cultivation of common workplace culture among employees.

Organization of African Unity (OAU): An organization of African nations that is more concerned with political than economic objectives.

Organization culture: The shared meaning and beliefs that shape how employees interpret information, make decisions, and implement actions.

Organization for Economic Cooperation and Development (OECD): A multilateral organization of industrialized and semi-industrialized countries that helps to formulate social and economic policies.

Organization of Petroleum Exporting Countries (OPEC): A producers' alliance among 12 petroleum-exporting countries that attempt to agree on oil production and pricing policies.

Organization structure: The formal arrangement of roles, responsibilities, and relationships within an organization.

Outright forward transaction: A forward contract that is not connected to a spot transaction.

Outsourcing: Where one company contracts with another company to perform certain functions, including manufacturing and back office operations. May be done in or close to the company's home country (nearshoring) or in another country (offshoring).

Over-the-counter (OTC) market: Trading in stocks, usually of smaller companies, that are not listed on one of the stock exchanges; also refers to how government and corporate bonds are traded, through dealers who quote bids and offers to buy and to sell "over the counter."

Par value: The benchmark value of a currency, originally quoted in terms of gold or the U.S. dollar and now quoted in terms of Special Drawing Rights.

Parliamentary democracy: A system of government where the people exercise their political power by electing representatives to parliament to make laws.

Passive income: Income from investments in tax-haven countries or sales and services income that involves buyers and sellers in other than the tax-haven country, where either the buyer or the seller must be part of the same organizational structure as the corporation that earns the income; also known as Subpart F income.

Patent: A right granted by a sovereign power or state for the protection of an invention or discovery against infringement.

Paternalism: Regulating conduct by satisfying needs of subordinates.

Payback period: The number of years required to recover the initial investment made.

Peg: To fix a currency's exchange rate to some benchmark, such as another currency.

Penetration strategy: A strategy of introducing a product at a low price to induce a maximum number of consumers to try it.

Perfect competition: Industry setting in which there are many firms with small market shares, all firms are price takers, identical products are sold by all firms, companies can freely enter and exit the industry, and there is perfect knowledge.

Piracy: The unauthorized duplication of goods protected by intellectual property law.

PLC: *See* Product life cycle theory.

Pluralism: Belief that there are multiple opinions about an issue, each of which contains part of the truth, but none that contain the entire truth.

Pluralistic societies: Societies in which different ideologies are held by various segments rather than one ideology being adhered to by all.

Political freedom: The right to participate freely in the political process.

Political ideology: The body of complex ideas, theories, and aims that constitute a sociopolitical program.

Political risk: Potential changes in political conditions that may cause a company's operating positions to deteriorate.

Political spectrum: A conceptual structure that specifies and organizes various types of political ideologies.

Political system: The system designed to integrate a society into a viable, functioning unit.

Polycentric framework: A staffing policy whereby a company relies on host country nationals to manage operations in their own country, while parent-country nationals staff corporate headquarters.

Polycentrism: Characteristic of an individual or organization that feels that it should act like locals or local companies.

Polychronic (approach to multitasking): A culture in which most people are more comfortable dealing simultaneously with multiple situations facing them.

Portfolio investment: An investment in the form of either debt or equity that does not give the investor a controlling interest.

Post-Christian society: A term describing northern European countries that do not adhere strongly to any religion, but which hold strong Christian values because of centuries of profound religious influence.

Poverty: Multidimensional condition in which a person or community lacks the essentials for a minimum standard of well-being and life.

Power distance: A measurement of preference for consultative versus autocratic styles of management.

PPP: *See* Purchasing power parity.

Pragmatism: Settling small issues before deciding on principles.

Premium (in foreign exchange): The difference between the spot and forward exchange rates in the forward market; a foreign currency sells at a premium when the forward rate exceeds the spot rate and when the domestic currency is quoted on a direct basis.

Premium (in foreign exchange) Primary activities: The steps and sequence of classic business functions that define the value chain of a company.

Principles-based accounting: A system of accounting that identifies key principles in a conceptual framework and establishes simple rules that conform to the key principles.

Private Technology Exchange (PTX): An online collaboration model that brings manufacturers, distributors, value-added resellers, and customers together to execute trading transactions and to share information about demand, production, availability, and more.

Product diversion: *See* Gray market.

Product division structure: A structure that assigns global responsibilities to each product division.

Product life cycle (PLC) theory: The theory that certain kinds of products go through a cycle consisting of four stages (introduction, growth, maturity, and decline) and that the location of production will shift internationally depending on the stage of the cycle.

Property rights: The legal rights to use goods, services, or resources.

Protectionism: Government restrictions on imports and occasionally on exports that frequently give direct or indirect subsidies to industries to enable them to compete with foreign production either at home or abroad.

Protestant ethic: A theory that there is more economic growth when work is viewed as a means of salvation and when people prefer to transform productivity gains into additional output rather than into additional leisure.

Pull: A promotion strategy that sells consumers before they reach the point of purchase, usually by relying on mass media.

Push: A promotion strategy that uses direct selling techniques.

Purchasing power parity (PPP): A theory that explains exchange-rate changes as being based on differences in price levels in different countries. Also, the number of units of a country's currency to buy the same products or services in the domestic market that U.S. $1 would buy in the United States.

Quality: Meeting or exceeding the expectations of a customer.

Quantity controls: Government limitations on the amount of foreign currency that can be used for specific purposes.

Quota: A limit on the quantitative amount of a product allowed to be exported from or imported into a country.

Quoted currency: When dealers quote currencies to their customers, they always quote the base currency first followed by the terms currency. A quote of USD/JPY refers to the number of Japanese yen for one U.S. dollar.

Rationalization: *See* Rationalized production.

Rationalized production: The specialization of production by product or process in different parts of the world to take advantage of varying costs of labor, capital, and raw materials.

Reciprocal quote: One divided by the direct quote in foreign exchange. Also known as the indirect quote.

Reconciliation: The process of a foreign country reconciling its home country GAAP with U.S. GAAP.

Reflation: The act of increasing the money supply.

Regional integration: A form of integration in which a group of countries located in the same geographic proximity decide to cooperate.

Relativism: A theory stating that ethical truths depend on the groups holding them, making intervention by outsiders unethical. The belief that behavior has meaning and can be judged only in its specific cultural context.

Repatriation: An expatriate's return to his or her home country.

Representative democracy: A type of government in which individual citizens elect representatives to make decisions governing the society.

Resource-based view (of the firm): A perspective that holds that each company has a unique combination of competencies.

Retaliation: A situation in which one country restricts imports from another country in response to that country's restrictions against its exports.

Revaluation: A formal change in an exchange rate by which the foreign-currency value of the reference currency rises, resulting in a strengthening of the reference currency.

Reverse culture shock: The experience of culture shock when returning to one's own country that is caused by having accepted what was experienced abroad.

Royalty: Payment for the use of intangible assets.

Rule of law: The principle that every member of a society must follow the same laws.

Rule of man: Notion that the word and whim, no matter how arbitrary, of the ruler are law.

Rules-based accounting: A legalistic accounting system filled with specific details in an attempt to address as many potential contingencies as possible.

Sales orientation: A company tries to sell abroad what it can sell domestically and in the same manner on the assumption that consumers are sufficiently similar globally.

Scale alliance: An alliance where firms aim at providing efficiency through the pooling of similar assets so that partners can carry out business activities in which they already have experience.

Scanning: Examining a variety of variables for different countries that may affect foreign investment alternatives.

SDR: *See* Special Drawing Right.

Securities and Exchange Commission (SEC): A U.S. government agency that regulates securities brokers, dealers, and markets.

Separate entity approach: A system for taxation of corporate income in which each unit is taxed when it receives income, with the result being double taxation.

Serendipity: Refers to a trigger of so-called accidental exporters who, responding to happenstance or odd circumstances, enter overseas markets by chance.

Service export: Internationally paid earnings other than those derived from exporting a tangible good.

Service import: International payments for an import other than for a tangible good.

Sight draft: A commercial bill of exchange that requires payment to be made as soon as it is presented to the party obligated to pay.

Silent language: The wide variety of cues other than formal language by which messages can be sent.

Single European Act: A 1987 act of the EU (then the EC) allowing all proposals except those relating to taxation, workers' rights, and immigration to be adopted by a weighted majority of member countries.

Singularity Principle: Forecasts a future during which the pace of technological change will be so rapid and its impact so deep, that human life and business practices will be irreversibly transformed.

Six Sigma: A highly focused system of quality control that uses data and rigorous statistical analysis to identify "defects" in a process or product, reduce variability, and achieve as close to zero defects as possible.

Skimming strategy: Charging a high price for a new product by aiming first at consumers willing to pay that price and then progressively lowering the price.

Small and medium-sized enterprise: Companies whose headcount or sale turnover falls below certain thresholds; in the United States, companies that employ fewer than 500 employees. Commonly expressed as "SME."

Smithsonian Agreement: A 1971 agreement among countries that resulted in the devaluation of the U.S. dollar, revaluation of other world currencies, a widening of exchange-rate flexibility, and a commitment on the part of all participating countries to reduce trade restrictions; superseded by the Jamaica Agreement of 1976.

Social stratification: The ranking of individuals in a society.

Socialism: A system based on public ownership of the means of production and distribution of wealth.

Social marketing orientation: Successful international marketing requires serious consideration of potential environmental, health, social, and work-related problems that may arise when selling or making their products abroad.

Society: A broad grouping of people having common traditions, institutions, and collective activities and interests; the term nation-state is often used in international business to denote a society.

Soft currency: *See* Weak currency.

Sogo shosha: Japanese trading companies that import and export merchandise.

Sourcing: The strategy that a company pursues in purchasing materials, components, and final products; sourcing can be from domestic and foreign locations and from inside and outside the company.

Sovereignty: A nation's intrinsic freedom from external (foreign) control.

Sovereign wealth fund: A pool of money from a country's reserve which is set aside for investment purposes.

Special Drawing Right (SDR): A unit of account issued to countries by the International Monetary Fund to expand their official reserves bases.

Specialization: A result of free trade policies that causes countries to concentrate on producing and exporting those products for which they have the greatest advantage and importing those for which they have less advantage.

Specific duty: A duty (tariff) assessed on a per-unit basis.

Speculation: The buying or selling of foreign currency with the prospect of great risk and high return.

Speculator: A person who takes positions in foreign exchange with the objective of earning a profit.

Spillover effect: Situation in which the marketing program in one country results in awareness of the product in other countries.

Spot market: The market in which an asset is traded for immediate delivery, as opposed to a market for forward or future deliveries.

Spot rate: An exchange rate quoted for immediate delivery of foreign currency, usually within two business days.

Spot transactions: Foreign exchange transactions involving the exchange of currency the second day after the date on which the two foreign-exchange traders agree to the transaction.

Spread: In the forward market, the difference between the spot rate and the forward rate; in the spot market, the difference between the bid (buy) and offer (sell) rates quoted by a foreign-exchange trader.

Stakeholders: The collection of groups, including stockholders, employees, customers, and society at large, that a company must satisfy to survive.

Standardization: The procedure of maintaining methods, equipment, and output as constant, no matter the location, as possible.

State capitalism: An economic system whereby the state decides how, when, and where assets will be valued and resources allocated.

Static effect: The shifting of resources from inefficient to efficient companies as trade barriers fall.

Strategic alliance: An agreement between companies that is of strategic importance to one or both companies' competitive viability.

Strategic marketing orientation: Most companies committed to continual rather than sporadic foreign sales adopt a strategy that combines production, sales, and customer orientations.

Strategic trade policy: The identification and development of target industries to be competitive internationally.

Strategy: Management's idea on how to best attract customers, operate efficiently, compete effectively, and create value. Guides building and sustaining the company's competitive position within its industry.

Subpart F income: Income of a CFC that comes from sources other than those connected with the active conduct of a trade or business, such as holding company income.

Subsidiary: A foreign operation that is legally separate from the parent company, even if wholly owned by it.

Subsidy: Direct assistance from governments to companies to make them more competitive.

Supply chain: The coordination of materials, information, and funds from the initial raw material supplier to the ultimate customer.

Supply-chaining: When a company decides to outsource its parts, or components, or products or even its manufacturing to an external company.

Support activities: The general infrastructure of the firm that anchors the day-to-day execution of the primary activities of the value chain.

Sustainable development: use of resources use that meet present needs while preserving ability of future generations to do the same.

Swap: A simultaneous spot and forward foreign-exchange transaction.

Syndication: Cooperation by a lead bank and several other banks to make a large loan to a public or private organization.

Tacit knowledge: Knowledge imbedded in people, which usually can be transferred only on a person-to-person basis rather than through printed material.

Tariff (or duty): A government tax levied on goods, usually imports, shipped internationally.

Tax credit: A dollar-for-dollar reduction of tax liability that must coincide with the recognition of income.

Tax deferral: Income is not taxed until it is remitted to the parent company as a dividend.

Tax-haven countries: Countries with low income taxes or no taxes on foreign-source income.

Tax-haven subsidiary: A subsidiary of a company established in a tax-haven country for the purpose of minimizing income tax.

Tax treaty: A treaty between two countries that generally results in the reciprocal reduction of dividend withholding taxes and the exemption of taxes or royalties and sometimes interest payments.

Technical forecasting: A forecasting tool that uses past trends in exchange rates themselves to spot future trends in rates.

Teleological approach: An approach based on the idea that decisions are made based on the consequences of the action.

Temporal method: A method of translating foreign-currency financial statements used when the functional currency is that of the parent company.

Terms currency: In a foreign exchange quote, the base currency is 1 and the terms currency gives you the number of units of that currency per one unit of the base currency. If a foreign exchange trader quotes USD/JPY, the dollar is the base currency and the yen is the terms currency. The quote will give you the number of Japanese yen per U.S. dollar. The quote is also shown as USDJPY=X.

Terms of trade: The quantity of imports that can be bought by a given quantity of a country's exports.

Theory of country size: *See* country size theory.

Third wave of democratization: Expression that captures the collective set of nations that moved from nondemocratic to democratic political systems during the 1970s through the 1990s.

Third-country nationals: Expatriates who are neither citizens of the country in which they are working nor citizens of the country where the company is headquartered.

Third-party logistics (3PL): Agents that develop state-of-the-art technology to help companies understand trade practices, identify opportunities, manage risks, and shepherd exports and imports from buyers to sellers.

Tied aid and loans: Aid and loans given by one government to another on the condition that the recipient country spend the money on products from the donor country.

Time draft: A commercial bill of exchange calling for payment to be made at some time after delivery.

TNC: *See* Transnational company.

Total quality management (TQM): The process that a company uses to achieve quality, where the goal is elimination of all defects.

Totalitarian system: A political system characterized by the absence of widespread participation in decision making and suppression of political and civil freedoms.

TQM: *See* Total quality management.

Trade creation: Production shifts to more efficient producers for reasons of comparative advantage, allowing consumers access to more goods at a lower price than would have been possible without integration.

Trade deficit: A situation in which a country imports more than it exports.

Trade diversion: A situation in which exports shift to a less efficient producing country because of preferential trade barriers.

Trade Related Aspects of Intellectual Property Rights (TRIPS): A provision from the Uruguay round of trade negotiations requiring countries to agree to enforce procedures under their national laws to protect intellectual property rights.

Trade sanctions: Tariffs and non-tariff barriers levied on another country, usually for political reasons.

Trade surplus: A situation in which a country exports more than it imports.

Trademark: A name or logo distinguishing a company or product.

Transaction cost theory: As applied to international business, the choice of operating based on the relative cost of doing business with a company's owned operations versus doing business with an independent company.

Transaction exposure: Foreign-exchange risk arising because a company has outstanding accounts receivable or accounts payable that are denominated in a foreign currency.

Transfer price: A price charged for goods or services between entities that are related to each other through stock ownership, such as between a parent and its subsidiaries or between subsidiaries owned by the same parent.

Transit tariff: A tax placed on goods passing through a country.

Translation: The restatement of foreign-currency financial statements into the currency of the parent company.

Translation exposure: Foreign-exchange risk that occurs because the parent company must translate foreign-currency financial statements into the reporting currency of the parent company.

Transnational: (1) An organization in which different capabilities and contributions among different country-operations are shared and integrated; (2) multinational enterprise; (3) company owned and managed by nationals from different countries.

Transnational company (TNC): Usually used as a term that is synonymous with multinational enterprise.

Transnational strategy: Configuring a value chain to exploit location economies as well as coordinate activities to leverage core competencies while simultaneously responding to local pressures.

Transparency: A characteristic of an accounting system that implies that companies disclose a great deal of information about accounting practices; more common in Anglo-Saxon countries (United States, United Kingdom).

Triad: Refers to the three major economic regions of the world—Europe, North America, and Asia.

TRIPS: *See* Trade Related Aspects of Intellectual Property Rights.

Turnkey operation: An operating facility that is constructed under contract and transferred to the owner when the facility is ready to begin operations.

Uncertainty avoidance: A cultural trait where individuals are uncomfortable with uncertainty and prefer structure to independence.

Underemployed: Those people who are working at less than their capacity.

Unfavorable balance of trade: An indication of a trade deficit—that is, imports are greater than exports. Also called deficit.

United Nations (UN): An international organization of countries formed in 1945 to promote world peace and security.

United Nations Conference on Trade and Development (UNCTAD): A UN body that has been especially active in dealing with the relationships between developing and industrialized countries with respect to trade.

Unity-of-command principle: An unbroken chain of command and communication should flow from the CEO to the entry-level worker.

Utilitarianism: A consequences-based approach to moral reasoning that judges an action to be right if it does the most good to the most people.

Value: A measure of a firm's capability to sell what it makes for more than the costs incurred to make it; the ultimate purpose of strategy.

Value-added tax (VAT): A tax that is a percentage of the value added to a product at each stage of the business process.

Value chain: The collective activities that occur as a product moves from raw materials through production to final distribution; the disaggregation of value creation.

VAT: *See* Value-added tax.

VER: *See* voluntary export control.

Vertical alliance: An alliance that links together elements in the value chain backward and forward, such as back to raw materials and forward to final distribution.

Vertical differentiation: The specification of the degrees of centralization and decentralization of decision-making in an organization.

Vertical integration: The control of the different stages as a product moves from raw materials through production to final distribution.

Virtual organization: A form of organization that acquires strategic capabilities by creating a temporary network of independent companies, suppliers, customers, and even rivals.

Visible exports: *See* Merchandise exports.

Visible imports: *See* Merchandise imports.

Voluntary export restraint (VER): A negotiated limitation of exports between an importing and an exporting country.

Weak (or soft) currency: A currency that is not fully convertible. However, even a hard currency can be weak relative to another currency because of the relative exchange rates over time.

World Bank: A multilateral lending institution that provides investment capital to countries.

World Trade Organization (WTO): A voluntary organization through which groups of countries negotiate trading agreements and which has authority to oversee trade disputes among countries.

WTO: *See* World Trade Organization.

Zero defects: The elimination of defects, which results in the reduction of manufacturing costs and an increase in consumer satisfaction.

company index and trademarks

Page references with "*f*" refer to figures, page references with "*m*" refer to maps, page references with "t" refer to tables, and page references with "n" refer to endnotes cited by number.

name index

Page references with "*f*" refer to figures, page references with "n" refer to endnotes cited by number, and page references with "*t*" refer to tables.

subject index

Page references with "*f*" refer to figures, page references with "*m*" refer to maps, page references with "*n*" refer to endnotes cited by number, and page references with "*t*" refer to tables.